America's Top-Rated Cities: A Statistical Handbook

Volume 2

2022

Twenty-ninth Edition

America's Top-Rated Cities: A Statistical Handbook

Volume 2: Western Region

Grey House Publishing

Cover image: Los Angeles, California

PUBLISHER: Leslie Mackenzie
EDITORIAL DIRECTOR: Stuart Paterson
SENIOR EDITOR: David Garoogian

RESEARCHER & WRITER: Jael Bridgemahon; Laura Mars
MARKETING DIRECTOR: Jessica Moody

Grey House Publishing, Inc.
4919 Route 22
Amenia, NY 12501
518.789.8700 • Fax 845.373.6390
www.greyhouse.com
books@greyhouse.com

Twenty-ninth Edition
Printed in Canada

Publisher's Cataloging-in-Publication Data
(Prepared by The Donohue Group, Inc.)

America's top-rated cities. Vol. 2, Western region : a statistical handbook. — 1992-

v. : ill. ; cm.
Annual, 1995-
Irregular, 1992-1993
ISSN: 1082-7102

1. Cities and towns--Ratings--Western States--Statistics--Periodicals. 2. Cities and towns--Western States--Statistics--Periodicals. 3. Social indicators--Western States--Periodicals. 4. Quality of life--Western States--Statistics--Periodicals. 5. Western States--Social conditions--Statistics--Periodicals. I. Title: America's top rated cities. II. Title: Western region

HT123.5.S6 A44
307.76/0973/05 95644648

4-Volume Set ISBN: 978-1-63700-132-5
Volume 1 ISBN: 978-1-63700-134-9
Volume 2 ISBN: 978-1-63700-135-6
Volume 3 ISBN: 978-1-63700-136-3
Volume 4 ISBN: 978-1-63700-137-0

Albuquerque, New Mexico

Anchorage, Alaska

Boise City, Idaho

Boulder, Colorado

Colorado Springs, Colorado

Denver, Colorado

Fort Collins, Colorado

Honolulu, Hawaii

Las Cruces, New Mexico

Las Vegas, Nevada

Los Angeles, California

Phoenix, Arizona

Portland, Oregon

Provo, Utah

Reno, Nevada

Riverside, California

Sacramento, California

Salt Lake City, Utah

San Diego, California

San Francisco, California

San Jose, California

Santa Rosa, California

Seattle, Washington

Tucson, Arizona

Appendices

Introduction

This twenty-ninth edition of *America's Top-Rated Cities* is a concise, statistical, 4-volume work identifying America's top-rated cities with estimated populations of approximately 100,000 or more. It profiles 100 cities that have received high marks for business and living from prominent sources such as *Forbes, Fortune, U.S. News & World Report, The Brookings Institution, U.S. Conference of Mayors, The Wall Street Journal,* and *CNNMoney.*

Each volume covers a different region of the country—Southern, Western, Central, Eastern—and includes a detailed Table of Contents, City Chapters, Appendices, and Maps. Each city chapter incorporates information from hundreds of resources to create the following major sections:

- **Background**—lively narrative of significant, up-to-date news for both businesses and residents. These combine historical facts with current developments, "known-for" annual events, and climate data.
- **Rankings**—fun-to-read, bulleted survey results from over 225 books, magazines, and online articles, ranging from general (Great Places to Live), to specific (Friendliest Cities), and everything in between.
- **Statistical Tables**—87 tables and detailed topics that offer an unparalleled view of each city's Business and Living Environments. They are carefully organized with data that is easy to read and understand.
- **Appendices**—five in all, appearing at the end of each volume. These range from listings of Metropolitan Statistical Areas to Comparative Statistics for all 100 cities.

This new edition of *America's Top-Rated Cities* includes cities that not only surveyed well, but ranked highest using our unique weighting system. We looked at violent crime, property crime, population growth, median household income, housing affordability, poverty, educational attainment, and unemployment. You'll find that we have included several American cities despite less-than-stellar numbers. New York, Los Angeles, and Miami remain world-class cities despite challenges faced by many large urban centers. Part of the criteria, in most cases, is that it be the "primary" city in a given metropolitan area. For example, if the metro area is Raleigh-Cary, NC, we would consider Raleigh, not Cary. This allows for a more equitable core city comparison. In general, the core city of a metro area is defined as having substantial influence on neighboring cities. A final consideration is location—we strive to include as many states in the country as possible.

New to this edition are:
Volume 2 - Las Cruces, NM
Volume 3 - St. Louis, MO
Volume 4 - Baltimore, MD; Buffalo, NY; Rochester, NY; Wilmington, NC

Praise for previous editions:

> *"...[ATRC] has...proven its worth to a wide audience...from businesspeople and corporations planning to launch, relocate, or expand their operations to market researchers, real estate professionals, urban planners, job-seekers, students...interested in...reliable, attractively presented statistical information about larger U.S. cities."*
>
> —ARBA

> *"...For individuals or businesses looking to relocate, this resource conveniently reports rankings from more than 300 sources for the top 100 US cities. Recommended..."*
>
> —Choice

> *"...While patrons are becoming increasingly comfortable locating statistical data online, there is still something to be said for the ease associated with such a compendium of otherwise scattered data. A well-organized and appropriate update...*
>
> —Library Journal

BACKGROUND

Each city begins with an informative Background that combines history with current events. These narratives often reflect changes that have occurred during the past year, and touch on the city's environment, politics, employment, cultural offerings, and climate, and include interesting trivia. For example: Peregrine Falcons were rehabilitated and released into the wild from Boise City's World Center for Birds of Prey; Grand Rapids was the first city to introduce fluoride into its drinking water in 1945; and Thomas Alva Edison discovered the phonograph and the light bulb in the city whose name was changed in 1954 from Raritan Township to Edison in his honor.

RANKINGS
This section has rankings from a possible 225 books, articles, and reports. For easy reference, these Rankings are categorized into 16 topics including Business/Finance, Dating/Romance, and Health/Fitness.

The Rankings are presented in an easy-to-read, bulleted format and include results from both annual surveys and one-shot studies. **Fastest-Growing Economies** . . . **Best Drivers** . . . **Most Well-Read** . . . **Most Wired** . . . **Healthiest for Women** . . . **Best for Minority Entrepreneurs** . . . **Safest** . . . **Best to Retire** . . . **Most Polite** . . . **Best for Moviemakers** . . . **Most Frugal** . . . **Best for Bikes** . . . **Most Cultured** . . . **Least Stressful** . . . **Best for Families** . . . **Most Romantic** . . . **Most Charitable** . . . **Best for Telecommuters** . . . **Best for Singles** . . . **Nerdiest** . . . **Fittest** . . . **Best for Dogs** . . . **Most Tattooed** . . . **Best for Wheelchair Users**, and more.

Sources for these Rankings include both well-known magazines and other media, including *Forbes, Fortune, USA Today, Condé Nast Traveler, Gallup, Kiplinger's Personal Finance, Men's Journal,* and *Travel + Leisure,* as well as *Asthma & Allergy Foundation of America, American Lung Association, League of American Bicyclists, The Advocate, National Civic League, National Alliance to End Homelessness, MovieMaker Magazine, National Insurance Crime Bureau, Center for Digital Government, National Association of Home Builders,* and *Milken Institute.*

Rankings cover a variety of geographic areas; see Appendix B for full geographic definitions.

STATISTICAL TABLES
Each city chapter includes a possible 87 tables and detailed topics—44 in Business and 43 in Living. Over 90% of statistical data has been updated.

Business Environment includes hard facts and figures on 8 major categories, including Demographics, Income, Economy, Employment, and Taxes. *Living Environment* includes 11 major categories, such as Cost of Living, Housing, Health, Education, Safety, and Climate.

To compile the Statistical Tables, editors have again turned to a wide range of sources, some well known, such as the *U.S. Census Bureau, U.S. Environmental Protection Agency, Bureau of Labor Statistics, Centers for Disease Control and Prevention,* and the *Federal Bureau of Investigation*, plus others like *The Council for Community and Economic Research, Texas A&M Transportation Institute,* and *Federation of Tax Administrators.*

APPENDIXES: Data for all cities appear in all volumes.

- **Appendix A**—*Comparative Statistics*
- **Appendix B**—*Metropolitan Area Definitions*
- **Appendix C**—*Government Type and County*
- **Appendix D**—*Chambers of Commerce and Economic Development Organizations*
- **Appendix E**—*State Departments of Labor and Employment*

Material provided by public and private agencies and organizations was supplemented by original research, numerous library sources and Internet sites. *America's Top-Rated Cities, 2022*, is designed for a wide range of readers: private individuals considering relocating a residence or business; professionals considering expanding their businesses or changing careers; corporations considering relocating, opening up additional offices or creating new divisions; government agencies; general and market researchers; real estate consultants; human resource personnel; urban planners; investors; and urban government students.

Customers who purchase the four-volume set receive free online access to *America's Top-Rated Cities* allowing them to download city reports and sort and rank by 50-plus data points.

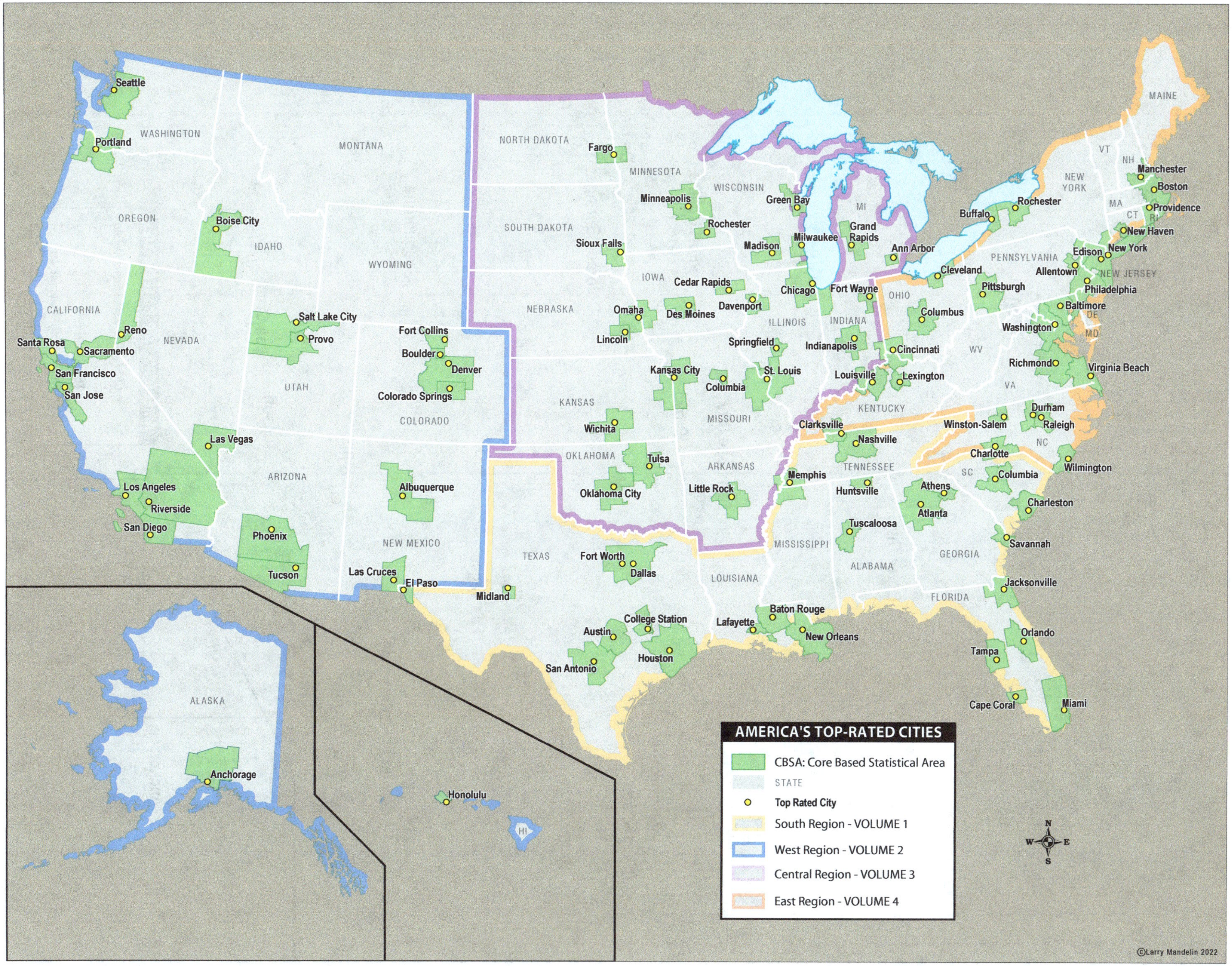
AMERICA'S TOP-RATED CITIES
CBSA: Core Based Statistical Area
STATE
Top Rated City
South Region - VOLUME 1
West Region - VOLUME 2
Central Region - VOLUME 3
East Region - VOLUME 4
WASHINGTON
OREGON
CALIFORNIA
NEVADA
IDAHO
MONTANA
WYOMING
UTAH
ARIZONA
COLORADO
NEW MEXICO
NORTH DAKOTA
SOUTH DAKOTA
NEBRASKA
KANSAS
OKLAHOMA
TEXAS
MINNESOTA
IOWA
MISSOURI
ARKANSAS
LOUISIANA
WISCONSIN
ILLINOIS
MI
INDIANA
OHIO
KENTUCKY
TENNESSEE
MISSISSIPPI
ALABAMA
GEORGIA
FLORIDA
SC
NC
VA
WV
PENNSYLVANIA
NEW YORK
NEW JERSEY
DE
MD
VT
NH
MA
CT
RI
MAINE
ALASKA
HI
Seattle
Portland
Boise City
Reno
Santa Rosa
Sacramento
San Francisco
San Jose
Las Vegas
Los Angeles
Riverside
San Diego
Phoenix
Tucson
Salt Lake City
Provo
Fort Collins
Boulder
Denver
Colorado Springs
Albuquerque
Las Cruces
El Paso
Midland
Fargo
Sioux Falls
Minneapolis
Rochester
Madison
Green Bay
Milwaukee
Grand Rapids
Ann Arbor
Chicago
Cedar Rapids
Davenport
Des Moines
Omaha
Lincoln
Kansas City
Columbia
Springfield
St. Louis
Wichita
Tulsa
Oklahoma City
Little Rock
Fort Worth
Dallas
Austin
San Antonio
College Station
Houston
Lafayette
Baton Rouge
New Orleans
Memphis
Clarksville
Nashville
Huntsville
Tuscaloosa
Indianapolis
Fort Wayne
Louisville
Lexington
Cincinnati
Columbus
Cleveland
Pittsburgh
Buffalo
Rochester
Manchester
Boston
Providence
New Haven
New York
Edison
Allentown
Philadelphia
Baltimore
Washington
Richmond
Virginia Beach
Durham
Raleigh
Winston-Salem
Charlotte
Columbia
Wilmington
Charleston
Athens
Atlanta
Savannah
Jacksonville
Orlando
Tampa
Cape Coral
Miami
Anchorage
Honolulu
N
S
E
W
©Larry Mandelin 2022

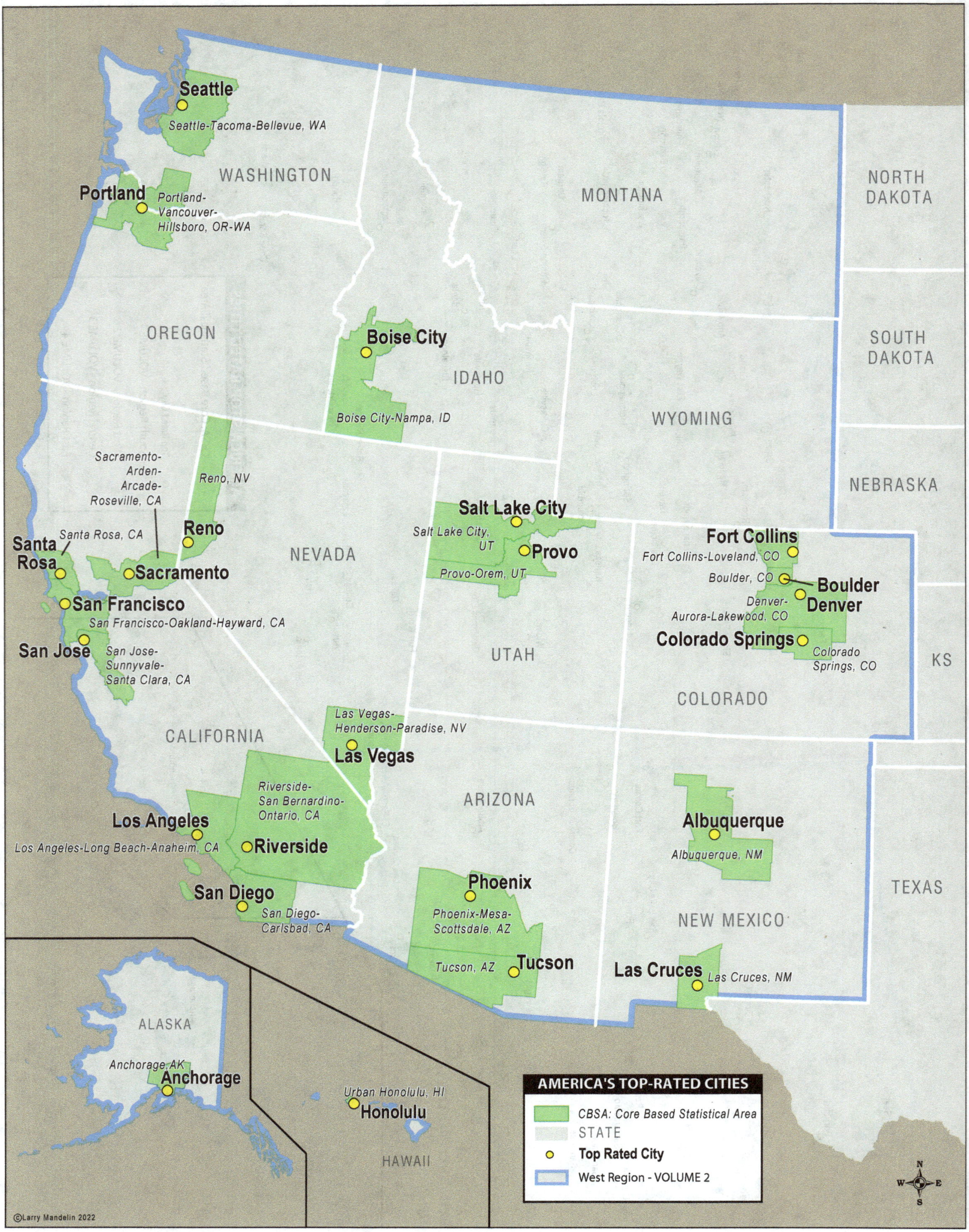

Seattle
Seattle-Tacoma-Bellevue, WA
WASHINGTON
Portland
Portland-
Vancouver-
Hillsboro, OR-WA
MONTANA
NORTH
DAKOTA
SOUTH
DAKOTA
OREGON
Boise City
IDAHO
Boise City-Nampa, ID
WYOMING
NEBRASKA
Sacramento-
Arden-
Arcade-
Roseville, CA
Reno, NV
Reno
Santa Rosa, CA
Santa
Rosa
Sacramento
NEVADA
Salt Lake City
Salt Lake City,
UT
Provo
Provo-Orem, UT
Fort Collins
Fort Collins-Loveland, CO
Boulder, CO
Boulder
Denver-
Aurora-Lakewood, CO
Denver
Colorado Springs
Colorado
Springs, CO
San Francisco
San Francisco-Oakland-Hayward, CA
San Jose
San Jose-
Sunnyvale-
Santa Clara, CA
UTAH
KS
COLORADO
CALIFORNIA
Las Vegas-
Henderson-Paradise, NV
Las Vegas
ARIZONA
Riverside-
San Bernardino-
Ontario, CA
Los Angeles
Los Angeles-Long Beach-Anaheim, CA
Riverside
Albuquerque
Albuquerque, NM
TEXAS
San Diego
San Diego-
Carlsbad, CA
Phoenix
Phoenix-Mesa-
Scottsdale, AZ
NEW MEXICO
Tucson, AZ
Tucson
Las Cruces
Las Cruces, NM
ALASKA
Anchorage, AK
Anchorage
Urban Honolulu, HI
Honolulu
HAWAII
AMERICA'S TOP-RATED CITIES
CBSA: Core Based Statistical Area
STATE
Top Rated City
West Region - VOLUME 2
N
W
E
S
©Larry Mandelin 2022

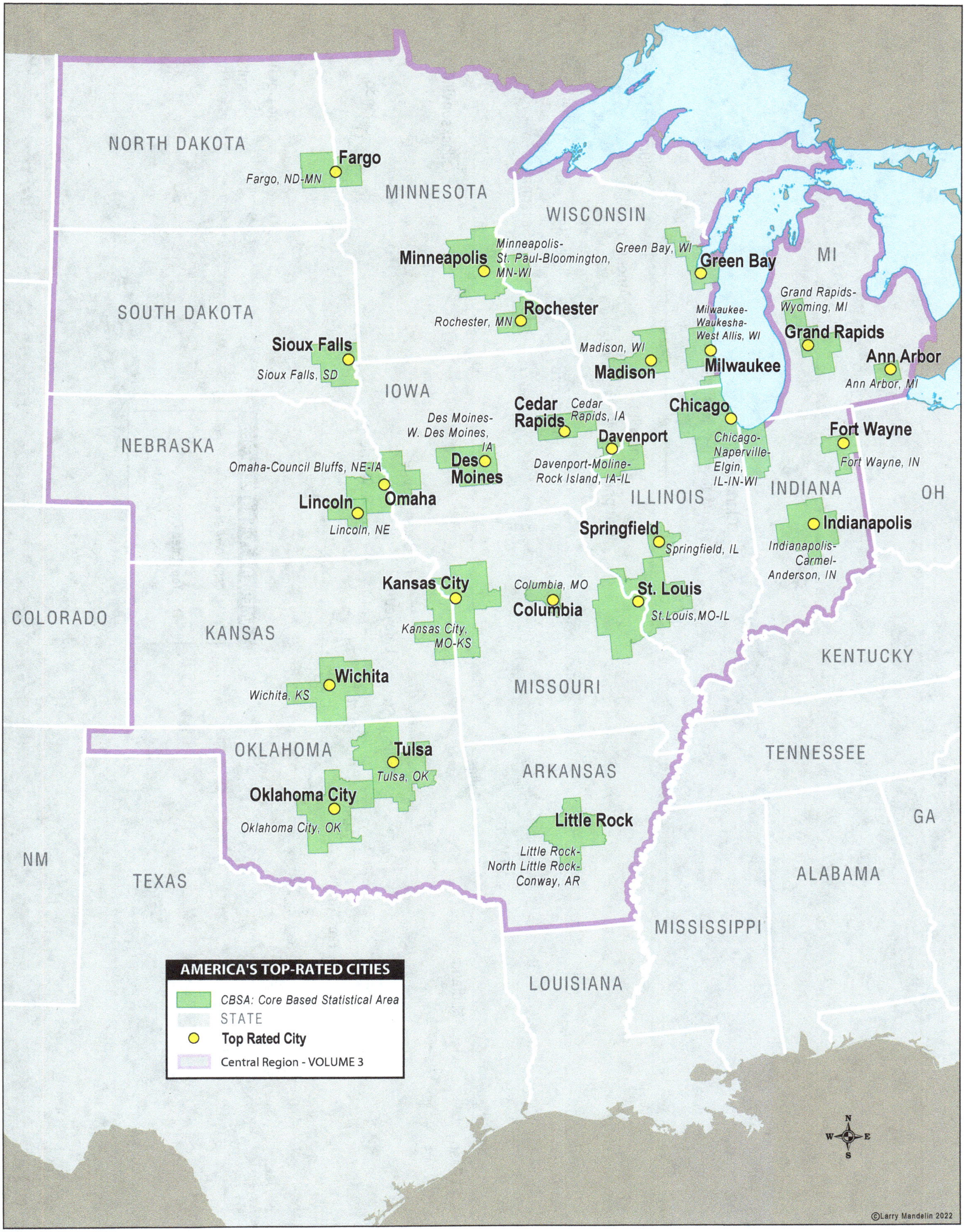
NORTH DAKOTA
Fargo
Fargo, ND-MN
MINNESOTA
WISCONSIN
Minneapolis
Minneapolis-St. Paul-Bloomington, MN-WI
Green Bay, WI
Green Bay
MI
SOUTH DAKOTA
Rochester
Rochester, MN
Grand Rapids-Wyoming, MI
Milwaukee-Waukesha-West Allis, WI
Grand Rapids
Sioux Falls
Sioux Falls, SD
Madison, WI
Madison
Milwaukee
Ann Arbor
Ann Arbor, MI
IOWA
Cedar Rapids
Cedar Rapids, IA
Chicago
Des Moines-W. Des Moines, IA
Des Moines
Davenport
Chicago-Naperville-Elgin, IL-IN-WI
Fort Wayne
Fort Wayne, IN
NEBRASKA
Omaha-Council Bluffs, NE-IA
Davenport-Moline-Rock Island, IA-IL
Omaha
Lincoln
Lincoln, NE
ILLINOIS
INDIANA
OH
Indianapolis
Indianapolis-Carmel-Anderson, IN
Springfield
Springfield, IL
Kansas City
Columbia, MO
Columbia
St. Louis
St. Louis, MO-IL
COLORADO
KANSAS
Kansas City, MO-KS
KENTUCKY
Wichita
Wichita, KS
MISSOURI
OKLAHOMA
Tulsa
Tulsa, OK
TENNESSEE
ARKANSAS
Oklahoma City
Oklahoma City, OK
Little Rock
Little Rock-North Little Rock-Conway, AR
GA
NM
TEXAS
ALABAMA
MISSISSIPPI
LOUISIANA
AMERICA'S TOP-RATED CITIES
CBSA: Core Based Statistical Area
STATE
Top Rated City
Central Region - VOLUME 3
N
W
E
S
©Larry Mandelin 2022

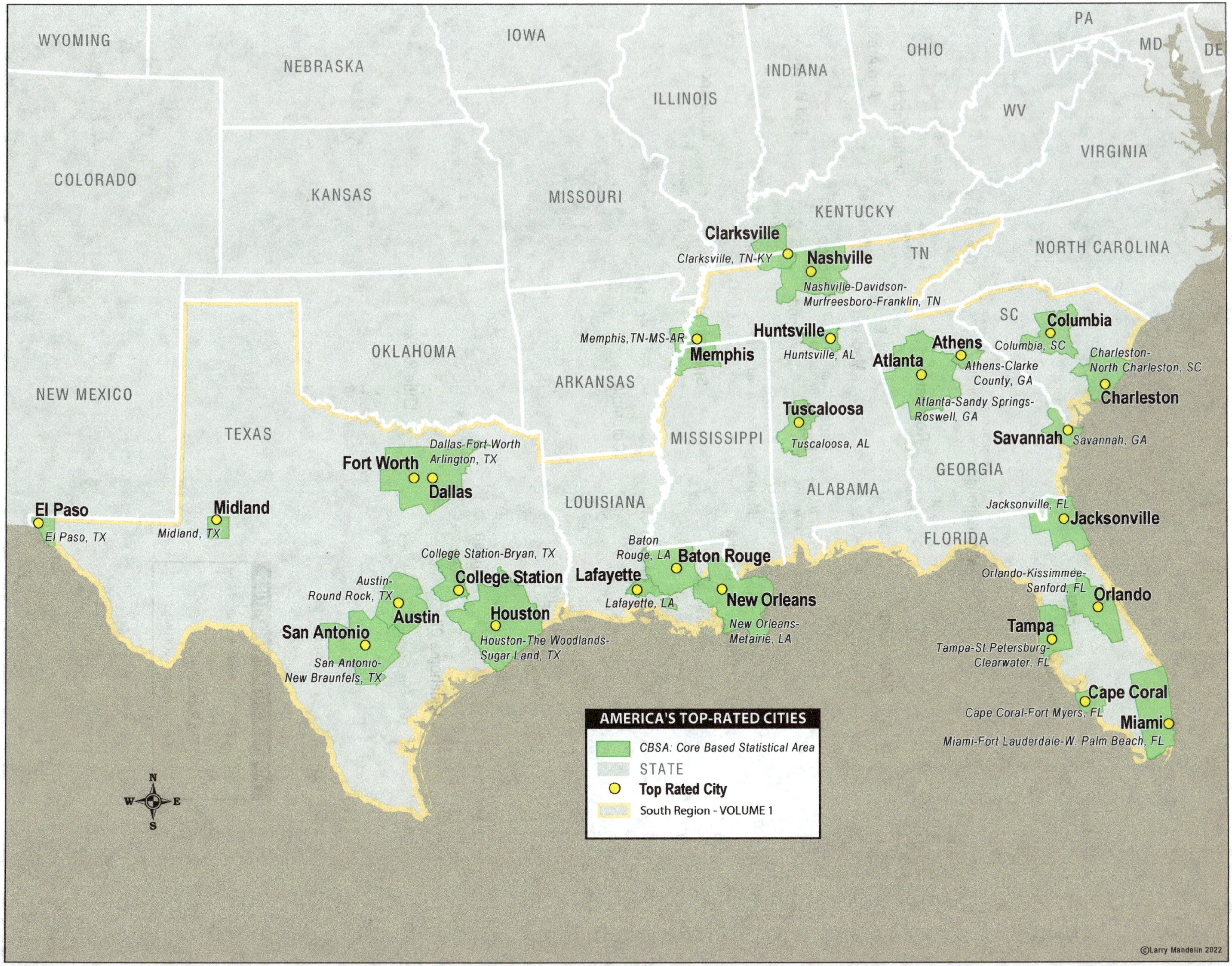
AMERICA'S TOP-RATED CITIES
CBSA: Core Based Statistical Area
STATE
Top Rated City
South Region - VOLUME 1
WYOMING
NEBRASKA
IOWA
ILLINOIS
INDIANA
OHIO
PA
MD
DE
WV
VIRGINIA
COLORADO
KANSAS
MISSOURI
KENTUCKY
NORTH CAROLINA
TN
SC
OKLAHOMA
ARKANSAS
NEW MEXICO
TEXAS
MISSISSIPPI
ALABAMA
GEORGIA
LOUISIANA
FLORIDA
Clarksville
Clarksville, TN-KY
Nashville
Nashville-Davidson-Murfreesboro-Franklin, TN
Memphis
Memphis, TN-MS-AR
Huntsville
Huntsville, AL
Atlanta
Atlanta-Sandy Springs-Roswell, GA
Athens
Athens-Clarke County, GA
Columbia
Columbia, SC
Charleston
Charleston-North Charleston, SC
Savannah
Savannah, GA
Tuscaloosa
Tuscaloosa, AL
Jacksonville
Jacksonville, FL
Orlando
Orlando-Kissimmee-Sanford, FL
Tampa
Tampa-St.Petersburg-Clearwater, FL
Cape Coral
Cape Coral-Fort Myers, FL
Miami
Miami-Fort Lauderdale-W. Palm Beach, FL
El Paso
El Paso, TX
Midland
Midland, TX
Fort Worth
Dallas
Dallas-Fort Worth Arlington, TX
College Station
College Station-Bryan, TX
Austin
Austin-Round Rock, TX
San Antonio
San Antonio-New Braunfels, TX
Houston
Houston-The Woodlands-Sugar Land, TX
Lafayette
Lafayette, LA
Baton Rouge
Baton Rouge, LA
New Orleans
New Orleans-Metairie, LA
N
S
E
W
©Larry Mandelin 2022

AMERICA'S TOP-RATED CITIES
CBSA: Core Based Statistical Area
STATE
Top Rated City
East Region - VOLUME 4
MAINE
VT
NH
NEW YORK
Manchester
Manchester-Nashua, NH
Boston-Cambridge-Newton, MA-NH
Boston
MA
Providence
CT
RI
Providence-Warwick, RI-MA
Rochester
Buffalo-Cheektowaga-Niagara Falls, NY
Rochester, NY
Buffalo
New Haven
New Haven-Milford, CT
MICHIGAN
Allentown-Bethlehem-Easton, PA-NJ
New York
PENNSYLVANIA
Allentown
Edison
New York-Newark-Jersey City, NY-NJ-PA
Cleveland
Cleveland-Elyria, OH
Pittsburgh
Philadelphia
Baltimore-Columbia-Towson, MD
NJ
Philadelphia-Camden-Wilmington, PA-NJ-DE-MD
OHIO
Pittsburgh, PA
Columbus
Baltimore
INDIANA
Washington
DE
Columbus, OH
MD
IL
Washington-Arlington-Alexandria, DC-VA-MD-WV
Cincinnati, OH-KY-IN
WV
Cincinnati
Richmond
VA
Virginia Beach-Norfolk-Newport News, VA-NC
Louisville/Jefferson County, KY-IN
Lexington
Richmond, VA
Virginia Beach
Louisville
Lexington-Fayette, KY
Durham-Chapel Hill, NC
Durham
KENTUCKY
Winston-Salem
Raleigh
Winston-Salem, NC
Raleigh, NC
Charlotte
TENNESSEE
NC
Wilmington, NC
Wilmington
Charlotte-Concord-Gastonia, NC-SC
N
W
E
S
S.CAROLINA
MS
ALABAMA
GEORGIA
©Larry Mandelin 2022

Albuquerque, New Mexico

Background

Pueblo Indians originally inhabited what is now the Albuquerque metropolitan area. In the sixteenth century, Spaniards began arriving from Mexico in search of riches, but it was not until 1706 that they founded the settlement, naming it after the viceroy of New Spain, San Francisco de Alburquerque, a duke whose permission was needed to set up the town. Eventually, the city's name would lose a consonant and become Albuquerque. The city earned the sobriquet "Duke City" because of its namesake.

In the early nineteenth century, Mexico secured her independence from Spanish rule and allowed Americans to enter the province of New Mexico to trade. During the Mexican War of the 1840s, Americans under the command of General Stephen Kearny captured the town, and New Mexico became part of the United States in the Treaty of Guadalupe Hidalgo, ending the war.

During the Civil War, Confederates held the town briefly before surrendering it to a besieging Union army. After the war, the railroad arrived in 1880, bringing with it people and business. In 1891 the town received a city charter. Albuquerque became an important site for tuberculosis sanatoriums during the next few decades because of the healing nature of the dry desert air.

World War II had a great impact on Albuquerque, as Kirtland Air Force Base became an important site for the manufacture of the atomic bomb. Sandia National Laboratories was founded in the city after the war and was important in defense-related research during the Cold War.

The defense industry is of prime significance to Albuquerque. Institutions in the city that were once dedicated to defense research are now involved in applying such technology to the private sector, making the city a perfect place for high-tech concerns. In addition to Sandia, the city hosts a branch of the Air Force Research Laboratories and the Los Alamos National Laboratory. Biotech and semiconductor industries also have had a positive impact on the city's economy.

Albuquerque and New Mexico have many programs to assist business. The state has property taxes that are among the lowest in the nation. The city consistently ranks high in business and engineering careers, and generally among best places to live. Additionally, traditional jobs, such as ranching, still have a large presence in the city.

Albuquerque is also a critical transportation center for the American Southwest, with two major interstates that intersect there. Its airport, Albuquerque International Sunport, is served by both major commercial and commuter carriers. The city is home to state-of-the-art manufacturing and shipping facilities and Mesa del Sol, a mixed-used development site connected to the airport by light-rail and a commuter rail line that also serves the region. The New Mexico Rail Runner Express system as well as the Rapid Ride bus service serves Albuquerque's residents. The city also gets high points for its walkability. According to 2022 figures, the city's Park Management Division maintains and manages more than 288 park sites.

There are various venues for higher education located in Albuquerque, the most significant of which is the University of New Mexico.

There are popular festive events scheduled throughout the year, including the annual International Albuquerque International Balloon Fiesta and the annual Gathering of Nations Powwow, an international event that is North America's biggest powwow. featuring over 3,000 indigenous Native American dancers and singers representing more than 500 tribes. The city is also the setting for television shows *Breaking Bad*, *Get Shorty*, and *Succession.* In 2018, the United Soccer League expanded into New Mexico with its headquarters in Albuquerque.

Albuquerque enjoys a dry, arid climate, with plenty of sunshine, low humidity, and scant rainfall. More than three-fourths of the daylight hours have sunshine, summer and winter. As in all desert climates, temperatures can fluctuate widely between day and night, all year round. Precipitation is meager during the winter, more abundant in summer with afternoon and evening thunderstorms.

Rankings

General Rankings

- For its "Best for Vets: Places to Live 2019" rankings, *Military Times* evaluated 599 cities (83 large, 234 medium, 282 small) and compared the locations across three broad categories: veteran and military culture/services; economic indicators; and livability factors such as health, crime, traffic, and school quality. Albuquerque ranked #14 out of the top 25, in the large city category (population of more than 250,000). Data points more specific to veterans and the military weighed more heavily than others. *rebootcamp.militarytimes.com, "Military Times Best Places to Live 2019," September 10, 2018*
- Albuquerque was selected as one of the best places to live in America by *Outside Magazine.* Criteria centered on diversity; sustainability; outdoor equity; and affordability. Local experts shared highlights from hands-on experience in each location. *Outside Magazine, "The 20 Most Livable Towns and Cities in America," October 15, 2021*

Business/Finance Rankings

- Albuquerque was the #13-ranked city for savers, according to a study by the finance site GOBankingRates, which considered the prospects for people trying to save money. Criteria: average monthly cost of grocery items; median home listing price; median rent; median income; transportation costs; gas prices; and the cost of eating out for an inexpensive and mid-range meal in 100 U.S. cities. *www.gobankingrates.com, "The 20 Best (and Worst) Places to Live If You're Trying to Save Money," August 27, 2019*
- Albuquerque was ranked #13 among 100 U.S. cities for most difficult conditions for savers, according to a study by the finance site GOBankingRates. Criteria: average monthly cost of grocery items; median home listing price; median rent; median income; transportation costs; gas prices; and the cost of eating out for an inexpensive and mid-range meal. *www.gobankingrates.com, "The 20 Best (and Worst) Places to Live If You're Trying to Save Money," August 27, 2019*
- The Brookings Institution ranked the nation's largest cities based on income inequality. Albuquerque was ranked #52 (#1 = greatest inequality). Criteria: the "95/20 ratio," a figure representing the income at which a household earns more than 95 percent of all other households, divided by the income at which a household earns more than only 20 percent of all other households. *Brookings Institution, "Household Income Inequality, Largest Cities of 97 Large U.S. Metro Areas, 2014-2016," February 5, 2018*
- The Brookings Institution ranked the 100 largest metro areas in the U.S. based on income inequality. Albuquerque was ranked #21 (#1 = greatest inequality). Criteria: the "95/20 ratio," a figure representing the income at which a household earns more than 95 percent of all other households, divided by the income at which a household earns more than only 20 percent of all other households. *Brookings Institution, "Household Income Inequality, 100 Largest U.S. Metro Areas, 2014-2016," February 5, 2018*
- The Albuquerque metro area appeared on the Milken Institute "2021 Best Performing Cities" list. Rank: #89 out of 200 large metro areas (population over 250,000). Criteria: job growth; wage and salary growth; high-tech output growth; housing affordability; household broadband access. *Milken Institute, "Best-Performing Cities 2021," February 16, 2021*
- *Forbes* ranked the 200 most populous metro areas to determine the nation's "Best Places for Business and Careers." The Albuquerque metro area was ranked #126. Criteria: costs (business and living); job growth (past and projected); income growth; quality of life; educational attainment (college and high school); projected economic growth; cultural and leisure opportunities; workplace tolerance laws; net migration patterns. *Forbes, "The Best Places for Business and Careers 2019: Seattle Still On Top," October 30, 2019*

Culture/Performing Arts Rankings

- Albuquerque was selected as one of the 25 best cities for moviemakers in North America. COVID-19 has spurred a quest for great film cities that offer more creative space, lower costs, and more great outdoors. NYC & LA were intentionally excluded. Criteria: longstanding reputations as film-friendly communities; film community and culture; work life balance; and efforts to deal with pandemic-specific challenges. The city was ranked #1. *MovieMaker Magazine, "Best Places to Live and Work as a Moviemaker in 2022," January 25, 2022*

Education Rankings

- Personal finance website *WalletHub* analyzed the 150 largest U.S. metropolitan statistical areas to determine where the most educated Americans are putting their degrees to work. Criteria: education levels; percentage of workers with degrees; education quality and attainment gap; public school quality rankings; quality and enrollment of each metro area's universities. Albuquerque was ranked #52 (#1 = most educated city). *www.WalletHub.com, "Most & Least Educated Cities in America," July 19, 2021*
- Albuquerque was selected as one of America's most literate cities. The city ranked #33 out of the 84 largest U.S. cities. Criteria: number of booksellers; library resources; Internet resources; educational attainment; periodical publishing resources; newspaper circulation. *Central Connecticut State University, "America's Most Literate Cities, 2018," February 2019*

Environmental Rankings

- Albuquerque was highlighted as one of the top 98 cleanest metro areas for short-term particle pollution (24-hour PM 2.5) in the U.S. during 2017 through 2019. Monitors in these cities reported no days with unhealthful PM 2.5 levels. *American Lung Association, "State of the Air 2021," April 21, 2021*

Health/Fitness Rankings

- For each of the 100 largest cities in the United States, the American Fitness Index®, published by the American College of Sports Medicine and the Anthem Foundation, evaluated community infrastructure and 34 health behaviors including preventive health, levels of chronic disease conditions, food insecurity, sleep quality, pedestrian safety, air quality, and community resources that support physical activity. Albuquerque ranked #27 for "community fitness." *americanfitnessindex.org, "2021 ACSM American Fitness Index Summary Report," July 13, 2021*
- Albuquerque was identified as a "2021 Spring Allergy Capital." The area ranked #79 out of 100. Three groups of factors were used to identify the most challenging cities for people with allergies during the spring season: annual spring pollen levels; over the counter medicine use; number of board-certified allergy specialists. *Asthma and Allergy Foundation of America, "Spring Allergy Capitals 2021," February 23, 2021*
- Albuquerque was identified as a "2021 Fall Allergy Capital." The area ranked #80 out of 100. Three groups of factors were used to identify the most challenging cities for people with allergies during the fall season: annual fall pollen levels; over the counter medicine use; number of board-certified allergy specialists. *Asthma and Allergy Foundation of America, "Fall Allergy Capitals 2021," February 23, 2021*
- Albuquerque was identified as a "2021 Asthma Capital." The area ranked #38 out of the nation's 100 largest metropolitan areas. Criteria: estimated asthma prevalence; asthma-related mortality; and ER visits due to asthma. Risk factors analyzed but not factored in the rankings: annual pollen score; annual air quality; public smoking laws; number of board-certified asthma specialists; rescue medication use; controller medication use; uninsured rate; poverty rate. *Asthma and Allergy Foundation of America, "Asthma Capitals 2021: The Most Challenging Places to Live With Asthma," May 5, 2021*

Real Estate Rankings

- *WalletHub* compared the most populated U.S. cities to determine which had the best markets for real estate agents. Albuquerque ranked #135 where demand was high and pay was the best. Criteria: sales per agent; annual median wage for real-estate agents; monthly average starting salary for real estate agents; real estate job density and competition; unemployment rate; home turnover rate; housing-market health index; and other relevant metrics. *www.WalletHub.com, "2021 Best Places to Be a Real Estate Agent," May 12, 2021*
- Albuquerque was ranked #129 out of 237 metro areas in terms of housing affordability in 2021 by the National Association of Home Builders (#1 = most affordable). Criteria: the share of homes sold in that area affordable to a family earning the local median income, based on standard mortgage underwriting criteria. *National Association of Home Builders®, NAHB-Wells Fargo Housing Opportunity Index, 4th Quarter 2021*

Safety Rankings

- To identify the most dangerous cities in America, 24/7 Wall Street focused on violent crime categories—murder, non-negligent manslaughter, rape, robbery, and aggravated assault—as reported for every 100,000 residents using data from the FBI's 2020 annual Uniform Crime Report. For cities with populations over 25,000, trim(city)+[was ranked #28. *247wallst.com, "America's Most Dangerous Cities" November 12, 2021*

- Allstate ranked the 200 largest cities in America in terms of driver safety. Albuquerque ranked #58. Criteria: internal property damage claims over a two-year period from January 2016 to December 2017. The report helps increase the importance of safety and awareness behind the wheel. *Allstate, "Allstate America's Best Drivers Report, 2019" June 24, 2019*
- Albuquerque was identified as one of the most dangerous cities in America by NeighborhoodScout. The city ranked #29 out of 100 (#1 = most dangerous). Criteria: number of violent crimes per 1,000 residents. The editors evaluated cities with 25,000 or more residents. *NeighborhoodScout.com, "2022 Top 100 Most Dangerous Cities in the U.S.," January 3, 2022*
- The National Insurance Crime Bureau ranked 390 metro areas in the U.S. in terms of per capita rates of vehicle theft. The Albuquerque metro area ranked #6 (#1 = highest rate). Criteria: number of vehicle theft offenses per 100,000 inhabitants in 2020. *National Insurance Crime Bureau, "Hot Spots 2020," August 31, 2021*

Seniors/Retirement Rankings

- From its Best Cities for Successful Aging indexes, the Milken Institute generated rankings for metropolitan areas, weighing data in nine categories—health care, wellness, living arrangements, transportation and convenience, financial characteristics, education, employment, community engagement, and overall livability. The Albuquerque metro area was ranked #87 overall in the large metro area category. *Milken Institute, "Best Cities for Successful Aging, 2017" March 14, 2017*
- Albuquerque was identified as #13 of 20 most popular places to retire in the Southwest region by *Topretirements.com*. The site separated its annual "Best Places to Retire" list by major U.S. regions for 2019. The list reflects the 20 cities that visitors to the website are most interested in for retirement, based on the number of times a city's review was viewed on the website. *Topretirements.com, "20 Most Popular Places to Retire in the Southwest for 2019," October 2, 2019*

Sports/Recreation Rankings

- Albuquerque was chosen as one of America's best cities for bicycling. The city ranked #47 out of 50. Criteria: cycling infrastructure that is safe and friendly for all ages; energy and bike culture. The editors evaluated cities with populations of 100,000 or more. *Bicycling, "The 50 Best Bike Cities in America," October 10, 2018*

Women/Minorities Rankings

- *Women's Health*, together with the site Yelp, identified the 15 "Wellthiest" spots in the U.S. Albuquerque appeared among the top for happiest, healthiest, outdoorsiest and Zen-iest. *Women's Health, "The 15 Wellthiest Cities in the U.S." July 5, 2017*
- Personal finance website *WalletHub* compared more than 180 U.S. cities across two key dimensions, "Hispanic Business-Friendliness" and "Hispanic Purchasing Power," to arrive at the most favorable conditions for Hispanic entrepreneurs. Albuquerque was ranked #39 out of 182. Criteria includes: share of Hispanic-Owned Businesses; Hispanic entrepreneurship rate to median annual income of Hispanics; Small Business-Friendliness score; cost of living; and number of Hispanics with at least a bachelor's degree. *WalletHub.com, "2019's Best Cities for Hispanic Entrepreneurs," May 1, 2019*

Miscellaneous Rankings

- Albuquerque was selected as a 2021 Digital Cities Survey winner. The city ranked #6 in the large city (500,000 or more population) category. The survey examined and assessed how city governments are utilizing technology to continue innovation, engage with residents, and persevere through the challenges of the pandemic. Survey questions focused on ten initiatives: cybersecurity; citizen experience; disaster recovery; business intelligence; IT personnel; data governance; budget control; IT governance; infrastructure modernization; and broadband connectivity. *Center for Digital Government, "2021 Digital Cities Survey," November 16, 2021*
- *WalletHub* compared the 150 most populated U.S. cities to determine their operating efficiency. A "Quality of City Services" score was constructed for each city and then divided by the total budget per capita to reveal which were managed the best. Albuquerque ranked #31. Criteria: financial stability; economy; education; safety; health; infrastructure and pollution. *www.WalletHub.com, "2021's Best- & Worst-Run Cities in America," June 22, 2021*

Business Environment

DEMOGRAPHICS

Population Growth

Area	1990 Census	2000 Census	2010 Census	2020* Estimate	Population Growth (%) 1990-2020	Population Growth (%) 2010-2020
City	388,375	448,607	545,852	560,447	44.3	2.7
MSA[1]	599,416	729,649	887,077	915,986	52.8	3.3
U.S.	248,709,873	281,421,906	308,745,538	326,569,308	31.3	5.8

Note: (1) Figures cover the Albuquerque, NM Metropolitan Statistical Area; (*) 2016-2020 5-year estimated population
Source: U.S. Census Bureau, 1990 Census, Census 2000, Census 2010, 2016-2020 American Community Survey 5-Year Estimates

Household Size

Area	Persons in Household (%)							Average Household Size
	One	Two	Three	Four	Five	Six	Seven or More	
City	35.9	33.3	13.8	10.4	4.7	1.3	0.7	2.40
MSA[1]	31.8	35.2	14.4	10.7	5.1	1.7	1.1	2.50
U.S.	28.0	33.9	15.5	12.9	6.0	2.3	1.4	2.60

Note: (1) Figures cover the Albuquerque, NM Metropolitan Statistical Area
Source: U.S. Census Bureau, 2016-2020 American Community Survey 5-Year Estimates

Race

Area	White Alone[2] (%)	Black Alone[2] (%)	Asian Alone[2] (%)	AIAN[3] Alone[2] (%)	NHOPI[4] Alone[2] (%)	Other Race Alone[2] (%)	Two or More Races (%)
City	70.3	3.1	3.0	4.5	0.1	9.8	9.2
MSA[1]	70.7	2.6	2.3	5.8	0.1	9.5	9.0
U.S.	70.4	12.6	5.6	0.8	0.2	5.1	5.2

Note: (1) Figures cover the Albuquerque, NM Metropolitan Statistical Area; (2) Alone is defined as not being in combination with one or more other races; (3) American Indian and Alaska Native; (4) Native Hawaiian and Other Pacific Islander
Source: U.S. Census Bureau, 2016-2020 American Community Survey 5-Year Estimates

Hispanic or Latino Origin

Area	Total (%)	Mexican (%)	Puerto Rican (%)	Cuban (%)	Other (%)
City	49.2	28.8	0.6	0.4	19.4
MSA[1]	49.4	28.5	0.6	0.4	20.0
U.S.	18.2	11.2	1.7	0.7	4.5

Note: Persons of Hispanic or Latino origin can be of any race; (1) Figures cover the Albuquerque, NM Metropolitan Statistical Area
Source: U.S. Census Bureau, 2016-2020 American Community Survey 5-Year Estimates

Ancestry

Area	German	Irish	English	American	Italian	Polish	French[2]	Scottish	Dutch
City	9.4	7.7	7.5	3.6	3.1	1.4	1.8	1.4	0.8
MSA[1]	9.0	7.1	7.3	4.2	3.0	1.3	1.7	1.5	0.7
U.S.	13.0	9.7	7.7	5.9	5.1	2.7	2.3	1.6	1.1

Note: Figures are the percentage of the total population reporting a particular ancestry. The nine most commonly reported ancestries in the U.S. are shown. Figures include multiple ancestries (e.g. if a person reported being Irish and Italian, they were included in both columns); (1) Figures cover the Albuquerque, NM Metropolitan Statistical Area; (2) Excludes Basque
Source: U.S. Census Bureau, 2016-2020 American Community Survey 5-Year Estimates

Foreign-born Population

Area	Percent of Population Born in								
	Any Foreign Country	Asia	Mexico	Europe	Caribbean	Central America[2]	South America	Africa	Canada
City	9.8	2.6	4.9	1.0	0.3	0.1	0.4	0.4	0.1
MSA[1]	8.9	1.9	4.9	0.8	0.2	0.1	0.4	0.4	0.1
U.S.	13.5	4.2	3.3	1.5	1.3	1.1	1.0	0.7	0.3

Note: (1) Figures cover the Albuquerque, NM Metropolitan Statistical Area; (2) Excludes Mexico.
Source: U.S. Census Bureau, 2016-2020 American Community Survey 5-Year Estimates

Marital Status

Area	Never Married	Now Married[2]	Separated	Widowed	Divorced
City	38.2	39.8	1.4	5.6	15.1
MSA[1]	35.5	43.4	1.4	5.7	14.0
U.S.	33.5	48.1	1.8	5.7	10.8

Note: Figures are percentages and cover the population 15 years of age and older; (1) Figures cover the Albuquerque, NM Metropolitan Statistical Area; (2) Excludes separated
Source: U.S. Census Bureau, 2016-2020 American Community Survey 5-Year Estimates

Disability by Age

Area	All Ages	Under 18 Years Old	18 to 64 Years Old	65 Years and Over
City	14.0	4.5	12.0	35.5
MSA[1]	15.0	4.3	12.9	36.9
U.S.	12.7	4.3	10.3	34.0

Note: Figures show percent of the civilian noninstitutionalized population that reported having a disability. Disability status is determined from six types of difficulty: vision, hearing, cognitive, ambulatory, self-care, and independent living. For children under 5 years old, hearing and vision difficulty are used to determine disability status. For children between the ages of 5 and 14, disability status is determined from hearing, vision, cognitive, ambulatory, and self-care difficulties. For people aged 15 years and older, they are considered to have a disability if they have difficulty with any one of the six difficulty types; Note: (1) Figures cover the Albuquerque, NM Metropolitan Statistical Area
Source: U.S. Census Bureau, 2016-2020 American Community Survey 5-Year Estimates

Age

Area	Percent of Population									Median Age
	Under Age 5	Age 5–19	Age 20–34	Age 35–44	Age 45–54	Age 55–64	Age 65–74	Age 75–84	Age 85+	
City	5.7	18.8	22.4	13.1	11.9	12.4	9.3	4.3	2.0	37.1
MSA[1]	5.5	19.0	20.5	12.8	12.1	13.1	10.1	4.7	1.9	38.5
U.S.	6.0	19.1	20.6	12.7	12.7	12.9	9.4	4.7	2.0	38.2

Note: (1) Figures cover the Albuquerque, NM Metropolitan Statistical Area
Source: U.S. Census Bureau, 2016-2020 American Community Survey 5-Year Estimates

Gender

Area	Males	Females	Males per 100 Females
City	273,056	287,391	95.0
MSA[1]	450,378	465,608	96.7
U.S.	160,818,530	165,750,778	97.0

Note: (1) Figures cover the Albuquerque, NM Metropolitan Statistical Area
Source: U.S. Census Bureau, 2016-2020 American Community Survey 5-Year Estimates

Religious Groups by Family

Area	Catholic	Baptist	Non-Den.	Methodist[2]	Lutheran	LDS[3]	Pente-costal	Presby-terian[4]	Muslim[5]	Judaism
MSA[1]	27.2	3.8	4.2	1.5	1.0	2.4	1.5	1.1	0.2	0.3
U.S.	19.1	9.3	4.0	4.0	2.3	2.0	1.9	1.6	0.8	0.7

Note: Figures are the number of adherents as a percentage of the total population; (1) Figures cover the Albuquerque, NM Metropolitan Statistical Area; (2) Methodist/Pietist; (3) Latter Day Saints; (4) Reformed; (5) Figures are estimates
Source: Association of Statisticians of American Religious Bodies, 2010 U.S. Religion Census: Religious Congregations & Membership Study

Religious Groups by Tradition

Area	Catholic	Evangelical Protestant	Mainline Protestant	Other Tradition	Black Protestant	Orthodox
MSA[1]	27.2	11.3	3.3	3.9	0.2	0.2
U.S.	19.1	16.2	7.3	4.3	1.6	0.3

Note: Figures are the number of adherents as a percentage of the total population; (1) Figures cover the Albuquerque, NM Metropolitan Statistical Area
Source: Association of Statisticians of American Religious Bodies, 2010 U.S. Religion Census: Religious Congregations & Membership Study

ECONOMY

Gross Metropolitan Product

Area	2017	2018	2019	2020	Rank[2]
MSA[1]	42.8	44.4	46.3	48.6	68

Note: Figures are in billions of dollars; (1) Figures cover the Albuquerque, NM Metropolitan Statistical Area; (2) Rank is based on 2018 data and ranges from 1 to 381
Source: U.S. Conference of Mayors, U.S. Metro Economies: GMP & Employment 2018-2020, September 2019

Economic Growth

Area	2015-17 (%)	2018 (%)	2019 (%)	2020 (%)	Rank[2]
MSA[1]	0.7	1.4	2.6	2.5	252
U.S.	1.9	2.9	2.3	2.1	–

Note: Figures are real gross metropolitan product (GMP) growth rates and represent average annual percent change; (1) Figures cover the Albuquerque, NM Metropolitan Statistical Area; (2) Rank is based on 2017 2-year average annual percent change and ranges from 1 to 381
Source: U.S. Conference of Mayors, U.S. Metro Economies: GMP & Employment 2018-2020, September 2019

Metropolitan Area Exports

Area	2015	2016	2017	2018	2019	2020	Rank[2]
MSA[1]	1,761.2	999.7	624.2	771.5	1,629.7	1,265.3	127

Note: Figures are in millions of dollars; (1) Figures cover the Albuquerque, NM Metropolitan Statistical Area; (2) Rank is based on 2020 data and ranges from 1 to 389
Source: U.S. Department of Commerce, International Trade Administration, Office of Trade and Economic Analysis, Industry and Analysis, Exports by Metropolitan Area, data extracted March 4, 2022

Building Permits

Area	Single-Family			Multi-Family			Total		
	2019	2020	Pct. Chg.	2019	2020	Pct. Chg.	2019	2020	Pct. Chg.
City	906	865	-4.5	188	0	-100.0	1,094	865	-20.9
MSA[1]	1,872	1,925	2.8	276	89	-67.8	2,148	2,014	-6.2
U.S.	862,100	979,400	13.6	523,900	491,700	-6.1	1,386,000	1,471,100	6.1

Note: (1) Figures cover the Albuquerque, NM Metropolitan Statistical Area; Figures represent new, privately-owned housing units authorized (unadjusted data); All permit data are based on estimates with imputation
Source: U.S. Census Bureau, Manufacturing, Mining, and Construction Statistics, Building Permits, 2019, 2020

Bankruptcy Filings

Area	Business Filings			Nonbusiness Filings		
	2020	2021	% Chg.	2020	2021	% Chg.
Bernalillo County	33	21	-36.4	872	560	-35.8
U.S.	21,655	14,347	-33.7	522,808	399,269	-23.6

Note: Business filings include Chapter 7, Chapter 9, Chapter 11, Chapter 12, Chapter 13, Chapter 15, and Section 304; Nonbusiness filings include Chapter 7, Chapter 11, and Chapter 13
Source: Administrative Office of the U.S. Courts, Business and Nonbusiness Bankruptcy, County Cases Commenced by Chapter of the Bankruptcy Code, During the 12-Month Period Ending December 31, 2020 and Business and Nonbusiness Bankruptcy, County Cases Commenced by Chapter of the Bankruptcy Code, During the 12-Month Period Ending December 31, 2021

Housing Vacancy Rates

Area	Gross Vacancy Rate[2] (%)			Year-Round Vacancy Rate[3] (%)			Rental Vacancy Rate[4] (%)			Homeowner Vacancy Rate[5] (%)		
	2019	2020	2021	2019	2020	2021	2019	2020	2021	2019	2020	2021
MSA[1]	7.9	5.1	5.3	7.4	4.9	5.1	6.5	5.4	6.4	1.9	1.4	0.5
U.S.	12.0	10.6	10.8	9.5	8.2	8.4	6.7	6.3	6.1	1.4	1.0	0.9

Note: (1) Figures cover the Albuquerque, NM Metropolitan Statistical Area; (2) The percentage of the total housing inventory that is vacant; (3) The percentage of the housing inventory (excluding seasonal units) that is year-round vacant; (4) The percentage of rental inventory that is vacant for rent; (5) The percentage of homeowner inventory that is vacant for sale
Source: U.S. Census Bureau, Housing Vacancies and Homeownership Annual Statistics: 2019, 2020, 2021

INCOME

Income

Area	Per Capita ($)	Median Household ($)	Average Household ($)
City	31,103	53,936	72,426
MSA[1]	30,397	55,370	74,226
U.S.	35,384	64,994	91,547

Note: (1) Figures cover the Albuquerque, NM Metropolitan Statistical Area
Source: U.S. Census Bureau, 2016-2020 American Community Survey 5-Year Estimates

Household Income Distribution

Area	Percent of Households Earning							
	Under $15,000	$15,000 -$24,999	$25,000 -$34,999	$35,000 -$49,999	$50,000 -$74,999	$75,000 -$99,999	$100,000 -$149,999	$150,000 and up
City	13.3	9.9	10.0	13.4	18.1	12.3	13.6	9.4
MSA[1]	12.4	9.8	9.7	13.4	18.2	12.7	13.7	10.0
U.S.	9.9	8.5	8.6	12.0	17.2	12.8	15.6	15.4

Note: (1) Figures cover the Albuquerque, NM Metropolitan Statistical Area
Source: U.S. Census Bureau, 2016-2020 American Community Survey 5-Year Estimates

Poverty Rate

Area	All Ages	Under 18 Years Old	18 to 64 Years Old	65 Years and Over
City	16.0	21.7	15.2	10.9
MSA[1]	15.5	21.0	14.8	10.8
U.S.	12.8	17.5	12.1	9.3

Note: Figures are percentage of people whose income during the past 12 months was below the poverty level; (1) Figures cover the Albuquerque, NM Metropolitan Statistical Area
Source: U.S. Census Bureau, 2016-2020 American Community Survey 5-Year Estimates

CITY FINANCES

City Government Finances

Component	2019 ($000)	2019 ($ per capita)
Total Revenues	1,205,381	2,158
Total Expenditures	1,085,168	1,943
Debt Outstanding	1,321,810	2,367
Cash and Securities[1]	839,213	1,502

Note: (1) Cash and security holdings of a government at the close of its fiscal year, including those of its dependent agencies, utilities, and liquor stores.
Source: U.S. Census Bureau, State & Local Government Finances 2019

City Government Revenue by Source

Source	2019 ($000)	2019 ($ per capita)	2019 (%)
General Revenue			
From Federal Government	28,331	51	2.4
From State Government	232,677	417	19.3
From Local Governments	3,029	5	0.3
Taxes			
Property	154,958	277	12.9
Sales and Gross Receipts	287,093	514	23.8
Personal Income	0	0	0.0
Corporate Income	0	0	0.0
Motor Vehicle License	0	0	0.0
Other Taxes	14,775	26	1.2
Current Charges	266,830	478	22.1
Liquor Store	0	0	0.0
Utility	152,378	273	12.6

Source: U.S. Census Bureau, State & Local Government Finances 2019

City Government Expenditures by Function

Function	2019 ($000)	2019 ($ per capita)	2019 (%)
General Direct Expenditures			
Air Transportation	43,629	78	4.0
Corrections	0	0	0.0
Education	0	0	0.0
Employment Security Administration	0	0	0.0
Financial Administration	24,192	43	2.2
Fire Protection	85,521	153	7.9
General Public Buildings	20,080	36	1.9
Governmental Administration, Other	37,743	67	3.5
Health	27,615	49	2.5
Highways	48,490	86	4.5
Hospitals	0	0	0.0
Housing and Community Development	8,335	14	0.8
Interest on General Debt	34,246	61	3.2
Judicial and Legal	5,678	10	0.5
Libraries	16,298	29	1.5
Parking	4,299	7	0.4
Parks and Recreation	102,892	184	9.5
Police Protection	204,800	366	18.9
Public Welfare	20,959	37	1.9
Sewerage	79,011	141	7.3
Solid Waste Management	68,792	123	6.3
Veterans' Services	0	0	0.0
Liquor Store	0	0	0.0
Utility	202,681	362	18.7

Source: U.S. Census Bureau, State & Local Government Finances 2019

EMPLOYMENT

Labor Force and Employment

Area	Civilian Labor Force			Workers Employed		
	Dec. 2020	Dec. 2021	% Chg.	Dec. 2020	Dec. 2021	% Chg.
City	283,911	282,488	-0.5	260,865	269,987	3.5
MSA[1]	440,283	438,957	-0.3	404,900	418,975	3.5
U.S.	160,017,000	161,696,000	1.0	149,613,000	155,732,000	4.1

Note: Data is not seasonally adjusted and covers workers 16 years of age and older; (1) Figures cover the Albuquerque, NM Metropolitan Statistical Area
Source: Bureau of Labor Statistics, Local Area Unemployment Statistics

Unemployment Rate

Area	2021											
	Jan.	Feb.	Mar.	Apr.	May	Jun.	Jul.	Aug.	Sep.	Oct.	Nov.	Dec.
City	8.6	7.7	7.3	7.1	6.9	7.9	7.3	5.9	5.4	4.9	4.9	4.4
MSA[1]	8.6	7.8	7.4	7.2	7.0	8.0	7.4	6.0	5.6	5.0	5.0	4.6
U.S.	6.8	6.6	6.2	5.7	5.5	6.1	5.7	5.3	4.6	4.3	3.9	3.7

Note: Data is not seasonally adjusted and covers workers 16 years of age and older; (1) Figures cover the Albuquerque, NM Metropolitan Statistical Area
Source: Bureau of Labor Statistics, Local Area Unemployment Statistics

Average Wages

Occupation	$/Hr.	Occupation	$/Hr.
Accountants and Auditors	35.64	Maintenance and Repair Workers	19.77
Automotive Mechanics	21.75	Marketing Managers	53.28
Bookkeepers	19.93	Network and Computer Systems Admin.	38.85
Carpenters	22.11	Nurses, Licensed Practical	27.06
Cashiers	12.69	Nurses, Registered	38.25
Computer Programmers	37.36	Nursing Assistants	15.54
Computer Systems Analysts	37.61	Office Clerks, General	14.66
Computer User Support Specialists	23.60	Physical Therapists	46.27
Construction Laborers	16.88	Physicians	124.08
Cooks, Restaurant	14.15	Plumbers, Pipefitters and Steamfitters	24.80
Customer Service Representatives	16.91	Police and Sheriff's Patrol Officers	27.32
Dentists	90.15	Postal Service Mail Carriers	25.43
Electricians	25.39	Real Estate Sales Agents	22.51
Engineers, Electrical	56.62	Retail Salespersons	14.34
Fast Food and Counter Workers	11.91	Sales Representatives, Technical/Scientific	36.71
Financial Managers	59.98	Secretaries, Exc. Legal/Medical/Executive	19.08
First-Line Supervisors of Office Workers	26.92	Security Guards	15.54
General and Operations Managers	52.87	Surgeons	154.18
Hairdressers/Cosmetologists	12.14	Teacher Assistants, Exc. Postsecondary*	12.11
Home Health and Personal Care Aides	12.66	Teachers, Secondary School, Exc. Sp. Ed.*	28.98
Janitors and Cleaners	13.25	Telemarketers	18.27
Landscaping/Groundskeeping Workers	15.74	Truck Drivers, Heavy/Tractor-Trailer	21.54
Lawyers	57.83	Truck Drivers, Light/Delivery Services	19.08
Maids and Housekeeping Cleaners	12.04	Waiters and Waitresses	13.13

Note: Wage data covers the Albuquerque, NM Metropolitan Statistical Area; (*) Hourly wages were calculated from annual wage data based on a 40 hour work week; n/a not available.
Source: Bureau of Labor Statistics, Metro Area Occupational Employment & Wage Estimates, May 2021

Employment by Industry

Sector	MSA[1]		U.S.
	Number of Employees	Percent of Total	Percent of Total
Construction, Mining, and Logging	26,200	6.6	5.3
Education and Health Services	66,700	16.7	16.0
Financial Activities	19,000	4.8	5.9
Government	81,800	20.5	14.9
Information	5,400	1.4	1.9
Leisure and Hospitality	41,300	10.3	9.8
Manufacturing	16,900	4.2	8.4
Other Services	11,200	2.8	3.7
Professional and Business Services	63,700	15.9	14.6
Retail Trade	43,700	10.9	10.7
Transportation, Warehousing, and Utilities	12,700	3.2	4.8
Wholesale Trade	11,100	2.8	3.8

Note: Figures are non-farm employment as of December 2021. Figures are not seasonally adjusted and include workers 16 years of age and older; (1) Figures cover the Albuquerque, NM Metropolitan Statistical Area
Source: Bureau of Labor Statistics, Current Employment Statistics, Employment, Hours, and Earnings

Employment by Occupation

Occupation Classification	City (%)	MSA[1] (%)	U.S. (%)
Management, Business, Science, and Arts	43.2	41.1	39.5
Natural Resources, Construction, and Maintenance	7.1	8.7	8.7
Production, Transportation, and Material Moving	7.6	8.7	13.1
Sales and Office	23.1	22.9	21.3
Service	18.9	18.6	17.4

Note: Figures cover employed civilians 16 years of age and older; (1) Figures cover the Albuquerque, NM Metropolitan Statistical Area
Source: U.S. Census Bureau, 2016-2020 American Community Survey 5-Year Estimates

Occupations with Greatest Projected Employment Growth: 2021 – 2023

Occupation[1]	2021 Employment	2023 Projected Employment	Numeric Employment Change	Percent Employment Change
Roustabouts, Oil and Gas	2,630	3,890	1,260	47.9
Fast Food and Counter Workers	21,960	23,180	1,220	5.6
Heavy and Tractor-Trailer Truck Drivers	11,480	12,610	1,130	9.8
Light Truck or Delivery Services Drivers	5,120	6,100	980	19.1
Laborers and Freight, Stock, and Material Movers, Hand	9,410	10,370	960	10.2
Cooks, Restaurant	6,360	7,140	780	12.3
Service Unit Operators, Oil, Gas, and Mining	2,260	3,020	760	33.6
Construction Laborers	11,940	12,670	730	6.1
Waiters and Waitresses	11,110	11,830	720	6.5
First-Line Supervisors of Construction Trades and Extraction Workers	6,820	7,530	710	10.4

Note: Projections cover New Mexico; (1) Sorted by numeric employment change
Source: www.projectionscentral.com, State Occupational Projections, 2021–2023 Short-Term Projections

Fastest-Growing Occupations: 2021 – 2023

Occupation[1]	2021 Employment	2023 Projected Employment	Numeric Employment Change	Percent Employment Change
Derrick Operators, Oil and Gas	540	810	270	50.0
Roustabouts, Oil and Gas	2,630	3,890	1,260	47.9
Rotary Drill Operators, Oil and Gas	720	1,050	330	45.8
Service Unit Operators, Oil, Gas, and Mining	2,260	3,020	760	33.6
Helpers—Extraction Workers	150	200	50	33.3
Ushers, Lobby Attendants, and Ticket Takers	260	340	80	30.8
Light Truck or Delivery Services Drivers	5,120	6,100	980	19.1
Wellhead Pumpers	280	330	50	17.9
Petroleum Engineers	340	400	60	17.6
Hotel, Motel, and Resort Desk Clerks	1,330	1,560	230	17.3

Note: Projections cover New Mexico; (1) Sorted by percent employment change and excludes occupations with numeric employment change less than 50
Source: www.projectionscentral.com, State Occupational Projections, 2021–2023 Short-Term Projections

TAXES

State Corporate Income Tax Rates

State	Tax Rate (%)	Income Brackets ($)	Num. of Brackets	Financial Institution Tax Rate (%)[a]	Federal Income Tax Ded.
New Mexico	4.8 - 5.9	500,000	2	4.8 - 5.9	No

Note: Tax rates as of January 1, 2022; (a) Rates listed are the corporate income tax rate applied to financial institutions or excise taxes based on income. Some states have other taxes based upon the value of deposits or shares.
Source: Federation of Tax Administrators, State Corporate Income Tax Rates, January 1, 2022

State Individual Income Tax Rates

State	Tax Rate (%)	Income Brackets ($)	Personal Exemptions ($)			Standard Ded. ($)	
			Single	Married	Depend.	Single	Married
New Mexico	1.7 - 5.9	5,500 - 210,000 (q)	(d)	(d)	(d)	12,950	25,900 (d)

Note: Tax rates as of January 1, 2022; Local- and county-level taxes are not included; Federal income tax is not deductible on state income tax returns; (d) These states use the personal exemption/standard deduction amounts provided in the federal Internal Revenue Code; (q) The income brackets reported for New Mexico are for single individuals. For married couples filing jointly, the same tax rates apply to income brackets ranging from $8,000 to $315,000.
Source: Federation of Tax Administrators, State Individual Income Tax Rates, January 1, 2022

Various State Sales and Excise Tax Rates

State	State Sales Tax (%)	Gasoline[1] (¢/gal.)	Cigarette[2] ($/pack)	Spirits[3] ($/gal.)	Wine[4] ($/gal.)	Beer[5] ($/gal.)	Recreational Marijuana (%)
New Mexico	5.125	18.88	2	6.06	1.7	0.41	(n)

Note: All tax rates as of January 1, 2022; (1) The American Petroleum Institute has developed a methodology for determining the average tax rate on a gallon of fuel. Rates may include any of the following: excise taxes, environmental fees, storage tank fees, other fees or taxes, general sales tax, and local taxes; (2) The federal excise tax of $1.0066 per pack and local taxes are not included; (3) Rates are those applicable to off-premise sales of 40% alcohol by volume (a.b.v.) distilled spirits in 750ml containers. Local excise taxes are excluded; (4) Rates are those applicable to off-premise sales of 11% a.b.v. non-carbonated wine in 750ml containers; (5) Rates are those applicable to off-premise sales of 4.7% a.b.v. beer in 12 ounce containers; (n) 12% excise tax (retail price)
Source: Tax Foundation, 2022 Facts & Figures: How Does Your State Compare?

State Business Tax Climate Index Rankings

State	Overall Rank	Corporate Tax Rank	Individual Income Tax Rank	Sales Tax Rank	Property Tax Rank	Unemployment Insurance Tax Rank
New Mexico	28	12	36	41	2	8

Note: The index is a measure of how each state's tax laws affect economic performance. The lower the rank, the more favorable a state's tax system is for business. States without a given tax are given a ranking of 1. The scores/rankings for the District of Columbia do not affect other states. The 2022 index represents the tax climate as of July 1, 2021.
Source: Tax Foundation, State Business Tax Climate Index 2022

TRANSPORTATION

Means of Transportation to Work

Area	Car/Truck/Van		Public Transportation			Bicycle	Walked	Other Means	Worked at Home
	Drove Alone	Car-pooled	Bus	Subway	Railroad				
City	78.5	9.5	1.6	0.0	0.1	1.0	1.9	1.1	6.5
MSA[1]	78.8	9.7	1.2	0.0	0.2	0.7	1.6	1.1	6.8
U.S.	74.9	8.9	2.2	1.7	0.5	0.5	2.6	1.4	7.3

Note: Figures are percentages and cover workers 16 years of age and older; (1) Figures cover the Albuquerque, NM Metropolitan Statistical Area
Source: U.S. Census Bureau, 2016-2020 American Community Survey 5-Year Estimates

Travel Time to Work

Area	Less Than 10 Minutes	10 to 19 Minutes	20 to 29 Minutes	30 to 44 Minutes	45 to 59 Minutes	60 to 89 Minutes	90 Minutes or More
City	11.0	35.6	27.9	18.0	3.2	2.8	1.4
MSA[1]	10.7	31.5	26.0	20.5	5.9	3.7	1.7
U.S.	12.3	28.4	20.9	20.9	8.3	6.4	2.9

Note: Note: Figures are percentages and include workers 16 years old and over; (1) Figures cover the Albuquerque, NM Metropolitan Statistical Area
Source: U.S. Census Bureau, 2016-2020 American Community Survey 5-Year Estimates

Key Congestion Measures

Measure	1990	2000	2010	2015	2020
Annual Hours of Delay, Total (000)	6,255	15,165	16,874	19,390	10,229
Annual Hours of Delay, Per Auto Commuter	21	39	37	43	22
Annual Congestion Cost, Per Auto Commuter ($)	406	620	877	944	516

Note: Covers the Albuquerque NM urban area
Source: Texas A&M Transportation Institute, 2021 Urban Mobility Report

Freeway Travel Time Index

Measure	1985	1990	1995	2000	2005	2010	2015	2020
Urban Area Index[1]	1.07	1.07	1.11	1.14	1.14	1.15	1.16	1.06
Urban Area Rank[1,2]	48	74	66	62	73	65	57	75

Note: Freeway Travel Time Index—the ratio of travel time in the peak period to the travel time at free-flow conditions. For example, a value of 1.30 indicates a 20-minute free-flow trip takes 26 minutes in the peak (20 minutes x 1.30 = 26 minutes); (1) Covers the Albuquerque NM urban area; (2) Rank is based on 101 larger urban areas (#1 = highest travel time index)
Source: Texas A&M Transportation Institute, 2021 Urban Mobility Report

Public Transportation

Agency Name / Mode of Transportation	Vehicles Operated in Maximum Service[1]	Annual Unlinked Passenger Trips[2] (in thous.)	Annual Passenger Miles[3] (in thous.)
ABQ Ride			
Bus (directly operated)	131	6,824.4	24,138.0
Bus Rapid Transit (directly operated)	16	824.9	3,241.8
Demand Response (directly operated)	62	196.4	2,110.8

Note: (1) Number of revenue vehicles operated by the given mode and type of service to meet the annual maximum service requirement. This is the revenue vehicle count during the peak season of the year; on the week and day that maximum service is provided. Vehicles operated in maximum service (VOMS) exclude atypical days and one-time special events; (2) Number of passengers who boarded public transportation vehicles. Passengers are counted each time they board a vehicle no matter how many vehicles they use to travel from their origin to their destination. (3) Sum of the distances ridden by all passengers during the entire fiscal year.
Source: Federal Transit Administration, National Transit Database, 2020

Air Transportation

Airport Name and Code / Type of Service	Passenger Airlines[1]	Passenger Enplanements	Freight Carriers[2]	Freight (lbs)
Albuquerque International (ABQ)				
Domestic service (U.S. carriers - 2021)	24	1,711,715	13	62,826,513
International service (U.S. carriers - 2020)	1	2	0	0

Note: (1) Includes all U.S.-based major, minor and commuter airlines that carried at least one passenger during the year; (2) Includes all U.S.-based airlines and freight carriers that transported at least one pound of freight during the year.
Source: Bureau of Transportation Statistics, The Intermodal Transportation Database, Air Carriers: T-100 Domestic Market (U.S. Carriers), 2021; Bureau of Transportation Statistics, The Intermodal Transportation Database, Air Carriers: T-100 International Market (U.S. Carriers), 2020

BUSINESSES

Major Business Headquarters

Company Name	Industry	Rankings	
		Fortune[1]	Forbes[2]
No companies listed	-	-	-

Note: (1) Companies that produce a 10-K are ranked 1 to 500 based on 2020 revenue; (2) All private companies with at least $2 billion in annual revenue through the end of their most current fiscal year are ranked 1 to 225; companies listed are headquartered in the city; dashes indicate no ranking
Source: Fortune, "Fortune 500," 2021; Forbes, "America's Largest Private Companies," 2021

Fastest-Growing Businesses

According to *Inc.*, Albuquerque is home to one of America's 500 fastest-growing private companies: **BrandCentric Ecommerce** (#288). Criteria: must be an independent, privately-held, for-profit, U.S. corporation, proprietorship or partnership as of December 31, 2020; revenues must be at least $100,000 in 2017 and $2 million in 2020; must have four-year operating/sales history. *Inc., "America's 500 Fastest-Growing Private Companies," 2021*

According to *Initiative for a Competitive Inner City (ICIC)*, Albuquerque is home to one of America's 100 fastest-growing "inner city" companies: **Environment Control of Bernalillo County** (#31). Criteria for inclusion: company must be headquartered in or have 51 percent or more of its physical operations in an economically distressed urban area; must be an independent, for-profit corporation, partnership or proprietorship; must have 10 or more employees and have a five-year sales history that includes sales of at least $200,000 in the base year and at least $1 million in the current year with no decrease in sales over the two most recent years. Companies were ranked overall by revenue growth over the five-year period between 2016 and 2020. *Initiative for a Competitive Inner City (ICIC), "Inner City 100 Companies," 2021*

According to Deloitte, Albuquerque is home to one of North America's 500 fastest-growing high-technology companies: **RS21** (#478). Companies are ranked by percentage growth in revenue over a four-year period. Criteria for inclusion: company must be headquartered within North America; must own proprietary intellectual property or technology that is sold to customers in products that contributes to a significant portion of the company's operating revenue; must have been in business for a minumum of four years with 2017 operating revenues of at least $50,000 USD/CD and 2020 operating revenues of at least $5 million USD/CD. *Deloitte, 2021 Technology Fast 500™*

Living Environment

COST OF LIVING

Cost of Living Index

Composite Index	Groceries	Housing	Utilities	Trans-portation	Health Care	Misc. Goods/ Services
93.1	90.5	88.4	93.2	99.9	95.0	97.6

Note: The Cost of Living Index measures regional differences in the cost of consumer goods and services, excluding taxes and non-consumer expenditures, for professional and managerial households in the top income quintile. It is based on more than 50,000 prices covering almost 60 different items for which prices are collected three times a year by chambers of commerce, economic development organizations or university applied economic centers in each participating urban area. The numbers shown should be read as a percentage above or below the national average of 100. For example, a value of 115.4 in the groceries column indicates that grocery prices are 15.4% higher than the national average. Small differences in the index numbers should not be interpreted as significant; Figures cover the Albuquerque NM urban area.
Source: The Council for Community and Economic Research, Cost of Living Index, 2021

Grocery Prices

Area[1]	T-Bone Steak ($/pound)	Frying Chicken ($/pound)	Whole Milk ($/half gal.)	Eggs ($/dozen)	Orange Juice ($/64 oz.)	Coffee ($/11.5 oz.)
City[2]	12.04	1.09	1.81	1.49	3.60	4.14
Avg.	12.82	1.40	2.22	1.57	3.59	4.30
Min.	8.91	0.91	1.29	0.75	2.87	3.02
Max.	21.35	2.69	3.92	3.86	5.49	8.11

Note: (1) Values for the local area are compared with the average, minimum and maximum values for all 285 areas in the Cost of Living Index; (2) Figures cover the Albuquerque NM urban area; ***T-Bone Steak*** *(price per pound);* ***Frying Chicken*** *(price per pound, whole fryer);* ***Whole Milk*** *(half gallon carton);* ***Eggs*** *(price per dozen, Grade A, large);* ***Orange Juice*** *(64 oz. Tropicana or Florida Natural);* ***Coffee*** *(11.5 oz. can, vacuum-packed, Maxwell House, Hills Bros, or Folgers).*
Source: The Council for Community and Economic Research, Cost of Living Index, 2021

Housing and Utility Costs

Area[1]	New Home Price ($)	Apartment Rent ($/month)	All Electric ($/month)	Part Electric ($/month)	Other Energy ($/month)	Telephone ($/month)
City[2]	365,948	951	-	106.17	44.01	187.47
Avg.	398,393	1,217	171.38	100.83	69.67	187.75
Min.	212,799	534	96.71	31.56	27.15	173.01
Max.	2,354,006	4,438	369.53	277.33	303.87	206.73

Note: (1) Values for the local area are compared with the average, minimum and maximum values for all 285 areas in the Cost of Living Index; (2) Figures cover the Albuquerque NM urban area; ***New Home Price*** *(2,400 sf living area, 8,000 sf lot, in urban area with full utilities);* ***Apartment Rent*** *(950 sf 2 bedroom/1.5 or 2 bath, unfurnished, excluding all utilities except water);* ***All Electric*** *(average monthly cost for an all-electric home);* ***Part Electric*** *(average monthly cost for a part-electric home);* ***Other Energy*** *(average monthly cost for natural gas, fuel oil, coal, wood, and any other forms of energy except electricity);* ***Telephone*** *(price includes the base monthly rate plus taxes and fees for three lines of mobile phone service).*
Source: The Council for Community and Economic Research, Cost of Living Index, 2021

Health Care, Transportation, and Other Costs

Area[1]	Doctor ($/visit)	Dentist ($/visit)	Optometrist ($/visit)	Gasoline ($/gallon)	Beauty Salon ($/visit)	Men's Shirt ($)
City[2]	107.50	99.30	108.72	2.77	42.21	26.60
Avg.	118.16	101.04	109.44	2.71	40.63	30.77
Min.	35.04	55.56	51.17	2.17	18.59	11.32
Max.	231.10	165.12	256.81	4.11	85.33	63.03

Note: (1) Values for the local area are compared with the average, minimum and maximum values for all 285 areas in the Cost of Living Index; (2) Figures cover the Albuquerque NM urban area; ***Doctor*** *(general practitioners routine exam of an established patient);* ***Dentist*** *(adult teeth cleaning and periodic oral examination);* ***Optometrist*** *(full vision eye exam for established adult patient);* ***Gasoline*** *(one gallon regular unleaded, national brand, including all taxes, cash price at self-service pump if available);* ***Beauty Salon*** *(woman's shampoo, trim, and blow-dry);* ***Men's Shirt*** *(cotton/polyester dress shirt, pinpoint weave, long sleeves).*
Source: The Council for Community and Economic Research, Cost of Living Index, 2021

HOUSING

Homeownership Rate

Area	2013 (%)	2014 (%)	2015 (%)	2016 (%)	2017 (%)	2018 (%)	2019 (%)	2020 (%)	2021 (%)
MSA[1]	65.9	64.4	64.3	66.9	67.0	67.9	70.0	69.5	66.5
U.S.	65.1	64.5	63.7	63.4	63.9	64.4	64.6	66.6	65.5

Note: (1) Figures cover the Albuquerque, NM Metropolitan Statistical Area
Source: U.S. Census Bureau, Housing Vacancies and Homeownership Annual Statistics: 2013-2021

House Price Index (HPI)

Area	National Ranking²	Quarterly Change (%)	One-Year Change (%)	Five-Year Change (%)	Since 1991Q1 (%)
MSA¹	109	3.52	18.66	43.07	212.14
U.S.³	–	3.33	17.54	54.45	258.04

Note: The HPI is a weighted repeat sales index. It measures average price changes in repeat sales or refinancings on the same properties. This information is obtained by reviewing repeat mortgage transactions on single-family properties whose mortgages have been purchased or securitized by Fannie Mae or Freddie Mac since January 1975; (1) Figures cover the Albuquerque, NM Metropolitan Statistical Area; (2) Rankings are based on annual percentage change for all metro areas containing at least 15,000 transactions over the last 10 years and ranges from 1 to 268; (3) figures based on a weighted average of Census Division estimates using a seasonally adjusted, purchase-only index; all figures are for the period ending December 31, 2021
Source: Federal Housing Finance Agency, Change in FHFA Metropolitan Area House Price Indexes, 2021Q4

Median Single-Family Home Prices

Area	2019	2020	2021ᵖ	Percent Change 2020 to 2021
MSA¹	225.0	248.1	292.5	17.9
U.S. Average	274.6	300.2	353.4	17.7

Note: Figures are median sales prices of existing single-family homes in thousands of dollars; (p) preliminary; (1) Figures cover the Albuquerque, NM Metropolitan Statistical Area
Source: National Association of Realtors, Median Sales Price of Existing Single-Family Homes for Metropolitan Areas, 4th Quarter 2021

Qualifying Income Based on Median Sales Price of Existing Single-Family Homes

Area	With 5% Down ($)	With 10% Down ($)	With 20% Down ($)
MSA¹	60,602	57,413	51,034
U.S. Average	70,699	66,978	59,536

Note: Figures are preliminary; Qualifying income is based on a mortgage rate of 3.13%. Monthly principal and interest payment is limited to 25% of income; (1) Figures cover the Albuquerque, NM Metropolitan Statistical Area
Source: National Association of Realtors, Qualifying Income Based on Median Sales Price of Existing Single-Family Homes for Metropolitan Areas, 4th Quarter 2021

Home Value Distribution

Area	Under $50,000	$50,000 -$99,999	$100,000 -$149,999	$150,000 -$199,999	$200,000 -$299,999	$300,000 -$499,999	$500,000 -$999,999	$1,000,000 or more
City	4.6	4.0	15.5	24.4	31.2	16.6	3.4	0.4
MSA¹	6.0	6.7	15.3	22.2	27.4	16.4	5.1	1.0
U.S.	6.6	11.0	12.3	13.6	20.0	20.5	12.3	3.7

Note: Figures are percentages and cover owner-occupied housing units; (1) Figures cover the Albuquerque, NM Metropolitan Statistical Area
Source: U.S. Census Bureau, 2016-2020 American Community Survey 5-Year Estimates

Year Housing Structure Built

Area	2010 or Later	2000 -2009	1990 -1999	1980 -1989	1970 -1979	1960 -1969	1950 -1959	1940 -1949	Before 1940	Median Year
City	4.8	15.7	15.4	15.2	19.3	10.1	11.8	4.5	3.0	1981
MSA¹	4.9	16.9	18.1	16.8	18.0	9.0	9.3	3.8	3.2	1984
U.S.	6.2	13.6	13.9	13.4	15.0	10.5	10.2	4.8	12.4	1978

Note: Figures are percentages except for Median Year; Note: (1) Figures cover the Albuquerque, NM Metropolitan Statistical Area
Source: U.S. Census Bureau, 2016-2020 American Community Survey 5-Year Estimates

Gross Monthly Rent

Area	Under $500	$500 -$999	$1,000 -$1,499	$1,500 -$1,999	$2,000 -$2,499	$2,500 -$2,999	$3,000 and up	Median ($)
City	8.5	52.7	30.1	6.9	1.0	0.3	0.4	889
MSA¹	8.5	50.9	31.2	7.7	1.1	0.3	0.4	908
U.S.	8.9	34.3	30.2	14.9	6.2	2.6	2.8	1,096

Note: Figures are percentages except for Median; Gross rent is the contract rent plus the estimated average monthly cost of utilities (electricity, gas, and water and sewer) and fuels (oil, coal, kerosene, wood, etc.) if these are paid by the renter (or paid for the renter by someone else); (1) Figures cover the Albuquerque, NM Metropolitan Statistical Area
Source: U.S. Census Bureau, 2016-2020 American Community Survey 5-Year Estimates

HEALTH

Health Risk Factors

Category	MSA[1] (%)	U.S. (%)
Adults aged 18–64 who have any kind of health care coverage	87.4	86.8
Adults who reported being in good or better health	87.1	86.7
Adults who are current smokers	16.5	15.5
Adults who currently use chewing tobacco, snuff, or snus	2.5	3.7
Adults who are heavy drinkers[2]	7.5	6.7
Adults who are binge drinkers[3]	16.1	15.7
Adults who are overweight (BMI 25.0 - 29.9)	36.2	35.2
Adults who are obese (BMI 30.0 - 99.8)	29.5	31.9
Adults who participated in any physical activities in the past month	79.2	77.6
Adults who always or nearly always wears a seat belt	96.6	94.2

Note: (1) Figures cover the Albuquerque, NM Metropolitan Statistical Area; (2) Heavy drinkers are classified as adult men having more than 14 drinks per week and adult women having more than 7 drinks per week; (3) Binge drinkers are classified as males having five or more drinks on one occasion or females having four or more drinks on one occasion
Source: Centers for Disease Control and Prevention, Behaviorial Risk Factor Surveillance System, SMART: Selected Metropolitan Area Risk Trends, 2020

Acute and Chronic Health Conditions

Category	MSA[1] (%)	U.S. (%)
Adults who have ever been told they had a heart attack	3.8	4.3
Adults who have ever been told they have angina or coronary heart disease	3.7	4.0
Adults who have ever been told they had a stroke	2.5	2.8
Adults who have ever been told they have asthma	15.1	14.2
Adults who have ever been told they have arthritis	24.9	24.5
Adults who have ever been told they have diabetes[2]	11.9	10.6
Adults who have ever been told they had skin cancer	6.1	6.4
Adults who have ever been told they had any other types of cancer	5.4	6.8
Adults who have ever been told they have COPD	4.8	6.2
Adults who have ever been told they have kidney disease	2.7	2.9
Adults who have ever been told they have a form of depression	19.4	19.6

Note: (1) Figures cover the Albuquerque, NM Metropolitan Statistical Area; (2) Figures do not include pregnancy-related, borderline, or pre-diabetes
Source: Centers for Disease Control and Prevention, Behaviorial Risk Factor Surveillance System, SMART: Selected Metropolitan Area Risk Trends, 2020

Health Screening and Vaccination Rates

Category	MSA[1] (%)	U.S. (%)
Adults 50-75 who have had a blood stool test within the past year	9.0	9.3
Adults aged 65+ who have had flu shot within the past year	70.7	67.9
Adults aged 65+ who have ever had a pneumonia vaccination	76.9	72.2
Adults who have ever been tested for HIV	35.5	37.1
Women aged 21-65 who have had a pap test in the past three years	76.2	77.7
Men aged 40+ who have had a PSA test within the past two years	25.9	31.8
Women aged 40+ who have had a mammogram within the past two years	68.5	71.5

Note: (1) Figures cover the Albuquerque, NM Metropolitan Statistical Area.
Source: Centers for Disease Control and Prevention, Behaviorial Risk Factor Surveillance System, SMART: Selected Metropolitan Area Risk Trends, 2020

Disability Status

Category	MSA[1] (%)	U.S. (%)
Adults who reported being deaf	6.7	6.8
Are you blind or have serious difficulty seeing, even when wearing glasses?	5.3	4.7
Do you have difficulty doing errands alone?	7.0	6.3
Do you have difficulty dressing or bathing?	3.4	3.0
Do you have serious difficulty concentrating/remembering/making decisions?	10.4	10.8
Do you have serious difficulty walking or climbing stairs?	12.5	11.9

Note: (1) Figures cover the Albuquerque, NM Metropolitan Statistical Area.
Source: Centers for Disease Control and Prevention, Behaviorial Risk Factor Surveillance System, SMART: Selected Metropolitan Area Risk Trends, 2020

Mortality Rates for the Top 10 Causes of Death in the U.S.

ICD-10[a] Sub-Chapter	ICD-10[a] Code	Age-Adjusted Mortality Rate[1] per 100,000 population	
		County[2]	U.S.
Malignant neoplasms	C00-C97	130.0	146.4
Ischaemic heart diseases	I20-I25	109.9	90.2
Other forms of heart disease	I30-I51	35.5	51.9
Other degenerative diseases of the nervous system	G30-G31	32.2	39.7
Other external causes of accidental injury	W00-X59	63.2	38.7
Chronic lower respiratory diseases	J40-J47	39.5	38.1
Cerebrovascular diseases	I60-I69	37.6	37.6
Organic, including symptomatic, mental disorders	F01-F09	26.3	29.4
Hypertensive diseases	I10-I15	12.9	26.1
Diabetes mellitus	E10-E14	19.5	22.6

Note: (a) ICD-10 = International Classification of Diseases 10th Revision; (1) Mortality rates are a three-year average covering 2018-2020; (2) Figures cover Bernalillo County.
Source: Centers for Disease Control and Prevention, National Center for Health Statistics. Underlying Cause of Death 1999-2020 on CDC WONDER Online Database

Mortality Rates for Selected Causes of Death

ICD-10[a] Sub-Chapter	ICD-10[a] Code	Age-Adjusted Mortality Rate[1] per 100,000 population	
		County[2]	U.S.
Assault	X85-Y09	12.4	6.5
Diseases of the liver	K70-K76	29.0	15.3
Human immunodeficiency virus (HIV) disease	B20-B24	1.4	1.4
Influenza and pneumonia	J09-J18	12.0	13.4
Intentional self-harm	X60-X84	23.4	13.9
Malnutrition	E40-E46	11.1	2.9
Obesity and other hyperalimentation	E65-E68	3.1	2.4
Renal failure	N17-N19	9.5	12.5
Transport accidents	V01-V99	16.4	12.5
Viral hepatitis	B15-B19	1.7	1.0

Note: (a) ICD-10 = International Classification of Diseases 10th Revision; (1) Mortality rates are a three-year average covering 2018-2020; (2) Figures cover Bernalillo County; Data are suppressed when the data meet the criteria for confidentiality constraints; Mortality rates are flagged as unreliable when the rate would be calculated with a numerator of 20 or less.
Source: Centers for Disease Control and Prevention, National Center for Health Statistics. Underlying Cause of Death 1999-2020 on CDC WONDER Online Database

Health Insurance Coverage

Area	With Health Insurance	With Private Health Insurance	With Public Health Insurance	Without Health Insurance	Population Under Age 19 Without Health Insurance
City	92.5	60.8	44.1	7.5	3.8
MSA[1]	92.1	60.2	45.3	7.9	4.6
U.S.	91.3	68.1	35.3	8.7	5.2

Note: Figures are percentages that cover the civilian noninstitutionalized population; (1) Figures cover the Albuquerque, NM Metropolitan Statistical Area
Source: U.S. Census Bureau, 2016-2020 American Community Survey 5-Year Estimates

Number of Medical Professionals

Area	MDs[3]	DOs[3,4]	Dentists	Podiatrists	Chiropractors	Optometrists
County[1] (number)	3,143	141	583	64	169	113
County[1] (rate[2])	464.6	20.8	86.2	9.5	25.0	16.7
U.S. (rate[2])	285.1	23.0	71.1	6.2	28.2	17.0

35001
Note: Data as of 2020 unless noted; (1) Data covers Bernalillo County; (2) Rate per 100,000 population; (3) Data as of 2019 and includes all active, non-federal physicians; (4) Doctor of Osteopathic Medicine
Source: U.S. Department of Health and Human Services, Health Resources and Services Administration, Bureau of Health Professions, Area Resource File (ARF) 2020-2021

EDUCATION

Public School District Statistics

District Name	Schls	Pupils	Pupil/ Teacher Ratio	Minority Pupils[1] (%)	LEP/ELL[2] (%)	IEP[3] (%)
Albuquerque Public Schools	175	88,312	14.3	78.9	17.3	18.5

Note: Table includes school districts with 2,000 or more students; (1) Percentage of students that are not non-Hispanic white; (2) Percentage of students that are Limited English Proficient (LEP) or English Language Learners (ELL) (2018-19); (3) Percentage of students that have an Individualized Education Program (IEP).
Source: U.S. Department of Education, National Center for Education Statistics, Common Core of Data, Local Education Agency (School District) Universe Survey: School Year 2019-2020

Best High Schools

According to *U.S. News,* Albuquerque is home to two of the top 500 high schools in the U.S.: **Albuquerque Institute of Math and Science** (#82); **Cottonwood Classical Prep** (#283). Nearly 18,000 public, magnet and charter schools were ranked based on their performance on state assessments and how well they prepare students for college. *U.S. News & World Report, "Best High Schools 2021"*

Highest Level of Education

Area	Less than H.S.	H.S. Diploma	Some College, No Deg.	Associate Degree	Bachelor's Degree	Master's Degree	Prof. School Degree	Doctorate Degree
City	9.1	22.3	23.3	8.8	20.4	10.9	2.7	2.4
MSA[1]	10.4	24.3	23.4	8.9	18.5	10.1	2.3	2.1
U.S.	11.5	26.7	20.3	8.6	20.2	9.1	2.2	1.5

Note: Figures cover persons age 25 and over; (1) Figures cover the Albuquerque, NM Metropolitan Statistical Area
Source: U.S. Census Bureau, 2016-2020 American Community Survey 5-Year Estimates

Educational Attainment by Race

Area	High School Graduate or Higher (%)					Bachelor's Degree or Higher (%)				
	Total	White	Black	Asian	Hisp.[2]	Total	White	Black	Asian	Hisp.[2]
City	90.9	92.4	92.9	87.9	85.0	36.5	39.3	35.2	52.7	23.5
MSA[1]	89.6	91.5	91.5	89.4	83.1	33.0	36.1	34.0	52.3	20.7
U.S.	88.5	90.7	86.7	87.3	70.3	32.9	34.4	22.6	55.0	17.6

Note: Figures shown cover persons 25 years old and over; (1) Figures cover the Albuquerque, NM Metropolitan Statistical Area; (2) People of Hispanic origin can be of any race
Source: U.S. Census Bureau, 2016-2020 American Community Survey 5-Year Estimates

School Enrollment by Grade and Control

Area	Preschool (%)		Kindergarten (%)		Grades 1 - 4 (%)		Grades 5 - 8 (%)		Grades 9 - 12 (%)	
	Public	Private	Public	Private	Public	Private	Public	Private	Public	Private
City	59.5	40.5	84.5	15.5	89.3	10.7	91.1	8.9	91.3	8.7
MSA[1]	60.9	39.1	82.9	17.1	87.7	12.3	89.9	10.1	91.0	9.0
U.S.	58.9	41.1	86.9	13.1	89.0	11.0	89.0	11.0	89.7	10.3

Note: Figures shown cover persons 3 years old and over; (1) Figures cover the Albuquerque, NM Metropolitan Statistical Area
Source: U.S. Census Bureau, 2016-2020 American Community Survey 5-Year Estimates

Higher Education

Four-Year Colleges			Two-Year Colleges			Medical Schools[1]	Law Schools[2]	Voc/ Tech[3]
Public	Private Non-profit	Private For-profit	Public	Private Non-profit	Private For-profit			
1	0	4	3	0	3	1	1	6

Note: Figures cover institutions located within the Albuquerque, NM Metropolitan Statistical Area and include main campuses only; (1) includes schools accredited by the Liaison Committee on Medical Education and the American Osteopathic Association's Commission on Osteopathic College Accreditation; (2) includes ABA-accredited schools, schools with provisional ABA accreditation, and state accredited schools; (3) includes all schools with programs that are less than 2 years.
Source: National Center for Education Statistics, Integrated Postsecondary Education System (IPEDS), 2020-21; Wikipedia, List of Medical Schools in the United States, accessed April 11, 2022; Wikipedia, List of Law Schools in the United States, accessed April 11, 2022

According to *U.S. News & World Report,* the Albuquerque, NM metro area is home to one of the top 200 national universities in the U.S.: **University of New Mexico** (#196 tie). The indicators used to capture academic quality fall into a number of categories: assessment by administrators at peer institutions; retention of students; faculty resources; student selectivity; financial resources; alumni giving; high school counselor ratings of colleges; and graduation rate. *U.S. News & World Report, "America's Best Colleges 2022"*

EMPLOYERS

Major Employers

Company Name	Industry
Central New Mexico Community College	Vocational schools
City of Albuquerque	Municipal government
City of Albuquerque Police Department	Municipal police
Jack Henry & Associates	Computers
Laguna Development Corporation	Grocery stores, independent
Mediplex of Massachusetts	Nursing home, exc skilled & intermediate care facility
Sandia Corporation	Noncommercial research organizations
The Boeing Company	Aircraft
U.S. Fish and Wildlife Service	Fish & wildlife conservation agency, government
United States Department of Energy	Energy development & conservation agency, government
United States Department of the Air Force	Testing laboratories
University of New Mexico	University
University of New Mexico Hospital	General medical & surgical hospitals
USAF	U.S. military
Veterans Health Administration	Administration of veterans' affiars
Veterans Hospital	General medical & surgical hospitals

Note: Companies shown are located within the Albuquerque, NM Metropolitan Statistical Area.
Source: Hoovers.com; Wikipedia

PUBLIC SAFETY

Crime Rate

Area	Total Crime	Violent Crime Rate				Property Crime Rate		
		Murder	Rape[3]	Robbery	Aggrav. Assault	Burglary	Larceny -Theft	Motor Vehicle Theft
City	6,355.7	14.2	78.5	256.0	994.9	902.9	3,225.8	883.3
Suburbs[1]	2,025.9	1.9	34.6	40.4	405.3	354.2	870.1	319.4
Metro[2]	4,660.5	9.4	61.3	171.6	764.1	688.1	2,303.5	662.5
U.S.	2,356.7	6.5	38.4	73.9	279.7	314.2	1,398.0	246.0

Note: Figures are crimes per 100,000 population; (1) All areas within the metro area that are located outside the city limits; (2) Figures cover the Albuquerque, NM Metropolitan Statistical Area; (3) All figures shown were reported using the revised Uniform Crime Reporting (UCR) definition of rape.
Source: FBI Uniform Crime Reports, 2020

Hate Crimes

Area	Number of Quarters Reported	Number of Incidents per Bias Motivation					
		Race/Ethnicity/ Ancestry	Religion	Sexual Orientation	Disability	Gender	Gender Identity
City[1]	4	26	3	9	1	2	2
U.S.	4	5,227	1,244	1,110	130	75	266

Note: (1) Figures include one incident reported with more than one bias motivation.
Source: Federal Bureau of Investigation, Hate Crime Statistics 2020

Identity Theft Consumer Reports

Area	Reports	Reports per 100,000 Population	Rank[2]
MSA[1]	2,513	274	152
U.S.	1,434,676	432	-

Note: (1) Figures cover the Albuquerque, NM Metropolitan Statistical Area; (2) Rank ranges from 1 to 391 where 1 indicates greatest number of identity theft reports per 100,000 population
Source: Federal Trade Commission, Consumer Sentinel Network Data Book 2021

Fraud and Other Consumer Reports

Area	Reports	Reports per 100,000 Population	Rank[2]
MSA[1]	9,126	994	113
U.S.	4,328,977	1,304	-

Note: (1) Figures cover the Albuquerque, NM Metropolitan Statistical Area; (2) Rank ranges from 1 to 391 where 1 indicates greatest number of fraud and other consumer reports per 100,000 population
Source: Federal Trade Commission, Consumer Sentinel Network Data Book 2021

POLITICS

2020 Presidential Election Results

Area	Biden	Trump	Jorgensen	Hawkins	Other
Bernalillo County	61.0	36.6	1.5	0.5	0.4
U.S.	51.3	46.8	1.2	0.3	0.5

Note: Results are percentages and may not add to 100% due to rounding
Source: Dave Leip's Atlas of U.S. Presidential Elections

SPORTS

Professional Sports Teams

Team Name	League	Year Established
No teams are located in the metro area		

Source: Wikipedia, Major Professional Sports Teams of the United States and Canada, April 6, 2022

CLIMATE

Average and Extreme Temperatures

Temperature	Jan	Feb	Mar	Apr	May	Jun	Jul	Aug	Sep	Oct	Nov	Dec	Yr.
Extreme High (°F)	69	76	85	89	98	105	105	101	100	91	77	72	105
Average High (°F)	47	53	61	71	80	90	92	89	83	72	57	48	70
Average Temp. (°F)	35	40	47	56	65	75	79	76	70	58	45	36	57
Average Low (°F)	23	27	33	41	50	59	65	63	56	44	31	24	43
Extreme Low (°F)	-17	-5	8	19	28	40	52	50	37	21	-7	-7	-17

Note: Figures cover the years 1948-1992
Source: National Climatic Data Center, International Station Meteorological Climate Summary, 9/96

Average Precipitation/Snowfall/Humidity

Precip./Humidity	Jan	Feb	Mar	Apr	May	Jun	Jul	Aug	Sep	Oct	Nov	Dec	Yr.
Avg. Precip. (in.)	0.4	0.4	0.5	0.4	0.5	0.5	1.4	1.5	0.9	0.9	0.4	0.5	8.5
Avg. Snowfall (in.)	3	2	2	1	Tr	0	0	0	Tr	Tr	1	3	11
Avg. Rel. Hum. 5am (%)	68	64	55	48	48	45	60	65	61	60	63	68	59
Avg. Rel. Hum. 5pm (%)	41	33	25	20	19	18	27	30	29	29	35	43	29

Note: Figures cover the years 1948-1992; Tr = Trace amounts (<0.05 in. of rain; <0.5 in. of snow)
Source: National Climatic Data Center, International Station Meteorological Climate Summary, 9/96

Weather Conditions

Temperature			Daytime Sky			Precipitation		
10°F & below	32°F & below	90°F & above	Clear	Partly cloudy	Cloudy	0.01 inch or more precip.	0.1 inch or more snow/ice	Thunder-storms
4	114	65	140	160	65	60	9	38

Note: Figures are average number of days per year and cover the years 1948-1992
Source: National Climatic Data Center, International Station Meteorological Climate Summary, 9/96

HAZARDOUS WASTE

Superfund Sites

The Albuquerque, NM metro area is home to three sites on the EPA's Superfund National Priorities List: **AT&SF (Albuquerque)** (final); **Fruit Avenue Plume** (final); **South Valley** (final). There are a total of 1,165 Superfund sites with a status of proposed or final on the list in the U.S. *U.S. Environmental Protection Agency, National Priorities List, April 6, 2022*

AIR QUALITY

Air Quality Trends: Ozone

	1990	1995	2000	2005	2010	2016	2017	2018	2019	2020
MSA[1]	0.072	0.070	0.072	0.073	0.066	0.066	0.069	0.074	0.067	0.071
U.S.	0.090	0.091	0.082	0.080	0.074	0.070	0.069	0.070	0.066	0.068

Note: (1) Data covers the Albuquerque, NM Metropolitan Statistical Area. The values shown are the composite ozone concentration averages among trend sites based on the highest fourth daily maximum 8-hour concentration in parts per million. These trends are based on sites having an adequate record of monitoring data during the trend period. Data from exceptional events are included.
Source: U.S. Environmental Protection Agency, Air Quality Monitoring Information, "Air Quality Trends by City, 1990-2020"

Air Quality Index

Area	Percent of Days when Air Quality was...[2]					AQI Statistics[2]	
	Good	Moderate	Unhealthy for Sensitive Groups	Unhealthy	Very Unhealthy	Maximum	Median
MSA[1]	35.8	61.5	2.2	0.3	0.3	214	54

Note: (1) Data covers the Albuquerque, NM Metropolitan Statistical Area; (2) Based on 366 days with AQI data in 2020. Air Quality Index (AQI) is an index for reporting daily air quality. EPA calculates the AQI for five major air pollutants regulated by the Clean Air Act: ground-level ozone, particle pollution (aka particulate matter), carbon monoxide, sulfur dioxide, and nitrogen dioxide. The AQI runs from 0 to 500. The higher the AQI value, the greater the level of air pollution and the greater the health concern. There are six AQI categories: "Good" AQI is between 0 and 50. Air quality is considered satisfactory; "Moderate" AQI is between 51 and 100. Air quality is acceptable; "Unhealthy for Sensitive Groups" When AQI values are between 101 and 150, members of sensitive groups may experience health effects; "Unhealthy" When AQI values are between 151 and 200 everyone may begin to experience health effects; "Very Unhealthy" AQI values between 201 and 300 trigger a health alert; "Hazardous" AQI values over 300 trigger warnings of emergency conditions (not shown).
Source: U.S. Environmental Protection Agency, Air Quality Index Report, 2020

Air Quality Index Pollutants

Area	Percent of Days when AQI Pollutant was...[2]					
	Carbon Monoxide	Nitrogen Dioxide	Ozone	Sulfur Dioxide	Particulate Matter 2.5	Particulate Matter 10
MSA[1]	0.0	0.0	55.2	0.0	22.1	22.7

Note: (1) Data covers the Albuquerque, NM Metropolitan Statistical Area; (2) Based on 366 days with AQI data in 2020. The Air Quality Index (AQI) is an index for reporting daily air quality. EPA calculates the AQI for five major air pollutants regulated by the Clean Air Act: ground-level ozone, particle pollution (also known as particulate matter), carbon monoxide, sulfur dioxide, and nitrogen dioxide. The AQI runs from 0 to 500. The higher the AQI value, the greater the level of air pollution and the greater the health concern.
Source: U.S. Environmental Protection Agency, Air Quality Index Report, 2020

Maximum Air Pollutant Concentrations: Particulate Matter, Ozone, CO and Lead

	Particulate Matter 10 (ug/m^3)	Particulate Matter 2.5 Wtd AM (ug/m^3)	Particulate Matter 2.5 24-Hr (ug/m^3)	Ozone (ppm)	Carbon Monoxide (ppm)	Lead (ug/m^3)
MSA[1] Level	349	9.4	25	0.074	1	n/a
NAAQS[2]	150	15	35	0.075	9	0.15
Met NAAQS[2]	No	Yes	Yes	Yes	Yes	n/a

Note: (1) Data covers the Albuquerque, NM Metropolitan Statistical Area; Data from exceptional events are included; (2) National Ambient Air Quality Standards; ppm = parts per million; ug/m^3 = micrograms per cubic meter; n/a not available.
Concentrations: Particulate Matter 10 (coarse particulate)—highest second maximum 24-hour concentration; Particulate Matter 2.5 Wtd AM (fine particulate)—highest weighted annual mean concentration; Particulate Matter 2.5 24-Hour (fine particulate)—highest 98th percentile 24-hour concentration; Ozone—highest fourth daily maximum 8-hour concentration; Carbon Monoxide—highest second maximum non-overlapping 8-hour concentration; Lead—maximum running 3-month average
Source: U.S. Environmental Protection Agency, Air Quality Monitoring Information, "Air Quality Statistics by City, 2020"

Maximum Air Pollutant Concentrations: Nitrogen Dioxide and Sulfur Dioxide

	Nitrogen Dioxide AM (ppb)	Nitrogen Dioxide 1-Hr (ppb)	Sulfur Dioxide AM (ppb)	Sulfur Dioxide 1-Hr (ppb)	Sulfur Dioxide 24-Hr (ppb)
MSA[1] Level	8	41	n/a	3	n/a
NAAQS[2]	53	100	30	75	140
Met NAAQS[2]	Yes	Yes	n/a	Yes	n/a

Note: (1) Data covers the Albuquerque, NM Metropolitan Statistical Area; Data from exceptional events are included; (2) National Ambient Air Quality Standards; ppm = parts per million; ug/m^3 = micrograms per cubic meter; n/a not available.
Concentrations: Nitrogen Dioxide AM—highest arithmetic mean concentration; Nitrogen Dioxide 1-Hr—highest 98th percentile 1-hour daily maximum concentration; Sulfur Dioxide AM—highest annual mean concentration; Sulfur Dioxide 1-Hr—highest 99th percentile 1-hour daily maximum concentration; Sulfur Dioxide 24-Hr—highest second maximum 24-hour concentration
Source: U.S. Environmental Protection Agency, Air Quality Monitoring Information, "Air Quality Statistics by City, 2020"

Anchorage, Alaska

Background

Anchorage, in south central Alaska, is the state's largest city and a center for the state's communication, transportation, health care, and finance industries. Originally powered by the railroads and the fishing industry, Anchorage's economy has in more recent times been closely tied to petroleum production, which accounts for more than 20 percent of the nation's oil reserves.

This modern city lies in a spectacular natural setting, with the Chugach Mountain Range across its eastern skyline and the waters of the Cook Inlet to the west. The city boasts all the advantages of a dynamic urban center, while its residents enjoy a natural environment that teems with bear, moose, caribou, fox, eagles, wolves, Dall sheep, orcas, and beluga whales.

The city was incorporated in 1920 and grew slowly for several decades. During World War II, when airfields and roads were constructed to aid in the war effort, the population expanded dramatically; by 1946, Anchorage was home to more than 40,000 people.

In 1964, the region was hit by the strongest earthquake ever to strike North America. There was extensive damage and some loss of life, but the city was quickly rebuilt; in fact, reconstruction was so prompt, efficient, and successful that many look back on the period with considerable civic pride. Earthquakes are not uncommon to the region, and a moderate 5.7 event occurred in Anchorage in January 2009.

In 1951, Anchorage International Airport, now Ted Stevens International Airport (ANC), was completed, and the city became vital to the emerging air transport industry as new routes were created. Ted Stevens International Airport flies nearly 600 transcontinental cargo flights each week and is the busiest cargo airport in the country. Elmendorf Air Force Base at the northeast end of town, and Anchorage's pioneering development of bush aviation, which serves the entire interior of Alaska, further testify to the importance of air travel to the city's development. Also located at the airport are Fort Richardson Army Post and Kulis Air National Guard Base that together employ 8,500.

Oil in Alaska was first discovered in 1957, and 17 oil companies subsequently set up headquarters in Anchorage, giving the city a tremendous economic boost. In 1968, the large North Slope field was discovered, Anchorage was again a major beneficiary. With the completion of the Trans-Alaskan Pipeline System in 1977, Anchorage entered its contemporary period of sustained population growth and dynamic economic development.

Tourism accounts for 1 in 9 jobs in Anchorage. More than $30 million is collected in local hotel and car rental taxes alone, and visitors spend hundreds of millions in Anchorage annually. Anchorage is also known as a tax-friendly city, with no sales or personal income tax.

The city's cultural amenities include the Anchorage Museum at Rasmuson Center and the Alaska Aviation Heritage Museum, which chronicles the story of Alaska's early and pioneering air transport system. Near the city is the Potter Section House Railway Museum, which pays homage to the state's vital rail industry. The city also boasts the Alaska Center for the Performing Arts and the Alaska Botanical Garden. Delaney Park, also known as the Park Strip, is a venerable and valued recreational resource in the city's business district, and its ongoing improvement looks toward a year-round "Central Park" for Anchorage. The Alaska State Fair has been recognized as one of the Top 100 Events in North America.

The city is an educational center with two universities and many technical, vocational, and private schools. A campus of the University of Alaska has been in Anchorage since 1954, and the city is also home to Alaska Pacific University.

The natural environment of Anchorage is spectacular, and at nearby Portage Glacier, one can watch the glacier "calving," as huge blocks of ice crash into the lake below. Anchorage is also located at one end of the famous annual Iditarod Trail Sled Dog Race.

Because of its long summer days and relatively mild temperatures, Anchorage is called "The City of Lights and Flowers," and open grassy expanses are adorned throughout the summer season with lights and flowers. Summer also brings out a friendly competition among the city's residents, who plant colorful flowers along streets, in parks, private gardens, window boxes, and lobbies.

The weather in Anchorage, contrary to what many believe, is not savagely cold. It is tempered by the city's location on the coast and by the Alaska Mountain Range, which acts as a barrier to very cold air from the north. Snow season lasts from October to May. Summers can bring fog and rain.

Rankings

General Rankings

- For its "Best for Vets: Places to Live 2019" rankings, *Military Times* evaluated 599 cities (83 large, 234 medium, 282 small) and compared the locations across three broad categories: veteran and military culture/services; economic indicators; and livability factors such as health, crime, traffic, and school quality. Anchorage ranked #15 out of the top 25, in the large city category (population of more than 250,000). Data points more specific to veterans and the military weighed more heavily than others. *rebootcamp.militarytimes.com, "Military Times Best Places to Live 2019," September 10, 2018*
- In their eigth annual survey, Livability.com looked at data for more than 1,000 small to mid-sized U.S. cities to determine the rankings for Livability's "Top 100 Best Places to Live" in 2021. Anchorage ranked #100. Criteria: housing and economy; sustainability; social and civic engagement; education; demographics; health care options; transportation & infrastructure; and community amenities. *Livability.com, "Top 100 Best Places to Live 2021" October 12, 2021*

Business/Finance Rankings

- For its annual survey of the "Most Expensive U.S. Cities to Live In," Kiplinger applied Cost of Living Index statistics developed by the Council for Community and Economic Research to U.S. Census Bureau population and median household income data for 256 urban areas. Anchorage was among the 20 most expensive in the country. *Kiplinger.com, "The 20 Most Expensive Cities in the U.S.," March 16, 2022*
- The Anchorage metro area appeared on the Milken Institute "2021 Best Performing Cities" list. Rank: #174 out of 200 large metro areas (population over 250,000). Criteria: job growth; wage and salary growth; high-tech output growth; housing affordability; household broadband access. *Milken Institute, "Best-Performing Cities 2021," February 16, 2021*
- *Forbes* ranked the 200 most populous metro areas to determine the nation's "Best Places for Business and Careers." The Anchorage metro area was ranked #185. Criteria: costs (business and living); job growth (past and projected); income growth; quality of life; educational attainment (college and high school); projected economic growth; cultural and leisure opportunities; workplace tolerance laws; net migration patterns. *Forbes, "The Best Places for Business and Careers 2019: Seattle Still On Top," October 30, 2019*

Education Rankings

- Personal finance website *WalletHub* analyzed the 150 largest U.S. metropolitan statistical areas to determine where the most educated Americans are putting their degrees to work. Criteria: education levels; percentage of workers with degrees; education quality and attainment gap; public school quality rankings; quality and enrollment of each metro area's universities. Anchorage was ranked #54 (#1 = most educated city). *www.WalletHub.com, "Most & Least Educated Cities in America," July 19, 2021*
- Anchorage was selected as one of America's most literate cities. The city ranked #52 out of the 84 largest U.S. cities. Criteria: number of booksellers; library resources; Internet resources; educational attainment; periodical publishing resources; newspaper circulation. *Central Connecticut State University, "America's Most Literate Cities, 2018," February 2019*

Environmental Rankings

- Anchorage was highlighted as one of the top 25 cleanest metro areas for year-round particle pollution (Annual PM 2.5) in the U.S. during 2017 through 2019. The area ranked #22. *American Lung Association, "State of the Air 2021," April 21, 2021*

Health/Fitness Rankings

- For each of the 100 largest cities in the United States, the American Fitness Index®, published by the American College of Sports Medicine and the Anthem Foundation, evaluated community infrastructure and 34 health behaviors including preventive health, levels of chronic disease conditions, food insecurity, sleep quality, pedestrian safety, air quality, and community resources that support physical activity. Anchorage ranked #44 for "community fitness." *americanfitnessindex.org, "2021 ACSM American Fitness Index Summary Report," July 13, 2021*

Real Estate Rankings

- *WalletHub* compared the most populated U.S. cities to determine which had the best markets for real estate agents. Anchorage ranked #140 where demand was high and pay was the best. Criteria: sales per agent; annual median wage for real-estate agents; monthly average starting salary for real estate agents; real estate job density and competition; unemployment rate; home turnover rate; housing-market health index; and other relevant metrics. *www.WalletHub.com, "2021 Best Places to Be a Real Estate Agent," May 12, 2021*
- Anchorage was ranked #43 out of 237 metro areas in terms of housing affordability in 2021 by the National Association of Home Builders (#1 = most affordable). Criteria: the share of homes sold in that area affordable to a family earning the local median income, based on standard mortgage underwriting criteria. *National Association of Home Builders®, NAHB-Wells Fargo Housing Opportunity Index, 4th Quarter 2021*

Safety Rankings

- To identify the most dangerous cities in America, 24/7 Wall Street focused on violent crime categories—murder, non-negligent manslaughter, rape, robbery, and aggravated assault—as reported for every 100,000 residents using data from the FBI's 2020 annual Uniform Crime Report. For cities with populations over 25,000, trim(city)+[was ranked #38. *247wallst.com, "America's Most Dangerous Cities" November 12, 2021*
- Allstate ranked the 200 largest cities in America in terms of driver safety. Anchorage ranked #27. Criteria: internal property damage claims over a two-year period from January 2016 to December 2017. The report helps increase the importance of safety and awareness behind the wheel. *Allstate, "Allstate America's Best Drivers Report, 2019" June 24, 2019*
- Anchorage was identified as one of the most dangerous cities in America by NeighborhoodScout. The city ranked #40 out of 100 (#1 = most dangerous). Criteria: number of violent crimes per 1,000 residents. The editors evaluated cities with 25,000 or more residents. *NeighborhoodScout.com, "2022 Top 100 Most Dangerous Cities in the U.S.," January 3, 2022*
- The National Insurance Crime Bureau ranked 390 metro areas in the U.S. in terms of per capita rates of vehicle theft. The Anchorage metro area ranked #58 (#1 = highest rate). Criteria: number of vehicle theft offenses per 100,000 inhabitants in 2020. *National Insurance Crime Bureau, "Hot Spots 2020," August 31, 2021*

Seniors/Retirement Rankings

- From its Best Cities for Successful Aging indexes, the Milken Institute generated rankings for metropolitan areas, weighing data in nine categories—health care, wellness, living arrangements, transportation and convenience, financial characteristics, education, employment, community engagement, and overall livability. The Anchorage metro area was ranked #52 overall in the small metro area category. *Milken Institute, "Best Cities for Successful Aging, 2017" March 14, 2017*

Sports/Recreation Rankings

- Anchorage was chosen as a bicycle friendly community by the League of American Bicyclists. A "Bicycle Friendly Community" welcomes cyclists by providing safe and supportive accommodation for cycling and encouraging people to bike for transportation and recreation. There are five award levels: Diamond; Platinum; Gold; Silver; and Bronze. The community achieved an award level of Silver. *League of American Bicyclists, "Fall 2021 Awards-New & Renewing Bicycle Friendly Communities List," December 8, 2021*

Women/Minorities Rankings

- *Women's Health*, together with the site Yelp, identified the 15 "Wellthiest" spots in the U.S. Anchorage appeared among the top for happiest, healthiest, outdoorsiest and Zen-iest. *Women's Health, "The 15 Wellthiest Cities in the U.S." July 5, 2017*
- Anchorage was selected as one of the gayest cities in America by *The Advocate.* The city ranked #20 out of 25. Criteria, among many: Trans Pride parades/festivals; gay rugby teams; lesbian bars; LGBT centers; theater screenings of "Moonlight"; LGBT-inclusive nondiscrimination ordinances; and gay bowling teams. *The Advocate, "Queerest Cities in America 2017" January 12, 2017*
- Personal finance website *WalletHub* compared more than 180 U.S. cities across two key dimensions, "Hispanic Business-Friendliness" and "Hispanic Purchasing Power," to arrive at the most favorable conditions for Hispanic entrepreneurs. Anchorage was ranked #49 out of 182. Criteria includes: share of Hispanic-Owned Businesses; Hispanic entrepreneurship rate to median annual income of Hispanics; Small Business-Friendliness score; cost of living; and number of Hispanics with at least a bachelor's degree. *WalletHub.com, "2019's Best Cities for Hispanic Entrepreneurs," May 1, 2019*

Miscellaneous Rankings

- *WalletHub* compared the 150 most populated U.S. cities to determine their operating efficiency. A "Quality of City Services" score was constructed for each city and then divided by the total budget per capita to reveal which were managed the best. Anchorage ranked #75. Criteria: financial stability; economy; education; safety; health; infrastructure and pollution. *www.WalletHub.com, "2021's Best- & Worst-Run Cities in America," June 22, 2021*

Business Environment

DEMOGRAPHICS

Population Growth

Area	1990 Census	2000 Census	2010 Census	2020* Estimate	Population Growth (%) 1990-2020	2010-2020
City	226,338	260,283	291,826	292,090	29.1	0.1
MSA[1]	266,021	319,605	380,821	399,450	50.2	4.9
U.S.	248,709,873	281,421,906	308,745,538	326,569,308	31.3	5.8

Note: (1) Figures cover the Anchorage, AK Metropolitan Statistical Area; (*) 2016-2020 5-year estimated population
Source: U.S. Census Bureau, 1990 Census, Census 2000, Census 2010, 2016-2020 American Community Survey 5-Year Estimates

Household Size

Area	Persons in Household (%) One	Two	Three	Four	Five	Six	Seven or More	Average Household Size
City	25.9	33.3	16.1	13.6	6.4	2.5	2.2	2.70
MSA[1]	25.3	33.7	15.8	13.5	6.6	2.7	2.3	2.80
U.S.	28.0	33.9	15.5	12.9	6.0	2.3	1.4	2.60

Note: (1) Figures cover the Anchorage, AK Metropolitan Statistical Area
Source: U.S. Census Bureau, 2016-2020 American Community Survey 5-Year Estimates

Race

Area	White Alone[2] (%)	Black Alone[2] (%)	Asian Alone[2] (%)	AIAN[3] Alone[2] (%)	NHOPI[4] Alone[2] (%)	Other Race Alone[2] (%)	Two or More Races (%)
City	61.2	5.3	9.8	7.5	2.9	2.4	11.0
MSA[1]	66.7	4.3	7.6	7.1	2.2	1.9	10.3
U.S.	70.4	12.6	5.6	0.8	0.2	5.1	5.2

Note: (1) Figures cover the Anchorage, AK Metropolitan Statistical Area; (2) Alone is defined as not being in combination with one or more other races; (3) American Indian and Alaska Native; (4) Native Hawaiian and Other Pacific Islander
Source: U.S. Census Bureau, 2016-2020 American Community Survey 5-Year Estimates

Hispanic or Latino Origin

Area	Total (%)	Mexican (%)	Puerto Rican (%)	Cuban (%)	Other (%)
City	9.4	5.0	1.4	0.2	2.8
MSA[1]	8.3	4.3	1.2	0.2	2.5
U.S.	18.2	11.2	1.7	0.7	4.5

Note: Persons of Hispanic or Latino origin can be of any race; (1) Figures cover the Anchorage, AK Metropolitan Statistical Area
Source: U.S. Census Bureau, 2016-2020 American Community Survey 5-Year Estimates

Ancestry

Area	German	Irish	English	American	Italian	Polish	French[2]	Scottish	Dutch
City	13.8	9.1	7.8	3.8	3.2	2.0	2.3	2.1	1.4
MSA[1]	14.7	9.8	8.2	4.1	3.2	2.0	2.5	2.2	1.6
U.S.	13.0	9.7	7.7	5.9	5.1	2.7	2.3	1.6	1.1

Note: Figures are the percentage of the total population reporting a particular ancestry. The nine most commonly reported ancestries in the U.S. are shown. Figures include multiple ancestries (e.g. if a person reported being Irish and Italian, they were included in both columns); (1) Figures cover the Anchorage, AK Metropolitan Statistical Area; (2) Excludes Basque
Source: U.S. Census Bureau, 2016-2020 American Community Survey 5-Year Estimates

Foreign-born Population

Area	Percent of Population Born in: Any Foreign Country	Asia	Mexico	Europe	Caribbean	Central America[2]	South America	Africa	Canada
City	10.8	6.0	0.8	1.1	0.5	0.1	0.5	0.6	0.4
MSA[1]	8.8	4.7	0.7	1.1	0.4	0.1	0.4	0.4	0.4
U.S.	13.5	4.2	3.3	1.5	1.3	1.1	1.0	0.7	0.3

Note: (1) Figures cover the Anchorage, AK Metropolitan Statistical Area; (2) Excludes Mexico.
Source: U.S. Census Bureau, 2016-2020 American Community Survey 5-Year Estimates

Marital Status

Area	Never Married	Now Married[2]	Separated	Widowed	Divorced
City	33.8	49.5	1.7	3.5	11.5
MSA[1]	33.3	49.4	1.7	3.8	11.8
U.S.	33.5	48.1	1.8	5.7	10.8

Note: Figures are percentages and cover the population 15 years of age and older; (1) Figures cover the Anchorage, AK Metropolitan Statistical Area; (2) Excludes separated
Source: U.S. Census Bureau, 2016-2020 American Community Survey 5-Year Estimates

Disability by Age

Area	All Ages	Under 18 Years Old	18 to 64 Years Old	65 Years and Over
City	11.2	3.4	10.0	35.2
MSA[1]	12.0	3.6	11.0	36.1
U.S.	12.7	4.3	10.3	34.0

Note: Figures show percent of the civilian noninstitutionalized population that reported having a disability. Disability status is determined from six types of difficulty: vision, hearing, cognitive, ambulatory, self-care, and independent living. For children under 5 years old, hearing and vision difficulty are used to determine disability status. For children between the ages of 5 and 14, disability status is determined from hearing, vision, cognitive, ambulatory, and self-care difficulties. For people aged 15 years and older, they are considered to have a disability if they have difficulty with any one of the six difficulty types; Note: (1) Figures cover the Anchorage, AK Metropolitan Statistical Area
Source: U.S. Census Bureau, 2016-2020 American Community Survey 5-Year Estimates

Age

Area	Percent of Population									Median Age
	Under Age 5	Age 5–19	Age 20–34	Age 35–44	Age 45–54	Age 55–64	Age 65–74	Age 75–84	Age 85+	
City	7.1	19.4	25.0	13.1	12.2	12.0	7.3	2.8	1.0	33.9
MSA[1]	7.1	20.1	23.8	13.2	12.2	12.4	7.5	2.8	1.0	34.3
U.S.	6.0	19.1	20.6	12.7	12.7	12.9	9.4	4.7	2.0	38.2

Note: (1) Figures cover the Anchorage, AK Metropolitan Statistical Area
Source: U.S. Census Bureau, 2016-2020 American Community Survey 5-Year Estimates

Gender

Area	Males	Females	Males per 100 Females
City	148,954	143,136	104.1
MSA[1]	204,725	194,725	105.1
U.S.	160,818,530	165,750,778	97.0

Note: (1) Figures cover the Anchorage, AK Metropolitan Statistical Area
Source: U.S. Census Bureau, 2016-2020 American Community Survey 5-Year Estimates

Religious Groups by Family

Area	Catholic	Baptist	Non-Den.	Methodist[2]	Lutheran	LDS[3]	Pente-costal	Presby-terian[4]	Muslim[5]	Judaism
MSA[1]	6.9	5.0	6.4	1.4	1.9	5.1	1.9	0.7	0.2	0.1
U.S.	19.1	9.3	4.0	4.0	2.3	2.0	1.9	1.6	0.8	0.7

Note: Figures are the number of adherents as a percentage of the total population; (1) Figures cover the Anchorage, AK Metropolitan Statistical Area; (2) Methodist/Pietist; (3) Latter Day Saints; (4) Reformed; (5) Figures are estimates
Source: Association of Statisticians of American Religious Bodies, 2010 U.S. Religion Census: Religious Congregations & Membership Study

Religious Groups by Tradition

Area	Catholic	Evangelical Protestant	Mainline Protestant	Other Tradition	Black Protestant	Orthodox
MSA[1]	6.9	15.7	3.6	6.8	0.3	0.6
U.S.	19.1	16.2	7.3	4.3	1.6	0.3

Note: Figures are the number of adherents as a percentage of the total population; (1) Figures cover the Anchorage, AK Metropolitan Statistical Area
Source: Association of Statisticians of American Religious Bodies, 2010 U.S. Religion Census: Religious Congregations & Membership Study

ECONOMY

Gross Metropolitan Product

Area	2017	2018	2019	2020	Rank[2]
MSA[1]	27.4	28.3	29.3	30.6	102

Note: Figures are in billions of dollars; (1) Figures cover the Anchorage, AK Metropolitan Statistical Area; (2) Rank is based on 2018 data and ranges from 1 to 381
Source: U.S. Conference of Mayors, U.S. Metro Economies: GMP & Employment 2018-2020, September 2019

Economic Growth

Area	2015-17 (%)	2018 (%)	2019 (%)	2020 (%)	Rank[2]
MSA[1]	-1.5	-0.9	2.4	0.6	353
U.S.	1.9	2.9	2.3	2.1	–

Note: Figures are real gross metropolitan product (GMP) growth rates and represent average annual percent change; (1) Figures cover the Anchorage, AK Metropolitan Statistical Area; (2) Rank is based on 2017 2-year average annual percent change and ranges from 1 to 381
Source: U.S. Conference of Mayors, U.S. Metro Economies: GMP & Employment 2018-2020, September 2019

Metropolitan Area Exports

Area	2015	2016	2017	2018	2019	2020	Rank[2]
MSA[1]	421.9	1,215.4	1,675.9	1,510.8	1,348.0	990.9	145

Note: Figures are in millions of dollars; (1) Figures cover the Anchorage, AK Metropolitan Statistical Area; (2) Rank is based on 2020 data and ranges from 1 to 389
Source: U.S. Department of Commerce, International Trade Administration, Office of Trade and Economic Analysis, Industry and Analysis, Exports by Metropolitan Area, data extracted March 4, 2022

Building Permits

Area	Single-Family			Multi-Family			Total		
	2019	2020	Pct. Chg.	2019	2020	Pct. Chg.	2019	2020	Pct. Chg.
City	838	735	-12.3	221	235	6.3	1,059	970	-8.4
MSA[1]	878	771	-12.2	285	259	-9.1	1,163	1,030	-11.4
U.S.	862,100	979,400	13.6	523,900	491,700	-6.1	1,386,000	1,471,100	6.1

Note: (1) Figures cover the Anchorage, AK Metropolitan Statistical Area; Figures represent new, privately-owned housing units authorized (unadjusted data); All permit data are based on estimates with imputation
Source: U.S. Census Bureau, Manufacturing, Mining, and Construction Statistics, Building Permits, 2019, 2020

Bankruptcy Filings

Area	Business Filings			Nonbusiness Filings		
	2020	2021	% Chg.	2020	2021	% Chg.
Anchorage Borough	20	12	-40.0	137	116	-15.3
U.S.	21,655	14,347	-33.7	522,808	399,269	-23.6

Note: Business filings include Chapter 7, Chapter 9, Chapter 11, Chapter 12, Chapter 13, Chapter 15, and Section 304; Nonbusiness filings include Chapter 7, Chapter 11, and Chapter 13
Source: Administrative Office of the U.S. Courts, Business and Nonbusiness Bankruptcy, County Cases Commenced by Chapter of the Bankruptcy Code, During the 12-Month Period Ending December 31, 2020 and Business and Nonbusiness Bankruptcy, County Cases Commenced by Chapter of the Bankruptcy Code, During the 12-Month Period Ending December 31, 2021

Housing Vacancy Rates

Area	Gross Vacancy Rate[2] (%)			Year-Round Vacancy Rate[3] (%)			Rental Vacancy Rate[4] (%)			Homeowner Vacancy Rate[5] (%)		
	2019	2020	2021	2019	2020	2021	2019	2020	2021	2019	2020	2021
MSA[1]	n/a	n/a	n/a	n/a	n/a	n/a	n/a	n/a	n/a	n/a	n/a	n/a
U.S.	12.0	10.6	10.8	9.5	8.2	8.4	6.7	6.3	6.1	1.4	1.0	0.9

Note: (1) Figures cover the Anchorage, AK Metropolitan Statistical Area; (2) The percentage of the total housing inventory that is vacant; (3) The percentage of the housing inventory (excluding seasonal units) that is year-round vacant; (4) The percentage of rental inventory that is vacant for rent; (5) The percentage of homeowner inventory that is vacant for sale; n/a not available
Source: U.S. Census Bureau, Housing Vacancies and Homeownership Annual Statistics: 2019, 2020, 2021

INCOME

Income

Area	Per Capita ($)	Median Household ($)	Average Household ($)
City	41,127	84,813	108,393
MSA[1]	38,664	82,890	105,130
U.S.	35,384	64,994	91,547

Note: (1) Figures cover the Anchorage, AK Metropolitan Statistical Area
Source: U.S. Census Bureau, 2016-2020 American Community Survey 5-Year Estimates

Household Income Distribution

Area	Percent of Households Earning							
	Under $15,000	$15,000 -$24,999	$25,000 -$34,999	$35,000 -$49,999	$50,000 -$74,999	$75,000 -$99,999	$100,000 -$149,999	$150,000 and up
City	5.3	4.9	6.3	9.2	18.2	14.3	20.2	21.6
MSA[1]	6.2	5.4	6.5	9.3	17.9	14.0	20.1	20.8
U.S.	9.9	8.5	8.6	12.0	17.2	12.8	15.6	15.4

Note: (1) Figures cover the Anchorage, AK Metropolitan Statistical Area
Source: U.S. Census Bureau, 2016-2020 American Community Survey 5-Year Estimates

Poverty Rate

Area	All Ages	Under 18 Years Old	18 to 64 Years Old	65 Years and Over
City	8.8	11.5	8.3	6.1
MSA[1]	9.2	11.6	8.7	7.0
U.S.	12.8	17.5	12.1	9.3

Note: Figures are percentage of people whose income during the past 12 months was below the poverty level; (1) Figures cover the Anchorage, AK Metropolitan Statistical Area
Source: U.S. Census Bureau, 2016-2020 American Community Survey 5-Year Estimates

CITY FINANCES

City Government Finances

Component	2019 ($000)	2019 ($ per capita)
Total Revenues	1,663,051	5,650
Total Expenditures	1,622,977	5,514
Debt Outstanding	1,630,250	5,538
Cash and Securities[1]	714,515	2,427

Note: (1) Cash and security holdings of a government at the close of its fiscal year, including those of its dependent agencies, utilities, and liquor stores.
Source: U.S. Census Bureau, State & Local Government Finances 2019

City Government Revenue by Source

Source	2019 ($000)	2019 ($ per capita)	2019 (%)
General Revenue			
From Federal Government	46,446	158	2.8
From State Government	541,465	1,839	32.6
From Local Governments	0	0	0.0
Taxes			
Property	554,032	1,882	33.3
Sales and Gross Receipts	70,320	239	4.2
Personal Income	0	0	0.0
Corporate Income	0	0	0.0
Motor Vehicle License	16,964	58	1.0
Other Taxes	9,088	31	0.5
Current Charges	143,673	488	8.6
Liquor Store	0	0	0.0
Utility	242,707	825	14.6

Source: U.S. Census Bureau, State & Local Government Finances 2019

City Government Expenditures by Function

Function	2019 ($000)	2019 ($ per capita)	2019 (%)
General Direct Expenditures			
Air Transportation	13,589	46	0.8
Corrections	0	0	0.0
Education	672,943	2,286	41.5
Employment Security Administration	0	0	0.0
Financial Administration	20,850	70	1.3
Fire Protection	109,115	370	6.7
General Public Buildings	0	0	0.0
Governmental Administration, Other	16,056	54	1.0
Health	22,956	78	1.4
Highways	91,612	311	5.6
Hospitals	0	0	0.0
Housing and Community Development	12,591	42	0.8
Interest on General Debt	29,462	100	1.8
Judicial and Legal	7,477	25	0.5
Libraries	8,056	27	0.5
Parking	0	0	0.0
Parks and Recreation	37,340	126	2.3
Police Protection	140,796	478	8.7
Public Welfare	777	2	0.0
Sewerage	62,245	211	3.8
Solid Waste Management	33,246	112	2.0
Veterans' Services	0	0	0.0
Liquor Store	0	0	0.0
Utility	240,987	818	14.8

Source: U.S. Census Bureau, State & Local Government Finances 2019

EMPLOYMENT

Labor Force and Employment

Area	Civilian Labor Force			Workers Employed		
	Dec. 2020	Dec. 2021	% Chg.	Dec. 2020	Dec. 2021	% Chg.
City	152,457	152,303	-0.1	143,093	145,581	1.7
MSA[1]	201,421	201,824	0.2	188,820	192,144	1.8
U.S.	160,017,000	161,696,000	1.0	149,613,000	155,732,000	4.1

Note: Data is not seasonally adjusted and covers workers 16 years of age and older; (1) Figures cover the Anchorage, AK Metropolitan Statistical Area
Source: Bureau of Labor Statistics, Local Area Unemployment Statistics

Unemployment Rate

Area	2021											
	Jan.	Feb.	Mar.	Apr.	May	Jun.	Jul.	Aug.	Sep.	Oct.	Nov.	Dec.
City	6.3	6.5	6.8	6.5	5.9	6.1	5.6	4.8	4.9	4.7	4.7	4.4
MSA[1]	6.6	6.8	7.1	6.7	6.1	6.3	5.8	4.9	5.0	4.9	5.0	4.8
U.S.	6.8	6.6	6.2	5.7	5.5	6.1	5.7	5.3	4.6	4.3	3.9	3.7

Note: Data is not seasonally adjusted and covers workers 16 years of age and older; (1) Figures cover the Anchorage, AK Metropolitan Statistical Area
Source: Bureau of Labor Statistics, Local Area Unemployment Statistics

Average Wages

Occupation	$/Hr.	Occupation	$/Hr.
Accountants and Auditors	37.91	Maintenance and Repair Workers	24.74
Automotive Mechanics	28.37	Marketing Managers	50.92
Bookkeepers	24.38	Network and Computer Systems Admin.	42.14
Carpenters	34.05	Nurses, Licensed Practical	30.49
Cashiers	15.16	Nurses, Registered	46.23
Computer Programmers	43.83	Nursing Assistants	19.99
Computer Systems Analysts	46.58	Office Clerks, General	20.94
Computer User Support Specialists	29.27	Physical Therapists	45.65
Construction Laborers	25.56	Physicians	123.16
Cooks, Restaurant	16.22	Plumbers, Pipefitters and Steamfitters	41.42
Customer Service Representatives	20.25	Police and Sheriff's Patrol Officers	46.53
Dentists	79.32	Postal Service Mail Carriers	25.28
Electricians	37.45	Real Estate Sales Agents	33.30
Engineers, Electrical	50.53	Retail Salespersons	17.29
Fast Food and Counter Workers	13.37	Sales Representatives, Technical/Scientific	39.23
Financial Managers	58.02	Secretaries, Exc. Legal/Medical/Executive	20.55
First-Line Supervisors of Office Workers	31.62	Security Guards	23.15
General and Operations Managers	50.16	Surgeons	n/a
Hairdressers/Cosmetologists	13.55	Teacher Assistants, Exc. Postsecondary*	16.48
Home Health and Personal Care Aides	16.58	Teachers, Secondary School, Exc. Sp. Ed.*	37.13
Janitors and Cleaners	16.77	Telemarketers	n/a
Landscaping/Groundskeeping Workers	19.32	Truck Drivers, Heavy/Tractor-Trailer	26.31
Lawyers	54.45	Truck Drivers, Light/Delivery Services	24.05
Maids and Housekeeping Cleaners	14.52	Waiters and Waitresses	13.74

Note: Wage data covers the Anchorage, AK Metropolitan Statistical Area; (*) Hourly wages were calculated from annual wage data based on a 40 hour work week; n/a not available.
Source: Bureau of Labor Statistics, Metro Area Occupational Employment & Wage Estimates, May 2021

Employment by Industry

Sector	MSA[1]		U.S.
	Number of Employees	Percent of Total	Percent of Total
Construction	9,000	5.3	5.0
Education and Health Services	32,100	19.0	16.0
Financial Activities	7,700	4.6	5.9
Government	34,000	20.1	14.9
Information	3,300	2.0	1.9
Leisure and Hospitality	16,900	10.0	9.8
Manufacturing	2,400	1.4	8.4
Mining and Logging	1,900	1.1	0.4
Other Services	6,100	3.6	3.7
Professional and Business Services	17,900	10.6	14.6
Retail Trade	19,600	11.6	10.7
Transportation, Warehousing, and Utilities	13,000	7.7	4.8
Wholesale Trade	5,000	3.0	3.8

Note: Figures are non-farm employment as of December 2021. Figures are not seasonally adjusted and include workers 16 years of age and older; (1) Figures cover the Anchorage, AK Metropolitan Statistical Area
Source: Bureau of Labor Statistics, Current Employment Statistics, Employment, Hours, and Earnings

Employment by Occupation

Occupation Classification	City (%)	MSA[1] (%)	U.S. (%)
Management, Business, Science, and Arts	41.5	39.5	39.5
Natural Resources, Construction, and Maintenance	8.5	10.3	8.7
Production, Transportation, and Material Moving	11.0	11.2	13.1
Sales and Office	21.8	21.3	21.3
Service	17.2	17.6	17.4

Note: Figures cover employed civilians 16 years of age and older; (1) Figures cover the Anchorage, AK Metropolitan Statistical Area
Source: U.S. Census Bureau, 2016-2020 American Community Survey 5-Year Estimates

Occupations with Greatest Projected Employment Growth: 2021 – 2023

Occupation[1]	2021 Employment	2023 Projected Employment	Numeric Employment Change	Percent Employment Change
Fast Food and Counter Workers	6,180	7,020	840	13.6
Waiters and Waitresses	4,170	4,860	690	16.5
Maids and Housekeeping Cleaners	3,020	3,540	520	17.2
Food Preparation Workers	3,560	4,000	440	12.4
Cooks, Restaurant	2,280	2,670	390	17.1
Retail Salespersons	12,680	13,030	350	2.8
Meat, Poultry, and Fish Cutters and Trimmers	6,240	6,580	340	5.4
Operating Engineers and Other Construction Equipment Operators	2,590	2,910	320	12.4
General and Operations Managers	4,150	4,430	280	6.7
Cashiers	6,770	7,050	280	4.1

Note: Projections cover Alaska; (1) Sorted by numeric employment change
Source: www.projectionscentral.com, State Occupational Projections, 2021–2023 Short-Term Projections

Fastest-Growing Occupations: 2021 – 2023

Occupation[1]	2021 Employment	2023 Projected Employment	Numeric Employment Change	Percent Employment Change
Concierges	70	120	50	71.4
Rotary Drill Operators, Oil and Gas	110	180	70	63.6
Travel Agents	90	140	50	55.6
Roustabouts, Oil and Gas	330	500	170	51.5
Service Unit Operators, Oil, Gas, and Mining	740	1,000	260	35.1
Tour and Travel Guides	730	960	230	31.5
Hotel, Motel, and Resort Desk Clerks	770	1,000	230	29.9
Bus Drivers, Transit and Intercity (SOC 2018)	780	1,000	220	28.2
Fitness Trainers and Aerobics Instructors	620	770	150	24.2
Ushers, Lobby Attendants, and Ticket Takers	250	310	60	24.0

Note: Projections cover Alaska; (1) Sorted by percent employment change and excludes occupations with numeric employment change less than 50
Source: www.projectionscentral.com, State Occupational Projections, 2021–2023 Short-Term Projections

TAXES

State Corporate Income Tax Rates

State	Tax Rate (%)	Income Brackets ($)	Num. of Brackets	Financial Institution Tax Rate (%)[a]	Federal Income Tax Ded.
Alaska	0 - 9.4	25,000 - 222,000	10	0 - 9.4	No

Note: Tax rates as of January 1, 2022; (a) Rates listed are the corporate income tax rate applied to financial institutions or excise taxes based on income. Some states have other taxes based upon the value of deposits or shares.
Source: Federation of Tax Administrators, State Corporate Income Tax Rates, January 1, 2022

State Individual Income Tax Rates

State	Tax Rate (%)	Income Brackets ($)	Personal Exemptions ($)			Standard Ded. ($)	
			Single	Married	Depend.	Single	Married
Alaska	– No state income tax –						

Note: Tax rates as of January 1, 2022; Local- and county-level taxes are not included
Source: Federation of Tax Administrators, State Individual Income Tax Rates, January 1, 2022

Various State Sales and Excise Tax Rates

State	State Sales Tax (%)	Gasoline[1] (¢/gal.)	Cigarette[2] ($/pack)	Spirits[3] ($/gal.)	Wine[4] ($/gal.)	Beer[5] ($/gal.)	Recreational Marijuana (%)
Alaska	None	15.13	2	12.8	2.5	1.07	(a)

Note: All tax rates as of January 1, 2022; (1) The American Petroleum Institute has developed a methodology for determining the average tax rate on a gallon of fuel. Rates may include any of the following: excise taxes, environmental fees, storage tank fees, other fees or taxes, general sales tax, and local taxes; (2) The federal excise tax of $1.0066 per pack and local taxes are not included; (3) Rates are those applicable to off-premise sales of 40% alcohol by volume (a.b.v.) distilled spirits in 750ml containers. Local excise taxes are excluded; (4) Rates are those applicable to off-premise sales of 11% a.b.v. non-carbonated wine in 750ml containers; (5) Rates are those applicable to off-premise sales of 4.7% a.b.v. beer in 12 ounce containers; (a) $50/oz. mature flowers; $25/oz. immature flowers; $15/oz. trim, $1 per clone
Source: Tax Foundation, 2022 Facts & Figures: How Does Your State Compare?

State Business Tax Climate Index Rankings

State	Overall Rank	Corporate Tax Rank	Individual Income Tax Rank	Sales Tax Rank	Property Tax Rank	Unemployment Insurance Tax Rank
Alaska	3	28	1	5	24	43

Note: The index is a measure of how each state's tax laws affect economic performance. The lower the rank, the more favorable a state's tax system is for business. States without a given tax are given a ranking of 1. The scores/rankings for the District of Columbia do not affect other states. The 2022 index represents the tax climate as of July 1, 2021.
Source: Tax Foundation, State Business Tax Climate Index 2022

TRANSPORTATION

Means of Transportation to Work

Area	Car/Truck/Van		Public Transportation			Bicycle	Walked	Other Means	Worked at Home
	Drove Alone	Car-pooled	Bus	Subway	Railroad				
City	75.0	12.4	1.5	0.0	0.0	1.1	2.6	1.9	5.5
MSA[1]	74.6	11.9	1.3	0.0	0.0	0.9	2.5	2.8	6.0
U.S.	74.9	8.9	2.2	1.7	0.5	0.5	2.6	1.4	7.3

Note: Figures are percentages and cover workers 16 years of age and older; (1) Figures cover the Anchorage, AK Metropolitan Statistical Area
Source: U.S. Census Bureau, 2016-2020 American Community Survey 5-Year Estimates

Travel Time to Work

Area	Less Than 10 Minutes	10 to 19 Minutes	20 to 29 Minutes	30 to 44 Minutes	45 to 59 Minutes	60 to 89 Minutes	90 Minutes or More
City	16.0	45.2	23.6	10.4	2.2	1.3	1.3
MSA[1]	15.3	41.3	21.9	10.8	4.4	4.0	2.3
U.S.	12.3	28.4	20.9	20.9	8.3	6.4	2.9

Note: Note: Figures are percentages and include workers 16 years old and over; (1) Figures cover the Anchorage, AK Metropolitan Statistical Area
Source: U.S. Census Bureau, 2016-2020 American Community Survey 5-Year Estimates

Key Congestion Measures

Measure	1990	2000	2010	2015	2020
Annual Hours of Delay, Total (000)	1,848	3,973	5,279	6,397	3,080
Annual Hours of Delay, Per Auto Commuter	19	32	37	41	18
Annual Congestion Cost, Per Auto Commuter ($)	566	917	974	1,088	563

Note: Covers the Anchorage AK urban area
Source: Texas A&M Transportation Institute, 2021 Urban Mobility Report

Freeway Travel Time Index

Measure	1985	1990	1995	2000	2005	2010	2015	2020
Urban Area Index[1]	1.03	1.07	1.10	1.14	1.16	1.16	1.18	1.07
Urban Area Rank[1,2]	89	74	72	62	57	54	41	57

Note: Freeway Travel Time Index—the ratio of travel time in the peak period to the travel time at free-flow conditions. For example, a value of 1.30 indicates a 20-minute free-flow trip takes 26 minutes in the peak (20 minutes x 1.30 = 26 minutes); (1) Covers the Anchorage AK urban area; (2) Rank is based on 101 larger urban areas (#1 = highest travel time index)
Source: Texas A&M Transportation Institute, 2021 Urban Mobility Report

Public Transportation

Agency Name / Mode of Transportation	Vehicles Operated in Maximum Service[1]	Annual Unlinked Passenger Trips[2] (in thous.)	Annual Passenger Miles[3] (in thous.)
Municipality of Anchorage, dba Public Transportation			
Bus (directly operated)	45	1,710.1	7,737.8
Demand Response (purchased transportation)	37	78.0	425.2
Vanpool (purchased transportation)	80	146.1	5,906.8

Note: (1) Number of revenue vehicles operated by the given mode and type of service to meet the annual maximum service requirement. This is the revenue vehicle count during the peak season of the year; on the week and day that maximum service is provided. Vehicles operated in maximum service (VOMS) exclude atypical days and one-time special events; (2) Number of passengers who boarded public transportation vehicles. Passengers are counted each time they board a vehicle no matter how many vehicles they use to travel from their origin to their destination. (3) Sum of the distances ridden by all passengers during the entire fiscal year.
Source: Federal Transit Administration, National Transit Database, 2020

Air Transportation

Airport Name and Code / Type of Service	Passenger Airlines[1]	Passenger Enplanements	Freight Carriers[2]	Freight (lbs)
Anchorage International (ANC)				
Domestic service (U.S. carriers - 2021)	24	2,164,378	30	2,694,750,566
International service (U.S. carriers - 2020)	3	494	12	462,951,386

Note: (1) Includes all U.S.-based major, minor and commuter airlines that carried at least one passenger during the year; (2) Includes all U.S.-based airlines and freight carriers that transported at least one pound of freight during the year.
Source: Bureau of Transportation Statistics, The Intermodal Transportation Database, Air Carriers: T-100 Domestic Market (U.S. Carriers), 2021; Bureau of Transportation Statistics, The Intermodal Transportation Database, Air Carriers: T-100 International Market (U.S. Carriers), 2020

BUSINESSES

Major Business Headquarters

Company Name	Industry	Rankings	
		Fortune[1]	Forbes[2]
No companies listed	-	-	-

Note: (1) Companies that produce a 10-K are ranked 1 to 500 based on 2020 revenue; (2) All private companies with at least $2 billion in annual revenue through the end of their most current fiscal year are ranked 1 to 225; companies listed are headquartered in the city; dashes indicate no ranking
Source: Fortune, "Fortune 500," 2021; Forbes, "America's Largest Private Companies," 2021

Living Environment

COST OF LIVING

Cost of Living Index

Composite Index	Groceries	Housing	Utilities	Trans-portation	Health Care	Misc. Goods/ Services
126.0	124.3	137.1	129.9	111.0	146.8	114.8

Note: The Cost of Living Index measures regional differences in the cost of consumer goods and services, excluding taxes and non-consumer expenditures, for professional and managerial households in the top income quintile. It is based on more than 50,000 prices covering almost 60 different items for which prices are collected three times a year by chambers of commerce, economic development organizations or university applied economic centers in each participating urban area. The numbers shown should be read as a percentage above or below the national average of 100. For example, a value of 115.4 in the groceries column indicates that grocery prices are 15.4% higher than the national average. Small differences in the index numbers should not be interpreted as significant; Figures cover the Anchorage AK urban area.
Source: The Council for Community and Economic Research, Cost of Living Index, 2021

Grocery Prices

Area[1]	T-Bone Steak ($/pound)	Frying Chicken ($/pound)	Whole Milk ($/half gal.)	Eggs ($/dozen)	Orange Juice ($/64 oz.)	Coffee ($/11.5 oz.)
City[2]	14.13	1.88	3.02	2.19	4.02	5.16
Avg.	12.82	1.40	2.22	1.57	3.59	4.30
Min.	8.91	0.91	1.29	0.75	2.87	3.02
Max.	21.35	2.69	3.92	3.86	5.49	8.11

Note: (1) Values for the local area are compared with the average, minimum and maximum values for all 285 areas in the Cost of Living Index; (2) Figures cover the Anchorage AK urban area; ***T-Bone Steak*** *(price per pound);* ***Frying Chicken*** *(price per pound, whole fryer);* ***Whole Milk*** *(half gallon carton);* ***Eggs*** *(price per dozen, Grade A, large);* ***Orange Juice*** *(64 oz. Tropicana or Florida Natural);* ***Coffee*** *(11.5 oz. can, vacuum-packed, Maxwell House, Hills Bros, or Folgers).*
Source: The Council for Community and Economic Research, Cost of Living Index, 2021

Housing and Utility Costs

Area[1]	New Home Price ($)	Apartment Rent ($/month)	All Electric ($/month)	Part Electric ($/month)	Other Energy ($/month)	Telephone ($/month)
City[2]	594,678	1,312	-	129.09	131.80	187.80
Avg.	398,393	1,217	171.38	100.83	69.67	187.75
Min.	212,799	534	96.71	31.56	27.15	173.01
Max.	2,354,006	4,438	369.53	277.33	303.87	206.73

Note: (1) Values for the local area are compared with the average, minimum and maximum values for all 285 areas in the Cost of Living Index; (2) Figures cover the Anchorage AK urban area; ***New Home Price*** *(2,400 sf living area, 8,000 sf lot, in urban area with full utilities);* ***Apartment Rent*** *(950 sf 2 bedroom/1.5 or 2 bath, unfurnished, excluding all utilities except water);* ***All Electric*** *(average monthly cost for an all-electric home);* ***Part Electric*** *(average monthly cost for a part-electric home);* ***Other Energy*** *(average monthly cost for natural gas, fuel oil, coal, wood, and any other forms of energy except electricity);* ***Telephone*** *(price includes the base monthly rate plus taxes and fees for three lines of mobile phone service).*
Source: The Council for Community and Economic Research, Cost of Living Index, 2021

Health Care, Transportation, and Other Costs

Area[1]	Doctor ($/visit)	Dentist ($/visit)	Optometrist ($/visit)	Gasoline ($/gallon)	Beauty Salon ($/visit)	Men's Shirt ($)
City[2]	211.00	145.68	228.22	3.12	50.83	19.59
Avg.	118.16	101.04	109.44	2.71	40.63	30.77
Min.	35.04	55.56	51.17	2.17	18.59	11.32
Max.	231.10	165.12	256.81	4.11	85.33	63.03

Note: (1) Values for the local area are compared with the average, minimum and maximum values for all 285 areas in the Cost of Living Index; (2) Figures cover the Anchorage AK urban area; ***Doctor*** *(general practitioners routine exam of an established patient);* ***Dentist*** *(adult teeth cleaning and periodic oral examination);* ***Optometrist*** *(full vision eye exam for established adult patient);* ***Gasoline*** *(one gallon regular unleaded, national brand, including all taxes, cash price at self-service pump if available);* ***Beauty Salon*** *(woman's shampoo, trim, and blow-dry);* ***Men's Shirt*** *(cotton/polyester dress shirt, pinpoint weave, long sleeves).*
Source: The Council for Community and Economic Research, Cost of Living Index, 2021

HOUSING

Homeownership Rate

Area	2013 (%)	2014 (%)	2015 (%)	2016 (%)	2017 (%)	2018 (%)	2019 (%)	2020 (%)	2021 (%)
MSA[1]	n/a	n/a	n/a	n/a	n/a	n/a	n/a	n/a	n/a
U.S.	65.1	64.5	63.7	63.4	63.9	64.4	64.6	66.6	65.5

Note: (1) Figures cover the Anchorage, AK Metropolitan Statistical Area; n/a not available
Source: U.S. Census Bureau, Housing Vacancies and Homeownership Annual Statistics: 2013-2021

House Price Index (HPI)

Area	National Ranking[2]	Quarterly Change (%)	One-Year Change (%)	Five-Year Change (%)	Since 1991Q1 (%)
MSA[1]	261	0.74	9.95	19.44	210.38
U.S.[3]	–	3.33	17.54	54.45	258.04

Note: The HPI is a weighted repeat sales index. It measures average price changes in repeat sales or refinancings on the same properties. This information is obtained by reviewing repeat mortgage transactions on single-family properties whose mortgages have been purchased or securitized by Fannie Mae or Freddie Mac since January 1975; (1) Figures cover the Anchorage, AK Metropolitan Statistical Area; (2) Rankings are based on annual percentage change for all metro areas containing at least 15,000 transactions over the last 10 years and ranges from 1 to 268; (3) figures based on a weighted average of Census Division estimates using a seasonally adjusted, purchase-only index; all figures are for the period ending December 31, 2021
Source: Federal Housing Finance Agency, Change in FHFA Metropolitan Area House Price Indexes, 2021Q4

Median Single-Family Home Prices

Area	2019	2020	2021[p]	Percent Change 2020 to 2021
MSA[1]	n/a	n/a	n/a	n/a
U.S. Average	274.6	300.2	353.4	17.7

Note: Figures are median sales prices of existing single-family homes in thousands of dollars; (p) preliminary; n/a not available; (1) Figures cover the Anchorage, AK Metropolitan Statistical Area
Source: National Association of Realtors, Median Sales Price of Existing Single-Family Homes for Metropolitan Areas, 4th Quarter 2021

Qualifying Income Based on Median Sales Price of Existing Single-Family Homes

Area	With 5% Down ($)	With 10% Down ($)	With 20% Down ($)
MSA[1]	n/a	n/a	n/a
U.S. Average	70,699	66,978	59,536

Note: Figures are preliminary; Qualifying income is based on a mortgage rate of 3.13%. Monthly principal and interest payment is limited to 25% of income; n/a not available; (1) Figures cover the Anchorage, AK Metropolitan Statistical Area
Source: National Association of Realtors, Qualifying Income Based on Median Sales Price of Existing Single-Family Homes for Metropolitan Areas, 4th Quarter 2021

Home Value Distribution

Area	Under $50,000	$50,000 -$99,999	$100,000 -$149,999	$150,000 -$199,999	$200,000 -$299,999	$300,000 -$499,999	$500,000 -$999,999	$1,000,000 or more
City	5.3	1.9	4.2	6.2	26.7	41.1	13.3	1.1
MSA[1]	4.8	2.5	4.7	8.2	29.5	38.0	11.3	1.0
U.S.	6.6	11.0	12.3	13.6	20.0	20.5	12.3	3.7

Note: Figures are percentages and cover owner-occupied housing units; (1) Figures cover the Anchorage, AK Metropolitan Statistical Area
Source: U.S. Census Bureau, 2016-2020 American Community Survey 5-Year Estimates

Year Housing Structure Built

Area	2010 or Later	2000 -2009	1990 -1999	1980 -1989	1970 -1979	1960 -1969	1950 -1959	1940 -1949	Before 1940	Median Year
City	3.9	11.9	12.2	26.4	27.7	10.2	6.0	1.2	0.5	1982
MSA[1]	5.1	16.7	13.5	25.6	24.0	8.6	4.9	1.0	0.5	1984
U.S.	6.2	13.6	13.9	13.4	15.0	10.5	10.2	4.8	12.4	1978

Note: Figures are percentages except for Median Year; Note: (1) Figures cover the Anchorage, AK Metropolitan Statistical Area
Source: U.S. Census Bureau, 2016-2020 American Community Survey 5-Year Estimates

Gross Monthly Rent

Area	Under $500	$500 -$999	$1,000 -$1,499	$1,500 -$1,999	$2,000 -$2,499	$2,500 -$2,999	$3,000 and up	Median ($)
City	4.4	21.8	37.4	19.5	11.8	3.4	1.6	1,310
MSA[1]	4.9	23.3	37.2	19.4	10.8	3.0	1.4	1,277
U.S.	8.9	34.3	30.2	14.9	6.2	2.6	2.8	1,096

Note: Figures are percentages except for Median; Gross rent is the contract rent plus the estimated average monthly cost of utilities (electricity, gas, and water and sewer) and fuels (oil, coal, kerosene, wood, etc.) if these are paid by the renter (or paid for the renter by someone else); (1) Figures cover the Anchorage, AK Metropolitan Statistical Area
Source: U.S. Census Bureau, 2016-2020 American Community Survey 5-Year Estimates

HEALTH

Health Risk Factors

Category	MSA[1] (%)	U.S. (%)
Adults aged 18–64 who have any kind of health care coverage	86.9	86.8
Adults who reported being in good or better health	87.7	86.7
Adults who are current smokers	16.3	15.5
Adults who currently use chewing tobacco, snuff, or snus	5.8	3.7
Adults who are heavy drinkers[2]	9.4	6.7
Adults who are binge drinkers[3]	18.3	15.7
Adults who are overweight (BMI 25.0 - 29.9)	34.6	35.2
Adults who are obese (BMI 30.0 - 99.8)	32.6	31.9
Adults who participated in any physical activities in the past month	79.6	77.6
Adults who always or nearly always wears a seat belt	97.3	94.2

Note: (1) Figures cover the Anchorage, AK Metropolitan Statistical Area; (2) Heavy drinkers are classified as adult men having more than 14 drinks per week and adult women having more than 7 drinks per week; (3) Binge drinkers are classified as males having five or more drinks on one occasion or females having four or more drinks on one occasion

Source: Centers for Disease Control and Prevention, Behaviorial Risk Factor Surveillance System, SMART: Selected Metropolitan Area Risk Trends, 2020

Acute and Chronic Health Conditions

Category	MSA[1] (%)	U.S. (%)
Adults who have ever been told they had a heart attack	2.3	4.3
Adults who have ever been told they have angina or coronary heart disease	4.0	4.0
Adults who have ever been told they had a stroke	n/a	2.8
Adults who have ever been told they have asthma	16.1	14.2
Adults who have ever been told they have arthritis	22.3	24.5
Adults who have ever been told they have diabetes[2]	8.4	10.6
Adults who have ever been told they had skin cancer	4.5	6.4
Adults who have ever been told they had any other types of cancer	6.1	6.8
Adults who have ever been told they have COPD	4.4	6.2
Adults who have ever been told they have kidney disease	2.4	2.9
Adults who have ever been told they have a form of depression	16.6	19.6

Note: (1) Figures cover the Anchorage, AK Metropolitan Statistical Area; (2) Figures do not include pregnancy-related, borderline, or pre-diabetes

Source: Centers for Disease Control and Prevention, Behaviorial Risk Factor Surveillance System, SMART: Selected Metropolitan Area Risk Trends, 2020

Health Screening and Vaccination Rates

Category	MSA[1] (%)	U.S. (%)
Adults 50-75 who have had a blood stool test within the past year	7.0	9.3
Adults aged 65+ who have had flu shot within the past year	58.9	67.9
Adults aged 65+ who have ever had a pneumonia vaccination	65.5	72.2
Adults who have ever been tested for HIV	42.6	37.1
Women aged 21-65 who have had a pap test in the past three years	74.3	77.7
Men aged 40+ who have had a PSA test within the past two years	33.9	31.8
Women aged 40+ who have had a mammogram within the past two years	63.5	71.5

Note: (1) Figures cover the Anchorage, AK Metropolitan Statistical Area.

Source: Centers for Disease Control and Prevention, Behaviorial Risk Factor Surveillance System, SMART: Selected Metropolitan Area Risk Trends, 2020

Disability Status

Category	MSA[1] (%)	U.S. (%)
Adults who reported being deaf	6.0	6.8
Are you blind or have serious difficulty seeing, even when wearing glasses?	3.5	4.7
Do you have difficulty doing errands alone?	4.4	6.3
Do you have difficulty dressing or bathing?	1.6	3.0
Do you have serious difficulty concentrating/remembering/making decisions?	6.9	10.8
Do you have serious difficulty walking or climbing stairs?	9.4	11.9

Note: (1) Figures cover the Anchorage, AK Metropolitan Statistical Area.

Source: Centers for Disease Control and Prevention, Behaviorial Risk Factor Surveillance System, SMART: Selected Metropolitan Area Risk Trends, 2020

Mortality Rates for the Top 10 Causes of Death in the U.S.

ICD-10[a] Sub-Chapter	ICD-10[a] Code	Age-Adjusted Mortality Rate[1] per 100,000 population	
		County[2]	U.S.
Malignant neoplasms	C00-C97	147.6	146.4
Ischaemic heart diseases	I20-I25	67.0	90.2
Other forms of heart disease	I30-I51	47.4	51.9
Other degenerative diseases of the nervous system	G30-G31	38.8	39.7
Other external causes of accidental injury	W00-X59	42.3	38.7
Chronic lower respiratory diseases	J40-J47	28.3	38.1
Cerebrovascular diseases	I60-I69	31.1	37.6
Organic, including symptomatic, mental disorders	F01-F09	38.5	29.4
Hypertensive diseases	I10-I15	19.3	26.1
Diabetes mellitus	E10-E14	20.5	22.6

Note: (a) ICD-10 = International Classification of Diseases 10th Revision; (1) Mortality rates are a three-year average covering 2018-2020; (2) Figures cover Anchorage Borough.
Source: Centers for Disease Control and Prevention, National Center for Health Statistics. Underlying Cause of Death 1999-2020 on CDC WONDER Online Database

Mortality Rates for Selected Causes of Death

ICD-10[a] Sub-Chapter	ICD-10[a] Code	Age-Adjusted Mortality Rate[1] per 100,000 population	
		County[2]	U.S.
Assault	X85-Y09	8.9	6.5
Diseases of the liver	K70-K76	21.9	15.3
Human immunodeficiency virus (HIV) disease	B20-B24	Suppressed	1.4
Influenza and pneumonia	J09-J18	8.8	13.4
Intentional self-harm	X60-X84	22.0	13.9
Malnutrition	E40-E46	3.5	2.9
Obesity and other hyperalimentation	E65-E68	Unreliable	2.4
Renal failure	N17-N19	10.0	12.5
Transport accidents	V01-V99	10.7	12.5
Viral hepatitis	B15-B19	Unreliable	1.0

Note: (a) ICD-10 = International Classification of Diseases 10th Revision; (1) Mortality rates are a three-year average covering 2018-2020; (2) Figures cover Anchorage Borough; Data are suppressed when the data meet the criteria for confidentiality constraints; Mortality rates are flagged as unreliable when the rate would be calculated with a numerator of 20 or less.
Source: Centers for Disease Control and Prevention, National Center for Health Statistics. Underlying Cause of Death 1999-2020 on CDC WONDER Online Database

Health Insurance Coverage

Area	With Health Insurance	With Private Health Insurance	With Public Health Insurance	Without Health Insurance	Population Under Age 19 Without Health Insurance
City	89.4	70.4	31.5	10.6	7.6
MSA[1]	88.4	68.1	32.8	11.6	8.9
U.S.	91.3	68.1	35.3	8.7	5.2

Note: Figures are percentages that cover the civilian noninstitutionalized population; (1) Figures cover the Anchorage, AK Metropolitan Statistical Area
Source: U.S. Census Bureau, 2016-2020 American Community Survey 5-Year Estimates

Number of Medical Professionals

Area	MDs[3]	DOs[3,4]	Dentists	Podiatrists	Chiropractors	Optometrists
Borough[1] (number)	1,081	132	370	15	185	90
Borough[1] (rate[2])	371.2	45.3	127.0	5.2	63.5	30.9
U.S. (rate[2])	285.1	23.0	71.1	6.2	28.2	17.0

02020
Note: Data as of 2020 unless noted; (1) Data covers Anchorage Borough; (2) Rate per 100,000 population; (3) Data as of 2019 and includes all active, non-federal physicians; (4) Doctor of Osteopathic Medicine
Source: U.S. Department of Health and Human Services, Health Resources and Services Administration, Bureau of Health Professions, Area Resource File (ARF) 2020-2021

Best Hospitals

According to *U.S. News,* the Anchorage, AK metro area is home to one of the best hospitals in the U.S.: **Providence Alaska Medical Center** (1 adult specialty). The hospital listed was nationally ranked in at least one of 15 adult or 10 pediatric specialties. Only 175 U.S. hospitals performed well enough to be nationally ranked in one or more specialties. Twenty hospitals in the U.S. made the Honor Roll. The Best Hospitals Honor Roll takes both the national rankings and the procedure and condition ratings into account. Hospitals received points if they were nationally ranked in one of the 15 adult specialties—the higher they ranked, the more points they got—and how many ratings of "high performing" they earned in the 17 procedures and conditions. *U.S. News Online, "America's Best Hospitals 2021-22"*

EDUCATION

Public School District Statistics

District Name	Schls	Pupils	Pupil/ Teacher Ratio	Minority Pupils[1] (%)	LEP/ELL[2] (%)	IEP[3] (%)
Anchorage School District	99	46,143	17.4	58.7	15.8	15.4

Note: Table includes school districts with 2,000 or more students; (1) Percentage of students that are not non-Hispanic white; (2) Percentage of students that are Limited English Proficient (LEP) or English Language Learners (ELL) (2018-19); (3) Percentage of students that have an Individualized Education Program (IEP).
Source: U.S. Department of Education, National Center for Education Statistics, Common Core of Data, Local Education Agency (School District) Universe Survey: School Year 2019-2020

Highest Level of Education

Area	Less than H.S.	H.S. Diploma	Some College, No Deg.	Associate Degree	Bachelor's Degree	Master's Degree	Prof. School Degree	Doctorate Degree
City	6.0	23.7	24.8	8.9	22.7	9.7	2.8	1.4
MSA[1]	6.1	26.4	25.5	9.2	20.5	8.6	2.4	1.2
U.S.	11.5	26.7	20.3	8.6	20.2	9.1	2.2	1.5

Note: Figures cover persons age 25 and over; (1) Figures cover the Anchorage, AK Metropolitan Statistical Area
Source: U.S. Census Bureau, 2016-2020 American Community Survey 5-Year Estimates

Educational Attainment by Race

Area	High School Graduate or Higher (%)					Bachelor's Degree or Higher (%)				
	Total	White	Black	Asian	Hisp.[2]	Total	White	Black	Asian	Hisp.[2]
City	94.0	96.4	92.5	85.8	84.5	36.6	43.6	20.1	25.5	23.3
MSA[1]	93.9	95.7	92.7	85.7	85.6	32.7	37.1	20.2	25.2	22.6
U.S.	88.5	90.7	86.7	87.3	70.3	32.9	34.4	22.6	55.0	17.6

Note: Figures shown cover persons 25 years old and over; (1) Figures cover the Anchorage, AK Metropolitan Statistical Area; (2) People of Hispanic origin can be of any race
Source: U.S. Census Bureau, 2016-2020 American Community Survey 5-Year Estimates

School Enrollment by Grade and Control

Area	Preschool (%)		Kindergarten (%)		Grades 1 - 4 (%)		Grades 5 - 8 (%)		Grades 9 - 12 (%)	
	Public	Private	Public	Private	Public	Private	Public	Private	Public	Private
City	53.5	46.5	91.8	8.2	90.8	9.2	90.3	9.7	94.1	5.9
MSA[1]	55.8	44.2	90.8	9.2	89.4	10.6	88.9	11.1	92.2	7.8
U.S.	58.9	41.1	86.9	13.1	89.0	11.0	89.0	11.0	89.7	10.3

Note: Figures shown cover persons 3 years old and over; (1) Figures cover the Anchorage, AK Metropolitan Statistical Area
Source: U.S. Census Bureau, 2016-2020 American Community Survey 5-Year Estimates

Higher Education

Four-Year Colleges			Two-Year Colleges			Medical Schools[1]	Law Schools[2]	Voc/ Tech[3]
Public	Private Non-profit	Private For-profit	Public	Private Non-profit	Private For-profit			
1	2	0	0	0	1	0	0	0

Note: Figures cover institutions located within the Anchorage, AK Metropolitan Statistical Area and include main campuses only; (1) includes schools accredited by the Liaison Committee on Medical Education and the American Osteopathic Association's Commission on Osteopathic College Accreditation; (2) includes ABA-accredited schools, schools with provisional ABA accreditation, and state accredited schools; (3) includes all schools with programs that are less than 2 years.
Source: National Center for Education Statistics, Integrated Postsecondary Education System (IPEDS), 2020-21; Wikipedia, List of Medical Schools in the United States, accessed April 11, 2022; Wikipedia, List of Law Schools in the United States, accessed April 11, 2022

EMPLOYERS

Major Employers

Company Name	Industry
ASRC Energy Services	Oil & gas field services
AT&T	Telephone communication, except radio
BP Transportation (Alaska)	Crude petroleum production
Bureau of Land Management	Information bureau
Carrs/Safeway	Grocery stores
Federal Aviation Administration	Aircraft regulating agencies
Federal Express Corporation	Air cargo carrier, scheduled
Fred Meyer	Retail
Galen Hospital Alaska	General medical & surgical hospitals
Indian Health Service	General medical & surgical hospitals
Municipality of Anchorage	Mayors' office
Nabors Alaska Drilling	Drilling oil & gas wells
Providence Health Services	Healthcare
U.S. Fish and Wildlife Service	Fish & wildlife conservation agency, government
United States Department of the Air Force	U.S. military
USPHS AK Native Medical Center	General medical & surgical hospitals
Wal-Mart Stores	Retail

Note: Companies shown are located within the Anchorage, AK Metropolitan Statistical Area.
Source: Hoovers.com; Wikipedia

PUBLIC SAFETY

Crime Rate

Area	Total Crime	Violent Crime Rate				Property Crime Rate		
		Murder	Rape[3]	Robbery	Aggrav. Assault	Burglary	Larceny -Theft	Motor Vehicle Theft
City	4,659.4	6.3	194.8	194.8	816.4	504.2	2,541.7	401.2
Suburbs[1]	3,312.3	0.0	63.6	42.4	445.2	233.2	2,247.1	280.9
Metro[2]	4,576.1	5.9	186.7	185.4	793.4	487.5	2,523.4	393.8
U.S.	2,356.7	6.5	38.4	73.9	279.7	314.2	1,398.0	246.0

Note: Figures are crimes per 100,000 population; (1) All areas within the metro area that are located outside the city limits; (2) Figures cover the Anchorage, AK Metropolitan Statistical Area; (3) All figures shown were reported using the revised Uniform Crime Reporting (UCR) definition of rape.
Source: FBI Uniform Crime Reports, 2020

Hate Crimes

Area	Number of Quarters Reported	Number of Incidents per Bias Motivation					
		Race/Ethnicity/ Ancestry	Religion	Sexual Orientation	Disability	Gender	Gender Identity
City	4	3	0	1	0	1	0
U.S.	4	5,227	1,244	1,110	130	75	266

Source: Federal Bureau of Investigation, Hate Crime Statistics 2020

Identity Theft Consumer Reports

Area	Reports	Reports per 100,000 Population	Rank[2]
MSA[1]	562	142	319
U.S.	1,434,676	432	-

Note: (1) Figures cover the Anchorage, AK Metropolitan Statistical Area; (2) Rank ranges from 1 to 391 where 1 indicates greatest number of identity theft reports per 100,000 population
Source: Federal Trade Commission, Consumer Sentinel Network Data Book 2021

Fraud and Other Consumer Reports

Area	Reports	Reports per 100,000 Population	Rank[2]
MSA[1]	4,958	1,251	30
U.S.	4,328,977	1,304	-

Note: (1) Figures cover the Anchorage, AK Metropolitan Statistical Area; (2) Rank ranges from 1 to 391 where 1 indicates greatest number of fraud and other consumer reports per 100,000 population
Source: Federal Trade Commission, Consumer Sentinel Network Data Book 2021

POLITICS

2020 Presidential Election Results

Area	Biden	Trump	Jorgensen	Hawkins	Other
Alaska	42.8	52.8	2.5	0.0	1.9
U.S.	51.3	46.8	1.2	0.3	0.5

Note: Results are percentages and may not add to 100% due to rounding
Source: Dave Leip's Atlas of U.S. Presidential Elections

SPORTS

Professional Sports Teams

Team Name	League	Year Established
No teams are located in the metro area		

Source: Wikipedia, Major Professional Sports Teams of the United States and Canada, April 6, 2022

CLIMATE

Average and Extreme Temperatures

Temperature	Jan	Feb	Mar	Apr	May	Jun	Jul	Aug	Sep	Oct	Nov	Dec	Yr.
Extreme High (°F)	50	48	51	65	77	85	82	82	73	61	53	48	85
Average High (°F)	22	25	33	43	55	62	65	63	55	41	28	22	43
Average Temp. (°F)	15	18	25	36	47	55	59	57	48	35	22	16	36
Average Low (°F)	8	11	17	28	39	47	51	49	41	28	15	10	29
Extreme Low (°F)	-34	-26	-24	-4	17	33	36	31	19	-5	-21	-30	-34

Note: Figures cover the years 1953-1995
Source: National Climatic Data Center, International Station Meteorological Climate Summary, 9/96

Average Precipitation/Snowfall/Humidity

Precip./Humidity	Jan	Feb	Mar	Apr	May	Jun	Jul	Aug	Sep	Oct	Nov	Dec	Yr.
Avg. Precip. (in.)	0.8	0.8	0.7	0.6	0.7	1.0	1.9	2.4	2.7	1.9	1.1	1.1	15.7
Avg. Snowfall (in.)	10	12	10	5	Tr	0	0	0	Tr	8	12	15	71
Avg. Rel. Hum. 6am (%)	74	74	72	75	73	74	80	84	84	78	78	78	77
Avg. Rel. Hum. 3pm (%)	73	67	57	54	50	55	62	64	64	67	74	76	64

Note: Figures cover the years 1953-1995; Tr = Trace amounts (<0.05 in. of rain; <0.5 in. of snow)
Source: National Climatic Data Center, International Station Meteorological Climate Summary, 9/96

Weather Conditions

Temperature			Daytime Sky			Precipitation		
0°F & below	32°F & below	65°F & above	Clear	Partly cloudy	Cloudy	0.01 inch or more precip.	0.1 inch or more snow/ice	Thunder-storms
32	194	41	50	115	200	113	49	2

Note: Figures are average number of days per year and cover the years 1953-1995
Source: National Climatic Data Center, International Station Meteorological Climate Summary, 9/96

HAZARDOUS WASTE

Superfund Sites

The Anchorage, AK metro area is home to two sites on the EPA's Superfund National Priorities List: **Elmendorf Air Force Base** (final); **Fort Richardson (USARMY)** (final). There are a total of 1,165 Superfund sites with a status of proposed or final on the list in the U.S. *U.S. Environmental Protection Agency, National Priorities List, April 6, 2022*

AIR QUALITY

Air Quality Trends: Ozone

	1990	1995	2000	2005	2010	2016	2017	2018	2019	2020
MSA[1]	n/a	n/a	n/a	n/a	n/a	n/a	n/a	n/a	n/a	n/a
U.S.	0.090	0.091	0.082	0.080	0.074	0.070	0.069	0.070	0.066	0.068

Note: (1) Data covers the Anchorage, AK Metropolitan Statistical Area; n/a not available. The values shown are the composite ozone concentration averages among trend sites based on the highest fourth daily maximum 8-hour concentration in parts per million. These trends are based on sites having an adequate record of monitoring data during the trend period. Data from exceptional events are included.
Source: U.S. Environmental Protection Agency, Air Quality Monitoring Information, "Air Quality Trends by City, 1990-2020"

Air Quality Index

Area	Percent of Days when Air Quality was...[2]					AQI Statistics[2]	
	Good	Moderate	Unhealthy for Sensitive Groups	Unhealthy	Very Unhealthy	Maximum	Median
MSA[1]	89.1	10.7	0.3	0.0	0.0	103	25

Note: (1) Data covers the Anchorage, AK Metropolitan Statistical Area; (2) Based on 366 days with AQI data in 2020. Air Quality Index (AQI) is an index for reporting daily air quality. EPA calculates the AQI for five major air pollutants regulated by the Clean Air Act: ground-level ozone, particle pollution (aka particulate matter), carbon monoxide, sulfur dioxide, and nitrogen dioxide. The AQI runs from 0 to 500. The higher the AQI value, the greater the level of air pollution and the greater the health concern. There are six AQI categories: "Good" AQI is between 0 and 50. Air quality is considered satisfactory; "Moderate" AQI is between 51 and 100. Air quality is acceptable; "Unhealthy for Sensitive Groups" When AQI values are between 101 and 150, members of sensitive groups may experience health effects; "Unhealthy" When AQI values are between 151 and 200 everyone may begin to experience health effects; "Very Unhealthy" AQI values between 201 and 300 trigger a health alert; "Hazardous" AQI values over 300 trigger warnings of emergency conditions (not shown).
Source: U.S. Environmental Protection Agency, Air Quality Index Report, 2020

Air Quality Index Pollutants

Area	Percent of Days when AQI Pollutant was...[2]					
	Carbon Monoxide	Nitrogen Dioxide	Ozone	Sulfur Dioxide	Particulate Matter 2.5	Particulate Matter 10
MSA[1]	1.1	0.0	0.0	0.0	67.8	31.1

Note: (1) Data covers the Anchorage, AK Metropolitan Statistical Area; (2) Based on 366 days with AQI data in 2020. The Air Quality Index (AQI) is an index for reporting daily air quality. EPA calculates the AQI for five major air pollutants regulated by the Clean Air Act: ground-level ozone, particle pollution (also known as particulate matter), carbon monoxide, sulfur dioxide, and nitrogen dioxide. The AQI runs from 0 to 500. The higher the AQI value, the greater the level of air pollution and the greater the health concern.
Source: U.S. Environmental Protection Agency, Air Quality Index Report, 2020

Maximum Air Pollutant Concentrations: Particulate Matter, Ozone, CO and Lead

	Particulate Matter 10 (ug/m^3)	Particulate Matter 2.5 Wtd AM (ug/m^3)	Particulate Matter 2.5 24-Hr (ug/m^3)	Ozone (ppm)	Carbon Monoxide (ppm)	Lead (ug/m^3)
MSA[1] Level	77	5.9	24	n/a	3	n/a
NAAQS[2]	150	15	35	0.075	9	0.15
Met NAAQS[2]	Yes	Yes	Yes	n/a	Yes	n/a

Note: (1) Data covers the Anchorage, AK Metropolitan Statistical Area; Data from exceptional events are included; (2) National Ambient Air Quality Standards; ppm = parts per million; ug/m^3 = micrograms per cubic meter; n/a not available.
Concentrations: Particulate Matter 10 (coarse particulate)—highest second maximum 24-hour concentration; Particulate Matter 2.5 Wtd AM (fine particulate)—highest weighted annual mean concentration; Particulate Matter 2.5 24-Hour (fine particulate)—highest 98th percentile 24-hour concentration; Ozone—highest fourth daily maximum 8-hour concentration; Carbon Monoxide—highest second maximum non-overlapping 8-hour concentration; Lead—maximum running 3-month average
Source: U.S. Environmental Protection Agency, Air Quality Monitoring Information, "Air Quality Statistics by City, 2020"

Maximum Air Pollutant Concentrations: Nitrogen Dioxide and Sulfur Dioxide

	Nitrogen Dioxide AM (ppb)	Nitrogen Dioxide 1-Hr (ppb)	Sulfur Dioxide AM (ppb)	Sulfur Dioxide 1-Hr (ppb)	Sulfur Dioxide 24-Hr (ppb)
MSA[1] Level	n/a	n/a	n/a	n/a	n/a
NAAQS[2]	53	100	30	75	140
Met NAAQS[2]	n/a	n/a	n/a	n/a	n/a

Note: (1) Data covers the Anchorage, AK Metropolitan Statistical Area; Data from exceptional events are included; (2) National Ambient Air Quality Standards; ppm = parts per million; ug/m^3 = micrograms per cubic meter; n/a not available.
Concentrations: Nitrogen Dioxide AM—highest arithmetic mean concentration; Nitrogen Dioxide 1-Hr—highest 98th percentile 1-hour daily maximum concentration; Sulfur Dioxide AM—highest annual mean concentration; Sulfur Dioxide 1-Hr—highest 99th percentile 1-hour daily maximum concentration; Sulfur Dioxide 24-Hr—highest second maximum 24-hour concentration
Source: U.S. Environmental Protection Agency, Air Quality Monitoring Information, "Air Quality Statistics by City, 2020"

Boise City, Idaho

Background

Boise (boy-see) is the capital and largest city in Idaho, lying along the Boise River adjacent to the foothills of the Rocky Mountains. The city is located southwest of the western slopes of the Rockies and is the site of a great system of natural warm water springs.

Boise's spectacular natural location is its most popular, and obvious, attraction, and this, coupled with its dynamic economic growth in recent decades, makes Boise an altogether remarkable city. The splendor of its surroundings, together with an average 18-minute drive to work, has allowed the city to combine pleasure and production in an enviable mix.

French-Canadian trappers were familiar with Boise and its environs by 1811, and the name of the city is an Anglicization of the French Les Bois—the trees. The first substantial European settlement dates to 1863 when, in the spring of that year, I.M. Coston built from pegged driftwood a great house that served as a hub for the activities of prospectors, traders, and Native Americans. In the same year, the U.S. Army built Fort Boise, and considerable deposits of gold and silver were discovered in the area. The U.S. Assay Office in Boise, in 1870-71 alone, is said to have valuated more than $75 million in precious metals.

The area is rich in gold rush lore, and there is still talk of buried treasure from that era: The eastbound stagecoach from Boise was said to have been waylaid by a robber, six miles above the city on the south side of the river, who, though wounded in the attack, managed to drag off a strongbox filled with $50,000 in gold. The robber died of his wounds and was discovered the next day, but the loot was never found.

The Boise area was subsequently developed for farming, as crops of grains, vegetables, and fruits, replaced the mines as its source of wealth. It became the territorial capital of Idaho in 1864 and the state capital in 1890. Education was served with the opening of a university in 1932, which became Boise State University in 1974 and now enrolls about 20,000 students.

The city's natural setting offers a great range of outdoor activities that are pursued energetically by its citizens. Its rivers, mountains, deserts, and lakes offer world-class skiing, hiking, camping, kayaking, river rafting, hunting, and fishing. Bike paths run throughout the city and into Boise's large outdoor trail network, the Boise River Greenbelt. Recreational wilderness exists extensively just outside the city's limits. The Word Center for Birds of Prey is located on the city's southern frontier and is the site of the Peregrine Falcon's rehabilitation and release into the wild.

Many large regional, national, and international companies are headquartered in Boise, including major call centers for DIRECTV and T-Mobile.

The city produces high- and low-tech products and everything in between: software, computer components, steel and sheet metal products, mobile homes, lumber products, farm machinery, packed meats, and processed foods. Increasingly an advanced technological center, it continues to serve as a trading center for the greater agricultural region.

By virtue of its history and geographical character, the city can be considered a presence on the Pacific Rim. In a more tangible vein, Boise, with nine airlines operating at its airport, is conveniently tied to the wider world.

Boise's Basque community is the largest in the United States and the third largest in the world outside Argentina and the Basque Country in Spain and France. A large Basque festival known as Jaialdi is held once every five years, with the next scheduled for 2025. Boise (along with Valley and Boise Counties) hosted the 2009 Special Olympics World Winter Games. More than 2,500 athletes from over 100 countries participated.

The city is protected by the mountains to the north in such a way that it is largely unbothered by the extreme blizzards that affect eastern Idaho and parts of neighboring states. Boise, and this section of western Idaho generally, is affected by climatic influences from the Pacific Ocean and exhibits an unusually mild climate for this latitude. Summers can be hot, but nights are almost always cool, and sunshine generally prevails.

Rankings

General Rankings

- For its "Best for Vets: Places to Live 2019" rankings, *Military Times* evaluated 599 cities (83 large, 234 medium, 282 small) and compared the locations across three broad categories: veteran and military culture/services; economic indicators; and livability factors such as health, crime, traffic, and school quality. Boise City ranked #13 out of the top 50, in the medium-sized city category (population of 100,000-249,999). Data points more specific to veterans and the military weighed more heavily than others. *rebootcamp.militarytimes.com, "Military Times Best Places to Live 2019," September 10, 2018*
- *US News & World Report* conducted a survey of more than 3,600 people and analyzed the 150 largest metropolitan areas to determine what matters most when selecting the next place to live. Boise City ranked #11 out of the top 25 as having the best combination of desirable factors. Criteria: cost of living; quality of life and education; net migration; job market; desirability; and other factors. *realestate.usnews.com, "The 25 Best Places to Live in the U.S. in 2021-2022," July 13, 2021*
- The Boise City metro area was identified as one of America's fastest-growing areas in terms of population and business growth by *MagnifyMoney.* The area ranked #8 out of 35. The 100 most populous metro areas in the U.S. were evaluated on their change from 2011 to 2016 in the following categories: people and housing; workforce and employment opportunities; growing industry. *www.businessinsider.com, "The 35 Cities in the US with the Biggest Influx of People, the Most Work Opportunities, and the Hottest Business Growth," August 12, 2018*
- The Boise City metro area was identified as one of America's fastest-growing areas in terms of population and economy by *Forbes.* The area ranked #1 out of 25. The 100 most populous metro areas in the U.S. were evaluated on the following criteria: estimated population growth; employment; economic output; wages; home values. *Forbes, "America's Fastest-Growing Cities 2018," February 28, 2018*
- Boise City was selected as one of the best places to live in the United States by *Money* magazine. The city ranked #13 out of 50. This year's list focused on cities with populations ranging from 25,000 through 500,000. Beginning with a pool of 1,300 candidates, editors looked at 100 metrics, organized into the these categories: income and personal finances, cost of living, economic opportunity and housing market, amenities, health and safety, education, racial diversity, and quality of life. *Money, "The 50 Best Places to Live in the U.S. in 2021-2022" September 14, 2021*
- In their eigth annual survey, Livability.com looked at data for more than 1,000 small to mid-sized U.S. cities to determine the rankings for Livability's "Top 100 Best Places to Live" in 2021. Boise City ranked #24. Criteria: housing and economy; sustainability; social and civic engagement; education; demographics; health care options; transportation & infrastructure; and community amenities. *Livability.com, "Top 100 Best Places to Live 2021" October 12, 2021*

Business/Finance Rankings

- The Brookings Institution ranked the nation's largest cities based on income inequality. Boise City was ranked #60 (#1 = greatest inequality). Criteria: the "95/20 ratio," a figure representing the income at which a household earns more than 95 percent of all other households, divided by the income at which a household earns more than only 20 percent of all other households. *Brookings Institution, "Household Income Inequality, Largest Cities of 97 Large U.S. Metro Areas, 2014-2016," February 5, 2018*
- The Brookings Institution ranked the 100 largest metro areas in the U.S. based on income inequality. Boise City was ranked #89 (#1 = greatest inequality). Criteria: the "95/20 ratio," a figure representing the income at which a household earns more than 95 percent of all other households, divided by the income at which a household earns more than only 20 percent of all other households. *Brookings Institution, "Household Income Inequality, 100 Largest U.S. Metro Areas, 2014-2016," February 5, 2018*
- The Boise City metro area appeared on the Milken Institute "2021 Best Performing Cities" list. Rank: #6 out of 200 large metro areas (population over 250,000). Criteria: job growth; wage and salary growth; high-tech output growth; housing affordability; household broadband access. *Milken Institute, "Best-Performing Cities 2021," February 16, 2021*
- *Forbes* ranked the 200 most populous metro areas to determine the nation's "Best Places for Business and Careers." The Boise City metro area was ranked #29. Criteria: costs (business and living); job growth (past and projected); income growth; quality of life; educational attainment (college and high school); projected economic growth; cultural and leisure opportunities; workplace tolerance laws; net migration patterns. *Forbes, "The Best Places for Business and Careers 2019: Seattle Still On Top," October 30, 2019*

Dating/Romance Rankings

- Boise City was ranked #3 out of 25 cities that stood out for inspiring romance and attracting diners on the website OpenTable.com. Criteria: percentage of people who dined out on Valentine's Day in 2018; percentage of romantic restaurants as rated by OpenTable diner reviews; and percentage of tables seated for two. *OpenTable, "25 Most Romantic Cities in America for 2019," February 7, 2019*

Education Rankings

- Personal finance website *WalletHub* analyzed the 150 largest U.S. metropolitan statistical areas to determine where the most educated Americans are putting their degrees to work. Criteria: education levels; percentage of workers with degrees; education quality and attainment gap; public school quality rankings; quality and enrollment of each metro area's universities. Boise City was ranked #58 (#1 = most educated city). *www.WalletHub.com, "Most & Least Educated Cities in America," July 19, 2021*

Food/Drink Rankings

- Boise City was selected as one of America's 10 most vegan-friendly areas. The city was ranked #5. Criteria now includes smaller urban areas, following the migration to smaller cities due to the pandemic. *People for the Ethical Treatment of Animals, "Top 10 Vegan-Friendly Towns and Small Cities of 2020," December 14, 2020*

Health/Fitness Rankings

- For each of the 100 largest cities in the United States, the American Fitness Index®, published by the American College of Sports Medicine and the Anthem Foundation, evaluated community infrastructure and 34 health behaviors including preventive health, levels of chronic disease conditions, food insecurity, sleep quality, pedestrian safety, air quality, and community resources that support physical activity. Boise City ranked #17 for "community fitness." *americanfitnessindex.org, "2021 ACSM American Fitness Index Summary Report," July 13, 2021*
- Boise City was identified as a "2021 Spring Allergy Capital." The area ranked #82 out of 100. Three groups of factors were used to identify the most challenging cities for people with allergies during the spring season: annual spring pollen levels; over the counter medicine use; number of board-certified allergy specialists. *Asthma and Allergy Foundation of America, "Spring Allergy Capitals 2021," February 23, 2021*
- Boise City was identified as a "2021 Fall Allergy Capital." The area ranked #85 out of 100. Three groups of factors were used to identify the most challenging cities for people with allergies during the fall season: annual fall pollen levels; over the counter medicine use; number of board-certified allergy specialists. *Asthma and Allergy Foundation of America, "Fall Allergy Capitals 2021," February 23, 2021*
- Boise City was identified as a "2021 Asthma Capital." The area ranked #75 out of the nation's 100 largest metropolitan areas. Criteria: estimated asthma prevalence; asthma-related mortality; and ER visits due to asthma. Risk factors analyzed but not factored in the rankings: annual pollen score; annual air quality; public smoking laws; number of board-certified asthma specialists; rescue medication use; controller medication use; uninsured rate; poverty rate. *Asthma and Allergy Foundation of America, "Asthma Capitals 2021: The Most Challenging Places to Live With Asthma," May 5, 2021*

Real Estate Rankings

- *WalletHub* compared the most populated U.S. cities to determine which had the best markets for real estate agents. Boise City ranked #107 where demand was high and pay was the best. Criteria: sales per agent; annual median wage for real-estate agents; monthly average starting salary for real estate agents; real estate job density and competition; unemployment rate; home turnover rate; housing-market health index; and other relevant metrics. *www.WalletHub.com, "2021 Best Places to Be a Real Estate Agent," May 12, 2021*
- The Boise City metro area appeared on Realtor.com's list of hot housing markets to watch in 2022. The area ranked #2. Criteria: forecasted home price and sales growth; overall economy; population trends. *Realtor.com®, "Top 10 Housing Markets Positioned for Growth in 2022," December 7, 2021*
- Boise City was ranked #9 in the top 20 out of the 100 largest metro areas in terms of house price appreciation in 2021 (#1 = highest rate). *Federal Housing Finance Agency, House Price Index, 4th Quarter 2021*

- The Boise City metro area was identified as one of the 20 best housing markets in the U.S. in 2021. The area ranked #10 out of 184 markets. Criteria: year-over-year change of median sales price of existing single-family homes between the 4th quarter of 2020 and the 4th quarter of 2021. *National Association of Realtors®, Median Sales Price of Existing Single-Family Homes for Metropolitan Areas, 4th Quarter 2021*
- Boise City was ranked #222 out of 237 metro areas in terms of housing affordability in 2021 by the National Association of Home Builders (#1 = most affordable). Criteria: the share of homes sold in that area affordable to a family earning the local median income, based on standard mortgage underwriting criteria. *National Association of Home Builders®, NAHB-Wells Fargo Housing Opportunity Index, 4th Quarter 2021*

Safety Rankings

- Allstate ranked the 200 largest cities in America in terms of driver safety. Boise City ranked #2. Criteria: internal property damage claims over a two-year period from January 2016 to December 2017. The report helps increase the importance of safety and awareness behind the wheel. *Allstate, "Allstate America's Best Drivers Report, 2019" June 24, 2019*
- The National Insurance Crime Bureau ranked 390 metro areas in the U.S. in terms of per capita rates of vehicle theft. The Boise City metro area ranked #297 (#1 = highest rate). Criteria: number of vehicle theft offenses per 100,000 inhabitants in 2020. *National Insurance Crime Bureau, "Hot Spots 2020," August 31, 2021*

Seniors/Retirement Rankings

- From its Best Cities for Successful Aging indexes, the Milken Institute generated rankings for metropolitan areas, weighing data in nine categories—health care, wellness, living arrangements, transportation and convenience, financial characteristics, education, employment, community engagement, and overall livability. The Boise City metro area was ranked #34 overall in the large metro area category. *Milken Institute, "Best Cities for Successful Aging, 2017" March 14, 2017*
- Boise City was identified as #13 of 20 most popular places to retire in the Western region by *Topretirements.com*. The site separated its annual "Best Places to Retire" list by major U.S. regions for 2019. The list reflects the 20 cities that visitors to the website are most interested in for retirement, based on the number of times a city's review was viewed on the website. *Topretirements.com, "20 Best Places to Retire in the West-2019," November 11, 2019*

Sports/Recreation Rankings

- Boise City was chosen as one of America's best cities for bicycling. The city ranked #21 out of 50. Criteria: cycling infrastructure that is safe and friendly for all ages; energy and bike culture. The editors evaluated cities with populations of 100,000 or more. *Bicycling, "The 50 Best Bike Cities in America," October 10, 2018*

Women/Minorities Rankings

- Personal finance website *WalletHub* compared more than 180 U.S. cities across two key dimensions, "Hispanic Business-Friendliness" and "Hispanic Purchasing Power," to arrive at the most favorable conditions for Hispanic entrepreneurs. Boise City was ranked #35 out of 182. Criteria includes: share of Hispanic-Owned Businesses; Hispanic entrepreneurship rate to median annual income of Hispanics; Small Business-Friendliness score; cost of living; and number of Hispanics with at least a bachelor's degree. *WalletHub.com, "2019's Best Cities for Hispanic Entrepreneurs," May 1, 2019*

Miscellaneous Rankings

- *WalletHub* compared the 150 most populated U.S. cities to determine their operating efficiency. A "Quality of City Services" score was constructed for each city and then divided by the total budget per capita to reveal which were managed the best. Boise City ranked #2. Criteria: financial stability; economy; education; safety; health; infrastructure and pollution. *www.WalletHub.com, "2021's Best- & Worst-Run Cities in America," June 22, 2021*

Business Environment

DEMOGRAPHICS

Population Growth

Area	1990 Census	2000 Census	2010 Census	2020* Estimate	Population Growth (%) 1990-2020	Population Growth (%) 2010-2020
City	144,317	185,787	205,671	228,057	58.0	10.9
MSA[1]	319,596	464,840	616,561	730,483	128.6	18.5
U.S.	248,709,873	281,421,906	308,745,538	326,569,308	31.3	5.8

Note: (1) Figures cover the Boise City, ID Metropolitan Statistical Area; (*) 2016-2020 5-year estimated population
Source: U.S. Census Bureau, 1990 Census, Census 2000, Census 2010, 2016-2020 American Community Survey 5-Year Estimates

Household Size

Area	Persons in Household (%) One	Two	Three	Four	Five	Six	Seven or More	Average Household Size
City	33.4	35.7	14.3	10.3	4.5	1.2	0.7	2.40
MSA[1]	26.1	35.8	14.7	12.4	6.5	2.8	1.6	2.70
U.S.	28.0	33.9	15.5	12.9	6.0	2.3	1.4	2.60

Note: (1) Figures cover the Boise City, ID Metropolitan Statistical Area
Source: U.S. Census Bureau, 2016-2020 American Community Survey 5-Year Estimates

Race

Area	White Alone[2] (%)	Black Alone[2] (%)	Asian Alone[2] (%)	AIAN[3] Alone[2] (%)	NHOPI[4] Alone[2] (%)	Other Race Alone[2] (%)	Two or More Races (%)
City	88.0	1.6	3.1	0.7	0.2	2.1	4.3
MSA[1]	86.5	0.9	1.9	0.7	0.2	4.9	4.7
U.S.	70.4	12.6	5.6	0.8	0.2	5.1	5.2

Note: (1) Figures cover the Boise City, ID Metropolitan Statistical Area; (2) Alone is defined as not being in combination with one or more other races; (3) American Indian and Alaska Native; (4) Native Hawaiian and Other Pacific Islander
Source: U.S. Census Bureau, 2016-2020 American Community Survey 5-Year Estimates

Hispanic or Latino Origin

Area	Total (%)	Mexican (%)	Puerto Rican (%)	Cuban (%)	Other (%)
City	9.0	6.8	0.4	0.0	1.8
MSA[1]	13.9	11.5	0.4	0.1	1.9
U.S.	18.2	11.2	1.7	0.7	4.5

Note: Persons of Hispanic or Latino origin can be of any race; (1) Figures cover the Boise City, ID Metropolitan Statistical Area
Source: U.S. Census Bureau, 2016-2020 American Community Survey 5-Year Estimates

Ancestry

Area	German	Irish	English	American	Italian	Polish	French[2]	Scottish	Dutch
City	16.6	11.6	19.3	4.5	4.1	2.1	2.1	3.4	1.6
MSA[1]	16.3	9.7	17.7	5.0	3.3	1.5	2.4	3.1	1.9
U.S.	13.0	9.7	7.7	5.9	5.1	2.7	2.3	1.6	1.1

Note: Figures are the percentage of the total population reporting a particular ancestry. The nine most commonly reported ancestries in the U.S. are shown. Figures include multiple ancestries (e.g. if a person reported being Irish and Italian, they were included in both columns); (1) Figures cover the Boise City, ID Metropolitan Statistical Area; (2) Excludes Basque
Source: U.S. Census Bureau, 2016-2020 American Community Survey 5-Year Estimates

Foreign-born Population

Area	Percent of Population Born in: Any Foreign Country	Asia	Mexico	Europe	Caribbean	Central America[2]	South America	Africa	Canada
City	6.6	2.8	1.0	1.3	0.0	0.1	0.2	0.6	0.4
MSA[1]	6.4	1.6	2.6	1.1	0.0	0.2	0.3	0.3	0.3
U.S.	13.5	4.2	3.3	1.5	1.3	1.1	1.0	0.7	0.3

Note: (1) Figures cover the Boise City, ID Metropolitan Statistical Area; (2) Excludes Mexico.
Source: U.S. Census Bureau, 2016-2020 American Community Survey 5-Year Estimates

Marital Status

Area	Never Married	Now Married[2]	Separated	Widowed	Divorced
City	34.9	46.6	1.0	4.3	13.2
MSA[1]	29.1	53.2	1.1	4.4	12.3
U.S.	33.5	48.1	1.8	5.7	10.8

Note: Figures are percentages and cover the population 15 years of age and older; (1) Figures cover the Boise City, ID Metropolitan Statistical Area; (2) Excludes separated
Source: U.S. Census Bureau, 2016-2020 American Community Survey 5-Year Estimates

Disability by Age

Area	All Ages	Under 18 Years Old	18 to 64 Years Old	65 Years and Over
City	11.1	4.1	9.3	29.3
MSA[1]	11.9	4.1	10.5	31.5
U.S.	12.7	4.3	10.3	34.0

Note: Figures show percent of the civilian noninstitutionalized population that reported having a disability. Disability status is determined from six types of difficulty: vision, hearing, cognitive, ambulatory, self-care, and independent living. For children under 5 years old, hearing and vision difficulty are used to determine disability status. For children between the ages of 5 and 14, disability status is determined from hearing, vision, cognitive, ambulatory, and self-care difficulties. For people aged 15 years and older, they are considered to have a disability if they have difficulty with any one of the six difficulty types; Note: (1) Figures cover the Boise City, ID Metropolitan Statistical Area
Source: U.S. Census Bureau, 2016-2020 American Community Survey 5-Year Estimates

Age

Area	Percent of Population									Median Age
	Under Age 5	Age 5–19	Age 20–34	Age 35–44	Age 45–54	Age 55–64	Age 65–74	Age 75–84	Age 85+	
City	4.8	18.2	23.3	13.9	12.8	12.4	8.6	4.2	1.8	37.5
MSA[1]	6.2	21.5	20.0	13.5	12.4	11.9	9.0	4.2	1.4	36.6
U.S.	6.0	19.1	20.6	12.7	12.7	12.9	9.4	4.7	2.0	38.2

Note: (1) Figures cover the Boise City, ID Metropolitan Statistical Area
Source: U.S. Census Bureau, 2016-2020 American Community Survey 5-Year Estimates

Gender

Area	Males	Females	Males per 100 Females
City	114,385	113,672	100.6
MSA[1]	364,989	365,494	99.9
U.S.	160,818,530	165,750,778	97.0

Note: (1) Figures cover the Boise City, ID Metropolitan Statistical Area
Source: U.S. Census Bureau, 2016-2020 American Community Survey 5-Year Estimates

Religious Groups by Family

Area	Catholic	Baptist	Non-Den.	Methodist[2]	Lutheran	LDS[3]	Pente-costal	Presby-terian[4]	Muslim[5]	Judaism
MSA[1]	8.0	2.9	4.2	2.1	1.2	15.9	2.3	0.6	0.1	0.1
U.S.	19.1	9.3	4.0	4.0	2.3	2.0	1.9	1.6	0.8	0.7

Note: Figures are the number of adherents as a percentage of the total population; (1) Figures cover the Boise City, ID Metropolitan Statistical Area; (2) Methodist/Pietist; (3) Latter Day Saints; (4) Reformed; (5) Figures are estimates
Source: Association of Statisticians of American Religious Bodies, 2010 U.S. Religion Census: Religious Congregations & Membership Study

Religious Groups by Tradition

Area	Catholic	Evangelical Protestant	Mainline Protestant	Other Tradition	Black Protestant	Orthodox
MSA[1]	8.0	13.0	4.4	16.7	<0.1	0.1
U.S.	19.1	16.2	7.3	4.3	1.6	0.3

Note: Figures are the number of adherents as a percentage of the total population; (1) Figures cover the Boise City, ID Metropolitan Statistical Area
Source: Association of Statisticians of American Religious Bodies, 2010 U.S. Religion Census: Religious Congregations & Membership Study

ECONOMY

Gross Metropolitan Product

Area	2017	2018	2019	2020	Rank[2]
MSA[1]	33.9	36.5	38.7	40.8	79

Note: Figures are in billions of dollars; (1) Figures cover the Boise City, ID Metropolitan Statistical Area; (2) Rank is based on 2018 data and ranges from 1 to 381
Source: U.S. Conference of Mayors, U.S. Metro Economies: GMP & Employment 2018-2020, September 2019

Economic Growth

Area	2015-17 (%)	2018 (%)	2019 (%)	2020 (%)	Rank[2]
MSA[1]	3.7	5.5	4.1	3.2	45
U.S.	1.9	2.9	2.3	2.1	–

Note: Figures are real gross metropolitan product (GMP) growth rates and represent average annual percent change; (1) Figures cover the Boise City, ID Metropolitan Statistical Area; (2) Rank is based on 2017 2-year average annual percent change and ranges from 1 to 381
Source: U.S. Conference of Mayors, U.S. Metro Economies: GMP & Employment 2018-2020, September 2019

Metropolitan Area Exports

Area	2015	2016	2017	2018	2019	2020	Rank[2]
MSA[1]	2,668.0	3,021.7	2,483.3	2,771.7	2,062.8	1,632.9	109

Note: Figures are in millions of dollars; (1) Figures cover the Boise City, ID Metropolitan Statistical Area; (2) Rank is based on 2020 data and ranges from 1 to 389
Source: U.S. Department of Commerce, International Trade Administration, Office of Trade and Economic Analysis, Industry and Analysis, Exports by Metropolitan Area, data extracted March 4, 2022

Building Permits

Area	Single-Family			Multi-Family			Total		
	2019	2020	Pct. Chg.	2019	2020	Pct. Chg.	2019	2020	Pct. Chg.
City	698	756	8.3	883	369	-58.2	1,581	1,125	-28.8
MSA[1]	7,570	8,158	7.8	3,062	1,604	-47.6	10,632	9,762	-8.2
U.S.	862,100	979,400	13.6	523,900	491,700	-6.1	1,386,000	1,471,100	6.1

Note: (1) Figures cover the Boise City, ID Metropolitan Statistical Area; Figures represent new, privately-owned housing units authorized (unadjusted data); All permit data are based on estimates with imputation
Source: U.S. Census Bureau, Manufacturing, Mining, and Construction Statistics, Building Permits, 2019, 2020

Bankruptcy Filings

Area	Business Filings			Nonbusiness Filings		
	2020	2021	% Chg.	2020	2021	% Chg.
Ada County	19	13	-31.6	589	393	-33.3
U.S.	21,655	14,347	-33.7	522,808	399,269	-23.6

Note: Business filings include Chapter 7, Chapter 9, Chapter 11, Chapter 12, Chapter 13, Chapter 15, and Section 304; Nonbusiness filings include Chapter 7, Chapter 11, and Chapter 13
Source: Administrative Office of the U.S. Courts, Business and Nonbusiness Bankruptcy, County Cases Commenced by Chapter of the Bankruptcy Code, During the 12-Month Period Ending December 31, 2020 and Business and Nonbusiness Bankruptcy, County Cases Commenced by Chapter of the Bankruptcy Code, During the 12-Month Period Ending December 31, 2021

Housing Vacancy Rates

Area	Gross Vacancy Rate[2] (%)			Year-Round Vacancy Rate[3] (%)			Rental Vacancy Rate[4] (%)			Homeowner Vacancy Rate[5] (%)		
	2019	2020	2021	2019	2020	2021	2019	2020	2021	2019	2020	2021
MSA[1]	n/a	n/a	n/a	n/a	n/a	n/a	n/a	n/a	n/a	n/a	n/a	n/a
U.S.	12.0	10.6	10.8	9.5	8.2	8.4	6.7	6.3	6.1	1.4	1.0	0.9

Note: (1) Figures cover the Boise City, ID Metropolitan Statistical Area; (2) The percentage of the total housing inventory that is vacant; (3) The percentage of the housing inventory (excluding seasonal units) that is year-round vacant; (4) The percentage of rental inventory that is vacant for rent; (5) The percentage of homeowner inventory that is vacant for sale; n/a not available
Source: U.S. Census Bureau, Housing Vacancies and Homeownership Annual Statistics: 2019, 2020, 2021

INCOME

Income

Area	Per Capita ($)	Median Household ($)	Average Household ($)
City	37,191	63,778	86,841
MSA[1]	32,704	64,717	85,592
U.S.	35,384	64,994	91,547

Note: (1) Figures cover the Boise City, ID Metropolitan Statistical Area
Source: U.S. Census Bureau, 2016-2020 American Community Survey 5-Year Estimates

Household Income Distribution

Area	Percent of Households Earning							
	Under $15,000	$15,000 -$24,999	$25,000 -$34,999	$35,000 -$49,999	$50,000 -$74,999	$75,000 -$99,999	$100,000 -$149,999	$150,000 and up
City	8.6	8.2	9.4	12.9	19.2	12.9	14.9	13.9
MSA[1]	8.0	7.5	8.4	13.1	21.2	13.8	16.0	12.1
U.S.	9.9	8.5	8.6	12.0	17.2	12.8	15.6	15.4

Note: (1) Figures cover the Boise City, ID Metropolitan Statistical Area
Source: U.S. Census Bureau, 2016-2020 American Community Survey 5-Year Estimates

Poverty Rate

Area	All Ages	Under 18 Years Old	18 to 64 Years Old	65 Years and Over
City	12.0	14.1	12.0	9.3
MSA[1]	10.5	11.8	10.5	8.2
U.S.	12.8	17.5	12.1	9.3

Note: Figures are percentage of people whose income during the past 12 months was below the poverty level; (1) Figures cover the Boise City, ID Metropolitan Statistical Area
Source: U.S. Census Bureau, 2016-2020 American Community Survey 5-Year Estimates

CITY FINANCES

City Government Finances

Component	2019 ($000)	2019 ($ per capita)
Total Revenues	411,975	1,818
Total Expenditures	376,069	1,660
Debt Outstanding	98,800	436
Cash and Securities[1]	290,761	1,283

Note: (1) Cash and security holdings of a government at the close of its fiscal year, including those of its dependent agencies, utilities, and liquor stores.
Source: U.S. Census Bureau, State & Local Government Finances 2019

City Government Revenue by Source

Source	2019 ($000)	2019 ($ per capita)	2019 (%)
General Revenue			
From Federal Government	2,979	13	0.7
From State Government	25,394	112	6.2
From Local Governments	655	3	0.2
Taxes			
Property	168,253	743	40.8
Sales and Gross Receipts	8,709	38	2.1
Personal Income	0	0	0.0
Corporate Income	0	0	0.0
Motor Vehicle License	0	0	0.0
Other Taxes	9,346	41	2.3
Current Charges	174,198	769	42.3
Liquor Store	0	0	0.0
Utility	0	0	0.0

Source: U.S. Census Bureau, State & Local Government Finances 2019

City Government Expenditures by Function

Function	2019 ($000)	2019 ($ per capita)	2019 (%)
General Direct Expenditures			
Air Transportation	23,760	104	6.3
Corrections	0	0	0.0
Education	0	0	0.0
Employment Security Administration	0	0	0.0
Financial Administration	4,327	19	1.2
Fire Protection	53,812	237	14.3
General Public Buildings	2,856	12	0.8
Governmental Administration, Other	13,862	61	3.7
Health	1,187	5	0.3
Highways	1,968	8	0.5
Hospitals	0	0	0.0
Housing and Community Development	4,699	20	1.2
Interest on General Debt	3,587	15	1.0
Judicial and Legal	6,154	27	1.6
Libraries	11,573	51	3.1
Parking	0	0	0.0
Parks and Recreation	39,133	172	10.4
Police Protection	61,749	272	16.4
Public Welfare	0	0	0.0
Sewerage	33,125	146	8.8
Solid Waste Management	36,359	160	9.7
Veterans' Services	0	0	0.0
Liquor Store	0	0	0.0
Utility	0	0	0.0

Source: U.S. Census Bureau, State & Local Government Finances 2019

EMPLOYMENT

Labor Force and Employment

Area	Civilian Labor Force			Workers Employed		
	Dec. 2020	Dec. 2021	% Chg.	Dec. 2020	Dec. 2021	% Chg.
City	133,110	133,310	0.2	127,984	131,155	2.5
MSA[1]	385,310	386,259	0.2	369,979	379,345	2.5
U.S.	160,017,000	161,696,000	1.0	149,613,000	155,732,000	4.1

Note: Data is not seasonally adjusted and covers workers 16 years of age and older; (1) Figures cover the Boise City, ID Metropolitan Statistical Area
Source: Bureau of Labor Statistics, Local Area Unemployment Statistics

Unemployment Rate

Area	2021											
	Jan.	Feb.	Mar.	Apr.	May	Jun.	Jul.	Aug.	Sep.	Oct.	Nov.	Dec.
City	4.1	4.1	3.6	3.1	2.8	3.0	2.7	2.5	2.0	1.8	1.8	1.6
MSA[1]	4.3	4.3	3.8	3.3	2.9	3.3	3.0	2.7	2.2	2.0	1.9	1.8
U.S.	6.8	6.6	6.2	5.7	5.5	6.1	5.7	5.3	4.6	4.3	3.9	3.7

Note: Data is not seasonally adjusted and covers workers 16 years of age and older; (1) Figures cover the Boise City, ID Metropolitan Statistical Area
Source: Bureau of Labor Statistics, Local Area Unemployment Statistics

Average Wages

Occupation	$/Hr.	Occupation	$/Hr.
Accountants and Auditors	34.78	Maintenance and Repair Workers	19.25
Automotive Mechanics	20.64	Marketing Managers	51.68
Bookkeepers	19.42	Network and Computer Systems Admin.	37.62
Carpenters	19.72	Nurses, Licensed Practical	24.66
Cashiers	12.23	Nurses, Registered	36.30
Computer Programmers	36.09	Nursing Assistants	15.18
Computer Systems Analysts	41.20	Office Clerks, General	17.28
Computer User Support Specialists	24.62	Physical Therapists	41.63
Construction Laborers	17.84	Physicians	144.79
Cooks, Restaurant	13.20	Plumbers, Pipefitters and Steamfitters	24.58
Customer Service Representatives	16.69	Police and Sheriff's Patrol Officers	31.03
Dentists	57.66	Postal Service Mail Carriers	26.37
Electricians	25.20	Real Estate Sales Agents	18.41
Engineers, Electrical	55.32	Retail Salespersons	15.99
Fast Food and Counter Workers	10.42	Sales Representatives, Technical/Scientific	37.00
Financial Managers	56.49	Secretaries, Exc. Legal/Medical/Executive	17.54
First-Line Supervisors of Office Workers	27.13	Security Guards	16.62
General and Operations Managers	38.16	Surgeons	n/a
Hairdressers/Cosmetologists	14.36	Teacher Assistants, Exc. Postsecondary*	13.12
Home Health and Personal Care Aides	13.37	Teachers, Secondary School, Exc. Sp. Ed.*	26.51
Janitors and Cleaners	13.47	Telemarketers	n/a
Landscaping/Groundskeeping Workers	16.81	Truck Drivers, Heavy/Tractor-Trailer	24.17
Lawyers	51.74	Truck Drivers, Light/Delivery Services	22.32
Maids and Housekeeping Cleaners	12.99	Waiters and Waitresses	11.86

Note: Wage data covers the Boise City, ID Metropolitan Statistical Area; (*) Hourly wages were calculated from annual wage data based on a 40 hour work week; n/a not available.
Source: Bureau of Labor Statistics, Metro Area Occupational Employment & Wage Estimates, May 2021

Employment by Industry

Sector	MSA[1]		U.S.
	Number of Employees	Percent of Total	Percent of Total
Construction, Mining, and Logging	30,000	8.0	5.3
Education and Health Services	54,100	14.5	16.0
Financial Activities	21,500	5.8	5.9
Government	49,200	13.2	14.9
Information	4,000	1.1	1.9
Leisure and Hospitality	36,700	9.8	9.8
Manufacturing	28,800	7.7	8.4
Other Services	12,700	3.4	3.7
Professional and Business Services	57,000	15.3	14.6
Retail Trade	42,200	11.3	10.7
Transportation, Warehousing, and Utilities	18,600	5.0	4.8
Wholesale Trade	18,700	5.0	3.8

Note: Figures are non-farm employment as of December 2021. Figures are not seasonally adjusted and include workers 16 years of age and older; (1) Figures cover the Boise City, ID Metropolitan Statistical Area
Source: Bureau of Labor Statistics, Current Employment Statistics, Employment, Hours, and Earnings

Employment by Occupation

Occupation Classification	City (%)	MSA[1] (%)	U.S. (%)
Management, Business, Science, and Arts	46.3	39.5	39.5
Natural Resources, Construction, and Maintenance	7.6	10.7	8.7
Production, Transportation, and Material Moving	8.6	11.1	13.1
Sales and Office	20.7	22.5	21.3
Service	16.8	16.2	17.4

Note: Figures cover employed civilians 16 years of age and older; (1) Figures cover the Boise City, ID Metropolitan Statistical Area
Source: U.S. Census Bureau, 2016-2020 American Community Survey 5-Year Estimates

Occupations with Greatest Projected Employment Growth: 2021 – 2023

Occupation[1]	2021 Employment	2023 Projected Employment	Numeric Employment Change	Percent Employment Change
Fast Food and Counter Workers	14,830	15,890	1,060	7.1
Waiters and Waitresses	13,020	13,960	940	7.2
Home Health and Personal Care Aides	17,650	18,450	800	4.5
Registered Nurses	15,850	16,520	670	4.2
Office Clerks, General	19,480	20,110	630	3.2
Cooks, Fast Food	7,530	8,110	580	7.7
Carpenters	8,760	9,340	580	6.6
Customer Service Representatives	19,180	19,750	570	3.0
Cooks, Restaurant	7,250	7,770	520	7.2
General and Operations Managers	14,740	15,210	470	3.2

Note: Projections cover Idaho; (1) Sorted by numeric employment change
Source: www.projectionscentral.com, State Occupational Projections, 2021–2023 Short-Term Projections

Fastest-Growing Occupations: 2021 – 2023

Occupation[1]	2021 Employment	2023 Projected Employment	Numeric Employment Change	Percent Employment Change
Semiconductor Processors	880	950	70	8.0
Hosts and Hostesses, Restaurant, Lounge, and Coffee Shop	2,280	2,460	180	7.9
Food Service Managers	1,040	1,120	80	7.7
Cooks, Fast Food	7,530	8,110	580	7.7
Electronics Engineers, Except Computer	1,880	2,020	140	7.4
Bartenders	2,890	3,100	210	7.3
Dining Room and Cafeteria Attendants and Bartender Helpers	1,500	1,610	110	7.3
Cooks, Restaurant	7,250	7,770	520	7.2
Waiters and Waitresses	13,020	13,960	940	7.2
Fast Food and Counter Workers	14,830	15,890	1,060	7.1

Note: Projections cover Idaho; (1) Sorted by percent employment change and excludes occupations with numeric employment change less than 50
Source: www.projectionscentral.com, State Occupational Projections, 2021–2023 Short-Term Projections

TAXES

State Corporate Income Tax Rates

State	Tax Rate (%)	Income Brackets ($)	Num. of Brackets	Financial Institution Tax Rate (%)[a]	Federal Income Tax Ded.
Idaho	6.5 (f)	Flat rate	1	6.5 (f)	No

Note: Tax rates as of January 1, 2022; (a) Rates listed are the corporate income tax rate applied to financial institutions or excise taxes based on income. Some states have other taxes based upon the value of deposits or shares; (f) Idaho's minimum tax on a corporation is $20. The $10 Permanent Building Fund Tax must be paid by each corporation in a unitary group filing a combined return. Taxpayers with gross sales in Idaho under $100,000, and with no property or payroll in Idaho, may elect to pay 1% on such sales (instead of the tax on net income).
Source: Federation of Tax Administrators, State Corporate Income Tax Rates, January 1, 2022

State Individual Income Tax Rates

State	Tax Rate (%)	Income Brackets ($)	Personal Exemptions ($)			Standard Ded. ($)	
			Single	Married	Depend.	Single	Married
Idaho (a)	1.125 - 6.5	1,568 - 7,939 (b)	(d)	(d)	(d)	12,950	25,900 (d)

Note: Tax rates as of January 1, 2022; Local- and county-level taxes are not included; Federal income tax is not deductible on state income tax returns; (a) 19 states have statutory provision for automatically adjusting to the rate of inflation the dollar values of the income tax brackets, standard deductions, and/or personal exemptions. Michigan indexes the personal exemption only. Oregon does not index the income brackets for $125,000 and over; (b) For joint returns, taxes are twice the tax on half the couple's income; (d) These states use the personal exemption/standard deduction amounts provided in the federal Internal Revenue Code.
Source: Federation of Tax Administrators, State Individual Income Tax Rates, January 1, 2022

Various State Sales and Excise Tax Rates

State	State Sales Tax (%)	Gasoline[1] (¢/gal.)	Cigarette[2] ($/pack)	Spirits[3] ($/gal.)	Wine[4] ($/gal.)	Beer[5] ($/gal.)	Recreational Marijuana (%)
Idaho	6	33	0.57	10.9	0.45	0.15	Not legal

Note: All tax rates as of January 1, 2022; (1) The American Petroleum Institute has developed a methodology for determining the average tax rate on a gallon of fuel. Rates may include any of the following: excise taxes, environmental fees, storage tank fees, other fees or taxes, general sales tax, and local taxes; (2) The federal excise tax of $1.0066 per pack and local taxes are not included; (3) Rates are those applicable to off-premise sales of 40% alcohol by volume (a.b.v.) distilled spirits in 750ml containers. Local excise taxes are excluded; (4) Rates are those applicable to off-premise sales of 11% a.b.v. non-carbonated wine in 750ml containers; (5) Rates are those applicable to off-premise sales of 4.7% a.b.v. beer in 12 ounce containers.
Source: Tax Foundation, 2022 Facts & Figures: How Does Your State Compare?

State Business Tax Climate Index Rankings

State	Overall Rank	Corporate Tax Rank	Individual Income Tax Rank	Sales Tax Rank	Property Tax Rank	Unemployment Insurance Tax Rank
Idaho	17	29	20	9	3	47

Note: The index is a measure of how each state's tax laws affect economic performance. The lower the rank, the more favorable a state's tax system is for business. States without a given tax are given a ranking of 1. The scores/rankings for the District of Columbia do not affect other states. The 2022 index represents the tax climate as of July 1, 2021.
Source: Tax Foundation, State Business Tax Climate Index 2022

TRANSPORTATION

Means of Transportation to Work

Area	Car/Truck/Van		Public Transportation			Bicycle	Walked	Other Means	Worked at Home
	Drove Alone	Car-pooled	Bus	Subway	Railroad				
City	76.5	7.1	0.5	0.0	0.0	2.7	3.2	1.5	8.5
MSA[1]	78.1	8.3	0.3	0.0	0.0	1.2	1.9	1.3	8.9
U.S.	74.9	8.9	2.2	1.7	0.5	0.5	2.6	1.4	7.3

Note: Figures are percentages and cover workers 16 years of age and older; (1) Figures cover the Boise City, ID Metropolitan Statistical Area
Source: U.S. Census Bureau, 2016-2020 American Community Survey 5-Year Estimates

Travel Time to Work

Area	Less Than 10 Minutes	10 to 19 Minutes	20 to 29 Minutes	30 to 44 Minutes	45 to 59 Minutes	60 to 89 Minutes	90 Minutes or More
City	13.7	46.0	25.7	10.6	1.5	1.3	1.3
MSA[1]	12.7	34.2	25.4	18.7	5.1	2.3	1.5
U.S.	12.3	28.4	20.9	20.9	8.3	6.4	2.9

Note: Note: Figures are percentages and include workers 16 years old and over; (1) Figures cover the Boise City, ID Metropolitan Statistical Area
Source: U.S. Census Bureau, 2016-2020 American Community Survey 5-Year Estimates

Key Congestion Measures

Measure	1990	2000	2010	2015	2020
Annual Hours of Delay, Total (000)	1,913	5,019	9,599	10,855	5,102
Annual Hours of Delay, Per Auto Commuter	16	28	35	43	18
Annual Congestion Cost, Per Auto Commuter ($)	229	451	692	720	341

Note: Covers the Boise ID urban area
Source: Texas A&M Transportation Institute, 2021 Urban Mobility Report

Freeway Travel Time Index

Measure	1985	1990	1995	2000	2005	2010	2015	2020
Urban Area Index[1]	1.01	1.04	1.06	1.11	1.15	1.15	1.15	1.05
Urban Area Rank[1,2]	100	94	93	79	68	65	67	85

Note: Freeway Travel Time Index—the ratio of travel time in the peak period to the travel time at free-flow conditions. For example, a value of 1.30 indicates a 20-minute free-flow trip takes 26 minutes in the peak (20 minutes x 1.30 = 26 minutes); (1) Covers the Boise ID urban area; (2) Rank is based on 101 larger urban areas (#1 = highest travel time index)
Source: Texas A&M Transportation Institute, 2021 Urban Mobility Report

Public Transportation

Agency Name / Mode of Transportation	Vehicles Operated in Maximum Service[1]	Annual Unlinked Passenger Trips[2] (in thous.)	Annual Passenger Miles[3] (in thous.)
Ada County Highway District, dba ACHD Commuteride			
Vanpool (directly operated)	79	117.9	7,378.1
Boise State University			
Bus (directly operated)	9	178.1	n/a

Note: (1) Number of revenue vehicles operated by the given mode and type of service to meet the annual maximum service requirement. This is the revenue vehicle count during the peak season of the year; on the week and day that maximum service is provided. Vehicles operated in maximum service (VOMS) exclude atypical days and one-time special events; (2) Number of passengers who boarded public transportation vehicles. Passengers are counted each time they board a vehicle no matter how many vehicles they use to travel from their origin to their destination. (3) Sum of the distances ridden by all passengers during the entire fiscal year.
Source: Federal Transit Administration, National Transit Database, 2020

Air Transportation

Airport Name and Code / Type of Service	Passenger Airlines[1]	Passenger Enplanements	Freight Carriers[2]	Freight (lbs)
Boise Air Terminal-Gowen Field (BOI)				
Domestic service (U.S. carriers - 2021)	20	1,815,549	11	58,124,061
International service (U.S. carriers - 2020)	0	0	0	0

Note: (1) Includes all U.S.-based major, minor and commuter airlines that carried at least one passenger during the year; (2) Includes all U.S.-based airlines and freight carriers that transported at least one pound of freight during the year.
Source: Bureau of Transportation Statistics, The Intermodal Transportation Database, Air Carriers: T-100 Domestic Market (U.S. Carriers), 2021; Bureau of Transportation Statistics, The Intermodal Transportation Database, Air Carriers: T-100 International Market (U.S. Carriers), 2020

BUSINESSES

Major Business Headquarters

Company Name	Industry	Rankings	
		Fortune[1]	Forbes[2]
Albertsons	Food and Drug Stores	52	-
Boise Cascade	Wholesalers: Diversified	493	-
JR Simplot	Food, Drink & Tobacco	-	54
Micron Technology	Semiconductors and Other Electronic Components	135	-
WinCo Foods	Food Markets	-	46

Note: (1) Companies that produce a 10-K are ranked 1 to 500 based on 2020 revenue; (2) All private companies with at least $2 billion in annual revenue through the end of their most current fiscal year are ranked 1 to 225; companies listed are headquartered in the city; dashes indicate no ranking
Source: Fortune, "Fortune 500," 2021; Forbes, "America's Largest Private Companies," 2021

Fastest-Growing Businesses

According to *Inc.*, Boise City is home to one of America's 500 fastest-growing private companies: **Proud Source Water** (#59). Criteria: must be an independent, privately-held, for-profit, U.S. corporation, proprietorship or partnership as of December 31, 2020; revenues must be at least $100,000 in 2017 and $2 million in 2020; must have four-year operating/sales history. *Inc., "America's 500 Fastest-Growing Private Companies," 2021*

Living Environment

COST OF LIVING

Cost of Living Index

Composite Index	Groceries	Housing	Utilities	Trans-portation	Health Care	Misc. Goods/ Services
102.1	93.8	110.5	82.3	111.4	102.5	102.7

Note: The Cost of Living Index measures regional differences in the cost of consumer goods and services, excluding taxes and non-consumer expenditures, for professional and managerial households in the top income quintile. It is based on more than 50,000 prices covering almost 60 different items for which prices are collected three times a year by chambers of commerce, economic development organizations or university applied economic centers in each participating urban area. The numbers shown should be read as a percentage above or below the national average of 100. For example, a value of 115.4 in the groceries column indicates that grocery prices are 15.4% higher than the national average. Small differences in the index numbers should not be interpreted as significant; Figures cover the Boise ID urban area.
Source: The Council for Community and Economic Research, Cost of Living Index, 2021

Grocery Prices

Area[1]	T-Bone Steak ($/pound)	Frying Chicken ($/pound)	Whole Milk ($/half gal.)	Eggs ($/dozen)	Orange Juice ($/64 oz.)	Coffee ($/11.5 oz.)
City[2]	13.01	1.55	1.90	1.17	3.49	4.45
Avg.	12.82	1.40	2.22	1.57	3.59	4.30
Min.	8.91	0.91	1.29	0.75	2.87	3.02
Max.	21.35	2.69	3.92	3.86	5.49	8.11

*Note: (1) Values for the local area are compared with the average, minimum and maximum values for all 285 areas in the Cost of Living Index; (2) Figures cover the Boise ID urban area; **T-Bone Steak** (price per pound); **Frying Chicken** (price per pound, whole fryer); **Whole Milk** (half gallon carton); **Eggs** (price per dozen, Grade A, large); **Orange Juice** (64 oz. Tropicana or Florida Natural); **Coffee** (11.5 oz. can, vacuum-packed, Maxwell House, Hills Bros, or Folgers).*
Source: The Council for Community and Economic Research, Cost of Living Index, 2021

Housing and Utility Costs

Area[1]	New Home Price ($)	Apartment Rent ($/month)	All Electric ($/month)	Part Electric ($/month)	Other Energy ($/month)	Telephone ($/month)
City[2]	437,890	1,410	-	63.81	63.35	173.61
Avg.	398,393	1,217	171.38	100.83	69.67	187.75
Min.	212,799	534	96.71	31.56	27.15	173.01
Max.	2,354,006	4,438	369.53	277.33	303.87	206.73

*Note: (1) Values for the local area are compared with the average, minimum and maximum values for all 285 areas in the Cost of Living Index; (2) Figures cover the Boise ID urban area; **New Home Price** (2,400 sf living area, 8,000 sf lot, in urban area with full utilities); **Apartment Rent** (950 sf 2 bedroom/1.5 or 2 bath, unfurnished, excluding all utilities except water); **All Electric** (average monthly cost for an all-electric home); **Part Electric** (average monthly cost for a part-electric home); **Other Energy** (average monthly cost for natural gas, fuel oil, coal, wood, and any other forms of energy except electricity); **Telephone** (price includes the base monthly rate plus taxes and fees for three lines of mobile phone service).*
Source: The Council for Community and Economic Research, Cost of Living Index, 2021

Health Care, Transportation, and Other Costs

Area[1]	Doctor ($/visit)	Dentist ($/visit)	Optometrist ($/visit)	Gasoline ($/gallon)	Beauty Salon ($/visit)	Men's Shirt ($)
City[2]	138.86	88.67	134.62	3.04	36.66	36.23
Avg.	118.16	101.04	109.44	2.71	40.63	30.77
Min.	35.04	55.56	51.17	2.17	18.59	11.32
Max.	231.10	165.12	256.81	4.11	85.33	63.03

*Note: (1) Values for the local area are compared with the average, minimum and maximum values for all 285 areas in the Cost of Living Index; (2) Figures cover the Boise ID urban area; **Doctor** (general practitioners routine exam of an established patient); **Dentist** (adult teeth cleaning and periodic oral examination); **Optometrist** (full vision eye exam for established adult patient); **Gasoline** (one gallon regular unleaded, national brand, including all taxes, cash price at self-service pump if available); **Beauty Salon** (woman's shampoo, trim, and blow-dry); **Men's Shirt** (cotton/polyester dress shirt, pinpoint weave, long sleeves).*
Source: The Council for Community and Economic Research, Cost of Living Index, 2021

HOUSING

Homeownership Rate

Area	2013 (%)	2014 (%)	2015 (%)	2016 (%)	2017 (%)	2018 (%)	2019 (%)	2020 (%)	2021 (%)
MSA[1]	n/a	n/a	n/a	n/a	n/a	n/a	n/a	n/a	n/a
U.S.	65.1	64.5	63.7	63.4	63.9	64.4	64.6	66.6	65.5

Note: (1) Figures cover the Boise City, ID Metropolitan Statistical Area; n/a not available
Source: U.S. Census Bureau, Housing Vacancies and Homeownership Annual Statistics: 2013-2021

House Price Index (HPI)

Area	National Ranking[2]	Quarterly Change (%)	One-Year Change (%)	Five-Year Change (%)	Since 1991Q1 (%)
MSA[1]	4	2.08	31.29	117.06	493.84
U.S.[3]	–	3.33	17.54	54.45	258.04

Note: The HPI is a weighted repeat sales index. It measures average price changes in repeat sales or refinancings on the same properties. This information is obtained by reviewing repeat mortgage transactions on single-family properties whose mortgages have been purchased or securitized by Fannie Mae or Freddie Mac since January 1975; (1) Figures cover the Boise City, ID Metropolitan Statistical Area; (2) Rankings are based on annual percentage change for all metro areas containing at least 15,000 transactions over the last 10 years and ranges from 1 to 268; (3) figures based on a weighted average of Census Division estimates using a seasonally adjusted, purchase-only index; all figures are for the period ending December 31, 2021
Source: Federal Housing Finance Agency, Change in FHFA Metropolitan Area House Price Indexes, 2021Q4

Median Single-Family Home Prices

Area	2019	2020	2021[p]	Percent Change 2020 to 2021
MSA[1]	294.2	353.9	468.6	32.4
U.S. Average	274.6	300.2	353.4	17.7

Note: Figures are median sales prices of existing single-family homes in thousands of dollars; (p) preliminary; (1) Figures cover the Boise City, ID Metropolitan Statistical Area
Source: National Association of Realtors, Median Sales Price of Existing Single-Family Homes for Metropolitan Areas, 4th Quarter 2021

Qualifying Income Based on Median Sales Price of Existing Single-Family Homes

Area	With 5% Down ($)	With 10% Down ($)	With 20% Down ($)
MSA[1]	93,407	88,491	78,659
U.S. Average	70,699	66,978	59,536

Note: Figures are preliminary; Qualifying income is based on a mortgage rate of 3.13%. Monthly principal and interest payment is limited to 25% of income; (1) Figures cover the Boise City, ID Metropolitan Statistical Area
Source: National Association of Realtors, Qualifying Income Based on Median Sales Price of Existing Single-Family Homes for Metropolitan Areas, 4th Quarter 2021

Home Value Distribution

Area	Under $50,000	$50,000 -$99,999	$100,000 -$149,999	$150,000 -$199,999	$200,000 -$299,999	$300,000 -$499,999	$500,000 -$999,999	$1,000,000 or more
City	3.7	1.4	5.8	13.5	30.8	31.6	11.9	1.3
MSA[1]	4.2	3.2	7.7	14.4	29.6	29.6	9.9	1.4
U.S.	6.6	11.0	12.3	13.6	20.0	20.5	12.3	3.7

Note: Figures are percentages and cover owner-occupied housing units; (1) Figures cover the Boise City, ID Metropolitan Statistical Area
Source: U.S. Census Bureau, 2016-2020 American Community Survey 5-Year Estimates

Year Housing Structure Built

Area	2010 or Later	2000 -2009	1990 -1999	1980 -1989	1970 -1979	1960 -1969	1950 -1959	1940 -1949	Before 1940	Median Year
City	7.9	10.9	23.4	15.9	17.7	7.6	6.8	3.9	6.0	1985
MSA[1]	12.6	23.6	21.3	10.2	14.9	5.1	4.4	2.8	5.0	1994
U.S.	6.2	13.6	13.9	13.4	15.0	10.5	10.2	4.8	12.4	1978

Note: Figures are percentages except for Median Year; Note: (1) Figures cover the Boise City, ID Metropolitan Statistical Area
Source: U.S. Census Bureau, 2016-2020 American Community Survey 5-Year Estimates

Gross Monthly Rent

Area	Under $500	$500 -$999	$1,000 -$1,499	$1,500 -$1,999	$2,000 -$2,499	$2,500 -$2,999	$3,000 and up	Median ($)
City	4.3	44.8	38.0	10.2	1.4	0.6	0.7	1,009
MSA[1]	7.4	42.1	37.2	10.7	1.6	0.5	0.5	1,005
U.S.	8.9	34.3	30.2	14.9	6.2	2.6	2.8	1,096

Note: Figures are percentages except for Median; Gross rent is the contract rent plus the estimated average monthly cost of utilities (electricity, gas, and water and sewer) and fuels (oil, coal, kerosene, wood, etc.) if these are paid by the renter (or paid for the renter by someone else); (1) Figures cover the Boise City, ID Metropolitan Statistical Area
Source: U.S. Census Bureau, 2016-2020 American Community Survey 5-Year Estimates

HEALTH

Health Risk Factors

Category	MSA[1] (%)	U.S. (%)
Adults aged 18–64 who have any kind of health care coverage	83.1	86.8
Adults who reported being in good or better health	87.8	86.7
Adults who are current smokers	13.5	15.5
Adults who currently use chewing tobacco, snuff, or snus	4.1	3.7
Adults who are heavy drinkers[2]	7.1	6.7
Adults who are binge drinkers[3]	15.7	15.7
Adults who are overweight (BMI 25.0 - 29.9)	34.0	35.2
Adults who are obese (BMI 30.0 - 99.8)	29.4	31.9
Adults who participated in any physical activities in the past month	83.0	77.6
Adults who always or nearly always wears a seat belt	94.1	94.2

Note: (1) Figures cover the Boise City, ID Metropolitan Statistical Area; (2) Heavy drinkers are classified as adult men having more than 14 drinks per week and adult women having more than 7 drinks per week; (3) Binge drinkers are classified as males having five or more drinks on one occasion or females having four or more drinks on one occasion
Source: Centers for Disease Control and Prevention, Behaviorial Risk Factor Surveillance System, SMART: Selected Metropolitan Area Risk Trends, 2020

Acute and Chronic Health Conditions

Category	MSA[1] (%)	U.S. (%)
Adults who have ever been told they had a heart attack	4.7	4.3
Adults who have ever been told they have angina or coronary heart disease	3.6	4.0
Adults who have ever been told they had a stroke	2.6	2.8
Adults who have ever been told they have asthma	15.0	14.2
Adults who have ever been told they have arthritis	20.7	24.5
Adults who have ever been told they have diabetes[2]	7.9	10.6
Adults who have ever been told they had skin cancer	8.5	6.4
Adults who have ever been told they had any other types of cancer	5.1	6.8
Adults who have ever been told they have COPD	5.6	6.2
Adults who have ever been told they have kidney disease	3.4	2.9
Adults who have ever been told they have a form of depression	19.7	19.6

Note: (1) Figures cover the Boise City, ID Metropolitan Statistical Area; (2) Figures do not include pregnancy-related, borderline, or pre-diabetes
Source: Centers for Disease Control and Prevention, Behaviorial Risk Factor Surveillance System, SMART: Selected Metropolitan Area Risk Trends, 2020

Health Screening and Vaccination Rates

Category	MSA[1] (%)	U.S. (%)
Adults 50-75 who have had a blood stool test within the past year	7.6	9.3
Adults aged 65+ who have had flu shot within the past year	68.1	67.9
Adults aged 65+ who have ever had a pneumonia vaccination	75.0	72.2
Adults who have ever been tested for HIV	32.6	37.1
Women aged 21-65 who have had a pap test in the past three years	75.0	77.7
Men aged 40+ who have had a PSA test within the past two years	29.8	31.8
Women aged 40+ who have had a mammogram within the past two years	67.6	71.5

Note: (1) Figures cover the Boise City, ID Metropolitan Statistical Area.
Source: Centers for Disease Control and Prevention, Behaviorial Risk Factor Surveillance System, SMART: Selected Metropolitan Area Risk Trends, 2020

Disability Status

Category	MSA[1] (%)	U.S. (%)
Adults who reported being deaf	7.8	6.8
Are you blind or have serious difficulty seeing, even when wearing glasses?	5.7	4.7
Do you have difficulty doing errands alone?	6.0	6.3
Do you have difficulty dressing or bathing?	3.1	3.0
Do you have serious difficulty concentrating/remembering/making decisions?	12.9	10.8
Do you have serious difficulty walking or climbing stairs?	11.1	11.9

Note: (1) Figures cover the Boise City, ID Metropolitan Statistical Area.
Source: Centers for Disease Control and Prevention, Behaviorial Risk Factor Surveillance System, SMART: Selected Metropolitan Area Risk Trends, 2020

Mortality Rates for the Top 10 Causes of Death in the U.S.

ICD-10[a] Sub-Chapter	ICD-10[a] Code	Age-Adjusted Mortality Rate[1] per 100,000 population	
		County[2]	U.S.
Malignant neoplasms	C00-C97	133.0	146.4
Ischaemic heart diseases	I20-I25	62.6	90.2
Other forms of heart disease	I30-I51	55.7	51.9
Other degenerative diseases of the nervous system	G30-G31	53.9	39.7
Other external causes of accidental injury	W00-X59	30.3	38.7
Chronic lower respiratory diseases	J40-J47	36.1	38.1
Cerebrovascular diseases	I60-I69	37.1	37.6
Organic, including symptomatic, mental disorders	F01-F09	24.4	29.4
Hypertensive diseases	I10-I15	17.4	26.1
Diabetes mellitus	E10-E14	14.6	22.6

Note: (a) ICD-10 = International Classification of Diseases 10th Revision; (1) Mortality rates are a three-year average covering 2018-2020; (2) Figures cover Ada County.
Source: Centers for Disease Control and Prevention, National Center for Health Statistics. Underlying Cause of Death 1999-2020 on CDC WONDER Online Database

Mortality Rates for Selected Causes of Death

ICD-10[a] Sub-Chapter	ICD-10[a] Code	Age-Adjusted Mortality Rate[1] per 100,000 population	
		County[2]	U.S.
Assault	X85-Y09	Unreliable	6.5
Diseases of the liver	K70-K76	13.1	15.3
Human immunodeficiency virus (HIV) disease	B20-B24	Suppressed	1.4
Influenza and pneumonia	J09-J18	7.7	13.4
Intentional self-harm	X60-X84	18.5	13.9
Malnutrition	E40-E46	4.8	2.9
Obesity and other hyperalimentation	E65-E68	1.5	2.4
Renal failure	N17-N19	5.9	12.5
Transport accidents	V01-V99	8.5	12.5
Viral hepatitis	B15-B19	Unreliable	1.0

Note: (a) ICD-10 = International Classification of Diseases 10th Revision; (1) Mortality rates are a three-year average covering 2018-2020; (2) Figures cover Ada County; Data are suppressed when the data meet the criteria for confidentiality constraints; Mortality rates are flagged as unreliable when the rate would be calculated with a numerator of 20 or less.
Source: Centers for Disease Control and Prevention, National Center for Health Statistics. Underlying Cause of Death 1999-2020 on CDC WONDER Online Database

Health Insurance Coverage

Area	With Health Insurance	With Private Health Insurance	With Public Health Insurance	Without Health Insurance	Population Under Age 19 Without Health Insurance
City	91.3	76.4	26.7	8.7	4.3
MSA[1]	90.1	72.6	29.9	9.9	4.8
U.S.	91.3	68.1	35.3	8.7	5.2

Note: Figures are percentages that cover the civilian noninstitutionalized population; (1) Figures cover the Boise City, ID Metropolitan Statistical Area
Source: U.S. Census Bureau, 2016-2020 American Community Survey 5-Year Estimates

Number of Medical Professionals

Area	MDs[3]	DOs[3,4]	Dentists	Podiatrists	Chiropractors	Optometrists
County[1] (number)	1,396	163	398	19	267	98
County[1] (rate[2])	282.0	32.9	80.4	3.8	53.9	19.8
U.S. (rate[2])	285.1	23.0	71.1	6.2	28.2	17.0

16001
Note: Data as of 2020 unless noted; (1) Data covers Ada County; (2) Rate per 100,000 population; (3) Data as of 2019 and includes all active, non-federal physicians; (4) Doctor of Osteopathic Medicine
Source: U.S. Department of Health and Human Services, Health Resources and Services Administration, Bureau of Health Professions, Area Resource File (ARF) 2020-2021

EDUCATION

Public School District Statistics

District Name	Schls	Pupils	Pupil/Teacher Ratio	Minority Pupils[1] (%)	LEP/ELL[2] (%)	IEP[3] (%)
Boise Independent District	50	25,673	16.3	26.0	9.3	12.6

Note: Table includes school districts with 2,000 or more students; (1) Percentage of students that are not non-Hispanic white; (2) Percentage of students that are Limited English Proficient (LEP) or English Language Learners (ELL) (2018-19); (3) Percentage of students that have an Individualized Education Program (IEP).
Source: U.S. Department of Education, National Center for Education Statistics, Common Core of Data, Local Education Agency (School District) Universe Survey: School Year 2019-2020

Highest Level of Education

Area	Less than H.S.	H.S. Diploma	Some College, No Deg.	Associate Degree	Bachelor's Degree	Master's Degree	Prof. School Degree	Doctorate Degree
City	5.0	20.4	23.2	8.8	27.6	10.2	2.7	2.2
MSA[1]	7.8	24.5	25.3	9.2	22.3	7.7	1.8	1.4
U.S.	11.5	26.7	20.3	8.6	20.2	9.1	2.2	1.5

Note: Figures cover persons age 25 and over; (1) Figures cover the Boise City, ID Metropolitan Statistical Area
Source: U.S. Census Bureau, 2016-2020 American Community Survey 5-Year Estimates

Educational Attainment by Race

Area	High School Graduate or Higher (%)					Bachelor's Degree or Higher (%)				
	Total	White	Black	Asian	Hisp.[2]	Total	White	Black	Asian	Hisp.[2]
City	95.0	95.8	81.0	91.5	82.9	42.7	42.9	34.0	55.1	22.3
MSA[1]	92.2	94.0	86.6	88.6	71.0	33.2	34.2	27.6	49.2	14.8
U.S.	88.5	90.7	86.7	87.3	70.3	32.9	34.4	22.6	55.0	17.6

Note: Figures shown cover persons 25 years old and over; (1) Figures cover the Boise City, ID Metropolitan Statistical Area; (2) People of Hispanic origin can be of any race
Source: U.S. Census Bureau, 2016-2020 American Community Survey 5-Year Estimates

School Enrollment by Grade and Control

Area	Preschool (%)		Kindergarten (%)		Grades 1 - 4 (%)		Grades 5 - 8 (%)		Grades 9 - 12 (%)	
	Public	Private	Public	Private	Public	Private	Public	Private	Public	Private
City	32.7	67.3	80.7	19.3	92.9	7.1	92.0	8.0	89.4	10.6
MSA[1]	35.1	64.9	87.8	12.2	90.5	9.5	91.0	9.0	89.9	10.1
U.S.	58.9	41.1	86.9	13.1	89.0	11.0	89.0	11.0	89.7	10.3

Note: Figures shown cover persons 3 years old and over; (1) Figures cover the Boise City, ID Metropolitan Statistical Area
Source: U.S. Census Bureau, 2016-2020 American Community Survey 5-Year Estimates

Higher Education

Four-Year Colleges			Two-Year Colleges			Medical Schools[1]	Law Schools[2]	Voc/ Tech[3]
Public	Private Non-profit	Private For-profit	Public	Private Non-profit	Private For-profit			
1	4	2	1	0	2	1	1	6

Note: Figures cover institutions located within the Boise City, ID Metropolitan Statistical Area and include main campuses only; (1) includes schools accredited by the Liaison Committee on Medical Education and the American Osteopathic Association's Commission on Osteopathic College Accreditation; (2) includes ABA-accredited schools, schools with provisional ABA accreditation, and state accredited schools; (3) includes all schools with programs that are less than 2 years.
Source: National Center for Education Statistics, Integrated Postsecondary Education System (IPEDS), 2020-21; Wikipedia, List of Medical Schools in the United States, accessed April 11, 2022; Wikipedia, List of Law Schools in the United States, accessed April 11, 2022

EMPLOYERS

Major Employers

Company Name	Industry
Ada County	Administration - local government
Albertsons Companies	Retail grocery
Boise City ISD #1	Education - local government
Boise State University	Education - state government
City of Boise	Municipal government
DirectTV Customer Service	Administrative & waste service
Hewlett-Packard Co.	Manufacturing
Idaho Power Co	Utilities
J R Simplot Co	Manufacturing
McDonalds	Accommodation & food services
Meridian JSD #2	Education - local government
Micron Technology	Manufacturing
Nampa School District #13	Education - local government
St. Alphonsus Regional Medical Center	Health care
St. Lukes Health Systems	Health care
State of Idaho Department of Health	State government
State of Idaho Dept of Corrections	State government
U.S. Postal Service	Transportation & warehousing
U.S. Veterans Administration	Federal government, health care
Wal-Mart Stores	Retail trade
WDS Global	Administrative & waste service
Wells Fargo	Finance & insurance

Note: Companies shown are located within the Boise City, ID Metropolitan Statistical Area.
Source: Hoovers.com; Wikipedia

PUBLIC SAFETY

Crime Rate

Area	Total Crime	Violent Crime Rate				Property Crime Rate		
		Murder	Rape[3]	Robbery	Aggrav. Assault	Burglary	Larceny -Theft	Motor Vehicle Theft
City	1,933.2	1.7	73.5	23.8	193.8	207.2	1,312.6	120.7
Suburbs[1]	1,206.5	1.9	52.0	6.9	189.1	178.4	674.0	104.3
Metro[2]	1,424.4	1.8	58.5	11.9	190.5	187.0	865.5	109.2
U.S.	2,356.7	6.5	38.4	73.9	279.7	314.2	1,398.0	246.0

Note: Figures are crimes per 100,000 population; (1) All areas within the metro area that are located outside the city limits; (2) Figures cover the Boise City, ID Metropolitan Statistical Area; (3) All figures shown were reported using the revised Uniform Crime Reporting (UCR) definition of rape.
Source: FBI Uniform Crime Reports, 2020

Hate Crimes

Area	Number of Quarters Reported	Number of Incidents per Bias Motivation					
		Race/Ethnicity/ Ancestry	Religion	Sexual Orientation	Disability	Gender	Gender Identity
City	4	10	5	2	0	1	1
U.S.	4	5,227	1,244	1,110	130	75	266

Source: Federal Bureau of Investigation, Hate Crime Statistics 2020

Identity Theft Consumer Reports

Area	Reports	Reports per 100,000 Population	Rank[2]
MSA[1]	1,402	187	245
U.S.	1,434,676	432	-

Note: (1) Figures cover the Boise City, ID Metropolitan Statistical Area; (2) Rank ranges from 1 to 391 where 1 indicates greatest number of identity theft reports per 100,000 population
Source: Federal Trade Commission, Consumer Sentinel Network Data Book 2021

Fraud and Other Consumer Reports

Area	Reports	Reports per 100,000 Population	Rank[2]
MSA[1]	6,775	904	177
U.S.	4,328,977	1,304	-

Note: (1) Figures cover the Boise City, ID Metropolitan Statistical Area; (2) Rank ranges from 1 to 391 where 1 indicates greatest number of fraud and other consumer reports per 100,000 population
Source: Federal Trade Commission, Consumer Sentinel Network Data Book 2021

POLITICS

2020 Presidential Election Results

Area	Biden	Trump	Jorgensen	Hawkins	Other
Ada County	46.1	50.0	2.0	0.1	1.8
U.S.	51.3	46.8	1.2	0.3	0.5

Note: Results are percentages and may not add to 100% due to rounding
Source: Dave Leip's Atlas of U.S. Presidential Elections

SPORTS

Professional Sports Teams

Team Name	League	Year Established
No teams are located in the metro area		

Source: Wikipedia, Major Professional Sports Teams of the United States and Canada, April 6, 2022

CLIMATE

Average and Extreme Temperatures

Temperature	Jan	Feb	Mar	Apr	May	Jun	Jul	Aug	Sep	Oct	Nov	Dec	Yr.
Extreme High (°F)	63	70	81	92	98	105	111	110	101	94	74	65	111
Average High (°F)	36	44	53	62	71	80	90	88	78	65	48	38	63
Average Temp. (°F)	29	36	42	49	58	66	74	73	63	52	40	31	51
Average Low (°F)	22	27	31	37	44	52	58	57	48	39	30	23	39
Extreme Low (°F)	-17	-15	6	19	22	31	35	34	23	11	-3	-25	-25

Note: Figures cover the years 1948-1995
Source: National Climatic Data Center, International Station Meteorological Climate Summary, 9/96

Average Precipitation/Snowfall/Humidity

Precip./Humidity	Jan	Feb	Mar	Apr	May	Jun	Jul	Aug	Sep	Oct	Nov	Dec	Yr.
Avg. Precip. (in.)	1.4	1.1	1.2	1.2	1.2	0.9	0.3	0.3	0.6	0.7	1.4	1.4	11.8
Avg. Snowfall (in.)	7	4	2	1	Tr	Tr	0	0	0	Tr	2	6	22
Avg. Rel. Hum. 7am (%)	81	80	75	69	65	59	48	50	58	67	77	81	68
Avg. Rel. Hum. 4pm (%)	68	58	45	35	34	29	22	23	28	36	55	67	42

Note: Figures cover the years 1948-1995; Tr = Trace amounts (<0.05 in. of rain; <0.5 in. of snow)
Source: National Climatic Data Center, International Station Meteorological Climate Summary, 9/96

Weather Conditions

Temperature			Daytime Sky			Precipitation		
5°F & below	32°F & below	90°F & above	Clear	Partly cloudy	Cloudy	0.01 inch or more precip.	0.1 inch or more snow/ice	Thunder-storms
6	124	45	106	133	126	91	22	14

Note: Figures are average number of days per year and cover the years 1948-1995
Source: National Climatic Data Center, International Station Meteorological Climate Summary, 9/96

HAZARDOUS WASTE

Superfund Sites

The Boise City, ID metro area has no sites on the EPA's Superfund Final National Priorities List. There are a total of 1,165 Superfund sites with a status of proposed or final on the list in the U.S. *U.S. Environmental Protection Agency, National Priorities List, April 6, 2022*

AIR QUALITY

Air Quality Trends: Ozone

	1990	1995	2000	2005	2010	2016	2017	2018	2019	2020
MSA[1]	n/a	n/a	n/a	n/a	n/a	n/a	n/a	n/a	n/a	n/a
U.S.	0.090	0.091	0.082	0.080	0.074	0.070	0.069	0.070	0.066	0.068

Note: (1) Data covers the Boise City, ID Metropolitan Statistical Area; n/a not available. The values shown are the composite ozone concentration averages among trend sites based on the highest fourth daily maximum 8-hour concentration in parts per million. These trends are based on sites having an adequate record of monitoring data during the trend period. Data from exceptional events are included.
Source: U.S. Environmental Protection Agency, Air Quality Monitoring Information, "Air Quality Trends by City, 1990-2020"

Air Quality Index

Area	Percent of Days when Air Quality was...[2]					AQI Statistics[2]	
	Good	Moderate	Unhealthy for Sensitive Groups	Unhealthy	Very Unhealthy	Maximum	Median
MSA[1]	57.7	36.6	2.7	3.0	0.0	198	47

Note: (1) Data covers the Boise City, ID Metropolitan Statistical Area; (2) Based on 366 days with AQI data in 2020. Air Quality Index (AQI) is an index for reporting daily air quality. EPA calculates the AQI for five major air pollutants regulated by the Clean Air Act: ground-level ozone, particle pollution (aka particulate matter), carbon monoxide, sulfur dioxide, and nitrogen dioxide. The AQI runs from 0 to 500. The higher the AQI value, the greater the level of air pollution and the greater the health concern. There are six AQI categories: "Good" AQI is between 0 and 50. Air quality is considered satisfactory; "Moderate" AQI is between 51 and 100. Air quality is acceptable; "Unhealthy for Sensitive Groups" When AQI values are between 101 and 150, members of sensitive groups may experience health effects; "Unhealthy" When AQI values are between 151 and 200 everyone may begin to experience health effects; "Very Unhealthy" AQI values between 201 and 300 trigger a health alert; "Hazardous" AQI values over 300 trigger warnings of emergency conditions (not shown).
Source: U.S. Environmental Protection Agency, Air Quality Index Report, 2020

Air Quality Index Pollutants

Area	Percent of Days when AQI Pollutant was...[2]					
	Carbon Monoxide	Nitrogen Dioxide	Ozone	Sulfur Dioxide	Particulate Matter 2.5	Particulate Matter 10
MSA[1]	0.0	0.5	39.9	0.0	57.7	1.9

Note: (1) Data covers the Boise City, ID Metropolitan Statistical Area; (2) Based on 366 days with AQI data in 2020. The Air Quality Index (AQI) is an index for reporting daily air quality. EPA calculates the AQI for five major air pollutants regulated by the Clean Air Act: ground-level ozone, particle pollution (also known as particulate matter), carbon monoxide, sulfur dioxide, and nitrogen dioxide. The AQI runs from 0 to 500. The higher the AQI value, the greater the level of air pollution and the greater the health concern.
Source: U.S. Environmental Protection Agency, Air Quality Index Report, 2020

Maximum Air Pollutant Concentrations: Particulate Matter, Ozone, CO and Lead

	Particulate Matter 10 (ug/m^3)	Particulate Matter 2.5 Wtd AM (ug/m^3)	Particulate Matter 2.5 24-Hr (ug/m^3)	Ozone (ppm)	Carbon Monoxide (ppm)	Lead (ug/m^3)
MSA[1] Level	142	10.6	49	0.065	2	n/a
NAAQS[2]	150	15	35	0.075	9	0.15
Met NAAQS[2]	Yes	Yes	No	Yes	Yes	n/a

Note: (1) Data covers the Boise City, ID Metropolitan Statistical Area; Data from exceptional events are included; (2) National Ambient Air Quality Standards; ppm = parts per million; ug/m^3 = micrograms per cubic meter; n/a not available.

Concentrations: Particulate Matter 10 (coarse particulate)—highest second maximum 24-hour concentration; Particulate Matter 2.5 Wtd AM (fine particulate)—highest weighted annual mean concentration; Particulate Matter 2.5 24-Hour (fine particulate)—highest 98th percentile 24-hour concentration; Ozone—highest fourth daily maximum 8-hour concentration; Carbon Monoxide—highest second maximum non-overlapping 8-hour concentration; Lead—maximum running 3-month average

Source: U.S. Environmental Protection Agency, Air Quality Monitoring Information, "Air Quality Statistics by City, 2020"

Maximum Air Pollutant Concentrations: Nitrogen Dioxide and Sulfur Dioxide

	Nitrogen Dioxide AM (ppb)	Nitrogen Dioxide 1-Hr (ppb)	Sulfur Dioxide AM (ppb)	Sulfur Dioxide 1-Hr (ppb)	Sulfur Dioxide 24-Hr (ppb)
MSA[1] Level	10	43	n/a	2	n/a
NAAQS[2]	53	100	30	75	140
Met NAAQS[2]	Yes	Yes	n/a	Yes	n/a

Note: (1) Data covers the Boise City, ID Metropolitan Statistical Area; Data from exceptional events are included; (2) National Ambient Air Quality Standards; ppm = parts per million; ug/m^3 = micrograms per cubic meter; n/a not available.

Concentrations: Nitrogen Dioxide AM—highest arithmetic mean concentration; Nitrogen Dioxide 1-Hr—highest 98th percentile 1-hour daily maximum concentration; Sulfur Dioxide AM—highest annual mean concentration; Sulfur Dioxide 1-Hr—highest 99th percentile 1-hour daily maximum concentration; Sulfur Dioxide 24-Hr—highest second maximum 24-hour concentration

Source: U.S. Environmental Protection Agency, Air Quality Monitoring Information, "Air Quality Statistics by City, 2020"

Boulder, Colorado

Background

Boulder lies at the foot of the Rocky Mountains in Boulder County. It is the eighth largest city in Colorado. Tourism is a major industry in Boulder, which offers spectacular views from its elevation of 5,430 feet and many outdoor recreation opportunities in over 31,000 acres of open space.

Boulder Valley originally was home to the Southern Arapahoe tribe. The first white settlement was established by gold miners in 1858 near the entrance to Boulder Canyon at Red Rocks. In 1859, the Boulder City Town Company was formed. The town's first schoolhouse was built in 1860, and in 1874 the University of Colorado opened.

Boulder was incorporated as a town in 1871 and as a city in 1882. By 1890, the railroad provided service from Boulder to Golden, Denver, and the western mining camps. In 1905, amidst a weakening economy, Boulder began promoting tourism to boost its finances. The city raised money to construct a first-class hotel, which was completed in 1908 and named Hotel Boulderado.

Although tourism remained strong until the late 1930s, it had begun to decline by World War II. The U.S. Navy's Japanese language school, housed at the city's University of Colorado, proved to be an impressive introduction to the area and students, professionals, and veterans attending the university on the GI Bill, returned to Boulder. Consequently, Boulder's population grew from 12,958 in 1940 to 20,000 in 1950. To accommodate this huge increase, new public buildings, highways, residential areas, and shopping centers developed, spurring further economic expansion.

Many major tech companies have operations in Boulder, as does NOAA, the National Oceanic and Atmospheric Administration.

Boulder is home to the University of Colorado, which houses a robust research park. Cultural venues in the city include the Boulder Dushanbe Teahouse, a gift to the city from its sister city of Dushanbe in Tajikistan, and the Pearl Street Mall, an open-air walkway that was the city's original downtown and is rich with restaurants, cafes, bookstores, and street entertainers. Boulder offers many scenic opportunities for outdoor activities, with parks, recreation areas, and hiking trails. The city boasts hundreds of miles of bike trails, lanes, and paths as a part of their renowned network of citywide bikeways. Boulder has been recognized by the League of American Bicyclists as a leading bicyclist-friendly city.

Keeping with Boulder's tradition of outdoor recreation, BOLDERBoulder, a popular race for over 50,000 runners, joggers, walkers, and wheelers, is returning on Memorial Day weekend, 2022, after a COVID hiatus. Over 100,000 spectators are expected.

Annual attractions include the Creek Festival in May, Art Fair in July, Fall Festival, and Lights of December Parade. The annual Boulder International Film Festival (BIFF) is held in February and has created a name for itself in the international film community.

Like the rest of Colorado, Boulder enjoys a cool, dry highland continental climate. In winter, the mountains to the west shield the city from the coldest temperatures. Humidity is generally low. Winter storms moving east from the Pacific drop most of their moisture on the mountains to the west, while summer precipitation comes from scattered thunderstorms.

Rankings

General Rankings

- *US News & World Report* conducted a survey of more than 3,600 people and analyzed the 150 largest metropolitan areas to determine what matters most when selecting the next place to live. Boulder ranked #1 out of the top 25 as having the best combination of desirable factors. Criteria: cost of living; quality of life and education; net migration; job market; desirability; and other factors. *realestate.usnews.com, "The 25 Best Places to Live in the U.S. in 2021-2022," July 13, 2021*

Business/Finance Rankings

- According to *Business Insider*, the Boulder metro area is a prime place to run a startup or move an existing business to. The area ranked #4. More than 300 metro areas were analyzed for factors that were of top concern to new business owners. Data was based on the 2019 U.S. Census Bureau American Community Survey, statistics from the CDC, Bureau of Labor Statistics employment report, and University of Chicago analysis. Criteria: business formations; percentage of vaccinated population; percentage of households with internet subscriptions; median household income; and share of work that can be done from home. *www.businessinsider.com, "The 20 Best Cities for Starting a Business in 2022 Include Baltimore, Boulder, and Boston," January 5, 2022*
- 24/7 Wall Street used metro data from the Bureau of Labor Statistics' Occupational Employment database to identify the cities with the highest percentage of those employed in jobs requiring knowledge in the science, technology, engineering, and math (STEM) fields as well as average wages for STEM jobs. The Boulder metro area was #4. *247wallst.com, "15 Cities with the Most High-Tech Jobs," January 11, 2020*
- The Boulder metro area appeared on the Milken Institute "2021 Best Performing Cities" list. Rank: #44 out of 200 large metro areas (population over 250,000). Criteria: job growth; wage and salary growth; high-tech output growth; housing affordability; household broadband access. *Milken Institute, "Best-Performing Cities 2021," February 16, 2021*
- *Forbes* ranked the 200 most populous metro areas to determine the nation's "Best Places for Business and Careers." The Boulder metro area was ranked #25. Criteria: costs (business and living); job growth (past and projected); income growth; quality of life; educational attainment (college and high school); projected economic growth; cultural and leisure opportunities; workplace tolerance laws; net migration patterns. *Forbes, "The Best Places for Business and Careers 2019: Seattle Still On Top," October 30, 2019*

Environmental Rankings

- Niche compiled a list of the nation's snowiest cities, based on the National Oceanic and Atmospheric Administration's 30-year average snowfall data. Among cities with a population of at least 50,000, Boulder ranked #6. *Niche.com, Top 25 Snowiest Cities in America, December 10, 2018*
- The U.S. Environmental Protection Agency (EPA) released its list of mid-size U.S. metropolitan areas with the most ENERGY STAR certified buildings in 2020. The Boulder metro area was ranked #8 out of 10. *U.S. Environmental Protection Agency, "2021 Energy Star Top Cities," June 15, 2021*

Health/Fitness Rankings

- The Sharecare Community Well-Being Index evaluates 10 individual and social health factors in order to measure what matters to Americans in the communities in which they live. The Boulder metro area ranked #10 in the top 10 across all 10 domains. Criteria: access to healthcare, food, and community resources; housng and transportation; economic security; feeling of purpose; physical, financial, social, and community well-being. *www.sharecare.com, "Community Well-Being Index: 2020 Metro Area & County Rankings Report," August 30, 2021*

Real Estate Rankings

- The Boulder metro area was identified as one of the nations's 20 hottest housing markets in 2022. Criteria: listing views as an indicator of demand and median days on the market as an indicator of supply. The area ranked #5. *Realtor.com, "January 2022 Top 20 Hottest Housing Markets," February 15, 2022*
- The Boulder metro area was identified as one of the 20 least affordable housing markets in the U.S. in 2021. The area ranked #177 out of 183 markets. Criteria: qualification for a mortgage loan with a 10 percent down payment on a typical home. *National Association of Realtors®, Qualifying Income Based on Sales Price of Existing Single-Family Homes for Metropolitan Areas, 2021*

- Boulder was ranked #173 out of 237 metro areas in terms of housing affordability in 2021 by the National Association of Home Builders (#1 = most affordable). Criteria: the share of homes sold in that area affordable to a family earning the local median income, based on standard mortgage underwriting criteria. *National Association of Home Builders®, NAHB-Wells Fargo Housing Opportunity Index, 4th Quarter 2021*

Safety Rankings

- The National Insurance Crime Bureau ranked 390 metro areas in the U.S. in terms of per capita rates of vehicle theft. The Boulder metro area ranked #115 (#1 = highest rate). Criteria: number of vehicle theft offenses per 100,000 inhabitants in 2020. *National Insurance Crime Bureau, "Hot Spots 2020," August 31, 2021*

Seniors/Retirement Rankings

- From its Best Cities for Successful Aging indexes, the Milken Institute generated rankings for metropolitan areas, weighing data in nine categories—health care, wellness, living arrangements, transportation and convenience, financial characteristics, education, employment, community engagement, and overall livability. The Boulder metro area was ranked #11 overall in the small metro area category. *Milken Institute, "Best Cities for Successful Aging, 2017" March 14, 2017*
- Boulder was identified as #11 of 20 most popular places to retire in the Western region by *Topretirements.com*. The site separated its annual "Best Places to Retire" list by major U.S. regions for 2019. The list reflects the 20 cities that visitors to the website are most interested in for retirement, based on the number of times a city's review was viewed on the website. *Topretirements.com, "20 Best Places to Retire in the West-2019," November 11, 2019*

Sports/Recreation Rankings

- Boulder was chosen as one of America's best cities for bicycling. The city ranked #12 out of 50. Criteria: cycling infrastructure that is safe and friendly for all ages; energy and bike culture. The editors evaluated cities with populations of 100,000 or more. *Bicycling, "The 50 Best Bike Cities in America," October 10, 2018*

Women/Minorities Rankings

- *Travel + Leisure* listed the best cities in and around the US for a memorable and fun girls' trip, even on a budget. Whether it is for a special occasion or just to get away, Boulder is sure to have something for all the ladies in your tribe. *Travel + Leisure, "25 Girls' Weekend Getaways That Won't Break the Bank," June 8, 2020*
- *Women's Health*, together with the site Yelp, identified the 15 "Wellthiest" spots in the U.S. Boulder appeared among the top for happiest, healthiest, outdoorsiest and Zen-iest. *Women's Health, "The 15 Wellthiest Cities in the U.S." July 5, 2017*

Business Environment

DEMOGRAPHICS

Population Growth

Area	1990 Census	2000 Census	2010 Census	2020* Estimate	Population Growth (%)	
					1990-2020	2010-2020
City	87,737	94,673	97,385	108,777	24.0	11.7
MSA[1]	208,898	269,758	294,567	324,682	55.4	10.2
U.S.	248,709,873	281,421,906	308,745,538	326,569,308	31.3	5.8

Note: (1) Figures cover the Boulder, CO Metropolitan Statistical Area; (*) 2016-2020 5-year estimated population
Source: U.S. Census Bureau, 1990 Census, Census 2000, Census 2010, 2016-2020 American Community Survey 5-Year Estimates

Household Size

Area	Persons in Household (%)							Average Household Size
	One	Two	Three	Four	Five	Six	Seven or More	
City	36.2	35.3	14.5	10.4	2.8	0.5	0.3	2.30
MSA[1]	29.3	35.9	15.6	13.0	4.4	1.3	0.4	2.50
U.S.	28.0	33.9	15.5	12.9	6.0	2.3	1.4	2.60

Note: (1) Figures cover the Boulder, CO Metropolitan Statistical Area
Source: U.S. Census Bureau, 2016-2020 American Community Survey 5-Year Estimates

Race

Area	White Alone[2] (%)	Black Alone[2] (%)	Asian Alone[2] (%)	AIAN[3] Alone[2] (%)	NHOPI[4] Alone[2] (%)	Other Race Alone[2] (%)	Two or More Races (%)
City	86.3	1.1	5.9	0.3	0.1	1.7	4.8
MSA[1]	87.2	0.9	4.9	0.5	0.1	2.1	4.4
U.S.	70.4	12.6	5.6	0.8	0.2	5.1	5.2

Note: (1) Figures cover the Boulder, CO Metropolitan Statistical Area; (2) Alone is defined as not being in combination with one or more other races; (3) American Indian and Alaska Native; (4) Native Hawaiian and Other Pacific Islander
Source: U.S. Census Bureau, 2016-2020 American Community Survey 5-Year Estimates

Hispanic or Latino Origin

Area	Total (%)	Mexican (%)	Puerto Rican (%)	Cuban (%)	Other (%)
City	10.3	6.3	0.3	0.4	3.3
MSA[1]	13.8	10.0	0.4	0.3	3.1
U.S.	18.2	11.2	1.7	0.7	4.5

Note: Persons of Hispanic or Latino origin can be of any race; (1) Figures cover the Boulder, CO Metropolitan Statistical Area
Source: U.S. Census Bureau, 2016-2020 American Community Survey 5-Year Estimates

Ancestry

Area	German	Irish	English	American	Italian	Polish	French[2]	Scottish	Dutch
City	16.8	11.8	11.4	2.5	6.1	3.5	2.5	3.2	1.3
MSA[1]	19.0	11.7	12.5	3.1	5.3	3.2	2.7	3.2	1.7
U.S.	13.0	9.7	7.7	5.9	5.1	2.7	2.3	1.6	1.1

Note: Figures are the percentage of the total population reporting a particular ancestry. The nine most commonly reported ancestries in the U.S. are shown. Figures include multiple ancestries (e.g. if a person reported being Irish and Italian, they were included in both columns); (1) Figures cover the Boulder, CO Metropolitan Statistical Area; (2) Excludes Basque
Source: U.S. Census Bureau, 2016-2020 American Community Survey 5-Year Estimates

Foreign-born Population

Area	Percent of Population Born in								
	Any Foreign Country	Asia	Mexico	Europe	Caribbean	Central America[2]	South America	Africa	Canada
City	10.5	4.5	1.2	2.8	0.1	0.3	0.8	0.2	0.4
MSA[1]	10.1	3.6	2.5	2.2	0.1	0.3	0.6	0.2	0.4
U.S.	13.5	4.2	3.3	1.5	1.3	1.1	1.0	0.7	0.3

Note: (1) Figures cover the Boulder, CO Metropolitan Statistical Area; (2) Excludes Mexico.
Source: U.S. Census Bureau, 2016-2020 American Community Survey 5-Year Estimates

Marital Status

Area	Never Married	Now Married[2]	Separated	Widowed	Divorced
City	55.5	31.6	0.7	2.7	9.6
MSA[1]	38.2	45.8	0.9	3.8	11.3
U.S.	33.5	48.1	1.8	5.7	10.8

Note: Figures are percentages and cover the population 15 years of age and older; (1) Figures cover the Boulder, CO Metropolitan Statistical Area; (2) Excludes separated
Source: U.S. Census Bureau, 2016-2020 American Community Survey 5-Year Estimates

Disability by Age

Area	All Ages	Under 18 Years Old	18 to 64 Years Old	65 Years and Over
City	6.3	2.7	4.4	22.9
MSA[1]	8.1	2.9	6.0	25.4
U.S.	12.7	4.3	10.3	34.0

Note: Figures show percent of the civilian noninstitutionalized population that reported having a disability. Disability status is determined from six types of difficulty: vision, hearing, cognitive, ambulatory, self-care, and independent living. For children under 5 years old, hearing and vision difficulty are used to determine disability status. For children between the ages of 5 and 14, disability status is determined from hearing, vision, cognitive, ambulatory, and self-care difficulties. For people aged 15 years and older, they are considered to have a disability if they have difficulty with any one of the six difficulty types; Note: (1) Figures cover the Boulder, CO Metropolitan Statistical Area
Source: U.S. Census Bureau, 2016-2020 American Community Survey 5-Year Estimates

Age

Area	Percent of Population									Median Age
	Under Age 5	Age 5–19	Age 20–34	Age 35–44	Age 45–54	Age 55–64	Age 65–74	Age 75–84	Age 85+	
City	3.0	18.3	37.5	10.2	10.1	9.4	6.8	3.0	1.8	28.8
MSA[1]	4.4	18.8	24.3	12.6	12.9	12.6	8.9	3.7	1.8	36.9
U.S.	6.0	19.1	20.6	12.7	12.7	12.9	9.4	4.7	2.0	38.2

Note: (1) Figures cover the Boulder, CO Metropolitan Statistical Area
Source: U.S. Census Bureau, 2016-2020 American Community Survey 5-Year Estimates

Gender

Area	Males	Females	Males per 100 Females
City	56,091	52,686	106.5
MSA[1]	163,343	161,339	101.2
U.S.	160,818,530	165,750,778	97.0

Note: (1) Figures cover the Boulder, CO Metropolitan Statistical Area
Source: U.S. Census Bureau, 2016-2020 American Community Survey 5-Year Estimates

Religious Groups by Family

Area	Catholic	Baptist	Non-Den.	Methodist[2]	Lutheran	LDS[3]	Pente-costal	Presby-terian[4]	Muslim[5]	Judaism
MSA[1]	20.1	2.4	4.8	1.8	3.1	3.0	0.5	2.0	0.1	0.8
U.S.	19.1	9.3	4.0	4.0	2.3	2.0	1.9	1.6	0.8	0.7

Note: Figures are the number of adherents as a percentage of the total population; (1) Figures cover the Boulder, CO Metropolitan Statistical Area; (2) Methodist/Pietist; (3) Latter Day Saints; (4) Reformed; (5) Figures are estimates
Source: Association of Statisticians of American Religious Bodies, 2010 U.S. Religion Census: Religious Congregations & Membership Study

Religious Groups by Tradition

Area	Catholic	Evangelical Protestant	Mainline Protestant	Other Tradition	Black Protestant	Orthodox
MSA[1]	20.1	9.8	6.5	4.9	<0.1	0.2
U.S.	19.1	16.2	7.3	4.3	1.6	0.3

Note: Figures are the number of adherents as a percentage of the total population; (1) Figures cover the Boulder, CO Metropolitan Statistical Area
Source: Association of Statisticians of American Religious Bodies, 2010 U.S. Religion Census: Religious Congregations & Membership Study

ECONOMY

Gross Metropolitan Product

Area	2017	2018	2019	2020	Rank[2]
MSA[1]	25.6	27.2	28.7	29.9	107

Note: Figures are in billions of dollars; (1) Figures cover the Boulder, CO Metropolitan Statistical Area; (2) Rank is based on 2018 data and ranges from 1 to 381
Source: U.S. Conference of Mayors, U.S. Metro Economies: GMP & Employment 2018-2020, September 2019

Economic Growth

Area	2015-17 (%)	2018 (%)	2019 (%)	2020 (%)	Rank[2]
MSA[1]	2.5	4.1	3.9	2.1	98
U.S.	1.9	2.9	2.3	2.1	–

Note: Figures are real gross metropolitan product (GMP) growth rates and represent average annual percent change; (1) Figures cover the Boulder, CO Metropolitan Statistical Area; (2) Rank is based on 2017 2-year average annual percent change and ranges from 1 to 381
Source: U.S. Conference of Mayors, U.S. Metro Economies: GMP & Employment 2018-2020, September 2019

Metropolitan Area Exports

Area	2015	2016	2017	2018	2019	2020	Rank[2]
MSA[1]	1,039.1	956.3	1,012.0	1,044.1	1,014.9	1,110.4	139

Note: Figures are in millions of dollars; (1) Figures cover the Boulder, CO Metropolitan Statistical Area; (2) Rank is based on 2020 data and ranges from 1 to 389
Source: U.S. Department of Commerce, International Trade Administration, Office of Trade and Economic Analysis, Industry and Analysis, Exports by Metropolitan Area, data extracted March 4, 2022

Building Permits

Area	Single-Family			Multi-Family			Total		
	2019	2020	Pct. Chg.	2019	2020	Pct. Chg.	2019	2020	Pct. Chg.
City	41	40	-2.4	286	276	-3.5	327	316	-3.4
MSA[1]	742	573	-22.8	908	1,061	16.9	1,650	1,634	-1.0
U.S.	862,100	979,400	13.6	523,900	491,700	-6.1	1,386,000	1,471,100	6.1

Note: (1) Figures cover the Boulder, CO Metropolitan Statistical Area; Figures represent new, privately-owned housing units authorized (unadjusted data); All permit data are based on estimates with imputation
Source: U.S. Census Bureau, Manufacturing, Mining, and Construction Statistics, Building Permits, 2019, 2020

Bankruptcy Filings

Area	Business Filings			Nonbusiness Filings		
	2020	2021	% Chg.	2020	2021	% Chg.
Boulder County	42	13	-69.0	286	216	-24.5
U.S.	21,655	14,347	-33.7	522,808	399,269	-23.6

Note: Business filings include Chapter 7, Chapter 9, Chapter 11, Chapter 12, Chapter 13, Chapter 15, and Section 304; Nonbusiness filings include Chapter 7, Chapter 11, and Chapter 13
Source: Administrative Office of the U.S. Courts, Business and Nonbusiness Bankruptcy, County Cases Commenced by Chapter of the Bankruptcy Code, During the 12-Month Period Ending December 31, 2020 and Business and Nonbusiness Bankruptcy, County Cases Commenced by Chapter of the Bankruptcy Code, During the 12-Month Period Ending December 31, 2021

Housing Vacancy Rates

Area	Gross Vacancy Rate[2] (%)			Year-Round Vacancy Rate[3] (%)			Rental Vacancy Rate[4] (%)			Homeowner Vacancy Rate[5] (%)		
	2019	2020	2021	2019	2020	2021	2019	2020	2021	2019	2020	2021
MSA[1]	n/a	n/a	n/a	n/a	n/a	n/a	n/a	n/a	n/a	n/a	n/a	n/a
U.S.	12.0	10.6	10.8	9.5	8.2	8.4	6.7	6.3	6.1	1.4	1.0	0.9

Note: (1) Figures cover the Boulder, CO Metropolitan Statistical Area; (2) The percentage of the total housing inventory that is vacant; (3) The percentage of the housing inventory (excluding seasonal units) that is year-round vacant; (4) The percentage of rental inventory that is vacant for rent; (5) The percentage of homeowner inventory that is vacant for sale; n/a not available
Source: U.S. Census Bureau, Housing Vacancies and Homeownership Annual Statistics: 2019, 2020, 2021

INCOME

Income

Area	Per Capita ($)	Median Household ($)	Average Household ($)
City	49,050	72,279	117,554
MSA[1]	48,776	87,476	121,262
U.S.	35,384	64,994	91,547

Note: (1) Figures cover the Boulder, CO Metropolitan Statistical Area
Source: U.S. Census Bureau, 2016-2020 American Community Survey 5-Year Estimates

Household Income Distribution

Area	Percent of Households Earning							
	Under $15,000	$15,000 -$24,999	$25,000 -$34,999	$35,000 -$49,999	$50,000 -$74,999	$75,000 -$99,999	$100,000 -$149,999	$150,000 and up
City	13.9	7.1	7.2	9.4	13.4	9.9	13.7	25.4
MSA[1]	8.5	5.9	6.1	9.2	14.0	12.1	17.7	26.5
U.S.	9.9	8.5	8.6	12.0	17.2	12.8	15.6	15.4

Note: (1) Figures cover the Boulder, CO Metropolitan Statistical Area
Source: U.S. Census Bureau, 2016-2020 American Community Survey 5-Year Estimates

Poverty Rate

Area	All Ages	Under 18 Years Old	18 to 64 Years Old	65 Years and Over
City	20.3	5.6	25.1	7.4
MSA[1]	11.2	6.4	13.6	6.3
U.S.	12.8	17.5	12.1	9.3

Note: Figures are percentage of people whose income during the past 12 months was below the poverty level; (1) Figures cover the Boulder, CO Metropolitan Statistical Area
Source: U.S. Census Bureau, 2016-2020 American Community Survey 5-Year Estimates

CITY FINANCES

City Government Finances

Component	2019 ($000)	2019 ($ per capita)
Total Revenues	441,536	4,122
Total Expenditures	399,109	3,726
Debt Outstanding	86,521	808
Cash and Securities[1]	326,237	3,045

Note: (1) Cash and security holdings of a government at the close of its fiscal year, including those of its dependent agencies, utilities, and liquor stores.
Source: U.S. Census Bureau, State & Local Government Finances 2019

City Government Revenue by Source

Source	2019 ($000)	2019 ($ per capita)	2019 (%)
General Revenue			
From Federal Government	2,248	21	0.5
From State Government	23,783	222	5.4
From Local Governments	4,277	40	1.0
Taxes			
Property	45,038	420	10.2
Sales and Gross Receipts	183,904	1,717	41.7
Personal Income	0	0	0.0
Corporate Income	0	0	0.0
Motor Vehicle License	0	0	0.0
Other Taxes	9,758	91	2.2
Current Charges	39,471	368	8.9
Liquor Store	0	0	0.0
Utility	26,379	246	6.0

Source: U.S. Census Bureau, State & Local Government Finances 2019

City Government Expenditures by Function

Function	2019 ($000)	2019 ($ per capita)	2019 (%)
General Direct Expenditures			
Air Transportation	563	5	0.1
Corrections	0	0	0.0
Education	0	0	0.0
Employment Security Administration	0	0	0.0
Financial Administration	10,790	100	2.7
Fire Protection	27,975	261	7.0
General Public Buildings	6,320	59	1.6
Governmental Administration, Other	25,277	236	6.3
Health	0	0	0.0
Highways	76,623	715	19.2
Hospitals	0	0	0.0
Housing and Community Development	17,094	159	4.3
Interest on General Debt	8,289	77	2.1
Judicial and Legal	4,655	43	1.2
Libraries	14,362	134	3.6
Parking	9,395	87	2.4
Parks and Recreation	62,264	581	15.6
Police Protection	41,582	388	10.4
Public Welfare	0	0	0.0
Sewerage	30,002	280	7.5
Solid Waste Management	1,990	18	0.5
Veterans' Services	0	0	0.0
Liquor Store	0	0	0.0
Utility	16,503	154	4.1

Source: U.S. Census Bureau, State & Local Government Finances 2019

EMPLOYMENT

Labor Force and Employment

Area	Civilian Labor Force			Workers Employed		
	Dec. 2020	Dec. 2021	% Chg.	Dec. 2020	Dec. 2021	% Chg.
City	63,840	65,584	2.7	60,404	63,755	5.5
MSA[1]	194,211	199,627	2.8	182,991	193,142	5.5
U.S.	160,017,000	161,696,000	1.0	149,613,000	155,732,000	4.1

Note: Data is not seasonally adjusted and covers workers 16 years of age and older; (1) Figures cover the Boulder, CO Metropolitan Statistical Area
Source: Bureau of Labor Statistics, Local Area Unemployment Statistics

Unemployment Rate

Area	2021											
	Jan.	Feb.	Mar.	Apr.	May	Jun.	Jul.	Aug.	Sep.	Oct.	Nov.	Dec.
City	5.4	5.1	5.1	4.8	4.4	5.3	4.4	4.0	3.2	3.1	3.1	2.8
MSA[1]	6.0	5.6	5.5	5.3	4.8	5.5	4.9	4.4	3.7	3.5	3.5	3.2
U.S.	6.8	6.6	6.2	5.7	5.5	6.1	5.7	5.3	4.6	4.3	3.9	3.7

Note: Data is not seasonally adjusted and covers workers 16 years of age and older; (1) Figures cover the Boulder, CO Metropolitan Statistical Area
Source: Bureau of Labor Statistics, Local Area Unemployment Statistics

Average Wages

Occupation	$/Hr.	Occupation	$/Hr.
Accountants and Auditors	43.69	Maintenance and Repair Workers	23.65
Automotive Mechanics	26.64	Marketing Managers	81.78
Bookkeepers	23.39	Network and Computer Systems Admin.	45.72
Carpenters	26.61	Nurses, Licensed Practical	27.32
Cashiers	15.73	Nurses, Registered	40.88
Computer Programmers	57.20	Nursing Assistants	17.84
Computer Systems Analysts	53.93	Office Clerks, General	23.23
Computer User Support Specialists	34.92	Physical Therapists	43.04
Construction Laborers	19.55	Physicians	139.68
Cooks, Restaurant	18.13	Plumbers, Pipefitters and Steamfitters	27.80
Customer Service Representatives	20.40	Police and Sheriff's Patrol Officers	40.99
Dentists	96.97	Postal Service Mail Carriers	26.37
Electricians	27.79	Real Estate Sales Agents	37.69
Engineers, Electrical	54.64	Retail Salespersons	17.87
Fast Food and Counter Workers	15.17	Sales Representatives, Technical/Scientific	56.70
Financial Managers	87.34	Secretaries, Exc. Legal/Medical/Executive	21.25
First-Line Supervisors of Office Workers	33.09	Security Guards	20.67
General and Operations Managers	68.52	Surgeons	169.91
Hairdressers/Cosmetologists	20.61	Teacher Assistants, Exc. Postsecondary*	17.55
Home Health and Personal Care Aides	16.65	Teachers, Secondary School, Exc. Sp. Ed.*	34.47
Janitors and Cleaners	17.63	Telemarketers	15.29
Landscaping/Groundskeeping Workers	20.13	Truck Drivers, Heavy/Tractor-Trailer	26.75
Lawyers	n/a	Truck Drivers, Light/Delivery Services	22.94
Maids and Housekeeping Cleaners	16.02	Waiters and Waitresses	18.30

Note: Wage data covers the Boulder, CO Metropolitan Statistical Area; (*) Hourly wages were calculated from annual wage data based on a 40 hour work week; n/a not available.
Source: Bureau of Labor Statistics, Metro Area Occupational Employment & Wage Estimates, May 2021

Employment by Industry

Sector	MSA[1]		U.S.
	Number of Employees	Percent of Total	Percent of Total
Construction, Mining, and Logging	5,700	2.8	5.3
Education and Health Services	25,900	12.9	16.0
Financial Activities	7,600	3.8	5.9
Government	37,200	18.5	14.9
Information	9,200	4.6	1.9
Leisure and Hospitality	18,700	9.3	9.8
Manufacturing	21,300	10.6	8.4
Other Services	6,500	3.2	3.7
Professional and Business Services	41,600	20.7	14.6
Retail Trade	18,400	9.1	10.7
Transportation, Warehousing, and Utilities	2,200	1.1	4.8
Wholesale Trade	6,900	3.4	3.8

Note: Figures are non-farm employment as of December 2021. Figures are not seasonally adjusted and include workers 16 years of age and older; (1) Figures cover the Boulder, CO Metropolitan Statistical Area
Source: Bureau of Labor Statistics, Current Employment Statistics, Employment, Hours, and Earnings

Employment by Occupation

Occupation Classification	City (%)	MSA[1] (%)	U.S. (%)
Management, Business, Science, and Arts	58.6	54.9	39.5
Natural Resources, Construction, and Maintenance	2.6	5.6	8.7
Production, Transportation, and Material Moving	6.0	7.5	13.1
Sales and Office	16.8	17.8	21.3
Service	16.0	14.3	17.4

Note: Figures cover employed civilians 16 years of age and older; (1) Figures cover the Boulder, CO Metropolitan Statistical Area
Source: U.S. Census Bureau, 2016-2020 American Community Survey 5-Year Estimates

Occupations with Greatest Projected Employment Growth: 2021 – 2023

Occupation[1]	2021 Employment	2023 Projected Employment	Numeric Employment Change	Percent Employment Change
Software Developers and Software Quality Assurance Analysts and Testers	62,100	66,810	4,710	7.6
Fast Food and Counter Workers	72,270	76,700	4,430	6.1
Cooks, Restaurant	30,360	34,250	3,890	12.8
Waiters and Waitresses	40,230	43,230	3,000	7.5
Retail Salespersons	77,680	80,550	2,870	3.7
Maids and Housekeeping Cleaners	22,930	25,680	2,750	12.0
Project Management Specialists and Business Operations Specialists, All Other	66,210	68,800	2,590	3.9
Home Health and Personal Care Aides	39,930	42,460	2,530	6.3
Stockers and Order Fillers	46,970	49,310	2,340	5.0
General and Operations Managers	37,390	39,420	2,030	5.4

Note: Projections cover Colorado; (1) Sorted by numeric employment change
Source: www.projectionscentral.com, State Occupational Projections, 2021–2023 Short-Term Projections

Fastest-Growing Occupations: 2021 – 2023

Occupation[1]	2021 Employment	2023 Projected Employment	Numeric Employment Change	Percent Employment Change
Motion Picture Projectionists	100	160	60	60.0
Rotary Drill Operators, Oil and Gas	240	340	100	41.7
Athletes and Sports Competitors	420	590	170	40.5
Roustabouts, Oil and Gas	1,780	2,490	710	39.9
Musicians and Singers	710	960	250	35.2
Fine Artists, Including Painters, Sculptors, and Illustrators	310	410	100	32.3
Actors	650	820	170	26.2
Service Unit Operators, Oil, Gas, and Mining	2,020	2,550	530	26.2
Dancers	320	400	80	25.0
Pump Operators, Except Wellhead Pumpers	200	250	50	25.0

Note: Projections cover Colorado; (1) Sorted by percent employment change and excludes occupations with numeric employment change less than 50
Source: www.projectionscentral.com, State Occupational Projections, 2021–2023 Short-Term Projections

TAXES

State Corporate Income Tax Rates

State	Tax Rate (%)	Income Brackets ($)	Num. of Brackets	Financial Institution Tax Rate (%)[a]	Federal Income Tax Ded.
Colorado	4.55	Flat rate	1	4.55	No

Note: Tax rates as of January 1, 2022; (a) Rates listed are the corporate income tax rate applied to financial institutions or excise taxes based on income. Some states have other taxes based upon the value of deposits or shares.
Source: Federation of Tax Administrators, State Corporate Income Tax Rates, January 1, 2022

State Individual Income Tax Rates

State	Tax Rate (%)	Income Brackets ($)	Personal Exemptions ($)			Standard Ded. ($)	
			Single	Married	Depend.	Single	Married
Colorado	4.55	Flat rate	(d)	(d)	(d)	12,950	25,900 (d)

Note: Tax rates as of January 1, 2022; Local- and county-level taxes are not included; Federal income tax is not deductible on state income tax returns; (d) These states use the personal exemption/standard deduction amounts provided in the federal Internal Revenue Code.
Source: Federation of Tax Administrators, State Individual Income Tax Rates, January 1, 2022

Various State Sales and Excise Tax Rates

State	State Sales Tax (%)	Gasoline[1] (¢/gal.)	Cigarette[2] ($/pack)	Spirits[3] ($/gal.)	Wine[4] ($/gal.)	Beer[5] ($/gal.)	Recreational Marijuana (%)
Colorado	2.9	22	1.94	2.28	0.32	0.08	(d)

Note: All tax rates as of January 1, 2022; (1) The American Petroleum Institute has developed a methodology for determining the average tax rate on a gallon of fuel. Rates may include any of the following: excise taxes, environmental fees, storage tank fees, other fees or taxes, general sales tax, and local taxes; (2) The federal excise tax of $1.0066 per pack and local taxes are not included; (3) Rates are those applicable to off-premise sales of 40% alcohol by volume (a.b.v.) distilled spirits in 750ml containers. Local excise taxes are excluded; (4) Rates are those applicable to off-premise sales of 11% a.b.v. non-carbonated wine in 750ml containers; (5) Rates are those applicable to off-premise sales of 4.7% a.b.v. beer in 12 ounce containers; (d) 15% excise tax (levied on wholesale at average market rate); 15% excise tax (retail price)
Source: Tax Foundation, 2022 Facts & Figures: How Does Your State Compare?

State Business Tax Climate Index Rankings

State	Overall Rank	Corporate Tax Rank	Individual Income Tax Rank	Sales Tax Rank	Property Tax Rank	Unemployment Insurance Tax Rank
Colorado	20	6	14	38	34	41

Note: The index is a measure of how each state's tax laws affect economic performance. The lower the rank, the more favorable a state's tax system is for business. States without a given tax are given a ranking of 1. The scores/rankings for the District of Columbia do not affect other states. The 2022 index represents the tax climate as of July 1, 2021.
Source: Tax Foundation, State Business Tax Climate Index 2022

TRANSPORTATION

Means of Transportation to Work

Area	Car/Truck/Van		Public Transportation			Bicycle	Walked	Other Means	Worked at Home
	Drove Alone	Car-pooled	Bus	Subway	Railroad				
City	48.5	4.7	7.5	0.0	0.0	9.1	10.2	1.4	18.7
MSA[1]	62.7	7.0	4.6	0.0	0.0	4.0	4.6	1.0	16.1
U.S.	74.9	8.9	2.2	1.7	0.5	0.5	2.6	1.4	7.3

Note: Figures are percentages and cover workers 16 years of age and older; (1) Figures cover the Boulder, CO Metropolitan Statistical Area
Source: U.S. Census Bureau, 2016-2020 American Community Survey 5-Year Estimates

Travel Time to Work

Area	Less Than 10 Minutes	10 to 19 Minutes	20 to 29 Minutes	30 to 44 Minutes	45 to 59 Minutes	60 to 89 Minutes	90 Minutes or More
City	18.9	44.3	16.4	10.2	5.6	3.6	1.1
MSA[1]	14.2	33.6	21.3	17.5	7.1	4.9	1.4
U.S.	12.3	28.4	20.9	20.9	8.3	6.4	2.9

Note: Note: Figures are percentages and include workers 16 years old and over; (1) Figures cover the Boulder, CO Metropolitan Statistical Area
Source: U.S. Census Bureau, 2016-2020 American Community Survey 5-Year Estimates

Key Congestion Measures

Measure	1990	2000	2010	2015	2020
Annual Hours of Delay, Total (000)	997	2,194	3,362	4,092	2,312
Annual Hours of Delay, Per Auto Commuter	17	30	37	43	23
Annual Congestion Cost, Per Auto Commuter ($)	326	539	660	744	436

Note: Covers the Boulder CO urban area
Source: Texas A&M Transportation Institute, 2021 Urban Mobility Report

Freeway Travel Time Index

Measure	1985	1990	1995	2000	2005	2010	2015	2020
Urban Area Index[1]	1.04	1.08	1.13	1.17	1.20	1.21	1.21	1.08
Urban Area Rank[1,2]	81	62	47	36	36	33	36	44

Note: Freeway Travel Time Index—the ratio of travel time in the peak period to the travel time at free-flow conditions. For example, a value of 1.30 indicates a 20-minute free-flow trip takes 26 minutes in the peak (20 minutes x 1.30 = 26 minutes); (1) Covers the Boulder CO urban area; (2) Rank is based on 101 larger urban areas (#1 = highest travel time index)
Source: Texas A&M Transportation Institute, 2021 Urban Mobility Report

Public Transportation

Agency Name / Mode of Transportation	Vehicles Operated in Maximum Service[1]	Annual Unlinked Passenger Trips[2] (in thous.)	Annual Passenger Miles[3] (in thous.)
Community Transit Network			
Bus (directly operated)	472	23,818.2	106,209.8
Bus (purchased transportation)	342	12,540.5	50,971.5
Commuter Rail (directly operated)	8	173.8	1,496.7
Commuter Rail (purchased transportation)	44	4,780.4	55,053.9
Demand Response (purchased transportation)	409	537.1	4,100.4
Light Rail (directly operated)	156	10,464.7	72,911.0

Note: (1) Number of revenue vehicles operated by the given mode and type of service to meet the annual maximum service requirement. This is the revenue vehicle count during the peak season of the year; on the week and day that maximum service is provided. Vehicles operated in maximum service (VOMS) exclude atypical days and one-time special events; (2) Number of passengers who boarded public transportation vehicles. Passengers are counted each time they board a vehicle no matter how many vehicles they use to travel from their origin to their destination. (3) Sum of the distances ridden by all passengers during the entire fiscal year.
Source: Federal Transit Administration, National Transit Database, 2020

Air Transportation

Airport Name and Code / Type of Service	Passenger Airlines[1]	Passenger Enplanements	Freight Carriers[2]	Freight (lbs)
Denver International (40 miles) (DEN)				
Domestic service (U.S. carriers - 2021)	22	27,776,445	15	266,792,807
International service (U.S. carriers - 2020)	7	311,343	3	1,986,377

Note: (1) Includes all U.S.-based major, minor and commuter airlines that carried at least one passenger during the year; (2) Includes all U.S.-based airlines and freight carriers that transported at least one pound of freight during the year.
Source: Bureau of Transportation Statistics, The Intermodal Transportation Database, Air Carriers: T-100 Domestic Market (U.S. Carriers), 2021; Bureau of Transportation Statistics, The Intermodal Transportation Database, Air Carriers: T-100 International Market (U.S. Carriers), 2020

BUSINESSES

Major Business Headquarters

Company Name	Industry	Rankings	
		Fortune[1]	Forbes[2]
No companies listed	-	-	-

Note: (1) Companies that produce a 10-K are ranked 1 to 500 based on 2020 revenue; (2) All private companies with at least $2 billion in annual revenue through the end of their most current fiscal year are ranked 1 to 225; companies listed are headquartered in the city; dashes indicate no ranking
Source: Fortune, "Fortune 500," 2021; Forbes, "America's Largest Private Companies," 2021

Fastest-Growing Businesses

According to *Inc.*, Boulder is home to one of America's 500 fastest-growing private companies: **Ivy.ai** (#168). Criteria: must be an independent, privately-held, for-profit, U.S. corporation, proprietorship or partnership as of December 31, 2020; revenues must be at least $100,000 in 2017 and $2 million in 2020; must have four-year operating/sales history. *Inc., "America's 500 Fastest-Growing Private Companies," 2021*

Living Environment

COST OF LIVING

Cost of Living Index

Composite Index	Groceries	Housing	Utilities	Trans-portation	Health Care	Misc. Goods/ Services
n/a	n/a	n/a	n/a	n/a	n/a	n/a

Note: The Cost of Living Index measures regional differences in the cost of consumer goods and services, excluding taxes and non-consumer expenditures, for professional and managerial households in the top income quintile. It is based on more than 50,000 prices covering almost 60 different items for which prices are collected three times a year by chambers of commerce, economic development organizations or university applied economic centers in each participating urban area. The numbers shown should be read as a percentage above or below the national average of 100. For example, a value of 115.4 in the groceries column indicates that grocery prices are 15.4% higher than the national average. Small differences in the index numbers should not be interpreted as significant; n/a not available.
Source: The Council for Community and Economic Research, Cost of Living Index, 2021

Grocery Prices

Area[1]	T-Bone Steak ($/pound)	Frying Chicken ($/pound)	Whole Milk ($/half gal.)	Eggs ($/dozen)	Orange Juice ($/64 oz.)	Coffee ($/11.5 oz.)
City[2]	n/a	n/a	n/a	n/a	n/a	n/a
Avg.	12.82	1.40	2.22	1.57	3.59	4.30
Min.	8.91	0.91	1.29	0.75	2.87	3.02
Max.	21.35	2.69	3.92	3.86	5.49	8.11

Note: (1) Values for the local area are compared with the average, minimum and maximum values for all 285 areas in the Cost of Living Index; (2) Figures cover the Boulder CO urban area; n/a not available; ***T-Bone Steak*** *(price per pound);* ***Frying Chicken*** *(price per pound, whole fryer);* ***Whole Milk*** *(half gallon carton);* ***Eggs*** *(price per dozen, Grade A, large);* ***Orange Juice*** *(64 oz. Tropicana or Florida Natural);* ***Coffee*** *(11.5 oz. can, vacuum-packed, Maxwell House, Hills Bros, or Folgers).*
Source: The Council for Community and Economic Research, Cost of Living Index, 2021

Housing and Utility Costs

Area[1]	New Home Price ($)	Apartment Rent ($/month)	All Electric ($/month)	Part Electric ($/month)	Other Energy ($/month)	Telephone ($/month)
City[2]	n/a	n/a	n/a	n/a	n/a	n/a
Avg.	398,393	1,217	171.38	100.83	69.67	187.75
Min.	212,799	534	96.71	31.56	27.15	173.01
Max.	2,354,006	4,438	369.53	277.33	303.87	206.73

Note: (1) Values for the local area are compared with the average, minimum and maximum values for all 285 areas in the Cost of Living Index; (2) Figures cover the Boulder CO urban area; n/a not available; ***New Home Price*** *(2,400 sf living area, 8,000 sf lot, in urban area with full utilities);* ***Apartment Rent*** *(950 sf 2 bedroom/1.5 or 2 bath, unfurnished, excluding all utilities except water);* ***All Electric*** *(average monthly cost for an all-electric home);* ***Part Electric*** *(average monthly cost for a part-electric home);* ***Other Energy*** *(average monthly cost for natural gas, fuel oil, coal, wood, and any other forms of energy except electricity);* ***Telephone*** *(price includes the base monthly rate plus taxes and fees for three lines of mobile phone service).*
Source: The Council for Community and Economic Research, Cost of Living Index, 2021

Health Care, Transportation, and Other Costs

Area[1]	Doctor ($/visit)	Dentist ($/visit)	Optometrist ($/visit)	Gasoline ($/gallon)	Beauty Salon ($/visit)	Men's Shirt ($)
City[2]	n/a	n/a	n/a	n/a	n/a	n/a
Avg.	118.16	101.04	109.44	2.71	40.63	30.77
Min.	35.04	55.56	51.17	2.17	18.59	11.32
Max.	231.10	165.12	256.81	4.11	85.33	63.03

Note: (1) Values for the local area are compared with the average, minimum and maximum values for all 285 areas in the Cost of Living Index; (2) Figures cover the Boulder CO urban area; n/a not available; ***Doctor*** *(general practitioners routine exam of an established patient);* ***Dentist*** *(adult teeth cleaning and periodic oral examination);* ***Optometrist*** *(full vision eye exam for established adult patient);* ***Gasoline*** *(one gallon regular unleaded, national brand, including all taxes, cash price at self-service pump if available);* ***Beauty Salon*** *(woman's shampoo, trim, and blow-dry);* ***Men's Shirt*** *(cotton/polyester dress shirt, pinpoint weave, long sleeves).*
Source: The Council for Community and Economic Research, Cost of Living Index, 2021

HOUSING

Homeownership Rate

Area	2013 (%)	2014 (%)	2015 (%)	2016 (%)	2017 (%)	2018 (%)	2019 (%)	2020 (%)	2021 (%)
MSA[1]	n/a	n/a	n/a	n/a	n/a	n/a	n/a	n/a	n/a
U.S.	65.1	64.5	63.7	63.4	63.9	64.4	64.6	66.6	65.5

Note: (1) Figures cover the Boulder, CO Metropolitan Statistical Area; n/a not available
Source: U.S. Census Bureau, Housing Vacancies and Homeownership Annual Statistics: 2013-2021

House Price Index (HPI)

Area	National Ranking[2]	Quarterly Change (%)	One-Year Change (%)	Five-Year Change (%)	Since 1991Q1 (%)
MSA[1]	153	1.19	16.72	43.62	521.25
U.S.[3]	–	3.33	17.54	54.45	258.04

Note: The HPI is a weighted repeat sales index. It measures average price changes in repeat sales or refinancings on the same properties. This information is obtained by reviewing repeat mortgage transactions on single-family properties whose mortgages have been purchased or securitized by Fannie Mae or Freddie Mac since January 1975; (1) Figures cover the Boulder, CO Metropolitan Statistical Area; (2) Rankings are based on annual percentage change for all metro areas containing at least 15,000 transactions over the last 10 years and ranges from 1 to 268; (3) figures based on a weighted average of Census Division estimates using a seasonally adjusted, purchase-only index; all figures are for the period ending December 31, 2021
Source: Federal Housing Finance Agency, Change in FHFA Metropolitan Area House Price Indexes, 2021Q4

Median Single-Family Home Prices

Area	2019	2020	2021[p]	Percent Change 2020 to 2021
MSA[1]	618.6	645.9	782.7	21.2
U.S. Average	274.6	300.2	353.4	17.7

Note: Figures are median sales prices of existing single-family homes in thousands of dollars; (p) preliminary; (1) Figures cover the Boulder, CO Metropolitan Statistical Area
Source: National Association of Realtors, Median Sales Price of Existing Single-Family Homes for Metropolitan Areas, 4th Quarter 2021

Qualifying Income Based on Median Sales Price of Existing Single-Family Homes

Area	With 5% Down ($)	With 10% Down ($)	With 20% Down ($)
MSA[1]	152,807	144,765	128,680
U.S. Average	70,699	66,978	59,536

Note: Figures are preliminary; Qualifying income is based on a mortgage rate of 3.13%. Monthly principal and interest payment is limited to 25% of income; (1) Figures cover the Boulder, CO Metropolitan Statistical Area
Source: National Association of Realtors, Qualifying Income Based on Median Sales Price of Existing Single-Family Homes for Metropolitan Areas, 4th Quarter 2021

Home Value Distribution

Area	Under $50,000	$50,000 -$99,999	$100,000 -$149,999	$150,000 -$199,999	$200,000 -$299,999	$300,000 -$499,999	$500,000 -$999,999	$1,000,000 or more
City	3.1	2.3	1.4	2.1	4.1	13.3	47.1	26.5
MSA[1]	2.7	1.2	0.9	1.8	7.7	31.3	41.6	12.7
U.S.	6.6	11.0	12.3	13.6	20.0	20.5	12.3	3.7

Note: Figures are percentages and cover owner-occupied housing units; (1) Figures cover the Boulder, CO Metropolitan Statistical Area
Source: U.S. Census Bureau, 2016-2020 American Community Survey 5-Year Estimates

Year Housing Structure Built

Area	2010 or Later	2000 -2009	1990 -1999	1980 -1989	1970 -1979	1960 -1969	1950 -1959	1940 -1949	Before 1940	Median Year
City	7.6	7.3	11.3	16.3	19.9	18.2	9.5	1.7	7.9	1976
MSA[1]	8.0	11.8	19.6	16.3	20.0	11.2	5.1	1.4	6.6	1984
U.S.	6.2	13.6	13.9	13.4	15.0	10.5	10.2	4.8	12.4	1978

Note: Figures are percentages except for Median Year; Note: (1) Figures cover the Boulder, CO Metropolitan Statistical Area
Source: U.S. Census Bureau, 2016-2020 American Community Survey 5-Year Estimates

Gross Monthly Rent

Area	Under $500	$500 -$999	$1,000 -$1,499	$1,500 -$1,999	$2,000 -$2,499	$2,500 -$2,999	$3,000 and up	Median ($)
City	2.8	8.2	34.4	26.5	14.2	6.2	7.8	1,588
MSA[1]	3.7	9.5	32.0	29.2	13.7	5.7	6.1	1,582
U.S.	8.9	34.3	30.2	14.9	6.2	2.6	2.8	1,096

Note: Figures are percentages except for Median; Gross rent is the contract rent plus the estimated average monthly cost of utilities (electricity, gas, and water and sewer) and fuels (oil, coal, kerosene, wood, etc.) if these are paid by the renter (or paid for the renter by someone else); (1) Figures cover the Boulder, CO Metropolitan Statistical Area
Source: U.S. Census Bureau, 2016-2020 American Community Survey 5-Year Estimates

HEALTH

Health Risk Factors

Category	MSA[1] (%)	U.S. (%)
Adults aged 18–64 who have any kind of health care coverage	n/a	86.8
Adults who reported being in good or better health	n/a	86.7
Adults who are current smokers	n/a	15.5
Adults who currently use chewing tobacco, snuff, or snus	n/a	3.7
Adults who are heavy drinkers[2]	n/a	6.7
Adults who are binge drinkers[3]	n/a	15.7
Adults who are overweight (BMI 25.0 - 29.9)	n/a	35.2
Adults who are obese (BMI 30.0 - 99.8)	n/a	31.9
Adults who participated in any physical activities in the past month	n/a	77.6
Adults who always or nearly always wears a seat belt	n/a	94.2

Note: (1) Figures for the Boulder, CO Metropolitan Statistical Area were not available. (2) Heavy drinkers are classified as adult men having more than 14 drinks per week and adult women having more than 7 drinks per week; (3) Binge drinkers are classified as males having five or more drinks on one occasion or females having four or more drinks on one occasion
Source: Centers for Disease Control and Prevention, Behaviorial Risk Factor Surveillance System, SMART: Selected Metropolitan Area Risk Trends, 2020

Acute and Chronic Health Conditions

Category	MSA[1] (%)	U.S. (%)
Adults who have ever been told they had a heart attack	n/a	4.3
Adults who have ever been told they have angina or coronary heart disease	n/a	4.0
Adults who have ever been told they had a stroke	n/a	2.8
Adults who have ever been told they have asthma	n/a	14.2
Adults who have ever been told they have arthritis	n/a	24.5
Adults who have ever been told they have diabetes[2]	n/a	10.6
Adults who have ever been told they had skin cancer	n/a	6.4
Adults who have ever been told they had any other types of cancer	n/a	6.8
Adults who have ever been told they have COPD	n/a	6.2
Adults who have ever been told they have kidney disease	n/a	2.9
Adults who have ever been told they have a form of depression	n/a	19.6

Note: (1) Figures for the Boulder, CO Metropolitan Statistical Area were not available. (2) Figures do not include pregnancy-related, borderline, or pre-diabetes
Source: Centers for Disease Control and Prevention, Behaviorial Risk Factor Surveillance System, SMART: Selected Metropolitan Area Risk Trends, 2020

Health Screening and Vaccination Rates

Category	MSA[1] (%)	U.S. (%)
Adults 50-75 who have had a blood stool test within the past year	n/a	9.3
Adults aged 65+ who have had flu shot within the past year	n/a	67.9
Adults aged 65+ who have ever had a pneumonia vaccination	n/a	72.2
Adults who have ever been tested for HIV	n/a	37.1
Women aged 21-65 who have had a pap test in the past three years	n/a	77.7
Men aged 40+ who have had a PSA test within the past two years	n/a	31.8
Women aged 40+ who have had a mammogram within the past two years	n/a	71.5

Note: (1) Figures for the Boulder, CO Metropolitan Statistical Area were not available.
Source: Centers for Disease Control and Prevention, Behaviorial Risk Factor Surveillance System, SMART: Selected Metropolitan Area Risk Trends, 2020

Disability Status

Category	MSA[1] (%)	U.S. (%)
Adults who reported being deaf	n/a	6.8
Are you blind or have serious difficulty seeing, even when wearing glasses?	n/a	4.7
Do you have difficulty doing errands alone?	n/a	6.3
Do you have difficulty dressing or bathing?	n/a	3.0
Do you have serious difficulty concentrating/remembering/making decisions?	n/a	10.8
Do you have serious difficulty walking or climbing stairs?	n/a	11.9

Note: (1) Figures for the Boulder, CO Metropolitan Statistical Area were not available.
Source: Centers for Disease Control and Prevention, Behaviorial Risk Factor Surveillance System, SMART: Selected Metropolitan Area Risk Trends, 2020

Mortality Rates for the Top 10 Causes of Death in the U.S.

ICD-10[a] Sub-Chapter	ICD-10[a] Code	Age-Adjusted Mortality Rate[1] per 100,000 population	
		County[2]	U.S.
Malignant neoplasms	C00-C97	120.0	146.4
Ischaemic heart diseases	I20-I25	48.5	90.2
Other forms of heart disease	I30-I51	38.1	51.9
Other degenerative diseases of the nervous system	G30-G31	40.1	39.7
Other external causes of accidental injury	W00-X59	34.4	38.7
Chronic lower respiratory diseases	J40-J47	27.8	38.1
Cerebrovascular diseases	I60-I69	37.1	37.6
Organic, including symptomatic, mental disorders	F01-F09	26.4	29.4
Hypertensive diseases	I10-I15	15.0	26.1
Diabetes mellitus	E10-E14	9.8	22.6

Note: (a) ICD-10 = International Classification of Diseases 10th Revision; (1) Mortality rates are a three-year average covering 2018-2020; (2) Figures cover Boulder County.
Source: Centers for Disease Control and Prevention, National Center for Health Statistics. Underlying Cause of Death 1999-2020 on CDC WONDER Online Database

Mortality Rates for Selected Causes of Death

ICD-10[a] Sub-Chapter	ICD-10[a] Code	Age-Adjusted Mortality Rate[1] per 100,000 population	
		County[2]	U.S.
Assault	X85-Y09	Unreliable	6.5
Diseases of the liver	K70-K76	11.4	15.3
Human immunodeficiency virus (HIV) disease	B20-B24	Suppressed	1.4
Influenza and pneumonia	J09-J18	9.2	13.4
Intentional self-harm	X60-X84	17.2	13.9
Malnutrition	E40-E46	6.0	2.9
Obesity and other hyperalimentation	E65-E68	Unreliable	2.4
Renal failure	N17-N19	5.8	12.5
Transport accidents	V01-V99	8.3	12.5
Viral hepatitis	B15-B19	Suppressed	1.0

Note: (a) ICD-10 = International Classification of Diseases 10th Revision; (1) Mortality rates are a three-year average covering 2018-2020; (2) Figures cover Boulder County; Data are suppressed when the data meet the criteria for confidentiality constraints; Mortality rates are flagged as unreliable when the rate would be calculated with a numerator of 20 or less.
Source: Centers for Disease Control and Prevention, National Center for Health Statistics. Underlying Cause of Death 1999-2020 on CDC WONDER Online Database

Health Insurance Coverage

Area	With Health Insurance	With Private Health Insurance	With Public Health Insurance	Without Health Insurance	Population Under Age 19 Without Health Insurance
City	95.9	83.8	21.0	4.1	1.2
MSA[1]	95.5	80.4	25.4	4.5	1.9
U.S.	91.3	68.1	35.3	8.7	5.2

Note: Figures are percentages that cover the civilian noninstitutionalized population; (1) Figures cover the Boulder, CO Metropolitan Statistical Area
Source: U.S. Census Bureau, 2016-2020 American Community Survey 5-Year Estimates

Number of Medical Professionals

Area	MDs[3]	DOs[3,4]	Dentists	Podiatrists	Chiropractors	Optometrists
County[1] (number)	1,175	105	349	20	266	87
County[1] (rate[2])	355.2	31.7	105.5	6.0	80.4	26.3
U.S. (rate[2])	285.1	23.0	71.1	6.2	28.2	17.0

08013
Note: Data as of 2020 unless noted; (1) Data covers Boulder County; (2) Rate per 100,000 population; (3) Data as of 2019 and includes all active, non-federal physicians; (4) Doctor of Osteopathic Medicine
Source: U.S. Department of Health and Human Services, Health Resources and Services Administration, Bureau of Health Professions, Area Resource File (ARF) 2020-2021

EDUCATION

Public School District Statistics

District Name	Schls	Pupils	Pupil/ Teacher Ratio	Minority Pupils[1] (%)	LEP/ELL[2] (%)	IEP[3] (%)
Boulder Valley SD No. Re2	56	31,000	17.7	32.0	6.3	n/a

Note: Table includes school districts with 2,000 or more students; (1) Percentage of students that are not non-Hispanic white; (2) Percentage of students that are Limited English Proficient (LEP) or English Language Learners (ELL) (2018-19); (3) Percentage of students that have an Individualized Education Program (IEP).
Source: U.S. Department of Education, National Center for Education Statistics, Common Core of Data, Local Education Agency (School District) Universe Survey: School Year 2019-2020

Best High Schools

According to *U.S. News,* Boulder is home to one of the top 500 high schools in the U.S.: **Fairview High School** (#457). Nearly 18,000 public, magnet and charter schools were ranked based on their performance on state assessments and how well they prepare students for college. *U.S. News & World Report, "Best High Schools 2021"*

Highest Level of Education

Area	Less than H.S.	H.S. Diploma	Some College, No Deg.	Associate Degree	Bachelor's Degree	Master's Degree	Prof. School Degree	Doctorate Degree
City	2.7	5.7	11.2	3.6	37.1	24.6	6.4	8.6
MSA[1]	4.5	11.3	14.8	6.4	34.6	19.0	4.2	5.2
U.S.	11.5	26.7	20.3	8.6	20.2	9.1	2.2	1.5

Note: Figures cover persons age 25 and over; (1) Figures cover the Boulder, CO Metropolitan Statistical Area
Source: U.S. Census Bureau, 2016-2020 American Community Survey 5-Year Estimates

Educational Attainment by Race

Area	High School Graduate or Higher (%)					Bachelor's Degree or Higher (%)				
	Total	White	Black	Asian	Hisp.[2]	Total	White	Black	Asian	Hisp.[2]
City	97.3	98.0	89.3	95.0	80.5	76.7	77.4	33.3	81.6	51.8
MSA[1]	95.5	96.6	88.7	93.4	75.1	63.0	64.0	24.7	73.3	30.2
U.S.	88.5	90.7	86.7	87.3	70.3	32.9	34.4	22.6	55.0	17.6

Note: Figures shown cover persons 25 years old and over; (1) Figures cover the Boulder, CO Metropolitan Statistical Area; (2) People of Hispanic origin can be of any race
Source: U.S. Census Bureau, 2016-2020 American Community Survey 5-Year Estimates

School Enrollment by Grade and Control

Area	Preschool (%)		Kindergarten (%)		Grades 1 - 4 (%)		Grades 5 - 8 (%)		Grades 9 - 12 (%)	
	Public	Private	Public	Private	Public	Private	Public	Private	Public	Private
City	49.7	50.3	87.0	13.0	87.8	12.2	93.2	6.8	92.2	7.8
MSA[1]	54.1	45.9	86.9	13.1	90.3	9.7	90.8	9.2	95.0	5.0
U.S.	58.9	41.1	86.9	13.1	89.0	11.0	89.0	11.0	89.7	10.3

Note: Figures shown cover persons 3 years old and over; (1) Figures cover the Boulder, CO Metropolitan Statistical Area
Source: U.S. Census Bureau, 2016-2020 American Community Survey 5-Year Estimates

Higher Education

Four-Year Colleges			Two-Year Colleges			Medical Schools[1]	Law Schools[2]	Voc/ Tech[3]
Public	Private Non-profit	Private For-profit	Public	Private Non-profit	Private For-profit			
1	3	1	0	0	1	0	1	1

Note: Figures cover institutions located within the Boulder, CO Metropolitan Statistical Area and include main campuses only; (1) includes schools accredited by the Liaison Committee on Medical Education and the American Osteopathic Association's Commission on Osteopathic College Accreditation; (2) includes ABA-accredited schools, schools with provisional ABA accreditation, and state accredited schools; (3) includes all schools with programs that are less than 2 years.
Source: National Center for Education Statistics, Integrated Postsecondary Education System (IPEDS), 2020-21; Wikipedia, List of Medical Schools in the United States, accessed April 11, 2022; Wikipedia, List of Law Schools in the United States, accessed April 11, 2022

According to *U.S. News & World Report,* the Boulder, CO metro area is home to one of the top 200 national universities in the U.S.: **University of Colorado Boulder** (#99 tie). The indicators used to capture academic quality fall into a number of categories: assessment by administrators at peer institutions; retention of students; faculty resources; student selectivity; financial resources; alumni giving; high school counselor ratings of colleges; and graduation rate. *U.S. News & World Report, "America's Best Colleges 2022"*

According to *U.S. News & World Report,* the Boulder, CO metro area is home to one of the top 100 law schools in the U.S.: **University of Colorado—Boulder** (#48 tie). The rankings are based on a weighted average of 12 measures of quality: peer assessment score; assessment score by lawyers/judges; median LSAT scores; median undergrad GPA; acceptance rate; employment rates for graduates; placement success; bar passage rate; faculty resources; expenditures per student; student/faculty ratio; and library resources. *U.S. News & World Report, "America's Best Graduate Schools, Law, 2022"*

According to *U.S. News & World Report,* the Boulder, CO metro area is home to one of the top 75 business schools in the U.S.: **University of Colorado—Boulder (Leeds)** (#74 tie). The rankings are based on a weighted average of the following nine measures: quality assessment; peer assessment; recruiter assessment; placement success; mean starting salary and bonus; student selectivity; mean

GMAT and GRE scores; mean undergraduate GPA; and acceptance rate. *U.S. News & World Report, "America's Best Graduate Schools, Business, 2022"*

EMPLOYERS

Major Employers

Company Name	Industry
Agilent Technologies	Instruments to measure electricity
America's Note Network	Mortgage bankers & loan correspondents
Ball Aerospace & Technologies Corp.	Search & navigation equipment
Ball Corporation	Space research & technology
Corden Pharma Colorado	Pharmaceutical preparations
County of Boulder	County government
Crispin Porter Bogusky	Business services at non-commercial site
Health Carechain	Medical field-related associations
IBM	Magnetic storage devices, computer
Lockheed Martin Corporation	Search & navigation equipment
Micro Motion	Liquid meters
National Oceanic and Atmospheric Admin	Environmental protection agency, government
Natl Inst of Standards & Technology	Commercial physical research
Qualcomm Incorporated	Integrated circuits, semiconductor networks
Staffing Solutions Southwest	Temporary help services
The Regents of the University of Colorado	Noncommercial research organizations
Tyco Healthcare Group	Medical instruments & equipment, blood & bone work
University Corp for Atmospheric Research	Noncommercial research organizations
University of Colorado	Colleges & universities
Wall Street On Demand	Financial services
Whole Foods Market	Grocery stores

Note: Companies shown are located within the Boulder, CO Metropolitan Statistical Area.
Source: Hoovers.com; Wikipedia

PUBLIC SAFETY

Crime Rate

Area	Total Crime	Violent Crime Rate				Property Crime Rate		
		Murder	Rape[3]	Robbery	Aggrav. Assault	Burglary	Larceny -Theft	Motor Vehicle Theft
City	4,092.0	1.9	29.1	67.5	223.3	613.5	2,808.7	348.0
Suburbs[1]	2,552.6	0.9	66.0	30.7	181.8	304.8	1,686.2	282.2
Metro[2]	3,053.3	1.2	54.0	42.7	195.3	405.2	2,051.3	303.6
U.S.	2,356.7	6.5	38.4	73.9	279.7	314.2	1,398.0	246.0

Note: Figures are crimes per 100,000 population; (1) All areas within the metro area that are located outside the city limits; (2) Figures cover the Boulder, CO Metropolitan Statistical Area; (3) All figures shown were reported using the revised Uniform Crime Reporting (UCR) definition of rape.
Source: FBI Uniform Crime Reports, 2020

Hate Crimes

Area	Number of Quarters Reported	Number of Incidents per Bias Motivation					
		Race/Ethnicity/ Ancestry	Religion	Sexual Orientation	Disability	Gender	Gender Identity
City	4	8	1	1	0	0	0
U.S.	4	5,227	1,244	1,110	130	75	266

Source: Federal Bureau of Investigation, Hate Crime Statistics 2020

Identity Theft Consumer Reports

Area	Reports	Reports per 100,000 Population	Rank[2]
MSA[1]	2,046	627	32
U.S.	1,434,676	432	-

Note: (1) Figures cover the Boulder, CO Metropolitan Statistical Area; (2) Rank ranges from 1 to 391 where 1 indicates greatest number of identity theft reports per 100,000 population
Source: Federal Trade Commission, Consumer Sentinel Network Data Book 2021

Fraud and Other Consumer Reports

Area	Reports	Reports per 100,000 Population	Rank[2]
MSA[1]	3,815	1,170	51
U.S.	4,328,977	1,304	-

Note: (1) Figures cover the Boulder, CO Metropolitan Statistical Area; (2) Rank ranges from 1 to 391 where 1 indicates greatest number of fraud and other consumer reports per 100,000 population
Source: Federal Trade Commission, Consumer Sentinel Network Data Book 2021

POLITICS

2020 Presidential Election Results

Area	Biden	Trump	Jorgensen	Hawkins	Other
Boulder County	77.2	20.6	1.2	0.3	0.6
U.S.	51.3	46.8	1.2	0.3	0.5

Note: Results are percentages and may not add to 100% due to rounding
Source: Dave Leip's Atlas of U.S. Presidential Elections

SPORTS

Professional Sports Teams

Team Name	League	Year Established
No teams are located in the metro area		

Source: Wikipedia, Major Professional Sports Teams of the United States and Canada, April 6, 2022

CLIMATE

Average and Extreme Temperatures

Temperature	Jan	Feb	Mar	Apr	May	Jun	Jul	Aug	Sep	Oct	Nov	Dec	Yr.
Extreme High (°F)	73	76	84	90	93	102	103	100	97	89	79	75	103
Average High (°F)	43	47	52	62	71	81	88	86	77	67	52	45	64
Average Temp. (°F)	30	34	39	48	58	67	73	72	63	52	39	32	51
Average Low (°F)	16	20	25	34	44	53	59	57	48	37	25	18	37
Extreme Low (°F)	-25	-25	-10	-2	22	30	43	41	17	3	-8	-25	-25

Note: Figures cover the years 1948-1992
Source: National Climatic Data Center, International Station Meteorological Climate Summary, 9/96

Average Precipitation/Snowfall/Humidity

Precip./Humidity	Jan	Feb	Mar	Apr	May	Jun	Jul	Aug	Sep	Oct	Nov	Dec	Yr.
Avg. Precip. (in.)	0.6	0.6	1.3	1.7	2.5	1.7	1.9	1.5	1.1	1.0	0.9	0.6	15.5
Avg. Snowfall (in.)	9	7	14	9	2	Tr	0	0	2	4	9	8	63
Avg. Rel. Hum. 5am (%)	62	65	67	66	70	68	67	68	66	63	66	63	66
Avg. Rel. Hum. 5pm (%)	49	44	40	35	38	34	34	34	32	34	47	50	39

Note: Figures cover the years 1948-1992; Tr = Trace amounts (<0.05 in. of rain; <0.5 in. of snow)
Source: National Climatic Data Center, International Station Meteorological Climate Summary, 9/96

Weather Conditions

Temperature			Daytime Sky			Precipitation		
10°F & below	32°F & below	90°F & above	Clear	Partly cloudy	Cloudy	0.01 inch or more precip.	0.1 inch or more snow/ice	Thunder-storms
24	155	33	99	177	89	90	38	39

Note: Figures are average number of days per year and cover the years 1948-1992
Source: National Climatic Data Center, International Station Meteorological Climate Summary, 9/96

HAZARDOUS WASTE

Superfund Sites

The Boulder, CO metro area is home to two sites on the EPA's Superfund National Priorities List: **Captain Jack Mill** (final); **Marshall Landfill** (final). There are a total of 1,165 Superfund sites with a status of proposed or final on the list in the U.S. *U.S. Environmental Protection Agency, National Priorities List, April 6, 2022*

AIR QUALITY

Air Quality Trends: Ozone

	1990	1995	2000	2005	2010	2016	2017	2018	2019	2020
MSA[1]	n/a	n/a	n/a	n/a	n/a	n/a	n/a	n/a	n/a	n/a
U.S.	0.090	0.091	0.082	0.080	0.074	0.070	0.069	0.070	0.066	0.068

Note: (1) Data covers the Boulder, CO Metropolitan Statistical Area; n/a not available. The values shown are the composite ozone concentration averages among trend sites based on the highest fourth daily maximum 8-hour concentration in parts per million. These trends are based on sites having an adequate record of monitoring data during the trend period. Data from exceptional events are included.
Source: U.S. Environmental Protection Agency, Air Quality Monitoring Information, "Air Quality Trends by City, 1990-2020"

Air Quality Index

Area	Percent of Days when Air Quality was...[2]					AQI Statistics[2]	
	Good	Moderate	Unhealthy for Sensitive Groups	Unhealthy	Very Unhealthy	Maximum	Median
MSA[1]	59.3	35.0	5.2	0.5	0.0	173	47

Note: (1) Data covers the Boulder, CO Metropolitan Statistical Area; (2) Based on 366 days with AQI data in 2020. Air Quality Index (AQI) is an index for reporting daily air quality. EPA calculates the AQI for five major air pollutants regulated by the Clean Air Act: ground-level ozone, particle pollution (aka particulate matter), carbon monoxide, sulfur dioxide, and nitrogen dioxide. The AQI runs from 0 to 500. The higher the AQI value, the greater the level of air pollution and the greater the health concern. There are six AQI categories: "Good" AQI is between 0 and 50. Air quality is considered satisfactory; "Moderate" AQI is between 51 and 100. Air quality is acceptable; "Unhealthy for Sensitive Groups" When AQI values are between 101 and 150, members of sensitive groups may experience health effects; "Unhealthy" When AQI values are between 151 and 200 everyone may begin to experience health effects; "Very Unhealthy" AQI values between 201 and 300 trigger a health alert; "Hazardous" AQI values over 300 trigger warnings of emergency conditions (not shown).
Source: U.S. Environmental Protection Agency, Air Quality Index Report, 2020

Air Quality Index Pollutants

Area	Percent of Days when AQI Pollutant was...[2]					
	Carbon Monoxide	Nitrogen Dioxide	Ozone	Sulfur Dioxide	Particulate Matter 2.5	Particulate Matter 10
MSA[1]	0.0	0.0	68.0	0.0	31.7	0.3

Note: (1) Data covers the Boulder, CO Metropolitan Statistical Area; (2) Based on 366 days with AQI data in 2020. The Air Quality Index (AQI) is an index for reporting daily air quality. EPA calculates the AQI for five major air pollutants regulated by the Clean Air Act: ground-level ozone, particle pollution (also known as particulate matter), carbon monoxide, sulfur dioxide, and nitrogen dioxide. The AQI runs from 0 to 500. The higher the AQI value, the greater the level of air pollution and the greater the health concern.
Source: U.S. Environmental Protection Agency, Air Quality Index Report, 2020

Maximum Air Pollutant Concentrations: Particulate Matter, Ozone, CO and Lead

	Particulate Matter 10 (ug/m^3)	Particulate Matter 2.5 Wtd AM (ug/m^3)	Particulate Matter 2.5 24-Hr (ug/m^3)	Ozone (ppm)	Carbon Monoxide (ppm)	Lead (ug/m^3)
MSA[1] Level	74	9.5	52	0.076	n/a	n/a
NAAQS[2]	150	15	35	0.075	9	0.15
Met NAAQS[2]	Yes	Yes	No	No	n/a	n/a

Note: (1) Data covers the Boulder, CO Metropolitan Statistical Area; Data from exceptional events are included; (2) National Ambient Air Quality Standards; ppm = parts per million; ug/m^3 = micrograms per cubic meter; n/a not available.
Concentrations: Particulate Matter 10 (coarse particulate)—highest second maximum 24-hour concentration; Particulate Matter 2.5 Wtd AM (fine particulate)—highest weighted annual mean concentration; Particulate Matter 2.5 24-Hour (fine particulate)—highest 98th percentile 24-hour concentration; Ozone—highest fourth daily maximum 8-hour concentration; Carbon Monoxide—highest second maximum non-overlapping 8-hour concentration; Lead—maximum running 3-month average
Source: U.S. Environmental Protection Agency, Air Quality Monitoring Information, "Air Quality Statistics by City, 2020"

Maximum Air Pollutant Concentrations: Nitrogen Dioxide and Sulfur Dioxide

	Nitrogen Dioxide AM (ppb)	Nitrogen Dioxide 1-Hr (ppb)	Sulfur Dioxide AM (ppb)	Sulfur Dioxide 1-Hr (ppb)	Sulfur Dioxide 24-Hr (ppb)
MSA[1] Level	n/a	n/a	n/a	n/a	n/a
NAAQS[2]	53	100	30	75	140
Met NAAQS[2]	n/a	n/a	n/a	n/a	n/a

Note: (1) Data covers the Boulder, CO Metropolitan Statistical Area; Data from exceptional events are included; (2) National Ambient Air Quality Standards; ppm = parts per million; ug/m^3 = micrograms per cubic meter; n/a not available.
Concentrations: Nitrogen Dioxide AM—highest arithmetic mean concentration; Nitrogen Dioxide 1-Hr—highest 98th percentile 1-hour daily maximum concentration; Sulfur Dioxide AM—highest annual mean concentration; Sulfur Dioxide 1-Hr—highest 99th percentile 1-hour daily maximum concentration; Sulfur Dioxide 24-Hr—highest second maximum 24-hour concentration
Source: U.S. Environmental Protection Agency, Air Quality Monitoring Information, "Air Quality Statistics by City, 2020"

Colorado Springs, Colorado

Background

Colorado Springs is the seat of El Paso County in central Colorado and sits at the foot of Pike's Peak, the highest summit of the Southern Front Range of the Rock Mountains in North America. A dynamic and growing city, its economy is based on health care, high-tech manufacturing, tourism, and sports, with strong employment links to nearby military installations. With its economy and gorgeous surroundings, it is no wonder that Colorado Springs ranks as one of the fastest-growing cities in the country.

In 1806, Lieutenant Zebulon Pike visited the site and the mountain that now bears his name, but settlement did not begin in earnest until gold was discovered in 1859 and miners flooded into the area.

In 1871, General William Jackson Palmer, a railroad tycoon, purchased the site for $10,000 and began promoting the area as a health and recreation resort. Pike's Peak was already well known as a scenic landmark, and very soon the Garden of the Gods, Seven Falls, Cheyenne Mountain, and Manitou Springs were widely known for their spectacular natural beauty. Perhaps the highest testimonial came from Katherine Lee Bates, who, after a trip to Pike's Peak in 1893, wrote "America the Beautiful."

The planned community of Colorado Springs was incorporated in 1876. As a resort, it was wildly successful, hosting the likes of Oscar Wilde and John D. Rockefeller. It became a special favorite of English visitors, one of whom made the claim that there were two "civilized" places between the Atlantic and the Pacific—Chicago and Colorado Springs.

The English were so enamored of the place, in fact, that it came to be called "Little London," as English visitors settled in the area, introducing golf, cricket, polo, and fox hunting. Since there were no local foxes, an artificial scent was spread out for the hounds, or sometimes a coyote was substituted. Several sumptuous hotels were built during this period, as was an elegantly appointed opera house.

In 1891, gold was again discovered, and the city's population tripled to 35,000 in the following decade. Sufficient gold deposits allowed a lucky few to amass considerable fortunes and build huge houses north of the city. However, not all the newly minted millionaires were inclined toward conspicuous display; Winfield Scott Stratton, "Midas of the Rockies," bruised emerging aesthetic sensibilities by constructing a crude wooden frame house near the business district.

After the 1890s rush ended, Colorado Springs resumed a more measured pace of growth. World War II caused saw considerable development as Fort Carson and the Peterson Air Force Base were established, followed by the North American Aerospace Defense Command (NORAD) and the U.S. Air Force Academy in the 1950s. Today NORAD is primarily concerned with the tracking of Intercontinental Ballistic Missiles (ICBM) and celebrated its 61st anniversary in 2019. The city's military connection has contributed in large part to the economic base of the area, and its highly educated and technically skilled workforce. In late 2008, Fort Carson became the home station of the 4th Infantry Division, nearly doubling the population of the base.

Colorado Springs is the site of the headquarters of the United States Olympics Committee, which maintains an important Olympic training center there. The U.S. Olympic and Paralympic Museum opened in 2020.

The city is also home to the World Figure Skating Museum and Hall of Fame, the Pro Rodeo Hall of Fame, and Museum of the American Cowboy. The state-of-the-art Pikes Peak Summit Center opened in 2021, and includes a visitor center, utilities facility, and high-altitude research laboratory.

The city hosts several institutions of higher learning, including Colorado College (1874), the U.S. Air Force Academy (1954), a campus of the University of Colorado (1965), and Nazarene Bible College (1967). Cultural amenities include the Fine Arts Center and Theatreworks at the University of Colorado.

Although recreational marijuana is legal in Colorado, the Colorado Springs city council has yet to approve retail shops in the city. In 2022, while hundreds of medical marijuana dispensaries operate in the city, there are no recreational cannabis shops.

The region enjoys four seasons, with plenty of sunshine—300 days each year. Rainfall is relatively minimal, but snow can pile up.

Rankings

General Rankings

- For its "Best for Vets: Places to Live 2019" rankings, *Military Times* evaluated 599 cities (83 large, 234 medium, 282 small) and compared the locations across three broad categories: veteran and military culture/services; economic indicators; and livability factors such as health, crime, traffic, and school quality. Colorado Springs ranked #1 out of the top 25, in the large city category (population of more than 250,000). Data points more specific to veterans and the military weighed more heavily than others. *rebootcamp.militarytimes.com, "Military Times Best Places to Live 2019," September 10, 2018*
- *US News & World Report* conducted a survey of more than 3,600 people and analyzed the 150 largest metropolitan areas to determine what matters most when selecting the next place to live. Colorado Springs ranked #6 out of the top 25 as having the best combination of desirable factors. Criteria: cost of living; quality of life and education; net migration; job market; desirability; and other factors. *realestate.usnews.com, "The 25 Best Places to Live in the U.S. in 2021-2022," July 13, 2021*
- The Colorado Springs metro area was identified as one of America's fastest-growing areas in terms of population and business growth by *MagnifyMoney.* The area ranked #23 out of 35. The 100 most populous metro areas in the U.S. were evaluated on their change from 2011 to 2016 in the following categories: people and housing; workforce and employment opportunities; growing industry. *www.businessinsider.com, "The 35 Cities in the US with the Biggest Influx of People, the Most Work Opportunities, and the Hottest Business Growth," August 12, 2018*
- The Colorado Springs metro area was identified as one of America's fastest-growing areas in terms of population and economy by *Forbes.* The area ranked #18 out of 25. The 100 most populous metro areas in the U.S. were evaluated on the following criteria: estimated population growth; employment; economic output; wages; home values. *Forbes, "America's Fastest-Growing Cities 2018," February 28, 2018*
- In their eigth annual survey, Livability.com looked at data for more than 1,000 small to mid-sized U.S. cities to determine the rankings for Livability's "Top 100 Best Places to Live" in 2021. Colorado Springs ranked #9. Criteria: housing and economy; sustainability; social and civic engagement; education; demographics; health care options; transportation & infrastructure; and community amenities. *Livability.com, "Top 100 Best Places to Live 2021" October 12, 2021*

Business/Finance Rankings

- WalletHub's latest report ranked over 2,500 cities by the average credit score of its residents. Colorado Springs was ranked #2,564 among the ten cities with the lowest average credit score, based on TransUnion data as of September 2021. *www.wallethub.com, "2022's Cities With the Highest & Lowest Credit Scores," February 16, 2022*
- The Brookings Institution ranked the nation's largest cities based on income inequality. Colorado Springs was ranked #87 (#1 = greatest inequality). Criteria: the "95/20 ratio," a figure representing the income at which a household earns more than 95 percent of all other households, divided by the income at which a household earns more than only 20 percent of all other households. *Brookings Institution, "Household Income Inequality, Largest Cities of 97 Large U.S. Metro Areas, 2014-2016," February 5, 2018*
- The Brookings Institution ranked the 100 largest metro areas in the U.S. based on income inequality. Colorado Springs was ranked #94 (#1 = greatest inequality). Criteria: the "95/20 ratio," a figure representing the income at which a household earns more than 95 percent of all other households, divided by the income at which a household earns more than only 20 percent of all other households. *Brookings Institution, "Household Income Inequality, 100 Largest U.S. Metro Areas, 2014-2016," February 5, 2018*
- The Colorado Springs metro area appeared on the Milken Institute "2021 Best Performing Cities" list. Rank: #17 out of 200 large metro areas (population over 250,000). Criteria: job growth; wage and salary growth; high-tech output growth; housing affordability; household broadband access. *Milken Institute, "Best-Performing Cities 2021," February 16, 2021*
- *Forbes* ranked the 200 most populous metro areas to determine the nation's "Best Places for Business and Careers." The Colorado Springs metro area was ranked #19. Criteria: costs (business and living); job growth (past and projected); income growth; quality of life; educational attainment (college and high school); projected economic growth; cultural and leisure opportunities; workplace tolerance laws; net migration patterns. *Forbes, "The Best Places for Business and Careers 2019: Seattle Still On Top," October 30, 2019*

Education Rankings

- Personal finance website *WalletHub* analyzed the 150 largest U.S. metropolitan statistical areas to determine where the most educated Americans are putting their degrees to work. Criteria: education levels; percentage of workers with degrees; education quality and attainment gap; public school quality rankings; quality and enrollment of each metro area's universities. Colorado Springs was ranked #13 (#1 = most educated city). *www.WalletHub.com, "Most & Least Educated Cities in America," July 19, 2021*
- Colorado Springs was selected as one of America's most literate cities. The city ranked #21 out of the 84 largest U.S. cities. Criteria: number of booksellers; library resources; Internet resources; educational attainment; periodical publishing resources; newspaper circulation. *Central Connecticut State University, "America's Most Literate Cities, 2018," February 2019*

Environmental Rankings

- Colorado Springs was highlighted as one of the top 25 cleanest metro areas for year-round particle pollution (Annual PM 2.5) in the U.S. during 2017 through 2019. The area ranked #14. *American Lung Association, "State of the Air 2021," April 21, 2021*

Health/Fitness Rankings

- For each of the 100 largest cities in the United States, the American Fitness Index®, published by the American College of Sports Medicine and the Anthem Foundation, evaluated community infrastructure and 34 health behaviors including preventive health, levels of chronic disease conditions, food insecurity, sleep quality, pedestrian safety, air quality, and community resources that support physical activity. Colorado Springs ranked #51 for "community fitness." *americanfitnessindex.org, "2021 ACSM American Fitness Index Summary Report," July 13, 2021*
- Colorado Springs was identified as a "2021 Spring Allergy Capital." The area ranked #78 out of 100. Three groups of factors were used to identify the most challenging cities for people with allergies during the spring season: annual spring pollen levels; over the counter medicine use; number of board-certified allergy specialists. *Asthma and Allergy Foundation of America, "Spring Allergy Capitals 2021," February 23, 2021*
- Colorado Springs was identified as a "2021 Fall Allergy Capital." The area ranked #70 out of 100. Three groups of factors were used to identify the most challenging cities for people with allergies during the fall season: annual fall pollen levels; over the counter medicine use; number of board-certified allergy specialists. *Asthma and Allergy Foundation of America, "Fall Allergy Capitals 2021," February 23, 2021*
- Colorado Springs was identified as a "2021 Asthma Capital." The area ranked #95 out of the nation's 100 largest metropolitan areas. Criteria: estimated asthma prevalence; asthma-related mortality; and ER visits due to asthma. Risk factors analyzed but not factored in the rankings: annual pollen score; annual air quality; public smoking laws; number of board-certified asthma specialists; rescue medication use; controller medication use; uninsured rate; poverty rate. *Asthma and Allergy Foundation of America, "Asthma Capitals 2021: The Most Challenging Places to Live With Asthma," May 5, 2021*

Real Estate Rankings

- *WalletHub* compared the most populated U.S. cities to determine which had the best markets for real estate agents. Colorado Springs ranked #38 where demand was high and pay was the best. Criteria: sales per agent; annual median wage for real-estate agents; monthly average starting salary for real estate agents; real estate job density and competition; unemployment rate; home turnover rate; housing-market health index; and other relevant metrics. *www.WalletHub.com, "2021 Best Places to Be a Real Estate Agent," May 12, 2021*
- The Colorado Springs metro area was identified as one of the nations's 20 hottest housing markets in 2022. Criteria: listing views as an indicator of demand and median days on the market as an indicator of supply. The area ranked #20. *Realtor.com, "January 2022 Top 20 Hottest Housing Markets," February 15, 2022*
- Colorado Springs was ranked #177 out of 237 metro areas in terms of housing affordability in 2021 by the National Association of Home Builders (#1 = most affordable). Criteria: the share of homes sold in that area affordable to a family earning the local median income, based on standard mortgage underwriting criteria. *National Association of Home Builders®, NAHB-Wells Fargo Housing Opportunity Index, 4th Quarter 2021*

Safety Rankings

- Allstate ranked the 200 largest cities in America in terms of driver safety. Colorado Springs ranked #13. Criteria: internal property damage claims over a two-year period from January 2016 to December 2017. The report helps increase the importance of safety and awareness behind the wheel. *Allstate, "Allstate America's Best Drivers Report, 2019" June 24, 2019*
- The National Insurance Crime Bureau ranked 390 metro areas in the U.S. in terms of per capita rates of vehicle theft. The Colorado Springs metro area ranked #61 (#1 = highest rate). Criteria: number of vehicle theft offenses per 100,000 inhabitants in 2020. *National Insurance Crime Bureau, "Hot Spots 2020," August 31, 2021*

Seniors/Retirement Rankings

- From its Best Cities for Successful Aging indexes, the Milken Institute generated rankings for metropolitan areas, weighing data in nine categories—health care, wellness, living arrangements, transportation and convenience, financial characteristics, education, employment, community engagement, and overall livability. The Colorado Springs metro area was ranked #46 overall in the large metro area category. *Milken Institute, "Best Cities for Successful Aging, 2017" March 14, 2017*
- Colorado Springs was identified as #16 of 20 most popular places to retire in the Western region by *Topretirements.com*. The site separated its annual "Best Places to Retire" list by major U.S. regions for 2019. The list reflects the 20 cities that visitors to the website are most interested in for retirement, based on the number of times a city's review was viewed on the website. *Topretirements.com, "20 Best Places to Retire in the West-2019," November 11, 2019*

Sports/Recreation Rankings

- Colorado Springs was chosen as one of America's best cities for bicycling. The city ranked #28 out of 50. Criteria: cycling infrastructure that is safe and friendly for all ages; energy and bike culture. The editors evaluated cities with populations of 100,000 or more. *Bicycling, "The 50 Best Bike Cities in America," October 10, 2018*

Women/Minorities Rankings

- Personal finance website *WalletHub* compared more than 180 U.S. cities across two key dimensions, "Hispanic Business-Friendliness" and "Hispanic Purchasing Power," to arrive at the most favorable conditions for Hispanic entrepreneurs. Colorado Springs was ranked #93 out of 182. Criteria includes: share of Hispanic-Owned Businesses; Hispanic entrepreneurship rate to median annual income of Hispanics; Small Business-Friendliness score; cost of living; and number of Hispanics with at least a bachelor's degree. *WalletHub.com, "2019's Best Cities for Hispanic Entrepreneurs," May 1, 2019*

Miscellaneous Rankings

- The watchdog site, Charity Navigator, conducted a study of charities in major markets both to analyze statistical differences in their financial, accountability, and transparency practices and to track year-to-year variations in individual philanthropic communities. The Colorado Springs metro area was ranked #28 among the 30 metro markets in the rating category of Overall Score. *www.charitynavigator.org, "2017 Metro Market Study," May 1, 2017*
- *WalletHub* compared the 150 most populated U.S. cities to determine their operating efficiency. A "Quality of City Services" score was constructed for each city and then divided by the total budget per capita to reveal which were managed the best. Colorado Springs ranked #50. Criteria: financial stability; economy; education; safety; health; infrastructure and pollution. *www.WalletHub.com, "2021's Best- & Worst-Run Cities in America," June 22, 2021*

Business Environment

DEMOGRAPHICS

Population Growth

Area	1990 Census	2000 Census	2010 Census	2020* Estimate	Population Growth (%) 1990-2020	Population Growth (%) 2010-2020
City	283,798	360,890	416,427	471,686	66.2	13.3
MSA[1]	409,482	537,484	645,613	735,480	79.6	13.9
U.S.	248,709,873	281,421,906	308,745,538	326,569,308	31.3	5.8

Note: (1) Figures cover the Colorado Springs, CO Metropolitan Statistical Area; (*) 2016-2020 5-year estimated population
Source: U.S. Census Bureau, 1990 Census, Census 2000, Census 2010, 2016-2020 American Community Survey 5-Year Estimates

Household Size

Area	Persons in Household (%) One	Two	Three	Four	Five	Six	Seven or More	Average Household Size
City	28.0	35.5	14.8	12.5	5.8	2.2	1.2	2.50
MSA[1]	24.9	35.4	15.8	13.3	6.8	2.3	1.5	2.60
U.S.	28.0	33.9	15.5	12.9	6.0	2.3	1.4	2.60

Note: (1) Figures cover the Colorado Springs, CO Metropolitan Statistical Area
Source: U.S. Census Bureau, 2016-2020 American Community Survey 5-Year Estimates

Race

Area	White Alone[2] (%)	Black Alone[2] (%)	Asian Alone[2] (%)	AIAN[3] Alone[2] (%)	NHOPI[4] Alone[2] (%)	Other Race Alone[2] (%)	Two or More Races (%)
City	77.3	6.3	2.8	0.9	0.3	4.6	7.9
MSA[1]	78.8	6.1	2.6	0.8	0.3	3.7	7.7
U.S.	70.4	12.6	5.6	0.8	0.2	5.1	5.2

Note: (1) Figures cover the Colorado Springs, CO Metropolitan Statistical Area; (2) Alone is defined as not being in combination with one or more other races; (3) American Indian and Alaska Native; (4) Native Hawaiian and Other Pacific Islander
Source: U.S. Census Bureau, 2016-2020 American Community Survey 5-Year Estimates

Hispanic or Latino Origin

Area	Total (%)	Mexican (%)	Puerto Rican (%)	Cuban (%)	Other (%)
City	18.0	11.6	1.3	0.4	4.7
MSA[1]	17.1	10.4	1.6	0.4	4.7
U.S.	18.2	11.2	1.7	0.7	4.5

Note: Persons of Hispanic or Latino origin can be of any race; (1) Figures cover the Colorado Springs, CO Metropolitan Statistical Area
Source: U.S. Census Bureau, 2016-2020 American Community Survey 5-Year Estimates

Ancestry

Area	German	Irish	English	American	Italian	Polish	French[2]	Scottish	Dutch
City	18.1	10.6	10.8	4.3	4.8	2.3	2.8	2.7	1.5
MSA[1]	18.2	10.6	10.3	4.4	4.7	2.3	2.6	2.7	1.5
U.S.	13.0	9.7	7.7	5.9	5.1	2.7	2.3	1.6	1.1

Note: Figures are the percentage of the total population reporting a particular ancestry. The nine most commonly reported ancestries in the U.S. are shown. Figures include multiple ancestries (e.g. if a person reported being Irish and Italian, they were included in both columns); (1) Figures cover the Colorado Springs, CO Metropolitan Statistical Area; (2) Excludes Basque
Source: U.S. Census Bureau, 2016-2020 American Community Survey 5-Year Estimates

Foreign-born Population

Area	Percent of Population Born in: Any Foreign Country	Asia	Mexico	Europe	Caribbean	Central America[2]	South America	Africa	Canada
City	7.5	2.1	2.0	1.5	0.3	0.3	0.4	0.4	0.3
MSA[1]	6.8	1.8	1.7	1.5	0.3	0.3	0.4	0.3	0.3
U.S.	13.5	4.2	3.3	1.5	1.3	1.1	1.0	0.7	0.3

Note: (1) Figures cover the Colorado Springs, CO Metropolitan Statistical Area; (2) Excludes Mexico.
Source: U.S. Census Bureau, 2016-2020 American Community Survey 5-Year Estimates

Marital Status

Area	Never Married	Now Married[2]	Separated	Widowed	Divorced
City	31.1	49.9	1.5	4.5	13.0
MSA[1]	29.5	53.2	1.4	4.1	11.8
U.S.	33.5	48.1	1.8	5.7	10.8

Note: Figures are percentages and cover the population 15 years of age and older; (1) Figures cover the Colorado Springs, CO Metropolitan Statistical Area; (2) Excludes separated
Source: U.S. Census Bureau, 2016-2020 American Community Survey 5-Year Estimates

Disability by Age

Area	All Ages	Under 18 Years Old	18 to 64 Years Old	65 Years and Over
City	13.0	4.8	11.8	32.2
MSA[1]	12.5	4.8	11.3	31.9
U.S.	12.7	4.3	10.3	34.0

Note: Figures show percent of the civilian noninstitutionalized population that reported having a disability. Disability status is determined from six types of difficulty: vision, hearing, cognitive, ambulatory, self-care, and independent living. For children under 5 years old, hearing and vision difficulty are used to determine disability status. For children between the ages of 5 and 14, disability status is determined from hearing, vision, cognitive, ambulatory, and self-care difficulties. For people aged 15 years and older, they are considered to have a disability if they have difficulty with any one of the six difficulty types; Note: (1) Figures cover the Colorado Springs, CO Metropolitan Statistical Area
Source: U.S. Census Bureau, 2016-2020 American Community Survey 5-Year Estimates

Age

Area	Percent of Population									Median Age
	Under Age 5	Age 5–19	Age 20–34	Age 35–44	Age 45–54	Age 55–64	Age 65–74	Age 75–84	Age 85+	
City	6.3	19.3	24.9	12.7	11.7	11.5	8.2	3.6	1.8	34.7
MSA[1]	6.5	20.0	23.7	12.7	11.8	12.0	8.2	3.5	1.5	34.8
U.S.	6.0	19.1	20.6	12.7	12.7	12.9	9.4	4.7	2.0	38.2

Note: (1) Figures cover the Colorado Springs, CO Metropolitan Statistical Area
Source: U.S. Census Bureau, 2016-2020 American Community Survey 5-Year Estimates

Gender

Area	Males	Females	Males per 100 Females
City	236,066	235,620	100.2
MSA[1]	371,410	364,070	102.0
U.S.	160,818,530	165,750,778	97.0

Note: (1) Figures cover the Colorado Springs, CO Metropolitan Statistical Area
Source: U.S. Census Bureau, 2016-2020 American Community Survey 5-Year Estimates

Religious Groups by Family

Area	Catholic	Baptist	Non-Den.	Methodist[2]	Lutheran	LDS[3]	Pente-costal	Presby-terian[4]	Muslim[5]	Judaism
MSA[1]	8.4	4.3	7.4	2.4	2.0	3.0	1.1	2.1	0.1	0.1
U.S.	19.1	9.3	4.0	4.0	2.3	2.0	1.9	1.6	0.8	0.7

Note: Figures are the number of adherents as a percentage of the total population; (1) Figures cover the Colorado Springs, CO Metropolitan Statistical Area; (2) Methodist/Pietist; (3) Latter Day Saints; (4) Reformed; (5) Figures are estimates
Source: Association of Statisticians of American Religious Bodies, 2010 U.S. Religion Census: Religious Congregations & Membership Study

Religious Groups by Tradition

Area	Catholic	Evangelical Protestant	Mainline Protestant	Other Tradition	Black Protestant	Orthodox
MSA[1]	8.4	15.2	5.4	3.7	0.4	0.1
U.S.	19.1	16.2	7.3	4.3	1.6	0.3

Note: Figures are the number of adherents as a percentage of the total population; (1) Figures cover the Colorado Springs, CO Metropolitan Statistical Area
Source: Association of Statisticians of American Religious Bodies, 2010 U.S. Religion Census: Religious Congregations & Membership Study

ECONOMY

Gross Metropolitan Product

Area	2017	2018	2019	2020	Rank[2]
MSA[1]	33.1	34.9	36.6	38.5	84

Note: Figures are in billions of dollars; (1) Figures cover the Colorado Springs, CO Metropolitan Statistical Area; (2) Rank is based on 2018 data and ranges from 1 to 381
Source: U.S. Conference of Mayors, U.S. Metro Economies: GMP & Employment 2018-2020, September 2019

Economic Growth

Area	2015-17 (%)	2018 (%)	2019 (%)	2020 (%)	Rank[2]
MSA[1]	2.9	3.1	3.0	2.8	73
U.S.	1.9	2.9	2.3	2.1	–

Note: Figures are real gross metropolitan product (GMP) growth rates and represent average annual percent change; (1) Figures cover the Colorado Springs, CO Metropolitan Statistical Area; (2) Rank is based on 2017 2-year average annual percent change and ranges from 1 to 381
Source: U.S. Conference of Mayors, U.S. Metro Economies: GMP & Employment 2018-2020, September 2019

Metropolitan Area Exports

Area	2015	2016	2017	2018	2019	2020	Rank[2]
MSA[1]	832.4	786.9	819.7	850.6	864.2	979.2	146

Note: Figures are in millions of dollars; (1) Figures cover the Colorado Springs, CO Metropolitan Statistical Area; (2) Rank is based on 2020 data and ranges from 1 to 389
Source: U.S. Department of Commerce, International Trade Administration, Office of Trade and Economic Analysis, Industry and Analysis, Exports by Metropolitan Area, data extracted March 4, 2022

Building Permits

Area	Single-Family			Multi-Family			Total		
	2019	2020	Pct. Chg.	2019	2020	Pct. Chg.	2019	2020	Pct. Chg.
City	n/a	n/a	n/a	n/a	n/a	n/a	n/a	n/a	n/a
MSA[1]	4,051	5,039	24.4	1,457	1,893	29.9	5,508	6,932	25.9
U.S.	862,100	979,400	13.6	523,900	491,700	-6.1	1,386,000	1,471,100	6.1

Note: (1) Figures cover the Colorado Springs, CO Metropolitan Statistical Area; Figures represent new, privately-owned housing units authorized (unadjusted data); All permit data are based on estimates with imputation
Source: U.S. Census Bureau, Manufacturing, Mining, and Construction Statistics, Building Permits, 2019, 2020

Bankruptcy Filings

Area	Business Filings			Nonbusiness Filings		
	2020	2021	% Chg.	2020	2021	% Chg.
El Paso County	30	22	-26.7	1,154	728	-36.9
U.S.	21,655	14,347	-33.7	522,808	399,269	-23.6

Note: Business filings include Chapter 7, Chapter 9, Chapter 11, Chapter 12, Chapter 13, Chapter 15, and Section 304; Nonbusiness filings include Chapter 7, Chapter 11, and Chapter 13
Source: Administrative Office of the U.S. Courts, Business and Nonbusiness Bankruptcy, County Cases Commenced by Chapter of the Bankruptcy Code, During the 12-Month Period Ending December 31, 2020 and Business and Nonbusiness Bankruptcy, County Cases Commenced by Chapter of the Bankruptcy Code, During the 12-Month Period Ending December 31, 2021

Housing Vacancy Rates

Area	Gross Vacancy Rate[2] (%)			Year-Round Vacancy Rate[3] (%)			Rental Vacancy Rate[4] (%)			Homeowner Vacancy Rate[5] (%)		
	2019	2020	2021	2019	2020	2021	2019	2020	2021	2019	2020	2021
MSA[1]	n/a	n/a	n/a	n/a	n/a	n/a	n/a	n/a	n/a	n/a	n/a	n/a
U.S.	12.0	10.6	10.8	9.5	8.2	8.4	6.7	6.3	6.1	1.4	1.0	0.9

Note: (1) Figures cover the Colorado Springs, CO Metropolitan Statistical Area; (2) The percentage of the total housing inventory that is vacant; (3) The percentage of the housing inventory (excluding seasonal units) that is year-round vacant; (4) The percentage of rental inventory that is vacant for rent; (5) The percentage of homeowner inventory that is vacant for sale; n/a not available
Source: U.S. Census Bureau, Housing Vacancies and Homeownership Annual Statistics: 2019, 2020, 2021

INCOME

Income

Area	Per Capita ($)	Median Household ($)	Average Household ($)
City	35,506	67,719	88,315
MSA[1]	35,155	71,171	91,541
U.S.	35,384	64,994	91,547

Note: (1) Figures cover the Colorado Springs, CO Metropolitan Statistical Area
Source: U.S. Census Bureau, 2016-2020 American Community Survey 5-Year Estimates

Household Income Distribution

Area	Percent of Households Earning							
	Under $15,000	$15,000 -$24,999	$25,000 -$34,999	$35,000 -$49,999	$50,000 -$74,999	$75,000 -$99,999	$100,000 -$149,999	$150,000 and up
City	8.5	7.7	8.2	12.3	18.7	13.9	16.7	14.1
MSA[1]	7.6	6.9	7.7	11.7	18.8	14.1	17.7	15.3
U.S.	9.9	8.5	8.6	12.0	17.2	12.8	15.6	15.4

Note: (1) Figures cover the Colorado Springs, CO Metropolitan Statistical Area
Source: U.S. Census Bureau, 2016-2020 American Community Survey 5-Year Estimates

Poverty Rate

Area	All Ages	Under 18 Years Old	18 to 64 Years Old	65 Years and Over
City	11.3	14.7	11.0	7.1
MSA[1]	9.8	12.6	9.5	6.5
U.S.	12.8	17.5	12.1	9.3

Note: Figures are percentage of people whose income during the past 12 months was below the poverty level; (1) Figures cover the Colorado Springs, CO Metropolitan Statistical Area
Source: U.S. Census Bureau, 2016-2020 American Community Survey 5-Year Estimates

CITY FINANCES

City Government Finances

Component	2019 ($000)	2019 ($ per capita)
Total Revenues	1,547,363	3,331
Total Expenditures	1,427,509	3,073
Debt Outstanding	2,617,234	5,635
Cash and Securities[1]	661,359	1,424

Note: (1) Cash and security holdings of a government at the close of its fiscal year, including those of its dependent agencies, utilities, and liquor stores.
Source: U.S. Census Bureau, State & Local Government Finances 2019

City Government Revenue by Source

Source	2019 ($000)	2019 ($ per capita)	2019 (%)
General Revenue			
From Federal Government	62,324	134	4.0
From State Government	6,115	13	0.4
From Local Governments	1,009	2	0.1
Taxes			
Property	51,780	111	3.3
Sales and Gross Receipts	318,282	685	20.6
Personal Income	0	0	0.0
Corporate Income	0	0	0.0
Motor Vehicle License	0	0	0.0
Other Taxes	3,266	7	0.2
Current Charges	122,360	263	7.9
Liquor Store	0	0	0.0
Utility	820,237	1,766	53.0

Source: U.S. Census Bureau, State & Local Government Finances 2019

City Government Expenditures by Function

Function	2019 ($000)	2019 ($ per capita)	2019 (%)
General Direct Expenditures			
Air Transportation	15,697	33	1.1
Corrections	0	0	0.0
Education	0	0	0.0
Employment Security Administration	0	0	0.0
Financial Administration	37,162	80	2.6
Fire Protection	53,430	115	3.7
General Public Buildings	0	0	0.0
Governmental Administration, Other	24,142	52	1.7
Health	0	0	0.0
Highways	157,685	339	11.0
Hospitals	0	0	0.0
Housing and Community Development	40,005	86	2.8
Interest on General Debt	23,480	50	1.6
Judicial and Legal	8,876	19	0.6
Libraries	0	0	0.0
Parking	2,405	5	0.2
Parks and Recreation	26,854	57	1.9
Police Protection	100,924	217	7.1
Public Welfare	0	0	0.0
Sewerage	50,907	109	3.6
Solid Waste Management	0	0	0.0
Veterans' Services	0	0	0.0
Liquor Store	0	0	0.0
Utility	797,458	1,716	55.9

Source: U.S. Census Bureau, State & Local Government Finances 2019

EMPLOYMENT

Labor Force and Employment

Area	Civilian Labor Force			Workers Employed		
	Dec. 2020	Dec. 2021	% Chg.	Dec. 2020	Dec. 2021	% Chg.
City	243,833	249,831	2.5	225,146	239,206	6.2
MSA[1]	362,171	372,478	2.8	335,526	356,536	6.3
U.S.	160,017,000	161,696,000	1.0	149,613,000	155,732,000	4.1

Note: Data is not seasonally adjusted and covers workers 16 years of age and older; (1) Figures cover the Colorado Springs, CO Metropolitan Statistical Area
Source: Bureau of Labor Statistics, Local Area Unemployment Statistics

Unemployment Rate

Area	2021											
	Jan.	Feb.	Mar.	Apr.	May	Jun.	Jul.	Aug.	Sep.	Oct.	Nov.	Dec.
City	7.2	7.0	6.7	6.4	5.8	6.4	6.2	5.5	4.9	4.6	4.5	4.3
MSA[1]	7.1	7.0	6.7	6.4	5.8	6.5	6.2	5.6	4.9	4.6	4.6	4.3
U.S.	6.8	6.6	6.2	5.7	5.5	6.1	5.7	5.3	4.6	4.3	3.9	3.7

Note: Data is not seasonally adjusted and covers workers 16 years of age and older; (1) Figures cover the Colorado Springs, CO Metropolitan Statistical Area
Source: Bureau of Labor Statistics, Local Area Unemployment Statistics

Average Wages

Occupation	$/Hr.	Occupation	$/Hr.
Accountants and Auditors	38.11	Maintenance and Repair Workers	21.14
Automotive Mechanics	24.49	Marketing Managers	77.39
Bookkeepers	20.35	Network and Computer Systems Admin.	43.42
Carpenters	23.91	Nurses, Licensed Practical	26.52
Cashiers	14.30	Nurses, Registered	37.75
Computer Programmers	43.09	Nursing Assistants	16.32
Computer Systems Analysts	50.29	Office Clerks, General	21.32
Computer User Support Specialists	30.02	Physical Therapists	41.33
Construction Laborers	18.94	Physicians	143.62
Cooks, Restaurant	16.32	Plumbers, Pipefitters and Steamfitters	25.37
Customer Service Representatives	18.23	Police and Sheriff's Patrol Officers	34.59
Dentists	77.91	Postal Service Mail Carriers	25.23
Electricians	25.94	Real Estate Sales Agents	29.87
Engineers, Electrical	49.66	Retail Salespersons	16.01
Fast Food and Counter Workers	14.04	Sales Representatives, Technical/Scientific	45.53
Financial Managers	77.12	Secretaries, Exc. Legal/Medical/Executive	18.76
First-Line Supervisors of Office Workers	30.14	Security Guards	16.96
General and Operations Managers	59.45	Surgeons	132.43
Hairdressers/Cosmetologists	18.13	Teacher Assistants, Exc. Postsecondary*	14.73
Home Health and Personal Care Aides	15.18	Teachers, Secondary School, Exc. Sp. Ed.*	26.79
Janitors and Cleaners	15.58	Telemarketers	18.92
Landscaping/Groundskeeping Workers	19.21	Truck Drivers, Heavy/Tractor-Trailer	23.88
Lawyers	51.23	Truck Drivers, Light/Delivery Services	20.28
Maids and Housekeeping Cleaners	15.00	Waiters and Waitresses	17.43

Note: Wage data covers the Colorado Springs, CO Metropolitan Statistical Area; (*) Hourly wages were calculated from annual wage data based on a 40 hour work week; n/a not available.
Source: Bureau of Labor Statistics, Metro Area Occupational Employment & Wage Estimates, May 2021

Employment by Industry

Sector	MSA[1]		U.S.
	Number of Employees	Percent of Total	Percent of Total
Construction, Mining, and Logging	18,500	6.0	5.3
Education and Health Services	43,000	13.9	16.0
Financial Activities	18,900	6.1	5.9
Government	55,000	17.8	14.9
Information	5,300	1.7	1.9
Leisure and Hospitality	37,700	12.2	9.8
Manufacturing	11,700	3.8	8.4
Other Services	18,700	6.0	3.7
Professional and Business Services	51,300	16.6	14.6
Retail Trade	34,100	11.0	10.7
Transportation, Warehousing, and Utilities	9,000	2.9	4.8
Wholesale Trade	6,100	2.0	3.8

Note: Figures are non-farm employment as of December 2021. Figures are not seasonally adjusted and include workers 16 years of age and older; (1) Figures cover the Colorado Springs, CO Metropolitan Statistical Area
Source: Bureau of Labor Statistics, Current Employment Statistics, Employment, Hours, and Earnings

Employment by Occupation

Occupation Classification	City (%)	MSA[1] (%)	U.S. (%)
Management, Business, Science, and Arts	43.3	42.8	39.5
Natural Resources, Construction, and Maintenance	8.0	8.6	8.7
Production, Transportation, and Material Moving	9.2	9.4	13.1
Sales and Office	21.4	21.4	21.3
Service	18.1	17.7	17.4

Note: Figures cover employed civilians 16 years of age and older; (1) Figures cover the Colorado Springs, CO Metropolitan Statistical Area
Source: U.S. Census Bureau, 2016-2020 American Community Survey 5-Year Estimates

Occupations with Greatest Projected Employment Growth: 2021 – 2023

Occupation[1]	2021 Employment	2023 Projected Employment	Numeric Employment Change	Percent Employment Change
Software Developers and Software Quality Assurance Analysts and Testers	62,100	66,810	4,710	7.6
Fast Food and Counter Workers	72,270	76,700	4,430	6.1
Cooks, Restaurant	30,360	34,250	3,890	12.8
Waiters and Waitresses	40,230	43,230	3,000	7.5
Retail Salespersons	77,680	80,550	2,870	3.7
Maids and Housekeeping Cleaners	22,930	25,680	2,750	12.0
Project Management Specialists and Business Operations Specialists, All Other	66,210	68,800	2,590	3.9
Home Health and Personal Care Aides	39,930	42,460	2,530	6.3
Stockers and Order Fillers	46,970	49,310	2,340	5.0
General and Operations Managers	37,390	39,420	2,030	5.4

Note: Projections cover Colorado; (1) Sorted by numeric employment change
Source: www.projectionscentral.com, State Occupational Projections, 2021–2023 Short-Term Projections

Fastest-Growing Occupations: 2021 – 2023

Occupation[1]	2021 Employment	2023 Projected Employment	Numeric Employment Change	Percent Employment Change
Motion Picture Projectionists	100	160	60	60.0
Rotary Drill Operators, Oil and Gas	240	340	100	41.7
Athletes and Sports Competitors	420	590	170	40.5
Roustabouts, Oil and Gas	1,780	2,490	710	39.9
Musicians and Singers	710	960	250	35.2
Fine Artists, Including Painters, Sculptors, and Illustrators	310	410	100	32.3
Actors	650	820	170	26.2
Service Unit Operators, Oil, Gas, and Mining	2,020	2,550	530	26.2
Dancers	320	400	80	25.0
Pump Operators, Except Wellhead Pumpers	200	250	50	25.0

Note: Projections cover Colorado; (1) Sorted by percent employment change and excludes occupations with numeric employment change less than 50
Source: www.projectionscentral.com, State Occupational Projections, 2021–2023 Short-Term Projections

TAXES

State Corporate Income Tax Rates

State	Tax Rate (%)	Income Brackets ($)	Num. of Brackets	Financial Institution Tax Rate (%)[a]	Federal Income Tax Ded.
Colorado	4.55	Flat rate	1	4.55	No

Note: Tax rates as of January 1, 2022; (a) Rates listed are the corporate income tax rate applied to financial institutions or excise taxes based on income. Some states have other taxes based upon the value of deposits or shares.
Source: Federation of Tax Administrators, State Corporate Income Tax Rates, January 1, 2022

State Individual Income Tax Rates

State	Tax Rate (%)	Income Brackets ($)	Personal Exemptions ($)			Standard Ded. ($)	
			Single	Married	Depend.	Single	Married
Colorado	4.55	Flat rate	(d)	(d)	(d)	12,950	25,900 (d)

Note: Tax rates as of January 1, 2022; Local- and county-level taxes are not included; Federal income tax is not deductible on state income tax returns; (d) These states use the personal exemption/standard deduction amounts provided in the federal Internal Revenue Code.
Source: Federation of Tax Administrators, State Individual Income Tax Rates, January 1, 2022

Various State Sales and Excise Tax Rates

State	State Sales Tax (%)	Gasoline[1] (¢/gal.)	Cigarette[2] ($/pack)	Spirits[3] ($/gal.)	Wine[4] ($/gal.)	Beer[5] ($/gal.)	Recreational Marijuana (%)
Colorado	2.9	22	1.94	2.28	0.32	0.08	(d)

Note: All tax rates as of January 1, 2022; (1) The American Petroleum Institute has developed a methodology for determining the average tax rate on a gallon of fuel. Rates may include any of the following: excise taxes, environmental fees, storage tank fees, other fees or taxes, general sales tax, and local taxes; (2) The federal excise tax of $1.0066 per pack and local taxes are not included; (3) Rates are those applicable to off-premise sales of 40% alcohol by volume (a.b.v.) distilled spirits in 750ml containers. Local excise taxes are excluded; (4) Rates are those applicable to off-premise sales of 11% a.b.v. non-carbonated wine in 750ml containers; (5) Rates are those applicable to off-premise sales of 4.7% a.b.v. beer in 12 ounce containers; (d) 15% excise tax (levied on wholesale at average market rate); 15% excise tax (retail price)
Source: Tax Foundation, 2022 Facts & Figures: How Does Your State Compare?

State Business Tax Climate Index Rankings

State	Overall Rank	Corporate Tax Rank	Individual Income Tax Rank	Sales Tax Rank	Property Tax Rank	Unemployment Insurance Tax Rank
Colorado	20	6	14	38	34	41

Note: The index is a measure of how each state's tax laws affect economic performance. The lower the rank, the more favorable a state's tax system is for business. States without a given tax are given a ranking of 1. The scores/rankings for the District of Columbia do not affect other states. The 2022 index represents the tax climate as of July 1, 2021.
Source: Tax Foundation, State Business Tax Climate Index 2022

TRANSPORTATION

Means of Transportation to Work

Area	Car/Truck/Van		Public Transportation			Bicycle	Walked	Other Means	Worked at Home
	Drove Alone	Car-pooled	Bus	Subway	Railroad				
City	76.2	10.4	0.8	0.1	0.0	0.5	1.9	1.0	9.1
MSA[1]	75.1	10.2	0.6	0.0	0.0	0.4	3.4	1.0	9.2
U.S.	74.9	8.9	2.2	1.7	0.5	0.5	2.6	1.4	7.3

Note: Figures are percentages and cover workers 16 years of age and older; (1) Figures cover the Colorado Springs, CO Metropolitan Statistical Area
Source: U.S. Census Bureau, 2016-2020 American Community Survey 5-Year Estimates

Travel Time to Work

Area	Less Than 10 Minutes	10 to 19 Minutes	20 to 29 Minutes	30 to 44 Minutes	45 to 59 Minutes	60 to 89 Minutes	90 Minutes or More
City	11.3	35.5	28.1	16.3	3.4	2.9	2.6
MSA[1]	11.8	32.2	26.9	18.2	4.9	3.5	2.5
U.S.	12.3	28.4	20.9	20.9	8.3	6.4	2.9

Note: Note: Figures are percentages and include workers 16 years old and over; (1) Figures cover the Colorado Springs, CO Metropolitan Statistical Area
Source: U.S. Census Bureau, 2016-2020 American Community Survey 5-Year Estimates

Key Congestion Measures

Measure	1990	2000	2010	2015	2020
Annual Hours of Delay, Total (000)	4,139	11,169	15,234	17,103	12,116
Annual Hours of Delay, Per Auto Commuter	20	34	36	40	29
Annual Congestion Cost, Per Auto Commuter ($)	346	704	763	793	582

Note: Covers the Colorado Springs CO urban area
Source: Texas A&M Transportation Institute, 2021 Urban Mobility Report

Freeway Travel Time Index

Measure	1985	1990	1995	2000	2005	2010	2015	2020
Urban Area Index[1]	1.04	1.09	1.12	1.15	1.16	1.15	1.15	1.08
Urban Area Rank[1,2]	81	56	57	53	57	65	67	44

Note: Freeway Travel Time Index—the ratio of travel time in the peak period to the travel time at free-flow conditions. For example, a value of 1.30 indicates a 20-minute free-flow trip takes 26 minutes in the peak (20 minutes x 1.30 = 26 minutes); (1) Covers the Colorado Springs CO urban area; (2) Rank is based on 101 larger urban areas (#1 = highest travel time index)
Source: Texas A&M Transportation Institute, 2021 Urban Mobility Report

Public Transportation

Agency Name / Mode of Transportation	Vehicles Operated in Maximum Service[1]	Annual Unlinked Passenger Trips[2] (in thous.)	Annual Passenger Miles[3] (in thous.)
Colorado Springs Transit System			
Bus (purchased transportation)	50	1,975.0	7,399.1
Demand Response (purchased transportation)	34	73.7	605.5
Demand Response - Taxi	13	1.5	6.7
Vanpool (directly operated)	25	13.3	816.1

Note: (1) Number of revenue vehicles operated by the given mode and type of service to meet the annual maximum service requirement. This is the revenue vehicle count during the peak season of the year; on the week and day that maximum service is provided. Vehicles operated in maximum service (VOMS) exclude atypical days and one-time special events; (2) Number of passengers who boarded public transportation vehicles. Passengers are counted each time they board a vehicle no matter how many vehicles they use to travel from their origin to their destination. (3) Sum of the distances ridden by all passengers during the entire fiscal year.
Source: Federal Transit Administration, National Transit Database, 2020

Air Transportation

Airport Name and Code / Type of Service	Passenger Airlines[1]	Passenger Enplanements	Freight Carriers[2]	Freight (lbs)
City of Colorado Springs Municipal (COS)				
Domestic service (U.S. carriers - 2021)	21	943,223	3	8,088,358
International service (U.S. carriers - 2020)	1	6	0	0

Note: (1) Includes all U.S.-based major, minor and commuter airlines that carried at least one passenger during the year; (2) Includes all U.S.-based airlines and freight carriers that transported at least one pound of freight during the year.
Source: Bureau of Transportation Statistics, The Intermodal Transportation Database, Air Carriers: T-100 Domestic Market (U.S. Carriers), 2021; Bureau of Transportation Statistics, The Intermodal Transportation Database, Air Carriers: T-100 International Market (U.S. Carriers), 2020

BUSINESSES

Major Business Headquarters

Company Name	Industry	Rankings	
		Fortune[1]	Forbes[2]
No companies listed	-	-	-

Note: (1) Companies that produce a 10-K are ranked 1 to 500 based on 2020 revenue; (2) All private companies with at least $2 billion in annual revenue through the end of their most current fiscal year are ranked 1 to 225; companies listed are headquartered in the city; dashes indicate no ranking
Source: Fortune, "Fortune 500," 2021; Forbes, "America's Largest Private Companies," 2021

Fastest-Growing Businesses

According to *Inc.*, Colorado Springs is home to one of America's 500 fastest-growing private companies: **Smith Plumbing** (#498). Criteria: must be an independent, privately-held, for-profit, U.S. corporation, proprietorship or partnership as of December 31, 2020; revenues must be at least $100,000 in 2017 and $2 million in 2020; must have four-year operating/sales history. *Inc., "America's 500 Fastest-Growing Private Companies," 2021*

According to Deloitte, Colorado Springs is home to one of North America's 500 fastest-growing high-technology companies: **Quantum Metric** (#158). Companies are ranked by percentage growth in revenue over a four-year period. Criteria for inclusion: company must be headquartered within North America; must own proprietary intellectual property or technology that is sold to customers in products that contributes to a significant portion of the company's operating revenue; must have been in business for a minumum of four years with 2017 operating revenues of at least $50,000 USD/CD and 2020 operating revenues of at least $5 million USD/CD. *Deloitte, 2021 Technology Fast 500™*

Living Environment

COST OF LIVING

Cost of Living Index

Composite Index	Groceries	Housing	Utilities	Trans-portation	Health Care	Misc. Goods/ Services
108.2	101.0	115.9	99.1	102.9	100.0	110.2

Note: The Cost of Living Index measures regional differences in the cost of consumer goods and services, excluding taxes and non-consumer expenditures, for professional and managerial households in the top income quintile. It is based on more than 50,000 prices covering almost 60 different items for which prices are collected three times a year by chambers of commerce, economic development organizations or university applied economic centers in each participating urban area. The numbers shown should be read as a percentage above or below the national average of 100. For example, a value of 115.4 in the groceries column indicates that grocery prices are 15.4% higher than the national average. Small differences in the index numbers should not be interpreted as significant; Figures cover the Colorado Springs CO urban area.
Source: The Council for Community and Economic Research, Cost of Living Index, 2021

Grocery Prices

Area[1]	T-Bone Steak ($/pound)	Frying Chicken ($/pound)	Whole Milk ($/half gal.)	Eggs ($/dozen)	Orange Juice ($/64 oz.)	Coffee ($/11.5 oz.)
City[2]	14.08	1.19	1.75	1.25	3.48	4.68
Avg.	12.82	1.40	2.22	1.57	3.59	4.30
Min.	8.91	0.91	1.29	0.75	2.87	3.02
Max.	21.35	2.69	3.92	3.86	5.49	8.11

Note: (1) Values for the local area are compared with the average, minimum and maximum values for all 285 areas in the Cost of Living Index; (2) Figures cover the Colorado Springs CO urban area; ***T-Bone Steak*** *(price per pound);* ***Frying Chicken*** *(price per pound, whole fryer);* ***Whole Milk*** *(half gallon carton);* ***Eggs*** *(price per dozen, Grade A, large);* ***Orange Juice*** *(64 oz. Tropicana or Florida Natural);* ***Coffee*** *(11.5 oz. can, vacuum-packed, Maxwell House, Hills Bros, or Folgers).*
Source: The Council for Community and Economic Research, Cost of Living Index, 2021

Housing and Utility Costs

Area[1]	New Home Price ($)	Apartment Rent ($/month)	All Electric ($/month)	Part Electric ($/month)	Other Energy ($/month)	Telephone ($/month)
City[2]	445,666	1,568	-	96.11	73.34	185.54
Avg.	398,393	1,217	171.38	100.83	69.67	187.75
Min.	212,799	534	96.71	31.56	27.15	173.01
Max.	2,354,006	4,438	369.53	277.33	303.87	206.73

Note: (1) Values for the local area are compared with the average, minimum and maximum values for all 285 areas in the Cost of Living Index; (2) Figures cover the Colorado Springs CO urban area; ***New Home Price*** *(2,400 sf living area, 8,000 sf lot, in urban area with full utilities);* ***Apartment Rent*** *(950 sf 2 bedroom/1.5 or 2 bath, unfurnished, excluding all utilities except water);* ***All Electric*** *(average monthly cost for an all-electric home);* ***Part Electric*** *(average monthly cost for a part-electric home);* ***Other Energy*** *(average monthly cost for natural gas, fuel oil, coal, wood, and any other forms of energy except electricity);* ***Telephone*** *(price includes the base monthly rate plus taxes and fees for three lines of mobile phone service).*
Source: The Council for Community and Economic Research, Cost of Living Index, 2021

Health Care, Transportation, and Other Costs

Area[1]	Doctor ($/visit)	Dentist ($/visit)	Optometrist ($/visit)	Gasoline ($/gallon)	Beauty Salon ($/visit)	Men's Shirt ($)
City[2]	119.60	100.70	112.79	2.81	45.60	31.79
Avg.	118.16	101.04	109.44	2.71	40.63	30.77
Min.	35.04	55.56	51.17	2.17	18.59	11.32
Max.	231.10	165.12	256.81	4.11	85.33	63.03

Note: (1) Values for the local area are compared with the average, minimum and maximum values for all 285 areas in the Cost of Living Index; (2) Figures cover the Colorado Springs CO urban area; ***Doctor*** *(general practitioners routine exam of an established patient);* ***Dentist*** *(adult teeth cleaning and periodic oral examination);* ***Optometrist*** *(full vision eye exam for established adult patient);* ***Gasoline*** *(one gallon regular unleaded, national brand, including all taxes, cash price at self-service pump if available);* ***Beauty Salon*** *(woman's shampoo, trim, and blow-dry);* ***Men's Shirt*** *(cotton/polyester dress shirt, pinpoint weave, long sleeves).*
Source: The Council for Community and Economic Research, Cost of Living Index, 2021

HOUSING

Homeownership Rate

Area	2013 (%)	2014 (%)	2015 (%)	2016 (%)	2017 (%)	2018 (%)	2019 (%)	2020 (%)	2021 (%)
MSA[1]	n/a	n/a	n/a	n/a	n/a	n/a	n/a	n/a	n/a
U.S.	65.1	64.5	63.7	63.4	63.9	64.4	64.6	66.6	65.5

Note: (1) Figures cover the Colorado Springs, CO Metropolitan Statistical Area; n/a not available
Source: U.S. Census Bureau, Housing Vacancies and Homeownership Annual Statistics: 2013-2021

House Price Index (HPI)

Area	National Ranking[2]	Quarterly Change (%)	One-Year Change (%)	Five-Year Change (%)	Since 1991Q1 (%)
MSA[1]	48	3.24	22.26	71.49	392.05
U.S.[3]	–	3.33	17.54	54.45	258.04

Note: The HPI is a weighted repeat sales index. It measures average price changes in repeat sales or refinancings on the same properties. This information is obtained by reviewing repeat mortgage transactions on single-family properties whose mortgages have been purchased or securitized by Fannie Mae or Freddie Mac since January 1975; (1) Figures cover the Colorado Springs, CO Metropolitan Statistical Area; (2) Rankings are based on annual percentage change for all metro areas containing at least 15,000 transactions over the last 10 years and ranges from 1 to 268; (3) figures based on a weighted average of Census Division estimates using a seasonally adjusted, purchase-only index; all figures are for the period ending December 31, 2021
Source: Federal Housing Finance Agency, Change in FHFA Metropolitan Area House Price Indexes, 2021Q4

Median Single-Family Home Prices

Area	2019	2020	2021p	Percent Change 2020 to 2021
MSA[1]	320.5	361.7	432.9	19.7
U.S. Average	274.6	300.2	353.4	17.7

Note: Figures are median sales prices of existing single-family homes in thousands of dollars; (p) preliminary; (1) Figures cover the Colorado Springs, CO Metropolitan Statistical Area
Source: National Association of Realtors, Median Sales Price of Existing Single-Family Homes for Metropolitan Areas, 4th Quarter 2021

Qualifying Income Based on Median Sales Price of Existing Single-Family Homes

Area	With 5% Down ($)	With 10% Down ($)	With 20% Down ($)
MSA[1]	87,276	82,683	73,496
U.S. Average	70,699	66,978	59,536

Note: Figures are preliminary; Qualifying income is based on a mortgage rate of 3.13%. Monthly principal and interest payment is limited to 25% of income; (1) Figures cover the Colorado Springs, CO Metropolitan Statistical Area
Source: National Association of Realtors, Qualifying Income Based on Median Sales Price of Existing Single-Family Homes for Metropolitan Areas, 4th Quarter 2021

Home Value Distribution

Area	Under $50,000	$50,000 -$99,999	$100,000 -$149,999	$150,000 -$199,999	$200,000 -$299,999	$300,000 -$499,999	$500,000 -$999,999	$1,000,000 or more
City	3.0	1.9	4.6	11.0	31.3	36.7	10.3	1.2
MSA[1]	3.1	1.7	4.4	10.9	29.9	36.2	12.6	1.4
U.S.	6.6	11.0	12.3	13.6	20.0	20.5	12.3	3.7

Note: Figures are percentages and cover owner-occupied housing units; (1) Figures cover the Colorado Springs, CO Metropolitan Statistical Area
Source: U.S. Census Bureau, 2016-2020 American Community Survey 5-Year Estimates

Year Housing Structure Built

Area	2010 or Later	2000 -2009	1990 -1999	1980 -1989	1970 -1979	1960 -1969	1950 -1959	1940 -1949	Before 1940	Median Year
City	8.2	14.9	15.6	19.1	17.7	9.5	7.3	1.9	5.7	1984
MSA[1]	9.2	18.0	16.7	17.9	16.6	8.2	6.5	1.6	5.3	1987
U.S.	6.2	13.6	13.9	13.4	15.0	10.5	10.2	4.8	12.4	1978

Note: Figures are percentages except for Median Year; Note: (1) Figures cover the Colorado Springs, CO Metropolitan Statistical Area
Source: U.S. Census Bureau, 2016-2020 American Community Survey 5-Year Estimates

Gross Monthly Rent

Area	Under $500	$500 -$999	$1,000 -$1,499	$1,500 -$1,999	$2,000 -$2,499	$2,500 -$2,999	$3,000 and up	Median ($)
City	3.5	28.9	40.0	19.8	4.7	2.3	0.9	1,196
MSA[1]	3.5	27.4	37.6	23.6	5.1	2.1	0.8	1,232
U.S.	8.9	34.3	30.2	14.9	6.2	2.6	2.8	1,096

Note: Figures are percentages except for Median; Gross rent is the contract rent plus the estimated average monthly cost of utilities (electricity, gas, and water and sewer) and fuels (oil, coal, kerosene, wood, etc.) if these are paid by the renter (or paid for the renter by someone else); (1) Figures cover the Colorado Springs, CO Metropolitan Statistical Area
Source: U.S. Census Bureau, 2016-2020 American Community Survey 5-Year Estimates

HEALTH

Health Risk Factors

Category	MSA[1] (%)	U.S. (%)
Adults aged 18–64 who have any kind of health care coverage	86.1	86.8
Adults who reported being in good or better health	88.6	86.7
Adults who are current smokers	15.0	15.5
Adults who currently use chewing tobacco, snuff, or snus	4.4	3.7
Adults who are heavy drinkers[2]	5.5	6.7
Adults who are binge drinkers[3]	12.9	15.7
Adults who are overweight (BMI 25.0 - 29.9)	33.3	35.2
Adults who are obese (BMI 30.0 - 99.8)	27.8	31.9
Adults who participated in any physical activities in the past month	81.3	77.6
Adults who always or nearly always wears a seat belt	95.2	94.2

Note: (1) Figures cover the Colorado Springs, CO Metropolitan Statistical Area; (2) Heavy drinkers are classified as adult men having more than 14 drinks per week and adult women having more than 7 drinks per week; (3) Binge drinkers are classified as males having five or more drinks on one occasion or females having four or more drinks on one occasion
Source: Centers for Disease Control and Prevention, Behaviorial Risk Factor Surveillance System, SMART: Selected Metropolitan Area Risk Trends, 2020

Acute and Chronic Health Conditions

Category	MSA[1] (%)	U.S. (%)
Adults who have ever been told they had a heart attack	3.0	4.3
Adults who have ever been told they have angina or coronary heart disease	2.4	4.0
Adults who have ever been told they had a stroke	2.6	2.8
Adults who have ever been told they have asthma	14.4	14.2
Adults who have ever been told they have arthritis	23.3	24.5
Adults who have ever been told they have diabetes[2]	7.3	10.6
Adults who have ever been told they had skin cancer	7.0	6.4
Adults who have ever been told they had any other types of cancer	6.5	6.8
Adults who have ever been told they have COPD	5.4	6.2
Adults who have ever been told they have kidney disease	3.4	2.9
Adults who have ever been told they have a form of depression	20.9	19.6

Note: (1) Figures cover the Colorado Springs, CO Metropolitan Statistical Area; (2) Figures do not include pregnancy-related, borderline, or pre-diabetes
Source: Centers for Disease Control and Prevention, Behaviorial Risk Factor Surveillance System, SMART: Selected Metropolitan Area Risk Trends, 2020

Health Screening and Vaccination Rates

Category	MSA[1] (%)	U.S. (%)
Adults 50-75 who have had a blood stool test within the past year	6.8	9.3
Adults aged 65+ who have had flu shot within the past year	69.9	67.9
Adults aged 65+ who have ever had a pneumonia vaccination	80.2	72.2
Adults who have ever been tested for HIV	41.4	37.1
Women aged 21-65 who have had a pap test in the past three years	73.2	77.7
Men aged 40+ who have had a PSA test within the past two years	26.0	31.8
Women aged 40+ who have had a mammogram within the past two years	61.2	71.5

Note: (1) Figures cover the Colorado Springs, CO Metropolitan Statistical Area.
Source: Centers for Disease Control and Prevention, Behaviorial Risk Factor Surveillance System, SMART: Selected Metropolitan Area Risk Trends, 2020

Disability Status

Category	MSA[1] (%)	U.S. (%)
Adults who reported being deaf	5.6	6.8
Are you blind or have serious difficulty seeing, even when wearing glasses?	4.0	4.7
Do you have difficulty doing errands alone?	4.9	6.3
Do you have difficulty dressing or bathing?	2.9	3.0
Do you have serious difficulty concentrating/remembering/making decisions?	10.2	10.8
Do you have serious difficulty walking or climbing stairs?	9.4	11.9

Note: (1) Figures cover the Colorado Springs, CO Metropolitan Statistical Area.
Source: Centers for Disease Control and Prevention, Behaviorial Risk Factor Surveillance System, SMART: Selected Metropolitan Area Risk Trends, 2020

Mortality Rates for the Top 10 Causes of Death in the U.S.

ICD-10[a] Sub-Chapter	ICD-10[a] Code	Age-Adjusted Mortality Rate[1] per 100,000 population	
		County[2]	U.S.
Malignant neoplasms	C00-C97	138.9	146.4
Ischaemic heart diseases	I20-I25	67.2	90.2
Other forms of heart disease	I30-I51	40.6	51.9
Other degenerative diseases of the nervous system	G30-G31	49.8	39.7
Other external causes of accidental injury	W00-X59	51.4	38.7
Chronic lower respiratory diseases	J40-J47	46.9	38.1
Cerebrovascular diseases	I60-I69	39.9	37.6
Organic, including symptomatic, mental disorders	F01-F09	27.0	29.4
Hypertensive diseases	I10-I15	36.9	26.1
Diabetes mellitus	E10-E14	21.1	22.6

Note: (a) ICD-10 = International Classification of Diseases 10th Revision; (1) Mortality rates are a three-year average covering 2018-2020; (2) Figures cover El Paso County.
Source: Centers for Disease Control and Prevention, National Center for Health Statistics. Underlying Cause of Death 1999-2020 on CDC WONDER Online Database

Mortality Rates for Selected Causes of Death

ICD-10[a] Sub-Chapter	ICD-10[a] Code	Age-Adjusted Mortality Rate[1] per 100,000 population	
		County[2]	U.S.
Assault	X85-Y09	7.5	6.5
Diseases of the liver	K70-K76	20.5	15.3
Human immunodeficiency virus (HIV) disease	B20-B24	Unreliable	1.4
Influenza and pneumonia	J09-J18	7.9	13.4
Intentional self-harm	X60-X84	27.1	13.9
Malnutrition	E40-E46	4.3	2.9
Obesity and other hyperalimentation	E65-E68	2.9	2.4
Renal failure	N17-N19	8.5	12.5
Transport accidents	V01-V99	16.3	12.5
Viral hepatitis	B15-B19	1.5	1.0

Note: (a) ICD-10 = International Classification of Diseases 10th Revision; (1) Mortality rates are a three-year average covering 2018-2020; (2) Figures cover El Paso County; Data are suppressed when the data meet the criteria for confidentiality constraints; Mortality rates are flagged as unreliable when the rate would be calculated with a numerator of 20 or less.
Source: Centers for Disease Control and Prevention, National Center for Health Statistics. Underlying Cause of Death 1999-2020 on CDC WONDER Online Database

Health Insurance Coverage

Area	With Health Insurance	With Private Health Insurance	With Public Health Insurance	Without Health Insurance	Population Under Age 19 Without Health Insurance
City	92.2	68.9	36.9	7.8	4.3
MSA[1]	92.8	71.0	35.8	7.2	4.5
U.S.	91.3	68.1	35.3	8.7	5.2

Note: Figures are percentages that cover the civilian noninstitutionalized population; (1) Figures cover the Colorado Springs, CO Metropolitan Statistical Area
Source: U.S. Census Bureau, 2016-2020 American Community Survey 5-Year Estimates

Number of Medical Professionals

Area	MDs[3]	DOs[3,4]	Dentists	Podiatrists	Chiropractors	Optometrists
County[1] (number)	1,484	229	762	32	325	177
County[1] (rate[2])	203.2	31.4	104.3	4.4	44.5	24.2
U.S. (rate[2])	285.1	23.0	71.1	6.2	28.2	17.0

08041
Note: Data as of 2020 unless noted; (1) Data covers El Paso County; (2) Rate per 100,000 population; (3) Data as of 2019 and includes all active, non-federal physicians; (4) Doctor of Osteopathic Medicine
Source: U.S. Department of Health and Human Services, Health Resources and Services Administration, Bureau of Health Professions, Area Resource File (ARF) 2020-2021

EDUCATION

Public School District Statistics

District Name	Schls	Pupils	Pupil/ Teacher Ratio	Minority Pupils[1] (%)	LEP/ELL[2] (%)	IEP[3] (%)
Academy School District No. 20	40	26,603	16.6	29.5	1.9	n/a
Cheyenne Mountain SD No. 12	11	5,309	14.7	31.4	2.1	n/a
Colorado Springs SD No. 11	56	26,040	16.6	49.5	6.3	n/a
Harrison School District No. 2	27	11,543	15.2	76.3	12.0	n/a
School District No. 3	17	9,669	16.3	52.0	1.4	n/a

Note: Table includes school districts with 2,000 or more students; (1) Percentage of students that are not non-Hispanic white; (2) Percentage of students that are Limited English Proficient (LEP) or English Language Learners (ELL) (2018-19); (3) Percentage of students that have an Individualized Education Program (IEP).
Source: U.S. Department of Education, National Center for Education Statistics, Common Core of Data, Local Education Agency (School District) Universe Survey: School Year 2019-2020

Best High Schools

According to *U.S. News,* Colorado Springs is home to one of the top 500 high schools in the U.S.: **The Vanguard School** (#306). Nearly 18,000 public, magnet and charter schools were ranked based on their performance on state assessments and how well they prepare students for college. *U.S. News & World Report, "Best High Schools 2021"*

Highest Level of Education

Area	Less than H.S.	H.S. Diploma	Some College, No Deg.	Associate Degree	Bachelor's Degree	Master's Degree	Prof. School Degree	Doctorate Degree
City	6.0	19.4	24.1	10.8	23.9	11.9	2.2	1.6
MSA[1]	5.4	20.2	24.5	11.3	23.3	11.8	1.9	1.6
U.S.	11.5	26.7	20.3	8.6	20.2	9.1	2.2	1.5

Note: Figures cover persons age 25 and over; (1) Figures cover the Colorado Springs, CO Metropolitan Statistical Area
Source: U.S. Census Bureau, 2016-2020 American Community Survey 5-Year Estimates

Educational Attainment by Race

Area	High School Graduate or Higher (%)					Bachelor's Degree or Higher (%)				
	Total	White	Black	Asian	Hisp.[2]	Total	White	Black	Asian	Hisp.[2]
City	94.0	95.3	94.1	84.3	82.6	39.6	42.7	24.4	42.6	19.7
MSA[1]	94.6	95.6	94.9	86.0	84.7	38.6	40.8	27.4	41.5	20.8
U.S.	88.5	90.7	86.7	87.3	70.3	32.9	34.4	22.6	55.0	17.6

Note: Figures shown cover persons 25 years old and over; (1) Figures cover the Colorado Springs, CO Metropolitan Statistical Area; (2) People of Hispanic origin can be of any race
Source: U.S. Census Bureau, 2016-2020 American Community Survey 5-Year Estimates

School Enrollment by Grade and Control

Area	Preschool (%)		Kindergarten (%)		Grades 1 - 4 (%)		Grades 5 - 8 (%)		Grades 9 - 12 (%)	
	Public	Private	Public	Private	Public	Private	Public	Private	Public	Private
City	55.7	44.3	88.8	11.2	89.7	10.3	90.6	9.4	91.9	8.1
MSA[1]	58.9	41.1	88.0	12.0	89.7	10.3	90.9	9.1	91.4	8.6
U.S.	58.9	41.1	86.9	13.1	89.0	11.0	89.0	11.0	89.7	10.3

Note: Figures shown cover persons 3 years old and over; (1) Figures cover the Colorado Springs, CO Metropolitan Statistical Area
Source: U.S. Census Bureau, 2016-2020 American Community Survey 5-Year Estimates

Higher Education

Four-Year Colleges			Two-Year Colleges			Medical Schools[1]	Law Schools[2]	Voc/ Tech[3]
Public	Private Non-profit	Private For-profit	Public	Private Non-profit	Private For-profit			
3	2	2	0	0	5	0	0	3

Note: Figures cover institutions located within the Colorado Springs, CO Metropolitan Statistical Area and include main campuses only; (1) includes schools accredited by the Liaison Committee on Medical Education and the American Osteopathic Association's Commission on Osteopathic College Accreditation; (2) includes ABA-accredited schools, schools with provisional ABA accreditation, and state accredited schools; (3) includes all schools with programs that are less than 2 years.
Source: National Center for Education Statistics, Integrated Postsecondary Education System (IPEDS), 2020-21; Wikipedia, List of Medical Schools in the United States, accessed April 11, 2022; Wikipedia, List of Law Schools in the United States, accessed April 11, 2022

According to *U.S. News & World Report,* the Colorado Springs, CO metro area is home to two of the top 100 liberal arts colleges in the U.S.: **United States Air Force Academy** (#22 tie); **Colorado College** (#26). The indicators used to capture academic quality fall into a number of categories: assessment by administrators at peer institutions; retention of students; faculty resources; student selectivity; financial resources; alumni giving; high school counselor ratings of colleges; and graduation rate. *U.S. News & World Report, "America's Best Colleges 2022"*

EMPLOYERS

Major Employers

Company Name	Industry
Children's Hospital Colorado	Healthcare
Colorado State University	Education
Community Hospital Assn	Healthcare
Denver International Airport	Airports
Exempla St Joseph Hospital	Healthcare
Great-West Funds Inc	Financial services
Great-West Life & Annuity Ins	Insurance
Keystone Resort	Recreation association
Level 3 Communications Inc	Communications
Lockheed Martin Corp	Technology
Lockheed Martin Space Systems	Defense systems & equipment
Memorial Hospital North	Healthcare
Penrose Hospital	Healthcare
Peterson AFB	U.S. military
Poudre Valley Hospital	Healthcare
Schriever Air Force Base	U.S. military
Terumo	Healthcare
University of Boulder	Education
University of Colorado Health	Healthcare
University of Colorado-Boulder	Education
University of Northern Colorado	Education
Verizon Wireless	Wireless communcations
Western Union Co	Payment services

Note: Companies shown are located within the Colorado Springs, CO Metropolitan Statistical Area.
Source: Hoovers.com; Wikipedia

PUBLIC SAFETY

Crime Rate

Area	Total Crime	Violent Crime Rate				Property Crime Rate		
		Murder	Rape³	Robbery	Aggrav. Assault	Burglary	Larceny -Theft	Motor Vehicle Theft
City	3,976.6	7.4	82.5	77.5	429.6	533.5	2,344.8	501.4
Suburbs¹	1,620.4	4.1	66.6	24.3	191.2	193.8	966.8	173.6
Metro²	3,139.6	6.2	76.8	58.6	344.9	412.8	1,855.2	384.9
U.S.	2,356.7	6.5	38.4	73.9	279.7	314.2	1,398.0	246.0

Note: Figures are crimes per 100,000 population; (1) All areas within the metro area that are located outside the city limits; (2) Figures cover the Colorado Springs, CO Metropolitan Statistical Area; (3) All figures shown were reported using the revised Uniform Crime Reporting (UCR) definition of rape.
Source: FBI Uniform Crime Reports, 2020

Hate Crimes

Area	Number of Quarters Reported	Number of Incidents per Bias Motivation					
		Race/Ethnicity/ Ancestry	Religion	Sexual Orientation	Disability	Gender	Gender Identity
City	4	15	2	3	0	0	0
U.S.	4	5,227	1,244	1,110	130	75	266

Source: Federal Bureau of Investigation, Hate Crime Statistics 2020

Identity Theft Consumer Reports

Area	Reports	Reports per 100,000 Population	Rank²
MSA¹	4,385	588	36
U.S.	1,434,676	432	-

Note: (1) Figures cover the Colorado Springs, CO Metropolitan Statistical Area; (2) Rank ranges from 1 to 391 where 1 indicates greatest number of identity theft reports per 100,000 population
Source: Federal Trade Commission, Consumer Sentinel Network Data Book 2021

Fraud and Other Consumer Reports

Area	Reports	Reports per 100,000 Population	Rank²
MSA¹	9,090	1,219	37
U.S.	4,328,977	1,304	-

Note: (1) Figures cover the Colorado Springs, CO Metropolitan Statistical Area; (2) Rank ranges from 1 to 391 where 1 indicates greatest number of fraud and other consumer reports per 100,000 population
Source: Federal Trade Commission, Consumer Sentinel Network Data Book 2021

POLITICS

2020 Presidential Election Results

Area	Biden	Trump	Jorgensen	Hawkins	Other
El Paso County	42.7	53.5	2.4	0.3	1.0
U.S.	51.3	46.8	1.2	0.3	0.5

Note: Results are percentages and may not add to 100% due to rounding
Source: Dave Leip's Atlas of U.S. Presidential Elections

SPORTS

Professional Sports Teams

Team Name	League	Year Established
No teams are located in the metro area		

Source: Wikipedia, Major Professional Sports Teams of the United States and Canada, April 6, 2022

CLIMATE

Average and Extreme Temperatures

Temperature	Jan	Feb	Mar	Apr	May	Jun	Jul	Aug	Sep	Oct	Nov	Dec	Yr.
Extreme High (°F)	71	72	78	87	93	99	98	97	94	86	78	75	99
Average High (°F)	41	44	51	61	68	79	85	81	75	63	49	41	62
Average Temp. (°F)	29	32	39	48	55	66	71	69	61	50	37	30	49
Average Low (°F)	17	20	26	34	42	52	57	55	48	36	24	17	36
Extreme Low (°F)	-20	-19	-3	8	22	36	48	39	22	7	-5	-24	-24

Note: Figures cover the years 1948-1993
Source: National Climatic Data Center, International Station Meteorological Climate Summary, 9/96

Average Precipitation/Snowfall/Humidity

Precip./Humidity	Jan	Feb	Mar	Apr	May	Jun	Jul	Aug	Sep	Oct	Nov	Dec	Yr.
Avg. Precip. (in.)	0.3	0.4	1.3	1.3	2.6	2.1	2.6	3.4	1.0	0.9	0.6	0.5	17.0
Avg. Snowfall (in.)	6	6	10	5	2	0	0	0	Tr	3	7	8	48
Avg. Rel. Hum. 5am (%)	57	60	62	62	69	67	66	71	66	59	60	59	63
Avg. Rel. Hum. 5pm (%)	48	43	39	34	39	36	36	43	36	36	45	52	41

Note: Figures cover the years 1948-1993; Tr = Trace amounts (<0.05 in. of rain; <0.5 in. of snow)
Source: National Climatic Data Center, International Station Meteorological Climate Summary, 9/96

Weather Conditions

Temperature			Daytime Sky			Precipitation		
10°F & below	32°F & below	90°F & above	Clear	Partly cloudy	Cloudy	0.01 inch or more precip.	0.1 inch or more snow/ice	Thunder-storms
21	161	18	108	157	100	98	33	49

Note: Figures are average number of days per year and cover the years 1948-1993
Source: National Climatic Data Center, International Station Meteorological Climate Summary, 9/96

HAZARDOUS WASTE

Superfund Sites

The Colorado Springs, CO metro area has no sites on the EPA's Superfund Final National Priorities List. There are a total of 1,165 Superfund sites with a status of proposed or final on the list in the U.S.
U.S. Environmental Protection Agency, National Priorities List, April 6, 2022

AIR QUALITY

Air Quality Trends: Ozone

	1990	1995	2000	2005	2010	2016	2017	2018	2019	2020
MSA[1]	n/a	n/a	n/a	n/a	n/a	n/a	n/a	n/a	n/a	n/a
U.S.	0.090	0.091	0.082	0.080	0.074	0.070	0.069	0.070	0.066	0.068

Note: (1) Data covers the Colorado Springs, CO Metropolitan Statistical Area; n/a not available. The values shown are the composite ozone concentration averages among trend sites based on the highest fourth daily maximum 8-hour concentration in parts per million. These trends are based on sites having an adequate record of monitoring data during the trend period. Data from exceptional events are included.
Source: U.S. Environmental Protection Agency, Air Quality Monitoring Information, "Air Quality Trends by City, 1990-2020"

Air Quality Index

Area	Percent of Days when Air Quality was...[2]					AQI Statistics[2]	
	Good	Moderate	Unhealthy for Sensitive Groups	Unhealthy	Very Unhealthy	Maximum	Median
MSA[1]	69.7	28.4	1.6	0.3	0.0	151	45

Note: (1) Data covers the Colorado Springs, CO Metropolitan Statistical Area; (2) Based on 366 days with AQI data in 2020. Air Quality Index (AQI) is an index for reporting daily air quality. EPA calculates the AQI for five major air pollutants regulated by the Clean Air Act: ground-level ozone, particle pollution (aka particulate matter), carbon monoxide, sulfur dioxide, and nitrogen dioxide. The AQI runs from 0 to 500. The higher the AQI value, the greater the level of air pollution and the greater the health concern. There are six AQI categories: "Good" AQI is between 0 and 50. Air quality is considered satisfactory; "Moderate" AQI is between 51 and 100. Air quality is acceptable; "Unhealthy for Sensitive Groups" When AQI values are between 101 and 150, members of sensitive groups may experience health effects; "Unhealthy" When AQI values are between 151 and 200 everyone may begin to experience health effects; "Very Unhealthy" AQI values between 201 and 300 trigger a health alert; "Hazardous" AQI values over 300 trigger warnings of emergency conditions (not shown).
Source: U.S. Environmental Protection Agency, Air Quality Index Report, 2020

Air Quality Index Pollutants

Area	Percent of Days when AQI Pollutant was...[2]					
	Carbon Monoxide	Nitrogen Dioxide	Ozone	Sulfur Dioxide	Particulate Matter 2.5	Particulate Matter 10
MSA[1]	0.0	0.0	92.9	0.0	7.1	0.0

Note: (1) Data covers the Colorado Springs, CO Metropolitan Statistical Area; (2) Based on 366 days with AQI data in 2020. The Air Quality Index (AQI) is an index for reporting daily air quality. EPA calculates the AQI for five major air pollutants regulated by the Clean Air Act: ground-level ozone, particle pollution (also known as particulate matter), carbon monoxide, sulfur dioxide, and nitrogen dioxide. The AQI runs from 0 to 500. The higher the AQI value, the greater the level of air pollution and the greater the health concern.
Source: U.S. Environmental Protection Agency, Air Quality Index Report, 2020

Maximum Air Pollutant Concentrations: Particulate Matter, Ozone, CO and Lead

	Particulate Matter 10 (ug/m^3)	Particulate Matter 2.5 Wtd AM (ug/m^3)	Particulate Matter 2.5 24-Hr (ug/m^3)	Ozone (ppm)	Carbon Monoxide (ppm)	Lead (ug/m^3)
MSA[1] Level	50	6	21	0.079	1	n/a
NAAQS[2]	150	15	35	0.075	9	0.15
Met NAAQS[2]	Yes	Yes	Yes	No	Yes	n/a

Note: (1) Data covers the Colorado Springs, CO Metropolitan Statistical Area; Data from exceptional events are included; (2) National Ambient Air Quality Standards; ppm = parts per million; ug/m^3 = micrograms per cubic meter; n/a not available.
Concentrations: Particulate Matter 10 (coarse particulate)—highest second maximum 24-hour concentration; Particulate Matter 2.5 Wtd AM (fine particulate)—highest weighted annual mean concentration; Particulate Matter 2.5 24-Hour (fine particulate)—highest 98th percentile 24-hour concentration; Ozone—highest fourth daily maximum 8-hour concentration; Carbon Monoxide—highest second maximum non-overlapping 8-hour concentration; Lead—maximum running 3-month average
Source: U.S. Environmental Protection Agency, Air Quality Monitoring Information, "Air Quality Statistics by City, 2020"

Maximum Air Pollutant Concentrations: Nitrogen Dioxide and Sulfur Dioxide

	Nitrogen Dioxide AM (ppb)	Nitrogen Dioxide 1-Hr (ppb)	Sulfur Dioxide AM (ppb)	Sulfur Dioxide 1-Hr (ppb)	Sulfur Dioxide 24-Hr (ppb)
MSA[1] Level	n/a	n/a	n/a	9	n/a
NAAQS[2]	53	100	30	75	140
Met NAAQS[2]	n/a	n/a	n/a	Yes	n/a

Note: (1) Data covers the Colorado Springs, CO Metropolitan Statistical Area; Data from exceptional events are included; (2) National Ambient Air Quality Standards; ppm = parts per million; ug/m^3 = micrograms per cubic meter; n/a not available.
Concentrations: Nitrogen Dioxide AM—highest arithmetic mean concentration; Nitrogen Dioxide 1-Hr—highest 98th percentile 1-hour daily maximum concentration; Sulfur Dioxide AM—highest annual mean concentration; Sulfur Dioxide 1-Hr—highest 99th percentile 1-hour daily maximum concentration; Sulfur Dioxide 24-Hr—highest second maximum 24-hour concentration
Source: U.S. Environmental Protection Agency, Air Quality Monitoring Information, "Air Quality Statistics by City, 2020"

Denver, Colorado

Background

From almost anywhere in Denver, you can command a breathtaking view of the 14,000-foot Rocky Mountains. The early settlers of Denver, however, were not attracted to the city because of its vistas, but because of its gold.

In 1858, there were rumors that gold had been discovered in Denver's Cherry Creek. It wasn't until 1867, however, that its gold and silver can be said to have established Denver on its way to the sparkling, dramatic skyline, and steel towers of the modern city.

Today's Denver bears little resemblance to the dusty frontier village of the nineteenth century. The "Mile High City" has become a manufacturing, distribution, and transportation center that serves not only the western regions of the United States, but the entire nation. Denver is also home to many companies that are engaged in alternative fuel research and development.

Denver has been the host city of the Democratic National Convention twice, first in 1908 and again in 2008. The city also hosted the international G7 (now G8) summit in 1997. These events bolstered Denver's international reputation both on a political and socioeconomic level.

The massively renovated Colorado Convention Center—now 584,000 square feet—is a magnet for regional and national conferences and shows and is enhanced by the 5,000-seat Wells Fargo Theatre and new Light Rail Train Station. The renovated historic Denver Union Station operates as a mixed-use retail and multi-modal transportation hub. Another architecturally interesting building is the Jeppesen Terminal at Denver's airport, the largest international hub in the United States. The unique roof is made of heat- and light-reflecting tension fabric. The airport is huge, with 53 square miles and 6 million square feet of public space and 93 gates.

The city is also home to a lively cultural, recreational, and educational scene, including concerts at the Boettcher Concert Hall and seasonal drives through the Denver Mountain Park Circle Drive. Awesome skiing and hiking the Rockies is just 90 minutes away. Other area attractions include the Denver Museum of Nature and Science, Colorado History Museum, Denver Art Museum, and the recently built condominiums, Museum Residences. In 2020 one of the city's many neighborhoods changed its name from Stapleton (a KKK member) to Central Park.

The city's multibillion-dollar public transportation expansion plan, FasTracks, is under construction in metropolitan Denver. New bus service, and several light rail and commuter rail lines have been completed, as has a $200 million renovation to Denver Union Station. Completion of all phases of the project is anticipated in 2050.

The city also has its share of offbeat, distinctive places, including the hip Capitol Hill district, which offers small music venues and dank bars that appeal to University of Denver students. Sports fans have the Colorado Avalanche hockey team, the Denver Nuggets basketball team, the Colorado Rockies baseball team, and the Denver Broncos football team. In 2019, the Denver Bandits became part of the Women's National Football League and the first professional women's football team in the state.

In 2005, Denver became the first major city in the U.S. to legalize the private possession of marijuana. In 2012, Colorado Amendment 64 was signed into law by Governor John Hickenlooper, in 2014 Colorado became the first state to allow the sale of marijuana for recreational use, and in 2019, Denver became the first U.S. city to decriminalize psilocybin mushrooms.

The Denver Zoo is open year-round and houses nearly 4,000 animals representing 700 species, including the okapi, red-bellied lemur, Amur leopard, black rhino, and Siberian tiger. The zoo continues to implement its master modernization plan of habitats, having recently completed Predator Ridge, home to 14 African species of mammals, birds and reptiles, and an indoor tropical rain forest.

The University of Denver, Community College of Denver, Metropolitan State College, and the University of Colorado at Denver are only a few of the many excellent educational opportunities available in the city.

Denver's invigorating climate matches much of the central Rocky Mountain region, without the frigidly cold mornings of the higher elevations during winter, or the hot afternoons of summer at lower altitudes. Extreme cold and heat are generally short-lived. Low relative humidity, light precipitation, and abundant sunshine characterize Denver's weather. Spring is the cloudiest, wettest, and windiest season, while autumn is the most pleasant. Air pollution remains challenging.

Rankings

General Rankings

- *US News & World Report* conducted a survey of more than 3,600 people and analyzed the 150 largest metropolitan areas to determine what matters most when selecting the next place to live. Denver ranked #14 out of the top 25 as having the best combination of desirable factors. Criteria: cost of living; quality of life and education; net migration; job market; desirability; and other factors. *realestate.usnews.com, "The 25 Best Places to Live in the U.S. in 2021-2022," July 13, 2021*
- The Denver metro area was identified as one of America's fastest-growing areas in terms of population and business growth by *MagnifyMoney.* The area ranked #6 out of 35. The 100 most populous metro areas in the U.S. were evaluated on their change from 2011 to 2016 in the following categories: people and housing; workforce and employment opportunities; growing industry. *www.businessinsider.com, "The 35 Cities in the US with the Biggest Influx of People, the Most Work Opportunities, and the Hottest Business Growth," August 12, 2018*

Business/Finance Rankings

- According to *Business Insider*, the Denver metro area is a prime place to run a startup or move an existing business to. The area ranked #11. More than 300 metro areas were analyzed for factors that were of top concern to new business owners. Data was based on the 2019 U.S. Census Bureau American Community Survey, statistics from the CDC, Bureau of Labor Statistics employment report, and University of Chicago analysis. Criteria: business formations; percentage of vaccinated population; percentage of households with internet subscriptions; median household income; and share of work that can be done from home. *www.businessinsider.com, "The 20 Best Cities for Starting a Business in 2022 Include Baltimore, Boulder, and Boston," January 5, 2022*
- 24/7 Wall Street used metro data from the Bureau of Labor Statistics' Occupational Employment database to identify the cities with the highest percentage of those employed in jobs requiring knowledge in the science, technology, engineering, and math (STEM) fields as well as average wages for STEM jobs. The Denver metro area was #15. *247wallst.com, "15 Cities with the Most High-Tech Jobs," January 11, 2020*
- The Brookings Institution ranked the nation's largest cities based on income inequality. Denver was ranked #29 (#1 = greatest inequality). Criteria: the "95/20 ratio," a figure representing the income at which a household earns more than 95 percent of all other households, divided by the income at which a household earns more than only 20 percent of all other households. *Brookings Institution, "Household Income Inequality, Largest Cities of 97 Large U.S. Metro Areas, 2014-2016," February 5, 2018*
- The Brookings Institution ranked the 100 largest metro areas in the U.S. based on income inequality. Denver was ranked #59 (#1 = greatest inequality). Criteria: the "95/20 ratio," a figure representing the income at which a household earns more than 95 percent of all other households, divided by the income at which a household earns more than only 20 percent of all other households. *Brookings Institution, "Household Income Inequality, 100 Largest U.S. Metro Areas, 2014-2016," February 5, 2018*
- Payscale.com ranked the 32 largest metro areas in terms of wage growth. The Denver metro area ranked #17. Criteria: private-sector and education professional wage growth between the 4th quarter of 2019 and the 4th quarter of 2020. *PayScale, "Wage Trends by Metro Area-4th Quarter," January 11, 2021*
- The Denver metro area was identified as one of the most debt-ridden places in America by the finance site Credit.com. The metro area was ranked #10. Criteria: residents' average credit card debt as well as median income. *Credit.com, "25 Cities With the Most Credit Card Debt," February 28, 2018*
- Denver was identified as one of the unhappiest cities to work in by CareerBliss.com, an online community for career advancement. The city ranked #1 out of 5. Criteria: an employee's relationship with his or her boss and co-workers; general work environment; compensation; opportunities for advancement; company culture and job reputation; and resources. *Businesswire.com, "CareerBliss Unhappiest Cities to Work 2019," February 12, 2019*
- The Denver metro area appeared on the Milken Institute "2021 Best Performing Cities" list. Rank: #11 out of 200 large metro areas (population over 250,000). Criteria: job growth; wage and salary growth; high-tech output growth; housing affordability; household broadband access. *Milken Institute, "Best-Performing Cities 2021," February 16, 2021*

- *Forbes* ranked the 200 most populous metro areas to determine the nation's "Best Places for Business and Careers." The Denver metro area was ranked #4. Criteria: costs (business and living); job growth (past and projected); income growth; quality of life; educational attainment (college and high school); projected economic growth; cultural and leisure opportunities; workplace tolerance laws; net migration patterns. *Forbes, "The Best Places for Business and Careers 2019: Seattle Still On Top," October 30, 2019*

Dating/Romance Rankings

- *Apartment List* conducted its annual survey of renters for cities that have the best opportunities for dating. More than 11,000 single respondents rated their current city or neighborhood for opportunities to date. Denver ranked #7 out of 86 where single residents were very satisfied or somewhat satisfied, making it among the ten best areas for dating opportunities. Other criteria analyzed included gender and education levels of renters. *Apartment List, "The Best & Worst Metros for Dating 2020," February 4, 2020*
- Denver was selected as one of America's best cities for singles by the readers of *Travel + Leisure* in their annual "America's Favorite Cities" survey. Criteria included good-looking locals, cool shopping, an active bar scene and hipster-magnet coffee bars. *Travel + Leisure, "Best Cities in America for Singles," July 21, 2017*

Education Rankings

- Personal finance website *WalletHub* analyzed the 150 largest U.S. metropolitan statistical areas to determine where the most educated Americans are putting their degrees to work. Criteria: education levels; percentage of workers with degrees; education quality and attainment gap; public school quality rankings; quality and enrollment of each metro area's universities. Denver was ranked #14 (#1 = most educated city). *www.WalletHub.com, "Most & Least Educated Cities in America," July 19, 2021*
- Denver was selected as one of America's most literate cities. The city ranked #8 out of the 84 largest U.S. cities. Criteria: number of booksellers; library resources; Internet resources; educational attainment; periodical publishing resources; newspaper circulation. *Central Connecticut State University, "America's Most Literate Cities, 2018," February 2019*

Environmental Rankings

- Niche compiled a list of the nation's snowiest cities, based on the National Oceanic and Atmospheric Administration's 30-year average snowfall data. Among cities with a population of at least 50,000, Denver ranked #25. *Niche.com, Top 25 Snowiest Cities in America, December 10, 2018*
- The U.S. Environmental Protection Agency (EPA) released its list of U.S. metropolitan areas with the most ENERGY STAR certified buildings in 2020. The Denver metro area was ranked #10 out of 25. *U.S. Environmental Protection Agency, "2021 Energy Star Top Cities," June 15, 2021*
- Denver was highlighted as one of the 25 most ozone-polluted metro areas in the U.S. during 2017 through 2019. The area ranked #8. *American Lung Association, "State of the Air 2021," April 21, 2021*

Food/Drink Rankings

- The U.S. Chamber of Commerce Foundation conducted an in-depth study on local food truck regulations, surveyed 288 food truck owners, and ranked 20 major American cities based on how friendly they are for operating a food truck. The compiled index assessed the following: procedures for obtaining permits and licenses; complying with restrictions; and financial obligations associated with operating a food truck. Denver ranked #2 overall (1 being the best). *www.foodtrucknation.us, "Food Truck Nation," March 20, 2018*

Health/Fitness Rankings

- For each of the 100 largest cities in the United States, the American Fitness Index®, published by the American College of Sports Medicine and the Anthem Foundation, evaluated community infrastructure and 34 health behaviors including preventive health, levels of chronic disease conditions, food insecurity, sleep quality, pedestrian safety, air quality, and community resources that support physical activity. Denver ranked #4 for "community fitness." *americanfitnessindex.org, "2021 ACSM American Fitness Index Summary Report," July 13, 2021*
- The Denver metro area was identified as one of the worst cities for bed bugs in America by pest control company Orkin. The area ranked #17 out of 50 based on the number of bed bug treatments Orkin performed from December 2020 to November 2021. *Orkin, "Chicago Takes Another Top Spot for Pests, This Time Ranking #1 On Orkin's Bed Bug Cities List," January 10, 2022*

- Denver was identified as a "2021 Spring Allergy Capital." The area ranked #98 out of 100. Three groups of factors were used to identify the most challenging cities for people with allergies during the spring season: annual spring pollen levels; over the counter medicine use; number of board-certified allergy specialists. *Asthma and Allergy Foundation of America, "Spring Allergy Capitals 2021," February 23, 2021*
- Denver was identified as a "2021 Fall Allergy Capital." The area ranked #91 out of 100. Three groups of factors were used to identify the most challenging cities for people with allergies during the fall season: annual fall pollen levels; over the counter medicine use; number of board-certified allergy specialists. *Asthma and Allergy Foundation of America, "Fall Allergy Capitals 2021," February 23, 2021*
- Denver was identified as a "2021 Asthma Capital." The area ranked #86 out of the nation's 100 largest metropolitan areas. Criteria: estimated asthma prevalence; asthma-related mortality; and ER visits due to asthma. Risk factors analyzed but not factored in the rankings: annual pollen score; annual air quality; public smoking laws; number of board-certified asthma specialists; rescue medication use; controller medication use; uninsured rate; poverty rate. *Asthma and Allergy Foundation of America, "Asthma Capitals 2021: The Most Challenging Places to Live With Asthma," May 5, 2021*

Pet Rankings

- Denver appeared on *The Dogington Post* site as one of the top cities for dog lovers, ranking #1 out of 15. The real estate marketplace, Zillow® and Rover, the largest pet sitter and dog walker network, introduced a new list of "Top Emerging Dog-Friendly Cities" for 2021. Criteria: number of new dog accounts on the Rover platform; and rentals and listings that mention features that attract dog owners (fenced-in yards, dog houses, dog door or proximity to a dog park). *www.dogingtonpost.com, "15 Cities Emerging as Dog-Friendliest in 2021," May 11, 2021*

Real Estate Rankings

- *WalletHub* compared the most populated U.S. cities to determine which had the best markets for real estate agents. Denver ranked #5 where demand was high and pay was the best. Criteria: sales per agent; annual median wage for real-estate agents; monthly average starting salary for real estate agents; real estate job density and competition; unemployment rate; home turnover rate; housing-market health index; and other relevant metrics. *www.WalletHub.com, "2021 Best Places to Be a Real Estate Agent," May 12, 2021*
- According to Penske Truck Rental, the Denver metro area was named the #3 moving destination in 2020, based on one-way consumer truck rental reservations made through Penske's website, rental locations, and reservations call center. *gopenske.com/blog, "Penske Truck Rental's 2020 Top Moving Destinations," May 3, 2021*
- The Denver metro area was identified as one of the 20 least affordable housing markets in the U.S. in 2021. The area ranked #171 out of 183 markets. Criteria: qualification for a mortgage loan with a 10 percent down payment on a typical home. *National Association of Realtors®, Qualifying Income Based on Sales Price of Existing Single-Family Homes for Metropolitan Areas, 2021*
- Denver was ranked #158 out of 237 metro areas in terms of housing affordability in 2021 by the National Association of Home Builders (#1 = most affordable). Criteria: the share of homes sold in that area affordable to a family earning the local median income, based on standard mortgage underwriting criteria. *National Association of Home Builders®, NAHB-Wells Fargo Housing Opportunity Index, 4th Quarter 2021*

Safety Rankings

- Allstate ranked the 200 largest cities in America in terms of driver safety. Denver ranked #83. Criteria: internal property damage claims over a two-year period from January 2016 to December 2017. The report helps increase the importance of safety and awareness behind the wheel. *Allstate, "Allstate America's Best Drivers Report, 2019" June 24, 2019*
- The National Insurance Crime Bureau ranked 390 metro areas in the U.S. in terms of per capita rates of vehicle theft. The Denver metro area ranked #3 (#1 = highest rate). Criteria: number of vehicle theft offenses per 100,000 inhabitants in 2020. *National Insurance Crime Bureau, "Hot Spots 2020," August 31, 2021*

Seniors/Retirement Rankings

- From its Best Cities for Successful Aging indexes, the Milken Institute generated rankings for metropolitan areas, weighing data in nine categories—health care, wellness, living arrangements, transportation and convenience, financial characteristics, education, employment, community engagement, and overall livability. The Denver metro area was ranked #12 overall in the large metro area category. *Milken Institute, "Best Cities for Successful Aging, 2017" March 14, 2017*

Sports/Recreation Rankings

- Denver was chosen as one of America's best cities for bicycling. The city ranked #14 out of 50. Criteria: cycling infrastructure that is safe and friendly for all ages; energy and bike culture. The editors evaluated cities with populations of 100,000 or more. *Bicycling, "The 50 Best Bike Cities in America," October 10, 2018*

Transportation Rankings

- According to the INRIX "2021 Global Traffic Scorecard," Denver was identified as one of the most congested metro areas in the U.S. The area ranked #15 out of 25. Criteria: average annual time spent in traffic and average cost of congestion per motorist. *Inrix.com, "Americans Lost 3.4 Billion Hours Due to Congestion in 2021, 42% Below Pre-COVID," December 7, 2021*

Women/Minorities Rankings

- The *Houston Chronicle* listed the Denver metro area as #3 in top places for young Latinos to live in the U.S. Research was largely based on housing and occupational data from the largest metropolitan areas performed by *Forbes* and NBC Universo. Criteria: percentage of 18-34 year-olds; Latino college grad rates; and diversity. *blog.chron.com, "The 15 Best Big Cities for Latino Millenials," January 26, 2016*
- Personal finance website *WalletHub* compared more than 180 U.S. cities across two key dimensions, "Hispanic Business-Friendliness" and "Hispanic Purchasing Power," to arrive at the most favorable conditions for Hispanic entrepreneurs. Denver was ranked #41 out of 182. Criteria includes: share of Hispanic-Owned Businesses; Hispanic entrepreneurship rate to median annual income of Hispanics; Small Business-Friendliness score; cost of living; and number of Hispanics with at least a bachelor's degree. *WalletHub.com, "2019's Best Cities for Hispanic Entrepreneurs," May 1, 2019*

Miscellaneous Rankings

- The watchdog site, Charity Navigator, conducted a study of charities in major markets both to analyze statistical differences in their financial, accountability, and transparency practices and to track year-to-year variations in individual philanthropic communities. The Denver metro area was ranked #22 among the 30 metro markets in the rating category of Overall Score. *www.charitynavigator.org, "2017 Metro Market Study," May 1, 2017*
- *WalletHub* compared the 150 most populated U.S. cities to determine their operating efficiency. A "Quality of City Services" score was constructed for each city and then divided by the total budget per capita to reveal which were managed the best. Denver ranked #130. Criteria: financial stability; economy; education; safety; health; infrastructure and pollution. *www.WalletHub.com, "2021's Best- & Worst-Run Cities in America," June 22, 2021*
- Denver was selected as one of "America's Friendliest Cities." The city ranked #20 in the "Friendliest" category. Respondents to an online survey were asked to rate 38 top urban destinations in the United States as to general friendliness, as well as manners, politeness and warm disposition. *Travel + Leisure, "America's Friendliest Cities," October 20, 2017*
- The National Alliance to End Homelessness listed the 25 most populous metro areas with the highest rate of homelessness. The Denver metro area had a high rate of homelessness. Criteria: number of homeless people per 10,000 population in 2016. *National Alliance to End Homelessness, "Homelessness in the 25 Most Populous U.S. Metro Areas," September 1, 2017*

Business Environment

DEMOGRAPHICS

Population Growth

Area	1990 Census	2000 Census	2010 Census	2020* Estimate	Population Growth (%) 1990-2020	Population Growth (%) 2010-2020
City	467,153	554,636	600,158	715,878	53.2	19.3
MSA[1]	1,666,935	2,179,296	2,543,482	2,928,437	75.7	15.1
U.S.	248,709,873	281,421,906	308,745,538	326,569,308	31.3	5.8

Note: (1) Figures cover the Denver-Aurora-Lakewood, CO Metropolitan Statistical Area; (*) 2016-2020 5-year estimated population
Source: U.S. Census Bureau, 1990 Census, Census 2000, Census 2010, 2016-2020 American Community Survey 5-Year Estimates

Household Size

Area	Persons in Household (%)							Average Household Size
	One	Two	Three	Four	Five	Six	Seven or More	
City	38.4	33.1	11.9	9.6	4.2	1.6	1.2	2.40
MSA[1]	28.4	34.2	15.0	13.3	5.6	2.2	1.3	2.60
U.S.	28.0	33.9	15.5	12.9	6.0	2.3	1.4	2.60

Note: (1) Figures cover the Denver-Aurora-Lakewood, CO Metropolitan Statistical Area
Source: U.S. Census Bureau, 2016-2020 American Community Survey 5-Year Estimates

Race

Area	White Alone[2] (%)	Black Alone[2] (%)	Asian Alone[2] (%)	AIAN[3] Alone[2] (%)	NHOPI[4] Alone[2] (%)	Other Race Alone[2] (%)	Two or More Races (%)
City	72.2	9.2	3.6	0.8	0.2	6.9	7.1
MSA[1]	78.0	5.7	4.3	0.7	0.1	4.8	6.3
U.S.	70.4	12.6	5.6	0.8	0.2	5.1	5.2

Note: (1) Figures cover the Denver-Aurora-Lakewood, CO Metropolitan Statistical Area; (2) Alone is defined as not being in combination with one or more other races; (3) American Indian and Alaska Native; (4) Native Hawaiian and Other Pacific Islander
Source: U.S. Census Bureau, 2016-2020 American Community Survey 5-Year Estimates

Hispanic or Latino Origin

Area	Total (%)	Mexican (%)	Puerto Rican (%)	Cuban (%)	Other (%)
City	29.5	22.9	0.6	0.2	5.8
MSA[1]	23.1	17.4	0.6	0.2	4.9
U.S.	18.2	11.2	1.7	0.7	4.5

Note: Persons of Hispanic or Latino origin can be of any race; (1) Figures cover the Denver-Aurora-Lakewood, CO Metropolitan Statistical Area
Source: U.S. Census Bureau, 2016-2020 American Community Survey 5-Year Estimates

Ancestry

Area	German	Irish	English	American	Italian	Polish	French[2]	Scottish	Dutch
City	13.8	10.1	8.4	2.8	4.7	2.7	2.2	2.0	1.2
MSA[1]	17.3	10.7	9.9	3.5	5.0	2.4	2.5	2.3	1.5
U.S.	13.0	9.7	7.7	5.9	5.1	2.7	2.3	1.6	1.1

Note: Figures are the percentage of the total population reporting a particular ancestry. The nine most commonly reported ancestries in the U.S. are shown. Figures include multiple ancestries (e.g. if a person reported being Irish and Italian, they were included in both columns); (1) Figures cover the Denver-Aurora-Lakewood, CO Metropolitan Statistical Area; (2) Excludes Basque
Source: U.S. Census Bureau, 2016-2020 American Community Survey 5-Year Estimates

Foreign-born Population

Area	Percent of Population Born in								
	Any Foreign Country	Asia	Mexico	Europe	Caribbean	Central America[2]	South America	Africa	Canada
City	14.0	2.9	6.8	1.4	0.2	0.6	0.6	1.2	0.3
MSA[1]	11.8	3.3	4.7	1.3	0.1	0.5	0.5	1.0	0.3
U.S.	13.5	4.2	3.3	1.5	1.3	1.1	1.0	0.7	0.3

Note: (1) Figures cover the Denver-Aurora-Lakewood, CO Metropolitan Statistical Area; (2) Excludes Mexico.
Source: U.S. Census Bureau, 2016-2020 American Community Survey 5-Year Estimates

Marital Status

Area	Never Married	Now Married[2]	Separated	Widowed	Divorced
City	44.4	37.8	1.8	3.9	12.1
MSA[1]	34.0	48.7	1.4	4.0	11.8
U.S.	33.5	48.1	1.8	5.7	10.8

Note: Figures are percentages and cover the population 15 years of age and older; (1) Figures cover the Denver-Aurora-Lakewood, CO Metropolitan Statistical Area; (2) Excludes separated
Source: U.S. Census Bureau, 2016-2020 American Community Survey 5-Year Estimates

Disability by Age

Area	All Ages	Under 18 Years Old	18 to 64 Years Old	65 Years and Over
City	9.7	3.4	7.6	33.0
MSA[1]	9.7	3.2	7.7	30.6
U.S.	12.7	4.3	10.3	34.0

Note: Figures show percent of the civilian noninstitutionalized population that reported having a disability. Disability status is determined from six types of difficulty: vision, hearing, cognitive, ambulatory, self-care, and independent living. For children under 5 years old, hearing and vision difficulty are used to determine disability status. For children between the ages of 5 and 14, disability status is determined from hearing, vision, cognitive, ambulatory, and self-care difficulties. For people aged 15 years and older, they are considered to have a disability if they have difficulty with any one of the six difficulty types; Note: (1) Figures cover the Denver-Aurora-Lakewood, CO Metropolitan Statistical Area
Source: U.S. Census Bureau, 2016-2020 American Community Survey 5-Year Estimates

Age

Area	Percent of Population									Median Age
	Under Age 5	Age 5–19	Age 20–34	Age 35–44	Age 45–54	Age 55–64	Age 65–74	Age 75–84	Age 85+	
City	5.9	15.5	29.4	16.1	11.6	9.8	7.2	3.1	1.5	34.6
MSA[1]	5.9	18.7	22.7	14.7	13.0	12.0	8.1	3.4	1.5	36.7
U.S.	6.0	19.1	20.6	12.7	12.7	12.9	9.4	4.7	2.0	38.2

Note: (1) Figures cover the Denver-Aurora-Lakewood, CO Metropolitan Statistical Area
Source: U.S. Census Bureau, 2016-2020 American Community Survey 5-Year Estimates

Gender

Area	Males	Females	Males per 100 Females
City	358,669	357,209	100.4
MSA[1]	1,464,957	1,463,480	100.1
U.S.	160,818,530	165,750,778	97.0

Note: (1) Figures cover the Denver-Aurora-Lakewood, CO Metropolitan Statistical Area
Source: U.S. Census Bureau, 2016-2020 American Community Survey 5-Year Estimates

Religious Groups by Family

Area	Catholic	Baptist	Non-Den.	Methodist[2]	Lutheran	LDS[3]	Pente-costal	Presby-terian[4]	Muslim[5]	Judaism
MSA[1]	16.1	3.0	4.6	1.7	2.1	2.4	1.2	1.6	0.6	0.6
U.S.	19.1	9.3	4.0	4.0	2.3	2.0	1.9	1.6	0.8	0.7

Note: Figures are the number of adherents as a percentage of the total population; (1) Figures cover the Denver-Aurora-Lakewood, CO Metropolitan Statistical Area; (2) Methodist/Pietist; (3) Latter Day Saints; (4) Reformed; (5) Figures are estimates
Source: Association of Statisticians of American Religious Bodies, 2010 U.S. Religion Census: Religious Congregations & Membership Study

Religious Groups by Tradition

Area	Catholic	Evangelical Protestant	Mainline Protestant	Other Tradition	Black Protestant	Orthodox
MSA[1]	16.1	11.1	4.5	4.6	0.4	0.3
U.S.	19.1	16.2	7.3	4.3	1.6	0.3

Note: Figures are the number of adherents as a percentage of the total population; (1) Figures cover the Denver-Aurora-Lakewood, CO Metropolitan Statistical Area
Source: Association of Statisticians of American Religious Bodies, 2010 U.S. Religion Census: Religious Congregations & Membership Study

ECONOMY

Gross Metropolitan Product

Area	2017	2018	2019	2020	Rank[2]
MSA[1]	211.6	225.3	235.8	246.9	18

Note: Figures are in billions of dollars; (1) Figures cover the Denver-Aurora-Lakewood, CO Metropolitan Statistical Area; (2) Rank is based on 2018 data and ranges from 1 to 381
Source: U.S. Conference of Mayors, U.S. Metro Economies: GMP & Employment 2018-2020, September 2019

Economic Growth

Area	2015-17 (%)	2018 (%)	2019 (%)	2020 (%)	Rank[2]
MSA[1]	2.6	3.7	3.0	1.9	89
U.S.	1.9	2.9	2.3	2.1	–

Note: Figures are real gross metropolitan product (GMP) growth rates and represent average annual percent change; (1) Figures cover the Denver-Aurora-Lakewood, CO Metropolitan Statistical Area; (2) Rank is based on 2017 2-year average annual percent change and ranges from 1 to 381
Source: U.S. Conference of Mayors, U.S. Metro Economies: GMP & Employment 2018-2020, September 2019

Metropolitan Area Exports

Area	2015	2016	2017	2018	2019	2020	Rank[2]
MSA[1]	3,909.5	3,649.3	3,954.7	4,544.3	4,555.6	4,604.4	57

Note: Figures are in millions of dollars; (1) Figures cover the Denver-Aurora-Lakewood, CO Metropolitan Statistical Area; (2) Rank is based on 2020 data and ranges from 1 to 389
Source: U.S. Department of Commerce, International Trade Administration, Office of Trade and Economic Analysis, Industry and Analysis, Exports by Metropolitan Area, data extracted March 4, 2022

Building Permits

Area	Single-Family			Multi-Family			Total		
	2019	2020	Pct. Chg.	2019	2020	Pct. Chg.	2019	2020	Pct. Chg.
City	2,257	1,167	-48.3	5,073	3,892	-23.3	7,330	5,059	-31.0
MSA[1]	11,081	11,234	1.4	8,227	8,498	3.3	19,308	19,732	2.2
U.S.	862,100	979,400	13.6	523,900	491,700	-6.1	1,386,000	1,471,100	6.1

Note: (1) Figures cover the Denver-Aurora-Lakewood, CO Metropolitan Statistical Area; Figures represent new, privately-owned housing units authorized (unadjusted data); All permit data are based on estimates with imputation
Source: U.S. Census Bureau, Manufacturing, Mining, and Construction Statistics, Building Permits, 2019, 2020

Bankruptcy Filings

Area	Business Filings			Nonbusiness Filings		
	2020	2021	% Chg.	2020	2021	% Chg.
Denver County	91	72	-20.9	1,029	764	-25.8
U.S.	21,655	14,347	-33.7	522,808	399,269	-23.6

Note: Business filings include Chapter 7, Chapter 9, Chapter 11, Chapter 12, Chapter 13, Chapter 15, and Section 304; Nonbusiness filings include Chapter 7, Chapter 11, and Chapter 13
Source: Administrative Office of the U.S. Courts, Business and Nonbusiness Bankruptcy, County Cases Commenced by Chapter of the Bankruptcy Code, During the 12-Month Period Ending December 31, 2020 and Business and Nonbusiness Bankruptcy, County Cases Commenced by Chapter of the Bankruptcy Code, During the 12-Month Period Ending December 31, 2021

Housing Vacancy Rates

Area	Gross Vacancy Rate[2] (%)			Year-Round Vacancy Rate[3] (%)			Rental Vacancy Rate[4] (%)			Homeowner Vacancy Rate[5] (%)		
	2019	2020	2021	2019	2020	2021	2019	2020	2021	2019	2020	2021
MSA[1]	7.5	5.8	6.5	7.0	5.1	5.3	4.7	4.8	4.6	1.0	0.5	1.0
U.S.	12.0	10.6	10.8	9.5	8.2	8.4	6.7	6.3	6.1	1.4	1.0	0.9

Note: (1) Figures cover the Denver-Aurora-Lakewood, CO Metropolitan Statistical Area; (2) The percentage of the total housing inventory that is vacant; (3) The percentage of the housing inventory (excluding seasonal units) that is year-round vacant; (4) The percentage of rental inventory that is vacant for rent; (5) The percentage of homeowner inventory that is vacant for sale
Source: U.S. Census Bureau, Housing Vacancies and Homeownership Annual Statistics: 2019, 2020, 2021

INCOME

Income

Area	Per Capita ($)	Median Household ($)	Average Household ($)
City	45,636	72,661	105,901
MSA[1]	43,427	83,289	110,927
U.S.	35,384	64,994	91,547

Note: (1) Figures cover the Denver-Aurora-Lakewood, CO Metropolitan Statistical Area
Source: U.S. Census Bureau, 2016-2020 American Community Survey 5-Year Estimates

Household Income Distribution

Area	Percent of Households Earning							
	Under $15,000	$15,000 -$24,999	$25,000 -$34,999	$35,000 -$49,999	$50,000 -$74,999	$75,000 -$99,999	$100,000 -$149,999	$150,000 and up
City	8.9	6.7	7.2	10.9	17.5	12.3	16.4	20.1
MSA[1]	6.2	5.4	6.3	10.1	16.9	13.5	19.6	21.8
U.S.	9.9	8.5	8.6	12.0	17.2	12.8	15.6	15.4

Note: (1) Figures cover the Denver-Aurora-Lakewood, CO Metropolitan Statistical Area
Source: U.S. Census Bureau, 2016-2020 American Community Survey 5-Year Estimates

Poverty Rate

Area	All Ages	Under 18 Years Old	18 to 64 Years Old	65 Years and Over
City	11.9	16.2	10.8	10.6
MSA[1]	8.3	10.3	7.8	7.1
U.S.	12.8	17.5	12.1	9.3

Note: Figures are percentage of people whose income during the past 12 months was below the poverty level; (1) Figures cover the Denver-Aurora-Lakewood, CO Metropolitan Statistical Area
Source: U.S. Census Bureau, 2016-2020 American Community Survey 5-Year Estimates

CITY FINANCES

City Government Finances

Component	2019 ($000)	2019 ($ per capita)
Total Revenues	4,079,180	5,789
Total Expenditures	3,542,595	5,028
Debt Outstanding	8,478,807	12,033
Cash and Securities[1]	6,842,843	9,711

Note: (1) Cash and security holdings of a government at the close of its fiscal year, including those of its dependent agencies, utilities, and liquor stores.
Source: U.S. Census Bureau, State & Local Government Finances 2019

City Government Revenue by Source

Source	2019 ($000)	2019 ($ per capita)	2019 (%)
General Revenue			
From Federal Government	24,964	35	0.6
From State Government	282,693	401	6.9
From Local Governments	52,961	75	1.3
Taxes			
Property	477,547	678	11.7
Sales and Gross Receipts	908,117	1,289	22.3
Personal Income	0	0	0.0
Corporate Income	0	0	0.0
Motor Vehicle License	30,654	44	0.8
Other Taxes	121,363	172	3.0
Current Charges	1,548,455	2,198	38.0
Liquor Store	0	0	0.0
Utility	294,780	418	7.2

Source: U.S. Census Bureau, State & Local Government Finances 2019

City Government Expenditures by Function

Function	2019 ($000)	2019 ($ per capita)	2019 (%)
General Direct Expenditures			
Air Transportation	712,254	1,010	20.1
Corrections	144,534	205	4.1
Education	0	0	0.0
Employment Security Administration	0	0	0.0
Financial Administration	80,823	114	2.3
Fire Protection	140,593	199	4.0
General Public Buildings	46,853	66	1.3
Governmental Administration, Other	99,124	140	2.8
Health	84,340	119	2.4
Highways	141,525	200	4.0
Hospitals	0	0	0.0
Housing and Community Development	156,479	222	4.4
Interest on General Debt	307,429	436	8.7
Judicial and Legal	84,442	119	2.4
Libraries	52,395	74	1.5
Parking	15,019	21	0.4
Parks and Recreation	354,710	503	10.0
Police Protection	256,597	364	7.2
Public Welfare	168,061	238	4.7
Sewerage	219,914	312	6.2
Solid Waste Management	13,042	18	0.4
Veterans' Services	0	0	0.0
Liquor Store	0	0	0.0
Utility	207,856	295	5.9

Source: U.S. Census Bureau, State & Local Government Finances 2019

EMPLOYMENT

Labor Force and Employment

Area	Civilian Labor Force			Workers Employed		
	Dec. 2020	Dec. 2021	% Chg.	Dec. 2020	Dec. 2021	% Chg.
City	428,037	436,110	1.9	394,814	416,130	5.4
MSA[1]	1,688,119	1,725,927	2.2	1,568,519	1,653,017	5.4
U.S.	160,017,000	161,696,000	1.0	149,613,000	155,732,000	4.1

Note: Data is not seasonally adjusted and covers workers 16 years of age and older; (1) Figures cover the Denver-Aurora-Lakewood, CO Metropolitan Statistical Area
Source: Bureau of Labor Statistics, Local Area Unemployment Statistics

Unemployment Rate

Area	2021											
	Jan.	Feb.	Mar.	Apr.	May	Jun.	Jul.	Aug.	Sep.	Oct.	Nov.	Dec.
City	7.7	7.3	7.1	7.0	6.4	6.7	6.6	5.9	5.2	5.0	4.8	4.6
MSA[1]	7.0	6.7	6.7	6.4	5.9	6.3	6.1	5.5	4.8	4.6	4.5	4.2
U.S.	6.8	6.6	6.2	5.7	5.5	6.1	5.7	5.3	4.6	4.3	3.9	3.7

Note: Data is not seasonally adjusted and covers workers 16 years of age and older; (1) Figures cover the Denver-Aurora-Lakewood, CO Metropolitan Statistical Area
Source: Bureau of Labor Statistics, Local Area Unemployment Statistics

Average Wages

Occupation	$/Hr.	Occupation	$/Hr.
Accountants and Auditors	42.42	Maintenance and Repair Workers	22.84
Automotive Mechanics	25.21	Marketing Managers	78.36
Bookkeepers	23.30	Network and Computer Systems Admin.	46.41
Carpenters	25.29	Nurses, Licensed Practical	27.98
Cashiers	15.03	Nurses, Registered	39.84
Computer Programmers	51.14	Nursing Assistants	17.45
Computer Systems Analysts	53.87	Office Clerks, General	23.49
Computer User Support Specialists	31.72	Physical Therapists	44.51
Construction Laborers	19.70	Physicians	118.01
Cooks, Restaurant	17.67	Plumbers, Pipefitters and Steamfitters	28.56
Customer Service Representatives	20.48	Police and Sheriff's Patrol Officers	42.33
Dentists	60.38	Postal Service Mail Carriers	26.13
Electricians	28.78	Real Estate Sales Agents	36.10
Engineers, Electrical	49.49	Retail Salespersons	17.22
Fast Food and Counter Workers	14.67	Sales Representatives, Technical/Scientific	53.64
Financial Managers	86.86	Secretaries, Exc. Legal/Medical/Executive	20.99
First-Line Supervisors of Office Workers	33.52	Security Guards	18.52
General and Operations Managers	66.83	Surgeons	135.07
Hairdressers/Cosmetologists	17.65	Teacher Assistants, Exc. Postsecondary*	16.83
Home Health and Personal Care Aides	15.58	Teachers, Secondary School, Exc. Sp. Ed.*	32.01
Janitors and Cleaners	16.38	Telemarketers	16.66
Landscaping/Groundskeeping Workers	19.22	Truck Drivers, Heavy/Tractor-Trailer	26.77
Lawyers	69.18	Truck Drivers, Light/Delivery Services	21.78
Maids and Housekeeping Cleaners	15.89	Waiters and Waitresses	16.59

Note: Wage data covers the Denver-Aurora-Lakewood, CO Metropolitan Statistical Area; (*) Hourly wages were calculated from annual wage data based on a 40 hour work week; n/a not available.
Source: Bureau of Labor Statistics, Metro Area Occupational Employment & Wage Estimates, May 2021

Employment by Industry

Sector	MSA[1]		U.S.
	Number of Employees	Percent of Total	Percent of Total
Construction, Mining, and Logging	107,900	7.0	5.3
Education and Health Services	192,700	12.4	16.0
Financial Activities	117,600	7.6	5.9
Government	200,600	12.9	14.9
Information	53,500	3.4	1.9
Leisure and Hospitality	156,700	10.1	9.8
Manufacturing	70,700	4.6	8.4
Other Services	59,200	3.8	3.7
Professional and Business Services	297,400	19.2	14.6
Retail Trade	141,800	9.1	10.7
Transportation, Warehousing, and Utilities	77,800	5.0	4.8
Wholesale Trade	75,500	4.9	3.8

Note: Figures are non-farm employment as of December 2021. Figures are not seasonally adjusted and include workers 16 years of age and older; (1) Figures cover the Denver-Aurora-Lakewood, CO Metropolitan Statistical Area
Source: Bureau of Labor Statistics, Current Employment Statistics, Employment, Hours, and Earnings

Employment by Occupation

Occupation Classification	City (%)	MSA[1] (%)	U.S. (%)
Management, Business, Science, and Arts	49.6	45.6	39.5
Natural Resources, Construction, and Maintenance	7.3	8.1	8.7
Production, Transportation, and Material Moving	8.1	9.5	13.1
Sales and Office	19.6	21.5	21.3
Service	15.5	15.3	17.4

Note: Figures cover employed civilians 16 years of age and older; (1) Figures cover the Denver-Aurora-Lakewood, CO Metropolitan Statistical Area
Source: U.S. Census Bureau, 2016-2020 American Community Survey 5-Year Estimates

Occupations with Greatest Projected Employment Growth: 2021 – 2023

Occupation[1]	2021 Employment	2023 Projected Employment	Numeric Employment Change	Percent Employment Change
Software Developers and Software Quality Assurance Analysts and Testers	62,100	66,810	4,710	7.6
Fast Food and Counter Workers	72,270	76,700	4,430	6.1
Cooks, Restaurant	30,360	34,250	3,890	12.8
Waiters and Waitresses	40,230	43,230	3,000	7.5
Retail Salespersons	77,680	80,550	2,870	3.7
Maids and Housekeeping Cleaners	22,930	25,680	2,750	12.0
Project Management Specialists and Business Operations Specialists, All Other	66,210	68,800	2,590	3.9
Home Health and Personal Care Aides	39,930	42,460	2,530	6.3
Stockers and Order Fillers	46,970	49,310	2,340	5.0
General and Operations Managers	37,390	39,420	2,030	5.4

Note: Projections cover Colorado; (1) Sorted by numeric employment change
Source: www.projectionscentral.com, State Occupational Projections, 2021–2023 Short-Term Projections

Fastest-Growing Occupations: 2021 – 2023

Occupation[1]	2021 Employment	2023 Projected Employment	Numeric Employment Change	Percent Employment Change
Motion Picture Projectionists	100	160	60	60.0
Rotary Drill Operators, Oil and Gas	240	340	100	41.7
Athletes and Sports Competitors	420	590	170	40.5
Roustabouts, Oil and Gas	1,780	2,490	710	39.9
Musicians and Singers	710	960	250	35.2
Fine Artists, Including Painters, Sculptors, and Illustrators	310	410	100	32.3
Actors	650	820	170	26.2
Service Unit Operators, Oil, Gas, and Mining	2,020	2,550	530	26.2
Dancers	320	400	80	25.0
Pump Operators, Except Wellhead Pumpers	200	250	50	25.0

Note: Projections cover Colorado; (1) Sorted by percent employment change and excludes occupations with numeric employment change less than 50
Source: www.projectionscentral.com, State Occupational Projections, 2021–2023 Short-Term Projections

TAXES

State Corporate Income Tax Rates

State	Tax Rate (%)	Income Brackets ($)	Num. of Brackets	Financial Institution Tax Rate (%)[a]	Federal Income Tax Ded.
Colorado	4.55	Flat rate	1	4.55	No

Note: Tax rates as of January 1, 2022; (a) Rates listed are the corporate income tax rate applied to financial institutions or excise taxes based on income. Some states have other taxes based upon the value of deposits or shares.
Source: Federation of Tax Administrators, State Corporate Income Tax Rates, January 1, 2022

State Individual Income Tax Rates

State	Tax Rate (%)	Income Brackets ($)	Personal Exemptions ($)			Standard Ded. ($)	
			Single	Married	Depend.	Single	Married
Colorado	4.55	Flat rate	(d)	(d)	(d)	12,950	25,900 (d)

Note: Tax rates as of January 1, 2022; Local- and county-level taxes are not included; Federal income tax is not deductible on state income tax returns; (d) These states use the personal exemption/standard deduction amounts provided in the federal Internal Revenue Code.
Source: Federation of Tax Administrators, State Individual Income Tax Rates, January 1, 2022

Various State Sales and Excise Tax Rates

State	State Sales Tax (%)	Gasoline[1] (¢/gal.)	Cigarette[2] ($/pack)	Spirits[3] ($/gal.)	Wine[4] ($/gal.)	Beer[5] ($/gal.)	Recreational Marijuana (%)
Colorado	2.9	22	1.94	2.28	0.32	0.08	(d)

Note: All tax rates as of January 1, 2022; (1) The American Petroleum Institute has developed a methodology for determining the average tax rate on a gallon of fuel. Rates may include any of the following: excise taxes, environmental fees, storage tank fees, other fees or taxes, general sales tax, and local taxes; (2) The federal excise tax of $1.0066 per pack and local taxes are not included; (3) Rates are those applicable to off-premise sales of 40% alcohol by volume (a.b.v.) distilled spirits in 750ml containers. Local excise taxes are excluded; (4) Rates are those applicable to off-premise sales of 11% a.b.v. non-carbonated wine in 750ml containers; (5) Rates are those applicable to off-premise sales of 4.7% a.b.v. beer in 12 ounce containers; (d) 15% excise tax (levied on wholesale at average market rate); 15% excise tax (retail price)
Source: Tax Foundation, 2022 Facts & Figures: How Does Your State Compare?

State Business Tax Climate Index Rankings

State	Overall Rank	Corporate Tax Rank	Individual Income Tax Rank	Sales Tax Rank	Property Tax Rank	Unemployment Insurance Tax Rank
Colorado	20	6	14	38	34	41

Note: The index is a measure of how each state's tax laws affect economic performance. The lower the rank, the more favorable a state's tax system is for business. States without a given tax are given a ranking of 1. The scores/rankings for the District of Columbia do not affect other states. The 2022 index represents the tax climate as of July 1, 2021.
Source: Tax Foundation, State Business Tax Climate Index 2022

TRANSPORTATION

Means of Transportation to Work

Area	Car/Truck/Van		Public Transportation			Bicycle	Walked	Other Means	Worked at Home
	Drove Alone	Car-pooled	Bus	Subway	Railroad				
City	66.1	7.3	4.1	0.8	0.5	2.1	4.7	2.2	12.4
MSA[1]	72.7	7.9	2.5	0.5	0.3	0.8	2.2	1.6	11.4
U.S.	74.9	8.9	2.2	1.7	0.5	0.5	2.6	1.4	7.3

Note: Figures are percentages and cover workers 16 years of age and older; (1) Figures cover the Denver-Aurora-Lakewood, CO Metropolitan Statistical Area
Source: U.S. Census Bureau, 2016-2020 American Community Survey 5-Year Estimates

Travel Time to Work

Area	Less Than 10 Minutes	10 to 19 Minutes	20 to 29 Minutes	30 to 44 Minutes	45 to 59 Minutes	60 to 89 Minutes	90 Minutes or More
City	7.7	28.8	24.7	25.8	7.6	3.9	1.5
MSA[1]	8.2	24.9	23.0	26.5	9.9	5.7	1.8
U.S.	12.3	28.4	20.9	20.9	8.3	6.4	2.9

Note: Note: Figures are percentages and include workers 16 years old and over; (1) Figures cover the Denver-Aurora-Lakewood, CO Metropolitan Statistical Area
Source: U.S. Census Bureau, 2016-2020 American Community Survey 5-Year Estimates

Key Congestion Measures

Measure	1990	2000	2010	2015	2020
Annual Hours of Delay, Total (000)	21,111	58,062	87,604	103,318	46,181
Annual Hours of Delay, Per Auto Commuter	23	44	50	58	26
Annual Congestion Cost, Per Auto Commuter ($)	437	903	1,083	1,180	545

Note: Covers the Denver-Aurora CO urban area
Source: Texas A&M Transportation Institute, 2021 Urban Mobility Report

Freeway Travel Time Index

Measure	1985	1990	1995	2000	2005	2010	2015	2020
Urban Area Index[1]	1.13	1.14	1.19	1.27	1.32	1.29	1.31	1.09
Urban Area Rank[1,2]	19	26	23	10	8	13	15	40

Note: Freeway Travel Time Index—the ratio of travel time in the peak period to the travel time at free-flow conditions. For example, a value of 1.30 indicates a 20-minute free-flow trip takes 26 minutes in the peak (20 minutes x 1.30 = 26 minutes); (1) Covers the Denver-Aurora CO urban area; (2) Rank is based on 101 larger urban areas (#1 = highest travel time index)
Source: Texas A&M Transportation Institute, 2021 Urban Mobility Report

Public Transportation

Agency Name / Mode of Transportation	Vehicles Operated in Maximum Service[1]	Annual Unlinked Passenger Trips[2] (in thous.)	Annual Passenger Miles[3] (in thous.)
Denver Regional Transportation District (RTD)			
Bus (directly operated)	472	23,818.2	106,209.8
Bus (purchased transportation)	342	12,540.5	50,971.5
Commuter Rail (directly operated)	8	173.8	1,496.7
Commuter Rail (purchased transportation)	44	4,780.4	55,053.9
Demand Response (purchased transportation)	409	537.1	4,100.4
Light Rail (directly operated)	156	10,464.7	72,911.0

Note: (1) Number of revenue vehicles operated by the given mode and type of service to meet the annual maximum service requirement. This is the revenue vehicle count during the peak season of the year; on the week and day that maximum service is provided. Vehicles operated in maximum service (VOMS) exclude atypical days and one-time special events; (2) Number of passengers who boarded public transportation vehicles. Passengers are counted each time they board a vehicle no matter how many vehicles they use to travel from their origin to their destination. (3) Sum of the distances ridden by all passengers during the entire fiscal year.
Source: Federal Transit Administration, National Transit Database, 2020

Air Transportation

Airport Name and Code / Type of Service	Passenger Airlines[1]	Passenger Enplanements	Freight Carriers[2]	Freight (lbs)
Denver International (DEN)				
Domestic service (U.S. carriers - 2021)	22	27,776,445	15	266,792,807
International service (U.S. carriers - 2020)	7	311,343	3	1,986,377

Note: (1) Includes all U.S.-based major, minor and commuter airlines that carried at least one passenger during the year; (2) Includes all U.S.-based airlines and freight carriers that transported at least one pound of freight during the year.
Source: Bureau of Transportation Statistics, The Intermodal Transportation Database, Air Carriers: T-100 Domestic Market (U.S. Carriers), 2021; Bureau of Transportation Statistics, The Intermodal Transportation Database, Air Carriers: T-100 International Market (U.S. Carriers), 2020

BUSINESSES

Major Business Headquarters

Company Name	Industry	Rankings	
		Fortune[1]	Forbes[2]
DCP Midstream	Pipelines	442	-
DaVita	Health Care, Medical Facilities	271	-
Leprino Foods	Food, Drink & Tobacco	-	130
Molson Coors Beverage	Beverages	314	-
Optiv Security	Business Services & Supplies	-	183
Ovintiv	Mining, Crude-Oil Production	458	-

Note: (1) Companies that produce a 10-K are ranked 1 to 500 based on 2020 revenue; (2) All private companies with at least $2 billion in annual revenue through the end of their most current fiscal year are ranked 1 to 225; companies listed are headquartered in the city; dashes indicate no ranking
Source: Fortune, "Fortune 500," 2021; Forbes, "America's Largest Private Companies," 2021

Fastest-Growing Businesses

According to *Inc.*, Denver is home to 12 of America's 500 fastest-growing private companies: **Brumate** (#71); **CyberGRX** (#97); **Eon** (#128); **Edison Interactive Holdings** (#144); **Maxwell Financial Labs** (#154); **Willow Industries** (#205); **The Dingman Group** (#212); **Raincatcher** (#376); **Raincatcher** (#376); **Complement** (#382); **RxRevu** (#384); **Point Solutions Group** (#486). Criteria: must be an independent, privately-held, for-profit, U.S. corporation, proprietorship or partnership as of December 31, 2020; revenues must be at least $100,000 in 2017 and $2 million in 2020; must have four-year operating/sales history. *Inc., "America's 500 Fastest-Growing Private Companies," 2021*

According to Deloitte, Denver is home to four of North America's 500 fastest-growing high-technology companies: **Maxwell** (#65); **Red Canary** (#252); **Evolve** (#276); **AdCellerant** (#472). Companies are ranked by percentage growth in revenue over a four-year period. Criteria for inclusion: company must be headquartered within North America; must own proprietary intellectual property or technology that is sold to customers in products that contributes to a significant portion of the company's operating revenue; must have been in business for a minumum of four years with 2017 operating revenues of at least $50,000 USD/CD and 2020 operating revenues of at least $5 million USD/CD. *Deloitte, 2021 Technology Fast 500™*

Living Environment

COST OF LIVING

Cost of Living Index

Composite Index	Groceries	Housing	Utilities	Trans-portation	Health Care	Misc. Goods/ Services
113.5	95.0	138.3	82.2	111.4	102.4	111.4

Note: The Cost of Living Index measures regional differences in the cost of consumer goods and services, excluding taxes and non-consumer expenditures, for professional and managerial households in the top income quintile. It is based on more than 50,000 prices covering almost 60 different items for which prices are collected three times a year by chambers of commerce, economic development organizations or university applied economic centers in each participating urban area. The numbers shown should be read as a percentage above or below the national average of 100. For example, a value of 115.4 in the groceries column indicates that grocery prices are 15.4% higher than the national average. Small differences in the index numbers should not be interpreted as significant; Figures cover the Denver CO urban area.
Source: The Council for Community and Economic Research, Cost of Living Index, 2021

Grocery Prices

Area[1]	T-Bone Steak ($/pound)	Frying Chicken ($/pound)	Whole Milk ($/half gal.)	Eggs ($/dozen)	Orange Juice ($/64 oz.)	Coffee ($/11.5 oz.)
City[2]	12.86	1.24	1.79	1.49	3.58	4.10
Avg.	12.82	1.40	2.22	1.57	3.59	4.30
Min.	8.91	0.91	1.29	0.75	2.87	3.02
Max.	21.35	2.69	3.92	3.86	5.49	8.11

*Note: (1) Values for the local area are compared with the average, minimum and maximum values for all 285 areas in the Cost of Living Index; (2) Figures cover the Denver CO urban area; **T-Bone Steak** (price per pound); **Frying Chicken** (price per pound, whole fryer); **Whole Milk** (half gallon carton); **Eggs** (price per dozen, Grade A, large); **Orange Juice** (64 oz. Tropicana or Florida Natural); **Coffee** (11.5 oz. can, vacuum-packed, Maxwell House, Hills Bros, or Folgers).*
Source: The Council for Community and Economic Research, Cost of Living Index, 2021

Housing and Utility Costs

Area[1]	New Home Price ($)	Apartment Rent ($/month)	All Electric ($/month)	Part Electric ($/month)	Other Energy ($/month)	Telephone ($/month)
City[2]	575,410	1,619	-	60.85	57.04	186.45
Avg.	398,393	1,217	171.38	100.83	69.67	187.75
Min.	212,799	534	96.71	31.56	27.15	173.01
Max.	2,354,006	4,438	369.53	277.33	303.87	206.73

*Note: (1) Values for the local area are compared with the average, minimum and maximum values for all 285 areas in the Cost of Living Index; (2) Figures cover the Denver CO urban area; **New Home Price** (2,400 sf living area, 8,000 sf lot, in urban area with full utilities); **Apartment Rent** (950 sf 2 bedroom/1.5 or 2 bath, unfurnished, excluding all utilities except water); **All Electric** (average monthly cost for an all-electric home); **Part Electric** (average monthly cost for a part-electric home); **Other Energy** (average monthly cost for natural gas, fuel oil, coal, wood, and any other forms of energy except electricity); **Telephone** (price includes the base monthly rate plus taxes and fees for three lines of mobile phone service).*
Source: The Council for Community and Economic Research, Cost of Living Index, 2021

Health Care, Transportation, and Other Costs

Area[1]	Doctor ($/visit)	Dentist ($/visit)	Optometrist ($/visit)	Gasoline ($/gallon)	Beauty Salon ($/visit)	Men's Shirt ($)
City[2]	113.95	111.41	110.56	2.94	44.79	36.47
Avg.	118.16	101.04	109.44	2.71	40.63	30.77
Min.	35.04	55.56	51.17	2.17	18.59	11.32
Max.	231.10	165.12	256.81	4.11	85.33	63.03

*Note: (1) Values for the local area are compared with the average, minimum and maximum values for all 285 areas in the Cost of Living Index; (2) Figures cover the Denver CO urban area; **Doctor** (general practitioners routine exam of an established patient); **Dentist** (adult teeth cleaning and periodic oral examination); **Optometrist** (full vision eye exam for established adult patient); **Gasoline** (one gallon regular unleaded, national brand, including all taxes, cash price at self-service pump if available); **Beauty Salon** (woman's shampoo, trim, and blow-dry); **Men's Shirt** (cotton/polyester dress shirt, pinpoint weave, long sleeves).*
Source: The Council for Community and Economic Research, Cost of Living Index, 2021

HOUSING

Homeownership Rate

Area	2013 (%)	2014 (%)	2015 (%)	2016 (%)	2017 (%)	2018 (%)	2019 (%)	2020 (%)	2021 (%)
MSA[1]	61.0	61.9	61.6	61.6	59.3	60.1	63.5	62.9	62.8
U.S.	65.1	64.5	63.7	63.4	63.9	64.4	64.6	66.6	65.5

Note: (1) Figures cover the Denver-Aurora-Lakewood, CO Metropolitan Statistical Area
Source: U.S. Census Bureau, Housing Vacancies and Homeownership Annual Statistics: 2013-2021

House Price Index (HPI)

Area	National Ranking[2]	Quarterly Change (%)	One-Year Change (%)	Five-Year Change (%)	Since 1991Q1 (%)
MSA[1]	95	2.51	19.44	53.94	500.40
U.S.[3]	–	3.33	17.54	54.45	258.04

Note: The HPI is a weighted repeat sales index. It measures average price changes in repeat sales or refinancings on the same properties. This information is obtained by reviewing repeat mortgage transactions on single-family properties whose mortgages have been purchased or securitized by Fannie Mae or Freddie Mac since January 1975; (1) Figures cover the Denver-Aurora-Lakewood, CO Metropolitan Statistical Area; (2) Rankings are based on annual percentage change for all metro areas containing at least 15,000 transactions over the last 10 years and ranges from 1 to 268; (3) figures based on a weighted average of Census Division estimates using a seasonally adjusted, purchase-only index; all figures are for the period ending December 31, 2021
Source: Federal Housing Finance Agency, Change in FHFA Metropolitan Area House Price Indexes, 2021Q4

Median Single-Family Home Prices

Area	2019	2020	2021[p]	Percent Change 2020 to 2021
MSA[1]	462.1	492.7	607.1	23.2
U.S. Average	274.6	300.2	353.4	17.7

Note: Figures are median sales prices of existing single-family homes in thousands of dollars; (p) preliminary; (1) Figures cover the Denver-Aurora-Lakewood, CO Metropolitan Statistical Area
Source: National Association of Realtors, Median Sales Price of Existing Single-Family Homes for Metropolitan Areas, 4th Quarter 2021

Qualifying Income Based on Median Sales Price of Existing Single-Family Homes

Area	With 5% Down ($)	With 10% Down ($)	With 20% Down ($)
MSA[1]	121,757	115,349	102,532
U.S. Average	70,699	66,978	59,536

Note: Figures are preliminary; Qualifying income is based on a mortgage rate of 3.13%. Monthly principal and interest payment is limited to 25% of income; (1) Figures cover the Denver-Aurora-Lakewood, CO Metropolitan Statistical Area
Source: National Association of Realtors, Qualifying Income Based on Median Sales Price of Existing Single-Family Homes for Metropolitan Areas, 4th Quarter 2021

Home Value Distribution

Area	Under $50,000	$50,000 -$99,999	$100,000 -$149,999	$150,000 -$199,999	$200,000 -$299,999	$300,000 -$499,999	$500,000 -$999,999	$1,000,000 or more
City	1.2	1.0	2.0	4.7	16.1	37.1	31.3	6.4
MSA[1]	2.0	1.0	1.5	3.6	15.3	44.9	27.5	4.0
U.S.	6.6	11.0	12.3	13.6	20.0	20.5	12.3	3.7

Note: Figures are percentages and cover owner-occupied housing units; (1) Figures cover the Denver-Aurora-Lakewood, CO Metropolitan Statistical Area
Source: U.S. Census Bureau, 2016-2020 American Community Survey 5-Year Estimates

Year Housing Structure Built

Area	2010 or Later	2000 -2009	1990 -1999	1980 -1989	1970 -1979	1960 -1969	1950 -1959	1940 -1949	Before 1940	Median Year
City	10.8	11.1	6.6	7.6	13.5	11.0	14.8	6.1	18.6	1970
MSA[1]	9.0	16.2	15.4	14.1	17.9	9.2	9.1	2.7	6.5	1983
U.S.	6.2	13.6	13.9	13.4	15.0	10.5	10.2	4.8	12.4	1978

Note: Figures are percentages except for Median Year; Note: (1) Figures cover the Denver-Aurora-Lakewood, CO Metropolitan Statistical Area
Source: U.S. Census Bureau, 2016-2020 American Community Survey 5-Year Estimates

Gross Monthly Rent

Area	Under $500	$500 -$999	$1,000 -$1,499	$1,500 -$1,999	$2,000 -$2,499	$2,500 -$2,999	$3,000 and up	Median ($)
City	7.6	14.4	35.3	25.9	11.2	3.7	1.9	1,397
MSA[1]	4.8	13.2	36.2	29.0	11.5	3.5	1.8	1,446
U.S.	8.9	34.3	30.2	14.9	6.2	2.6	2.8	1,096

Note: Figures are percentages except for Median; Gross rent is the contract rent plus the estimated average monthly cost of utilities (electricity, gas, and water and sewer) and fuels (oil, coal, kerosene, wood, etc.) if these are paid by the renter (or paid for the renter by someone else); (1) Figures cover the Denver-Aurora-Lakewood, CO Metropolitan Statistical Area
Source: U.S. Census Bureau, 2016-2020 American Community Survey 5-Year Estimates

HEALTH

Health Risk Factors

Category	MSA[1] (%)	U.S. (%)
Adults aged 18–64 who have any kind of health care coverage	86.1	86.8
Adults who reported being in good or better health	90.4	86.7
Adults who are current smokers	11.8	15.5
Adults who currently use chewing tobacco, snuff, or snus	2.8	3.7
Adults who are heavy drinkers[2]	8.2	6.7
Adults who are binge drinkers[3]	19.0	15.7
Adults who are overweight (BMI 25.0 - 29.9)	36.3	35.2
Adults who are obese (BMI 30.0 - 99.8)	23.6	31.9
Adults who participated in any physical activities in the past month	84.6	77.6
Adults who always or nearly always wears a seat belt	95.5	94.2

Note: (1) Figures cover the Denver-Aurora-Lakewood, CO Metropolitan Statistical Area; (2) Heavy drinkers are classified as adult men having more than 14 drinks per week and adult women having more than 7 drinks per week; (3) Binge drinkers are classified as males having five or more drinks on one occasion or females having four or more drinks on one occasion

Source: Centers for Disease Control and Prevention, Behaviorial Risk Factor Surveillance System, SMART: Selected Metropolitan Area Risk Trends, 2020

Acute and Chronic Health Conditions

Category	MSA[1] (%)	U.S. (%)
Adults who have ever been told they had a heart attack	2.8	4.3
Adults who have ever been told they have angina or coronary heart disease	2.8	4.0
Adults who have ever been told they had a stroke	2.2	2.8
Adults who have ever been told they have asthma	13.8	14.2
Adults who have ever been told they have arthritis	19.7	24.5
Adults who have ever been told they have diabetes[2]	7.5	10.6
Adults who have ever been told they had skin cancer	6.5	6.4
Adults who have ever been told they had any other types of cancer	5.8	6.8
Adults who have ever been told they have COPD	3.8	6.2
Adults who have ever been told they have kidney disease	1.9	2.9
Adults who have ever been told they have a form of depression	17.5	19.6

Note: (1) Figures cover the Denver-Aurora-Lakewood, CO Metropolitan Statistical Area; (2) Figures do not include pregnancy-related, borderline, or pre-diabetes

Source: Centers for Disease Control and Prevention, Behaviorial Risk Factor Surveillance System, SMART: Selected Metropolitan Area Risk Trends, 2020

Health Screening and Vaccination Rates

Category	MSA[1] (%)	U.S. (%)
Adults 50-75 who have had a blood stool test within the past year	12.5	9.3
Adults aged 65+ who have had flu shot within the past year	72.9	67.9
Adults aged 65+ who have ever had a pneumonia vaccination	78.0	72.2
Adults who have ever been tested for HIV	39.6	37.1
Women aged 21-65 who have had a pap test in the past three years	76.7	77.7
Men aged 40+ who have had a PSA test within the past two years	25.2	31.8
Women aged 40+ who have had a mammogram within the past two years	67.9	71.5

Note: (1) Figures cover the Denver-Aurora-Lakewood, CO Metropolitan Statistical Area.

Source: Centers for Disease Control and Prevention, Behaviorial Risk Factor Surveillance System, SMART: Selected Metropolitan Area Risk Trends, 2020

Disability Status

Category	MSA[1] (%)	U.S. (%)
Adults who reported being deaf	4.2	6.8
Are you blind or have serious difficulty seeing, even when wearing glasses?	3.4	4.7
Do you have difficulty doing errands alone?	4.2	6.3
Do you have difficulty dressing or bathing?	2.2	3.0
Do you have serious difficulty concentrating/remembering/making decisions?	7.3	10.8
Do you have serious difficulty walking or climbing stairs?	7.2	11.9

Note: (1) Figures cover the Denver-Aurora-Lakewood, CO Metropolitan Statistical Area.

Source: Centers for Disease Control and Prevention, Behaviorial Risk Factor Surveillance System, SMART: Selected Metropolitan Area Risk Trends, 2020

Mortality Rates for the Top 10 Causes of Death in the U.S.

ICD-10[a] Sub-Chapter	ICD-10[a] Code	Age-Adjusted Mortality Rate[1] per 100,000 population	
		County[2]	U.S.
Malignant neoplasms	C00-C97	131.4	146.4
Ischaemic heart diseases	I20-I25	63.7	90.2
Other forms of heart disease	I30-I51	36.9	51.9
Other degenerative diseases of the nervous system	G30-G31	35.2	39.7
Other external causes of accidental injury	W00-X59	48.1	38.7
Chronic lower respiratory diseases	J40-J47	42.5	38.1
Cerebrovascular diseases	I60-I69	35.7	37.6
Organic, including symptomatic, mental disorders	F01-F09	28.4	29.4
Hypertensive diseases	I10-I15	30.5	26.1
Diabetes mellitus	E10-E14	20.5	22.6

Note: (a) ICD-10 = International Classification of Diseases 10th Revision; (1) Mortality rates are a three-year average covering 2018-2020; (2) Figures cover Denver County.
Source: Centers for Disease Control and Prevention, National Center for Health Statistics. Underlying Cause of Death 1999-2020 on CDC WONDER Online Database

Mortality Rates for Selected Causes of Death

ICD-10[a] Sub-Chapter	ICD-10[a] Code	Age-Adjusted Mortality Rate[1] per 100,000 population	
		County[2]	U.S.
Assault	X85-Y09	8.1	6.5
Diseases of the liver	K70-K76	25.6	15.3
Human immunodeficiency virus (HIV) disease	B20-B24	1.9	1.4
Influenza and pneumonia	J09-J18	8.6	13.4
Intentional self-harm	X60-X84	20.7	13.9
Malnutrition	E40-E46	6.6	2.9
Obesity and other hyperalimentation	E65-E68	2.7	2.4
Renal failure	N17-N19	9.6	12.5
Transport accidents	V01-V99	10.1	12.5
Viral hepatitis	B15-B19	1.9	1.0

Note: (a) ICD-10 = International Classification of Diseases 10th Revision; (1) Mortality rates are a three-year average covering 2018-2020; (2) Figures cover Denver County; Data are suppressed when the data meet the criteria for confidentiality constraints; Mortality rates are flagged as unreliable when the rate would be calculated with a numerator of 20 or less.
Source: Centers for Disease Control and Prevention, National Center for Health Statistics. Underlying Cause of Death 1999-2020 on CDC WONDER Online Database

Health Insurance Coverage

Area	With Health Insurance	With Private Health Insurance	With Public Health Insurance	Without Health Insurance	Population Under Age 19 Without Health Insurance
City	90.4	65.8	32.4	9.6	4.9
MSA[1]	92.3	72.5	29.3	7.7	4.5
U.S.	91.3	68.1	35.3	8.7	5.2

Note: Figures are percentages that cover the civilian noninstitutionalized population; (1) Figures cover the Denver-Aurora-Lakewood, CO Metropolitan Statistical Area
Source: U.S. Census Bureau, 2016-2020 American Community Survey 5-Year Estimates

Number of Medical Professionals

Area	MDs[3]	DOs[3,4]	Dentists	Podiatrists	Chiropractors	Optometrists
County[1] (number)	4,300	233	570	45	266	121
County[1] (rate[2])	601.0	32.6	79.7	6.3	37.2	16.9
U.S. (rate[2])	285.1	23.0	71.1	6.2	28.2	17.0

08031
Note: Data as of 2020 unless noted; (1) Data covers Denver County; (2) Rate per 100,000 population; (3) Data as of 2019 and includes all active, non-federal physicians; (4) Doctor of Osteopathic Medicine
Source: U.S. Department of Health and Human Services, Health Resources and Services Administration, Bureau of Health Professions, Area Resource File (ARF) 2020-2021

Best Hospitals

According to *U.S. News*, the Denver-Aurora-Lakewood, CO metro area is home to four of the best hospitals in the U.S.: **Craig Hospital** (1 adult specialty); **National Jewish Health, Denver-University of Colorado Hospital** (1 adult specialty); **UCHealth University of Colorado Hospital** (8 adult specialties); **University of Colorado Cancer Center-UCHealth University of Colorado H** (8 adult specialties). The hospitals listed were nationally ranked in at least one of 15 adult or 10 pediatric specialties. Only 175 U.S. hospitals performed well enough to be nationally ranked in one or more specialties. Twenty hospitals in the U.S. made the Honor Roll. The Best Hospitals Honor Roll takes both the national rankings and the procedure and condition ratings into account. Hospitals received points if they were nationally ranked in one of the 15 adult specialties—the higher they ranked, the more points they got—and how many ratings of "high performing" they earned in the 17 procedures and conditions. *U.S. News Online, "America's Best Hospitals 2021-22"*

According to *U.S. News,* the Denver-Aurora-Lakewood, CO metro area is home to one of the best children's hospitals in the U.S.: **Children's Hospital Colorado** (Honor Roll/10 pediatric specialties). The hospital listed was highly ranked in at least one of 10 pediatric specialties. Ninety-two children's hospitals in the U.S. were nationally ranked in at least one specialty. Hospitals received points for being ranked in a specialty, and the 10 hospitals with the most points across the 10 specialties make up the Honor Roll. *U.S. News Online, "America's Best Children's Hospitals 2021-22"*

EDUCATION

Public School District Statistics

District Name	Schls	Pupils	Pupil/ Teacher Ratio	Minority Pupils[1] (%)	LEP/ELL[2] (%)	IEP[3] (%)
Mapleton School District No. 1	19	9,149	20.9	73.9	22.8	n/a
School District No. 1	207	92,143	15.0	74.5	27.4	n/a
State Charter School Institute	41	18,275	17.4	50.5	13.1	n/a

Note: Table includes school districts with 2,000 or more students; (1) Percentage of students that are not non-Hispanic white; (2) Percentage of students that are Limited English Proficient (LEP) or English Language Learners (ELL) (2018-19); (3) Percentage of students that have an Individualized Education Program (IEP).
Source: U.S. Department of Education, National Center for Education Statistics, Common Core of Data, Local Education Agency (School District) Universe Survey: School Year 2019-2020

Best High Schools

According to *U.S. News,* Denver is home to five of the top 500 high schools in the U.S.: **D'Evelyn Junior/Senior High School** (#67); **Denver School of the Arts** (#176); **DSST: Stapleton High School** (#266); **KIPP Denver Collegiate High School** (#329); **DSST: Green Valley Ranch High School** (#347). Nearly 18,000 public, magnet and charter schools were ranked based on their performance on state assessments and how well they prepare students for college. *U.S. News & World Report, "Best High Schools 2021"*

Highest Level of Education

Area	Less than H.S.	H.S. Diploma	Some College, No Deg.	Associate Degree	Bachelor's Degree	Master's Degree	Prof. School Degree	Doctorate Degree
City	10.9	17.2	16.1	5.6	31.0	13.1	4.2	1.9
MSA[1]	8.4	19.9	19.3	7.7	28.4	12.0	2.6	1.6
U.S.	11.5	26.7	20.3	8.6	20.2	9.1	2.2	1.5

Note: Figures cover persons age 25 and over; (1) Figures cover the Denver-Aurora-Lakewood, CO Metropolitan Statistical Area
Source: U.S. Census Bureau, 2016-2020 American Community Survey 5-Year Estimates

Educational Attainment by Race

Area	High School Graduate or Higher (%)					Bachelor's Degree or Higher (%)				
	Total	White	Black	Asian	Hisp.[2]	Total	White	Black	Asian	Hisp.[2]
City	89.1	92.0	88.2	85.5	67.4	50.3	56.8	27.3	54.7	16.8
MSA[1]	91.6	93.7	90.0	84.4	73.1	44.7	47.9	28.3	51.2	17.9
U.S.	88.5	90.7	86.7	87.3	70.3	32.9	34.4	22.6	55.0	17.6

Note: Figures shown cover persons 25 years old and over; (1) Figures cover the Denver-Aurora-Lakewood, CO Metropolitan Statistical Area; (2) People of Hispanic origin can be of any race
Source: U.S. Census Bureau, 2016-2020 American Community Survey 5-Year Estimates

School Enrollment by Grade and Control

Area	Preschool (%)		Kindergarten (%)		Grades 1 - 4 (%)		Grades 5 - 8 (%)		Grades 9 - 12 (%)	
	Public	Private	Public	Private	Public	Private	Public	Private	Public	Private
City	60.0	40.0	86.1	13.9	90.2	9.8	90.2	9.8	91.8	8.2
MSA[1]	58.0	42.0	89.0	11.0	91.3	8.7	91.7	8.3	92.0	8.0
U.S.	58.9	41.1	86.9	13.1	89.0	11.0	89.0	11.0	89.7	10.3

Note: Figures shown cover persons 3 years old and over; (1) Figures cover the Denver-Aurora-Lakewood, CO Metropolitan Statistical Area
Source: U.S. Census Bureau, 2016-2020 American Community Survey 5-Year Estimates

Higher Education

Four-Year Colleges			Two-Year Colleges			Medical Schools[1]	Law Schools[2]	Voc/ Tech[3]
Public	Private Non-profit	Private For-profit	Public	Private Non-profit	Private For-profit			
8	6	9	2	0	8	2	1	16

Note: Figures cover institutions located within the Denver-Aurora-Lakewood, CO Metropolitan Statistical Area and include main campuses only; (1) includes schools accredited by the Liaison Committee on Medical Education and the American Osteopathic Association's Commission on Osteopathic College Accreditation; (2) includes ABA-accredited schools, schools with provisional ABA accreditation, and state accredited schools; (3) includes all schools with programs that are less than 2 years.
Source: National Center for Education Statistics, Integrated Postsecondary Education System (IPEDS), 2020-21; Wikipedia, List of Medical Schools in the United States, accessed April 11, 2022; Wikipedia, List of Law Schools in the United States, accessed April 11, 2022

According to *U.S. News & World Report,* the Denver-Aurora-Lakewood, CO metro area is home to two of the top 200 national universities in the U.S.: **Colorado School of Mines** (#83 tie); **University of Denver** (#93 tie). The indicators used to capture academic quality fall into a number of categories: assessment by administrators at peer institutions; retention of students; faculty resources; student selectivity; financial resources; alumni giving; high school counselor ratings of colleges; and graduation rate. *U.S. News & World Report, "America's Best Colleges 2022"*

According to *U.S. News & World Report,* the Denver-Aurora-Lakewood, CO metro area is home to one of the top 100 law schools in the U.S.: **University of Denver (Sturm)** (#78 tie). The rankings are based on a weighted average of 12 measures of quality: peer assessment score; assessment score by lawyers/judges; median LSAT scores; median undergrad GPA; acceptance rate; employment rates for graduates; placement success; bar passage rate; faculty resources; expenditures per student; student/faculty ratio; and library resources. *U.S. News & World Report, "America's Best Graduate Schools, Law, 2022"*

According to *U.S. News & World Report,* the Denver-Aurora-Lakewood, CO metro area is home to one of the top 75 medical schools for research in the U.S.: **University of Colorado** (#27 tie). The rankings are based on a weighted average of 11 measures of quality: quality assessment; peer assessment score; assessment score by residency directors; research activity; total research activity; average research activity per faculty member; student selectivity; median MCAT total score; median undergraduate GPA; acceptance rate; and faculty resources. *U.S. News & World Report, "America's Best Graduate Schools, Medical, 2022"*

EMPLOYERS

Major Employers

Company Name	Industry
Arvada House Preservation	Apartment building operators
Centura Health Corporation	General medical & surgical hospitals
Colorado Department of Transportation	Regulation, administration of transportation
County of Jefferson	County government
DISH Network Corporation	Cable & other pay television services
Gart Bros Sporting Goods Company	Sporting goods & bicycle shops
HCA Healthone	General medical & surgical hospitals
IBM	Printers, computer
Level 3 Communications	Telephone communication, except radio
Lockheed Martin Corporation	Aircraft & space vehicles
Mormon Church	Mormon church
MWH/Fni Joint Venture	Engineering services
Newmont Gold Company	Gold ores mining
Noodles and Company	Eating places
Strasburg Telephone Company	Telephone communication, except radio
Synergy Services	Payroll accounting service
TW Telecom Holdings	Telephone communication, except radio
Western Union Financial Services	Electronic funds transfer network, including switching

Note: Companies shown are located within the Denver-Aurora-Lakewood, CO Metropolitan Statistical Area.
Source: Hoovers.com; Wikipedia

PUBLIC SAFETY

Crime Rate

Area	Total Crime	Violent Crime Rate				Property Crime Rate		
		Murder	Rape[3]	Robbery	Aggrav. Assault	Burglary	Larceny -Theft	Motor Vehicle Theft
City	5,506.6	13.1	90.8	165.1	588.9	708.0	2,800.8	1,139.9
Suburbs[1]	3,233.8	3.8	57.7	70.7	238.2	357.6	1,904.0	601.8
Metro[2]	3,793.1	6.1	65.8	93.9	324.5	443.9	2,124.7	734.2
U.S.	2,356.7	6.5	38.4	73.9	279.7	314.2	1,398.0	246.0

Note: Figures are crimes per 100,000 population; (1) All areas within the metro area that are located outside the city limits; (2) Figures cover the Denver-Aurora-Lakewood, CO Metropolitan Statistical Area; (3) All figures shown were reported using the revised Uniform Crime Reporting (UCR) definition of rape.
Source: FBI Uniform Crime Reports, 2020

Hate Crimes

Area	Number of Quarters Reported	Number of Incidents per Bias Motivation					
		Race/Ethnicity/ Ancestry	Religion	Sexual Orientation	Disability	Gender	Gender Identity
City	4	47	7	21	1	0	4
U.S.	4	5,227	1,244	1,110	130	75	266

Source: Federal Bureau of Investigation, Hate Crime Statistics 2020

Identity Theft Consumer Reports

Area	Reports	Reports per 100,000 Population	Rank[2]
MSA[1]	18,786	633	28
U.S.	1,434,676	432	-

Note: (1) Figures cover the Denver-Aurora-Lakewood, CO Metropolitan Statistical Area; (2) Rank ranges from 1 to 391 where 1 indicates greatest number of identity theft reports per 100,000 population
Source: Federal Trade Commission, Consumer Sentinel Network Data Book 2021

Fraud and Other Consumer Reports

Area	Reports	Reports per 100,000 Population	Rank[2]
MSA[1]	34,412	1,160	55
U.S.	4,328,977	1,304	-

Note: (1) Figures cover the Denver-Aurora-Lakewood, CO Metropolitan Statistical Area; (2) Rank ranges from 1 to 391 where 1 indicates greatest number of fraud and other consumer reports per 100,000 population
Source: Federal Trade Commission, Consumer Sentinel Network Data Book 2021

POLITICS

2020 Presidential Election Results

Area	Biden	Trump	Jorgensen	Hawkins	Other
Denver County	79.6	18.2	1.2	0.3	0.7
U.S.	51.3	46.8	1.2	0.3	0.5

Note: Results are percentages and may not add to 100% due to rounding
Source: Dave Leip's Atlas of U.S. Presidential Elections

SPORTS

Professional Sports Teams

Team Name	League	Year Established
Colorado Avalanche	National Hockey League (NHL)	1995
Colorado Rapids	Major League Soccer (MLS)	1996
Colorado Rockies	Major League Baseball (MLB)	1993
Denver Broncos	National Football League (NFL)	1960
Denver Nuggets	National Basketball Association (NBA)	1967

Note: Includes teams located in the Denver-Aurora-Lakewood, CO Metropolitan Statistical Area.
Source: Wikipedia, Major Professional Sports Teams of the United States and Canada, April 6, 2022

CLIMATE

Average and Extreme Temperatures

Temperature	Jan	Feb	Mar	Apr	May	Jun	Jul	Aug	Sep	Oct	Nov	Dec	Yr.
Extreme High (°F)	73	76	84	90	93	102	103	100	97	89	79	75	103
Average High (°F)	43	47	52	62	71	81	88	86	77	67	52	45	64
Average Temp. (°F)	30	34	39	48	58	67	73	72	63	52	39	32	51
Average Low (°F)	16	20	25	34	44	53	59	57	48	37	25	18	37
Extreme Low (°F)	-25	-25	-10	-2	22	30	43	41	17	3	-8	-25	-25

Note: Figures cover the years 1948-1992
Source: National Climatic Data Center, International Station Meteorological Climate Summary, 9/96

Average Precipitation/Snowfall/Humidity

Precip./Humidity	Jan	Feb	Mar	Apr	May	Jun	Jul	Aug	Sep	Oct	Nov	Dec	Yr.
Avg. Precip. (in.)	0.6	0.6	1.3	1.7	2.5	1.7	1.9	1.5	1.1	1.0	0.9	0.6	15.5
Avg. Snowfall (in.)	9	7	14	9	2	Tr	0	0	2	4	9	8	63
Avg. Rel. Hum. 5am (%)	62	65	67	66	70	68	67	68	66	63	66	63	66
Avg. Rel. Hum. 5pm (%)	49	44	40	35	38	34	34	34	32	34	47	50	39

Note: Figures cover the years 1948-1992; Tr = Trace amounts (<0.05 in. of rain; <0.5 in. of snow)
Source: National Climatic Data Center, International Station Meteorological Climate Summary, 9/96

Weather Conditions

Temperature			Daytime Sky			Precipitation		
10°F & below	32°F & below	90°F & above	Clear	Partly cloudy	Cloudy	0.01 inch or more precip.	0.1 inch or more snow/ice	Thunder-storms
24	155	33	99	177	89	90	38	39

Note: Figures are average number of days per year and cover the years 1948-1992
Source: National Climatic Data Center, International Station Meteorological Climate Summary, 9/96

HAZARDOUS WASTE

Superfund Sites

The Denver-Aurora-Lakewood, CO metro area is home to eight sites on the EPA's Superfund National Priorities List: **Air Force Plant PJKS** (final); **Broderick Wood Products** (final); **Central City, Clear Creek** (final); **Chemical Sales Co.** (final); **Denver Radium Site** (final); **Lowry Landfill** (final); **Rocky Flats Plant (USDOE)** (final); **Rocky Mountain Arsenal (USARMY)** (final). There are a total of 1,165 Superfund sites with a status of proposed or final on the list in the U.S. *U.S. Environmental Protection Agency, National Priorities List, April 6, 2022*

AIR QUALITY

Air Quality Trends: Ozone

	1990	1995	2000	2005	2010	2016	2017	2018	2019	2020
MSA[1]	0.077	0.070	0.069	0.072	0.070	0.073	0.072	0.071	0.068	0.079
U.S.	0.090	0.091	0.082	0.080	0.074	0.070	0.069	0.070	0.066	0.068

Note: (1) Data covers the Denver-Aurora-Lakewood, CO Metropolitan Statistical Area. The values shown are the composite ozone concentration averages among trend sites based on the highest fourth daily maximum 8-hour concentration in parts per million. These trends are based on sites having an adequate record of monitoring data during the trend period. Data from exceptional events are included.
Source: U.S. Environmental Protection Agency, Air Quality Monitoring Information, "Air Quality Trends by City, 1990-2020"

Air Quality Index

Area	Percent of Days when Air Quality was...[2]					AQI Statistics[2]	
	Good	Moderate	Unhealthy for Sensitive Groups	Unhealthy	Very Unhealthy	Maximum	Median
MSA[1]	32.5	58.2	8.2	1.1	0.0	161	58

Note: (1) Data covers the Denver-Aurora-Lakewood, CO Metropolitan Statistical Area; (2) Based on 366 days with AQI data in 2020. Air Quality Index (AQI) is an index for reporting daily air quality. EPA calculates the AQI for five major air pollutants regulated by the Clean Air Act: ground-level ozone, particle pollution (aka particulate matter), carbon monoxide, sulfur dioxide, and nitrogen dioxide. The AQI runs from 0 to 500. The higher the AQI value, the greater the level of air pollution and the greater the health concern. There are six AQI categories: "Good" AQI is between 0 and 50. Air quality is considered satisfactory; "Moderate" AQI is between 51 and 100. Air quality is acceptable; "Unhealthy for Sensitive Groups" When AQI values are between 101 and 150, members of sensitive groups may experience health effects; "Unhealthy" When AQI values are between 151 and 200 everyone may begin to experience health effects; "Very Unhealthy" AQI values between 201 and 300 trigger a health alert; "Hazardous" AQI values over 300 trigger warnings of emergency conditions (not shown).
Source: U.S. Environmental Protection Agency, Air Quality Index Report, 2020

Air Quality Index Pollutants

Area	Percent of Days when AQI Pollutant was...[2]					
	Carbon Monoxide	Nitrogen Dioxide	Ozone	Sulfur Dioxide	Particulate Matter 2.5	Particulate Matter 10
MSA[1]	0.0	18.6	58.2	0.0	19.1	4.1

Note: (1) Data covers the Denver-Aurora-Lakewood, CO Metropolitan Statistical Area; (2) Based on 366 days with AQI data in 2020. The Air Quality Index (AQI) is an index for reporting daily air quality. EPA calculates the AQI for five major air pollutants regulated by the Clean Air Act: ground-level ozone, particle pollution (also known as particulate matter), carbon monoxide, sulfur dioxide, and nitrogen dioxide. The AQI runs from 0 to 500. The higher the AQI value, the greater the level of air pollution and the greater the health concern.
Source: U.S. Environmental Protection Agency, Air Quality Index Report, 2020

Maximum Air Pollutant Concentrations: Particulate Matter, Ozone, CO and Lead

	Particulate Matter 10 (ug/m^3)	Particulate Matter 2.5 Wtd AM (ug/m^3)	Particulate Matter 2.5 24-Hr (ug/m^3)	Ozone (ppm)	Carbon Monoxide (ppm)	Lead (ug/m^3)
MSA[1] Level	113	10.5	42	0.087	2	n/a
NAAQS[2]	150	15	35	0.075	9	0.15
Met NAAQS[2]	Yes	Yes	No	No	Yes	n/a

Note: (1) Data covers the Denver-Aurora-Lakewood, CO Metropolitan Statistical Area; Data from exceptional events are included; (2) National Ambient Air Quality Standards; ppm = parts per million; ug/m^3 = micrograms per cubic meter; n/a not available.

Concentrations: Particulate Matter 10 (coarse particulate)—highest second maximum 24-hour concentration; Particulate Matter 2.5 Wtd AM (fine particulate)—highest weighted annual mean concentration; Particulate Matter 2.5 24-Hour (fine particulate)—highest 98th percentile 24-hour concentration; Ozone—highest fourth daily maximum 8-hour concentration; Carbon Monoxide—highest second maximum non-overlapping 8-hour concentration; Lead—maximum running 3-month average

Source: U.S. Environmental Protection Agency, Air Quality Monitoring Information, "Air Quality Statistics by City, 2020"

Maximum Air Pollutant Concentrations: Nitrogen Dioxide and Sulfur Dioxide

	Nitrogen Dioxide AM (ppb)	Nitrogen Dioxide 1-Hr (ppb)	Sulfur Dioxide AM (ppb)	Sulfur Dioxide 1-Hr (ppb)	Sulfur Dioxide 24-Hr (ppb)
MSA[1] Level	25	71	n/a	7	n/a
NAAQS[2]	53	100	30	75	140
Met NAAQS[2]	Yes	Yes	n/a	Yes	n/a

Note: (1) Data covers the Denver-Aurora-Lakewood, CO Metropolitan Statistical Area; Data from exceptional events are included; (2) National Ambient Air Quality Standards; ppm = parts per million; ug/m^3 = micrograms per cubic meter; n/a not available.

Concentrations: Nitrogen Dioxide AM—highest arithmetic mean concentration; Nitrogen Dioxide 1-Hr—highest 98th percentile 1-hour daily maximum concentration; Sulfur Dioxide AM—highest annual mean concentration; Sulfur Dioxide 1-Hr—highest 99th percentile 1-hour daily maximum concentration; Sulfur Dioxide 24-Hr—highest second maximum 24-hour concentration

Source: U.S. Environmental Protection Agency, Air Quality Monitoring Information, "Air Quality Statistics by City, 2020"

Fort Collins, Colorado

Background

At 4,985 feet, Fort Collins lies high in the eastern base of the Rocky Mountains' front range along the Cache la Poudre River about one hour from Denver. Although not quite as large as Denver, Fort Collins, home to Colorado State University and its own symphony orchestra, offers virtually everything its citizens need with a spectacular landscape, strong economy, and world-class outdoor adventure opportunities.

Fort Collins owes its name to Colonel William Collins of the Civil War era, who was sent with a regiment of Union soldiers to guard farmers and ranchers scattered throughout the valley, and to provide security for the Overland Stage trail. Originally called Camp Collins, the place remained a military reservation until 1866 and was incorporated in 1879.

The early economy of the town depended first on lumber, and then on the raising of livestock and produce, with alfalfa, grain, and sugar beets as the chief crops. Sugar refineries, dairies, and meatpacking plants bolstered the wealth of the town, as did the products of mining and quarrying. Fort Collins is still the commercial center for a rich agricultural region that produces hay, barley, and sugar beets.

Colorado State University, the land grant University of Colorado, was established in Fort Collins in 1879, and offers innumerable cultural, economic, and educational benefits to residents. More than 32,000 students are enrolled at CSU, which is the largest employer in the city. CSU offers a world-class range of undergraduate and graduate programs, and is an internationally recognized center for forestry, agricultural science, veterinary medicine, and civil engineering.

Fort Collins' businesses produce motion-picture film, combustion engines, prefabricated metal buildings, arc welders and rods, cement products, dental hygiene appliances, and miscellaneous plastics.

The Fort Collins public school system, within the Poudre School District, is one of the area's largest employers. The latest addition was the city's 32nd elementary school. The city's public library system, Poudre River Public Libraries, operates three branches.

Gateway Natural Area, 15 miles from Fort Collins, offers several recreation opportunities, including a quarter-mile nature trail and a designated boat launch. Lakes are easily accessible for all water sports, and the Cache La Poudre River offers some of the best trout fishing in Colorado. For hunters, the area is a paradise, with ample supplies of antelope, black bear, deer, elk, mountain lion, and small game.

Fort Collins also offers a great range of cultural amenities. The city's Lincoln Center presents year-round performances by a variety of artists. Old Town, a historic downtown shopping district, hosts several large festivals each year. Fort Collins Symphony, the Larimer Chorale, Open Stage Theatre, and the Canyon Concert Ballet call Fort Collins their home. The city also cultivates the visual arts, with "Art in Public Places" sponsored by the city, and provides exhibits at the Lincoln Center, Fort Collins Museum, and private galleries.

Transportation in and around the city is convenient. The municipality operates its own bus service, and interstate bus service is available. Residents are served by three nearby airports—Fort Collins/Loveland Airport, Cheyenne Municipal Airport, and Denver International Airport, one of the nation's busiest airports.

Fort Collins features four distinct seasons and, though high in the foothills, is buffered from both summer and winter temperature extremes. A typical day in Fort Collins is warm and dry with mild nights. The town enjoys on average more than 300 sunny days per year, and an annual snowfall of 51 inches, with far less rainfall. Summers are comfortable, while winters are cold.

Rankings

General Rankings

- *US News & World Report* conducted a survey of more than 3,600 people and analyzed the 150 largest metropolitan areas to determine what matters most when selecting the next place to live. Fort Collins ranked #17 out of the top 25 as having the best combination of desirable factors. Criteria: cost of living; quality of life and education; net migration; job market; desirability; and other factors. *realestate.usnews.com, "The 25 Best Places to Live in the U.S. in 2021-2022," July 13, 2021*
- In their eigth annual survey, Livability.com looked at data for more than 1,000 small to mid-sized U.S. cities to determine the rankings for Livability's "Top 100 Best Places to Live" in 2021. Fort Collins ranked #42. Criteria: housing and economy; sustainability; social and civic engagement; education; demographics; health care options; transportation & infrastructure; and community amenities. *Livability.com, "Top 100 Best Places to Live 2021" October 12, 2021*

Business/Finance Rankings

- The Fort Collins metro area appeared on the Milken Institute "2021 Best Performing Cities" list. Rank: #12 out of 200 large metro areas (population over 250,000). Criteria: job growth; wage and salary growth; high-tech output growth; housing affordability; household broadband access. *Milken Institute, "Best-Performing Cities 2021," February 16, 2021*
- *Forbes* ranked the 200 most populous metro areas to determine the nation's "Best Places for Business and Careers." The Fort Collins metro area was ranked #27. Criteria: costs (business and living); job growth (past and projected); income growth; quality of life; educational attainment (college and high school); projected economic growth; cultural and leisure opportunities; workplace tolerance laws; net migration patterns. *Forbes, "The Best Places for Business and Careers 2019: Seattle Still On Top," October 30, 2019*

Children/Family Rankings

- Fort Collins was selected as one of the most playful cities in the U.S. by KaBOOM! The organization's Playful City USA initiative honors cities and towns across the nation that have made their communities more playable. Criteria: pledging to integrate play as a solution to challenges in their communities; making it easy for children to get active and balanced play; creating more family-friendly and innovative communities as a result. *KaBOOM! National Campaign for Play, "2017 Playful City USA Communities"*
- Fort Collins was selected as one of the best cities for newlyweds by *Rent.com*. The city ranked #13 of 15. Criteria: cost of living; availability of affordable rental inventory; annual household income; activities and restaurant options; percentage of married couples; concentration of millennials; safety. *Rent.com, "The 15 Best Cities for Newlyweds," December 11, 2018*

Environmental Rankings

- Fort Collins was highlighted as one of the 25 most ozone-polluted metro areas in the U.S. during 2017 through 2019. The area ranked #17. *American Lung Association, "State of the Air 2021," April 21, 2021*

Real Estate Rankings

- The Fort Collins metro area was identified as one of the 20 least affordable housing markets in the U.S. in 2021. The area ranked #167 out of 183 markets. Criteria: qualification for a mortgage loan with a 10 percent down payment on a typical home. *National Association of Realtors®, Qualifying Income Based on Sales Price of Existing Single-Family Homes for Metropolitan Areas, 2021*
- Fort Collins was ranked #153 out of 237 metro areas in terms of housing affordability in 2021 by the National Association of Home Builders (#1 = most affordable). Criteria: the share of homes sold in that area affordable to a family earning the local median income, based on standard mortgage underwriting criteria. *National Association of Home Builders®, NAHB-Wells Fargo Housing Opportunity Index, 4th Quarter 2021*

Safety Rankings

- Allstate ranked the 200 largest cities in America in terms of driver safety. Fort Collins ranked #7. Criteria: internal property damage claims over a two-year period from January 2016 to December 2017. The report helps increase the importance of safety and awareness behind the wheel. *Allstate, "Allstate America's Best Drivers Report, 2019" June 24, 2019*

- The National Insurance Crime Bureau ranked 390 metro areas in the U.S. in terms of per capita rates of vehicle theft. The Fort Collins metro area ranked #248 (#1 = highest rate). Criteria: number of vehicle theft offenses per 100,000 inhabitants in 2020. *National Insurance Crime Bureau, "Hot Spots 2020," August 31, 2021*

Seniors/Retirement Rankings

- From its Best Cities for Successful Aging indexes, the Milken Institute generated rankings for metropolitan areas, weighing data in nine categories—health care, wellness, living arrangements, transportation and convenience, financial characteristics, education, employment, community engagement, and overall livability. The Fort Collins metro area was ranked #88 overall in the small metro area category. *Milken Institute, "Best Cities for Successful Aging, 2017" March 14, 2017*
- Fort Collins was identified as #9 of 20 most popular places to retire in the Western region by *Topretirements.com*. The site separated its annual "Best Places to Retire" list by major U.S. regions for 2019. The list reflects the 20 cities that visitors to the website are most interested in for retirement, based on the number of times a city's review was viewed on the website. *Topretirements.com, "20 Best Places to Retire in the West-2019," November 11, 2019*

Sports/Recreation Rankings

- Fort Collins was chosen as a bicycle friendly community by the League of American Bicyclists. A "Bicycle Friendly Community" welcomes cyclists by providing safe and supportive accommodation for cycling and encouraging people to bike for transportation and recreation. There are five award levels: Diamond; Platinum; Gold; Silver; and Bronze. The community achieved an award level of Platinum. *League of American Bicyclists, "Fall 2021 Awards-New & Renewing Bicycle Friendly Communities List," December 8, 2021*
- Fort Collins was chosen as one of America's best cities for bicycling. The city ranked #3 out of 50. Criteria: cycling infrastructure that is safe and friendly for all ages; energy and bike culture. The editors evaluated cities with populations of 100,000 or more. *Bicycling, "The 50 Best Bike Cities in America," October 10, 2018*

Miscellaneous Rankings

- *MoveHub* ranked 446 hipster cities across 20 countries, using its *alternative* Hipster Index and Fort Collins came out as #48 among the top 50. Criteria: population over 150,000; number of vintage boutiques; density of tattoo parlors; vegan places to eat; coffee shops; and density of vinyl record stores. *www.movehub.com, "The Hipster Index: Brighton Pips Portland to Global Top Spot," July 28, 2021*
- Fort Collins was selected as a 2021 Digital Cities Survey winner. The city ranked #6 in the mid-sized city (125,000 to 249,999 population) category. The survey examined and assessed how city governments are utilizing technology to continue innovation, engage with residents, and persevere through the challenges of the pandemic. Survey questions focused on ten initiatives: cybersecurity; citizen experience; disaster recovery; business intelligence; IT personnel; data governance; budget control; IT governance; infrastructure modernization; and broadband connectivity. *Center for Digital Government, "2021 Digital Cities Survey," November 16, 2021*

Business Environment

DEMOGRAPHICS

Population Growth

Area	1990 Census	2000 Census	2010 Census	2020* Estimate	Population Growth (%) 1990-2020	Population Growth (%) 2010-2020
City	89,555	118,652	143,986	166,069	85.4	15.3
MSA[1]	186,136	251,494	299,630	350,523	88.3	17.0
U.S.	248,709,873	281,421,906	308,745,538	326,569,308	31.3	5.8

Note: (1) Figures cover the Fort Collins, CO Metropolitan Statistical Area; (*) 2016-2020 5-year estimated population
Source: U.S. Census Bureau, 1990 Census, Census 2000, Census 2010, 2016-2020 American Community Survey 5-Year Estimates

Household Size

Area	Persons in Household (%) One	Two	Three	Four	Five	Six	Seven or More	Average Household Size
City	25.1	37.4	17.5	14.4	4.0	1.1	0.5	2.60
MSA[1]	24.6	39.9	15.9	12.4	4.9	1.4	0.9	2.50
U.S.	28.0	33.9	15.5	12.9	6.0	2.3	1.4	2.60

Note: (1) Figures cover the Fort Collins, CO Metropolitan Statistical Area
Source: U.S. Census Bureau, 2016-2020 American Community Survey 5-Year Estimates

Race

Area	White Alone[2] (%)	Black Alone[2] (%)	Asian Alone[2] (%)	AIAN[3] Alone[2] (%)	NHOPI[4] Alone[2] (%)	Other Race Alone[2] (%)	Two or More Races (%)
City	86.3	1.5	3.4	0.9	0.1	1.7	6.1
MSA[1]	89.2	1.0	2.2	0.7	0.1	1.8	5.0
U.S.	70.4	12.6	5.6	0.8	0.2	5.1	5.2

Note: (1) Figures cover the Fort Collins, CO Metropolitan Statistical Area; (2) Alone is defined as not being in combination with one or more other races; (3) American Indian and Alaska Native; (4) Native Hawaiian and Other Pacific Islander
Source: U.S. Census Bureau, 2016-2020 American Community Survey 5-Year Estimates

Hispanic or Latino Origin

Area	Total (%)	Mexican (%)	Puerto Rican (%)	Cuban (%)	Other (%)
City	12.3	8.8	0.4	0.1	2.9
MSA[1]	11.7	8.5	0.4	0.2	2.6
U.S.	18.2	11.2	1.7	0.7	4.5

Note: Persons of Hispanic or Latino origin can be of any race; (1) Figures cover the Fort Collins, CO Metropolitan Statistical Area
Source: U.S. Census Bureau, 2016-2020 American Community Survey 5-Year Estimates

Ancestry

Area	German	Irish	English	American	Italian	Polish	French[2]	Scottish	Dutch
City	23.0	12.8	12.5	3.7	5.4	3.1	3.4	3.3	1.8
MSA[1]	24.9	13.0	13.7	4.3	4.8	2.6	3.3	3.5	2.0
U.S.	13.0	9.7	7.7	5.9	5.1	2.7	2.3	1.6	1.1

Note: Figures are the percentage of the total population reporting a particular ancestry. The nine most commonly reported ancestries in the U.S. are shown. Figures include multiple ancestries (e.g. if a person reported being Irish and Italian, they were included in both columns); (1) Figures cover the Fort Collins, CO Metropolitan Statistical Area; (2) Excludes Basque
Source: U.S. Census Bureau, 2016-2020 American Community Survey 5-Year Estimates

Foreign-born Population

Area	Percent of Population Born in: Any Foreign Country	Asia	Mexico	Europe	Caribbean	Central America[2]	South America	Africa	Canada
City	6.9	3.1	1.2	1.4	0.1	0.2	0.4	0.3	0.2
MSA[1]	5.7	1.9	1.4	1.2	0.1	0.2	0.4	0.3	0.2
U.S.	13.5	4.2	3.3	1.5	1.3	1.1	1.0	0.7	0.3

Note: (1) Figures cover the Fort Collins, CO Metropolitan Statistical Area; (2) Excludes Mexico.
Source: U.S. Census Bureau, 2016-2020 American Community Survey 5-Year Estimates

Marital Status

Area	Never Married	Now Married[2]	Separated	Widowed	Divorced
City	47.2	39.7	0.7	3.4	9.0
MSA[1]	35.6	49.2	0.8	4.0	10.4
U.S.	33.5	48.1	1.8	5.7	10.8

Note: Figures are percentages and cover the population 15 years of age and older; (1) Figures cover the Fort Collins, CO Metropolitan Statistical Area; (2) Excludes separated
Source: U.S. Census Bureau, 2016-2020 American Community Survey 5-Year Estimates

Disability by Age

Area	All Ages	Under 18 Years Old	18 to 64 Years Old	65 Years and Over
City	8.4	2.6	6.4	30.9
MSA[1]	10.1	2.7	7.8	29.5
U.S.	12.7	4.3	10.3	34.0

Note: Figures show percent of the civilian noninstitutionalized population that reported having a disability. Disability status is determined from six types of difficulty: vision, hearing, cognitive, ambulatory, self-care, and independent living. For children under 5 years old, hearing and vision difficulty are used to determine disability status. For children between the ages of 5 and 14, disability status is determined from hearing, vision, cognitive, ambulatory, and self-care difficulties. For people aged 15 years and older, they are considered to have a disability if they have difficulty with any one of the six difficulty types; Note: (1) Figures cover the Fort Collins, CO Metropolitan Statistical Area
Source: U.S. Census Bureau, 2016-2020 American Community Survey 5-Year Estimates

Age

Area	Percent of Population									Median Age
	Under Age 5	Age 5–19	Age 20–34	Age 35–44	Age 45–54	Age 55–64	Age 65–74	Age 75–84	Age 85+	
City	4.6	18.9	34.1	11.9	9.7	9.8	6.5	2.9	1.5	29.9
MSA[1]	5.0	18.3	25.2	12.4	11.0	12.5	9.7	4.0	1.9	36.2
U.S.	6.0	19.1	20.6	12.7	12.7	12.9	9.4	4.7	2.0	38.2

Note: (1) Figures cover the Fort Collins, CO Metropolitan Statistical Area
Source: U.S. Census Bureau, 2016-2020 American Community Survey 5-Year Estimates

Gender

Area	Males	Females	Males per 100 Females
City	83,149	82,920	100.3
MSA[1]	174,652	175,871	99.3
U.S.	160,818,530	165,750,778	97.0

Note: (1) Figures cover the Fort Collins, CO Metropolitan Statistical Area
Source: U.S. Census Bureau, 2016-2020 American Community Survey 5-Year Estimates

Religious Groups by Family

Area	Catholic	Baptist	Non-Den.	Methodist[2]	Lutheran	LDS[3]	Pente-costal	Presby-terian[4]	Muslim[5]	Judaism
MSA[1]	11.8	2.2	6.4	4.4	3.5	3.0	4.7	1.9	0.1	<0.1
U.S.	19.1	9.3	4.0	4.0	2.3	2.0	1.9	1.6	0.8	0.7

Note: Figures are the number of adherents as a percentage of the total population; (1) Figures cover the Fort Collins, CO Metropolitan Statistical Area; (2) Methodist/Pietist; (3) Latter Day Saints; (4) Reformed; (5) Figures are estimates
Source: Association of Statisticians of American Religious Bodies, 2010 U.S. Religion Census: Religious Congregations & Membership Study

Religious Groups by Tradition

Area	Catholic	Evangelical Protestant	Mainline Protestant	Other Tradition	Black Protestant	Orthodox
MSA[1]	11.8	18.8	5.9	4.0	<0.1	0.1
U.S.	19.1	16.2	7.3	4.3	1.6	0.3

Note: Figures are the number of adherents as a percentage of the total population; (1) Figures cover the Fort Collins, CO Metropolitan Statistical Area
Source: Association of Statisticians of American Religious Bodies, 2010 U.S. Religion Census: Religious Congregations & Membership Study

ECONOMY

Gross Metropolitan Product

Area	2017	2018	2019	2020	Rank[2]
MSA[1]	17.4	18.4	19.7	20.7	139

Note: Figures are in billions of dollars; (1) Figures cover the Fort Collins, CO Metropolitan Statistical Area; (2) Rank is based on 2018 data and ranges from 1 to 381
Source: U.S. Conference of Mayors, U.S. Metro Economies: GMP & Employment 2018-2020, September 2019

Economic Growth

Area	2015-17 (%)	2018 (%)	2019 (%)	2020 (%)	Rank[2]
MSA[1]	5.3	3.7	4.7	3.1	14
U.S.	1.9	2.9	2.3	2.1	–

Note: Figures are real gross metropolitan product (GMP) growth rates and represent average annual percent change; (1) Figures cover the Fort Collins, CO Metropolitan Statistical Area; (2) Rank is based on 2017 2-year average annual percent change and ranges from 1 to 381
Source: U.S. Conference of Mayors, U.S. Metro Economies: GMP & Employment 2018-2020, September 2019

Metropolitan Area Exports

Area	2015	2016	2017	2018	2019	2020	Rank[2]
MSA[1]	990.7	993.8	1,034.1	1,021.8	1,060.0	1,092.5	140

Note: Figures are in millions of dollars; (1) Figures cover the Fort Collins, CO Metropolitan Statistical Area; (2) Rank is based on 2020 data and ranges from 1 to 389
Source: U.S. Department of Commerce, International Trade Administration, Office of Trade and Economic Analysis, Industry and Analysis, Exports by Metropolitan Area, data extracted March 4, 2022

Building Permits

Area	Single-Family			Multi-Family			Total		
	2019	2020	Pct. Chg.	2019	2020	Pct. Chg.	2019	2020	Pct. Chg.
City	316	453	43.4	632	174	-72.5	948	627	-33.9
MSA[1]	1,580	2,190	38.6	910	375	-58.8	2,490	2,565	3.0
U.S.	862,100	979,400	13.6	523,900	491,700	-6.1	1,386,000	1,471,100	6.1

Note: (1) Figures cover the Fort Collins, CO Metropolitan Statistical Area; Figures represent new, privately-owned housing units authorized (unadjusted data); All permit data are based on estimates with imputation
Source: U.S. Census Bureau, Manufacturing, Mining, and Construction Statistics, Building Permits, 2019, 2020

Bankruptcy Filings

Area	Business Filings			Nonbusiness Filings		
	2020	2021	% Chg.	2020	2021	% Chg.
Larimer County	28	14	-50.0	404	306	-24.3
U.S.	21,655	14,347	-33.7	522,808	399,269	-23.6

Note: Business filings include Chapter 7, Chapter 9, Chapter 11, Chapter 12, Chapter 13, Chapter 15, and Section 304; Nonbusiness filings include Chapter 7, Chapter 11, and Chapter 13
Source: Administrative Office of the U.S. Courts, Business and Nonbusiness Bankruptcy, County Cases Commenced by Chapter of the Bankruptcy Code, During the 12-Month Period Ending December 31, 2020 and Business and Nonbusiness Bankruptcy, County Cases Commenced by Chapter of the Bankruptcy Code, During the 12-Month Period Ending December 31, 2021

Housing Vacancy Rates

Area	Gross Vacancy Rate[2] (%)			Year-Round Vacancy Rate[3] (%)			Rental Vacancy Rate[4] (%)			Homeowner Vacancy Rate[5] (%)		
	2019	2020	2021	2019	2020	2021	2019	2020	2021	2019	2020	2021
MSA[1]	n/a	n/a	n/a	n/a	n/a	n/a	n/a	n/a	n/a	n/a	n/a	n/a
U.S.	12.0	10.6	10.8	9.5	8.2	8.4	6.7	6.3	6.1	1.4	1.0	0.9

Note: (1) Figures cover the Fort Collins, CO Metropolitan Statistical Area; (2) The percentage of the total housing inventory that is vacant; (3) The percentage of the housing inventory (excluding seasonal units) that is year-round vacant; (4) The percentage of rental inventory that is vacant for rent; (5) The percentage of homeowner inventory that is vacant for sale; n/a not available
Source: U.S. Census Bureau, Housing Vacancies and Homeownership Annual Statistics: 2019, 2020, 2021

INCOME

Income

Area	Per Capita ($)	Median Household ($)	Average Household ($)
City	35,489	70,528	91,635
MSA[1]	38,142	76,366	97,178
U.S.	35,384	64,994	91,547

Note: (1) Figures cover the Fort Collins, CO Metropolitan Statistical Area
Source: U.S. Census Bureau, 2016-2020 American Community Survey 5-Year Estimates

Household Income Distribution

Area	Percent of Households Earning							
	Under $15,000	$15,000 -$24,999	$25,000 -$34,999	$35,000 -$49,999	$50,000 -$74,999	$75,000 -$99,999	$100,000 -$149,999	$150,000 and up
City	9.7	7.7	7.6	11.5	16.4	13.7	16.6	16.8
MSA[1]	7.9	7.2	7.0	10.5	16.5	14.8	18.4	17.6
U.S.	9.9	8.5	8.6	12.0	17.2	12.8	15.6	15.4

Note: (1) Figures cover the Fort Collins, CO Metropolitan Statistical Area
Source: U.S. Census Bureau, 2016-2020 American Community Survey 5-Year Estimates

Poverty Rate

Area	All Ages	Under 18 Years Old	18 to 64 Years Old	65 Years and Over
City	15.9	9.3	19.0	7.4
MSA[1]	11.1	8.6	13.0	6.4
U.S.	12.8	17.5	12.1	9.3

Note: Figures are percentage of people whose income during the past 12 months was below the poverty level; (1) Figures cover the Fort Collins, CO Metropolitan Statistical Area
Source: U.S. Census Bureau, 2016-2020 American Community Survey 5-Year Estimates

CITY FINANCES

City Government Finances

Component	2019 ($000)	2019 ($ per capita)
Total Revenues	671,021	4,065
Total Expenditures	767,787	4,651
Debt Outstanding	257,459	1,560
Cash and Securities[1]	563,405	3,413

Note: (1) Cash and security holdings of a government at the close of its fiscal year, including those of its dependent agencies, utilities, and liquor stores.
Source: U.S. Census Bureau, State & Local Government Finances 2019

City Government Revenue by Source

Source	2019 ($000)	2019 ($ per capita)	2019 (%)
General Revenue			
From Federal Government	102,908	623	15.3
From State Government	57,923	351	8.6
From Local Governments	350	2	0.1
Taxes			
Property	33,973	206	5.1
Sales and Gross Receipts	134,506	815	20.0
Personal Income	0	0	0.0
Corporate Income	0	0	0.0
Motor Vehicle License	0	0	0.0
Other Taxes	4,451	27	0.7
Current Charges	100,973	612	15.0
Liquor Store	0	0	0.0
Utility	178,299	1,080	26.6

Source: U.S. Census Bureau, State & Local Government Finances 2019

City Government Expenditures by Function

Function	2019 ($000)	2019 ($ per capita)	2019 (%)
General Direct Expenditures			
Air Transportation	0	0	0.0
Corrections	0	0	0.0
Education	0	0	0.0
Employment Security Administration	0	0	0.0
Financial Administration	4,529	27	0.6
Fire Protection	28,145	170	3.7
General Public Buildings	0	0	0.0
Governmental Administration, Other	7,433	45	1.0
Health	0	0	0.0
Highways	67,402	408	8.8
Hospitals	0	0	0.0
Housing and Community Development	47,305	286	6.2
Interest on General Debt	4,802	29	0.6
Judicial and Legal	0	0	0.0
Libraries	0	0	0.0
Parking	3,528	21	0.5
Parks and Recreation	48,414	293	6.3
Police Protection	46,904	284	6.1
Public Welfare	0	0	0.0
Sewerage	22,098	133	2.9
Solid Waste Management	0	0	0.0
Veterans' Services	0	0	0.0
Liquor Store	0	0	0.0
Utility	354,431	2,147	46.2

Source: U.S. Census Bureau, State & Local Government Finances 2019

EMPLOYMENT

Labor Force and Employment

Area	Civilian Labor Force			Workers Employed		
	Dec. 2020	Dec. 2021	% Chg.	Dec. 2020	Dec. 2021	% Chg.
City	102,741	102,230	-0.5	96,111	99,065	3.1
MSA[1]	207,120	207,229	0.1	193,967	199,929	3.1
U.S.	160,017,000	161,696,000	1.0	149,613,000	155,732,000	4.1

Note: Data is not seasonally adjusted and covers workers 16 years of age and older; (1) Figures cover the Fort Collins, CO Metropolitan Statistical Area
Source: Bureau of Labor Statistics, Local Area Unemployment Statistics

Unemployment Rate

Area	2021											
	Jan.	Feb.	Mar.	Apr.	May	Jun.	Jul.	Aug.	Sep.	Oct.	Nov.	Dec.
City	6.1	5.7	5.6	5.3	4.8	5.5	5.0	4.4	3.6	3.5	3.4	3.1
MSA[1]	6.4	6.0	5.8	5.4	4.9	5.5	5.2	4.7	3.9	3.8	3.8	3.5
U.S.	6.8	6.6	6.2	5.7	5.5	6.1	5.7	5.3	4.6	4.3	3.9	3.7

Note: Data is not seasonally adjusted and covers workers 16 years of age and older; (1) Figures cover the Fort Collins, CO Metropolitan Statistical Area
Source: Bureau of Labor Statistics, Local Area Unemployment Statistics

Average Wages

Occupation	$/Hr.	Occupation	$/Hr.
Accountants and Auditors	38.19	Maintenance and Repair Workers	21.76
Automotive Mechanics	25.13	Marketing Managers	80.61
Bookkeepers	21.49	Network and Computer Systems Admin.	40.88
Carpenters	24.18	Nurses, Licensed Practical	25.82
Cashiers	14.83	Nurses, Registered	37.82
Computer Programmers	30.17	Nursing Assistants	16.55
Computer Systems Analysts	46.29	Office Clerks, General	21.42
Computer User Support Specialists	28.95	Physical Therapists	40.46
Construction Laborers	19.71	Physicians	130.44
Cooks, Restaurant	16.66	Plumbers, Pipefitters and Steamfitters	27.57
Customer Service Representatives	17.87	Police and Sheriff's Patrol Officers	42.17
Dentists	92.60	Postal Service Mail Carriers	25.64
Electricians	27.54	Real Estate Sales Agents	32.04
Engineers, Electrical	52.55	Retail Salespersons	16.16
Fast Food and Counter Workers	14.28	Sales Representatives, Technical/Scientific	44.82
Financial Managers	77.74	Secretaries, Exc. Legal/Medical/Executive	19.46
First-Line Supervisors of Office Workers	30.32	Security Guards	17.41
General and Operations Managers	59.28	Surgeons	n/a
Hairdressers/Cosmetologists	18.64	Teacher Assistants, Exc. Postsecondary*	15.88
Home Health and Personal Care Aides	15.57	Teachers, Secondary School, Exc. Sp. Ed.*	29.95
Janitors and Cleaners	16.06	Telemarketers	17.07
Landscaping/Groundskeeping Workers	18.81	Truck Drivers, Heavy/Tractor-Trailer	23.54
Lawyers	63.75	Truck Drivers, Light/Delivery Services	20.90
Maids and Housekeeping Cleaners	15.57	Waiters and Waitresses	17.45

Note: Wage data covers the Fort Collins, CO Metropolitan Statistical Area; (*) Hourly wages were calculated from annual wage data based on a 40 hour work week; n/a not available.
Source: Bureau of Labor Statistics, Metro Area Occupational Employment & Wage Estimates, May 2021

Employment by Industry

Sector	MSA[1]		U.S.
	Number of Employees	Percent of Total	Percent of Total
Construction, Mining, and Logging	12,100	6.9	5.3
Education and Health Services	18,700	10.6	16.0
Financial Activities	7,000	4.0	5.9
Government	42,400	24.0	14.9
Information	2,700	1.5	1.9
Leisure and Hospitality	20,300	11.5	9.8
Manufacturing	15,100	8.6	8.4
Other Services	6,900	3.9	3.7
Professional and Business Services	20,800	11.8	14.6
Retail Trade	20,600	11.7	10.7
Transportation, Warehousing, and Utilities	4,400	2.5	4.8
Wholesale Trade	5,500	3.1	3.8

Note: Figures are non-farm employment as of December 2021. Figures are not seasonally adjusted and include workers 16 years of age and older; (1) Figures cover the Fort Collins, CO Metropolitan Statistical Area
Source: Bureau of Labor Statistics, Current Employment Statistics, Employment, Hours, and Earnings

Employment by Occupation

Occupation Classification	City (%)	MSA[1] (%)	U.S. (%)
Management, Business, Science, and Arts	48.3	45.2	39.5
Natural Resources, Construction, and Maintenance	6.3	8.2	8.7
Production, Transportation, and Material Moving	7.7	9.4	13.1
Sales and Office	19.6	20.3	21.3
Service	18.0	16.8	17.4

Note: Figures cover employed civilians 16 years of age and older; (1) Figures cover the Fort Collins, CO Metropolitan Statistical Area
Source: U.S. Census Bureau, 2016-2020 American Community Survey 5-Year Estimates

Occupations with Greatest Projected Employment Growth: 2021 – 2023

Occupation[1]	2021 Employment	2023 Projected Employment	Numeric Employment Change	Percent Employment Change
Software Developers and Software Quality Assurance Analysts and Testers	62,100	66,810	4,710	7.6
Fast Food and Counter Workers	72,270	76,700	4,430	6.1
Cooks, Restaurant	30,360	34,250	3,890	12.8
Waiters and Waitresses	40,230	43,230	3,000	7.5
Retail Salespersons	77,680	80,550	2,870	3.7
Maids and Housekeeping Cleaners	22,930	25,680	2,750	12.0
Project Management Specialists and Business Operations Specialists, All Other	66,210	68,800	2,590	3.9
Home Health and Personal Care Aides	39,930	42,460	2,530	6.3
Stockers and Order Fillers	46,970	49,310	2,340	5.0
General and Operations Managers	37,390	39,420	2,030	5.4

Note: Projections cover Colorado; (1) Sorted by numeric employment change
Source: www.projectionscentral.com, State Occupational Projections, 2021–2023 Short-Term Projections

Fastest-Growing Occupations: 2021 – 2023

Occupation[1]	2021 Employment	2023 Projected Employment	Numeric Employment Change	Percent Employment Change
Motion Picture Projectionists	100	160	60	60.0
Rotary Drill Operators, Oil and Gas	240	340	100	41.7
Athletes and Sports Competitors	420	590	170	40.5
Roustabouts, Oil and Gas	1,780	2,490	710	39.9
Musicians and Singers	710	960	250	35.2
Fine Artists, Including Painters, Sculptors, and Illustrators	310	410	100	32.3
Actors	650	820	170	26.2
Service Unit Operators, Oil, Gas, and Mining	2,020	2,550	530	26.2
Dancers	320	400	80	25.0
Pump Operators, Except Wellhead Pumpers	200	250	50	25.0

Note: Projections cover Colorado; (1) Sorted by percent employment change and excludes occupations with numeric employment change less than 50
Source: www.projectionscentral.com, State Occupational Projections, 2021–2023 Short-Term Projections

TAXES

State Corporate Income Tax Rates

State	Tax Rate (%)	Income Brackets ($)	Num. of Brackets	Financial Institution Tax Rate (%)[a]	Federal Income Tax Ded.
Colorado	4.55	Flat rate	1	4.55	No

Note: Tax rates as of January 1, 2022; (a) Rates listed are the corporate income tax rate applied to financial institutions or excise taxes based on income. Some states have other taxes based upon the value of deposits or shares.
Source: Federation of Tax Administrators, State Corporate Income Tax Rates, January 1, 2022

State Individual Income Tax Rates

State	Tax Rate (%)	Income Brackets ($)	Personal Exemptions ($)			Standard Ded. ($)	
			Single	Married	Depend.	Single	Married
Colorado	4.55	Flat rate	(d)	(d)	(d)	12,950	25,900 (d)

Note: Tax rates as of January 1, 2022; Local- and county-level taxes are not included; Federal income tax is not deductible on state income tax returns; (d) These states use the personal exemption/standard deduction amounts provided in the federal Internal Revenue Code.
Source: Federation of Tax Administrators, State Individual Income Tax Rates, January 1, 2022

Various State Sales and Excise Tax Rates

State	State Sales Tax (%)	Gasoline[1] (¢/gal.)	Cigarette[2] ($/pack)	Spirits[3] ($/gal.)	Wine[4] ($/gal.)	Beer[5] ($/gal.)	Recreational Marijuana (%)
Colorado	2.9	22	1.94	2.28	0.32	0.08	(d)

Note: All tax rates as of January 1, 2022; (1) The American Petroleum Institute has developed a methodology for determining the average tax rate on a gallon of fuel. Rates may include any of the following: excise taxes, environmental fees, storage tank fees, other fees or taxes, general sales tax, and local taxes; (2) The federal excise tax of $1.0066 per pack and local taxes are not included; (3) Rates are those applicable to off-premise sales of 40% alcohol by volume (a.b.v.) distilled spirits in 750ml containers. Local excise taxes are excluded; (4) Rates are those applicable to off-premise sales of 11% a.b.v. non-carbonated wine in 750ml containers; (5) Rates are those applicable to off-premise sales of 4.7% a.b.v. beer in 12 ounce containers; (d) 15% excise tax (levied on wholesale at average market rate); 15% excise tax (retail price)
Source: Tax Foundation, 2022 Facts & Figures: How Does Your State Compare?

State Business Tax Climate Index Rankings

State	Overall Rank	Corporate Tax Rank	Individual Income Tax Rank	Sales Tax Rank	Property Tax Rank	Unemployment Insurance Tax Rank
Colorado	20	6	14	38	34	41

Note: The index is a measure of how each state's tax laws affect economic performance. The lower the rank, the more favorable a state's tax system is for business. States without a given tax are given a ranking of 1. The scores/rankings for the District of Columbia do not affect other states. The 2022 index represents the tax climate as of July 1, 2021.
Source: Tax Foundation, State Business Tax Climate Index 2022

TRANSPORTATION

Means of Transportation to Work

Area	Car/Truck/Van		Public Transportation			Bicycle	Walked	Other Means	Worked at Home
	Drove Alone	Car-pooled	Bus	Subway	Railroad				
City	69.7	6.7	1.9	0.0	0.0	4.9	4.2	0.9	11.6
MSA[1]	73.0	7.3	1.3	0.1	0.0	2.7	2.8	1.1	11.7
U.S.	74.9	8.9	2.2	1.7	0.5	0.5	2.6	1.4	7.3

Note: Figures are percentages and cover workers 16 years of age and older; (1) Figures cover the Fort Collins, CO Metropolitan Statistical Area
Source: U.S. Census Bureau, 2016-2020 American Community Survey 5-Year Estimates

Travel Time to Work

Area	Less Than 10 Minutes	10 to 19 Minutes	20 to 29 Minutes	30 to 44 Minutes	45 to 59 Minutes	60 to 89 Minutes	90 Minutes or More
City	15.7	43.3	20.9	10.2	4.8	3.6	1.5
MSA[1]	13.7	35.5	22.0	15.8	5.9	5.0	2.1
U.S.	12.3	28.4	20.9	20.9	8.3	6.4	2.9

Note: Note: Figures are percentages and include workers 16 years old and over; (1) Figures cover the Fort Collins, CO Metropolitan Statistical Area
Source: U.S. Census Bureau, 2016-2020 American Community Survey 5-Year Estimates

Key Congestion Measures

Measure	1990	2000	2010	2015	2020
Annual Hours of Delay, Total (000)	n/a	n/a	n/a	5,902	3,465
Annual Hours of Delay, Per Auto Commuter	n/a	n/a	n/a	21	12
Annual Congestion Cost, Per Auto Commuter ($)	n/a	n/a	n/a	421	256

Note: n/a not available
Source: Texas A&M Transportation Institute, 2021 Urban Mobility Report

Freeway Travel Time Index

Measure	1985	1990	1995	2000	2005	2010	2015	2020
Urban Area Index[1]	n/a	n/a	n/a	n/a	n/a	n/a	1.10	1.07
Urban Area Rank[1,2]	n/a	n/a	n/a	n/a	n/a	n/a	n/a	n/a

Note: Freeway Travel Time Index—the ratio of travel time in the peak period to the travel time at free-flow conditions. For example, a value of 1.30 indicates a 20-minute free-flow trip takes 26 minutes in the peak (20 minutes x 1.30 = 26 minutes); (1) Covers the Fort Collins CO urban area; (2) Rank is based on 101 larger urban areas (#1 = highest travel time index); n/a not available
Source: Texas A&M Transportation Institute, 2021 Urban Mobility Report

Public Transportation

Agency Name / Mode of Transportation	Vehicles Operated in Maximum Service[1]	Annual Unlinked Passenger Trips[2] (in thous.)	Annual Passenger Miles[3] (in thous.)
Transfort			
Bus (directly operated)	32	1,171.6	4,717.6
Bus (purchased transportation)	2	5.0	21.9
Bus Rapid Transit (directly operated)	6	597.3	1,718.8
Demand Response (purchased transportation)	2	3.2	27.6
Demand Response - Taxi	10	19.9	98.4

Note: (1) Number of revenue vehicles operated by the given mode and type of service to meet the annual maximum service requirement. This is the revenue vehicle count during the peak season of the year; on the week and day that maximum service is provided. Vehicles operated in maximum service (VOMS) exclude atypical days and one-time special events; (2) Number of passengers who boarded public transportation vehicles. Passengers are counted each time they board a vehicle no matter how many vehicles they use to travel from their origin to their destination. (3) Sum of the distances ridden by all passengers during the entire fiscal year.
Source: Federal Transit Administration, National Transit Database, 2020

Air Transportation

Airport Name and Code / Type of Service	Passenger Airlines[1]	Passenger Enplanements	Freight Carriers[2]	Freight (lbs)
Denver International (60 miles) (DEN)				
Domestic service (U.S. carriers - 2021)	22	27,776,445	15	266,792,807
International service (U.S. carriers - 2020)	7	311,343	3	1,986,377

Note: (1) Includes all U.S.-based major, minor and commuter airlines that carried at least one passenger during the year; (2) Includes all U.S.-based airlines and freight carriers that transported at least one pound of freight during the year.
Source: Bureau of Transportation Statistics, The Intermodal Transportation Database, Air Carriers: T-100 Domestic Market (U.S. Carriers), 2021; Bureau of Transportation Statistics, The Intermodal Transportation Database, Air Carriers: T-100 International Market (U.S. Carriers), 2020

BUSINESSES

Major Business Headquarters

Company Name	Industry	Rankings	
		Fortune[1]	Forbes[2]
No companies listed	-	-	-

Note: (1) Companies that produce a 10-K are ranked 1 to 500 based on 2020 revenue; (2) All private companies with at least $2 billion in annual revenue through the end of their most current fiscal year are ranked 1 to 225; companies listed are headquartered in the city; dashes indicate no ranking
Source: Fortune, "Fortune 500," 2021; Forbes, "America's Largest Private Companies," 2021

Living Environment

COST OF LIVING

Cost of Living Index

Composite Index	Groceries	Housing	Utilities	Trans-portation	Health Care	Misc. Goods/ Services
n/a	n/a	n/a	n/a	n/a	n/a	n/a

Note: The Cost of Living Index measures regional differences in the cost of consumer goods and services, excluding taxes and non-consumer expenditures, for professional and managerial households in the top income quintile. It is based on more than 50,000 prices covering almost 60 different items for which prices are collected three times a year by chambers of commerce, economic development organizations or university applied economic centers in each participating urban area. The numbers shown should be read as a percentage above or below the national average of 100. For example, a value of 115.4 in the groceries column indicates that grocery prices are 15.4% higher than the national average. Small differences in the index numbers should not be interpreted as significant; n/a not available.
Source: The Council for Community and Economic Research, Cost of Living Index, 2021

Grocery Prices

Area[1]	T-Bone Steak ($/pound)	Frying Chicken ($/pound)	Whole Milk ($/half gal.)	Eggs ($/dozen)	Orange Juice ($/64 oz.)	Coffee ($/11.5 oz.)
City[2]	n/a	n/a	n/a	n/a	n/a	n/a
Avg.	12.82	1.40	2.22	1.57	3.59	4.30
Min.	8.91	0.91	1.29	0.75	2.87	3.02
Max.	21.35	2.69	3.92	3.86	5.49	8.11

Note: (1) Values for the local area are compared with the average, minimum and maximum values for all 285 areas in the Cost of Living Index; (2) Figures cover the Fort Collins CO urban area; n/a not available; ***T-Bone Steak*** *(price per pound);* ***Frying Chicken*** *(price per pound, whole fryer);* ***Whole Milk*** *(half gallon carton);* ***Eggs*** *(price per dozen, Grade A, large);* ***Orange Juice*** *(64 oz. Tropicana or Florida Natural);* ***Coffee*** *(11.5 oz. can, vacuum-packed, Maxwell House, Hills Bros, or Folgers).*
Source: The Council for Community and Economic Research, Cost of Living Index, 2021

Housing and Utility Costs

Area[1]	New Home Price ($)	Apartment Rent ($/month)	All Electric ($/month)	Part Electric ($/month)	Other Energy ($/month)	Telephone ($/month)
City[2]	n/a	n/a	n/a	n/a	n/a	n/a
Avg.	398,393	1,217	171.38	100.83	69.67	187.75
Min.	212,799	534	96.71	31.56	27.15	173.01
Max.	2,354,006	4,438	369.53	277.33	303.87	206.73

Note: (1) Values for the local area are compared with the average, minimum and maximum values for all 285 areas in the Cost of Living Index; (2) Figures cover the Fort Collins CO urban area; n/a not available; ***New Home Price*** *(2,400 sf living area, 8,000 sf lot, in urban area with full utilities);* ***Apartment Rent*** *(950 sf 2 bedroom/1.5 or 2 bath, unfurnished, excluding all utilities except water);* ***All Electric*** *(average monthly cost for an all-electric home);* ***Part Electric*** *(average monthly cost for a part-electric home);* ***Other Energy*** *(average monthly cost for natural gas, fuel oil, coal, wood, and any other forms of energy except electricity);* ***Telephone*** *(price includes the base monthly rate plus taxes and fees for three lines of mobile phone service).*
Source: The Council for Community and Economic Research, Cost of Living Index, 2021

Health Care, Transportation, and Other Costs

Area[1]	Doctor ($/visit)	Dentist ($/visit)	Optometrist ($/visit)	Gasoline ($/gallon)	Beauty Salon ($/visit)	Men's Shirt ($)
City[2]	n/a	n/a	n/a	n/a	n/a	n/a
Avg.	118.16	101.04	109.44	2.71	40.63	30.77
Min.	35.04	55.56	51.17	2.17	18.59	11.32
Max.	231.10	165.12	256.81	4.11	85.33	63.03

Note: (1) Values for the local area are compared with the average, minimum and maximum values for all 285 areas in the Cost of Living Index; (2) Figures cover the Fort Collins CO urban area; n/a not available; ***Doctor*** *(general practitioners routine exam of an established patient);* ***Dentist*** *(adult teeth cleaning and periodic oral examination);* ***Optometrist*** *(full vision eye exam for established adult patient);* ***Gasoline*** *(one gallon regular unleaded, national brand, including all taxes, cash price at self-service pump if available);* ***Beauty Salon*** *(woman's shampoo, trim, and blow-dry);* ***Men's Shirt*** *(cotton/polyester dress shirt, pinpoint weave, long sleeves).*
Source: The Council for Community and Economic Research, Cost of Living Index, 2021

HOUSING

Homeownership Rate

Area	2013 (%)	2014 (%)	2015 (%)	2016 (%)	2017 (%)	2018 (%)	2019 (%)	2020 (%)	2021 (%)
MSA[1]	n/a	n/a	n/a	n/a	n/a	n/a	n/a	n/a	n/a
U.S.	65.1	64.5	63.7	63.4	63.9	64.4	64.6	66.6	65.5

Note: (1) Figures cover the Fort Collins, CO Metropolitan Statistical Area; n/a not available
Source: U.S. Census Bureau, Housing Vacancies and Homeownership Annual Statistics: 2013-2021

House Price Index (HPI)

Area	National Ranking[2]	Quarterly Change (%)	One-Year Change (%)	Five-Year Change (%)	Since 1991Q1 (%)
MSA[1]	126	2.95	17.86	47.46	448.11
U.S.[3]	–	3.33	17.54	54.45	258.04

Note: The HPI is a weighted repeat sales index. It measures average price changes in repeat sales or refinancings on the same properties. This information is obtained by reviewing repeat mortgage transactions on single-family properties whose mortgages have been purchased or securitized by Fannie Mae or Freddie Mac since January 1975; (1) Figures cover the Fort Collins, CO Metropolitan Statistical Area; (2) Rankings are based on annual percentage change for all metro areas containing at least 15,000 transactions over the last 10 years and ranges from 1 to 268; (3) figures based on a weighted average of Census Division estimates using a seasonally adjusted, purchase-only index; all figures are for the period ending December 31, 2021
Source: Federal Housing Finance Agency, Change in FHFA Metropolitan Area House Price Indexes, 2021Q4

Median Single-Family Home Prices

Area	2019	2020	2021[p]	Percent Change 2020 to 2021
MSA[1]	420.8	446.0	514.3	15.3
U.S. Average	274.6	300.2	353.4	17.7

Note: Figures are median sales prices of existing single-family homes in thousands of dollars; (p) preliminary; (1) Figures cover the Fort Collins, CO Metropolitan Statistical Area
Source: National Association of Realtors, Median Sales Price of Existing Single-Family Homes for Metropolitan Areas, 4th Quarter 2021

Qualifying Income Based on Median Sales Price of Existing Single-Family Homes

Area	With 5% Down ($)	With 10% Down ($)	With 20% Down ($)
MSA[1]	109,632	103,862	92,322
U.S. Average	70,699	66,978	59,536

Note: Figures are preliminary; Qualifying income is based on a mortgage rate of 3.13%. Monthly principal and interest payment is limited to 25% of income; (1) Figures cover the Fort Collins, CO Metropolitan Statistical Area
Source: National Association of Realtors, Qualifying Income Based on Median Sales Price of Existing Single-Family Homes for Metropolitan Areas, 4th Quarter 2021

Home Value Distribution

Area	Under $50,000	$50,000 -$99,999	$100,000 -$149,999	$150,000 -$199,999	$200,000 -$299,999	$300,000 -$499,999	$500,000 -$999,999	$1,000,000 or more
City	2.9	0.9	1.3	2.4	13.9	55.5	21.6	1.5
MSA[1]	3.8	1.3	1.1	2.9	15.7	49.5	23.0	2.6
U.S.	6.6	11.0	12.3	13.6	20.0	20.5	12.3	3.7

Note: Figures are percentages and cover owner-occupied housing units; (1) Figures cover the Fort Collins, CO Metropolitan Statistical Area
Source: U.S. Census Bureau, 2016-2020 American Community Survey 5-Year Estimates

Year Housing Structure Built

Area	2010 or Later	2000 -2009	1990 -1999	1980 -1989	1970 -1979	1960 -1969	1950 -1959	1940 -1949	Before 1940	Median Year
City	11.6	18.4	22.2	14.9	16.8	7.0	2.9	1.6	4.7	1991
MSA[1]	11.9	18.7	20.3	12.8	18.4	7.0	3.5	1.8	5.6	1990
U.S.	6.2	13.6	13.9	13.4	15.0	10.5	10.2	4.8	12.4	1978

Note: Figures are percentages except for Median Year; Note: (1) Figures cover the Fort Collins, CO Metropolitan Statistical Area
Source: U.S. Census Bureau, 2016-2020 American Community Survey 5-Year Estimates

Gross Monthly Rent

Area	Under $500	$500 -$999	$1,000 -$1,499	$1,500 -$1,999	$2,000 -$2,499	$2,500 -$2,999	$3,000 and up	Median ($)
City	2.9	19.2	37.8	28.5	9.0	1.5	1.0	1,373
MSA[1]	3.9	21.1	36.3	27.3	8.0	2.2	1.2	1,340
U.S.	8.9	34.3	30.2	14.9	6.2	2.6	2.8	1,096

Note: Figures are percentages except for Median; Gross rent is the contract rent plus the estimated average monthly cost of utilities (electricity, gas, and water and sewer) and fuels (oil, coal, kerosene, wood, etc.) if these are paid by the renter (or paid for the renter by someone else); (1) Figures cover the Fort Collins, CO Metropolitan Statistical Area
Source: U.S. Census Bureau, 2016-2020 American Community Survey 5-Year Estimates

HEALTH

Health Risk Factors

Category	MSA[1] (%)	U.S. (%)
Adults aged 18–64 who have any kind of health care coverage	n/a	86.8
Adults who reported being in good or better health	n/a	86.7
Adults who are current smokers	n/a	15.5
Adults who currently use chewing tobacco, snuff, or snus	n/a	3.7
Adults who are heavy drinkers[2]	n/a	6.7
Adults who are binge drinkers[3]	n/a	15.7
Adults who are overweight (BMI 25.0 - 29.9)	n/a	35.2
Adults who are obese (BMI 30.0 - 99.8)	n/a	31.9
Adults who participated in any physical activities in the past month	n/a	77.6
Adults who always or nearly always wears a seat belt	n/a	94.2

Note: (1) Figures for the Fort Collins, CO Metropolitan Statistical Area were not available. (2) Heavy drinkers are classified as adult men having more than 14 drinks per week and adult women having more than 7 drinks per week; (3) Binge drinkers are classified as males having five or more drinks on one occasion or females having four or more drinks on one occasion
Source: Centers for Disease Control and Prevention, Behaviorial Risk Factor Surveillance System, SMART: Selected Metropolitan Area Risk Trends, 2020

Acute and Chronic Health Conditions

Category	MSA[1] (%)	U.S. (%)
Adults who have ever been told they had a heart attack	n/a	4.3
Adults who have ever been told they have angina or coronary heart disease	n/a	4.0
Adults who have ever been told they had a stroke	n/a	2.8
Adults who have ever been told they have asthma	n/a	14.2
Adults who have ever been told they have arthritis	n/a	24.5
Adults who have ever been told they have diabetes[2]	n/a	10.6
Adults who have ever been told they had skin cancer	n/a	6.4
Adults who have ever been told they had any other types of cancer	n/a	6.8
Adults who have ever been told they have COPD	n/a	6.2
Adults who have ever been told they have kidney disease	n/a	2.9
Adults who have ever been told they have a form of depression	n/a	19.6

Note: (1) Figures for the Fort Collins, CO Metropolitan Statistical Area were not available. (2) Figures do not include pregnancy-related, borderline, or pre-diabetes
Source: Centers for Disease Control and Prevention, Behaviorial Risk Factor Surveillance System, SMART: Selected Metropolitan Area Risk Trends, 2020

Health Screening and Vaccination Rates

Category	MSA[1] (%)	U.S. (%)
Adults 50-75 who have had a blood stool test within the past year	n/a	9.3
Adults aged 65+ who have had flu shot within the past year	n/a	67.9
Adults aged 65+ who have ever had a pneumonia vaccination	n/a	72.2
Adults who have ever been tested for HIV	n/a	37.1
Women aged 21-65 who have had a pap test in the past three years	n/a	77.7
Men aged 40+ who have had a PSA test within the past two years	n/a	31.8
Women aged 40+ who have had a mammogram within the past two years	n/a	71.5

Note: (1) Figures for the Fort Collins, CO Metropolitan Statistical Area were not available.
Source: Centers for Disease Control and Prevention, Behaviorial Risk Factor Surveillance System, SMART: Selected Metropolitan Area Risk Trends, 2020

Disability Status

Category	MSA[1] (%)	U.S. (%)
Adults who reported being deaf	n/a	6.8
Are you blind or have serious difficulty seeing, even when wearing glasses?	n/a	4.7
Do you have difficulty doing errands alone?	n/a	6.3
Do you have difficulty dressing or bathing?	n/a	3.0
Do you have serious difficulty concentrating/remembering/making decisions?	n/a	10.8
Do you have serious difficulty walking or climbing stairs?	n/a	11.9

Note: (1) Figures for the Fort Collins, CO Metropolitan Statistical Area were not available.
Source: Centers for Disease Control and Prevention, Behaviorial Risk Factor Surveillance System, SMART: Selected Metropolitan Area Risk Trends, 2020

Mortality Rates for the Top 10 Causes of Death in the U.S.

ICD-10[a] Sub-Chapter	ICD-10[a] Code	Age-Adjusted Mortality Rate[1] per 100,000 population	
		County[2]	U.S.
Malignant neoplasms	C00-C97	115.5	146.4
Ischaemic heart diseases	I20-I25	49.2	90.2
Other forms of heart disease	I30-I51	40.8	51.9
Other degenerative diseases of the nervous system	G30-G31	45.7	39.7
Other external causes of accidental injury	W00-X59	30.1	38.7
Chronic lower respiratory diseases	J40-J47	29.6	38.1
Cerebrovascular diseases	I60-I69	36.8	37.6
Organic, including symptomatic, mental disorders	F01-F09	31.9	29.4
Hypertensive diseases	I10-I15	23.2	26.1
Diabetes mellitus	E10-E14	14.4	22.6

Note: (a) ICD-10 = International Classification of Diseases 10th Revision; (1) Mortality rates are a three-year average covering 2018-2020; (2) Figures cover Larimer County.
Source: Centers for Disease Control and Prevention, National Center for Health Statistics. Underlying Cause of Death 1999-2020 on CDC WONDER Online Database

Mortality Rates for Selected Causes of Death

ICD-10[a] Sub-Chapter	ICD-10[a] Code	Age-Adjusted Mortality Rate[1] per 100,000 population	
		County[2]	U.S.
Assault	X85-Y09	Unreliable	6.5
Diseases of the liver	K70-K76	14.4	15.3
Human immunodeficiency virus (HIV) disease	B20-B24	Suppressed	1.4
Influenza and pneumonia	J09-J18	7.7	13.4
Intentional self-harm	X60-X84	21.9	13.9
Malnutrition	E40-E46	2.2	2.9
Obesity and other hyperalimentation	E65-E68	Unreliable	2.4
Renal failure	N17-N19	7.7	12.5
Transport accidents	V01-V99	10.5	12.5
Viral hepatitis	B15-B19	Suppressed	1.0

Note: (a) ICD-10 = International Classification of Diseases 10th Revision; (1) Mortality rates are a three-year average covering 2018-2020; (2) Figures cover Larimer County; Data are suppressed when the data meet the criteria for confidentiality constraints; Mortality rates are flagged as unreliable when the rate would be calculated with a numerator of 20 or less.
Source: Centers for Disease Control and Prevention, National Center for Health Statistics. Underlying Cause of Death 1999-2020 on CDC WONDER Online Database

Health Insurance Coverage

Area	With Health Insurance	With Private Health Insurance	With Public Health Insurance	Without Health Insurance	Population Under Age 19 Without Health Insurance
City	94.0	78.5	24.2	6.0	4.7
MSA[1]	94.0	75.7	29.6	6.0	4.5
U.S.	91.3	68.1	35.3	8.7	5.2

Note: Figures are percentages that cover the civilian noninstitutionalized population; (1) Figures cover the Fort Collins, CO Metropolitan Statistical Area
Source: U.S. Census Bureau, 2016-2020 American Community Survey 5-Year Estimates

Number of Medical Professionals

Area	MDs[3]	DOs[3,4]	Dentists	Podiatrists	Chiropractors	Optometrists
County[1] (number)	881	112	295	22	198	77
County[1] (rate[2])	245.4	31.2	82.2	6.1	55.1	21.4
U.S. (rate[2])	285.1	23.0	71.1	6.2	28.2	17.0

08069
Note: Data as of 2020 unless noted; (1) Data covers Larimer County; (2) Rate per 100,000 population; (3) Data as of 2019 and includes all active, non-federal physicians; (4) Doctor of Osteopathic Medicine
Source: U.S. Department of Health and Human Services, Health Resources and Services Administration, Bureau of Health Professions, Area Resource File (ARF) 2020-2021

Best Hospitals

According to *U.S. News*, the Fort Collins, CO metro area is home to one of the best hospitals in the U.S.: **UCHealth Poudre Valley Hospital** (1 adult specialty). The hospital listed was nationally ranked in at least one of 15 adult or 10 pediatric specialties. Only 175 U.S. hospitals performed well enough to be nationally ranked in one or more specialties. Twenty hospitals in the U.S. made the Honor Roll. The Best Hospitals Honor Roll takes both the national rankings and the procedure and condition ratings into account. Hospitals received points if they were nationally ranked in one of the 15 adult specialties—the higher they ranked, the more points they got—and how many ratings of "high performing" they earned in the 17 procedures and conditions. *U.S. News Online, "America's Best Hospitals 2021-22"*

EDUCATION

Public School District Statistics

District Name	Schls	Pupils	Pupil/ Teacher Ratio	Minority Pupils[1] (%)	LEP/ELL[2] (%)	IEP[3] (%)
Poudre School District R-1	51	30,754	17.1	27.1	4.3	n/a

Note: Table includes school districts with 2,000 or more students; (1) Percentage of students that are not non-Hispanic white; (2) Percentage of students that are Limited English Proficient (LEP) or English Language Learners (ELL) (2018-19); (3) Percentage of students that have an Individualized Education Program (IEP).
Source: U.S. Department of Education, National Center for Education Statistics, Common Core of Data, Local Education Agency (School District) Universe Survey: School Year 2019-2020

Best High Schools

According to *U.S. News,* Fort Collins is home to one of the top 500 high schools in the U.S.: **Liberty Common Charter School** (#141). Nearly 18,000 public, magnet and charter schools were ranked based on their performance on state assessments and how well they prepare students for college. *U.S. News & World Report, "Best High Schools 2021"*

Highest Level of Education

Area	Less than H.S.	H.S. Diploma	Some College, No Deg.	Associate Degree	Bachelor's Degree	Master's Degree	Prof. School Degree	Doctorate Degree
City	3.3	15.0	17.2	8.9	31.9	17.5	2.4	3.8
MSA[1]	3.8	18.6	20.6	9.3	28.1	14.4	2.3	2.9
U.S.	11.5	26.7	20.3	8.6	20.2	9.1	2.2	1.5

Note: Figures cover persons age 25 and over; (1) Figures cover the Fort Collins, CO Metropolitan Statistical Area
Source: U.S. Census Bureau, 2016-2020 American Community Survey 5-Year Estimates

Educational Attainment by Race

Area	High School Graduate or Higher (%)					Bachelor's Degree or Higher (%)				
	Total	White	Black	Asian	Hisp.[2]	Total	White	Black	Asian	Hisp.[2]
City	96.7	97.3	94.0	91.4	85.9	55.6	56.7	33.9	69.7	33.6
MSA[1]	96.2	96.7	95.5	90.3	84.1	47.7	48.4	32.8	57.6	26.9
U.S.	88.5	90.7	86.7	87.3	70.3	32.9	34.4	22.6	55.0	17.6

Note: Figures shown cover persons 25 years old and over; (1) Figures cover the Fort Collins, CO Metropolitan Statistical Area; (2) People of Hispanic origin can be of any race
Source: U.S. Census Bureau, 2016-2020 American Community Survey 5-Year Estimates

School Enrollment by Grade and Control

Area	Preschool (%)		Kindergarten (%)		Grades 1 - 4 (%)		Grades 5 - 8 (%)		Grades 9 - 12 (%)	
	Public	Private	Public	Private	Public	Private	Public	Private	Public	Private
City	42.2	57.8	91.2	8.8	94.4	5.6	93.5	6.5	93.2	6.8
MSA[1]	44.2	55.8	91.4	8.6	90.5	9.5	88.1	11.9	88.6	11.4
U.S.	58.9	41.1	86.9	13.1	89.0	11.0	89.0	11.0	89.7	10.3

Note: Figures shown cover persons 3 years old and over; (1) Figures cover the Fort Collins, CO Metropolitan Statistical Area
Source: U.S. Census Bureau, 2016-2020 American Community Survey 5-Year Estimates

Higher Education

Four-Year Colleges			Two-Year Colleges			Medical Schools[1]	Law Schools[2]	Voc/ Tech[3]
Public	Private Non-profit	Private For-profit	Public	Private Non-profit	Private For-profit			
1	0	0	0	0	1	0	0	1

Note: Figures cover institutions located within the Fort Collins, CO Metropolitan Statistical Area and include main campuses only; (1) includes schools accredited by the Liaison Committee on Medical Education and the American Osteopathic Association's Commission on Osteopathic College Accreditation; (2) includes ABA-accredited schools, schools with provisional ABA accreditation, and state accredited schools; (3) includes all schools with programs that are less than 2 years.
Source: National Center for Education Statistics, Integrated Postsecondary Education System (IPEDS), 2020-21; Wikipedia, List of Medical Schools in the United States, accessed April 11, 2022; Wikipedia, List of Law Schools in the United States, accessed April 11, 2022

According to *U.S. News & World Report,* the Fort Collins, CO metro area is home to one of the top 200 national universities in the U.S.: **Colorado State University** (#148 tie). The indicators used to capture academic quality fall into a number of categories: assessment by administrators at peer institutions; retention of students; faculty resources; student selectivity; financial resources; alumni giving; high school counselor ratings of colleges; and graduation rate. *U.S. News & World Report, "America's Best Colleges 2022"*

EMPLOYERS

Major Employers

Company Name	Industry
Advanced Energy Industrials	Special industry machinery
Anheuser Busch	Malt beverages
Animal and Plant Health Inspection	Management services
Aramark Corporation	Food/bars
Center Partners	Business services
City of Loveland	Municipal government
Colorado State University	Colleges & universities
Contibeef	Beef cattle feedlots
Deere and Company	Farm machinery/equipment
Hach Company	Analytical instruments
Hewlett-Packard Co.	Electronic computers
Medical Center of the Rockies	General medical & surgical hospitals
Poudre School District	Building cleaning service
Poudre Valley Health Systems	General medical & surgical hospitals
Woodward	Aircraft engines & engine parts

Note: Companies shown are located within the Fort Collins, CO Metropolitan Statistical Area.
Source: Hoovers.com; Wikipedia

PUBLIC SAFETY

Crime Rate

Area	Total Crime	Violent Crime Rate				Property Crime Rate		
		Murder	Rape[3]	Robbery	Aggrav. Assault	Burglary	Larceny -Theft	Motor Vehicle Theft
City	2,389.9	0.6	24.0	21.1	171.5	204.8	1,834.5	133.4
Suburbs[1]	1,855.9	1.1	44.9	14.6	189.3	184.4	1,296.7	124.9
Metro[2]	2,112.3	0.8	34.8	17.7	180.7	194.2	1,555.0	129.0
U.S.	2,510.4	5.1	42.6	81.8	250.4	340.5	1,569.2	220.8

Note: Figures are crimes per 100,000 population; (1) All areas within the metro area that are located outside the city limits; (2) Figures cover the Fort Collins, CO Metropolitan Statistical Area; (3) All figures shown were reported using the revised Uniform Crime Reporting (UCR) definition of rape.
Source: FBI Uniform Crime Reports, 2019 (data for 2020 was not available)

Hate Crimes

Area	Number of Quarters Reported	Number of Incidents per Bias Motivation					
		Race/Ethnicity/ Ancestry	Religion	Sexual Orientation	Disability	Gender	Gender Identity
City	4	2	1	0	0	0	0
U.S.	4	5,227	1,244	1,110	130	75	266

Source: Federal Bureau of Investigation, Hate Crime Statistics 2020

Identity Theft Consumer Reports

Area	Reports	Reports per 100,000 Population	Rank[2]
MSA[1]	2,272	637	26
U.S.	1,434,676	432	-

Note: (1) Figures cover the Fort Collins, CO Metropolitan Statistical Area; (2) Rank ranges from 1 to 391 where 1 indicates greatest number of identity theft reports per 100,000 population
Source: Federal Trade Commission, Consumer Sentinel Network Data Book 2021

Fraud and Other Consumer Reports

Area	Reports	Reports per 100,000 Population	Rank[2]
MSA[1]	3,731	1,045	88
U.S.	4,328,977	1,304	-

Note: (1) Figures cover the Fort Collins, CO Metropolitan Statistical Area; (2) Rank ranges from 1 to 391 where 1 indicates greatest number of fraud and other consumer reports per 100,000 population
Source: Federal Trade Commission, Consumer Sentinel Network Data Book 2021

POLITICS

2020 Presidential Election Results

Area	Biden	Trump	Jorgensen	Hawkins	Other
Larimer County	56.2	40.8	1.8	0.3	0.9
U.S.	51.3	46.8	1.2	0.3	0.5

Note: Results are percentages and may not add to 100% due to rounding
Source: Dave Leip's Atlas of U.S. Presidential Elections

SPORTS

Professional Sports Teams

Team Name	League	Year Established
No teams are located in the metro area		

Source: Wikipedia, Major Professional Sports Teams of the United States and Canada, April 6, 2022

CLIMATE

Average and Extreme Temperatures

Temperature	Jan	Feb	Mar	Apr	May	Jun	Jul	Aug	Sep	Oct	Nov	Dec	Yr.
Extreme High (°F)	73	76	84	90	93	102	103	100	97	89	79	75	103
Average High (°F)	43	47	52	62	71	81	88	86	77	67	52	45	64
Average Temp. (°F)	30	34	39	48	58	67	73	72	63	52	39	32	51
Average Low (°F)	16	20	25	34	44	53	59	57	48	37	25	18	37
Extreme Low (°F)	-25	-25	-10	-2	22	30	43	41	17	3	-8	-25	-25

Note: Figures cover the years 1948-1992
Source: National Climatic Data Center, International Station Meteorological Climate Summary, 9/96

Average Precipitation/Snowfall/Humidity

Precip./Humidity	Jan	Feb	Mar	Apr	May	Jun	Jul	Aug	Sep	Oct	Nov	Dec	Yr.
Avg. Precip. (in.)	0.6	0.6	1.3	1.7	2.5	1.7	1.9	1.5	1.1	1.0	0.9	0.6	15.5
Avg. Snowfall (in.)	9	7	14	9	2	Tr	0	0	2	4	9	8	63
Avg. Rel. Hum. 5am (%)	62	65	67	66	70	68	67	68	66	63	66	63	66
Avg. Rel. Hum. 5pm (%)	49	44	40	35	38	34	34	34	32	34	47	50	39

Note: Figures cover the years 1948-1992; Tr = Trace amounts (<0.05 in. of rain; <0.5 in. of snow)
Source: National Climatic Data Center, International Station Meteorological Climate Summary, 9/96

Weather Conditions

Temperature			Daytime Sky			Precipitation		
10°F & below	32°F & below	90°F & above	Clear	Partly cloudy	Cloudy	0.01 inch or more precip.	0.1 inch or more snow/ice	Thunder-storms
24	155	33	99	177	89	90	38	39

Note: Figures are average number of days per year and cover the years 1948-1992
Source: National Climatic Data Center, International Station Meteorological Climate Summary, 9/96

HAZARDOUS WASTE

Superfund Sites

The Fort Collins, CO metro area has no sites on the EPA's Superfund Final National Priorities List. There are a total of 1,165 Superfund sites with a status of proposed or final on the list in the U.S. *U.S. Environmental Protection Agency, National Priorities List, April 6, 2022*

AIR QUALITY

Air Quality Trends: Ozone

	1990	1995	2000	2005	2010	2016	2017	2018	2019	2020
MSA[1]	0.066	0.072	0.074	0.076	0.072	0.069	0.067	0.073	0.065	0.070
U.S.	0.090	0.091	0.082	0.080	0.074	0.070	0.069	0.070	0.066	0.068

Note: (1) Data covers the Fort Collins, CO Metropolitan Statistical Area. The values shown are the composite ozone concentration averages among trend sites based on the highest fourth daily maximum 8-hour concentration in parts per million. These trends are based on sites having an adequate record of monitoring data during the trend period. Data from exceptional events are included.
Source: U.S. Environmental Protection Agency, Air Quality Monitoring Information, "Air Quality Trends by City, 1990-2020"

Air Quality Index

Area	Percent of Days when Air Quality was...[2]					AQI Statistics[2]	
	Good	Moderate	Unhealthy for Sensitive Groups	Unhealthy	Very Unhealthy	Maximum	Median
MSA[1]	60.7	34.2	4.6	0.5	0.0	157	48

Note: (1) Data covers the Fort Collins, CO Metropolitan Statistical Area; (2) Based on 366 days with AQI data in 2020. Air Quality Index (AQI) is an index for reporting daily air quality. EPA calculates the AQI for five major air pollutants regulated by the Clean Air Act: ground-level ozone, particle pollution (aka particulate matter), carbon monoxide, sulfur dioxide, and nitrogen dioxide. The AQI runs from 0 to 500. The higher the AQI value, the greater the level of air pollution and the greater the health concern. There are six AQI categories: "Good" AQI is between 0 and 50. Air quality is considered satisfactory; "Moderate" AQI is between 51 and 100. Air quality is acceptable; "Unhealthy for Sensitive Groups" When AQI values are between 101 and 150, members of sensitive groups may experience health effects; "Unhealthy" When AQI values are between 151 and 200 everyone may begin to experience health effects; "Very Unhealthy" AQI values between 201 and 300 trigger a health alert; "Hazardous" AQI values over 300 trigger warnings of emergency conditions (not shown).
Source: U.S. Environmental Protection Agency, Air Quality Index Report, 2020

Air Quality Index Pollutants

Area	Percent of Days when AQI Pollutant was...[2]					
	Carbon Monoxide	Nitrogen Dioxide	Ozone	Sulfur Dioxide	Particulate Matter 2.5	Particulate Matter 10
MSA[1]	0.0	0.0	86.3	0.0	13.7	0.0

Note: (1) Data covers the Fort Collins, CO Metropolitan Statistical Area; (2) Based on 366 days with AQI data in 2020. The Air Quality Index (AQI) is an index for reporting daily air quality. EPA calculates the AQI for five major air pollutants regulated by the Clean Air Act: ground-level ozone, particle pollution (also known as particulate matter), carbon monoxide, sulfur dioxide, and nitrogen dioxide. The AQI runs from 0 to 500. The higher the AQI value, the greater the level of air pollution and the greater the health concern.
Source: U.S. Environmental Protection Agency, Air Quality Index Report, 2020

Maximum Air Pollutant Concentrations: Particulate Matter, Ozone, CO and Lead

	Particulate Matter 10 (ug/m^3)	Particulate Matter 2.5 Wtd AM (ug/m^3)	Particulate Matter 2.5 24-Hr (ug/m^3)	Ozone (ppm)	Carbon Monoxide (ppm)	Lead (ug/m^3)
MSA[1] Level	n/a	8.1	47	0.075	1	n/a
NAAQS[2]	150	15	35	0.075	9	0.15
Met NAAQS[2]	n/a	Yes	No	Yes	Yes	n/a

Note: (1) Data covers the Fort Collins, CO Metropolitan Statistical Area; Data from exceptional events are included; (2) National Ambient Air Quality Standards; ppm = parts per million; ug/m^3 = micrograms per cubic meter; n/a not available.
Concentrations: Particulate Matter 10 (coarse particulate)—highest second maximum 24-hour concentration; Particulate Matter 2.5 Wtd AM (fine particulate)—highest weighted annual mean concentration; Particulate Matter 2.5 24-Hour (fine particulate)—highest 98th percentile 24-hour concentration; Ozone—highest fourth daily maximum 8-hour concentration; Carbon Monoxide—highest second maximum non-overlapping 8-hour concentration; Lead—maximum running 3-month average
Source: U.S. Environmental Protection Agency, Air Quality Monitoring Information, "Air Quality Statistics by City, 2020"

Maximum Air Pollutant Concentrations: Nitrogen Dioxide and Sulfur Dioxide

	Nitrogen Dioxide AM (ppb)	Nitrogen Dioxide 1-Hr (ppb)	Sulfur Dioxide AM (ppb)	Sulfur Dioxide 1-Hr (ppb)	Sulfur Dioxide 24-Hr (ppb)
MSA[1] Level	n/a	n/a	n/a	n/a	n/a
NAAQS[2]	53	100	30	75	140
Met NAAQS[2]	n/a	n/a	n/a	n/a	n/a

Note: (1) Data covers the Fort Collins, CO Metropolitan Statistical Area; Data from exceptional events are included; (2) National Ambient Air Quality Standards; ppm = parts per million; ug/m^3 = micrograms per cubic meter; n/a not available.
Concentrations: Nitrogen Dioxide AM—highest arithmetic mean concentration; Nitrogen Dioxide 1-Hr—highest 98th percentile 1-hour daily maximum concentration; Sulfur Dioxide AM—highest annual mean concentration; Sulfur Dioxide 1-Hr—highest 99th percentile 1-hour daily maximum concentration; Sulfur Dioxide 24-Hr—highest second maximum 24-hour concentration
Source: U.S. Environmental Protection Agency, Air Quality Monitoring Information, "Air Quality Statistics by City, 2020"

Honolulu, Hawaii

Background

Honolulu, whose name means "sheltered harbor," is the capital of Hawaii and the seat of Honolulu County. The city sits in one of the most famously attractive areas of the world, on the island of Oahu, home to the extinct volcano Diamond Head, Waikiki Beach, and two mountain ranges, the Koolau and the Waianae. Honolulu is the economic hub of Hawaii and a major seaport. In 2017, the city saw 9.4 million visitors spend $16 billion. COVID-19 has significantly impacted those numbers, but Hawaii Tourism Authority sees tourism on the upswing.

Traditionally home to fishing and horticultural tribal groups, the Hawaiian Islands were politically united under the reign of King Kamehameha I, who first moved his triumphant court to Waikiki and subsequently to a site in what is now downtown Honolulu (1804). It was during his time that the port became a center for the sandalwood trade, thus establishing the region as an international presence even before the political interventions of non-Hawaiians.

European activity dates from 1794, when the English sea captain William Brown entered Honolulu, dubbing it Fair Harbor. Two decades later, the first missionaries arrived. American Congregationalists were followed by French Catholics and, later, Mormons and Anglicans. By the end of the nineteenth century, non-Hawaiians owned most of the land. In 1898 Hawaii was annexed by the U.S.

As is true for many strategically located cities, the events of World War II had a profound effect on Honolulu. The Japanese attack on December 7, 1941, forever etched the name of Pearl Harbor into the national memory. During the war, existing military bases were expanded, and new bases built, providing considerable economic stimuli. The Vietnam War also had a dramatic effect on Honolulu and by the end of the twentieth century, military families accounted for 10 percent of the population.

Today, the U.S. military employs more than 45,000 throughout the state. Fruit, primarily pineapple, processing and light manufacturing are also important to the economy. Aquaculture, which includes cultivated species of shellfish, finfish, and algae, has grown in recent years, as has biotechnology.

Tourism, however, has been the private-sector mainstay of Honolulu's economy, with most of the millions of tourists who visit Hawaii annually coming through its port or airport. Honolulu is a required stop for any holiday ship cruising these waters, and it is also the center for the inter-island air services that ferry tourists to various resort locations.

The center of Honolulu's downtown district is dominated by the Iolani Palace, once home to Hawaii's original royal family. Nearby are the State Capitol Building and the State Supreme Court Building, known as Ali'iolani Hall. The Aloha Tower Development Corporation continues to modernize the mixed-use space in and around the Aloha Tower Complex along the city's piers.

Construction of the Honolulu High-Capacity Transit Corridor Project, including a new rail line connecting Kapolei in West Oahu to the University of Hawaii at Manoa was completed in 2018.

Honolulu, as it has grown along the southern coast of Oahu, has established a mix of residential zones, with single-family dwellings and relatively small multi-unit buildings. The result is that large parts of what is a major metropolitan area feel like cozy neighborhoods. In fact, Honolulu is governed in part through a Neighborhood Board System, which insures maximal local input with regard to planning decisions and city services.

Cultural amenities include the Bishop Museum, the Honolulu Academy of Arts, and the Contemporary Museum, which together offer world-class collections in Polynesian art and artifacts, Japanese, Chinese, and Korean art, and modern art from the world over. Honolulu also hosts a symphony orchestra, the oldest U.S. symphony orchestra west of the Rocky Mountains, which performs at the Neal S. Blaisdell Center.

Barack Obama, the United States' 44th president, is the first president from Hawaii. Obama was born in Honolulu, causing the city a fair amount of attention during the 2008 presidential election.

Honolulu's weather is subtropical, with temperatures moderated by the surrounding ocean and the trade winds. There are only slight variations in temperature from summer to winter. Rain is moderate, though heavier in summer, when it sometimes comes in the form of quick showers while the sun is shining— known locally as "liquid sunshine."

Rankings

General Rankings

- For its "Best for Vets: Places to Live 2019" rankings, *Military Times* evaluated 599 cities (83 large, 234 medium, 282 small) and compared the locations across three broad categories: veteran and military culture/services; economic indicators; and livability factors such as health, crime, traffic, and school quality. Honolulu ranked #5 out of the top 25, in the large city category (population of more than 250,000). Data points more specific to veterans and the military weighed more heavily than others. *rebootcamp.militarytimes.com, "Military Times Best Places to Live 2019," September 10, 2018*
- The human resources consulting firm Mercer ranked 231 major cities worldwide in terms of overall quality of life. Honolulu ranked #37. Criteria: political, social, economic, and socio-cultural factors; medical and health considerations; schools and education; public services and transportation; recreation; consumer goods; housing; and natural environment. *Mercer, "Mercer 2019 Quality of Living Survey," March 13, 2019*
- Honolulu appeared on *Travel + Leisure's* list of the 15 best cities in the United States. The city was ranked #10. Criteria: sights/landmarks; culture; food; friendliness; shopping; and overall value. *Travel + Leisure, "The World's Best Awards 2021" September 8, 2021*
- For its 34th annual "Readers' Choice Awards" survey, *Condé Nast Traveler* ranked its readers' favorite cities in the U.S. Whether it be a longed for visit or a first on the list, these are the places that inspired a return to travel. The list was broken into large cities and cities under 250,000. Honolulu ranked #9 in the big city category. *Condé Nast Traveler, Readers' Choice Awards 2021, "Best Big Cities in the U.S." October 5, 2021*

Business/Finance Rankings

- The Brookings Institution ranked the nation's largest cities based on income inequality. Honolulu was ranked #54 (#1 = greatest inequality). Criteria: the "95/20 ratio," a figure representing the income at which a household earns more than 95 percent of all other households, divided by the income at which a household earns more than only 20 percent of all other households. *Brookings Institution, "Household Income Inequality, Largest Cities of 97 Large U.S. Metro Areas, 2014-2016," February 5, 2018*
- The Brookings Institution ranked the 100 largest metro areas in the U.S. based on income inequality. Honolulu was ranked #79 (#1 = greatest inequality). Criteria: the "95/20 ratio," a figure representing the income at which a household earns more than 95 percent of all other households, divided by the income at which a household earns more than only 20 percent of all other households. *Brookings Institution, "Household Income Inequality, 100 Largest U.S. Metro Areas, 2014-2016," February 5, 2018*
- For its annual survey of the "Most Expensive U.S. Cities to Live In," Kiplinger applied Cost of Living Index statistics developed by the Council for Community and Economic Research to U.S. Census Bureau population and median household income data for 256 urban areas. Honolulu was among the 20 most expensive in the country. *Kiplinger.com, "The 20 Most Expensive Cities in the U.S.," March 16, 2022*
- The Honolulu metro area appeared on the Milken Institute "2021 Best Performing Cities" list. Rank: #196 out of 200 large metro areas (population over 250,000). Criteria: job growth; wage and salary growth; high-tech output growth; housing affordability; household broadband access. *Milken Institute, "Best-Performing Cities 2021," February 16, 2021*
- *Forbes* ranked the 200 most populous metro areas to determine the nation's "Best Places for Business and Careers." The Honolulu metro area was ranked #162. Criteria: costs (business and living); job growth (past and projected); income growth; quality of life; educational attainment (college and high school); projected economic growth; cultural and leisure opportunities; workplace tolerance laws; net migration patterns. *Forbes, "The Best Places for Business and Careers 2019: Seattle Still On Top," October 30, 2019*
- Mercer Human Resources Consulting ranked 209 cities worldwide in terms of cost-of-living. Honolulu ranked #43 (the lower the ranking, the higher the cost-of-living). The survey measured the comparative cost of over 200 items (such as housing, food, clothing, household goods, transportation, and entertainment) in each location. *Mercer, "2021 Cost of Living City Ranking," June 22, 2021*

Education Rankings

- Personal finance website *WalletHub* analyzed the 150 largest U.S. metropolitan statistical areas to determine where the most educated Americans are putting their degrees to work. Criteria: education levels; percentage of workers with degrees; education quality and attainment gap; public school quality rankings; quality and enrollment of each metro area's universities. Honolulu was ranked #28 (#1 = most educated city). *www.WalletHub.com, "Most & Least Educated Cities in America," July 19, 2021*
- Honolulu was selected as one of America's most literate cities. The city ranked #30 out of the 84 largest U.S. cities. Criteria: number of booksellers; library resources; Internet resources; educational attainment; periodical publishing resources; newspaper circulation. *Central Connecticut State University, "America's Most Literate Cities, 2018," February 2019*

Environmental Rankings

- Honolulu was highlighted as one of the cleanest metro areas for ozone air pollution in the U.S. during 2017 through 2019. The list represents cities with no monitored ozone air pollution in unhealthful ranges. *American Lung Association, "State of the Air 2021," April 21, 2021*
- Honolulu was highlighted as one of the top 25 cleanest metro areas for year-round particle pollution (Annual PM 2.5) in the U.S. during 2017 through 2019. The area ranked #1. *American Lung Association, "State of the Air 2021," April 21, 2021*
- Honolulu was highlighted as one of the top 98 cleanest metro areas for short-term particle pollution (24-hour PM 2.5) in the U.S. during 2017 through 2019. Monitors in these cities reported no days with unhealthful PM 2.5 levels. *American Lung Association, "State of the Air 2021," April 21, 2021*

Health/Fitness Rankings

- For each of the 100 largest cities in the United States, the American Fitness Index®, published by the American College of Sports Medicine and the Anthem Foundation, evaluated community infrastructure and 34 health behaviors including preventive health, levels of chronic disease conditions, food insecurity, sleep quality, pedestrian safety, air quality, and community resources that support physical activity. Honolulu ranked #23 for "community fitness." *americanfitnessindex.org, "2021 ACSM American Fitness Index Summary Report," July 13, 2021*
- The Sharecare Community Well-Being Index evaluates 10 individual and social health factors in order to measure what matters to Americans in the communities in which they live. The Honolulu metro area ranked #6 in the top 10 across all 10 domains. Criteria: access to healthcare, food, and community resources; housng and transportation; economic security; feeling of purpose; physical, financial, social, and community well-being. *www.sharecare.com, "Community Well-Being Index: 2020 Metro Area & County Rankings Report," August 30, 2021*

Real Estate Rankings

- *WalletHub* compared the most populated U.S. cities to determine which had the best markets for real estate agents. Honolulu ranked #41 where demand was high and pay was the best. Criteria: sales per agent; annual median wage for real-estate agents; monthly average starting salary for real estate agents; real estate job density and competition; unemployment rate; home turnover rate; housing-market health index; and other relevant metrics. *www.WalletHub.com, "2021 Best Places to Be a Real Estate Agent," May 12, 2021*
- The Honolulu metro area was identified as one of the 20 least affordable housing markets in the U.S. in 2021. The area ranked #180 out of 183 markets. Criteria: qualification for a mortgage loan with a 10 percent down payment on a typical home. *National Association of Realtors®, Qualifying Income Based on Sales Price of Existing Single-Family Homes for Metropolitan Areas, 2021*
- Honolulu was ranked #186 out of 237 metro areas in terms of housing affordability in 2021 by the National Association of Home Builders (#1 = most affordable). Criteria: the share of homes sold in that area affordable to a family earning the local median income, based on standard mortgage underwriting criteria. *National Association of Home Builders®, NAHB-Wells Fargo Housing Opportunity Index, 4th Quarter 2021*

Safety Rankings

- Allstate ranked the 200 largest cities in America in terms of driver safety. Honolulu ranked #94. Criteria: internal property damage claims over a two-year period from January 2016 to December 2017. The report helps increase the importance of safety and awareness behind the wheel. *Allstate, "Allstate America's Best Drivers Report, 2019" June 24, 2019*

- The National Insurance Crime Bureau ranked 390 metro areas in the U.S. in terms of per capita rates of vehicle theft. The Honolulu metro area ranked #101 (#1 = highest rate). Criteria: number of vehicle theft offenses per 100,000 inhabitants in 2020. *National Insurance Crime Bureau, "Hot Spots 2020," August 31, 2021*

Seniors/Retirement Rankings

- From its Best Cities for Successful Aging indexes, the Milken Institute generated rankings for metropolitan areas, weighing data in nine categories—health care, wellness, living arrangements, transportation and convenience, financial characteristics, education, employment, community engagement, and overall livability. The Honolulu metro area was ranked #24 overall in the large metro area category. *Milken Institute, "Best Cities for Successful Aging, 2017" March 14, 2017*

Transportation Rankings

- Honolulu was identified as one of the most congested metro areas in the U.S. The area ranked #7 out of 10. Criteria: yearly delay per auto commuter in hours. *Texas A&M Transportation Institute, "2021 Urban Mobility Report," June 2021*

Women/Minorities Rankings

- Personal finance website *WalletHub* compared more than 180 U.S. cities across two key dimensions, "Hispanic Business-Friendliness" and "Hispanic Purchasing Power," to arrive at the most favorable conditions for Hispanic entrepreneurs. Honolulu was ranked #151 out of 182. Criteria includes: share of Hispanic-Owned Businesses; Hispanic entrepreneurship rate to median annual income of Hispanics; Small Business-Friendliness score; cost of living; and number of Hispanics with at least a bachelor's degree. *WalletHub.com, "2019's Best Cities for Hispanic Entrepreneurs," May 1, 2019*

Miscellaneous Rankings

- *MoveHub* ranked 446 hipster cities across 20 countries, using its *alternative* Hipster Index and Honolulu came out as #45 among the top 50. Criteria: population over 150,000; number of vintage boutiques; density of tattoo parlors; vegan places to eat; coffee shops; and density of vinyl record stores. *www.movehub.com, "The Hipster Index: Brighton Pips Portland to Global Top Spot," July 28, 2021*
- Honolulu was selected as one of "America's Friendliest Cities." The city ranked #19 in the "Friendliest" category. Respondents to an online survey were asked to rate 38 top urban destinations in the United States as to general friendliness, as well as manners, politeness and warm disposition. *Travel + Leisure, "America's Friendliest Cities," October 20, 2017*

Business Environment

DEMOGRAPHICS

Population Growth

Area	1990 Census	2000 Census	2010 Census	2020* Estimate	Population Growth (%) 1990-2020	Population Growth (%) 2010-2020
City	376,465	371,657	337,256	347,181	-7.8	2.9
MSA[1]	836,231	876,156	953,207	979,682	17.2	2.8
U.S.	248,709,873	281,421,906	308,745,538	326,569,308	31.3	5.8

Note: (1) Figures cover the Urban Honolulu, HI Metropolitan Statistical Area; (*) 2016-2020 5-year estimated population
Source: U.S. Census Bureau, 1990 Census, Census 2000, Census 2010, 2016-2020 American Community Survey 5-Year Estimates

Household Size

Area	Persons in Household (%) One	Two	Three	Four	Five	Six	Seven or More	Average Household Size
City	34.7	30.8	14.2	10.4	5.0	2.2	2.7	2.60
MSA[1]	24.5	30.5	16.8	13.3	7.4	3.6	3.9	3.00
U.S.	28.0	33.9	15.5	12.9	6.0	2.3	1.4	2.60

Note: (1) Figures cover the Urban Honolulu, HI Metropolitan Statistical Area
Source: U.S. Census Bureau, 2016-2020 American Community Survey 5-Year Estimates

Race

Area	White Alone[2] (%)	Black Alone[2] (%)	Asian Alone[2] (%)	AIAN[3] Alone[2] (%)	NHOPI[4] Alone[2] (%)	Other Race Alone[2] (%)	Two or More Races (%)
City	16.9	2.0	53.1	0.2	8.3	1.0	18.6
MSA[1]	20.2	2.5	42.6	0.2	10.0	1.2	23.3
U.S.	70.4	12.6	5.6	0.8	0.2	5.1	5.2

Note: (1) Figures cover the Urban Honolulu, HI Metropolitan Statistical Area; (2) Alone is defined as not being in combination with one or more other races; (3) American Indian and Alaska Native; (4) Native Hawaiian and Other Pacific Islander
Source: U.S. Census Bureau, 2016-2020 American Community Survey 5-Year Estimates

Hispanic or Latino Origin

Area	Total (%)	Mexican (%)	Puerto Rican (%)	Cuban (%)	Other (%)
City	7.2	2.1	1.8	0.1	3.1
MSA[1]	10.0	3.0	3.3	0.1	3.6
U.S.	18.2	11.2	1.7	0.7	4.5

Note: Persons of Hispanic or Latino origin can be of any race; (1) Figures cover the Urban Honolulu, HI Metropolitan Statistical Area
Source: U.S. Census Bureau, 2016-2020 American Community Survey 5-Year Estimates

Ancestry

Area	German	Irish	English	American	Italian	Polish	French[2]	Scottish	Dutch
City	4.2	3.2	2.9	1.3	1.6	0.8	0.8	0.6	0.3
MSA[1]	5.3	3.9	3.4	1.3	1.9	0.9	1.1	0.8	0.4
U.S.	13.0	9.7	7.7	5.9	5.1	2.7	2.3	1.6	1.1

Note: Figures are the percentage of the total population reporting a particular ancestry. The nine most commonly reported ancestries in the U.S. are shown. Figures include multiple ancestries (e.g. if a person reported being Irish and Italian, they were included in both columns); (1) Figures cover the Urban Honolulu, HI Metropolitan Statistical Area; (2) Excludes Basque
Source: U.S. Census Bureau, 2016-2020 American Community Survey 5-Year Estimates

Foreign-born Population

Area	Percent of Population Born in: Any Foreign Country	Asia	Mexico	Europe	Caribbean	Central America[2]	South America	Africa	Canada
City	27.5	22.9	0.2	0.9	0.2	0.1	0.2	0.1	0.2
MSA[1]	19.5	15.7	0.2	0.7	0.2	0.1	0.2	0.1	0.2
U.S.	13.5	4.2	3.3	1.5	1.3	1.1	1.0	0.7	0.3

Note: (1) Figures cover the Urban Honolulu, HI Metropolitan Statistical Area; (2) Excludes Mexico.
Source: U.S. Census Bureau, 2016-2020 American Community Survey 5-Year Estimates

Marital Status

Area	Never Married	Now Married[2]	Separated	Widowed	Divorced
City	37.0	45.0	1.3	7.0	9.7
MSA[1]	34.2	49.7	1.2	6.4	8.5
U.S.	33.5	48.1	1.8	5.7	10.8

Note: Figures are percentages and cover the population 15 years of age and older; (1) Figures cover the Urban Honolulu, HI Metropolitan Statistical Area; (2) Excludes separated
Source: U.S. Census Bureau, 2016-2020 American Community Survey 5-Year Estimates

Disability by Age

Area	All Ages	Under 18 Years Old	18 to 64 Years Old	65 Years and Over
City	11.4	2.9	6.9	32.5
MSA[1]	11.2	3.0	7.4	33.6
U.S.	12.7	4.3	10.3	34.0

Note: Figures show percent of the civilian noninstitutionalized population that reported having a disability. Disability status is determined from six types of difficulty: vision, hearing, cognitive, ambulatory, self-care, and independent living. For children under 5 years old, hearing and vision difficulty are used to determine disability status. For children between the ages of 5 and 14, disability status is determined from hearing, vision, cognitive, ambulatory, and self-care difficulties. For people aged 15 years and older, they are considered to have a disability if they have difficulty with any one of the six difficulty types; Note: (1) Figures cover the Urban Honolulu, HI Metropolitan Statistical Area
Source: U.S. Census Bureau, 2016-2020 American Community Survey 5-Year Estimates

Age

Area	Percent of Population									Median Age
	Under Age 5	Age 5–19	Age 20–34	Age 35–44	Age 45–54	Age 55–64	Age 65–74	Age 75–84	Age 85+	
City	5.0	14.3	21.6	13.2	12.7	12.8	10.8	5.7	3.9	41.7
MSA[1]	6.4	16.9	22.3	12.7	11.9	11.9	9.6	5.1	3.1	38.2
U.S.	6.0	19.1	20.6	12.7	12.7	12.9	9.4	4.7	2.0	38.2

Note: (1) Figures cover the Urban Honolulu, HI Metropolitan Statistical Area
Source: U.S. Census Bureau, 2016-2020 American Community Survey 5-Year Estimates

Gender

Area	Males	Females	Males per 100 Females
City	174,117	173,064	100.6
MSA[1]	493,534	486,148	101.5
U.S.	160,818,530	165,750,778	97.0

Note: (1) Figures cover the Urban Honolulu, HI Metropolitan Statistical Area
Source: U.S. Census Bureau, 2016-2020 American Community Survey 5-Year Estimates

Religious Groups by Family

Area	Catholic	Baptist	Non-Den.	Methodist[2]	Lutheran	LDS[3]	Pente-costal	Presby-terian[4]	Muslim[5]	Judaism
MSA[1]	18.2	1.9	2.2	0.8	0.3	5.1	4.2	1.5	<0.1	0.1
U.S.	19.1	9.3	4.0	4.0	2.3	2.0	1.9	1.6	0.8	0.7

Note: Figures are the number of adherents as a percentage of the total population; (1) Figures cover the Urban Honolulu, HI Metropolitan Statistical Area; (2) Methodist/Pietist; (3) Latter Day Saints; (4) Reformed; (5) Figures are estimates
Source: Association of Statisticians of American Religious Bodies, 2010 U.S. Religion Census: Religious Congregations & Membership Study

Religious Groups by Tradition

Area	Catholic	Evangelical Protestant	Mainline Protestant	Other Tradition	Black Protestant	Orthodox
MSA[1]	18.2	9.7	2.9	8.4	<0.1	<0.1
U.S.	19.1	16.2	7.3	4.3	1.6	0.3

Note: Figures are the number of adherents as a percentage of the total population; (1) Figures cover the Urban Honolulu, HI Metropolitan Statistical Area
Source: Association of Statisticians of American Religious Bodies, 2010 U.S. Religion Census: Religious Congregations & Membership Study

ECONOMY

Gross Metropolitan Product

Area	2017	2018	2019	2020	Rank[2]
MSA[1]	68.2	70.5	73.2	75.5	50

Note: Figures are in billions of dollars; (1) Figures cover the Urban Honolulu, HI Metropolitan Statistical Area; (2) Rank is based on 2018 data and ranges from 1 to 381
Source: U.S. Conference of Mayors, U.S. Metro Economies: GMP & Employment 2018-2020, September 2019

Economic Growth

Area	2015-17 (%)	2018 (%)	2019 (%)	2020 (%)	Rank[2]
MSA[1]	1.6	1.0	1.9	0.9	165
U.S.	1.9	2.9	2.3	2.1	–

Note: Figures are real gross metropolitan product (GMP) growth rates and represent average annual percent change; (1) Figures cover the Urban Honolulu, HI Metropolitan Statistical Area; (2) Rank is based on 2017 2-year average annual percent change and ranges from 1 to 381
Source: U.S. Conference of Mayors, U.S. Metro Economies: GMP & Employment 2018-2020, September 2019

Metropolitan Area Exports

Area	2015	2016	2017	2018	2019	2020	Rank[2]
MSA[1]	446.4	330.3	393.6	438.9	308.6	169.0	296

Note: Figures are in millions of dollars; (1) Figures cover the Urban Honolulu, HI Metropolitan Statistical Area; (2) Rank is based on 2020 data and ranges from 1 to 389
Source: U.S. Department of Commerce, International Trade Administration, Office of Trade and Economic Analysis, Industry and Analysis, Exports by Metropolitan Area, data extracted March 4, 2022

Building Permits

Area	Single-Family			Multi-Family			Total		
	2019	2020	Pct. Chg.	2019	2020	Pct. Chg.	2019	2020	Pct. Chg.
City	n/a	n/a	n/a	n/a	n/a	n/a	n/a	n/a	n/a
MSA[1]	912	862	-5.5	1,367	759	-44.5	2,279	1,621	-28.9
U.S.	862,100	979,400	13.6	523,900	491,700	-6.1	1,386,000	1,471,100	6.1

Note: (1) Figures cover the Urban Honolulu, HI Metropolitan Statistical Area; Figures represent new, privately-owned housing units authorized (unadjusted data); All permit data are based on estimates with imputation
Source: U.S. Census Bureau, Manufacturing, Mining, and Construction Statistics, Building Permits, 2019, 2020

Bankruptcy Filings

Area	Business Filings			Nonbusiness Filings		
	2020	2021	% Chg.	2020	2021	% Chg.
Honolulu County	46	28	-39.1	1,106	830	-25.0
U.S.	21,655	14,347	-33.7	522,808	399,269	-23.6

Note: Business filings include Chapter 7, Chapter 9, Chapter 11, Chapter 12, Chapter 13, Chapter 15, and Section 304; Nonbusiness filings include Chapter 7, Chapter 11, and Chapter 13
Source: Administrative Office of the U.S. Courts, Business and Nonbusiness Bankruptcy, County Cases Commenced by Chapter of the Bankruptcy Code, During the 12-Month Period Ending December 31, 2020 and Business and Nonbusiness Bankruptcy, County Cases Commenced by Chapter of the Bankruptcy Code, During the 12-Month Period Ending December 31, 2021

Housing Vacancy Rates

Area	Gross Vacancy Rate[2] (%)			Year-Round Vacancy Rate[3] (%)			Rental Vacancy Rate[4] (%)			Homeowner Vacancy Rate[5] (%)		
	2019	2020	2021	2019	2020	2021	2019	2020	2021	2019	2020	2021
MSA[1]	11.7	10.0	10.6	10.9	9.6	10.1	5.7	5.5	5.1	1.8	1.0	0.6
U.S.	12.0	10.6	10.8	9.5	8.2	8.4	6.7	6.3	6.1	1.4	1.0	0.9

Note: (1) Figures cover the Urban Honolulu, HI Metropolitan Statistical Area; (2) The percentage of the total housing inventory that is vacant; (3) The percentage of the housing inventory (excluding seasonal units) that is year-round vacant; (4) The percentage of rental inventory that is vacant for rent; (5) The percentage of homeowner inventory that is vacant for sale
Source: U.S. Census Bureau, Housing Vacancies and Homeownership Annual Statistics: 2019, 2020, 2021

INCOME

Income

Area	Per Capita ($)	Median Household ($)	Average Household ($)
City	39,235	72,454	99,703
MSA[1]	38,288	87,722	112,641
U.S.	35,384	64,994	91,547

Note: (1) Figures cover the Urban Honolulu, HI Metropolitan Statistical Area
Source: U.S. Census Bureau, 2016-2020 American Community Survey 5-Year Estimates

Household Income Distribution

Area	Percent of Households Earning							
	Under $15,000	$15,000 -$24,999	$25,000 -$34,999	$35,000 -$49,999	$50,000 -$74,999	$75,000 -$99,999	$100,000 -$149,999	$150,000 and up
City	9.6	6.4	6.4	12.1	17.4	12.9	16.7	18.5
MSA[1]	6.8	4.7	5.7	9.6	15.9	13.5	19.9	24.0
U.S.	9.9	8.5	8.6	12.0	17.2	12.8	15.6	15.4

Note: (1) Figures cover the Urban Honolulu, HI Metropolitan Statistical Area
Source: U.S. Census Bureau, 2016-2020 American Community Survey 5-Year Estimates

Poverty Rate

Area	All Ages	Under 18 Years Old	18 to 64 Years Old	65 Years and Over
City	10.7	13.3	9.9	10.9
MSA[1]	8.4	10.8	7.7	8.1
U.S.	12.8	17.5	12.1	9.3

Note: Figures are percentage of people whose income during the past 12 months was below the poverty level; (1) Figures cover the Urban Honolulu, HI Metropolitan Statistical Area
Source: U.S. Census Bureau, 2016-2020 American Community Survey 5-Year Estimates

CITY FINANCES

City Government Finances

Component	2019 ($000)	2019 ($ per capita)
Total Revenues	3,373,969	3,378
Total Expenditures	3,190,371	3,194
Debt Outstanding	6,512,796	6,521
Cash and Securities[1]	3,245,646	3,250

Note: (1) Cash and security holdings of a government at the close of its fiscal year, including those of its dependent agencies, utilities, and liquor stores.
Source: U.S. Census Bureau, State & Local Government Finances 2019

City Government Revenue by Source

Source	2019 ($000)	2019 ($ per capita)	2019 (%)
General Revenue			
From Federal Government	117,653	118	3.5
From State Government	166,770	167	4.9
From Local Governments	536	1	0.0
Taxes			
Property	1,288,798	1,290	38.2
Sales and Gross Receipts	464,244	465	13.8
Personal Income	0	0	0.0
Corporate Income	0	0	0.0
Motor Vehicle License	173,351	174	5.1
Other Taxes	35,424	35	1.0
Current Charges	663,099	664	19.7
Liquor Store	0	0	0.0
Utility	285,541	286	8.5

Source: U.S. Census Bureau, State & Local Government Finances 2019

City Government Expenditures by Function

Function	2019 ($000)	2019 ($ per capita)	2019 (%)
General Direct Expenditures			
Air Transportation	0	0	0.0
Corrections	0	0	0.0
Education	0	0	0.0
Employment Security Administration	0	0	0.0
Financial Administration	44,152	44	1.4
Fire Protection	144,192	144	4.5
General Public Buildings	31,609	31	1.0
Governmental Administration, Other	84,149	84	2.6
Health	43,530	43	1.4
Highways	133,950	134	4.2
Hospitals	0	0	0.0
Housing and Community Development	98,008	98	3.1
Interest on General Debt	207,013	207	6.5
Judicial and Legal	30,346	30	1.0
Libraries	0	0	0.0
Parking	139	< 1	< 0.1
Parks and Recreation	144,515	144	4.5
Police Protection	294,917	295	9.2
Public Welfare	13,188	13	0.4
Sewerage	354,076	354	11.1
Solid Waste Management	197,321	197	6.2
Veterans' Services	0	0	0.0
Liquor Store	0	0	0.0
Utility	1,075,480	1,076	33.7

Source: U.S. Census Bureau, State & Local Government Finances 2019

EMPLOYMENT

Labor Force and Employment

Area	Civilian Labor Force			Workers Employed		
	Dec. 2020	Dec. 2021	% Chg.	Dec. 2020	Dec. 2021	% Chg.
City	446,117	449,039	0.7	408,943	428,507	4.8
MSA[1]	446,117	449,039	0.7	408,943	428,507	4.8
U.S.	160,017,000	161,696,000	1.0	149,613,000	155,732,000	4.1

Note: Data is not seasonally adjusted and covers workers 16 years of age and older; (1) Figures cover the Urban Honolulu, HI Metropolitan Statistical Area
Source: Bureau of Labor Statistics, Local Area Unemployment Statistics

Unemployment Rate

Area	2021											
	Jan.	Feb.	Mar.	Apr.	May	Jun.	Jul.	Aug.	Sep.	Oct.	Nov.	Dec.
City	8.9	7.7	7.7	7.1	6.7	7.1	6.2	6.1	5.9	5.4	5.0	4.6
MSA[1]	8.9	7.7	7.7	7.1	6.7	7.1	6.2	6.1	5.9	5.4	5.0	4.6
U.S.	6.8	6.6	6.2	5.7	5.5	6.1	5.7	5.3	4.6	4.3	3.9	3.7

Note: Data is not seasonally adjusted and covers workers 16 years of age and older; (1) Figures cover the Urban Honolulu, HI Metropolitan Statistical Area
Source: Bureau of Labor Statistics, Local Area Unemployment Statistics

Average Wages

Occupation	$/Hr.	Occupation	$/Hr.
Accountants and Auditors	33.88	Maintenance and Repair Workers	23.94
Automotive Mechanics	25.18	Marketing Managers	54.25
Bookkeepers	22.42	Network and Computer Systems Admin.	43.34
Carpenters	39.29	Nurses, Licensed Practical	26.08
Cashiers	14.60	Nurses, Registered	51.77
Computer Programmers	45.28	Nursing Assistants	17.68
Computer Systems Analysts	42.10	Office Clerks, General	19.62
Computer User Support Specialists	30.11	Physical Therapists	44.80
Construction Laborers	28.96	Physicians	126.41
Cooks, Restaurant	17.56	Plumbers, Pipefitters and Steamfitters	35.40
Customer Service Representatives	19.59	Police and Sheriff's Patrol Officers	39.26
Dentists	82.15	Postal Service Mail Carriers	26.11
Electricians	38.72	Real Estate Sales Agents	24.72
Engineers, Electrical	52.64	Retail Salespersons	16.88
Fast Food and Counter Workers	13.62	Sales Representatives, Technical/Scientific	44.50
Financial Managers	59.93	Secretaries, Exc. Legal/Medical/Executive	22.86
First-Line Supervisors of Office Workers	29.39	Security Guards	17.49
General and Operations Managers	53.15	Surgeons	146.73
Hairdressers/Cosmetologists	21.03	Teacher Assistants, Exc. Postsecondary*	15.46
Home Health and Personal Care Aides	14.60	Teachers, Secondary School, Exc. Sp. Ed.*	31.27
Janitors and Cleaners	15.99	Telemarketers	16.72
Landscaping/Groundskeeping Workers	18.67	Truck Drivers, Heavy/Tractor-Trailer	26.14
Lawyers	49.23	Truck Drivers, Light/Delivery Services	19.61
Maids and Housekeeping Cleaners	19.61	Waiters and Waitresses	19.46

Note: Wage data covers the Urban Honolulu, HI Metropolitan Statistical Area; (*) Hourly wages were calculated from annual wage data based on a 40 hour work week; n/a not available.
Source: Bureau of Labor Statistics, Metro Area Occupational Employment & Wage Estimates, May 2021

Employment by Industry

Sector	MSA[1]		U.S.
	Number of Employees	Percent of Total	Percent of Total
Construction, Mining, and Logging	26,200	6.0	5.3
Education and Health Services	64,000	14.6	16.0
Financial Activities	21,400	4.9	5.9
Government	94,500	21.6	14.9
Information	7,000	1.6	1.9
Leisure and Hospitality	62,800	14.4	9.8
Manufacturing	9,300	2.1	8.4
Other Services	18,500	4.2	3.7
Professional and Business Services	53,500	12.2	14.6
Retail Trade	43,600	10.0	10.7
Transportation, Warehousing, and Utilities	23,300	5.3	4.8
Wholesale Trade	13,000	3.0	3.8

Note: Figures are non-farm employment as of December 2021. Figures are not seasonally adjusted and include workers 16 years of age and older; (1) Figures cover the Urban Honolulu, HI Metropolitan Statistical Area
Source: Bureau of Labor Statistics, Current Employment Statistics, Employment, Hours, and Earnings

Employment by Occupation

Occupation Classification	City (%)	MSA[1] (%)	U.S. (%)
Management, Business, Science, and Arts	38.2	37.5	39.5
Natural Resources, Construction, and Maintenance	6.2	8.6	8.7
Production, Transportation, and Material Moving	9.1	9.3	13.1
Sales and Office	23.7	23.5	21.3
Service	22.9	21.1	17.4

Note: Figures cover employed civilians 16 years of age and older; (1) Figures cover the Urban Honolulu, HI Metropolitan Statistical Area
Source: U.S. Census Bureau, 2016-2020 American Community Survey 5-Year Estimates

Occupations with Greatest Projected Employment Growth: 2021 – 2023

Occupation[1]	2021 Employment	2023 Projected Employment	Numeric Employment Change	Percent Employment Change
Maids and Housekeeping Cleaners	8,640	12,800	4,160	48.1
Waiters and Waitresses	12,200	16,160	3,960	32.5
Fast Food and Counter Workers	15,100	18,160	3,060	20.3
Cooks, Restaurant	7,110	9,750	2,640	37.1
Retail Salespersons	19,600	22,020	2,420	12.3
First-Line Supervisors of Food Preparation and Serving Workers	5,130	6,410	1,280	25.0
Food Preparation Workers	7,590	8,870	1,280	16.9
Security Guards	7,830	9,040	1,210	15.5
Dining Room and Cafeteria Attendants and Bartender Helpers	2,850	4,020	1,170	41.1
Maintenance and Repair Workers, General	5,940	7,110	1,170	19.7

Note: Projections cover Hawaii; (1) Sorted by numeric employment change
Source: www.projectionscentral.com, State Occupational Projections, 2021–2023 Short-Term Projections

Fastest-Growing Occupations: 2021 – 2023

Occupation[1]	2021 Employment	2023 Projected Employment	Numeric Employment Change	Percent Employment Change
Hotel, Motel, and Resort Desk Clerks	1,550	2,680	1,130	72.9
Locker Room, Coatroom, and Dressing Room Attendants	110	180	70	63.6
Baggage Porters and Bellhops	780	1,270	490	62.8
Concierges	540	820	280	51.9
Lodging Managers	340	510	170	50.0
Maids and Housekeeping Cleaners	8,640	12,800	4,160	48.1
Passenger Vehicle Drivers, Except Bus Drivers, Transit and Intercity	1,780	2,560	780	43.8
Captains, Mates, and Pilots of Water Vessels	400	570	170	42.5
Dining Room and Cafeteria Attendants and Bartender Helpers	2,850	4,020	1,170	41.1
Bartenders	2,080	2,890	810	38.9

Note: Projections cover Hawaii; (1) Sorted by percent employment change and excludes occupations with numeric employment change less than 50
Source: www.projectionscentral.com, State Occupational Projections, 2021–2023 Short-Term Projections

TAXES

State Corporate Income Tax Rates

State	Tax Rate (%)	Income Brackets ($)	Num. of Brackets	Financial Institution Tax Rate (%)[a]	Federal Income Tax Ded.
Hawaii	4.4 - 6.4 (e)	25,000 - 100,001	3	7.92 (f)	No

Note: Tax rates as of January 1, 2022; (a) Rates listed are the corporate income tax rate applied to financial institutions or excise taxes based on income. Some states have other taxes based upon the value of deposits or shares; (e) Hawaii taxes capital gains at 4%. Financial institutions pay a franchise tax of 7.92% of taxable income (in lieu of the corporate income tax and general excise taxes); (f) Idaho's minimum tax on a corporation is $20. The $10 Permanent Building Fund Tax must be paid by each corporation in a unitary group filing a combined return. Taxpayers with gross sales in Idaho under $100,000, and with no property or payroll in Idaho, may elect to pay 1% on such sales (instead of the tax on net income).
Source: Federation of Tax Administrators, State Corporate Income Tax Rates, January 1, 2022

State Individual Income Tax Rates

State	Tax Rate (%)	Income Brackets ($)	Personal Exemptions ($)			Standard Ded. ($)	
			Single	Married	Depend.	Single	Married
Hawaii	1.4 - 11.0	2,400 - 200,000 (b)	1,144	2,288	1,144	2,200	4,400

Note: Tax rates as of January 1, 2022; Local- and county-level taxes are not included; Federal income tax is not deductible on state income tax returns; (b) For joint returns, taxes are twice the tax on half the couple's income.
Source: Federation of Tax Administrators, State Individual Income Tax Rates, January 1, 2022

Various State Sales and Excise Tax Rates

State	State Sales Tax (%)	Gasoline[1] (¢/gal.)	Cigarette[2] ($/pack)	Spirits[3] ($/gal.)	Wine[4] ($/gal.)	Beer[5] ($/gal.)	Recreational Marijuana (%)
Hawaii	4	51.69	3.2	5.98	1.38	0.93	Not legal

Note: All tax rates as of January 1, 2022; (1) The American Petroleum Institute has developed a methodology for determining the average tax rate on a gallon of fuel. Rates may include any of the following: excise taxes, environmental fees, storage tank fees, other fees or taxes, general sales tax, and local taxes; (2) The federal excise tax of $1.0066 per pack and local taxes are not included; (3) Rates are those applicable to off-premise sales of 40% alcohol by volume (a.b.v.) distilled spirits in 750ml containers. Local excise taxes are excluded; (4) Rates are those applicable to off-premise sales of 11% a.b.v. non-carbonated wine in 750ml containers; (5) Rates are those applicable to off-premise sales of 4.7% a.b.v. beer in 12 ounce containers.
Source: Tax Foundation, 2022 Facts & Figures: How Does Your State Compare?

State Business Tax Climate Index Rankings

State	Overall Rank	Corporate Tax Rank	Individual Income Tax Rank	Sales Tax Rank	Property Tax Rank	Unemployment Insurance Tax Rank
Hawaii	41	19	46	28	30	29

Note: The index is a measure of how each state's tax laws affect economic performance. The lower the rank, the more favorable a state's tax system is for business. States without a given tax are given a ranking of 1. The scores/rankings for the District of Columbia do not affect other states. The 2022 index represents the tax climate as of July 1, 2021.
Source: Tax Foundation, State Business Tax Climate Index 2022

TRANSPORTATION

Means of Transportation to Work

Area	Car/Truck/Van		Public Transportation			Bicycle	Walked	Other Means	Worked at Home
	Drove Alone	Car-pooled	Bus	Subway	Railroad				
City	57.9	12.8	10.4	0.0	0.0	1.7	8.3	3.9	5.0
MSA[1]	65.2	13.4	7.1	0.0	0.0	0.9	5.6	2.7	5.1
U.S.	74.9	8.9	2.2	1.7	0.5	0.5	2.6	1.4	7.3

Note: Figures are percentages and cover workers 16 years of age and older; (1) Figures cover the Urban Honolulu, HI Metropolitan Statistical Area
Source: U.S. Census Bureau, 2016-2020 American Community Survey 5-Year Estimates

Travel Time to Work

Area	Less Than 10 Minutes	10 to 19 Minutes	20 to 29 Minutes	30 to 44 Minutes	45 to 59 Minutes	60 to 89 Minutes	90 Minutes or More
City	8.5	36.6	23.0	21.6	5.3	3.6	1.4
MSA[1]	9.7	25.4	19.8	25.0	9.6	7.7	2.8
U.S.	12.3	28.4	20.9	20.9	8.3	6.4	2.9

Note: Note: Figures are percentages and include workers 16 years old and over; (1) Figures cover the Urban Honolulu, HI Metropolitan Statistical Area
Source: U.S. Census Bureau, 2016-2020 American Community Survey 5-Year Estimates

Key Congestion Measures

Measure	1990	2000	2010	2015	2020
Annual Hours of Delay, Total (000)	11,789	18,787	27,593	32,628	13,365
Annual Hours of Delay, Per Auto Commuter	31	44	55	60	24
Annual Congestion Cost, Per Auto Commuter ($)	849	1,023	1,191	1,302	562

Note: Covers the Honolulu HI urban area
Source: Texas A&M Transportation Institute, 2021 Urban Mobility Report

Freeway Travel Time Index

Measure	1985	1990	1995	2000	2005	2010	2015	2020
Urban Area Index[1]	1.18	1.23	1.28	1.32	1.37	1.38	1.40	1.11
Urban Area Rank[1,2]	8	4	4	4	3	3	4	20

Note: Freeway Travel Time Index—the ratio of travel time in the peak period to the travel time at free-flow conditions. For example, a value of 1.30 indicates a 20-minute free-flow trip takes 26 minutes in the peak (20 minutes x 1.30 = 26 minutes); (1) Covers the Honolulu HI urban area; (2) Rank is based on 101 larger urban areas (#1 = highest travel time index)
Source: Texas A&M Transportation Institute, 2021 Urban Mobility Report

Public Transportation

Agency Name / Mode of Transportation	Vehicles Operated in Maximum Service[1]	Annual Unlinked Passenger Trips[2] (in thous.)	Annual Passenger Miles[3] (in thous.)
City and County of Honolulu Dept. of Transportation Services (DTS)			
Bus (purchased transportation)	453	48,536.0	220,965.4
Demand Response (purchased transportation)	223	987.8	10,657.5
Demand Response - Taxi	121	178.3	1,431.6
Vanpool (purchased transportation)	58	178.3	2,950.8

Note: (1) Number of revenue vehicles operated by the given mode and type of service to meet the annual maximum service requirement. This is the revenue vehicle count during the peak season of the year; on the week and day that maximum service is provided. Vehicles operated in maximum service (VOMS) exclude atypical days and one-time special events; (2) Number of passengers who boarded public transportation vehicles. Passengers are counted each time they board a vehicle no matter how many vehicles they use to travel from their origin to their destination. (3) Sum of the distances ridden by all passengers during the entire fiscal year.
Source: Federal Transit Administration, National Transit Database, 2020

Air Transportation

Airport Name and Code / Type of Service	Passenger Airlines[1]	Passenger Enplanements	Freight Carriers[2]	Freight (lbs)
Honolulu International (HNL)				
Domestic service (U.S. carriers - 2021)	15	5,772,275	19	351,112,342
International service (U.S. carriers - 2020)	6	206,317	9	143,490,600

Note: (1) Includes all U.S.-based major, minor and commuter airlines that carried at least one passenger during the year; (2) Includes all U.S.-based airlines and freight carriers that transported at least one pound of freight during the year.
Source: Bureau of Transportation Statistics, The Intermodal Transportation Database, Air Carriers: T-100 Domestic Market (U.S. Carriers), 2021; Bureau of Transportation Statistics, The Intermodal Transportation Database, Air Carriers: T-100 International Market (U.S. Carriers), 2020

BUSINESSES

Major Business Headquarters

Company Name	Industry	Rankings: Fortune[1]	Rankings: Forbes[2]
No companies listed	-	-	-

Note: (1) Companies that produce a 10-K are ranked 1 to 500 based on 2020 revenue; (2) All private companies with at least $2 billion in annual revenue through the end of their most current fiscal year are ranked 1 to 225; companies listed are headquartered in the city; dashes indicate no ranking
Source: Fortune, "Fortune 500," 2021; Forbes, "America's Largest Private Companies," 2021

Living Environment

COST OF LIVING

Cost of Living Index

Composite Index	Groceries	Housing	Utilities	Trans-portation	Health Care	Misc. Goods/ Services
193.4	153.0	315.3	164.4	133.4	115.0	126.7

Note: The Cost of Living Index measures regional differences in the cost of consumer goods and services, excluding taxes and non-consumer expenditures, for professional and managerial households in the top income quintile. It is based on more than 50,000 prices covering almost 60 different items for which prices are collected three times a year by chambers of commerce, economic development organizations or university applied economic centers in each participating urban area. The numbers shown should be read as a percentage above or below the national average of 100. For example, a value of 115.4 in the groceries column indicates that grocery prices are 15.4% higher than the national average. Small differences in the index numbers should not be interpreted as significant; Figures cover the Honolulu HI urban area.
Source: The Council for Community and Economic Research, Cost of Living Index, 2021

Grocery Prices

Area[1]	T-Bone Steak ($/pound)	Frying Chicken ($/pound)	Whole Milk ($/half gal.)	Eggs ($/dozen)	Orange Juice ($/64 oz.)	Coffee ($/11.5 oz.)
City[2]	16.01	2.24	3.92	3.86	5.09	8.11
Avg.	12.82	1.40	2.22	1.57	3.59	4.30
Min.	8.91	0.91	1.29	0.75	2.87	3.02
Max.	21.35	2.69	3.92	3.86	5.49	8.11

Note: (1) Values for the local area are compared with the average, minimum and maximum values for all 285 areas in the Cost of Living Index; (2) Figures cover the Honolulu HI urban area; ***T-Bone Steak*** *(price per pound);* ***Frying Chicken*** *(price per pound, whole fryer);* ***Whole Milk*** *(half gallon carton);* ***Eggs*** *(price per dozen, Grade A, large);* ***Orange Juice*** *(64 oz. Tropicana or Florida Natural);* ***Coffee*** *(11.5 oz. can, vacuum-packed, Maxwell House, Hills Bros, or Folgers).*
Source: The Council for Community and Economic Research, Cost of Living Index, 2021

Housing and Utility Costs

Area[1]	New Home Price ($)	Apartment Rent ($/month)	All Electric ($/month)	Part Electric ($/month)	Other Energy ($/month)	Telephone ($/month)
City[2]	1,399,439	3,190	369.53	-	-	181.65
Avg.	398,393	1,217	171.38	100.83	69.67	187.75
Min.	212,799	534	96.71	31.56	27.15	173.01
Max.	2,354,006	4,438	369.53	277.33	303.87	206.73

Note: (1) Values for the local area are compared with the average, minimum and maximum values for all 285 areas in the Cost of Living Index; (2) Figures cover the Honolulu HI urban area; ***New Home Price*** *(2,400 sf living area, 8,000 sf lot, in urban area with full utilities);* ***Apartment Rent*** *(950 sf 2 bedroom/1.5 or 2 bath, unfurnished, excluding all utilities except water);* ***All Electric*** *(average monthly cost for an all-electric home);* ***Part Electric*** *(average monthly cost for a part-electric home);* ***Other Energy*** *(average monthly cost for natural gas, fuel oil, coal, wood, and any other forms of energy except electricity);* ***Telephone*** *(price includes the base monthly rate plus taxes and fees for three lines of mobile phone service).*
Source: The Council for Community and Economic Research, Cost of Living Index, 2021

Health Care, Transportation, and Other Costs

Area[1]	Doctor ($/visit)	Dentist ($/visit)	Optometrist ($/visit)	Gasoline ($/gallon)	Beauty Salon ($/visit)	Men's Shirt ($)
City[2]	151.37	85.30	205.02	3.67	66.60	60.31
Avg.	118.16	101.04	109.44	2.71	40.63	30.77
Min.	35.04	55.56	51.17	2.17	18.59	11.32
Max.	231.10	165.12	256.81	4.11	85.33	63.03

Note: (1) Values for the local area are compared with the average, minimum and maximum values for all 285 areas in the Cost of Living Index; (2) Figures cover the Honolulu HI urban area; ***Doctor*** *(general practitioners routine exam of an established patient);* ***Dentist*** *(adult teeth cleaning and periodic oral examination);* ***Optometrist*** *(full vision eye exam for established adult patient);* ***Gasoline*** *(one gallon regular unleaded, national brand, including all taxes, cash price at self-service pump if available);* ***Beauty Salon*** *(woman's shampoo, trim, and blow-dry);* ***Men's Shirt*** *(cotton/polyester dress shirt, pinpoint weave, long sleeves).*
Source: The Council for Community and Economic Research, Cost of Living Index, 2021

HOUSING

Homeownership Rate

Area	2013 (%)	2014 (%)	2015 (%)	2016 (%)	2017 (%)	2018 (%)	2019 (%)	2020 (%)	2021 (%)
MSA[1]	57.9	58.2	59.6	57.9	53.8	57.7	59.0	56.9	55.9
U.S.	65.1	64.5	63.7	63.4	63.9	64.4	64.6	66.6	65.5

Note: (1) Figures cover the Urban Honolulu, HI Metropolitan Statistical Area
Source: U.S. Census Bureau, Housing Vacancies and Homeownership Annual Statistics: 2013-2021

House Price Index (HPI)

Area	National Ranking[2]	Quarterly Change (%)	One-Year Change (%)	Five-Year Change (%)	Since 1991Q1 (%)
MSA[1]	219	5.43	14.02	23.26	189.27
U.S.[3]	–	3.33	17.54	54.45	258.04

Note: The HPI is a weighted repeat sales index. It measures average price changes in repeat sales or refinancings on the same properties. This information is obtained by reviewing repeat mortgage transactions on single-family properties whose mortgages have been purchased or securitized by Fannie Mae or Freddie Mac since January 1975; (1) Figures cover the Urban Honolulu, HI Metropolitan Statistical Area; (2) Rankings are based on annual percentage change for all metro areas containing at least 15,000 transactions over the last 10 years and ranges from 1 to 268; (3) figures based on a weighted average of Census Division estimates using a seasonally adjusted, purchase-only index; all figures are for the period ending December 31, 2021
Source: Federal Housing Finance Agency, Change in FHFA Metropolitan Area House Price Indexes, 2021Q4

Median Single-Family Home Prices

Area	2019	2020	2021[p]	Percent Change 2020 to 2021
MSA[1]	802.5	851.5	996.2	17.0
U.S. Average	274.6	300.2	353.4	17.7

Note: Figures are median sales prices of existing single-family homes in thousands of dollars; (p) preliminary; (1) Figures cover the Urban Honolulu, HI Metropolitan Statistical Area
Source: National Association of Realtors, Median Sales Price of Existing Single-Family Homes for Metropolitan Areas, 4th Quarter 2021

Qualifying Income Based on Median Sales Price of Existing Single-Family Homes

Area	With 5% Down ($)	With 10% Down ($)	With 20% Down ($)
MSA[1]	207,890	196,948	175,065
U.S. Average	70,699	66,978	59,536

Note: Figures are preliminary; Qualifying income is based on a mortgage rate of 3.13%. Monthly principal and interest payment is limited to 25% of income; (1) Figures cover the Urban Honolulu, HI Metropolitan Statistical Area
Source: National Association of Realtors, Qualifying Income Based on Median Sales Price of Existing Single-Family Homes for Metropolitan Areas, 4th Quarter 2021

Home Value Distribution

Area	Under $50,000	$50,000 -$99,999	$100,000 -$149,999	$150,000 -$199,999	$200,000 -$299,999	$300,000 -$499,999	$500,000 -$999,999	$1,000,000 or more
City	1.0	0.6	0.8	1.0	6.4	22.3	42.2	25.7
MSA[1]	0.7	0.6	0.7	0.9	4.3	18.9	54.3	19.5
U.S.	6.6	11.0	12.3	13.6	20.0	20.5	12.3	3.7

Note: Figures are percentages and cover owner-occupied housing units; (1) Figures cover the Urban Honolulu, HI Metropolitan Statistical Area
Source: U.S. Census Bureau, 2016-2020 American Community Survey 5-Year Estimates

Year Housing Structure Built

Area	2010 or Later	2000 -2009	1990 -1999	1980 -1989	1970 -1979	1960 -1969	1950 -1959	1940 -1949	Before 1940	Median Year
City	5.0	6.7	8.2	10.1	25.5	21.6	12.2	5.5	5.1	1972
MSA[1]	6.0	9.7	11.5	12.6	24.2	18.4	10.4	4.0	3.3	1976
U.S.	6.2	13.6	13.9	13.4	15.0	10.5	10.2	4.8	12.4	1978

Note: Figures are percentages except for Median Year; Note: (1) Figures cover the Urban Honolulu, HI Metropolitan Statistical Area
Source: U.S. Census Bureau, 2016-2020 American Community Survey 5-Year Estimates

Gross Monthly Rent

Area	Under $500	$500 -$999	$1,000 -$1,499	$1,500 -$1,999	$2,000 -$2,499	$2,500 -$2,999	$3,000 and up	Median ($)
City	7.3	11.6	30.2	22.4	12.2	6.8	9.4	1,520
MSA[1]	5.7	9.6	23.4	20.1	14.8	10.8	15.5	1,779
U.S.	8.9	34.3	30.2	14.9	6.2	2.6	2.8	1,096

Note: Figures are percentages except for Median; Gross rent is the contract rent plus the estimated average monthly cost of utilities (electricity, gas, and water and sewer) and fuels (oil, coal, kerosene, wood, etc.) if these are paid by the renter (or paid for the renter by someone else); (1) Figures cover the Urban Honolulu, HI Metropolitan Statistical Area
Source: U.S. Census Bureau, 2016-2020 American Community Survey 5-Year Estimates

HEALTH

Health Risk Factors

Category	MSA[1] (%)	U.S. (%)
Adults aged 18–64 who have any kind of health care coverage	n/a	86.8
Adults who reported being in good or better health	n/a	86.7
Adults who are current smokers	n/a	15.5
Adults who currently use chewing tobacco, snuff, or snus	n/a	3.7
Adults who are heavy drinkers[2]	n/a	6.7
Adults who are binge drinkers[3]	n/a	15.7
Adults who are overweight (BMI 25.0 - 29.9)	n/a	35.2
Adults who are obese (BMI 30.0 - 99.8)	n/a	31.9
Adults who participated in any physical activities in the past month	n/a	77.6
Adults who always or nearly always wears a seat belt	n/a	94.2

Note: (1) Figures for the Urban Honolulu, HI Metropolitan Statistical Area were not available.
(2) Heavy drinkers are classified as adult men having more than 14 drinks per week and adult women having more than 7 drinks per week; (3) Binge drinkers are classified as males having five or more drinks on one occasion or females having four or more drinks on one occasion
Source: Centers for Disease Control and Prevention, Behaviorial Risk Factor Surveillance System, SMART: Selected Metropolitan Area Risk Trends, 2020

Acute and Chronic Health Conditions

Category	MSA[1] (%)	U.S. (%)
Adults who have ever been told they had a heart attack	n/a	4.3
Adults who have ever been told they have angina or coronary heart disease	n/a	4.0
Adults who have ever been told they had a stroke	n/a	2.8
Adults who have ever been told they have asthma	n/a	14.2
Adults who have ever been told they have arthritis	n/a	24.5
Adults who have ever been told they have diabetes[2]	n/a	10.6
Adults who have ever been told they had skin cancer	n/a	6.4
Adults who have ever been told they had any other types of cancer	n/a	6.8
Adults who have ever been told they have COPD	n/a	6.2
Adults who have ever been told they have kidney disease	n/a	2.9
Adults who have ever been told they have a form of depression	n/a	19.6

Note: (1) Figures for the Urban Honolulu, HI Metropolitan Statistical Area were not available.
(2) Figures do not include pregnancy-related, borderline, or pre-diabetes
Source: Centers for Disease Control and Prevention, Behaviorial Risk Factor Surveillance System, SMART: Selected Metropolitan Area Risk Trends, 2020

Health Screening and Vaccination Rates

Category	MSA[1] (%)	U.S. (%)
Adults 50-75 who have had a blood stool test within the past year	n/a	9.3
Adults aged 65+ who have had flu shot within the past year	n/a	67.9
Adults aged 65+ who have ever had a pneumonia vaccination	n/a	72.2
Adults who have ever been tested for HIV	n/a	37.1
Women aged 21-65 who have had a pap test in the past three years	n/a	77.7
Men aged 40+ who have had a PSA test within the past two years	n/a	31.8
Women aged 40+ who have had a mammogram within the past two years	n/a	71.5

Note: (1) Figures for the Urban Honolulu, HI Metropolitan Statistical Area were not available.
Source: Centers for Disease Control and Prevention, Behaviorial Risk Factor Surveillance System, SMART: Selected Metropolitan Area Risk Trends, 2020

Disability Status

Category	MSA[1] (%)	U.S. (%)
Adults who reported being deaf	n/a	6.8
Are you blind or have serious difficulty seeing, even when wearing glasses?	n/a	4.7
Do you have difficulty doing errands alone?	n/a	6.3
Do you have difficulty dressing or bathing?	n/a	3.0
Do you have serious difficulty concentrating/remembering/making decisions?	n/a	10.8
Do you have serious difficulty walking or climbing stairs?	n/a	11.9

Note: (1) Figures for the Urban Honolulu, HI Metropolitan Statistical Area were not available.
Source: Centers for Disease Control and Prevention, Behaviorial Risk Factor Surveillance System, SMART: Selected Metropolitan Area Risk Trends, 2020

Mortality Rates for the Top 10 Causes of Death in the U.S.

ICD-10[a] Sub-Chapter	ICD-10[a] Code	Age-Adjusted Mortality Rate[1] per 100,000 population	
		County[2]	U.S.
Malignant neoplasms	C00-C97	123.6	146.4
Ischaemic heart diseases	I20-I25	62.0	90.2
Other forms of heart disease	I30-I51	38.6	51.9
Other degenerative diseases of the nervous system	G30-G31	23.5	39.7
Other external causes of accidental injury	W00-X59	31.6	38.7
Chronic lower respiratory diseases	J40-J47	15.9	38.1
Cerebrovascular diseases	I60-I69	37.7	37.6
Organic, including symptomatic, mental disorders	F01-F09	31.9	29.4
Hypertensive diseases	I10-I15	23.1	26.1
Diabetes mellitus	E10-E14	16.1	22.6

Note: (a) ICD-10 = International Classification of Diseases 10th Revision; (1) Mortality rates are a three-year average covering 2018-2020; (2) Figures cover Honolulu County.
Source: Centers for Disease Control and Prevention, National Center for Health Statistics. Underlying Cause of Death 1999-2020 on CDC WONDER Online Database

Mortality Rates for Selected Causes of Death

ICD-10[a] Sub-Chapter	ICD-10[a] Code	Age-Adjusted Mortality Rate[1] per 100,000 population	
		County[2]	U.S.
Assault	X85-Y09	2.8	6.5
Diseases of the liver	K70-K76	8.6	15.3
Human immunodeficiency virus (HIV) disease	B20-B24	0.6	1.4
Influenza and pneumonia	J09-J18	19.6	13.4
Intentional self-harm	X60-X84	11.0	13.9
Malnutrition	E40-E46	0.8	2.9
Obesity and other hyperalimentation	E65-E68	0.9	2.4
Renal failure	N17-N19	10.0	12.5
Transport accidents	V01-V99	6.5	12.5
Viral hepatitis	B15-B19	0.8	1.0

Note: (a) ICD-10 = International Classification of Diseases 10th Revision; (1) Mortality rates are a three-year average covering 2018-2020; (2) Figures cover Honolulu County; Data are suppressed when the data meet the criteria for confidentiality constraints; Mortality rates are flagged as unreliable when the rate would be calculated with a numerator of 20 or less.
Source: Centers for Disease Control and Prevention, National Center for Health Statistics. Underlying Cause of Death 1999-2020 on CDC WONDER Online Database

Health Insurance Coverage

Area	With Health Insurance	With Private Health Insurance	With Public Health Insurance	Without Health Insurance	Population Under Age 19 Without Health Insurance
City	96.3	77.6	35.5	3.7	2.2
MSA[1]	96.6	80.0	33.3	3.4	2.3
U.S.	91.3	68.1	35.3	8.7	5.2

Note: Figures are percentages that cover the civilian noninstitutionalized population; (1) Figures cover the Urban Honolulu, HI Metropolitan Statistical Area
Source: U.S. Census Bureau, 2016-2020 American Community Survey 5-Year Estimates

Number of Medical Professionals

Area	MDs[3]	DOs[3,4]	Dentists	Podiatrists	Chiropractors	Optometrists
County[1] (number)	3,516	165	970	33	196	235
County[1] (rate[2])	345.9	16.2	95.4	3.2	19.3	23.1
U.S. (rate[2])	285.1	23.0	71.1	6.2	28.2	17.0

15003
Note: Data as of 2020 unless noted; (1) Data covers Honolulu County; (2) Rate per 100,000 population; (3) Data as of 2019 and includes all active, non-federal physicians; (4) Doctor of Osteopathic Medicine
Source: U.S. Department of Health and Human Services, Health Resources and Services Administration, Bureau of Health Professions, Area Resource File (ARF) 2020-2021

Best Hospitals

According to *U.S. News,* the Urban Honolulu, HI metro area is home to one of the best hospitals in the U.S.: **Queen's Medical Center** (1 adult specialty). The hospital listed was nationally ranked in at least one of 15 adult or 10 pediatric specialties. Only 175 U.S. hospitals performed well enough to be nationally ranked in one or more specialties. Twenty hospitals in the U.S. made the Honor Roll. The Best Hospitals Honor Roll takes both the national rankings and the procedure and condition ratings into account. Hospitals received points if they were nationally ranked in one of the 15 adult specialties—the higher they ranked, the more points they got—and how many ratings of "high performing" they earned in the 17 procedures and conditions. *U.S. News Online, "America's Best Hospitals 2021-22"*

EDUCATION

Public School District Statistics

District Name	Schls	Pupils	Pupil/ Teacher Ratio	Minority Pupils[1] (%)	LEP/ELL[2] (%)	IEP[3] (%)
Hawaii Department of Education	295	181,088	14.8	88.2	9.2	11.1

Note: Table includes school districts with 2,000 or more students; (1) Percentage of students that are not non-Hispanic white; (2) Percentage of students that are Limited English Proficient (LEP) or English Language Learners (ELL) (2018-19); (3) Percentage of students that have an Individualized Education Program (IEP).
Source: U.S. Department of Education, National Center for Education Statistics, Common Core of Data, Local Education Agency (School District) Universe Survey: School Year 2019-2020

Highest Level of Education

Area	Less than H.S.	H.S. Diploma	Some College, No Deg.	Associate Degree	Bachelor's Degree	Master's Degree	Prof. School Degree	Doctorate Degree
City	10.2	23.3	18.2	10.5	23.9	8.7	3.1	2.1
MSA[1]	7.6	25.7	20.1	10.9	23.1	8.5	2.5	1.6
U.S.	11.5	26.7	20.3	8.6	20.2	9.1	2.2	1.5

Note: Figures cover persons age 25 and over; (1) Figures cover the Urban Honolulu, HI Metropolitan Statistical Area
Source: U.S. Census Bureau, 2016-2020 American Community Survey 5-Year Estimates

Educational Attainment by Race

Area	High School Graduate or Higher (%)					Bachelor's Degree or Higher (%)				
	Total	White	Black	Asian	Hisp.[2]	Total	White	Black	Asian	Hisp.[2]
City	89.8	97.7	95.1	86.7	92.9	37.8	53.0	31.1	37.5	29.8
MSA[1]	92.4	97.5	96.7	89.8	94.3	35.7	48.5	31.2	37.2	26.9
U.S.	88.5	90.7	86.7	87.3	70.3	32.9	34.4	22.6	55.0	17.6

Note: Figures shown cover persons 25 years old and over; (1) Figures cover the Urban Honolulu, HI Metropolitan Statistical Area; (2) People of Hispanic origin can be of any race
Source: U.S. Census Bureau, 2016-2020 American Community Survey 5-Year Estimates

School Enrollment by Grade and Control

Area	Preschool (%)		Kindergarten (%)		Grades 1 - 4 (%)		Grades 5 - 8 (%)		Grades 9 - 12 (%)	
	Public	Private	Public	Private	Public	Private	Public	Private	Public	Private
City	36.4	63.6	73.2	26.8	81.9	18.1	76.2	23.8	73.9	26.1
MSA[1]	37.9	62.1	78.3	21.7	85.0	15.0	79.3	20.7	76.1	23.9
U.S.	58.9	41.1	86.9	13.1	89.0	11.0	89.0	11.0	89.7	10.3

Note: Figures shown cover persons 3 years old and over; (1) Figures cover the Urban Honolulu, HI Metropolitan Statistical Area
Source: U.S. Census Bureau, 2016-2020 American Community Survey 5-Year Estimates

Higher Education

Four-Year Colleges			Two-Year Colleges			Medical Schools[1]	Law Schools[2]	Voc/ Tech[3]
Public	Private Non-profit	Private For-profit	Public	Private Non-profit	Private For-profit			
2	4	2	4	0	2	0	0	2

Note: Figures cover institutions located within the Urban Honolulu, HI Metropolitan Statistical Area and include main campuses only; (1) includes schools accredited by the Liaison Committee on Medical Education and the American Osteopathic Association's Commission on Osteopathic College Accreditation; (2) includes ABA-accredited schools, schools with provisional ABA accreditation, and state accredited schools; (3) includes all schools with programs that are less than 2 years.
Source: National Center for Education Statistics, Integrated Postsecondary Education System (IPEDS), 2020-21; Wikipedia, List of Medical Schools in the United States, accessed April 11, 2022; Wikipedia, List of Law Schools in the United States, accessed April 11, 2022

EMPLOYERS

Major Employers

Company Name	Industry
City and County of Honolulu	Civil service/commission government
First Hawaiin Bank	State commercial banks
Hawaii Dept of Health	Administration of public health programs
Hawaii Dept of Transportation	Administration of transportation
Hawaii Mediacal Services Assoc	Hospital & medical services plans
Hawaii Pacific Health	General medical & surgical hospitals
Hawaiian Telecom	Local & long distance telephone
KYO YA Hotels and Resorts	Hotels & motels
Mormon Church	Misc denominational church
OAHU transit Services	Bus line operations
St. Francis Healthcare Sys of Hawaii	Skilled nursing facility
State of Hawaii	State government
The Boeing Company	Airplanes, fixed or rotary wing
The Queens Medical Center	General medical & surgical hospitals
Trustess of the Estate of Bernice Bishop	Private elementary/secondary schools
University of Hawaii System	Colleges & universities

Note: Companies shown are located within the Urban Honolulu, HI Metropolitan Statistical Area.
Source: Hoovers.com; Wikipedia

PUBLIC SAFETY

Crime Rate

Area	Total Crime	Violent Crime Rate				Property Crime Rate		
		Murder	Rape[3]	Robbery	Aggrav. Assault	Burglary	Larceny -Theft	Motor Vehicle Theft
City	3,272.2	2.8	34.9	97.9	135.1	396.3	2,211.7	393.6
Suburbs[1]	n/a	n/a	n/a	n/a	n/a	n/a	n/a	n/a
Metro[2]	n/a	n/a	n/a	n/a	n/a	n/a	n/a	n/a
U.S.	2,510.4	5.1	42.6	81.8	250.4	340.5	1,569.2	220.8

Note: Figures are crimes per 100,000 population; (1) All areas within the metro area that are located outside the city limits; (2) Figures cover the Urban Honolulu, HI Metropolitan Statistical Area; n/a not available; (3) All figures shown were reported using the revised Uniform Crime Reporting (UCR) definition of rape.
Source: FBI Uniform Crime Reports, 2019 (data for 2020 was not available)

Hate Crimes

Area	Number of Quarters Reported	Number of Incidents per Bias Motivation					
		Race/Ethnicity/ Ancestry	Religion	Sexual Orientation	Disability	Gender	Gender Identity
City	4	31	0	5	0	0	0
U.S.	4	5,227	1,244	1,110	130	75	266

Source: Federal Bureau of Investigation, Hate Crime Statistics 2020

Identity Theft Consumer Reports

Area	Reports	Reports per 100,000 Population	Rank[2]
MSA[1]	2,194	225	197
U.S.	1,434,676	432	-

Note: (1) Figures cover the Urban Honolulu, HI Metropolitan Statistical Area; (2) Rank ranges from 1 to 391 where 1 indicates greatest number of identity theft reports per 100,000 population
Source: Federal Trade Commission, Consumer Sentinel Network Data Book 2021

Fraud and Other Consumer Reports

Area	Reports	Reports per 100,000 Population	Rank[2]
MSA[1]	8,072	828	229
U.S.	4,328,977	1,304	-

Note: (1) Figures cover the Urban Honolulu, HI Metropolitan Statistical Area; (2) Rank ranges from 1 to 391 where 1 indicates greatest number of fraud and other consumer reports per 100,000 population
Source: Federal Trade Commission, Consumer Sentinel Network Data Book 2021

POLITICS

2020 Presidential Election Results

Area	Biden	Trump	Jorgensen	Hawkins	Other
Honolulu County	62.5	35.7	0.9	0.6	0.4
U.S.	51.3	46.8	1.2	0.3	0.5

Note: Results are percentages and may not add to 100% due to rounding
Source: Dave Leip's Atlas of U.S. Presidential Elections

SPORTS

Professional Sports Teams

Team Name	League	Year Established
No teams are located in the metro area		

Source: Wikipedia, Major Professional Sports Teams of the United States and Canada, April 6, 2022

CLIMATE

Average and Extreme Temperatures

Temperature	Jan	Feb	Mar	Apr	May	Jun	Jul	Aug	Sep	Oct	Nov	Dec	Yr.
Extreme High (°F)	87	88	89	89	93	92	92	93	94	94	93	89	94
Average High (°F)	80	80	81	82	84	86	87	88	88	86	84	81	84
Average Temp. (°F)	73	73	74	76	77	79	80	81	81	79	77	74	77
Average Low (°F)	66	66	67	69	70	72	73	74	73	72	70	67	70
Extreme Low (°F)	52	53	55	56	60	65	66	67	66	64	57	54	52

Note: Figures cover the years 1949-1990
Source: National Climatic Data Center, International Station Meteorological Climate Summary, 9/96

Average Precipitation/Snowfall/Humidity

Precip./Humidity	Jan	Feb	Mar	Apr	May	Jun	Jul	Aug	Sep	Oct	Nov	Dec	Yr.
Avg. Precip. (in.)	3.7	2.5	2.8	1.4	1.0	0.4	0.5	0.6	0.7	2.0	2.8	3.7	22.4
Avg. Snowfall (in.)	0	0	0	0	0	0	0	0	0	0	0	0	0
Avg. Rel. Hum. 5am (%)	82	80	78	77	76	75	75	75	76	78	79	80	78
Avg. Rel. Hum. 5pm (%)	66	64	62	61	60	58	58	58	60	63	66	66	62

Note: Figures cover the years 1949-1990; Tr = Trace amounts (<0.05 in. of rain; <0.5 in. of snow)
Source: National Climatic Data Center, International Station Meteorological Climate Summary, 9/96

Weather Conditions

Temperature			Daytime Sky			Precipitation		
32°F & below	45°F & below	90°F & above	Clear	Partly cloudy	Cloudy	0.01 inch or more precip.	0.1 inch or more snow/ice	Thunder-storms
0	0	23	25	286	54	98	0	7

Note: Figures are average number of days per year and cover the years 1949-1990
Source: National Climatic Data Center, International Station Meteorological Climate Summary, 9/96

HAZARDOUS WASTE

Superfund Sites

The Urban Honolulu, HI metro area is home to three sites on the EPA's Superfund National Priorities List: **Del Monte Corp. (Oahu Plantation)** (final); **Naval Computer and Telecommunications Area Master Station Eastern Pacific** (final); **Pearl Harbor Naval Complex** (final). There are a total of 1,165 Superfund sites with a status of proposed or final on the list in the U.S. *U.S. Environmental Protection Agency, National Priorities List, April 6, 2022*

AIR QUALITY

Air Quality Trends: Ozone

	1990	1995	2000	2005	2010	2016	2017	2018	2019	2020
MSA[1]	0.034	0.049	0.044	0.042	0.046	0.048	0.046	0.046	0.053	0.044
U.S.	0.090	0.091	0.082	0.080	0.074	0.070	0.069	0.070	0.066	0.068

Note: (1) Data covers the Urban Honolulu, HI Metropolitan Statistical Area. The values shown are the composite ozone concentration averages among trend sites based on the highest fourth daily maximum 8-hour concentration in parts per million. These trends are based on sites having an adequate record of monitoring data during the trend period. Data from exceptional events are included.
Source: U.S. Environmental Protection Agency, Air Quality Monitoring Information, "Air Quality Trends by City, 1990-2020"

Air Quality Index

Area	Percent of Days when Air Quality was...[2]					AQI Statistics[2]	
	Good	Moderate	Unhealthy for Sensitive Groups	Unhealthy	Very Unhealthy	Maximum	Median
MSA[1]	97.0	3.0	0.0	0.0	0.0	92	26

Note: (1) Data covers the Urban Honolulu, HI Metropolitan Statistical Area; (2) Based on 366 days with AQI data in 2020. Air Quality Index (AQI) is an index for reporting daily air quality. EPA calculates the AQI for five major air pollutants regulated by the Clean Air Act: ground-level ozone, particle pollution (aka particulate matter), carbon monoxide, sulfur dioxide, and nitrogen dioxide. The AQI runs from 0 to 500. The higher the AQI value, the greater the level of air pollution and the greater the health concern. There are six AQI categories: "Good" AQI is between 0 and 50. Air quality is considered satisfactory; "Moderate" AQI is between 51 and 100. Air quality is acceptable; "Unhealthy for Sensitive Groups" When AQI values are between 101 and 150, members of sensitive groups may experience health effects; "Unhealthy" When AQI values are between 151 and 200 everyone may begin to experience health effects; "Very Unhealthy" AQI values between 201 and 300 trigger a health alert; "Hazardous" AQI values over 300 trigger warnings of emergency conditions (not shown).
Source: U.S. Environmental Protection Agency, Air Quality Index Report, 2020

Air Quality Index Pollutants

Area	Percent of Days when AQI Pollutant was...[2]					
	Carbon Monoxide	Nitrogen Dioxide	Ozone	Sulfur Dioxide	Particulate Matter 2.5	Particulate Matter 10
MSA[1]	0.0	0.3	76.0	9.6	13.4	0.8

Note: (1) Data covers the Urban Honolulu, HI Metropolitan Statistical Area; (2) Based on 366 days with AQI data in 2020. The Air Quality Index (AQI) is an index for reporting daily air quality. EPA calculates the AQI for five major air pollutants regulated by the Clean Air Act: ground-level ozone, particle pollution (also known as particulate matter), carbon monoxide, sulfur dioxide, and nitrogen dioxide. The AQI runs from 0 to 500. The higher the AQI value, the greater the level of air pollution and the greater the health concern.
Source: U.S. Environmental Protection Agency, Air Quality Index Report, 2020

Maximum Air Pollutant Concentrations: Particulate Matter, Ozone, CO and Lead

	Particulate Matter 10 (ug/m^3)	Particulate Matter 2.5 Wtd AM (ug/m^3)	Particulate Matter 2.5 24-Hr (ug/m^3)	Ozone (ppm)	Carbon Monoxide (ppm)	Lead (ug/m^3)
MSA[1] Level	38	3.9	7	0.045	1	n/a
NAAQS[2]	150	15	35	0.075	9	0.15
Met NAAQS[2]	Yes	Yes	Yes	Yes	Yes	n/a

Note: (1) Data covers the Urban Honolulu, HI Metropolitan Statistical Area; Data from exceptional events are included; (2) National Ambient Air Quality Standards; ppm = parts per million; ug/m^3 = micrograms per cubic meter; n/a not available.
Concentrations: Particulate Matter 10 (coarse particulate)—highest second maximum 24-hour concentration; Particulate Matter 2.5 Wtd AM (fine particulate)—highest weighted annual mean concentration; Particulate Matter 2.5 24-Hour (fine particulate)—highest 98th percentile 24-hour concentration; Ozone—highest fourth daily maximum 8-hour concentration; Carbon Monoxide—highest second maximum non-overlapping 8-hour concentration; Lead—maximum running 3-month average
Source: U.S. Environmental Protection Agency, Air Quality Monitoring Information, "Air Quality Statistics by City, 2020"

Maximum Air Pollutant Concentrations: Nitrogen Dioxide and Sulfur Dioxide

	Nitrogen Dioxide AM (ppb)	Nitrogen Dioxide 1-Hr (ppb)	Sulfur Dioxide AM (ppb)	Sulfur Dioxide 1-Hr (ppb)	Sulfur Dioxide 24-Hr (ppb)
MSA[1] Level	3	26	n/a	57	n/a
NAAQS[2]	53	100	30	75	140
Met NAAQS[2]	Yes	Yes	n/a	Yes	n/a

Note: (1) Data covers the Urban Honolulu, HI Metropolitan Statistical Area; Data from exceptional events are included; (2) National Ambient Air Quality Standards; ppm = parts per million; ug/m^3 = micrograms per cubic meter; n/a not available.
Concentrations: Nitrogen Dioxide AM—highest arithmetic mean concentration; Nitrogen Dioxide 1-Hr—highest 98th percentile 1-hour daily maximum concentration; Sulfur Dioxide AM—highest annual mean concentration; Sulfur Dioxide 1-Hr—highest 99th percentile 1-hour daily maximum concentration; Sulfur Dioxide 24-Hr—highest second maximum 24-hour concentration
Source: U.S. Environmental Protection Agency, Air Quality Monitoring Information, "Air Quality Statistics by City, 2020"

Las Cruces, New Mexico

Background

"People helping people" is the motto of the city of Las Cruces which is also known as "City of Crosses." The seat of Doña Ana County, Las Cruces has experienced a rich history filled with war, growth, and renewal. Like other sunbelt communities, its economy is booming, mainly due to its major research university, an abundance of government jobs, and popularity with retirees. With a younger-than-national-average median age, the city has a prime, mostly bilingual labor force.

Las Cruces was officially founded in 1849 when the US Army laid out the town plans. It sits 3,908 feet above sea level, 225 miles south of Albuquerque, with Doña Ana Mountains to the north and the Organ Mountains to the east. West of Las Cruces is the Rio Grande River, which supplies irrigation water for the extensive agriculture in the region.

Las Cruces is part of the Borderplex Region which, together with El Paso TX and Ciudad Juarez Mexico represent the seventh largest manufacturing center in North America. The city is a top aerospace research, testing, and development center and home to divisions of Boeing, General Dynamics, Honeywell, Raytheon, and NASA. The nation's first purpose-built commercial space facility, Spaceport America, is just north of the city and has completed several successful manned, sub-orbital space flights; Virgin Galactic is the spaceport's anchor tenant and neighbors with other top commercial space and research firms.

The city's major research institution New Mexico State University (NMSU) is home to The Physical Science Laboratory—an aerospace and defense-oriented organization that provides cutting-edge research. Long standing government organizations—White Sands Missile Range providing research and experiment support, and White Sands Test Facility providing testing of spacecraft materials and propulsion systems—provide many NMSU graduates with high-paying jobs. Other significant areas of concentration at NMSU include creative media and agriculture.

The city is also home to other major employers including Las Cruces Public Schools, Memorial Medical Center, and NASA. Renewable energy from biofuels and solar energy generation is a growing industry in the region, which is in the nation's top-rated solar resource aera for flat-plate solar energy collectors.

Ongoing planned development in the city's east side provides multiple living and recreational options, and its historic downtown offers museums, art galleries, restaurants, and theaters up and down Main Street. Las Cruces hosts a variety of annual cultural events, including celebrations of the Day of the Dead and Cinco de Mayo—a testament to the city's Spanish roots.

Due to its stunning physical location, many films have been set in Las Cruces including *Hang 'Em High* (1968), *Lost in America* (1985), *Due Date* (2010), *Captain Fantastic* (2016), *The Mule* (2018), and *All the World Is Sleeping* (2021),

Las Cruces offers an arid climate, with mild winters and hot summers. Winter frost with light snow dusting can occur, usually only for a few hours. Summers often see extended periods of 100-plus degrees, with high humidity and frequent afternoon thunderstorms late in the season. The wettest single day in Las Cruces was in 1935, with 6.49 inches of rain.

Rankings

Business/Finance Rankings

- The Las Cruces metro area appeared on the Milken Institute "2021 Best Performing Cities" list. Rank: #96 out of 201 small metro areas (population over 60,000). Criteria: job growth; wage and salary growth; high-tech output growth; housing affordability; household broadband access. *Milken Institute, "Best-Performing Cities 2021," February 16, 2021*
- *Forbes* ranked 203 smaller metro areas (population under 268,000) to determine the nation's "Best Small Places for Business and Careers." The Las Cruces metro area was ranked #122. Criteria: costs (business and living); job growth (past and projected); income growth; quality of life; educational attainment (college and high school); projected economic growth; cultural and leisure opportunities; workplace tolerance laws; net migration patterns. *Forbes, "The Best Small Places for Business and Careers 2019," October 30, 2019*

Children/Family Rankings

- Las Cruces was selected as one of the most playful cities in the U.S. by KaBOOM! The organization's Playful City USA initiative honors cities and towns across the nation that have made their communities more playable. Criteria: pledging to integrate play as a solution to challenges in their communities; making it easy for children to get active and balanced play; creating more family-friendly and innovative communities as a result. *KaBOOM! National Campaign for Play, "2017 Playful City USA Communities"*

Health/Fitness Rankings

- The Sharecare Community Well-Being Index evaluates 10 individual and social health factors in order to measure what matters to Americans in the communities in which they live. The Las Cruces metro area ranked #380 in the bottom 10 across all 10 domains. Criteria: access to healthcare, food, and community resources; housng and transportation; economic security; feeling of purpose; physical, financial, social, and community well-being. *www.sharecare.com, "Community Well-Being Index: 2020 Metro Area & County Rankings Report," August 30, 2021*

Real Estate Rankings

- *WalletHub* compared the most populated U.S. cities to determine which had the best markets for real estate agents. Las Cruces ranked #178 where demand was high and pay was the best. Criteria: sales per agent; annual median wage for real-estate agents; monthly average starting salary for real estate agents; real estate job density and competition; unemployment rate; home turnover rate; housing-market health index; and other relevant metrics. *www.WalletHub.com, "2021 Best Places to Be a Real Estate Agent," May 12, 2021*

Safety Rankings

- The National Insurance Crime Bureau ranked 390 metro areas in the U.S. in terms of per capita rates of vehicle theft. The Las Cruces metro area ranked #78 (#1 = highest rate). Criteria: number of vehicle theft offenses per 100,000 inhabitants in 2020. *National Insurance Crime Bureau, "Hot Spots 2020," August 31, 2021*

Seniors/Retirement Rankings

- From its Best Cities for Successful Aging indexes, the Milken Institute generated rankings for metropolitan areas, weighing data in nine categories—health care, wellness, living arrangements, transportation and convenience, financial characteristics, education, employment, community engagement, and overall livability. The Las Cruces metro area was ranked #227 overall in the small metro area category. *Milken Institute, "Best Cities for Successful Aging, 2017" March 14, 2017*
- Las Cruces was identified as #3 of 20 most captivating places to retire in the U.S. by *Topretirements.com*. After consulting its visitor logs, the list primarily reflects the 20 cities that members are most interested in for retirement, based on which reviews were visited the most. *Topretirements.com, "20 Most Captivating Places to Retire for 2022," January 12, 2022*
- Las Cruces was identified as #5 of 20 most popular places to retire in the Southwest region by *Topretirements.com*. The site separated its annual "Best Places to Retire" list by major U.S. regions for 2019. The list reflects the 20 cities that visitors to the website are most interested in for retirement, based on the number of times a city's review was viewed on the website. *Topretirements.com, "20 Most Popular Places to Retire in the Southwest for 2019," October 2, 2019*

Women/Minorities Rankings

- Personal finance website *WalletHub* compared more than 180 U.S. cities across two key dimensions, "Hispanic Business-Friendliness" and "Hispanic Purchasing Power," to arrive at the most favorable conditions for Hispanic entrepreneurs. Las Cruces was ranked #45 out of 182. Criteria includes: share of Hispanic-Owned Businesses; Hispanic entrepreneurship rate to median annual income of Hispanics; Small Business-Friendliness score; cost of living; and number of Hispanics with at least a bachelor's degree. *WalletHub.com, "2019's Best Cities for Hispanic Entrepreneurs," May 1, 2019*

Miscellaneous Rankings

- *WalletHub* compared the 150 most populated U.S. cities to determine their operating efficiency. A "Quality of City Services" score was constructed for each city and then divided by the total budget per capita to reveal which were managed the best. Las Cruces ranked #9. Criteria: financial stability; economy; education; safety; health; infrastructure and pollution. *www.WalletHub.com, "2021's Best- & Worst-Run Cities in America," June 22, 2021*

Business Environment

DEMOGRAPHICS

Population Growth

Area	1990 Census	2000 Census	2010 Census	2020* Estimate	Population Growth (%) 1990-2020	2010-2020
City	63,267	74,267	97,618	102,950	62.7	5.5
MSA[1]	135,510	174,682	209,233	217,696	60.6	4.0
U.S.	248,709,873	281,421,906	308,745,538	326,569,308	31.3	5.8

Note: (1) Figures cover the Las Cruces, NM Metropolitan Statistical Area; (*) 2016-2020 5-year estimated population
Source: U.S. Census Bureau, 1990 Census, Census 2000, Census 2010, 2016-2020 American Community Survey 5-Year Estimates

Household Size

Area	Persons in Household (%) One	Two	Three	Four	Five	Six	Seven or More	Average Household Size
City	31.5	31.8	16.5	12.7	4.8	1.8	1.0	2.50
MSA[1]	26.4	32.6	16.8	14.1	5.7	2.5	1.9	2.70
U.S.	28.0	33.9	15.5	12.9	6.0	2.3	1.4	2.60

Note: (1) Figures cover the Las Cruces, NM Metropolitan Statistical Area
Source: U.S. Census Bureau, 2016-2020 American Community Survey 5-Year Estimates

Race

Area	White Alone[2] (%)	Black Alone[2] (%)	Asian Alone[2] (%)	AIAN[3] Alone[2] (%)	NHOPI[4] Alone[2] (%)	Other Race Alone[2] (%)	Two or More Races (%)
City	78.7	2.8	1.7	1.1	0.1	7.5	8.1
MSA[1]	78.5	1.8	1.1	1.0	0.1	9.0	8.5
U.S.	70.4	12.6	5.6	0.8	0.2	5.1	5.2

Note: (1) Figures cover the Las Cruces, NM Metropolitan Statistical Area; (2) Alone is defined as not being in combination with one or more other races; (3) American Indian and Alaska Native; (4) Native Hawaiian and Other Pacific Islander
Source: U.S. Census Bureau, 2016-2020 American Community Survey 5-Year Estimates

Hispanic or Latino Origin

Area	Total (%)	Mexican (%)	Puerto Rican (%)	Cuban (%)	Other (%)
City	60.2	51.1	0.6	0.3	8.2
MSA[1]	68.6	61.7	0.3	0.2	6.3
U.S.	18.2	11.2	1.7	0.7	4.5

Note: Persons of Hispanic or Latino origin can be of any race; (1) Figures cover the Las Cruces, NM Metropolitan Statistical Area
Source: U.S. Census Bureau, 2016-2020 American Community Survey 5-Year Estimates

Ancestry

Area	German	Irish	English	American	Italian	Polish	French[2]	Scottish	Dutch
City	7.1	4.9	6.5	2.6	2.4	1.0	1.3	1.1	1.0
MSA[1]	6.3	4.3	5.0	2.5	1.7	0.7	1.2	1.1	0.8
U.S.	13.0	9.7	7.7	5.9	5.1	2.7	2.3	1.6	1.1

Note: Figures are the percentage of the total population reporting a particular ancestry. The nine most commonly reported ancestries in the U.S. are shown. Figures include multiple ancestries (e.g. if a person reported being Irish and Italian, they were included in both columns); (1) Figures cover the Las Cruces, NM Metropolitan Statistical Area; (2) Excludes Basque
Source: U.S. Census Bureau, 2016-2020 American Community Survey 5-Year Estimates

Foreign-born Population

Area	Percent of Population Born in: Any Foreign Country	Asia	Mexico	Europe	Caribbean	Central America[2]	South America	Africa	Canada
City	11.5	2.5	7.6	0.5	0.1	0.1	0.1	0.4	0.1
MSA[1]	16.5	1.5	14.0	0.5	0.1	0.1	0.1	0.2	0.1
U.S.	13.5	4.2	3.3	1.5	1.3	1.1	1.0	0.7	0.3

Note: (1) Figures cover the Las Cruces, NM Metropolitan Statistical Area; (2) Excludes Mexico.
Source: U.S. Census Bureau, 2016-2020 American Community Survey 5-Year Estimates

Marital Status

Area	Never Married	Now Married[2]	Separated	Widowed	Divorced
City	41.8	39.3	1.9	4.7	12.3
MSA[1]	38.2	44.2	2.1	4.8	10.6
U.S.	33.5	48.1	1.8	5.7	10.8

Note: Figures are percentages and cover the population 15 years of age and older; (1) Figures cover the Las Cruces, NM Metropolitan Statistical Area; (2) Excludes separated
Source: U.S. Census Bureau, 2016-2020 American Community Survey 5-Year Estimates

Disability by Age

Area	All Ages	Under 18 Years Old	18 to 64 Years Old	65 Years and Over
City	15.5	6.9	12.8	38.1
MSA[1]	14.6	5.6	12.6	36.3
U.S.	12.7	4.3	10.3	34.0

Note: Figures show percent of the civilian noninstitutionalized population that reported having a disability. Disability status is determined from six types of difficulty: vision, hearing, cognitive, ambulatory, self-care, and independent living. For children under 5 years old, hearing and vision difficulty are used to determine disability status. For children between the ages of 5 and 14, disability status is determined from hearing, vision, cognitive, ambulatory, and self-care difficulties. For people aged 15 years and older, they are considered to have a disability if they have difficulty with any one of the six difficulty types; Note: (1) Figures cover the Las Cruces, NM Metropolitan Statistical Area
Source: U.S. Census Bureau, 2016-2020 American Community Survey 5-Year Estimates

Age

Area	Percent of Population									Median Age
	Under Age 5	Age 5–19	Age 20–34	Age 35–44	Age 45–54	Age 55–64	Age 65–74	Age 75–84	Age 85+	
City	5.9	20.4	26.9	11.1	9.9	9.7	9.2	4.6	2.3	32.5
MSA[1]	6.4	21.9	23.7	11.0	10.2	11.1	9.0	5.0	1.7	33.3
U.S.	6.0	19.1	20.6	12.7	12.7	12.9	9.4	4.7	2.0	38.2

Note: (1) Figures cover the Las Cruces, NM Metropolitan Statistical Area
Source: U.S. Census Bureau, 2016-2020 American Community Survey 5-Year Estimates

Gender

Area	Males	Females	Males per 100 Females
City	50,889	52,061	97.7
MSA[1]	106,990	110,706	96.6
U.S.	160,818,530	165,750,778	97.0

Note: (1) Figures cover the Las Cruces, NM Metropolitan Statistical Area
Source: U.S. Census Bureau, 2016-2020 American Community Survey 5-Year Estimates

Religious Groups by Family

Area	Catholic	Baptist	Non-Den.	Methodist[2]	Lutheran	LDS[3]	Pente-costal	Presby-terian[4]	Muslim[5]	Judaism
MSA[1]	31.8	5.8	1.2	2.1	0.5	2.1	2.7	0.6	0.3	0.2
U.S.	19.1	9.3	4.0	4.0	2.3	2.0	1.9	1.6	0.8	0.7

Note: Figures are the number of adherents as a percentage of the total population; (1) Figures cover the Las Cruces, NM Metropolitan Statistical Area; (2) Methodist/Pietist; (3) Latter Day Saints; (4) Reformed; (5) Figures are estimates
Source: Association of Statisticians of American Religious Bodies, 2010 U.S. Religion Census: Religious Congregations & Membership Study

Religious Groups by Tradition

Area	Catholic	Evangelical Protestant	Mainline Protestant	Other Tradition	Black Protestant	Orthodox
MSA[1]	31.8	10.6	3.2	3.2	0.2	<0.1
U.S.	19.1	16.2	7.3	4.3	1.6	0.3

Note: Figures are the number of adherents as a percentage of the total population; (1) Figures cover the Las Cruces, NM Metropolitan Statistical Area
Source: Association of Statisticians of American Religious Bodies, 2010 U.S. Religion Census: Religious Congregations & Membership Study

ECONOMY

Gross Metropolitan Product

Area	2017	2018	2019	2020	Rank[2]
MSA[1]	7.0	7.3	7.7	8.1	257

Note: Figures are in billions of dollars; (1) Figures cover the Las Cruces, NM Metropolitan Statistical Area; (2) Rank is based on 2018 data and ranges from 1 to 381
Source: U.S. Conference of Mayors, U.S. Metro Economies: GMP & Employment 2018-2020, September 2019

Economic Growth

Area	2015-17 (%)	2018 (%)	2019 (%)	2020 (%)	Rank[2]
MSA[1]	1.0	1.7	2.7	2.5	228
U.S.	1.9	2.9	2.3	2.1	–

Note: Figures are real gross metropolitan product (GMP) growth rates and represent average annual percent change; (1) Figures cover the Las Cruces, NM Metropolitan Statistical Area; (2) Rank is based on 2017 2-year average annual percent change and ranges from 1 to 381
Source: U.S. Conference of Mayors, U.S. Metro Economies: GMP & Employment 2018-2020, September 2019

Metropolitan Area Exports

Area	2015	2016	2017	2018	2019	2020	Rank[2]
MSA[1]	1,593.7	1,568.6	1,390.2	1,467.5	n/a	2,149.5	91

Note: Figures are in millions of dollars; (1) Figures cover the Las Cruces, NM Metropolitan Statistical Area; (2) Rank is based on 2020 data and ranges from 1 to 389
Source: U.S. Department of Commerce, International Trade Administration, Office of Trade and Economic Analysis, Industry and Analysis, Exports by Metropolitan Area, data extracted March 4, 2022

Building Permits

Area	Single-Family			Multi-Family			Total		
	2019	2020	Pct. Chg.	2019	2020	Pct. Chg.	2019	2020	Pct. Chg.
City	584	737	26.2	102	76	-25.5	686	813	18.5
MSA[1]	876	1,033	17.9	102	76	-25.5	978	1,109	13.4
U.S.	862,100	979,400	13.6	523,900	491,700	-6.1	1,386,000	1,471,100	6.1

Note: (1) Figures cover the Las Cruces, NM Metropolitan Statistical Area; Figures represent new, privately-owned housing units authorized (unadjusted data); All permit data are based on estimates with imputation
Source: U.S. Census Bureau, Manufacturing, Mining, and Construction Statistics, Building Permits, 2019, 2020

Bankruptcy Filings

Area	Business Filings			Nonbusiness Filings		
	2020	2021	% Chg.	2020	2021	% Chg.
Dona Ana County	6	8	33.3	322	187	-41.9
U.S.	21,655	14,347	-33.7	522,808	399,269	-23.6

Note: Business filings include Chapter 7, Chapter 9, Chapter 11, Chapter 12, Chapter 13, Chapter 15, and Section 304; Nonbusiness filings include Chapter 7, Chapter 11, and Chapter 13
Source: Administrative Office of the U.S. Courts, Business and Nonbusiness Bankruptcy, County Cases Commenced by Chapter of the Bankruptcy Code, During the 12-Month Period Ending December 31, 2020 and Business and Nonbusiness Bankruptcy, County Cases Commenced by Chapter of the Bankruptcy Code, During the 12-Month Period Ending December 31, 2021

Housing Vacancy Rates

Area	Gross Vacancy Rate[2] (%)			Year-Round Vacancy Rate[3] (%)			Rental Vacancy Rate[4] (%)			Homeowner Vacancy Rate[5] (%)		
	2019	2020	2021	2019	2020	2021	2019	2020	2021	2019	2020	2021
MSA[1]	n/a	n/a	n/a	n/a	n/a	n/a	n/a	n/a	n/a	n/a	n/a	n/a
U.S.	12.0	10.6	10.8	9.5	8.2	8.4	6.7	6.3	6.1	1.4	1.0	0.9

Note: (1) Figures cover the Las Cruces, NM Metropolitan Statistical Area; (2) The percentage of the total housing inventory that is vacant; (3) The percentage of the housing inventory (excluding seasonal units) that is year-round vacant; (4) The percentage of rental inventory that is vacant for rent; (5) The percentage of homeowner inventory that is vacant for sale; n/a not available
Source: U.S. Census Bureau, Housing Vacancies and Homeownership Annual Statistics: 2019, 2020, 2021

INCOME

Income

Area	Per Capita ($)	Median Household ($)	Average Household ($)
City	24,674	45,140	60,220
MSA[1]	22,772	44,024	60,780
U.S.	35,384	64,994	91,547

Note: (1) Figures cover the Las Cruces, NM Metropolitan Statistical Area
Source: U.S. Census Bureau, 2016-2020 American Community Survey 5-Year Estimates

Household Income Distribution

Area	Percent of Households Earning							
	Under $15,000	$15,000 -$24,999	$25,000 -$34,999	$35,000 -$49,999	$50,000 -$74,999	$75,000 -$99,999	$100,000 -$149,999	$150,000 and up
City	18.7	13.4	10.5	11.7	17.7	10.6	11.7	5.8
MSA[1]	17.5	14.6	10.7	12.0	17.9	9.5	12.1	5.7
U.S.	9.9	8.5	8.6	12.0	17.2	12.8	15.6	15.4

Note: (1) Figures cover the Las Cruces, NM Metropolitan Statistical Area
Source: U.S. Census Bureau, 2016-2020 American Community Survey 5-Year Estimates

Poverty Rate

Area	All Ages	Under 18 Years Old	18 to 64 Years Old	65 Years and Over
City	23.6	30.0	24.3	11.6
MSA[1]	24.8	34.7	23.5	14.4
U.S.	12.8	17.5	12.1	9.3

Note: Figures are percentage of people whose income during the past 12 months was below the poverty level; (1) Figures cover the Las Cruces, NM Metropolitan Statistical Area
Source: U.S. Census Bureau, 2016-2020 American Community Survey 5-Year Estimates

CITY FINANCES

City Government Finances

Component	2019 ($000)	2019 ($ per capita)
Total Revenues	221,487	2,178
Total Expenditures	228,122	2,243
Debt Outstanding	259,243	2,549
Cash and Securities[1]	283,353	2,786

Note: (1) Cash and security holdings of a government at the close of its fiscal year, including those of its dependent agencies, utilities, and liquor stores.
Source: U.S. Census Bureau, State & Local Government Finances 2019

City Government Revenue by Source

Source	2019 ($000)	2019 ($ per capita)	2019 (%)
General Revenue			
From Federal Government	4,769	47	2.2
From State Government	8,288	81	3.7
From Local Governments	4,683	46	2.1
Taxes			
Property	21,609	212	9.8
Sales and Gross Receipts	97,331	957	43.9
Personal Income	0	0	0.0
Corporate Income	0	0	0.0
Motor Vehicle License	647	6	0.3
Other Taxes	3,301	32	1.5
Current Charges	37,605	370	17.0
Liquor Store	0	0	0.0
Utility	39,000	383	17.6

Source: U.S. Census Bureau, State & Local Government Finances 2019

City Government Expenditures by Function

Function	2019 ($000)	2019 ($ per capita)	2019 (%)
General Direct Expenditures			
Air Transportation	2,296	22	1.0
Corrections	0	0	0.0
Education	0	0	0.0
Employment Security Administration	0	0	0.0
Financial Administration	3,459	34	1.5
Fire Protection	18,308	180	8.0
General Public Buildings	14,301	140	6.3
Governmental Administration, Other	3,705	36	1.6
Health	1,059	10	0.5
Highways	10,747	105	4.7
Hospitals	0	0	0.0
Housing and Community Development	1,043	10	0.5
Interest on General Debt	5,356	52	2.3
Judicial and Legal	111	1	0.0
Libraries	2,246	22	1.0
Parking	0	0	0.0
Parks and Recreation	13,024	128	5.7
Police Protection	27,412	269	12.0
Public Welfare	0	0	0.0
Sewerage	20,952	206	9.2
Solid Waste Management	13,811	135	6.1
Veterans' Services	0	0	0.0
Liquor Store	0	0	0.0
Utility	66,398	652	29.1

Source: U.S. Census Bureau, State & Local Government Finances 2019

EMPLOYMENT

Labor Force and Employment

Area	Civilian Labor Force			Workers Employed		
	Dec. 2020	Dec. 2021	% Chg.	Dec. 2020	Dec. 2021	% Chg.
City	48,527	47,528	-2.1	44,666	45,495	1.9
MSA[1]	99,084	97,888	-1.2	91,359	93,054	1.9
U.S.	160,017,000	161,696,000	1.0	149,613,000	155,732,000	4.1

Note: Data is not seasonally adjusted and covers workers 16 years of age and older; (1) Figures cover the Las Cruces, NM Metropolitan Statistical Area
Source: Bureau of Labor Statistics, Local Area Unemployment Statistics

Unemployment Rate

Area	2021											
	Jan.	Feb.	Mar.	Apr.	May	Jun.	Jul.	Aug.	Sep.	Oct.	Nov.	Dec.
City	8.5	7.4	7.1	6.9	6.7	7.9	7.6	6.2	5.8	5.3	4.8	4.3
MSA[1]	8.7	8.0	8.0	7.6	7.2	8.4	7.8	6.3	5.7	5.2	5.4	4.9
U.S.	6.8	6.6	6.2	5.7	5.5	6.1	5.7	5.3	4.6	4.3	3.9	3.7

Note: Data is not seasonally adjusted and covers workers 16 years of age and older; (1) Figures cover the Las Cruces, NM Metropolitan Statistical Area
Source: Bureau of Labor Statistics, Local Area Unemployment Statistics

Average Wages

Occupation	$/Hr.	Occupation	$/Hr.
Accountants and Auditors	30.88	Maintenance and Repair Workers	17.22
Automotive Mechanics	19.20	Marketing Managers	n/a
Bookkeepers	17.90	Network and Computer Systems Admin.	38.34
Carpenters	19.98	Nurses, Licensed Practical	25.10
Cashiers	11.62	Nurses, Registered	34.07
Computer Programmers	33.37	Nursing Assistants	13.30
Computer Systems Analysts	35.38	Office Clerks, General	13.47
Computer User Support Specialists	20.62	Physical Therapists	45.42
Construction Laborers	16.10	Physicians	134.17
Cooks, Restaurant	12.73	Plumbers, Pipefitters and Steamfitters	22.00
Customer Service Representatives	14.45	Police and Sheriff's Patrol Officers	27.10
Dentists	81.76	Postal Service Mail Carriers	25.53
Electricians	22.49	Real Estate Sales Agents	21.37
Engineers, Electrical	45.77	Retail Salespersons	13.23
Fast Food and Counter Workers	11.42	Sales Representatives, Technical/Scientific	43.89
Financial Managers	48.61	Secretaries, Exc. Legal/Medical/Executive	17.34
First-Line Supervisors of Office Workers	25.05	Security Guards	14.98
General and Operations Managers	45.03	Surgeons	n/a
Hairdressers/Cosmetologists	12.51	Teacher Assistants, Exc. Postsecondary*	11.72
Home Health and Personal Care Aides	11.38	Teachers, Secondary School, Exc. Sp. Ed.*	28.83
Janitors and Cleaners	12.50	Telemarketers	n/a
Landscaping/Groundskeeping Workers	14.80	Truck Drivers, Heavy/Tractor-Trailer	20.14
Lawyers	56.69	Truck Drivers, Light/Delivery Services	18.37
Maids and Housekeeping Cleaners	11.23	Waiters and Waitresses	12.31

Note: Wage data covers the Las Cruces, NM Metropolitan Statistical Area; (*) Hourly wages were calculated from annual wage data based on a 40 hour work week; n/a not available.
Source: Bureau of Labor Statistics, Metro Area Occupational Employment & Wage Estimates, May 2021

Employment by Industry

Sector	MSA[1]		U.S.
	Number of Employees	Percent of Total	Percent of Total
Construction, Mining, and Logging	3,900	5.2	5.3
Education and Health Services	16,800	22.3	16.0
Financial Activities	2,300	3.1	5.9
Government	20,000	26.5	14.9
Information	500	0.7	1.9
Leisure and Hospitality	8,600	11.4	9.8
Manufacturing	3,000	4.0	8.4
Other Services	1,400	1.9	3.7
Professional and Business Services	7,100	9.4	14.6
Retail Trade	7,600	10.1	10.7
Transportation, Warehousing, and Utilities	2,700	3.6	4.8
Wholesale Trade	1,500	2.0	3.8

Note: Figures are non-farm employment as of December 2021. Figures are not seasonally adjusted and include workers 16 years of age and older; (1) Figures cover the Las Cruces, NM Metropolitan Statistical Area
Source: Bureau of Labor Statistics, Current Employment Statistics, Employment, Hours, and Earnings

Employment by Occupation

Occupation Classification	City (%)	MSA[1] (%)	U.S. (%)
Management, Business, Science, and Arts	40.4	35.2	39.5
Natural Resources, Construction, and Maintenance	8.0	10.7	8.7
Production, Transportation, and Material Moving	5.9	9.1	13.1
Sales and Office	23.0	21.9	21.3
Service	22.8	23.1	17.4

Note: Figures cover employed civilians 16 years of age and older; (1) Figures cover the Las Cruces, NM Metropolitan Statistical Area
Source: U.S. Census Bureau, 2016-2020 American Community Survey 5-Year Estimates

Occupations with Greatest Projected Employment Growth: 2021 – 2023

Occupation[1]	2021 Employment	2023 Projected Employment	Numeric Employment Change	Percent Employment Change
Roustabouts, Oil and Gas	2,630	3,890	1,260	47.9
Fast Food and Counter Workers	21,960	23,180	1,220	5.6
Heavy and Tractor-Trailer Truck Drivers	11,480	12,610	1,130	9.8
Light Truck or Delivery Services Drivers	5,120	6,100	980	19.1
Laborers and Freight, Stock, and Material Movers, Hand	9,410	10,370	960	10.2
Cooks, Restaurant	6,360	7,140	780	12.3
Service Unit Operators, Oil, Gas, and Mining	2,260	3,020	760	33.6
Construction Laborers	11,940	12,670	730	6.1
Waiters and Waitresses	11,110	11,830	720	6.5
First-Line Supervisors of Construction Trades and Extraction Workers	6,820	7,530	710	10.4

Note: Projections cover New Mexico; (1) Sorted by numeric employment change
Source: www.projectionscentral.com, State Occupational Projections, 2021–2023 Short-Term Projections

Fastest-Growing Occupations: 2021 – 2023

Occupation[1]	2021 Employment	2023 Projected Employment	Numeric Employment Change	Percent Employment Change
Derrick Operators, Oil and Gas	540	810	270	50.0
Roustabouts, Oil and Gas	2,630	3,890	1,260	47.9
Rotary Drill Operators, Oil and Gas	720	1,050	330	45.8
Service Unit Operators, Oil, Gas, and Mining	2,260	3,020	760	33.6
Helpers—Extraction Workers	150	200	50	33.3
Ushers, Lobby Attendants, and Ticket Takers	260	340	80	30.8
Light Truck or Delivery Services Drivers	5,120	6,100	980	19.1
Wellhead Pumpers	280	330	50	17.9
Petroleum Engineers	340	400	60	17.6
Hotel, Motel, and Resort Desk Clerks	1,330	1,560	230	17.3

Note: Projections cover New Mexico; (1) Sorted by percent employment change and excludes occupations with numeric employment change less than 50
Source: www.projectionscentral.com, State Occupational Projections, 2021–2023 Short-Term Projections

TAXES

State Corporate Income Tax Rates

State	Tax Rate (%)	Income Brackets ($)	Num. of Brackets	Financial Institution Tax Rate (%)[a]	Federal Income Tax Ded.
New Mexico	4.8 - 5.9	500,000	2	4.8 - 5.9	No

Note: Tax rates as of January 1, 2022; (a) Rates listed are the corporate income tax rate applied to financial institutions or excise taxes based on income. Some states have other taxes based upon the value of deposits or shares.
Source: Federation of Tax Administrators, State Corporate Income Tax Rates, January 1, 2022

State Individual Income Tax Rates

State	Tax Rate (%)	Income Brackets ($)	Personal Exemptions ($)			Standard Ded. ($)	
			Single	Married	Depend.	Single	Married
New Mexico	1.7 - 5.9	5,500 - 210,000 (q)	(d)	(d)	(d)	12,950	25,900 (d)

Note: Tax rates as of January 1, 2022; Local- and county-level taxes are not included; Federal income tax is not deductible on state income tax returns; (d) These states use the personal exemption/standard deduction amounts provided in the federal Internal Revenue Code; (q) The income brackets reported for New Mexico are for single individuals. For married couples filing jointly, the same tax rates apply to income brackets ranging from $8,000 to $315,000.
Source: Federation of Tax Administrators, State Individual Income Tax Rates, January 1, 2022

Various State Sales and Excise Tax Rates

State	State Sales Tax (%)	Gasoline[1] (¢/gal.)	Cigarette[2] ($/pack)	Spirits[3] ($/gal.)	Wine[4] ($/gal.)	Beer[5] ($/gal.)	Recreational Marijuana (%)
New Mexico	5.125	18.88	2	6.06	1.7	0.41	(n)

Note: All tax rates as of January 1, 2022; (1) The American Petroleum Institute has developed a methodology for determining the average tax rate on a gallon of fuel. Rates may include any of the following: excise taxes, environmental fees, storage tank fees, other fees or taxes, general sales tax, and local taxes; (2) The federal excise tax of $1.0066 per pack and local taxes are not included; (3) Rates are those applicable to off-premise sales of 40% alcohol by volume (a.b.v.) distilled spirits in 750ml containers. Local excise taxes are excluded; (4) Rates are those applicable to off-premise sales of 11% a.b.v. non-carbonated wine in 750ml containers; (5) Rates are those applicable to off-premise sales of 4.7% a.b.v. beer in 12 ounce containers; (n) 12% excise tax (retail price)
Source: Tax Foundation, 2022 Facts & Figures: How Does Your State Compare?

State Business Tax Climate Index Rankings

State	Overall Rank	Corporate Tax Rank	Individual Income Tax Rank	Sales Tax Rank	Property Tax Rank	Unemployment Insurance Tax Rank
New Mexico	28	12	36	41	2	8

Note: The index is a measure of how each state's tax laws affect economic performance. The lower the rank, the more favorable a state's tax system is for business. States without a given tax are given a ranking of 1. The scores/rankings for the District of Columbia do not affect other states. The 2022 index represents the tax climate as of July 1, 2021.
Source: Tax Foundation, State Business Tax Climate Index 2022

TRANSPORTATION

Means of Transportation to Work

Area	Car/Truck/Van		Public Transportation			Bicycle	Walked	Other Means	Worked at Home
	Drove Alone	Car-pooled	Bus	Subway	Railroad				
City	77.1	11.5	0.6	0.0	0.0	1.7	2.2	0.8	6.0
MSA[1]	79.2	11.2	0.4	0.0	0.0	0.9	1.8	0.8	5.6
U.S.	74.9	8.9	2.2	1.7	0.5	0.5	2.6	1.4	7.3

Note: Figures are percentages and cover workers 16 years of age and older; (1) Figures cover the Las Cruces, NM Metropolitan Statistical Area
Source: U.S. Census Bureau, 2016-2020 American Community Survey 5-Year Estimates

Travel Time to Work

Area	Less Than 10 Minutes	10 to 19 Minutes	20 to 29 Minutes	30 to 44 Minutes	45 to 59 Minutes	60 to 89 Minutes	90 Minutes or More
City	17.0	49.0	17.3	8.6	3.5	4.0	0.7
MSA[1]	14.5	39.0	21.5	13.5	5.3	4.5	1.7
U.S.	12.3	28.4	20.9	20.9	8.3	6.4	2.9

Note: Note: Figures are percentages and include workers 16 years old and over; (1) Figures cover the Las Cruces, NM Metropolitan Statistical Area
Source: U.S. Census Bureau, 2016-2020 American Community Survey 5-Year Estimates

Key Congestion Measures

Measure	1990	2000	2010	2015	2020
Annual Hours of Delay, Total (000)	n/a	n/a	n/a	2,651	1,236
Annual Hours of Delay, Per Auto Commuter	n/a	n/a	n/a	18	8
Annual Congestion Cost, Per Auto Commuter ($)	n/a	n/a	n/a	383	187

Note: n/a not available
Source: Texas A&M Transportation Institute, 2021 Urban Mobility Report

Freeway Travel Time Index

Measure	1985	1990	1995	2000	2005	2010	2015	2020
Urban Area Index[1]	n/a	n/a	n/a	n/a	n/a	n/a	1.07	1.04
Urban Area Rank[1,2]	n/a	n/a	n/a	n/a	n/a	n/a	n/a	n/a

Note: Freeway Travel Time Index—the ratio of travel time in the peak period to the travel time at free-flow conditions. For example, a value of 1.30 indicates a 20-minute free-flow trip takes 26 minutes in the peak (20 minutes x 1.30 = 26 minutes); (1) Covers the Las Cruces NM urban area; (2) Rank is based on 101 larger urban areas (#1 = highest travel time index); n/a not available
Source: Texas A&M Transportation Institute, 2021 Urban Mobility Report

Public Transportation

Agency Name / Mode of Transportation	Vehicles Operated in Maximum Service[1]	Annual Unlinked Passenger Trips[2] (in thous.)	Annual Passenger Miles[3] (in thous.)
Las Cruces Area Transit			
Bus (directly operated)	13	505.2	n/a
Demand Response (directly operated)	15	41.9	n/a

Note: (1) Number of revenue vehicles operated by the given mode and type of service to meet the annual maximum service requirement. This is the revenue vehicle count during the peak season of the year; on the week and day that maximum service is provided. Vehicles operated in maximum service (VOMS) exclude atypical days and one-time special events; (2) Number of passengers who boarded public transportation vehicles. Passengers are counted each time they board a vehicle no matter how many vehicles they use to travel from their origin to their destination. (3) Sum of the distances ridden by all passengers during the entire fiscal year.
Source: Federal Transit Administration, National Transit Database, 2020

Air Transportation

Airport Name and Code / Type of Service	Passenger Airlines[1]	Passenger Enplanements	Freight Carriers[2]	Freight (lbs)
El Paso International (52 miles) (ELP)				
Domestic service (U.S. carriers - 2021)	25	1,450,402	19	103,629,587
International service (U.S. carriers - 2020)	2	14,462	6	804,487

Note: (1) Includes all U.S.-based major, minor and commuter airlines that carried at least one passenger during the year; (2) Includes all U.S.-based airlines and freight carriers that transported at least one pound of freight during the year.
Source: Bureau of Transportation Statistics, The Intermodal Transportation Database, Air Carriers: T-100 Domestic Market (U.S. Carriers), 2021; Bureau of Transportation Statistics, The Intermodal Transportation Database, Air Carriers: T-100 International Market (U.S. Carriers), 2020

BUSINESSES

Major Business Headquarters

Company Name	Industry	Rankings	
		Fortune[1]	Forbes[2]
No companies listed	-	-	-

Note: (1) Companies that produce a 10-K are ranked 1 to 500 based on 2020 revenue; (2) All private companies with at least $2 billion in annual revenue through the end of their most current fiscal year are ranked 1 to 225; companies listed are headquartered in the city; dashes indicate no ranking
Source: Fortune, "Fortune 500," 2021; Forbes, "America's Largest Private Companies," 2021

Living Environment

COST OF LIVING

Cost of Living Index

Composite Index	Groceries	Housing	Utilities	Trans-portation	Health Care	Misc. Goods/ Services
86.9	97.0	75.8	82.5	100.9	99.7	88.5

Note: The Cost of Living Index measures regional differences in the cost of consumer goods and services, excluding taxes and non-consumer expenditures, for professional and managerial households in the top income quintile. It is based on more than 50,000 prices covering almost 60 different items for which prices are collected three times a year by chambers of commerce, economic development organizations or university applied economic centers in each participating urban area. The numbers shown should be read as a percentage above or below the national average of 100. For example, a value of 115.4 in the groceries column indicates that grocery prices are 15.4% higher than the national average. Small differences in the index numbers should not be interpreted as significant; Figures cover the Las Cruces NM urban area.
Source: The Council for Community and Economic Research, Cost of Living Index, 2021

Grocery Prices

Area[1]	T-Bone Steak ($/pound)	Frying Chicken ($/pound)	Whole Milk ($/half gal.)	Eggs ($/dozen)	Orange Juice ($/64 oz.)	Coffee ($/11.5 oz.)
City[2]	13.27	1.05	3.31	1.97	3.64	4.63
Avg.	12.82	1.40	2.22	1.57	3.59	4.30
Min.	8.91	0.91	1.29	0.75	2.87	3.02
Max.	21.35	2.69	3.92	3.86	5.49	8.11

*Note: (1) Values for the local area are compared with the average, minimum and maximum values for all 285 areas in the Cost of Living Index; (2) Figures cover the Las Cruces NM urban area; **T-Bone Steak** (price per pound); **Frying Chicken** (price per pound, whole fryer); **Whole Milk** (half gallon carton); **Eggs** (price per dozen, Grade A, large); **Orange Juice** (64 oz. Tropicana or Florida Natural); **Coffee** (11.5 oz. can, vacuum-packed, Maxwell House, Hills Bros, or Folgers).*
Source: The Council for Community and Economic Research, Cost of Living Index, 2021

Housing and Utility Costs

Area[1]	New Home Price ($)	Apartment Rent ($/month)	All Electric ($/month)	Part Electric ($/month)	Other Energy ($/month)	Telephone ($/month)
City[2]	316,391	814	-	77.22	40.12	188.36
Avg.	398,393	1,217	171.38	100.83	69.67	187.75
Min.	212,799	534	96.71	31.56	27.15	173.01
Max.	2,354,006	4,438	369.53	277.33	303.87	206.73

*Note: (1) Values for the local area are compared with the average, minimum and maximum values for all 285 areas in the Cost of Living Index; (2) Figures cover the Las Cruces NM urban area; **New Home Price** (2,400 sf living area, 8,000 sf lot, in urban area with full utilities); **Apartment Rent** (950 sf 2 bedroom/1.5 or 2 bath, unfurnished, excluding all utilities except water); **All Electric** (average monthly cost for an all-electric home); **Part Electric** (average monthly cost for a part-electric home); **Other Energy** (average monthly cost for natural gas, fuel oil, coal, wood, and any other forms of energy except electricity); **Telephone** (price includes the base monthly rate plus taxes and fees for three lines of mobile phone service).*
Source: The Council for Community and Economic Research, Cost of Living Index, 2021

Health Care, Transportation, and Other Costs

Area[1]	Doctor ($/visit)	Dentist ($/visit)	Optometrist ($/visit)	Gasoline ($/gallon)	Beauty Salon ($/visit)	Men's Shirt ($)
City[2]	106.77	99.67	107.20	2.88	36.83	25.82
Avg.	118.16	101.04	109.44	2.71	40.63	30.77
Min.	35.04	55.56	51.17	2.17	18.59	11.32
Max.	231.10	165.12	256.81	4.11	85.33	63.03

*Note: (1) Values for the local area are compared with the average, minimum and maximum values for all 285 areas in the Cost of Living Index; (2) Figures cover the Las Cruces NM urban area; **Doctor** (general practitioners routine exam of an established patient); **Dentist** (adult teeth cleaning and periodic oral examination); **Optometrist** (full vision eye exam for established adult patient); **Gasoline** (one gallon regular unleaded, national brand, including all taxes, cash price at self-service pump if available); **Beauty Salon** (woman's shampoo, trim, and blow-dry); **Men's Shirt** (cotton/polyester dress shirt, pinpoint weave, long sleeves).*
Source: The Council for Community and Economic Research, Cost of Living Index, 2021

HOUSING

Homeownership Rate

Area	2013 (%)	2014 (%)	2015 (%)	2016 (%)	2017 (%)	2018 (%)	2019 (%)	2020 (%)	2021 (%)
MSA[1]	n/a	n/a	n/a	n/a	n/a	n/a	n/a	n/a	n/a
U.S.	65.1	64.5	63.7	63.4	63.9	64.4	64.6	66.6	65.5

Note: (1) Figures cover the Las Cruces, NM Metropolitan Statistical Area; n/a not available
Source: U.S. Census Bureau, Housing Vacancies and Homeownership Annual Statistics: 2013-2021

House Price Index (HPI)

Area	National Ranking[2]	Quarterly Change (%)	One-Year Change (%)	Five-Year Change (%)	Since 1991Q1 (%)
MSA[1]	97	3.27	19.28	42.47	157.99
U.S.[3]	–	3.33	17.54	54.45	258.04

Note: The HPI is a weighted repeat sales index. It measures average price changes in repeat sales or refinancings on the same properties. This information is obtained by reviewing repeat mortgage transactions on single-family properties whose mortgages have been purchased or securitized by Fannie Mae or Freddie Mac since January 1975; (1) Figures cover the Las Cruces, NM Metropolitan Statistical Area; (2) Rankings are based on annual percentage change for all metro areas containing at least 15,000 transactions over the last 10 years and ranges from 1 to 268; (3) figures based on a weighted average of Census Division estimates using a seasonally adjusted, purchase-only index; all figures are for the period ending December 31, 2021
Source: Federal Housing Finance Agency, Change in FHFA Metropolitan Area House Price Indexes, 2021Q4

Median Single-Family Home Prices

Area	2019	2020	2021p	Percent Change 2020 to 2021
MSA[1]	n/a	n/a	n/a	n/a
U.S. Average	274.6	300.2	353.4	17.7

Note: Figures are median sales prices of existing single-family homes in thousands of dollars; (p) preliminary; n/a not available; (1) Figures cover the Las Cruces, NM Metropolitan Statistical Area
Source: National Association of Realtors, Median Sales Price of Existing Single-Family Homes for Metropolitan Areas, 4th Quarter 2021

Qualifying Income Based on Median Sales Price of Existing Single-Family Homes

Area	With 5% Down ($)	With 10% Down ($)	With 20% Down ($)
MSA[1]	n/a	n/a	n/a
U.S. Average	70,699	66,978	59,536

Note: Figures are preliminary; Qualifying income is based on a mortgage rate of 3.13%. Monthly principal and interest payment is limited to 25% of income; n/a not available; (1) Figures cover the Las Cruces, NM Metropolitan Statistical Area
Source: National Association of Realtors, Qualifying Income Based on Median Sales Price of Existing Single-Family Homes for Metropolitan Areas, 4th Quarter 2021

Home Value Distribution

Area	Under $50,000	$50,000 -$99,999	$100,000 -$149,999	$150,000 -$199,999	$200,000 -$299,999	$300,000 -$499,999	$500,000 -$999,999	$1,000,000 or more
City	7.2	11.7	24.6	26.3	20.6	7.7	1.7	0.3
MSA[1]	11.4	17.2	19.8	20.1	18.5	9.9	2.9	0.3
U.S.	6.6	11.0	12.3	13.6	20.0	20.5	12.3	3.7

Note: Figures are percentages and cover owner-occupied housing units; (1) Figures cover the Las Cruces, NM Metropolitan Statistical Area
Source: U.S. Census Bureau, 2016-2020 American Community Survey 5-Year Estimates

Year Housing Structure Built

Area	2010 or Later	2000 -2009	1990 -1999	1980 -1989	1970 -1979	1960 -1969	1950 -1959	1940 -1949	Before 1940	Median Year
City	10.2	20.0	14.7	17.8	14.9	8.2	9.6	2.2	2.3	1987
MSA[1]	9.6	17.5	19.9	19.1	14.7	7.4	6.7	2.2	2.8	1988
U.S.	6.2	13.6	13.9	13.4	15.0	10.5	10.2	4.8	12.4	1978

Note: Figures are percentages except for Median Year; Note: (1) Figures cover the Las Cruces, NM Metropolitan Statistical Area
Source: U.S. Census Bureau, 2016-2020 American Community Survey 5-Year Estimates

Gross Monthly Rent

Area	Under $500	$500 -$999	$1,000 -$1,499	$1,500 -$1,999	$2,000 -$2,499	$2,500 -$2,999	$3,000 and up	Median ($)
City	13.6	58.4	24.0	2.9	1.0	0.0	0.2	805
MSA[1]	16.3	58.2	20.6	3.5	1.2	0.1	0.1	765
U.S.	8.9	34.3	30.2	14.9	6.2	2.6	2.8	1,096

Note: Figures are percentages except for Median; Gross rent is the contract rent plus the estimated average monthly cost of utilities (electricity, gas, and water and sewer) and fuels (oil, coal, kerosene, wood, etc.) if these are paid by the renter (or paid for the renter by someone else); (1) Figures cover the Las Cruces, NM Metropolitan Statistical Area
Source: U.S. Census Bureau, 2016-2020 American Community Survey 5-Year Estimates

HEALTH

Health Risk Factors

Category	MSA[1] (%)	U.S. (%)
Adults aged 18–64 who have any kind of health care coverage	n/a	86.8
Adults who reported being in good or better health	n/a	86.7
Adults who are current smokers	n/a	15.5
Adults who currently use chewing tobacco, snuff, or snus	n/a	3.7
Adults who are heavy drinkers[2]	n/a	6.7
Adults who are binge drinkers[3]	n/a	15.7
Adults who are overweight (BMI 25.0 - 29.9)	n/a	35.2
Adults who are obese (BMI 30.0 - 99.8)	n/a	31.9
Adults who participated in any physical activities in the past month	n/a	77.6
Adults who always or nearly always wears a seat belt	n/a	94.2

Note: (1) Figures for the Las Cruces, NM Metropolitan Statistical Area were not available.
(2) Heavy drinkers are classified as adult men having more than 14 drinks per week and adult women having more than 7 drinks per week; (3) Binge drinkers are classified as males having five or more drinks on one occasion or females having four or more drinks on one occasion
Source: Centers for Disease Control and Prevention, Behaviorial Risk Factor Surveillance System, SMART: Selected Metropolitan Area Risk Trends, 2020

Acute and Chronic Health Conditions

Category	MSA[1] (%)	U.S. (%)
Adults who have ever been told they had a heart attack	n/a	4.3
Adults who have ever been told they have angina or coronary heart disease	n/a	4.0
Adults who have ever been told they had a stroke	n/a	2.8
Adults who have ever been told they have asthma	n/a	14.2
Adults who have ever been told they have arthritis	n/a	24.5
Adults who have ever been told they have diabetes[2]	n/a	10.6
Adults who have ever been told they had skin cancer	n/a	6.4
Adults who have ever been told they had any other types of cancer	n/a	6.8
Adults who have ever been told they have COPD	n/a	6.2
Adults who have ever been told they have kidney disease	n/a	2.9
Adults who have ever been told they have a form of depression	n/a	19.6

Note: (1) Figures for the Las Cruces, NM Metropolitan Statistical Area were not available.
(2) Figures do not include pregnancy-related, borderline, or pre-diabetes
Source: Centers for Disease Control and Prevention, Behaviorial Risk Factor Surveillance System, SMART: Selected Metropolitan Area Risk Trends, 2020

Health Screening and Vaccination Rates

Category	MSA[1] (%)	U.S. (%)
Adults 50-75 who have had a blood stool test within the past year	n/a	9.3
Adults aged 65+ who have had flu shot within the past year	n/a	67.9
Adults aged 65+ who have ever had a pneumonia vaccination	n/a	72.2
Adults who have ever been tested for HIV	n/a	37.1
Women aged 21-65 who have had a pap test in the past three years	n/a	77.7
Men aged 40+ who have had a PSA test within the past two years	n/a	31.8
Women aged 40+ who have had a mammogram within the past two years	n/a	71.5

Note: (1) Figures for the Las Cruces, NM Metropolitan Statistical Area were not available.
Source: Centers for Disease Control and Prevention, Behaviorial Risk Factor Surveillance System, SMART: Selected Metropolitan Area Risk Trends, 2020

Disability Status

Category	MSA[1] (%)	U.S. (%)
Adults who reported being deaf	n/a	6.8
Are you blind or have serious difficulty seeing, even when wearing glasses?	n/a	4.7
Do you have difficulty doing errands alone?	n/a	6.3
Do you have difficulty dressing or bathing?	n/a	3.0
Do you have serious difficulty concentrating/remembering/making decisions?	n/a	10.8
Do you have serious difficulty walking or climbing stairs?	n/a	11.9

Note: (1) Figures for the Las Cruces, NM Metropolitan Statistical Area were not available.
Source: Centers for Disease Control and Prevention, Behaviorial Risk Factor Surveillance System, SMART: Selected Metropolitan Area Risk Trends, 2020

Mortality Rates for the Top 10 Causes of Death in the U.S.

ICD-10[a] Sub-Chapter	ICD-10[a] Code	Age-Adjusted Mortality Rate[1] per 100,000 population	
		County[2]	U.S.
Malignant neoplasms	C00-C97	130.8	146.4
Ischaemic heart diseases	I20-I25	88.8	90.2
Other forms of heart disease	I30-I51	32.5	51.9
Other degenerative diseases of the nervous system	G30-G31	28.3	39.7
Other external causes of accidental injury	W00-X59	37.5	38.7
Chronic lower respiratory diseases	J40-J47	34.1	38.1
Cerebrovascular diseases	I60-I69	38.6	37.6
Organic, including symptomatic, mental disorders	F01-F09	34.5	29.4
Hypertensive diseases	I10-I15	13.6	26.1
Diabetes mellitus	E10-E14	29.6	22.6

Note: (a) ICD-10 = International Classification of Diseases 10th Revision; (1) Mortality rates are a three-year average covering 2018-2020; (2) Figures cover Dona Ana County.
Source: Centers for Disease Control and Prevention, National Center for Health Statistics. Underlying Cause of Death 1999-2020 on CDC WONDER Online Database

Mortality Rates for Selected Causes of Death

ICD-10[a] Sub-Chapter	ICD-10[a] Code	Age-Adjusted Mortality Rate[1] per 100,000 population	
		County[2]	U.S.
Assault	X85-Y09	6.3	6.5
Diseases of the liver	K70-K76	26.5	15.3
Human immunodeficiency virus (HIV) disease	B20-B24	Unreliable	1.4
Influenza and pneumonia	J09-J18	15.5	13.4
Intentional self-harm	X60-X84	17.0	13.9
Malnutrition	E40-E46	2.7	2.9
Obesity and other hyperalimentation	E65-E68	Unreliable	2.4
Renal failure	N17-N19	18.2	12.5
Transport accidents	V01-V99	13.7	12.5
Viral hepatitis	B15-B19	Unreliable	1.0

Note: (a) ICD-10 = International Classification of Diseases 10th Revision; (1) Mortality rates are a three-year average covering 2018-2020; (2) Figures cover Dona Ana County; Data are suppressed when the data meet the criteria for confidentiality constraints; Mortality rates are flagged as unreliable when the rate would be calculated with a numerator of 20 or less.
Source: Centers for Disease Control and Prevention, National Center for Health Statistics. Underlying Cause of Death 1999-2020 on CDC WONDER Online Database

Health Insurance Coverage

Area	With Health Insurance	With Private Health Insurance	With Public Health Insurance	Without Health Insurance	Population Under Age 19 Without Health Insurance
City	93.1	56.1	51.3	6.9	2.0
MSA[1]	89.4	48.6	52.4	10.6	5.5
U.S.	91.3	68.1	35.3	8.7	5.2

Note: Figures are percentages that cover the civilian noninstitutionalized population; (1) Figures cover the Las Cruces, NM Metropolitan Statistical Area
Source: U.S. Census Bureau, 2016-2020 American Community Survey 5-Year Estimates

Number of Medical Professionals

Area	MDs[3]	DOs[3,4]	Dentists	Podiatrists	Chiropractors	Optometrists
County[1] (number)	367	30	136	13	40	20
County[1] (rate[2])	167.2	13.7	61.9	5.9	18.2	9.1
U.S. (rate[2])	285.1	23.0	71.1	6.2	28.2	17.0

35013
Note: Data as of 2020 unless noted; (1) Data covers Dona Ana County; (2) Rate per 100,000 population; (3) Data as of 2019 and includes all active, non-federal physicians; (4) Doctor of Osteopathic Medicine
Source: U.S. Department of Health and Human Services, Health Resources and Services Administration, Bureau of Health Professions, Area Resource File (ARF) 2020-2021

EDUCATION

Public School District Statistics

District Name	Schls	Pupils	Pupil/ Teacher Ratio	Minority Pupils[1] (%)	LEP/ELL[2] (%)	IEP[3] (%)
Las Cruces Public Schools	40	24,517	16.1	81.8	13.0	15.3

Note: Table includes school districts with 2,000 or more students; (1) Percentage of students that are not non-Hispanic white; (2) Percentage of students that are Limited English Proficient (LEP) or English Language Learners (ELL) (2018-19); (3) Percentage of students that have an Individualized Education Program (IEP).
Source: U.S. Department of Education, National Center for Education Statistics, Common Core of Data, Local Education Agency (School District) Universe Survey: School Year 2019-2020

Highest Level of Education

Area	Less than H.S.	H.S. Diploma	Some College, No Deg.	Associate Degree	Bachelor's Degree	Master's Degree	Prof. School Degree	Doctorate Degree
City	11.5	19.7	23.2	8.8	20.5	12.0	2.4	1.9
MSA[1]	19.4	21.5	21.4	8.1	17.3	9.0	1.7	1.5
U.S.	11.5	26.7	20.3	8.6	20.2	9.1	2.2	1.5

Note: Figures cover persons age 25 and over; (1) Figures cover the Las Cruces, NM Metropolitan Statistical Area
Source: U.S. Census Bureau, 2016-2020 American Community Survey 5-Year Estimates

Educational Attainment by Race

Area	High School Graduate or Higher (%)					Bachelor's Degree or Higher (%)				
	Total	White	Black	Asian	Hisp.[2]	Total	White	Black	Asian	Hisp.[2]
City	88.5	89.8	86.9	89.6	82.9	36.8	37.5	48.4	66.3	23.6
MSA[1]	80.6	81.6	88.1	91.9	72.5	29.5	30.1	48.8	62.5	18.3
U.S.	88.5	90.7	86.7	87.3	70.3	32.9	34.4	22.6	55.0	17.6

Note: Figures shown cover persons 25 years old and over; (1) Figures cover the Las Cruces, NM Metropolitan Statistical Area; (2) People of Hispanic origin can be of any race
Source: U.S. Census Bureau, 2016-2020 American Community Survey 5-Year Estimates

School Enrollment by Grade and Control

Area	Preschool (%)		Kindergarten (%)		Grades 1 - 4 (%)		Grades 5 - 8 (%)		Grades 9 - 12 (%)	
	Public	Private	Public	Private	Public	Private	Public	Private	Public	Private
City	79.6	20.4	89.8	10.2	93.6	6.4	97.2	2.8	96.8	3.2
MSA[1]	82.9	17.1	92.6	7.4	91.4	8.6	96.5	3.5	96.4	3.6
U.S.	58.9	41.1	86.9	13.1	89.0	11.0	89.0	11.0	89.7	10.3

Note: Figures shown cover persons 3 years old and over; (1) Figures cover the Las Cruces, NM Metropolitan Statistical Area
Source: U.S. Census Bureau, 2016-2020 American Community Survey 5-Year Estimates

Higher Education

Four-Year Colleges			Two-Year Colleges			Medical Schools[1]	Law Schools[2]	Voc/ Tech[3]
Public	Private Non-profit	Private For-profit	Public	Private Non-profit	Private For-profit			
1	0	1	1	0	0	1	0	1

Note: Figures cover institutions located within the Las Cruces, NM Metropolitan Statistical Area and include main campuses only; (1) includes schools accredited by the Liaison Committee on Medical Education and the American Osteopathic Association's Commission on Osteopathic College Accreditation; (2) includes ABA-accredited schools, schools with provisional ABA accreditation, and state accredited schools; (3) includes all schools with programs that are less than 2 years.
Source: National Center for Education Statistics, Integrated Postsecondary Education System (IPEDS), 2020-21; Wikipedia, List of Medical Schools in the United States, accessed April 11, 2022; Wikipedia, List of Law Schools in the United States, accessed April 11, 2022

EMPLOYERS

Major Employers

Company Name	Industry
City of Las Cruces	Municipal government
Doña Ana Co. Independent School Districts	School districts
Doña Ana Community College	Community college
Doña Ana County	County government
Memorial Medical Center	Medical center
Mountain View Regional Medical Center	Medical center
NASA White Sands Test Facility	Government test facility
New Mexico State University	State universities
SiTel/Client Logic	Telemarketing
State of New Mexico	State government
Tresco	Early intervention services
U.S. Postal Service	Mail and package delivery
Wal-Mart Stores	Retail

Note: Companies shown are located within the Las Cruces, NM Metropolitan Statistical Area.
Source: Hoovers.com; Wikipedia

PUBLIC SAFETY

Crime Rate

Area	Total Crime	Violent Crime Rate				Property Crime Rate		
		Murder	Rape[3]	Robbery	Aggrav. Assault	Burglary	Larceny -Theft	Motor Vehicle Theft
City	4,077.5	9.7	61.8	55.1	370.0	631.8	2,652.6	296.6
Suburbs[1]	1,781.8	1.7	52.3	10.5	546.8	362.8	699.5	108.1
Metro[2]	2,871.0	5.5	56.8	31.6	462.9	490.4	1,626.2	197.5
U.S.	2,510.4	5.1	42.6	81.8	250.4	340.5	1,569.2	220.8

Note: Figures are crimes per 100,000 population; (1) All areas within the metro area that are located outside the city limits; (2) Figures cover the Las Cruces, NM Metropolitan Statistical Area; (3) All figures shown were reported using the revised Uniform Crime Reporting (UCR) definition of rape.
Source: FBI Uniform Crime Reports, 2019 (data for 2020 was not available)

Hate Crimes

Area	Number of Quarters Reported	Number of Incidents per Bias Motivation					
		Race/Ethnicity/ Ancestry	Religion	Sexual Orientation	Disability	Gender	Gender Identity
City	4	0	0	0	0	0	0
U.S.	4	5,227	1,244	1,110	130	75	266

Source: Federal Bureau of Investigation, Hate Crime Statistics 2020

Identity Theft Consumer Reports

Area	Reports	Reports per 100,000 Population	Rank[2]
MSA[1]	489	224	198
U.S.	1,434,676	432	-

Note: (1) Figures cover the Las Cruces, NM Metropolitan Statistical Area; (2) Rank ranges from 1 to 391 where 1 indicates greatest number of identity theft reports per 100,000 population
Source: Federal Trade Commission, Consumer Sentinel Network Data Book 2021

Fraud and Other Consumer Reports

Area	Reports	Reports per 100,000 Population	Rank[2]
MSA[1]	1,697	778	268
U.S.	4,328,977	1,304	-

Note: (1) Figures cover the Las Cruces, NM Metropolitan Statistical Area; (2) Rank ranges from 1 to 391 where 1 indicates greatest number of fraud and other consumer reports per 100,000 population
Source: Federal Trade Commission, Consumer Sentinel Network Data Book 2021

POLITICS

2020 Presidential Election Results

Area	Biden	Trump	Jorgensen	Hawkins	Other
Dona Ana County	58.0	39.7	1.4	0.5	0.4
U.S.	51.3	46.8	1.2	0.3	0.5

Note: Results are percentages and may not add to 100% due to rounding
Source: Dave Leip's Atlas of U.S. Presidential Elections

SPORTS

Professional Sports Teams

Team Name	League	Year Established
No teams are located in the metro area		

Source: Wikipedia, Major Professional Sports Teams of the United States and Canada, April 6, 2022

CLIMATE

Average and Extreme Temperatures

Temperature	Jan	Feb	Mar	Apr	May	Jun	Jul	Aug	Sep	Oct	Nov	Dec	Yr.
Extreme High (°F)	80	83	89	98	104	114	112	108	104	96	87	80	114
Average High (°F)	57	63	70	79	87	96	95	93	88	79	66	58	78
Average Temp. (°F)	44	49	56	64	73	81	83	81	75	65	52	45	64
Average Low (°F)	31	35	41	49	58	66	70	68	62	50	38	32	50
Extreme Low (°F)	-8	8	14	23	31	46	57	56	42	25	1	5	-8

Note: Figures cover the years 1948-1995
Source: National Climatic Data Center, International Station Meteorological Climate Summary, 9/96

Average Precipitation/Snowfall/Humidity

Precip./Humidity	Jan	Feb	Mar	Apr	May	Jun	Jul	Aug	Sep	Oct	Nov	Dec	Yr.
Avg. Precip. (in.)	0.4	0.4	0.3	0.2	0.3	0.7	1.6	1.5	1.4	0.7	0.3	0.6	8.6
Avg. Snowfall (in.)	1	1	Tr	Tr	0	0	0	0	0	Tr	1	2	6
Avg. Rel. Hum. 6am (%)	68	60	50	43	44	46	63	69	72	66	63	68	59
Avg. Rel. Hum. 3pm (%)	34	27	21	17	17	17	28	30	32	29	30	36	26

Note: Figures cover the years 1948-1995; Tr = Trace amounts (<0.05 in. of rain; <0.5 in. of snow)
Source: National Climatic Data Center, International Station Meteorological Climate Summary, 9/96

Weather Conditions

Temperature			Daytime Sky			Precipitation		
10°F & below	32°F & below	90°F & above	Clear	Partly cloudy	Cloudy	0.01 inch or more precip.	0.1 inch or more snow/ice	Thunder-storms
1	59	106	147	164	54	49	3	35

Note: Figures are average number of days per year and cover the years 1948-1995
Source: National Climatic Data Center, International Station Meteorological Climate Summary, 9/96

HAZARDOUS WASTE

Superfund Sites

The Las Cruces, NM metro area has no sites on the EPA's Superfund Final National Priorities List. There are a total of 1,165 Superfund sites with a status of proposed or final on the list in the U.S. *U.S. Environmental Protection Agency, National Priorities List, April 6, 2022*

AIR QUALITY

Air Quality Trends: Ozone

	1990	1995	2000	2005	2010	2016	2017	2018	2019	2020
MSA[1]	0.073	0.075	0.075	0.070	0.060	0.070	0.071	0.072	0.068	0.071
U.S.	0.090	0.091	0.082	0.080	0.074	0.070	0.069	0.070	0.066	0.068

Note: (1) Data covers the Las Cruces, NM Metropolitan Statistical Area. The values shown are the composite ozone concentration averages among trend sites based on the highest fourth daily maximum 8-hour concentration in parts per million. These trends are based on sites having an adequate record of monitoring data during the trend period. Data from exceptional events are included.
Source: U.S. Environmental Protection Agency, Air Quality Monitoring Information, "Air Quality Trends by City, 1990-2020"

Air Quality Index

Area	Percent of Days when Air Quality was...[2]					AQI Statistics[2]	
	Good	Moderate	Unhealthy for Sensitive Groups	Unhealthy	Very Unhealthy	Maximum	Median
MSA[1]	45.9	48.4	4.1	0.8	0.3	400	53

Note: (1) Data covers the Las Cruces, NM Metropolitan Statistical Area; (2) Based on 366 days with AQI data in 2020. Air Quality Index (AQI) is an index for reporting daily air quality. EPA calculates the AQI for five major air pollutants regulated by the Clean Air Act: ground-level ozone, particle pollution (aka particulate matter), carbon monoxide, sulfur dioxide, and nitrogen dioxide. The AQI runs from 0 to 500. The higher the AQI value, the greater the level of air pollution and the greater the health concern. There are six AQI categories: "Good" AQI is between 0 and 50. Air quality is considered satisfactory; "Moderate" AQI is between 51 and 100. Air quality is acceptable; "Unhealthy for Sensitive Groups" When AQI values are between 101 and 150, members of sensitive groups may experience health effects; "Unhealthy" When AQI values are between 151 and 200 everyone may begin to experience health effects; "Very Unhealthy" AQI values between 201 and 300 trigger a health alert; "Hazardous" AQI values over 300 trigger warnings of emergency conditions (not shown).
Source: U.S. Environmental Protection Agency, Air Quality Index Report, 2020

Air Quality Index Pollutants

Area	Percent of Days when AQI Pollutant was...[2]					
	Carbon Monoxide	Nitrogen Dioxide	Ozone	Sulfur Dioxide	Particulate Matter 2.5	Particulate Matter 10
MSA[1]	0.0	1.9	64.8	0.0	10.7	22.7

Note: (1) Data covers the Las Cruces, NM Metropolitan Statistical Area; (2) Based on 366 days with AQI data in 2020. The Air Quality Index (AQI) is an index for reporting daily air quality. EPA calculates the AQI for five major air pollutants regulated by the Clean Air Act: ground-level ozone, particle pollution (also known as particulate matter), carbon monoxide, sulfur dioxide, and nitrogen dioxide. The AQI runs from 0 to 500. The higher the AQI value, the greater the level of air pollution and the greater the health concern.
Source: U.S. Environmental Protection Agency, Air Quality Index Report, 2020

Maximum Air Pollutant Concentrations: Particulate Matter, Ozone, CO and Lead

	Particulate Matter 10 (ug/m^3)	Particulate Matter 2.5 Wtd AM (ug/m^3)	Particulate Matter 2.5 24-Hr (ug/m^3)	Ozone (ppm)	Carbon Monoxide (ppm)	Lead (ug/m^3)
MSA[1] Level	367	9	21	0.077	n/a	n/a
NAAQS[2]	150	15	35	0.075	9	0.15
Met NAAQS[2]	No	Yes	Yes	No	n/a	n/a

Note: (1) Data covers the Las Cruces, NM Metropolitan Statistical Area; Data from exceptional events are included; (2) National Ambient Air Quality Standards; ppm = parts per million; ug/m^3 = micrograms per cubic meter; n/a not available.

Concentrations: Particulate Matter 10 (coarse particulate)—highest second maximum 24-hour concentration; Particulate Matter 2.5 Wtd AM (fine particulate)—highest weighted annual mean concentration; Particulate Matter 2.5 24-Hour (fine particulate)—highest 98th percentile 24-hour concentration; Ozone—highest fourth daily maximum 8-hour concentration; Carbon Monoxide—highest second maximum non-overlapping 8-hour concentration; Lead—maximum running 3-month average

Source: U.S. Environmental Protection Agency, Air Quality Monitoring Information, "Air Quality Statistics by City, 2020"

Maximum Air Pollutant Concentrations: Nitrogen Dioxide and Sulfur Dioxide

	Nitrogen Dioxide AM (ppb)	Nitrogen Dioxide 1-Hr (ppb)	Sulfur Dioxide AM (ppb)	Sulfur Dioxide 1-Hr (ppb)	Sulfur Dioxide 24-Hr (ppb)
MSA[1] Level	8	49	n/a	n/a	n/a
NAAQS[2]	53	100	30	75	140
Met NAAQS[2]	Yes	Yes	n/a	n/a	n/a

Note: (1) Data covers the Las Cruces, NM Metropolitan Statistical Area; Data from exceptional events are included; (2) National Ambient Air Quality Standards; ppm = parts per million; ug/m^3 = micrograms per cubic meter; n/a not available.

Concentrations: Nitrogen Dioxide AM—highest arithmetic mean concentration; Nitrogen Dioxide 1-Hr—highest 98th percentile 1-hour daily maximum concentration; Sulfur Dioxide AM—highest annual mean concentration; Sulfur Dioxide 1-Hr—highest 99th percentile 1-hour daily maximum concentration; Sulfur Dioxide 24-Hr—highest second maximum 24-hour concentration

Source: U.S. Environmental Protection Agency, Air Quality Monitoring Information, "Air Quality Statistics by City, 2020"

Las Vegas, Nevada

Background

Upright citizens can accuse Las Vegas of many vices, but not of hypocrisy. Back in 1931, the city officials of this desert town, located 225 miles northeast of Los Angeles, saw gambling to be a growing popular pastime. To capitalize upon that trend, the city simply legalized it. Gambling, combined with spectacular, neon-lit entertainment, lured more than 36.4 million visitors annually during pre-COVID years; 2021 saw 32.2 million as the city anticipates increased 2022 numbers to fill its 143,000 hotel rooms and 60 casinos in its Strip area.

Before celebrities and tourists flocked to Las Vegas, it was a temporary stopping place for a diverse group of people. In the early 1880s, Las Vegas was a watering hole for those on the trail to California. Areas of the Las Vegas Valley contained artesian wells that supported extensive green meadows, or *vega* in Spanish, hence the name Las Vegas. In 1855 the area was settled by Mormon missionaries, but they left two years later. In the late 1800s the land was used for ranching.

In the beginning of the twentieth century, the seeds of the present Las Vegas began to sprout. In 1905 the arrival of the Union Pacific Railroad came with businesses, saloons, and gambling houses sprinkled along it tracks and the city was formally founded on May 15, 1905.

During the Great Depression, men working on the nearby Hoover Dam spent their extra money in the city's establishments, and gambling was quickly legalized. Hydroelectric power from the Hoover Dam lit the city in neon, and hotels began to compete for the brightest stars and the plushest surroundings. Las Vegas was an overnight success, luring many people with get-rich-quick dreams. The dream has thus far endured, and in 2005 the city celebrated its centennial with a suitably festive media blitz, special events, and the world's largest, 130,000-pound, birthday cake.

Las Vegas is home to the World Series of Poker, which consists of 101 events. Winners have pocketed more than $12 million.

For the past 25 years, senior citizens have constituted the fastest-growing segment of the Las Vegas population, taking advantage of the dry climate, reasonably priced housing, low property taxes, no sales tax, and plenty of entertainment. Nevada continues to lead the nation in growth of its senior citizen population. Many programs exist to ensure their comfort and welfare, including quality economic, legal, and medical plans.

The city's World Market Center, a furniture wholesale showroom and marketplace, was built to compete with current furniture market capital of High Point, North Carolina. Megahotels and smaller projects continue to be developed. Billions have been spent have on hotel and casino construction. At its peak, some 3,000 people moved to the city each month, most of them in construction and casino-related work. The Durango Drive Improvement project has helped to ease traffic congestion with new ramps, a trails system underpass, new auxiliary lanes, and a new traffic signal system.

Since 2012, hundreds of millions of dollars' worth of projects have been completed. They include The Smith Center for the Performing Arts and DISCOVERY Children's Museum, Mob Museum, Neon Museum, City Hall complex and a new Zappos.com corporate headquarters in the old City Hall building.

Las Vegas valley is home to three major professional sports teams: Vegas Golden Knights (NHL); Las Vegas Raiders (NFL); and Las Vegas Aces (WNBA).

One of the more serious problems facing the fast-growing city is its diminishing water supply. It's estimated that Las Vegas gets up to 90 percent of its water from Lake Mead, whose levels are falling, not only due to usage (219 gallons daily person, more than most U.S. cities), but also due to climate change. The city employs reuse and recycle programs and encourages conservation by homeowners and businesses through desert landscaping.

The city made national headlines in October 2017 when a gunman opened fire on a crowd of concert goers on Las Vegas Boulevard, killing 58 people and injuring 800. This mass shooting, and others in recent years, contributed to the ongoing national debate on gun control.

Las Vegas is located near the center of a broad desert valley, which is nearly surrounded by mountains ranging from 2,000 to 10,000 feet. The four seasons are well defined. Summers display desert conditions with extreme high temperatures, but nights are relatively cool due to the closeness of the mountains. For about two weeks almost every summer, warm, moist air predominates, causing higher-than-average humidity and scattered, severe thunderstorms. Winters are generally mild and pleasant with clear skies prevailing. Strong winds, associated with major storms, usually reach the valley from the southwest or through the pass from the northwest. Winds over 50 miles per hour are infrequent but troublesome because of the dust and sand they stir up.

Rankings

General Rankings

- The Las Vegas metro area was identified as one of America's fastest-growing areas in terms of population and business growth by *MagnifyMoney.* The area ranked #26 out of 35. The 100 most populous metro areas in the U.S. were evaluated on their change from 2011 to 2016 in the following categories: people and housing; workforce and employment opportunities; growing industry. *www.businessinsider.com, "The 35 Cities in the US with the Biggest Influx of People, the Most Work Opportunities, and the Hottest Business Growth," August 12, 2018*
- The Las Vegas metro area was identified as one of America's fastest-growing areas in terms of population and economy by *Forbes.* The area ranked #6 out of 25. The 100 most populous metro areas in the U.S. were evaluated on the following criteria: estimated population growth; employment; economic output; wages; home values. *Forbes, "America's Fastest-Growing Cities 2018," February 28, 2018*

Business/Finance Rankings

- WalletHub's latest report ranked over 2,500 cities by the average credit score of its residents. Las Vegas was ranked #2,568 among the ten cities with the lowest average credit score, based on TransUnion data as of September 2021. *www.wallethub.com, "2022's Cities With the Highest & Lowest Credit Scores," February 16, 2022*
- The Brookings Institution ranked the nation's largest cities based on income inequality. Las Vegas was ranked #80 (#1 = greatest inequality). Criteria: the "95/20 ratio," a figure representing the income at which a household earns more than 95 percent of all other households, divided by the income at which a household earns more than only 20 percent of all other households. *Brookings Institution, "Household Income Inequality, Largest Cities of 97 Large U.S. Metro Areas, 2014-2016," February 5, 2018*
- The Brookings Institution ranked the 100 largest metro areas in the U.S. based on income inequality. Las Vegas was ranked #86 (#1 = greatest inequality). Criteria: the "95/20 ratio," a figure representing the income at which a household earns more than 95 percent of all other households, divided by the income at which a household earns more than only 20 percent of all other households. *Brookings Institution, "Household Income Inequality, 100 Largest U.S. Metro Areas, 2014-2016," February 5, 2018*
- Las Vegas was identified as one of America's most frugal metro areas by *Coupons.com.* The city ranked #21 out of 25. Criteria: digital coupon usage. *Coupons.com, "America's Most Frugal Cities of 2017," March 22, 2018*
- The Las Vegas metro area appeared on the Milken Institute "2021 Best Performing Cities" list. Rank: #88 out of 200 large metro areas (population over 250,000). Criteria: job growth; wage and salary growth; high-tech output growth; housing affordability; household broadband access. *Milken Institute, "Best-Performing Cities 2021," February 16, 2021*
- *Forbes* ranked the 200 most populous metro areas to determine the nation's "Best Places for Business and Careers." The Las Vegas metro area was ranked #49. Criteria: costs (business and living); job growth (past and projected); income growth; quality of life; educational attainment (college and high school); projected economic growth; cultural and leisure opportunities; workplace tolerance laws; net migration patterns. *Forbes, "The Best Places for Business and Careers 2019: Seattle Still On Top," October 30, 2019*

Culture/Performing Arts Rankings

- Las Vegas was selected as one of "America's Favorite Cities." The city ranked #13 in the "Architecture " category. Respondents to an online survey were asked to rate their favorite place (population over 100,000) in over 65 categories. *Travelandleisure.com, "America's Favorite Cities for Architecture 2016," March 2, 2017*

Dating/Romance Rankings

- Las Vegas was selected as one of America's best cities for singles by the readers of *Travel + Leisure* in their annual "America's Favorite Cities" survey. Criteria included good-looking locals, cool shopping, an active bar scene and hipster-magnet coffee bars. *Travel + Leisure, "Best Cities in America for Singles," July 21, 2017*
- Las Vegas was selected as one of the nation's most romantic cities with 100,000 or more residents by Amazon.com. The city ranked #17 of 20. Criteria: per capita sales of romance novels, relationship books, romantic comedy movies, romantic music, and sexual wellness products. *Amazon.com, "Top 20 Most Romantic Cities in the U.S.," February 1, 2017*

Education Rankings

- Personal finance website *WalletHub* analyzed the 150 largest U.S. metropolitan statistical areas to determine where the most educated Americans are putting their degrees to work. Criteria: education levels; percentage of workers with degrees; education quality and attainment gap; public school quality rankings; quality and enrollment of each metro area's universities. Las Vegas was ranked #120 (#1 = most educated city). *www.WalletHub.com, "Most & Least Educated Cities in America," July 19, 2021*
- Las Vegas was selected as one of America's most literate cities. The city ranked #54 out of the 84 largest U.S. cities. Criteria: number of booksellers; library resources; Internet resources; educational attainment; periodical publishing resources; newspaper circulation. *Central Connecticut State University, "America's Most Literate Cities, 2018," February 2019*

Environmental Rankings

- Las Vegas was highlighted as one of the 25 most ozone-polluted metro areas in the U.S. during 2017 through 2019. The area ranked #12. *American Lung Association, "State of the Air 2021," April 21, 2021*
- Las Vegas was highlighted as one of the 25 metro areas most polluted by short-term particle pollution (24-hour PM 2.5) in the U.S. during 2017 through 2019. The area ranked #25. *American Lung Association, "State of the Air 2021," April 21, 2021*

Health/Fitness Rankings

- For each of the 100 largest cities in the United States, the American Fitness Index®, published by the American College of Sports Medicine and the Anthem Foundation, evaluated community infrastructure and 34 health behaviors including preventive health, levels of chronic disease conditions, food insecurity, sleep quality, pedestrian safety, air quality, and community resources that support physical activity. Las Vegas ranked #88 for "community fitness." *americanfitnessindex.org, "2021 ACSM American Fitness Index Summary Report," July 13, 2021*
- Las Vegas was identified as a "2021 Spring Allergy Capital." The area ranked #22 out of 100. Three groups of factors were used to identify the most challenging cities for people with allergies during the spring season: annual spring pollen levels; over the counter medicine use; number of board-certified allergy specialists. *Asthma and Allergy Foundation of America, "Spring Allergy Capitals 2021," February 23, 2021*
- Las Vegas was identified as a "2021 Fall Allergy Capital." The area ranked #20 out of 100. Three groups of factors were used to identify the most challenging cities for people with allergies during the fall season: annual fall pollen levels; over the counter medicine use; number of board-certified allergy specialists. *Asthma and Allergy Foundation of America, "Fall Allergy Capitals 2021," February 23, 2021*
- Las Vegas was identified as a "2021 Asthma Capital." The area ranked #43 out of the nation's 100 largest metropolitan areas. Criteria: estimated asthma prevalence; asthma-related mortality; and ER visits due to asthma. Risk factors analyzed but not factored in the rankings: annual pollen score; annual air quality; public smoking laws; number of board-certified asthma specialists; rescue medication use; controller medication use; uninsured rate; poverty rate. *Asthma and Allergy Foundation of America, "Asthma Capitals 2021: The Most Challenging Places to Live With Asthma," May 5, 2021*

Real Estate Rankings

- *WalletHub* compared the most populated U.S. cities to determine which had the best markets for real estate agents. Las Vegas ranked #87 where demand was high and pay was the best. Criteria: sales per agent; annual median wage for real-estate agents; monthly average starting salary for real estate agents; real estate job density and competition; unemployment rate; home turnover rate; housing-market health index; and other relevant metrics. *www.WalletHub.com, "2021 Best Places to Be a Real Estate Agent," May 12, 2021*
- According to Penske Truck Rental, the Las Vegas metro area was named the #1 moving destination in 2020, based on one-way consumer truck rental reservations made through Penske's website, rental locations, and reservations call center. *gopenske.com/blog, "Penske Truck Rental's 2020 Top Moving Destinations," May 3, 2021*
- Las Vegas was ranked #7 in the top 20 out of the 100 largest metro areas in terms of house price appreciation in 2021 (#1 = highest rate). *Federal Housing Finance Agency, House Price Index, 4th Quarter 2021*

- The Las Vegas metro area was identified as one of the 20 best housing markets in the U.S. in 2021. The area ranked #8 out of 184 markets. Criteria: year-over-year change of median sales price of existing single-family homes between the 4th quarter of 2020 and the 4th quarter of 2021. *National Association of Realtors®, Median Sales Price of Existing Single-Family Homes for Metropolitan Areas, 4th Quarter 2021*
- The Las Vegas metro area was identified as one of the 10 best condo markets in the U.S. in 2021. The area ranked #9 out of 63 markets. Criteria: year-over-year change of median sales price of existing apartment condo-coop homes between the 4th quarter of 2020 and the 4th quarter of 2021. *National Association of Realtors®, Median Sales Price of Existing Apartment Condo-Coops Homes for Metropolitan Areas, 4th Quarter 2021*
- Las Vegas was ranked #183 out of 237 metro areas in terms of housing affordability in 2021 by the National Association of Home Builders (#1 = most affordable). Criteria: the share of homes sold in that area affordable to a family earning the local median income, based on standard mortgage underwriting criteria. *National Association of Home Builders®, NAHB-Wells Fargo Housing Opportunity Index, 4th Quarter 2021*
- The nation's largest metro areas were analyzed in terms of the percentage of households entering some stage of foreclosure in 2021. The Las Vegas metro area ranked #2 out of 8 (#1 = highest foreclosure rate). *ATTOM Data Solutions, "2021 Year-End U.S. Foreclosure Market Report™," January 13, 2022*

Safety Rankings

- Allstate ranked the 200 largest cities in America in terms of driver safety. Las Vegas ranked #129. Criteria: internal property damage claims over a two-year period from January 2016 to December 2017. The report helps increase the importance of safety and awareness behind the wheel. *Allstate, "Allstate America's Best Drivers Report, 2019" June 24, 2019*
- The National Insurance Crime Bureau ranked 390 metro areas in the U.S. in terms of per capita rates of vehicle theft. The Las Vegas metro area ranked #40 (#1 = highest rate). Criteria: number of vehicle theft offenses per 100,000 inhabitants in 2020. *National Insurance Crime Bureau, "Hot Spots 2020," August 31, 2021*

Seniors/Retirement Rankings

- From its Best Cities for Successful Aging indexes, the Milken Institute generated rankings for metropolitan areas, weighing data in nine categories—health care, wellness, living arrangements, transportation and convenience, financial characteristics, education, employment, community engagement, and overall livability. The Las Vegas metro area was ranked #77 overall in the large metro area category. *Milken Institute, "Best Cities for Successful Aging, 2017" March 14, 2017*

Transportation Rankings

- According to the INRIX "2021 Global Traffic Scorecard," Las Vegas was identified as one of the most congested metro areas in the U.S. The area ranked #22 out of 25. Criteria: average annual time spent in traffic and average cost of congestion per motorist. *Inrix.com, "Americans Lost 3.4 Billion Hours Due to Congestion in 2021, 42% Below Pre-COVID," December 7, 2021*

Women/Minorities Rankings

- *Travel + Leisure* listed the best cities in and around the US for a memorable and fun girls' trip, even on a budget. Whether it is for a special occasion or just to get away, Las Vegas is sure to have something for all the ladies in your tribe. *Travel + Leisure, "25 Girls' Weekend Getaways That Won't Break the Bank," June 8, 2020*
- The *Houston Chronicle* listed the Las Vegas metro area as #15 in top places for young Latinos to live in the U.S. Research was largely based on housing and occupational data from the largest metropolitan areas performed by *Forbes* and NBC Universo. Criteria: percentage of 18-34 year-olds; Latino college grad rates; and diversity. *blog.chron.com, "The 15 Best Big Cities for Latino Millenials," January 26, 2016*
- Personal finance website *WalletHub* compared more than 180 U.S. cities across two key dimensions, "Hispanic Business-Friendliness" and "Hispanic Purchasing Power," to arrive at the most favorable conditions for Hispanic entrepreneurs. Las Vegas was ranked #78 out of 182. Criteria includes: share of Hispanic-Owned Businesses; Hispanic entrepreneurship rate to median annual income of Hispanics; Small Business-Friendliness score; cost of living; and number of Hispanics with at least a bachelor's degree. *WalletHub.com, "2019's Best Cities for Hispanic Entrepreneurs," May 1, 2019*

Miscellaneous Rankings

- *MoveHub* ranked 446 hipster cities across 20 countries, using its *alternative* Hipster Index and Las Vegas came out as #19 among the top 50. Criteria: population over 150,000; number of vintage boutiques; density of tattoo parlors; vegan places to eat; coffee shops; and density of vinyl record stores. *www.movehub.com, "The Hipster Index: Brighton Pips Portland to Global Top Spot," July 28, 2021*
- Las Vegas was selected as a 2021 Digital Cities Survey winner. The city ranked #9 in the large city (500,000 or more population) category. The survey examined and assessed how city governments are utilizing technology to continue innovation, engage with residents, and persevere through the challenges of the pandemic. Survey questions focused on ten initiatives: cybersecurity; citizen experience; disaster recovery; business intelligence; IT personnel; data governance; budget control; IT governance; infrastructure modernization; and broadband connectivity. *Center for Digital Government, "2021 Digital Cities Survey," November 16, 2021*
- The financial planning site SmartAsset has compiled its annual study on the best places for Halloween in the U.S. for 2021. 210 cities were compared to determine that Las Vegas ranked #23 out of 35 for still being able to enjoy the festivities despite the COVID-19 pandemic. Metrics included: safety, family-friendliness, percentage of children in the population, concentration of candy and costume shops, weather and COVID infection rates. *www.smartasset.com, "2021 Edition-Best Places to Celebrate Halloween," October 20, 2021*
- *WalletHub* compared the 150 most populated U.S. cities to determine their operating efficiency. A "Quality of City Services" score was constructed for each city and then divided by the total budget per capita to reveal which were managed the best. Las Vegas ranked #52. Criteria: financial stability; economy; education; safety; health; infrastructure and pollution. *www.WalletHub.com, "2021's Best- & Worst-Run Cities in America," June 22, 2021*

Business Environment

DEMOGRAPHICS

Population Growth

Area	1990 Census	2000 Census	2010 Census	2020* Estimate	Population Growth (%) 1990-2020	2010-2020
City	261,374	478,434	583,756	644,594	146.6	10.4
MSA[1]	741,459	1,375,765	1,951,269	2,228,866	200.6	14.2
U.S.	248,709,873	281,421,906	308,745,538	326,569,308	31.3	5.8

Note: (1) Figures cover the Las Vegas-Henderson-Paradise, NV Metropolitan Statistical Area; (*) 2016-2020 5-year estimated population
Source: U.S. Census Bureau, 1990 Census, Census 2000, Census 2010, 2016-2020 American Community Survey 5-Year Estimates

Household Size

Area	Persons in Household (%) One	Two	Three	Four	Five	Six	Seven or More	Average Household Size
City	30.0	31.5	15.4	12.1	6.4	2.8	1.8	2.70
MSA[1]	28.2	32.9	15.3	12.3	6.8	2.7	1.8	2.70
U.S.	28.0	33.9	15.5	12.9	6.0	2.3	1.4	2.60

Note: (1) Figures cover the Las Vegas-Henderson-Paradise, NV Metropolitan Statistical Area
Source: U.S. Census Bureau, 2016-2020 American Community Survey 5-Year Estimates

Race

Area	White Alone[2] (%)	Black Alone[2] (%)	Asian Alone[2] (%)	AIAN[3] Alone[2] (%)	NHOPI[4] Alone[2] (%)	Other Race Alone[2] (%)	Two or More Races (%)
City	58.5	12.1	6.7	1.0	0.9	12.6	8.2
MSA[1]	56.6	11.9	9.9	0.9	0.8	11.9	8.1
U.S.	70.4	12.6	5.6	0.8	0.2	5.1	5.2

Note: (1) Figures cover the Las Vegas-Henderson-Paradise, NV Metropolitan Statistical Area; (2) Alone is defined as not being in combination with one or more other races; (3) American Indian and Alaska Native; (4) Native Hawaiian and Other Pacific Islander
Source: U.S. Census Bureau, 2016-2020 American Community Survey 5-Year Estimates

Hispanic or Latino Origin

Area	Total (%)	Mexican (%)	Puerto Rican (%)	Cuban (%)	Other (%)
City	33.2	24.9	1.1	1.4	5.8
MSA[1]	31.3	23.1	1.1	1.5	5.6
U.S.	18.2	11.2	1.7	0.7	4.5

Note: Persons of Hispanic or Latino origin can be of any race; (1) Figures cover the Las Vegas-Henderson-Paradise, NV Metropolitan Statistical Area
Source: U.S. Census Bureau, 2016-2020 American Community Survey 5-Year Estimates

Ancestry

Area	German	Irish	English	American	Italian	Polish	French[2]	Scottish	Dutch
City	8.7	7.6	5.9	3.3	5.3	2.0	1.7	1.3	0.7
MSA[1]	8.5	7.1	6.0	3.2	5.0	1.9	1.6	1.2	0.7
U.S.	13.0	9.7	7.7	5.9	5.1	2.7	2.3	1.6	1.1

Note: Figures are the percentage of the total population reporting a particular ancestry. The nine most commonly reported ancestries in the U.S. are shown. Figures include multiple ancestries (e.g. if a person reported being Irish and Italian, they were included in both columns); (1) Figures cover the Las Vegas-Henderson-Paradise, NV Metropolitan Statistical Area; (2) Excludes Basque
Source: U.S. Census Bureau, 2016-2020 American Community Survey 5-Year Estimates

Foreign-born Population

Area	Percent of Population Born in: Any Foreign Country	Asia	Mexico	Europe	Caribbean	Central America[2]	South America	Africa	Canada
City	20.6	5.3	8.8	1.5	1.1	2.2	0.7	0.4	0.4
MSA[1]	22.1	7.3	7.9	1.6	1.2	1.9	0.8	0.9	0.4
U.S.	13.5	4.2	3.3	1.5	1.3	1.1	1.0	0.7	0.3

Note: (1) Figures cover the Las Vegas-Henderson-Paradise, NV Metropolitan Statistical Area; (2) Excludes Mexico.
Source: U.S. Census Bureau, 2016-2020 American Community Survey 5-Year Estimates

Marital Status

Area	Never Married	Now Married[2]	Separated	Widowed	Divorced
City	35.3	43.8	2.0	5.2	13.8
MSA[1]	34.9	44.1	2.2	5.1	13.7
U.S.	33.5	48.1	1.8	5.7	10.8

Note: Figures are percentages and cover the population 15 years of age and older; (1) Figures cover the Las Vegas-Henderson-Paradise, NV Metropolitan Statistical Area; (2) Excludes separated
Source: U.S. Census Bureau, 2016-2020 American Community Survey 5-Year Estimates

Disability by Age

Area	All Ages	Under 18 Years Old	18 to 64 Years Old	65 Years and Over
City	12.8	3.8	10.8	35.1
MSA[1]	12.1	3.9	9.9	34.5
U.S.	12.7	4.3	10.3	34.0

Note: Figures show percent of the civilian noninstitutionalized population that reported having a disability. Disability status is determined from six types of difficulty: vision, hearing, cognitive, ambulatory, self-care, and independent living. For children under 5 years old, hearing and vision difficulty are used to determine disability status. For children between the ages of 5 and 14, disability status is determined from hearing, vision, cognitive, ambulatory, and self-care difficulties. For people aged 15 years and older, they are considered to have a disability if they have difficulty with any one of the six difficulty types; Note: (1) Figures cover the Las Vegas-Henderson-Paradise, NV Metropolitan Statistical Area
Source: U.S. Census Bureau, 2016-2020 American Community Survey 5-Year Estimates

Age

Area	Percent of Population									Median Age
	Under Age 5	Age 5–19	Age 20–34	Age 35–44	Age 45–54	Age 55–64	Age 65–74	Age 75–84	Age 85+	
City	6.3	19.5	20.4	13.6	13.1	12.1	9.0	4.3	1.5	37.7
MSA[1]	6.2	19.0	21.0	13.8	13.2	11.8	9.1	4.3	1.4	37.5
U.S.	6.0	19.1	20.6	12.7	12.7	12.9	9.4	4.7	2.0	38.2

Note: (1) Figures cover the Las Vegas-Henderson-Paradise, NV Metropolitan Statistical Area
Source: U.S. Census Bureau, 2016-2020 American Community Survey 5-Year Estimates

Gender

Area	Males	Females	Males per 100 Females
City	321,537	323,057	99.5
MSA[1]	1,111,677	1,117,189	99.5
U.S.	160,818,530	165,750,778	97.0

Note: (1) Figures cover the Las Vegas-Henderson-Paradise, NV Metropolitan Statistical Area
Source: U.S. Census Bureau, 2016-2020 American Community Survey 5-Year Estimates

Religious Groups by Family

Area	Catholic	Baptist	Non-Den.	Methodist[2]	Lutheran	LDS[3]	Pente-costal	Presby-terian[4]	Muslim[5]	Judaism
MSA[1]	18.1	3.0	3.1	0.4	0.7	6.4	1.5	0.2	0.1	0.3
U.S.	19.1	9.3	4.0	4.0	2.3	2.0	1.9	1.6	0.8	0.7

Note: Figures are the number of adherents as a percentage of the total population; (1) Figures cover the Las Vegas-Henderson-Paradise, NV Metropolitan Statistical Area; (2) Methodist/Pietist; (3) Latter Day Saints; (4) Reformed; (5) Figures are estimates
Source: Association of Statisticians of American Religious Bodies, 2010 U.S. Religion Census: Religious Congregations & Membership Study

Religious Groups by Tradition

Area	Catholic	Evangelical Protestant	Mainline Protestant	Other Tradition	Black Protestant	Orthodox
MSA[1]	18.1	7.7	1.4	7.6	0.4	0.4
U.S.	19.1	16.2	7.3	4.3	1.6	0.3

Note: Figures are the number of adherents as a percentage of the total population; (1) Figures cover the Las Vegas-Henderson-Paradise, NV Metropolitan Statistical Area
Source: Association of Statisticians of American Religious Bodies, 2010 U.S. Religion Census: Religious Congregations & Membership Study

ECONOMY

Gross Metropolitan Product

Area	2017	2018	2019	2020	Rank[2]
MSA[1]	112.8	119.1	124.1	130.3	36

Note: Figures are in billions of dollars; (1) Figures cover the Las Vegas-Henderson-Paradise, NV Metropolitan Statistical Area; (2) Rank is based on 2018 data and ranges from 1 to 381
Source: U.S. Conference of Mayors, U.S. Metro Economies: GMP & Employment 2018-2020, September 2019

Economic Growth

Area	2015-17 (%)	2018 (%)	2019 (%)	2020 (%)	Rank[2]
MSA[1]	1.5	3.1	2.3	2.7	182
U.S.	1.9	2.9	2.3	2.1	–

Note: Figures are real gross metropolitan product (GMP) growth rates and represent average annual percent change; (1) Figures cover the Las Vegas-Henderson-Paradise, NV Metropolitan Statistical Area; (2) Rank is based on 2017 2-year average annual percent change and ranges from 1 to 381
Source: U.S. Conference of Mayors, U.S. Metro Economies: GMP & Employment 2018-2020, September 2019

Metropolitan Area Exports

Area	2015	2016	2017	2018	2019	2020	Rank[2]
MSA[1]	2,916.2	2,312.3	2,710.6	2,240.6	2,430.8	1,705.9	106

Note: Figures are in millions of dollars; (1) Figures cover the Las Vegas-Henderson-Paradise, NV Metropolitan Statistical Area; (2) Rank is based on 2020 data and ranges from 1 to 389
Source: U.S. Department of Commerce, International Trade Administration, Office of Trade and Economic Analysis, Industry and Analysis, Exports by Metropolitan Area, data extracted March 4, 2022

Building Permits

Area	Single-Family			Multi-Family			Total		
	2019	2020	Pct. Chg.	2019	2020	Pct. Chg.	2019	2020	Pct. Chg.
City	1,885	1,941	3.0	780	1,415	81.4	2,665	3,356	25.9
MSA[1]	10,042	10,038	0.0	3,861	4,062	5.2	13,903	14,100	1.4
U.S.	862,100	979,400	13.6	523,900	491,700	-6.1	1,386,000	1,471,100	6.1

Note: (1) Figures cover the Las Vegas-Henderson-Paradise, NV Metropolitan Statistical Area; Figures represent new, privately-owned housing units authorized (unadjusted data); All permit data are based on estimates with imputation
Source: U.S. Census Bureau, Manufacturing, Mining, and Construction Statistics, Building Permits, 2019, 2020

Bankruptcy Filings

Area	Business Filings			Nonbusiness Filings		
	2020	2021	% Chg.	2020	2021	% Chg.
Clark County	204	181	-11.3	6,529	5,825	-10.8
U.S.	21,655	14,347	-33.7	522,808	399,269	-23.6

Note: Business filings include Chapter 7, Chapter 9, Chapter 11, Chapter 12, Chapter 13, Chapter 15, and Section 304; Nonbusiness filings include Chapter 7, Chapter 11, and Chapter 13
Source: Administrative Office of the U.S. Courts, Business and Nonbusiness Bankruptcy, County Cases Commenced by Chapter of the Bankruptcy Code, During the 12-Month Period Ending December 31, 2020 and Business and Nonbusiness Bankruptcy, County Cases Commenced by Chapter of the Bankruptcy Code, During the 12-Month Period Ending December 31, 2021

Housing Vacancy Rates

Area	Gross Vacancy Rate[2] (%)			Year-Round Vacancy Rate[3] (%)			Rental Vacancy Rate[4] (%)			Homeowner Vacancy Rate[5] (%)		
	2019	2020	2021	2019	2020	2021	2019	2020	2021	2019	2020	2021
MSA[1]	10.2	7.8	7.7	9.5	7.1	7.1	5.5	5.0	3.7	2.0	1.1	0.9
U.S.	12.0	10.6	10.8	9.5	8.2	8.4	6.7	6.3	6.1	1.4	1.0	0.9

Note: (1) Figures cover the Las Vegas-Henderson-Paradise, NV Metropolitan Statistical Area; (2) The percentage of the total housing inventory that is vacant; (3) The percentage of the housing inventory (excluding seasonal units) that is year-round vacant; (4) The percentage of rental inventory that is vacant for rent; (5) The percentage of homeowner inventory that is vacant for sale
Source: U.S. Census Bureau, Housing Vacancies and Homeownership Annual Statistics: 2019, 2020, 2021

INCOME

Income

Area	Per Capita ($)	Median Household ($)	Average Household ($)
City	31,521	58,377	81,840
MSA[1]	31,651	61,048	83,343
U.S.	35,384	64,994	91,547

Note: (1) Figures cover the Las Vegas-Henderson-Paradise, NV Metropolitan Statistical Area
Source: U.S. Census Bureau, 2016-2020 American Community Survey 5-Year Estimates

Household Income Distribution

Area	Percent of Households Earning							
	Under $15,000	$15,000 -$24,999	$25,000 -$34,999	$35,000 -$49,999	$50,000 -$74,999	$75,000 -$99,999	$100,000 -$149,999	$150,000 and up
City	11.6	8.7	9.4	13.6	17.7	12.8	14.6	11.6
MSA[1]	9.8	8.4	9.3	13.7	18.4	13.6	15.0	11.8
U.S.	9.9	8.5	8.6	12.0	17.2	12.8	15.6	15.4

Note: (1) Figures cover the Las Vegas-Henderson-Paradise, NV Metropolitan Statistical Area
Source: U.S. Census Bureau, 2016-2020 American Community Survey 5-Year Estimates

Poverty Rate

Area	All Ages	Under 18 Years Old	18 to 64 Years Old	65 Years and Over
City	14.9	21.3	13.5	10.8
MSA[1]	13.4	18.7	12.3	9.3
U.S.	12.8	17.5	12.1	9.3

Note: Figures are percentage of people whose income during the past 12 months was below the poverty level; (1) Figures cover the Las Vegas-Henderson-Paradise, NV Metropolitan Statistical Area
Source: U.S. Census Bureau, 2016-2020 American Community Survey 5-Year Estimates

CITY FINANCES

City Government Finances

Component	2019 ($000)	2019 ($ per capita)
Total Revenues	1,020,256	1,590
Total Expenditures	925,853	1,443
Debt Outstanding	810,287	1,263
Cash and Securities[1]	1,142,979	1,781

Note: (1) Cash and security holdings of a government at the close of its fiscal year, including those of its dependent agencies, utilities, and liquor stores.
Source: U.S. Census Bureau, State & Local Government Finances 2019

City Government Revenue by Source

Source	2019 ($000)	2019 ($ per capita)	2019 (%)
General Revenue			
From Federal Government	36,977	58	3.6
From State Government	332,075	518	32.5
From Local Governments	138,478	216	13.6
Taxes			
Property	129,823	202	12.7
Sales and Gross Receipts	75,670	118	7.4
Personal Income	0	0	0.0
Corporate Income	0	0	0.0
Motor Vehicle License	0	0	0.0
Other Taxes	53,404	83	5.2
Current Charges	165,432	258	16.2
Liquor Store	0	0	0.0
Utility	87	0	0.0

Source: U.S. Census Bureau, State & Local Government Finances 2019

City Government Expenditures by Function

Function	2019 ($000)	2019 ($ per capita)	2019 (%)
General Direct Expenditures			
Air Transportation	0	0	0.0
Corrections	63,391	98	6.8
Education	0	0	0.0
Employment Security Administration	0	0	0.0
Financial Administration	9,586	14	1.0
Fire Protection	152,368	237	16.5
General Public Buildings	33,210	51	3.6
Governmental Administration, Other	33,671	52	3.6
Health	4,953	7	0.5
Highways	104,788	163	11.3
Hospitals	0	0	0.0
Housing and Community Development	20,280	31	2.2
Interest on General Debt	34,059	53	3.7
Judicial and Legal	33,615	52	3.6
Libraries	0	0	0.0
Parking	9,991	15	1.1
Parks and Recreation	51,294	79	5.5
Police Protection	14,428	22	1.6
Public Welfare	0	0	0.0
Sewerage	61,138	95	6.6
Solid Waste Management	7,366	11	0.8
Veterans' Services	0	0	0.0
Liquor Store	0	0	0.0
Utility	0	0	0.0

Source: U.S. Census Bureau, State & Local Government Finances 2019

EMPLOYMENT

Labor Force and Employment

Area	Civilian Labor Force			Workers Employed		
	Dec. 2020	Dec. 2021	% Chg.	Dec. 2020	Dec. 2021	% Chg.
City	303,291	310,246	2.3	274,574	291,433	6.1
MSA[1]	1,097,286	1,120,967	2.2	992,442	1,053,379	6.1
U.S.	160,017,000	161,696,000	1.0	149,613,000	155,732,000	4.1

Note: Data is not seasonally adjusted and covers workers 16 years of age and older; (1) Figures cover the Las Vegas-Henderson-Paradise, NV Metropolitan Statistical Area
Source: Bureau of Labor Statistics, Local Area Unemployment Statistics

Unemployment Rate

Area	2021											
	Jan.	Feb.	Mar.	Apr.	May	Jun.	Jul.	Aug.	Sep.	Oct.	Nov.	Dec.
City	9.7	9.3	8.9	9.1	8.9	9.7	9.5	8.2	7.4	6.6	6.4	6.1
MSA[1]	9.8	9.2	8.8	9.1	8.9	9.6	9.3	8.2	7.4	6.6	6.3	6.0
U.S.	6.8	6.6	6.2	5.7	5.5	6.1	5.7	5.3	4.6	4.3	3.9	3.7

Note: Data is not seasonally adjusted and covers workers 16 years of age and older; (1) Figures cover the Las Vegas-Henderson-Paradise, NV Metropolitan Statistical Area
Source: Bureau of Labor Statistics, Local Area Unemployment Statistics

Average Wages

Occupation	$/Hr.	Occupation	$/Hr.
Accountants and Auditors	30.92	Maintenance and Repair Workers	21.01
Automotive Mechanics	23.43	Marketing Managers	58.31
Bookkeepers	20.47	Network and Computer Systems Admin.	45.09
Carpenters	29.70	Nurses, Licensed Practical	29.09
Cashiers	12.21	Nurses, Registered	43.38
Computer Programmers	39.00	Nursing Assistants	17.45
Computer Systems Analysts	44.90	Office Clerks, General	18.91
Computer User Support Specialists	22.84	Physical Therapists	50.32
Construction Laborers	20.72	Physicians	126.33
Cooks, Restaurant	15.84	Plumbers, Pipefitters and Steamfitters	31.03
Customer Service Representatives	17.99	Police and Sheriff's Patrol Officers	37.51
Dentists	80.56	Postal Service Mail Carriers	26.19
Electricians	32.48	Real Estate Sales Agents	30.73
Engineers, Electrical	48.49	Retail Salespersons	14.95
Fast Food and Counter Workers	11.20	Sales Representatives, Technical/Scientific	46.38
Financial Managers	54.48	Secretaries, Exc. Legal/Medical/Executive	20.02
First-Line Supervisors of Office Workers	26.95	Security Guards	15.30
General and Operations Managers	48.61	Surgeons	n/a
Hairdressers/Cosmetologists	12.37	Teacher Assistants, Exc. Postsecondary*	16.02
Home Health and Personal Care Aides	12.24	Teachers, Secondary School, Exc. Sp. Ed.*	30.04
Janitors and Cleaners	14.65	Telemarketers	11.60
Landscaping/Groundskeeping Workers	16.40	Truck Drivers, Heavy/Tractor-Trailer	24.20
Lawyers	65.53	Truck Drivers, Light/Delivery Services	19.49
Maids and Housekeeping Cleaners	16.12	Waiters and Waitresses	11.59

Note: Wage data covers the Las Vegas-Henderson-Paradise, NV Metropolitan Statistical Area; (*) Hourly wages were calculated from annual wage data based on a 40 hour work week; n/a not available.
Source: Bureau of Labor Statistics, Metro Area Occupational Employment & Wage Estimates, May 2021

Employment by Industry

Sector	MSA[1]		U.S.
	Number of Employees	Percent of Total	Percent of Total
Construction	66,900	6.4	5.0
Education and Health Services	112,100	10.8	16.0
Financial Activities	55,800	5.4	5.9
Government	105,600	10.2	14.9
Information	11,600	1.1	1.9
Leisure and Hospitality	266,000	25.6	9.8
Manufacturing	26,600	2.6	8.4
Mining and Logging	400	<0.1	0.4
Other Services	28,200	2.7	3.7
Professional and Business Services	154,700	14.9	14.6
Retail Trade	116,000	11.2	10.7
Transportation, Warehousing, and Utilities	70,700	6.8	4.8
Wholesale Trade	24,200	2.3	3.8

Note: Figures are non-farm employment as of December 2021. Figures are not seasonally adjusted and include workers 16 years of age and older; (1) Figures cover the Las Vegas-Henderson-Paradise, NV Metropolitan Statistical Area
Source: Bureau of Labor Statistics, Current Employment Statistics, Employment, Hours, and Earnings

Employment by Occupation

Occupation Classification	City (%)	MSA[1] (%)	U.S. (%)
Management, Business, Science, and Arts	30.6	29.8	39.5
Natural Resources, Construction, and Maintenance	8.7	8.2	8.7
Production, Transportation, and Material Moving	10.8	11.3	13.1
Sales and Office	23.7	23.5	21.3
Service	26.2	27.3	17.4

Note: Figures cover employed civilians 16 years of age and older; (1) Figures cover the Las Vegas-Henderson-Paradise, NV Metropolitan Statistical Area
Source: U.S. Census Bureau, 2016-2020 American Community Survey 5-Year Estimates

Occupations with Greatest Projected Employment Growth: 2021 – 2023

Occupation[1]	2021 Employment	2023 Projected Employment	Numeric Employment Change	Percent Employment Change
Laborers and Freight, Stock, and Material Movers, Hand	37,280	44,490	7,210	19.3
Retail Salespersons	42,730	46,100	3,370	7.9
Stockers and Order Fillers	24,080	27,450	3,370	14.0
Fast Food and Counter Workers	42,350	44,540	2,190	5.2
Cooks, Restaurant	18,590	20,670	2,080	11.2
Waiters and Waitresses	29,200	31,250	2,050	7.0
Security Guards	20,470	22,220	1,750	8.5
Janitors and Cleaners, Except Maids and Housekeeping Cleaners	26,000	27,750	1,750	6.7
Customer Service Representatives	28,270	29,910	1,640	5.8
General and Operations Managers	21,570	23,170	1,600	7.4

Note: Projections cover Nevada; (1) Sorted by numeric employment change
Source: www.projectionscentral.com, State Occupational Projections, 2021–2023 Short-Term Projections

Fastest-Growing Occupations: 2021 – 2023

Occupation[1]	2021 Employment	2023 Projected Employment	Numeric Employment Change	Percent Employment Change
Conveyor Operators and Tenders	180	230	50	27.8
Industrial Truck and Tractor Operators	6,320	7,720	1,400	22.2
Laborers and Freight, Stock, and Material Movers, Hand	37,280	44,490	7,210	19.3
Light Truck or Delivery Services Drivers	7,960	9,490	1,530	19.2
Transportation, Storage, and Distribution Managers	1,180	1,380	200	16.9
Weighers, Measurers, Checkers, and Samplers, Recordkeeping	780	910	130	16.7
Electrical, Electronic, and Electromechanical Assemblers, Except Coil Winders, Tapers, and Fini	3,550	4,110	560	15.8
Logisticians	640	740	100	15.6
Bus Drivers, Transit and Intercity (SOC 2018)	1,800	2,070	270	15.0
Industrial Engineers	810	930	120	14.8

Note: Projections cover Nevada; (1) Sorted by percent employment change and excludes occupations with numeric employment change less than 50
Source: www.projectionscentral.com, State Occupational Projections, 2021–2023 Short-Term Projections

TAXES

State Corporate Income Tax Rates

State	Tax Rate (%)	Income Brackets ($)	Num. of Brackets	Financial Institution Tax Rate (%)[a]	Federal Income Tax Ded.
Nevada	None	–	–	–	–

Note: Tax rates as of January 1, 2022; (a) Rates listed are the corporate income tax rate applied to financial institutions or excise taxes based on income. Some states have other taxes based upon the value of deposits or shares.
Source: Federation of Tax Administrators, State Corporate Income Tax Rates, January 1, 2022

State Individual Income Tax Rates

State	Tax Rate (%)	Income Brackets ($)	Personal Exemptions ($)			Standard Ded. ($)	
			Single	Married	Depend.	Single	Married
Nevada	– No state income tax –						

Note: Tax rates as of January 1, 2022; Local- and county-level taxes are not included
Source: Federation of Tax Administrators, State Individual Income Tax Rates, January 1, 2022

Various State Sales and Excise Tax Rates

State	State Sales Tax (%)	Gasoline[1] (¢/gal.)	Cigarette[2] ($/pack)	Spirits[3] ($/gal.)	Wine[4] ($/gal.)	Beer[5] ($/gal.)	Recreational Marijuana (%)
Nevada	6.85	50.48	1.8	3.6	0.7	0.16	(k)

Note: All tax rates as of January 1, 2022; (1) The American Petroleum Institute has developed a methodology for determining the average tax rate on a gallon of fuel. Rates may include any of the following: excise taxes, environmental fees, storage tank fees, other fees or taxes, general sales tax, and local taxes; (2) The federal excise tax of $1.0066 per pack and local taxes are not included; (3) Rates are those applicable to off-premise sales of 40% alcohol by volume (a.b.v.) distilled spirits in 750ml containers. Local excise taxes are excluded; (4) Rates are those applicable to off-premise sales of 11% a.b.v. non-carbonated wine in 750ml containers; (5) Rates are those applicable to off-premise sales of 4.7% a.b.v. beer in 12 ounce containers; (k) 15% excise tax (fair market value at wholesale); 10% excise tax (retail price)
Source: Tax Foundation, 2022 Facts & Figures: How Does Your State Compare?

State Business Tax Climate Index Rankings

State	Overall Rank	Corporate Tax Rank	Individual Income Tax Rank	Sales Tax Rank	Property Tax Rank	Unemployment Insurance Tax Rank
Nevada	7	25	5	44	5	45

Note: The index is a measure of how each state's tax laws affect economic performance. The lower the rank, the more favorable a state's tax system is for business. States without a given tax are given a ranking of 1. The scores/rankings for the District of Columbia do not affect other states. The 2022 index represents the tax climate as of July 1, 2021.
Source: Tax Foundation, State Business Tax Climate Index 2022

TRANSPORTATION

Means of Transportation to Work

Area	Car/Truck/Van		Public Transportation			Bicycle	Walked	Other Means	Worked at Home
	Drove Alone	Car-pooled	Bus	Subway	Railroad				
City	76.7	10.3	3.1	0.0	0.0	0.2	1.4	2.7	5.6
MSA[1]	77.5	10.1	3.0	0.0	0.0	0.2	1.3	2.2	5.6
U.S.	74.9	8.9	2.2	1.7	0.5	0.5	2.6	1.4	7.3

Note: Figures are percentages and cover workers 16 years of age and older; (1) Figures cover the Las Vegas-Henderson-Paradise, NV Metropolitan Statistical Area
Source: U.S. Census Bureau, 2016-2020 American Community Survey 5-Year Estimates

Travel Time to Work

Area	Less Than 10 Minutes	10 to 19 Minutes	20 to 29 Minutes	30 to 44 Minutes	45 to 59 Minutes	60 to 89 Minutes	90 Minutes or More
City	7.3	24.6	29.7	27.8	6.2	2.6	1.8
MSA[1]	7.7	27.6	29.1	25.7	5.4	2.6	1.9
U.S.	12.3	28.4	20.9	20.9	8.3	6.4	2.9

Note: Note: Figures are percentages and include workers 16 years old and over; (1) Figures cover the Las Vegas-Henderson-Paradise, NV Metropolitan Statistical Area
Source: U.S. Census Bureau, 2016-2020 American Community Survey 5-Year Estimates

Key Congestion Measures

Measure	1990	2000	2010	2015	2020
Annual Hours of Delay, Total (000)	9,793	31,658	48,936	56,055	21,702
Annual Hours of Delay, Per Auto Commuter	28	41	44	49	18
Annual Congestion Cost, Per Auto Commuter ($)	291	708	871	922	363

Note: Covers the Las Vegas-Henderson NV urban area
Source: Texas A&M Transportation Institute, 2021 Urban Mobility Report

Freeway Travel Time Index

Measure	1985	1990	1995	2000	2005	2010	2015	2020
Urban Area Index[1]	1.10	1.16	1.21	1.24	1.27	1.25	1.24	1.07
Urban Area Rank[1,2]	27	19	16	18	18	21	26	57

Note: Freeway Travel Time Index—the ratio of travel time in the peak period to the travel time at free-flow conditions. For example, a value of 1.30 indicates a 20-minute free-flow trip takes 26 minutes in the peak (20 minutes x 1.30 = 26 minutes); (1) Covers the Las Vegas-Henderson NV urban area; (2) Rank is based on 101 larger urban areas (#1 = highest travel time index)
Source: Texas A&M Transportation Institute, 2021 Urban Mobility Report

Public Transportation

Agency Name / Mode of Transportation	Vehicles Operated in Maximum Service[1]	Annual Unlinked Passenger Trips[2] (in thous.)	Annual Passenger Miles[3] (in thous.)
Regional Transportation Commission of Southern Nevada (RTC)			
Bus (purchased transportation)	309	55,719.6	213,418.1
Demand Response (purchased transportation)	364	1,176.9	12,309.9

Note: (1) Number of revenue vehicles operated by the given mode and type of service to meet the annual maximum service requirement. This is the revenue vehicle count during the peak season of the year; on the week and day that maximum service is provided. Vehicles operated in maximum service (VOMS) exclude atypical days and one-time special events; (2) Number of passengers who boarded public transportation vehicles. Passengers are counted each time they board a vehicle no matter how many vehicles they use to travel from their origin to their destination. (3) Sum of the distances ridden by all passengers during the entire fiscal year.
Source: Federal Transit Administration, National Transit Database, 2020

Air Transportation

Airport Name and Code / Type of Service	Passenger Airlines[1]	Passenger Enplanements	Freight Carriers[2]	Freight (lbs)
McCarran International (LAS)				
Domestic service (U.S. carriers - 2021)	29	18,808,558	14	107,154,406
International service (U.S. carriers - 2020)	5	6,154	2	17,829

Note: (1) Includes all U.S.-based major, minor and commuter airlines that carried at least one passenger during the year; (2) Includes all U.S.-based airlines and freight carriers that transported at least one pound of freight during the year.
Source: Bureau of Transportation Statistics, The Intermodal Transportation Database, Air Carriers: T-100 Domestic Market (U.S. Carriers), 2021; Bureau of Transportation Statistics, The Intermodal Transportation Database, Air Carriers: T-100 International Market (U.S. Carriers), 2020

BUSINESSES

Major Business Headquarters

Company Name	Industry	Rankings	
		Fortune[1]	Forbes[2]
No companies listed	-	-	-

Note: (1) Companies that produce a 10-K are ranked 1 to 500 based on 2020 revenue; (2) All private companies with at least $2 billion in annual revenue through the end of their most current fiscal year are ranked 1 to 225; companies listed are headquartered in the city; dashes indicate no ranking
Source: Fortune, "Fortune 500," 2021; Forbes, "America's Largest Private Companies," 2021

Fastest-Growing Businesses

According to *Inc.*, Las Vegas is home to three of America's 500 fastest-growing private companies: **Peak Performance Life** (#187); **Doughp** (#274); **Hemper** (#492). Criteria: must be an independent, privately-held, for-profit, U.S. corporation, proprietorship or partnership as of December 31, 2020; revenues must be at least $100,000 in 2017 and $2 million in 2020; must have four-year operating/sales history. *Inc., "America's 500 Fastest-Growing Private Companies," 2021*

According to Deloitte, Las Vegas is home to one of North America's 500 fastest-growing high-technology companies: **Sightline Payments** (#217). Companies are ranked by percentage growth in revenue over a four-year period. Criteria for inclusion: company must be headquartered within North America; must own proprietary intellectual property or technology that is sold to customers in products that contributes to a significant portion of the company's operating revenue; must have been in business for a minumum of four years with 2017 operating revenues of at least $50,000 USD/CD and 2020 operating revenues of at least $5 million USD/CD. *Deloitte, 2021 Technology Fast 500™*

Living Environment

COST OF LIVING

Cost of Living Index

Composite Index	Groceries	Housing	Utilities	Trans- portation	Health Care	Misc. Goods/ Services
104.3	108.7	109.4	94.3	120.2	98.1	96.8

Note: The Cost of Living Index measures regional differences in the cost of consumer goods and services, excluding taxes and non-consumer expenditures, for professional and managerial households in the top income quintile. It is based on more than 50,000 prices covering almost 60 different items for which prices are collected three times a year by chambers of commerce, economic development organizations or university applied economic centers in each participating urban area. The numbers shown should be read as a percentage above or below the national average of 100. For example, a value of 115.4 in the groceries column indicates that grocery prices are 15.4% higher than the national average. Small differences in the index numbers should not be interpreted as significant; Figures cover the Las Vegas NV urban area.
Source: The Council for Community and Economic Research, Cost of Living Index, 2021

Grocery Prices

Area[1]	T-Bone Steak ($/pound)	Frying Chicken ($/pound)	Whole Milk ($/half gal.)	Eggs ($/dozen)	Orange Juice ($/64 oz.)	Coffee ($/11.5 oz.)
City[2]	12.62	1.70	2.79	2.22	3.76	6.03
Avg.	12.82	1.40	2.22	1.57	3.59	4.30
Min.	8.91	0.91	1.29	0.75	2.87	3.02
Max.	21.35	2.69	3.92	3.86	5.49	8.11

Note: (1) Values for the local area are compared with the average, minimum and maximum values for all 285 areas in the Cost of Living Index; (2) Figures cover the Las Vegas NV urban area; ***T-Bone Steak*** *(price per pound);* ***Frying Chicken*** *(price per pound, whole fryer);* ***Whole Milk*** *(half gallon carton);* ***Eggs*** *(price per dozen, Grade A, large);* ***Orange Juice*** *(64 oz. Tropicana or Florida Natural);* ***Coffee*** *(11.5 oz. can, vacuum-packed, Maxwell House, Hills Bros, or Folgers).*
Source: The Council for Community and Economic Research, Cost of Living Index, 2021

Housing and Utility Costs

Area[1]	New Home Price ($)	Apartment Rent ($/month)	All Electric ($/month)	Part Electric ($/month)	Other Energy ($/month)	Telephone ($/month)
City[2]	439,033	1,325	-	116.97	42.69	178.82
Avg.	398,393	1,217	171.38	100.83	69.67	187.75
Min.	212,799	534	96.71	31.56	27.15	173.01
Max.	2,354,006	4,438	369.53	277.33	303.87	206.73

Note: (1) Values for the local area are compared with the average, minimum and maximum values for all 285 areas in the Cost of Living Index; (2) Figures cover the Las Vegas NV urban area; ***New Home Price*** *(2,400 sf living area, 8,000 sf lot, in urban area with full utilities);* ***Apartment Rent*** *(950 sf 2 bedroom/1.5 or 2 bath, unfurnished, excluding all utilities except water);* ***All Electric*** *(average monthly cost for an all-electric home);* ***Part Electric*** *(average monthly cost for a part-electric home);* ***Other Energy*** *(average monthly cost for natural gas, fuel oil, coal, wood, and any other forms of energy except electricity);* ***Telephone*** *(price includes the base monthly rate plus taxes and fees for three lines of mobile phone service).*
Source: The Council for Community and Economic Research, Cost of Living Index, 2021

Health Care, Transportation, and Other Costs

Area[1]	Doctor ($/visit)	Dentist ($/visit)	Optometrist ($/visit)	Gasoline ($/gallon)	Beauty Salon ($/visit)	Men's Shirt ($)
City[2]	109.27	102.27	103.80	3.24	46.03	23.03
Avg.	118.16	101.04	109.44	2.71	40.63	30.77
Min.	35.04	55.56	51.17	2.17	18.59	11.32
Max.	231.10	165.12	256.81	4.11	85.33	63.03

Note: (1) Values for the local area are compared with the average, minimum and maximum values for all 285 areas in the Cost of Living Index; (2) Figures cover the Las Vegas NV urban area; ***Doctor*** *(general practitioners routine exam of an established patient);* ***Dentist*** *(adult teeth cleaning and periodic oral examination);* ***Optometrist*** *(full vision eye exam for established adult patient);* ***Gasoline*** *(one gallon regular unleaded, national brand, including all taxes, cash price at self-service pump if available);* ***Beauty Salon*** *(woman's shampoo, trim, and blow-dry);* ***Men's Shirt*** *(cotton/polyester dress shirt, pinpoint weave, long sleeves).*
Source: The Council for Community and Economic Research, Cost of Living Index, 2021

HOUSING

Homeownership Rate

Area	2013 (%)	2014 (%)	2015 (%)	2016 (%)	2017 (%)	2018 (%)	2019 (%)	2020 (%)	2021 (%)
MSA[1]	52.8	53.2	52.1	51.3	54.4	58.1	56.0	57.3	57.7
U.S.	65.1	64.5	63.7	63.4	63.9	64.4	64.6	66.6	65.5

Note: (1) Figures cover the Las Vegas-Henderson-Paradise, NV Metropolitan Statistical Area
Source: U.S. Census Bureau, Housing Vacancies and Homeownership Annual Statistics: 2013-2021

House Price Index (HPI)

Area	National Ranking[2]	Quarterly Change (%)	One-Year Change (%)	Five-Year Change (%)	Since 1991Q1 (%)
MSA[1]	32	5.02	23.96	74.24	226.18
U.S.[3]	–	3.33	17.54	54.45	258.04

Note: The HPI is a weighted repeat sales index. It measures average price changes in repeat sales or refinancings on the same properties. This information is obtained by reviewing repeat mortgage transactions on single-family properties whose mortgages have been purchased or securitized by Fannie Mae or Freddie Mac since January 1975; (1) Figures cover the Las Vegas-Henderson-Paradise, NV Metropolitan Statistical Area; (2) Rankings are based on annual percentage change for all metro areas containing at least 15,000 transactions over the last 10 years and ranges from 1 to 268; (3) figures based on a weighted average of Census Division estimates using a seasonally adjusted, purchase-only index; all figures are for the period ending December 31, 2021
Source: Federal Housing Finance Agency, Change in FHFA Metropolitan Area House Price Indexes, 2021Q4

Median Single-Family Home Prices

Area	2019	2020	2021[p]	Percent Change 2020 to 2021
MSA[1]	306.0	331.0	397.0	19.9
U.S. Average	274.6	300.2	353.4	17.7

Note: Figures are median sales prices of existing single-family homes in thousands of dollars; (p) preliminary; (1) Figures cover the Las Vegas-Henderson-Paradise, NV Metropolitan Statistical Area
Source: National Association of Realtors, Median Sales Price of Existing Single-Family Homes for Metropolitan Areas, 4th Quarter 2021

Qualifying Income Based on Median Sales Price of Existing Single-Family Homes

Area	With 5% Down ($)	With 10% Down ($)	With 20% Down ($)
MSA[1]	84,457	80,012	71,122
U.S. Average	70,699	66,978	59,536

Note: Figures are preliminary; Qualifying income is based on a mortgage rate of 3.13%. Monthly principal and interest payment is limited to 25% of income; (1) Figures cover the Las Vegas-Henderson-Paradise, NV Metropolitan Statistical Area
Source: National Association of Realtors, Qualifying Income Based on Median Sales Price of Existing Single-Family Homes for Metropolitan Areas, 4th Quarter 2021

Home Value Distribution

Area	Under $50,000	$50,000 -$99,999	$100,000 -$149,999	$150,000 -$199,999	$200,000 -$299,999	$300,000 -$499,999	$500,000 -$999,999	$1,000,000 or more
City	2.5	2.7	6.5	12.4	32.5	31.0	10.6	1.8
MSA[1]	3.4	3.0	6.2	10.9	31.4	33.4	9.8	1.9
U.S.	6.6	11.0	12.3	13.6	20.0	20.5	12.3	3.7

Note: Figures are percentages and cover owner-occupied housing units; (1) Figures cover the Las Vegas-Henderson-Paradise, NV Metropolitan Statistical Area
Source: U.S. Census Bureau, 2016-2020 American Community Survey 5-Year Estimates

Year Housing Structure Built

Area	2010 or Later	2000 -2009	1990 -1999	1980 -1989	1970 -1979	1960 -1969	1950 -1959	1940 -1949	Before 1940	Median Year
City	6.0	21.9	32.2	16.3	10.0	7.5	4.3	1.3	0.5	1993
MSA[1]	8.6	29.0	28.8	14.6	10.6	5.0	2.2	0.7	0.4	1996
U.S.	6.2	13.6	13.9	13.4	15.0	10.5	10.2	4.8	12.4	1978

Note: Figures are percentages except for Median Year; Note: (1) Figures cover the Las Vegas-Henderson-Paradise, NV Metropolitan Statistical Area
Source: U.S. Census Bureau, 2016-2020 American Community Survey 5-Year Estimates

Gross Monthly Rent

Area	Under $500	$500 -$999	$1,000 -$1,499	$1,500 -$1,999	$2,000 -$2,499	$2,500 -$2,999	$3,000 and up	Median ($)
City	4.5	31.1	43.1	16.0	3.7	0.9	0.7	1,153
MSA[1]	2.7	30.0	43.0	18.5	4.1	0.9	0.7	1,181
U.S.	8.9	34.3	30.2	14.9	6.2	2.6	2.8	1,096

Note: Figures are percentages except for Median; Gross rent is the contract rent plus the estimated average monthly cost of utilities (electricity, gas, and water and sewer) and fuels (oil, coal, kerosene, wood, etc.) if these are paid by the renter (or paid for the renter by someone else); (1) Figures cover the Las Vegas-Henderson-Paradise, NV Metropolitan Statistical Area
Source: U.S. Census Bureau, 2016-2020 American Community Survey 5-Year Estimates

HEALTH

Health Risk Factors

Category	MSA[1] (%)	U.S. (%)
Adults aged 18–64 who have any kind of health care coverage	n/a	86.8
Adults who reported being in good or better health	n/a	86.7
Adults who are current smokers	n/a	15.5
Adults who currently use chewing tobacco, snuff, or snus	n/a	3.7
Adults who are heavy drinkers[2]	n/a	6.7
Adults who are binge drinkers[3]	n/a	15.7
Adults who are overweight (BMI 25.0 - 29.9)	n/a	35.2
Adults who are obese (BMI 30.0 - 99.8)	n/a	31.9
Adults who participated in any physical activities in the past month	n/a	77.6
Adults who always or nearly always wears a seat belt	n/a	94.2

Note: (1) Figures for the Las Vegas-Henderson-Paradise, NV Metropolitan Statistical Area were not available. (2) Heavy drinkers are classified as adult men having more than 14 drinks per week and adult women having more than 7 drinks per week; (3) Binge drinkers are classified as males having five or more drinks on one occasion or females having four or more drinks on one occasion
Source: Centers for Disease Control and Prevention, Behaviorial Risk Factor Surveillance System, SMART: Selected Metropolitan Area Risk Trends, 2020

Acute and Chronic Health Conditions

Category	MSA[1] (%)	U.S. (%)
Adults who have ever been told they had a heart attack	n/a	4.3
Adults who have ever been told they have angina or coronary heart disease	n/a	4.0
Adults who have ever been told they had a stroke	n/a	2.8
Adults who have ever been told they have asthma	n/a	14.2
Adults who have ever been told they have arthritis	n/a	24.5
Adults who have ever been told they have diabetes[2]	n/a	10.6
Adults who have ever been told they had skin cancer	n/a	6.4
Adults who have ever been told they had any other types of cancer	n/a	6.8
Adults who have ever been told they have COPD	n/a	6.2
Adults who have ever been told they have kidney disease	n/a	2.9
Adults who have ever been told they have a form of depression	n/a	19.6

Note: (1) Figures for the Las Vegas-Henderson-Paradise, NV Metropolitan Statistical Area were not available. (2) Figures do not include pregnancy-related, borderline, or pre-diabetes
Source: Centers for Disease Control and Prevention, Behaviorial Risk Factor Surveillance System, SMART: Selected Metropolitan Area Risk Trends, 2020

Health Screening and Vaccination Rates

Category	MSA[1] (%)	U.S. (%)
Adults 50-75 who have had a blood stool test within the past year	n/a	9.3
Adults aged 65+ who have had flu shot within the past year	n/a	67.9
Adults aged 65+ who have ever had a pneumonia vaccination	n/a	72.2
Adults who have ever been tested for HIV	n/a	37.1
Women aged 21-65 who have had a pap test in the past three years	n/a	77.7
Men aged 40+ who have had a PSA test within the past two years	n/a	31.8
Women aged 40+ who have had a mammogram within the past two years	n/a	71.5

Note: (1) Figures for the Las Vegas-Henderson-Paradise, NV Metropolitan Statistical Area were not available.
Source: Centers for Disease Control and Prevention, Behaviorial Risk Factor Surveillance System, SMART: Selected Metropolitan Area Risk Trends, 2020

Disability Status

Category	MSA[1] (%)	U.S. (%)
Adults who reported being deaf	n/a	6.8
Are you blind or have serious difficulty seeing, even when wearing glasses?	n/a	4.7
Do you have difficulty doing errands alone?	n/a	6.3
Do you have difficulty dressing or bathing?	n/a	3.0
Do you have serious difficulty concentrating/remembering/making decisions?	n/a	10.8
Do you have serious difficulty walking or climbing stairs?	n/a	11.9

Note: (1) Figures for the Las Vegas-Henderson-Paradise, NV Metropolitan Statistical Area were not available.
Source: Centers for Disease Control and Prevention, Behaviorial Risk Factor Surveillance System, SMART: Selected Metropolitan Area Risk Trends, 2020

Mortality Rates for the Top 10 Causes of Death in the U.S.

ICD-10[a] Sub-Chapter	ICD-10[a] Code	Age-Adjusted Mortality Rate[1] per 100,000 population	
		County[2]	U.S.
Malignant neoplasms	C00-C97	147.3	146.4
Ischaemic heart diseases	I20-I25	98.0	90.2
Other forms of heart disease	I30-I51	68.6	51.9
Other degenerative diseases of the nervous system	G30-G31	45.1	39.7
Other external causes of accidental injury	W00-X59	34.2	38.7
Chronic lower respiratory diseases	J40-J47	44.7	38.1
Cerebrovascular diseases	I60-I69	35.7	37.6
Organic, including symptomatic, mental disorders	F01-F09	18.5	29.4
Hypertensive diseases	I10-I15	39.0	26.1
Diabetes mellitus	E10-E14	21.7	22.6

Note: (a) ICD-10 = International Classification of Diseases 10th Revision; (1) Mortality rates are a three-year average covering 2018-2020; (2) Figures cover Clark County.
Source: Centers for Disease Control and Prevention, National Center for Health Statistics. Underlying Cause of Death 1999-2020 on CDC WONDER Online Database

Mortality Rates for Selected Causes of Death

ICD-10[a] Sub-Chapter	ICD-10[a] Code	Age-Adjusted Mortality Rate[1] per 100,000 population	
		County[2]	U.S.
Assault	X85-Y09	7.2	6.5
Diseases of the liver	K70-K76	16.0	15.3
Human immunodeficiency virus (HIV) disease	B20-B24	2.0	1.4
Influenza and pneumonia	J09-J18	14.1	13.4
Intentional self-harm	X60-X84	18.0	13.9
Malnutrition	E40-E46	4.1	2.9
Obesity and other hyperalimentation	E65-E68	2.3	2.4
Renal failure	N17-N19	8.0	12.5
Transport accidents	V01-V99	9.7	12.5
Viral hepatitis	B15-B19	1.4	1.0

Note: (a) ICD-10 = International Classification of Diseases 10th Revision; (1) Mortality rates are a three-year average covering 2018-2020; (2) Figures cover Clark County; Data are suppressed when the data meet the criteria for confidentiality constraints; Mortality rates are flagged as unreliable when the rate would be calculated with a numerator of 20 or less.
Source: Centers for Disease Control and Prevention, National Center for Health Statistics. Underlying Cause of Death 1999-2020 on CDC WONDER Online Database

Health Insurance Coverage

Area	With Health Insurance	With Private Health Insurance	With Public Health Insurance	Without Health Insurance	Population Under Age 19 Without Health Insurance
City	87.5	61.4	35.9	12.5	7.9
MSA[1]	88.3	63.9	34.3	11.7	7.6
U.S.	91.3	68.1	35.3	8.7	5.2

Note: Figures are percentages that cover the civilian noninstitutionalized population; (1) Figures cover the Las Vegas-Henderson-Paradise, NV Metropolitan Statistical Area
Source: U.S. Census Bureau, 2016-2020 American Community Survey 5-Year Estimates

Number of Medical Professionals

Area	MDs[3]	DOs[3,4]	Dentists	Podiatrists	Chiropractors	Optometrists
County[1] (number)	4,076	788	1,454	99	452	311
County[1] (rate[2])	179.9	34.8	64.2	4.4	20.0	13.7
U.S. (rate[2])	285.1	23.0	71.1	6.2	28.2	17.0

32003
Note: Data as of 2020 unless noted; (1) Data covers Clark County; (2) Rate per 100,000 population; (3) Data as of 2019 and includes all active, non-federal physicians; (4) Doctor of Osteopathic Medicine
Source: U.S. Department of Health and Human Services, Health Resources and Services Administration, Bureau of Health Professions, Area Resource File (ARF) 2020-2021

EDUCATION

Public School District Statistics

District Name	Schls	Pupils	Pupil/ Teacher Ratio	Minority Pupils[1] (%)	LEP/ELL[2] (%)	IEP[3] (%)
Clark County School District	384	328,991	20.0	76.2	16.9	12.9

Note: Table includes school districts with 2,000 or more students; (1) Percentage of students that are not non-Hispanic white; (2) Percentage of students that are Limited English Proficient (LEP) or English Language Learners (ELL) (2018-19); (3) Percentage of students that have an Individualized Education Program (IEP).
Source: U.S. Department of Education, National Center for Education Statistics, Common Core of Data, Local Education Agency (School District) Universe Survey: School Year 2019-2020

Best High Schools

According to *U.S. News,* Las Vegas is home to two of the top 500 high schools in the U.S.: **Advanced Technologies Academy** (#135); **West Career and Technical Academy** (#481). Nearly 18,000 public, magnet and charter schools were ranked based on their performance on state assessments and how well they prepare students for college. *U.S. News & World Report, "Best High Schools 2021"*

Highest Level of Education

Area	Less than H.S.	H.S. Diploma	Some College, No Deg.	Associate Degree	Bachelor's Degree	Master's Degree	Prof. School Degree	Doctorate Degree
City	14.7	27.6	24.5	7.9	16.4	6.1	2.0	0.8
MSA[1]	13.7	28.3	24.7	8.1	16.7	6.0	1.7	0.9
U.S.	11.5	26.7	20.3	8.6	20.2	9.1	2.2	1.5

Note: Figures cover persons age 25 and over; (1) Figures cover the Las Vegas-Henderson-Paradise, NV Metropolitan Statistical Area
Source: U.S. Census Bureau, 2016-2020 American Community Survey 5-Year Estimates

Educational Attainment by Race

Area	High School Graduate or Higher (%)					Bachelor's Degree or Higher (%)				
	Total	White	Black	Asian	Hisp.[2]	Total	White	Black	Asian	Hisp.[2]
City	85.3	88.6	88.7	91.5	65.4	25.2	27.9	18.6	42.6	10.5
MSA[1]	86.3	89.1	90.1	90.7	67.6	25.2	26.9	18.8	40.7	11.0
U.S.	88.5	90.7	86.7	87.3	70.3	32.9	34.4	22.6	55.0	17.6

Note: Figures shown cover persons 25 years old and over; (1) Figures cover the Las Vegas-Henderson-Paradise, NV Metropolitan Statistical Area; (2) People of Hispanic origin can be of any race
Source: U.S. Census Bureau, 2016-2020 American Community Survey 5-Year Estimates

School Enrollment by Grade and Control

Area	Preschool (%)		Kindergarten (%)		Grades 1 - 4 (%)		Grades 5 - 8 (%)		Grades 9 - 12 (%)	
	Public	Private	Public	Private	Public	Private	Public	Private	Public	Private
City	63.9	36.1	90.4	9.6	91.3	8.7	91.9	8.1	93.1	6.9
MSA[1]	60.1	39.9	89.3	10.7	92.3	7.7	92.9	7.1	93.0	7.0
U.S.	58.9	41.1	86.9	13.1	89.0	11.0	89.0	11.0	89.7	10.3

Note: Figures shown cover persons 3 years old and over; (1) Figures cover the Las Vegas-Henderson-Paradise, NV Metropolitan Statistical Area
Source: U.S. Census Bureau, 2016-2020 American Community Survey 5-Year Estimates

Higher Education

Four-Year Colleges			Two-Year Colleges			Medical Schools[1]	Law Schools[2]	Voc/ Tech[3]
Public	Private Non-profit	Private For-profit	Public	Private Non-profit	Private For-profit			
3	3	4	0	0	6	2	1	10

Note: Figures cover institutions located within the Las Vegas-Henderson-Paradise, NV Metropolitan Statistical Area and include main campuses only; (1) includes schools accredited by the Liaison Committee on Medical Education and the American Osteopathic Association's Commission on Osteopathic College Accreditation; (2) includes ABA-accredited schools, schools with provisional ABA accreditation, and state accredited schools; (3) includes all schools with programs that are less than 2 years.
Source: National Center for Education Statistics, Integrated Postsecondary Education System (IPEDS), 2020-21; Wikipedia, List of Medical Schools in the United States, accessed April 11, 2022; Wikipedia, List of Law Schools in the United States, accessed April 11, 2022

According to *U.S. News & World Report,* the Las Vegas-Henderson-Paradise, NV metro area is home to one of the top 100 law schools in the U.S.: **University of Nevada—Las Vegas** (#60 tie). The rankings are based on a weighted average of 12 measures of quality: peer assessment score; assessment score by lawyers/judges; median LSAT scores; median undergrad GPA; acceptance rate; employment rates for graduates; placement success; bar passage rate; faculty resources; expenditures per student; student/faculty ratio; and library resources. *U.S. News & World Report, "America's Best Graduate Schools, Law, 2022"*

EMPLOYERS

Major Employers

Company Name	Industry
American Casino & Entertainment	Hospitality
Blackstone Group	Hospitality
Boyd Gaming Corporation	Hospitality
Caesars Entertainment	Hospitality
Cannery Casino Resorts	Hospitality
City of Henderson	Municipal government
City of Las Vegas	Municipal government
Clark County	County government
Clark County School District	K-12 public education
Dignity Health	Health care
Landry's	Hospitality
Las Vegas Metropolitan Police Department	Police protection
Las Vegas Sands Corporation	Hospitality
MGM Resorts International	Hospitality
Nellis & Creech AFB	National security
Southwest Airlines	Air transportation, scheduled
Stations Casinos	Hospitality
Sunrise Health System	Health care
University Medical Center	Health care
University of Nevada Las Vegas	Higher education
Valley Health System	Health care
Wynn Resorts	Hospitality
Yellow Checker Star Transportation	Taxi/limo service

Note: Companies shown are located within the Las Vegas-Henderson-Paradise, NV Metropolitan Statistical Area.
Source: Hoovers.com; Wikipedia

PUBLIC SAFETY

Crime Rate

Area	Total Crime	Violent Crime Rate				Property Crime Rate		
		Murder	Rape[3]	Robbery	Aggrav. Assault	Burglary	Larceny -Theft	Motor Vehicle Theft
City	2,738.2	5.7	63.1	100.8	358.1	416.8	1,390.7	403.0
Suburbs[1]	1,944.4	5.0	31.6	99.0	209.5	261.9	1,057.0	280.4
Metro[2]	2,525.2	5.5	54.6	100.3	318.2	375.2	1,301.2	370.1
U.S.	2,356.7	6.5	38.4	73.9	279.7	314.2	1,398.0	246.0

Note: Figures are crimes per 100,000 population; (1) All areas within the metro area that are located outside the city limits; (2) Figures cover the Las Vegas-Henderson-Paradise, NV Metropolitan Statistical Area; (3) All figures shown were reported using the revised Uniform Crime Reporting (UCR) definition of rape.
Source: FBI Uniform Crime Reports, 2020

Hate Crimes

Area	Number of Quarters Reported	Number of Incidents per Bias Motivation					
		Race/Ethnicity/ Ancestry	Religion	Sexual Orientation	Disability	Gender	Gender Identity
City	4	27	1	9	1	0	1
U.S.	4	5,227	1,244	1,110	130	75	266

Source: Federal Bureau of Investigation, Hate Crime Statistics 2020

Identity Theft Consumer Reports

Area	Reports	Reports per 100,000 Population	Rank[2]
MSA[1]	15,055	664	22
U.S.	1,434,676	432	-

Note: (1) Figures cover the Las Vegas-Henderson-Paradise, NV Metropolitan Statistical Area; (2) Rank ranges from 1 to 391 where 1 indicates greatest number of identity theft reports per 100,000 population
Source: Federal Trade Commission, Consumer Sentinel Network Data Book 2021

Fraud and Other Consumer Reports

Area	Reports	Reports per 100,000 Population	Rank[2]
MSA[1]	34,173	1,508	9
U.S.	4,328,977	1,304	-

Note: (1) Figures cover the Las Vegas-Henderson-Paradise, NV Metropolitan Statistical Area; (2) Rank ranges from 1 to 391 where 1 indicates greatest number of fraud and other consumer reports per 100,000 population
Source: Federal Trade Commission, Consumer Sentinel Network Data Book 2021

POLITICS

2020 Presidential Election Results

Area	Biden	Trump	Jorgensen	Hawkins	Other
Clark County	53.7	44.3	0.9	0.0	1.1
U.S.	51.3	46.8	1.2	0.3	0.5

Note: Results are percentages and may not add to 100% due to rounding
Source: Dave Leip's Atlas of U.S. Presidential Elections

SPORTS

Professional Sports Teams

Team Name	League	Year Established
Las Vegas Raiders	National Football League (NFL)	2020
Vegas Golden Nights	National Hockey League (NHL)	2017

Note: Includes teams located in the Las Vegas-Henderson-Paradise, NV Metropolitan Statistical Area.
Source: Wikipedia, Major Professional Sports Teams of the United States and Canada, April 6, 2022

CLIMATE

Average and Extreme Temperatures

Temperature	Jan	Feb	Mar	Apr	May	Jun	Jul	Aug	Sep	Oct	Nov	Dec	Yr.
Extreme High (°F)	77	87	91	99	109	115	116	116	113	103	87	77	116
Average High (°F)	56	62	69	78	88	99	104	102	94	81	66	57	80
Average Temp. (°F)	45	50	56	65	74	84	90	88	80	68	54	46	67
Average Low (°F)	33	38	43	51	60	69	76	74	66	54	41	34	53
Extreme Low (°F)	8	16	23	31	40	49	60	56	43	26	21	11	8

Note: Figures cover the years 1948-1990
Source: National Climatic Data Center, International Station Meteorological Climate Summary, 9/96

Average Precipitation/Snowfall/Humidity

Precip./Humidity	Jan	Feb	Mar	Apr	May	Jun	Jul	Aug	Sep	Oct	Nov	Dec	Yr.
Avg. Precip. (in.)	0.5	0.4	0.4	0.2	0.2	0.1	0.4	0.5	0.3	0.2	0.4	0.3	4.0
Avg. Snowfall (in.)	1	Tr	Tr	Tr	0	0	0	0	0	0	Tr	Tr	1
Avg. Rel. Hum. 7am (%)	59	52	41	31	26	20	26	31	30	36	47	56	38
Avg. Rel. Hum. 4pm (%)	32	25	20	15	13	10	14	16	16	18	26	31	20

Note: Figures cover the years 1948-1990; Tr = Trace amounts (<0.05 in. of rain; <0.5 in. of snow)
Source: National Climatic Data Center, International Station Meteorological Climate Summary, 9/96

Weather Conditions

Temperature			Daytime Sky			Precipitation		
10°F & below	32°F & below	90°F & above	Clear	Partly cloudy	Cloudy	0.01 inch or more precip.	0.1 inch or more snow/ice	Thunder-storms
< 1	37	134	185	132	48	27	2	13

Note: Figures are average number of days per year and cover the years 1948-1990
Source: National Climatic Data Center, International Station Meteorological Climate Summary, 9/96

HAZARDOUS WASTE

Superfund Sites

The Las Vegas-Henderson-Paradise, NV metro area has no sites on the EPA's Superfund Final National Priorities List. There are a total of 1,165 Superfund sites with a status of proposed or final on the list in the U.S. *U.S. Environmental Protection Agency, National Priorities List, April 6, 2022*

AIR QUALITY

Air Quality Trends: Ozone

	1990	1995	2000	2005	2010	2016	2017	2018	2019	2020
MSA[1]	n/a	n/a	n/a	n/a	n/a	n/a	n/a	n/a	n/a	n/a
U.S.	0.090	0.091	0.082	0.080	0.074	0.070	0.069	0.070	0.066	0.068

Note: (1) Data covers the Las Vegas-Henderson-Paradise, NV Metropolitan Statistical Area; n/a not available. The values shown are the composite ozone concentration averages among trend sites based on the highest fourth daily maximum 8-hour concentration in parts per million. These trends are based on sites having an adequate record of monitoring data during the trend period. Data from exceptional events are included.
Source: U.S. Environmental Protection Agency, Air Quality Monitoring Information, "Air Quality Trends by City, 1990-2020"

Air Quality Index

Area	Percent of Days when Air Quality was...[2]					AQI Statistics[2]	
	Good	Moderate	Unhealthy for Sensitive Groups	Unhealthy	Very Unhealthy	Maximum	Median
MSA[1]	29.5	63.7	6.0	0.8	0.0	174	61

Note: (1) Data covers the Las Vegas-Henderson-Paradise, NV Metropolitan Statistical Area; (2) Based on 366 days with AQI data in 2020. Air Quality Index (AQI) is an index for reporting daily air quality. EPA calculates the AQI for five major air pollutants regulated by the Clean Air Act: ground-level ozone, particle pollution (aka particulate matter), carbon monoxide, sulfur dioxide, and nitrogen dioxide. The AQI runs from 0 to 500. The higher the AQI value, the greater the level of air pollution and the greater the health concern. There are six AQI categories: "Good" AQI is between 0 and 50. Air quality is considered satisfactory; "Moderate" AQI is between 51 and 100. Air quality is acceptable; "Unhealthy for Sensitive Groups" When AQI values are between 101 and 150, members of sensitive groups may experience health effects; "Unhealthy" When AQI values are between 151 and 200 everyone may begin to experience health effects; "Very Unhealthy" AQI values between 201 and 300 trigger a health alert; "Hazardous" AQI values over 300 trigger warnings of emergency conditions (not shown).
Source: U.S. Environmental Protection Agency, Air Quality Index Report, 2020

Air Quality Index Pollutants

Area	Percent of Days when AQI Pollutant was...[2]					
	Carbon Monoxide	Nitrogen Dioxide	Ozone	Sulfur Dioxide	Particulate Matter 2.5	Particulate Matter 10
MSA[1]	0.0	4.6	58.5	0.0	33.6	3.3

Note: (1) Data covers the Las Vegas-Henderson-Paradise, NV Metropolitan Statistical Area; (2) Based on 366 days with AQI data in 2020. The Air Quality Index (AQI) is an index for reporting daily air quality. EPA calculates the AQI for five major air pollutants regulated by the Clean Air Act: ground-level ozone, particle pollution (also known as particulate matter), carbon monoxide, sulfur dioxide, and nitrogen dioxide. The AQI runs from 0 to 500. The higher the AQI value, the greater the level of air pollution and the greater the health concern.
Source: U.S. Environmental Protection Agency, Air Quality Index Report, 2020

Maximum Air Pollutant Concentrations: Particulate Matter, Ozone, CO and Lead

	Particulate Matter 10 (ug/m^3)	Particulate Matter 2.5 Wtd AM (ug/m^3)	Particulate Matter 2.5 24-Hr (ug/m^3)	Ozone (ppm)	Carbon Monoxide (ppm)	Lead (ug/m^3)
MSA[1] Level	210	12.2	33	0.078	2	n/a
NAAQS[2]	150	15	35	0.075	9	0.15
Met NAAQS[2]	No	Yes	Yes	No	Yes	n/a

Note: (1) Data covers the Las Vegas-Henderson-Paradise, NV Metropolitan Statistical Area; Data from exceptional events are included; (2) National Ambient Air Quality Standards; ppm = parts per million; ug/m^3 = micrograms per cubic meter; n/a not available.
Concentrations: Particulate Matter 10 (coarse particulate)—highest second maximum 24-hour concentration; Particulate Matter 2.5 Wtd AM (fine particulate)—highest weighted annual mean concentration; Particulate Matter 2.5 24-Hour (fine particulate)—highest 98th percentile 24-hour concentration; Ozone—highest fourth daily maximum 8-hour concentration; Carbon Monoxide—highest second maximum non-overlapping 8-hour concentration; Lead—maximum running 3-month average
Source: U.S. Environmental Protection Agency, Air Quality Monitoring Information, "Air Quality Statistics by City, 2020"

Maximum Air Pollutant Concentrations: Nitrogen Dioxide and Sulfur Dioxide

	Nitrogen Dioxide AM (ppb)	Nitrogen Dioxide 1-Hr (ppb)	Sulfur Dioxide AM (ppb)	Sulfur Dioxide 1-Hr (ppb)	Sulfur Dioxide 24-Hr (ppb)
MSA[1] Level	23	57	n/a	5	n/a
NAAQS[2]	53	100	30	75	140
Met NAAQS[2]	Yes	Yes	n/a	Yes	n/a

Note: (1) Data covers the Las Vegas-Henderson-Paradise, NV Metropolitan Statistical Area; Data from exceptional events are included; (2) National Ambient Air Quality Standards; ppm = parts per million; ug/m^3 = micrograms per cubic meter; n/a not available.
Concentrations: Nitrogen Dioxide AM—highest arithmetic mean concentration; Nitrogen Dioxide 1-Hr—highest 98th percentile 1-hour daily maximum concentration; Sulfur Dioxide AM—highest annual mean concentration; Sulfur Dioxide 1-Hr—highest 99th percentile 1-hour daily maximum concentration; Sulfur Dioxide 24-Hr—highest second maximum 24-hour concentration
Source: U.S. Environmental Protection Agency, Air Quality Monitoring Information, "Air Quality Statistics by City, 2020"

Los Angeles, California

Background

There is as much to say about Los Angeles as there are municipalities under its jurisdiction. The city is immense, and as the saying goes, "If you want a life in LA, you need a car."

Los Angeles acquired its many neighborhoods and communities such as Hollywood, Glendale, Burbank, and Alhambra when those cities wanted to share in the water piped into Los Angeles from the Owens River. To obtain it, the cities were required to join the Los Angeles municipal system. Due to those annexations, Los Angeles is now one of the largest U.S. cities in both acreage and population. It is also one of the most racially diverse.

The city's communities are connected through a complex system of freeways which gives Los Angeles its reputation as a congested, car-oriented culture, where people must schedule their days around the three-hour rush hour.

Despite these challenges, Los Angeles is a city with a diversified economy and an average of 325 days of sunshine a year. What was founded in 1781 as a sleepy pueblo of 44 people, with chickens roaming the footpaths, is now a city leading the nation in commerce, transportation, finance, and, especially, entertainment—with most of all motion pictures made in the United States still produced in the Los Angeles area, and headquarters of such major studios as MGM and Universal located in "municipalities" unto themselves.

Playa Vista, the first new community to be established on the west side of Los Angeles in more than 50 years, was built in 2002 on the former site of the Hughes Aircraft Company. It is home to Electronic Arts, the world's leading video game publisher, Belkin and others. Lincoln Properties built office buildings totaling more than 820,000 square feet in the eastern portion of Playa Vista community known as "The Campus at Playa Vista." The National Basketball Association Clippers has a training facility at the Campus, which is also home to a basketball-themed public park, a fitting way to celebrate the 2011 NBA champion Lakers.

The arts are center stage in Los Angeles. The Getty Center and Museum, an architectural masterpiece designed by Richard Meier built on a commanding hill, is a dramatic venue for visual arts and other events. The Los Angeles Opera, under the direction of Placido Domingo, offers a lively season of operas as well as recitals by such luminaries as Cecilia Bartoli and Renee Fleming. The Los Angeles Philharmonic performs in the Walt Disney Concert Hall, designed by Frank Gehry, famous as the architect of the Guggenheim Museum at Bilbao. The city's iconic music venue, The Hollywood Bowl, celebrates its 100th anniversary in 2022.

The downtown's first modern industrial park, Los Angeles World Trade Center, is a 20-acre project that is downtown's only foreign trade zone.

Los Angeles has hosted the Olympic and Paralympic Games twice and will again in 2028. Los Angeles will be the third city after London and Paris to host the Olympic Games three times. Major league baseball's Los Angeles Dodgers won the World Series in 2020, ending a 32-year drought. Super Bowl LVI was played at the newly built SoFi Stadium in neighboring Inglewood in 2022.

Inland and up foothill slopes, both high and low temperatures become more extreme and the relative humidity, which is frequently high near the coast, drops. Most rain falls November through March, while the summers are very dry. Destructive flash floods occasionally develop in and below some mountain canyons. Snow is often visible on the nearby mountains in the winter but is extremely rare in the coastal basin. Thunderstorms are infrequent.

The climate of Los Angeles is normally pleasant and mild throughout the year, with unusual differences in temperature, humidity, cloudiness, fog, rain, and sunshine over short distances in the metro area. Low clouds are common at night and in the morning along the coast during spring and summer. Near the foothills, clouds form later in the day and clear earlier. Annual percentages of fog and cloudiness are greatest near the ocean. Sunshine totals are highest on the inland side of the city.

At times, high concentrations of air pollution affect the Los Angeles coastal basin and adjacent areas, when lack of air movement combines with an atmospheric inversion. In fall and winter, the Santa Ana winds pick up considerable amounts of dust and can blow strongly in the northern and eastern sections of the city and in outlying areas in the north and east, increasing the threat of wildfires in the region. The Woolsey Fire in 2018 burned 96,949 acres of land in Los Angeles and Ventura Counties.

Rankings

General Rankings

- The human resources consulting firm Mercer ranked 231 major cities worldwide in terms of overall quality of life. Los Angeles ranked #66. Criteria: political, social, economic, and socio-cultural factors; medical and health considerations; schools and education; public services and transportation; recreation; consumer goods; housing; and natural environment. *Mercer, "Mercer 2019 Quality of Living Survey," March 13, 2019*

Business/Finance Rankings

- According to *Business Insider*, the Los Angeles metro area is a prime place to run a startup or move an existing business to. The area ranked #9. More than 300 metro areas were analyzed for factors that were of top concern to new business owners. Data was based on the 2019 U.S. Census Bureau American Community Survey, statistics from the CDC, Bureau of Labor Statistics employment report, and University of Chicago analysis. Criteria: business formations; percentage of vaccinated population; percentage of households with internet subscriptions; median household income; and share of work that can be done from home. *www.businessinsider.com, "The 20 Best Cities for Starting a Business in 2022 Include Baltimore, Boulder, and Boston," January 5, 2022*
- The Brookings Institution ranked the nation's largest cities based on income inequality. Los Angeles was ranked #15 (#1 = greatest inequality). Criteria: the "95/20 ratio," a figure representing the income at which a household earns more than 95 percent of all other households, divided by the income at which a household earns more than only 20 percent of all other households. *Brookings Institution, "Household Income Inequality, Largest Cities of 97 Large U.S. Metro Areas, 2014-2016," February 5, 2018*
- The Brookings Institution ranked the 100 largest metro areas in the U.S. based on income inequality. Los Angeles was ranked #4 (#1 = greatest inequality). Criteria: the "95/20 ratio," a figure representing the income at which a household earns more than 95 percent of all other households, divided by the income at which a household earns more than only 20 percent of all other households. *Brookings Institution, "Household Income Inequality, 100 Largest U.S. Metro Areas, 2014-2016," February 5, 2018*
- Payscale.com ranked the 32 largest metro areas in terms of wage growth. The Los Angeles metro area ranked #13. Criteria: private-sector and education professional wage growth between the 4th quarter of 2019 and the 4th quarter of 2020. *PayScale, "Wage Trends by Metro Area-4th Quarter," January 11, 2021*
- The Los Angeles metro area was identified as one of the most debt-ridden places in America by the finance site Credit.com. The metro area was ranked #13. Criteria: residents' average credit card debt as well as median income. *Credit.com, "25 Cities With the Most Credit Card Debt," February 28, 2018*
- For its annual survey of the "Most Expensive U.S. Cities to Live In," Kiplinger applied Cost of Living Index statistics developed by the Council for Community and Economic Research to U.S. Census Bureau population and median household income data for 256 urban areas. Los Angeles was among the 20 most expensive in the country. *Kiplinger.com, "The 20 Most Expensive Cities in the U.S.," March 16, 2022*
- Los Angeles was cited as one of America's top metros for total major capital investment facility projects in 2021. The area ranked #8 in the large metro area category (population over 1 million). *Site Selection, "Top Metros of 2021," March 2022*
- The Los Angeles metro area appeared on the Milken Institute "2021 Best Performing Cities" list. Rank: #93 out of 200 large metro areas (population over 250,000). Criteria: job growth; wage and salary growth; high-tech output growth; housing affordability; household broadband access. *Milken Institute, "Best-Performing Cities 2021," February 16, 2021*
- *Forbes* ranked the 200 most populous metro areas to determine the nation's "Best Places for Business and Careers." The Los Angeles metro area was ranked #113. Criteria: costs (business and living); job growth (past and projected); income growth; quality of life; educational attainment (college and high school); projected economic growth; cultural and leisure opportunities; workplace tolerance laws; net migration patterns. *Forbes, "The Best Places for Business and Careers 2019: Seattle Still On Top," October 30, 2019*
- Mercer Human Resources Consulting ranked 209 cities worldwide in terms of cost-of-living. Los Angeles ranked #20 (the lower the ranking, the higher the cost-of-living). The survey measured the comparative cost of over 200 items (such as housing, food, clothing, household goods, transportation, and entertainment) in each location. *Mercer, "2021 Cost of Living City Ranking," June 22, 2021*

Education Rankings

- Personal finance website *WalletHub* analyzed the 150 largest U.S. metropolitan statistical areas to determine where the most educated Americans are putting their degrees to work. Criteria: education levels; percentage of workers with degrees; education quality and attainment gap; public school quality rankings; quality and enrollment of each metro area's universities. Los Angeles was ranked #92 (#1 = most educated city). *www.WalletHub.com, "Most & Least Educated Cities in America," July 19, 2021*
- Los Angeles was selected as one of America's most literate cities. The city ranked #62 out of the 84 largest U.S. cities. Criteria: number of booksellers; library resources; Internet resources; educational attainment; periodical publishing resources; newspaper circulation. *Central Connecticut State University, "America's Most Literate Cities, 2018," February 2019*

Environmental Rankings

- The U.S. Environmental Protection Agency (EPA) released its list of U.S. metropolitan areas with the most ENERGY STAR certified buildings in 2020. The Los Angeles metro area was ranked #1 out of 25. *U.S. Environmental Protection Agency, "2021 Energy Star Top Cities," June 15, 2021*
- Los Angeles was highlighted as one of the 25 most ozone-polluted metro areas in the U.S. during 2017 through 2019. The area ranked #1. *American Lung Association, "State of the Air 2021," April 21, 2021*
- Los Angeles was highlighted as one of the 25 metro areas most polluted by year-round particle pollution (Annual PM 2.5) in the U.S. during 2017 through 2019. The area ranked #4. *American Lung Association, "State of the Air 2021," April 21, 2021*
- Los Angeles was highlighted as one of the 25 metro areas most polluted by short-term particle pollution (24-hour PM 2.5) in the U.S. during 2017 through 2019. The area ranked #6. *American Lung Association, "State of the Air 2021," April 21, 2021*

Food/Drink Rankings

- The U.S. Chamber of Commerce Foundation conducted an in-depth study on local food truck regulations, surveyed 288 food truck owners, and ranked 20 major American cities based on how friendly they are for operating a food truck. The compiled index assessed the following: procedures for obtaining permits and licenses; complying with restrictions; and financial obligations associated with operating a food truck. Los Angeles ranked #8 overall (1 being the best). *www.foodtrucknation.us, "Food Truck Nation," March 20, 2018*
- Los Angeles was identified as one of the cities in America ordering the most vegan food options by GrubHub.com. The city ranked #1 out of 5. Criteria: percentage of vegan, vegetarian and plant-based food orders compared to the overall number of orders. *GrubHub.com, "State of the Plate Report 2021: Top Cities for Vegans," June 20, 2021*
- Dodger stadium was selected as one of PETA's "Top 10 Vegan-Friendly Ballparks" for 2019. The park ranked #7. *People for the Ethical Treatment of Animals, "Top 10 Vegan-Friendly Ballparks," May 23, 2019*

Health/Fitness Rankings

- For each of the 100 largest cities in the United States, the American Fitness Index®, published by the American College of Sports Medicine and the Anthem Foundation, evaluated community infrastructure and 34 health behaviors including preventive health, levels of chronic disease conditions, food insecurity, sleep quality, pedestrian safety, air quality, and community resources that support physical activity. Los Angeles ranked #39 for "community fitness." *americanfitnessindex.org, "2021 ACSM American Fitness Index Summary Report," July 13, 2021*
- The Los Angeles metro area was identified as one of the worst cities for bed bugs in America by pest control company Orkin. The area ranked #12 out of 50 based on the number of bed bug treatments Orkin performed from December 2020 to November 2021. *Orkin, "Chicago Takes Another Top Spot for Pests, This Time Ranking #1 On Orkin's Bed Bug Cities List," January 10, 2022*
- Los Angeles was identified as a "2021 Spring Allergy Capital." The area ranked #67 out of 100. Three groups of factors were used to identify the most challenging cities for people with allergies during the spring season: annual spring pollen levels; over the counter medicine use; number of board-certified allergy specialists. *Asthma and Allergy Foundation of America, "Spring Allergy Capitals 2021," February 23, 2021*

- Los Angeles was identified as a "2021 Fall Allergy Capital." The area ranked #66 out of 100. Three groups of factors were used to identify the most challenging cities for people with allergies during the fall season: annual fall pollen levels; over the counter medicine use; number of board-certified allergy specialists. *Asthma and Allergy Foundation of America, "Fall Allergy Capitals 2021," February 23, 2021*
- Los Angeles was identified as a "2021 Asthma Capital." The area ranked #90 out of the nation's 100 largest metropolitan areas. Criteria: estimated asthma prevalence; asthma-related mortality; and ER visits due to asthma. Risk factors analyzed but not factored in the rankings: annual pollen score; annual air quality; public smoking laws; number of board-certified asthma specialists; rescue medication use; controller medication use; uninsured rate; poverty rate. *Asthma and Allergy Foundation of America, "Asthma Capitals 2021: The Most Challenging Places to Live With Asthma," May 5, 2021*

Real Estate Rankings

- *WalletHub* compared the most populated U.S. cities to determine which had the best markets for real estate agents. Los Angeles ranked #40 where demand was high and pay was the best. Criteria: sales per agent; annual median wage for real-estate agents; monthly average starting salary for real estate agents; real estate job density and competition; unemployment rate; home turnover rate; housing-market health index; and other relevant metrics. *www.WalletHub.com, "2021 Best Places to Be a Real Estate Agent," May 12, 2021*
- The Los Angeles metro area was identified as one of the 20 least affordable housing markets in the U.S. in 2021. The area ranked #178 out of 183 markets. Criteria: qualification for a mortgage loan with a 10 percent down payment on a typical home. *National Association of Realtors®, Qualifying Income Based on Sales Price of Existing Single-Family Homes for Metropolitan Areas, 2021*
- Los Angeles was ranked #237 out of 237 metro areas in terms of housing affordability in 2021 by the National Association of Home Builders (#1 = most affordable). Criteria: the share of homes sold in that area affordable to a family earning the local median income, based on standard mortgage underwriting criteria. *National Association of Home Builders®, NAHB-Wells Fargo Housing Opportunity Index, 4th Quarter 2021*

Safety Rankings

- Allstate ranked the 200 largest cities in America in terms of driver safety. Los Angeles ranked #195. Criteria: internal property damage claims over a two-year period from January 2016 to December 2017. The report helps increase the importance of safety and awareness behind the wheel. *Allstate, "Allstate America's Best Drivers Report, 2019" June 24, 2019*
- The National Insurance Crime Bureau ranked 390 metro areas in the U.S. in terms of per capita rates of vehicle theft. The Los Angeles metro area ranked #21 (#1 = highest rate). Criteria: number of vehicle theft offenses per 100,000 inhabitants in 2020. *National Insurance Crime Bureau, "Hot Spots 2020," August 31, 2021*

Seniors/Retirement Rankings

- From its Best Cities for Successful Aging indexes, the Milken Institute generated rankings for metropolitan areas, weighing data in nine categories—health care, wellness, living arrangements, transportation and convenience, financial characteristics, education, employment, community engagement, and overall livability. The Los Angeles metro area was ranked #56 overall in the large metro area category. *Milken Institute, "Best Cities for Successful Aging, 2017" March 14, 2017*

Transportation Rankings

- Los Angeles was identified as one of the most congested metro areas in the U.S. The area ranked #1 out of 10. Criteria: yearly delay per auto commuter in hours. *Texas A&M Transportation Institute, "2021 Urban Mobility Report," June 2021*
- According to the INRIX "2021 Global Traffic Scorecard," Los Angeles was identified as one of the most congested metro areas in the U.S. The area ranked #6 out of 25. Criteria: average annual time spent in traffic and average cost of congestion per motorist. *Inrix.com, "Americans Lost 3.4 Billion Hours Due to Congestion in 2021, 42% Below Pre-COVID," December 7, 2021*

Women/Minorities Rankings

- The *Houston Chronicle* listed the Los Angeles metro area as #6 in top places for young Latinos to live in the U.S. Research was largely based on housing and occupational data from the largest metropolitan areas performed by *Forbes* and NBC Universo. Criteria: percentage of 18-34 year-olds; Latino college grad rates; and diversity. *blog.chron.com, "The 15 Best Big Cities for Latino Millenials," January 26, 2016*

- Personal finance website *WalletHub* compared more than 180 U.S. cities across two key dimensions, "Hispanic Business-Friendliness" and "Hispanic Purchasing Power," to arrive at the most favorable conditions for Hispanic entrepreneurs. Los Angeles was ranked #123 out of 182. Criteria includes: share of Hispanic-Owned Businesses; Hispanic entrepreneurship rate to median annual income of Hispanics; Small Business-Friendliness score; cost of living; and number of Hispanics with at least a bachelor's degree. *WalletHub.com, "2019's Best Cities for Hispanic Entrepreneurs," May 1, 2019*

Miscellaneous Rankings

- Los Angeles was selected as a 2021 Digital Cities Survey winner. The city ranked #2 in the large city (500,000 or more population) category. The survey examined and assessed how city governments are utilizing technology to continue innovation, engage with residents, and persevere through the challenges of the pandemic. Survey questions focused on ten initiatives: cybersecurity; citizen experience; disaster recovery; business intelligence; IT personnel; data governance; budget control; IT governance; infrastructure modernization; and broadband connectivity. *Center for Digital Government, "2021 Digital Cities Survey," November 16, 2021*
- The watchdog site, Charity Navigator, conducted a study of charities in major markets both to analyze statistical differences in their financial, accountability, and transparency practices and to track year-to-year variations in individual philanthropic communities. The Los Angeles metro area was ranked #14 among the 30 metro markets in the rating category of Overall Score. *www.charitynavigator.org, "2017 Metro Market Study," May 1, 2017*
- *WalletHub* compared the 150 most populated U.S. cities to determine their operating efficiency. A "Quality of City Services" score was constructed for each city and then divided by the total budget per capita to reveal which were managed the best. Los Angeles ranked #134. Criteria: financial stability; economy; education; safety; health; infrastructure and pollution. *www.WalletHub.com, "2021's Best- & Worst-Run Cities in America," June 22, 2021*
- The National Alliance to End Homelessness listed the 25 most populous metro areas with the highest rate of homelessness. The Los Angeles metro area had a high rate of homelessness. Criteria: number of homeless people per 10,000 population in 2016. *National Alliance to End Homelessness, "Homelessness in the 25 Most Populous U.S. Metro Areas," September 1, 2017*

Business Environment

DEMOGRAPHICS

Population Growth

Area	1990 Census	2000 Census	2010 Census	2020* Estimate	Population Growth (%) 1990-2020	Population Growth (%) 2010-2020
City	3,487,671	3,694,820	3,792,621	3,973,278	13.9	4.8
MSA[1]	11,273,720	12,365,627	12,828,837	13,211,027	17.2	3.0
U.S.	248,709,873	281,421,906	308,745,538	326,569,308	31.3	5.8

Note: (1) Figures cover the Los Angeles-Long Beach-Anaheim, CA Metropolitan Statistical Area; (*) 2016-2020 5-year estimated population
Source: U.S. Census Bureau, 1990 Census, Census 2000, Census 2010, 2016-2020 American Community Survey 5-Year Estimates

Household Size

Area	Persons in Household (%) One	Two	Three	Four	Five	Six	Seven or More	Average Household Size
City	30.5	28.9	15.3	13.0	6.8	2.9	2.6	2.80
MSA[1]	24.7	28.7	17.0	15.4	7.9	3.4	2.9	3.00
U.S.	28.0	33.9	15.5	12.9	6.0	2.3	1.4	2.60

Note: (1) Figures cover the Los Angeles-Long Beach-Anaheim, CA Metropolitan Statistical Area
Source: U.S. Census Bureau, 2016-2020 American Community Survey 5-Year Estimates

Race

Area	White Alone[2] (%)	Black Alone[2] (%)	Asian Alone[2] (%)	AIAN[3] Alone[2] (%)	NHOPI[4] Alone[2] (%)	Other Race Alone[2] (%)	Two or More Races (%)
City	48.9	8.8	11.8	0.7	0.2	22.7	7.0
MSA[1]	50.1	6.5	16.3	0.7	0.3	18.9	7.2
U.S.	70.4	12.6	5.6	0.8	0.2	5.1	5.2

Note: (1) Figures cover the Los Angeles-Long Beach-Anaheim, CA Metropolitan Statistical Area; (2) Alone is defined as not being in combination with one or more other races; (3) American Indian and Alaska Native; (4) Native Hawaiian and Other Pacific Islander
Source: U.S. Census Bureau, 2016-2020 American Community Survey 5-Year Estimates

Hispanic or Latino Origin

Area	Total (%)	Mexican (%)	Puerto Rican (%)	Cuban (%)	Other (%)
City	48.1	31.6	0.5	0.4	15.5
MSA[1]	44.8	34.5	0.5	0.4	9.5
U.S.	18.2	11.2	1.7	0.7	4.5

Note: Persons of Hispanic or Latino origin can be of any race; (1) Figures cover the Los Angeles-Long Beach-Anaheim, CA Metropolitan Statistical Area
Source: U.S. Census Bureau, 2016-2020 American Community Survey 5-Year Estimates

Ancestry

Area	German	Irish	English	American	Italian	Polish	French[2]	Scottish	Dutch
City	3.9	3.6	3.0	3.8	2.7	1.4	1.1	0.7	0.4
MSA[1]	5.1	4.3	4.0	3.5	2.9	1.2	1.3	0.9	0.6
U.S.	13.0	9.7	7.7	5.9	5.1	2.7	2.3	1.6	1.1

Note: Figures are the percentage of the total population reporting a particular ancestry. The nine most commonly reported ancestries in the U.S. are shown. Figures include multiple ancestries (e.g. if a person reported being Irish and Italian, they were included in both columns); (1) Figures cover the Los Angeles-Long Beach-Anaheim, CA Metropolitan Statistical Area; (2) Excludes Basque
Source: U.S. Census Bureau, 2016-2020 American Community Survey 5-Year Estimates

Foreign-born Population

Area	Percent of Population Born in: Any Foreign Country	Asia	Mexico	Europe	Caribbean	Central America[2]	South America	Africa	Canada
City	36.3	11.0	12.1	2.4	0.3	8.2	1.1	0.7	0.4
MSA[1]	32.7	12.8	11.7	1.7	0.3	4.2	0.9	0.6	0.3
U.S.	13.5	4.2	3.3	1.5	1.3	1.1	1.0	0.7	0.3

Note: (1) Figures cover the Los Angeles-Long Beach-Anaheim, CA Metropolitan Statistical Area; (2) Excludes Mexico.
Source: U.S. Census Bureau, 2016-2020 American Community Survey 5-Year Estimates

Marital Status

Area	Never Married	Now Married[2]	Separated	Widowed	Divorced
City	45.7	39.1	2.5	4.6	8.1
MSA[1]	40.1	44.6	2.0	4.9	8.4
U.S.	33.5	48.1	1.8	5.7	10.8

Note: Figures are percentages and cover the population 15 years of age and older; (1) Figures cover the Los Angeles-Long Beach-Anaheim, CA Metropolitan Statistical Area; (2) Excludes separated
Source: U.S. Census Bureau, 2016-2020 American Community Survey 5-Year Estimates

Disability by Age

Area	All Ages	Under 18 Years Old	18 to 64 Years Old	65 Years and Over
City	10.3	3.2	7.4	37.3
MSA[1]	9.8	3.1	6.9	33.8
U.S.	12.7	4.3	10.3	34.0

Note: Figures show percent of the civilian noninstitutionalized population that reported having a disability. Disability status is determined from six types of difficulty: vision, hearing, cognitive, ambulatory, self-care, and independent living. For children under 5 years old, hearing and vision difficulty are used to determine disability status. For children between the ages of 5 and 14, disability status is determined from hearing, vision, cognitive, ambulatory, and self-care difficulties. For people aged 15 years and older, they are considered to have a disability if they have difficulty with any one of the six difficulty types; Note: (1) Figures cover the Los Angeles-Long Beach-Anaheim, CA Metropolitan Statistical Area
Source: U.S. Census Bureau, 2016-2020 American Community Survey 5-Year Estimates

Age

Area	Percent of Population									Median Age
	Under Age 5	Age 5–19	Age 20–34	Age 35–44	Age 45–54	Age 55–64	Age 65–74	Age 75–84	Age 85+	
City	5.7	17.3	25.6	14.4	13.0	11.2	7.3	3.6	1.9	35.9
MSA[1]	5.9	18.4	22.7	13.5	13.5	12.1	7.9	4.0	2.0	37.1
U.S.	6.0	19.1	20.6	12.7	12.7	12.9	9.4	4.7	2.0	38.2

Note: (1) Figures cover the Los Angeles-Long Beach-Anaheim, CA Metropolitan Statistical Area
Source: U.S. Census Bureau, 2016-2020 American Community Survey 5-Year Estimates

Gender

Area	Males	Females	Males per 100 Females
City	1,966,568	2,006,710	98.0
MSA[1]	6,514,142	6,696,885	97.3
U.S.	160,818,530	165,750,778	97.0

Note: (1) Figures cover the Los Angeles-Long Beach-Anaheim, CA Metropolitan Statistical Area
Source: U.S. Census Bureau, 2016-2020 American Community Survey 5-Year Estimates

Religious Groups by Family

Area	Catholic	Baptist	Non-Den.	Methodist[2]	Lutheran	LDS[3]	Pente-costal	Presby-terian[4]	Muslim[5]	Judaism
MSA[1]	33.8	2.8	3.6	1.1	0.7	1.7	1.8	0.9	0.7	1.0
U.S.	19.1	9.3	4.0	4.0	2.3	2.0	1.9	1.6	0.8	0.7

Note: Figures are the number of adherents as a percentage of the total population; (1) Figures cover the Los Angeles-Long Beach-Anaheim, CA Metropolitan Statistical Area; (2) Methodist/Pietist; (3) Latter Day Saints; (4) Reformed; (5) Figures are estimates
Source: Association of Statisticians of American Religious Bodies, 2010 U.S. Religion Census: Religious Congregations & Membership Study

Religious Groups by Tradition

Area	Catholic	Evangelical Protestant	Mainline Protestant	Other Tradition	Black Protestant	Orthodox
MSA[1]	33.8	9.0	2.4	4.6	0.9	0.6
U.S.	19.1	16.2	7.3	4.3	1.6	0.3

Note: Figures are the number of adherents as a percentage of the total population; (1) Figures cover the Los Angeles-Long Beach-Anaheim, CA Metropolitan Statistical Area
Source: Association of Statisticians of American Religious Bodies, 2010 U.S. Religion Census: Religious Congregations & Membership Study

ECONOMY

Gross Metropolitan Product

Area	2017	2018	2019	2020	Rank[2]
MSA[1]	1,067.7	1,125.5	1,164.2	1,207.3	2

Note: Figures are in billions of dollars; (1) Figures cover the Los Angeles-Long Beach-Anaheim, CA Metropolitan Statistical Area; (2) Rank is based on 2018 data and ranges from 1 to 381
Source: U.S. Conference of Mayors, U.S. Metro Economies: GMP & Employment 2018-2020, September 2019

Economic Growth

Area	2015-17 (%)	2018 (%)	2019 (%)	2020 (%)	Rank[2]
MSA[1]	2.3	3.5	1.8	1.6	110
U.S.	1.9	2.9	2.3	2.1	–

Note: Figures are real gross metropolitan product (GMP) growth rates and represent average annual percent change; (1) Figures cover the Los Angeles-Long Beach-Anaheim, CA Metropolitan Statistical Area; (2) Rank is based on 2017 2-year average annual percent change and ranges from 1 to 381
Source: U.S. Conference of Mayors, U.S. Metro Economies: GMP & Employment 2018-2020, September 2019

Metropolitan Area Exports

Area	2015	2016	2017	2018	2019	2020	Rank[2]
MSA[1]	61,758.7	61,245.7	63,752.9	64,814.6	61,041.1	50,185.4	3

Note: Figures are in millions of dollars; (1) Figures cover the Los Angeles-Long Beach-Anaheim, CA Metropolitan Statistical Area; (2) Rank is based on 2020 data and ranges from 1 to 389
Source: U.S. Department of Commerce, International Trade Administration, Office of Trade and Economic Analysis, Industry and Analysis, Exports by Metropolitan Area, data extracted March 4, 2022

Building Permits

Area	Single-Family			Multi-Family			Total		
	2019	2020	Pct. Chg.	2019	2020	Pct. Chg.	2019	2020	Pct. Chg.
City	2,647	1,854	-30.0	11,740	10,438	-11.1	14,387	12,292	-14.6
MSA[1]	9,306	9,737	4.6	21,248	17,193	-19.1	30,554	26,930	-11.9
U.S.	862,100	979,400	13.6	523,900	491,700	-6.1	1,386,000	1,471,100	6.1

Note: (1) Figures cover the Los Angeles-Long Beach-Anaheim, CA Metropolitan Statistical Area; Figures represent new, privately-owned housing units authorized (unadjusted data); All permit data are based on estimates with imputation
Source: U.S. Census Bureau, Manufacturing, Mining, and Construction Statistics, Building Permits, 2019, 2020

Bankruptcy Filings

Area	Business Filings			Nonbusiness Filings		
	2020	2021	% Chg.	2020	2021	% Chg.
Los Angeles County	857	672	-21.6	13,323	11,316	-15.1
U.S.	21,655	14,347	-33.7	522,808	399,269	-23.6

Note: Business filings include Chapter 7, Chapter 9, Chapter 11, Chapter 12, Chapter 13, Chapter 15, and Section 304; Nonbusiness filings include Chapter 7, Chapter 11, and Chapter 13
Source: Administrative Office of the U.S. Courts, Business and Nonbusiness Bankruptcy, County Cases Commenced by Chapter of the Bankruptcy Code, During the 12-Month Period Ending December 31, 2020 and Business and Nonbusiness Bankruptcy, County Cases Commenced by Chapter of the Bankruptcy Code, During the 12-Month Period Ending December 31, 2021

Housing Vacancy Rates

Area	Gross Vacancy Rate[2] (%)			Year-Round Vacancy Rate[3] (%)			Rental Vacancy Rate[4] (%)			Homeowner Vacancy Rate[5] (%)		
	2019	2020	2021	2019	2020	2021	2019	2020	2021	2019	2020	2021
MSA[1]	6.3	5.5	6.4	5.8	4.8	5.9	4.0	3.6	4.6	1.1	0.6	0.7
U.S.	12.0	10.6	10.8	9.5	8.2	8.4	6.7	6.3	6.1	1.4	1.0	0.9

Note: (1) Figures cover the Los Angeles-Long Beach-Anaheim, CA Metropolitan Statistical Area; (2) The percentage of the total housing inventory that is vacant; (3) The percentage of the housing inventory (excluding seasonal units) that is year-round vacant; (4) The percentage of rental inventory that is vacant for rent; (5) The percentage of homeowner inventory that is vacant for sale
Source: U.S. Census Bureau, Housing Vacancies and Homeownership Annual Statistics: 2019, 2020, 2021

INCOME

Income

Area	Per Capita ($)	Median Household ($)	Average Household ($)
City	37,143	65,290	101,006
MSA[1]	37,452	76,399	108,889
U.S.	35,384	64,994	91,547

Note: (1) Figures cover the Los Angeles-Long Beach-Anaheim, CA Metropolitan Statistical Area
Source: U.S. Census Bureau, 2016-2020 American Community Survey 5-Year Estimates

Household Income Distribution

Area	Percent of Households Earning							
	Under $15,000	$15,000 -$24,999	$25,000 -$34,999	$35,000 -$49,999	$50,000 -$74,999	$75,000 -$99,999	$100,000 -$149,999	$150,000 and up
City	12.1	8.6	8.1	11.1	15.4	11.4	14.9	18.3
MSA[1]	9.2	7.1	7.2	10.2	15.4	12.4	17.1	21.4
U.S.	9.9	8.5	8.6	12.0	17.2	12.8	15.6	15.4

Note: (1) Figures cover the Los Angeles-Long Beach-Anaheim, CA Metropolitan Statistical Area
Source: U.S. Census Bureau, 2016-2020 American Community Survey 5-Year Estimates

Poverty Rate

Area	All Ages	Under 18 Years Old	18 to 64 Years Old	65 Years and Over
City	16.9	23.6	15.0	15.8
MSA[1]	13.2	17.9	11.8	12.2
U.S.	12.8	17.5	12.1	9.3

Note: Figures are percentage of people whose income during the past 12 months was below the poverty level; (1) Figures cover the Los Angeles-Long Beach-Anaheim, CA Metropolitan Statistical Area
Source: U.S. Census Bureau, 2016-2020 American Community Survey 5-Year Estimates

CITY FINANCES

City Government Finances

Component	2019 ($000)	2019 ($ per capita)
Total Revenues	17,886,000	4,472
Total Expenditures	16,337,968	4,085
Debt Outstanding	35,174,050	8,794
Cash and Securities[1]	9,158,261	2,290

Note: (1) Cash and security holdings of a government at the close of its fiscal year, including those of its dependent agencies, utilities, and liquor stores.
Source: U.S. Census Bureau, State & Local Government Finances 2019

City Government Revenue by Source

Source	2019 ($000)	2019 ($ per capita)	2019 (%)
General Revenue			
From Federal Government	389,827	97	2.2
From State Government	622,572	156	3.5
From Local Governments	408,951	102	2.3
Taxes			
Property	2,225,977	557	12.4
Sales and Gross Receipts	2,056,788	514	11.5
Personal Income	0	0	0.0
Corporate Income	0	0	0.0
Motor Vehicle License	0	0	0.0
Other Taxes	1,058,905	265	5.9
Current Charges	4,742,462	1,186	26.5
Liquor Store	0	0	0.0
Utility	5,078,772	1,270	28.4

Source: U.S. Census Bureau, State & Local Government Finances 2019

City Government Expenditures by Function

Function	2019 ($000)	2019 ($ per capita)	2019 (%)
General Direct Expenditures			
Air Transportation	2,110,838	527	12.9
Corrections	0	0	0.0
Education	0	0	0.0
Employment Security Administration	0	0	0.0
Financial Administration	141,999	35	0.9
Fire Protection	542,617	135	3.3
General Public Buildings	0	0	0.0
Governmental Administration, Other	176,513	44	1.1
Health	405,252	101	2.5
Highways	530,679	132	3.2
Hospitals	0	0	0.0
Housing and Community Development	208,862	52	1.3
Interest on General Debt	664,626	166	4.1
Judicial and Legal	146,756	36	0.9
Libraries	194,130	48	1.2
Parking	38,755	9	0.2
Parks and Recreation	527,729	131	3.2
Police Protection	2,366,330	591	14.5
Public Welfare	0	0	0.0
Sewerage	695,674	173	4.3
Solid Waste Management	573,128	143	3.5
Veterans' Services	0	0	0.0
Liquor Store	0	0	0.0
Utility	5,467,886	1,367	33.5

Source: U.S. Census Bureau, State & Local Government Finances 2019

EMPLOYMENT

Labor Force and Employment

Area	Civilian Labor Force			Workers Employed		
	Dec. 2020	Dec. 2021	% Chg.	Dec. 2020	Dec. 2021	% Chg.
City	1,982,385	2,049,462	3.4	1,741,791	1,919,116	10.2
MD[1]	4,894,787	4,980,229	1.7	4,354,871	4,701,381	8.0
U.S.	160,017,000	161,696,000	1.0	149,613,000	155,732,000	4.1

Note: Data is not seasonally adjusted and covers workers 16 years of age and older; (1) Figures cover the Los Angeles-Long Beach-Glendale, CA Metropolitan Division
Source: Bureau of Labor Statistics, Local Area Unemployment Statistics

Unemployment Rate

Area	2021											
	Jan.	Feb.	Mar.	Apr.	May	Jun.	Jul.	Aug.	Sep.	Oct.	Nov.	Dec.
City	12.6	10.6	10.8	11.1	10.2	10.3	10.2	9.7	8.2	7.9	7.2	6.4
MD[1]	11.2	10.7	10.4	10.3	9.5	10.0	9.6	8.9	7.6	7.1	6.2	5.6
U.S.	6.8	6.6	6.2	5.7	5.5	6.1	5.7	5.3	4.6	4.3	3.9	3.7

Note: Data is not seasonally adjusted and covers workers 16 years of age and older; (1) Figures cover the Los Angeles-Long Beach-Glendale, CA Metropolitan Division
Source: Bureau of Labor Statistics, Local Area Unemployment Statistics

Average Wages

Occupation	$/Hr.	Occupation	$/Hr.
Accountants and Auditors	43.13	Maintenance and Repair Workers	23.74
Automotive Mechanics	25.40	Marketing Managers	77.77
Bookkeepers	24.26	Network and Computer Systems Admin.	46.28
Carpenters	30.58	Nurses, Licensed Practical	30.77
Cashiers	15.34	Nurses, Registered	55.82
Computer Programmers	50.13	Nursing Assistants	18.60
Computer Systems Analysts	55.04	Office Clerks, General	21.13
Computer User Support Specialists	31.32	Physical Therapists	45.64
Construction Laborers	24.70	Physicians	113.29
Cooks, Restaurant	18.32	Plumbers, Pipefitters and Steamfitters	32.17
Customer Service Representatives	20.84	Police and Sheriff's Patrol Officers	49.72
Dentists	72.86	Postal Service Mail Carriers	27.29
Electricians	34.83	Real Estate Sales Agents	35.97
Engineers, Electrical	59.67	Retail Salespersons	17.29
Fast Food and Counter Workers	15.33	Sales Representatives, Technical/Scientific	46.52
Financial Managers	77.35	Secretaries, Exc. Legal/Medical/Executive	22.40
First-Line Supervisors of Office Workers	33.40	Security Guards	17.75
General and Operations Managers	63.48	Surgeons	n/a
Hairdressers/Cosmetologists	20.20	Teacher Assistants, Exc. Postsecondary*	19.48
Home Health and Personal Care Aides	15.02	Teachers, Secondary School, Exc. Sp. Ed.*	46.47
Janitors and Cleaners	17.58	Telemarketers	16.92
Landscaping/Groundskeeping Workers	18.89	Truck Drivers, Heavy/Tractor-Trailer	24.61
Lawyers	85.36	Truck Drivers, Light/Delivery Services	21.93
Maids and Housekeeping Cleaners	17.03	Waiters and Waitresses	17.49

Note: Wage data covers the Los Angeles-Long Beach-Anaheim, CA Metropolitan Statistical Area; (*) Hourly wages were calculated from annual wage data based on a 40 hour work week; n/a not available.
Source: Bureau of Labor Statistics, Metro Area Occupational Employment & Wage Estimates, May 2021

Employment by Industry

Sector	MD[1]		U.S.
	Number of Employees	Percent of Total	Percent of Total
Construction	153,600	3.4	5.0
Education and Health Services	862,300	19.3	16.0
Financial Activities	211,500	4.7	5.9
Government	570,200	12.7	14.9
Information	227,800	5.1	1.9
Leisure and Hospitality	475,100	10.6	9.8
Manufacturing	314,500	7.0	8.4
Mining and Logging	1,600	<0.1	0.4
Other Services	145,000	3.2	3.7
Professional and Business Services	660,000	14.7	14.6
Retail Trade	425,000	9.5	10.7
Transportation, Warehousing, and Utilities	227,400	5.1	4.8
Wholesale Trade	205,300	4.6	3.8

Note: Figures are non-farm employment as of December 2021. Figures are not seasonally adjusted and include workers 16 years of age and older; (1) Figures cover the Los Angeles-Long Beach-Glendale, CA Metropolitan Division
Source: Bureau of Labor Statistics, Current Employment Statistics, Employment, Hours, and Earnings

Employment by Occupation

Occupation Classification	City (%)	MSA[1] (%)	U.S. (%)
Management, Business, Science, and Arts	40.1	39.9	39.5
Natural Resources, Construction, and Maintenance	7.4	7.2	8.7
Production, Transportation, and Material Moving	12.0	12.6	13.1
Sales and Office	20.4	22.1	21.3
Service	20.2	18.2	17.4

Note: Figures cover employed civilians 16 years of age and older; (1) Figures cover the Los Angeles-Long Beach-Anaheim, CA Metropolitan Statistical Area
Source: U.S. Census Bureau, 2016-2020 American Community Survey 5-Year Estimates

Occupations with Greatest Projected Employment Growth: 2021 – 2023

Occupation[1]	2021 Employment	2023 Projected Employment	Numeric Employment Change	Percent Employment Change
Fast Food and Counter Workers	383,500	457,000	73,500	19.2
Home Health and Personal Care Aides	663,400	716,600	53,200	8.0
Waiters and Waitresses	208,500	257,600	49,100	23.5
Cooks, Restaurant	136,700	175,300	38,600	28.2
Laborers and Freight, Stock, and Material Movers, Hand	401,500	431,600	30,100	7.5
Software Developers and Software Quality Assurance Analysts and Testers	311,600	336,800	25,200	8.1
Janitors and Cleaners, Except Maids and Housekeeping Cleaners	232,200	252,400	20,200	8.7
Cooks, Fast Food	109,600	128,200	18,600	17.0
Stockers and Order Fillers	273,000	290,400	17,400	6.4
First-Line Supervisors of Food Preparation and Serving Workers	81,700	98,600	16,900	20.7

Note: Projections cover California; (1) Sorted by numeric employment change
Source: www.projectionscentral.com, State Occupational Projections, 2021–2023 Short-Term Projections

Fastest-Growing Occupations: 2021 – 2023

Occupation[1]	2021 Employment	2023 Projected Employment	Numeric Employment Change	Percent Employment Change
Manicurists and Pedicurists	23,400	33,500	10,100	43.2
Cooks, All Other	3,900	5,400	1,500	38.5
Miscellaneous Entertainers and Performers, Sports and Related Workers	5,900	8,100	2,200	37.3
Barbers	1,900	2,600	700	36.8
Gaming Change Persons and Booth Cashiers	2,200	3,000	800	36.4
Gaming Service Workers, All Other	1,400	1,900	500	35.7
Gaming Dealers	12,200	16,500	4,300	35.2
First-Line Supervisors of Gambling Services Workers	2,900	3,900	1,000	34.5
Massage Therapists	18,000	24,200	6,200	34.4
Costume Attendants	1,500	2,000	500	33.3

Note: Projections cover California; (1) Sorted by percent employment change and excludes occupations with numeric employment change less than 50
Source: www.projectionscentral.com, State Occupational Projections, 2021–2023 Short-Term Projections

TAXES

State Corporate Income Tax Rates

State	Tax Rate (%)	Income Brackets ($)	Num. of Brackets	Financial Institution Tax Rate (%)[a]	Federal Income Tax Ded.
California	8.84 (b)	Flat rate	1	10.84 (b)	No

Note: Tax rates as of January 1, 2022; (a) Rates listed are the corporate income tax rate applied to financial institutions or excise taxes based on income. Some states have other taxes based upon the value of deposits or shares; (b) Minimum tax is $800 in California, $250 in District of Columbia, $50 in Arizona and North Dakota (banks), $400 ($100 banks) in Rhode Island, $200 per location in South Dakota (banks), $100 in Utah, $300 in Vermont.
Source: Federation of Tax Administrators, State Corporate Income Tax Rates, January 1, 2022

State Individual Income Tax Rates

State	Tax Rate (%)	Income Brackets ($)	Personal Exemptions ($)			Standard Ded. ($)	
			Single	Married	Depend.	Single	Married
California (a)	1.0 - 12.3 (g)	9,325 - 625,369 (b)	129	258	400 (c)	4,803	9,606 (a)

Note: Tax rates as of January 1, 2022; Local- and county-level taxes are not included; Federal income tax is not deductible on state income tax returns; (a) 19 states have statutory provision for automatically adjusting to the rate of inflation the dollar values of the income tax brackets, standard deductions, and/or personal exemptions. Michigan indexes the personal exemption only. Oregon does not index the income brackets for $125,000 and over; (b) For joint returns, taxes are twice the tax on half the couple's income; (c) The personal exemption takes the form of a tax credit instead of a deduction; (g) California imposes an additional 1% tax on taxable income over $1 million, making the maximum rate 13.3% over $1 million.
Source: Federation of Tax Administrators, State Individual Income Tax Rates, January 1, 2022

Various State Sales and Excise Tax Rates

State	State Sales Tax (%)	Gasoline[1] (¢/gal.)	Cigarette[2] ($/pack)	Spirits[3] ($/gal.)	Wine[4] ($/gal.)	Beer[5] ($/gal.)	Recreational Marijuana (%)
California	7.25	68.15	2.87	3.3	0.2	0.2	(c)

Note: All tax rates as of January 1, 2022; (1) The American Petroleum Institute has developed a methodology for determining the average tax rate on a gallon of fuel. Rates may include any of the following: excise taxes, environmental fees, storage tank fees, other fees or taxes, general sales tax, and local taxes; (2) The federal excise tax of $1.0066 per pack and local taxes are not included; (3) Rates are those applicable to off-premise sales of 40% alcohol by volume (a.b.v.) distilled spirits in 750ml containers. Local excise taxes are excluded; (4) Rates are those applicable to off-premise sales of 11% a.b.v. non-carbonated wine in 750ml containers; (5) Rates are those applicable to off-premise sales of 4.7% a.b.v. beer in 12 ounce containers; (c) 15% excise tax (levied on wholesale at average market rate); $10.08/oz. flowers & $3/oz. leaves cultivation tax; $1.41/oz fresh cannabis plant
Source: Tax Foundation, 2022 Facts & Figures: How Does Your State Compare?

State Business Tax Climate Index Rankings

State	Overall Rank	Corporate Tax Rank	Individual Income Tax Rank	Sales Tax Rank	Property Tax Rank	Unemployment Insurance Tax Rank
California	48	46	49	47	14	23

Note: The index is a measure of how each state's tax laws affect economic performance. The lower the rank, the more favorable a state's tax system is for business. States without a given tax are given a ranking of 1. The scores/rankings for the District of Columbia do not affect other states. The 2022 index represents the tax climate as of July 1, 2021.
Source: Tax Foundation, State Business Tax Climate Index 2022

TRANSPORTATION

Means of Transportation to Work

Area	Car/Truck/Van		Public Transportation			Bicycle	Walked	Other Means	Worked at Home
	Drove Alone	Car-pooled	Bus	Subway	Railroad				
City	67.7	8.9	7.1	0.9	0.1	0.8	3.3	2.0	9.2
MSA[1]	73.1	9.5	3.7	0.4	0.2	0.6	2.4	1.7	8.3
U.S.	74.9	8.9	2.2	1.7	0.5	0.5	2.6	1.4	7.3

Note: Figures are percentages and cover workers 16 years of age and older; (1) Figures cover the Los Angeles-Long Beach-Anaheim, CA Metropolitan Statistical Area
Source: U.S. Census Bureau, 2016-2020 American Community Survey 5-Year Estimates

Travel Time to Work

Area	Less Than 10 Minutes	10 to 19 Minutes	20 to 29 Minutes	30 to 44 Minutes	45 to 59 Minutes	60 to 89 Minutes	90 Minutes or More
City	5.8	21.8	19.2	28.3	10.8	10.3	3.8
MSA[1]	7.0	24.5	19.6	25.4	10.2	9.6	3.7
U.S.	12.3	28.4	20.9	20.9	8.3	6.4	2.9

Note: Note: Figures are percentages and include workers 16 years old and over; (1) Figures cover the Los Angeles-Long Beach-Anaheim, CA Metropolitan Statistical Area
Source: U.S. Census Bureau, 2016-2020 American Community Survey 5-Year Estimates

Key Congestion Measures

Measure	1990	2000	2010	2015	2020
Annual Hours of Delay, Total (000)	472,274	673,878	812,204	924,196	365,543
Annual Hours of Delay, Per Auto Commuter	70	84	97	113	46
Annual Congestion Cost, Per Auto Commuter ($)	2,423	2,596	2,487	2,688	1,142

Note: Covers the Los Angeles-Long Beach-Anaheim CA urban area
Source: Texas A&M Transportation Institute, 2021 Urban Mobility Report

Freeway Travel Time Index

Measure	1985	1990	1995	2000	2005	2010	2015	2020
Urban Area Index[1]	1.31	1.34	1.38	1.41	1.45	1.45	1.49	1.16
Urban Area Rank[1,2]	1	1	1	1	1	1	1	2

Note: Freeway Travel Time Index—the ratio of travel time in the peak period to the travel time at free-flow conditions. For example, a value of 1.30 indicates a 20-minute free-flow trip takes 26 minutes in the peak (20 minutes x 1.30 = 26 minutes); (1) Covers the Los Angeles-Long Beach-Anaheim CA urban area; (2) Rank is based on 101 larger urban areas (#1 = highest travel time index)
Source: Texas A&M Transportation Institute, 2021 Urban Mobility Report

Public Transportation

Agency Name / Mode of Transportation	Vehicles Operated in Maximum Service[1]	Annual Unlinked Passenger Trips[2] (in thous.)	Annual Passenger Miles[3] (in thous.)
Los Angeles Co. Metro Transportation Authority (LACMTA)			
Bus (directly operated)	1,784	211,875.3	844,757.7
Bus (purchased transportation)	134	10,303.6	46,736.3
Bus Rapid Transit (directly operated)	26	5,398.5	33,978.7
Heavy Rail (directly operated)	68	33,668.3	162,927.5
Light Rail (directly operated)	203	42,098.3	318,737.7
Vanpool (purchased transportation)	1,267	2,563.2	116,497.4
City of Los Angeles Department of Transportation (LADOT)			
Bus (purchased transportation)	169	12,899.6	22,828.1
Commuter Bus (purchased transportation)	91	1,109.8	18,358.1
Demand Response (purchased transportation)	93	171.1	939.4
Demand Response - Taxi	9	90.3	204.9

Note: (1) Number of revenue vehicles operated by the given mode and type of service to meet the annual maximum service requirement. This is the revenue vehicle count during the peak season of the year; on the week and day that maximum service is provided. Vehicles operated in maximum service (VOMS) exclude atypical days and one-time special events; (2) Number of passengers who boarded public transportation vehicles. Passengers are counted each time they board a vehicle no matter how many vehicles they use to travel from their origin to their destination. (3) Sum of the distances ridden by all passengers during the entire fiscal year.
Source: Federal Transit Administration, National Transit Database, 2020

Air Transportation

Airport Name and Code / Type of Service	Passenger Airlines[1]	Passenger Enplanements	Freight Carriers[2]	Freight (lbs)
Los Angeles International (LAX)				
Domestic service (U.S. carriers - 2021)	25	20,184,764	23	1,038,237,271
International service (U.S. carriers - 2020)	13	826,240	12	256,517,595

Note: (1) Includes all U.S.-based major, minor and commuter airlines that carried at least one passenger during the year; (2) Includes all U.S.-based airlines and freight carriers that transported at least one pound of freight during the year.
Source: Bureau of Transportation Statistics, The Intermodal Transportation Database, Air Carriers: T-100 Domestic Market (U.S. Carriers), 2021; Bureau of Transportation Statistics, The Intermodal Transportation Database, Air Carriers: T-100 International Market (U.S. Carriers), 2020

BUSINESSES

Major Business Headquarters

Company Name	Industry	Rankings	
		Fortune[1]	Forbes[2]
AECOM	Engineering, Construction	189	-
CBRE Group	Real Estate	122	-
Capital Group Companies	Diversified Financials	-	49
Gibson, Dunn & Crutcher	Services	-	211
Reliance Steel & Aluminum	Metals	343	-
The Wonderful Company	Multicompany	-	96

Note: (1) Companies that produce a 10-K are ranked 1 to 500 based on 2020 revenue; (2) All private companies with at least $2 billion in annual revenue through the end of their most current fiscal year are ranked 1 to 225; companies listed are headquartered in the city; dashes indicate no ranking
Source: Fortune, "Fortune 500," 2021; Forbes, "America's Largest Private Companies," 2021

Fastest-Growing Businesses

According to *Inc.*, Los Angeles is home to 11 of America's 500 fastest-growing private companies: **Dave** (#5); **Your Super** (#25); **Alpine Solutions Group** (#115); **Caulipower** (#260); **Yedi Houseware Appliances** (#309); **Resecurity** (#317); **sourceM** (#322); **AvantStay** (#332); **Vital Pet Life** (#348); **Kitsch** (#370); **YENSA beauty** (#443). Criteria: must be an independent, privately-held, for-profit, U.S. corporation, proprietorship or partnership as of December 31, 2020; revenues must be at least $100,000 in 2017 and $2 million in 2020; must have four-year operating/sales history. *Inc., "America's 500 Fastest-Growing Private Companies," 2021*

According to *Fortune*, Los Angeles is home to one of the 100 fastest-growing companies in the world: **B. Riley Financial** (#2). Companies were ranked by their revenue growth rate; their EPS growth rate; and their three-year annualized total return to investors for the period ending June 30, 2021. Criteria for inclusion: a company, foreign or domestic, must trade on a major U.S. stock exchange; must file quarterly reports with the SEC; must have a minimum market capitalization of $250 million; must have a stock price of at least $5 on June 30, 2021; must have been trading continuously since June 30, 2018; must have revenue and net income for the four quarters ended on or before April 30, 2021, of at least $50 million and $10 million, respectively; and must have posted a compound annual growth in revenue and earnings per share of at least 15% annually over the three years ending on or before April 30, 2021. Real estate investment trusts, limited-liability companies, limited parterships, business development companies, closed-end investment firms, companies about to be acquired, and companies that lost money in the quarter ending April 30, 2021 were excluded. *Fortune, "100 Fastest-Growing Companies," 2021*

According to *Initiative for a Competitive Inner City (ICIC)*, Los Angeles is home to two of America's 100 fastest-growing "inner city" companies: **City Design Studio** (#24); **Giroux Glass** (#85). Criteria for inclusion: company must be headquartered in or have 51 percent or more of its physical operations in an economically distressed urban area; must be an independent, for-profit corporation, partnership or proprietorship; must have 10 or more employees and have a five-year sales history that includes sales of at least $200,000 in the base year and at least $1 million in the current year with no decrease in sales over the two most recent years. Companies were ranked overall by revenue growth over the five-year period between 2016 and 2020. *Initiative for a Competitive Inner City (ICIC), "Inner City 100 Companies," 2021*

According to Deloitte, Los Angeles is home to five of North America's 500 fastest-growing high-technology companies: **Therabody** (#61); **HAAWK** (#100); **14th Round** (#130); **Puma Biotechnology** (#193); **FloQast** (#229). Companies are ranked by percentage growth in revenue over a four-year period. Criteria for inclusion: company must be headquartered within North America; must own proprietary intellectual property or technology that is sold to customers in products that contributes to a significant portion of the company's operating revenue; must have been in business for a minumum of four years with 2017 operating revenues of at least $50,000 USD/CD and 2020 operating revenues of at least $5 million USD/CD. *Deloitte, 2021 Technology Fast 500™*

Living Environment

COST OF LIVING

Cost of Living Index

Composite Index	Groceries	Housing	Utilities	Trans-portation	Health Care	Misc. Goods/ Services
149.4	112.7	228.5	106.9	127.3	110.6	114.5

Note: The Cost of Living Index measures regional differences in the cost of consumer goods and services, excluding taxes and non-consumer expenditures, for professional and managerial households in the top income quintile. It is based on more than 50,000 prices covering almost 60 different items for which prices are collected three times a year by chambers of commerce, economic development organizations or university applied economic centers in each participating urban area. The numbers shown should be read as a percentage above or below the national average of 100. For example, a value of 115.4 in the groceries column indicates that grocery prices are 15.4% higher than the national average. Small differences in the index numbers should not be interpreted as significant; Figures cover the Los Angeles-Long Beach CA urban area.
Source: The Council for Community and Economic Research, Cost of Living Index, 2021

Grocery Prices

Area[1]	T-Bone Steak ($/pound)	Frying Chicken ($/pound)	Whole Milk ($/half gal.)	Eggs ($/dozen)	Orange Juice ($/64 oz.)	Coffee ($/11.5 oz.)
City[2]	12.66	1.79	2.30	2.95	3.76	5.47
Avg.	12.82	1.40	2.22	1.57	3.59	4.30
Min.	8.91	0.91	1.29	0.75	2.87	3.02
Max.	21.35	2.69	3.92	3.86	5.49	8.11

*Note: (1) Values for the local area are compared with the average, minimum and maximum values for all 285 areas in the Cost of Living Index; (2) Figures cover the Los Angeles-Long Beach CA urban area; **T-Bone Steak** (price per pound); **Frying Chicken** (price per pound, whole fryer); **Whole Milk** (half gallon carton); **Eggs** (price per dozen, Grade A, large); **Orange Juice** (64 oz. Tropicana or Florida Natural); **Coffee** (11.5 oz. can, vacuum-packed, Maxwell House, Hills Bros, or Folgers).*
Source: The Council for Community and Economic Research, Cost of Living Index, 2021

Housing and Utility Costs

Area[1]	New Home Price ($)	Apartment Rent ($/month)	All Electric ($/month)	Part Electric ($/month)	Other Energy ($/month)	Telephone ($/month)
City[2]	917,683	2,770	-	120.13	71.51	187.64
Avg.	398,393	1,217	171.38	100.83	69.67	187.75
Min.	212,799	534	96.71	31.56	27.15	173.01
Max.	2,354,006	4,438	369.53	277.33	303.87	206.73

*Note: (1) Values for the local area are compared with the average, minimum and maximum values for all 285 areas in the Cost of Living Index; (2) Figures cover the Los Angeles-Long Beach CA urban area; **New Home Price** (2,400 sf living area, 8,000 sf lot, in urban area with full utilities); **Apartment Rent** (950 sf 2 bedroom/1.5 or 2 bath, unfurnished, excluding all utilities except water); **All Electric** (average monthly cost for an all-electric home); **Part Electric** (average monthly cost for a part-electric home); **Other Energy** (average monthly cost for natural gas, fuel oil, coal, wood, and any other forms of energy except electricity); **Telephone** (price includes the base monthly rate plus taxes and fees for three lines of mobile phone service).*
Source: The Council for Community and Economic Research, Cost of Living Index, 2021

Health Care, Transportation, and Other Costs

Area[1]	Doctor ($/visit)	Dentist ($/visit)	Optometrist ($/visit)	Gasoline ($/gallon)	Beauty Salon ($/visit)	Men's Shirt ($)
City[2]	126.33	115.69	123.18	3.91	85.33	32.77
Avg.	118.16	101.04	109.44	2.71	40.63	30.77
Min.	35.04	55.56	51.17	2.17	18.59	11.32
Max.	231.10	165.12	256.81	4.11	85.33	63.03

*Note: (1) Values for the local area are compared with the average, minimum and maximum values for all 285 areas in the Cost of Living Index; (2) Figures cover the Los Angeles-Long Beach CA urban area; **Doctor** (general practitioners routine exam of an established patient); **Dentist** (adult teeth cleaning and periodic oral examination); **Optometrist** (full vision eye exam for established adult patient); **Gasoline** (one gallon regular unleaded, national brand, including all taxes, cash price at self-service pump if available); **Beauty Salon** (woman's shampoo, trim, and blow-dry); **Men's Shirt** (cotton/polyester dress shirt, pinpoint weave, long sleeves).*
Source: The Council for Community and Economic Research, Cost of Living Index, 2021

HOUSING

Homeownership Rate

Area	2013 (%)	2014 (%)	2015 (%)	2016 (%)	2017 (%)	2018 (%)	2019 (%)	2020 (%)	2021 (%)
MSA[1]	48.7	49.0	49.1	47.1	49.1	49.5	48.2	48.5	47.9
U.S.	65.1	64.5	63.7	63.4	63.9	64.4	64.6	66.6	65.5

Note: (1) Figures cover the Los Angeles-Long Beach-Anaheim, CA Metropolitan Statistical Area
Source: U.S. Census Bureau, Housing Vacancies and Homeownership Annual Statistics: 2013-2021

House Price Index (HPI)

Area	National Ranking[2]	Quarterly Change (%)	One-Year Change (%)	Five-Year Change (%)	Since 1991Q1 (%)
MD[1]	141	3.58	17.03	43.63	266.91
U.S.[3]	–	3.33	17.54	54.45	258.04

Note: The HPI is a weighted repeat sales index. It measures average price changes in repeat sales or refinancings on the same properties. This information is obtained by reviewing repeat mortgage transactions on single-family properties whose mortgages have been purchased or securitized by Fannie Mae or Freddie Mac since January 1975; (1) Figures cover the Los Angeles-Long Beach-Glendale, CA Metropolitan Division; (2) Rankings are based on annual percentage change for all metro areas containing at least 15,000 transactions over the last 10 years and ranges from 1 to 268; (3) figures based on a weighted average of Census Division estimates using a seasonally adjusted, purchase-only index; all figures are for the period ending December 31, 2021

Source: Federal Housing Finance Agency, Change in FHFA Metropolitan Area House Price Indexes, 2021Q4

Median Single-Family Home Prices

Area	2019	2020	2021p	Percent Change 2020 to 2021
MD[1]	611.2	673.1	801.3	19.0
U.S. Average	274.6	300.2	353.4	17.7

Note: Figures are median sales prices of existing single-family homes in thousands of dollars; (p) preliminary; (1) Figures cover the Los Angeles-Long Beach-Glendale, CA Metropolitan Division

Source: National Association of Realtors, Median Sales Price of Existing Single-Family Homes for Metropolitan Areas, 4th Quarter 2021

Qualifying Income Based on Median Sales Price of Existing Single-Family Homes

Area	With 5% Down ($)	With 10% Down ($)	With 20% Down ($)
MD[1]	157,302	149,023	132,465
U.S. Average	70,699	66,978	59,536

Note: Figures are preliminary; Qualifying income is based on a mortgage rate of 3.13%. Monthly principal and interest payment is limited to 25% of income; (1) Figures cover the Los Angeles-Long Beach-Glendale, CA Metropolitan Division

Source: National Association of Realtors, Qualifying Income Based on Median Sales Price of Existing Single-Family Homes for Metropolitan Areas, 4th Quarter 2021

Home Value Distribution

Area	Under $50,000	$50,000 -$99,999	$100,000 -$149,999	$150,000 -$199,999	$200,000 -$299,999	$300,000 -$499,999	$500,000 -$999,999	$1,000,000 or more
City	1.2	0.9	0.6	0.6	3.3	21.6	47.6	24.2
MSA[1]	1.8	1.4	0.9	1.0	3.9	22.2	50.3	18.5
U.S.	6.6	11.0	12.3	13.6	20.0	20.5	12.3	3.7

Note: Figures are percentages and cover owner-occupied housing units; (1) Figures cover the Los Angeles-Long Beach-Anaheim, CA Metropolitan Statistical Area

Source: U.S. Census Bureau, 2016-2020 American Community Survey 5-Year Estimates

Year Housing Structure Built

Area	2010 or Later	2000 -2009	1990 -1999	1980 -1989	1970 -1979	1960 -1969	1950 -1959	1940 -1949	Before 1940	Median Year
City	4.0	5.4	6.0	10.6	13.7	13.9	17.1	9.5	19.8	1963
MSA[1]	3.6	5.9	7.7	12.4	16.1	15.8	18.5	8.2	11.8	1967
U.S.	6.2	13.6	13.9	13.4	15.0	10.5	10.2	4.8	12.4	1978

Note: Figures are percentages except for Median Year; Note: (1) Figures cover the Los Angeles-Long Beach-Anaheim, CA Metropolitan Statistical Area

Source: U.S. Census Bureau, 2016-2020 American Community Survey 5-Year Estimates

Gross Monthly Rent

Area	Under $500	$500 -$999	$1,000 -$1,499	$1,500 -$1,999	$2,000 -$2,499	$2,500 -$2,999	$3,000 and up	Median ($)
City	5.2	13.8	30.0	23.6	13.4	7.0	7.1	1,523
MSA[1]	4.1	11.0	28.3	26.3	15.4	7.6	7.3	1,624
U.S.	8.9	34.3	30.2	14.9	6.2	2.6	2.8	1,096

Note: Figures are percentages except for Median; Gross rent is the contract rent plus the estimated average monthly cost of utilities (electricity, gas, and water and sewer) and fuels (oil, coal, kerosene, wood, etc.) if these are paid by the renter (or paid for the renter by someone else); (1) Figures cover the Los Angeles-Long Beach-Anaheim, CA Metropolitan Statistical Area

Source: U.S. Census Bureau, 2016-2020 American Community Survey 5-Year Estimates

HEALTH

Health Risk Factors

Category	MSA[1] (%)	U.S. (%)
Adults aged 18–64 who have any kind of health care coverage	85.9	86.8
Adults who reported being in good or better health	85.1	86.7
Adults who are current smokers	9.4	15.5
Adults who currently use chewing tobacco, snuff, or snus	1.6	3.7
Adults who are heavy drinkers[2]	5.3	6.7
Adults who are binge drinkers[3]	14.8	15.7
Adults who are overweight (BMI 25.0 - 29.9)	32.4	35.2
Adults who are obese (BMI 30.0 - 99.8)	29.8	31.9
Adults who participated in any physical activities in the past month	78.0	77.6
Adults who always or nearly always wears a seat belt	97.3	94.2

Note: (1) Figures cover the Los Angeles-Long Beach-Anaheim, CA Metropolitan Statistical Area; (2) Heavy drinkers are classified as adult men having more than 14 drinks per week and adult women having more than 7 drinks per week; (3) Binge drinkers are classified as males having five or more drinks on one occasion or females having four or more drinks on one occasion
Source: Centers for Disease Control and Prevention, Behaviorial Risk Factor Surveillance System, SMART: Selected Metropolitan Area Risk Trends, 2020

Acute and Chronic Health Conditions

Category	MSA[1] (%)	U.S. (%)
Adults who have ever been told they had a heart attack	3.0	4.3
Adults who have ever been told they have angina or coronary heart disease	3.8	4.0
Adults who have ever been told they had a stroke	n/a	2.8
Adults who have ever been told they have asthma	14.0	14.2
Adults who have ever been told they have arthritis	16.7	24.5
Adults who have ever been told they have diabetes[2]	9.2	10.6
Adults who have ever been told they had skin cancer	5.0	6.4
Adults who have ever been told they had any other types of cancer	5.8	6.8
Adults who have ever been told they have COPD	6.8	6.2
Adults who have ever been told they have kidney disease	2.8	2.9
Adults who have ever been told they have a form of depression	13.2	19.6

Note: (1) Figures cover the Los Angeles-Long Beach-Anaheim, CA Metropolitan Statistical Area; (2) Figures do not include pregnancy-related, borderline, or pre-diabetes
Source: Centers for Disease Control and Prevention, Behaviorial Risk Factor Surveillance System, SMART: Selected Metropolitan Area Risk Trends, 2020

Health Screening and Vaccination Rates

Category	MSA[1] (%)	U.S. (%)
Adults 50-75 who have had a blood stool test within the past year	15.6	9.3
Adults aged 65+ who have had flu shot within the past year	69.2	67.9
Adults aged 65+ who have ever had a pneumonia vaccination	67.3	72.2
Adults who have ever been tested for HIV	42.3	37.1
Women aged 21-65 who have had a pap test in the past three years	82.0	77.7
Men aged 40+ who have had a PSA test within the past two years	25.6	31.8
Women aged 40+ who have had a mammogram within the past two years	66.3	71.5

Note: (1) Figures cover the Los Angeles-Long Beach-Anaheim, CA Metropolitan Statistical Area.
Source: Centers for Disease Control and Prevention, Behaviorial Risk Factor Surveillance System, SMART: Selected Metropolitan Area Risk Trends, 2020

Disability Status

Category	MSA[1] (%)	U.S. (%)
Adults who reported being deaf	4.4	6.8
Are you blind or have serious difficulty seeing, even when wearing glasses?	6.0	4.7
Do you have difficulty doing errands alone?	6.6	6.3
Do you have difficulty dressing or bathing?	3.2	3.0
Do you have serious difficulty concentrating/remembering/making decisions?	10.7	10.8
Do you have serious difficulty walking or climbing stairs?	10.9	11.9

Note: (1) Figures cover the Los Angeles-Long Beach-Anaheim, CA Metropolitan Statistical Area.
Source: Centers for Disease Control and Prevention, Behaviorial Risk Factor Surveillance System, SMART: Selected Metropolitan Area Risk Trends, 2020

Mortality Rates for the Top 10 Causes of Death in the U.S.

ICD-10[a] Sub-Chapter	ICD-10[a] Code	Age-Adjusted Mortality Rate[1] per 100,000 population	
		County[2]	U.S.
Malignant neoplasms	C00-C97	130.7	146.4
Ischaemic heart diseases	I20-I25	101.0	90.2
Other forms of heart disease	I30-I51	33.8	51.9
Other degenerative diseases of the nervous system	G30-G31	41.7	39.7
Other external causes of accidental injury	W00-X59	20.5	38.7
Chronic lower respiratory diseases	J40-J47	26.6	38.1
Cerebrovascular diseases	I60-I69	34.3	37.6
Organic, including symptomatic, mental disorders	F01-F09	10.2	29.4
Hypertensive diseases	I10-I15	27.4	26.1
Diabetes mellitus	E10-E14	27.4	22.6

Note: (a) ICD-10 = International Classification of Diseases 10th Revision; (1) Mortality rates are a three-year average covering 2018-2020; (2) Figures cover Los Angeles County.
Source: Centers for Disease Control and Prevention, National Center for Health Statistics. Underlying Cause of Death 1999-2020 on CDC WONDER Online Database

Mortality Rates for Selected Causes of Death

ICD-10[a] Sub-Chapter	ICD-10[a] Code	Age-Adjusted Mortality Rate[1] per 100,000 population	
		County[2]	U.S.
Assault	X85-Y09	5.8	6.5
Diseases of the liver	K70-K76	15.0	15.3
Human immunodeficiency virus (HIV) disease	B20-B24	1.9	1.4
Influenza and pneumonia	J09-J18	18.1	13.4
Intentional self-harm	X60-X84	8.3	13.9
Malnutrition	E40-E46	1.0	2.9
Obesity and other hyperalimentation	E65-E68	2.0	2.4
Renal failure	N17-N19	12.3	12.5
Transport accidents	V01-V99	9.0	12.5
Viral hepatitis	B15-B19	1.2	1.0

Note: (a) ICD-10 = International Classification of Diseases 10th Revision; (1) Mortality rates are a three-year average covering 2018-2020; (2) Figures cover Los Angeles County; Data are suppressed when the data meet the criteria for confidentiality constraints; Mortality rates are flagged as unreliable when the rate would be calculated with a numerator of 20 or less.
Source: Centers for Disease Control and Prevention, National Center for Health Statistics. Underlying Cause of Death 1999-2020 on CDC WONDER Online Database

Health Insurance Coverage

Area	With Health Insurance	With Private Health Insurance	With Public Health Insurance	Without Health Insurance	Population Under Age 19 Without Health Insurance
City	89.3	55.2	40.7	10.7	3.8
MSA[1]	91.3	61.1	37.6	8.7	3.6
U.S.	91.3	68.1	35.3	8.7	5.2

Note: Figures are percentages that cover the civilian noninstitutionalized population; (1) Figures cover the Los Angeles-Long Beach-Anaheim, CA Metropolitan Statistical Area
Source: U.S. Census Bureau, 2016-2020 American Community Survey 5-Year Estimates

Number of Medical Professionals

Area	MDs[3]	DOs[3,4]	Dentists	Podiatrists	Chiropractors	Optometrists
County[1] (number)	30,911	1,421	9,060	640	2,991	1,895
County[1] (rate[2])	308.7	14.2	90.5	6.4	29.9	18.9
U.S. (rate[2])	285.1	23.0	71.1	6.2	28.2	17.0

06037
Note: Data as of 2020 unless noted; (1) Data covers Los Angeles County; (2) Rate per 100,000 population; (3) Data as of 2019 and includes all active, non-federal physicians; (4) Doctor of Osteopathic Medicine
Source: U.S. Department of Health and Human Services, Health Resources and Services Administration, Bureau of Health Professions, Area Resource File (ARF) 2020-2021

Best Hospitals

According to *U.S. News,* the Los Angeles-Long Beach-Glendale, CA metro area is home to 11 of the best hospitals in the U.S.: **Cedars-Sinai Medical Center** (Honor Roll/11 adult specialties); **City of Hope Comprehensive Cancer Center** (1 adult specialty); **Huntington Hospital** (1 adult specialty); **Keck Medical Center of USC** (12 adult specialties); **MemorialCare Long Beach Medical Center** (1 adult specialty); **Providence Saint John's Health Center** (1 adult specialty); **Resnick Neuropsychiatric Hospital at UCLA** (1 adult specialty); **Santa Monica-UCLA Medical Center and Orthopedic Hospital** (1 adult specialty); **UCLA Medical Center** (Honor Roll/14 adult specialties and 6 pediatric specialties); **USC Norris Cancer Hospital-Keck Medical Center of USC** (1 adult specialty); **USC Roski Eye Institute** (12 adult specialties). The hospitals listed were nationally ranked in at least one of 15 adult or 10 pediatric specialties. Only 175 U.S. hospitals performed well enough to be nationally ranked in one or more specialties. Twenty hospitals in the U.S. made the Honor Roll. The Best Hospitals Honor Roll takes both the national rankings and the procedure and condition ratings into account. Hospitals received points if they were nationally ranked in one of the 15 adult specialties—the higher they ranked, the more points they got—and how many ratings of "high performing" they earned in the 17 procedures and conditions. *U.S. News Online, "America's Best Hospitals 2021-22"*

According to *U.S. News,* the Los Angeles-Long Beach-Glendale, CA metro area is home to three of the best children's hospitals in the U.S.: **Children's Hospital Los Angeles** (Honor Roll/10 pediatric specialties); **MemorialCare Miller Children's and Women's Hospital Long Beach** (1 pediatric specialty); **UCLA Mattel Children's Hospital** (6 pediatric specialties). The hospitals listed were highly ranked in at least one of 10 pediatric specialties. Ninety-two children's hospitals in the U.S. were nationally ranked in at least one specialty. Hospitals received points for being ranked in a specialty, and the 10 hospitals with the most points across the 10 specialties make up the Honor Roll. *U.S. News Online, "America's Best Children's Hospitals 2021-22"*

EDUCATION

Public School District Statistics

District Name	Schls	Pupils	Pupil/ Teacher Ratio	Minority Pupils[1] (%)	LEP/ELL[2] (%)	IEP[3] (%)
Los Angeles Unified	785	483,234	n/a	89.4	21.1	16.1

Note: Table includes school districts with 2,000 or more students; (1) Percentage of students that are not non-Hispanic white; (2) Percentage of students that are Limited English Proficient (LEP) or English Language Learners (ELL) (2018-19); (3) Percentage of students that have an Individualized Education Program (IEP).
Source: U.S. Department of Education, National Center for Education Statistics, Common Core of Data, Local Education Agency (School District) Universe Survey: School Year 2019-2020

Best High Schools

According to *U.S. News,* Los Angeles is home to seven of the top 500 high schools in the U.S.: **Harbor Teacher Preparation Academy** (#84); **Los Angeles Center for Enriched Studies** (#190); **Downtown Business High** (#226); **Alliance Ted K. Tajima High School** (#272); **Francisco Bravo Medical Magnet High** (#335); **Alliance Gertz-Ressler Richard Merkin 6-12 Complex** (#359); **Alliance Marc and Eva Stern Math and Science** (#397). Nearly 18,000 public, magnet and charter schools were ranked based on their performance on state assessments and how well they prepare students for college. *U.S. News & World Report, "Best High Schools 2021"*

Highest Level of Education

Area	Less than H.S.	H.S. Diploma	Some College, No Deg.	Associate Degree	Bachelor's Degree	Master's Degree	Prof. School Degree	Doctorate Degree
City	21.7	18.8	17.5	6.3	23.3	7.9	3.0	1.4
MSA[1]	18.7	19.6	19.1	7.2	22.9	8.4	2.6	1.4
U.S.	11.5	26.7	20.3	8.6	20.2	9.1	2.2	1.5

Note: Figures cover persons age 25 and over; (1) Figures cover the Los Angeles-Long Beach-Anaheim, CA Metropolitan Statistical Area
Source: U.S. Census Bureau, 2016-2020 American Community Survey 5-Year Estimates

Educational Attainment by Race

Area	High School Graduate or Higher (%)					Bachelor's Degree or Higher (%)				
	Total	White	Black	Asian	Hisp.[2]	Total	White	Black	Asian	Hisp.[2]
City	78.3	82.8	89.0	90.7	57.8	35.6	42.3	28.4	55.6	13.5
MSA[1]	81.3	84.9	90.1	88.4	63.7	35.4	38.5	28.9	53.9	14.4
U.S.	88.5	90.7	86.7	87.3	70.3	32.9	34.4	22.6	55.0	17.6

Note: Figures shown cover persons 25 years old and over; (1) Figures cover the Los Angeles-Long Beach-Anaheim, CA Metropolitan Statistical Area; (2) People of Hispanic origin can be of any race
Source: U.S. Census Bureau, 2016-2020 American Community Survey 5-Year Estimates

School Enrollment by Grade and Control

Area	Preschool (%)		Kindergarten (%)		Grades 1 - 4 (%)		Grades 5 - 8 (%)		Grades 9 - 12 (%)	
	Public	Private	Public	Private	Public	Private	Public	Private	Public	Private
City	57.3	42.7	86.9	13.1	88.6	11.4	88.3	11.7	89.2	10.8
MSA[1]	56.4	43.6	87.8	12.2	90.3	9.7	90.5	9.5	91.2	8.8
U.S.	58.9	41.1	86.9	13.1	89.0	11.0	89.0	11.0	89.7	10.3

Note: Figures shown cover persons 3 years old and over; (1) Figures cover the Los Angeles-Long Beach-Anaheim, CA Metropolitan Statistical Area
Source: U.S. Census Bureau, 2016-2020 American Community Survey 5-Year Estimates

Higher Education

Four-Year Colleges			Two-Year Colleges			Medical Schools[1]	Law Schools[2]	Voc/ Tech[3]
Public	Private Non-profit	Private For-profit	Public	Private Non-profit	Private For-profit			
14	76	35	28	1	30	6	22	73

Note: Figures cover institutions located within the Los Angeles-Long Beach-Anaheim, CA Metropolitan Statistical Area and include main campuses only; (1) includes schools accredited by the Liaison Committee on Medical Education and the American Osteopathic Association's Commission on Osteopathic College Accreditation; (2) includes ABA-accredited schools, schools with provisional ABA accreditation, and state accredited schools; (3) includes all schools with programs that are less than 2 years.
Source: National Center for Education Statistics, Integrated Postsecondary Education System (IPEDS), 2020-21; Wikipedia, List of Medical Schools in the United States, accessed April 11, 2022; Wikipedia, List of Law Schools in the United States, accessed April 11, 2022

According to *U.S. News & World Report,* the Los Angeles-Long Beach-Glendale, CA metro division is home to seven of the top 200 national universities in the U.S.: **California Institute of Technology** (#9 tie); **University of California—Los Angeles** (#20); **University of Southern California** (#27); **Pepperdine University** (#49 tie); **Loyola Marymount University** (#75 tie); **University of La Verne** (#136 tie); **Biola University** (#196 tie). The indicators used to capture academic quality fall into a number of categories: assessment by administrators at peer institutions; retention of students; faculty resources; student selectivity; financial resources; alumni giving; high school counselor ratings of colleges; and graduation rate. *U.S. News & World Report, "America's Best Colleges 2022"*

According to *U.S. News & World Report,* the Los Angeles-Long Beach-Glendale, CA metro division is home to six of the top 100 liberal arts colleges in the U.S.: **Pomona College** (#4); **Claremont McKenna College** (#8); **Harvey Mudd College** (#28); **Scripps College** (#30 tie); **Pitzer College** (#35 tie); **Occidental College** (#42 tie). The indicators used to capture academic quality fall into a number of categories: assessment by administrators at peer institutions; retention of students; faculty resources; student selectivity; financial resources; alumni giving; high school counselor ratings of colleges; and graduation rate. *U.S. News & World Report, "America's Best Colleges 2022"*

According to *U.S. News & World Report,* the Los Angeles-Long Beach-Glendale, CA metro division is home to four of the top 100 law schools in the U.S.: **University of California—Los Angeles** (#14); **University of Southern California (Gould)** (#19); **Pepperdine University Caruso** (#46 tie); **Loyola Marymount University** (#72 tie). The rankings are based on a weighted average of 12 measures of quality: peer assessment score; assessment score by lawyers/judges; median LSAT scores; median undergrad GPA; acceptance rate; employment rates for graduates; placement success; bar passage rate; faculty resources; expenditures per student; student/faculty ratio; and library resources. *U.S. News & World Report, "America's Best Graduate Schools, Law, 2022"*

According to *U.S. News & World Report,* the Los Angeles-Long Beach-Glendale, CA metro division is home to two of the top 75 medical schools for research in the U.S.: **University of California—Los Angeles (Geffen)** (#21); **University of Southern California (Keck)** (#29). The rankings are based on a weighted average of 11 measures of quality: quality assessment; peer assessment score; assessment score by residency directors; research activity; total research activity; average research activity per faculty member; student selectivity; median MCAT total score; median undergraduate GPA; acceptance rate; and faculty resources. *U.S. News & World Report, "America's Best Graduate Schools, Medical, 2022"*

According to *U.S. News & World Report,* the Los Angeles-Long Beach-Glendale, CA metro division is home to three of the top 75 business schools in the U.S.: **University of Southern California (Marshall)** (#16 tie); **University of California—Los Angeles (Anderson)** (#18); **Pepperdine University (Graziadio)** (#68 tie). The rankings are based on a weighted average of the following nine measures: quality assessment; peer assessment; recruiter assessment; placement success; mean starting salary and bonus; student selectivity; mean GMAT and GRE scores; mean undergraduate GPA; and acceptance rate. *U.S. News & World Report, "America's Best Graduate Schools, Business, 2022"*

EMPLOYERS

Major Employers

Company Name	Industry
City of Los Angeles	Municipal government
County of Los Angeles	County government
Decton	Employment agencies
Disney Enterprises	Motion picture production & distribution
Disney Worldwide Services	Telecommunication equipment repair, excl telephones
Electronic Arts	Home entertainment computer software
King Holding Corporation	Bolts, nuts, rivets, & washers
Securitas Security Services USA	Security guard service
Team-One Employment Specialists	Employment agencies
The Boeing Company	Aircraft
The Walt Disney Company	Television broadcasting stations
UCLA Health System	Home health care services
UCLA Medical Group	Medical centers
University of California, Irvine	University
University of Southern California	Colleges & universities
Veterans Health Administration	Administration of veterans' affairs
Warner Bros. Entertainment	Motion picture production & distribution

Note: Companies shown are located within the Los Angeles-Long Beach-Anaheim, CA Metropolitan Statistical Area.
Source: Hoovers.com; Wikipedia

PUBLIC SAFETY

Crime Rate

Area	Total Crime	Violent Crime Rate				Property Crime Rate		
		Murder	Rape[3]	Robbery	Aggrav. Assault	Burglary	Larceny -Theft	Motor Vehicle Theft
City	2,869.9	8.8	49.6	200.3	463.3	344.3	1,274.6	529.1
Suburbs[1]	2,435.2	4.2	28.0	102.7	228.4	355.9	1,303.4	412.7
Metro[2]	2,567.7	5.6	34.6	132.5	300.0	352.3	1,294.6	448.2
U.S.	2,356.7	6.5	38.4	73.9	279.7	314.2	1,398.0	246.0

Note: Figures are crimes per 100,000 population; (1) All areas within the metro area that are located outside the city limits; (2) Figures cover the Los Angeles-Long Beach-Glendale, CA Metropolitan Division; (3) All figures shown were reported using the revised Uniform Crime Reporting (UCR) definition of rape.
Source: FBI Uniform Crime Reports, 2020

Hate Crimes

Area	Number of Quarters Reported	Number of Incidents per Bias Motivation					
		Race/Ethnicity/ Ancestry	Religion	Sexual Orientation	Disability	Gender	Gender Identity
City[1]	4	187	67	81	1	2	31
U.S.	4	5,227	1,244	1,110	130	75	266

Note: (1) Figures include one incident reported with more than one bias motivation.
Source: Federal Bureau of Investigation, Hate Crime Statistics 2020

Identity Theft Consumer Reports

Area	Reports	Reports per 100,000 Population	Rank[2]
MSA[1]	67,258	509	49
U.S.	1,434,676	432	-

Note: (1) Figures cover the Los Angeles-Long Beach-Anaheim, CA Metropolitan Statistical Area; (2) Rank ranges from 1 to 391 where 1 indicates greatest number of identity theft reports per 100,000 population
Source: Federal Trade Commission, Consumer Sentinel Network Data Book 2021

Fraud and Other Consumer Reports

Area	Reports	Reports per 100,000 Population	Rank[2]
MSA[1]	136,827	1,035	92
U.S.	4,328,977	1,304	-

Note: (1) Figures cover the Los Angeles-Long Beach-Anaheim, CA Metropolitan Statistical Area; (2) Rank ranges from 1 to 391 where 1 indicates greatest number of fraud and other consumer reports per 100,000 population
Source: Federal Trade Commission, Consumer Sentinel Network Data Book 2021

POLITICS

2020 Presidential Election Results

Area	Biden	Trump	Jorgensen	Hawkins	Other
Los Angeles County	71.0	26.9	0.8	0.5	0.8
U.S.	51.3	46.8	1.2	0.3	0.5

Note: Results are percentages and may not add to 100% due to rounding
Source: Dave Leip's Atlas of U.S. Presidential Elections

SPORTS

Professional Sports Teams

Team Name	League	Year Established
Anaheim Ducks	National Hockey League (NHL)	1993
C.D. Chivas USA	Major League Soccer (MLS)	2004
Los Angeles Angels of Anaheim	Major League Baseball (MLB)	1961
Los Angeles Chargers	National Football League (NFL)	2017
Los Angeles Clippers	National Basketball Association (NBA)	1984
Los Angeles Dodgers	Major League Baseball (MLB)	1958
Los Angeles FC	Major League Soccer (MLS)	2018
Los Angeles Galaxy	Major League Soccer (MLS)	1996
Los Angeles Kings	National Hockey League (NHL)	1967
Los Angeles Lakers	National Basketball Association (NBA)	1960
Los Angeles Rams	National Football League (NFL)	2016

Note: Includes teams located in the Los Angeles-Long Beach-Anaheim, CA Metropolitan Statistical Area.
Source: Wikipedia, Major Professional Sports Teams of the United States and Canada, April 6, 2022

CLIMATE

Average and Extreme Temperatures

Temperature	Jan	Feb	Mar	Apr	May	Jun	Jul	Aug	Sep	Oct	Nov	Dec	Yr.
Extreme High (°F)	88	92	95	102	97	104	97	98	110	106	101	94	110
Average High (°F)	65	66	65	67	69	72	75	76	76	74	71	66	70
Average Temp. (°F)	56	57	58	60	63	66	69	70	70	67	62	57	63
Average Low (°F)	47	49	50	53	56	59	63	64	63	59	52	48	55
Extreme Low (°F)	27	34	37	43	45	48	52	51	47	43	38	32	27

Note: Figures cover the years 1947-1990
Source: National Climatic Data Center, International Station Meteorological Climate Summary, 9/96

Average Precipitation/Snowfall/Humidity

Precip./Humidity	Jan	Feb	Mar	Apr	May	Jun	Jul	Aug	Sep	Oct	Nov	Dec	Yr.
Avg. Precip. (in.)	2.6	2.3	1.8	0.8	0.1	Tr	Tr	0.1	0.2	0.3	1.5	1.5	11.3
Avg. Snowfall (in.)	Tr	0	0	0	0	0	0	0	0	0	0	0	Tr
Avg. Rel. Hum. 7am (%)	69	72	76	76	77	80	80	81	80	76	69	67	75
Avg. Rel. Hum. 4pm (%)	60	62	64	64	66	67	67	68	67	66	61	60	64

Note: Figures cover the years 1947-1990; Tr = Trace amounts (<0.05 in. of rain; <0.5 in. of snow)
Source: National Climatic Data Center, International Station Meteorological Climate Summary, 9/96

Weather Conditions

Temperature			Daytime Sky			Precipitation		
10°F & below	32°F & below	90°F & above	Clear	Partly cloudy	Cloudy	0.01 inch or more precip.	0.1 inch or more snow/ice	Thunder-storms
0	< 1	5	131	125	109	34	0	1

Note: Figures are average number of days per year and cover the years 1947-1990
Source: National Climatic Data Center, International Station Meteorological Climate Summary, 9/96

HAZARDOUS WASTE

Superfund Sites

The Los Angeles-Long Beach-Glendale, CA metro division is home to 15 sites on the EPA's Superfund National Priorities List: **Cooper Drum Co.** (final); **Del Amo** (final); **Jervis B. Webb Co.** (final); **Jet Propulsion Laboratory (NASA)** (final); **Montrose Chemical Corp.** (final); **Omega Chemical Corporation** (final); **Operating Industries, Inc., Landfill** (final); **Pemaco Maywood** (final); **San Fernando Valley (Area 1)** (final); **San Fernando Valley (Area 2)** (final); **San Fernando Valley (Area 4)** (final); **San Gabriel Valley (Area 1)** (final); **San Gabriel Valley (Area 2)** (final); **San Gabriel Valley (Area 3)** (final); **San Gabriel Valley (Area 4)** (final). There are a total of 1,165 Superfund sites with a status of proposed or final on the list in the U.S. *U.S. Environmental Protection Agency, National Priorities List, April 6, 2022*

AIR QUALITY

Air Quality Trends: Ozone

	1990	1995	2000	2005	2010	2016	2017	2018	2019	2020
MSA[1]	0.134	0.114	0.091	0.085	0.076	0.083	0.093	0.084	0.080	0.100
U.S.	0.090	0.091	0.082	0.080	0.074	0.070	0.069	0.070	0.066	0.068

Note: (1) Data covers the Los Angeles-Long Beach-Anaheim, CA Metropolitan Statistical Area. The values shown are the composite ozone concentration averages among trend sites based on the highest fourth daily maximum 8-hour concentration in parts per million. These trends are based on sites having an adequate record of monitoring data during the trend period. Data from exceptional events are included.
Source: U.S. Environmental Protection Agency, Air Quality Monitoring Information, "Air Quality Trends by City, 1990-2020"

Air Quality Index

Area	Percent of Days when Air Quality was...[2]					AQI Statistics[2]	
	Good	Moderate	Unhealthy for Sensitive Groups	Unhealthy	Very Unhealthy	Maximum	Median
MSA[1]	16.4	44.8	21.6	12.8	4.4	235	84

Note: (1) Data covers the Los Angeles-Long Beach-Anaheim, CA Metropolitan Statistical Area; (2) Based on 366 days with AQI data in 2020. Air Quality Index (AQI) is an index for reporting daily air quality. EPA calculates the AQI for five major air pollutants regulated by the Clean Air Act: ground-level ozone, particle pollution (aka particulate matter), carbon monoxide, sulfur dioxide, and nitrogen dioxide. The AQI runs from 0 to 500. The higher the AQI value, the greater the level of air pollution and the greater the health concern. There are six AQI categories: "Good" AQI is between 0 and 50. Air quality is considered satisfactory; "Moderate" AQI is between 51 and 100. Air quality is acceptable; "Unhealthy for Sensitive Groups" When AQI values are between 101 and 150, members of sensitive groups may experience health effects; "Unhealthy" When AQI values are between 151 and 200 everyone may begin to experience health effects; "Very Unhealthy" AQI values between 201 and 300 trigger a health alert; "Hazardous" AQI values over 300 trigger warnings of emergency conditions (not shown).

Source: U.S. Environmental Protection Agency, Air Quality Index Report, 2020

Air Quality Index Pollutants

Area	Percent of Days when AQI Pollutant was...[2]					
	Carbon Monoxide	Nitrogen Dioxide	Ozone	Sulfur Dioxide	Particulate Matter 2.5	Particulate Matter 10
MSA[1]	0.0	6.3	57.4	0.0	35.0	1.4

Note: (1) Data covers the Los Angeles-Long Beach-Anaheim, CA Metropolitan Statistical Area; (2) Based on 366 days with AQI data in 2020. The Air Quality Index (AQI) is an index for reporting daily air quality. EPA calculates the AQI for five major air pollutants regulated by the Clean Air Act: ground-level ozone, particle pollution (also known as particulate matter), carbon monoxide, sulfur dioxide, and nitrogen dioxide. The AQI runs from 0 to 500. The higher the AQI value, the greater the level of air pollution and the greater the health concern.

Source: U.S. Environmental Protection Agency, Air Quality Index Report, 2020

Maximum Air Pollutant Concentrations: Particulate Matter, Ozone, CO and Lead

	Particulate Matter 10 (ug/m^3)	Particulate Matter 2.5 Wtd AM (ug/m^3)	Particulate Matter 2.5 24-Hr (ug/m^3)	Ozone (ppm)	Carbon Monoxide (ppm)	Lead (ug/m^3)
MSA[1] Level	169	14.8	53	0.124	3	0.02
NAAQS[2]	150	15	35	0.075	9	0.15
Met NAAQS[2]	No	Yes	No	No	Yes	Yes

Note: (1) Data covers the Los Angeles-Long Beach-Anaheim, CA Metropolitan Statistical Area; Data from exceptional events are included; (2) National Ambient Air Quality Standards; ppm = parts per million; ug/m^3 = micrograms per cubic meter; n/a not available.

Concentrations: Particulate Matter 10 (coarse particulate)—highest second maximum 24-hour concentration; Particulate Matter 2.5 Wtd AM (fine particulate)—highest weighted annual mean concentration; Particulate Matter 2.5 24-Hour (fine particulate)—highest 98th percentile 24-hour concentration; Ozone—highest fourth daily maximum 8-hour concentration; Carbon Monoxide—highest second maximum non-overlapping 8-hour concentration; Lead—maximum running 3-month average

Source: U.S. Environmental Protection Agency, Air Quality Monitoring Information, "Air Quality Statistics by City, 2020"

Maximum Air Pollutant Concentrations: Nitrogen Dioxide and Sulfur Dioxide

	Nitrogen Dioxide AM (ppb)	Nitrogen Dioxide 1-Hr (ppb)	Sulfur Dioxide AM (ppb)	Sulfur Dioxide 1-Hr (ppb)	Sulfur Dioxide 24-Hr (ppb)
MSA[1] Level	23	86	n/a	3	n/a
NAAQS[2]	53	100	30	75	140
Met NAAQS[2]	Yes	Yes	n/a	Yes	n/a

Note: (1) Data covers the Los Angeles-Long Beach-Anaheim, CA Metropolitan Statistical Area; Data from exceptional events are included; (2) National Ambient Air Quality Standards; ppm = parts per million; ug/m^3 = micrograms per cubic meter; n/a not available.

Concentrations: Nitrogen Dioxide AM—highest arithmetic mean concentration; Nitrogen Dioxide 1-Hr—highest 98th percentile 1-hour daily maximum concentration; Sulfur Dioxide AM—highest annual mean concentration; Sulfur Dioxide 1-Hr—highest 99th percentile 1-hour daily maximum concentration; Sulfur Dioxide 24-Hr—highest second maximum 24-hour concentration

Source: U.S. Environmental Protection Agency, Air Quality Monitoring Information, "Air Quality Statistics by City, 2020"

Phoenix, Arizona

Background

Phoenix, the arid "Valley of the Sun," and the capital of Arizona, was named by the English soldier and prospector, "Lord Darell" Duppa for the mythical bird of ancient Greek/Phoenician lore. According to the legend, the Phoenix was a beautiful bird that destroyed itself with its own flames. When nothing remained but embers, it would rise again from the ashes, more awesome and beautiful than before. Like the romantic tale, Duppa hoped that his city of Phoenix would rise again from the mysteriously abandoned Hohokam village which occupied the Phoenix area for 2,000 years.

Many might agree that Phoenix fulfilled Duppa's wish. Within 15 years after its second founding in 1867, Phoenix had grown to be an important supply point for the mining districts of north-central Arizona, as well as an important trading site for farmers, cattlemen, and prospectors.

Around this time, Phoenix entered its Wild West phase, complete with stagecoaches, saloons, gambling houses, soldiers, cowboys, miners, and the pungent air of outlawry. Two public hangings near the end of the 1800s set a dramatic example and helped turn the tide.

Today, Phoenix is just as exciting as ever, but more law-abiding, and many continue to be attracted to Phoenix's natural beauty. Despite occasional sprawling suburbs and shopping malls, the sophisticated blend of Spanish, Native American, and cowboy culture is obvious in the city's architecture, arts, and crafts. Downtown Phoenix underwent a major renaissance in the 1990s with the completion of a history museum, expanded art museum, new central library, Arizona Science Center, and a renovated concert hall. Today it also features the 20,000 square foot Musical Instrument Museum featuring musical instruments from around the world. More than 300 arts and entertainment venues are in the Phoenix region, as well as five professional sports teams. Phoenix Concept 2000 split the city into 15 urban villages, each with its own height and density permits, further shaping the city's free-market development culture.

Phoenix is the country's fifth-largest city, with more than one million people, while the Phoenix metro area population has grown to nearly four million. This increase in population continues to make Phoenix an attractive location for companies that are expanding in the fields of electronics and communications. Renewable energy, biomedicine, advanced business services, manufacturing and distribution, aerospace and aviation, and emerging technologies from start-ups are key industries in the region, as are insurance, healthcare, and technology.

Phoenix is home to several professional sports franchises. The Phoenix Suns of the NBA and the Phoenix Mercury of the WNBA both play at Talking Stick Resort Arena. The Mercury have won the WNBA championships three times: in 2007, 2009, and 2014. The Arizona Diamondbacks of Major League Baseball play their home games in Chase Field, the second-highest stadium in the country, and defeated the New York Yankees in 2001 to claim the World Series title. The Arizona Cardinals is the oldest continuously run professional football franchise in the nation, though they originated in Chicago. They play at the University of Phoenix Stadium in Glendale, 20 miles from Phoenix, which hosted Super Bowl in 2008, 2015 and will host again in 2023.

The Valley Metro Rail light rail eco-friendly transit system hopes to complete its 60-mile expansion in 2023, to accommodate the visitors expected to the area for the game.

In 1981, Phoenix resident Sandra Day O'Connor broke the gender barrier on the U.S. Supreme Court when she was sworn in as the first female justice. The influx of refugees - most recently about 450 Afghans — has resulted in more than 100 languages being spoken in local schools.

Temperatures in Phoenix are mild in winter and very hot in summer. The low humidity makes the summer heat somewhat more bearable than one might expect. Rainfall is slight and comes in two seasons: winter rain comes on winds from the Pacific, ending by April; summer, rains, with severe thunderstorms come from the southeast.

Rankings

General Rankings

- For its "Best for Vets: Places to Live 2019" rankings, *Military Times* evaluated 599 cities (83 large, 234 medium, 282 small) and compared the locations across three broad categories: veteran and military culture/services; economic indicators; and livability factors such as health, crime, traffic, and school quality. Phoenix ranked #21 out of the top 25, in the large city category (population of more than 250,000). Data points more specific to veterans and the military weighed more heavily than others. *rebootcamp.militarytimes.com, "Military Times Best Places to Live 2019," September 10, 2018*
- The Phoenix metro area was identified as one of America's fastest-growing areas in terms of population and business growth by *MagnifyMoney.* The area ranked #28 out of 35. The 100 most populous metro areas in the U.S. were evaluated on their change from 2011 to 2016 in the following categories: people and housing; workforce and employment opportunities; growing industry. *www.businessinsider.com, "The 35 Cities in the US with the Biggest Influx of People, the Most Work Opportunities, and the Hottest Business Growth," August 12, 2018*
- The Phoenix metro area was identified as one of America's fastest-growing areas in terms of population and economy by *Forbes.* The area ranked #11 out of 25. The 100 most populous metro areas in the U.S. were evaluated on the following criteria: estimated population growth; employment; economic output; wages; home values. *Forbes, "America's Fastest-Growing Cities 2018," February 28, 2018*

Business/Finance Rankings

- The Brookings Institution ranked the nation's largest cities based on income inequality. Phoenix was ranked #62 (#1 = greatest inequality). Criteria: the "95/20 ratio," a figure representing the income at which a household earns more than 95 percent of all other households, divided by the income at which a household earns more than only 20 percent of all other households. *Brookings Institution, "Household Income Inequality, Largest Cities of 97 Large U.S. Metro Areas, 2014-2016," February 5, 2018*
- The Brookings Institution ranked the 100 largest metro areas in the U.S. based on income inequality. Phoenix was ranked #61 (#1 = greatest inequality). Criteria: the "95/20 ratio," a figure representing the income at which a household earns more than 95 percent of all other households, divided by the income at which a household earns more than only 20 percent of all other households. *Brookings Institution, "Household Income Inequality, 100 Largest U.S. Metro Areas, 2014-2016," February 5, 2018*
- Payscale.com ranked the 32 largest metro areas in terms of wage growth. The Phoenix metro area ranked #1. Criteria: private-sector and education professional wage growth between the 4th quarter of 2019 and the 4th quarter of 2020. *PayScale, "Wage Trends by Metro Area-4th Quarter," January 11, 2021*
- The Phoenix metro area was identified as one of the most debt-ridden places in America by the finance site Credit.com. The metro area was ranked #17. Criteria: residents' average credit card debt as well as median income. *Credit.com, "25 Cities With the Most Credit Card Debt," February 28, 2018*
- Phoenix was identified as one of America's most frugal metro areas by *Coupons.com.* The city ranked #16 out of 25. Criteria: digital coupon usage. *Coupons.com, "America's Most Frugal Cities of 2017," March 22, 2018*
- Phoenix was identified as one of the happiest cities to work in by CareerBliss.com, an online community for career advancement. The city ranked #4 out of 10. Criteria: an employee's relationship with his or her boss and co-workers; daily tasks; general work environment; compensation; opportunities for advancement; company culture and job reputation; and resources. *Businesswire.com, "CareerBliss Happiest Cities to Work 2019," February 12, 2019*
- The Phoenix metro area appeared on the Milken Institute "2021 Best Performing Cities" list. Rank: #7 out of 200 large metro areas (population over 250,000). Criteria: job growth; wage and salary growth; high-tech output growth; housing affordability; household broadband access. *Milken Institute, "Best-Performing Cities 2021," February 16, 2021*
- *Forbes* ranked the 200 most populous metro areas to determine the nation's "Best Places for Business and Careers." The Phoenix metro area was ranked #26. Criteria: costs (business and living); job growth (past and projected); income growth; quality of life; educational attainment (college and high school); projected economic growth; cultural and leisure opportunities; workplace tolerance laws; net migration patterns. *Forbes, "The Best Places for Business and Careers 2019: Seattle Still On Top," October 30, 2019*

Education Rankings

- Personal finance website *WalletHub* analyzed the 150 largest U.S. metropolitan statistical areas to determine where the most educated Americans are putting their degrees to work. Criteria: education levels; percentage of workers with degrees; education quality and attainment gap; public school quality rankings; quality and enrollment of each metro area's universities. Phoenix was ranked #80 (#1 = most educated city). *www.WalletHub.com, "Most & Least Educated Cities in America," July 19, 2021*
- Phoenix was selected as one of America's most literate cities. The city ranked #74 out of the 84 largest U.S. cities. Criteria: number of booksellers; library resources; Internet resources; educational attainment; periodical publishing resources; newspaper circulation. *Central Connecticut State University, "America's Most Literate Cities, 2018," February 2019*

Environmental Rankings

- Sperling's BestPlaces assessed the 50 largest metropolitan areas of the United States for the likelihood of dangerously extreme weather events or earthquakes. In general the Southeast and South-Central regions have the highest risk of weather extremes and earthquakes, while the Pacific Northwest enjoys the lowest risk. Of the most risky metropolitan areas, the Phoenix metro area was ranked #9. *www.bestplaces.net, "Avoid Natural Disasters: BestPlaces Reveals The Top 10 Safest Places to Live," October 25, 2017*
- The U.S. Environmental Protection Agency (EPA) released its list of U.S. metropolitan areas with the most ENERGY STAR certified buildings in 2020. The Phoenix metro area was ranked #16 out of 25. *U.S. Environmental Protection Agency, "2021 Energy Star Top Cities," June 15, 2021*
- Phoenix was highlighted as one of the 25 most ozone-polluted metro areas in the U.S. during 2017 through 2019. The area ranked #5. *American Lung Association, "State of the Air 2021," April 21, 2021*
- Phoenix was highlighted as one of the 25 metro areas most polluted by year-round particle pollution (Annual PM 2.5) in the U.S. during 2017 through 2019. The area ranked #8. *American Lung Association, "State of the Air 2021," April 21, 2021*
- Phoenix was highlighted as one of the 25 metro areas most polluted by short-term particle pollution (24-hour PM 2.5) in the U.S. during 2017 through 2019. The area ranked #13. *American Lung Association, "State of the Air 2021," April 21, 2021*

Food/Drink Rankings

- The U.S. Chamber of Commerce Foundation conducted an in-depth study on local food truck regulations, surveyed 288 food truck owners, and ranked 20 major American cities based on how friendly they are for operating a food truck. The compiled index assessed the following: procedures for obtaining permits and licenses; complying with restrictions; and financial obligations associated with operating a food truck. Phoenix ranked #14 overall (1 being the best). *www.foodtrucknation.us, "Food Truck Nation," March 20, 2018*
- Chase Field was selected as one of PETA's "Top 10 Vegan-Friendly Ballparks" for 2019. The park ranked #10. *People for the Ethical Treatment of Animals, "Top 10 Vegan-Friendly Ballparks," May 23, 2019*

Health/Fitness Rankings

- For each of the 100 largest cities in the United States, the American Fitness Index®, published by the American College of Sports Medicine and the Anthem Foundation, evaluated community infrastructure and 34 health behaviors including preventive health, levels of chronic disease conditions, food insecurity, sleep quality, pedestrian safety, air quality, and community resources that support physical activity. Phoenix ranked #70 for "community fitness." *americanfitnessindex.org, "2021 ACSM American Fitness Index Summary Report," July 13, 2021*
- Phoenix was identified as a "2021 Spring Allergy Capital." The area ranked #97 out of 100. Three groups of factors were used to identify the most challenging cities for people with allergies during the spring season: annual spring pollen levels; over the counter medicine use; number of board-certified allergy specialists. *Asthma and Allergy Foundation of America, "Spring Allergy Capitals 2021," February 23, 2021*
- Phoenix was identified as a "2021 Fall Allergy Capital." The area ranked #90 out of 100. Three groups of factors were used to identify the most challenging cities for people with allergies during the fall season: annual fall pollen levels; over the counter medicine use; number of board-certified allergy specialists. *Asthma and Allergy Foundation of America, "Fall Allergy Capitals 2021," February 23, 2021*

- Phoenix was identified as a "2021 Asthma Capital." The area ranked #52 out of the nation's 100 largest metropolitan areas. Criteria: estimated asthma prevalence; asthma-related mortality; and ER visits due to asthma. Risk factors analyzed but not factored in the rankings: annual pollen score; annual air quality; public smoking laws; number of board-certified asthma specialists; rescue medication use; controller medication use; uninsured rate; poverty rate. *Asthma and Allergy Foundation of America, "Asthma Capitals 2021: The Most Challenging Places to Live With Asthma," May 5, 2021*

Real Estate Rankings

- *WalletHub* compared the most populated U.S. cities to determine which had the best markets for real estate agents. Phoenix ranked #45 where demand was high and pay was the best. Criteria: sales per agent; annual median wage for real-estate agents; monthly average starting salary for real estate agents; real estate job density and competition; unemployment rate; home turnover rate; housing-market health index; and other relevant metrics. *www.WalletHub.com, "2021 Best Places to Be a Real Estate Agent," May 12, 2021*
- According to Penske Truck Rental, the Phoenix metro area was named the #2 moving destination in 2020, based on one-way consumer truck rental reservations made through Penske's website, rental locations, and reservations call center. *gopenske.com/blog, "Penske Truck Rental's 2020 Top Moving Destinations," May 3, 2021*
- Phoenix was ranked #4 in the top 20 out of the 100 largest metro areas in terms of house price appreciation in 2021 (#1 = highest rate). *Federal Housing Finance Agency, House Price Index, 4th Quarter 2021*
- The Phoenix metro area was identified as one of the 20 best housing markets in the U.S. in 2021. The area ranked #4 out of 184 markets. Criteria: year-over-year change of median sales price of existing single-family homes between the 4th quarter of 2020 and the 4th quarter of 2021. *National Association of Realtors®, Median Sales Price of Existing Single-Family Homes for Metropolitan Areas, 4th Quarter 2021*
- The Phoenix metro area was identified as one of the 10 best condo markets in the U.S. in 2021. The area ranked #1 out of 63 markets. Criteria: year-over-year change of median sales price of existing apartment condo-coop homes between the 4th quarter of 2020 and the 4th quarter of 2021. *National Association of Realtors®, Median Sales Price of Existing Apartment Condo-Coops Homes for Metropolitan Areas, 4th Quarter 2021*
- Phoenix was ranked #174 out of 237 metro areas in terms of housing affordability in 2021 by the National Association of Home Builders (#1 = most affordable). Criteria: the share of homes sold in that area affordable to a family earning the local median income, based on standard mortgage underwriting criteria. *National Association of Home Builders®, NAHB-Wells Fargo Housing Opportunity Index, 4th Quarter 2021*

Safety Rankings

- Allstate ranked the 200 largest cities in America in terms of driver safety. Phoenix ranked #84. Criteria: internal property damage claims over a two-year period from January 2016 to December 2017. The report helps increase the importance of safety and awareness behind the wheel. *Allstate, "Allstate America's Best Drivers Report, 2019" June 24, 2019*
- The National Insurance Crime Bureau ranked 390 metro areas in the U.S. in terms of per capita rates of vehicle theft. The Phoenix metro area ranked #109 (#1 = highest rate). Criteria: number of vehicle theft offenses per 100,000 inhabitants in 2020. *National Insurance Crime Bureau, "Hot Spots 2020," August 31, 2021*

Seniors/Retirement Rankings

- From its Best Cities for Successful Aging indexes, the Milken Institute generated rankings for metropolitan areas, weighing data in nine categories—health care, wellness, living arrangements, transportation and convenience, financial characteristics, education, employment, community engagement, and overall livability. The Phoenix metro area was ranked #88 overall in the large metro area category. *Milken Institute, "Best Cities for Successful Aging, 2017" March 14, 2017*

Transportation Rankings

- According to the INRIX "2021 Global Traffic Scorecard," Phoenix was identified as one of the most congested metro areas in the U.S. The area ranked #25 out of 25. Criteria: average annual time spent in traffic and average cost of congestion per motorist. *Inrix.com, "Americans Lost 3.4 Billion Hours Due to Congestion in 2021, 42% Below Pre-COVID," December 7, 2021*

Women/Minorities Rankings

- The *Houston Chronicle* listed the Phoenix metro area as #5 in top places for young Latinos to live in the U.S. Research was largely based on housing and occupational data from the largest metropolitan areas performed by *Forbes* and NBC Universo. Criteria: percentage of 18-34 year-olds; Latino college grad rates; and diversity. *blog.chron.com, "The 15 Best Big Cities for Latino Millenials," January 26, 2016*
- *Women's Health*, together with the site Yelp, identified the 15 "Wellthiest" spots in the U.S. Phoenix appeared among the top for happiest, healthiest, outdoorsiest and Zen-iest. *Women's Health, "The 15 Wellthiest Cities in the U.S." July 5, 2017*
- Personal finance website *WalletHub* compared more than 180 U.S. cities across two key dimensions, "Hispanic Business-Friendliness" and "Hispanic Purchasing Power," to arrive at the most favorable conditions for Hispanic entrepreneurs. Phoenix was ranked #77 out of 182. Criteria includes: share of Hispanic-Owned Businesses; Hispanic entrepreneurship rate to median annual income of Hispanics; Small Business-Friendliness score; cost of living; and number of Hispanics with at least a bachelor's degree. *WalletHub.com, "2019's Best Cities for Hispanic Entrepreneurs," May 1, 2019*

Miscellaneous Rankings

- Phoenix was selected as a 2021 Digital Cities Survey winner. The city ranked #7 in the large city (500,000 or more population) category. The survey examined and assessed how city governments are utilizing technology to continue innovation, engage with residents, and persevere through the challenges of the pandemic. Survey questions focused on ten initiatives: cybersecurity; citizen experience; disaster recovery; business intelligence; IT personnel; data governance; budget control; IT governance; infrastructure modernization; and broadband connectivity. *Center for Digital Government, "2021 Digital Cities Survey," November 16, 2021*
- The watchdog site, Charity Navigator, conducted a study of charities in major markets both to analyze statistical differences in their financial, accountability, and transparency practices and to track year-to-year variations in individual philanthropic communities. The Phoenix metro area was ranked #12 among the 30 metro markets in the rating category of Overall Score. *www.charitynavigator.org, "2017 Metro Market Study," May 1, 2017*
- *WalletHub* compared the 150 most populated U.S. cities to determine their operating efficiency. A "Quality of City Services" score was constructed for each city and then divided by the total budget per capita to reveal which were managed the best. Phoenix ranked #36. Criteria: financial stability; economy; education; safety; health; infrastructure and pollution. *www.WalletHub.com, "2021's Best- & Worst-Run Cities in America," June 22, 2021*
- The National Alliance to End Homelessness listed the 25 most populous metro areas with the highest rate of homelessness. The Phoenix metro area had a high rate of homelessness. Criteria: number of homeless people per 10,000 population in 2016. *National Alliance to End Homelessness, "Homelessness in the 25 Most Populous U.S. Metro Areas," September 1, 2017*

Business Environment

DEMOGRAPHICS

Population Growth

Area	1990 Census	2000 Census	2010 Census	2020* Estimate	Population Growth (%) 1990-2020	Population Growth (%) 2010-2020
City	989,873	1,321,045	1,445,632	1,658,422	67.5	14.7
MSA[1]	2,238,480	3,251,876	4,192,887	4,860,338	117.1	15.9
U.S.	248,709,873	281,421,906	308,745,538	326,569,308	31.3	5.8

Note: (1) Figures cover the Phoenix-Mesa-Scottsdale, AZ Metropolitan Statistical Area; (*) 2016-2020 5-year estimated population
Source: U.S. Census Bureau, 1990 Census, Census 2000, Census 2010, 2016-2020 American Community Survey 5-Year Estimates

Household Size

Area	Persons in Household (%) One	Two	Three	Four	Five	Six	Seven or More	Average Household Size
City	28.2	29.6	15.2	13.0	7.3	3.8	2.9	2.80
MSA[1]	26.3	34.6	14.4	12.6	6.8	3.0	2.3	2.70
U.S.	28.0	33.9	15.5	12.9	6.0	2.3	1.4	2.60

Note: (1) Figures cover the Phoenix-Mesa-Scottsdale, AZ Metropolitan Statistical Area
Source: U.S. Census Bureau, 2016-2020 American Community Survey 5-Year Estimates

Race

Area	White Alone[2] (%)	Black Alone[2] (%)	Asian Alone[2] (%)	AIAN[3] Alone[2] (%)	NHOPI[4] Alone[2] (%)	Other Race Alone[2] (%)	Two or More Races (%)
City	68.2	7.1	3.9	2.0	0.2	10.3	8.3
MSA[1]	74.1	5.6	4.0	2.2	0.2	6.9	7.1
U.S.	70.4	12.6	5.6	0.8	0.2	5.1	5.2

Note: (1) Figures cover the Phoenix-Mesa-Scottsdale, AZ Metropolitan Statistical Area; (2) Alone is defined as not being in combination with one or more other races; (3) American Indian and Alaska Native; (4) Native Hawaiian and Other Pacific Islander
Source: U.S. Census Bureau, 2016-2020 American Community Survey 5-Year Estimates

Hispanic or Latino Origin

Area	Total (%)	Mexican (%)	Puerto Rican (%)	Cuban (%)	Other (%)
City	42.6	38.0	0.8	0.3	3.5
MSA[1]	31.1	27.0	0.7	0.3	3.1
U.S.	18.2	11.2	1.7	0.7	4.5

Note: Persons of Hispanic or Latino origin can be of any race; (1) Figures cover the Phoenix-Mesa-Scottsdale, AZ Metropolitan Statistical Area
Source: U.S. Census Bureau, 2016-2020 American Community Survey 5-Year Estimates

Ancestry

Area	German	Irish	English	American	Italian	Polish	French[2]	Scottish	Dutch
City	10.0	7.4	6.0	2.8	3.9	1.8	1.6	1.2	0.9
MSA[1]	12.6	8.5	8.2	3.8	4.5	2.3	2.0	1.6	1.1
U.S.	13.0	9.7	7.7	5.9	5.1	2.7	2.3	1.6	1.1

Note: Figures are the percentage of the total population reporting a particular ancestry. The nine most commonly reported ancestries in the U.S. are shown. Figures include multiple ancestries (e.g. if a person reported being Irish and Italian, they were included in both columns); (1) Figures cover the Phoenix-Mesa-Scottsdale, AZ Metropolitan Statistical Area; (2) Excludes Basque
Source: U.S. Census Bureau, 2016-2020 American Community Survey 5-Year Estimates

Foreign-born Population

Area	Percent of Population Born in: Any Foreign Country	Asia	Mexico	Europe	Caribbean	Central America[2]	South America	Africa	Canada
City	19.3	3.3	11.8	1.4	0.3	0.8	0.4	0.8	0.4
MSA[1]	14.2	3.3	7.1	1.4	0.3	0.6	0.3	0.5	0.7
U.S.	13.5	4.2	3.3	1.5	1.3	1.1	1.0	0.7	0.3

Note: (1) Figures cover the Phoenix-Mesa-Scottsdale, AZ Metropolitan Statistical Area; (2) Excludes Mexico.
Source: U.S. Census Bureau, 2016-2020 American Community Survey 5-Year Estimates

Marital Status

Area	Never Married	Now Married[2]	Separated	Widowed	Divorced
City	38.9	42.3	2.1	4.3	12.3
MSA[1]	34.0	47.4	1.6	5.0	11.9
U.S.	33.5	48.1	1.8	5.7	10.8

Note: Figures are percentages and cover the population 15 years of age and older; (1) Figures cover the Phoenix-Mesa-Scottsdale, AZ Metropolitan Statistical Area; (2) Excludes separated
Source: U.S. Census Bureau, 2016-2020 American Community Survey 5-Year Estimates

Disability by Age

Area	All Ages	Under 18 Years Old	18 to 64 Years Old	65 Years and Over
City	10.8	4.3	9.5	34.0
MSA[1]	11.8	4.1	9.6	32.3
U.S.	12.7	4.3	10.3	34.0

Note: Figures show percent of the civilian noninstitutionalized population that reported having a disability. Disability status is determined from six types of difficulty: vision, hearing, cognitive, ambulatory, self-care, and independent living. For children under 5 years old, hearing and vision difficulty are used to determine disability status. For children between the ages of 5 and 14, disability status is determined from hearing, vision, cognitive, ambulatory, and self-care difficulties. For people aged 15 years and older, they are considered to have a disability if they have difficulty with any one of the six difficulty types; Note: (1) Figures cover the Phoenix-Mesa-Scottsdale, AZ Metropolitan Statistical Area
Source: U.S. Census Bureau, 2016-2020 American Community Survey 5-Year Estimates

Age

Area	Percent of Population									Median Age
	Under Age 5	Age 5–19	Age 20–34	Age 35–44	Age 45–54	Age 55–64	Age 65–74	Age 75–84	Age 85+	
City	7.0	21.3	23.3	13.9	12.6	10.9	6.8	3.0	1.3	33.9
MSA[1]	6.2	20.1	21.0	13.0	12.4	11.5	9.1	4.8	1.8	36.9
U.S.	6.0	19.1	20.6	12.7	12.7	12.9	9.4	4.7	2.0	38.2

Note: (1) Figures cover the Phoenix-Mesa-Scottsdale, AZ Metropolitan Statistical Area
Source: U.S. Census Bureau, 2016-2020 American Community Survey 5-Year Estimates

Gender

Area	Males	Females	Males per 100 Females
City	828,085	830,337	99.7
MSA[1]	2,414,389	2,445,949	98.7
U.S.	160,818,530	165,750,778	97.0

Note: (1) Figures cover the Phoenix-Mesa-Scottsdale, AZ Metropolitan Statistical Area
Source: U.S. Census Bureau, 2016-2020 American Community Survey 5-Year Estimates

Religious Groups by Family

Area	Catholic	Baptist	Non-Den.	Methodist[2]	Lutheran	LDS[3]	Pente-costal	Presby-terian[4]	Muslim[5]	Judaism
MSA[1]	13.4	3.5	5.2	1.0	1.6	6.1	2.9	0.6	0.2	0.3
U.S.	19.1	9.3	4.0	4.0	2.3	2.0	1.9	1.6	0.8	0.7

Note: Figures are the number of adherents as a percentage of the total population; (1) Figures cover the Phoenix-Mesa-Scottsdale, AZ Metropolitan Statistical Area; (2) Methodist/Pietist; (3) Latter Day Saints; (4) Reformed; (5) Figures are estimates
Source: Association of Statisticians of American Religious Bodies, 2010 U.S. Religion Census: Religious Congregations & Membership Study

Religious Groups by Tradition

Area	Catholic	Evangelical Protestant	Mainline Protestant	Other Tradition	Black Protestant	Orthodox
MSA[1]	13.4	13.2	2.6	7.8	0.2	0.3
U.S.	19.1	16.2	7.3	4.3	1.6	0.3

Note: Figures are the number of adherents as a percentage of the total population; (1) Figures cover the Phoenix-Mesa-Scottsdale, AZ Metropolitan Statistical Area
Source: Association of Statisticians of American Religious Bodies, 2010 U.S. Religion Census: Religious Congregations & Membership Study

ECONOMY

Gross Metropolitan Product

Area	2017	2018	2019	2020	Rank[2]
MSA[1]	248.0	264.9	280.3	294.0	16

Note: Figures are in billions of dollars; (1) Figures cover the Phoenix-Mesa-Scottsdale, AZ Metropolitan Statistical Area; (2) Rank is based on 2018 data and ranges from 1 to 381
Source: U.S. Conference of Mayors, U.S. Metro Economies: GMP & Employment 2018-2020, September 2019

Economic Growth

Area	2015-17 (%)	2018 (%)	2019 (%)	2020 (%)	Rank[2]
MSA[1]	3.3	4.5	4.0	2.7	54
U.S.	1.9	2.9	2.3	2.1	–

Note: Figures are real gross metropolitan product (GMP) growth rates and represent average annual percent change; (1) Figures cover the Phoenix-Mesa-Scottsdale, AZ Metropolitan Statistical Area; (2) Rank is based on 2017 2-year average annual percent change and ranges from 1 to 381
Source: U.S. Conference of Mayors, U.S. Metro Economies: GMP & Employment 2018-2020, September 2019

Metropolitan Area Exports

Area	2015	2016	2017	2018	2019	2020	Rank[2]
MSA[1]	13,821.5	12,838.2	13,223.1	13,614.9	15,136.6	11,073.9	29

Note: Figures are in millions of dollars; (1) Figures cover the Phoenix-Mesa-Scottsdale, AZ Metropolitan Statistical Area; (2) Rank is based on 2020 data and ranges from 1 to 389
Source: U.S. Department of Commerce, International Trade Administration, Office of Trade and Economic Analysis, Industry and Analysis, Exports by Metropolitan Area, data extracted March 4, 2022

Building Permits

Area	Single-Family			Multi-Family			Total		
	2019	2020	Pct. Chg.	2019	2020	Pct. Chg.	2019	2020	Pct. Chg.
City	4,175	4,666	11.8	5,723	6,981	22.0	9,898	11,647	17.7
MSA[1]	25,026	31,658	26.5	10,847	16,561	52.7	35,873	48,219	34.4
U.S.	862,100	979,400	13.6	523,900	491,700	-6.1	1,386,000	1,471,100	6.1

Note: (1) Figures cover the Phoenix-Mesa-Scottsdale, AZ Metropolitan Statistical Area; Figures represent new, privately-owned housing units authorized (unadjusted data); All permit data are based on estimates with imputation
Source: U.S. Census Bureau, Manufacturing, Mining, and Construction Statistics, Building Permits, 2019, 2020

Bankruptcy Filings

Area	Business Filings			Nonbusiness Filings		
	2020	2021	% Chg.	2020	2021	% Chg.
Maricopa County	261	223	-14.6	8,954	6,402	-28.5
U.S.	21,655	14,347	-33.7	522,808	399,269	-23.6

Note: Business filings include Chapter 7, Chapter 9, Chapter 11, Chapter 12, Chapter 13, Chapter 15, and Section 304; Nonbusiness filings include Chapter 7, Chapter 11, and Chapter 13
Source: Administrative Office of the U.S. Courts, Business and Nonbusiness Bankruptcy, County Cases Commenced by Chapter of the Bankruptcy Code, During the 12-Month Period Ending December 31, 2020 and Business and Nonbusiness Bankruptcy, County Cases Commenced by Chapter of the Bankruptcy Code, During the 12-Month Period Ending December 31, 2021

Housing Vacancy Rates

Area	Gross Vacancy Rate[2] (%)			Year-Round Vacancy Rate[3] (%)			Rental Vacancy Rate[4] (%)			Homeowner Vacancy Rate[5] (%)		
	2019	2020	2021	2019	2020	2021	2019	2020	2021	2019	2020	2021
MSA[1]	10.3	8.9	9.0	6.2	5.3	5.6	5.0	4.9	4.9	1.0	0.7	0.6
U.S.	12.0	10.6	10.8	9.5	8.2	8.4	6.7	6.3	6.1	1.4	1.0	0.9

Note: (1) Figures cover the Phoenix-Mesa-Scottsdale, AZ Metropolitan Statistical Area; (2) The percentage of the total housing inventory that is vacant; (3) The percentage of the housing inventory (excluding seasonal units) that is year-round vacant; (4) The percentage of rental inventory that is vacant for rent; (5) The percentage of homeowner inventory that is vacant for sale
Source: U.S. Census Bureau, Housing Vacancies and Homeownership Annual Statistics: 2019, 2020, 2021

INCOME

Income

Area	Per Capita ($)	Median Household ($)	Average Household ($)
City	31,427	60,914	85,527
MSA[1]	34,378	67,068	91,834
U.S.	35,384	64,994	91,547

Note: (1) Figures cover the Phoenix-Mesa-Scottsdale, AZ Metropolitan Statistical Area
Source: U.S. Census Bureau, 2016-2020 American Community Survey 5-Year Estimates

Household Income Distribution

Area	Percent of Households Earning							
	Under $15,000	$15,000 -$24,999	$25,000 -$34,999	$35,000 -$49,999	$50,000 -$74,999	$75,000 -$99,999	$100,000 -$149,999	$150,000 and up
City	9.2	8.3	9.3	14.2	19.0	13.0	14.1	12.9
MSA[1]	8.2	7.4	8.3	12.8	18.6	13.6	16.5	14.6
U.S.	9.9	8.5	8.6	12.0	17.2	12.8	15.6	15.4

Note: (1) Figures cover the Phoenix-Mesa-Scottsdale, AZ Metropolitan Statistical Area
Source: U.S. Census Bureau, 2016-2020 American Community Survey 5-Year Estimates

CITY FINANCES

Poverty Rate

Area	All Ages	Under 18 Years Old	18 to 64 Years Old	65 Years and Over
City	16.2	24.0	14.0	10.5
MSA[1]	12.7	18.1	11.7	8.1
U.S.	12.8	17.5	12.1	9.3

Note: Figures are percentage of people whose income during the past 12 months was below the poverty level; (1) Figures cover the Phoenix-Mesa-Scottsdale, AZ Metropolitan Statistical Area
Source: U.S. Census Bureau, 2016-2020 American Community Survey 5-Year Estimates

City Government Finances

Component	2019 ($000)	2019 ($ per capita)
Total Revenues	3,978,771	2,447
Total Expenditures	3,337,307	2,052
Debt Outstanding	7,275,403	4,474
Cash and Securities[1]	5,188,556	3,191

Note: (1) Cash and security holdings of a government at the close of its fiscal year, including those of its dependent agencies, utilities, and liquor stores.
Source: U.S. Census Bureau, State & Local Government Finances 2019

City Government Revenue by Source

Source	2019 ($000)	2019 ($ per capita)	2019 (%)
General Revenue			
From Federal Government	183,656	113	4.6
From State Government	716,731	441	18.0
From Local Governments	28,290	17	0.7
Taxes			
Property	365,400	225	9.2
Sales and Gross Receipts	969,661	596	24.4
Personal Income	0	0	0.0
Corporate Income	0	0	0.0
Motor Vehicle License	0	0	0.0
Other Taxes	112,780	69	2.8
Current Charges	928,433	571	23.3
Liquor Store	0	0	0.0
Utility	447,540	275	11.2

Source: U.S. Census Bureau, State & Local Government Finances 2019

City Government Expenditures by Function

Function	2019 ($000)	2019 ($ per capita)	2019 (%)
General Direct Expenditures			
Air Transportation	565,871	348	17.0
Corrections	0	0	0.0
Education	2,710	1	0.1
Employment Security Administration	0	0	0.0
Financial Administration	40,280	24	1.2
Fire Protection	350,923	215	10.5
General Public Buildings	8,658	5	0.3
Governmental Administration, Other	16,383	10	0.5
Health	0	0	0.0
Highways	159,980	98	4.8
Hospitals	0	0	0.0
Housing and Community Development	137,212	84	4.1
Interest on General Debt	268,211	164	8.0
Judicial and Legal	45,094	27	1.4
Libraries	35,988	22	1.1
Parking	1,390	< 1	< 0.1
Parks and Recreation	180,398	110	5.4
Police Protection	479,661	295	14.4
Public Welfare	208	< 1	< 0.1
Sewerage	99,927	61	3.0
Solid Waste Management	129,130	79	3.9
Veterans' Services	0	0	0.0
Liquor Store	0	0	0.0
Utility	637,328	391	19.1

Source: U.S. Census Bureau, State & Local Government Finances 2019

EMPLOYMENT

Labor Force and Employment

Area	Civilian Labor Force			Workers Employed		
	Dec. 2020	Dec. 2021	% Chg.	Dec. 2020	Dec. 2021	% Chg.
City	879,665	899,909	2.3	817,499	876,739	7.2
MSA[1]	2,529,507	2,601,855	2.9	2,367,440	2,538,519	7.2
U.S.	160,017,000	161,696,000	1.0	149,613,000	155,732,000	4.1

Note: Data is not seasonally adjusted and covers workers 16 years of age and older; (1) Figures cover the Phoenix-Mesa-Scottsdale, AZ Metropolitan Statistical Area
Source: Bureau of Labor Statistics, Local Area Unemployment Statistics

Unemployment Rate

Area	2021											
	Jan.	Feb.	Mar.	Apr.	May	Jun.	Jul.	Aug.	Sep.	Oct.	Nov.	Dec.
City	7.2	7.3	6.6	6.6	6.7	7.1	6.2	5.2	4.2	3.5	3.0	2.6
MSA[1]	6.6	6.7	6.1	6.1	6.2	6.6	5.7	4.7	3.8	3.2	2.8	2.4
U.S.	6.8	6.6	6.2	5.7	5.5	6.1	5.7	5.3	4.6	4.3	3.9	3.7

Note: Data is not seasonally adjusted and covers workers 16 years of age and older; (1) Figures cover the Phoenix-Mesa-Scottsdale, AZ Metropolitan Statistical Area
Source: Bureau of Labor Statistics, Local Area Unemployment Statistics

Average Wages

Occupation	$/Hr.	Occupation	$/Hr.
Accountants and Auditors	38.88	Maintenance and Repair Workers	21.54
Automotive Mechanics	23.07	Marketing Managers	63.45
Bookkeepers	21.64	Network and Computer Systems Admin.	43.62
Carpenters	23.77	Nurses, Licensed Practical	28.14
Cashiers	14.34	Nurses, Registered	39.72
Computer Programmers	39.02	Nursing Assistants	16.94
Computer Systems Analysts	47.79	Office Clerks, General	20.37
Computer User Support Specialists	26.83	Physical Therapists	45.87
Construction Laborers	19.70	Physicians	123.85
Cooks, Restaurant	16.11	Plumbers, Pipefitters and Steamfitters	27.19
Customer Service Representatives	18.74	Police and Sheriff's Patrol Officers	34.65
Dentists	87.75	Postal Service Mail Carriers	26.85
Electricians	24.53	Real Estate Sales Agents	24.19
Engineers, Electrical	48.89	Retail Salespersons	16.62
Fast Food and Counter Workers	15.27	Sales Representatives, Technical/Scientific	45.15
Financial Managers	66.61	Secretaries, Exc. Legal/Medical/Executive	19.83
First-Line Supervisors of Office Workers	29.45	Security Guards	16.17
General and Operations Managers	50.20	Surgeons	n/a
Hairdressers/Cosmetologists	19.51	Teacher Assistants, Exc. Postsecondary*	14.59
Home Health and Personal Care Aides	14.23	Teachers, Secondary School, Exc. Sp. Ed.*	27.99
Janitors and Cleaners	15.02	Telemarketers	15.88
Landscaping/Groundskeeping Workers	16.57	Truck Drivers, Heavy/Tractor-Trailer	24.44
Lawyers	63.06	Truck Drivers, Light/Delivery Services	21.56
Maids and Housekeeping Cleaners	14.71	Waiters and Waitresses	19.59

Note: Wage data covers the Phoenix-Mesa-Scottsdale, AZ Metropolitan Statistical Area; (*) Hourly wages were calculated from annual wage data based on a 40 hour work week; n/a not available.
Source: Bureau of Labor Statistics, Metro Area Occupational Employment & Wage Estimates, May 2021

Employment by Industry

Sector	MSA[1]		U.S.
	Number of Employees	Percent of Total	Percent of Total
Construction	139,900	6.1	5.0
Education and Health Services	351,900	15.4	16.0
Financial Activities	217,200	9.5	5.9
Government	244,000	10.7	14.9
Information	41,600	1.8	1.9
Leisure and Hospitality	224,700	9.8	9.8
Manufacturing	139,100	6.1	8.4
Mining and Logging	2,900	0.1	0.4
Other Services	70,900	3.1	3.7
Professional and Business Services	385,800	16.9	14.6
Retail Trade	260,200	11.4	10.7
Transportation, Warehousing, and Utilities	122,500	5.4	4.8
Wholesale Trade	85,900	3.8	3.8

Note: Figures are non-farm employment as of December 2021. Figures are not seasonally adjusted and include workers 16 years of age and older; (1) Figures cover the Phoenix-Mesa-Scottsdale, AZ Metropolitan Statistical Area
Source: Bureau of Labor Statistics, Current Employment Statistics, Employment, Hours, and Earnings

Employment by Occupation

Occupation Classification	City (%)	MSA[1] (%)	U.S. (%)
Management, Business, Science, and Arts	35.7	38.8	39.5
Natural Resources, Construction, and Maintenance	9.6	8.4	8.7
Production, Transportation, and Material Moving	12.3	11.0	13.1
Sales and Office	23.7	24.4	21.3
Service	18.7	17.5	17.4

Note: Figures cover employed civilians 16 years of age and older; (1) Figures cover the Phoenix-Mesa-Scottsdale, AZ Metropolitan Statistical Area
Source: U.S. Census Bureau, 2016-2020 American Community Survey 5-Year Estimates

Occupations with Greatest Projected Employment Growth: 2021 – 2023

Occupation[1]	2021 Employment	2023 Projected Employment	Numeric Employment Change	Percent Employment Change
Home Health and Personal Care Aides	73,830	83,930	10,100	13.7
Laborers and Freight, Stock, and Material Movers, Hand	61,750	68,460	6,710	10.9
Customer Service Representatives	108,520	114,910	6,390	5.9
Stockers and Order Fillers	56,260	62,630	6,370	11.3
Waiters and Waitresses	45,830	51,130	5,300	11.6
Fast Food and Counter Workers	54,000	59,140	5,140	9.5
Cooks, Restaurant	31,160	36,290	5,130	16.5
Software Developers and Software Quality Assurance Analysts and Testers	40,110	45,180	5,070	12.6
Registered Nurses	58,640	63,090	4,450	7.6
General and Operations Managers	54,050	58,370	4,320	8.0

Note: Projections cover Arizona; (1) Sorted by numeric employment change
Source: www.projectionscentral.com, State Occupational Projections, 2021–2023 Short-Term Projections

Fastest-Growing Occupations: 2021 – 2023

Occupation[1]	2021 Employment	2023 Projected Employment	Numeric Employment Change	Percent Employment Change
Hotel, Motel, and Resort Desk Clerks	4,850	6,120	1,270	26.2
Ushers, Lobby Attendants, and Ticket Takers	1,000	1,250	250	25.0
Lodging Managers	1,300	1,620	320	24.6
Baggage Porters and Bellhops	750	910	160	21.3
Locker Room, Coatroom, and Dressing Room Attendants	240	290	50	20.8
Conveyor Operators and Tenders	290	350	60	20.7
Athletes and Sports Competitors	830	1,000	170	20.5
Barbers	780	940	160	20.5
Fine Artists, Including Painters, Sculptors, and Illustrators	490	590	100	20.4
Musicians and Singers	1,620	1,950	330	20.4

Note: Projections cover Arizona; (1) Sorted by percent employment change and excludes occupations with numeric employment change less than 50
Source: www.projectionscentral.com, State Occupational Projections, 2021–2023 Short-Term Projections

TAXES

State Corporate Income Tax Rates

State	Tax Rate (%)	Income Brackets ($)	Num. of Brackets	Financial Institution Tax Rate (%)[a]	Federal Income Tax Ded.
Arizona	4.9 (b)	Flat rate	1	4.9 (b)	No

Note: Tax rates as of January 1, 2022; (a) Rates listed are the corporate income tax rate applied to financial institutions or excise taxes based on income. Some states have other taxes based upon the value of deposits or shares; (b) Minimum tax is $800 in California, $250 in District of Columbia, $50 in Arizona and North Dakota (banks), $400 ($100 banks) in Rhode Island, $200 per location in South Dakota (banks), $100 in Utah, $300 in Vermont.
Source: Federation of Tax Administrators, State Corporate Income Tax Rates, January 1, 2022

State Individual Income Tax Rates

State	Tax Rate (%)	Income Brackets ($)	Personal Exemptions ($)			Standard Ded. ($)	
			Single	Married	Depend.	Single	Married
Arizona (a)	2.59 - 4.5	27,808 - 166,843 (b)	–	–	100 (c)	12,550	25,100

Note: Tax rates as of January 1, 2022; Local- and county-level taxes are not included; Federal income tax is not deductible on state income tax returns; (a) 19 states have statutory provision for automatically adjusting to the rate of inflation the dollar values of the income tax brackets, standard deductions, and/or personal exemptions. Michigan indexes the personal exemption only. Oregon does not index the income brackets for $125,000 and over; (b) For joint returns, taxes are twice the tax on half the couple's income; (c) The personal exemption takes the form of a tax credit instead of a deduction
Source: Federation of Tax Administrators, State Individual Income Tax Rates, January 1, 2022

Various State Sales and Excise Tax Rates

State	State Sales Tax (%)	Gasoline[1] (¢/gal.)	Cigarette[2] ($/pack)	Spirits[3] ($/gal.)	Wine[4] ($/gal.)	Beer[5] ($/gal.)	Recreational Marijuana (%)
Arizona	5.6	19	2	3	0.84	0.16	(b)

Note: All tax rates as of January 1, 2022; (1) The American Petroleum Institute has developed a methodology for determining the average tax rate on a gallon of fuel. Rates may include any of the following: excise taxes, environmental fees, storage tank fees, other fees or taxes, general sales tax, and local taxes; (2) The federal excise tax of $1.0066 per pack and local taxes are not included; (3) Rates are those applicable to off-premise sales of 40% alcohol by volume (a.b.v.) distilled spirits in 750ml containers. Local excise taxes are excluded; (4) Rates are those applicable to off-premise sales of 11% a.b.v. non-carbonated wine in 750ml containers; (5) Rates are those applicable to off-premise sales of 4.7% a.b.v. beer in 12 ounce containers; (b) 16% excise tax (retail price)
Source: Tax Foundation, 2022 Facts & Figures: How Does Your State Compare?

State Business Tax Climate Index Rankings

State	Overall Rank	Corporate Tax Rank	Individual Income Tax Rank	Sales Tax Rank	Property Tax Rank	Unemployment Insurance Tax Rank
Arizona	23	23	18	40	11	11

Note: The index is a measure of how each state's tax laws affect economic performance. The lower the rank, the more favorable a state's tax system is for business. States without a given tax are given a ranking of 1. The scores/rankings for the District of Columbia do not affect other states. The 2022 index represents the tax climate as of July 1, 2021.
Source: Tax Foundation, State Business Tax Climate Index 2022

TRANSPORTATION

Means of Transportation to Work

Area	Car/Truck/Van		Public Transportation			Bicycle	Walked	Other Means	Worked at Home
	Drove Alone	Car-pooled	Bus	Subway	Railroad				
City	72.9	12.2	2.4	0.1	0.0	0.6	1.5	2.0	8.3
MSA[1]	73.9	10.8	1.5	0.0	0.0	0.6	1.5	1.9	9.7
U.S.	74.9	8.9	2.2	1.7	0.5	0.5	2.6	1.4	7.3

Note: Figures are percentages and cover workers 16 years of age and older; (1) Figures cover the Phoenix-Mesa-Scottsdale, AZ Metropolitan Statistical Area
Source: U.S. Census Bureau, 2016-2020 American Community Survey 5-Year Estimates

Travel Time to Work

Area	Less Than 10 Minutes	10 to 19 Minutes	20 to 29 Minutes	30 to 44 Minutes	45 to 59 Minutes	60 to 89 Minutes	90 Minutes or More
City	8.8	26.5	25.7	24.9	7.6	4.8	1.9
MSA[1]	9.9	26.1	23.7	23.7	8.9	5.8	1.9
U.S.	12.3	28.4	20.9	20.9	8.3	6.4	2.9

Note: Note: Figures are percentages and include workers 16 years old and over; (1) Figures cover the Phoenix-Mesa-Scottsdale, AZ Metropolitan Statistical Area
Source: U.S. Census Bureau, 2016-2020 American Community Survey 5-Year Estimates

Key Congestion Measures

Measure	1990	2000	2010	2015	2020
Annual Hours of Delay, Total (000)	42,716	86,505	133,493	156,520	68,645
Annual Hours of Delay, Per Auto Commuter	41	45	50	59	25
Annual Congestion Cost, Per Auto Commuter ($)	544	829	1,017	1,102	489

Note: Covers the Phoenix-Mesa AZ urban area
Source: Texas A&M Transportation Institute, 2021 Urban Mobility Report

Freeway Travel Time Index

Measure	1985	1990	1995	2000	2005	2010	2015	2020
Urban Area Index[1]	1.20	1.21	1.22	1.25	1.28	1.28	1.27	1.08
Urban Area Rank[1,2]	5	7	13	16	14	16	20	44

Note: Freeway Travel Time Index—the ratio of travel time in the peak period to the travel time at free-flow conditions. For example, a value of 1.30 indicates a 20-minute free-flow trip takes 26 minutes in the peak (20 minutes x 1.30 = 26 minutes); (1) Covers the Phoenix-Mesa AZ urban area; (2) Rank is based on 101 larger urban areas (#1 = highest travel time index)
Source: Texas A&M Transportation Institute, 2021 Urban Mobility Report

Public Transportation

Agency Name / Mode of Transportation	Vehicles Operated in Maximum Service[1]	Annual Unlinked Passenger Trips[2] (in thous.)	Annual Passenger Miles[3] (in thous.)
City of Phoenix Public Transit Dept. (Valley Metro)			
Bus (purchased transportation)	419	30,330.7	107,447.9
Demand Response (purchased transportation)	112	299.8	2,274.5

Note: (1) Number of revenue vehicles operated by the given mode and type of service to meet the annual maximum service requirement. This is the revenue vehicle count during the peak season of the year; on the week and day that maximum service is provided. Vehicles operated in maximum service (VOMS) exclude atypical days and one-time special events; (2) Number of passengers who boarded public transportation vehicles. Passengers are counted each time they board a vehicle no matter how many vehicles they use to travel from their origin to their destination. (3) Sum of the distances ridden by all passengers during the entire fiscal year.
Source: Federal Transit Administration, National Transit Database, 2020

Air Transportation

Airport Name and Code / Type of Service	Passenger Airlines[1]	Passenger Enplanements	Freight Carriers[2]	Freight (lbs)
Phoenix Sky Harbor International (PHX)				
Domestic service (U.S. carriers - 2021)	28	18,797,074	20	400,960,194
International service (U.S. carriers - 2020)	7	239,386	2	241,145

Note: (1) Includes all U.S.-based major, minor and commuter airlines that carried at least one passenger during the year; (2) Includes all U.S.-based airlines and freight carriers that transported at least one pound of freight during the year.
Source: Bureau of Transportation Statistics, The Intermodal Transportation Database, Air Carriers: T-100 Domestic Market (U.S. Carriers), 2021; Bureau of Transportation Statistics, The Intermodal Transportation Database, Air Carriers: T-100 International Market (U.S. Carriers), 2020

BUSINESSES

Major Business Headquarters

Company Name	Industry	Rankings	
		Fortune[1]	Forbes[2]
Avnet	Wholesalers, Electronics and Office Equipment	168	-
Freeport-McMoRan	Mining, Crude-Oil Production	215	-
Petsmart	Retailing	-	52
Republic Services	Waste Management	297	-
Shamrock Foods	Food, Drink & Tobacco	-	155
Sprouts Farmers Market	Food and Drugstores	437	-

Note: (1) Companies that produce a 10-K are ranked 1 to 500 based on 2020 revenue; (2) All private companies with at least $2 billion in annual revenue through the end of their most current fiscal year are ranked 1 to 225; companies listed are headquartered in the city; dashes indicate no ranking
Source: Fortune, "Fortune 500," 2021; Forbes, "America's Largest Private Companies," 2021

Fastest-Growing Businesses

According to *Inc.*, Phoenix is home to four of America's 500 fastest-growing private companies: **BIM Designs** (#148); **Paradigm Laboratories** (#224); **RallyUp** (#323); **me4kidz** (#346). Criteria: must be an independent, privately-held, for-profit, U.S. corporation, proprietorship or partnership as of December 31, 2020; revenues must be at least $100,000 in 2017 and $2 million in 2020; must have four-year operating/sales history. *Inc., "America's 500 Fastest-Growing Private Companies," 2021*

According to *Initiative for a Competitive Inner City (ICIC)*, Phoenix is home to one of America's 100 fastest-growing "inner city" companies: **WebPT** (#33). Criteria for inclusion: company must be headquartered in or have 51 percent or more of its physical operations in an economically distressed urban area; must be an independent, for-profit corporation, partnership or proprietorship; must have 10 or more employees and have a five-year sales history that includes sales of at least $200,000 in the base year and at least $1 million in the current year with no decrease in sales over the two most recent years. Companies were ranked overall by revenue growth over the five-year period between 2016 and 2020. *Initiative for a Competitive Inner City (ICIC), "Inner City 100 Companies," 2021*

Living Environment

COST OF LIVING

Cost of Living Index

Composite Index	Groceries	Housing	Utilities	Trans-portation	Health Care	Misc. Goods/ Services
103.9	99.2	117.0	105.9	102.8	92.9	94.2

Note: The Cost of Living Index measures regional differences in the cost of consumer goods and services, excluding taxes and non-consumer expenditures, for professional and managerial households in the top income quintile. It is based on more than 50,000 prices covering almost 60 different items for which prices are collected three times a year by chambers of commerce, economic development organizations or university applied economic centers in each participating urban area. The numbers shown should be read as a percentage above or below the national average of 100. For example, a value of 115.4 in the groceries column indicates that grocery prices are 15.4% higher than the national average. Small differences in the index numbers should not be interpreted as significant; Figures cover the Phoenix AZ urban area.
Source: The Council for Community and Economic Research, Cost of Living Index, 2021

Grocery Prices

Area[1]	T-Bone Steak ($/pound)	Frying Chicken ($/pound)	Whole Milk ($/half gal.)	Eggs ($/dozen)	Orange Juice ($/64 oz.)	Coffee ($/11.5 oz.)
City[2]	13.76	1.61	1.82	1.78	3.78	4.69
Avg.	12.82	1.40	2.22	1.57	3.59	4.30
Min.	8.91	0.91	1.29	0.75	2.87	3.02
Max.	21.35	2.69	3.92	3.86	5.49	8.11

*Note: (1) Values for the local area are compared with the average, minimum and maximum values for all 285 areas in the Cost of Living Index; (2) Figures cover the Phoenix AZ urban area; **T-Bone Steak** (price per pound); **Frying Chicken** (price per pound, whole fryer); **Whole Milk** (half gallon carton); **Eggs** (price per dozen, Grade A, large); **Orange Juice** (64 oz. Tropicana or Florida Natural); **Coffee** (11.5 oz. can, vacuum-packed, Maxwell House, Hills Bros, or Folgers).*
Source: The Council for Community and Economic Research, Cost of Living Index, 2021

Housing and Utility Costs

Area[1]	New Home Price ($)	Apartment Rent ($/month)	All Electric ($/month)	Part Electric ($/month)	Other Energy ($/month)	Telephone ($/month)
City[2]	394,309	1,745	192.55	-	-	181.87
Avg.	398,393	1,217	171.38	100.83	69.67	187.75
Min.	212,799	534	96.71	31.56	27.15	173.01
Max.	2,354,006	4,438	369.53	277.33	303.87	206.73

*Note: (1) Values for the local area are compared with the average, minimum and maximum values for all 285 areas in the Cost of Living Index; (2) Figures cover the Phoenix AZ urban area; **New Home Price** (2,400 sf living area, 8,000 sf lot, in urban area with full utilities); **Apartment Rent** (950 sf 2 bedroom/1.5 or 2 bath, unfurnished, excluding all utilities except water); **All Electric** (average monthly cost for an all-electric home); **Part Electric** (average monthly cost for a part-electric home); **Other Energy** (average monthly cost for natural gas, fuel oil, coal, wood, and any other forms of energy except electricity); **Telephone** (price includes the base monthly rate plus taxes and fees for three lines of mobile phone service).*
Source: The Council for Community and Economic Research, Cost of Living Index, 2021

Health Care, Transportation, and Other Costs

Area[1]	Doctor ($/visit)	Dentist ($/visit)	Optometrist ($/visit)	Gasoline ($/gallon)	Beauty Salon ($/visit)	Men's Shirt ($)
City[2]	99.00	92.00	111.72	2.88	40.00	25.85
Avg.	118.16	101.04	109.44	2.71	40.63	30.77
Min.	35.04	55.56	51.17	2.17	18.59	11.32
Max.	231.10	165.12	256.81	4.11	85.33	63.03

*Note: (1) Values for the local area are compared with the average, minimum and maximum values for all 285 areas in the Cost of Living Index; (2) Figures cover the Phoenix AZ urban area; **Doctor** (general practitioners routine exam of an established patient); **Dentist** (adult teeth cleaning and periodic oral examination); **Optometrist** (full vision eye exam for established adult patient); **Gasoline** (one gallon regular unleaded, national brand, including all taxes, cash price at self-service pump if available); **Beauty Salon** (woman's shampoo, trim, and blow-dry); **Men's Shirt** (cotton/polyester dress shirt, pinpoint weave, long sleeves).*
Source: The Council for Community and Economic Research, Cost of Living Index, 2021

HOUSING

Homeownership Rate

Area	2013 (%)	2014 (%)	2015 (%)	2016 (%)	2017 (%)	2018 (%)	2019 (%)	2020 (%)	2021 (%)
MSA[1]	62.2	61.9	61.0	62.6	64.0	65.3	65.9	67.9	65.2
U.S.	65.1	64.5	63.7	63.4	63.9	64.4	64.6	66.6	65.5

Note: (1) Figures cover the Phoenix-Mesa-Scottsdale, AZ Metropolitan Statistical Area
Source: U.S. Census Bureau, Housing Vacancies and Homeownership Annual Statistics: 2013-2021

House Price Index (HPI)

Area	National Ranking[2]	Quarterly Change (%)	One-Year Change (%)	Five-Year Change (%)	Since 1991Q1 (%)
MSA[1]	11	5.33	29.26	77.70	397.18
U.S.[3]	–	3.33	17.54	54.45	258.04

Note: The HPI is a weighted repeat sales index. It measures average price changes in repeat sales or refinancings on the same properties. This information is obtained by reviewing repeat mortgage transactions on single-family properties whose mortgages have been purchased or securitized by Fannie Mae or Freddie Mac since January 1975; (1) Figures cover the Phoenix-Mesa-Scottsdale, AZ Metropolitan Statistical Area; (2) Rankings are based on annual percentage change for all metro areas containing at least 15,000 transactions over the last 10 years and ranges from 1 to 268; (3) figures based on a weighted average of Census Division estimates using a seasonally adjusted, purchase-only index; all figures are for the period ending December 31, 2021

Source: Federal Housing Finance Agency, Change in FHFA Metropolitan Area House Price Indexes, 2021Q4

Median Single-Family Home Prices

Area	2019	2020	2021[p]	Percent Change 2020 to 2021
MSA[1]	287.1	333.0	415.4	24.7
U.S. Average	274.6	300.2	353.4	17.7

Note: Figures are median sales prices of existing single-family homes in thousands of dollars; (p) preliminary; (1) Figures cover the Phoenix-Mesa-Scottsdale, AZ Metropolitan Statistical Area

Source: National Association of Realtors, Median Sales Price of Existing Single-Family Homes for Metropolitan Areas, 4th Quarter 2021

Qualifying Income Based on Median Sales Price of Existing Single-Family Homes

Area	With 5% Down ($)	With 10% Down ($)	With 20% Down ($)
MSA[1]	87,887	83,262	74,010
U.S. Average	70,699	66,978	59,536

Note: Figures are preliminary; Qualifying income is based on a mortgage rate of 3.13%. Monthly principal and interest payment is limited to 25% of income; (1) Figures cover the Phoenix-Mesa-Scottsdale, AZ Metropolitan Statistical Area

Source: National Association of Realtors, Qualifying Income Based on Median Sales Price of Existing Single-Family Homes for Metropolitan Areas, 4th Quarter 2021

Home Value Distribution

Area	Under $50,000	$50,000 -$99,999	$100,000 -$149,999	$150,000 -$199,999	$200,000 -$299,999	$300,000 -$499,999	$500,000 -$999,999	$1,000,000 or more
City	4.2	4.4	8.4	16.2	28.8	24.8	11.3	1.9
MSA[1]	5.4	4.0	6.8	13.3	28.9	28.1	11.0	2.5
U.S.	6.6	11.0	12.3	13.6	20.0	20.5	12.3	3.7

Note: Figures are percentages and cover owner-occupied housing units; (1) Figures cover the Phoenix-Mesa-Scottsdale, AZ Metropolitan Statistical Area

Source: U.S. Census Bureau, 2016-2020 American Community Survey 5-Year Estimates

Year Housing Structure Built

Area	2010 or Later	2000 -2009	1990 -1999	1980 -1989	1970 -1979	1960 -1969	1950 -1959	1940 -1949	Before 1940	Median Year
City	5.3	16.3	16.2	17.3	19.6	11.5	9.6	2.4	1.9	1983
MSA[1]	8.1	24.7	20.0	17.1	15.9	7.2	4.8	1.2	0.9	1991
U.S.	6.2	13.6	13.9	13.4	15.0	10.5	10.2	4.8	12.4	1978

Note: Figures are percentages except for Median Year; Note: (1) Figures cover the Phoenix-Mesa-Scottsdale, AZ Metropolitan Statistical Area

Source: U.S. Census Bureau, 2016-2020 American Community Survey 5-Year Estimates

Gross Monthly Rent

Area	Under $500	$500 -$999	$1,000 -$1,499	$1,500 -$1,999	$2,000 -$2,499	$2,500 -$2,999	$3,000 and up	Median ($)
City	4.3	35.7	42.0	14.0	2.8	0.7	0.5	1,100
MSA[1]	3.4	29.6	41.8	18.2	4.5	1.2	1.3	1,177
U.S.	8.9	34.3	30.2	14.9	6.2	2.6	2.8	1,096

Note: Figures are percentages except for Median; Gross rent is the contract rent plus the estimated average monthly cost of utilities (electricity, gas, and water and sewer) and fuels (oil, coal, kerosene, wood, etc.) if these are paid by the renter (or paid for the renter by someone else); (1) Figures cover the Phoenix-Mesa-Scottsdale, AZ Metropolitan Statistical Area

Source: U.S. Census Bureau, 2016-2020 American Community Survey 5-Year Estimates

HEALTH

Health Risk Factors

Category	MSA[1] (%)	U.S. (%)
Adults aged 18–64 who have any kind of health care coverage	80.5	86.8
Adults who reported being in good or better health	85.6	86.7
Adults who are current smokers	12.4	15.5
Adults who currently use chewing tobacco, snuff, or snus	2.7	3.7
Adults who are heavy drinkers[2]	6.4	6.7
Adults who are binge drinkers[3]	14.1	15.7
Adults who are overweight (BMI 25.0 - 29.9)	35.0	35.2
Adults who are obese (BMI 30.0 - 99.8)	31.2	31.9
Adults who participated in any physical activities in the past month	78.2	77.6
Adults who always or nearly always wears a seat belt	94.4	94.2

Note: (1) Figures cover the Phoenix-Mesa-Scottsdale, AZ Metropolitan Statistical Area; (2) Heavy drinkers are classified as adult men having more than 14 drinks per week and adult women having more than 7 drinks per week; (3) Binge drinkers are classified as males having five or more drinks on one occasion or females having four or more drinks on one occasion

Source: Centers for Disease Control and Prevention, Behaviorial Risk Factor Surveillance System, SMART: Selected Metropolitan Area Risk Trends, 2020

Acute and Chronic Health Conditions

Category	MSA[1] (%)	U.S. (%)
Adults who have ever been told they had a heart attack	4.1	4.3
Adults who have ever been told they have angina or coronary heart disease	3.4	4.0
Adults who have ever been told they had a stroke	2.7	2.8
Adults who have ever been told they have asthma	14.5	14.2
Adults who have ever been told they have arthritis	21.3	24.5
Adults who have ever been told they have diabetes[2]	10.7	10.6
Adults who have ever been told they had skin cancer	7.7	6.4
Adults who have ever been told they had any other types of cancer	6.1	6.8
Adults who have ever been told they have COPD	5.6	6.2
Adults who have ever been told they have kidney disease	3.6	2.9
Adults who have ever been told they have a form of depression	16.7	19.6

Note: (1) Figures cover the Phoenix-Mesa-Scottsdale, AZ Metropolitan Statistical Area; (2) Figures do not include pregnancy-related, borderline, or pre-diabetes

Source: Centers for Disease Control and Prevention, Behaviorial Risk Factor Surveillance System, SMART: Selected Metropolitan Area Risk Trends, 2020

Health Screening and Vaccination Rates

Category	MSA[1] (%)	U.S. (%)
Adults 50-75 who have had a blood stool test within the past year	12.5	9.3
Adults aged 65+ who have had flu shot within the past year	66.9	67.9
Adults aged 65+ who have ever had a pneumonia vaccination	73.2	72.2
Adults who have ever been tested for HIV	36.2	37.1
Women aged 21-65 who have had a pap test in the past three years	75.6	77.7
Men aged 40+ who have had a PSA test within the past two years	30.1	31.8
Women aged 40+ who have had a mammogram within the past two years	68.1	71.5

Note: (1) Figures cover the Phoenix-Mesa-Scottsdale, AZ Metropolitan Statistical Area.

Source: Centers for Disease Control and Prevention, Behaviorial Risk Factor Surveillance System, SMART: Selected Metropolitan Area Risk Trends, 2020

Disability Status

Category	MSA[1] (%)	U.S. (%)
Adults who reported being deaf	5.7	6.8
Are you blind or have serious difficulty seeing, even when wearing glasses?	4.6	4.7
Do you have difficulty doing errands alone?	5.4	6.3
Do you have difficulty dressing or bathing?	2.9	3.0
Do you have serious difficulty concentrating/remembering/making decisions?	9.2	10.8
Do you have serious difficulty walking or climbing stairs?	11.1	11.9

Note: (1) Figures cover the Phoenix-Mesa-Scottsdale, AZ Metropolitan Statistical Area.

Source: Centers for Disease Control and Prevention, Behaviorial Risk Factor Surveillance System, SMART: Selected Metropolitan Area Risk Trends, 2020

Mortality Rates for the Top 10 Causes of Death in the U.S.

ICD-10[a] Sub-Chapter	ICD-10[a] Code	Age-Adjusted Mortality Rate[1] per 100,000 population	
		County[2]	U.S.
Malignant neoplasms	C00-C97	127.0	146.4
Ischaemic heart diseases	I20-I25	78.0	90.2
Other forms of heart disease	I30-I51	34.1	51.9
Other degenerative diseases of the nervous system	G30-G31	52.5	39.7
Other external causes of accidental injury	W00-X59	46.1	38.7
Chronic lower respiratory diseases	J40-J47	36.2	38.1
Cerebrovascular diseases	I60-I69	31.3	37.6
Organic, including symptomatic, mental disorders	F01-F09	14.6	29.4
Hypertensive diseases	I10-I15	30.6	26.1
Diabetes mellitus	E10-E14	23.1	22.6

Note: (a) ICD-10 = International Classification of Diseases 10th Revision; (1) Mortality rates are a three-year average covering 2018-2020; (2) Figures cover Maricopa County.
Source: Centers for Disease Control and Prevention, National Center for Health Statistics. Underlying Cause of Death 1999-2020 on CDC WONDER Online Database

Mortality Rates for Selected Causes of Death

ICD-10[a] Sub-Chapter	ICD-10[a] Code	Age-Adjusted Mortality Rate[1] per 100,000 population	
		County[2]	U.S.
Assault	X85-Y09	6.2	6.5
Diseases of the liver	K70-K76	15.4	15.3
Human immunodeficiency virus (HIV) disease	B20-B24	1.0	1.4
Influenza and pneumonia	J09-J18	10.9	13.4
Intentional self-harm	X60-X84	15.7	13.9
Malnutrition	E40-E46	3.1	2.9
Obesity and other hyperalimentation	E65-E68	2.3	2.4
Renal failure	N17-N19	6.4	12.5
Transport accidents	V01-V99	11.9	12.5
Viral hepatitis	B15-B19	1.2	1.0

Note: (a) ICD-10 = International Classification of Diseases 10th Revision; (1) Mortality rates are a three-year average covering 2018-2020; (2) Figures cover Maricopa County; Data are suppressed when the data meet the criteria for confidentiality constraints; Mortality rates are flagged as unreliable when the rate would be calculated with a numerator of 20 or less.
Source: Centers for Disease Control and Prevention, National Center for Health Statistics. Underlying Cause of Death 1999-2020 on CDC WONDER Online Database

Health Insurance Coverage

Area	With Health Insurance	With Private Health Insurance	With Public Health Insurance	Without Health Insurance	Population Under Age 19 Without Health Insurance
City	85.7	57.4	35.5	14.3	9.6
MSA[1]	89.3	65.4	34.7	10.7	8.5
U.S.	91.3	68.1	35.3	8.7	5.2

Note: Figures are percentages that cover the civilian noninstitutionalized population; (1) Figures cover the Phoenix-Mesa-Scottsdale, AZ Metropolitan Statistical Area
Source: U.S. Census Bureau, 2016-2020 American Community Survey 5-Year Estimates

Number of Medical Professionals

Area	MDs[3]	DOs[3,4]	Dentists	Podiatrists	Chiropractors	Optometrists
County[1] (number)	11,186	1,441	3,128	304	1,509	720
County[1] (rate[2])	253.0	32.6	70.8	6.9	34.1	16.3
U.S. (rate[2])	285.1	23.0	71.1	6.2	28.2	17.0

04013
Note: Data as of 2020 unless noted; (1) Data covers Maricopa County; (2) Rate per 100,000 population; (3) Data as of 2019 and includes all active, non-federal physicians; (4) Doctor of Osteopathic Medicine
Source: U.S. Department of Health and Human Services, Health Resources and Services Administration, Bureau of Health Professions, Area Resource File (ARF) 2020-2021

Best Hospitals

According to *U.S. News,* the Phoenix-Mesa-Scottsdale, AZ metro area is home to four of the best hospitals in the U.S.: **Banner Boswell Medical Center** (1 adult specialty); **Banner Del E. Webb Medical Center** (1 adult specialty); **Barrow Neurological Institute** (1 adult specialty); **Mayo Clinic-Phoenix** (Honor Roll/10 adult specialties). The hospitals listed were nationally ranked in at least one of 15 adult or 10 pediatric specialties. Only 175 U.S. hospitals performed well enough to be nationally ranked in one or more specialties. Twenty hospitals in the U.S. made the Honor Roll. The Best Hospitals Honor Roll takes both the national rankings and the procedure and condition ratings into account. Hospitals received points if they were nationally ranked in one of the 15 adult specialties—the higher they ranked, the more points they got—and how many ratings of "high performing"

they earned in the 17 procedures and conditions. *U.S. News Online, "America's Best Hospitals 2021-22"*

According to *U.S. News,* the Phoenix-Mesa-Scottsdale, AZ metro area is home to one of the best children's hospitals in the U.S.: **Phoenix Children's Hospital** (10 pediatric specialties). The hospital listed was highly ranked in at least one of 10 pediatric specialties. Ninety-two children's hospitals in the U.S. were nationally ranked in at least one specialty. Hospitals received points for being ranked in a specialty, and the 10 hospitals with the most points across the 10 specialties make up the Honor Roll. *U.S. News Online, "America's Best Children's Hospitals 2021-22"*

EDUCATION

Public School District Statistics

District Name	Schls	Pupils	Pupil/ Teacher Ratio	Minority Pupils[1] (%)	LEP/ELL[2] (%)	IEP[3] (%)
Alhambra Elementary District	16	12,307	20.9	95.0	21.4	11.5
Balsz Elementary District	5	2,289	17.8	92.7	23.7	15.2
Cartwright Elementary District	21	16,060	21.3	96.9	23.3	10.7
Creighton Elementary District	10	5,771	17.9	92.9	24.9	12.2
Deer Valley Unified District	39	34,645	18.5	31.8	2.2	12.6
Fowler Elementary District	7	4,428	21.1	89.4	18.7	10.9
Isaac Elementary District	12	6,149	19.9	98.6	35.5	13.4
Madison Elementary District	8	5,971	20.0	52.1	4.4	9.2
Osborn Elementary District	6	2,854	19.1	88.2	13.2	16.0
Paradise Valley Unified District	44	30,999	17.8	44.3	6.1	11.2
Pendergast Elementary District	14	9,161	19.1	90.1	11.4	13.9
Phoenix Elementary District	16	6,239	17.1	93.4	15.9	12.9
Phoenix Union High SD	18	27,603	18.5	94.7	9.9	11.5
Portable Practical Ed. Prep.	2	4,932	n/a	52.1	1.0	17.7
Roosevelt Elementary District	19	8,660	17.5	97.0	21.5	14.2

Note: Table includes school districts with 2,000 or more students; (1) Percentage of students that are not non-Hispanic white; (2) Percentage of students that are Limited English Proficient (LEP) or English Language Learners (ELL) (2018-19); (3) Percentage of students that have an Individualized Education Program (IEP).
Source: U.S. Department of Education, National Center for Education Statistics, Common Core of Data, Local Education Agency (School District) Universe Survey: School Year 2019-2020

Best High Schools

According to *U.S. News,* Phoenix is home to two of the top 500 high schools in the U.S.: **BASIS Ahwatukee** (#45); **BASIS Phoenix** (#52). Nearly 18,000 public, magnet and charter schools were ranked based on their performance on state assessments and how well they prepare students for college. *U.S. News & World Report, "Best High Schools 2021"*

Highest Level of Education

Area	Less than H.S.	H.S. Diploma	Some College, No Deg.	Associate Degree	Bachelor's Degree	Master's Degree	Prof. School Degree	Doctorate Degree
City	17.1	23.4	22.2	7.9	18.5	7.7	2.0	1.2
MSA[1]	11.7	23.1	24.1	8.8	20.4	8.6	2.0	1.3
U.S.	11.5	26.7	20.3	8.6	20.2	9.1	2.2	1.5

Note: Figures cover persons age 25 and over; (1) Figures cover the Phoenix-Mesa-Scottsdale, AZ Metropolitan Statistical Area
Source: U.S. Census Bureau, 2016-2020 American Community Survey 5-Year Estimates

Educational Attainment by Race

Area	High School Graduate or Higher (%)					Bachelor's Degree or Higher (%)				
	Total	White	Black	Asian	Hisp.[2]	Total	White	Black	Asian	Hisp.[2]
City	82.9	85.9	89.0	85.7	64.2	29.4	31.9	24.1	58.6	11.1
MSA[1]	88.3	90.5	90.9	88.4	70.5	32.2	33.7	26.2	58.9	14.0
U.S.	88.5	90.7	86.7	87.3	70.3	32.9	34.4	22.6	55.0	17.6

Note: Figures shown cover persons 25 years old and over; (1) Figures cover the Phoenix-Mesa-Scottsdale, AZ Metropolitan Statistical Area; (2) People of Hispanic origin can be of any race
Source: U.S. Census Bureau, 2016-2020 American Community Survey 5-Year Estimates

School Enrollment by Grade and Control

Area	Preschool (%)		Kindergarten (%)		Grades 1 - 4 (%)		Grades 5 - 8 (%)		Grades 9 - 12 (%)	
	Public	Private	Public	Private	Public	Private	Public	Private	Public	Private
City	61.8	38.2	86.7	13.3	91.3	8.7	91.2	8.8	92.9	7.1
MSA[1]	60.3	39.7	87.0	13.0	90.6	9.4	91.3	8.7	92.8	7.2
U.S.	58.9	41.1	86.9	13.1	89.0	11.0	89.0	11.0	89.7	10.3

Note: Figures shown cover persons 3 years old and over; (1) Figures cover the Phoenix-Mesa-Scottsdale, AZ Metropolitan Statistical Area
Source: U.S. Census Bureau, 2016-2020 American Community Survey 5-Year Estimates

Higher Education

Four-Year Colleges			Two-Year Colleges			Medical Schools[1]	Law Schools[2]	Voc/ Tech[3]
Public	Private Non-profit	Private For-profit	Public	Private Non-profit	Private For-profit			
2	9	13	12	0	12	4	1	25

Note: Figures cover institutions located within the Phoenix-Mesa-Scottsdale, AZ Metropolitan Statistical Area and include main campuses only; (1) includes schools accredited by the Liaison Committee on Medical Education and the American Osteopathic Association's Commission on Osteopathic College Accreditation; (2) includes ABA-accredited schools, schools with provisional ABA accreditation, and state accredited schools; (3) includes all schools with programs that are less than 2 years.
Source: National Center for Education Statistics, Integrated Postsecondary Education System (IPEDS), 2020-21; Wikipedia, List of Medical Schools in the United States, accessed April 11, 2022; Wikipedia, List of Law Schools in the United States, accessed April 11, 2022

According to *U.S. News & World Report,* the Phoenix-Mesa-Scottsdale, AZ metro area is home to one of the top 200 national universities in the U.S.: **Arizona State University** (#117 tie). The indicators used to capture academic quality fall into a number of categories: assessment by administrators at peer institutions; retention of students; faculty resources; student selectivity; financial resources; alumni giving; high school counselor ratings of colleges; and graduation rate. *U.S. News & World Report, "America's Best Colleges 2022"*

According to *U.S. News & World Report,* the Phoenix-Mesa-Scottsdale, AZ metro area is home to one of the top 100 law schools in the U.S.: **Arizona State University (O'Connor)** (#25 tie). The rankings are based on a weighted average of 12 measures of quality: peer assessment score; assessment score by lawyers/judges; median LSAT scores; median undergrad GPA; acceptance rate; employment rates for graduates; placement success; bar passage rate; faculty resources; expenditures per student; student/faculty ratio; and library resources. *U.S. News & World Report, "America's Best Graduate Schools, Law, 2022"*

According to *U.S. News & World Report,* the Phoenix-Mesa-Scottsdale, AZ metro area is home to one of the top 75 business schools in the U.S.: **Arizona State University (W.P. Carey)** (#30). The rankings are based on a weighted average of the following nine measures: quality assessment; peer assessment; recruiter assessment; placement success; mean starting salary and bonus; student selectivity; mean GMAT and GRE scores; mean undergraduate GPA; and acceptance rate. *U.S. News & World Report, "America's Best Graduate Schools, Business, 2022"*

EMPLOYERS

Major Employers

Company Name	Industry
Arizona Dept of Transportation	Regulation, administration of transportation
Arizona State University	University
Avnet	Electronic parts & equipment, nec
Carter & Burgess	Engineering services
Chase Bankcard Services	State commercial banks
City of Mesa	Municipal government
City of Phoenix	Municipal government
General Dynamics C4 Systems	Communications equipment, nec
Grand Canyon Education	Colleges & universities
Honeywell International	Aircraft engines & engine parts
Lockheed Martin Corporation	Search & navigation equipment
Paramount Building Solutions	Janitorial service, contract basis
Salt River Pima-Maricopa Indian Community	Casino resort
Scottsdale Healthcare Osborn Med Ctr	General medical & surgical hospitals
Swift Transportation Company	Trucking, except local
The Boeing Company	Helicopters
Veterans Health Administration	General medical & surgical hospitals

Note: Companies shown are located within the Phoenix-Mesa-Scottsdale, AZ Metropolitan Statistical Area.
Source: Hoovers.com; Wikipedia

Best Companies to Work For

Banner Health, headquartered in Phoenix, is among the "100 Best Places to Work in IT." To qualify, companies had to be U.S.-based organizations or be non-U.S.-based employers that met the following criteria: have a minimum of 300 total employees at a U.S. headquarters and a minimum of 30 IT employees in the U.S., with at least 50% of their IT employees based in the U.S. The best places to work were selected based on compensation, benefits, work/life balance, employee morale, and satisfaction with training and development programs. In addition, *InsiderPro* and *Computerworld* looked at retention efforts, programs for recognizing and rewarding outstanding performances, and benefits such as flextime, elder care and child care, and reimbursement for college tuition and the cost of pursuing technology certifications. *InsiderPro and Computerworld, "100 Best Places to Work in IT," 2021*

PUBLIC SAFETY

Crime Rate

Area	Total Crime	Violent Crime Rate				Property Crime Rate		
		Murder	Rape[3]	Robbery	Aggrav. Assault	Burglary	Larceny -Theft	Motor Vehicle Theft
City	3,788.0	10.9	62.5	191.8	533.2	433.4	2,121.4	434.7
Suburbs[1]	2,118.2	3.8	35.2	43.8	211.2	276.5	1,380.4	167.3
Metro[2]	2,681.7	6.2	44.4	93.8	319.9	329.5	1,630.4	257.5
U.S.	2,356.7	6.5	38.4	73.9	279.7	314.2	1,398.0	246.0

Note: Figures are crimes per 100,000 population; (1) All areas within the metro area that are located outside the city limits; (2) Figures cover the Phoenix-Mesa-Scottsdale, AZ Metropolitan Statistical Area; (3) All figures shown were reported using the revised Uniform Crime Reporting (UCR) definition of rape.
Source: FBI Uniform Crime Reports, 2020

Hate Crimes

Area	Number of Quarters Reported	Number of Incidents per Bias Motivation					
		Race/Ethnicity/ Ancestry	Religion	Sexual Orientation	Disability	Gender	Gender Identity
City[1]	4	140	17	28	0	1	3
U.S.	4	5,227	1,244	1,110	130	75	266

Note: (1) Figures include one incident reported with more than one bias motivation.
Source: Federal Bureau of Investigation, Hate Crime Statistics 2020

Identity Theft Consumer Reports

Area	Reports	Reports per 100,000 Population	Rank[2]
MSA[1]	21,302	430	69
U.S.	1,434,676	432	-

Note: (1) Figures cover the Phoenix-Mesa-Scottsdale, AZ Metropolitan Statistical Area; (2) Rank ranges from 1 to 391 where 1 indicates greatest number of identity theft reports per 100,000 population
Source: Federal Trade Commission, Consumer Sentinel Network Data Book 2021

Fraud and Other Consumer Reports

Area	Reports	Reports per 100,000 Population	Rank[2]
MSA[1]	54,762	1,107	72
U.S.	4,328,977	1,304	-

Note: (1) Figures cover the Phoenix-Mesa-Scottsdale, AZ Metropolitan Statistical Area; (2) Rank ranges from 1 to 391 where 1 indicates greatest number of fraud and other consumer reports per 100,000 population
Source: Federal Trade Commission, Consumer Sentinel Network Data Book 2021

POLITICS

2020 Presidential Election Results

Area	Biden	Trump	Jorgensen	Hawkins	Other
Maricopa County	50.1	48.0	1.5	0.0	0.3
U.S.	51.3	46.8	1.2	0.3	0.5

Note: Results are percentages and may not add to 100% due to rounding
Source: Dave Leip's Atlas of U.S. Presidential Elections

SPORTS

Professional Sports Teams

Team Name	League	Year Established
Arizona Cardinals	National Football League (NFL)	1988
Arizona Diamondbacks	Major League Baseball (MLB)	1998
Phoenix Coyotes	National Hockey League (NHL)	1996
Phoenix Suns	National Basketball Association (NBA)	1968

Note: Includes teams located in the Phoenix-Mesa-Scottsdale, AZ Metropolitan Statistical Area.
Source: Wikipedia, Major Professional Sports Teams of the United States and Canada, April 6, 2022

CLIMATE

Average and Extreme Temperatures

Temperature	Jan	Feb	Mar	Apr	May	Jun	Jul	Aug	Sep	Oct	Nov	Dec	Yr.
Extreme High (°F)	88	92	100	105	113	122	118	116	118	107	93	88	122
Average High (°F)	66	70	75	84	93	103	105	103	99	88	75	67	86
Average Temp. (°F)	53	57	62	70	78	88	93	91	85	74	62	54	72
Average Low (°F)	40	44	48	55	63	72	80	78	72	60	48	41	59
Extreme Low (°F)	17	22	25	37	40	51	66	61	47	34	27	22	17

Note: Figures cover the years 1948-1990
Source: National Climatic Data Center, International Station Meteorological Climate Summary, 9/96

Average Precipitation/Snowfall/Humidity

Precip./Humidity	Jan	Feb	Mar	Apr	May	Jun	Jul	Aug	Sep	Oct	Nov	Dec	Yr.
Avg. Precip. (in.)	0.7	0.6	0.8	0.3	0.1	0.1	0.8	1.0	0.7	0.6	0.6	0.9	7.3
Avg. Snowfall (in.)	Tr	Tr	0	0	0	0	0	0	0	0	0	Tr	Tr
Avg. Rel. Hum. 5am (%)	68	63	56	45	37	33	47	53	50	53	59	66	53
Avg. Rel. Hum. 5pm (%)	34	28	24	17	14	12	21	24	23	24	28	34	24

Note: Figures cover the years 1948-1990; Tr = Trace amounts (<0.05 in. of rain; <0.5 in. of snow)
Source: National Climatic Data Center, International Station Meteorological Climate Summary, 9/96

Weather Conditions

Temperature			Daytime Sky			Precipitation		
10°F & below	32°F & below	90°F & above	Clear	Partly cloudy	Cloudy	0.01 inch or more precip.	0.1 inch or more snow/ice	Thunder-storms
0	10	167	186	125	54	37	< 1	23

Note: Figures are average number of days per year and cover the years 1948-1990
Source: National Climatic Data Center, International Station Meteorological Climate Summary, 9/96

HAZARDOUS WASTE

Superfund Sites

The Phoenix-Mesa-Scottsdale, AZ metro area is home to four sites on the EPA's Superfund National Priorities List: **Hassayampa Landfill** (final); **Indian Bend Wash Area** (final); **Motorola, Inc. (52nd Street Plant)** (final); **Phoenix-Goodyear Airport Area** (final). There are a total of 1,165 Superfund sites with a status of proposed or final on the list in the U.S. *U.S. Environmental Protection Agency, National Priorities List, April 6, 2022*

AIR QUALITY

Air Quality Trends: Ozone

	1990	1995	2000	2005	2010	2016	2017	2018	2019	2020
MSA[1]	0.080	0.087	0.082	0.077	0.076	0.072	0.075	0.074	0.071	0.080
U.S.	0.090	0.091	0.082	0.080	0.074	0.070	0.069	0.070	0.066	0.068

Note: (1) Data covers the Phoenix-Mesa-Scottsdale, AZ Metropolitan Statistical Area. The values shown are the composite ozone concentration averages among trend sites based on the highest fourth daily maximum 8-hour concentration in parts per million. These trends are based on sites having an adequate record of monitoring data during the trend period. Data from exceptional events are included.
Source: U.S. Environmental Protection Agency, Air Quality Monitoring Information, "Air Quality Trends by City, 1990-2020"

Air Quality Index

Area	Percent of Days when Air Quality was...[2]					AQI Statistics[2]	
	Good	Moderate	Unhealthy for Sensitive Groups	Unhealthy	Very Unhealthy	Maximum	Median
MSA[1]	3.0	34.2	23.2	18.9	20.2	1124	119

Note: (1) Data covers the Phoenix-Mesa-Scottsdale, AZ Metropolitan Statistical Area; (2) Based on 366 days with AQI data in 2020. Air Quality Index (AQI) is an index for reporting daily air quality. EPA calculates the AQI for five major air pollutants regulated by the Clean Air Act: ground-level ozone, particle pollution (aka particulate matter), carbon monoxide, sulfur dioxide, and nitrogen dioxide. The AQI runs from 0 to 500. The higher the AQI value, the greater the level of air pollution and the greater the health concern. There are six AQI categories: "Good" AQI is between 0 and 50. Air quality is considered satisfactory; "Moderate" AQI is between 51 and 100. Air quality is acceptable; "Unhealthy for Sensitive Groups" When AQI values are between 101 and 150, members of sensitive groups may experience health effects; "Unhealthy" When AQI values are between 151 and 200 everyone may begin to experience health effects; "Very Unhealthy" AQI values between 201 and 300 trigger a health alert; "Hazardous" AQI values over 300 trigger warnings of emergency conditions (not shown).
Source: U.S. Environmental Protection Agency, Air Quality Index Report, 2020

Air Quality Index Pollutants

Area	Percent of Days when AQI Pollutant was...[2]					
	Carbon Monoxide	Nitrogen Dioxide	Ozone	Sulfur Dioxide	Particulate Matter 2.5	Particulate Matter 10
MSA[1]	0.0	0.0	61.5	0.0	16.7	21.9

Note: (1) Data covers the Phoenix-Mesa-Scottsdale, AZ Metropolitan Statistical Area; (2) Based on 366 days with AQI data in 2020. The Air Quality Index (AQI) is an index for reporting daily air quality. EPA calculates the AQI for five major air pollutants regulated by the Clean Air Act: ground-level ozone, particle pollution (also known as particulate matter), carbon monoxide, sulfur dioxide, and nitrogen dioxide. The AQI runs from 0 to 500. The higher the AQI value, the greater the level of air pollution and the greater the health concern.
Source: U.S. Environmental Protection Agency, Air Quality Index Report, 2020

Maximum Air Pollutant Concentrations: Particulate Matter, Ozone, CO and Lead

	Particulate Matter 10 (ug/m³)	Particulate Matter 2.5 Wtd AM (ug/m³)	Particulate Matter 2.5 24-Hr (ug/m³)	Ozone (ppm)	Carbon Monoxide (ppm)	Lead (ug/m³)
MSA[1] Level	624	15.5	41	0.087	3	n/a
NAAQS[2]	150	15	35	0.075	9	0.15
Met NAAQS[2]	No	No	No	No	Yes	n/a

Note: (1) Data covers the Phoenix-Mesa-Scottsdale, AZ Metropolitan Statistical Area; Data from exceptional events are included; (2) National Ambient Air Quality Standards; ppm = parts per million; ug/m³ = micrograms per cubic meter; n/a not available.
Concentrations: Particulate Matter 10 (coarse particulate)—highest second maximum 24-hour concentration; Particulate Matter 2.5 Wtd AM (fine particulate)—highest weighted annual mean concentration; Particulate Matter 2.5 24-Hour (fine particulate)—highest 98th percentile 24-hour concentration; Ozone—highest fourth daily maximum 8-hour concentration; Carbon Monoxide—highest second maximum non-overlapping 8-hour concentration; Lead—maximum running 3-month average
Source: U.S. Environmental Protection Agency, Air Quality Monitoring Information, "Air Quality Statistics by City, 2020"

Maximum Air Pollutant Concentrations: Nitrogen Dioxide and Sulfur Dioxide

	Nitrogen Dioxide AM (ppb)	Nitrogen Dioxide 1-Hr (ppb)	Sulfur Dioxide AM (ppb)	Sulfur Dioxide 1-Hr (ppb)	Sulfur Dioxide 24-Hr (ppb)
MSA[1] Level	25	57	n/a	7	n/a
NAAQS[2]	53	100	30	75	140
Met NAAQS[2]	Yes	Yes	n/a	Yes	n/a

Note: (1) Data covers the Phoenix-Mesa-Scottsdale, AZ Metropolitan Statistical Area; Data from exceptional events are included; (2) National Ambient Air Quality Standards; ppm = parts per million; ug/m³ = micrograms per cubic meter; n/a not available.
Concentrations: Nitrogen Dioxide AM—highest arithmetic mean concentration; Nitrogen Dioxide 1-Hr—highest 98th percentile 1-hour daily maximum concentration; Sulfur Dioxide AM—highest annual mean concentration; Sulfur Dioxide 1-Hr—highest 99th percentile 1-hour daily maximum concentration; Sulfur Dioxide 24-Hr—highest second maximum 24-hour concentration
Source: U.S. Environmental Protection Agency, Air Quality Monitoring Information, "Air Quality Statistics by City, 2020"

Portland, Oregon

Background

Portland is the kind of city that inspires civic pride and the desire to preserve. It offers magnificent views of the Cascade Mountains, a mild climate, and an attractive combination of historical brick structures and contemporary architecture.

Nature is the undisputed queen of Portland and embodied in Portlandia, the city's statue of an earth mother kneeling among her animal children. The number of activities, such as fishing, skiing, and hunting, as well as the number of outdoor zoological gardens, attest to the mindset of the typical Portlander.

Portland is a major industrial and commercial center that boasts clean air and water within its city limits, as many of the factories use the electricity generated by mountain rivers; thus, little soot or smoke is belched out. Manufacturing specializing in high-tech electronics and specialty metal fabrication is leading industry in city, and major employers include Intel, NIKE, US Bank, and Precision Castparts. Health services and the highly-rated University of Portland also make a significant impact in the city.

The city is a major cultural center, with art museums such as the Portland Art Museum and the Oregon Museum of Science and Industry, and educational institutions including Reed College and the University of Portland. In 2001, Portland's PGE Park sports stadium had a multi-million-dollar face-lift, with a field level bar and grill and pavilion suites, all state-of-the-art and seismic code compliant.

The Portland area's metro region includes 24 cities and parts of three counties. Established in the late 1970s, it is the nation's first and only elected regional government. It attempts to control growth by using its authority over land use, transportation, and the environment. This experiment in urban planning is designed to protect farms, forests, and open space. Portland today has a downtown area that caters to pedestrians and includes a heavily used city park. Visible from the air is a clear line against sprawl—with cities on one side and open spaces on the other.

Portland is Oregon's biggest city, and is a shining example of effective sprawl control, a "role model for twenty-first century urban development." The city's well-organized mass-transit system makes living there more enjoyable, and Portland Streetcar recently added more track and three additional streetcars in 2021 with more improvements on the way.

In 2000, the Portland Art Museum completed its "Program for the Millennium," a multi-stage expansion program that brought total exhibition space to 240,000 square feet. In 2005, restoration of the North Building, a former Masonic Temple, was completed. While preserving the historical integrity, the restoration provides space for the Portland Art Museum's Center for Modern and Contemporary Art.

The Portland metropolitan area had a significant LGBTQ population throughout the late 20th and early 21st century. In 2015, it had the second highest percentage of LGBTQ residents in the United States, at 5.4 percent, second only to San Francisco. The city held its first pride festival in 1975 on the Portland State University campus.

Many films have been shot in Portland, from independents to big-budget productions. The city has been featured in various television programs, most notably the comedy series *Portlandia*, which ran 2011 to 2018. Shot on location in Portland, it lovingly satirized the city as a hub of liberal politics, organic food, alternative lifestyles, and anti-establishment attitudes.

Portland has a very definite winter rainfall climate, with the most rain falling October through May in relatively mild temperatures. Summer produces pleasant, mild temperatures with very little precipitation. Fall and spring are transitional. Fall and early winter bring the most frequent fog. Destructive storms are infrequent, with thunderstorms occurring once a month through the spring and summer.

Rankings

General Rankings

- *US News & World Report* conducted a survey of more than 3,600 people and analyzed the 150 largest metropolitan areas to determine what matters most when selecting the next place to live. Portland ranked #10 out of the top 25 as having the best combination of desirable factors. Criteria: cost of living; quality of life and education; net migration; job market; desirability; and other factors. *realestate.usnews.com, "The 25 Best Places to Live in the U.S. in 2021-2022," July 13, 2021*
- The Portland metro area was identified as one of America's fastest-growing areas in terms of population and business growth by *MagnifyMoney.* The area ranked #21 out of 35. The 100 most populous metro areas in the U.S. were evaluated on their change from 2011 to 2016 in the following categories: people and housing; workforce and employment opportunities; growing industry. *www.businessinsider.com, "The 35 Cities in the US with the Biggest Influx of People, the Most Work Opportunities, and the Hottest Business Growth," August 12, 2018*
- The Portland metro area was identified as one of America's fastest-growing areas in terms of population and economy by *Forbes.* The area ranked #17 out of 25. The 100 most populous metro areas in the U.S. were evaluated on the following criteria: estimated population growth; employment; economic output; wages; home values. *Forbes, "America's Fastest-Growing Cities 2018," February 28, 2018*
- In its eighth annual survey, *Travel + Leisure* readers nominated their favorite cities and towns in America—voting on numerous attractive features in categories including culture, food and drink, quality of life, style, and people. After 50,000 votes, Portland was ranked #17 among the proposed favorites. *www.travelandleisure.com, "America's Favorite Cities," October 20, 2017*
- For its 34th annual "Readers' Choice Awards" survey, *Condé Nast Traveler* ranked its readers' favorite cities in the U.S. Whether it be a longed for visit or a first on the list, these are the places that inspired a return to travel. The list was broken into large cities and cities under 250,000. Portland ranked #8 in the big city category. *Condé Nast Traveler, Readers' Choice Awards 2021, "Best Big Cities in the U.S." October 5, 2021*

Business/Finance Rankings

- The Brookings Institution ranked the nation's largest cities based on income inequality. Portland was ranked #48 (#1 = greatest inequality). Criteria: the "95/20 ratio," a figure representing the income at which a household earns more than 95 percent of all other households, divided by the income at which a household earns more than only 20 percent of all other households. *Brookings Institution, "Household Income Inequality, Largest Cities of 97 Large U.S. Metro Areas, 2014-2016," February 5, 2018*
- The Brookings Institution ranked the 100 largest metro areas in the U.S. based on income inequality. Portland was ranked #83 (#1 = greatest inequality). Criteria: the "95/20 ratio," a figure representing the income at which a household earns more than 95 percent of all other households, divided by the income at which a household earns more than only 20 percent of all other households. *Brookings Institution, "Household Income Inequality, 100 Largest U.S. Metro Areas, 2014-2016," February 5, 2018*
- Payscale.com ranked the 32 largest metro areas in terms of wage growth. The Portland metro area ranked #17. Criteria: private-sector and education professional wage growth between the 4th quarter of 2019 and the 4th quarter of 2020. *PayScale, "Wage Trends by Metro Area-4th Quarter," January 11, 2021*
- The Portland metro area was identified as one of the most debt-ridden places in America by the finance site Credit.com. The metro area was ranked #21. Criteria: residents' average credit card debt as well as median income. *Credit.com, "25 Cities With the Most Credit Card Debt," February 28, 2018*
- For its annual survey of the "Most Expensive U.S. Cities to Live In," Kiplinger applied Cost of Living Index statistics developed by the Council for Community and Economic Research to U.S. Census Bureau population and median household income data for 256 urban areas. Portland was among the 20 most expensive in the country. *Kiplinger.com, "The 20 Most Expensive Cities in the U.S.," March 16, 2022*
- The Portland metro area appeared on the Milken Institute "2021 Best Performing Cities" list. Rank: #38 out of 200 large metro areas (population over 250,000). Criteria: job growth; wage and salary growth; high-tech output growth; housing affordability; household broadband access. *Milken Institute, "Best-Performing Cities 2021," February 16, 2021*

- *Forbes* ranked the 200 most populous metro areas to determine the nation's "Best Places for Business and Careers." The Portland metro area was ranked #5. Criteria: costs (business and living); job growth (past and projected); income growth; quality of life; educational attainment (college and high school); projected economic growth; cultural and leisure opportunities; workplace tolerance laws; net migration patterns. *Forbes, "The Best Places for Business and Careers 2019: Seattle Still On Top," October 30, 2019*
- Mercer Human Resources Consulting ranked 209 cities worldwide in terms of cost-of-living. Portland ranked #106 (the lower the ranking, the higher the cost-of-living). The survey measured the comparative cost of over 200 items (such as housing, food, clothing, household goods, transportation, and entertainment) in each location. *Mercer, "2021 Cost of Living City Ranking," June 22, 2021*

Culture/Performing Arts Rankings

- Portland was selected as one of the 25 best cities for moviemakers in North America. COVID-19 has spurred a quest for great film cities that offer more creative space, lower costs, and more great outdoors. NYC & LA were intentionally excluded. Criteria: longstanding reputations as film-friendly communities; film community and culture; work life balance; and efforts to deal with pandemic-specific challenges. The city was ranked #21. *MovieMaker Magazine, "Best Places to Live and Work as a Moviemaker in 2022," January 25, 2022*

Dating/Romance Rankings

- Portland was selected as one of the nation's most romantic cities with 100,000 or more residents by Amazon.com. The city ranked #18 of 20. Criteria: per capita sales of romance novels, relationship books, romantic comedy movies, romantic music, and sexual wellness products. *Amazon.com, "Top 20 Most Romantic Cities in the U.S.," February 1, 2017*

Education Rankings

- Personal finance website *WalletHub* analyzed the 150 largest U.S. metropolitan statistical areas to determine where the most educated Americans are putting their degrees to work. Criteria: education levels; percentage of workers with degrees; education quality and attainment gap; public school quality rankings; quality and enrollment of each metro area's universities. Portland was ranked #16 (#1 = most educated city). *www.WalletHub.com, "Most & Least Educated Cities in America," July 19, 2021*
- Portland was selected as one of America's most literate cities. The city ranked #5 out of the 84 largest U.S. cities. Criteria: number of booksellers; library resources; Internet resources; educational attainment; periodical publishing resources; newspaper circulation. *Central Connecticut State University, "America's Most Literate Cities, 2018," February 2019*

Environmental Rankings

- Sperling's BestPlaces assessed the 50 largest metropolitan areas of the United States for the likelihood of dangerously extreme weather events or earthquakes. In general the Southeast and South-Central regions have the highest risk of weather extremes and earthquakes, while the Pacific Northwest enjoys the lowest risk. Of the least risky metropolitan areas, the Portland metro area was ranked #1. *www.bestplaces.net, "Avoid Natural Disasters: BestPlaces Reveals The Top 10 Safest Places to Live," October 25, 2017*
- The U.S. Environmental Protection Agency (EPA) released its list of U.S. metropolitan areas with the most ENERGY STAR certified buildings in 2020. The Portland metro area was ranked #23 out of 25. *U.S. Environmental Protection Agency, "2021 Energy Star Top Cities," June 15, 2021*
- Portland was highlighted as one of the 25 metro areas most polluted by short-term particle pollution (24-hour PM 2.5) in the U.S. during 2017 through 2019. The area ranked #23. *American Lung Association, "State of the Air 2021," April 21, 2021*

Food/Drink Rankings

- The U.S. Chamber of Commerce Foundation conducted an in-depth study on local food truck regulations, surveyed 288 food truck owners, and ranked 20 major American cities based on how friendly they are for operating a food truck. The compiled index assessed the following: procedures for obtaining permits and licenses; complying with restrictions; and financial obligations associated with operating a food truck. Portland ranked #1 overall (1 being the best). *www.foodtrucknation.us, "Food Truck Nation," March 20, 2018*
- Portland was identified as one of the cities in America ordering the most vegan food options by GrubHub.com. The city ranked #3 out of 5. Criteria: percentage of vegan, vegetarian and plant-based food orders compared to the overall number of orders. *GrubHub.com, "State of the Plate Report 2021: Top Cities for Vegans," June 20, 2021*

Health/Fitness Rankings

- For each of the 100 largest cities in the United States, the American Fitness Index®, published by the American College of Sports Medicine and the Anthem Foundation, evaluated community infrastructure and 34 health behaviors including preventive health, levels of chronic disease conditions, food insecurity, sleep quality, pedestrian safety, air quality, and community resources that support physical activity. Portland ranked #9 for "community fitness." *americanfitnessindex.org, "2021 ACSM American Fitness Index Summary Report," July 13, 2021*
- Portland was identified as a "2021 Spring Allergy Capital." The area ranked #91 out of 100. Three groups of factors were used to identify the most challenging cities for people with allergies during the spring season: annual spring pollen levels; over the counter medicine use; number of board-certified allergy specialists. *Asthma and Allergy Foundation of America, "Spring Allergy Capitals 2021," February 23, 2021*
- Portland was identified as a "2021 Fall Allergy Capital." The area ranked #95 out of 100. Three groups of factors were used to identify the most challenging cities for people with allergies during the fall season: annual fall pollen levels; over the counter medicine use; number of board-certified allergy specialists. *Asthma and Allergy Foundation of America, "Fall Allergy Capitals 2021," February 23, 2021*
- Portland was identified as a "2021 Asthma Capital." The area ranked #50 out of the nation's 100 largest metropolitan areas. Criteria: estimated asthma prevalence; asthma-related mortality; and ER visits due to asthma. Risk factors analyzed but not factored in the rankings: annual pollen score; annual air quality; public smoking laws; number of board-certified asthma specialists; rescue medication use; controller medication use; uninsured rate; poverty rate. *Asthma and Allergy Foundation of America, "Asthma Capitals 2021: The Most Challenging Places to Live With Asthma," May 5, 2021*

Real Estate Rankings

- *WalletHub* compared the most populated U.S. cities to determine which had the best markets for real estate agents. Portland ranked #16 where demand was high and pay was the best. Criteria: sales per agent; annual median wage for real-estate agents; monthly average starting salary for real estate agents; real estate job density and competition; unemployment rate; home turnover rate; housing-market health index; and other relevant metrics. *www.WalletHub.com, "2021 Best Places to Be a Real Estate Agent," May 12, 2021*
- The Portland metro area was identified as one of the 20 least affordable housing markets in the U.S. in 2021. The area ranked #166 out of 183 markets. Criteria: qualification for a mortgage loan with a 10 percent down payment on a typical home. *National Association of Realtors®, Qualifying Income Based on Sales Price of Existing Single-Family Homes for Metropolitan Areas, 2021*
- Portland was ranked #184 out of 237 metro areas in terms of housing affordability in 2021 by the National Association of Home Builders (#1 = most affordable). Criteria: the share of homes sold in that area affordable to a family earning the local median income, based on standard mortgage underwriting criteria. *National Association of Home Builders®, NAHB-Wells Fargo Housing Opportunity Index, 4th Quarter 2021*

Safety Rankings

- Allstate ranked the 200 largest cities in America in terms of driver safety. Portland ranked #181. Criteria: internal property damage claims over a two-year period from January 2016 to December 2017. The report helps increase the importance of safety and awareness behind the wheel. *Allstate, "Allstate America's Best Drivers Report, 2019" June 24, 2019*
- The National Insurance Crime Bureau ranked 390 metro areas in the U.S. in terms of per capita rates of vehicle theft. The Portland metro area ranked #19 (#1 = highest rate). Criteria: number of vehicle theft offenses per 100,000 inhabitants in 2020. *National Insurance Crime Bureau, "Hot Spots 2020," August 31, 2021*

Seniors/Retirement Rankings

- From its Best Cities for Successful Aging indexes, the Milken Institute generated rankings for metropolitan areas, weighing data in nine categories—health care, wellness, living arrangements, transportation and convenience, financial characteristics, education, employment, community engagement, and overall livability. The Portland metro area was ranked #40 overall in the large metro area category. *Milken Institute, "Best Cities for Successful Aging, 2017" March 14, 2017*

Sports/Recreation Rankings

- Portland was chosen as one of America's best cities for bicycling. The city ranked #5 out of 50. Criteria: cycling infrastructure that is safe and friendly for all ages; energy and bike culture. The editors evaluated cities with populations of 100,000 or more. *Bicycling, "The 50 Best Bike Cities in America," October 10, 2018*

Transportation Rankings

- Business Insider presented an AllTransit Performance Score ranking of public transportation in major U.S. cities and towns, with populations over 250,000, in which Portland earned the #13-ranked "Transit Score," awarded for frequency of service, access to jobs, quality and number of stops, and affordability. *www.businessinsider.com, "The 17 Major U.S. Cities with the Best Public Transportation," April 17, 2018*
- According to the INRIX "2021 Global Traffic Scorecard," Portland was identified as one of the most congested metro areas in the U.S. The area ranked #11 out of 25. Criteria: average annual time spent in traffic and average cost of congestion per motorist. *Inrix.com, "Americans Lost 3.4 Billion Hours Due to Congestion in 2021, 42% Below Pre-COVID," December 7, 2021*

Women/Minorities Rankings

- *Women's Health*, together with the site Yelp, identified the 15 "Wellthiest" spots in the U.S. Portland appeared among the top for happiest, healthiest, outdoorsiest and Zen-iest. *Women's Health, "The 15 Wellthiest Cities in the U.S." July 5, 2017*
- Personal finance website *WalletHub* compared more than 180 U.S. cities across two key dimensions, "Hispanic Business-Friendliness" and "Hispanic Purchasing Power," to arrive at the most favorable conditions for Hispanic entrepreneurs. Portland was ranked #95 out of 182. Criteria includes: share of Hispanic-Owned Businesses; Hispanic entrepreneurship rate to median annual income of Hispanics; Small Business-Friendliness score; cost of living; and number of Hispanics with at least a bachelor's degree. *WalletHub.com, "2019's Best Cities for Hispanic Entrepreneurs," May 1, 2019*

Miscellaneous Rankings

- While the majority of travel ground to a halt in 2020, plugged-in travel influencers and experts were able to rediscover their local regions. Portland appeared on a *Forbes* list of 15 U.S. cities that provided solace as well as local inspiration. Whether it be quirky things to see and do, delicious take out, outdoor exploring and daytrips, these places are must-see destinations. *Forbes, "Bucket List Travel: The 15 Best U.S. Destinations For 2021," January 1, 2021*
- *MoveHub* ranked 446 hipster cities across 20 countries, using its *alternative* Hipster Index and Portland came out as #2 among the top 50. Criteria: population over 150,000; number of vintage boutiques; density of tattoo parlors; vegan places to eat; coffee shops; and density of vinyl record stores. *www.movehub.com, "The Hipster Index: Brighton Pips Portland to Global Top Spot," July 28, 2021*
- The watchdog site, Charity Navigator, conducted a study of charities in major markets both to analyze statistical differences in their financial, accountability, and transparency practices and to track year-to-year variations in individual philanthropic communities. The Portland metro area was ranked #10 among the 30 metro markets in the rating category of Overall Score. *www.charitynavigator.org, "2017 Metro Market Study," May 1, 2017*
- *WalletHub* compared the 150 most populated U.S. cities to determine their operating efficiency. A "Quality of City Services" score was constructed for each city and then divided by the total budget per capita to reveal which were managed the best. Portland ranked #69. Criteria: financial stability; economy; education; safety; health; infrastructure and pollution. *www.WalletHub.com, "2021's Best- & Worst-Run Cities in America," June 22, 2021*
- The National Alliance to End Homelessness listed the 25 most populous metro areas with the highest rate of homelessness. The Portland metro area had a high rate of homelessness. Criteria: number of homeless people per 10,000 population in 2016. *National Alliance to End Homelessness, "Homelessness in the 25 Most Populous U.S. Metro Areas," September 1, 2017*

Business Environment

DEMOGRAPHICS

Population Growth

Area	1990 Census	2000 Census	2010 Census	2020* Estimate	Population Growth (%) 1990-2020	Population Growth (%) 2010-2020
City	485,833	529,121	583,776	650,380	33.9	11.4
MSA[1]	1,523,741	1,927,881	2,226,009	2,472,774	62.3	11.1
U.S.	248,709,873	281,421,906	308,745,538	326,569,308	31.3	5.8

Note: (1) Figures cover the Portland-Vancouver-Hillsboro, OR-WA Metropolitan Statistical Area; (*) 2016-2020 5-year estimated population
Source: U.S. Census Bureau, 1990 Census, Census 2000, Census 2010, 2016-2020 American Community Survey 5-Year Estimates

Household Size

Area	Persons in Household (%) One	Two	Three	Four	Five	Six	Seven or More	Average Household Size
City	34.1	35.2	14.3	10.5	3.8	1.4	0.8	2.30
MSA[1]	26.7	35.5	15.6	13.4	5.3	2.1	1.3	2.50
U.S.	28.0	33.9	15.5	12.9	6.0	2.3	1.4	2.60

Note: (1) Figures cover the Portland-Vancouver-Hillsboro, OR-WA Metropolitan Statistical Area
Source: U.S. Census Bureau, 2016-2020 American Community Survey 5-Year Estimates

Race

Area	White Alone[2] (%)	Black Alone[2] (%)	Asian Alone[2] (%)	AIAN[3] Alone[2] (%)	NHOPI[4] Alone[2] (%)	Other Race Alone[2] (%)	Two or More Races (%)
City	75.3	5.9	8.7	0.8	0.7	2.3	6.4
MSA[1]	79.3	2.9	6.9	0.7	0.5	3.3	6.4
U.S.	70.4	12.6	5.6	0.8	0.2	5.1	5.2

Note: (1) Figures cover the Portland-Vancouver-Hillsboro, OR-WA Metropolitan Statistical Area; (2) Alone is defined as not being in combination with one or more other races; (3) American Indian and Alaska Native; (4) Native Hawaiian and Other Pacific Islander
Source: U.S. Census Bureau, 2016-2020 American Community Survey 5-Year Estimates

Hispanic or Latino Origin

Area	Total (%)	Mexican (%)	Puerto Rican (%)	Cuban (%)	Other (%)
City	9.8	6.8	0.5	0.4	2.1
MSA[1]	12.2	9.4	0.4	0.2	2.2
U.S.	18.2	11.2	1.7	0.7	4.5

Note: Persons of Hispanic or Latino origin can be of any race; (1) Figures cover the Portland-Vancouver-Hillsboro, OR-WA Metropolitan Statistical Area
Source: U.S. Census Bureau, 2016-2020 American Community Survey 5-Year Estimates

Ancestry

Area	German	Irish	English	American	Italian	Polish	French[2]	Scottish	Dutch
City	15.7	11.1	11.2	4.6	4.4	2.2	2.9	2.9	1.9
MSA[1]	17.0	10.6	11.0	4.6	3.8	1.8	2.7	2.8	1.8
U.S.	13.0	9.7	7.7	5.9	5.1	2.7	2.3	1.6	1.1

Note: Figures are the percentage of the total population reporting a particular ancestry. The nine most commonly reported ancestries in the U.S. are shown. Figures include multiple ancestries (e.g. if a person reported being Irish and Italian, they were included in both columns); (1) Figures cover the Portland-Vancouver-Hillsboro, OR-WA Metropolitan Statistical Area; (2) Excludes Basque
Source: U.S. Census Bureau, 2016-2020 American Community Survey 5-Year Estimates

Foreign-born Population

Area	Percent of Population Born in: Any Foreign Country	Asia	Mexico	Europe	Caribbean	Central America[2]	South America	Africa	Canada
City	13.4	6.0	2.0	2.7	0.2	0.3	0.3	1.0	0.5
MSA[1]	12.7	5.1	3.1	2.4	0.2	0.4	0.3	0.6	0.4
U.S.	13.5	4.2	3.3	1.5	1.3	1.1	1.0	0.7	0.3

Note: (1) Figures cover the Portland-Vancouver-Hillsboro, OR-WA Metropolitan Statistical Area; (2) Excludes Mexico.
Source: U.S. Census Bureau, 2016-2020 American Community Survey 5-Year Estimates

Marital Status

Area	Never Married	Now Married[2]	Separated	Widowed	Divorced
City	41.3	41.2	1.4	3.7	12.5
MSA[1]	32.3	49.9	1.3	4.5	12.0
U.S.	33.5	48.1	1.8	5.7	10.8

Note: Figures are percentages and cover the population 15 years of age and older; (1) Figures cover the Portland-Vancouver-Hillsboro, OR-WA Metropolitan Statistical Area; (2) Excludes separated
Source: U.S. Census Bureau, 2016-2020 American Community Survey 5-Year Estimates

Disability by Age

Area	All Ages	Under 18 Years Old	18 to 64 Years Old	65 Years and Over
City	11.9	4.4	9.6	34.0
MSA[1]	11.9	4.0	9.6	33.3
U.S.	12.7	4.3	10.3	34.0

Note: Figures show percent of the civilian noninstitutionalized population that reported having a disability. Disability status is determined from six types of difficulty: vision, hearing, cognitive, ambulatory, self-care, and independent living. For children under 5 years old, hearing and vision difficulty are used to determine disability status. For children between the ages of 5 and 14, disability status is determined from hearing, vision, cognitive, ambulatory, and self-care difficulties. For people aged 15 years and older, they are considered to have a disability if they have difficulty with any one of the six difficulty types; Note: (1) Figures cover the Portland-Vancouver-Hillsboro, OR-WA Metropolitan Statistical Area
Source: U.S. Census Bureau, 2016-2020 American Community Survey 5-Year Estimates

Age

Area	Percent of Population									Median Age
	Under Age 5	Age 5–19	Age 20–34	Age 35–44	Age 45–54	Age 55–64	Age 65–74	Age 75–84	Age 85+	
City	4.9	14.5	25.6	17.3	13.3	11.1	8.3	3.4	1.5	37.5
MSA[1]	5.6	17.9	21.4	14.7	13.2	12.3	9.2	3.9	1.8	38.3
U.S.	6.0	19.1	20.6	12.7	12.7	12.9	9.4	4.7	2.0	38.2

Note: (1) Figures cover the Portland-Vancouver-Hillsboro, OR-WA Metropolitan Statistical Area
Source: U.S. Census Bureau, 2016-2020 American Community Survey 5-Year Estimates

Gender

Area	Males	Females	Males per 100 Females
City	322,445	327,935	98.3
MSA[1]	1,224,427	1,248,347	98.1
U.S.	160,818,530	165,750,778	97.0

Note: (1) Figures cover the Portland-Vancouver-Hillsboro, OR-WA Metropolitan Statistical Area
Source: U.S. Census Bureau, 2016-2020 American Community Survey 5-Year Estimates

Religious Groups by Family

Area	Catholic	Baptist	Non-Den.	Methodist[2]	Lutheran	LDS[3]	Pente-costal	Presby-terian[4]	Muslim[5]	Judaism
MSA[1]	10.6	2.3	4.5	1.0	1.6	3.8	2.0	1.0	0.1	0.3
U.S.	19.1	9.3	4.0	4.0	2.3	2.0	1.9	1.6	0.8	0.7

Note: Figures are the number of adherents as a percentage of the total population; (1) Figures cover the Portland-Vancouver-Hillsboro, OR-WA Metropolitan Statistical Area; (2) Methodist/Pietist; (3) Latter Day Saints; (4) Reformed; (5) Figures are estimates
Source: Association of Statisticians of American Religious Bodies, 2010 U.S. Religion Census: Religious Congregations & Membership Study

Religious Groups by Tradition

Area	Catholic	Evangelical Protestant	Mainline Protestant	Other Tradition	Black Protestant	Orthodox
MSA[1]	10.6	11.7	3.7	5.2	0.2	0.3
U.S.	19.1	16.2	7.3	4.3	1.6	0.3

Note: Figures are the number of adherents as a percentage of the total population; (1) Figures cover the Portland-Vancouver-Hillsboro, OR-WA Metropolitan Statistical Area
Source: Association of Statisticians of American Religious Bodies, 2010 U.S. Religion Census: Religious Congregations & Membership Study

ECONOMY

Gross Metropolitan Product

Area	2017	2018	2019	2020	Rank[2]
MSA[1]	165.9	175.7	183.8	191.1	21

Note: Figures are in billions of dollars; (1) Figures cover the Portland-Vancouver-Hillsboro, OR-WA Metropolitan Statistical Area; (2) Rank is based on 2018 data and ranges from 1 to 381
Source: U.S. Conference of Mayors, U.S. Metro Economies: GMP & Employment 2018-2020, September 2019

Economic Growth

Area	2015-17 (%)	2018 (%)	2019 (%)	2020 (%)	Rank[2]
MSA[1]	3.9	3.5	2.6	1.6	42
U.S.	1.9	2.9	2.3	2.1	–

Note: Figures are real gross metropolitan product (GMP) growth rates and represent average annual percent change; (1) Figures cover the Portland-Vancouver-Hillsboro, OR-WA Metropolitan Statistical Area; (2) Rank is based on 2017 2-year average annual percent change and ranges from 1 to 381
Source: U.S. Conference of Mayors, U.S. Metro Economies: GMP & Employment 2018-2020, September 2019

Metropolitan Area Exports

Area	2015	2016	2017	2018	2019	2020	Rank[2]
MSA[1]	18,847.8	20,256.8	20,788.8	21,442.9	23,761.9	27,824.7	10

Note: Figures are in millions of dollars; (1) Figures cover the Portland-Vancouver-Hillsboro, OR-WA Metropolitan Statistical Area; (2) Rank is based on 2020 data and ranges from 1 to 389
Source: U.S. Department of Commerce, International Trade Administration, Office of Trade and Economic Analysis, Industry and Analysis, Exports by Metropolitan Area, data extracted March 4, 2022

Building Permits

Area	Single-Family			Multi-Family			Total		
	2019	2020	Pct. Chg.	2019	2020	Pct. Chg.	2019	2020	Pct. Chg.
City	703	584	-16.9	4,391	1,195	-72.8	5,094	1,779	-65.1
MSA[1]	7,688	7,513	-2.3	9,127	5,933	-35.0	16,815	13,446	-20.0
U.S.	862,100	979,400	13.6	523,900	491,700	-6.1	1,386,000	1,471,100	6.1

Note: (1) Figures cover the Portland-Vancouver-Hillsboro, OR-WA Metropolitan Statistical Area; Figures represent new, privately-owned housing units authorized (unadjusted data); All permit data are based on estimates with imputation
Source: U.S. Census Bureau, Manufacturing, Mining, and Construction Statistics, Building Permits, 2019, 2020

Bankruptcy Filings

Area	Business Filings			Nonbusiness Filings		
	2020	2021	% Chg.	2020	2021	% Chg.
Multnomah County	59	33	-44.1	1,147	802	-30.1
U.S.	21,655	14,347	-33.7	522,808	399,269	-23.6

Note: Business filings include Chapter 7, Chapter 9, Chapter 11, Chapter 12, Chapter 13, Chapter 15, and Section 304; Nonbusiness filings include Chapter 7, Chapter 11, and Chapter 13
Source: Administrative Office of the U.S. Courts, Business and Nonbusiness Bankruptcy, County Cases Commenced by Chapter of the Bankruptcy Code, During the 12-Month Period Ending December 31, 2020 and Business and Nonbusiness Bankruptcy, County Cases Commenced by Chapter of the Bankruptcy Code, During the 12-Month Period Ending December 31, 2021

Housing Vacancy Rates

Area	Gross Vacancy Rate[2] (%)			Year-Round Vacancy Rate[3] (%)			Rental Vacancy Rate[4] (%)			Homeowner Vacancy Rate[5] (%)		
	2019	2020	2021	2019	2020	2021	2019	2020	2021	2019	2020	2021
MSA[1]	6.6	5.5	6.0	5.6	4.9	5.6	4.4	4.3	5.2	0.9	0.8	0.9
U.S.	12.0	10.6	10.8	9.5	8.2	8.4	6.7	6.3	6.1	1.4	1.0	0.9

Note: (1) Figures cover the Portland-Vancouver-Hillsboro, OR-WA Metropolitan Statistical Area; (2) The percentage of the total housing inventory that is vacant; (3) The percentage of the housing inventory (excluding seasonal units) that is year-round vacant; (4) The percentage of rental inventory that is vacant for rent; (5) The percentage of homeowner inventory that is vacant for sale
Source: U.S. Census Bureau, Housing Vacancies and Homeownership Annual Statistics: 2019, 2020, 2021

INCOME

Income

Area	Per Capita ($)	Median Household ($)	Average Household ($)
City	43,811	73,159	100,369
MSA[1]	40,138	77,511	101,594
U.S.	35,384	64,994	91,547

Note: (1) Figures cover the Portland-Vancouver-Hillsboro, OR-WA Metropolitan Statistical Area
Source: U.S. Census Bureau, 2016-2020 American Community Survey 5-Year Estimates

Household Income Distribution

Area	Percent of Households Earning							
	Under $15,000	$15,000 -$24,999	$25,000 -$34,999	$35,000 -$49,999	$50,000 -$74,999	$75,000 -$99,999	$100,000 -$149,999	$150,000 and up
City	10.1	6.8	7.4	10.3	16.4	12.6	16.9	19.5
MSA[1]	7.3	6.2	6.9	10.7	17.2	13.6	19.0	19.0
U.S.	9.9	8.5	8.6	12.0	17.2	12.8	15.6	15.4

Note: (1) Figures cover the Portland-Vancouver-Hillsboro, OR-WA Metropolitan Statistical Area
Source: U.S. Census Bureau, 2016-2020 American Community Survey 5-Year Estimates

Poverty Rate

Area	All Ages	Under 18 Years Old	18 to 64 Years Old	65 Years and Over
City	13.1	15.1	12.9	11.1
MSA[1]	10.1	12.2	9.9	8.0
U.S.	12.8	17.5	12.1	9.3

Note: Figures are percentage of people whose income during the past 12 months was below the poverty level; (1) Figures cover the Portland-Vancouver-Hillsboro, OR-WA Metropolitan Statistical Area
Source: U.S. Census Bureau, 2016-2020 American Community Survey 5-Year Estimates

CITY FINANCES

City Government Finances

Component	2019 ($000)	2019 ($ per capita)
Total Revenues	2,193,814	3,387
Total Expenditures	1,801,476	2,781
Debt Outstanding	3,434,781	5,302
Cash and Securities[1]	1,660,301	2,563

Note: (1) Cash and security holdings of a government at the close of its fiscal year, including those of its dependent agencies, utilities, and liquor stores.
Source: U.S. Census Bureau, State & Local Government Finances 2019

City Government Revenue by Source

Source	2019 ($000)	2019 ($ per capita)	2019 (%)
General Revenue			
From Federal Government	27,126	42	1.2
From State Government	98,407	152	4.5
From Local Governments	114,019	176	5.2
Taxes			
Property	625,310	965	28.5
Sales and Gross Receipts	202,969	313	9.3
Personal Income	0	0	0.0
Corporate Income	0	0	0.0
Motor Vehicle License	0	0	0.0
Other Taxes	224,792	347	10.2
Current Charges	637,099	983	29.0
Liquor Store	0	0	0.0
Utility	200,762	310	9.2

Source: U.S. Census Bureau, State & Local Government Finances 2019

City Government Expenditures by Function

Function	2019 ($000)	2019 ($ per capita)	2019 (%)
General Direct Expenditures			
Air Transportation	0	0	0.0
Corrections	0	0	0.0
Education	0	0	0.0
Employment Security Administration	0	0	0.0
Financial Administration	51,994	80	2.9
Fire Protection	125,865	194	7.0
General Public Buildings	23,449	36	1.3
Governmental Administration, Other	41,234	63	2.3
Health	0	0	0.0
Highways	222,609	343	12.4
Hospitals	0	0	0.0
Housing and Community Development	85,036	131	4.7
Interest on General Debt	118,483	182	6.6
Judicial and Legal	12,471	19	0.7
Libraries	0	0	0.0
Parking	17,907	27	1.0
Parks and Recreation	160,998	248	8.9
Police Protection	222,464	343	12.3
Public Welfare	0	0	0.0
Sewerage	291,348	449	16.2
Solid Waste Management	4,166	6	0.2
Veterans' Services	0	0	0.0
Liquor Store	0	0	0.0
Utility	224,591	346	12.5

Source: U.S. Census Bureau, State & Local Government Finances 2019

EMPLOYMENT

Labor Force and Employment

Area	Civilian Labor Force			Workers Employed		
	Dec. 2020	Dec. 2021	% Chg.	Dec. 2020	Dec. 2021	% Chg.
City	381,311	390,784	2.5	355,432	376,716	6.0
MSA[1]	1,323,921	1,372,904	3.7	1,241,677	1,325,954	6.8
U.S.	160,017,000	161,696,000	1.0	149,613,000	155,732,000	4.1

Note: Data is not seasonally adjusted and covers workers 16 years of age and older; (1) Figures cover the Portland-Vancouver-Hillsboro, OR-WA Metropolitan Statistical Area
Source: Bureau of Labor Statistics, Local Area Unemployment Statistics

Unemployment Rate

Area	2021											
	Jan.	Feb.	Mar.	Apr.	May	Jun.	Jul.	Aug.	Sep.	Oct.	Nov.	Dec.
City	7.4	6.9	7.0	6.2	5.5	5.4	5.0	4.6	4.3	3.5	3.5	3.6
MSA[1]	6.7	6.4	6.4	5.7	5.1	5.0	4.6	4.4	4.0	3.4	3.3	3.4
U.S.	6.8	6.6	6.2	5.7	5.5	6.1	5.7	5.3	4.6	4.3	3.9	3.7

Note: Data is not seasonally adjusted and covers workers 16 years of age and older; (1) Figures cover the Portland-Vancouver-Hillsboro, OR-WA Metropolitan Statistical Area
Source: Bureau of Labor Statistics, Local Area Unemployment Statistics

Average Wages

Occupation	$/Hr.	Occupation	$/Hr.
Accountants and Auditors	39.17	Maintenance and Repair Workers	22.93
Automotive Mechanics	25.93	Marketing Managers	64.96
Bookkeepers	23.24	Network and Computer Systems Admin.	45.42
Carpenters	28.95	Nurses, Licensed Practical	29.52
Cashiers	15.55	Nurses, Registered	48.90
Computer Programmers	50.00	Nursing Assistants	19.04
Computer Systems Analysts	51.45	Office Clerks, General	20.23
Computer User Support Specialists	29.02	Physical Therapists	44.33
Construction Laborers	23.45	Physicians	93.93
Cooks, Restaurant	17.48	Plumbers, Pipefitters and Steamfitters	40.80
Customer Service Representatives	20.24	Police and Sheriff's Patrol Officers	40.26
Dentists	104.00	Postal Service Mail Carriers	26.00
Electricians	40.05	Real Estate Sales Agents	27.87
Engineers, Electrical	50.79	Retail Salespersons	17.03
Fast Food and Counter Workers	15.10	Sales Representatives, Technical/Scientific	54.99
Financial Managers	67.59	Secretaries, Exc. Legal/Medical/Executive	23.43
First-Line Supervisors of Office Workers	31.56	Security Guards	17.34
General and Operations Managers	56.48	Surgeons	147.47
Hairdressers/Cosmetologists	17.10	Teacher Assistants, Exc. Postsecondary*	18.49
Home Health and Personal Care Aides	15.92	Teachers, Secondary School, Exc. Sp. Ed.*	41.20
Janitors and Cleaners	16.88	Telemarketers	17.77
Landscaping/Groundskeeping Workers	19.37	Truck Drivers, Heavy/Tractor-Trailer	26.96
Lawyers	71.10	Truck Drivers, Light/Delivery Services	21.32
Maids and Housekeeping Cleaners	16.43	Waiters and Waitresses	17.10

Note: Wage data covers the Portland-Vancouver-Hillsboro, OR-WA Metropolitan Statistical Area; (*) Hourly wages were calculated from annual wage data based on a 40 hour work week; n/a not available.
Source: Bureau of Labor Statistics, Metro Area Occupational Employment & Wage Estimates, May 2021

Employment by Industry

Sector	MSA[1]		U.S.
	Number of Employees	Percent of Total	Percent of Total
Construction	75,900	6.3	5.0
Education and Health Services	181,600	15.0	16.0
Financial Activities	75,300	6.2	5.9
Government	150,200	12.4	14.9
Information	27,500	2.3	1.9
Leisure and Hospitality	109,700	9.1	9.8
Manufacturing	124,100	10.3	8.4
Mining and Logging	1,200	0.1	0.4
Other Services	39,000	3.2	3.7
Professional and Business Services	190,400	15.7	14.6
Retail Trade	121,700	10.1	10.7
Transportation, Warehousing, and Utilities	54,900	4.5	4.8
Wholesale Trade	57,700	4.8	3.8

Note: Figures are non-farm employment as of December 2021. Figures are not seasonally adjusted and include workers 16 years of age and older; (1) Figures cover the Portland-Vancouver-Hillsboro, OR-WA Metropolitan Statistical Area
Source: Bureau of Labor Statistics, Current Employment Statistics, Employment, Hours, and Earnings

Employment by Occupation

Occupation Classification	City (%)	MSA[1] (%)	U.S. (%)
Management, Business, Science, and Arts	51.0	44.1	39.5
Natural Resources, Construction, and Maintenance	5.1	7.6	8.7
Production, Transportation, and Material Moving	9.7	12.2	13.1
Sales and Office	18.5	20.4	21.3
Service	15.7	15.7	17.4

Note: Figures cover employed civilians 16 years of age and older; (1) Figures cover the Portland-Vancouver-Hillsboro, OR-WA Metropolitan Statistical Area
Source: U.S. Census Bureau, 2016-2020 American Community Survey 5-Year Estimates

Occupations with Greatest Projected Employment Growth: 2021 – 2023

Occupation[1]	2021 Employment	2023 Projected Employment	Numeric Employment Change	Percent Employment Change
Fast Food and Counter Workers	64,740	72,090	7,350	11.4
Cooks, Restaurant	19,990	23,030	3,040	15.2
Waiters and Waitresses	25,240	28,020	2,780	11.0
Retail Salespersons	54,130	55,970	1,840	3.4
Laborers and Freight, Stock, and Material Movers, Hand	25,960	27,670	1,710	6.6
General and Operations Managers	35,450	37,100	1,650	4.7
Home Health and Personal Care Aides	31,340	32,850	1,510	4.8
Stockers and Order Fillers	39,010	40,500	1,490	3.8
Registered Nurses	42,490	43,860	1,370	3.2
First-Line Supervisors of Food Preparation and Serving Workers	12,650	13,930	1,280	10.1

Note: Projections cover Oregon; (1) Sorted by numeric employment change
Source: www.projectionscentral.com, State Occupational Projections, 2021–2023 Short-Term Projections

Fastest-Growing Occupations: 2021 – 2023

Occupation[1]	2021 Employment	2023 Projected Employment	Numeric Employment Change	Percent Employment Change
Film and Video Editors	350	410	60	17.1
Cooks, Restaurant	19,990	23,030	3,040	15.2
Amusement and Recreation Attendants	2,180	2,490	310	14.2
Fitness Trainers and Aerobics Instructors	4,590	5,240	650	14.2
Multimedia Artists and Animators	780	890	110	14.1
Bartenders	8,070	9,170	1,100	13.6
Tour and Travel Guides	540	610	70	13.0
Manicurists and Pedicurists	2,090	2,350	260	12.4
Food Preparation and Serving Related Workers, All Other	990	1,110	120	12.1
Fine Artists, Including Painters, Sculptors, and Illustrators	590	660	70	11.9

Note: Projections cover Oregon; (1) Sorted by percent employment change and excludes occupations with numeric employment change less than 50
Source: www.projectionscentral.com, State Occupational Projections, 2021–2023 Short-Term Projections

TAXES

State Corporate Income Tax Rates

State	Tax Rate (%)	Income Brackets ($)	Num. of Brackets	Financial Institution Tax Rate (%)[a]	Federal Income Tax Ded.
Oregon	6.6 - 7.6 (u)	1 million	2	6.6 - 7.6 (u)	No

Note: Tax rates as of January 1, 2022; (a) Rates listed are the corporate income tax rate applied to financial institutions or excise taxes based on income. Some states have other taxes based upon the value of deposits or shares; (u) South Carolina taxes savings and loans at a 6% rate.
Source: Federation of Tax Administrators, State Corporate Income Tax Rates, January 1, 2022

State Individual Income Tax Rates

State	Tax Rate (%)	Income Brackets ($)	Personal Exemptions ($)			Standard Ded. ($)	
			Single	Married	Depend.	Single	Married
Oregon (a)	4.75 - 9.9	3,750 -125,000 (b)	219	438	219 (c)	2,420	4,840

Note: Tax rates as of January 1, 2022; Local- and county-level taxes are not included; The deduction for federal income tax is limited to $5,000 for individuals and $10,000 for joint returns in Missouri and Montana, and to $6,500 for all filers in Oregon; (a) 19 states have statutory provision for automatically adjusting to the rate of inflation the dollar values of the income tax brackets, standard deductions, and/or personal exemptions. Michigan indexes the personal exemption only. Oregon does not index the income brackets for $125,000 and over; (b) For joint returns, taxes are twice the tax on half the couple's income; (c) The personal exemption takes the form of a tax credit instead of a deduction
Source: Federation of Tax Administrators, State Individual Income Tax Rates, January 1, 2022

Various State Sales and Excise Tax Rates

State	State Sales Tax (%)	Gasoline[1] (¢/gal.)	Cigarette[2] ($/pack)	Spirits[3] ($/gal.)	Wine[4] ($/gal.)	Beer[5] ($/gal.)	Recreational Marijuana (%)
Oregon	None	38.83	3.33	21.94	0.67	0.08	(p)

Note: All tax rates as of January 1, 2022; (1) The American Petroleum Institute has developed a methodology for determining the average tax rate on a gallon of fuel. Rates may include any of the following: excise taxes, environmental fees, storage tank fees, other fees or taxes, general sales tax, and local taxes; (2) The federal excise tax of $1.0066 per pack and local taxes are not included; (3) Rates are those applicable to off-premise sales of 40% alcohol by volume (a.b.v.) distilled spirits in 750ml containers. Local excise taxes are excluded; (4) Rates are those applicable to off-premise sales of 11% a.b.v. non-carbonated wine in 750ml containers; (5) Rates are those applicable to off-premise sales of 4.7% a.b.v. beer in 12 ounce containers; (p) 17% excise tax (retail price)
Source: Tax Foundation, 2022 Facts & Figures: How Does Your State Compare?

State Business Tax Climate Index Rankings

State	Overall Rank	Corporate Tax Rank	Individual Income Tax Rank	Sales Tax Rank	Property Tax Rank	Unemployment Insurance Tax Rank
Oregon	22	49	42	4	17	39

Note: The index is a measure of how each state's tax laws affect economic performance. The lower the rank, the more favorable a state's tax system is for business. States without a given tax are given a ranking of 1. The scores/rankings for the District of Columbia do not affect other states. The 2022 index represents the tax climate as of July 1, 2021.
Source: Tax Foundation, State Business Tax Climate Index 2022

TRANSPORTATION

Means of Transportation to Work

Area	Car/Truck/Van		Public Transportation			Bicycle	Walked	Other Means	Worked at Home
	Drove Alone	Car-pooled	Bus	Subway	Railroad				
City	55.7	7.9	8.6	0.7	0.3	5.4	5.5	3.2	12.7
MSA[1]	68.6	8.8	4.2	0.5	0.2	2.0	3.3	2.1	10.4
U.S.	74.9	8.9	2.2	1.7	0.5	0.5	2.6	1.4	7.3

Note: Figures are percentages and cover workers 16 years of age and older; (1) Figures cover the Portland-Vancouver-Hillsboro, OR-WA Metropolitan Statistical Area
Source: U.S. Census Bureau, 2016-2020 American Community Survey 5-Year Estimates

Travel Time to Work

Area	Less Than 10 Minutes	10 to 19 Minutes	20 to 29 Minutes	30 to 44 Minutes	45 to 59 Minutes	60 to 89 Minutes	90 Minutes or More
City	7.9	27.0	26.6	24.6	7.7	4.5	1.7
MSA[1]	10.5	26.9	22.8	22.9	9.3	5.5	2.1
U.S.	12.3	28.4	20.9	20.9	8.3	6.4	2.9

Note: Note: Figures are percentages and include workers 16 years old and over; (1) Figures cover the Portland-Vancouver-Hillsboro, OR-WA Metropolitan Statistical Area
Source: U.S. Census Bureau, 2016-2020 American Community Survey 5-Year Estimates

Key Congestion Measures

Measure	1990	2000	2010	2015	2020
Annual Hours of Delay, Total (000)	16,712	37,832	57,165	71,704	36,065
Annual Hours of Delay, Per Auto Commuter	28	44	51	62	31
Annual Congestion Cost, Per Auto Commuter ($)	553	941	1,130	1,308	690

Note: Covers the Portland OR-WA urban area
Source: Texas A&M Transportation Institute, 2021 Urban Mobility Report

Freeway Travel Time Index

Measure	1985	1990	1995	2000	2005	2010	2015	2020
Urban Area Index[1]	1.16	1.19	1.25	1.30	1.32	1.32	1.36	1.10
Urban Area Rank[1,2]	10	12	6	5	8	8	6	29

Note: Freeway Travel Time Index—the ratio of travel time in the peak period to the travel time at free-flow conditions. For example, a value of 1.30 indicates a 20-minute free-flow trip takes 26 minutes in the peak (20 minutes x 1.30 = 26 minutes); (1) Covers the Portland OR-WA urban area; (2) Rank is based on 101 larger urban areas (#1 = highest travel time index)
Source: Texas A&M Transportation Institute, 2021 Urban Mobility Report

Public Transportation

Agency Name / Mode of Transportation	Vehicles Operated in Maximum Service[1]	Annual Unlinked Passenger Trips[2] (in thous.)	Annual Passenger Miles[3] (in thous.)
Tri-County Metropolitan Transportation District of Oregon (Tri-Met)			
Bus (directly operated)	589	46,845.6	160,875.2
Demand Response (purchased transportation)	223	648.4	5,776.3
Demand Response - Taxi	50	74.2	860.5
Hybrid Rail (purchased transportation)	4	272.3	2,231.7
Light Rail (directly operated)	116	30,343.3	159,458.5
Ride Connection, Inc.			
Bus (directly operated)	7	120.0	386.5
Demand Response (directly operated)	38	73.9	178.5
Demand Response - Taxi	42	74.3	366.2
City of Portland			
Aerial Tramway (purchased transportation)	2	1,623.2	1,038.9
Streetcar Rail (purchased transportation)	13	3,154.5	4,100.8
Special Mobility Services			
Bus (directly operated)	5	5.3	n/a
Demand Response (directly operated)	1	1.6	n/a

Note: (1) Number of revenue vehicles operated by the given mode and type of service to meet the annual maximum service requirement. This is the revenue vehicle count during the peak season of the year; on the week and day that maximum service is provided. Vehicles operated in maximum service (VOMS) exclude atypical days and one-time special events; (2) Number of passengers who boarded public transportation vehicles. Passengers are counted each time they board a vehicle no matter how many vehicles they use to travel from their origin to their destination. (3) Sum of the distances ridden by all passengers during the entire fiscal year.
Source: Federal Transit Administration, National Transit Database, 2020

Air Transportation

Airport Name and Code / Type of Service	Passenger Airlines[1]	Passenger Enplanements	Freight Carriers[2]	Freight (lbs)
Portland International (PDX)				
Domestic service (U.S. carriers - 2021)	20	5,674,716	19	337,445,563
International service (U.S. carriers - 2020)	6	52,440	4	483,597

Note: (1) Includes all U.S.-based major, minor and commuter airlines that carried at least one passenger during the year; (2) Includes all U.S.-based airlines and freight carriers that transported at least one pound of freight during the year.
Source: Bureau of Transportation Statistics, The Intermodal Transportation Database, Air Carriers: T-100 Domestic Market (U.S. Carriers), 2021; Bureau of Transportation Statistics, The Intermodal Transportation Database, Air Carriers: T-100 International Market (U.S. Carriers), 2020

BUSINESSES

Major Business Headquarters

Company Name	Industry	Rankings	
		Fortune[1]	Forbes[2]
Hoffman	Construction	-	179

Note: (1) Companies that produce a 10-K are ranked 1 to 500 based on 2020 revenue; (2) All private companies with at least $2 billion in annual revenue through the end of their most current fiscal year are ranked 1 to 225; companies listed are headquartered in the city; dashes indicate no ranking
Source: Fortune, "Fortune 500," 2021; Forbes, "America's Largest Private Companies," 2021

Fastest-Growing Businesses

According to *Inc.*, Portland is home to one of America's 500 fastest-growing private companies: **A&M Communications** (#355). Criteria: must be an independent, privately-held, for-profit, U.S. corporation, proprietorship or partnership as of December 31, 2020; revenues must be at least $100,000 in 2017 and $2 million in 2020; must have four-year operating/sales history. *Inc., "America's 500 Fastest-Growing Private Companies," 2021*

According to *Initiative for a Competitive Inner City (ICIC)*, Portland is home to one of America's 100 fastest-growing "inner city" companies: **Pepper Foster Consulting** (#23). Criteria for inclusion: company must be headquartered in or have 51 percent or more of its physical operations in an economically distressed urban area; must be an independent, for-profit corporation, partnership or proprietorship; must have 10 or more employees and have a five-year sales history that includes sales of at least $200,000 in the base year and at least $1 million in the current year with no decrease in sales over the two most recent years. Companies were ranked overall by revenue growth over the five-year period between 2016 and 2020. *Initiative for a Competitive Inner City (ICIC), "Inner City 100 Companies," 2021*

According to Deloitte, Portland is home to three of North America's 500 fastest-growing high-technology companies: **PayRange** (#170); **SheerID** (#316); **Foureyes** (#456). Companies are ranked by percentage growth in revenue over a four-year period. Criteria for inclusion: company must be headquartered within North America; must own proprietary intellectual property or technology that is sold to customers in products that contributes to a significant portion of the company's operating revenue; must have been in business for a minumum of four years with 2017 operating revenues of at least $50,000 USD/CD and 2020 operating revenues of at least $5 million USD/CD. *Deloitte, 2021 Technology Fast 500™*

Living Environment

COST OF LIVING

Cost of Living Index

Composite Index	Groceries	Housing	Utilities	Trans-portation	Health Care	Misc. Goods/ Services
130.1	107.9	172.7	90.3	125.6	115.4	115.6

Note: The Cost of Living Index measures regional differences in the cost of consumer goods and services, excluding taxes and non-consumer expenditures, for professional and managerial households in the top income quintile. It is based on more than 50,000 prices covering almost 60 different items for which prices are collected three times a year by chambers of commerce, economic development organizations or university applied economic centers in each participating urban area. The numbers shown should be read as a percentage above or below the national average of 100. For example, a value of 115.4 in the groceries column indicates that grocery prices are 15.4% higher than the national average. Small differences in the index numbers should not be interpreted as significant; Figures cover the Portland OR urban area.
Source: The Council for Community and Economic Research, Cost of Living Index, 2021

Grocery Prices

Area[1]	T-Bone Steak ($/pound)	Frying Chicken ($/pound)	Whole Milk ($/half gal.)	Eggs ($/dozen)	Orange Juice ($/64 oz.)	Coffee ($/11.5 oz.)
City[2]	12.57	1.58	2.61	2.04	3.93	5.63
Avg.	12.82	1.40	2.22	1.57	3.59	4.30
Min.	8.91	0.91	1.29	0.75	2.87	3.02
Max.	21.35	2.69	3.92	3.86	5.49	8.11

Note: (1) Values for the local area are compared with the average, minimum and maximum values for all 285 areas in the Cost of Living Index; (2) Figures cover the Portland OR urban area; ***T-Bone Steak*** *(price per pound);* ***Frying Chicken*** *(price per pound, whole fryer);* ***Whole Milk*** *(half gallon carton);* ***Eggs*** *(price per dozen, Grade A, large);* ***Orange Juice*** *(64 oz. Tropicana or Florida Natural);* ***Coffee*** *(11.5 oz. can, vacuum-packed, Maxwell House, Hills Bros, or Folgers).*
Source: The Council for Community and Economic Research, Cost of Living Index, 2021

Housing and Utility Costs

Area[1]	New Home Price ($)	Apartment Rent ($/month)	All Electric ($/month)	Part Electric ($/month)	Other Energy ($/month)	Telephone ($/month)
City[2]	628,508	2,544	-	80.74	67.49	177.93
Avg.	398,393	1,217	171.38	100.83	69.67	187.75
Min.	212,799	534	96.71	31.56	27.15	173.01
Max.	2,354,006	4,438	369.53	277.33	303.87	206.73

Note: (1) Values for the local area are compared with the average, minimum and maximum values for all 285 areas in the Cost of Living Index; (2) Figures cover the Portland OR urban area; ***New Home Price*** *(2,400 sf living area, 8,000 sf lot, in urban area with full utilities);* ***Apartment Rent*** *(950 sf 2 bedroom/1.5 or 2 bath, unfurnished, excluding all utilities except water);* ***All Electric*** *(average monthly cost for an all-electric home);* ***Part Electric*** *(average monthly cost for a part-electric home);* ***Other Energy*** *(average monthly cost for natural gas, fuel oil, coal, wood, and any other forms of energy except electricity);* ***Telephone*** *(price includes the base monthly rate plus taxes and fees for three lines of mobile phone service).*
Source: The Council for Community and Economic Research, Cost of Living Index, 2021

Health Care, Transportation, and Other Costs

Area[1]	Doctor ($/visit)	Dentist ($/visit)	Optometrist ($/visit)	Gasoline ($/gallon)	Beauty Salon ($/visit)	Men's Shirt ($)
City[2]	168.67	101.75	146.25	3.31	60.28	43.30
Avg.	118.16	101.04	109.44	2.71	40.63	30.77
Min.	35.04	55.56	51.17	2.17	18.59	11.32
Max.	231.10	165.12	256.81	4.11	85.33	63.03

Note: (1) Values for the local area are compared with the average, minimum and maximum values for all 285 areas in the Cost of Living Index; (2) Figures cover the Portland OR urban area; ***Doctor*** *(general practitioners routine exam of an established patient);* ***Dentist*** *(adult teeth cleaning and periodic oral examination);* ***Optometrist*** *(full vision eye exam for established adult patient);* ***Gasoline*** *(one gallon regular unleaded, national brand, including all taxes, cash price at self-service pump if available);* ***Beauty Salon*** *(woman's shampoo, trim, and blow-dry);* ***Men's Shirt*** *(cotton/polyester dress shirt, pinpoint weave, long sleeves).*
Source: The Council for Community and Economic Research, Cost of Living Index, 2021

HOUSING

Homeownership Rate

Area	2013 (%)	2014 (%)	2015 (%)	2016 (%)	2017 (%)	2018 (%)	2019 (%)	2020 (%)	2021 (%)
MSA[1]	60.9	59.8	58.9	61.8	61.1	59.2	60.0	62.5	64.1
U.S.	65.1	64.5	63.7	63.4	63.9	64.4	64.6	66.6	65.5

Note: (1) Figures cover the Portland-Vancouver-Hillsboro, OR-WA Metropolitan Statistical Area
Source: U.S. Census Bureau, Housing Vacancies and Homeownership Annual Statistics: 2013-2021

House Price Index (HPI)

Area	National Ranking[2]	Quarterly Change (%)	One-Year Change (%)	Five-Year Change (%)	Since 1991Q1 (%)
MSA[1]	116	2.32	18.40	46.02	467.52
U.S.[3]	–	3.33	17.54	54.45	258.04

Note: The HPI is a weighted repeat sales index. It measures average price changes in repeat sales or refinancings on the same properties. This information is obtained by reviewing repeat mortgage transactions on single-family properties whose mortgages have been purchased or securitized by Fannie Mae or Freddie Mac since January 1975; (1) Figures cover the Portland-Vancouver-Hillsboro, OR-WA Metropolitan Statistical Area; (2) Rankings are based on annual percentage change for all metro areas containing at least 15,000 transactions over the last 10 years and ranges from 1 to 268; (3) figures based on a weighted average of Census Division estimates using a seasonally adjusted, purchase-only index; all figures are for the period ending December 31, 2021
Source: Federal Housing Finance Agency, Change in FHFA Metropolitan Area House Price Indexes, 2021Q4

Median Single-Family Home Prices

Area	2019	2020	2021[p]	Percent Change 2020 to 2021
MSA[1]	409.3	451.0	536.4	18.9
U.S. Average	274.6	300.2	353.4	17.7

Note: Figures are median sales prices of existing single-family homes in thousands of dollars; (p) preliminary; (1) Figures cover the Portland-Vancouver-Hillsboro, OR-WA Metropolitan Statistical Area
Source: National Association of Realtors, Median Sales Price of Existing Single-Family Homes for Metropolitan Areas, 4th Quarter 2021

Qualifying Income Based on Median Sales Price of Existing Single-Family Homes

Area	With 5% Down ($)	With 10% Down ($)	With 20% Down ($)
MSA[1]	107,779	102,107	90,762
U.S. Average	70,699	66,978	59,536

Note: Figures are preliminary; Qualifying income is based on a mortgage rate of 3.13%. Monthly principal and interest payment is limited to 25% of income; (1) Figures cover the Portland-Vancouver-Hillsboro, OR-WA Metropolitan Statistical Area
Source: National Association of Realtors, Qualifying Income Based on Median Sales Price of Existing Single-Family Homes for Metropolitan Areas, 4th Quarter 2021

Home Value Distribution

Area	Under $50,000	$50,000 -$99,999	$100,000 -$149,999	$150,000 -$199,999	$200,000 -$299,999	$300,000 -$499,999	$500,000 -$999,999	$1,000,000 or more
City	1.7	0.8	0.8	3.0	13.0	42.6	34.4	3.7
MSA[1]	2.9	1.2	1.6	3.5	16.5	46.2	25.2	3.0
U.S.	6.6	11.0	12.3	13.6	20.0	20.5	12.3	3.7

Note: Figures are percentages and cover owner-occupied housing units; (1) Figures cover the Portland-Vancouver-Hillsboro, OR-WA Metropolitan Statistical Area
Source: U.S. Census Bureau, 2016-2020 American Community Survey 5-Year Estimates

Year Housing Structure Built

Area	2010 or Later	2000 -2009	1990 -1999	1980 -1989	1970 -1979	1960 -1969	1950 -1959	1940 -1949	Before 1940	Median Year
City	7.5	10.1	8.5	6.7	10.7	8.8	11.5	8.1	28.1	1963
MSA[1]	7.9	14.0	18.1	11.4	16.9	8.3	7.0	4.6	11.9	1981
U.S.	6.2	13.6	13.9	13.4	15.0	10.5	10.2	4.8	12.4	1978

Note: Figures are percentages except for Median Year; Note: (1) Figures cover the Portland-Vancouver-Hillsboro, OR-WA Metropolitan Statistical Area
Source: U.S. Census Bureau, 2016-2020 American Community Survey 5-Year Estimates

Gross Monthly Rent

Area	Under $500	$500 -$999	$1,000 -$1,499	$1,500 -$1,999	$2,000 -$2,499	$2,500 -$2,999	$3,000 and up	Median ($)
City	6.1	18.0	38.5	23.2	9.1	3.3	1.8	1,325
MSA[1]	4.4	16.7	41.6	24.8	8.4	2.5	1.6	1,345
U.S.	8.9	34.3	30.2	14.9	6.2	2.6	2.8	1,096

Note: Figures are percentages except for Median; Gross rent is the contract rent plus the estimated average monthly cost of utilities (electricity, gas, and water and sewer) and fuels (oil, coal, kerosene, wood, etc.) if these are paid by the renter (or paid for the renter by someone else); (1) Figures cover the Portland-Vancouver-Hillsboro, OR-WA Metropolitan Statistical Area
Source: U.S. Census Bureau, 2016-2020 American Community Survey 5-Year Estimates

HEALTH

Health Risk Factors

Category	MSA[1] (%)	U.S. (%)
Adults aged 18–64 who have any kind of health care coverage	90.2	86.8
Adults who reported being in good or better health	88.4	86.7
Adults who are current smokers	11.7	15.5
Adults who currently use chewing tobacco, snuff, or snus	2.5	3.7
Adults who are heavy drinkers[2]	8.2	6.7
Adults who are binge drinkers[3]	15.8	15.7
Adults who are overweight (BMI 25.0 - 29.9)	36.3	35.2
Adults who are obese (BMI 30.0 - 99.8)	28.2	31.9
Adults who participated in any physical activities in the past month	83.7	77.6
Adults who always or nearly always wears a seat belt	97.8	94.2

Note: (1) Figures cover the Portland-Vancouver-Hillsboro, OR-WA Metropolitan Statistical Area; (2) Heavy drinkers are classified as adult men having more than 14 drinks per week and adult women having more than 7 drinks per week; (3) Binge drinkers are classified as males having five or more drinks on one occasion or females having four or more drinks on one occasion
Source: Centers for Disease Control and Prevention, Behaviorial Risk Factor Surveillance System, SMART: Selected Metropolitan Area Risk Trends, 2020

Acute and Chronic Health Conditions

Category	MSA[1] (%)	U.S. (%)
Adults who have ever been told they had a heart attack	2.6	4.3
Adults who have ever been told they have angina or coronary heart disease	2.8	4.0
Adults who have ever been told they had a stroke	2.4	2.8
Adults who have ever been told they have asthma	14.9	14.2
Adults who have ever been told they have arthritis	21.3	24.5
Adults who have ever been told they have diabetes[2]	8.8	10.6
Adults who have ever been told they had skin cancer	6.6	6.4
Adults who have ever been told they had any other types of cancer	6.2	6.8
Adults who have ever been told they have COPD	5.1	6.2
Adults who have ever been told they have kidney disease	1.8	2.9
Adults who have ever been told they have a form of depression	22.0	19.6

Note: (1) Figures cover the Portland-Vancouver-Hillsboro, OR-WA Metropolitan Statistical Area; (2) Figures do not include pregnancy-related, borderline, or pre-diabetes
Source: Centers for Disease Control and Prevention, Behaviorial Risk Factor Surveillance System, SMART: Selected Metropolitan Area Risk Trends, 2020

Health Screening and Vaccination Rates

Category	MSA[1] (%)	U.S. (%)
Adults 50-75 who have had a blood stool test within the past year	16.4	9.3
Adults aged 65+ who have had flu shot within the past year	70.4	67.9
Adults aged 65+ who have ever had a pneumonia vaccination	76.1	72.2
Adults who have ever been tested for HIV	39.9	37.1
Women aged 21-65 who have had a pap test in the past three years	77.8	77.7
Men aged 40+ who have had a PSA test within the past two years	25.3	31.8
Women aged 40+ who have had a mammogram within the past two years	69.6	71.5

Note: (1) Figures cover the Portland-Vancouver-Hillsboro, OR-WA Metropolitan Statistical Area.
Source: Centers for Disease Control and Prevention, Behaviorial Risk Factor Surveillance System, SMART: Selected Metropolitan Area Risk Trends, 2020

Disability Status

Category	MSA[1] (%)	U.S. (%)
Adults who reported being deaf	6.0	6.8
Are you blind or have serious difficulty seeing, even when wearing glasses?	3.9	4.7
Do you have difficulty doing errands alone?	5.0	6.3
Do you have difficulty dressing or bathing?	2.7	3.0
Do you have serious difficulty concentrating/remembering/making decisions?	10.2	10.8
Do you have serious difficulty walking or climbing stairs?	9.5	11.9

Note: (1) Figures cover the Portland-Vancouver-Hillsboro, OR-WA Metropolitan Statistical Area.
Source: Centers for Disease Control and Prevention, Behaviorial Risk Factor Surveillance System, SMART: Selected Metropolitan Area Risk Trends, 2020

Mortality Rates for the Top 10 Causes of Death in the U.S.

ICD-10[a] Sub-Chapter	ICD-10[a] Code	Age-Adjusted Mortality Rate[1] per 100,000 population	
		County[2]	U.S.
Malignant neoplasms	C00-C97	145.3	146.4
Ischaemic heart diseases	I20-I25	57.6	90.2
Other forms of heart disease	I30-I51	54.9	51.9
Other degenerative diseases of the nervous system	G30-G31	46.2	39.7
Other external causes of accidental injury	W00-X59	40.9	38.7
Chronic lower respiratory diseases	J40-J47	30.3	38.1
Cerebrovascular diseases	I60-I69	42.6	37.6
Organic, including symptomatic, mental disorders	F01-F09	34.1	29.4
Hypertensive diseases	I10-I15	24.7	26.1
Diabetes mellitus	E10-E14	23.9	22.6

Note: (a) ICD-10 = International Classification of Diseases 10th Revision; (1) Mortality rates are a three-year average covering 2018-2020; (2) Figures cover Multnomah County.
Source: Centers for Disease Control and Prevention, National Center for Health Statistics. Underlying Cause of Death 1999-2020 on CDC WONDER Online Database

Mortality Rates for Selected Causes of Death

ICD-10[a] Sub-Chapter	ICD-10[a] Code	Age-Adjusted Mortality Rate[1] per 100,000 population	
		County[2]	U.S.
Assault	X85-Y09	4.3	6.5
Diseases of the liver	K70-K76	15.7	15.3
Human immunodeficiency virus (HIV) disease	B20-B24	1.5	1.4
Influenza and pneumonia	J09-J18	10.2	13.4
Intentional self-harm	X60-X84	17.6	13.9
Malnutrition	E40-E46	2.3	2.9
Obesity and other hyperalimentation	E65-E68	2.4	2.4
Renal failure	N17-N19	8.1	12.5
Transport accidents	V01-V99	8.7	12.5
Viral hepatitis	B15-B19	2.0	1.0

Note: (a) ICD-10 = International Classification of Diseases 10th Revision; (1) Mortality rates are a three-year average covering 2018-2020; (2) Figures cover Multnomah County; Data are suppressed when the data meet the criteria for confidentiality constraints; Mortality rates are flagged as unreliable when the rate would be calculated with a numerator of 20 or less.
Source: Centers for Disease Control and Prevention, National Center for Health Statistics. Underlying Cause of Death 1999-2020 on CDC WONDER Online Database

Health Insurance Coverage

Area	With Health Insurance	With Private Health Insurance	With Public Health Insurance	Without Health Insurance	Population Under Age 19 Without Health Insurance
City	93.8	72.3	31.6	6.2	2.5
MSA[1]	94.0	73.4	32.7	6.0	2.9
U.S.	91.3	68.1	35.3	8.7	5.2

Note: Figures are percentages that cover the civilian noninstitutionalized population; (1) Figures cover the Portland-Vancouver-Hillsboro, OR-WA Metropolitan Statistical Area
Source: U.S. Census Bureau, 2016-2020 American Community Survey 5-Year Estimates

Number of Medical Professionals

Area	MDs[3]	DOs[3,4]	Dentists	Podiatrists	Chiropractors	Optometrists
County[1] (number)	5,203	258	804	40	611	189
County[1] (rate[2])	638.1	31.6	98.6	4.9	74.9	23.2
U.S. (rate[2])	285.1	23.0	71.1	6.2	28.2	17.0

41051

Note: Data as of 2020 unless noted; (1) Data covers Multnomah County; (2) Rate per 100,000 population; (3) Data as of 2019 and includes all active, non-federal physicians; (4) Doctor of Osteopathic Medicine
Source: U.S. Department of Health and Human Services, Health Resources and Services Administration, Bureau of Health Professions, Area Resource File (ARF) 2020-2021

Best Hospitals

According to *U.S. News*, the Portland-Vancouver-Hillsboro, OR-WA metro area is home to two of the best hospitals in the U.S.: **Legacy Good Samaritan Medical Center** (1 adult specialty); **OHSU Hospital** (6 adult specialties and 5 pediatric specialties). The hospitals listed were nationally ranked in at least one of 15 adult or 10 pediatric specialties. Only 175 U.S. hospitals performed well enough to be nationally ranked in one or more specialties. Twenty hospitals in the U.S. made the Honor Roll. The Best Hospitals Honor Roll takes both the national rankings and the procedure and condition ratings into account. Hospitals received points if they were nationally ranked in one of the 15 adult specialties—the higher they ranked, the more points they got—and how many ratings of "high performing"

they earned in the 17 procedures and conditions. *U.S. News Online, "America's Best Hospitals 2021-22"*

According to *U.S. News,* the Portland-Vancouver-Hillsboro, OR-WA metro area is home to one of the best children's hospitals in the U.S.: **Doernbecher Children's Hospital at Oregon Health and Science University** (5 pediatric specialties). The hospital listed was highly ranked in at least one of 10 pediatric specialties. Ninety-two children's hospitals in the U.S. were nationally ranked in at least one specialty. Hospitals received points for being ranked in a specialty, and the 10 hospitals with the most points across the 10 specialties make up the Honor Roll. *U.S. News Online, "America's Best Children's Hospitals 2021-22"*

EDUCATION

Public School District Statistics

District Name	Schls	Pupils	Pupil/ Teacher Ratio	Minority Pupils[1] (%)	LEP/ELL[2] (%)	IEP[3] (%)
Centennial SD 28J	10	6,095	20.8	59.0	19.6	16.1
David Douglas SD 40	14	9,818	19.2	64.2	21.1	13.7
Parkrose SD 3	6	3,124	21.2	68.1	14.4	18.6
Portland SD 1J	86	48,601	17.6	43.2	7.4	17.6
Reynolds SD 7	19	11,071	19.3	68.7	25.6	18.4

Note: Table includes school districts with 2,000 or more students; (1) Percentage of students that are not non-Hispanic white; (2) Percentage of students that are Limited English Proficient (LEP) or English Language Learners (ELL) (2018-19); (3) Percentage of students that have an Individualized Education Program (IEP).
Source: U.S. Department of Education, National Center for Education Statistics, Common Core of Data, Local Education Agency (School District) Universe Survey: School Year 2019-2020

Highest Level of Education

Area	Less than H.S.	H.S. Diploma	Some College, No Deg.	Associate Degree	Bachelor's Degree	Master's Degree	Prof. School Degree	Doctorate Degree
City	7.1	15.5	19.7	6.8	30.7	13.7	4.2	2.4
MSA[1]	7.5	20.0	23.2	8.9	25.2	10.5	2.7	2.0
U.S.	11.5	26.7	20.3	8.6	20.2	9.1	2.2	1.5

Note: Figures cover persons age 25 and over; (1) Figures cover the Portland-Vancouver-Hillsboro, OR-WA Metropolitan Statistical Area
Source: U.S. Census Bureau, 2016-2020 American Community Survey 5-Year Estimates

Educational Attainment by Race

Area	High School Graduate or Higher (%)					Bachelor's Degree or Higher (%)				
	Total	White	Black	Asian	Hisp.[2]	Total	White	Black	Asian	Hisp.[2]
City	92.9	95.3	85.7	78.9	77.9	51.0	54.9	23.9	43.6	33.0
MSA[1]	92.5	94.1	88.7	87.2	70.8	40.4	40.9	28.8	53.7	20.5
U.S.	88.5	90.7	86.7	87.3	70.3	32.9	34.4	22.6	55.0	17.6

Note: Figures shown cover persons 25 years old and over; (1) Figures cover the Portland-Vancouver-Hillsboro, OR-WA Metropolitan Statistical Area; (2) People of Hispanic origin can be of any race
Source: U.S. Census Bureau, 2016-2020 American Community Survey 5-Year Estimates

School Enrollment by Grade and Control

Area	Preschool (%)		Kindergarten (%)		Grades 1 - 4 (%)		Grades 5 - 8 (%)		Grades 9 - 12 (%)	
	Public	Private	Public	Private	Public	Private	Public	Private	Public	Private
City	40.5	59.5	83.9	16.1	87.6	12.4	87.5	12.5	84.7	15.3
MSA[1]	43.0	57.0	84.9	15.1	88.4	11.6	89.2	10.8	89.8	10.2
U.S.	58.9	41.1	86.9	13.1	89.0	11.0	89.0	11.0	89.7	10.3

Note: Figures shown cover persons 3 years old and over; (1) Figures cover the Portland-Vancouver-Hillsboro, OR-WA Metropolitan Statistical Area
Source: U.S. Census Bureau, 2016-2020 American Community Survey 5-Year Estimates

Higher Education

Four-Year Colleges			Two-Year Colleges			Medical Schools[1]	Law Schools[2]	Voc/ Tech[3]
Public	Private Non-profit	Private For-profit	Public	Private Non-profit	Private For-profit			
3	17	3	3	1	10	1	2	4

Note: Figures cover institutions located within the Portland-Vancouver-Hillsboro, OR-WA Metropolitan Statistical Area and include main campuses only; (1) includes schools accredited by the Liaison Committee on Medical Education and the American Osteopathic Association's Commission on Osteopathic College Accreditation; (2) includes ABA-accredited schools, schools with provisional ABA accreditation, and state accredited schools; (3) includes all schools with programs that are less than 2 years.
Source: National Center for Education Statistics, Integrated Postsecondary Education System (IPEDS), 2020-21; Wikipedia, List of Medical Schools in the United States, accessed April 11, 2022; Wikipedia, List of Law Schools in the United States, accessed April 11, 2022

According to *U.S. News & World Report,* the Portland-Vancouver-Hillsboro, OR-WA metro area is home to one of the top 200 national universities in the U.S.: **Pacific University** (#187 tie). The indicators used to capture academic quality fall into a number of categories: assessment by administrators at peer institutions; retention of students; faculty resources; student selectivity; financial resources; alumni giving; high school counselor ratings of colleges; and graduation rate. *U.S. News & World Report, "America's Best Colleges 2022"*

According to *U.S. News & World Report,* the Portland-Vancouver-Hillsboro, OR-WA metro area is home to two of the top 100 liberal arts colleges in the U.S.: **Reed College** (#62 tie); **Lewis & Clark College** (#82 tie). The indicators used to capture academic quality fall into a number of categories: assessment by administrators at peer institutions; retention of students; faculty resources; student selectivity; financial resources; alumni giving; high school counselor ratings of colleges; and graduation rate. *U.S. News & World Report, "America's Best Colleges 2022"*

According to *U.S. News & World Report,* the Portland-Vancouver-Hillsboro, OR-WA metro area is home to one of the top 100 law schools in the U.S.: **Lewis & Clark College (Northwestern)** (#88 tie). The rankings are based on a weighted average of 12 measures of quality: peer assessment score; assessment score by lawyers/judges; median LSAT scores; median undergrad GPA; acceptance rate; employment rates for graduates; placement success; bar passage rate; faculty resources; expenditures per student; student/faculty ratio; and library resources. *U.S. News & World Report, "America's Best Graduate Schools, Law, 2022"*

According to *U.S. News & World Report,* the Portland-Vancouver-Hillsboro, OR-WA metro area is home to one of the top 75 medical schools for research in the U.S.: **Oregon Health and Science University** (#29 tie). The rankings are based on a weighted average of 11 measures of quality: quality assessment; peer assessment score; assessment score by residency directors; research activity; total research activity; average research activity per faculty member; student selectivity; median MCAT total score; median undergraduate GPA; acceptance rate; and faculty resources. *U.S. News & World Report, "America's Best Graduate Schools, Medical, 2022"*

EMPLOYERS

Major Employers

Company Name	Industry
Children's Creative Learning Center	Child day care services
Clackamas Community College	Community college
Coho Distributing	Liquor
Con-Way Enterprise Services	Accounting, auditing, & bookkeeping
Legacy Emanuel Hospital and Health Center	General medical & surgical hospitals
Nike	Rubber & plastics footwear
Oregon Health & Science University	Colleges & universities
PCC Structurals	Aircraft parts & equipment, nec
Portland Adventist Medical Center	General medical & surgical hospitals
Portland Community College	Community college
Portland State University	Colleges & universities
Providence Health & Services - Oregon	Skilled nursing facility
School Dist 1 Multnomah County	Public elementary & secondary schools
Shilo Management Corp.	Hotels & motels
Southwest Washington Medical Center	General medical & surgical hospitals
Stancorp Mortgage Investors	Life insurance
SW Washington Hospital	General medical & surgical hospitals
Tektronix	Instruments to measure elasticity
The Evergreen Aviation and Space Museum	Museums & art galleries
Veterans Health Administration	Administration of veterans' affairs

Note: Companies shown are located within the Portland-Vancouver-Hillsboro, OR-WA Metropolitan Statistical Area.
Source: Hoovers.com; Wikipedia

Best Companies to Work For

Portland State University, headquartered in Portland, is among the "100 Best Places to Work in IT." To qualify, companies had to be U.S.-based organizations or be non-U.S.-based employers that met the following criteria: have a minimum of 300 total employees at a U.S. headquarters and a minimum of 30 IT employees in the U.S., with at least 50% of their IT employees based in the U.S. The best places to work were selected based on compensation, benefits, work/life balance, employee morale, and satisfaction with training and development programs. In addition, *InsiderPro* and *Computerworld* looked at retention efforts, programs for recognizing and rewarding outstanding performances, and benefits such as flextime, elder care and child care, and reimbursement for college tuition and the cost of pursuing technology certifications. *InsiderPro and Computerworld, "100 Best Places to Work in IT," 2021*

PUBLIC SAFETY

Crime Rate

Area	Total Crime	Violent Crime Rate				Property Crime Rate		
		Murder	Rape[3]	Robbery	Aggrav. Assault	Burglary	Larceny -Theft	Motor Vehicle Theft
City	5,261.6	8.0	39.5	121.7	353.4	567.0	3,211.0	960.9
Suburbs[1]	n/a	n/a	41.7	37.9	150.0	262.3	1,381.0	296.2
Metro[2]	n/a	n/a	41.1	60.0	203.7	342.7	1,864.0	471.6
U.S.	2,356.7	6.5	38.4	73.9	279.7	314.2	1,398.0	246.0

Note: Figures are crimes per 100,000 population; (1) All areas within the metro area that are located outside the city limits; (2) Figures cover the Portland-Vancouver-Hillsboro, OR-WA Metropolitan Statistical Area; (3) All figures shown were reported using the revised Uniform Crime Reporting (UCR) definition of rape.
Source: FBI Uniform Crime Reports, 2020

Hate Crimes

Area	Number of Quarters Reported	Number of Incidents per Bias Motivation					
		Race/Ethnicity/ Ancestry	Religion	Sexual Orientation	Disability	Gender	Gender Identity
City[1]	4	28	2	9	0	1	0
U.S.	4	5,227	1,244	1,110	130	75	266

Note: (1) Figures include one incident reported with more than one bias motivation.
Source: Federal Bureau of Investigation, Hate Crime Statistics 2020

Identity Theft Consumer Reports

Area	Reports	Reports per 100,000 Population	Rank[2]
MSA[1]	5,344	214	206
U.S.	1,434,676	432	-

Note: (1) Figures cover the Portland-Vancouver-Hillsboro, OR-WA Metropolitan Statistical Area; (2) Rank ranges from 1 to 391 where 1 indicates greatest number of identity theft reports per 100,000 population
Source: Federal Trade Commission, Consumer Sentinel Network Data Book 2021

Fraud and Other Consumer Reports

Area	Reports	Reports per 100,000 Population	Rank[2]
MSA[1]	25,469	1,022	98
U.S.	4,328,977	1,304	-

Note: (1) Figures cover the Portland-Vancouver-Hillsboro, OR-WA Metropolitan Statistical Area; (2) Rank ranges from 1 to 391 where 1 indicates greatest number of fraud and other consumer reports per 100,000 population
Source: Federal Trade Commission, Consumer Sentinel Network Data Book 2021

POLITICS

2020 Presidential Election Results

Area	Biden	Trump	Jorgensen	Hawkins	Other
Multnomah County	79.2	17.9	1.2	0.6	1.0
U.S.	51.3	46.8	1.2	0.3	0.5

Note: Results are percentages and may not add to 100% due to rounding
Source: Dave Leip's Atlas of U.S. Presidential Elections

SPORTS

Professional Sports Teams

Team Name	League	Year Established
Portland Timbers	Major League Soccer (MLS)	2011
Portland Trail Blazers	National Basketball Association (NBA)	1970

Note: Includes teams located in the Portland-Vancouver-Hillsboro, OR-WA Metropolitan Statistical Area.
Source: Wikipedia, Major Professional Sports Teams of the United States and Canada, April 6, 2022

CLIMATE

Average and Extreme Temperatures

Temperature	Jan	Feb	Mar	Apr	May	Jun	Jul	Aug	Sep	Oct	Nov	Dec	Yr.
Extreme High (°F)	65	71	83	93	100	102	107	107	105	92	73	64	107
Average High (°F)	45	50	56	61	68	73	80	79	74	64	53	46	62
Average Temp. (°F)	39	43	48	52	58	63	68	68	63	55	46	41	54
Average Low (°F)	34	36	39	42	48	53	57	57	52	46	40	36	45
Extreme Low (°F)	-2	-3	19	29	29	39	43	44	34	26	13	6	-3

Note: Figures cover the years 1926-1992
Source: National Climatic Data Center, International Station Meteorological Climate Summary, 9/96

Average Precipitation/Snowfall/Humidity

Precip./Humidity	Jan	Feb	Mar	Apr	May	Jun	Jul	Aug	Sep	Oct	Nov	Dec	Yr.
Avg. Precip. (in.)	5.5	4.2	3.8	2.4	2.0	1.5	0.5	0.9	1.7	3.0	5.5	6.6	37.5
Avg. Snowfall (in.)	3	1	1	Tr	Tr	0	0	0	0	0	1	2	7
Avg. Rel. Hum. 7am (%)	85	86	86	84	80	78	77	81	87	90	88	87	84
Avg. Rel. Hum. 4pm (%)	75	67	60	55	53	50	45	45	49	61	74	79	59

Note: Figures cover the years 1926-1992; Tr = Trace amounts (<0.05 in. of rain; <0.5 in. of snow)
Source: National Climatic Data Center, International Station Meteorological Climate Summary, 9/96

Weather Conditions

Temperature			Daytime Sky			Precipitation		
5°F & below	32°F & below	90°F & above	Clear	Partly cloudy	Cloudy	0.01 inch or more precip.	0.1 inch or more snow/ice	Thunder-storms
< 1	37	11	67	116	182	152	4	7

Note: Figures are average number of days per year and cover the years 1926-1992
Source: National Climatic Data Center, International Station Meteorological Climate Summary, 9/96

HAZARDOUS WASTE

Superfund Sites

The Portland-Vancouver-Hillsboro, OR-WA metro area is home to six sites on the EPA's Superfund National Priorities List: **Boomsnub/Airco** (final); **Bradford Island** (final); **McCormick & Baxter Creosoting Co. (Portland Plant)** (final); **Northwest Pipe & Casing/Hall Process Company** (final); **Portland Harbor** (final); **Reynolds Metals Company** (final). There are a total of 1,165 Superfund sites with a status of proposed or final on the list in the U.S. *U.S. Environmental Protection Agency, National Priorities List, April 6, 2022*

AIR QUALITY

Air Quality Trends: Ozone

	1990	1995	2000	2005	2010	2016	2017	2018	2019	2020
MSA[1]	0.081	0.065	0.059	0.059	0.056	0.064	0.073	0.062	0.058	0.058
U.S.	0.090	0.091	0.082	0.080	0.074	0.070	0.069	0.070	0.066	0.068

Note: (1) Data covers the Portland-Vancouver-Hillsboro, OR-WA Metropolitan Statistical Area. The values shown are the composite ozone concentration averages among trend sites based on the highest fourth daily maximum 8-hour concentration in parts per million. These trends are based on sites having an adequate record of monitoring data during the trend period. Data from exceptional events are included.
Source: U.S. Environmental Protection Agency, Air Quality Monitoring Information, "Air Quality Trends by City, 1990-2020"

Air Quality Index

Area	Percent of Days when Air Quality was...[2]					AQI Statistics[2]	
	Good	Moderate	Unhealthy for Sensitive Groups	Unhealthy	Very Unhealthy	Maximum	Median
MSA[1]	78.1	18.0	1.6	0.0	0.8	509	37

Note: (1) Data covers the Portland-Vancouver-Hillsboro, OR-WA Metropolitan Statistical Area; (2) Based on 366 days with AQI data in 2020. Air Quality Index (AQI) is an index for reporting daily air quality. EPA calculates the AQI for five major air pollutants regulated by the Clean Air Act: ground-level ozone, particle pollution (aka particulate matter), carbon monoxide, sulfur dioxide, and nitrogen dioxide. The AQI runs from 0 to 500. The higher the AQI value, the greater the level of air pollution and the greater the health concern. There are six AQI categories: "Good" AQI is between 0 and 50. Air quality is considered satisfactory; "Moderate" AQI is between 51 and 100. Air quality is acceptable; "Unhealthy for Sensitive Groups" When AQI values are between 101 and 150, members of sensitive groups may experience health effects; "Unhealthy" When AQI values are between 151 and 200 everyone may begin to experience health effects; "Very Unhealthy" AQI values between 201 and 300 trigger a health alert; "Hazardous" AQI values over 300 trigger warnings of emergency conditions (not shown).
Source: U.S. Environmental Protection Agency, Air Quality Index Report, 2020

Air Quality Index Pollutants

Area	Percent of Days when AQI Pollutant was...[2]					
	Carbon Monoxide	Nitrogen Dioxide	Ozone	Sulfur Dioxide	Particulate Matter 2.5	Particulate Matter 10
MSA[1]	0.0	0.5	59.6	0.0	39.9	0.0

Note: (1) Data covers the Portland-Vancouver-Hillsboro, OR-WA Metropolitan Statistical Area; (2) Based on 366 days with AQI data in 2020. The Air Quality Index (AQI) is an index for reporting daily air quality. EPA calculates the AQI for five major air pollutants regulated by the Clean Air Act: ground-level ozone, particle pollution (also known as particulate matter), carbon monoxide, sulfur dioxide, and nitrogen dioxide. The AQI runs from 0 to 500. The higher the AQI value, the greater the level of air pollution and the greater the health concern.
Source: U.S. Environmental Protection Agency, Air Quality Index Report, 2020

Maximum Air Pollutant Concentrations: Particulate Matter, Ozone, CO and Lead

	Particulate Matter 10 (ug/m³)	Particulate Matter 2.5 Wtd AM (ug/m³)	Particulate Matter 2.5 24-Hr (ug/m³)	Ozone (ppm)	Carbon Monoxide (ppm)	Lead (ug/m³)
MSA[1] Level	35	13.9	147	0.07	14	n/a
NAAQS[2]	150	15	35	0.075	9	0.15
Met NAAQS[2]	Yes	Yes	No	Yes	No	n/a

Note: (1) Data covers the Portland-Vancouver-Hillsboro, OR-WA Metropolitan Statistical Area; Data from exceptional events are included; (2) National Ambient Air Quality Standards; ppm = parts per million; ug/m³ = micrograms per cubic meter; n/a not available.

Concentrations: Particulate Matter 10 (coarse particulate)—highest second maximum 24-hour concentration; Particulate Matter 2.5 Wtd AM (fine particulate)—highest weighted annual mean concentration; Particulate Matter 2.5 24-Hour (fine particulate)—highest 98th percentile 24-hour concentration; Ozone—highest fourth daily maximum 8-hour concentration; Carbon Monoxide—highest second maximum non-overlapping 8-hour concentration; Lead—maximum running 3-month average

Source: U.S. Environmental Protection Agency, Air Quality Monitoring Information, "Air Quality Statistics by City, 2020"

Maximum Air Pollutant Concentrations: Nitrogen Dioxide and Sulfur Dioxide

	Nitrogen Dioxide AM (ppb)	Nitrogen Dioxide 1-Hr (ppb)	Sulfur Dioxide AM (ppb)	Sulfur Dioxide 1-Hr (ppb)	Sulfur Dioxide 24-Hr (ppb)
MSA[1] Level	10	30	n/a	2	n/a
NAAQS[2]	53	100	30	75	140
Met NAAQS[2]	Yes	Yes	n/a	Yes	n/a

Note: (1) Data covers the Portland-Vancouver-Hillsboro, OR-WA Metropolitan Statistical Area; Data from exceptional events are included; (2) National Ambient Air Quality Standards; ppm = parts per million; ug/m³ = micrograms per cubic meter; n/a not available.

Concentrations: Nitrogen Dioxide AM—highest arithmetic mean concentration; Nitrogen Dioxide 1-Hr—highest 98th percentile 1-hour daily maximum concentration; Sulfur Dioxide AM—highest annual mean concentration; Sulfur Dioxide 1-Hr—highest 99th percentile 1-hour daily maximum concentration; Sulfur Dioxide 24-Hr—highest second maximum 24-hour concentration

Source: U.S. Environmental Protection Agency, Air Quality Monitoring Information, "Air Quality Statistics by City, 2020"

Provo, Utah

Background

Provo is situated on the Provo River at a site that was, prehistorically, under the waters of Lake Bonneville. Today, Provo enjoys one of the country's highest employment rates, a growing high-tech economy, a low crime rate, and a magnificent natural environment. The seat of Utah County, it lies at the base of the steep Wasatch Mountains, with Provo Peak rising to a height of 11,054 feet just east of the city, making Provo convenient to many of Utah's famed ski areas and to the Uinta National Forest.

Spanish missionaries Francisco Silvestre Velez de Escalante and Francisco Atanasio Dominguez, exploring for a more direct route from present-day New Mexico to California, were likely the first Europeans to view the area. They did not establish a permanent mission but did note that the area could easily be irrigated and developed into an important agricultural settlement. Etienne Prevot, a Canadian trapper and explorer, likewise visited but did not settle, though he too remarked on the beauty and potential of the site. These early explorers also met, and conflicted with, the area's original inhabitants, the Ute Indians, who held an important fish festival on the river every spring.

Permanent European settlement of Provo is strongly linked to Mormon history. In 1849, John S. Higbee, with 30 families in a wagon train, left the larger Salt Lake City community to move north. As they arrived in the region, they confronted a group of Ute, with whom white settlers had already been in some conflict. A short-lived peace agreement gave way to further conflict and a series of battles, after which the Indians agreed to resettlement. Peace ensued, and Provo was subject to long periods of peaceful relations with the Indians, different from many other young Western towns.

Irrigation has been central to Provo's success, and in the very year of Higbee's arrival, two large canals were dug, taking water from the Provo River. Grain mills were constructed to serve the needs of nearby farmers, and important rail links were completed in the 1870s connecting Provo to Salt Lake City and to the Union Pacific System, giving impetus to the region's agricultural and mining industries.

Provo's growth took off, with an electric generating plant built in 1890, and an interurban commuter rail service between Provo and Salt Lake City in 1914. The town had become a major regional industrial center, with ironworks, flourmills, and brickyards. Today, the area has the second largest concentration of software technology companies in the country and the third concentration of high-tech companies. Also important to the economy of the region are biotech companies, Nestle Frozen Foods, and NuSkin Enterprises.

Provo's industrial dynamism and creativity is reflected in the careers of two of its favorite sons. Dr. Harvey Fletcher, of Bell Laboratories, was the inventor of aids to the deaf and hearing-impaired, and an important early leader of the National Acoustic Association. Philo T. Farnsworth, born in Beaver but raised in Provo, developed the fundamental concepts of television in 1924 at the age of 18.

Provo is home to Farnsworth's alma mater, Brigham Young University (BYU), a private university operated by The Church of Jesus Christ of Latter-day Saints (LDS). Founded in 1875 it has earned national respect for everything from football and undergraduate liberal arts programs to its graduate programs in business and law. The Provo Tabernacle, destroyed by fire in 2010, was rebuilt as the Provo City Center Temple in 2016, making Provo the second city in the LDS Church to have two temples.

In 2001, Provo resident Larry H. Miller donated the Larry H. Miller Field to Brigham Young University, which is currently used as a training and competitive facility by various teams, including the Brigham Young Cougars. In 2009, the city of Provo implemented CITYWATCH, a city-wide emergency notification system. The Utah Valley Convention Center was completed in early 2012.

Provo hosts the annual America's Freedom Festival, a private, non-profit, non-political event, and one of the largest and longest (May to July) patriotic celebrations in the country. It's not without controversary, as it has prevented certain entities, namely Mormons and LGBTQ groups, from participating over the years.

The festivities have featured such notable figures as Bob Hope, David Hasselhoff, Reba McEntire, Mandy Moore, Huey Lewis and the News, Toby Keith, Sean Hannity, Fred Willard, Taylor Hicks, Journey, and Olivia Holt. Marie Osmond and Tim McGraw are part of the 2022 line up.

The climate of Provo is semi-arid continental. Summers are generally hot and dry. Winters are cold but not severe. Precipitation is generally light, with most of the rain falling in the spring.

Rankings

General Rankings

- The Provo metro area was identified as one of America's fastest-growing areas in terms of population and business growth by *MagnifyMoney.* The area ranked #2 out of 35. The 100 most populous metro areas in the U.S. were evaluated on their change from 2011 to 2016 in the following categories: people and housing; workforce and employment opportunities; growing industry. *www.businessinsider.com, "The 35 Cities in the US with the Biggest Influx of People, the Most Work Opportunities, and the Hottest Business Growth," August 12, 2018*

Business/Finance Rankings

- The Brookings Institution ranked the nation's largest cities based on income inequality. Provo was ranked #63 (#1 = greatest inequality). Criteria: the "95/20 ratio," a figure representing the income at which a household earns more than 95 percent of all other households, divided by the income at which a household earns more than only 20 percent of all other households. *Brookings Institution, "Household Income Inequality, Largest Cities of 97 Large U.S. Metro Areas, 2014-2016," February 5, 2018*
- The Brookings Institution ranked the 100 largest metro areas in the U.S. based on income inequality. Provo was ranked #99 (#1 = greatest inequality). Criteria: the "95/20 ratio," a figure representing the income at which a household earns more than 95 percent of all other households, divided by the income at which a household earns more than only 20 percent of all other households. *Brookings Institution, "Household Income Inequality, 100 Largest U.S. Metro Areas, 2014-2016," February 5, 2018*
- The Provo metro area appeared on the Milken Institute "2021 Best Performing Cities" list. Rank: #1 out of 200 large metro areas (population over 250,000). Criteria: job growth; wage and salary growth; high-tech output growth; housing affordability; household broadband access. *Milken Institute, "Best-Performing Cities 2021," February 16, 2021*
- *Forbes* ranked the 200 most populous metro areas to determine the nation's "Best Places for Business and Careers." The Provo metro area was ranked #6. Criteria: costs (business and living); job growth (past and projected); income growth; quality of life; educational attainment (college and high school); projected economic growth; cultural and leisure opportunities; workplace tolerance laws; net migration patterns. *Forbes, "The Best Places for Business and Careers 2019: Seattle Still On Top," October 30, 2019*

Dating/Romance Rankings

- *Apartment List* conducted its annual survey of renters for cities that have the best opportunities for dating. More than 11,000 single respondents rated their current city or neighborhood for opportunities to date. Provo ranked #1 out of 86 where single residents were very satisfied or somewhat satisfied, making it among the ten best areas for dating opportunities. Other criteria analyzed included gender and education levels of renters. *Apartment List, "The Best & Worst Metros for Dating 2020," February 4, 2020*

Education Rankings

- Personal finance website *WalletHub* analyzed the 150 largest U.S. metropolitan statistical areas to determine where the most educated Americans are putting their degrees to work. Criteria: education levels; percentage of workers with degrees; education quality and attainment gap; public school quality rankings; quality and enrollment of each metro area's universities. Provo was ranked #10 (#1 = most educated city). *www.WalletHub.com, "Most & Least Educated Cities in America," July 19, 2021*

Environmental Rankings

- Niche compiled a list of the nation's snowiest cities, based on the National Oceanic and Atmospheric Administration's 30-year average snowfall data. Among cities with a population of at least 50,000, Provo ranked #20. *Niche.com, Top 25 Snowiest Cities in America, December 10, 2018*

Health/Fitness Rankings

- Provo was identified as a "2021 Spring Allergy Capital." The area ranked #96 out of 100. Three groups of factors were used to identify the most challenging cities for people with allergies during the spring season: annual spring pollen levels; over the counter medicine use; number of board-certified allergy specialists. *Asthma and Allergy Foundation of America, "Spring Allergy Capitals 2021," February 23, 2021*

- Provo was identified as a "2021 Fall Allergy Capital." The area ranked #93 out of 100. Three groups of factors were used to identify the most challenging cities for people with allergies during the fall season: annual fall pollen levels; over the counter medicine use; number of board-certified allergy specialists. *Asthma and Allergy Foundation of America, "Fall Allergy Capitals 2021," February 23, 2021*
- Provo was identified as a "2021 Asthma Capital." The area ranked #98 out of the nation's 100 largest metropolitan areas. Criteria: estimated asthma prevalence; asthma-related mortality; and ER visits due to asthma. Risk factors analyzed but not factored in the rankings: annual pollen score; annual air quality; public smoking laws; number of board-certified asthma specialists; rescue medication use; controller medication use; uninsured rate; poverty rate. *Asthma and Allergy Foundation of America, "Asthma Capitals 2021: The Most Challenging Places to Live With Asthma," May 5, 2021*

Real Estate Rankings

- Provo was ranked #202 out of 237 metro areas in terms of housing affordability in 2021 by the National Association of Home Builders (#1 = most affordable). Criteria: the share of homes sold in that area affordable to a family earning the local median income, based on standard mortgage underwriting criteria. *National Association of Home Builders®, NAHB-Wells Fargo Housing Opportunity Index, 4th Quarter 2021*

Safety Rankings

- The National Insurance Crime Bureau ranked 390 metro areas in the U.S. in terms of per capita rates of vehicle theft. The Provo metro area ranked #307 (#1 = highest rate). Criteria: number of vehicle theft offenses per 100,000 inhabitants in 2020. *National Insurance Crime Bureau, "Hot Spots 2020," August 31, 2021*

Seniors/Retirement Rankings

- *AARP the Magazine* selected Provo as one of the great places in the United States for seniors, as well as younger generations, that represent "a place to call home." For the list, the magazine recognized the change in criteria due to the pandemic, and looked for cities with easy access to exercise/outdoors, quality healthcare, sense of community, relatively affordable housing costs, job markets that accommodate working from home, and reliable internet access. *www.aarp.org/magazine, "Best Places to Live and Retire Now," November 29, 2021*
- From its Best Cities for Successful Aging indexes, the Milken Institute generated rankings for metropolitan areas, weighing data in nine categories—health care, wellness, living arrangements, transportation and convenience, financial characteristics, education, employment, community engagement, and overall livability. The Provo metro area was ranked #1 overall in the large metro area category. *Milken Institute, "Best Cities for Successful Aging, 2017" March 14, 2017*

Miscellaneous Rankings

- *WalletHub* compared the 150 most populated U.S. cities to determine their operating efficiency. A "Quality of City Services" score was constructed for each city and then divided by the total budget per capita to reveal which were managed the best. Provo ranked #15. Criteria: financial stability; economy; education; safety; health; infrastructure and pollution. *www.WalletHub.com, "2021's Best- & Worst-Run Cities in America," June 22, 2021*

Business Environment

DEMOGRAPHICS

Population Growth

Area	1990 Census	2000 Census	2010 Census	2020* Estimate	Population Growth (%) 1990-2020	Population Growth (%) 2010-2020
City	87,148	105,166	112,488	116,886	34.1	3.9
MSA[1]	269,407	376,774	526,810	633,129	135.0	20.2
U.S.	248,709,873	281,421,906	308,745,538	326,569,308	31.3	5.8

Note: (1) Figures cover the Provo-Orem, UT Metropolitan Statistical Area; (*) 2016-2020 5-year estimated population
Source: U.S. Census Bureau, 1990 Census, Census 2000, Census 2010, 2016-2020 American Community Survey 5-Year Estimates

Household Size

Area	Persons in Household (%) One	Two	Three	Four	Five	Six	Seven or More	Average Household Size
City	14.5	34.3	17.9	15.5	7.4	7.2	3.2	3.10
MSA[1]	12.3	28.9	15.7	15.6	12.6	8.9	6.1	3.50
U.S.	28.0	33.9	15.5	12.9	6.0	2.3	1.4	2.60

Note: (1) Figures cover the Provo-Orem, UT Metropolitan Statistical Area
Source: U.S. Census Bureau, 2016-2020 American Community Survey 5-Year Estimates

Race

Area	White Alone[2] (%)	Black Alone[2] (%)	Asian Alone[2] (%)	AIAN[3] Alone[2] (%)	NHOPI[4] Alone[2] (%)	Other Race Alone[2] (%)	Two or More Races (%)
City	85.6	1.1	2.8	1.0	1.3	2.8	5.5
MSA[1]	90.2	0.6	1.4	0.6	0.8	2.1	4.3
U.S.	70.4	12.6	5.6	0.8	0.2	5.1	5.2

Note: (1) Figures cover the Provo-Orem, UT Metropolitan Statistical Area; (2) Alone is defined as not being in combination with one or more other races; (3) American Indian and Alaska Native; (4) Native Hawaiian and Other Pacific Islander
Source: U.S. Census Bureau, 2016-2020 American Community Survey 5-Year Estimates

Hispanic or Latino Origin

Area	Total (%)	Mexican (%)	Puerto Rican (%)	Cuban (%)	Other (%)
City	17.7	11.3	0.7	0.1	5.6
MSA[1]	11.8	7.6	0.3	0.1	3.9
U.S.	18.2	11.2	1.7	0.7	4.5

Note: Persons of Hispanic or Latino origin can be of any race; (1) Figures cover the Provo-Orem, UT Metropolitan Statistical Area
Source: U.S. Census Bureau, 2016-2020 American Community Survey 5-Year Estimates

Ancestry

Area	German	Irish	English	American	Italian	Polish	French[2]	Scottish	Dutch
City	10.1	4.5	24.0	2.6	1.8	0.8	1.5	4.4	1.4
MSA[1]	10.4	5.0	28.2	4.2	2.3	0.6	1.7	4.7	1.5
U.S.	13.0	9.7	7.7	5.9	5.1	2.7	2.3	1.6	1.1

Note: Figures are the percentage of the total population reporting a particular ancestry. The nine most commonly reported ancestries in the U.S. are shown. Figures include multiple ancestries (e.g. if a person reported being Irish and Italian, they were included in both columns); (1) Figures cover the Provo-Orem, UT Metropolitan Statistical Area; (2) Excludes Basque
Source: U.S. Census Bureau, 2016-2020 American Community Survey 5-Year Estimates

Foreign-born Population

Area	Percent of Population Born in: Any Foreign Country	Asia	Mexico	Europe	Caribbean	Central America[2]	South America	Africa	Canada
City	11.2	2.1	4.1	0.4	0.3	0.8	2.4	0.3	0.3
MSA[1]	7.2	1.1	2.5	0.5	0.1	0.5	1.6	0.2	0.4
U.S.	13.5	4.2	3.3	1.5	1.3	1.1	1.0	0.7	0.3

Note: (1) Figures cover the Provo-Orem, UT Metropolitan Statistical Area; (2) Excludes Mexico.
Source: U.S. Census Bureau, 2016-2020 American Community Survey 5-Year Estimates

Marital Status

Area	Never Married	Now Married[2]	Separated	Widowed	Divorced
City	48.6	44.0	0.9	2.2	4.3
MSA[1]	32.5	58.4	0.9	2.6	5.5
U.S.	33.5	48.1	1.8	5.7	10.8

Note: Figures are percentages and cover the population 15 years of age and older; (1) Figures cover the Provo-Orem, UT Metropolitan Statistical Area; (2) Excludes separated
Source: U.S. Census Bureau, 2016-2020 American Community Survey 5-Year Estimates

Disability by Age

Area	All Ages	Under 18 Years Old	18 to 64 Years Old	65 Years and Over
City	8.7	4.4	7.1	41.9
MSA[1]	8.2	3.6	7.5	32.6
U.S.	12.7	4.3	10.3	34.0

Note: Figures show percent of the civilian noninstitutionalized population that reported having a disability. Disability status is determined from six types of difficulty: vision, hearing, cognitive, ambulatory, self-care, and independent living. For children under 5 years old, hearing and vision difficulty are used to determine disability status. For children between the ages of 5 and 14, disability status is determined from hearing, vision, cognitive, ambulatory, and self-care difficulties. For people aged 15 years and older, they are considered to have a disability if they have difficulty with any one of the six difficulty types; Note: (1) Figures cover the Provo-Orem, UT Metropolitan Statistical Area
Source: U.S. Census Bureau, 2016-2020 American Community Survey 5-Year Estimates

Age

Area	Percent of Population									Median Age
	Under Age 5	Age 5–19	Age 20–34	Age 35–44	Age 45–54	Age 55–64	Age 65–74	Age 75–84	Age 85+	
City	6.6	20.2	48.0	8.3	5.6	5.0	3.3	2.0	0.9	23.7
MSA[1]	9.3	28.1	26.9	12.7	8.5	6.7	4.6	2.4	0.8	25.0
U.S.	6.0	19.1	20.6	12.7	12.7	12.9	9.4	4.7	2.0	38.2

Note: (1) Figures cover the Provo-Orem, UT Metropolitan Statistical Area
Source: U.S. Census Bureau, 2016-2020 American Community Survey 5-Year Estimates

Gender

Area	Males	Females	Males per 100 Females
City	57,710	59,176	97.5
MSA[1]	320,120	313,009	102.3
U.S.	160,818,530	165,750,778	97.0

Note: (1) Figures cover the Provo-Orem, UT Metropolitan Statistical Area
Source: U.S. Census Bureau, 2016-2020 American Community Survey 5-Year Estimates

Religious Groups by Family

Area	Catholic	Baptist	Non-Den.	Methodist[2]	Lutheran	LDS[3]	Pentecostal	Presbyterian[4]	Muslim[5]	Judaism
MSA[1]	1.3	0.1	0.1	0.2	<0.1	88.6	0.1	0.1	<0.1	<0.1
U.S.	19.1	9.3	4.0	4.0	2.3	2.0	1.9	1.6	0.8	0.7

Note: Figures are the number of adherents as a percentage of the total population; (1) Figures cover the Provo-Orem, UT Metropolitan Statistical Area; (2) Methodist/Pietist; (3) Latter Day Saints; (4) Reformed; (5) Figures are estimates
Source: Association of Statisticians of American Religious Bodies, 2010 U.S. Religion Census: Religious Congregations & Membership Study

Religious Groups by Tradition

Area	Catholic	Evangelical Protestant	Mainline Protestant	Other Tradition	Black Protestant	Orthodox
MSA[1]	1.3	0.5	0.1	88.9	<0.1	<0.1
U.S.	19.1	16.2	7.3	4.3	1.6	0.3

Note: Figures are the number of adherents as a percentage of the total population; (1) Figures cover the Provo-Orem, UT Metropolitan Statistical Area
Source: Association of Statisticians of American Religious Bodies, 2010 U.S. Religion Census: Religious Congregations & Membership Study

ECONOMY

Gross Metropolitan Product

Area	2017	2018	2019	2020	Rank[2]
MSA[1]	25.7	27.9	29.5	31.2	104

Note: Figures are in billions of dollars; (1) Figures cover the Provo-Orem, UT Metropolitan Statistical Area; (2) Rank is based on 2018 data and ranges from 1 to 381
Source: U.S. Conference of Mayors, U.S. Metro Economies: GMP & Employment 2018-2020, September 2019

Economic Growth

Area	2015-17 (%)	2018 (%)	2019 (%)	2020 (%)	Rank[2]
MSA[1]	6.6	6.5	4.0	3.7	7
U.S.	1.9	2.9	2.3	2.1	–

Note: Figures are real gross metropolitan product (GMP) growth rates and represent average annual percent change; (1) Figures cover the Provo-Orem, UT Metropolitan Statistical Area; (2) Rank is based on 2017 2-year average annual percent change and ranges from 1 to 381
Source: U.S. Conference of Mayors, U.S. Metro Economies: GMP & Employment 2018-2020, September 2019

Metropolitan Area Exports

Area	2015	2016	2017	2018	2019	2020	Rank[2]
MSA[1]	2,216.4	1,894.8	2,065.3	1,788.1	1,783.7	1,888.5	100

Note: Figures are in millions of dollars; (1) Figures cover the Provo-Orem, UT Metropolitan Statistical Area; (2) Rank is based on 2020 data and ranges from 1 to 389
Source: U.S. Department of Commerce, International Trade Administration, Office of Trade and Economic Analysis, Industry and Analysis, Exports by Metropolitan Area, data extracted March 4, 2022

Building Permits

Area	Single-Family			Multi-Family			Total		
	2019	2020	Pct. Chg.	2019	2020	Pct. Chg.	2019	2020	Pct. Chg.
City	174	219	25.9	140	138	-1.4	314	357	13.7
MSA[1]	5,423	6,800	25.4	1,524	1,167	-23.4	6,947	7,967	14.7
U.S.	862,100	979,400	13.6	523,900	491,700	-6.1	1,386,000	1,471,100	6.1

Note: (1) Figures cover the Provo-Orem, UT Metropolitan Statistical Area; Figures represent new, privately-owned housing units authorized (unadjusted data); All permit data are based on estimates with imputation
Source: U.S. Census Bureau, Manufacturing, Mining, and Construction Statistics, Building Permits, 2019, 2020

Bankruptcy Filings

Area	Business Filings			Nonbusiness Filings		
	2020	2021	% Chg.	2020	2021	% Chg.
Utah County	31	22	-29.0	1,151	814	-29.3
U.S.	21,655	14,347	-33.7	522,808	399,269	-23.6

Note: Business filings include Chapter 7, Chapter 9, Chapter 11, Chapter 12, Chapter 13, Chapter 15, and Section 304; Nonbusiness filings include Chapter 7, Chapter 11, and Chapter 13
Source: Administrative Office of the U.S. Courts, Business and Nonbusiness Bankruptcy, County Cases Commenced by Chapter of the Bankruptcy Code, During the 12-Month Period Ending December 31, 2020 and Business and Nonbusiness Bankruptcy, County Cases Commenced by Chapter of the Bankruptcy Code, During the 12-Month Period Ending December 31, 2021

Housing Vacancy Rates

Area	Gross Vacancy Rate[2] (%)			Year-Round Vacancy Rate[3] (%)			Rental Vacancy Rate[4] (%)			Homeowner Vacancy Rate[5] (%)		
	2019	2020	2021	2019	2020	2021	2019	2020	2021	2019	2020	2021
MSA[1]	n/a	n/a	n/a	n/a	n/a	n/a	n/a	n/a	n/a	n/a	n/a	n/a
U.S.	12.0	10.6	10.8	9.5	8.2	8.4	6.7	6.3	6.1	1.4	1.0	0.9

Note: (1) Figures cover the Provo-Orem, UT Metropolitan Statistical Area; (2) The percentage of the total housing inventory that is vacant; (3) The percentage of the housing inventory (excluding seasonal units) that is year-round vacant; (4) The percentage of rental inventory that is vacant for rent; (5) The percentage of homeowner inventory that is vacant for sale; n/a not available
Source: U.S. Census Bureau, Housing Vacancies and Homeownership Annual Statistics: 2019, 2020, 2021

INCOME

Income

Area	Per Capita ($)	Median Household ($)	Average Household ($)
City	21,607	50,072	70,832
MSA[1]	27,293	76,864	96,434
U.S.	35,384	64,994	91,547

Note: (1) Figures cover the Provo-Orem, UT Metropolitan Statistical Area
Source: U.S. Census Bureau, 2016-2020 American Community Survey 5-Year Estimates

Household Income Distribution

Area	Percent of Households Earning							
	Under $15,000	$15,000 -$24,999	$25,000 -$34,999	$35,000 -$49,999	$50,000 -$74,999	$75,000 -$99,999	$100,000 -$149,999	$150,000 and up
City	12.0	11.4	13.1	13.5	18.8	11.9	10.7	8.6
MSA[1]	5.7	5.8	7.3	11.1	18.7	16.0	20.1	15.3
U.S.	9.9	8.5	8.6	12.0	17.2	12.8	15.6	15.4

Note: (1) Figures cover the Provo-Orem, UT Metropolitan Statistical Area
Source: U.S. Census Bureau, 2016-2020 American Community Survey 5-Year Estimates

Poverty Rate

Area	All Ages	Under 18 Years Old	18 to 64 Years Old	65 Years and Over
City	25.8	19.2	29.3	10.4
MSA[1]	10.1	8.7	11.5	5.6
U.S.	12.8	17.5	12.1	9.3

Note: Figures are percentage of people whose income during the past 12 months was below the poverty level; (1) Figures cover the Provo-Orem, UT Metropolitan Statistical Area
Source: U.S. Census Bureau, 2016-2020 American Community Survey 5-Year Estimates

CITY FINANCES

City Government Finances

Component	2019 ($000)	2019 ($ per capita)
Total Revenues	218,485	1,862
Total Expenditures	201,967	1,721
Debt Outstanding	169,209	1,442
Cash and Securities[1]	193,091	1,646

Note: (1) Cash and security holdings of a government at the close of its fiscal year, including those of its dependent agencies, utilities, and liquor stores.
Source: U.S. Census Bureau, State & Local Government Finances 2019

City Government Revenue by Source

Source	2019 ($000)	2019 ($ per capita)	2019 (%)
General Revenue			
From Federal Government	1,945	17	0.9
From State Government	5,723	49	2.6
From Local Governments	5,093	43	2.3
Taxes			
Property	13,727	117	6.3
Sales and Gross Receipts	31,183	266	14.3
Personal Income	0	0	0.0
Corporate Income	0	0	0.0
Motor Vehicle License	0	0	0.0
Other Taxes	1,782	15	0.8
Current Charges	54,122	461	24.8
Liquor Store	0	0	0.0
Utility	88,399	753	40.5

Source: U.S. Census Bureau, State & Local Government Finances 2019

City Government Expenditures by Function

Function	2019 ($000)	2019 ($ per capita)	2019 (%)
General Direct Expenditures			
Air Transportation	8,078	68	4.0
Corrections	0	0	0.0
Education	0	0	0.0
Employment Security Administration	0	0	0.0
Financial Administration	2,566	21	1.3
Fire Protection	10,038	85	5.0
General Public Buildings	0	0	0.0
Governmental Administration, Other	5,164	44	2.6
Health	488	4	0.2
Highways	5,749	49	2.8
Hospitals	0	0	0.0
Housing and Community Development	3,714	31	1.8
Interest on General Debt	2,918	24	1.4
Judicial and Legal	2,712	23	1.3
Libraries	3,835	32	1.9
Parking	231	2	0.1
Parks and Recreation	15,494	132	7.7
Police Protection	15,984	136	7.9
Public Welfare	0	0	0.0
Sewerage	26,750	228	13.2
Solid Waste Management	0	0	0.0
Veterans' Services	0	0	0.0
Liquor Store	0	0	0.0
Utility	75,649	644	37.5

Source: U.S. Census Bureau, State & Local Government Finances 2019

EMPLOYMENT

Labor Force and Employment

Area	Civilian Labor Force			Workers Employed		
	Dec. 2020	Dec. 2021	% Chg.	Dec. 2020	Dec. 2021	% Chg.
City	67,158	70,473	4.9	65,654	69,726	6.2
MSA[1]	322,546	337,804	4.7	314,394	333,883	6.2
U.S.	160,017,000	161,696,000	1.0	149,613,000	155,732,000	4.1

Note: Data is not seasonally adjusted and covers workers 16 years of age and older; (1) Figures cover the Provo-Orem, UT Metropolitan Statistical Area
Source: Bureau of Labor Statistics, Local Area Unemployment Statistics

Unemployment Rate

Area	2021											
	Jan.	Feb.	Mar.	Apr.	May	Jun.	Jul.	Aug.	Sep.	Oct.	Nov.	Dec.
City	2.6	2.7	2.1	2.1	2.1	2.7	2.1	2.1	1.1	1.1	1.1	1.1
MSA[1]	2.9	3.1	2.4	2.4	2.3	2.8	2.3	2.3	1.4	1.2	1.2	1.2
U.S.	6.8	6.6	6.2	5.7	5.5	6.1	5.7	5.3	4.6	4.3	3.9	3.7

Note: Data is not seasonally adjusted and covers workers 16 years of age and older; (1) Figures cover the Provo-Orem, UT Metropolitan Statistical Area
Source: Bureau of Labor Statistics, Local Area Unemployment Statistics

Average Wages

Occupation	$/Hr.	Occupation	$/Hr.
Accountants and Auditors	33.20	Maintenance and Repair Workers	20.67
Automotive Mechanics	22.18	Marketing Managers	56.64
Bookkeepers	20.57	Network and Computer Systems Admin.	41.93
Carpenters	21.23	Nurses, Licensed Practical	23.55
Cashiers	12.38	Nurses, Registered	33.61
Computer Programmers	45.65	Nursing Assistants	14.42
Computer Systems Analysts	55.42	Office Clerks, General	17.38
Computer User Support Specialists	25.51	Physical Therapists	42.30
Construction Laborers	18.10	Physicians	108.18
Cooks, Restaurant	14.67	Plumbers, Pipefitters and Steamfitters	24.27
Customer Service Representatives	17.07	Police and Sheriff's Patrol Officers	28.08
Dentists	62.68	Postal Service Mail Carriers	25.82
Electricians	26.19	Real Estate Sales Agents	22.96
Engineers, Electrical	44.41	Retail Salespersons	14.94
Fast Food and Counter Workers	11.73	Sales Representatives, Technical/Scientific	34.68
Financial Managers	58.84	Secretaries, Exc. Legal/Medical/Executive	18.18
First-Line Supervisors of Office Workers	27.36	Security Guards	16.06
General and Operations Managers	42.31	Surgeons	130.48
Hairdressers/Cosmetologists	13.30	Teacher Assistants, Exc. Postsecondary*	13.94
Home Health and Personal Care Aides	13.94	Teachers, Secondary School, Exc. Sp. Ed.*	31.63
Janitors and Cleaners	13.28	Telemarketers	14.48
Landscaping/Groundskeeping Workers	16.62	Truck Drivers, Heavy/Tractor-Trailer	23.79
Lawyers	69.48	Truck Drivers, Light/Delivery Services	18.92
Maids and Housekeeping Cleaners	13.58	Waiters and Waitresses	13.77

Note: Wage data covers the Provo-Orem, UT Metropolitan Statistical Area; (*) Hourly wages were calculated from annual wage data based on a 40 hour work week; n/a not available.
Source: Bureau of Labor Statistics, Metro Area Occupational Employment & Wage Estimates, May 2021

Employment by Industry

Sector	MSA[1]		U.S.
	Number of Employees	Percent of Total	Percent of Total
Construction, Mining, and Logging	27,800	9.2	5.3
Education and Health Services	60,000	19.9	16.0
Financial Activities	13,200	4.4	5.9
Government	34,500	11.5	14.9
Information	15,900	5.3	1.9
Leisure and Hospitality	25,400	8.4	9.8
Manufacturing	22,300	7.4	8.4
Other Services	6,300	2.1	3.7
Professional and Business Services	42,500	14.1	14.6
Retail Trade	39,900	13.2	10.7
Transportation, Warehousing, and Utilities	5,600	1.9	4.8
Wholesale Trade	7,900	2.6	3.8

Note: Figures are non-farm employment as of December 2021. Figures are not seasonally adjusted and include workers 16 years of age and older; (1) Figures cover the Provo-Orem, UT Metropolitan Statistical Area
Source: Bureau of Labor Statistics, Current Employment Statistics, Employment, Hours, and Earnings

Employment by Occupation

Occupation Classification	City (%)	MSA[1] (%)	U.S. (%)
Management, Business, Science, and Arts	41.5	42.5	39.5
Natural Resources, Construction, and Maintenance	5.2	7.7	8.7
Production, Transportation, and Material Moving	9.5	10.3	13.1
Sales and Office	24.5	24.7	21.3
Service	19.2	14.8	17.4

Note: Figures cover employed civilians 16 years of age and older; (1) Figures cover the Provo-Orem, UT Metropolitan Statistical Area
Source: U.S. Census Bureau, 2016-2020 American Community Survey 5-Year Estimates

Occupations with Greatest Projected Employment Growth: 2021 – 2023

Occupation[1]	2021 Employment	2023 Projected Employment	Numeric Employment Change	Percent Employment Change
General and Operations Managers	52,760	56,070	3,310	6.3
Fast Food and Counter Workers	47,350	50,490	3,140	6.6
Software Developers and Software Quality Assurance Analysts and Testers	20,880	23,330	2,450	11.7
Construction Laborers	23,190	25,200	2,010	8.7
Retail Salespersons	48,570	50,450	1,880	3.9
Customer Service Representatives	52,690	54,500	1,810	3.4
Laborers and Freight, Stock, and Material Movers, Hand	24,160	25,930	1,770	7.3
Janitors and Cleaners, Except Maids and Housekeeping Cleaners	24,190	25,670	1,480	6.1
Sales Representatives, Wholesale and Manufacturing, Except Technical and Scientific Products	22,530	23,900	1,370	6.1
Project Management Specialists and Business Operations Specialists, All Other	20,740	22,090	1,350	6.5

Note: Projections cover Utah; (1) Sorted by numeric employment change
Source: www.projectionscentral.com, State Occupational Projections, 2021–2023 Short-Term Projections

Fastest-Growing Occupations: 2021 – 2023

Occupation[1]	2021 Employment	2023 Projected Employment	Numeric Employment Change	Percent Employment Change
Travel Agents	570	700	130	22.8
Reservation and Transportation Ticket Agents and Travel Clerks	3,100	3,740	640	20.6
Hotel, Motel, and Resort Desk Clerks	3,360	3,900	540	16.1
Statisticians	540	620	80	14.8
Data Scientists and Mathematical Science Occupations, All Other	420	480	60	14.3
Health Specialties Teachers, Postsecondary	2,390	2,700	310	13.0
Lodging Managers	400	450	50	12.5
Reinforcing Iron and Rebar Workers	410	460	50	12.2
Concierges	420	470	50	11.9
Software Developers and Software Quality Assurance Analysts and Testers	20,880	23,330	2,450	11.7

Note: Projections cover Utah; (1) Sorted by percent employment change and excludes occupations with numeric employment change less than 50
Source: www.projectionscentral.com, State Occupational Projections, 2021–2023 Short-Term Projections

TAXES

State Corporate Income Tax Rates

State	Tax Rate (%)	Income Brackets ($)	Num. of Brackets	Financial Institution Tax Rate (%)[a]	Federal Income Tax Ded.
Utah	4.95 (b)	Flat rate	–	4.95 (b)	No

Note: Tax rates as of January 1, 2022; (a) Rates listed are the corporate income tax rate applied to financial institutions or excise taxes based on income. Some states have other taxes based upon the value of deposits or shares; (b) Minimum tax is $800 in California, $250 in District of Columbia, $50 in Arizona and North Dakota (banks), $400 ($100 banks) in Rhode Island, $200 per location in South Dakota (banks), $100 in Utah, $300 in Vermont.
Source: Federation of Tax Administrators, State Corporate Income Tax Rates, January 1, 2022

State Individual Income Tax Rates

State	Tax Rate (%)	Income Brackets ($)	Personal Exemptions ($)			Standard Ded. ($)	
			Single	Married	Depend.	Single	Married
Utah	4.95	Flat rate	None	None	None	(v)	(v)

Note: Tax rates as of January 1, 2022; Local- and county-level taxes are not included; Federal income tax is not deductible on state income tax returns; (v) Utah provides a tax credit equal to 6% of the federal personal exemption amounts (and applicable standard deduction).
Source: Federation of Tax Administrators, State Individual Income Tax Rates, January 1, 2022

Various State Sales and Excise Tax Rates

State	State Sales Tax (%)	Gasoline[1] (¢/gal.)	Cigarette[2] ($/pack)	Spirits[3] ($/gal.)	Wine[4] ($/gal.)	Beer[5] ($/gal.)	Recreational Marijuana (%)
Utah	6.1	31.91	1.7	15.91	0	0.41	Not legal

Note: All tax rates as of January 1, 2022; (1) The American Petroleum Institute has developed a methodology for determining the average tax rate on a gallon of fuel. Rates may include any of the following: excise taxes, environmental fees, storage tank fees, other fees or taxes, general sales tax, and local taxes; (2) The federal excise tax of $1.0066 per pack and local taxes are not included; (3) Rates are those applicable to off-premise sales of 40% alcohol by volume (a.b.v.) distilled spirits in 750ml containers. Local excise taxes are excluded; (4) Rates are those applicable to off-premise sales of 11% a.b.v. non-carbonated wine in 750ml containers; (5) Rates are those applicable to off-premise sales of 4.7% a.b.v. beer in 12 ounce containers.
Source: Tax Foundation, 2022 Facts & Figures: How Does Your State Compare?

State Business Tax Climate Index Rankings

State	Overall Rank	Corporate Tax Rank	Individual Income Tax Rank	Sales Tax Rank	Property Tax Rank	Unemployment Insurance Tax Rank
Utah	10	14	10	22	7	17

Note: The index is a measure of how each state's tax laws affect economic performance. The lower the rank, the more favorable a state's tax system is for business. States without a given tax are given a ranking of 1. The scores/rankings for the District of Columbia do not affect other states. The 2022 index represents the tax climate as of July 1, 2021.
Source: Tax Foundation, State Business Tax Climate Index 2022

TRANSPORTATION

Means of Transportation to Work

Area	Car/Truck/Van		Public Transportation			Bicycle	Walked	Other Means	Worked at Home
	Drove Alone	Car-pooled	Bus	Subway	Railroad				
City	59.8	11.5	3.1	0.2	1.1	2.1	13.1	1.4	7.7
MSA[1]	71.6	10.6	1.1	0.2	0.8	0.7	3.8	1.1	10.1
U.S.	74.9	8.9	2.2	1.7	0.5	0.5	2.6	1.4	7.3

Note: Figures are percentages and cover workers 16 years of age and older; (1) Figures cover the Provo-Orem, UT Metropolitan Statistical Area
Source: U.S. Census Bureau, 2016-2020 American Community Survey 5-Year Estimates

Travel Time to Work

Area	Less Than 10 Minutes	10 to 19 Minutes	20 to 29 Minutes	30 to 44 Minutes	45 to 59 Minutes	60 to 89 Minutes	90 Minutes or More
City	20.8	44.9	16.5	9.8	3.5	3.0	1.5
MSA[1]	17.1	35.8	19.7	15.9	6.0	3.9	1.6
U.S.	12.3	28.4	20.9	20.9	8.3	6.4	2.9

Note: Note: Figures are percentages and include workers 16 years old and over; (1) Figures cover the Provo-Orem, UT Metropolitan Statistical Area
Source: U.S. Census Bureau, 2016-2020 American Community Survey 5-Year Estimates

Key Congestion Measures

Measure	1990	2000	2010	2015	2020
Annual Hours of Delay, Total (000)	1,961	4,001	6,075	8,107	5,275
Annual Hours of Delay, Per Auto Commuter	12	18	21	23	15
Annual Congestion Cost, Per Auto Commuter ($)	203	311	379	466	309

Note: Covers the Provo-Orem UT urban area
Source: Texas A&M Transportation Institute, 2021 Urban Mobility Report

Freeway Travel Time Index

Measure	1985	1990	1995	2000	2005	2010	2015	2020
Urban Area Index[1]	1.05	1.07	1.08	1.10	1.12	1.11	1.11	1.05
Urban Area Rank[1,2]	64	74	84	85	86	93	96	85

Note: Freeway Travel Time Index—the ratio of travel time in the peak period to the travel time at free-flow conditions. For example, a value of 1.30 indicates a 20-minute free-flow trip takes 26 minutes in the peak (20 minutes x 1.30 = 26 minutes); (1) Covers the Provo-Orem UT urban area; (2) Rank is based on 101 larger urban areas (#1 = highest travel time index)
Source: Texas A&M Transportation Institute, 2021 Urban Mobility Report

Public Transportation

Agency Name / Mode of Transportation	Vehicles Operated in Maximum Service[1]	Annual Unlinked Passenger Trips[2] (in thous.)	Annual Passenger Miles[3] (in thous.)
Utah Transit Authority (UT)			
Bus (directly operated)	354	12,182.5	53,227.8
Bus (purchased transportation)	7	67.9	235.1
Commuter Bus (directly operated)	48	190.9	4,084.8
Commuter Rail (directly operated)	50	2,024.5	51,916.8
Demand Response (directly operated)	69	109.8	1,040.1
Demand Response (purchased transportation)	37	77.3	858.9
Light Rail (directly operated)	89	8,247.4	39,122.9
Vanpool (directly operated)	427	659.0	27,330.7

Note: (1) Number of revenue vehicles operated by the given mode and type of service to meet the annual maximum service requirement. This is the revenue vehicle count during the peak season of the year; on the week and day that maximum service is provided. Vehicles operated in maximum service (VOMS) exclude atypical days and one-time special events; (2) Number of passengers who boarded public transportation vehicles. Passengers are counted each time they board a vehicle no matter how many vehicles they use to travel from their origin to their destination. (3) Sum of the distances ridden by all passengers during the entire fiscal year.
Source: Federal Transit Administration, National Transit Database, 2020

Air Transportation

Airport Name and Code / Type of Service	Passenger Airlines[1]	Passenger Enplanements	Freight Carriers[2]	Freight (lbs)
Salt Lake City International (50 miles) (SLC)				
Domestic service (U.S. carriers - 2021)	23	10,529,068	19	220,323,350
International service (U.S. carriers - 2020)	4	146,251	1	761,140

Note: (1) Includes all U.S.-based major, minor and commuter airlines that carried at least one passenger during the year; (2) Includes all U.S.-based airlines and freight carriers that transported at least one pound of freight during the year.
Source: Bureau of Transportation Statistics, The Intermodal Transportation Database, Air Carriers: T-100 Domestic Market (U.S. Carriers), 2021; Bureau of Transportation Statistics, The Intermodal Transportation Database, Air Carriers: T-100 International Market (U.S. Carriers), 2020

BUSINESSES

Major Business Headquarters

Company Name	Industry	Rankings	
		Fortune[1]	Forbes[2]
No companies listed	-	-	-

Note: (1) Companies that produce a 10-K are ranked 1 to 500 based on 2020 revenue; (2) All private companies with at least $2 billion in annual revenue through the end of their most current fiscal year are ranked 1 to 225; companies listed are headquartered in the city; dashes indicate no ranking
Source: Fortune, "Fortune 500," 2021; Forbes, "America's Largest Private Companies," 2021

Fastest-Growing Businesses

According to *Inc.*, Provo is home to two of America's 500 fastest-growing private companies: **Awardco** (#310); **Thread Wallets** (#442). Criteria: must be an independent, privately-held, for-profit, U.S. corporation, proprietorship or partnership as of December 31, 2020; revenues must be at least $100,000 in 2017 and $2 million in 2020; must have four-year operating/sales history. *Inc., "America's 500 Fastest-Growing Private Companies," 2021*

According to Deloitte, Provo is home to one of North America's 500 fastest-growing high-technology companies: **Awardco** (#107). Companies are ranked by percentage growth in revenue over a four-year period. Criteria for inclusion: company must be headquartered within North America; must own proprietary intellectual property or technology that is sold to customers in products that contributes to a significant portion of the company's operating revenue; must have been in business for a minumum of four years with 2017 operating revenues of at least $50,000 USD/CD and 2020 operating revenues of at least $5 million USD/CD. *Deloitte, 2021 Technology Fast 500™*

Living Environment

COST OF LIVING

Cost of Living Index

Composite Index	Groceries	Housing	Utilities	Trans-portation	Health Care	Misc. Goods/ Services
100.0	97.7	103.3	86.7	105.1	90.1	102.7

Note: The Cost of Living Index measures regional differences in the cost of consumer goods and services, excluding taxes and non-consumer expenditures, for professional and managerial households in the top income quintile. It is based on more than 50,000 prices covering almost 60 different items for which prices are collected three times a year by chambers of commerce, economic development organizations or university applied economic centers in each participating urban area. The numbers shown should be read as a percentage above or below the national average of 100. For example, a value of 115.4 in the groceries column indicates that grocery prices are 15.4% higher than the national average. Small differences in the index numbers should not be interpreted as significant; Figures cover the Provo-Orem UT urban area.
Source: The Council for Community and Economic Research, Cost of Living Index, 2021

Grocery Prices

Area[1]	T-Bone Steak ($/pound)	Frying Chicken ($/pound)	Whole Milk ($/half gal.)	Eggs ($/dozen)	Orange Juice ($/64 oz.)	Coffee ($/11.5 oz.)
City[2]	11.47	1.42	1.76	1.43	4.08	5.22
Avg.	12.82	1.40	2.22	1.57	3.59	4.30
Min.	8.91	0.91	1.29	0.75	2.87	3.02
Max.	21.35	2.69	3.92	3.86	5.49	8.11

Note: (1) Values for the local area are compared with the average, minimum and maximum values for all 285 areas in the Cost of Living Index; (2) Figures cover the Provo-Orem UT urban area; ***T-Bone Steak*** *(price per pound);* ***Frying Chicken*** *(price per pound, whole fryer);* ***Whole Milk*** *(half gallon carton);* ***Eggs*** *(price per dozen, Grade A, large);* ***Orange Juice*** *(64 oz. Tropicana or Florida Natural);* ***Coffee*** *(11.5 oz. can, vacuum-packed, Maxwell House, Hills Bros, or Folgers).*
Source: The Council for Community and Economic Research, Cost of Living Index, 2021

Housing and Utility Costs

Area[1]	New Home Price ($)	Apartment Rent ($/month)	All Electric ($/month)	Part Electric ($/month)	Other Energy ($/month)	Telephone ($/month)
City[2]	444,696	1,186	-	67.96	60.58	190.47
Avg.	398,393	1,217	171.38	100.83	69.67	187.75
Min.	212,799	534	96.71	31.56	27.15	173.01
Max.	2,354,006	4,438	369.53	277.33	303.87	206.73

Note: (1) Values for the local area are compared with the average, minimum and maximum values for all 285 areas in the Cost of Living Index; (2) Figures cover the Provo-Orem UT urban area; ***New Home Price*** *(2,400 sf living area, 8,000 sf lot, in urban area with full utilities);* ***Apartment Rent*** *(950 sf 2 bedroom/1.5 or 2 bath, unfurnished, excluding all utilities except water);* ***All Electric*** *(average monthly cost for an all-electric home);* ***Part Electric*** *(average monthly cost for a part-electric home);* ***Other Energy*** *(average monthly cost for natural gas, fuel oil, coal, wood, and any other forms of energy except electricity);* ***Telephone*** *(price includes the base monthly rate plus taxes and fees for three lines of mobile phone service).*
Source: The Council for Community and Economic Research, Cost of Living Index, 2021

Health Care, Transportation, and Other Costs

Area[1]	Doctor ($/visit)	Dentist ($/visit)	Optometrist ($/visit)	Gasoline ($/gallon)	Beauty Salon ($/visit)	Men's Shirt ($)
City[2]	95.10	90.16	98.09	3.06	38.90	33.86
Avg.	118.16	101.04	109.44	2.71	40.63	30.77
Min.	35.04	55.56	51.17	2.17	18.59	11.32
Max.	231.10	165.12	256.81	4.11	85.33	63.03

Note: (1) Values for the local area are compared with the average, minimum and maximum values for all 285 areas in the Cost of Living Index; (2) Figures cover the Provo-Orem UT urban area; ***Doctor*** *(general practitioners routine exam of an established patient);* ***Dentist*** *(adult teeth cleaning and periodic oral examination);* ***Optometrist*** *(full vision eye exam for established adult patient);* ***Gasoline*** *(one gallon regular unleaded, national brand, including all taxes, cash price at self-service pump if available);* ***Beauty Salon*** *(woman's shampoo, trim, and blow-dry);* ***Men's Shirt*** *(cotton/polyester dress shirt, pinpoint weave, long sleeves).*
Source: The Council for Community and Economic Research, Cost of Living Index, 2021

HOUSING

Homeownership Rate

Area	2013 (%)	2014 (%)	2015 (%)	2016 (%)	2017 (%)	2018 (%)	2019 (%)	2020 (%)	2021 (%)
MSA[1]	n/a	n/a	n/a	n/a	n/a	n/a	n/a	n/a	n/a
U.S.	65.1	64.5	63.7	63.4	63.9	64.4	64.6	66.6	65.5

Note: (1) Figures cover the Provo-Orem, UT Metropolitan Statistical Area; n/a not available
Source: U.S. Census Bureau, Housing Vacancies and Homeownership Annual Statistics: 2013-2021

House Price Index (HPI)

Area	National Ranking[2]	Quarterly Change (%)	One-Year Change (%)	Five-Year Change (%)	Since 1991Q1 (%)
MSA[1]	15	3.82	28.09	75.93	464.66
U.S.[3]	–	3.33	17.54	54.45	258.04

Note: The HPI is a weighted repeat sales index. It measures average price changes in repeat sales or refinancings on the same properties. This information is obtained by reviewing repeat mortgage transactions on single-family properties whose mortgages have been purchased or securitized by Fannie Mae or Freddie Mac since January 1975; (1) Figures cover the Provo-Orem, UT Metropolitan Statistical Area; (2) Rankings are based on annual percentage change for all metro areas containing at least 15,000 transactions over the last 10 years and ranges from 1 to 268; (3) figures based on a weighted average of Census Division estimates using a seasonally adjusted, purchase-only index; all figures are for the period ending December 31, 2021
Source: Federal Housing Finance Agency, Change in FHFA Metropolitan Area House Price Indexes, 2021Q4

Median Single-Family Home Prices

Area	2019	2020	2021p	Percent Change 2020 to 2021
MSA[1]	n/a	n/a	n/a	n/a
U.S. Average	274.6	300.2	353.4	17.7

Note: Figures are median sales prices of existing single-family homes in thousands of dollars; (p) preliminary; n/a not available; (1) Figures cover the Provo-Orem, UT Metropolitan Statistical Area
Source: National Association of Realtors, Median Sales Price of Existing Single-Family Homes for Metropolitan Areas, 4th Quarter 2021

Qualifying Income Based on Median Sales Price of Existing Single-Family Homes

Area	With 5% Down ($)	With 10% Down ($)	With 20% Down ($)
MSA[1]	n/a	n/a	n/a
U.S. Average	70,699	66,978	59,536

Note: Figures are preliminary; Qualifying income is based on a mortgage rate of 3.13%. Monthly principal and interest payment is limited to 25% of income; n/a not available; (1) Figures cover the Provo-Orem, UT Metropolitan Statistical Area
Source: National Association of Realtors, Qualifying Income Based on Median Sales Price of Existing Single-Family Homes for Metropolitan Areas, 4th Quarter 2021

Home Value Distribution

Area	Under $50,000	$50,000 -$99,999	$100,000 -$149,999	$150,000 -$199,999	$200,000 -$299,999	$300,000 -$499,999	$500,000 -$999,999	$1,000,000 or more
City	3.8	1.3	4.1	9.4	32.1	35.7	11.4	2.3
MSA[1]	2.2	0.9	2.2	6.9	28.0	43.5	14.3	2.0
U.S.	6.6	11.0	12.3	13.6	20.0	20.5	12.3	3.7

Note: Figures are percentages and cover owner-occupied housing units; (1) Figures cover the Provo-Orem, UT Metropolitan Statistical Area
Source: U.S. Census Bureau, 2016-2020 American Community Survey 5-Year Estimates

Year Housing Structure Built

Area	2010 or Later	2000 -2009	1990 -1999	1980 -1989	1970 -1979	1960 -1969	1950 -1959	1940 -1949	Before 1940	Median Year
City	6.1	10.9	19.9	14.6	18.3	10.2	7.7	5.0	7.3	1981
MSA[1]	16.8	24.6	18.8	8.9	13.3	5.0	5.1	3.0	4.3	1995
U.S.	6.2	13.6	13.9	13.4	15.0	10.5	10.2	4.8	12.4	1978

Note: Figures are percentages except for Median Year; Note: (1) Figures cover the Provo-Orem, UT Metropolitan Statistical Area
Source: U.S. Census Bureau, 2016-2020 American Community Survey 5-Year Estimates

Gross Monthly Rent

Area	Under $500	$500 -$999	$1,000 -$1,499	$1,500 -$1,999	$2,000 -$2,499	$2,500 -$2,999	$3,000 and up	Median ($)
City	11.7	49.5	24.9	10.3	3.0	0.3	0.3	901
MSA[1]	6.0	37.0	33.9	16.9	4.5	0.8	0.9	1,095
U.S.	8.9	34.3	30.2	14.9	6.2	2.6	2.8	1,096

Note: Figures are percentages except for Median; Gross rent is the contract rent plus the estimated average monthly cost of utilities (electricity, gas, and water and sewer) and fuels (oil, coal, kerosene, wood, etc.) if these are paid by the renter (or paid for the renter by someone else); (1) Figures cover the Provo-Orem, UT Metropolitan Statistical Area
Source: U.S. Census Bureau, 2016-2020 American Community Survey 5-Year Estimates

HEALTH

Health Risk Factors

Category	MSA[1] (%)	U.S. (%)
Adults aged 18–64 who have any kind of health care coverage	87.7	86.8
Adults who reported being in good or better health	91.5	86.7
Adults who are current smokers	4.9	15.5
Adults who currently use chewing tobacco, snuff, or snus	3.3	3.7
Adults who are heavy drinkers[2]	2.9	6.7
Adults who are binge drinkers[3]	8.6	15.7
Adults who are overweight (BMI 25.0 - 29.9)	32.8	35.2
Adults who are obese (BMI 30.0 - 99.8)	25.3	31.9
Adults who participated in any physical activities in the past month	86.8	77.6
Adults who always or nearly always wears a seat belt	96.9	94.2

Note: (1) Figures cover the Provo-Orem, UT Metropolitan Statistical Area; (2) Heavy drinkers are classified as adult men having more than 14 drinks per week and adult women having more than 7 drinks per week; (3) Binge drinkers are classified as males having five or more drinks on one occasion or females having four or more drinks on one occasion
Source: Centers for Disease Control and Prevention, Behaviorial Risk Factor Surveillance System, SMART: Selected Metropolitan Area Risk Trends, 2020

Acute and Chronic Health Conditions

Category	MSA[1] (%)	U.S. (%)
Adults who have ever been told they had a heart attack	2.6	4.3
Adults who have ever been told they have angina or coronary heart disease	2.0	4.0
Adults who have ever been told they had a stroke	1.4	2.8
Adults who have ever been told they have asthma	14.9	14.2
Adults who have ever been told they have arthritis	16.3	24.5
Adults who have ever been told they have diabetes[2]	6.3	10.6
Adults who have ever been told they had skin cancer	5.9	6.4
Adults who have ever been told they had any other types of cancer	3.9	6.8
Adults who have ever been told they have COPD	2.9	6.2
Adults who have ever been told they have kidney disease	1.5	2.9
Adults who have ever been told they have a form of depression	22.6	19.6

Note: (1) Figures cover the Provo-Orem, UT Metropolitan Statistical Area; (2) Figures do not include pregnancy-related, borderline, or pre-diabetes
Source: Centers for Disease Control and Prevention, Behaviorial Risk Factor Surveillance System, SMART: Selected Metropolitan Area Risk Trends, 2020

Health Screening and Vaccination Rates

Category	MSA[1] (%)	U.S. (%)
Adults 50-75 who have had a blood stool test within the past year	4.2	9.3
Adults aged 65+ who have had flu shot within the past year	61.9	67.9
Adults aged 65+ who have ever had a pneumonia vaccination	67.3	72.2
Adults who have ever been tested for HIV	20.5	37.1
Women aged 21-65 who have had a pap test in the past three years	65.7	77.7
Men aged 40+ who have had a PSA test within the past two years	22.3	31.8
Women aged 40+ who have had a mammogram within the past two years	65.3	71.5

Note: (1) Figures cover the Provo-Orem, UT Metropolitan Statistical Area.
Source: Centers for Disease Control and Prevention, Behaviorial Risk Factor Surveillance System, SMART: Selected Metropolitan Area Risk Trends, 2020

Disability Status

Category	MSA[1] (%)	U.S. (%)
Adults who reported being deaf	4.5	6.8
Are you blind or have serious difficulty seeing, even when wearing glasses?	2.0	4.7
Do you have difficulty doing errands alone?	4.7	6.3
Do you have difficulty dressing or bathing?	1.5	3.0
Do you have serious difficulty concentrating/remembering/making decisions?	9.4	10.8
Do you have serious difficulty walking or climbing stairs?	6.1	11.9

Note: (1) Figures cover the Provo-Orem, UT Metropolitan Statistical Area.
Source: Centers for Disease Control and Prevention, Behaviorial Risk Factor Surveillance System, SMART: Selected Metropolitan Area Risk Trends, 2020

Mortality Rates for the Top 10 Causes of Death in the U.S.

ICD-10[a] Sub-Chapter	ICD-10[a] Code	Age-Adjusted Mortality Rate[1] per 100,000 population	
		County[2]	U.S.
Malignant neoplasms	C00-C97	112.9	146.4
Ischaemic heart diseases	I20-I25	62.3	90.2
Other forms of heart disease	I30-I51	76.4	51.9
Other degenerative diseases of the nervous system	G30-G31	50.9	39.7
Other external causes of accidental injury	W00-X59	33.2	38.7
Chronic lower respiratory diseases	J40-J47	20.2	38.1
Cerebrovascular diseases	I60-I69	37.1	37.6
Organic, including symptomatic, mental disorders	F01-F09	35.6	29.4
Hypertensive diseases	I10-I15	17.2	26.1
Diabetes mellitus	E10-E14	25.0	22.6

Note: (a) ICD-10 = International Classification of Diseases 10th Revision; (1) Mortality rates are a three-year average covering 2018-2020; (2) Figures cover Utah County.
Source: Centers for Disease Control and Prevention, National Center for Health Statistics. Underlying Cause of Death 1999-2020 on CDC WONDER Online Database

Mortality Rates for Selected Causes of Death

ICD-10[a] Sub-Chapter	ICD-10[a] Code	Age-Adjusted Mortality Rate[1] per 100,000 population	
		County[2]	U.S.
Assault	X85-Y09	1.3	6.5
Diseases of the liver	K70-K76	10.1	15.3
Human immunodeficiency virus (HIV) disease	B20-B24	Suppressed	1.4
Influenza and pneumonia	J09-J18	12.1	13.4
Intentional self-harm	X60-X84	18.1	13.9
Malnutrition	E40-E46	10.2	2.9
Obesity and other hyperalimentation	E65-E68	2.3	2.4
Renal failure	N17-N19	16.0	12.5
Transport accidents	V01-V99	7.2	12.5
Viral hepatitis	B15-B19	Suppressed	1.0

Note: (a) ICD-10 = International Classification of Diseases 10th Revision; (1) Mortality rates are a three-year average covering 2018-2020; (2) Figures cover Utah County; Data are suppressed when the data meet the criteria for confidentiality constraints; Mortality rates are flagged as unreliable when the rate would be calculated with a numerator of 20 or less.
Source: Centers for Disease Control and Prevention, National Center for Health Statistics. Underlying Cause of Death 1999-2020 on CDC WONDER Online Database

Health Insurance Coverage

Area	With Health Insurance	With Private Health Insurance	With Public Health Insurance	Without Health Insurance	Population Under Age 19 Without Health Insurance
City	89.5	78.5	17.3	10.5	10.2
MSA[1]	92.3	82.4	17.3	7.7	6.1
U.S.	91.3	68.1	35.3	8.7	5.2

Note: Figures are percentages that cover the civilian noninstitutionalized population; (1) Figures cover the Provo-Orem, UT Metropolitan Statistical Area
Source: U.S. Census Bureau, 2016-2020 American Community Survey 5-Year Estimates

Number of Medical Professionals

Area	MDs[3]	DOs[3,4]	Dentists	Podiatrists	Chiropractors	Optometrists
County[1] (number)	758	129	394	30	168	69
County[1] (rate[2])	115.0	19.6	59.8	4.5	25.5	10.5
U.S. (rate[2])	285.1	23.0	71.1	6.2	28.2	17.0

49049
Note: Data as of 2020 unless noted; (1) Data covers Utah County; (2) Rate per 100,000 population; (3) Data as of 2019 and includes all active, non-federal physicians; (4) Doctor of Osteopathic Medicine
Source: U.S. Department of Health and Human Services, Health Resources and Services Administration, Bureau of Health Professions, Area Resource File (ARF) 2020-2021

EDUCATION

Public School District Statistics

District Name	Schls	Pupils	Pupil/ Teacher Ratio	Minority Pupils[1] (%)	LEP/ELL[2] (%)	IEP[3] (%)
Provo District	23	17,005	24.3	35.6	13.3	10.8

Note: Table includes school districts with 2,000 or more students; (1) Percentage of students that are not non-Hispanic white; (2) Percentage of students that are Limited English Proficient (LEP) or English Language Learners (ELL) (2018-19); (3) Percentage of students that have an Individualized Education Program (IEP).
Source: U.S. Department of Education, National Center for Education Statistics, Common Core of Data, Local Education Agency (School District) Universe Survey: School Year 2019-2020

Highest Level of Education

Area	Less than H.S.	H.S. Diploma	Some College, No Deg.	Associate Degree	Bachelor's Degree	Master's Degree	Prof. School Degree	Doctorate Degree
City	6.9	15.1	26.1	9.0	30.1	8.6	1.7	2.6
MSA[1]	4.9	17.2	26.7	10.5	28.1	9.1	1.7	1.8
U.S.	11.5	26.7	20.3	8.6	20.2	9.1	2.2	1.5

Note: Figures cover persons age 25 and over; (1) Figures cover the Provo-Orem, UT Metropolitan Statistical Area
Source: U.S. Census Bureau, 2016-2020 American Community Survey 5-Year Estimates

Educational Attainment by Race

Area	High School Graduate or Higher (%)					Bachelor's Degree or Higher (%)				
	Total	White	Black	Asian	Hisp.[2]	Total	White	Black	Asian	Hisp.[2]
City	93.1	93.8	97.2	86.7	76.0	42.9	44.2	20.3	47.6	17.6
MSA[1]	95.1	95.5	96.1	93.5	78.8	40.7	41.2	29.4	54.3	22.0
U.S.	88.5	90.7	86.7	87.3	70.3	32.9	34.4	22.6	55.0	17.6

Note: Figures shown cover persons 25 years old and over; (1) Figures cover the Provo-Orem, UT Metropolitan Statistical Area; (2) People of Hispanic origin can be of any race
Source: U.S. Census Bureau, 2016-2020 American Community Survey 5-Year Estimates

School Enrollment by Grade and Control

Area	Preschool (%)		Kindergarten (%)		Grades 1 - 4 (%)		Grades 5 - 8 (%)		Grades 9 - 12 (%)	
	Public	Private	Public	Private	Public	Private	Public	Private	Public	Private
City	57.5	42.5	93.7	6.3	94.3	5.7	95.7	4.3	90.6	9.4
MSA[1]	53.5	46.5	88.7	11.3	92.4	7.6	93.9	6.1	94.9	5.1
U.S.	58.9	41.1	86.9	13.1	89.0	11.0	89.0	11.0	89.7	10.3

Note: Figures shown cover persons 3 years old and over; (1) Figures cover the Provo-Orem, UT Metropolitan Statistical Area
Source: U.S. Census Bureau, 2016-2020 American Community Survey 5-Year Estimates

Higher Education

Four-Year Colleges			Two-Year Colleges			Medical Schools[1]	Law Schools[2]	Voc/ Tech[3]
Public	Private Non-profit	Private For-profit	Public	Private Non-profit	Private For-profit			
1	2	3	0	0	0	1	1	10

Note: Figures cover institutions located within the Provo-Orem, UT Metropolitan Statistical Area and include main campuses only; (1) includes schools accredited by the Liaison Committee on Medical Education and the American Osteopathic Association's Commission on Osteopathic College Accreditation; (2) includes ABA-accredited schools, schools with provisional ABA accreditation, and state accredited schools; (3) includes all schools with programs that are less than 2 years.
Source: National Center for Education Statistics, Integrated Postsecondary Education System (IPEDS), 2020-21; Wikipedia, List of Medical Schools in the United States, accessed April 11, 2022; Wikipedia, List of Law Schools in the United States, accessed April 11, 2022

According to *U.S. News & World Report,* the Provo-Orem, UT metro area is home to one of the top 200 national universities in the U.S.: **Brigham Young University—Provo** (#79 tie). The indicators used to capture academic quality fall into a number of categories: assessment by administrators at peer institutions; retention of students; faculty resources; student selectivity; financial resources; alumni giving; high school counselor ratings of colleges; and graduation rate. *U.S. News & World Report, "America's Best Colleges 2022"*

According to *U.S. News & World Report,* the Provo-Orem, UT metro area is home to one of the top 100 law schools in the U.S.: **Brigham Young University (Clark)** (#29 tie). The rankings are based on a weighted average of 12 measures of quality: peer assessment score; assessment score by lawyers/judges; median LSAT scores; median undergrad GPA; acceptance rate; employment rates for graduates; placement success; bar passage rate; faculty resources; expenditures per student; student/faculty ratio; and library resources. *U.S. News & World Report, "America's Best Graduate Schools, Law, 2022"*

According to *U.S. News & World Report,* the Provo-Orem, UT metro area is home to one of the top 75 business schools in the U.S.: **Brigham Young University (Marriott)** (#31 tie). The rankings are based on a weighted average of the following nine measures: quality assessment; peer assessment; recruiter assessment; placement success; mean starting salary and bonus; student selectivity; mean GMAT and GRE scores; mean undergraduate GPA; and acceptance rate. *U.S. News & World Report, "America's Best Graduate Schools, Business, 2022"*

EMPLOYERS

Major Employers

Company Name	Industry
About Time Technologies	Movements, clock or watch
Ancestry.com	Communication services, nec
Brigham Young University	Colleges & universities
City of Provo	Municipal government
Intermountain Health Care	General medical & surgical hospitals
Morinda Holdings	Bottled & canned soft drinks
Novell	Prepackaged software
Nu Skin Enterprises United States	Drugs, proprietaries, & sundries
Nu Skin International	Toilet preparations
Phone Directories Company	Directories, phone: publish only, not printed on site
RBM Services	Building cleaning service
TPUSA	Telemarketing services
Utah Dept of Human Services	Mental hospital, except for the mentally retarded
Utah Valley University	Colleges & universities
Wal-Mart Stores	Department stores, discount
Wasatch Summit	Management consulting services
Xango	Drugs, proprietaries, & sundries

Note: Companies shown are located within the Provo-Orem, UT Metropolitan Statistical Area.
Source: Hoovers.com; Wikipedia

PUBLIC SAFETY

Crime Rate

Area	Total Crime	Violent Crime Rate				Property Crime Rate		
		Murder	Rape[3]	Robbery	Aggrav. Assault	Burglary	Larceny -Theft	Motor Vehicle Theft
City	1,623.0	0.9	37.5	11.1	65.7	139.1	1,259.5	109.2
Suburbs[1]	1,312.0	1.1	30.2	7.2	46.1	131.5	1,018.1	77.8
Metro[2]	1,368.4	1.1	31.6	7.9	49.6	132.9	1,061.8	83.5
U.S.	2,510.4	5.1	42.6	81.8	250.4	340.5	1,569.2	220.8

Note: Figures are crimes per 100,000 population; (1) All areas within the metro area that are located outside the city limits; (2) Figures cover the Provo-Orem, UT Metropolitan Statistical Area; (3) All figures shown were reported using the revised Uniform Crime Reporting (UCR) definition of rape.
Source: FBI Uniform Crime Reports, 2019 (data for 2020 was not available)

Hate Crimes

Area	Number of Quarters Reported	Number of Incidents per Bias Motivation					
		Race/Ethnicity/ Ancestry	Religion	Sexual Orientation	Disability	Gender	Gender Identity
City	1	0	0	0	0	0	0
U.S.	4	5,227	1,244	1,110	130	75	266

Source: Federal Bureau of Investigation, Hate Crime Statistics 2020

Identity Theft Consumer Reports

Area	Reports	Reports per 100,000 Population	Rank[2]
MSA[1]	1,199	185	248
U.S.	1,434,676	432	-

Note: (1) Figures cover the Provo-Orem, UT Metropolitan Statistical Area; (2) Rank ranges from 1 to 391 where 1 indicates greatest number of identity theft reports per 100,000 population
Source: Federal Trade Commission, Consumer Sentinel Network Data Book 2021

Fraud and Other Consumer Reports

Area	Reports	Reports per 100,000 Population	Rank[2]
MSA[1]	4,486	692	333
U.S.	4,328,977	1,304	-

Note: (1) Figures cover the Provo-Orem, UT Metropolitan Statistical Area; (2) Rank ranges from 1 to 391 where 1 indicates greatest number of fraud and other consumer reports per 100,000 population
Source: Federal Trade Commission, Consumer Sentinel Network Data Book 2021

POLITICS

2020 Presidential Election Results

Area	Biden	Trump	Jorgensen	Hawkins	Other
Utah County	26.3	66.7	3.6	0.3	3.1
U.S.	51.3	46.8	1.2	0.3	0.5

Note: Results are percentages and may not add to 100% due to rounding
Source: Dave Leip's Atlas of U.S. Presidential Elections

SPORTS

Professional Sports Teams

Team Name	League	Year Established
No teams are located in the metro area		

Source: Wikipedia, Major Professional Sports Teams of the United States and Canada, April 6, 2022

CLIMATE

Average and Extreme Temperatures

Temperature	Jan	Feb	Mar	Apr	May	Jun	Jul	Aug	Sep	Oct	Nov	Dec	Yr.
Extreme High (°F)	62	69	78	85	93	104	107	104	100	89	75	67	107
Average High (°F)	37	43	52	62	72	83	93	90	80	66	50	38	64
Average Temp. (°F)	28	34	41	50	59	69	78	76	65	53	40	30	52
Average Low (°F)	19	24	31	38	46	54	62	61	51	40	30	22	40
Extreme Low (°F)	-22	-14	2	15	25	35	40	37	27	16	-14	-15	-22

Note: Figures cover the years 1948-1990
Source: National Climatic Data Center, International Station Meteorological Climate Summary, 9/96

Average Precipitation/Snowfall/Humidity

Precip./Humidity	Jan	Feb	Mar	Apr	May	Jun	Jul	Aug	Sep	Oct	Nov	Dec	Yr.
Avg. Precip. (in.)	1.3	1.2	1.8	2.0	1.7	0.9	0.8	0.9	1.1	1.3	1.3	1.4	15.6
Avg. Snowfall (in.)	13	10	11	6	1	Tr	0	0	Tr	2	6	13	63
Avg. Rel. Hum. 5am (%)	79	77	71	67	66	60	53	54	60	68	75	79	67
Avg. Rel. Hum. 5pm (%)	69	59	47	38	33	26	22	23	28	40	59	71	43

Note: Figures cover the years 1948-1990; Tr = Trace amounts (<0.05 in. of rain; <0.5 in. of snow)
Source: National Climatic Data Center, International Station Meteorological Climate Summary, 9/96

Weather Conditions

Temperature			Daytime Sky			Precipitation		
5°F & below	32°F & below	90°F & above	Clear	Partly cloudy	Cloudy	0.01 inch or more precip.	0.1 inch or more snow/ice	Thunder-storms
7	128	56	94	152	119	92	38	38

Note: Figures are average number of days per year and cover the years 1948-1990
Source: National Climatic Data Center, International Station Meteorological Climate Summary, 9/96

HAZARDOUS WASTE

Superfund Sites

The Provo-Orem, UT metro area has no sites on the EPA's Superfund Final National Priorities List. There are a total of 1,165 Superfund sites with a status of proposed or final on the list in the U.S. *U.S. Environmental Protection Agency, National Priorities List, April 6, 2022*

AIR QUALITY

Air Quality Trends: Ozone

	1990	1995	2000	2005	2010	2016	2017	2018	2019	2020
MSA[1]	n/a	n/a	n/a	n/a	n/a	n/a	n/a	n/a	n/a	n/a
U.S.	0.090	0.091	0.082	0.080	0.074	0.070	0.069	0.070	0.066	0.068

Note: (1) Data covers the Provo-Orem, UT Metropolitan Statistical Area; n/a not available. The values shown are the composite ozone concentration averages among trend sites based on the highest fourth daily maximum 8-hour concentration in parts per million. These trends are based on sites having an adequate record of monitoring data during the trend period. Data from exceptional events are included.
Source: U.S. Environmental Protection Agency, Air Quality Monitoring Information, "Air Quality Trends by City, 1990-2020"

Air Quality Index

Area	Percent of Days when Air Quality was...[2]					AQI Statistics[2]	
	Good	Moderate	Unhealthy for Sensitive Groups	Unhealthy	Very Unhealthy	Maximum	Median
MSA[1]	64.8	33.9	1.4	0.0	0.0	150	45

Note: (1) Data covers the Provo-Orem, UT Metropolitan Statistical Area; (2) Based on 366 days with AQI data in 2020. Air Quality Index (AQI) is an index for reporting daily air quality. EPA calculates the AQI for five major air pollutants regulated by the Clean Air Act: ground-level ozone, particle pollution (aka particulate matter), carbon monoxide, sulfur dioxide, and nitrogen dioxide. The AQI runs from 0 to 500. The higher the AQI value, the greater the level of air pollution and the greater the health concern. There are six AQI categories: "Good" AQI is between 0 and 50. Air quality is considered satisfactory; "Moderate" AQI is between 51 and 100. Air quality is acceptable; "Unhealthy for Sensitive Groups" When AQI values are between 101 and 150, members of sensitive groups may experience health effects; "Unhealthy" When AQI values are between 151 and 200 everyone may begin to experience health effects; "Very Unhealthy" AQI values between 201 and 300 trigger a health alert; "Hazardous" AQI values over 300 trigger warnings of emergency conditions (not shown).
Source: U.S. Environmental Protection Agency, Air Quality Index Report, 2020

Air Quality Index Pollutants

Area	Percent of Days when AQI Pollutant was...[2]					
	Carbon Monoxide	Nitrogen Dioxide	Ozone	Sulfur Dioxide	Particulate Matter 2.5	Particulate Matter 10
MSA[1]	0.0	2.5	69.4	0.0	27.6	0.5

Note: (1) Data covers the Provo-Orem, UT Metropolitan Statistical Area; (2) Based on 366 days with AQI data in 2020. The Air Quality Index (AQI) is an index for reporting daily air quality. EPA calculates the AQI for five major air pollutants regulated by the Clean Air Act: ground-level ozone, particle pollution (also known as particulate matter), carbon monoxide, sulfur dioxide, and nitrogen dioxide. The AQI runs from 0 to 500. The higher the AQI value, the greater the level of air pollution and the greater the health concern.
Source: U.S. Environmental Protection Agency, Air Quality Index Report, 2020

Maximum Air Pollutant Concentrations: Particulate Matter, Ozone, CO and Lead

	Particulate Matter 10 (ug/m^3)	Particulate Matter 2.5 Wtd AM (ug/m^3)	Particulate Matter 2.5 24-Hr (ug/m^3)	Ozone (ppm)	Carbon Monoxide (ppm)	Lead (ug/m^3)
MSA[1] Level	90	7.9	26	0.07	1	n/a
NAAQS[2]	150	15	35	0.075	9	0.15
Met NAAQS[2]	Yes	Yes	Yes	Yes	Yes	n/a

Note: (1) Data covers the Provo-Orem, UT Metropolitan Statistical Area; Data from exceptional events are included; (2) National Ambient Air Quality Standards; ppm = parts per million; ug/m^3 = micrograms per cubic meter; n/a not available.
Concentrations: Particulate Matter 10 (coarse particulate)—highest second maximum 24-hour concentration; Particulate Matter 2.5 Wtd AM (fine particulate)—highest weighted annual mean concentration; Particulate Matter 2.5 24-Hour (fine particulate)—highest 98th percentile 24-hour concentration; Ozone—highest fourth daily maximum 8-hour concentration; Carbon Monoxide—highest second maximum non-overlapping 8-hour concentration; Lead—maximum running 3-month average
Source: U.S. Environmental Protection Agency, Air Quality Monitoring Information, "Air Quality Statistics by City, 2020"

Maximum Air Pollutant Concentrations: Nitrogen Dioxide and Sulfur Dioxide

	Nitrogen Dioxide AM (ppb)	Nitrogen Dioxide 1-Hr (ppb)	Sulfur Dioxide AM (ppb)	Sulfur Dioxide 1-Hr (ppb)	Sulfur Dioxide 24-Hr (ppb)
MSA[1] Level	10	43	n/a	n/a	n/a
NAAQS[2]	53	100	30	75	140
Met NAAQS[2]	Yes	Yes	n/a	n/a	n/a

Note: (1) Data covers the Provo-Orem, UT Metropolitan Statistical Area; Data from exceptional events are included; (2) National Ambient Air Quality Standards; ppm = parts per million; ug/m^3 = micrograms per cubic meter; n/a not available.
Concentrations: Nitrogen Dioxide AM—highest arithmetic mean concentration; Nitrogen Dioxide 1-Hr—highest 98th percentile 1-hour daily maximum concentration; Sulfur Dioxide AM—highest annual mean concentration; Sulfur Dioxide 1-Hr—highest 99th percentile 1-hour daily maximum concentration; Sulfur Dioxide 24-Hr—highest second maximum 24-hour concentration
Source: U.S. Environmental Protection Agency, Air Quality Monitoring Information, "Air Quality Statistics by City, 2020"

Reno, Nevada

Background

Dubbed the "Biggest Little City in the World," Reno is known as a mecca for tourists who want to gamble, but it is so much more. Native American Washoes and Paiutes roamed the area before white explorers led by the famed John C. Fremont arrived in the nineteenth century. Due to the Truckee River running through it, the area became a stopping point for people hurrying to California to take advantage of the 1849 gold rush. In 1859, prospectors discovered the Comstock Lode—a massive vein of gold and silver forty miles to the south of the Truckee.

Shrewd entrepreneur Charles Fuller built a hotel and a toll bridge across the river for prospectors desperate to reach the lode. Floods kept destroying Fuller's bridge, and he sold the land to Myron Lake in 1861, who constructed another bridge around which a settlement grew. Lake turned over to the Central Pacific Railroad several dozen acres of his land, on the condition that half of the transcontinental railroad would run through the area. Here, the town of Reno was founded in 1868 and named after Jesse Lee Reno, a valiant Union officer killed during the Civil War. Reno became an important shipping point for the mines of the Comstock Lode.

By 1900, the lode was in decline and Reno had to look to other commercial ventures. One was the quick divorce—a six weeks' residency requirement was approved by the state legislature in 1931. In a continuing effort to jumpstart the state's economy during the Great Depression, Nevada legalized gambling in 1931. As the number of gambling houses increased in Reno, so did its population.

The Reno Arch, emblazoned with the city's nickname—Biggest Little City in the World—welcomes tourists to an array of glittering casinos and hotels. The tourist and gambling industries are still quite important to the area's commerce, but other commercial ventures have been attracted to Reno's business-friendly environment, which includes no corporate or personal income taxes, and no inventory or franchise taxes. Key industries throughout the Greater Reno-Sparks-Tahoe area include manufacturing; distribution/logistics/internet fulfillment; back office/business support; financial and intangible assets; clean energy; and aerospace/aviation/defense. Companies with distribution and fulfillment operations in the city include Walmart, PetSmart, Urban Outfitters, and Barnes & Noble. Major employers include Amazon, Tesla, Wells Fargo, Target, and Home Depot.

The University of Nevada at Reno opened its Earthquake Engineering Laboratory in 2014, the largest seismic stimulation facility in the country and the second largest in the world. The city boasts significant renovated meeting space at both the Reno-Sparks Convention Center and Reno Events Center, a premier venue for concerts, community events, tradeshows, and sporting events. Reno is home to the National Bowling Stadium and the Reno-Sparks Livestock Events Center, which is looking forward to a major renovation in 2023. The Reno Aces play ball under the flag of the MLB-affiliated Pacific Coast League. The city hosts ArtTown, in which music, visual arts, film, dance, theater and historical tours are highlighted every year in July, for one of the country's largest visual and performing arts festivals.

Skiing and snowboarding are popular winter sports and draw many tourists. There are 18 ski resorts within a 98-mile radius of the Reno-Tahoe International Airport. In 2018, the city changed its flag to a colorful mountain graphic. Other popular winter activities include snowshoeing, ice skating, and snowmobiling, with many bike paths for summertime fun.

Located on a semi-arid plateau to the east of the Sierra Nevada mountains, Reno offers short, hot summers and relatively mild winters. Temperatures can vary widely from day to night. More than half of the city's precipitation falls as a rain-snow mixture during winter. Located at the edge of the Sierra Nevada, snow can pile up but tends to melt within a few days. Reno sees relatively little rain.

Rankings

General Rankings

- In their eigth annual survey, Livability.com looked at data for more than 1,000 small to mid-sized U.S. cities to determine the rankings for Livability's "Top 100 Best Places to Live" in 2021. Reno ranked #41. Criteria: housing and economy; sustainability; social and civic engagement; education; demographics; health care options; transportation & infrastructure; and community amenities. *Livability.com, "Top 100 Best Places to Live 2021" October 12, 2021*

Business/Finance Rankings

- The Reno metro area appeared on the Milken Institute "2021 Best Performing Cities" list. Rank: #18 out of 200 large metro areas (population over 250,000). Criteria: job growth; wage and salary growth; high-tech output growth; housing affordability; household broadband access. *Milken Institute, "Best-Performing Cities 2021," February 16, 2021*
- *Forbes* ranked the 200 most populous metro areas to determine the nation's "Best Places for Business and Careers." The Reno metro area was ranked #11. Criteria: costs (business and living); job growth (past and projected); income growth; quality of life; educational attainment (college and high school); projected economic growth; cultural and leisure opportunities; workplace tolerance laws; net migration patterns. *Forbes, "The Best Places for Business and Careers 2019: Seattle Still On Top," October 30, 2019*

Dating/Romance Rankings

- Reno was ranked #21 out of 25 cities that stood out for inspiring romance and attracting diners on the website OpenTable.com. Criteria: percentage of people who dined out on Valentine's Day in 2018; percentage of romantic restaurants as rated by OpenTable diner reviews; and percentage of tables seated for two. *OpenTable, "25 Most Romantic Cities in America for 2019," February 7, 2019*

Education Rankings

- Personal finance website *WalletHub* analyzed the 150 largest U.S. metropolitan statistical areas to determine where the most educated Americans are putting their degrees to work. Criteria: education levels; percentage of workers with degrees; education quality and attainment gap; public school quality rankings; quality and enrollment of each metro area's universities. Reno was ranked #64 (#1 = most educated city). *www.WalletHub.com, "Most & Least Educated Cities in America," July 19, 2021*

Environmental Rankings

- The U.S. Conference of Mayors and Walmart Stores sponsor the Mayors' Climate Protection Awards Program which recognize mayors for outstanding and innovative practices that mayors are taking to increase energy efficiency in their cities, reduce carbon emissions and expand renewable energy. Reno received an Honorable Mention in the large city category. *U.S. Conference of Mayors, "2021 Mayors' Climate Protection Awards," December 17, 2021*
- Reno was highlighted as one of the 25 metro areas most polluted by short-term particle pollution (24-hour PM 2.5) in the U.S. during 2017 through 2019. The area ranked #21. *American Lung Association, "State of the Air 2021," April 21, 2021*

Health/Fitness Rankings

- For each of the 100 largest cities in the United States, the American Fitness Index®, published by the American College of Sports Medicine and the Anthem Foundation, evaluated community infrastructure and 34 health behaviors including preventive health, levels of chronic disease conditions, food insecurity, sleep quality, pedestrian safety, air quality, and community resources that support physical activity. Reno ranked #52 for "community fitness." *americanfitnessindex.org, "2021 ACSM American Fitness Index Summary Report," July 13, 2021*

Real Estate Rankings

- *WalletHub* compared the most populated U.S. cities to determine which had the best markets for real estate agents. Reno ranked #12 where demand was high and pay was the best. Criteria: sales per agent; annual median wage for real-estate agents; monthly average starting salary for real estate agents; real estate job density and competition; unemployment rate; home turnover rate; housing-market health index; and other relevant metrics. *www.WalletHub.com, "2021 Best Places to Be a Real Estate Agent," May 12, 2021*

- The Reno metro area was identified as one of the 20 least affordable housing markets in the U.S. in 2021. The area ranked #168 out of 183 markets. Criteria: qualification for a mortgage loan with a 10 percent down payment on a typical home. *National Association of Realtors®, Qualifying Income Based on Sales Price of Existing Single-Family Homes for Metropolitan Areas, 2021*
- Reno was ranked #199 out of 237 metro areas in terms of housing affordability in 2021 by the National Association of Home Builders (#1 = most affordable). Criteria: the share of homes sold in that area affordable to a family earning the local median income, based on standard mortgage underwriting criteria. *National Association of Home Builders®, NAHB-Wells Fargo Housing Opportunity Index, 4th Quarter 2021*

Safety Rankings

- Allstate ranked the 200 largest cities in America in terms of driver safety. Reno ranked #25. Criteria: internal property damage claims over a two-year period from January 2016 to December 2017. The report helps increase the importance of safety and awareness behind the wheel. *Allstate, "Allstate America's Best Drivers Report, 2019" June 24, 2019*
- The National Insurance Crime Bureau ranked 390 metro areas in the U.S. in terms of per capita rates of vehicle theft. The Reno metro area ranked #85 (#1 = highest rate). Criteria: number of vehicle theft offenses per 100,000 inhabitants in 2020. *National Insurance Crime Bureau, "Hot Spots 2020," August 31, 2021*

Seniors/Retirement Rankings

- From its Best Cities for Successful Aging indexes, the Milken Institute generated rankings for metropolitan areas, weighing data in nine categories—health care, wellness, living arrangements, transportation and convenience, financial characteristics, education, employment, community engagement, and overall livability. The Reno metro area was ranked #101 overall in the small metro area category. *Milken Institute, "Best Cities for Successful Aging, 2017" March 14, 2017*
- Reno was identified as #15 of 20 most popular places to retire in the Western region by *Topretirements.com*. The site separated its annual "Best Places to Retire" list by major U.S. regions for 2019. The list reflects the 20 cities that visitors to the website are most interested in for retirement, based on the number of times a city's review was viewed on the website. *Topretirements.com, "20 Best Places to Retire in the West-2019," November 11, 2019*

Women/Minorities Rankings

- Personal finance website *WalletHub* compared more than 180 U.S. cities across two key dimensions, "Hispanic Business-Friendliness" and "Hispanic Purchasing Power," to arrive at the most favorable conditions for Hispanic entrepreneurs. Reno was ranked #102 out of 182. Criteria includes: share of Hispanic-Owned Businesses; Hispanic entrepreneurship rate to median annual income of Hispanics; Small Business-Friendliness score; cost of living; and number of Hispanics with at least a bachelor's degree. *WalletHub.com, "2019's Best Cities for Hispanic Entrepreneurs," May 1, 2019*

Miscellaneous Rankings

- *WalletHub* compared the 150 most populated U.S. cities to determine their operating efficiency. A "Quality of City Services" score was constructed for each city and then divided by the total budget per capita to reveal which were managed the best. Reno ranked #41. Criteria: financial stability; economy; education; safety; health; infrastructure and pollution. *www.WalletHub.com, "2021's Best- & Worst-Run Cities in America," June 22, 2021*

Business Environment

DEMOGRAPHICS

Population Growth

Area	1990 Census	2000 Census	2010 Census	2020* Estimate	Population Growth (%) 1990-2020	2010-2020
City	139,950	180,480	225,221	250,903	79.3	11.4
MSA[1]	257,193	342,885	425,417	468,268	82.1	10.1
U.S.	248,709,873	281,421,906	308,745,538	326,569,308	31.3	5.8

Note: (1) Figures cover the Reno, NV Metropolitan Statistical Area; (*) 2016-2020 5-year estimated population
Source: U.S. Census Bureau, 1990 Census, Census 2000, Census 2010, 2016-2020 American Community Survey 5-Year Estimates

Household Size

Area	Persons in Household (%) One	Two	Three	Four	Five	Six	Seven or More	Average Household Size
City	32.5	34.0	14.4	11.2	5.1	1.6	1.4	2.30
MSA[1]	27.7	35.3	15.3	12.3	5.6	2.2	1.5	2.50
U.S.	28.0	33.9	15.5	12.9	6.0	2.3	1.4	2.60

Note: (1) Figures cover the Reno, NV Metropolitan Statistical Area
Source: U.S. Census Bureau, 2016-2020 American Community Survey 5-Year Estimates

Race

Area	White Alone[2] (%)	Black Alone[2] (%)	Asian Alone[2] (%)	AIAN[3] Alone[2] (%)	NHOPI[4] Alone[2] (%)	Other Race Alone[2] (%)	Two or More Races (%)
City	72.2	3.2	7.2	1.1	0.8	9.2	6.3
MSA[1]	74.2	2.4	5.5	1.5	0.7	9.0	6.7
U.S.	70.4	12.6	5.6	0.8	0.2	5.1	5.2

Note: (1) Figures cover the Reno, NV Metropolitan Statistical Area; (2) Alone is defined as not being in combination with one or more other races; (3) American Indian and Alaska Native; (4) Native Hawaiian and Other Pacific Islander
Source: U.S. Census Bureau, 2016-2020 American Community Survey 5-Year Estimates

Hispanic or Latino Origin

Area	Total (%)	Mexican (%)	Puerto Rican (%)	Cuban (%)	Other (%)
City	24.0	18.5	0.6	0.3	4.6
MSA[1]	24.5	18.9	0.6	0.4	4.7
U.S.	18.2	11.2	1.7	0.7	4.5

Note: Persons of Hispanic or Latino origin can be of any race; (1) Figures cover the Reno, NV Metropolitan Statistical Area
Source: U.S. Census Bureau, 2016-2020 American Community Survey 5-Year Estimates

Ancestry

Area	German	Irish	English	American	Italian	Polish	French[2]	Scottish	Dutch
City	12.5	10.4	9.6	4.0	6.1	1.9	2.5	2.0	1.3
MSA[1]	13.2	10.6	10.2	3.8	6.6	1.8	2.6	2.0	1.3
U.S.	13.0	9.7	7.7	5.9	5.1	2.7	2.3	1.6	1.1

Note: Figures are the percentage of the total population reporting a particular ancestry. The nine most commonly reported ancestries in the U.S. are shown. Figures include multiple ancestries (e.g. if a person reported being Irish and Italian, they were included in both columns); (1) Figures cover the Reno, NV Metropolitan Statistical Area; (2) Excludes Basque
Source: U.S. Census Bureau, 2016-2020 American Community Survey 5-Year Estimates

Foreign-born Population

Area	Percent of Population Born in: Any Foreign Country	Asia	Mexico	Europe	Caribbean	Central America[2]	South America	Africa	Canada
City	16.4	5.6	5.9	1.5	0.2	1.6	0.5	0.5	0.4
MSA[1]	14.3	4.0	6.0	1.2	0.2	1.4	0.4	0.3	0.4
U.S.	13.5	4.2	3.3	1.5	1.3	1.1	1.0	0.7	0.3

Note: (1) Figures cover the Reno, NV Metropolitan Statistical Area; (2) Excludes Mexico.
Source: U.S. Census Bureau, 2016-2020 American Community Survey 5-Year Estimates

Marital Status

Area	Never Married	Now Married[2]	Separated	Widowed	Divorced
City	35.3	42.9	2.0	4.9	14.8
MSA[1]	31.1	48.6	1.8	5.0	13.5
U.S.	33.5	48.1	1.8	5.7	10.8

Note: Figures are percentages and cover the population 15 years of age and older; (1) Figures cover the Reno, NV Metropolitan Statistical Area; (2) Excludes separated
Source: U.S. Census Bureau, 2016-2020 American Community Survey 5-Year Estimates

Disability by Age

Area	All Ages	Under 18 Years Old	18 to 64 Years Old	65 Years and Over
City	11.8	4.5	10.0	29.8
MSA[1]	12.1	4.6	9.8	30.7
U.S.	12.7	4.3	10.3	34.0

Note: Figures show percent of the civilian noninstitutionalized population that reported having a disability. Disability status is determined from six types of difficulty: vision, hearing, cognitive, ambulatory, self-care, and independent living. For children under 5 years old, hearing and vision difficulty are used to determine disability status. For children between the ages of 5 and 14, disability status is determined from hearing, vision, cognitive, ambulatory, and self-care difficulties. For people aged 15 years and older, they are considered to have a disability if they have difficulty with any one of the six difficulty types; Note: (1) Figures cover the Reno, NV Metropolitan Statistical Area
Source: U.S. Census Bureau, 2016-2020 American Community Survey 5-Year Estimates

Age

Area	Percent of Population									Median Age
	Under Age 5	Age 5–19	Age 20–34	Age 35–44	Age 45–54	Age 55–64	Age 65–74	Age 75–84	Age 85+	
City	5.9	17.5	24.8	12.8	11.7	12.3	9.4	4.1	1.5	36.1
MSA[1]	5.9	18.0	21.6	12.4	12.5	13.2	10.4	4.5	1.6	38.6
U.S.	6.0	19.1	20.6	12.7	12.7	12.9	9.4	4.7	2.0	38.2

Note: (1) Figures cover the Reno, NV Metropolitan Statistical Area
Source: U.S. Census Bureau, 2016-2020 American Community Survey 5-Year Estimates

Gender

Area	Males	Females	Males per 100 Females
City	126,469	124,434	101.6
MSA[1]	236,059	232,209	101.7
U.S.	160,818,530	165,750,778	97.0

Note: (1) Figures cover the Reno, NV Metropolitan Statistical Area
Source: U.S. Census Bureau, 2016-2020 American Community Survey 5-Year Estimates

Religious Groups by Family

Area	Catholic	Baptist	Non-Den.	Methodist[2]	Lutheran	LDS[3]	Pente-costal	Presby-terian[4]	Muslim[5]	Judaism
MSA[1]	14.3	1.5	3.2	0.9	0.8	4.6	2.0	0.4	0.1	0.2
U.S.	19.1	9.3	4.0	4.0	2.3	2.0	1.9	1.6	0.8	0.7

Note: Figures are the number of adherents as a percentage of the total population; (1) Figures cover the Reno, NV Metropolitan Statistical Area; (2) Methodist/Pietist; (3) Latter Day Saints; (4) Reformed; (5) Figures are estimates
Source: Association of Statisticians of American Religious Bodies, 2010 U.S. Religion Census: Religious Congregations & Membership Study

Religious Groups by Tradition

Area	Catholic	Evangelical Protestant	Mainline Protestant	Other Tradition	Black Protestant	Orthodox
MSA[1]	14.3	7.7	1.9	5.1	0.2	0.1
U.S.	19.1	16.2	7.3	4.3	1.6	0.3

Note: Figures are the number of adherents as a percentage of the total population; (1) Figures cover the Reno, NV Metropolitan Statistical Area
Source: Association of Statisticians of American Religious Bodies, 2010 U.S. Religion Census: Religious Congregations & Membership Study

ECONOMY

Gross Metropolitan Product

Area	2017	2018	2019	2020	Rank[2]
MSA[1]	26.8	28.8	30.8	32.3	99

Note: Figures are in billions of dollars; (1) Figures cover the Reno, NV Metropolitan Statistical Area; (2) Rank is based on 2018 data and ranges from 1 to 381
Source: U.S. Conference of Mayors, U.S. Metro Economies: GMP & Employment 2018-2020, September 2019

Economic Growth

Area	2015-17 (%)	2018 (%)	2019 (%)	2020 (%)	Rank[2]
MSA[1]	4.3	5.3	4.9	2.5	27
U.S.	1.9	2.9	2.3	2.1	–

Note: Figures are real gross metropolitan product (GMP) growth rates and represent average annual percent change; (1) Figures cover the Reno, NV Metropolitan Statistical Area; (2) Rank is based on 2017 2-year average annual percent change and ranges from 1 to 381
Source: U.S. Conference of Mayors, U.S. Metro Economies: GMP & Employment 2018-2020, September 2019

Metropolitan Area Exports

Area	2015	2016	2017	2018	2019	2020	Rank[2]
MSA[1]	1,943.3	2,382.1	2,517.3	2,631.7	2,598.3	4,553.3	59

Note: Figures are in millions of dollars; (1) Figures cover the Reno, NV Metropolitan Statistical Area; (2) Rank is based on 2020 data and ranges from 1 to 389
Source: U.S. Department of Commerce, International Trade Administration, Office of Trade and Economic Analysis, Industry and Analysis, Exports by Metropolitan Area, data extracted March 4, 2022

Building Permits

Area	Single-Family			Multi-Family			Total		
	2019	2020	Pct. Chg.	2019	2020	Pct. Chg.	2019	2020	Pct. Chg.
City	1,176	1,330	13.1	2,144	1,871	-12.7	3,320	3,201	-3.6
MSA[1]	2,157	2,629	21.9	3,106	1,875	-39.6	5,263	4,504	-14.4
U.S.	862,100	979,400	13.6	523,900	491,700	-6.1	1,386,000	1,471,100	6.1

Note: (1) Figures cover the Reno, NV Metropolitan Statistical Area; Figures represent new, privately-owned housing units authorized (unadjusted data); All permit data are based on estimates with imputation
Source: U.S. Census Bureau, Manufacturing, Mining, and Construction Statistics, Building Permits, 2019, 2020

Bankruptcy Filings

Area	Business Filings			Nonbusiness Filings		
	2020	2021	% Chg.	2020	2021	% Chg.
Washoe County	44	25	-43.2	765	592	-22.6
U.S.	21,655	14,347	-33.7	522,808	399,269	-23.6

Note: Business filings include Chapter 7, Chapter 9, Chapter 11, Chapter 12, Chapter 13, Chapter 15, and Section 304; Nonbusiness filings include Chapter 7, Chapter 11, and Chapter 13
Source: Administrative Office of the U.S. Courts, Business and Nonbusiness Bankruptcy, County Cases Commenced by Chapter of the Bankruptcy Code, During the 12-Month Period Ending December 31, 2020 and Business and Nonbusiness Bankruptcy, County Cases Commenced by Chapter of the Bankruptcy Code, During the 12-Month Period Ending December 31, 2021

Housing Vacancy Rates

Area	Gross Vacancy Rate[2] (%)			Year-Round Vacancy Rate[3] (%)			Rental Vacancy Rate[4] (%)			Homeowner Vacancy Rate[5] (%)		
	2019	2020	2021	2019	2020	2021	2019	2020	2021	2019	2020	2021
MSA[1]	n/a	n/a	n/a	n/a	n/a	n/a	n/a	n/a	n/a	n/a	n/a	n/a
U.S.	12.0	10.6	10.8	9.5	8.2	8.4	6.7	6.3	6.1	1.4	1.0	0.9

Note: (1) Figures cover the Reno, NV Metropolitan Statistical Area; (2) The percentage of the total housing inventory that is vacant; (3) The percentage of the housing inventory (excluding seasonal units) that is year-round vacant; (4) The percentage of rental inventory that is vacant for rent; (5) The percentage of homeowner inventory that is vacant for sale; n/a not available
Source: U.S. Census Bureau, Housing Vacancies and Homeownership Annual Statistics: 2019, 2020, 2021

INCOME

Income

Area	Per Capita ($)	Median Household ($)	Average Household ($)
City	36,358	61,860	85,808
MSA[1]	37,707	68,214	93,405
U.S.	35,384	64,994	91,547

Note: (1) Figures cover the Reno, NV Metropolitan Statistical Area
Source: U.S. Census Bureau, 2016-2020 American Community Survey 5-Year Estimates

Household Income Distribution

Area	Percent of Households Earning							
	Under $15,000	$15,000 -$24,999	$25,000 -$34,999	$35,000 -$49,999	$50,000 -$74,999	$75,000 -$99,999	$100,000 -$149,999	$150,000 and up
City	8.8	9.4	8.7	13.7	18.1	12.5	16.0	12.8
MSA[1]	7.4	8.1	8.1	12.2	18.5	13.9	16.9	14.9
U.S.	9.9	8.5	8.6	12.0	17.2	12.8	15.6	15.4

Note: (1) Figures cover the Reno, NV Metropolitan Statistical Area
Source: U.S. Census Bureau, 2016-2020 American Community Survey 5-Year Estimates

Poverty Rate

Area	All Ages	Under 18 Years Old	18 to 64 Years Old	65 Years and Over
City	12.6	14.5	12.9	8.9
MSA[1]	10.9	13.4	10.7	8.5
U.S.	12.8	17.5	12.1	9.3

Note: Figures are percentage of people whose income during the past 12 months was below the poverty level; (1) Figures cover the Reno, NV Metropolitan Statistical Area
Source: U.S. Census Bureau, 2016-2020 American Community Survey 5-Year Estimates

CITY FINANCES

City Government Finances

Component	2019 ($000)	2019 ($ per capita)
Total Revenues	447,845	1,800
Total Expenditures	405,032	1,628
Debt Outstanding	685,162	2,753
Cash and Securities[1]	483,931	1,945

Note: (1) Cash and security holdings of a government at the close of its fiscal year, including those of its dependent agencies, utilities, and liquor stores.
Source: U.S. Census Bureau, State & Local Government Finances 2019

City Government Revenue by Source

Source	2019 ($000)	2019 ($ per capita)	2019 (%)
General Revenue			
From Federal Government	4,857	20	1.1
From State Government	89,571	360	20.0
From Local Governments	9,664	39	2.2
Taxes			
Property	70,587	284	15.8
Sales and Gross Receipts	38,266	154	8.5
Personal Income	0	0	0.0
Corporate Income	0	0	0.0
Motor Vehicle License	0	0	0.0
Other Taxes	43,078	173	9.6
Current Charges	142,355	572	31.8
Liquor Store	0	0	0.0
Utility	0	0	0.0

Source: U.S. Census Bureau, State & Local Government Finances 2019

City Government Expenditures by Function

Function	2019 ($000)	2019 ($ per capita)	2019 (%)
General Direct Expenditures			
Air Transportation	0	0	0.0
Corrections	0	0	0.0
Education	0	0	0.0
Employment Security Administration	0	0	0.0
Financial Administration	2,421	9	0.6
Fire Protection	55,164	221	13.6
General Public Buildings	0	0	0.0
Governmental Administration, Other	16,228	65	4.0
Health	0	0	0.0
Highways	26,283	105	6.5
Hospitals	0	0	0.0
Housing and Community Development	21,611	86	5.3
Interest on General Debt	23,923	96	5.9
Judicial and Legal	11,824	47	2.9
Libraries	0	0	0.0
Parking	659	2	0.2
Parks and Recreation	0	0	0.0
Police Protection	73,496	295	18.1
Public Welfare	0	0	0.0
Sewerage	67,305	270	16.6
Solid Waste Management	0	0	0.0
Veterans' Services	0	0	0.0
Liquor Store	0	0	0.0
Utility	0	0	0.0

Source: U.S. Census Bureau, State & Local Government Finances 2019

EMPLOYMENT

Labor Force and Employment

Area	Civilian Labor Force			Workers Employed		
	Dec. 2020	Dec. 2021	% Chg.	Dec. 2020	Dec. 2021	% Chg.
City	142,120	142,480	0.3	135,813	138,462	2.0
MSA[1]	264,095	264,813	0.3	252,360	257,292	2.0
U.S.	160,017,000	161,696,000	1.0	149,613,000	155,732,000	4.1

Note: Data is not seasonally adjusted and covers workers 16 years of age and older; (1) Figures cover the Reno, NV Metropolitan Statistical Area
Source: Bureau of Labor Statistics, Local Area Unemployment Statistics

Unemployment Rate

Area	2021											
	Jan.	Feb.	Mar.	Apr.	May	Jun.	Jul.	Aug.	Sep.	Oct.	Nov.	Dec.
City	4.8	4.9	4.6	4.9	4.7	5.0	5.0	4.3	3.6	3.2	2.9	2.8
MSA[1]	4.8	4.8	4.7	4.9	4.6	4.9	5.0	4.3	3.5	3.2	2.9	2.8
U.S.	6.8	6.6	6.2	5.7	5.5	6.1	5.7	5.3	4.6	4.3	3.9	3.7

Note: Data is not seasonally adjusted and covers workers 16 years of age and older; (1) Figures cover the Reno, NV Metropolitan Statistical Area
Source: Bureau of Labor Statistics, Local Area Unemployment Statistics

Average Wages

Occupation	$/Hr.	Occupation	$/Hr.
Accountants and Auditors	33.07	Maintenance and Repair Workers	23.16
Automotive Mechanics	24.44	Marketing Managers	54.05
Bookkeepers	21.88	Network and Computer Systems Admin.	38.60
Carpenters	28.25	Nurses, Licensed Practical	28.90
Cashiers	12.55	Nurses, Registered	40.67
Computer Programmers	43.95	Nursing Assistants	16.54
Computer Systems Analysts	46.69	Office Clerks, General	19.54
Computer User Support Specialists	23.61	Physical Therapists	49.12
Construction Laborers	21.87	Physicians	n/a
Cooks, Restaurant	14.96	Plumbers, Pipefitters and Steamfitters	31.87
Customer Service Representatives	17.78	Police and Sheriff's Patrol Officers	35.24
Dentists	58.47	Postal Service Mail Carriers	26.10
Electricians	30.31	Real Estate Sales Agents	26.33
Engineers, Electrical	47.85	Retail Salespersons	15.14
Fast Food and Counter Workers	11.60	Sales Representatives, Technical/Scientific	49.73
Financial Managers	55.75	Secretaries, Exc. Legal/Medical/Executive	20.93
First-Line Supervisors of Office Workers	27.64	Security Guards	15.79
General and Operations Managers	50.41	Surgeons	n/a
Hairdressers/Cosmetologists	13.98	Teacher Assistants, Exc. Postsecondary*	10.75
Home Health and Personal Care Aides	12.22	Teachers, Secondary School, Exc. Sp. Ed.*	27.00
Janitors and Cleaners	14.01	Telemarketers	13.24
Landscaping/Groundskeeping Workers	16.69	Truck Drivers, Heavy/Tractor-Trailer	24.77
Lawyers	65.89	Truck Drivers, Light/Delivery Services	19.76
Maids and Housekeeping Cleaners	14.51	Waiters and Waitresses	11.87

Note: Wage data covers the Reno, NV Metropolitan Statistical Area; (*) Hourly wages were calculated from annual wage data based on a 40 hour work week; n/a not available.
Source: Bureau of Labor Statistics, Metro Area Occupational Employment & Wage Estimates, May 2021

Employment by Industry

Sector	MSA[1]		U.S.
	Number of Employees	Percent of Total	Percent of Total
Construction	19,400	7.6	5.0
Education and Health Services	28,000	11.0	16.0
Financial Activities	11,200	4.4	5.9
Government	30,200	11.9	14.9
Information	3,000	1.2	1.9
Leisure and Hospitality	34,600	13.6	9.8
Manufacturing	29,000	11.4	8.4
Mining and Logging	300	0.1	0.4
Other Services	6,400	2.5	3.7
Professional and Business Services	32,600	12.9	14.6
Retail Trade	25,100	9.9	10.7
Transportation, Warehousing, and Utilities	23,900	9.4	4.8
Wholesale Trade	9,900	3.9	3.8

Note: Figures are non-farm employment as of December 2021. Figures are not seasonally adjusted and include workers 16 years of age and older; (1) Figures cover the Reno, NV Metropolitan Statistical Area
Source: Bureau of Labor Statistics, Current Employment Statistics, Employment, Hours, and Earnings

Employment by Occupation

Occupation Classification	City (%)	MSA[1] (%)	U.S. (%)
Management, Business, Science, and Arts	35.8	35.4	39.5
Natural Resources, Construction, and Maintenance	7.9	9.0	8.7
Production, Transportation, and Material Moving	13.4	13.9	13.1
Sales and Office	22.1	22.3	21.3
Service	20.7	19.3	17.4

Note: Figures cover employed civilians 16 years of age and older; (1) Figures cover the Reno, NV Metropolitan Statistical Area
Source: U.S. Census Bureau, 2016-2020 American Community Survey 5-Year Estimates

Occupations with Greatest Projected Employment Growth: 2021 – 2023

Occupation[1]	2021 Employment	2023 Projected Employment	Numeric Employment Change	Percent Employment Change
Laborers and Freight, Stock, and Material Movers, Hand	37,280	44,490	7,210	19.3
Retail Salespersons	42,730	46,100	3,370	7.9
Stockers and Order Fillers	24,080	27,450	3,370	14.0
Fast Food and Counter Workers	42,350	44,540	2,190	5.2
Cooks, Restaurant	18,590	20,670	2,080	11.2
Waiters and Waitresses	29,200	31,250	2,050	7.0
Security Guards	20,470	22,220	1,750	8.5
Janitors and Cleaners, Except Maids and Housekeeping Cleaners	26,000	27,750	1,750	6.7
Customer Service Representatives	28,270	29,910	1,640	5.8
General and Operations Managers	21,570	23,170	1,600	7.4

Note: Projections cover Nevada; (1) Sorted by numeric employment change
Source: www.projectionscentral.com, State Occupational Projections, 2021–2023 Short-Term Projections

Fastest-Growing Occupations: 2021 – 2023

Occupation[1]	2021 Employment	2023 Projected Employment	Numeric Employment Change	Percent Employment Change
Conveyor Operators and Tenders	180	230	50	27.8
Industrial Truck and Tractor Operators	6,320	7,720	1,400	22.2
Laborers and Freight, Stock, and Material Movers, Hand	37,280	44,490	7,210	19.3
Light Truck or Delivery Services Drivers	7,960	9,490	1,530	19.2
Transportation, Storage, and Distribution Managers	1,180	1,380	200	16.9
Weighers, Measurers, Checkers, and Samplers, Recordkeeping	780	910	130	16.7
Electrical, Electronic, and Electromechanical Assemblers, Except Coil Winders, Tapers, and Fini	3,550	4,110	560	15.8
Logisticians	640	740	100	15.6
Bus Drivers, Transit and Intercity (SOC 2018)	1,800	2,070	270	15.0
Industrial Engineers	810	930	120	14.8

Note: Projections cover Nevada; (1) Sorted by percent employment change and excludes occupations with numeric employment change less than 50
Source: www.projectionscentral.com, State Occupational Projections, 2021–2023 Short-Term Projections

TAXES

State Corporate Income Tax Rates

State	Tax Rate (%)	Income Brackets ($)	Num. of Brackets	Financial Institution Tax Rate (%)[a]	Federal Income Tax Ded.
Nevada	None	–	–	–	–

Note: Tax rates as of January 1, 2022; (a) Rates listed are the corporate income tax rate applied to financial institutions or excise taxes based on income. Some states have other taxes based upon the value of deposits or shares.
Source: Federation of Tax Administrators, State Corporate Income Tax Rates, January 1, 2022

State Individual Income Tax Rates

State	Tax Rate (%)	Income Brackets ($)	Personal Exemptions ($)			Standard Ded. ($)	
			Single	Married	Depend.	Single	Married
Nevada	– No state income tax –						

Note: Tax rates as of January 1, 2022; Local- and county-level taxes are not included
Source: Federation of Tax Administrators, State Individual Income Tax Rates, January 1, 2022

Various State Sales and Excise Tax Rates

State	State Sales Tax (%)	Gasoline[1] (¢/gal.)	Cigarette[2] ($/pack)	Spirits[3] ($/gal.)	Wine[4] ($/gal.)	Beer[5] ($/gal.)	Recreational Marijuana (%)
Nevada	6.85	50.48	1.8	3.6	0.7	0.16	(k)

Note: All tax rates as of January 1, 2022; (1) The American Petroleum Institute has developed a methodology for determining the average tax rate on a gallon of fuel. Rates may include any of the following: excise taxes, environmental fees, storage tank fees, other fees or taxes, general sales tax, and local taxes; (2) The federal excise tax of $1.0066 per pack and local taxes are not included; (3) Rates are those applicable to off-premise sales of 40% alcohol by volume (a.b.v.) distilled spirits in 750ml containers. Local excise taxes are excluded; (4) Rates are those applicable to off-premise sales of 11% a.b.v. non-carbonated wine in 750ml containers; (5) Rates are those applicable to off-premise sales of 4.7% a.b.v. beer in 12 ounce containers; (k) 15% excise tax (fair market value at wholesale); 10% excise tax (retail price)
Source: Tax Foundation, 2022 Facts & Figures: How Does Your State Compare?

State Business Tax Climate Index Rankings

State	Overall Rank	Corporate Tax Rank	Individual Income Tax Rank	Sales Tax Rank	Property Tax Rank	Unemployment Insurance Tax Rank
Nevada	7	25	5	44	5	45

Note: The index is a measure of how each state's tax laws affect economic performance. The lower the rank, the more favorable a state's tax system is for business. States without a given tax are given a ranking of 1. The scores/rankings for the District of Columbia do not affect other states. The 2022 index represents the tax climate as of July 1, 2021.
Source: Tax Foundation, State Business Tax Climate Index 2022

TRANSPORTATION

Means of Transportation to Work

Area	Car/Truck/Van		Public Transportation			Bicycle	Walked	Other Means	Worked at Home
	Drove Alone	Car-pooled	Bus	Subway	Railroad				
City	73.0	11.9	2.8	0.0	0.0	0.8	3.1	1.8	6.5
MSA[1]	75.1	11.8	2.1	0.0	0.0	0.5	2.2	1.5	6.7
U.S.	74.9	8.9	2.2	1.7	0.5	0.5	2.6	1.4	7.3

Note: Figures are percentages and cover workers 16 years of age and older; (1) Figures cover the Reno, NV Metropolitan Statistical Area
Source: U.S. Census Bureau, 2016-2020 American Community Survey 5-Year Estimates

Travel Time to Work

Area	Less Than 10 Minutes	10 to 19 Minutes	20 to 29 Minutes	30 to 44 Minutes	45 to 59 Minutes	60 to 89 Minutes	90 Minutes or More
City	15.1	41.3	22.2	12.8	4.4	2.7	1.5
MSA[1]	12.6	36.6	24.4	17.0	4.9	2.9	1.5
U.S.	12.3	28.4	20.9	20.9	8.3	6.4	2.9

Note: Note: Figures are percentages and include workers 16 years old and over; (1) Figures cover the Reno, NV Metropolitan Statistical Area
Source: U.S. Census Bureau, 2016-2020 American Community Survey 5-Year Estimates

Key Congestion Measures

Measure	1990	2000	2010	2015	2020
Annual Hours of Delay, Total (000)	n/a	n/a	n/a	10,688	4,936
Annual Hours of Delay, Per Auto Commuter	n/a	n/a	n/a	26	11
Annual Congestion Cost, Per Auto Commuter ($)	n/a	n/a	n/a	539	263

Note: n/a not available
Source: Texas A&M Transportation Institute, 2021 Urban Mobility Report

Freeway Travel Time Index

Measure	1985	1990	1995	2000	2005	2010	2015	2020
Urban Area Index[1]	n/a	n/a	n/a	n/a	n/a	n/a	1.13	1.07
Urban Area Rank[1,2]	n/a	n/a	n/a	n/a	n/a	n/a	n/a	n/a

Note: Freeway Travel Time Index—the ratio of travel time in the peak period to the travel time at free-flow conditions. For example, a value of 1.30 indicates a 20-minute free-flow trip takes 26 minutes in the peak (20 minutes x 1.30 = 26 minutes); (1) Covers the Reno NV-CA urban area; (2) Rank is based on 101 larger urban areas (#1 = highest travel time index); n/a not available
Source: Texas A&M Transportation Institute, 2021 Urban Mobility Report

Public Transportation

Agency Name / Mode of Transportation	Vehicles Operated in Maximum Service[1]	Annual Unlinked Passenger Trips[2] (in thous.)	Annual Passenger Miles[3] (in thous.)
Regional Transportation Commission of Washoe County (RTC)			
Bus (purchased transportation)	56	6,811.9	29,343.2
Commuter Bus (purchased transportation)	3	23.4	599.9
Demand Response (purchased transportation)	49	177.9	1,427.9
Vanpool (purchased transportation)	209	497.3	17,618.1

Note: (1) Number of revenue vehicles operated by the given mode and type of service to meet the annual maximum service requirement. This is the revenue vehicle count during the peak season of the year; on the week and day that maximum service is provided. Vehicles operated in maximum service (VOMS) exclude atypical days and one-time special events; (2) Number of passengers who boarded public transportation vehicles. Passengers are counted each time they board a vehicle no matter how many vehicles they use to travel from their origin to their destination. (3) Sum of the distances ridden by all passengers during the entire fiscal year.
Source: Federal Transit Administration, National Transit Database, 2020

Air Transportation

Airport Name and Code / Type of Service	Passenger Airlines[1]	Passenger Enplanements	Freight Carriers[2]	Freight (lbs)
Reno-Tahoe International (RNO)				
Domestic service (U.S. carriers - 2021)	24	1,772,772	10	92,865,682
International service (U.S. carriers - 2020)	2	337	0	0

Note: (1) Includes all U.S.-based major, minor and commuter airlines that carried at least one passenger during the year; (2) Includes all U.S.-based airlines and freight carriers that transported at least one pound of freight during the year.
Source: Bureau of Transportation Statistics, The Intermodal Transportation Database, Air Carriers: T-100 Domestic Market (U.S. Carriers), 2021; Bureau of Transportation Statistics, The Intermodal Transportation Database, Air Carriers: T-100 International Market (U.S. Carriers), 2020

BUSINESSES

Major Business Headquarters

Company Name	Industry	Rankings	
		Fortune[1]	Forbes[2]
No companies listed	-	-	-

Note: (1) Companies that produce a 10-K are ranked 1 to 500 based on 2020 revenue; (2) All private companies with at least $2 billion in annual revenue through the end of their most current fiscal year are ranked 1 to 225; companies listed are headquartered in the city; dashes indicate no ranking
Source: Fortune, "Fortune 500," 2021; Forbes, "America's Largest Private Companies," 2021

Living Environment

COST OF LIVING

Cost of Living Index

Composite Index	Groceries	Housing	Utilities	Trans-portation	Health Care	Misc. Goods/ Services
108.3	105.5	126.5	82.6	118.7	103.9	97.7

Note: The Cost of Living Index measures regional differences in the cost of consumer goods and services, excluding taxes and non-consumer expenditures, for professional and managerial households in the top income quintile. It is based on more than 50,000 prices covering almost 60 different items for which prices are collected three times a year by chambers of commerce, economic development organizations or university applied economic centers in each participating urban area. The numbers shown should be read as a percentage above or below the national average of 100. For example, a value of 115.4 in the groceries column indicates that grocery prices are 15.4% higher than the national average. Small differences in the index numbers should not be interpreted as significant; Figures cover the Reno-Sparks NV urban area.
Source: The Council for Community and Economic Research, Cost of Living Index, 2021

Grocery Prices

Area[1]	T-Bone Steak ($/pound)	Frying Chicken ($/pound)	Whole Milk ($/half gal.)	Eggs ($/dozen)	Orange Juice ($/64 oz.)	Coffee ($/11.5 oz.)
City[2]	12.76	1.32	2.81	1.70	3.50	5.53
Avg.	12.82	1.40	2.22	1.57	3.59	4.30
Min.	8.91	0.91	1.29	0.75	2.87	3.02
Max.	21.35	2.69	3.92	3.86	5.49	8.11

Note: (1) Values for the local area are compared with the average, minimum and maximum values for all 285 areas in the Cost of Living Index; (2) Figures cover the Reno-Sparks NV urban area; ***T-Bone Steak*** *(price per pound);* ***Frying Chicken*** *(price per pound, whole fryer);* ***Whole Milk*** *(half gallon carton);* ***Eggs*** *(price per dozen, Grade A, large);* ***Orange Juice*** *(64 oz. Tropicana or Florida Natural);* ***Coffee*** *(11.5 oz. can, vacuum-packed, Maxwell House, Hills Bros, or Folgers).*
Source: The Council for Community and Economic Research, Cost of Living Index, 2021

Housing and Utility Costs

Area[1]	New Home Price ($)	Apartment Rent ($/month)	All Electric ($/month)	Part Electric ($/month)	Other Energy ($/month)	Telephone ($/month)
City[2]	525,709	1,326	-	84.77	37.80	181.37
Avg.	398,393	1,217	171.38	100.83	69.67	187.75
Min.	212,799	534	96.71	31.56	27.15	173.01
Max.	2,354,006	4,438	369.53	277.33	303.87	206.73

Note: (1) Values for the local area are compared with the average, minimum and maximum values for all 285 areas in the Cost of Living Index; (2) Figures cover the Reno-Sparks NV urban area; ***New Home Price*** *(2,400 sf living area, 8,000 sf lot, in urban area with full utilities);* ***Apartment Rent*** *(950 sf 2 bedroom/1.5 or 2 bath, unfurnished, excluding all utilities except water);* ***All Electric*** *(average monthly cost for an all-electric home);* ***Part Electric*** *(average monthly cost for a part-electric home);* ***Other Energy*** *(average monthly cost for natural gas, fuel oil, coal, wood, and any other forms of energy except electricity);* ***Telephone*** *(price includes the base monthly rate plus taxes and fees for three lines of mobile phone service).*
Source: The Council for Community and Economic Research, Cost of Living Index, 2021

Health Care, Transportation, and Other Costs

Area[1]	Doctor ($/visit)	Dentist ($/visit)	Optometrist ($/visit)	Gasoline ($/gallon)	Beauty Salon ($/visit)	Men's Shirt ($)
City[2]	124.17	109.89	103.33	3.26	36.39	20.46
Avg.	118.16	101.04	109.44	2.71	40.63	30.77
Min.	35.04	55.56	51.17	2.17	18.59	11.32
Max.	231.10	165.12	256.81	4.11	85.33	63.03

Note: (1) Values for the local area are compared with the average, minimum and maximum values for all 285 areas in the Cost of Living Index; (2) Figures cover the Reno-Sparks NV urban area; ***Doctor*** *(general practitioners routine exam of an established patient);* ***Dentist*** *(adult teeth cleaning and periodic oral examination);* ***Optometrist*** *(full vision eye exam for established adult patient);* ***Gasoline*** *(one gallon regular unleaded, national brand, including all taxes, cash price at self-service pump if available);* ***Beauty Salon*** *(woman's shampoo, trim, and blow-dry);* ***Men's Shirt*** *(cotton/polyester dress shirt, pinpoint weave, long sleeves).*
Source: The Council for Community and Economic Research, Cost of Living Index, 2021

HOUSING

Homeownership Rate

Area	2013 (%)	2014 (%)	2015 (%)	2016 (%)	2017 (%)	2018 (%)	2019 (%)	2020 (%)	2021 (%)
MSA[1]	n/a	n/a	n/a	n/a	n/a	n/a	n/a	n/a	n/a
U.S.	65.1	64.5	63.7	63.4	63.9	64.4	64.6	66.6	65.5

Note: (1) Figures cover the Reno, NV Metropolitan Statistical Area; n/a not available
Source: U.S. Census Bureau, Housing Vacancies and Homeownership Annual Statistics: 2013-2021

House Price Index (HPI)

Area	National Ranking[2]	Quarterly Change (%)	One-Year Change (%)	Five-Year Change (%)	Since 1991Q1 (%)
MSA[1]	24	3.85	25.10	68.22	312.60
U.S.[3]	–	3.33	17.54	54.45	258.04

Note: The HPI is a weighted repeat sales index. It measures average price changes in repeat sales or refinancings on the same properties. This information is obtained by reviewing repeat mortgage transactions on single-family properties whose mortgages have been purchased or securitized by Fannie Mae or Freddie Mac since January 1975; (1) Figures cover the Reno, NV Metropolitan Statistical Area; (2) Rankings are based on annual percentage change for all metro areas containing at least 15,000 transactions over the last 10 years and ranges from 1 to 268; (3) figures based on a weighted average of Census Division estimates using a seasonally adjusted, purchase-only index; all figures are for the period ending December 31, 2021
Source: Federal Housing Finance Agency, Change in FHFA Metropolitan Area House Price Indexes, 2021Q4

Median Single-Family Home Prices

Area	2019	2020	2021[p]	Percent Change 2020 to 2021
MSA[1]	393.9	440.8	531.8	20.6
U.S. Average	274.6	300.2	353.4	17.7

Note: Figures are median sales prices of existing single-family homes in thousands of dollars; (p) preliminary; (1) Figures cover the Reno, NV Metropolitan Statistical Area
Source: National Association of Realtors, Median Sales Price of Existing Single-Family Homes for Metropolitan Areas, 4th Quarter 2021

Qualifying Income Based on Median Sales Price of Existing Single-Family Homes

Area	With 5% Down ($)	With 10% Down ($)	With 20% Down ($)
MSA[1]	111,505	105,637	93,899
U.S. Average	70,699	66,978	59,536

Note: Figures are preliminary; Qualifying income is based on a mortgage rate of 3.13%. Monthly principal and interest payment is limited to 25% of income; (1) Figures cover the Reno, NV Metropolitan Statistical Area
Source: National Association of Realtors, Qualifying Income Based on Median Sales Price of Existing Single-Family Homes for Metropolitan Areas, 4th Quarter 2021

Home Value Distribution

Area	Under $50,000	$50,000 -$99,999	$100,000 -$149,999	$150,000 -$199,999	$200,000 -$299,999	$300,000 -$499,999	$500,000 -$999,999	$1,000,000 or more
City	3.4	2.7	3.1	4.9	19.1	45.5	18.6	2.7
MSA[1]	3.1	2.5	3.5	5.3	20.4	41.1	19.1	4.9
U.S.	6.6	11.0	12.3	13.6	20.0	20.5	12.3	3.7

Note: Figures are percentages and cover owner-occupied housing units; (1) Figures cover the Reno, NV Metropolitan Statistical Area
Source: U.S. Census Bureau, 2016-2020 American Community Survey 5-Year Estimates

Year Housing Structure Built

Area	2010 or Later	2000 -2009	1990 -1999	1980 -1989	1970 -1979	1960 -1969	1950 -1959	1940 -1949	Before 1940	Median Year
City	8.8	19.7	18.2	13.4	18.2	9.0	6.4	2.9	3.4	1988
MSA[1]	7.6	20.9	19.5	14.8	18.9	8.8	5.0	2.1	2.5	1989
U.S.	6.2	13.6	13.9	13.4	15.0	10.5	10.2	4.8	12.4	1978

Note: Figures are percentages except for Median Year; Note: (1) Figures cover the Reno, NV Metropolitan Statistical Area
Source: U.S. Census Bureau, 2016-2020 American Community Survey 5-Year Estimates

Gross Monthly Rent

Area	Under $500	$500 -$999	$1,000 -$1,499	$1,500 -$1,999	$2,000 -$2,499	$2,500 -$2,999	$3,000 and up	Median ($)
City	6.0	35.5	35.8	17.0	4.4	0.5	0.7	1,107
MSA[1]	5.1	33.1	36.0	19.0	4.8	1.0	1.0	1,149
U.S.	8.9	34.3	30.2	14.9	6.2	2.6	2.8	1,096

Note: Figures are percentages except for Median; Gross rent is the contract rent plus the estimated average monthly cost of utilities (electricity, gas, and water and sewer) and fuels (oil, coal, kerosene, wood, etc.) if these are paid by the renter (or paid for the renter by someone else); (1) Figures cover the Reno, NV Metropolitan Statistical Area
Source: U.S. Census Bureau, 2016-2020 American Community Survey 5-Year Estimates

HEALTH

Health Risk Factors

Category	MSA[1] (%)	U.S. (%)
Adults aged 18–64 who have any kind of health care coverage	84.2	86.8
Adults who reported being in good or better health	88.6	86.7
Adults who are current smokers	16.0	15.5
Adults who currently use chewing tobacco, snuff, or snus	4.2	3.7
Adults who are heavy drinkers[2]	8.1	6.7
Adults who are binge drinkers[3]	20.2	15.7
Adults who are overweight (BMI 25.0 - 29.9)	36.4	35.2
Adults who are obese (BMI 30.0 - 99.8)	24.6	31.9
Adults who participated in any physical activities in the past month	80.6	77.6
Adults who always or nearly always wears a seat belt	95.7	94.2

Note: (1) Figures cover the Reno, NV Metropolitan Statistical Area; (2) Heavy drinkers are classified as adult men having more than 14 drinks per week and adult women having more than 7 drinks per week; (3) Binge drinkers are classified as males having five or more drinks on one occasion or females having four or more drinks on one occasion

Source: Centers for Disease Control and Prevention, Behaviorial Risk Factor Surveillance System, SMART: Selected Metropolitan Area Risk Trends, 2020

Acute and Chronic Health Conditions

Category	MSA[1] (%)	U.S. (%)
Adults who have ever been told they had a heart attack	5.5	4.3
Adults who have ever been told they have angina or coronary heart disease	4.2	4.0
Adults who have ever been told they had a stroke	2.6	2.8
Adults who have ever been told they have asthma	12.2	14.2
Adults who have ever been told they have arthritis	23.3	24.5
Adults who have ever been told they have diabetes[2]	7.2	10.6
Adults who have ever been told they had skin cancer	12.3	6.4
Adults who have ever been told they had any other types of cancer	6.8	6.8
Adults who have ever been told they have COPD	5.4	6.2
Adults who have ever been told they have kidney disease	n/a	2.9
Adults who have ever been told they have a form of depression	18.2	19.6

Note: (1) Figures cover the Reno, NV Metropolitan Statistical Area; (2) Figures do not include pregnancy-related, borderline, or pre-diabetes

Source: Centers for Disease Control and Prevention, Behaviorial Risk Factor Surveillance System, SMART: Selected Metropolitan Area Risk Trends, 2020

Health Screening and Vaccination Rates

Category	MSA[1] (%)	U.S. (%)
Adults 50-75 who have had a blood stool test within the past year	11.9	9.3
Adults aged 65+ who have had flu shot within the past year	65.6	67.9
Adults aged 65+ who have ever had a pneumonia vaccination	74.0	72.2
Adults who have ever been tested for HIV	38.1	37.1
Women aged 21-65 who have had a pap test in the past three years	77.3	77.7
Men aged 40+ who have had a PSA test within the past two years	32.9	31.8
Women aged 40+ who have had a mammogram within the past two years	69.4	71.5

Note: (1) Figures cover the Reno, NV Metropolitan Statistical Area.

Source: Centers for Disease Control and Prevention, Behaviorial Risk Factor Surveillance System, SMART: Selected Metropolitan Area Risk Trends, 2020

Disability Status

Category	MSA[1] (%)	U.S. (%)
Adults who reported being deaf	6.7	6.8
Are you blind or have serious difficulty seeing, even when wearing glasses?	4.1	4.7
Do you have difficulty doing errands alone?	7.1	6.3
Do you have difficulty dressing or bathing?	3.5	3.0
Do you have serious difficulty concentrating/remembering/making decisions?	11.4	10.8
Do you have serious difficulty walking or climbing stairs?	9.7	11.9

Note: (1) Figures cover the Reno, NV Metropolitan Statistical Area.

Source: Centers for Disease Control and Prevention, Behaviorial Risk Factor Surveillance System, SMART: Selected Metropolitan Area Risk Trends, 2020

Mortality Rates for the Top 10 Causes of Death in the U.S.

ICD-10[a] Sub-Chapter	ICD-10[a] Code	Age-Adjusted Mortality Rate[1] per 100,000 population	
		County[2]	U.S.
Malignant neoplasms	C00-C97	136.7	146.4
Ischaemic heart diseases	I20-I25	116.4	90.2
Other forms of heart disease	I30-I51	39.1	51.9
Other degenerative diseases of the nervous system	G30-G31	29.8	39.7
Other external causes of accidental injury	W00-X59	47.9	38.7
Chronic lower respiratory diseases	J40-J47	43.9	38.1
Cerebrovascular diseases	I60-I69	45.4	37.6
Organic, including symptomatic, mental disorders	F01-F09	18.7	29.4
Hypertensive diseases	I10-I15	29.2	26.1
Diabetes mellitus	E10-E14	21.0	22.6

Note: (a) ICD-10 = International Classification of Diseases 10th Revision; (1) Mortality rates are a three-year average covering 2018-2020; (2) Figures cover Washoe County.
Source: Centers for Disease Control and Prevention, National Center for Health Statistics. Underlying Cause of Death 1999-2020 on CDC WONDER Online Database

Mortality Rates for Selected Causes of Death

ICD-10[a] Sub-Chapter	ICD-10[a] Code	Age-Adjusted Mortality Rate[1] per 100,000 population	
		County[2]	U.S.
Assault	X85-Y09	5.1	6.5
Diseases of the liver	K70-K76	19.3	15.3
Human immunodeficiency virus (HIV) disease	B20-B24	1.5	1.4
Influenza and pneumonia	J09-J18	13.5	13.4
Intentional self-harm	X60-X84	19.9	13.9
Malnutrition	E40-E46	3.4	2.9
Obesity and other hyperalimentation	E65-E68	3.0	2.4
Renal failure	N17-N19	8.6	12.5
Transport accidents	V01-V99	12.1	12.5
Viral hepatitis	B15-B19	Unreliable	1.0

Note: (a) ICD-10 = International Classification of Diseases 10th Revision; (1) Mortality rates are a three-year average covering 2018-2020; (2) Figures cover Washoe County; Data are suppressed when the data meet the criteria for confidentiality constraints; Mortality rates are flagged as unreliable when the rate would be calculated with a numerator of 20 or less.
Source: Centers for Disease Control and Prevention, National Center for Health Statistics. Underlying Cause of Death 1999-2020 on CDC WONDER Online Database

Health Insurance Coverage

Area	With Health Insurance	With Private Health Insurance	With Public Health Insurance	Without Health Insurance	Population Under Age 19 Without Health Insurance
City	90.0	69.0	30.9	10.0	8.4
MSA[1]	90.3	69.9	31.6	9.7	8.2
U.S.	91.3	68.1	35.3	8.7	5.2

Note: Figures are percentages that cover the civilian noninstitutionalized population; (1) Figures cover the Reno, NV Metropolitan Statistical Area
Source: U.S. Census Bureau, 2016-2020 American Community Survey 5-Year Estimates

Number of Medical Professionals

Area	MDs[3]	DOs[3,4]	Dentists	Podiatrists	Chiropractors	Optometrists
County[1] (number)	1,414	96	333	19	141	115
County[1] (rate[2])	290.7	19.7	68.4	3.9	29.0	23.6
U.S. (rate[2])	285.1	23.0	71.1	6.2	28.2	17.0

32031
Note: Data as of 2020 unless noted; (1) Data covers Washoe County; (2) Rate per 100,000 population; (3) Data as of 2019 and includes all active, non-federal physicians; (4) Doctor of Osteopathic Medicine
Source: U.S. Department of Health and Human Services, Health Resources and Services Administration, Bureau of Health Professions, Area Resource File (ARF) 2020-2021

EDUCATION

Public School District Statistics

District Name	Schls	Pupils	Pupil/Teacher Ratio	Minority Pupils[1] (%)	LEP/ELL[2] (%)	IEP[3] (%)
Washoe County School District	115	67,301	17.4	56.5	15.0	14.2

Note: Table includes school districts with 2,000 or more students; (1) Percentage of students that are not non-Hispanic white; (2) Percentage of students that are Limited English Proficient (LEP) or English Language Learners (ELL) (2018-19); (3) Percentage of students that have an Individualized Education Program (IEP).
Source: U.S. Department of Education, National Center for Education Statistics, Common Core of Data, Local Education Agency (School District) Universe Survey: School Year 2019-2020

Best High Schools

According to *U.S. News,* Reno is home to one of the top 500 high schools in the U.S.: **The Davidson Academy of Nevada** (#3). Nearly 18,000 public, magnet and charter schools were ranked based on their performance on state assessments and how well they prepare students for college. *U.S. News & World Report, "Best High Schools 2021"*

Highest Level of Education

Area	Less than H.S.	H.S. Diploma	Some College, No Deg.	Associate Degree	Bachelor's Degree	Master's Degree	Prof. School Degree	Doctorate Degree
City	10.1	22.5	24.2	8.3	21.6	8.8	2.3	2.2
MSA[1]	11.1	23.7	25.0	8.6	19.7	8.2	2.1	1.7
U.S.	11.5	26.7	20.3	8.6	20.2	9.1	2.2	1.5

Note: Figures cover persons age 25 and over; (1) Figures cover the Reno, NV Metropolitan Statistical Area
Source: U.S. Census Bureau, 2016-2020 American Community Survey 5-Year Estimates

Educational Attainment by Race

Area	High School Graduate or Higher (%)					Bachelor's Degree or Higher (%)				
	Total	White	Black	Asian	Hisp.[2]	Total	White	Black	Asian	Hisp.[2]
City	89.9	92.6	94.1	91.9	67.0	34.8	36.5	30.2	52.2	13.5
MSA[1]	88.9	91.9	92.2	91.3	64.7	31.7	33.4	27.2	49.0	12.4
U.S.	88.5	90.7	86.7	87.3	70.3	32.9	34.4	22.6	55.0	17.6

Note: Figures shown cover persons 25 years old and over; (1) Figures cover the Reno, NV Metropolitan Statistical Area; (2) People of Hispanic origin can be of any race
Source: U.S. Census Bureau, 2016-2020 American Community Survey 5-Year Estimates

School Enrollment by Grade and Control

Area	Preschool (%)		Kindergarten (%)		Grades 1 - 4 (%)		Grades 5 - 8 (%)		Grades 9 - 12 (%)	
	Public	Private	Public	Private	Public	Private	Public	Private	Public	Private
City	61.7	38.3	89.7	10.3	94.1	5.9	92.6	7.4	95.1	4.9
MSA[1]	58.5	41.5	89.4	10.6	93.1	6.9	93.4	6.6	93.3	6.7
U.S.	58.9	41.1	86.9	13.1	89.0	11.0	89.0	11.0	89.7	10.3

Note: Figures shown cover persons 3 years old and over; (1) Figures cover the Reno, NV Metropolitan Statistical Area
Source: U.S. Census Bureau, 2016-2020 American Community Survey 5-Year Estimates

Higher Education

Four-Year Colleges			Two-Year Colleges			Medical Schools[1]	Law Schools[2]	Voc/ Tech[3]
Public	Private Non-profit	Private For-profit	Public	Private Non-profit	Private For-profit			
2	1	0	0	0	2	1	0	4

Note: Figures cover institutions located within the Reno, NV Metropolitan Statistical Area and include main campuses only; (1) includes schools accredited by the Liaison Committee on Medical Education and the American Osteopathic Association's Commission on Osteopathic College Accreditation; (2) includes ABA-accredited schools, schools with provisional ABA accreditation, and state accredited schools; (3) includes all schools with programs that are less than 2 years.
Source: National Center for Education Statistics, Integrated Postsecondary Education System (IPEDS), 2020-21; Wikipedia, List of Medical Schools in the United States, accessed April 11, 2022; Wikipedia, List of Law Schools in the United States, accessed April 11, 2022

EMPLOYERS

Major Employers

Company Name	Industry
Atlantis Casino Resort	Casino hotels
Bellagio	Casino hotels
Circus Circus Casinos - Reno	Casino hotels
City of Reno	Municipal government
Desert Palace	Casino hotels
Eldorado Hotel & Casino	Casino hotels
Grand Sierra Resort & Casino	Casino hotels
Harrahs Reno	Casino hotels
IGT	All other miscellaneous manufacturing
Integrity Staffing Solutions	Temporary help services
Mandalay Corp	Casino hotels
Peppermill Hotel Casino - Reno	Casino hotels
Renown Regional Medical Center	General medical & surgical hospitals
Saint Marys	General medical & surgical hospitals
Sierra Nevada Healthcare System	General medical & surgical hospitals
Silver Legacy Resort Casino	Casino hotels
Sparks Nugget	Casino hotels
Truckee Meadows Community Coll	Junior colleges
United Parcel Service	Package delivery services
University of Nevada-Reno	Colleges & universities
Washoe County Comptroller	Executive & legislative offices combined
Washoe County School District	Elementary & secondary schools
West Business Solutions	Telemarketing bureaus

Note: Companies shown are located within the Reno, NV Metropolitan Statistical Area.
Source: Hoovers.com; Wikipedia

PUBLIC SAFETY

Crime Rate

Area	Total Crime	Violent Crime Rate				Property Crime Rate		
		Murder	Rape[3]	Robbery	Aggrav. Assault	Burglary	Larceny -Theft	Motor Vehicle Theft
City	2,710.2	6.6	108.4	110.4	338.0	426.4	1,345.1	375.4
Suburbs[1]	1,808.3	4.5	59.7	39.2	243.4	304.1	959.0	198.4
Metro[2]	2,291.8	5.6	85.8	77.4	294.1	369.6	1,165.9	293.3
U.S.	2,356.7	6.5	38.4	73.9	279.7	314.2	1,398.0	246.0

Note: Figures are crimes per 100,000 population; (1) All areas within the metro area that are located outside the city limits; (2) Figures cover the Reno, NV Metropolitan Statistical Area; (3) All figures shown were reported using the revised Uniform Crime Reporting (UCR) definition of rape.
Source: FBI Uniform Crime Reports, 2020

Hate Crimes

Area	Number of Quarters Reported	Number of Incidents per Bias Motivation					
		Race/Ethnicity/ Ancestry	Religion	Sexual Orientation	Disability	Gender	Gender Identity
City	4	30	3	1	0	2	0
U.S.	4	5,227	1,244	1,110	130	75	266

Source: Federal Bureau of Investigation, Hate Crime Statistics 2020

Identity Theft Consumer Reports

Area	Reports	Reports per 100,000 Population	Rank[2]
MSA[1]	2,005	422	75
U.S.	1,434,676	432	-

Note: (1) Figures cover the Reno, NV Metropolitan Statistical Area; (2) Rank ranges from 1 to 391 where 1 indicates greatest number of identity theft reports per 100,000 population
Source: Federal Trade Commission, Consumer Sentinel Network Data Book 2021

Fraud and Other Consumer Reports

Area	Reports	Reports per 100,000 Population	Rank[2]
MSA[1]	5,455	1,147	59
U.S.	4,328,977	1,304	-

Note: (1) Figures cover the Reno, NV Metropolitan Statistical Area; (2) Rank ranges from 1 to 391 where 1 indicates greatest number of fraud and other consumer reports per 100,000 population
Source: Federal Trade Commission, Consumer Sentinel Network Data Book 2021

POLITICS

2020 Presidential Election Results

Area	Biden	Trump	Jorgensen	Hawkins	Other
Washoe County	50.8	46.3	1.4	0.0	1.5
U.S.	51.3	46.8	1.2	0.3	0.5

Note: Results are percentages and may not add to 100% due to rounding
Source: Dave Leip's Atlas of U.S. Presidential Elections

SPORTS

Professional Sports Teams

Team Name	League	Year Established
No teams are located in the metro area		

Source: Wikipedia, Major Professional Sports Teams of the United States and Canada, April 6, 2022

CLIMATE

Average and Extreme Temperatures

Temperature	Jan	Feb	Mar	Apr	May	Jun	Jul	Aug	Sep	Oct	Nov	Dec	Yr.
Extreme High (°F)	70	75	83	89	96	103	104	105	101	91	77	70	105
Average High (°F)	45	51	56	64	73	82	91	89	81	70	55	46	67
Average Temp. (°F)	32	38	41	48	56	63	70	68	61	51	40	33	50
Average Low (°F)	19	23	26	31	38	44	49	47	40	32	25	20	33
Extreme Low (°F)	-16	-16	0	13	18	25	33	24	20	8	1	-16	-16

Note: Figures cover the years 1949-1992
Source: National Climatic Data Center, International Station Meteorological Climate Summary, 9/96

Average Precipitation/Snowfall/Humidity

Precip./Humidity	Jan	Feb	Mar	Apr	May	Jun	Jul	Aug	Sep	Oct	Nov	Dec	Yr.
Avg. Precip. (in.)	1.0	0.9	0.7	0.4	0.7	0.4	0.3	0.2	0.3	0.4	0.8	1.0	7.2
Avg. Snowfall (in.)	6	5	4	1	1	Tr	0	0	Tr	Tr	2	4	24
Avg. Rel. Hum. 7am (%)	79	77	71	61	55	51	49	55	64	72	78	80	66
Avg. Rel. Hum. 4pm (%)	51	41	34	27	26	22	19	19	22	27	41	51	32

Note: Figures cover the years 1949-1992; Tr = Trace amounts (<0.05 in. of rain; <0.5 in. of snow)
Source: National Climatic Data Center, International Station Meteorological Climate Summary, 9/96

Weather Conditions

Temperature			Daytime Sky			Precipitation		
10°F & below	32°F & below	90°F & above	Clear	Partly cloudy	Cloudy	0.01 inch or more precip.	0.1 inch or more snow/ice	Thunderstorms
14	178	50	143	139	83	50	17	14

Note: Figures are average number of days per year and cover the years 1949-1992
Source: National Climatic Data Center, International Station Meteorological Climate Summary, 9/96

HAZARDOUS WASTE

Superfund Sites

The Reno, NV metro area has no sites on the EPA's Superfund Final National Priorities List. There are a total of 1,165 Superfund sites with a status of proposed or final on the list in the U.S. *U.S. Environmental Protection Agency, National Priorities List, April 6, 2022*

AIR QUALITY

Air Quality Trends: Ozone

	1990	1995	2000	2005	2010	2016	2017	2018	2019	2020
MSA[1]	0.074	0.069	0.067	0.069	0.068	0.071	0.068	0.077	0.063	0.071
U.S.	0.090	0.091	0.082	0.080	0.074	0.070	0.069	0.070	0.066	0.068

Note: (1) Data covers the Reno, NV Metropolitan Statistical Area. The values shown are the composite ozone concentration averages among trend sites based on the highest fourth daily maximum 8-hour concentration in parts per million. These trends are based on sites having an adequate record of monitoring data during the trend period. Data from exceptional events are included.
Source: U.S. Environmental Protection Agency, Air Quality Monitoring Information, "Air Quality Trends by City, 1990-2020"

Air Quality Index

Area	Percent of Days when Air Quality was...[2]					AQI Statistics[2]	
	Good	Moderate	Unhealthy for Sensitive Groups	Unhealthy	Very Unhealthy	Maximum	Median
MSA[1]	65.3	28.1	3.0	3.0	0.5	240	46

Note: (1) Data covers the Reno, NV Metropolitan Statistical Area; (2) Based on 366 days with AQI data in 2020. Air Quality Index (AQI) is an index for reporting daily air quality. EPA calculates the AQI for five major air pollutants regulated by the Clean Air Act: ground-level ozone, particle pollution (aka particulate matter), carbon monoxide, sulfur dioxide, and nitrogen dioxide. The AQI runs from 0 to 500. The higher the AQI value, the greater the level of air pollution and the greater the health concern. There are six AQI categories: "Good" AQI is between 0 and 50. Air quality is considered satisfactory; "Moderate" AQI is between 51 and 100. Air quality is acceptable; "Unhealthy for Sensitive Groups" When AQI values are between 101 and 150, members of sensitive groups may experience health effects; "Unhealthy" When AQI values are between 151 and 200 everyone may begin to experience health effects; "Very Unhealthy" AQI values between 201 and 300 trigger a health alert; "Hazardous" AQI values over 300 trigger warnings of emergency conditions (not shown).
Source: U.S. Environmental Protection Agency, Air Quality Index Report, 2020

Air Quality Index Pollutants

Area	Percent of Days when AQI Pollutant was...[2]					
	Carbon Monoxide	Nitrogen Dioxide	Ozone	Sulfur Dioxide	Particulate Matter 2.5	Particulate Matter 10
MSA[1]	0.0	1.1	70.8	0.0	26.2	1.9

Note: (1) Data covers the Reno, NV Metropolitan Statistical Area; (2) Based on 366 days with AQI data in 2020. The Air Quality Index (AQI) is an index for reporting daily air quality. EPA calculates the AQI for five major air pollutants regulated by the Clean Air Act: ground-level ozone, particle pollution (also known as particulate matter), carbon monoxide, sulfur dioxide, and nitrogen dioxide. The AQI runs from 0 to 500. The higher the AQI value, the greater the level of air pollution and the greater the health concern.
Source: U.S. Environmental Protection Agency, Air Quality Index Report, 2020

Maximum Air Pollutant Concentrations: Particulate Matter, Ozone, CO and Lead

	Particulate Matter 10 (ug/m^3)	Particulate Matter 2.5 Wtd AM (ug/m^3)	Particulate Matter 2.5 24-Hr (ug/m^3)	Ozone (ppm)	Carbon Monoxide (ppm)	Lead (ug/m^3)
MSA[1] Level	220	11.1	75	0.079	2	n/a
NAAQS[2]	150	15	35	0.075	9	0.15
Met NAAQS[2]	No	Yes	No	No	Yes	n/a

Note: (1) Data covers the Reno, NV Metropolitan Statistical Area; Data from exceptional events are included; (2) National Ambient Air Quality Standards; ppm = parts per million; ug/m^3 = micrograms per cubic meter; n/a not available.
Concentrations: Particulate Matter 10 (coarse particulate)—highest second maximum 24-hour concentration; Particulate Matter 2.5 Wtd AM (fine particulate)—highest weighted annual mean concentration; Particulate Matter 2.5 24-Hour (fine particulate)—highest 98th percentile 24-hour concentration; Ozone—highest fourth daily maximum 8-hour concentration; Carbon Monoxide—highest second maximum non-overlapping 8-hour concentration; Lead—maximum running 3-month average
Source: U.S. Environmental Protection Agency, Air Quality Monitoring Information, "Air Quality Statistics by City, 2020"

Maximum Air Pollutant Concentrations: Nitrogen Dioxide and Sulfur Dioxide

	Nitrogen Dioxide AM (ppb)	Nitrogen Dioxide 1-Hr (ppb)	Sulfur Dioxide AM (ppb)	Sulfur Dioxide 1-Hr (ppb)	Sulfur Dioxide 24-Hr (ppb)
MSA[1] Level	12	46	n/a	3	n/a
NAAQS[2]	53	100	30	75	140
Met NAAQS[2]	Yes	Yes	n/a	Yes	n/a

Note: (1) Data covers the Reno, NV Metropolitan Statistical Area; Data from exceptional events are included; (2) National Ambient Air Quality Standards; ppm = parts per million; ug/m^3 = micrograms per cubic meter; n/a not available.
Concentrations: Nitrogen Dioxide AM—highest arithmetic mean concentration; Nitrogen Dioxide 1-Hr—highest 98th percentile 1-hour daily maximum concentration; Sulfur Dioxide AM—highest annual mean concentration; Sulfur Dioxide 1-Hr—highest 99th percentile 1-hour daily maximum concentration; Sulfur Dioxide 24-Hr—highest second maximum 24-hour concentration
Source: U.S. Environmental Protection Agency, Air Quality Monitoring Information, "Air Quality Statistics by City, 2020"

Riverside, California

Background

The city of Riverside is in southern California in Riverside County. It is approximately 100 miles north of San Diego, on the banks of the Santa Ana River. The city is known for its agriculture and is considered by many to be the birthplace of the California citrus industry.

John W. North, a well-known pioneer from Tennessee who also founded the city of Northfield in Minnesota, founded Riverside in 1870, named for its location along the Santa Ana River. He envisioned Riverside as a place of culture and education and had the support of investors from both Canada and England. In 1871, a local woman named Eliza Tibbets received two Brazilian navel orange trees from a friend at the U.S. Department of Agriculture in Washington, D.C. Seemingly insignificant at the time, the trees thrived in the southern California climate, and the rest is history. By 1882, more than half a million citrus trees were planted in California, half of them in Riverside alone. Developments in irrigation and transportation, such as refrigerated railroad cars, also helped the industry to prosper.

The city's prosperity at the turn of the century led to the construction of the luxury hotels and resorts that made Riverside a popular destination for celebrities and wealthy tourists. One such hotel was the Glenwood Tavern, which later became the Mission Inn, modeled after the area's Spanish Mission. Today, the historic property is the upscale Mission Inn Hotel & Spa.

Riverside has always had relatively high populations of immigrants, especially from Mexico, China, Japan, and Korea. Many came to work the citrus harvest. In the days of Riverside's peak citrus production, immigrant communities sprung up along the railroad tracks on the outskirts of town, but today few remain. One of the city's most famous immigrants was Japanese-born Jukichi Harada who owned a restaurant in Riverside and, in 1915, purchased a home in the name of his American-born children so they would be eligible to attend the public schools. Residents protested that he violated the California Alien Land Law of 1913, which prohibited non-citizens from owning land. The case was heard by the California Supreme Court, which ruled in Harada's favor. The Harada house is now a National Historic Landmark and is owned by the Metropolitan Museum of Riverside.

The middle of the twentieth century saw the citrus industry partially give way to new commercial development. Urban shopping centers, industrial parks and residential communities replaced many original orange groves. In 2014, the city received state approval to sell or develop significant local properties as part of a Long-Range Property Management Plan affecting more than 80 parcels of land worth an estimated $5.9 million. Among the properties is the Stalder Building, Imperial Hardware, and Eastside Medical Center.

Riverside's economy consists largely of light industry and generates a wide range of products, including aircraft components, automotive parts, and electric equipment. American electronic company Bourns, Inc. is headquartered in the city. Several rail stations, Riverside Transit Agency's bus service, and the Riverside Municipal Airport serve the city.

Riverside is home to four institutions of higher learning: University of California Riverside, California Baptist University, La Sierra University and Riverside Community College. The University of California Riverside is also home to the UCR Botanic Gardens, which boasts three of the city's original orange trees and is a major tourist attraction. Other visitor hot spots include the Mission Inn and the Fox Theater, which hosted the first showing of *Gone With the Wind.* The heavily attended Riverside International Film Festival, established in 2002, is returning to a five-day in-person event, after a two-year COVID hiatus.

Riverside has a warm, dry climate that is appreciated by residents and citrus growers alike. Although summer days are generally very hot, low humidity prevents high temperatures from feeling oppressive. Evening temperatures are generally mild and often accompanied by a cool breeze. The city records most of its annual rainfall between September and April.

Rankings

General Rankings

- In their eigth annual survey, Livability.com looked at data for more than 1,000 small to mid-sized U.S. cities to determine the rankings for Livability's "Top 100 Best Places to Live" in 2021. Riverside ranked #82. Criteria: housing and economy; sustainability; social and civic engagement; education; demographics; health care options; transportation & infrastructure; and community amenities. *Livability.com, "Top 100 Best Places to Live 2021" October 12, 2021*

Business/Finance Rankings

- The Brookings Institution ranked the nation's largest cities based on income inequality. Riverside was ranked #89 (#1 = greatest inequality). Criteria: the "95/20 ratio," a figure representing the income at which a household earns more than 95 percent of all other households, divided by the income at which a household earns more than only 20 percent of all other households. *Brookings Institution, "Household Income Inequality, Largest Cities of 97 Large U.S. Metro Areas, 2014-2016," February 5, 2018*
- The Brookings Institution ranked the 100 largest metro areas in the U.S. based on income inequality. Riverside was ranked #68 (#1 = greatest inequality). Criteria: the "95/20 ratio," a figure representing the income at which a household earns more than 95 percent of all other households, divided by the income at which a household earns more than only 20 percent of all other households. *Brookings Institution, "Household Income Inequality, 100 Largest U.S. Metro Areas, 2014-2016," February 5, 2018*
- The Riverside metro area was identified as one of the most debt-ridden places in America by the finance site Credit.com. The metro area was ranked #25. Criteria: residents' average credit card debt as well as median income. *Credit.com, "25 Cities With the Most Credit Card Debt," February 28, 2018*
- The Riverside metro area appeared on the Milken Institute "2021 Best Performing Cities" list. Rank: #36 out of 200 large metro areas (population over 250,000). Criteria: job growth; wage and salary growth; high-tech output growth; housing affordability; household broadband access. *Milken Institute, "Best-Performing Cities 2021," February 16, 2021*
- *Forbes* ranked the 200 most populous metro areas to determine the nation's "Best Places for Business and Careers." The Riverside metro area was ranked #72. Criteria: costs (business and living); job growth (past and projected); income growth; quality of life; educational attainment (college and high school); projected economic growth; cultural and leisure opportunities; workplace tolerance laws; net migration patterns. *Forbes, "The Best Places for Business and Careers 2019: Seattle Still On Top," October 30, 2019*

Children/Family Rankings

- Riverside was selected as one of the most playful cities in the U.S. by KaBOOM! The organization's Playful City USA initiative honors cities and towns across the nation that have made their communities more playable. Criteria: pledging to integrate play as a solution to challenges in their communities; making it easy for children to get active and balanced play; creating more family-friendly and innovative communities as a result. *KaBOOM! National Campaign for Play, "2017 Playful City USA Communities"*

Education Rankings

- Personal finance website *WalletHub* analyzed the 150 largest U.S. metropolitan statistical areas to determine where the most educated Americans are putting their degrees to work. Criteria: education levels; percentage of workers with degrees; education quality and attainment gap; public school quality rankings; quality and enrollment of each metro area's universities. Riverside was ranked #137 (#1 = most educated city). *www.WalletHub.com, "Most & Least Educated Cities in America," July 19, 2021*
- Riverside was selected as one of America's most literate cities. The city ranked #61 out of the 84 largest U.S. cities. Criteria: number of booksellers; library resources; Internet resources; educational attainment; periodical publishing resources; newspaper circulation. *Central Connecticut State University, "America's Most Literate Cities, 2018," February 2019*

Environmental Rankings

- The U.S. Environmental Protection Agency (EPA) released its list of U.S. metropolitan areas with the most ENERGY STAR certified buildings in 2020. The Riverside metro area was ranked #13 out of 25. *U.S. Environmental Protection Agency, "2021 Energy Star Top Cities," June 15, 2021*

Health/Fitness Rankings

- For each of the 100 largest cities in the United States, the American Fitness Index®, published by the American College of Sports Medicine and the Anthem Foundation, evaluated community infrastructure and 34 health behaviors including preventive health, levels of chronic disease conditions, food insecurity, sleep quality, pedestrian safety, air quality, and community resources that support physical activity. Riverside ranked #73 for "community fitness." *americanfitnessindex.org, "2021 ACSM American Fitness Index Summary Report," July 13, 2021*
- Riverside was identified as a "2021 Spring Allergy Capital." The area ranked #28 out of 100. Three groups of factors were used to identify the most challenging cities for people with allergies during the spring season: annual spring pollen levels; over the counter medicine use; number of board-certified allergy specialists. *Asthma and Allergy Foundation of America, "Spring Allergy Capitals 2021," February 23, 2021*
- Riverside was identified as a "2021 Fall Allergy Capital." The area ranked #23 out of 100. Three groups of factors were used to identify the most challenging cities for people with allergies during the fall season: annual fall pollen levels; over the counter medicine use; number of board-certified allergy specialists. *Asthma and Allergy Foundation of America, "Fall Allergy Capitals 2021," February 23, 2021*
- Riverside was identified as a "2021 Asthma Capital." The area ranked #87 out of the nation's 100 largest metropolitan areas. Criteria: estimated asthma prevalence; asthma-related mortality; and ER visits due to asthma. Risk factors analyzed but not factored in the rankings: annual pollen score; annual air quality; public smoking laws; number of board-certified asthma specialists; rescue medication use; controller medication use; uninsured rate; poverty rate. *Asthma and Allergy Foundation of America, "Asthma Capitals 2021: The Most Challenging Places to Live With Asthma," May 5, 2021*

Real Estate Rankings

- *WalletHub* compared the most populated U.S. cities to determine which had the best markets for real estate agents. Riverside ranked #53 where demand was high and pay was the best. Criteria: sales per agent; annual median wage for real-estate agents; monthly average starting salary for real estate agents; real estate job density and competition; unemployment rate; home turnover rate; housing-market health index; and other relevant metrics. *www.WalletHub.com, "2021 Best Places to Be a Real Estate Agent," May 12, 2021*
- Riverside was ranked #10 in the top 20 out of the 100 largest metro areas in terms of house price appreciation in 2021 (#1 = highest rate). *Federal Housing Finance Agency, House Price Index, 4th Quarter 2021*
- Riverside was ranked #221 out of 237 metro areas in terms of housing affordability in 2021 by the National Association of Home Builders (#1 = most affordable). Criteria: the share of homes sold in that area affordable to a family earning the local median income, based on standard mortgage underwriting criteria. *National Association of Home Builders®, NAHB-Wells Fargo Housing Opportunity Index, 4th Quarter 2021*

Safety Rankings

- Allstate ranked the 200 largest cities in America in terms of driver safety. Riverside ranked #134. Criteria: internal property damage claims over a two-year period from January 2016 to December 2017. The report helps increase the importance of safety and awareness behind the wheel. *Allstate, "Allstate America's Best Drivers Report, 2019" June 24, 2019*
- The National Insurance Crime Bureau ranked 390 metro areas in the U.S. in terms of per capita rates of vehicle theft. The Riverside metro area ranked #17 (#1 = highest rate). Criteria: number of vehicle theft offenses per 100,000 inhabitants in 2020. *National Insurance Crime Bureau, "Hot Spots 2020," August 31, 2021*

Seniors/Retirement Rankings

- From its Best Cities for Successful Aging indexes, the Milken Institute generated rankings for metropolitan areas, weighing data in nine categories—health care, wellness, living arrangements, transportation and convenience, financial characteristics, education, employment, community engagement, and overall livability. The Riverside metro area was ranked #100 overall in the large metro area category. *Milken Institute, "Best Cities for Successful Aging, 2017" March 14, 2017*

Sports/Recreation Rankings

- Riverside was chosen as a bicycle friendly community by the League of American Bicyclists. A "Bicycle Friendly Community" welcomes cyclists by providing safe and supportive accommodation for cycling and encouraging people to bike for transportation and recreation. There are five award levels: Diamond; Platinum; Gold; Silver; and Bronze. The community achieved an award level of Bronze. *League of American Bicyclists, "Fall 2021 Awards-New & Renewing Bicycle Friendly Communities List," December 8, 2021*

Women/Minorities Rankings

- Personal finance website *WalletHub* compared more than 180 U.S. cities across two key dimensions, "Hispanic Business-Friendliness" and "Hispanic Purchasing Power," to arrive at the most favorable conditions for Hispanic entrepreneurs. Riverside was ranked #74 out of 182. Criteria includes: share of Hispanic-Owned Businesses; Hispanic entrepreneurship rate to median annual income of Hispanics; Small Business-Friendliness score; cost of living; and number of Hispanics with at least a bachelor's degree. *WalletHub.com, "2019's Best Cities for Hispanic Entrepreneurs," May 1, 2019*

Miscellaneous Rankings

- Riverside was selected as a 2021 Digital Cities Survey winner. The city ranked #6 in the large city (250,000 to 499,999 population) category. The survey examined and assessed how city governments are utilizing technology to continue innovation, engage with residents, and persevere through the challenges of the pandemic. Survey questions focused on ten initiatives: cybersecurity; citizen experience; disaster recovery; business intelligence; IT personnel; data governance; budget control; IT governance; infrastructure modernization; and broadband connectivity. *Center for Digital Government, "2021 Digital Cities Survey," November 16, 2021*
- The financial planning site SmartAsset has compiled its annual study on the best places for Halloween in the U.S. for 2021. 210 cities were compared to determine that Riverside ranked #35 out of 35 for still being able to enjoy the festivities despite the COVID-19 pandemic. Metrics included: safety, family-friendliness, percentage of children in the population, concentration of candy and costume shops, weather and COVID infection rates. *www.smartasset.com, "2021 Edition-Best Places to Celebrate Halloween," October 20, 2021*
- *WalletHub* compared the 150 most populated U.S. cities to determine their operating efficiency. A "Quality of City Services" score was constructed for each city and then divided by the total budget per capita to reveal which were managed the best. Riverside ranked #123. Criteria: financial stability; economy; education; safety; health; infrastructure and pollution. *www.WalletHub.com, "2021's Best- & Worst-Run Cities in America," June 22, 2021*
- The National Alliance to End Homelessness listed the 25 most populous metro areas with the highest rate of homelessness. The Riverside metro area had a high rate of homelessness. Criteria: number of homeless people per 10,000 population in 2016. *National Alliance to End Homelessness, "Homelessness in the 25 Most Populous U.S. Metro Areas," September 1, 2017*

Business Environment

DEMOGRAPHICS

Population Growth

Area	1990 Census	2000 Census	2010 Census	2020* Estimate	Population Growth (%) 1990-2020	2010-2020
City	226,232	255,166	303,871	327,569	44.8	7.8
MSA[1]	2,588,793	3,254,821	4,224,851	4,600,396	77.7	8.9
U.S.	248,709,873	281,421,906	308,745,538	326,569,308	31.3	5.8

Note: (1) Figures cover the Riverside-San Bernardino-Ontario, CA Metropolitan Statistical Area; (*) 2016-2020 5-year estimated population
Source: U.S. Census Bureau, 1990 Census, Census 2000, Census 2010, 2016-2020 American Community Survey 5-Year Estimates

Household Size

Area	Persons in Household (%) One	Two	Three	Four	Five	Six	Seven or More	Average Household Size
City	18.9	27.4	18.2	16.4	10.2	5.0	3.8	3.40
MSA[1]	19.9	28.4	16.6	16.4	10.1	4.8	3.8	3.30
U.S.	28.0	33.9	15.5	12.9	6.0	2.3	1.4	2.60

Note: (1) Figures cover the Riverside-San Bernardino-Ontario, CA Metropolitan Statistical Area
Source: U.S. Census Bureau, 2016-2020 American Community Survey 5-Year Estimates

Race

Area	White Alone[2] (%)	Black Alone[2] (%)	Asian Alone[2] (%)	AIAN[3] Alone[2] (%)	NHOPI[4] Alone[2] (%)	Other Race Alone[2] (%)	Two or More Races (%)
City	52.8	5.9	8.7	0.8	0.3	24.1	7.3
MSA[1]	55.9	7.3	7.1	0.8	0.3	20.1	8.5
U.S.	70.4	12.6	5.6	0.8	0.2	5.1	5.2

Note: (1) Figures cover the Riverside-San Bernardino-Ontario, CA Metropolitan Statistical Area; (2) Alone is defined as not being in combination with one or more other races; (3) American Indian and Alaska Native; (4) Native Hawaiian and Other Pacific Islander
Source: U.S. Census Bureau, 2016-2020 American Community Survey 5-Year Estimates

Hispanic or Latino Origin

Area	Total (%)	Mexican (%)	Puerto Rican (%)	Cuban (%)	Other (%)
City	53.6	46.2	0.9	0.3	6.2
MSA[1]	51.5	44.5	0.8	0.4	5.8
U.S.	18.2	11.2	1.7	0.7	4.5

Note: Persons of Hispanic or Latino origin can be of any race; (1) Figures cover the Riverside-San Bernardino-Ontario, CA Metropolitan Statistical Area
Source: U.S. Census Bureau, 2016-2020 American Community Survey 5-Year Estimates

Ancestry

Area	German	Irish	English	American	Italian	Polish	French[2]	Scottish	Dutch
City	5.8	4.9	4.5	3.3	3.0	1.0	1.3	0.8	0.7
MSA[1]	6.8	5.4	4.8	2.7	3.0	0.9	1.5	1.0	0.9
U.S.	13.0	9.7	7.7	5.9	5.1	2.7	2.3	1.6	1.1

Note: Figures are the percentage of the total population reporting a particular ancestry. The nine most commonly reported ancestries in the U.S. are shown. Figures include multiple ancestries (e.g. if a person reported being Irish and Italian, they were included in both columns); (1) Figures cover the Riverside-San Bernardino-Ontario, CA Metropolitan Statistical Area; (2) Excludes Basque
Source: U.S. Census Bureau, 2016-2020 American Community Survey 5-Year Estimates

Foreign-born Population

Area	Percent of Population Born in: Any Foreign Country	Asia	Mexico	Europe	Caribbean	Central America[2]	South America	Africa	Canada
City	22.7	5.7	12.5	0.8	0.2	1.9	0.8	0.5	0.2
MSA[1]	21.1	4.9	12.1	0.9	0.2	1.6	0.6	0.4	0.3
U.S.	13.5	4.2	3.3	1.5	1.3	1.1	1.0	0.7	0.3

Note: (1) Figures cover the Riverside-San Bernardino-Ontario, CA Metropolitan Statistical Area; (2) Excludes Mexico.
Source: U.S. Census Bureau, 2016-2020 American Community Survey 5-Year Estimates

Marital Status

Area	Never Married	Now Married[2]	Separated	Widowed	Divorced
City	42.6	42.0	2.2	4.5	8.6
MSA[1]	36.1	47.3	2.2	4.9	9.5
U.S.	33.5	48.1	1.8	5.7	10.8

Note: Figures are percentages and cover the population 15 years of age and older; (1) Figures cover the Riverside-San Bernardino-Ontario, CA Metropolitan Statistical Area; (2) Excludes separated
Source: U.S. Census Bureau, 2016-2020 American Community Survey 5-Year Estimates

Disability by Age

Area	All Ages	Under 18 Years Old	18 to 64 Years Old	65 Years and Over
City	11.2	4.2	8.7	41.6
MSA[1]	11.5	4.0	9.1	37.6
U.S.	12.7	4.3	10.3	34.0

Note: Figures show percent of the civilian noninstitutionalized population that reported having a disability. Disability status is determined from six types of difficulty: vision, hearing, cognitive, ambulatory, self-care, and independent living. For children under 5 years old, hearing and vision difficulty are used to determine disability status. For children between the ages of 5 and 14, disability status is determined from hearing, vision, cognitive, ambulatory, and self-care difficulties. For people aged 15 years and older, they are considered to have a disability if they have difficulty with any one of the six difficulty types; Note: (1) Figures cover the Riverside-San Bernardino-Ontario, CA Metropolitan Statistical Area
Source: U.S. Census Bureau, 2016-2020 American Community Survey 5-Year Estimates

Age

Area	Percent of Population									Median Age
	Under Age 5	Age 5–19	Age 20–34	Age 35–44	Age 45–54	Age 55–64	Age 65–74	Age 75–84	Age 85+	
City	6.1	22.5	25.8	12.8	11.7	10.0	6.6	3.1	1.4	31.8
MSA[1]	6.7	21.9	21.8	12.9	12.3	11.3	7.7	3.9	1.5	34.8
U.S.	6.0	19.1	20.6	12.7	12.7	12.9	9.4	4.7	2.0	38.2

Note: (1) Figures cover the Riverside-San Bernardino-Ontario, CA Metropolitan Statistical Area
Source: U.S. Census Bureau, 2016-2020 American Community Survey 5-Year Estimates

Gender

Area	Males	Females	Males per 100 Females
City	163,233	164,336	99.3
MSA[1]	2,291,834	2,308,562	99.3
U.S.	160,818,530	165,750,778	97.0

Note: (1) Figures cover the Riverside-San Bernardino-Ontario, CA Metropolitan Statistical Area
Source: U.S. Census Bureau, 2016-2020 American Community Survey 5-Year Estimates

Religious Groups by Family

Area	Catholic	Baptist	Non-Den.	Methodist[2]	Lutheran	LDS[3]	Pente-costal	Presby-terian[4]	Muslim[5]	Judaism
MSA[1]	24.8	2.6	5.5	0.6	0.5	2.5	1.6	0.6	0.6	0.1
U.S.	19.1	9.3	4.0	4.0	2.3	2.0	1.9	1.6	0.8	0.7

Note: Figures are the number of adherents as a percentage of the total population; (1) Figures cover the Riverside-San Bernardino-Ontario, CA Metropolitan Statistical Area; (2) Methodist/Pietist; (3) Latter Day Saints; (4) Reformed; (5) Figures are estimates
Source: Association of Statisticians of American Religious Bodies, 2010 U.S. Religion Census: Religious Congregations & Membership Study

Religious Groups by Tradition

Area	Catholic	Evangelical Protestant	Mainline Protestant	Other Tradition	Black Protestant	Orthodox
MSA[1]	24.8	11.5	1.3	3.7	0.8	0.2
U.S.	19.1	16.2	7.3	4.3	1.6	0.3

Note: Figures are the number of adherents as a percentage of the total population; (1) Figures cover the Riverside-San Bernardino-Ontario, CA Metropolitan Statistical Area
Source: Association of Statisticians of American Religious Bodies, 2010 U.S. Religion Census: Religious Congregations & Membership Study

ECONOMY

Gross Metropolitan Product

Area	2017	2018	2019	2020	Rank[2]
MSA[1]	161.6	171.0	178.3	186.9	22

Note: Figures are in billions of dollars; (1) Figures cover the Riverside-San Bernardino-Ontario, CA Metropolitan Statistical Area; (2) Rank is based on 2018 data and ranges from 1 to 381
Source: U.S. Conference of Mayors, U.S. Metro Economies: GMP & Employment 2018-2020, September 2019

Economic Growth

Area	2015-17 (%)	2018 (%)	2019 (%)	2020 (%)	Rank[2]
MSA[1]	3.0	3.4	2.3	2.6	65
U.S.	1.9	2.9	2.3	2.1	–

Note: Figures are real gross metropolitan product (GMP) growth rates and represent average annual percent change; (1) Figures cover the Riverside-San Bernardino-Ontario, CA Metropolitan Statistical Area; (2) Rank is based on 2017 2-year average annual percent change and ranges from 1 to 381
Source: U.S. Conference of Mayors, U.S. Metro Economies: GMP & Employment 2018-2020, September 2019

Metropolitan Area Exports

Area	2015	2016	2017	2018	2019	2020	Rank[2]
MSA[1]	8,970.0	10,211.6	8,782.3	9,745.7	9,737.6	8,459.8	35

Note: Figures are in millions of dollars; (1) Figures cover the Riverside-San Bernardino-Ontario, CA Metropolitan Statistical Area; (2) Rank is based on 2020 data and ranges from 1 to 389
Source: U.S. Department of Commerce, International Trade Administration, Office of Trade and Economic Analysis, Industry and Analysis, Exports by Metropolitan Area, data extracted March 4, 2022

Building Permits

Area	Single-Family			Multi-Family			Total		
	2019	2020	Pct. Chg.	2019	2020	Pct. Chg.	2019	2020	Pct. Chg.
City	170	180	5.9	509	164	-67.8	679	344	-49.3
MSA[1]	11,147	12,897	15.7	3,452	2,335	-32.4	14,599	15,232	4.3
U.S.	862,100	979,400	13.6	523,900	491,700	-6.1	1,386,000	1,471,100	6.1

Note: (1) Figures cover the Riverside-San Bernardino-Ontario, CA Metropolitan Statistical Area; Figures represent new, privately-owned housing units authorized (unadjusted data); All permit data are based on estimates with imputation
Source: U.S. Census Bureau, Manufacturing, Mining, and Construction Statistics, Building Permits, 2019, 2020

Bankruptcy Filings

Area	Business Filings			Nonbusiness Filings		
	2020	2021	% Chg.	2020	2021	% Chg.
Riverside County	145	105	-27.6	4,455	3,583	-19.6
U.S.	21,655	14,347	-33.7	522,808	399,269	-23.6

Note: Business filings include Chapter 7, Chapter 9, Chapter 11, Chapter 12, Chapter 13, Chapter 15, and Section 304; Nonbusiness filings include Chapter 7, Chapter 11, and Chapter 13
Source: Administrative Office of the U.S. Courts, Business and Nonbusiness Bankruptcy, County Cases Commenced by Chapter of the Bankruptcy Code, During the 12-Month Period Ending December 31, 2020 and Business and Nonbusiness Bankruptcy, County Cases Commenced by Chapter of the Bankruptcy Code, During the 12-Month Period Ending December 31, 2021

Housing Vacancy Rates

Area	Gross Vacancy Rate[2] (%)			Year-Round Vacancy Rate[3] (%)			Rental Vacancy Rate[4] (%)			Homeowner Vacancy Rate[5] (%)		
	2019	2020	2021	2019	2020	2021	2019	2020	2021	2019	2020	2021
MSA[1]	14.9	11.8	10.9	9.6	7.5	6.6	4.5	4.4	3.1	1.7	0.8	0.8
U.S.	12.0	10.6	10.8	9.5	8.2	8.4	6.7	6.3	6.1	1.4	1.0	0.9

Note: (1) Figures cover the Riverside-San Bernardino-Ontario, CA Metropolitan Statistical Area; (2) The percentage of the total housing inventory that is vacant; (3) The percentage of the housing inventory (excluding seasonal units) that is year-round vacant; (4) The percentage of rental inventory that is vacant for rent; (5) The percentage of homeowner inventory that is vacant for sale
Source: U.S. Census Bureau, Housing Vacancies and Homeownership Annual Statistics: 2019, 2020, 2021

INCOME

Income

Area	Per Capita ($)	Median Household ($)	Average Household ($)
City	27,144	72,738	90,520
MSA[1]	28,263	68,331	89,733
U.S.	35,384	64,994	91,547

Note: (1) Figures cover the Riverside-San Bernardino-Ontario, CA Metropolitan Statistical Area
Source: U.S. Census Bureau, 2016-2020 American Community Survey 5-Year Estimates

Household Income Distribution

Area	Percent of Households Earning							
	Under $15,000	$15,000 -$24,999	$25,000 -$34,999	$35,000 -$49,999	$50,000 -$74,999	$75,000 -$99,999	$100,000 -$149,999	$150,000 and up
City	8.3	7.0	8.0	11.0	17.3	13.8	19.0	15.6
MSA[1]	8.9	8.0	8.2	11.6	17.6	13.3	17.0	15.4
U.S.	9.9	8.5	8.6	12.0	17.2	12.8	15.6	15.4

Note: (1) Figures cover the Riverside-San Bernardino-Ontario, CA Metropolitan Statistical Area
Source: U.S. Census Bureau, 2016-2020 American Community Survey 5-Year Estimates

Poverty Rate

Area	All Ages	Under 18 Years Old	18 to 64 Years Old	65 Years and Over
City	13.2	16.0	12.7	10.4
MSA[1]	13.7	18.5	12.3	10.7
U.S.	12.8	17.5	12.1	9.3

Note: Figures are percentage of people whose income during the past 12 months was below the poverty level; (1) Figures cover the Riverside-San Bernardino-Ontario, CA Metropolitan Statistical Area
Source: U.S. Census Bureau, 2016-2020 American Community Survey 5-Year Estimates

CITY FINANCES

City Government Finances

Component	2019 ($000)	2019 ($ per capita)
Total Revenues	948,599	2,894
Total Expenditures	873,703	2,666
Debt Outstanding	1,867,534	5,698
Cash and Securities[1]	290,239	886

Note: (1) Cash and security holdings of a government at the close of its fiscal year, including those of its dependent agencies, utilities, and liquor stores.
Source: U.S. Census Bureau, State & Local Government Finances 2019

City Government Revenue by Source

Source	2019 ($000)	2019 ($ per capita)	2019 (%)
General Revenue			
From Federal Government	12,711	39	1.3
From State Government	31,850	97	3.4
From Local Governments	527	2	0.1
Taxes			
Property	65,315	199	6.9
Sales and Gross Receipts	177,485	542	18.7
Personal Income	0	0	0.0
Corporate Income	0	0	0.0
Motor Vehicle License	0	0	0.0
Other Taxes	18,441	56	1.9
Current Charges	137,153	418	14.5
Liquor Store	0	0	0.0
Utility	429,186	1,310	45.2

Source: U.S. Census Bureau, State & Local Government Finances 2019

City Government Expenditures by Function

Function	2019 ($000)	2019 ($ per capita)	2019 (%)
General Direct Expenditures			
Air Transportation	1,255	3	0.1
Corrections	0	0	0.0
Education	0	0	0.0
Employment Security Administration	0	0	0.0
Financial Administration	5,058	15	0.6
Fire Protection	65,913	201	7.5
General Public Buildings	0	0	0.0
Governmental Administration, Other	14,139	43	1.6
Health	4,599	14	0.5
Highways	19,257	58	2.2
Hospitals	0	0	0.0
Housing and Community Development	10,900	33	1.2
Interest on General Debt	53,150	162	6.1
Judicial and Legal	0	0	0.0
Libraries	7,931	24	0.9
Parking	3,557	10	0.4
Parks and Recreation	41,192	125	4.7
Police Protection	110,941	338	12.7
Public Welfare	0	0	0.0
Sewerage	62,773	191	7.2
Solid Waste Management	23,051	70	2.6
Veterans' Services	0	0	0.0
Liquor Store	0	0	0.0
Utility	417,700	1,274	47.8

Source: U.S. Census Bureau, State & Local Government Finances 2019

EMPLOYMENT

Labor Force and Employment

Area	Civilian Labor Force			Workers Employed		
	Dec. 2020	Dec. 2021	% Chg.	Dec. 2020	Dec. 2021	% Chg.
City	155,946	157,686	1.1	143,359	150,678	5.1
MSA[1]	2,097,412	2,121,275	1.1	1,914,226	2,012,478	5.1
U.S.	160,017,000	161,696,000	1.0	149,613,000	155,732,000	4.1

Note: Data is not seasonally adjusted and covers workers 16 years of age and older; (1) Figures cover the Riverside-San Bernardino-Ontario, CA Metropolitan Statistical Area
Source: Bureau of Labor Statistics, Local Area Unemployment Statistics

Unemployment Rate

Area	2021											
	Jan.	Feb.	Mar.	Apr.	May	Jun.	Jul.	Aug.	Sep.	Oct.	Nov.	Dec.
City	7.9	7.5	7.0	6.9	6.6	7.4	7.2	6.8	5.8	5.4	4.7	4.4
MSA[1]	8.6	8.1	7.7	7.5	7.2	8.0	7.9	7.6	6.6	6.3	5.4	5.1
U.S.	6.8	6.6	6.2	5.7	5.5	6.1	5.7	5.3	4.6	4.3	3.9	3.7

Note: Data is not seasonally adjusted and covers workers 16 years of age and older; (1) Figures cover the Riverside-San Bernardino-Ontario, CA Metropolitan Statistical Area
Source: Bureau of Labor Statistics, Local Area Unemployment Statistics

Average Wages

Occupation	$/Hr.	Occupation	$/Hr.
Accountants and Auditors	38.52	Maintenance and Repair Workers	23.19
Automotive Mechanics	25.03	Marketing Managers	63.83
Bookkeepers	22.34	Network and Computer Systems Admin.	43.39
Carpenters	28.56	Nurses, Licensed Practical	28.97
Cashiers	14.92	Nurses, Registered	53.70
Computer Programmers	42.54	Nursing Assistants	17.39
Computer Systems Analysts	45.59	Office Clerks, General	19.41
Computer User Support Specialists	28.71	Physical Therapists	51.63
Construction Laborers	23.87	Physicians	81.89
Cooks, Restaurant	16.31	Plumbers, Pipefitters and Steamfitters	31.48
Customer Service Representatives	19.92	Police and Sheriff's Patrol Officers	46.85
Dentists	79.35	Postal Service Mail Carriers	26.31
Electricians	33.67	Real Estate Sales Agents	24.46
Engineers, Electrical	47.98	Retail Salespersons	16.43
Fast Food and Counter Workers	15.06	Sales Representatives, Technical/Scientific	49.34
Financial Managers	66.09	Secretaries, Exc. Legal/Medical/Executive	21.59
First-Line Supervisors of Office Workers	30.12	Security Guards	17.26
General and Operations Managers	53.12	Surgeons	n/a
Hairdressers/Cosmetologists	18.17	Teacher Assistants, Exc. Postsecondary*	18.60
Home Health and Personal Care Aides	14.59	Teachers, Secondary School, Exc. Sp. Ed.*	49.03
Janitors and Cleaners	17.66	Telemarketers	16.07
Landscaping/Groundskeeping Workers	17.93	Truck Drivers, Heavy/Tractor-Trailer	24.78
Lawyers	72.68	Truck Drivers, Light/Delivery Services	21.58
Maids and Housekeeping Cleaners	16.24	Waiters and Waitresses	15.69

Note: Wage data covers the Riverside-San Bernardino-Ontario, CA Metropolitan Statistical Area; (*) Hourly wages were calculated from annual wage data based on a 40 hour work week; n/a not available.
Source: Bureau of Labor Statistics, Metro Area Occupational Employment & Wage Estimates, May 2021

Employment by Industry

Sector	MSA[1]		U.S.
	Number of Employees	Percent of Total	Percent of Total
Construction	105,600	6.5	5.0
Education and Health Services	254,300	15.6	16.0
Financial Activities	45,900	2.8	5.9
Government	253,700	15.5	14.9
Information	9,900	0.6	1.9
Leisure and Hospitality	172,900	10.6	9.8
Manufacturing	96,200	5.9	8.4
Mining and Logging	1,300	0.1	0.4
Other Services	43,900	2.7	3.7
Professional and Business Services	170,900	10.5	14.6
Retail Trade	187,800	11.5	10.7
Transportation, Warehousing, and Utilities	222,500	13.6	4.8
Wholesale Trade	67,600	4.1	3.8

Note: Figures are non-farm employment as of December 2021. Figures are not seasonally adjusted and include workers 16 years of age and older; (1) Figures cover the Riverside-San Bernardino-Ontario, CA Metropolitan Statistical Area
Source: Bureau of Labor Statistics, Current Employment Statistics, Employment, Hours, and Earnings

Employment by Occupation

Occupation Classification	City (%)	MSA[1] (%)	U.S. (%)
Management, Business, Science, and Arts	30.2	30.7	39.5
Natural Resources, Construction, and Maintenance	9.5	10.6	8.7
Production, Transportation, and Material Moving	17.4	16.6	13.1
Sales and Office	23.0	22.7	21.3
Service	19.9	19.4	17.4

Note: Figures cover employed civilians 16 years of age and older; (1) Figures cover the Riverside-San Bernardino-Ontario, CA Metropolitan Statistical Area
Source: U.S. Census Bureau, 2016-2020 American Community Survey 5-Year Estimates

Occupations with Greatest Projected Employment Growth: 2021 – 2023

Occupation[1]	2021 Employment	2023 Projected Employment	Numeric Employment Change	Percent Employment Change
Fast Food and Counter Workers	383,500	457,000	73,500	19.2
Home Health and Personal Care Aides	663,400	716,600	53,200	8.0
Waiters and Waitresses	208,500	257,600	49,100	23.5
Cooks, Restaurant	136,700	175,300	38,600	28.2
Laborers and Freight, Stock, and Material Movers, Hand	401,500	431,600	30,100	7.5
Software Developers and Software Quality Assurance Analysts and Testers	311,600	336,800	25,200	8.1
Janitors and Cleaners, Except Maids and Housekeeping Cleaners	232,200	252,400	20,200	8.7
Cooks, Fast Food	109,600	128,200	18,600	17.0
Stockers and Order Fillers	273,000	290,400	17,400	6.4
First-Line Supervisors of Food Preparation and Serving Workers	81,700	98,600	16,900	20.7

Note: Projections cover California; (1) Sorted by numeric employment change
Source: www.projectionscentral.com, State Occupational Projections, 2021–2023 Short-Term Projections

Fastest-Growing Occupations: 2021 – 2023

Occupation[1]	2021 Employment	2023 Projected Employment	Numeric Employment Change	Percent Employment Change
Manicurists and Pedicurists	23,400	33,500	10,100	43.2
Cooks, All Other	3,900	5,400	1,500	38.5
Miscellaneous Entertainers and Performers, Sports and Related Workers	5,900	8,100	2,200	37.3
Barbers	1,900	2,600	700	36.8
Gaming Change Persons and Booth Cashiers	2,200	3,000	800	36.4
Gaming Service Workers, All Other	1,400	1,900	500	35.7
Gaming Dealers	12,200	16,500	4,300	35.2
First-Line Supervisors of Gambling Services Workers	2,900	3,900	1,000	34.5
Massage Therapists	18,000	24,200	6,200	34.4
Costume Attendants	1,500	2,000	500	33.3

Note: Projections cover California; (1) Sorted by percent employment change and excludes occupations with numeric employment change less than 50
Source: www.projectionscentral.com, State Occupational Projections, 2021–2023 Short-Term Projections

TAXES

State Corporate Income Tax Rates

State	Tax Rate (%)	Income Brackets ($)	Num. of Brackets	Financial Institution Tax Rate (%)[a]	Federal Income Tax Ded.
California	8.84 (b)	Flat rate	1	10.84 (b)	No

Note: Tax rates as of January 1, 2022; (a) Rates listed are the corporate income tax rate applied to financial institutions or excise taxes based on income. Some states have other taxes based upon the value of deposits or shares; (b) Minimum tax is $800 in California, $250 in District of Columbia, $50 in Arizona and North Dakota (banks), $400 ($100 banks) in Rhode Island, $200 per location in South Dakota (banks), $100 in Utah, $300 in Vermont.
Source: Federation of Tax Administrators, State Corporate Income Tax Rates, January 1, 2022

State Individual Income Tax Rates

State	Tax Rate (%)	Income Brackets ($)	Personal Exemptions ($)			Standard Ded. ($)	
			Single	Married	Depend.	Single	Married
California (a)	1.0 - 12.3 (g)	9,325 - 625,369 (b)	129	258	400 (c)	4,803	9,606 (a)

Note: Tax rates as of January 1, 2022; Local- and county-level taxes are not included; Federal income tax is not deductible on state income tax returns; (a) 19 states have statutory provision for automatically adjusting to the rate of inflation the dollar values of the income tax brackets, standard deductions, and/or personal exemptions. Michigan indexes the personal exemption only. Oregon does not index the income brackets for $125,000 and over; (b) For joint returns, taxes are twice the tax on half the couple's income; (c) The personal exemption takes the form of a tax credit instead of a deduction; (g) California imposes an additional 1% tax on taxable income over $1 million, making the maximum rate 13.3% over $1 million.
Source: Federation of Tax Administrators, State Individual Income Tax Rates, January 1, 2022

Various State Sales and Excise Tax Rates

State	State Sales Tax (%)	Gasoline[1] (¢/gal.)	Cigarette[2] ($/pack)	Spirits[3] ($/gal.)	Wine[4] ($/gal.)	Beer[5] ($/gal.)	Recreational Marijuana (%)
California	7.25	68.15	2.87	3.3	0.2	0.2	(c)

Note: All tax rates as of January 1, 2022; (1) The American Petroleum Institute has developed a methodology for determining the average tax rate on a gallon of fuel. Rates may include any of the following: excise taxes, environmental fees, storage tank fees, other fees or taxes, general sales tax, and local taxes; (2) The federal excise tax of $1.0066 per pack and local taxes are not included; (3) Rates are those applicable to off-premise sales of 40% alcohol by volume (a.b.v.) distilled spirits in 750ml containers. Local excise taxes are excluded; (4) Rates are those applicable to off-premise sales of 11% a.b.v. non-carbonated wine in 750ml containers; (5) Rates are those applicable to off-premise sales of 4.7% a.b.v. beer in 12 ounce containers; (c) 15% excise tax (levied on wholesale at average market rate); $10.08/oz. flowers & $3/oz. leaves cultivation tax; $1.41/oz fresh cannabis plant
Source: Tax Foundation, 2022 Facts & Figures: How Does Your State Compare?

State Business Tax Climate Index Rankings

State	Overall Rank	Corporate Tax Rank	Individual Income Tax Rank	Sales Tax Rank	Property Tax Rank	Unemployment Insurance Tax Rank
California	48	46	49	47	14	23

Note: The index is a measure of how each state's tax laws affect economic performance. The lower the rank, the more favorable a state's tax system is for business. States without a given tax are given a ranking of 1. The scores/rankings for the District of Columbia do not affect other states. The 2022 index represents the tax climate as of July 1, 2021.
Source: Tax Foundation, State Business Tax Climate Index 2022

TRANSPORTATION

Means of Transportation to Work

Area	Car/Truck/Van		Public Transportation			Bicycle	Walked	Other Means	Worked at Home
	Drove Alone	Car-pooled	Bus	Subway	Railroad				
City	76.1	12.0	1.6	0.0	0.8	0.6	2.5	1.1	5.3
MSA[1]	78.2	11.5	0.7	0.1	0.3	0.2	1.4	1.4	6.3
U.S.	74.9	8.9	2.2	1.7	0.5	0.5	2.6	1.4	7.3

Note: Figures are percentages and cover workers 16 years of age and older; (1) Figures cover the Riverside-San Bernardino-Ontario, CA Metropolitan Statistical Area
Source: U.S. Census Bureau, 2016-2020 American Community Survey 5-Year Estimates

Travel Time to Work

Area	Less Than 10 Minutes	10 to 19 Minutes	20 to 29 Minutes	30 to 44 Minutes	45 to 59 Minutes	60 to 89 Minutes	90 Minutes or More
City	8.4	26.1	18.9	22.4	7.8	10.1	6.4
MSA[1]	9.0	25.9	18.6	20.0	8.8	10.5	7.3
U.S.	12.3	28.4	20.9	20.9	8.3	6.4	2.9

Note: Note: Figures are percentages and include workers 16 years old and over; (1) Figures cover the Riverside-San Bernardino-Ontario, CA Metropolitan Statistical Area
Source: U.S. Census Bureau, 2016-2020 American Community Survey 5-Year Estimates

Key Congestion Measures

Measure	1990	2000	2010	2015	2020
Annual Hours of Delay, Total (000)	27,398	53,748	90,943	103,091	38,687
Annual Hours of Delay, Per Auto Commuter	30	46	58	66	25
Annual Congestion Cost, Per Auto Commuter ($)	629	927	1,247	1,305	511

Note: Covers the Riverside-San Bernardino CA urban area
Source: Texas A&M Transportation Institute, 2021 Urban Mobility Report

Freeway Travel Time Index

Measure	1985	1990	1995	2000	2005	2010	2015	2020
Urban Area Index[1]	1.13	1.17	1.21	1.26	1.32	1.31	1.33	1.08
Urban Area Rank[1,2]	19	17	16	13	8	11	11	44

Note: Freeway Travel Time Index—the ratio of travel time in the peak period to the travel time at free-flow conditions. For example, a value of 1.30 indicates a 20-minute free-flow trip takes 26 minutes in the peak (20 minutes x 1.30 = 26 minutes); (1) Covers the Riverside-San Bernardino CA urban area; (2) Rank is based on 101 larger urban areas (#1 = highest travel time index)
Source: Texas A&M Transportation Institute, 2021 Urban Mobility Report

Public Transportation

Agency Name / Mode of Transportation	Vehicles Operated in Maximum Service[1]	Annual Unlinked Passenger Trips[2] (in thous.)	Annual Passenger Miles[3] (in thous.)
City of Riverside Special Transportation (City of Riverside)			
Demand Response (directly operated)	23	97.1	702.5
Riverside Transit Agency (RTA)			
Bus (directly operated)	101	5,235.0	34,191.7
Bus (purchased transportation)	52	1,137.4	11,435.7
Commuter Bus (directly operated)	20	271.1	8,148.9
Commuter Bus (purchased transportation)	12	50.0	1,342.3
Demand Response (purchased transportation)	97	275.4	2,226.6
Demand Response - Taxi	16	8.3	98.6

Note: (1) Number of revenue vehicles operated by the given mode and type of service to meet the annual maximum service requirement. This is the revenue vehicle count during the peak season of the year; on the week and day that maximum service is provided. Vehicles operated in maximum service (VOMS) exclude atypical days and one-time special events; (2) Number of passengers who boarded public transportation vehicles. Passengers are counted each time they board a vehicle no matter how many vehicles they use to travel from their origin to their destination. (3) Sum of the distances ridden by all passengers during the entire fiscal year.
Source: Federal Transit Administration, National Transit Database, 2020

Air Transportation

Airport Name and Code / Type of Service	Passenger Airlines[1]	Passenger Enplanements	Freight Carriers[2]	Freight (lbs)
Ontario International (ONT)				
Domestic service (U.S. carriers - 2021)	20	2,169,923	21	971,977,494
International service (U.S. carriers - 2020)	1	7	4	435,013

Note: (1) Includes all U.S.-based major, minor and commuter airlines that carried at least one passenger during the year; (2) Includes all U.S.-based airlines and freight carriers that transported at least one pound of freight during the year.
Source: Bureau of Transportation Statistics, The Intermodal Transportation Database, Air Carriers: T-100 Domestic Market (U.S. Carriers), 2021; Bureau of Transportation Statistics, The Intermodal Transportation Database, Air Carriers: T-100 International Market (U.S. Carriers), 2020

BUSINESSES

Major Business Headquarters

Company Name	Industry	Rankings	
		Fortune[1]	Forbes[2]
No companies listed	-	-	-

Note: (1) Companies that produce a 10-K are ranked 1 to 500 based on 2020 revenue; (2) All private companies with at least $2 billion in annual revenue through the end of their most current fiscal year are ranked 1 to 225; companies listed are headquartered in the city; dashes indicate no ranking
Source: Fortune, "Fortune 500," 2021; Forbes, "America's Largest Private Companies," 2021

Living Environment

COST OF LIVING

Cost of Living Index

Composite Index	Groceries	Housing	Utilities	Trans-portation	Health Care	Misc. Goods/ Services
n/a	n/a	n/a	n/a	n/a	n/a	n/a

Note: The Cost of Living Index measures regional differences in the cost of consumer goods and services, excluding taxes and non-consumer expenditures, for professional and managerial households in the top income quintile. It is based on more than 50,000 prices covering almost 60 different items for which prices are collected three times a year by chambers of commerce, economic development organizations or university applied economic centers in each participating urban area. The numbers shown should be read as a percentage above or below the national average of 100. For example, a value of 115.4 in the groceries column indicates that grocery prices are 15.4% higher than the national average. Small differences in the index numbers should not be interpreted as significant; n/a not available.
Source: The Council for Community and Economic Research, Cost of Living Index, 2021

Grocery Prices

Area[1]	T-Bone Steak ($/pound)	Frying Chicken ($/pound)	Whole Milk ($/half gal.)	Eggs ($/dozen)	Orange Juice ($/64 oz.)	Coffee ($/11.5 oz.)
City[2]	n/a	n/a	n/a	n/a	n/a	n/a
Avg.	12.82	1.40	2.22	1.57	3.59	4.30
Min.	8.91	0.91	1.29	0.75	2.87	3.02
Max.	21.35	2.69	3.92	3.86	5.49	8.11

Note: (1) Values for the local area are compared with the average, minimum and maximum values for all 285 areas in the Cost of Living Index; (2) Figures cover the Riverside CA urban area; n/a not available; ***T-Bone Steak*** *(price per pound);* ***Frying Chicken*** *(price per pound, whole fryer);* ***Whole Milk*** *(half gallon carton);* ***Eggs*** *(price per dozen, Grade A, large);* ***Orange Juice*** *(64 oz. Tropicana or Florida Natural);* ***Coffee*** *(11.5 oz. can, vacuum-packed, Maxwell House, Hills Bros, or Folgers).*
Source: The Council for Community and Economic Research, Cost of Living Index, 2021

Housing and Utility Costs

Area[1]	New Home Price ($)	Apartment Rent ($/month)	All Electric ($/month)	Part Electric ($/month)	Other Energy ($/month)	Telephone ($/month)
City[2]	n/a	n/a	n/a	n/a	n/a	n/a
Avg.	398,393	1,217	171.38	100.83	69.67	187.75
Min.	212,799	534	96.71	31.56	27.15	173.01
Max.	2,354,006	4,438	369.53	277.33	303.87	206.73

Note: (1) Values for the local area are compared with the average, minimum and maximum values for all 285 areas in the Cost of Living Index; (2) Figures cover the Riverside CA urban area; n/a not available; ***New Home Price*** *(2,400 sf living area, 8,000 sf lot, in urban area with full utilities);* ***Apartment Rent*** *(950 sf 2 bedroom/1.5 or 2 bath, unfurnished, excluding all utilities except water);* ***All Electric*** *(average monthly cost for an all-electric home);* ***Part Electric*** *(average monthly cost for a part-electric home);* ***Other Energy*** *(average monthly cost for natural gas, fuel oil, coal, wood, and any other forms of energy except electricity);* ***Telephone*** *(price includes the base monthly rate plus taxes and fees for three lines of mobile phone service).*
Source: The Council for Community and Economic Research, Cost of Living Index, 2021

Health Care, Transportation, and Other Costs

Area[1]	Doctor ($/visit)	Dentist ($/visit)	Optometrist ($/visit)	Gasoline ($/gallon)	Beauty Salon ($/visit)	Men's Shirt ($)
City[2]	n/a	n/a	n/a	n/a	n/a	n/a
Avg.	118.16	101.04	109.44	2.71	40.63	30.77
Min.	35.04	55.56	51.17	2.17	18.59	11.32
Max.	231.10	165.12	256.81	4.11	85.33	63.03

Note: (1) Values for the local area are compared with the average, minimum and maximum values for all 285 areas in the Cost of Living Index; (2) Figures cover the Riverside CA urban area; n/a not available; ***Doctor*** *(general practitioners routine exam of an established patient);* ***Dentist*** *(adult teeth cleaning and periodic oral examination);* ***Optometrist*** *(full vision eye exam for established adult patient);* ***Gasoline*** *(one gallon regular unleaded, national brand, including all taxes, cash price at self-service pump if available);* ***Beauty Salon*** *(woman's shampoo, trim, and blow-dry);* ***Men's Shirt*** *(cotton/polyester dress shirt, pinpoint weave, long sleeves).*
Source: The Council for Community and Economic Research, Cost of Living Index, 2021

HOUSING

Homeownership Rate

Area	2013 (%)	2014 (%)	2015 (%)	2016 (%)	2017 (%)	2018 (%)	2019 (%)	2020 (%)	2021 (%)
MSA[1]	56.3	56.8	61.1	62.9	59.9	62.3	64.4	65.8	62.4
U.S.	65.1	64.5	63.7	63.4	63.9	64.4	64.6	66.6	65.5

Note: (1) Figures cover the Riverside-San Bernardino-Ontario, CA Metropolitan Statistical Area
Source: U.S. Census Bureau, Housing Vacancies and Homeownership Annual Statistics: 2013-2021

House Price Index (HPI)

Area	National Ranking[2]	Quarterly Change (%)	One-Year Change (%)	Five-Year Change (%)	Since 1991Q1 (%)
MSA[1]	31	4.57	24.04	57.79	235.21
U.S.[3]	–	3.33	17.54	54.45	258.04

Note: The HPI is a weighted repeat sales index. It measures average price changes in repeat sales or refinancings on the same properties. This information is obtained by reviewing repeat mortgage transactions on single-family properties whose mortgages have been purchased or securitized by Fannie Mae or Freddie Mac since January 1975; (1) Figures cover the Riverside-San Bernardino-Ontario, CA Metropolitan Statistical Area; (2) Rankings are based on annual percentage change for all metro areas containing at least 15,000 transactions over the last 10 years and ranges from 1 to 268; (3) figures based on a weighted average of Census Division estimates using a seasonally adjusted, purchase-only index; all figures are for the period ending December 31, 2021
Source: Federal Housing Finance Agency, Change in FHFA Metropolitan Area House Price Indexes, 2021Q4

Median Single-Family Home Prices

Area	2019	2020	2021p	Percent Change 2020 to 2021
MSA[1]	378.5	422.6	510.0	20.7
U.S. Average	274.6	300.2	353.4	17.7

Note: Figures are median sales prices of existing single-family homes in thousands of dollars; (p) preliminary; (1) Figures cover the Riverside-San Bernardino-Ontario, CA Metropolitan Statistical Area
Source: National Association of Realtors, Median Sales Price of Existing Single-Family Homes for Metropolitan Areas, 4th Quarter 2021

Qualifying Income Based on Median Sales Price of Existing Single-Family Homes

Area	With 5% Down ($)	With 10% Down ($)	With 20% Down ($)
MSA[1]	104,487	98,988	87,989
U.S. Average	70,699	66,978	59,536

Note: Figures are preliminary; Qualifying income is based on a mortgage rate of 3.13%. Monthly principal and interest payment is limited to 25% of income; (1) Figures cover the Riverside-San Bernardino-Ontario, CA Metropolitan Statistical Area
Source: National Association of Realtors, Qualifying Income Based on Median Sales Price of Existing Single-Family Homes for Metropolitan Areas, 4th Quarter 2021

Home Value Distribution

Area	Under $50,000	$50,000 -$99,999	$100,000 -$149,999	$150,000 -$199,999	$200,000 -$299,999	$300,000 -$499,999	$500,000 -$999,999	$1,000,000 or more
City	2.8	1.7	1.2	1.9	11.7	58.6	20.0	1.9
MSA[1]	4.7	3.3	3.3	5.5	18.8	42.7	19.6	2.2
U.S.	6.6	11.0	12.3	13.6	20.0	20.5	12.3	3.7

Note: Figures are percentages and cover owner-occupied housing units; (1) Figures cover the Riverside-San Bernardino-Ontario, CA Metropolitan Statistical Area
Source: U.S. Census Bureau, 2016-2020 American Community Survey 5-Year Estimates

Year Housing Structure Built

Area	2010 or Later	2000 -2009	1990 -1999	1980 -1989	1970 -1979	1960 -1969	1950 -1959	1940 -1949	Before 1940	Median Year
City	3.2	12.4	10.7	16.5	17.8	11.6	16.3	4.4	7.1	1976
MSA[1]	5.2	20.2	14.6	21.5	15.6	8.9	8.5	2.7	2.8	1985
U.S.	6.2	13.6	13.9	13.4	15.0	10.5	10.2	4.8	12.4	1978

Note: Figures are percentages except for Median Year; Note: (1) Figures cover the Riverside-San Bernardino-Ontario, CA Metropolitan Statistical Area
Source: U.S. Census Bureau, 2016-2020 American Community Survey 5-Year Estimates

Gross Monthly Rent

Area	Under $500	$500 -$999	$1,000 -$1,499	$1,500 -$1,999	$2,000 -$2,499	$2,500 -$2,999	$3,000 and up	Median ($)
City	3.0	13.2	36.1	31.0	13.0	2.2	1.5	1,466
MSA[1]	3.9	19.9	33.5	25.2	11.3	4.1	2.1	1,387
U.S.	8.9	34.3	30.2	14.9	6.2	2.6	2.8	1,096

Note: Figures are percentages except for Median; Gross rent is the contract rent plus the estimated average monthly cost of utilities (electricity, gas, and water and sewer) and fuels (oil, coal, kerosene, wood, etc.) if these are paid by the renter (or paid for the renter by someone else); (1) Figures cover the Riverside-San Bernardino-Ontario, CA Metropolitan Statistical Area
Source: U.S. Census Bureau, 2016-2020 American Community Survey 5-Year Estimates

HEALTH

Health Risk Factors

Category	MSA[1] (%)	U.S. (%)
Adults aged 18–64 who have any kind of health care coverage	n/a	86.8
Adults who reported being in good or better health	n/a	86.7
Adults who are current smokers	n/a	15.5
Adults who currently use chewing tobacco, snuff, or snus	n/a	3.7
Adults who are heavy drinkers[2]	n/a	6.7
Adults who are binge drinkers[3]	n/a	15.7
Adults who are overweight (BMI 25.0 - 29.9)	n/a	35.2
Adults who are obese (BMI 30.0 - 99.8)	n/a	31.9
Adults who participated in any physical activities in the past month	n/a	77.6
Adults who always or nearly always wears a seat belt	n/a	94.2

Note: (1) Figures for the Riverside-San Bernardino-Ontario, CA Metropolitan Statistical Area were not available.
(2) Heavy drinkers are classified as adult men having more than 14 drinks per week and adult women having more than 7 drinks per week; (3) Binge drinkers are classified as males having five or more drinks on one occasion or females having four or more drinks on one occasion
Source: Centers for Disease Control and Prevention, Behaviorial Risk Factor Surveillance System, SMART: Selected Metropolitan Area Risk Trends, 2020

Acute and Chronic Health Conditions

Category	MSA[1] (%)	U.S. (%)
Adults who have ever been told they had a heart attack	n/a	4.3
Adults who have ever been told they have angina or coronary heart disease	n/a	4.0
Adults who have ever been told they had a stroke	n/a	2.8
Adults who have ever been told they have asthma	n/a	14.2
Adults who have ever been told they have arthritis	n/a	24.5
Adults who have ever been told they have diabetes[2]	n/a	10.6
Adults who have ever been told they had skin cancer	n/a	6.4
Adults who have ever been told they had any other types of cancer	n/a	6.8
Adults who have ever been told they have COPD	n/a	6.2
Adults who have ever been told they have kidney disease	n/a	2.9
Adults who have ever been told they have a form of depression	n/a	19.6

Note: (1) Figures for the Riverside-San Bernardino-Ontario, CA Metropolitan Statistical Area were not available.
(2) Figures do not include pregnancy-related, borderline, or pre-diabetes
Source: Centers for Disease Control and Prevention, Behaviorial Risk Factor Surveillance System, SMART: Selected Metropolitan Area Risk Trends, 2020

Health Screening and Vaccination Rates

Category	MSA[1] (%)	U.S. (%)
Adults 50-75 who have had a blood stool test within the past year	n/a	9.3
Adults aged 65+ who have had flu shot within the past year	n/a	67.9
Adults aged 65+ who have ever had a pneumonia vaccination	n/a	72.2
Adults who have ever been tested for HIV	n/a	37.1
Women aged 21-65 who have had a pap test in the past three years	n/a	77.7
Men aged 40+ who have had a PSA test within the past two years	n/a	31.8
Women aged 40+ who have had a mammogram within the past two years	n/a	71.5

Note: (1) Figures for the Riverside-San Bernardino-Ontario, CA Metropolitan Statistical Area were not available.
Source: Centers for Disease Control and Prevention, Behaviorial Risk Factor Surveillance System, SMART: Selected Metropolitan Area Risk Trends, 2020

Disability Status

Category	MSA[1] (%)	U.S. (%)
Adults who reported being deaf	n/a	6.8
Are you blind or have serious difficulty seeing, even when wearing glasses?	n/a	4.7
Do you have difficulty doing errands alone?	n/a	6.3
Do you have difficulty dressing or bathing?	n/a	3.0
Do you have serious difficulty concentrating/remembering/making decisions?	n/a	10.8
Do you have serious difficulty walking or climbing stairs?	n/a	11.9

Note: (1) Figures for the Riverside-San Bernardino-Ontario, CA Metropolitan Statistical Area were not available.
Source: Centers for Disease Control and Prevention, Behaviorial Risk Factor Surveillance System, SMART: Selected Metropolitan Area Risk Trends, 2020

Mortality Rates for the Top 10 Causes of Death in the U.S.

ICD-10[a] Sub-Chapter	ICD-10[a] Code	Age-Adjusted Mortality Rate[1] per 100,000 population	
		County[2]	U.S.
Malignant neoplasms	C00-C97	136.7	146.4
Ischaemic heart diseases	I20-I25	106.5	90.2
Other forms of heart disease	I30-I51	41.4	51.9
Other degenerative diseases of the nervous system	G30-G31	45.2	39.7
Other external causes of accidental injury	W00-X59	29.9	38.7
Chronic lower respiratory diseases	J40-J47	38.8	38.1
Cerebrovascular diseases	I60-I69	36.8	37.6
Organic, including symptomatic, mental disorders	F01-F09	9.2	29.4
Hypertensive diseases	I10-I15	33.7	26.1
Diabetes mellitus	E10-E14	19.4	22.6

Note: (a) ICD-10 = International Classification of Diseases 10th Revision; (1) Mortality rates are a three-year average covering 2018-2020; (2) Figures cover Riverside County.
Source: Centers for Disease Control and Prevention, National Center for Health Statistics. Underlying Cause of Death 1999-2020 on CDC WONDER Online Database

Mortality Rates for Selected Causes of Death

ICD-10[a] Sub-Chapter	ICD-10[a] Code	Age-Adjusted Mortality Rate[1] per 100,000 population	
		County[2]	U.S.
Assault	X85-Y09	5.1	6.5
Diseases of the liver	K70-K76	15.8	15.3
Human immunodeficiency virus (HIV) disease	B20-B24	1.8	1.4
Influenza and pneumonia	J09-J18	13.0	13.4
Intentional self-harm	X60-X84	11.7	13.9
Malnutrition	E40-E46	1.1	2.9
Obesity and other hyperalimentation	E65-E68	2.3	2.4
Renal failure	N17-N19	9.9	12.5
Transport accidents	V01-V99	13.7	12.5
Viral hepatitis	B15-B19	1.2	1.0

Note: (a) ICD-10 = International Classification of Diseases 10th Revision; (1) Mortality rates are a three-year average covering 2018-2020; (2) Figures cover Riverside County; Data are suppressed when the data meet the criteria for confidentiality constraints; Mortality rates are flagged as unreliable when the rate would be calculated with a numerator of 20 or less.
Source: Centers for Disease Control and Prevention, National Center for Health Statistics. Underlying Cause of Death 1999-2020 on CDC WONDER Online Database

Health Insurance Coverage

Area	With Health Insurance	With Private Health Insurance	With Public Health Insurance	Without Health Insurance	Population Under Age 19 Without Health Insurance
City	91.0	59.7	38.0	9.0	3.9
MSA[1]	91.6	57.9	42.0	8.4	4.1
U.S.	91.3	68.1	35.3	8.7	5.2

Note: Figures are percentages that cover the civilian noninstitutionalized population; (1) Figures cover the Riverside-San Bernardino-Ontario, CA Metropolitan Statistical Area
Source: U.S. Census Bureau, 2016-2020 American Community Survey 5-Year Estimates

Number of Medical Professionals

Area	MDs[3]	DOs[3,4]	Dentists	Podiatrists	Chiropractors	Optometrists
County[1] (number)	3,213	376	1,332	66	416	314
County[1] (rate[2])	132.9	15.5	55.1	2.7	17.2	13.0
U.S. (rate[2])	285.1	23.0	71.1	6.2	28.2	17.0

06065
Note: Data as of 2020 unless noted; (1) Data covers Riverside County; (2) Rate per 100,000 population; (3) Data as of 2019 and includes all active, non-federal physicians; (4) Doctor of Osteopathic Medicine
Source: U.S. Department of Health and Human Services, Health Resources and Services Administration, Bureau of Health Professions, Area Resource File (ARF) 2020-2021

Best Hospitals

According to *U.S. News,* the Riverside-San Bernardino-Ontario, CA metro area is home to one of the best hospitals in the U.S.: **Loma Linda University Medical Center** (1 adult specialty). The hospital listed was nationally ranked in at least one of 15 adult or 10 pediatric specialties. Only 175 U.S. hospitals performed well enough to be nationally ranked in one or more specialties. Twenty hospitals in the U.S. made the Honor Roll. The Best Hospitals Honor Roll takes both the national rankings and the procedure and condition ratings into account. Hospitals received points if they were nationally ranked in one of the 15 adult specialties—the higher they ranked, the more points they got—and how many ratings of "high performing" they earned in the 17 procedures and conditions. *U.S. News Online, "America's Best Hospitals 2021-22"*

According to *U.S. News,* the Riverside-San Bernardino-Ontario, CA metro area is home to one of the best children's hospitals in the U.S.: **Loma Linda University Children's Hospital** (1 pediatric specialty). The hospital listed was highly ranked in at least one of 10 pediatric specialties. Ninety-two children's hospitals in the U.S. were nationally ranked in at least one specialty. Hospitals received points for being ranked in a specialty, and the 10 hospitals with the most points across the 10 specialties make up the Honor Roll. *U.S. News Online, "America's Best Children's Hospitals 2021-22"*

EDUCATION

Public School District Statistics

District Name	Schls	Pupils	Pupil/ Teacher Ratio	Minority Pupils[1] (%)	LEP/ELL[2] (%)	IEP[3] (%)
Riverside Unified	49	40,204	n/a	80.1	17.0	12.3

Note: Table includes school districts with 2,000 or more students; (1) Percentage of students that are not non-Hispanic white; (2) Percentage of students that are Limited English Proficient (LEP) or English Language Learners (ELL) (2018-19); (3) Percentage of students that have an Individualized Education Program (IEP).
Source: U.S. Department of Education, National Center for Education Statistics, Common Core of Data, Local Education Agency (School District) Universe Survey: School Year 2019-2020

Best High Schools

According to *U.S. News,* Riverside is home to one of the top 500 high schools in the U.S.: **Riverside Stem Academy** (#62). Nearly 18,000 public, magnet and charter schools were ranked based on their performance on state assessments and how well they prepare students for college. *U.S. News & World Report, "Best High Schools 2021"*

Highest Level of Education

Area	Less than H.S.	H.S. Diploma	Some College, No Deg.	Associate Degree	Bachelor's Degree	Master's Degree	Prof. School Degree	Doctorate Degree
City	18.4	26.5	23.0	7.9	14.2	6.7	1.5	1.7
MSA[1]	18.2	26.5	24.4	8.5	14.5	5.7	1.4	0.9
U.S.	11.5	26.7	20.3	8.6	20.2	9.1	2.2	1.5

Note: Figures cover persons age 25 and over; (1) Figures cover the Riverside-San Bernardino-Ontario, CA Metropolitan Statistical Area
Source: U.S. Census Bureau, 2016-2020 American Community Survey 5-Year Estimates

Educational Attainment by Race

Area	High School Graduate or Higher (%)					Bachelor's Degree or Higher (%)				
	Total	White	Black	Asian	Hisp.[2]	Total	White	Black	Asian	Hisp.[2]
City	81.6	85.7	90.8	88.7	69.9	24.1	25.1	28.9	52.0	12.8
MSA[1]	81.8	85.1	89.9	90.2	69.1	22.4	23.0	24.2	49.2	11.7
U.S.	88.5	90.7	86.7	87.3	70.3	32.9	34.4	22.6	55.0	17.6

Note: Figures shown cover persons 25 years old and over; (1) Figures cover the Riverside-San Bernardino-Ontario, CA Metropolitan Statistical Area; (2) People of Hispanic origin can be of any race
Source: U.S. Census Bureau, 2016-2020 American Community Survey 5-Year Estimates

School Enrollment by Grade and Control

Area	Preschool (%)		Kindergarten (%)		Grades 1 - 4 (%)		Grades 5 - 8 (%)		Grades 9 - 12 (%)	
	Public	Private	Public	Private	Public	Private	Public	Private	Public	Private
City	64.8	35.2	90.6	9.4	92.0	8.0	93.4	6.6	94.6	5.4
MSA[1]	67.2	32.8	91.0	9.0	94.0	6.0	93.7	6.3	94.6	5.4
U.S.	58.9	41.1	86.9	13.1	89.0	11.0	89.0	11.0	89.7	10.3

Note: Figures shown cover persons 3 years old and over; (1) Figures cover the Riverside-San Bernardino-Ontario, CA Metropolitan Statistical Area
Source: U.S. Census Bureau, 2016-2020 American Community Survey 5-Year Estimates

Higher Education

Four-Year Colleges			Two-Year Colleges			Medical Schools[1]	Law Schools[2]	Voc/ Tech[3]
Public	Private Non-profit	Private For-profit	Public	Private Non-profit	Private For-profit			
2	7	5	12	3	14	3	3	26

Note: Figures cover institutions located within the Riverside-San Bernardino-Ontario, CA Metropolitan Statistical Area and include main campuses only; (1) includes schools accredited by the Liaison Committee on Medical Education and the American Osteopathic Association's Commission on Osteopathic College Accreditation; (2) includes ABA-accredited schools, schools with provisional ABA accreditation, and state accredited schools; (3) includes all schools with programs that are less than 2 years.
Source: National Center for Education Statistics, Integrated Postsecondary Education System (IPEDS), 2020-21; Wikipedia, List of Medical Schools in the United States, accessed April 11, 2022; Wikipedia, List of Law Schools in the United States, accessed April 11, 2022

According to *U.S. News & World Report,* the Riverside-San Bernardino-Ontario, CA metro area is home to one of the top 200 national universities in the U.S.: **University of California—Riverside** (#83 tie). The indicators used to capture academic quality fall into a number of categories: assessment by administrators at peer institutions; retention of students; faculty resources; student selectivity; financial resources; alumni giving; high school counselor ratings of colleges; and graduation rate. *U.S. News & World Report, "America's Best Colleges 2022"*

EMPLOYERS

Major Employers

Company Name	Industry
Agua Caliente Band of Cahuilla Indians	Casino resort
Amazon	E-Commerce
Cal Baptist University	University
City of Riverside	Municipal government
Corona-Norco Unified School District	School district
County of Riverside	County government
Desert Sands Unified School District	School district
Eisenhower Medical Center	Hospital
Hemet Unified School District	School district
Jurupa Unified School District	School district
JW Marriott Desert Springs Resort & Spa	Resort
Kaiser Permanente Riverside Medical Ctr	Hospital
Lake Elsinore Unified School District	School district
March Air Reserve Base	Military reserve base
Moreno Valley Unified School District	School district
Morongo Casino	Resort
Murrieta Valley Unified School District	School district
Palm Springs Unified School District	School district
Pechanga Resort & Casino	Casino resort
Riverside Community College District	Community college
Riverside Community Hospital	Hospital
Riverside Unified School District	School district
Ross Dress For Less	Department stores, discount
Stater Bros	Retail grocery
Temecula Valley Unified School District	School district
University of California	Riverside
Walmart	Department stores, discount

Note: Companies shown are located within the Riverside-San Bernardino-Ontario, CA Metropolitan Statistical Area.
Source: Hoovers.com; Wikipedia

PUBLIC SAFETY

Crime Rate

Area	Total Crime	Violent Crime Rate				Property Crime Rate		
		Murder	Rape[3]	Robbery	Aggrav. Assault	Burglary	Larceny -Theft	Motor Vehicle Theft
City	3,430.6	6.0	45.5	117.8	276.6	490.2	1,930.8	563.7
Suburbs[1]	2,337.0	7.3	26.5	90.0	306.2	359.1	1,123.2	424.8
Metro[2]	2,415.6	7.2	27.9	92.0	304.0	368.5	1,181.3	434.7
U.S.	2,356.7	6.5	38.4	73.9	279.7	314.2	1,398.0	246.0

Note: Figures are crimes per 100,000 population; (1) All areas within the metro area that are located outside the city limits; (2) Figures cover the Riverside-San Bernardino-Ontario, CA Metropolitan Statistical Area; (3) All figures shown were reported using the revised Uniform Crime Reporting (UCR) definition of rape.
Source: FBI Uniform Crime Reports, 2020

Hate Crimes

Area	Number of Quarters Reported	Number of Incidents per Bias Motivation					
		Race/Ethnicity/ Ancestry	Religion	Sexual Orientation	Disability	Gender	Gender Identity
City	4	9	2	3	0	0	0
U.S.	4	5,227	1,244	1,110	130	75	266

Source: Federal Bureau of Investigation, Hate Crime Statistics 2020

Identity Theft Consumer Reports

Area	Reports	Reports per 100,000 Population	Rank[2]
MSA[1]	16,145	347	98
U.S.	1,434,676	432	-

Note: (1) Figures cover the Riverside-San Bernardino-Ontario, CA Metropolitan Statistical Area; (2) Rank ranges from 1 to 391 where 1 indicates greatest number of identity theft reports per 100,000 population
Source: Federal Trade Commission, Consumer Sentinel Network Data Book 2021

Fraud and Other Consumer Reports

Area	Reports	Reports per 100,000 Population	Rank[2]
MSA[1]	43,854	943	151
U.S.	4,328,977	1,304	-

Note: (1) Figures cover the Riverside-San Bernardino-Ontario, CA Metropolitan Statistical Area; (2) Rank ranges from 1 to 391 where 1 indicates greatest number of fraud and other consumer reports per 100,000 population
Source: Federal Trade Commission, Consumer Sentinel Network Data Book 2021

POLITICS

2020 Presidential Election Results

Area	Biden	Trump	Jorgensen	Hawkins	Other
Riverside County	53.0	45.0	1.0	0.3	0.6
U.S.	51.3	46.8	1.2	0.3	0.5

Note: Results are percentages and may not add to 100% due to rounding
Source: Dave Leip's Atlas of U.S. Presidential Elections

SPORTS

Professional Sports Teams

Team Name	League	Year Established
No teams are located in the metro area		

Source: Wikipedia, Major Professional Sports Teams of the United States and Canada, April 6, 2022

CLIMATE

Average and Extreme Temperatures

Temperature	Jan	Feb	Mar	Apr	May	Jun	Jul	Aug	Sep	Oct	Nov	Dec	Yr.
Extreme High (°F)	90	89	97	110	107	114	114	114	112	110	95	99	114
Average High (°F)	66	68	68	75	79	86	92	92	89	83	73	67	78
Average Temp. (°F)	54	57	58	63	67	73	78	78	76	70	61	55	66
Average Low (°F)	42	45	47	50	55	59	63	64	62	56	47	42	53
Extreme Low (°F)	25	29	30	35	38	43	52	51	47	40	31	24	24

Note: Figures cover the years 1973-1993
Source: National Climatic Data Center, International Station Meteorological Climate Summary, 9/96

Average Precipitation/Snowfall/Humidity

Precip./Humidity	Jan	Feb	Mar	Apr	May	Jun	Jul	Aug	Sep	Oct	Nov	Dec	Yr.
Avg. Precip. (in.)	n/a	n/a	n/a	n/a	n/a	n/a	n/a	n/a	n/a	n/a	n/a	n/a	n/a
Avg. Snowfall (in.)	n/a	n/a	n/a	n/a	n/a	n/a	n/a	n/a	n/a	n/a	n/a	n/a	n/a
Avg. Rel. Hum. 6am (%)	45	44	50	42	44	39	35	36	38	37	36	39	40
Avg. Rel. Hum. 3pm (%)	74	75	79	75	77	76	73	72	71	73	69	70	74

Note: Figures cover the years 1973-1993
Source: National Climatic Data Center, International Station Meteorological Climate Summary, 9/96

Weather Conditions

Temperature			Daytime Sky			Precipitation		
10°F & below	32°F & below	90°F & above	Clear	Partly cloudy	Cloudy	0.01 inch or more precip.	0.1 inch or more snow/ice	Thunder-storms
0	4	82	124	178	63	n/a	n/a	5

Note: Figures are average number of days per year and cover the years 1973-1993
Source: National Climatic Data Center, International Station Meteorological Climate Summary, 9/96

HAZARDOUS WASTE

Superfund Sites

The Riverside-San Bernardino-Ontario, CA metro area is home to seven sites on the EPA's Superfund National Priorities List: **Alark Hard Chrome** (final); **Barstow Marine Corps Logistics Base** (final); **George Air Force Base** (final); **March Air Force Base** (final); **Newmark Ground Water Contamination** (final); **Norton Air Force Base (Landfill #2)** (final); **Rockets, Fireworks, and Flares Site** (final). There are a total of 1,165 Superfund sites with a status of proposed or final on the list in the U.S. *U.S. Environmental Protection Agency, National Priorities List, April 6, 2022*

AIR QUALITY

Air Quality Trends: Ozone

	1990	1995	2000	2005	2010	2016	2017	2018	2019	2020
MSA[1]	0.146	0.129	0.104	0.102	0.093	0.094	0.099	0.097	0.091	0.101
U.S.	0.090	0.091	0.082	0.080	0.074	0.070	0.069	0.070	0.066	0.068

Note: (1) Data covers the Riverside-San Bernardino-Ontario, CA Metropolitan Statistical Area. The values shown are the composite ozone concentration averages among trend sites based on the highest fourth daily maximum 8-hour concentration in parts per million. These trends are based on sites having an adequate record of monitoring data during the trend period. Data from exceptional events are included.
Source: U.S. Environmental Protection Agency, Air Quality Monitoring Information, "Air Quality Trends by City, 1990-2020"

Air Quality Index

Area	Percent of Days when Air Quality was...[2]					AQI Statistics[2]	
	Good	Moderate	Unhealthy for Sensitive Groups	Unhealthy	Very Unhealthy	Maximum	Median
MSA[1]	10.4	41.5	22.4	19.7	5.5	576	98

Note: (1) Data covers the Riverside-San Bernardino-Ontario, CA Metropolitan Statistical Area; (2) Based on 366 days with AQI data in 2020. Air Quality Index (AQI) is an index for reporting daily air quality. EPA calculates the AQI for five major air pollutants regulated by the Clean Air Act: ground-level ozone, particle pollution (aka particulate matter), carbon monoxide, sulfur dioxide, and nitrogen dioxide. The AQI runs from 0 to 500. The higher the AQI value, the greater the level of air pollution and the greater the health concern. There are six AQI categories: "Good" AQI is between 0 and 50. Air quality is considered satisfactory; "Moderate" AQI is between 51 and 100. Air quality is acceptable; "Unhealthy for Sensitive Groups" When AQI values are between 101 and 150, members of sensitive groups may experience health effects; "Unhealthy" When AQI values are between 151 and 200 everyone may begin to experience health effects; "Very Unhealthy" AQI values between 201 and 300 trigger a health alert; "Hazardous" AQI values over 300 trigger warnings of emergency conditions (not shown).
Source: U.S. Environmental Protection Agency, Air Quality Index Report, 2020

Air Quality Index Pollutants

Area	Percent of Days when AQI Pollutant was...[2]					
	Carbon Monoxide	Nitrogen Dioxide	Ozone	Sulfur Dioxide	Particulate Matter 2.5	Particulate Matter 10
MSA[1]	0.0	2.5	59.0	0.0	29.0	9.6

Note: (1) Data covers the Riverside-San Bernardino-Ontario, CA Metropolitan Statistical Area; (2) Based on 366 days with AQI data in 2020. The Air Quality Index (AQI) is an index for reporting daily air quality. EPA calculates the AQI for five major air pollutants regulated by the Clean Air Act: ground-level ozone, particle pollution (also known as particulate matter), carbon monoxide, sulfur dioxide, and nitrogen dioxide. The AQI runs from 0 to 500. The higher the AQI value, the greater the level of air pollution and the greater the health concern.
Source: U.S. Environmental Protection Agency, Air Quality Index Report, 2020

Maximum Air Pollutant Concentrations: Particulate Matter, Ozone, CO and Lead

	Particulate Matter 10 (ug/m^3)	Particulate Matter 2.5 Wtd AM (ug/m^3)	Particulate Matter 2.5 24-Hr (ug/m^3)	Ozone (ppm)	Carbon Monoxide (ppm)	Lead (ug/m^3)
MSA[1] Level	359	15.1	43	0.125	2	n/a
NAAQS[2]	150	15	35	0.075	9	0.15
Met NAAQS[2]	No	No	No	No	Yes	n/a

Note: (1) Data covers the Riverside-San Bernardino-Ontario, CA Metropolitan Statistical Area; Data from exceptional events are included; (2) National Ambient Air Quality Standards; ppm = parts per million; ug/m^3 = micrograms per cubic meter; n/a not available.
Concentrations: Particulate Matter 10 (coarse particulate)—highest second maximum 24-hour concentration; Particulate Matter 2.5 Wtd AM (fine particulate)—highest weighted annual mean concentration; Particulate Matter 2.5 24-Hour (fine particulate)—highest 98th percentile 24-hour concentration; Ozone—highest fourth daily maximum 8-hour concentration; Carbon Monoxide—highest second maximum non-overlapping 8-hour concentration; Lead—maximum running 3-month average
Source: U.S. Environmental Protection Agency, Air Quality Monitoring Information, "Air Quality Statistics by City, 2020"

Maximum Air Pollutant Concentrations: Nitrogen Dioxide and Sulfur Dioxide

	Nitrogen Dioxide AM (ppb)	Nitrogen Dioxide 1-Hr (ppb)	Sulfur Dioxide AM (ppb)	Sulfur Dioxide 1-Hr (ppb)	Sulfur Dioxide 24-Hr (ppb)
MSA[1] Level	29	78	n/a	5	n/a
NAAQS[2]	53	100	30	75	140
Met NAAQS[2]	Yes	Yes	n/a	Yes	n/a

Note: (1) Data covers the Riverside-San Bernardino-Ontario, CA Metropolitan Statistical Area; Data from exceptional events are included; (2) National Ambient Air Quality Standards; ppm = parts per million; ug/m^3 = micrograms per cubic meter; n/a not available.
Concentrations: Nitrogen Dioxide AM—highest arithmetic mean concentration; Nitrogen Dioxide 1-Hr—highest 98th percentile 1-hour daily maximum concentration; Sulfur Dioxide AM—highest annual mean concentration; Sulfur Dioxide 1-Hr—highest 99th percentile 1-hour daily maximum concentration; Sulfur Dioxide 24-Hr—highest second maximum 24-hour concentration
Source: U.S. Environmental Protection Agency, Air Quality Monitoring Information, "Air Quality Statistics by City, 2020"

Sacramento, California

Background

Sacramento is the capital of California, the seat of Sacramento County, and the sixth-largest city in the state. It was named after the Sacramento River which derived its name from the Catholic sacrament of the Holy Eucharist. It lies at the juncture of the Sacramento and American rivers.

A Swiss soldier, Captain John Augustus Sutter, settled Sacramento in 1839, when he received permission from the Mexican government to establish a new colony which became known as New Helvetia. The 50,000-acre land grant included a wide swath of the rich and fertile valley between the two rivers, and Sutter's ranch, trading post, and agricultural projects were soon productive and profitable. When, in 1846, American troops occupied the area, Sutter was well-positioned to take advantage, and his trade soon extended well up the northern coast.

In 1848, one of Sutter's employees, a carpenter named James W. Marshall, discovered gold at what became known as "Sutter's Mill" in the settlement of Coloma. The discovery brought an onslaught of prospectors and the beginning of the California Gold Rush. The prospectors overwhelmed New Helvetia resources and the havoc that followed destroyed the economic foundation of the town. The newcomers overran Sutter's land and claimed it as their own. Sutter tried to expand his business to include mining supplies but was only meagerly rewarded. He ceded land along the Sacramento River to his son, who founded the town that became the city we know today.

Sacramento supported miners with housing, food, banking, transportation and necessary mining equipment. One of Sacramento's most famous entrepreneurs is Levi Strauss who sold the ultimate mining pants known as "Levi's." Sacramento's economy was booming, but plagued by floods, fire, and a cholera epidemic. Today, flooding that is endemic to the area is controlled by a series of dams, which also supply a large amount of electricity to the area.

On April 3, 1860, the legendary Pony Express carried mail from Sacramento to St. Joseph, Missouri on horseback in record time. The ten-day journey of nearly 1,800 miles was unprofitable but caught the attention of the federal government and helped launch of our current postal system.

In the years since, the city has grown rapidly, passing 400,000 in 2000 and 500,000 in 2020. As befitting a state capital, government (state, county, and local) is the largest employer in the city, followed by the health industry, including UC David Health and Kaiser Permanente. Other notable companies located in the area include Sutter Health, Blue Diamond Growers, Aerojet Rocketdyne, and the McClatchey Company.

Sutter's Fort State Historical Monument features a restoration of John Sutter's original ranch and trading post, and a designated Old Sacramento Historical Area preserves many buildings from the gold rush period and thereafter. At the city's Crocker Art Museum, visitors can view an extensive collection of works by Michelangelo, Rembrandt, and Leonardo da Vinci. In October 2010, the Crocker completed a 100,000-ft. expansion that more than tripled its size.

Sacramento has been called America's most diverse city and the most hipster city in California.

The Wells Fargo Museum is a monument to the history of the Pony Express and the era of the gold rush. Housed in the original bank building that managed the Pony Express, its staff conducts tours dressed in period attire. The museum displays include tools, gold nuggets, documents, and other relevant artifacts

The Woodland Opera House opened in 1896 in nearby Woodland, California. It closed in 1913, when motion pictures took hold of the public's interest and the building stayed dormant until 1971 when Yolo County Historic Society saved it from demolition. They gave it to the state in 1980 and underwent a total renovation in 1982. Today it is a major entertainment venue and on the National Register of Historic Places.

Since 1985, Sacramento has hosted NBA basketball when the Kings relocated from Kansas City. The city fields a professional soccer team, the Sacramento Republic FC of the USL Championship League, and a minor league baseball team, the River Cats, the AAA affiliate of the San Francisco Giants. Golden 1 Center sports arena opened in 2016.

Sacramento has a mild climate with abundant sunshine. A nearly cloud-free sky prevails throughout the summer months, which are usually dry, with warm to hot afternoons and mostly mild nights.

Rankings

General Rankings

- Sacramento was selected as one of the best places to live in America by *Outside Magazine.* Criteria centered on diversity; sustainability; outdoor equity; and affordability. Local experts shared highlights from hands-on experience in each location. *Outside Magazine, "The 20 Most Livable Towns and Cities in America," October 15, 2021*

Business/Finance Rankings

- The Brookings Institution ranked the nation's largest cities based on income inequality. Sacramento was ranked #71 (#1 = greatest inequality). Criteria: the "95/20 ratio," a figure representing the income at which a household earns more than 95 percent of all other households, divided by the income at which a household earns more than only 20 percent of all other households. *Brookings Institution, "Household Income Inequality, Largest Cities of 97 Large U.S. Metro Areas, 2014-2016," February 5, 2018*
- The Brookings Institution ranked the 100 largest metro areas in the U.S. based on income inequality. Sacramento was ranked #33 (#1 = greatest inequality). Criteria: the "95/20 ratio," a figure representing the income at which a household earns more than 95 percent of all other households, divided by the income at which a household earns more than only 20 percent of all other households. *Brookings Institution, "Household Income Inequality, 100 Largest U.S. Metro Areas, 2014-2016," February 5, 2018*
- The Sacramento metro area appeared on the Milken Institute "2021 Best Performing Cities" list. Rank: #47 out of 200 large metro areas (population over 250,000). Criteria: job growth; wage and salary growth; high-tech output growth; housing affordability; household broadband access. *Milken Institute, "Best-Performing Cities 2021," February 16, 2021*
- *Forbes* ranked the 200 most populous metro areas to determine the nation's "Best Places for Business and Careers." The Sacramento metro area was ranked #56. Criteria: costs (business and living); job growth (past and projected); income growth; quality of life; educational attainment (college and high school); projected economic growth; cultural and leisure opportunities; workplace tolerance laws; net migration patterns. *Forbes, "The Best Places for Business and Careers 2019: Seattle Still On Top," October 30, 2019*

Education Rankings

- Personal finance website *WalletHub* analyzed the 150 largest U.S. metropolitan statistical areas to determine where the most educated Americans are putting their degrees to work. Criteria: education levels; percentage of workers with degrees; education quality and attainment gap; public school quality rankings; quality and enrollment of each metro area's universities. Sacramento was ranked #49 (#1 = most educated city). *www.WalletHub.com, "Most & Least Educated Cities in America," July 19, 2021*
- Sacramento was selected as one of America's most literate cities. The city ranked #42 out of the 84 largest U.S. cities. Criteria: number of booksellers; library resources; Internet resources; educational attainment; periodical publishing resources; newspaper circulation. *Central Connecticut State University, "America's Most Literate Cities, 2018," February 2019*

Environmental Rankings

- Sperling's BestPlaces assessed the 50 largest metropolitan areas of the United States for the likelihood of dangerously extreme weather events or earthquakes. In general the Southeast and South-Central regions have the highest risk of weather extremes and earthquakes, while the Pacific Northwest enjoys the lowest risk. Of the least risky metropolitan areas, the Sacramento metro area was ranked #3. *www.bestplaces.net, "Avoid Natural Disasters: BestPlaces Reveals The Top 10 Safest Places to Live," October 25, 2017*
- The U.S. Environmental Protection Agency (EPA) released its list of U.S. metropolitan areas with the most ENERGY STAR certified buildings in 2020. The Sacramento metro area was ranked #22 out of 25. *U.S. Environmental Protection Agency, "2021 Energy Star Top Cities," June 15, 2021*
- Sacramento was highlighted as one of the 25 most ozone-polluted metro areas in the U.S. during 2017 through 2019. The area ranked #6. *American Lung Association, "State of the Air 2021," April 21, 2021*
- Sacramento was highlighted as one of the 25 metro areas most polluted by year-round particle pollution (Annual PM 2.5) in the U.S. during 2017 through 2019. The area ranked #24. *American Lung Association, "State of the Air 2021," April 21, 2021*

- Sacramento was highlighted as one of the 25 metro areas most polluted by short-term particle pollution (24-hour PM 2.5) in the U.S. during 2017 through 2019. The area ranked #10. *American Lung Association, "State of the Air 2021," April 21, 2021*

Health/Fitness Rankings

- For each of the 100 largest cities in the United States, the American Fitness Index®, published by the American College of Sports Medicine and the Anthem Foundation, evaluated community infrastructure and 34 health behaviors including preventive health, levels of chronic disease conditions, food insecurity, sleep quality, pedestrian safety, air quality, and community resources that support physical activity. Sacramento ranked #18 for "community fitness." *americanfitnessindex.org, "2021 ACSM American Fitness Index Summary Report," July 13, 2021*
- Sacramento was identified as a "2021 Spring Allergy Capital." The area ranked #90 out of 100. Three groups of factors were used to identify the most challenging cities for people with allergies during the spring season: annual spring pollen levels; over the counter medicine use; number of board-certified allergy specialists. *Asthma and Allergy Foundation of America, "Spring Allergy Capitals 2021," February 23, 2021*
- Sacramento was identified as a "2021 Fall Allergy Capital." The area ranked #97 out of 100. Three groups of factors were used to identify the most challenging cities for people with allergies during the fall season: annual fall pollen levels; over the counter medicine use; number of board-certified allergy specialists. *Asthma and Allergy Foundation of America, "Fall Allergy Capitals 2021," February 23, 2021*
- Sacramento was identified as a "2021 Asthma Capital." The area ranked #66 out of the nation's 100 largest metropolitan areas. Criteria: estimated asthma prevalence; asthma-related mortality; and ER visits due to asthma. Risk factors analyzed but not factored in the rankings: annual pollen score; annual air quality; public smoking laws; number of board-certified asthma specialists; rescue medication use; controller medication use; uninsured rate; poverty rate. *Asthma and Allergy Foundation of America, "Asthma Capitals 2021: The Most Challenging Places to Live With Asthma," May 5, 2021*

Real Estate Rankings

- *WalletHub* compared the most populated U.S. cities to determine which had the best markets for real estate agents. Sacramento ranked #3 where demand was high and pay was the best. Criteria: sales per agent; annual median wage for real-estate agents; monthly average starting salary for real estate agents; real estate job density and competition; unemployment rate; home turnover rate; housing-market health index; and other relevant metrics. *www.WalletHub.com, "2021 Best Places to Be a Real Estate Agent," May 12, 2021*
- Sacramento was ranked #212 out of 237 metro areas in terms of housing affordability in 2021 by the National Association of Home Builders (#1 = most affordable). Criteria: the share of homes sold in that area affordable to a family earning the local median income, based on standard mortgage underwriting criteria. *National Association of Home Builders®, NAHB-Wells Fargo Housing Opportunity Index, 4th Quarter 2021*

Safety Rankings

- Allstate ranked the 200 largest cities in America in terms of driver safety. Sacramento ranked #163. Criteria: internal property damage claims over a two-year period from January 2016 to December 2017. The report helps increase the importance of safety and awareness behind the wheel. *Allstate, "Allstate America's Best Drivers Report, 2019" June 24, 2019*
- The National Insurance Crime Bureau ranked 390 metro areas in the U.S. in terms of per capita rates of vehicle theft. The Sacramento metro area ranked #63 (#1 = highest rate). Criteria: number of vehicle theft offenses per 100,000 inhabitants in 2020. *National Insurance Crime Bureau, "Hot Spots 2020," August 31, 2021*

Seniors/Retirement Rankings

- From its Best Cities for Successful Aging indexes, the Milken Institute generated rankings for metropolitan areas, weighing data in nine categories—health care, wellness, living arrangements, transportation and convenience, financial characteristics, education, employment, community engagement, and overall livability. The Sacramento metro area was ranked #82 overall in the large metro area category. *Milken Institute, "Best Cities for Successful Aging, 2017" March 14, 2017*

Sports/Recreation Rankings

- Sacramento was chosen as one of America's best cities for bicycling. The city ranked #32 out of 50. Criteria: cycling infrastructure that is safe and friendly for all ages; energy and bike culture. The editors evaluated cities with populations of 100,000 or more. *Bicycling, "The 50 Best Bike Cities in America," October 10, 2018*

Transportation Rankings

- According to the INRIX "2021 Global Traffic Scorecard," Sacramento was identified as one of the most congested metro areas in the U.S. The area ranked #23 out of 25. Criteria: average annual time spent in traffic and average cost of congestion per motorist. *Inrix.com, "Americans Lost 3.4 Billion Hours Due to Congestion in 2021, 42% Below Pre-COVID," December 7, 2021*

Women/Minorities Rankings

- Personal finance website *WalletHub* compared more than 180 U.S. cities across two key dimensions, "Hispanic Business-Friendliness" and "Hispanic Purchasing Power," to arrive at the most favorable conditions for Hispanic entrepreneurs. Sacramento was ranked #125 out of 182. Criteria includes: share of Hispanic-Owned Businesses; Hispanic entrepreneurship rate to median annual income of Hispanics; Small Business-Friendliness score; cost of living; and number of Hispanics with at least a bachelor's degree. *WalletHub.com, "2019's Best Cities for Hispanic Entrepreneurs," May 1, 2019*

Miscellaneous Rankings

- *MoveHub* ranked 446 hipster cities across 20 countries, using its *alternative* Hipster Index and Sacramento came out as #35 among the top 50. Criteria: population over 150,000; number of vintage boutiques; density of tattoo parlors; vegan places to eat; coffee shops; and density of vinyl record stores. *www.movehub.com, "The Hipster Index: Brighton Pips Portland to Global Top Spot," July 28, 2021*
- *WalletHub* compared the 150 most populated U.S. cities to determine their operating efficiency. A "Quality of City Services" score was constructed for each city and then divided by the total budget per capita to reveal which were managed the best. Sacramento ranked #120. Criteria: financial stability; economy; education; safety; health; infrastructure and pollution. *www.WalletHub.com, "2021's Best- & Worst-Run Cities in America," June 22, 2021*

Business Environment

DEMOGRAPHICS

Population Growth

Area	1990 Census	2000 Census	2010 Census	2020* Estimate	Population Growth (%) 1990-2020	Population Growth (%) 2010-2020
City	368,923	407,018	466,488	503,482	36.5	7.9
MSA[1]	1,481,126	1,796,857	2,149,127	2,338,866	57.9	8.8
U.S.	248,709,873	281,421,906	308,745,538	326,569,308	31.3	5.8

Note: (1) Figures cover the Sacramento—Arden-Arcade—Roseville, CA Metropolitan Statistical Area; (*) 2016-2020 5-year estimated population
Source: U.S. Census Bureau, 1990 Census, Census 2000, Census 2010, 2016-2020 American Community Survey 5-Year Estimates

Household Size

Area	Persons in Household (%) One	Two	Three	Four	Five	Six	Seven or More	Average Household Size
City	30.7	30.3	14.3	13.3	6.2	2.7	2.4	2.60
MSA[1]	24.9	33.0	15.9	14.7	6.8	2.7	1.9	2.70
U.S.	28.0	33.9	15.5	12.9	6.0	2.3	1.4	2.60

Note: (1) Figures cover the Sacramento—Arden-Arcade—Roseville, CA Metropolitan Statistical Area
Source: U.S. Census Bureau, 2016-2020 American Community Survey 5-Year Estimates

Race

Area	White Alone[2] (%)	Black Alone[2] (%)	Asian Alone[2] (%)	AIAN[3] Alone[2] (%)	NHOPI[4] Alone[2] (%)	Other Race Alone[2] (%)	Two or More Races (%)
City	43.5	13.5	19.3	0.8	1.7	11.6	9.6
MSA[1]	62.6	6.9	14.1	0.6	0.8	6.6	8.4
U.S.	70.4	12.6	5.6	0.8	0.2	5.1	5.2

Note: (1) Figures cover the Sacramento—Arden-Arcade—Roseville, CA Metropolitan Statistical Area; (2) Alone is defined as not being in combination with one or more other races; (3) American Indian and Alaska Native; (4) Native Hawaiian and Other Pacific Islander
Source: U.S. Census Bureau, 2016-2020 American Community Survey 5-Year Estimates

Hispanic or Latino Origin

Area	Total (%)	Mexican (%)	Puerto Rican (%)	Cuban (%)	Other (%)
City	28.3	23.9	0.8	0.2	3.4
MSA[1]	21.8	17.6	0.7	0.2	3.3
U.S.	18.2	11.2	1.7	0.7	4.5

Note: Persons of Hispanic or Latino origin can be of any race; (1) Figures cover the Sacramento—Arden-Arcade—Roseville, CA Metropolitan Statistical Area
Source: U.S. Census Bureau, 2016-2020 American Community Survey 5-Year Estimates

Ancestry

Area	German	Irish	English	American	Italian	Polish	French[2]	Scottish	Dutch
City	6.7	6.0	5.1	1.6	3.6	1.0	1.6	1.1	0.7
MSA[1]	10.3	8.1	8.3	2.6	4.7	1.3	2.1	1.6	1.0
U.S.	13.0	9.7	7.7	5.9	5.1	2.7	2.3	1.6	1.1

Note: Figures are the percentage of the total population reporting a particular ancestry. The nine most commonly reported ancestries in the U.S. are shown. Figures include multiple ancestries (e.g. if a person reported being Irish and Italian, they were included in both columns); (1) Figures cover the Sacramento—Arden-Arcade—Roseville, CA Metropolitan Statistical Area; (2) Excludes Basque
Source: U.S. Census Bureau, 2016-2020 American Community Survey 5-Year Estimates

Foreign-born Population

Area	Percent of Population Born in: Any Foreign Country	Asia	Mexico	Europe	Caribbean	Central America[2]	South America	Africa	Canada
City	21.3	10.8	6.0	1.5	0.1	0.7	0.2	0.6	0.1
MSA[1]	18.5	9.0	4.4	2.7	0.1	0.6	0.3	0.5	0.3
U.S.	13.5	4.2	3.3	1.5	1.3	1.1	1.0	0.7	0.3

Note: (1) Figures cover the Sacramento—Arden-Arcade—Roseville, CA Metropolitan Statistical Area; (2) Excludes Mexico.
Source: U.S. Census Bureau, 2016-2020 American Community Survey 5-Year Estimates

Marital Status

Area	Never Married	Now Married[2]	Separated	Widowed	Divorced
City	40.1	41.2	2.6	5.1	11.1
MSA[1]	33.5	48.5	2.0	5.1	10.8
U.S.	33.5	48.1	1.8	5.7	10.8

Note: Figures are percentages and cover the population 15 years of age and older; (1) Figures cover the Sacramento—Arden-Arcade—Roseville, CA Metropolitan Statistical Area; (2) Excludes separated
Source: U.S. Census Bureau, 2016-2020 American Community Survey 5-Year Estimates

Disability by Age

Area	All Ages	Under 18 Years Old	18 to 64 Years Old	65 Years and Over
City	11.8	3.2	9.5	37.9
MSA[1]	11.7	3.4	9.0	34.7
U.S.	12.7	4.3	10.3	34.0

Note: Figures show percent of the civilian noninstitutionalized population that reported having a disability. Disability status is determined from six types of difficulty: vision, hearing, cognitive, ambulatory, self-care, and independent living. For children under 5 years old, hearing and vision difficulty are used to determine disability status. For children between the ages of 5 and 14, disability status is determined from hearing, vision, cognitive, ambulatory, and self-care difficulties. For people aged 15 years and older, they are considered to have a disability if they have difficulty with any one of the six difficulty types; Note: (1) Figures cover the Sacramento—Arden-Arcade—Roseville, CA Metropolitan Statistical Area
Source: U.S. Census Bureau, 2016-2020 American Community Survey 5-Year Estimates

Age

Area	Percent of Population									Median Age
	Under Age 5	Age 5–19	Age 20–34	Age 35–44	Age 45–54	Age 55–64	Age 65–74	Age 75–84	Age 85+	
City	6.5	18.6	25.2	13.7	11.5	11.2	8.0	3.6	1.8	34.9
MSA[1]	6.0	19.5	21.0	13.0	12.5	12.6	9.1	4.3	2.0	37.6
U.S.	6.0	19.1	20.6	12.7	12.7	12.9	9.4	4.7	2.0	38.2

Note: (1) Figures cover the Sacramento—Arden-Arcade—Roseville, CA Metropolitan Statistical Area
Source: U.S. Census Bureau, 2016-2020 American Community Survey 5-Year Estimates

Gender

Area	Males	Females	Males per 100 Females
City	247,126	256,356	96.4
MSA[1]	1,144,264	1,194,602	95.8
U.S.	160,818,530	165,750,778	97.0

Note: (1) Figures cover the Sacramento—Arden-Arcade—Roseville, CA Metropolitan Statistical Area
Source: U.S. Census Bureau, 2016-2020 American Community Survey 5-Year Estimates

Religious Groups by Family

Area	Catholic	Baptist	Non-Den.	Methodist[2]	Lutheran	LDS[3]	Pente-costal	Presby-terian[4]	Muslim[5]	Judaism
MSA[1]	16.2	3.2	4.0	1.8	0.8	3.4	2.0	0.8	0.8	0.3
U.S.	19.1	9.3	4.0	4.0	2.3	2.0	1.9	1.6	0.8	0.7

Note: Figures are the number of adherents as a percentage of the total population; (1) Figures cover the Sacramento—Arden-Arcade—Roseville, CA Metropolitan Statistical Area; (2) Methodist/Pietist; (3) Latter Day Saints; (4) Reformed; (5) Figures are estimates
Source: Association of Statisticians of American Religious Bodies, 2010 U.S. Religion Census: Religious Congregations & Membership Study

Religious Groups by Tradition

Area	Catholic	Evangelical Protestant	Mainline Protestant	Other Tradition	Black Protestant	Orthodox
MSA[1]	16.2	11.4	2.2	5.8	0.6	0.3
U.S.	19.1	16.2	7.3	4.3	1.6	0.3

Note: Figures are the number of adherents as a percentage of the total population; (1) Figures cover the Sacramento—Arden-Arcade—Roseville, CA Metropolitan Statistical Area
Source: Association of Statisticians of American Religious Bodies, 2010 U.S. Religion Census: Religious Congregations & Membership Study

ECONOMY

Gross Metropolitan Product

Area	2017	2018	2019	2020	Rank[2]
MSA[1]	129.3	137.0	144.3	151.5	34

Note: Figures are in billions of dollars; (1) Figures cover the Sacramento—Arden-Arcade—Roseville, CA Metropolitan Statistical Area; (2) Rank is based on 2018 data and ranges from 1 to 381
Source: U.S. Conference of Mayors, U.S. Metro Economies: GMP & Employment 2018-2020, September 2019

Economic Growth

Area	2015-17 (%)	2018 (%)	2019 (%)	2020 (%)	Rank[2]
MSA[1]	2.6	3.6	3.4	2.7	90
U.S.	1.9	2.9	2.3	2.1	–

Note: Figures are real gross metropolitan product (GMP) growth rates and represent average annual percent change; (1) Figures cover the Sacramento—Arden-Arcade—Roseville, CA Metropolitan Statistical Area; (2) Rank is based on 2017 2-year average annual percent change and ranges from 1 to 381
Source: U.S. Conference of Mayors, U.S. Metro Economies: GMP & Employment 2018-2020, September 2019

Metropolitan Area Exports

Area	2015	2016	2017	2018	2019	2020	Rank[2]
MSA[1]	8,101.2	7,032.1	6,552.6	6,222.8	5,449.2	4,980.9	54

Note: Figures are in millions of dollars; (1) Figures cover the Sacramento—Arden-Arcade—Roseville, CA Metropolitan Statistical Area; (2) Rank is based on 2020 data and ranges from 1 to 389
Source: U.S. Department of Commerce, International Trade Administration, Office of Trade and Economic Analysis, Industry and Analysis, Exports by Metropolitan Area, data extracted March 4, 2022

Building Permits

Area	Single-Family			Multi-Family			Total		
	2019	2020	Pct. Chg.	2019	2020	Pct. Chg.	2019	2020	Pct. Chg.
City	1,538	935	-39.2	1,463	2,649	81.1	3,001	3,584	19.4
MSA[1]	7,184	7,279	1.3	2,247	3,885	72.9	9,431	11,164	18.4
U.S.	862,100	979,400	13.6	523,900	491,700	-6.1	1,386,000	1,471,100	6.1

Note: (1) Figures cover the Sacramento—Arden-Arcade—Roseville, CA Metropolitan Statistical Area; Figures represent new, privately-owned housing units authorized (unadjusted data); All permit data are based on estimates with imputation
Source: U.S. Census Bureau, Manufacturing, Mining, and Construction Statistics, Building Permits, 2019, 2020

Bankruptcy Filings

Area	Business Filings			Nonbusiness Filings		
	2020	2021	% Chg.	2020	2021	% Chg.
Sacramento County	124	80	-35.5	2,300	1,731	-24.7
U.S.	21,655	14,347	-33.7	522,808	399,269	-23.6

Note: Business filings include Chapter 7, Chapter 9, Chapter 11, Chapter 12, Chapter 13, Chapter 15, and Section 304; Nonbusiness filings include Chapter 7, Chapter 11, and Chapter 13
Source: Administrative Office of the U.S. Courts, Business and Nonbusiness Bankruptcy, County Cases Commenced by Chapter of the Bankruptcy Code, During the 12-Month Period Ending December 31, 2020 and Business and Nonbusiness Bankruptcy, County Cases Commenced by Chapter of the Bankruptcy Code, During the 12-Month Period Ending December 31, 2021

Housing Vacancy Rates

Area	Gross Vacancy Rate[2] (%)			Year-Round Vacancy Rate[3] (%)			Rental Vacancy Rate[4] (%)			Homeowner Vacancy Rate[5] (%)		
	2019	2020	2021	2019	2020	2021	2019	2020	2021	2019	2020	2021
MSA[1]	7.8	6.1	6.7	7.1	5.8	6.5	4.2	4.2	3.6	0.8	1.0	0.7
U.S.	12.0	10.6	10.8	9.5	8.2	8.4	6.7	6.3	6.1	1.4	1.0	0.9

Note: (1) Figures cover the Sacramento—Arden-Arcade—Roseville, CA Metropolitan Statistical Area; (2) The percentage of the total housing inventory that is vacant; (3) The percentage of the housing inventory (excluding seasonal units) that is year-round vacant; (4) The percentage of rental inventory that is vacant for rent; (5) The percentage of homeowner inventory that is vacant for sale
Source: U.S. Census Bureau, Housing Vacancies and Homeownership Annual Statistics: 2019, 2020, 2021

INCOME

Income

Area	Per Capita ($)	Median Household ($)	Average Household ($)
City	33,503	65,847	87,213
MSA[1]	37,122	75,533	100,554
U.S.	35,384	64,994	91,547

Note: (1) Figures cover the Sacramento—Arden-Arcade—Roseville, CA Metropolitan Statistical Area
Source: U.S. Census Bureau, 2016-2020 American Community Survey 5-Year Estimates

Household Income Distribution

Area	Percent of Households Earning							
	Under $15,000	$15,000 -$24,999	$25,000 -$34,999	$35,000 -$49,999	$50,000 -$74,999	$75,000 -$99,999	$100,000 -$149,999	$150,000 and up
City	10.8	7.8	8.0	11.4	17.6	13.2	16.2	14.9
MSA[1]	8.7	6.9	7.3	10.3	16.5	13.0	17.8	19.5
U.S.	9.9	8.5	8.6	12.0	17.2	12.8	15.6	15.4

Note: (1) Figures cover the Sacramento—Arden-Arcade—Roseville, CA Metropolitan Statistical Area
Source: U.S. Census Bureau, 2016-2020 American Community Survey 5-Year Estimates

Poverty Rate

Area	All Ages	Under 18 Years Old	18 to 64 Years Old	65 Years and Over
City	15.7	20.4	14.8	11.7
MSA[1]	12.7	15.8	12.6	8.6
U.S.	12.8	17.5	12.1	9.3

Note: Figures are percentage of people whose income during the past 12 months was below the poverty level;
(1) Figures cover the Sacramento—Arden-Arcade—Roseville, CA Metropolitan Statistical Area
Source: U.S. Census Bureau, 2016-2020 American Community Survey 5-Year Estimates

CITY FINANCES

City Government Finances

Component	2019 ($000)	2019 ($ per capita)
Total Revenues	1,353,946	2,698
Total Expenditures	1,195,322	2,382
Debt Outstanding	2,319,313	4,621
Cash and Securities[1]	993,144	1,979

Note: (1) Cash and security holdings of a government at the close of its fiscal year, including those of its dependent agencies, utilities, and liquor stores.
Source: U.S. Census Bureau, State & Local Government Finances 2019

City Government Revenue by Source

Source	2019 ($000)	2019 ($ per capita)	2019 (%)
General Revenue			
From Federal Government	34,130	68	2.5
From State Government	41,725	83	3.1
From Local Governments	5,146	10	0.4
Taxes			
Property	173,297	345	12.8
Sales and Gross Receipts	246,318	491	18.2
Personal Income	0	0	0.0
Corporate Income	0	0	0.0
Motor Vehicle License	0	0	0.0
Other Taxes	67,329	134	5.0
Current Charges	426,800	850	31.5
Liquor Store	0	0	0.0
Utility	127,868	255	9.4

Source: U.S. Census Bureau, State & Local Government Finances 2019

City Government Expenditures by Function

Function	2019 ($000)	2019 ($ per capita)	2019 (%)
General Direct Expenditures			
Air Transportation	0	0	0.0
Corrections	0	0	0.0
Education	0	0	0.0
Employment Security Administration	0	0	0.0
Financial Administration	10,236	20	0.9
Fire Protection	125,567	250	10.5
General Public Buildings	0	0	0.0
Governmental Administration, Other	116,135	231	9.7
Health	25,933	51	2.2
Highways	29,684	59	2.5
Hospitals	0	0	0.0
Housing and Community Development	44,254	88	3.7
Interest on General Debt	101,198	201	8.5
Judicial and Legal	4,940	9	0.4
Libraries	17,732	35	1.5
Parking	19,991	39	1.7
Parks and Recreation	66,194	131	5.5
Police Protection	181,274	361	15.2
Public Welfare	6,681	13	0.6
Sewerage	60,544	120	5.1
Solid Waste Management	55,503	110	4.6
Veterans' Services	0	0	0.0
Liquor Store	0	0	0.0
Utility	101,298	201	8.5

Source: U.S. Census Bureau, State & Local Government Finances 2019

EMPLOYMENT

Labor Force and Employment

Area	Civilian Labor Force			Workers Employed		
	Dec. 2020	Dec. 2021	% Chg.	Dec. 2020	Dec. 2021	% Chg.
City	237,986	238,610	0.3	216,868	226,597	4.5
MSA[1]	1,089,088	1,099,258	0.9	1,005,859	1,051,043	4.5
U.S.	160,017,000	161,696,000	1.0	149,613,000	155,732,000	4.1

Note: Data is not seasonally adjusted and covers workers 16 years of age and older; (1) Figures cover the Sacramento—Arden-Arcade—Roseville, CA Metropolitan Statistical Area
Source: Bureau of Labor Statistics, Local Area Unemployment Statistics

Unemployment Rate

Area	2021											
	Jan.	Feb.	Mar.	Apr.	May	Jun.	Jul.	Aug.	Sep.	Oct.	Nov.	Dec.
City	8.6	8.1	7.6	7.4	7.0	7.8	7.7	7.4	6.4	6.2	5.3	5.0
MSA[1]	7.6	7.1	6.8	6.6	6.2	6.9	6.7	6.4	5.5	5.3	4.7	4.4
U.S.	6.8	6.6	6.2	5.7	5.5	6.1	5.7	5.3	4.6	4.3	3.9	3.7

Note: Data is not seasonally adjusted and covers workers 16 years of age and older; (1) Figures cover the Sacramento—Arden-Arcade—Roseville, CA Metropolitan Statistical Area
Source: Bureau of Labor Statistics, Local Area Unemployment Statistics

Average Wages

Occupation	$/Hr.	Occupation	$/Hr.
Accountants and Auditors	40.35	Maintenance and Repair Workers	23.52
Automotive Mechanics	25.92	Marketing Managers	73.18
Bookkeepers	23.84	Network and Computer Systems Admin.	46.15
Carpenters	30.30	Nurses, Licensed Practical	31.77
Cashiers	15.42	Nurses, Registered	65.14
Computer Programmers	49.68	Nursing Assistants	19.19
Computer Systems Analysts	50.24	Office Clerks, General	20.76
Computer User Support Specialists	43.50	Physical Therapists	52.79
Construction Laborers	25.27	Physicians	135.69
Cooks, Restaurant	17.88	Plumbers, Pipefitters and Steamfitters	34.10
Customer Service Representatives	20.44	Police and Sheriff's Patrol Officers	47.89
Dentists	96.67	Postal Service Mail Carriers	27.18
Electricians	35.72	Real Estate Sales Agents	28.61
Engineers, Electrical	59.94	Retail Salespersons	17.18
Fast Food and Counter Workers	15.35	Sales Representatives, Technical/Scientific	48.77
Financial Managers	71.93	Secretaries, Exc. Legal/Medical/Executive	22.33
First-Line Supervisors of Office Workers	34.08	Security Guards	18.04
General and Operations Managers	57.73	Surgeons	n/a
Hairdressers/Cosmetologists	17.82	Teacher Assistants, Exc. Postsecondary*	18.57
Home Health and Personal Care Aides	15.11	Teachers, Secondary School, Exc. Sp. Ed.*	41.43
Janitors and Cleaners	17.50	Telemarketers	16.78
Landscaping/Groundskeeping Workers	19.08	Truck Drivers, Heavy/Tractor-Trailer	25.32
Lawyers	75.74	Truck Drivers, Light/Delivery Services	22.16
Maids and Housekeeping Cleaners	18.59	Waiters and Waitresses	16.81

Note: Wage data covers the Sacramento—Arden-Arcade—Roseville, CA Metropolitan Statistical Area; (*) Hourly wages were calculated from annual wage data based on a 40 hour work week; n/a not available.
Source: Bureau of Labor Statistics, Metro Area Occupational Employment & Wage Estimates, May 2021

Employment by Industry

Sector	MSA[1]		U.S.
	Number of Employees	Percent of Total	Percent of Total
Construction	72,600	7.0	5.0
Education and Health Services	170,300	16.5	16.0
Financial Activities	52,900	5.1	5.9
Government	243,500	23.6	14.9
Information	10,300	1.0	1.9
Leisure and Hospitality	99,400	9.6	9.8
Manufacturing	37,900	3.7	8.4
Mining and Logging	700	0.1	0.4
Other Services	32,200	3.1	3.7
Professional and Business Services	137,700	13.4	14.6
Retail Trade	106,000	10.3	10.7
Transportation, Warehousing, and Utilities	40,700	3.9	4.8
Wholesale Trade	26,400	2.6	3.8

Note: Figures are non-farm employment as of December 2021. Figures are not seasonally adjusted and include workers 16 years of age and older; (1) Figures cover the Sacramento—Arden-Arcade—Roseville, CA Metropolitan Statistical Area
Source: Bureau of Labor Statistics, Current Employment Statistics, Employment, Hours, and Earnings

Employment by Occupation

Occupation Classification	City (%)	MSA[1] (%)	U.S. (%)
Management, Business, Science, and Arts	41.3	42.1	39.5
Natural Resources, Construction, and Maintenance	7.1	7.7	8.7
Production, Transportation, and Material Moving	11.7	10.1	13.1
Sales and Office	21.7	21.8	21.3
Service	18.3	18.2	17.4

Note: Figures cover employed civilians 16 years of age and older; (1) Figures cover the Sacramento—Arden-Arcade—Roseville, CA Metropolitan Statistical Area
Source: U.S. Census Bureau, 2016-2020 American Community Survey 5-Year Estimates

Occupations with Greatest Projected Employment Growth: 2021 – 2023

Occupation[1]	2021 Employment	2023 Projected Employment	Numeric Employment Change	Percent Employment Change
Fast Food and Counter Workers	383,500	457,000	73,500	19.2
Home Health and Personal Care Aides	663,400	716,600	53,200	8.0
Waiters and Waitresses	208,500	257,600	49,100	23.5
Cooks, Restaurant	136,700	175,300	38,600	28.2
Laborers and Freight, Stock, and Material Movers, Hand	401,500	431,600	30,100	7.5
Software Developers and Software Quality Assurance Analysts and Testers	311,600	336,800	25,200	8.1
Janitors and Cleaners, Except Maids and Housekeeping Cleaners	232,200	252,400	20,200	8.7
Cooks, Fast Food	109,600	128,200	18,600	17.0
Stockers and Order Fillers	273,000	290,400	17,400	6.4
First-Line Supervisors of Food Preparation and Serving Workers	81,700	98,600	16,900	20.7

Note: Projections cover California; (1) Sorted by numeric employment change
Source: www.projectionscentral.com, State Occupational Projections, 2021–2023 Short-Term Projections

Fastest-Growing Occupations: 2021 – 2023

Occupation[1]	2021 Employment	2023 Projected Employment	Numeric Employment Change	Percent Employment Change
Manicurists and Pedicurists	23,400	33,500	10,100	43.2
Cooks, All Other	3,900	5,400	1,500	38.5
Miscellaneous Entertainers and Performers, Sports and Related Workers	5,900	8,100	2,200	37.3
Barbers	1,900	2,600	700	36.8
Gaming Change Persons and Booth Cashiers	2,200	3,000	800	36.4
Gaming Service Workers, All Other	1,400	1,900	500	35.7
Gaming Dealers	12,200	16,500	4,300	35.2
First-Line Supervisors of Gambling Services Workers	2,900	3,900	1,000	34.5
Massage Therapists	18,000	24,200	6,200	34.4
Costume Attendants	1,500	2,000	500	33.3

Note: Projections cover California; (1) Sorted by percent employment change and excludes occupations with numeric employment change less than 50
Source: www.projectionscentral.com, State Occupational Projections, 2021–2023 Short-Term Projections

TAXES

State Corporate Income Tax Rates

State	Tax Rate (%)	Income Brackets ($)	Num. of Brackets	Financial Institution Tax Rate (%)[a]	Federal Income Tax Ded.
California	8.84 (b)	Flat rate	1	10.84 (b)	No

Note: Tax rates as of January 1, 2022; (a) Rates listed are the corporate income tax rate applied to financial institutions or excise taxes based on income. Some states have other taxes based upon the value of deposits or shares; (b) Minimum tax is $800 in California, $250 in District of Columbia, $50 in Arizona and North Dakota (banks), $400 ($100 banks) in Rhode Island, $200 per location in South Dakota (banks), $100 in Utah, $300 in Vermont.
Source: Federation of Tax Administrators, State Corporate Income Tax Rates, January 1, 2022

State Individual Income Tax Rates

State	Tax Rate (%)	Income Brackets ($)	Personal Exemptions ($)			Standard Ded. ($)	
			Single	Married	Depend.	Single	Married
California (a)	1.0 - 12.3 (g)	9,325 - 625,369 (b)	129	258	400 (c)	4,803	9,606 (a)

Note: Tax rates as of January 1, 2022; Local- and county-level taxes are not included; Federal income tax is not deductible on state income tax returns; (a) 19 states have statutory provision for automatically adjusting to the rate of inflation the dollar values of the income tax brackets, standard deductions, and/or personal exemptions. Michigan indexes the personal exemption only. Oregon does not index the income brackets for $125,000 and over; (b) For joint returns, taxes are twice the tax on half the couple's income; (c) The personal exemption takes the form of a tax credit instead of a deduction; (g) California imposes an additional 1% tax on taxable income over $1 million, making the maximum rate 13.3% over $1 million.
Source: Federation of Tax Administrators, State Individual Income Tax Rates, January 1, 2022

Various State Sales and Excise Tax Rates

State	State Sales Tax (%)	Gasoline[1] (¢/gal.)	Cigarette[2] ($/pack)	Spirits[3] ($/gal.)	Wine[4] ($/gal.)	Beer[5] ($/gal.)	Recreational Marijuana (%)
California	7.25	68.15	2.87	3.3	0.2	0.2	(c)

Note: All tax rates as of January 1, 2022; (1) The American Petroleum Institute has developed a methodology for determining the average tax rate on a gallon of fuel. Rates may include any of the following: excise taxes, environmental fees, storage tank fees, other fees or taxes, general sales tax, and local taxes; (2) The federal excise tax of $1.0066 per pack and local taxes are not included; (3) Rates are those applicable to off-premise sales of 40% alcohol by volume (a.b.v.) distilled spirits in 750ml containers. Local excise taxes are excluded; (4) Rates are those applicable to off-premise sales of 11% a.b.v. non-carbonated wine in 750ml containers; (5) Rates are those applicable to off-premise sales of 4.7% a.b.v. beer in 12 ounce containers; (c) 15% excise tax (levied on wholesale at average market rate); $10.08/oz. flowers & $3/oz. leaves cultivation tax; $1.41/oz fresh cannabis plant
Source: Tax Foundation, 2022 Facts & Figures: How Does Your State Compare?

State Business Tax Climate Index Rankings

State	Overall Rank	Corporate Tax Rank	Individual Income Tax Rank	Sales Tax Rank	Property Tax Rank	Unemployment Insurance Tax Rank
California	48	46	49	47	14	23

Note: The index is a measure of how each state's tax laws affect economic performance. The lower the rank, the more favorable a state's tax system is for business. States without a given tax are given a ranking of 1. The scores/rankings for the District of Columbia do not affect other states. The 2022 index represents the tax climate as of July 1, 2021.
Source: Tax Foundation, State Business Tax Climate Index 2022

TRANSPORTATION

Means of Transportation to Work

Area	Car/Truck/Van		Public Transportation			Bicycle	Walked	Other Means	Worked at Home
	Drove Alone	Car-pooled	Bus	Subway	Railroad				
City	71.9	10.1	1.8	0.2	0.3	1.8	3.0	2.0	8.9
MSA[1]	74.7	9.1	1.4	0.1	0.2	1.3	1.7	1.6	9.9
U.S.	74.9	8.9	2.2	1.7	0.5	0.5	2.6	1.4	7.3

Note: Figures are percentages and cover workers 16 years of age and older; (1) Figures cover the Sacramento—Arden-Arcade—Roseville, CA Metropolitan Statistical Area
Source: U.S. Census Bureau, 2016-2020 American Community Survey 5-Year Estimates

Travel Time to Work

Area	Less Than 10 Minutes	10 to 19 Minutes	20 to 29 Minutes	30 to 44 Minutes	45 to 59 Minutes	60 to 89 Minutes	90 Minutes or More
City	8.1	31.2	25.7	22.0	5.7	4.1	3.2
MSA[1]	9.7	28.3	22.4	23.1	7.9	4.9	3.6
U.S.	12.3	28.4	20.9	20.9	8.3	6.4	2.9

Note: Note: Figures are percentages and include workers 16 years old and over; (1) Figures cover the Sacramento—Arden-Arcade—Roseville, CA Metropolitan Statistical Area
Source: U.S. Census Bureau, 2016-2020 American Community Survey 5-Year Estimates

Key Congestion Measures

Measure	1990	2000	2010	2015	2020
Annual Hours of Delay, Total (000)	17,833	37,073	59,264	68,922	47,492
Annual Hours of Delay, Per Auto Commuter	26	37	46	55	38
Annual Congestion Cost, Per Auto Commuter ($)	519	812	1,032	1,108	800

Note: Covers the Sacramento CA urban area
Source: Texas A&M Transportation Institute, 2021 Urban Mobility Report

Freeway Travel Time Index

Measure	1985	1990	1995	2000	2005	2010	2015	2020
Urban Area Index[1]	1.10	1.14	1.17	1.20	1.23	1.24	1.27	1.11
Urban Area Rank[1,2]	27	26	29	29	28	24	20	20

Note: Freeway Travel Time Index—the ratio of travel time in the peak period to the travel time at free-flow conditions. For example, a value of 1.30 indicates a 20-minute free-flow trip takes 26 minutes in the peak (20 minutes x 1.30 = 26 minutes); (1) Covers the Sacramento CA urban area; (2) Rank is based on 101 larger urban areas (#1 = highest travel time index)
Source: Texas A&M Transportation Institute, 2021 Urban Mobility Report

Public Transportation

Agency Name / Mode of Transportation	Vehicles Operated in Maximum Service[1]	Annual Unlinked Passenger Trips[2] (in thous.)	Annual Passenger Miles[3] (in thous.)
Sacramento Regional Transit District (Sacramento RT)			
Bus (directly operated)	162	8,448.8	30,592.7
Demand Response (directly operated)	100	126.1	415.3
Light Rail (directly operated)	69	8,988.8	53,131.3

Note: (1) Number of revenue vehicles operated by the given mode and type of service to meet the annual maximum service requirement. This is the revenue vehicle count during the peak season of the year; on the week and day that maximum service is provided. Vehicles operated in maximum service (VOMS) exclude atypical days and one-time special events; (2) Number of passengers who boarded public transportation vehicles. Passengers are counted each time they board a vehicle no matter how many vehicles they use to travel from their origin to their destination. (3) Sum of the distances ridden by all passengers during the entire fiscal year.
Source: Federal Transit Administration, National Transit Database, 2020

Air Transportation

Airport Name and Code / Type of Service	Passenger Airlines[1]	Passenger Enplanements	Freight Carriers[2]	Freight (lbs)
Sacramento International (SMF)				
Domestic service (U.S. carriers - 2021)	21	4,631,053	14	154,344,179
International service (U.S. carriers - 2020)	3	5,536	0	0

Note: (1) Includes all U.S.-based major, minor and commuter airlines that carried at least one passenger during the year; (2) Includes all U.S.-based airlines and freight carriers that transported at least one pound of freight during the year.
Source: Bureau of Transportation Statistics, The Intermodal Transportation Database, Air Carriers: T-100 Domestic Market (U.S. Carriers), 2021; Bureau of Transportation Statistics, The Intermodal Transportation Database, Air Carriers: T-100 International Market (U.S. Carriers), 2020

BUSINESSES

Major Business Headquarters

Company Name	Industry	Rankings	
		Fortune[1]	Forbes[2]
No companies listed	-	-	-

Note: (1) Companies that produce a 10-K are ranked 1 to 500 based on 2020 revenue; (2) All private companies with at least $2 billion in annual revenue through the end of their most current fiscal year are ranked 1 to 225; companies listed are headquartered in the city; dashes indicate no ranking
Source: Fortune, "Fortune 500," 2021; Forbes, "America's Largest Private Companies," 2021

Fastest-Growing Businesses

According to *Inc.*, Sacramento is home to one of America's 500 fastest-growing private companies: **RCG Logistics** (#485). Criteria: must be an independent, privately-held, for-profit, U.S. corporation, proprietorship or partnership as of December 31, 2020; revenues must be at least $100,000 in 2017 and $2 million in 2020; must have four-year operating/sales history. *Inc., "America's 500 Fastest-Growing Private Companies," 2021*

According to *Initiative for a Competitive Inner City (ICIC)*, Sacramento is home to one of America's 100 fastest-growing "inner city" companies: **24/7 MedStaff** (#75). Criteria for inclusion: company must be headquartered in or have 51 percent or more of its physical operations in an economically distressed urban area; must be an independent, for-profit corporation, partnership or proprietorship; must have 10 or more employees and have a five-year sales history that includes sales of at least $200,000 in the base year and at least $1 million in the current year with no decrease in sales over the two most recent years. Companies were ranked overall by revenue growth over the five-year period between 2016 and 2020. *Initiative for a Competitive Inner City (ICIC), "Inner City 100 Companies," 2021*

Living Environment

COST OF LIVING

Cost of Living Index

Composite Index	Groceries	Housing	Utilities	Trans-portation	Health Care	Misc. Goods/ Services
120.0	104.4	140.8	107.7	131.8	117.8	109.0

Note: The Cost of Living Index measures regional differences in the cost of consumer goods and services, excluding taxes and non-consumer expenditures, for professional and managerial households in the top income quintile. It is based on more than 50,000 prices covering almost 60 different items for which prices are collected three times a year by chambers of commerce, economic development organizations or university applied economic centers in each participating urban area. The numbers shown should be read as a percentage above or below the national average of 100. For example, a value of 115.4 in the groceries column indicates that grocery prices are 15.4% higher than the national average. Small differences in the index numbers should not be interpreted as significant; Figures cover the Sacramento CA urban area.
Source: The Council for Community and Economic Research, Cost of Living Index, 2021

Grocery Prices

Area[1]	T-Bone Steak ($/pound)	Frying Chicken ($/pound)	Whole Milk ($/half gal.)	Eggs ($/dozen)	Orange Juice ($/64 oz.)	Coffee ($/11.5 oz.)
City[2]	11.52	1.59	3.79	2.54	3.84	4.84
Avg.	12.82	1.40	2.22	1.57	3.59	4.30
Min.	8.91	0.91	1.29	0.75	2.87	3.02
Max.	21.35	2.69	3.92	3.86	5.49	8.11

Note: (1) Values for the local area are compared with the average, minimum and maximum values for all 285 areas in the Cost of Living Index; (2) Figures cover the Sacramento CA urban area; ***T-Bone Steak*** *(price per pound);* ***Frying Chicken*** *(price per pound, whole fryer);* ***Whole Milk*** *(half gallon carton);* ***Eggs*** *(price per dozen, Grade A, large);* ***Orange Juice*** *(64 oz. Tropicana or Florida Natural);* ***Coffee*** *(11.5 oz. can, vacuum-packed, Maxwell House, Hills Bros, or Folgers).*
Source: The Council for Community and Economic Research, Cost of Living Index, 2021

Housing and Utility Costs

Area[1]	New Home Price ($)	Apartment Rent ($/month)	All Electric ($/month)	Part Electric ($/month)	Other Energy ($/month)	Telephone ($/month)
City[2]	514,667	2,051	-	152.89	43.30	184.64
Avg.	398,393	1,217	171.38	100.83	69.67	187.75
Min.	212,799	534	96.71	31.56	27.15	173.01
Max.	2,354,006	4,438	369.53	277.33	303.87	206.73

Note: (1) Values for the local area are compared with the average, minimum and maximum values for all 285 areas in the Cost of Living Index; (2) Figures cover the Sacramento CA urban area; ***New Home Price*** *(2,400 sf living area, 8,000 sf lot, in urban area with full utilities);* ***Apartment Rent*** *(950 sf 2 bedroom/1.5 or 2 bath, unfurnished, excluding all utilities except water);* ***All Electric*** *(average monthly cost for an all-electric home);* ***Part Electric*** *(average monthly cost for a part-electric home);* ***Other Energy*** *(average monthly cost for natural gas, fuel oil, coal, wood, and any other forms of energy except electricity);* ***Telephone*** *(price includes the base monthly rate plus taxes and fees for three lines of mobile phone service).*
Source: The Council for Community and Economic Research, Cost of Living Index, 2021

Health Care, Transportation, and Other Costs

Area[1]	Doctor ($/visit)	Dentist ($/visit)	Optometrist ($/visit)	Gasoline ($/gallon)	Beauty Salon ($/visit)	Men's Shirt ($)
City[2]	188.58	96.32	146.32	4.11	62.33	29.93
Avg.	118.16	101.04	109.44	2.71	40.63	30.77
Min.	35.04	55.56	51.17	2.17	18.59	11.32
Max.	231.10	165.12	256.81	4.11	85.33	63.03

Note: (1) Values for the local area are compared with the average, minimum and maximum values for all 285 areas in the Cost of Living Index; (2) Figures cover the Sacramento CA urban area; ***Doctor*** *(general practitioners routine exam of an established patient);* ***Dentist*** *(adult teeth cleaning and periodic oral examination);* ***Optometrist*** *(full vision eye exam for established adult patient);* ***Gasoline*** *(one gallon regular unleaded, national brand, including all taxes, cash price at self-service pump if available);* ***Beauty Salon*** *(woman's shampoo, trim, and blow-dry);* ***Men's Shirt*** *(cotton/polyester dress shirt, pinpoint weave, long sleeves).*
Source: The Council for Community and Economic Research, Cost of Living Index, 2021

HOUSING

Homeownership Rate

Area	2013 (%)	2014 (%)	2015 (%)	2016 (%)	2017 (%)	2018 (%)	2019 (%)	2020 (%)	2021 (%)
MSA[1]	60.4	60.1	60.8	60.5	60.1	64.1	61.6	63.4	63.2
U.S.	65.1	64.5	63.7	63.4	63.9	64.4	64.6	66.6	65.5

Note: (1) Figures cover the Sacramento—Arden-Arcade—Roseville, CA Metropolitan Statistical Area
Source: U.S. Census Bureau, Housing Vacancies and Homeownership Annual Statistics: 2013-2021

House Price Index (HPI)

Area	National Ranking²	Quarterly Change (%)	One-Year Change (%)	Five-Year Change (%)	Since 1991Q1 (%)
MSA¹	76	3.18	20.94	53.71	223.68
U.S.³	–	3.33	17.54	54.45	258.04

Note: The HPI is a weighted repeat sales index. It measures average price changes in repeat sales or refinancings on the same properties. This information is obtained by reviewing repeat mortgage transactions on single-family properties whose mortgages have been purchased or securitized by Fannie Mae or Freddie Mac since January 1975; (1) Figures cover the Sacramento—Roseville—Arden-Arcade, CA Metropolitan Statistical Area; (2) Rankings are based on annual percentage change for all metro areas containing at least 15,000 transactions over the last 10 years and ranges from 1 to 268; (3) figures based on a weighted average of Census Division estimates using a seasonally adjusted, purchase-only index; all figures are for the period ending December 31, 2021
Source: Federal Housing Finance Agency, Change in FHFA Metropolitan Area House Price Indexes, 2021Q4

Median Single-Family Home Prices

Area	2019	2020	2021ᴾ	Percent Change 2020 to 2021
MSA¹	380.0	421.0	500.0	18.8
U.S. Average	274.6	300.2	353.4	17.7

Note: Figures are median sales prices of existing single-family homes in thousands of dollars; (p) preliminary; (1) Figures cover the Sacramento—Arden-Arcade—Roseville, CA Metropolitan Statistical Area
Source: National Association of Realtors, Median Sales Price of Existing Single-Family Homes for Metropolitan Areas, 4th Quarter 2021

Qualifying Income Based on Median Sales Price of Existing Single-Family Homes

Area	With 5% Down ($)	With 10% Down ($)	With 20% Down ($)
MSA¹	101,530	96,186	85,499
U.S. Average	70,699	66,978	59,536

Note: Figures are preliminary; Qualifying income is based on a mortgage rate of 3.13%. Monthly principal and interest payment is limited to 25% of income; (1) Figures cover the Sacramento—Arden-Arcade—Roseville, CA Metropolitan Statistical Area
Source: National Association of Realtors, Qualifying Income Based on Median Sales Price of Existing Single-Family Homes for Metropolitan Areas, 4th Quarter 2021

Home Value Distribution

Area	Under $50,000	$50,000 -$99,999	$100,000 -$149,999	$150,000 -$199,999	$200,000 -$299,999	$300,000 -$499,999	$500,000 -$999,999	$1,000,000 or more
City	2.6	1.6	2.6	4.8	22.9	42.9	20.1	2.5
MSA¹	2.7	1.5	1.8	3.1	14.7	43.5	29.1	3.6
U.S.	6.6	11.0	12.3	13.6	20.0	20.5	12.3	3.7

Note: Figures are percentages and cover owner-occupied housing units; (1) Figures cover the Sacramento—Arden-Arcade—Roseville, CA Metropolitan Statistical Area
Source: U.S. Census Bureau, 2016-2020 American Community Survey 5-Year Estimates

Year Housing Structure Built

Area	2010 or Later	2000 -2009	1990 -1999	1980 -1989	1970 -1979	1960 -1969	1950 -1959	1940 -1949	Before 1940	Median Year
City	3.3	14.9	9.1	15.5	14.3	11.7	12.4	7.4	11.4	1975
MSA¹	4.4	17.1	15.3	16.7	18.2	10.7	9.8	3.5	4.3	1982
U.S.	6.2	13.6	13.9	13.4	15.0	10.5	10.2	4.8	12.4	1978

Note: Figures are percentages except for Median Year; Note: (1) Figures cover the Sacramento—Arden-Arcade—Roseville, CA Metropolitan Statistical Area
Source: U.S. Census Bureau, 2016-2020 American Community Survey 5-Year Estimates

Gross Monthly Rent

Area	Under $500	$500 -$999	$1,000 -$1,499	$1,500 -$1,999	$2,000 -$2,499	$2,500 -$2,999	$3,000 and up	Median ($)
City	5.8	20.7	36.4	26.7	8.0	1.7	0.8	1,328
MSA¹	4.4	18.9	36.6	25.7	10.2	2.7	1.6	1,364
U.S.	8.9	34.3	30.2	14.9	6.2	2.6	2.8	1,096

Note: Figures are percentages except for Median; Gross rent is the contract rent plus the estimated average monthly cost of utilities (electricity, gas, and water and sewer) and fuels (oil, coal, kerosene, wood, etc.) if these are paid by the renter (or paid for the renter by someone else); (1) Figures cover the Sacramento—Arden-Arcade—Roseville, CA Metropolitan Statistical Area
Source: U.S. Census Bureau, 2016-2020 American Community Survey 5-Year Estimates

HEALTH

Health Risk Factors

Category	MSA[1] (%)	U.S. (%)
Adults aged 18–64 who have any kind of health care coverage	n/a	86.8
Adults who reported being in good or better health	n/a	86.7
Adults who are current smokers	n/a	15.5
Adults who currently use chewing tobacco, snuff, or snus	n/a	3.7
Adults who are heavy drinkers[2]	n/a	6.7
Adults who are binge drinkers[3]	n/a	15.7
Adults who are overweight (BMI 25.0 - 29.9)	n/a	35.2
Adults who are obese (BMI 30.0 - 99.8)	n/a	31.9
Adults who participated in any physical activities in the past month	n/a	77.6
Adults who always or nearly always wears a seat belt	n/a	94.2

Note: (1) Figures for the Sacramento—Arden-Arcade—Roseville, CA Metropolitan Statistical Area were not available.
(2) Heavy drinkers are classified as adult men having more than 14 drinks per week and adult women having more than 7 drinks per week; (3) Binge drinkers are classified as males having five or more drinks on one occasion or females having four or more drinks on one occasion
Source: Centers for Disease Control and Prevention, Behaviorial Risk Factor Surveillance System, SMART: Selected Metropolitan Area Risk Trends, 2020

Acute and Chronic Health Conditions

Category	MSA[1] (%)	U.S. (%)
Adults who have ever been told they had a heart attack	n/a	4.3
Adults who have ever been told they have angina or coronary heart disease	n/a	4.0
Adults who have ever been told they had a stroke	n/a	2.8
Adults who have ever been told they have asthma	n/a	14.2
Adults who have ever been told they have arthritis	n/a	24.5
Adults who have ever been told they have diabetes[2]	n/a	10.6
Adults who have ever been told they had skin cancer	n/a	6.4
Adults who have ever been told they had any other types of cancer	n/a	6.8
Adults who have ever been told they have COPD	n/a	6.2
Adults who have ever been told they have kidney disease	n/a	2.9
Adults who have ever been told they have a form of depression	n/a	19.6

Note: (1) Figures for the Sacramento—Arden-Arcade—Roseville, CA Metropolitan Statistical Area were not available.
(2) Figures do not include pregnancy-related, borderline, or pre-diabetes
Source: Centers for Disease Control and Prevention, Behaviorial Risk Factor Surveillance System, SMART: Selected Metropolitan Area Risk Trends, 2020

Health Screening and Vaccination Rates

Category	MSA[1] (%)	U.S. (%)
Adults 50-75 who have had a blood stool test within the past year	n/a	9.3
Adults aged 65+ who have had flu shot within the past year	n/a	67.9
Adults aged 65+ who have ever had a pneumonia vaccination	n/a	72.2
Adults who have ever been tested for HIV	n/a	37.1
Women aged 21-65 who have had a pap test in the past three years	n/a	77.7
Men aged 40+ who have had a PSA test within the past two years	n/a	31.8
Women aged 40+ who have had a mammogram within the past two years	n/a	71.5

Note: (1) Figures for the Sacramento—Arden-Arcade—Roseville, CA Metropolitan Statistical Area were not available.
Source: Centers for Disease Control and Prevention, Behaviorial Risk Factor Surveillance System, SMART: Selected Metropolitan Area Risk Trends, 2020

Disability Status

Category	MSA[1] (%)	U.S. (%)
Adults who reported being deaf	n/a	6.8
Are you blind or have serious difficulty seeing, even when wearing glasses?	n/a	4.7
Do you have difficulty doing errands alone?	n/a	6.3
Do you have difficulty dressing or bathing?	n/a	3.0
Do you have serious difficulty concentrating/remembering/making decisions?	n/a	10.8
Do you have serious difficulty walking or climbing stairs?	n/a	11.9

Note: (1) Figures for the Sacramento—Arden-Arcade—Roseville, CA Metropolitan Statistical Area were not available.
Source: Centers for Disease Control and Prevention, Behaviorial Risk Factor Surveillance System, SMART: Selected Metropolitan Area Risk Trends, 2020

Mortality Rates for the Top 10 Causes of Death in the U.S.

ICD-10[a] Sub-Chapter	ICD-10[a] Code	Age-Adjusted Mortality Rate[1] per 100,000 population	
		County[2]	U.S.
Malignant neoplasms	C00-C97	147.7	146.4
Ischaemic heart diseases	I20-I25	85.0	90.2
Other forms of heart disease	I30-I51	41.2	51.9
Other degenerative diseases of the nervous system	G30-G31	54.5	39.7
Other external causes of accidental injury	W00-X59	30.2	38.7
Chronic lower respiratory diseases	J40-J47	34.2	38.1
Cerebrovascular diseases	I60-I69	45.1	37.6
Organic, including symptomatic, mental disorders	F01-F09	22.8	29.4
Hypertensive diseases	I10-I15	29.8	26.1
Diabetes mellitus	E10-E14	28.8	22.6

Note: (a) ICD-10 = International Classification of Diseases 10th Revision; (1) Mortality rates are a three-year average covering 2018-2020; (2) Figures cover Sacramento County.
Source: Centers for Disease Control and Prevention, National Center for Health Statistics. Underlying Cause of Death 1999-2020 on CDC WONDER Online Database

Mortality Rates for Selected Causes of Death

ICD-10[a] Sub-Chapter	ICD-10[a] Code	Age-Adjusted Mortality Rate[1] per 100,000 population	
		County[2]	U.S.
Assault	X85-Y09	6.1	6.5
Diseases of the liver	K70-K76	15.3	15.3
Human immunodeficiency virus (HIV) disease	B20-B24	1.4	1.4
Influenza and pneumonia	J09-J18	14.4	13.4
Intentional self-harm	X60-X84	12.2	13.9
Malnutrition	E40-E46	3.2	2.9
Obesity and other hyperalimentation	E65-E68	2.9	2.4
Renal failure	N17-N19	3.9	12.5
Transport accidents	V01-V99	12.5	12.5
Viral hepatitis	B15-B19	2.4	1.0

Note: (a) ICD-10 = International Classification of Diseases 10th Revision; (1) Mortality rates are a three-year average covering 2018-2020; (2) Figures cover Sacramento County; Data are suppressed when the data meet the criteria for confidentiality constraints; Mortality rates are flagged as unreliable when the rate would be calculated with a numerator of 20 or less.
Source: Centers for Disease Control and Prevention, National Center for Health Statistics. Underlying Cause of Death 1999-2020 on CDC WONDER Online Database

Health Insurance Coverage

Area	With Health Insurance	With Private Health Insurance	With Public Health Insurance	Without Health Insurance	Population Under Age 19 Without Health Insurance
City	94.3	63.6	41.2	5.7	2.3
MSA[1]	95.0	69.9	38.2	5.0	2.5
U.S.	91.3	68.1	35.3	8.7	5.2

Note: Figures are percentages that cover the civilian noninstitutionalized population; (1) Figures cover the Sacramento—Arden-Arcade—Roseville, CA Metropolitan Statistical Area
Source: U.S. Census Bureau, 2016-2020 American Community Survey 5-Year Estimates

Number of Medical Professionals

Area	MDs[3]	DOs[3,4]	Dentists	Podiatrists	Chiropractors	Optometrists
County[1] (number)	5,075	252	1,250	72	344	286
County[1] (rate[2])	320.2	15.9	78.9	4.5	21.7	18.0
U.S. (rate[2])	285.1	23.0	71.1	6.2	28.2	17.0

06067
Note: Data as of 2020 unless noted; (1) Data covers Sacramento County; (2) Rate per 100,000 population; (3) Data as of 2019 and includes all active, non-federal physicians; (4) Doctor of Osteopathic Medicine
Source: U.S. Department of Health and Human Services, Health Resources and Services Administration, Bureau of Health Professions, Area Resource File (ARF) 2020-2021

Best Hospitals

According to *U.S. News*, the Sacramento—Arden-Arcade—Roseville, CA metro area is home to one of the best hospitals in the U.S.: **UC Davis Medical Center** (9 adult specialties and 4 pediatric specialties). The hospital listed was nationally ranked in at least one of 15 adult or 10 pediatric specialties. Only 175 U.S. hospitals performed well enough to be nationally ranked in one or more specialties. Twenty hospitals in the U.S. made the Honor Roll. The Best Hospitals Honor Roll takes both the national rankings and the procedure and condition ratings into account. Hospitals received points if they were nationally ranked in one of the 15 adult specialties—the higher they ranked, the more points they got—and how many ratings of "high performing" they earned in the 17 procedures and conditions. *U.S. News Online, "America's Best Hospitals 2021-22"*

According to *U.S. News,* the Sacramento—Arden-Arcade—Roseville, CA metro area is home to one of the best children's hospitals in the U.S.: **UC Davis Children's Hospital** (4 pediatric specialties). The hospital listed was highly ranked in at least one of 10 pediatric specialties. Ninety-two children's hospitals in the U.S. were nationally ranked in at least one specialty. Hospitals received points for being ranked in a specialty, and the 10 hospitals with the most points across the 10 specialties make up the Honor Roll. *U.S. News Online, "America's Best Children's Hospitals 2021-22"*

EDUCATION

Public School District Statistics

District Name	Schls	Pupils	Pupil/ Teacher Ratio	Minority Pupils[1] (%)	LEP/ELL[2] (%)	IEP[3] (%)
Natomas Unified	18	13,767	n/a	84.4	12.8	12.0
Robla Elementary	6	2,069	n/a	86.1	38.1	10.9
Sacramento City Unified	73	42,232	n/a	82.5	19.1	14.0

Note: Table includes school districts with 2,000 or more students; (1) Percentage of students that are not non-Hispanic white; (2) Percentage of students that are Limited English Proficient (LEP) or English Language Learners (ELL) (2018-19); (3) Percentage of students that have an Individualized Education Program (IEP).
Source: U.S. Department of Education, National Center for Education Statistics, Common Core of Data, Local Education Agency (School District) Universe Survey: School Year 2019-2020

Best High Schools

According to *U.S. News,* Sacramento is home to one of the top 500 high schools in the U.S.: **West Campus High School** (#222). Nearly 18,000 public, magnet and charter schools were ranked based on their performance on state assessments and how well they prepare students for college. *U.S. News & World Report, "Best High Schools 2021"*

Highest Level of Education

Area	Less than H.S.	H.S. Diploma	Some College, No Deg.	Associate Degree	Bachelor's Degree	Master's Degree	Prof. School Degree	Doctorate Degree
City	14.1	20.6	22.6	8.4	21.9	8.1	3.1	1.3
MSA[1]	10.3	20.9	24.5	10.0	22.0	8.1	2.8	1.5
U.S.	11.5	26.7	20.3	8.6	20.2	9.1	2.2	1.5

Note: Figures cover persons age 25 and over; (1) Figures cover the Sacramento—Arden-Arcade—Roseville, CA Metropolitan Statistical Area
Source: U.S. Census Bureau, 2016-2020 American Community Survey 5-Year Estimates

Educational Attainment by Race

Area	High School Graduate or Higher (%)					Bachelor's Degree or Higher (%)				
	Total	White	Black	Asian	Hisp.[2]	Total	White	Black	Asian	Hisp.[2]
City	85.9	90.5	91.1	80.6	73.8	34.3	41.2	24.0	38.4	19.9
MSA[1]	89.7	92.7	91.2	84.1	75.8	34.3	35.7	25.4	43.9	19.4
U.S.	88.5	90.7	86.7	87.3	70.3	32.9	34.4	22.6	55.0	17.6

Note: Figures shown cover persons 25 years old and over; (1) Figures cover the Sacramento—Arden-Arcade—Roseville, CA Metropolitan Statistical Area; (2) People of Hispanic origin can be of any race
Source: U.S. Census Bureau, 2016-2020 American Community Survey 5-Year Estimates

School Enrollment by Grade and Control

Area	Preschool (%)		Kindergarten (%)		Grades 1 - 4 (%)		Grades 5 - 8 (%)		Grades 9 - 12 (%)	
	Public	Private	Public	Private	Public	Private	Public	Private	Public	Private
City	66.4	33.6	92.9	7.1	93.6	6.4	92.9	7.1	91.4	8.6
MSA[1]	61.8	38.2	90.6	9.4	92.4	7.6	92.4	7.6	91.8	8.2
U.S.	58.9	41.1	86.9	13.1	89.0	11.0	89.0	11.0	89.7	10.3

Note: Figures shown cover persons 3 years old and over; (1) Figures cover the Sacramento—Arden-Arcade—Roseville, CA Metropolitan Statistical Area
Source: U.S. Census Bureau, 2016-2020 American Community Survey 5-Year Estimates

Higher Education

Four-Year Colleges			Two-Year Colleges			Medical Schools[1]	Law Schools[2]	Voc/ Tech[3]
Public	Private Non-profit	Private For-profit	Public	Private Non-profit	Private For-profit			
2	3	1	8	0	8	2	4	12

Note: Figures cover institutions located within the Sacramento—Arden-Arcade—Roseville, CA Metropolitan Statistical Area and include main campuses only; (1) includes schools accredited by the Liaison Committee on Medical Education and the American Osteopathic Association's Commission on Osteopathic College Accreditation; (2) includes ABA-accredited schools, schools with provisional ABA accreditation, and state accredited schools; (3) includes all schools with programs that are less than 2 years.
Source: National Center for Education Statistics, Integrated Postsecondary Education System (IPEDS), 2020-21; Wikipedia, List of Medical Schools in the United States, accessed April 11, 2022; Wikipedia, List of Law Schools in the United States, accessed April 11, 2022

According to *U.S. News & World Report,* the Sacramento—Arden-Arcade—Roseville, CA metro area is home to one of the top 200 national universities in the U.S.: **University of California—Davis** (#38 tie). The indicators used to capture academic quality fall into a number of categories: assessment by administrators at peer institutions; retention of students; faculty resources; student selectivity; financial resources; alumni giving; high school counselor ratings of colleges; and graduation rate. *U.S. News & World Report, "America's Best Colleges 2022"*

According to *U.S. News & World Report,* the Sacramento—Arden-Arcade—Roseville, CA metro area is home to one of the top 100 law schools in the U.S.: **University of California—Davis** (#35 tie). The rankings are based on a weighted average of 12 measures of quality: peer assessment score; assessment score by lawyers/judges; median LSAT scores; median undergrad GPA; acceptance rate; employment rates for graduates; placement success; bar passage rate; faculty resources; expenditures per student; student/faculty ratio; and library resources. *U.S. News & World Report, "America's Best Graduate Schools, Law, 2022"*

According to *U.S. News & World Report,* the Sacramento—Arden-Arcade—Roseville, CA metro area is home to one of the top 75 medical schools for research in the U.S.: **University of California—Davis** (#48 tie). The rankings are based on a weighted average of 11 measures of quality: quality assessment; peer assessment score; assessment score by residency directors; research activity; total research activity; average research activity per faculty member; student selectivity; median MCAT total score; median undergraduate GPA; acceptance rate; and faculty resources. *U.S. News & World Report, "America's Best Graduate Schools, Medical, 2022"*

According to *U.S. News & World Report,* the Sacramento—Arden-Arcade—Roseville, CA metro area is home to one of the top 75 business schools in the U.S.: **University of California—Davis** (#53 tie). The rankings are based on a weighted average of the following nine measures: quality assessment; peer assessment; recruiter assessment; placement success; mean starting salary and bonus; student selectivity; mean GMAT and GRE scores; mean undergraduate GPA; and acceptance rate. *U.S. News & World Report, "America's Best Graduate Schools, Business, 2022"*

EMPLOYERS

Major Employers

Company Name	Industry
Aerojet Rocketdyne	Aerospace industries, mfg
Agreeya Solutions	Information technology services
Ampac Fine Chemicals	Electronic equipment & supplies, mfg
Apple Distribution Center	Distribution centers, wholesale
California Department of Corrections	State govt-correctional institutions
California Prison Ind Auth	Government offices-state
California State Univercity-Sacramento	Schools-universities & colleges academic
Department of Transportation	Government offices-state
Disabled American Veterans	Veterans' & military organizations
Division of Fiscal Services	Services nec
Employment Development Dept	Government offices-state
Environmental Protection Agency	State government-environmental programs
Intel Corp	Semiconductor devices, mfg
Kaiser Permanente South	Hospitals
L A Care Health Plan	Health plans
Mercy General Hospital	Hospitals
Mercy San Juan Medical Center	Hospitals
Sacramento Municipal Utility	Electric contractors
Securitas Security Services USA	Security guard & patrol services
SMUD	Electric companies
State Compensation Insurance Fund	Insurance
Sutter Medical Center-Sacramento	Hospitals
United Loan Corp	Real estate
Water Resource Dept	Government offices-state

Note: Companies shown are located within the Sacramento—Arden-Arcade—Roseville, CA Metropolitan Statistical Area.
Source: Hoovers.com; Wikipedia

PUBLIC SAFETY

Crime Rate

Area	Total Crime	Violent Crime Rate				Property Crime Rate		
		Murder	Rape[3]	Robbery	Aggrav. Assault	Burglary	Larceny -Theft	Motor Vehicle Theft
City	3,428.4	8.1	24.1	169.3	481.8	546.0	1,715.2	483.8
Suburbs[1]	2,102.6	3.8	27.9	64.5	196.3	323.1	1,274.4	212.6
Metro[2]	2,393.6	4.8	27.0	87.5	259.0	372.0	1,371.2	272.1
U.S.	2,356.7	6.5	38.4	73.9	279.7	314.2	1,398.0	246.0

Note: Figures are crimes per 100,000 population; (1) All areas within the metro area that are located outside the city limits; (2) Figures cover the Sacramento—Arden-Arcade—Roseville, CA Metropolitan Statistical Area; (3) All figures shown were reported using the revised Uniform Crime Reporting (UCR) definition of rape.
Source: FBI Uniform Crime Reports, 2020

Hate Crimes

Area	Number of Quarters Reported	Number of Incidents per Bias Motivation					
		Race/Ethnicity/ Ancestry	Religion	Sexual Orientation	Disability	Gender	Gender Identity
City	4	8	0	2	0	0	0
U.S.	4	5,227	1,244	1,110	130	75	266

Source: Federal Bureau of Investigation, Hate Crime Statistics 2020

Identity Theft Consumer Reports

Area	Reports	Reports per 100,000 Population	Rank[2]
MSA[1]	6,231	264	159
U.S.	1,434,676	432	-

Note: (1) Figures cover the Sacramento—Arden-Arcade—Roseville, CA Metropolitan Statistical Area; (2) Rank ranges from 1 to 391 where 1 indicates greatest number of identity theft reports per 100,000 population
Source: Federal Trade Commission, Consumer Sentinel Network Data Book 2021

Fraud and Other Consumer Reports

Area	Reports	Reports per 100,000 Population	Rank[2]
MSA[1]	26,044	1,102	73
U.S.	4,328,977	1,304	-

Note: (1) Figures cover the Sacramento—Arden-Arcade—Roseville, CA Metropolitan Statistical Area; (2) Rank ranges from 1 to 391 where 1 indicates greatest number of fraud and other consumer reports per 100,000 population
Source: Federal Trade Commission, Consumer Sentinel Network Data Book 2021

POLITICS

2020 Presidential Election Results

Area	Biden	Trump	Jorgensen	Hawkins	Other
Sacramento County	61.4	36.1	1.4	0.5	0.7
U.S.	51.3	46.8	1.2	0.3	0.5

Note: Results are percentages and may not add to 100% due to rounding
Source: Dave Leip's Atlas of U.S. Presidential Elections

SPORTS

Professional Sports Teams

Team Name	League	Year Established
Sacramento Kings	National Basketball Association (NBA)	1985
Sacramento Republic FC	Major League Soccer (MLS)	2023

Note: Includes teams located in the Sacramento—Arden-Arcade—Roseville, CA Metropolitan Statistical Area.
Source: Wikipedia, Major Professional Sports Teams of the United States and Canada, April 6, 2022

CLIMATE

Average and Extreme Temperatures

Temperature	Jan	Feb	Mar	Apr	May	Jun	Jul	Aug	Sep	Oct	Nov	Dec	Yr.
Extreme High (°F)	70	76	88	93	105	115	114	109	108	101	87	72	115
Average High (°F)	53	60	64	71	80	87	93	91	87	78	63	53	73
Average Temp. (°F)	45	51	54	59	65	72	76	75	72	64	53	46	61
Average Low (°F)	38	41	43	46	50	55	58	58	56	50	43	38	48
Extreme Low (°F)	20	23	26	32	34	41	48	48	43	35	26	18	18

Note: Figures cover the years 1947-1990
Source: National Climatic Data Center, International Station Meteorological Climate Summary, 9/96

Average Precipitation/Snowfall/Humidity

Precip./Humidity	Jan	Feb	Mar	Apr	May	Jun	Jul	Aug	Sep	Oct	Nov	Dec	Yr.
Avg. Precip. (in.)	3.6	2.8	2.4	1.3	0.4	0.1	Tr	0.1	0.3	1.0	2.4	2.8	17.3
Avg. Snowfall (in.)	Tr	Tr	Tr	Tr	0	0	0	0	0	0	0	Tr	Tr
Avg. Rel. Hum. 7am (%)	90	88	84	78	71	67	68	73	75	80	87	90	79
Avg. Rel. Hum. 4pm (%)	70	59	51	43	36	31	28	29	31	39	57	70	45

Note: Figures cover the years 1947-1990; Tr = Trace amounts (<0.05 in. of rain; <0.5 in. of snow)
Source: National Climatic Data Center, International Station Meteorological Climate Summary, 9/96

Weather Conditions

Temperature			Daytime Sky			Precipitation		
10°F & below	32°F & below	90°F & above	Clear	Partly cloudy	Cloudy	0.01 inch or more precip.	0.1 inch or more snow/ice	Thunder-storms
0	21	73	175	111	79	58	< 1	2

Note: Figures are average number of days per year and cover the years 1947-1990
Source: National Climatic Data Center, International Station Meteorological Climate Summary, 9/96

HAZARDOUS WASTE

Superfund Sites

The Sacramento—Arden-Arcade—Roseville, CA metro area is home to five sites on the EPA's Superfund National Priorities List: **Aerojet General Corp.** (final); **Frontier Fertilizer** (final); **Mather Air Force Base (AC&W Disposal Site)** (final); **McClellan Air Force Base (Ground Water Contamination)** (final); **Sacramento Army Depot** (final). There are a total of 1,165 Superfund sites with a status of proposed or final on the list in the U.S. *U.S. Environmental Protection Agency, National Priorities List, April 6, 2022*

AIR QUALITY

Air Quality Trends: Ozone

	1990	1995	2000	2005	2010	2016	2017	2018	2019	2020
MSA[1]	0.087	0.093	0.086	0.085	0.074	0.074	0.072	0.075	0.067	0.073
U.S.	0.090	0.091	0.082	0.080	0.074	0.070	0.069	0.070	0.066	0.068

Note: (1) Data covers the Sacramento—Arden-Arcade—Roseville, CA Metropolitan Statistical Area. The values shown are the composite ozone concentration averages among trend sites based on the highest fourth daily maximum 8-hour concentration in parts per million. These trends are based on sites having an adequate record of monitoring data during the trend period. Data from exceptional events are included.
Source: U.S. Environmental Protection Agency, Air Quality Monitoring Information, "Air Quality Trends by City, 1990-2020"

Air Quality Index

Area	Percent of Days when Air Quality was...[2]					AQI Statistics[2]	
	Good	Moderate	Unhealthy for Sensitive Groups	Unhealthy	Very Unhealthy	Maximum	Median
MSA[1]	36.1	50.3	6.3	6.6	0.8	222	60

Note: (1) Data covers the Sacramento—Arden-Arcade—Roseville, CA Metropolitan Statistical Area; (2) Based on 366 days with AQI data in 2020. Air Quality Index (AQI) is an index for reporting daily air quality. EPA calculates the AQI for five major air pollutants regulated by the Clean Air Act: ground-level ozone, particle pollution (aka particulate matter), carbon monoxide, sulfur dioxide, and nitrogen dioxide. The AQI runs from 0 to 500. The higher the AQI value, the greater the level of air pollution and the greater the health concern. There are six AQI categories: "Good" AQI is between 0 and 50. Air quality is considered satisfactory; "Moderate" AQI is between 51 and 100. Air quality is acceptable; "Unhealthy for Sensitive Groups" When AQI values are between 101 and 150, members of sensitive groups may experience health effects; "Unhealthy" When AQI values are between 151 and 200 everyone may begin to experience health effects; "Very Unhealthy" AQI values between 201 and 300 trigger a health alert; "Hazardous" AQI values over 300 trigger warnings of emergency conditions (not shown).
Source: U.S. Environmental Protection Agency, Air Quality Index Report, 2020

Air Quality Index Pollutants

Area	Percent of Days when AQI Pollutant was...[2]					
	Carbon Monoxide	Nitrogen Dioxide	Ozone	Sulfur Dioxide	Particulate Matter 2.5	Particulate Matter 10
MSA[1]	0.0	0.3	54.6	0.0	42.6	2.5

Note: (1) Data covers the Sacramento—Arden-Arcade—Roseville, CA Metropolitan Statistical Area; (2) Based on 366 days with AQI data in 2020. The Air Quality Index (AQI) is an index for reporting daily air quality. EPA calculates the AQI for five major air pollutants regulated by the Clean Air Act: ground-level ozone, particle pollution (also known as particulate matter), carbon monoxide, sulfur dioxide, and nitrogen dioxide. The AQI runs from 0 to 500. The higher the AQI value, the greater the level of air pollution and the greater the health concern.
Source: U.S. Environmental Protection Agency, Air Quality Index Report, 2020

Maximum Air Pollutant Concentrations: Particulate Matter, Ozone, CO and Lead

	Particulate Matter 10 (ug/m³)	Particulate Matter 2.5 Wtd AM (ug/m³)	Particulate Matter 2.5 24-Hr (ug/m³)	Ozone (ppm)	Carbon Monoxide (ppm)	Lead (ug/m³)
MSA[1] Level	231	14.7	134	0.086	2	n/a
NAAQS[2]	150	15	35	0.075	9	0.15
Met NAAQS[2]	No	Yes	No	No	Yes	n/a

Note: (1) Data covers the Sacramento—Arden-Arcade—Roseville, CA Metropolitan Statistical Area; Data from exceptional events are included; (2) National Ambient Air Quality Standards; ppm = parts per million; ug/m³ = micrograms per cubic meter; n/a not available.

Concentrations: Particulate Matter 10 (coarse particulate)—highest second maximum 24-hour concentration; Particulate Matter 2.5 Wtd AM (fine particulate)—highest weighted annual mean concentration; Particulate Matter 2.5 24-Hour (fine particulate)—highest 98th percentile 24-hour concentration; Ozone—highest fourth daily maximum 8-hour concentration; Carbon Monoxide—highest second maximum non-overlapping 8-hour concentration; Lead—maximum running 3-month average

Source: U.S. Environmental Protection Agency, Air Quality Monitoring Information, "Air Quality Statistics by City, 2020"

Maximum Air Pollutant Concentrations: Nitrogen Dioxide and Sulfur Dioxide

	Nitrogen Dioxide AM (ppb)	Nitrogen Dioxide 1-Hr (ppb)	Sulfur Dioxide AM (ppb)	Sulfur Dioxide 1-Hr (ppb)	Sulfur Dioxide 24-Hr (ppb)
MSA[1] Level	11	46	n/a	3	n/a
NAAQS[2]	53	100	30	75	140
Met NAAQS[2]	Yes	Yes	n/a	Yes	n/a

Note: (1) Data covers the Sacramento—Arden-Arcade—Roseville, CA Metropolitan Statistical Area; Data from exceptional events are included; (2) National Ambient Air Quality Standards; ppm = parts per million; ug/m³ = micrograms per cubic meter; n/a not available.

Concentrations: Nitrogen Dioxide AM—highest arithmetic mean concentration; Nitrogen Dioxide 1-Hr—highest 98th percentile 1-hour daily maximum concentration; Sulfur Dioxide AM—highest annual mean concentration; Sulfur Dioxide 1-Hr—highest 99th percentile 1-hour daily maximum concentration; Sulfur Dioxide 24-Hr—highest second maximum 24-hour concentration

Source: U.S. Environmental Protection Agency, Air Quality Monitoring Information, "Air Quality Statistics by City, 2020"

Salt Lake City, Utah

Background

Salt Lake City, Utah's largest city and state capital, is known for its Mormon, or Church of Jesus Christ of Latter-day Saints, origins. The city was founded by Brigham Young on July 24, 1847, as a place of refuge from mainstream ostracism for the Mormon's polygamous lifestyle.

Brigham Young led his people to a "land that nobody wanted," so they could exercise their form of worship in peace. Two scouts, Orson Pratt and Erastus Snow located the site for Brigham Young, who declared: "This is the place." The site that was to be called Salt Lake City was breathtaking, bordered on the east and southwest by the dramatic peaks of the Wasatch Range, and on the northwest by the Great Salt Lake.

The land was too dry and hard for traditional farming, but Mormon industry diverted the flow of mountain streams to irrigate the land, and the valley turned into a prosperous agricultural region. More than 10 years after its incorporation as a city, the U.S. government was still suspicious of its Mormon residents. Fort Douglas, founded in 1862, was manned by federal troops to keep an eye on the Mormons and their polygamous practices. In 1869, the completion of the Transcontinental Railroad brought mining, industry, and other non-Mormon interests to Salt Lake City. As for polygamy, the Mormon Church made it illegal in 1890.

While mining played a major role in the early development of Salt Lake City, major industry sectors today include construction, trade, transportation, communications, finance, insurance, and real estate. The University of Utah Research Park, also known at Bionic Valley, is on the campus of the university and houses 48 companies, 18 university departments, and employs more than 14,000. Plans to update the Research Park include additional student housing, research innovation hub and additional locations for businesses.

Major efforts to revitalize the downtown area have included the $1 billion, 20-acre City Creek Center with residences, offices, and a mall; Salt Lake City Redevelopment Agency renovated retail space that is part of the Utah Theater, a former 1918 vaudeville theater on Main Street; Utah Performing Arts Center costing $116 million and holding 2,500.

The Utah Pride Festival is held in June each year. Since 1983, it has grown dramatically to a three-day festival with attendance over 20,000 and is one of the largest festivals in the country comprising hundreds of vendors, food, musical performers, a 5k run, a dyke and trans march, as well as an interfaith service by the Utah Pride Interfaith Coalition.

Salt Lake City International Airport is undergoing a huge redevelopment plan. Recently completed Phase 1 incudes a new concourse and terminal. Phase 2, which will be complete in 2025, includes more shops, restaurants, and gates, and a Central Tunnel with an art installation called The River Tunnel.

Salt Lake City was designated as a Silver-level Bicycle Friendly Community in 2010 by the League of American Bicyclists. Many streets in the city have bike lanes, and the city has published a bicycle map.

The NBA's Utah Jazz plays at the EnergySolutions Arena. The city is also home to Real Salt Lake of Major League Soccer.

The nearby mountain ranges and the Great Salt Lake greatly influence climatic conditions. Temperatures are moderated by the lake in winter, and storm activity is enhanced by both the lake and the mountains. Salt Lake City has a semi-arid continental climate with four well-defined seasons. Summers are hot and dry, while winters are cold, but not severe due to the mountains to the north and east that barricade the cold air. Periods of heavy fog can develop in winter and persist for several days.

Rankings

General Rankings

- *US News & World Report* conducted a survey of more than 3,600 people and analyzed the 150 largest metropolitan areas to determine what matters most when selecting the next place to live. Salt Lake City ranked #23 out of the top 25 as having the best combination of desirable factors. Criteria: cost of living; quality of life and education; net migration; job market; desirability; and other factors. *realestate.usnews.com, "The 25 Best Places to Live in the U.S. in 2021-2022," July 13, 2021*
- The Salt Lake City metro area was identified as one of America's fastest-growing areas in terms of population and business growth by *MagnifyMoney*. The area ranked #18 out of 35. The 100 most populous metro areas in the U.S. were evaluated on their change from 2011 to 2016 in the following categories: people and housing; workforce and employment opportunities; growing industry. *www.businessinsider.com, "The 35 Cities in the US with the Biggest Influx of People, the Most Work Opportunities, and the Hottest Business Growth," August 12, 2018*
- The Salt Lake City metro area was identified as one of America's fastest-growing areas in terms of population and economy by *Forbes*. The area ranked #24 out of 25. The 100 most populous metro areas in the U.S. were evaluated on the following criteria: estimated population growth; employment; economic output; wages; home values. *Forbes, "America's Fastest-Growing Cities 2018," February 28, 2018*
- In their eigth annual survey, Livability.com looked at data for more than 1,000 small to mid-sized U.S. cities to determine the rankings for Livability's "Top 100 Best Places to Live" in 2021. Salt Lake City ranked #30. Criteria: housing and economy; sustainability; social and civic engagement; education; demographics; health care options; transportation & infrastructure; and community amenities. *Livability.com, "Top 100 Best Places to Live 2021" October 12, 2021*

Business/Finance Rankings

- According to *Business Insider*, the Salt Lake City metro area is a prime place to run a startup or move an existing business to. The area ranked #19. More than 300 metro areas were analyzed for factors that were of top concern to new business owners. Data was based on the 2019 U.S. Census Bureau American Community Survey, statistics from the CDC, Bureau of Labor Statistics employment report, and University of Chicago analysis. Criteria: business formations; percentage of vaccinated population; percentage of households with internet subscriptions; median household income; and share of work that can be done from home. *www.businessinsider.com, "The 20 Best Cities for Starting a Business in 2022 Include Baltimore, Boulder, and Boston," January 5, 2022*
- The Brookings Institution ranked the nation's largest cities based on income inequality. Salt Lake City was ranked #57 (#1 = greatest inequality). Criteria: the "95/20 ratio," a figure representing the income at which a household earns more than 95 percent of all other households, divided by the income at which a household earns more than only 20 percent of all other households. *Brookings Institution, "Household Income Inequality, Largest Cities of 97 Large U.S. Metro Areas, 2014-2016," February 5, 2018*
- The Brookings Institution ranked the 100 largest metro areas in the U.S. based on income inequality. Salt Lake City was ranked #98 (#1 = greatest inequality). Criteria: the "95/20 ratio," a figure representing the income at which a household earns more than 95 percent of all other households, divided by the income at which a household earns more than only 20 percent of all other households. *Brookings Institution, "Household Income Inequality, 100 Largest U.S. Metro Areas, 2014-2016," February 5, 2018*
- The Salt Lake City metro area appeared on the Milken Institute "2021 Best Performing Cities" list. Rank: #4 out of 200 large metro areas (population over 250,000). Criteria: job growth; wage and salary growth; high-tech output growth; housing affordability; household broadband access. *Milken Institute, "Best-Performing Cities 2021," February 16, 2021*
- *Forbes* ranked the 200 most populous metro areas to determine the nation's "Best Places for Business and Careers." The Salt Lake City metro area was ranked #21. Criteria: costs (business and living); job growth (past and projected); income growth; quality of life; educational attainment (college and high school); projected economic growth; cultural and leisure opportunities; workplace tolerance laws; net migration patterns. *Forbes, "The Best Places for Business and Careers 2019: Seattle Still On Top," October 30, 2019*

Dating/Romance Rankings

- Salt Lake City was ranked #22 out of 25 cities that stood out for inspiring romance and attracting diners on the website OpenTable.com. Criteria: percentage of people who dined out on Valentine's Day in 2018; percentage of romantic restaurants as rated by OpenTable diner reviews; and percentage of tables seated for two. *OpenTable, "25 Most Romantic Cities in America for 2019," February 7, 2019*
- Salt Lake City was selected as one of the nation's most romantic cities with 100,000 or more residents by Amazon.com. The city ranked #5 of 20. Criteria: per capita sales of romance novels, relationship books, romantic comedy movies, romantic music, and sexual wellness products. *Amazon.com, "Top 20 Most Romantic Cities in the U.S.," February 1, 2017*

Education Rankings

- Personal finance website *WalletHub* analyzed the 150 largest U.S. metropolitan statistical areas to determine where the most educated Americans are putting their degrees to work. Criteria: education levels; percentage of workers with degrees; education quality and attainment gap; public school quality rankings; quality and enrollment of each metro area's universities. Salt Lake City was ranked #40 (#1 = most educated city). *www.WalletHub.com, "Most & Least Educated Cities in America," July 19, 2021*

Environmental Rankings

- Sperling's BestPlaces assessed the 50 largest metropolitan areas of the United States for the likelihood of dangerously extreme weather events or earthquakes. In general the Southeast and South-Central regions have the highest risk of weather extremes and earthquakes, while the Pacific Northwest enjoys the lowest risk. Of the least risky metropolitan areas, the Salt Lake City metro area was ranked #2. *www.bestplaces.net, "Avoid Natural Disasters: BestPlaces Reveals The Top 10 Safest Places to Live," October 25, 2017*
- Salt Lake City was highlighted as one of the 25 most ozone-polluted metro areas in the U.S. during 2017 through 2019. The area ranked #8. *American Lung Association, "State of the Air 2021," April 21, 2021*
- Salt Lake City was highlighted as one of the 25 metro areas most polluted by short-term particle pollution (24-hour PM 2.5) in the U.S. during 2017 through 2019. The area ranked #17. *American Lung Association, "State of the Air 2021," April 21, 2021*

Health/Fitness Rankings

- Trulia analyzed the 100 largest U.S. metro areas to identify the nation's best cities for weight loss, based on the percentage of adults who bike or walk to work, sporting goods stores, grocery stores, access to outdoor activities, weight-loss centers, gyms, and average space reserved for parks. Salt Lake City ranked #1. *Trulia.com, "Where to Live to Get in Shape in the New Year," January 4, 2018*
- Salt Lake City was identified as a "2021 Spring Allergy Capital." The area ranked #93 out of 100. Three groups of factors were used to identify the most challenging cities for people with allergies during the spring season: annual spring pollen levels; over the counter medicine use; number of board-certified allergy specialists. *Asthma and Allergy Foundation of America, "Spring Allergy Capitals 2021," February 23, 2021*
- Salt Lake City was identified as a "2021 Fall Allergy Capital." The area ranked #89 out of 100. Three groups of factors were used to identify the most challenging cities for people with allergies during the fall season: annual fall pollen levels; over the counter medicine use; number of board-certified allergy specialists. *Asthma and Allergy Foundation of America, "Fall Allergy Capitals 2021," February 23, 2021*
- Salt Lake City was identified as a "2021 Asthma Capital." The area ranked #62 out of the nation's 100 largest metropolitan areas. Criteria: estimated asthma prevalence; asthma-related mortality; and ER visits due to asthma. Risk factors analyzed but not factored in the rankings: annual pollen score; annual air quality; public smoking laws; number of board-certified asthma specialists; rescue medication use; controller medication use; uninsured rate; poverty rate. *Asthma and Allergy Foundation of America, "Asthma Capitals 2021: The Most Challenging Places to Live With Asthma," May 5, 2021*

Real Estate Rankings

- *WalletHub* compared the most populated U.S. cities to determine which had the best markets for real estate agents. Salt Lake City ranked #4 where demand was high and pay was the best. Criteria: sales per agent; annual median wage for real-estate agents; monthly average starting salary for real estate agents; real estate job density and competition; unemployment rate; home turnover rate; housing-market health index; and other relevant metrics. *www.WalletHub.com, "2021 Best Places to Be a Real Estate Agent," May 12, 2021*
- The Salt Lake City metro area appeared on Realtor.com's list of hot housing markets to watch in 2022. The area ranked #1. Criteria: forecasted home price and sales growth; overall economy; population trends. *Realtor.com®, "Top 10 Housing Markets Positioned for Growth in 2022," December 7, 2021*
- Salt Lake City was ranked #13 in the top 20 out of the 100 largest metro areas in terms of house price appreciation in 2021 (#1 = highest rate). *Federal Housing Finance Agency, House Price Index, 4th Quarter 2021*
- The Salt Lake City metro area was identified as one of the 20 best housing markets in the U.S. in 2021. The area ranked #9 out of 184 markets. Criteria: year-over-year change of median sales price of existing single-family homes between the 4th quarter of 2020 and the 4th quarter of 2021. *National Association of Realtors®, Median Sales Price of Existing Single-Family Homes for Metropolitan Areas, 4th Quarter 2021*
- The Salt Lake City metro area was identified as one of the 10 best condo markets in the U.S. in 2021. The area ranked #2 out of 63 markets. Criteria: year-over-year change of median sales price of existing apartment condo-coop homes between the 4th quarter of 2020 and the 4th quarter of 2021. *National Association of Realtors®, Median Sales Price of Existing Apartment Condo-Coops Homes for Metropolitan Areas, 4th Quarter 2021*
- Salt Lake City was ranked #160 out of 237 metro areas in terms of housing affordability in 2021 by the National Association of Home Builders (#1 = most affordable). Criteria: the share of homes sold in that area affordable to a family earning the local median income, based on standard mortgage underwriting criteria. *National Association of Home Builders®, NAHB-Wells Fargo Housing Opportunity Index, 4th Quarter 2021*

Safety Rankings

- Statistics drawn from the FBI's Uniform Crime Report were used to rank the cities where violent crime rose the most year over year from 2019 to 2020. Only cities with 25,000 or more residents were included. 24/7 Wall Street found that trim(city)+[placed #26 of those with a notable surge in incidents of violent crime. *247wallst.com, "American Cities Where Crime Is Soaring," March 4, 2022*
- Allstate ranked the 200 largest cities in America in terms of driver safety. Salt Lake City ranked #67. Criteria: internal property damage claims over a two-year period from January 2016 to December 2017. The report helps increase the importance of safety and awareness behind the wheel. *Allstate, "Allstate America's Best Drivers Report, 2019" June 24, 2019*
- Salt Lake City was identified as one of the most dangerous cities in America by NeighborhoodScout. The city ranked #80 out of 100 (#1 = most dangerous). Criteria: number of violent crimes per 1,000 residents. The editors evaluated cities with 25,000 or more residents. *NeighborhoodScout.com, "2022 Top 100 Most Dangerous Cities in the U.S.," January 3, 2022*
- The National Insurance Crime Bureau ranked 390 metro areas in the U.S. in terms of per capita rates of vehicle theft. The Salt Lake City metro area ranked #13 (#1 = highest rate). Criteria: number of vehicle theft offenses per 100,000 inhabitants in 2020. *National Insurance Crime Bureau, "Hot Spots 2020," August 31, 2021*

Seniors/Retirement Rankings

- From its Best Cities for Successful Aging indexes, the Milken Institute generated rankings for metropolitan areas, weighing data in nine categories—health care, wellness, living arrangements, transportation and convenience, financial characteristics, education, employment, community engagement, and overall livability. The Salt Lake City metro area was ranked #4 overall in the large metro area category. *Milken Institute, "Best Cities for Successful Aging, 2017" March 14, 2017*

Sports/Recreation Rankings

- Salt Lake City was chosen as one of America's best cities for bicycling. The city ranked #16 out of 50. Criteria: cycling infrastructure that is safe and friendly for all ages; energy and bike culture. The editors evaluated cities with populations of 100,000 or more. *Bicycling, "The 50 Best Bike Cities in America," October 10, 2018*

Women/Minorities Rankings

- Personal finance website *WalletHub* compared more than 180 U.S. cities across two key dimensions, "Hispanic Business-Friendliness" and "Hispanic Purchasing Power," to arrive at the most favorable conditions for Hispanic entrepreneurs. Salt Lake City was ranked #55 out of 182. Criteria includes: share of Hispanic-Owned Businesses; Hispanic entrepreneurship rate to median annual income of Hispanics; Small Business-Friendliness score; cost of living; and number of Hispanics with at least a bachelor's degree. *WalletHub.com, "2019's Best Cities for Hispanic Entrepreneurs," May 1, 2019*

Miscellaneous Rankings

- *MoveHub* ranked 446 hipster cities across 20 countries, using its *alternative* Hipster Index and Salt Lake City came out as #3 among the top 50. Criteria: population over 150,000; number of vintage boutiques; density of tattoo parlors; vegan places to eat; coffee shops; and density of vinyl record stores. *www.movehub.com, "The Hipster Index: Brighton Pips Portland to Global Top Spot," July 28, 2021*
- *WalletHub* compared the 150 most populated U.S. cities to determine their operating efficiency. A "Quality of City Services" score was constructed for each city and then divided by the total budget per capita to reveal which were managed the best. Salt Lake City ranked #74. Criteria: financial stability; economy; education; safety; health; infrastructure and pollution. *www.WalletHub.com, "2021's Best- & Worst-Run Cities in America," June 22, 2021*

Business Environment

DEMOGRAPHICS

Population Growth

Area	1990 Census	2000 Census	2010 Census	2020* Estimate	Population Growth (%) 1990-2020	2010-2020
City	159,796	181,743	186,440	200,133	25.2	7.3
MSA[1]	768,075	968,858	1,124,197	1,215,955	58.3	8.2
U.S.	248,709,873	281,421,906	308,745,538	326,569,308	31.3	5.8

Note: (1) Figures cover the Salt Lake City, UT Metropolitan Statistical Area; (*) 2016-2020 5-year estimated population
Source: U.S. Census Bureau, 1990 Census, Census 2000, Census 2010, 2016-2020 American Community Survey 5-Year Estimates

Household Size

Area	Persons in Household (%) One	Two	Three	Four	Five	Six	Seven or More	Average Household Size
City	37.3	33.0	12.3	9.5	4.1	2.0	1.8	2.40
MSA[1]	22.9	30.8	15.7	14.2	8.4	4.8	3.3	3.00
U.S.	28.0	33.9	15.5	12.9	6.0	2.3	1.4	2.60

Note: (1) Figures cover the Salt Lake City, UT Metropolitan Statistical Area
Source: U.S. Census Bureau, 2016-2020 American Community Survey 5-Year Estimates

Race

Area	White Alone[2] (%)	Black Alone[2] (%)	Asian Alone[2] (%)	AIAN[3] Alone[2] (%)	NHOPI[4] Alone[2] (%)	Other Race Alone[2] (%)	Two or More Races (%)
City	73.3	2.6	5.3	1.3	1.8	11.2	4.6
MSA[1]	78.2	1.9	3.9	0.8	1.5	9.0	4.7
U.S.	70.4	12.6	5.6	0.8	0.2	5.1	5.2

Note: (1) Figures cover the Salt Lake City, UT Metropolitan Statistical Area; (2) Alone is defined as not being in combination with one or more other races; (3) American Indian and Alaska Native; (4) Native Hawaiian and Other Pacific Islander
Source: U.S. Census Bureau, 2016-2020 American Community Survey 5-Year Estimates

Hispanic or Latino Origin

Area	Total (%)	Mexican (%)	Puerto Rican (%)	Cuban (%)	Other (%)
City	21.2	15.6	0.4	0.3	4.8
MSA[1]	18.2	13.1	0.5	0.1	4.5
U.S.	18.2	11.2	1.7	0.7	4.5

Note: Persons of Hispanic or Latino origin can be of any race; (1) Figures cover the Salt Lake City, UT Metropolitan Statistical Area
Source: U.S. Census Bureau, 2016-2020 American Community Survey 5-Year Estimates

Ancestry

Area	German	Irish	English	American	Italian	Polish	French[2]	Scottish	Dutch
City	10.8	6.9	16.9	3.4	3.8	1.4	2.2	3.4	1.8
MSA[1]	9.9	5.6	20.6	4.1	2.9	0.9	1.9	3.6	1.8
U.S.	13.0	9.7	7.7	5.9	5.1	2.7	2.3	1.6	1.1

Note: Figures are the percentage of the total population reporting a particular ancestry. The nine most commonly reported ancestries in the U.S. are shown. Figures include multiple ancestries (e.g. if a person reported being Irish and Italian, they were included in both columns); (1) Figures cover the Salt Lake City, UT Metropolitan Statistical Area; (2) Excludes Basque
Source: U.S. Census Bureau, 2016-2020 American Community Survey 5-Year Estimates

Foreign-born Population

Area	Percent of Population Born in: Any Foreign Country	Asia	Mexico	Europe	Caribbean	Central America[2]	South America	Africa	Canada
City	16.3	4.3	5.7	2.0	0.2	0.7	1.5	0.8	0.4
MSA[1]	12.3	3.1	4.3	1.2	0.1	0.7	1.5	0.5	0.3
U.S.	13.5	4.2	3.3	1.5	1.3	1.1	1.0	0.7	0.3

Note: (1) Figures cover the Salt Lake City, UT Metropolitan Statistical Area; (2) Excludes Mexico.
Source: U.S. Census Bureau, 2016-2020 American Community Survey 5-Year Estimates

Marital Status

Area	Never Married	Now Married[2]	Separated	Widowed	Divorced
City	43.0	41.3	1.4	3.4	10.9
MSA[1]	32.3	52.1	1.6	3.7	10.3
U.S.	33.5	48.1	1.8	5.7	10.8

Note: Figures are percentages and cover the population 15 years of age and older; (1) Figures cover the Salt Lake City, UT Metropolitan Statistical Area; (2) Excludes separated
Source: U.S. Census Bureau, 2016-2020 American Community Survey 5-Year Estimates

Disability by Age

Area	All Ages	Under 18 Years Old	18 to 64 Years Old	65 Years and Over
City	11.0	3.5	9.1	35.7
MSA[1]	9.5	3.7	8.3	31.3
U.S.	12.7	4.3	10.3	34.0

Note: Figures show percent of the civilian noninstitutionalized population that reported having a disability. Disability status is determined from six types of difficulty: vision, hearing, cognitive, ambulatory, self-care, and independent living. For children under 5 years old, hearing and vision difficulty are used to determine disability status. For children between the ages of 5 and 14, disability status is determined from hearing, vision, cognitive, ambulatory, and self-care difficulties. For people aged 15 years and older, they are considered to have a disability if they have difficulty with any one of the six difficulty types; Note: (1) Figures cover the Salt Lake City, UT Metropolitan Statistical Area
Source: U.S. Census Bureau, 2016-2020 American Community Survey 5-Year Estimates

Age

Area	Percent of Population									Median Age
	Under Age 5	Age 5–19	Age 20–34	Age 35–44	Age 45–54	Age 55–64	Age 65–74	Age 75–84	Age 85+	
City	5.9	16.5	32.0	14.1	9.8	10.0	6.9	3.4	1.3	32.5
MSA[1]	7.4	22.5	23.3	14.7	11.2	10.0	6.6	3.1	1.1	32.9
U.S.	6.0	19.1	20.6	12.7	12.7	12.9	9.4	4.7	2.0	38.2

Note: (1) Figures cover the Salt Lake City, UT Metropolitan Statistical Area
Source: U.S. Census Bureau, 2016-2020 American Community Survey 5-Year Estimates

Gender

Area	Males	Females	Males per 100 Females
City	102,985	97,148	106.0
MSA[1]	610,556	605,399	100.9
U.S.	160,818,530	165,750,778	97.0

Note: (1) Figures cover the Salt Lake City, UT Metropolitan Statistical Area
Source: U.S. Census Bureau, 2016-2020 American Community Survey 5-Year Estimates

Religious Groups by Family

Area	Catholic	Baptist	Non-Den.	Methodist[2]	Lutheran	LDS[3]	Pente-costal	Presby-terian[4]	Muslim[5]	Judaism
MSA[1]	8.9	0.8	0.5	0.5	0.5	58.9	0.7	0.4	0.4	0.1
U.S.	19.1	9.3	4.0	4.0	2.3	2.0	1.9	1.6	0.8	0.7

Note: Figures are the number of adherents as a percentage of the total population; (1) Figures cover the Salt Lake City, UT Metropolitan Statistical Area; (2) Methodist/Pietist; (3) Latter Day Saints; (4) Reformed; (5) Figures are estimates
Source: Association of Statisticians of American Religious Bodies, 2010 U.S. Religion Census: Religious Congregations & Membership Study

Religious Groups by Tradition

Area	Catholic	Evangelical Protestant	Mainline Protestant	Other Tradition	Black Protestant	Orthodox
MSA[1]	8.9	2.6	1.3	60.1	0.1	0.5
U.S.	19.1	16.2	7.3	4.3	1.6	0.3

Note: Figures are the number of adherents as a percentage of the total population; (1) Figures cover the Salt Lake City, UT Metropolitan Statistical Area
Source: Association of Statisticians of American Religious Bodies, 2010 U.S. Religion Census: Religious Congregations & Membership Study

ECONOMY

Gross Metropolitan Product

Area	2017	2018	2019	2020	Rank[2]
MSA[1]	87.9	93.6	97.8	102.5	41

Note: Figures are in billions of dollars; (1) Figures cover the Salt Lake City, UT Metropolitan Statistical Area; (2) Rank is based on 2018 data and ranges from 1 to 381
Source: U.S. Conference of Mayors, U.S. Metro Economies: GMP & Employment 2018-2020, September 2019

Economic Growth

Area	2015-17 (%)	2018 (%)	2019 (%)	2020 (%)	Rank[2]
MSA[1]	2.3	3.7	2.6	2.7	114
U.S.	1.9	2.9	2.3	2.1	–

Note: Figures are real gross metropolitan product (GMP) growth rates and represent average annual percent change; (1) Figures cover the Salt Lake City, UT Metropolitan Statistical Area; (2) Rank is based on 2017 2-year average annual percent change and ranges from 1 to 381
Source: U.S. Conference of Mayors, U.S. Metro Economies: GMP & Employment 2018-2020, September 2019

Metropolitan Area Exports

Area	2015	2016	2017	2018	2019	2020	Rank[2]
MSA[1]	10,380.5	8,653.7	7,916.9	9,748.6	13,273.9	13,565.5	23

Note: Figures are in millions of dollars; (1) Figures cover the Salt Lake City, UT Metropolitan Statistical Area; (2) Rank is based on 2020 data and ranges from 1 to 389
Source: U.S. Department of Commerce, International Trade Administration, Office of Trade and Economic Analysis, Industry and Analysis, Exports by Metropolitan Area, data extracted March 4, 2022

Building Permits

Area	Single-Family			Multi-Family			Total		
	2019	2020	Pct. Chg.	2019	2020	Pct. Chg.	2019	2020	Pct. Chg.
City	127	168	32.3	3,359	2,499	-25.6	3,486	2,667	-23.5
MSA[1]	4,760	5,203	9.3	5,920	5,830	-1.5	10,680	11,033	3.3
U.S.	862,100	979,400	13.6	523,900	491,700	-6.1	1,386,000	1,471,100	6.1

Note: (1) Figures cover the Salt Lake City, UT Metropolitan Statistical Area; Figures represent new, privately-owned housing units authorized (unadjusted data); All permit data are based on estimates with imputation
Source: U.S. Census Bureau, Manufacturing, Mining, and Construction Statistics, Building Permits, 2019, 2020

Bankruptcy Filings

Area	Business Filings			Nonbusiness Filings		
	2020	2021	% Chg.	2020	2021	% Chg.
Salt Lake County	60	27	-55.0	3,232	2,389	-26.1
U.S.	21,655	14,347	-33.7	522,808	399,269	-23.6

Note: Business filings include Chapter 7, Chapter 9, Chapter 11, Chapter 12, Chapter 13, Chapter 15, and Section 304; Nonbusiness filings include Chapter 7, Chapter 11, and Chapter 13
Source: Administrative Office of the U.S. Courts, Business and Nonbusiness Bankruptcy, County Cases Commenced by Chapter of the Bankruptcy Code, During the 12-Month Period Ending December 31, 2020 and Business and Nonbusiness Bankruptcy, County Cases Commenced by Chapter of the Bankruptcy Code, During the 12-Month Period Ending December 31, 2021

Housing Vacancy Rates

Area	Gross Vacancy Rate[2] (%)			Year-Round Vacancy Rate[3] (%)			Rental Vacancy Rate[4] (%)			Homeowner Vacancy Rate[5] (%)		
	2019	2020	2021	2019	2020	2021	2019	2020	2021	2019	2020	2021
MSA[1]	4.8	5.7	4.1	4.8	5.6	3.9	5.0	6.2	4.1	0.8	0.3	0.8
U.S.	12.0	10.6	10.8	9.5	8.2	8.4	6.7	6.3	6.1	1.4	1.0	0.9

Note: (1) Figures cover the Salt Lake City, UT Metropolitan Statistical Area; (2) The percentage of the total housing inventory that is vacant; (3) The percentage of the housing inventory (excluding seasonal units) that is year-round vacant; (4) The percentage of rental inventory that is vacant for rent; (5) The percentage of homeowner inventory that is vacant for sale
Source: U.S. Census Bureau, Housing Vacancies and Homeownership Annual Statistics: 2019, 2020, 2021

INCOME

Income

Area	Per Capita ($)	Median Household ($)	Average Household ($)
City	39,126	63,156	92,248
MSA[1]	34,242	77,102	99,517
U.S.	35,384	64,994	91,547

Note: (1) Figures cover the Salt Lake City, UT Metropolitan Statistical Area
Source: U.S. Census Bureau, 2016-2020 American Community Survey 5-Year Estimates

Household Income Distribution

Area	Percent of Households Earning							
	Under $15,000	$15,000 -$24,999	$25,000 -$34,999	$35,000 -$49,999	$50,000 -$74,999	$75,000 -$99,999	$100,000 -$149,999	$150,000 and up
City	12.0	7.7	8.4	12.3	17.5	12.7	14.9	14.4
MSA[1]	6.2	5.5	6.8	11.1	18.8	15.0	19.8	16.8
U.S.	9.9	8.5	8.6	12.0	17.2	12.8	15.6	15.4

Note: (1) Figures cover the Salt Lake City, UT Metropolitan Statistical Area
Source: U.S. Census Bureau, 2016-2020 American Community Survey 5-Year Estimates

Poverty Rate

Area	All Ages	Under 18 Years Old	18 to 64 Years Old	65 Years and Over
City	15.2	16.5	15.8	9.4
MSA[1]	8.4	9.7	8.3	6.3
U.S.	12.8	17.5	12.1	9.3

Note: Figures are percentage of people whose income during the past 12 months was below the poverty level; (1) Figures cover the Salt Lake City, UT Metropolitan Statistical Area
Source: U.S. Census Bureau, 2016-2020 American Community Survey 5-Year Estimates

CITY FINANCES

City Government Finances

Component	2019 ($000)	2019 ($ per capita)
Total Revenues	975,244	4,863
Total Expenditures	1,354,505	6,754
Debt Outstanding	2,302,090	11,479
Cash and Securities[1]	1,591,033	7,934

Note: (1) Cash and security holdings of a government at the close of its fiscal year, including those of its dependent agencies, utilities, and liquor stores.
Source: U.S. Census Bureau, State & Local Government Finances 2019

City Government Revenue by Source

Source	2019 ($000)	2019 ($ per capita)	2019 (%)
General Revenue			
From Federal Government	22,867	114	2.3
From State Government	8,246	41	0.8
From Local Governments	7,362	37	0.8
Taxes			
Property	141,977	708	14.6
Sales and Gross Receipts	133,211	664	13.7
Personal Income	0	0	0.0
Corporate Income	0	0	0.0
Motor Vehicle License	0	0	0.0
Other Taxes	13,752	69	1.4
Current Charges	446,489	2,226	45.8
Liquor Store	0	0	0.0
Utility	75,328	376	7.7

Source: U.S. Census Bureau, State & Local Government Finances 2019

City Government Expenditures by Function

Function	2019 ($000)	2019 ($ per capita)	2019 (%)
General Direct Expenditures			
Air Transportation	792,445	3,951	58.5
Corrections	0	0	0.0
Education	3,333	16	0.2
Employment Security Administration	0	0	0.0
Financial Administration	9,299	46	0.7
Fire Protection	43,698	217	3.2
General Public Buildings	465	2	0.0
Governmental Administration, Other	11,057	55	0.8
Health	47,616	237	3.5
Highways	31,034	154	2.3
Hospitals	0	0	0.0
Housing and Community Development	5,709	28	0.4
Interest on General Debt	21,549	107	1.6
Judicial and Legal	12,431	62	0.9
Libraries	14,061	70	1.0
Parking	2,213	11	0.2
Parks and Recreation	11,326	56	0.8
Police Protection	82,822	413	6.1
Public Welfare	101	< 1	< 0.1
Sewerage	45,926	229	3.4
Solid Waste Management	17,556	87	1.3
Veterans' Services	0	0	0.0
Liquor Store	0	0	0.0
Utility	97,032	483	7.2

Source: U.S. Census Bureau, State & Local Government Finances 2019

EMPLOYMENT

Labor Force and Employment

Area	Civilian Labor Force			Workers Employed		
	Dec. 2020	Dec. 2021	% Chg.	Dec. 2020	Dec. 2021	% Chg.
City	116,271	119,804	3.0	112,477	118,246	5.1
MSA[1]	674,466	696,167	3.2	653,349	686,805	5.1
U.S.	160,017,000	161,696,000	1.0	149,613,000	155,732,000	4.1

Note: Data is not seasonally adjusted and covers workers 16 years of age and older; (1) Figures cover the Salt Lake City, UT Metropolitan Statistical Area
Source: Bureau of Labor Statistics, Local Area Unemployment Statistics

Unemployment Rate

Area	2021											
	Jan.	Feb.	Mar.	Apr.	May	Jun.	Jul.	Aug.	Sep.	Oct.	Nov.	Dec.
City	3.6	3.7	2.9	2.9	2.8	3.1	2.9	2.5	1.6	1.4	1.4	1.3
MSA[1]	3.5	3.7	3.0	3.0	2.8	3.2	2.8	2.6	1.6	1.5	1.4	1.3
U.S.	6.8	6.6	6.2	5.7	5.5	6.1	5.7	5.3	4.6	4.3	3.9	3.7

Note: Data is not seasonally adjusted and covers workers 16 years of age and older; (1) Figures cover the Salt Lake City, UT Metropolitan Statistical Area
Source: Bureau of Labor Statistics, Local Area Unemployment Statistics

Average Wages

Occupation	$/Hr.	Occupation	$/Hr.
Accountants and Auditors	35.97	Maintenance and Repair Workers	22.76
Automotive Mechanics	24.99	Marketing Managers	59.66
Bookkeepers	22.18	Network and Computer Systems Admin.	44.66
Carpenters	24.24	Nurses, Licensed Practical	26.56
Cashiers	12.62	Nurses, Registered	36.33
Computer Programmers	48.03	Nursing Assistants	15.28
Computer Systems Analysts	44.89	Office Clerks, General	18.21
Computer User Support Specialists	28.49	Physical Therapists	43.21
Construction Laborers	18.79	Physicians	117.34
Cooks, Restaurant	15.20	Plumbers, Pipefitters and Steamfitters	28.79
Customer Service Representatives	19.08	Police and Sheriff's Patrol Officers	31.31
Dentists	66.94	Postal Service Mail Carriers	26.51
Electricians	28.52	Real Estate Sales Agents	31.65
Engineers, Electrical	51.10	Retail Salespersons	16.05
Fast Food and Counter Workers	12.37	Sales Representatives, Technical/Scientific	50.78
Financial Managers	62.34	Secretaries, Exc. Legal/Medical/Executive	19.19
First-Line Supervisors of Office Workers	28.73	Security Guards	17.58
General and Operations Managers	43.88	Surgeons	158.20
Hairdressers/Cosmetologists	14.78	Teacher Assistants, Exc. Postsecondary*	15.44
Home Health and Personal Care Aides	15.25	Teachers, Secondary School, Exc. Sp. Ed.*	31.75
Janitors and Cleaners	13.94	Telemarketers	14.70
Landscaping/Groundskeeping Workers	17.21	Truck Drivers, Heavy/Tractor-Trailer	25.50
Lawyers	63.20	Truck Drivers, Light/Delivery Services	20.36
Maids and Housekeeping Cleaners	14.47	Waiters and Waitresses	13.92

Note: Wage data covers the Salt Lake City, UT Metropolitan Statistical Area; (*) Hourly wages were calculated from annual wage data based on a 40 hour work week; n/a not available.
Source: Bureau of Labor Statistics, Metro Area Occupational Employment & Wage Estimates, May 2021

Employment by Industry

Sector	MSA[1]		U.S.
	Number of Employees	Percent of Total	Percent of Total
Construction, Mining, and Logging	54,200	6.9	5.3
Education and Health Services	91,500	11.6	16.0
Financial Activities	64,300	8.2	5.9
Government	108,100	13.7	14.9
Information	22,700	2.9	1.9
Leisure and Hospitality	61,800	7.9	9.8
Manufacturing	61,800	7.9	8.4
Other Services	22,400	2.8	3.7
Professional and Business Services	135,400	17.2	14.6
Retail Trade	83,400	10.6	10.7
Transportation, Warehousing, and Utilities	45,600	5.8	4.8
Wholesale Trade	35,300	4.5	3.8

Note: Figures are non-farm employment as of December 2021. Figures are not seasonally adjusted and include workers 16 years of age and older; (1) Figures cover the Salt Lake City, UT Metropolitan Statistical Area
Source: Bureau of Labor Statistics, Current Employment Statistics, Employment, Hours, and Earnings

Employment by Occupation

Occupation Classification	City (%)	MSA[1] (%)	U.S. (%)
Management, Business, Science, and Arts	48.6	40.9	39.5
Natural Resources, Construction, and Maintenance	6.2	8.2	8.7
Production, Transportation, and Material Moving	10.8	12.9	13.1
Sales and Office	18.8	23.9	21.3
Service	15.6	14.0	17.4

Note: Figures cover employed civilians 16 years of age and older; (1) Figures cover the Salt Lake City, UT Metropolitan Statistical Area
Source: U.S. Census Bureau, 2016-2020 American Community Survey 5-Year Estimates

Occupations with Greatest Projected Employment Growth: 2021 – 2023

Occupation[1]	2021 Employment	2023 Projected Employment	Numeric Employment Change	Percent Employment Change
General and Operations Managers	52,760	56,070	3,310	6.3
Fast Food and Counter Workers	47,350	50,490	3,140	6.6
Software Developers and Software Quality Assurance Analysts and Testers	20,880	23,330	2,450	11.7
Construction Laborers	23,190	25,200	2,010	8.7
Retail Salespersons	48,570	50,450	1,880	3.9
Customer Service Representatives	52,690	54,500	1,810	3.4
Laborers and Freight, Stock, and Material Movers, Hand	24,160	25,930	1,770	7.3
Janitors and Cleaners, Except Maids and Housekeeping Cleaners	24,190	25,670	1,480	6.1
Sales Representatives, Wholesale and Manufacturing, Except Technical and Scientific Products	22,530	23,900	1,370	6.1
Project Management Specialists and Business Operations Specialists, All Other	20,740	22,090	1,350	6.5

Note: Projections cover Utah; (1) Sorted by numeric employment change
Source: www.projectionscentral.com, State Occupational Projections, 2021–2023 Short-Term Projections

Fastest-Growing Occupations: 2021 – 2023

Occupation[1]	2021 Employment	2023 Projected Employment	Numeric Employment Change	Percent Employment Change
Travel Agents	570	700	130	22.8
Reservation and Transportation Ticket Agents and Travel Clerks	3,100	3,740	640	20.6
Hotel, Motel, and Resort Desk Clerks	3,360	3,900	540	16.1
Statisticians	540	620	80	14.8
Data Scientists and Mathematical Science Occupations, All Other	420	480	60	14.3
Health Specialties Teachers, Postsecondary	2,390	2,700	310	13.0
Lodging Managers	400	450	50	12.5
Reinforcing Iron and Rebar Workers	410	460	50	12.2
Concierges	420	470	50	11.9
Software Developers and Software Quality Assurance Analysts and Testers	20,880	23,330	2,450	11.7

Note: Projections cover Utah; (1) Sorted by percent employment change and excludes occupations with numeric employment change less than 50
Source: www.projectionscentral.com, State Occupational Projections, 2021–2023 Short-Term Projections

TAXES

State Corporate Income Tax Rates

State	Tax Rate (%)	Income Brackets ($)	Num. of Brackets	Financial Institution Tax Rate (%)[a]	Federal Income Tax Ded.
Utah	4.95 (b)	Flat rate	–	4.95 (b)	No

Note: Tax rates as of January 1, 2022; (a) Rates listed are the corporate income tax rate applied to financial institutions or excise taxes based on income. Some states have other taxes based upon the value of deposits or shares; (b) Minimum tax is $800 in California, $250 in District of Columbia, $50 in Arizona and North Dakota (banks), $400 ($100 banks) in Rhode Island, $200 per location in South Dakota (banks), $100 in Utah, $300 in Vermont.
Source: Federation of Tax Administrators, State Corporate Income Tax Rates, January 1, 2022

State Individual Income Tax Rates

State	Tax Rate (%)	Income Brackets ($)	Personal Exemptions ($)			Standard Ded. ($)	
			Single	Married	Depend.	Single	Married
Utah	4.95	Flat rate	None	None	None	(v)	(v)

Note: Tax rates as of January 1, 2022; Local- and county-level taxes are not included; Federal income tax is not deductible on state income tax returns; (v) Utah provides a tax credit equal to 6% of the federal personal exemption amounts (and applicable standard deduction).
Source: Federation of Tax Administrators, State Individual Income Tax Rates, January 1, 2022

Various State Sales and Excise Tax Rates

State	State Sales Tax (%)	Gasoline[1] (¢/gal.)	Cigarette[2] ($/pack)	Spirits[3] ($/gal.)	Wine[4] ($/gal.)	Beer[5] ($/gal.)	Recreational Marijuana (%)
Utah	6.1	31.91	1.7	15.91	0	0.41	Not legal

Note: All tax rates as of January 1, 2022; (1) The American Petroleum Institute has developed a methodology for determining the average tax rate on a gallon of fuel. Rates may include any of the following: excise taxes, environmental fees, storage tank fees, other fees or taxes, general sales tax, and local taxes; (2) The federal excise tax of $1.0066 per pack and local taxes are not included; (3) Rates are those applicable to off-premise sales of 40% alcohol by volume (a.b.v.) distilled spirits in 750ml containers. Local excise taxes are excluded; (4) Rates are those applicable to off-premise sales of 11% a.b.v. non-carbonated wine in 750ml containers; (5) Rates are those applicable to off-premise sales of 4.7% a.b.v. beer in 12 ounce containers.
Source: Tax Foundation, 2022 Facts & Figures: How Does Your State Compare?

State Business Tax Climate Index Rankings

State	Overall Rank	Corporate Tax Rank	Individual Income Tax Rank	Sales Tax Rank	Property Tax Rank	Unemployment Insurance Tax Rank
Utah	10	14	10	22	7	17

Note: The index is a measure of how each state's tax laws affect economic performance. The lower the rank, the more favorable a state's tax system is for business. States without a given tax are given a ranking of 1. The scores/rankings for the District of Columbia do not affect other states. The 2022 index represents the tax climate as of July 1, 2021.
Source: Tax Foundation, State Business Tax Climate Index 2022

TRANSPORTATION

Means of Transportation to Work

Area	Car/Truck/Van		Public Transportation			Bicycle	Walked	Other Means	Worked at Home
	Drove Alone	Car-pooled	Bus	Subway	Railroad				
City	66.0	9.5	4.3	0.3	0.7	2.1	4.9	3.1	9.1
MSA[1]	73.2	10.7	1.8	0.3	0.5	0.6	2.0	1.6	9.2
U.S.	74.9	8.9	2.2	1.7	0.5	0.5	2.6	1.4	7.3

Note: Figures are percentages and cover workers 16 years of age and older; (1) Figures cover the Salt Lake City, UT Metropolitan Statistical Area
Source: U.S. Census Bureau, 2016-2020 American Community Survey 5-Year Estimates

Travel Time to Work

Area	Less Than 10 Minutes	10 to 19 Minutes	20 to 29 Minutes	30 to 44 Minutes	45 to 59 Minutes	60 to 89 Minutes	90 Minutes or More
City	12.7	44.8	22.5	13.1	3.5	2.1	1.2
MSA[1]	10.7	33.2	27.0	19.6	5.6	2.9	1.1
U.S.	12.3	28.4	20.9	20.9	8.3	6.4	2.9

Note: Note: Figures are percentages and include workers 16 years old and over; (1) Figures cover the Salt Lake City, UT Metropolitan Statistical Area
Source: U.S. Census Bureau, 2016-2020 American Community Survey 5-Year Estimates

Key Congestion Measures

Measure	1990	2000	2010	2015	2020
Annual Hours of Delay, Total (000)	6,374	14,974	22,524	27,472	17,124
Annual Hours of Delay, Per Auto Commuter	15	28	36	43	26
Annual Congestion Cost, Per Auto Commuter ($)	352	623	746	840	544

Note: Covers the Salt Lake City-West Valley City UT urban area
Source: Texas A&M Transportation Institute, 2021 Urban Mobility Report

Freeway Travel Time Index

Measure	1985	1990	1995	2000	2005	2010	2015	2020
Urban Area Index[1]	1.06	1.07	1.10	1.14	1.17	1.17	1.18	1.06
Urban Area Rank[1,2]	53	74	72	62	49	41	41	75

Note: Freeway Travel Time Index—the ratio of travel time in the peak period to the travel time at free-flow conditions. For example, a value of 1.30 indicates a 20-minute free-flow trip takes 26 minutes in the peak (20 minutes x 1.30 = 26 minutes); (1) Covers the Salt Lake City-West Valley City UT urban area; (2) Rank is based on 101 larger urban areas (#1 = highest travel time index)
Source: Texas A&M Transportation Institute, 2021 Urban Mobility Report

Public Transportation

Agency Name / Mode of Transportation	Vehicles Operated in Maximum Service[1]	Annual Unlinked Passenger Trips[2] (in thous.)	Annual Passenger Miles[3] (in thous.)
Utah Transit Authority (UTA)			
Bus (directly operated)	354	12,182.5	53,227.8
Bus (purchased transportation)	7	67.9	235.1
Commuter Bus (directly operated)	48	190.9	4,084.8
Commuter Rail (directly operated)	50	2,024.5	51,916.8
Demand Response (directly operated)	69	109.8	1,040.1
Demand Response (purchased transportation)	37	77.3	858.9
Light Rail (directly operated)	89	8,247.4	39,122.9
Vanpool (directly operated)	427	659.0	27,330.7

Note: (1) Number of revenue vehicles operated by the given mode and type of service to meet the annual maximum service requirement. This is the revenue vehicle count during the peak season of the year; on the week and day that maximum service is provided. Vehicles operated in maximum service (VOMS) exclude atypical days and one-time special events; (2) Number of passengers who boarded public transportation vehicles. Passengers are counted each time they board a vehicle no matter how many vehicles they use to travel from their origin to their destination. (3) Sum of the distances ridden by all passengers during the entire fiscal year.
Source: Federal Transit Administration, National Transit Database, 2020

Air Transportation

Airport Name and Code / Type of Service	Passenger Airlines[1]	Passenger Enplanements	Freight Carriers[2]	Freight (lbs)
Salt Lake City International (SLC)				
Domestic service (U.S. carriers - 2021)	23	10,529,068	19	220,323,350
International service (U.S. carriers - 2020)	4	146,251	1	761,140

Note: (1) Includes all U.S.-based major, minor and commuter airlines that carried at least one passenger during the year; (2) Includes all U.S.-based airlines and freight carriers that transported at least one pound of freight during the year.
Source: Bureau of Transportation Statistics, The Intermodal Transportation Database, Air Carriers: T-100 Domestic Market (U.S. Carriers), 2021; Bureau of Transportation Statistics, The Intermodal Transportation Database, Air Carriers: T-100 International Market (U.S. Carriers), 2020

BUSINESSES

Major Business Headquarters

Company Name	Industry	Rankings	
		Fortune[1]	Forbes[2]
Huntsman	Chemicals	460	-
Sinclair Oil	Oil & Gas Operations	-	94

Note: (1) Companies that produce a 10-K are ranked 1 to 500 based on 2020 revenue; (2) All private companies with at least $2 billion in annual revenue through the end of their most current fiscal year are ranked 1 to 225; companies listed are headquartered in the city; dashes indicate no ranking
Source: Fortune, "Fortune 500," 2021; Forbes, "America's Largest Private Companies," 2021

Fastest-Growing Businesses

According to *Inc.*, Salt Lake City is home to two of America's 500 fastest-growing private companies: **Coldwater Capital** (#27); **Pit Viper** (#465). Criteria: must be an independent, privately-held, for-profit, U.S. corporation, proprietorship or partnership as of December 31, 2020; revenues must be at least $100,000 in 2017 and $2 million in 2020; must have four-year operating/sales history. *Inc., "America's 500 Fastest-Growing Private Companies," 2021*

According to Deloitte, Salt Lake City is home to one of North America's 500 fastest-growing high-technology companies: **Filevine** (#188). Companies are ranked by percentage growth in revenue over a four-year period. Criteria for inclusion: company must be headquartered within North America; must own proprietary intellectual property or technology that is sold to customers in products that contributes to a significant portion of the company's operating revenue; must have been in business for a minumum of four years with 2017 operating revenues of at least $50,000 USD/CD and 2020 operating revenues of at least $5 million USD/CD. *Deloitte, 2021 Technology Fast 500™*

Living Environment

COST OF LIVING

Cost of Living Index

Composite Index	Groceries	Housing	Utilities	Trans-portation	Health Care	Misc. Goods/ Services
102.1	101.2	103.8	90.6	111.8	97.5	102.9

Note: The Cost of Living Index measures regional differences in the cost of consumer goods and services, excluding taxes and non-consumer expenditures, for professional and managerial households in the top income quintile. It is based on more than 50,000 prices covering almost 60 different items for which prices are collected three times a year by chambers of commerce, economic development organizations or university applied economic centers in each participating urban area. The numbers shown should be read as a percentage above or below the national average of 100. For example, a value of 115.4 in the groceries column indicates that grocery prices are 15.4% higher than the national average. Small differences in the index numbers should not be interpreted as significant; Figures cover the Salt Lake City UT urban area.
Source: The Council for Community and Economic Research, Cost of Living Index, 2021

Grocery Prices

Area[1]	T-Bone Steak ($/pound)	Frying Chicken ($/pound)	Whole Milk ($/half gal.)	Eggs ($/dozen)	Orange Juice ($/64 oz.)	Coffee ($/11.5 oz.)
City[2]	12.10	1.56	1.78	1.40	3.60	4.44
Avg.	12.82	1.40	2.22	1.57	3.59	4.30
Min.	8.91	0.91	1.29	0.75	2.87	3.02
Max.	21.35	2.69	3.92	3.86	5.49	8.11

Note: (1) Values for the local area are compared with the average, minimum and maximum values for all 285 areas in the Cost of Living Index; (2) Figures cover the Salt Lake City UT urban area; ***T-Bone Steak*** *(price per pound);* ***Frying Chicken*** *(price per pound, whole fryer);* ***Whole Milk*** *(half gallon carton);* ***Eggs*** *(price per dozen, Grade A, large);* ***Orange Juice*** *(64 oz. Tropicana or Florida Natural);* ***Coffee*** *(11.5 oz. can, vacuum-packed, Maxwell House, Hills Bros, or Folgers).*
Source: The Council for Community and Economic Research, Cost of Living Index, 2021

Housing and Utility Costs

Area[1]	New Home Price ($)	Apartment Rent ($/month)	All Electric ($/month)	Part Electric ($/month)	Other Energy ($/month)	Telephone ($/month)
City[2]	436,783	1,251	-	77.49	62.29	191.06
Avg.	398,393	1,217	171.38	100.83	69.67	187.75
Min.	212,799	534	96.71	31.56	27.15	173.01
Max.	2,354,006	4,438	369.53	277.33	303.87	206.73

Note: (1) Values for the local area are compared with the average, minimum and maximum values for all 285 areas in the Cost of Living Index; (2) Figures cover the Salt Lake City UT urban area; ***New Home Price*** *(2,400 sf living area, 8,000 sf lot, in urban area with full utilities);* ***Apartment Rent*** *(950 sf 2 bedroom/1.5 or 2 bath, unfurnished, excluding all utilities except water);* ***All Electric*** *(average monthly cost for an all-electric home);* ***Part Electric*** *(average monthly cost for a part-electric home);* ***Other Energy*** *(average monthly cost for natural gas, fuel oil, coal, wood, and any other forms of energy except electricity);* ***Telephone*** *(price includes the base monthly rate plus taxes and fees for three lines of mobile phone service).*
Source: The Council for Community and Economic Research, Cost of Living Index, 2021

Health Care, Transportation, and Other Costs

Area[1]	Doctor ($/visit)	Dentist ($/visit)	Optometrist ($/visit)	Gasoline ($/gallon)	Beauty Salon ($/visit)	Men's Shirt ($)
City[2]	107.40	96.11	96.64	3.10	38.87	28.98
Avg.	118.16	101.04	109.44	2.71	40.63	30.77
Min.	35.04	55.56	51.17	2.17	18.59	11.32
Max.	231.10	165.12	256.81	4.11	85.33	63.03

Note: (1) Values for the local area are compared with the average, minimum and maximum values for all 285 areas in the Cost of Living Index; (2) Figures cover the Salt Lake City UT urban area; ***Doctor*** *(general practitioners routine exam of an established patient);* ***Dentist*** *(adult teeth cleaning and periodic oral examination);* ***Optometrist*** *(full vision eye exam for established adult patient);* ***Gasoline*** *(one gallon regular unleaded, national brand, including all taxes, cash price at self-service pump if available);* ***Beauty Salon*** *(woman's shampoo, trim, and blow-dry);* ***Men's Shirt*** *(cotton/polyester dress shirt, pinpoint weave, long sleeves).*
Source: The Council for Community and Economic Research, Cost of Living Index, 2021

HOUSING

Homeownership Rate

Area	2013 (%)	2014 (%)	2015 (%)	2016 (%)	2017 (%)	2018 (%)	2019 (%)	2020 (%)	2021 (%)
MSA[1]	66.8	68.2	69.1	69.2	68.1	69.5	69.2	68.0	64.1
U.S.	65.1	64.5	63.7	63.4	63.9	64.4	64.6	66.6	65.5

Note: (1) Figures cover the Salt Lake City, UT Metropolitan Statistical Area
Source: U.S. Census Bureau, Housing Vacancies and Homeownership Annual Statistics: 2013-2021

House Price Index (HPI)

Area	National Ranking[2]	Quarterly Change (%)	One-Year Change (%)	Five-Year Change (%)	Since 1991Q1 (%)
MSA[1]	23	3.19	25.65	74.98	540.19
U.S.[3]	–	3.33	17.54	54.45	258.04

Note: The HPI is a weighted repeat sales index. It measures average price changes in repeat sales or refinancings on the same properties. This information is obtained by reviewing repeat mortgage transactions on single-family properties whose mortgages have been purchased or securitized by Fannie Mae or Freddie Mac since January 1975; (1) Figures cover the Salt Lake City, UT Metropolitan Statistical Area; (2) Rankings are based on annual percentage change for all metro areas containing at least 15,000 transactions over the last 10 years and ranges from 1 to 268; (3) figures based on a weighted average of Census Division estimates using a seasonally adjusted, purchase-only index; all figures are for the period ending December 31, 2021
Source: Federal Housing Finance Agency, Change in FHFA Metropolitan Area House Price Indexes, 2021Q4

Median Single-Family Home Prices

Area	2019	2020	2021[p]	Percent Change 2020 to 2021
MSA[1]	355.2	391.0	486.1	24.3
U.S. Average	274.6	300.2	353.4	17.7

Note: Figures are median sales prices of existing single-family homes in thousands of dollars; (p) preliminary; (1) Figures cover the Salt Lake City, UT Metropolitan Statistical Area
Source: National Association of Realtors, Median Sales Price of Existing Single-Family Homes for Metropolitan Areas, 4th Quarter 2021

Qualifying Income Based on Median Sales Price of Existing Single-Family Homes

Area	With 5% Down ($)	With 10% Down ($)	With 20% Down ($)
MSA[1]	99,696	94,449	83,955
U.S. Average	70,699	66,978	59,536

Note: Figures are preliminary; Qualifying income is based on a mortgage rate of 3.13%. Monthly principal and interest payment is limited to 25% of income; (1) Figures cover the Salt Lake City, UT Metropolitan Statistical Area
Source: National Association of Realtors, Qualifying Income Based on Median Sales Price of Existing Single-Family Homes for Metropolitan Areas, 4th Quarter 2021

Home Value Distribution

Area	Under $50,000	$50,000 -$99,999	$100,000 -$149,999	$150,000 -$199,999	$200,000 -$299,999	$300,000 -$499,999	$500,000 -$999,999	$1,000,000 or more
City	2.6	1.2	5.1	9.4	23.4	31.7	22.3	4.3
MSA[1]	2.7	1.1	3.7	8.3	27.3	38.4	16.5	2.1
U.S.	6.6	11.0	12.3	13.6	20.0	20.5	12.3	3.7

Note: Figures are percentages and cover owner-occupied housing units; (1) Figures cover the Salt Lake City, UT Metropolitan Statistical Area
Source: U.S. Census Bureau, 2016-2020 American Community Survey 5-Year Estimates

Year Housing Structure Built

Area	2010 or Later	2000 -2009	1990 -1999	1980 -1989	1970 -1979	1960 -1969	1950 -1959	1940 -1949	Before 1940	Median Year
City	6.7	6.8	6.4	8.2	11.7	9.9	13.2	8.9	28.2	1960
MSA[1]	11.1	14.8	15.4	12.1	18.0	8.9	8.6	3.5	7.7	1983
U.S.	6.2	13.6	13.9	13.4	15.0	10.5	10.2	4.8	12.4	1978

Note: Figures are percentages except for Median Year; Note: (1) Figures cover the Salt Lake City, UT Metropolitan Statistical Area
Source: U.S. Census Bureau, 2016-2020 American Community Survey 5-Year Estimates

Gross Monthly Rent

Area	Under $500	$500 -$999	$1,000 -$1,499	$1,500 -$1,999	$2,000 -$2,499	$2,500 -$2,999	$3,000 and up	Median ($)
City	8.4	37.6	34.6	14.6	3.4	0.8	0.6	1,050
MSA[1]	5.0	28.2	43.4	17.8	3.8	1.0	0.8	1,171
U.S.	8.9	34.3	30.2	14.9	6.2	2.6	2.8	1,096

Note: Figures are percentages except for Median; Gross rent is the contract rent plus the estimated average monthly cost of utilities (electricity, gas, and water and sewer) and fuels (oil, coal, kerosene, wood, etc.) if these are paid by the renter (or paid for the renter by someone else); (1) Figures cover the Salt Lake City, UT Metropolitan Statistical Area
Source: U.S. Census Bureau, 2016-2020 American Community Survey 5-Year Estimates

HEALTH

Health Risk Factors

Category	MSA[1] (%)	U.S. (%)
Adults aged 18–64 who have any kind of health care coverage	85.2	86.8
Adults who reported being in good or better health	89.4	86.7
Adults who are current smokers	9.5	15.5
Adults who currently use chewing tobacco, snuff, or snus	2.2	3.7
Adults who are heavy drinkers[2]	5.2	6.7
Adults who are binge drinkers[3]	14.0	15.7
Adults who are overweight (BMI 25.0 - 29.9)	34.1	35.2
Adults who are obese (BMI 30.0 - 99.8)	29.8	31.9
Adults who participated in any physical activities in the past month	82.8	77.6
Adults who always or nearly always wears a seat belt	96.4	94.2

Note: (1) Figures cover the Salt Lake City, UT Metropolitan Statistical Area; (2) Heavy drinkers are classified as adult men having more than 14 drinks per week and adult women having more than 7 drinks per week; (3) Binge drinkers are classified as males having five or more drinks on one occasion or females having four or more drinks on one occasion

Source: Centers for Disease Control and Prevention, Behaviorial Risk Factor Surveillance System, SMART: Selected Metropolitan Area Risk Trends, 2020

Acute and Chronic Health Conditions

Category	MSA[1] (%)	U.S. (%)
Adults who have ever been told they had a heart attack	3.1	4.3
Adults who have ever been told they have angina or coronary heart disease	2.9	4.0
Adults who have ever been told they had a stroke	2.4	2.8
Adults who have ever been told they have asthma	15.9	14.2
Adults who have ever been told they have arthritis	19.9	24.5
Adults who have ever been told they have diabetes[2]	8.9	10.6
Adults who have ever been told they had skin cancer	7.7	6.4
Adults who have ever been told they had any other types of cancer	5.6	6.8
Adults who have ever been told they have COPD	4.6	6.2
Adults who have ever been told they have kidney disease	2.8	2.9
Adults who have ever been told they have a form of depression	23.6	19.6

Note: (1) Figures cover the Salt Lake City, UT Metropolitan Statistical Area; (2) Figures do not include pregnancy-related, borderline, or pre-diabetes

Source: Centers for Disease Control and Prevention, Behaviorial Risk Factor Surveillance System, SMART: Selected Metropolitan Area Risk Trends, 2020

Health Screening and Vaccination Rates

Category	MSA[1] (%)	U.S. (%)
Adults 50-75 who have had a blood stool test within the past year	6.0	9.3
Adults aged 65+ who have had flu shot within the past year	75.5	67.9
Adults aged 65+ who have ever had a pneumonia vaccination	77.9	72.2
Adults who have ever been tested for HIV	28.8	37.1
Women aged 21-65 who have had a pap test in the past three years	73.0	77.7
Men aged 40+ who have had a PSA test within the past two years	25.9	31.8
Women aged 40+ who have had a mammogram within the past two years	62.2	71.5

Note: (1) Figures cover the Salt Lake City, UT Metropolitan Statistical Area.

Source: Centers for Disease Control and Prevention, Behaviorial Risk Factor Surveillance System, SMART: Selected Metropolitan Area Risk Trends, 2020

Disability Status

Category	MSA[1] (%)	U.S. (%)
Adults who reported being deaf	5.0	6.8
Are you blind or have serious difficulty seeing, even when wearing glasses?	2.7	4.7
Do you have difficulty doing errands alone?	5.4	6.3
Do you have difficulty dressing or bathing?	1.9	3.0
Do you have serious difficulty concentrating/remembering/making decisions?	10.6	10.8
Do you have serious difficulty walking or climbing stairs?	8.4	11.9

Note: (1) Figures cover the Salt Lake City, UT Metropolitan Statistical Area.

Source: Centers for Disease Control and Prevention, Behaviorial Risk Factor Surveillance System, SMART: Selected Metropolitan Area Risk Trends, 2020

Mortality Rates for the Top 10 Causes of Death in the U.S.

ICD-10[a] Sub-Chapter	ICD-10[a] Code	Age-Adjusted Mortality Rate[1] per 100,000 population	
		County[2]	U.S.
Malignant neoplasms	C00-C97	122.6	146.4
Ischaemic heart diseases	I20-I25	64.1	90.2
Other forms of heart disease	I30-I51	64.2	51.9
Other degenerative diseases of the nervous system	G30-G31	51.1	39.7
Other external causes of accidental injury	W00-X59	38.2	38.7
Chronic lower respiratory diseases	J40-J47	33.3	38.1
Cerebrovascular diseases	I60-I69	35.5	37.6
Organic, including symptomatic, mental disorders	F01-F09	31.9	29.4
Hypertensive diseases	I10-I15	21.0	26.1
Diabetes mellitus	E10-E14	26.6	22.6

Note: (a) ICD-10 = International Classification of Diseases 10th Revision; (1) Mortality rates are a three-year average covering 2018-2020; (2) Figures cover Salt Lake County.
Source: Centers for Disease Control and Prevention, National Center for Health Statistics. Underlying Cause of Death 1999-2020 on CDC WONDER Online Database

Mortality Rates for Selected Causes of Death

ICD-10[a] Sub-Chapter	ICD-10[a] Code	Age-Adjusted Mortality Rate[1] per 100,000 population	
		County[2]	U.S.
Assault	X85-Y09	3.5	6.5
Diseases of the liver	K70-K76	14.6	15.3
Human immunodeficiency virus (HIV) disease	B20-B24	0.9	1.4
Influenza and pneumonia	J09-J18	9.6	13.4
Intentional self-harm	X60-X84	21.4	13.9
Malnutrition	E40-E46	12.2	2.9
Obesity and other hyperalimentation	E65-E68	3.0	2.4
Renal failure	N17-N19	10.1	12.5
Transport accidents	V01-V99	9.7	12.5
Viral hepatitis	B15-B19	1.1	1.0

Note: (a) ICD-10 = International Classification of Diseases 10th Revision; (1) Mortality rates are a three-year average covering 2018-2020; (2) Figures cover Salt Lake County; Data are suppressed when the data meet the criteria for confidentiality constraints; Mortality rates are flagged as unreliable when the rate would be calculated with a numerator of 20 or less.
Source: Centers for Disease Control and Prevention, National Center for Health Statistics. Underlying Cause of Death 1999-2020 on CDC WONDER Online Database

Health Insurance Coverage

Area	With Health Insurance	With Private Health Insurance	With Public Health Insurance	Without Health Insurance	Population Under Age 19 Without Health Insurance
City	87.7	73.0	22.3	12.3	11.2
MSA[1]	90.1	77.6	20.4	9.9	7.9
U.S.	91.3	68.1	35.3	8.7	5.2

Note: Figures are percentages that cover the civilian noninstitutionalized population; (1) Figures cover the Salt Lake City, UT Metropolitan Statistical Area
Source: U.S. Census Bureau, 2016-2020 American Community Survey 5-Year Estimates

Number of Medical Professionals

Area	MDs[3]	DOs[3,4]	Dentists	Podiatrists	Chiropractors	Optometrists
County[1] (number)	4,453	208	922	72	331	160
County[1] (rate[2])	375.7	17.5	77.8	6.1	27.9	13.5
U.S. (rate[2])	285.1	23.0	71.1	6.2	28.2	17.0

49035
Note: Data as of 2020 unless noted; (1) Data covers Salt Lake County; (2) Rate per 100,000 population; (3) Data as of 2019 and includes all active, non-federal physicians; (4) Doctor of Osteopathic Medicine
Source: U.S. Department of Health and Human Services, Health Resources and Services Administration, Bureau of Health Professions, Area Resource File (ARF) 2020-2021

Best Hospitals

According to *U.S. News*, the Salt Lake City, UT metro area is home to four of the best hospitals in the U.S.: **Craig H. Neilsen Rehabilitation Hospital** (2 adult specialties); **Huntsman Cancer Institute at the University of Utah** (2 adult specialties); **Huntsman Mental Health Institute** (2 adult specialties); **John A. Moran Eye Center, University of Utah Hospitals and Clinics** (2 adult specialties). The hospitals listed were nationally ranked in at least one of 15 adult or 10 pediatric specialties. Only 175 U.S. hospitals performed well enough to be nationally ranked in one or more specialties. Twenty hospitals in the U.S. made the Honor Roll. The Best Hospitals Honor Roll takes both the national rankings and the procedure and condition ratings into account. Hospitals received points if they were nationally ranked in one of the 15 adult specialties—the higher they ranked, the more points they got—and how many ratings of "high performing" they earned in the 17 procedures and conditions. *U.S. News Online, "America's Best Hospitals 2021-22"*

According to *U.S. News,* the Salt Lake City, UT metro area is home to one of the best children's hospitals in the U.S.: **Intermountain Primary Children's Hospital-University of Utah** (8 pediatric specialties). The hospital listed was highly ranked in at least one of 10 pediatric specialties. Ninety-two children's hospitals in the U.S. were nationally ranked in at least one specialty. Hospitals received points for being ranked in a specialty, and the 10 hospitals with the most points across the 10 specialties make up the Honor Roll. *U.S. News Online, "America's Best Children's Hospitals 2021-22"*

EDUCATION

Public School District Statistics

District Name	Schls	Pupils	Pupil/ Teacher Ratio	Minority Pupils[1] (%)	LEP/ELL[2] (%)	IEP[3] (%)
Granite District	92	66,276	23.6	50.3	21.9	12.6
Salt Lake District	42	22,571	19.8	56.0	21.3	13.1

Note: Table includes school districts with 2,000 or more students; (1) Percentage of students that are not non-Hispanic white; (2) Percentage of students that are Limited English Proficient (LEP) or English Language Learners (ELL) (2018-19); (3) Percentage of students that have an Individualized Education Program (IEP).
Source: U.S. Department of Education, National Center for Education Statistics, Common Core of Data, Local Education Agency (School District) Universe Survey: School Year 2019-2020

Highest Level of Education

Area	Less than H.S.	H.S. Diploma	Some College, No Deg.	Associate Degree	Bachelor's Degree	Master's Degree	Prof. School Degree	Doctorate Degree
City	10.0	16.5	18.0	6.7	27.3	13.1	4.6	3.7
MSA[1]	8.5	22.9	23.6	9.3	23.0	9.0	2.3	1.6
U.S.	11.5	26.7	20.3	8.6	20.2	9.1	2.2	1.5

Note: Figures cover persons age 25 and over; (1) Figures cover the Salt Lake City, UT Metropolitan Statistical Area
Source: U.S. Census Bureau, 2016-2020 American Community Survey 5-Year Estimates

Educational Attainment by Race

Area	High School Graduate or Higher (%)					Bachelor's Degree or Higher (%)				
	Total	White	Black	Asian	Hisp.[2]	Total	White	Black	Asian	Hisp.[2]
City	90.0	94.7	85.0	82.9	65.1	48.7	53.3	34.2	61.4	20.6
MSA[1]	91.5	94.6	85.3	86.6	72.4	35.8	38.0	23.8	51.0	16.6
U.S.	88.5	90.7	86.7	87.3	70.3	32.9	34.4	22.6	55.0	17.6

Note: Figures shown cover persons 25 years old and over; (1) Figures cover the Salt Lake City, UT Metropolitan Statistical Area; (2) People of Hispanic origin can be of any race
Source: U.S. Census Bureau, 2016-2020 American Community Survey 5-Year Estimates

School Enrollment by Grade and Control

Area	Preschool (%)		Kindergarten (%)		Grades 1 - 4 (%)		Grades 5 - 8 (%)		Grades 9 - 12 (%)	
	Public	Private	Public	Private	Public	Private	Public	Private	Public	Private
City	43.9	56.1	88.1	11.9	90.5	9.5	90.1	9.9	94.1	5.9
MSA[1]	54.5	45.5	87.0	13.0	91.1	8.9	93.4	6.6	93.4	6.6
U.S.	58.9	41.1	86.9	13.1	89.0	11.0	89.0	11.0	89.7	10.3

Note: Figures shown cover persons 3 years old and over; (1) Figures cover the Salt Lake City, UT Metropolitan Statistical Area
Source: U.S. Census Bureau, 2016-2020 American Community Survey 5-Year Estimates

Higher Education

Four-Year Colleges			Two-Year Colleges			Medical Schools[1]	Law Schools[2]	Voc/ Tech[3]
Public	Private Non-profit	Private For-profit	Public	Private Non-profit	Private For-profit			
1	5	6	1	1	1	1	1	13

Note: Figures cover institutions located within the Salt Lake City, UT Metropolitan Statistical Area and include main campuses only; (1) includes schools accredited by the Liaison Committee on Medical Education and the American Osteopathic Association's Commission on Osteopathic College Accreditation; (2) includes ABA-accredited schools, schools with provisional ABA accreditation, and state accredited schools; (3) includes all schools with programs that are less than 2 years.
Source: National Center for Education Statistics, Integrated Postsecondary Education System (IPEDS), 2020-21; Wikipedia, List of Medical Schools in the United States, accessed April 11, 2022; Wikipedia, List of Law Schools in the United States, accessed April 11, 2022

According to *U.S. News & World Report,* the Salt Lake City, UT metro area is home to one of the top 200 national universities in the U.S.: **University of Utah** (#99 tie). The indicators used to capture academic quality fall into a number of categories: assessment by administrators at peer institutions; retention of students; faculty resources; student selectivity; financial resources; alumni giving; high school counselor ratings of colleges; and graduation rate. *U.S. News & World Report, "America's Best Colleges 2022"*

According to *U.S. News & World Report,* the Salt Lake City, UT metro area is home to one of the top 100 law schools in the U.S.: **University of Utah (Quinney)** (#43 tie). The rankings are based on a weighted average of 12 measures of quality: peer assessment score; assessment score by lawyers/judges; median LSAT scores; median undergrad GPA; acceptance rate; employment rates for graduates; placement success; bar passage rate; faculty resources; expenditures per student; student/faculty ratio; and library resources. *U.S. News & World Report, "America's Best Graduate Schools, Law, 2022"*

According to *U.S. News & World Report,* the Salt Lake City, UT metro area is home to one of the top 75 medical schools for research in the U.S.: **University of Utah** (#41). The rankings are based on a weighted average of 11 measures of quality: quality assessment; peer assessment score; assessment score by residency directors; research activity; total research activity; average research activity per faculty member; student selectivity; median MCAT total score; median undergraduate GPA; acceptance rate; and faculty resources. *U.S. News & World Report, "America's Best Graduate Schools, Medical, 2022"*

According to *U.S. News & World Report,* the Salt Lake City, UT metro area is home to one of the top 75 business schools in the U.S.: **University of Utah (Eccles)** (#44 tie). The rankings are based on a weighted average of the following nine measures: quality assessment; peer assessment; recruiter assessment; placement success; mean starting salary and bonus; student selectivity; mean GMAT and GRE scores; mean undergraduate GPA; and acceptance rate. *U.S. News & World Report, "America's Best Graduate Schools, Business, 2022"*

EMPLOYERS

Major Employers

Company Name	Industry
ACS Commercial Solutions	Data entry service
Alsco	Laundry & garment services, nec
Boart Longyear Company	Test boring for nonmetallic minerals
Church of Jesus Christ of LDS	Mormon church
Comenity Capital Bank	State commercial banks
County of Salt Lake	County government
EnergySolutions	Nonresidential construction, nec
Executive Office of the State of Utah	Executive offices
Granite School District Aid Association	Public elementary & secondary schools
Huntsman Corporation	Plastics materials & resins
Huntsman Holdings	Polystyrene resins
Intermountain Health Care	General medical & surgical hospitals
Jordan School District	Public elementary & secondary schools
Longyear Holdings	Test boring for nonmetallic minerals
Sinclair Oil Corporation	Petroleum refining
Smith's Food & Drug Centers	Grocery stores
Sportsman's Warehouse Holdings	Hunting equipment
State of Utah	State government
The University of Utah	Colleges & universities
TPUSA	Telemarketing services
University of Utah Hospitals & Clinics	General medical & surgical hospitals
Utah Department of Human Services	Administration of social & manpower programs
Zions Bancorporation	Bank holding companies

Note: Companies shown are located within the Salt Lake City, UT Metropolitan Statistical Area.
Source: Hoovers.com; Wikipedia

Best Companies to Work For

O.C. Tanner, headquartered in Salt Lake City, is among "The 100 Best Companies to Work For." To pick the best companies, *Fortune* partnered with the Great Place to Work Institute. Two-thirds of a company's score is based on the results of the Institute's Trust Index survey, which is sent to a random sample of employees from each company. The questions related to attitudes about management's credibility, job satisfaction, and camaraderie. The other third of the scoring is based on the company's responses to the Institute's Culture Audit, which includes detailed questions about pay and benefit programs, and a series of open-ended questions about hiring practices, internal communication, training, recognition programs, and diversity efforts. Any company that is at least five years old with more than 1,000 U.S. employees is eligible. *Fortune, "The 100 Best Companies to Work For," 2021*

Health Catalyst; Primary Residential Mortgage, headquartered in Salt Lake City, are among "75 Best Large Workplaces for Women." To pick the best companies, *Fortune* partnered with the Great Place to Work Institute. Employees responded to over 60 survey questions describing the extent to which their organization creates a Great Place to Work For All. Eighty-five percent of the ranking is based on what women themselves report about their workplace, and how fairly those experiences compare to men's reports of the same workplaces. Fifteen percent of the remaining rank is based on how well represented women are in the workforce and throughout management, taking into account industry trends. To be considered, at a minimum, companies need to employ at least 50 women, at least 20% of their non-executive managers need to be female, and at least one of their executives needs to be female. *Fortune, "75 Best Large Workplaces for Women," 2021*

PUBLIC SAFETY

Crime Rate

Area	Total Crime	Violent Crime Rate				Property Crime Rate		
		Murder	Rape[3]	Robbery	Aggrav. Assault	Burglary	Larceny -Theft	Motor Vehicle Theft
City	8,274.5	8.4	137.0	240.9	536.1	764.1	5,503.8	1,084.1
Suburbs[1]	3,411.8	4.1	53.4	45.4	176.7	364.6	2,327.6	439.9
Metro[2]	4,200.7	4.8	67.0	77.1	235.0	429.5	2,842.9	544.4
U.S.	2,356.7	6.5	38.4	73.9	279.7	314.2	1,398.0	246.0

Note: Figures are crimes per 100,000 population; (1) All areas within the metro area that are located outside the city limits; (2) Figures cover the Salt Lake City, UT Metropolitan Statistical Area; (3) All figures shown were reported using the revised Uniform Crime Reporting (UCR) definition of rape.
Source: FBI Uniform Crime Reports, 2020

Hate Crimes

Area	Number of Quarters Reported	Number of Incidents per Bias Motivation					
		Race/Ethnicity/ Ancestry	Religion	Sexual Orientation	Disability	Gender	Gender Identity
City[1]	4	1	0	2	0	0	0
U.S.	4	5,227	1,244	1,110	130	75	266

Note: (1) Figures include one incident reported with more than one bias motivation.
Source: Federal Bureau of Investigation, Hate Crime Statistics 2020

Identity Theft Consumer Reports

Area	Reports	Reports per 100,000 Population	Rank[2]
MSA[1]	2,822	229	194
U.S.	1,434,676	432	-

Note: (1) Figures cover the Salt Lake City, UT Metropolitan Statistical Area; (2) Rank ranges from 1 to 391 where 1 indicates greatest number of identity theft reports per 100,000 population
Source: Federal Trade Commission, Consumer Sentinel Network Data Book 2021

Fraud and Other Consumer Reports

Area	Reports	Reports per 100,000 Population	Rank[2]
MSA[1]	11,293	916	169
U.S.	4,328,977	1,304	-

Note: (1) Figures cover the Salt Lake City, UT Metropolitan Statistical Area; (2) Rank ranges from 1 to 391 where 1 indicates greatest number of fraud and other consumer reports per 100,000 population
Source: Federal Trade Commission, Consumer Sentinel Network Data Book 2021

POLITICS

2020 Presidential Election Results

Area	Biden	Trump	Jorgensen	Hawkins	Other
Salt Lake County	53.0	42.1	2.2	0.4	2.2
U.S.	51.3	46.8	1.2	0.3	0.5

Note: Results are percentages and may not add to 100% due to rounding
Source: Dave Leip's Atlas of U.S. Presidential Elections

SPORTS

Professional Sports Teams

Team Name	League	Year Established
Real Salt Lake	Major League Soccer (MLS)	2005
Utah Jazz	National Basketball Association (NBA)	1979

Note: Includes teams located in the Salt Lake City, UT Metropolitan Statistical Area.
Source: Wikipedia, Major Professional Sports Teams of the United States and Canada, April 6, 2022

CLIMATE

Average and Extreme Temperatures

Temperature	Jan	Feb	Mar	Apr	May	Jun	Jul	Aug	Sep	Oct	Nov	Dec	Yr.
Extreme High (°F)	62	69	78	85	93	104	107	104	100	89	75	67	107
Average High (°F)	37	43	52	62	72	83	93	90	80	66	50	38	64
Average Temp. (°F)	28	34	41	50	59	69	78	76	65	53	40	30	52
Average Low (°F)	19	24	31	38	46	54	62	61	51	40	30	22	40
Extreme Low (°F)	-22	-14	2	15	25	35	40	37	27	16	-14	-15	-22

Note: Figures cover the years 1948-1990
Source: National Climatic Data Center, International Station Meteorological Climate Summary, 9/96

Average Precipitation/Snowfall/Humidity

Precip./Humidity	Jan	Feb	Mar	Apr	May	Jun	Jul	Aug	Sep	Oct	Nov	Dec	Yr.
Avg. Precip. (in.)	1.3	1.2	1.8	2.0	1.7	0.9	0.8	0.9	1.1	1.3	1.3	1.4	15.6
Avg. Snowfall (in.)	13	10	11	6	1	Tr	0	0	Tr	2	6	13	63
Avg. Rel. Hum. 5am (%)	79	77	71	67	66	60	53	54	60	68	75	79	67
Avg. Rel. Hum. 5pm (%)	69	59	47	38	33	26	22	23	28	40	59	71	43

Note: Figures cover the years 1948-1990; Tr = Trace amounts (<0.05 in. of rain; <0.5 in. of snow)
Source: National Climatic Data Center, International Station Meteorological Climate Summary, 9/96

Weather Conditions

Temperature			Daytime Sky			Precipitation		
5°F & below	32°F & below	90°F & above	Clear	Partly cloudy	Cloudy	0.01 inch or more precip.	0.1 inch or more snow/ice	Thunder-storms
7	128	56	94	152	119	92	38	38

Note: Figures are average number of days per year and cover the years 1948-1990
Source: National Climatic Data Center, International Station Meteorological Climate Summary, 9/96

HAZARDOUS WASTE

Superfund Sites

The Salt Lake City, UT metro area is home to five sites on the EPA's Superfund National Priorities List: **700 South 1600 East Pce Plume** (final); **Jacobs Smelter** (final); **Kennecott (North Zone)** (proposed); **Murray Smelter** (proposed); **Portland Cement (Kiln Dust 2 & 3)** (final). There are a total of 1,165 Superfund sites with a status of proposed or final on the list in the U.S. *U.S. Environmental Protection Agency, National Priorities List, April 6, 2022*

AIR QUALITY

Air Quality Trends: Ozone

	1990	1995	2000	2005	2010	2016	2017	2018	2019	2020
MSA[1]	n/a	n/a	n/a	n/a	n/a	n/a	n/a	n/a	n/a	n/a
U.S.	0.090	0.091	0.082	0.080	0.074	0.070	0.069	0.070	0.066	0.068

Note: (1) Data covers the Salt Lake City, UT Metropolitan Statistical Area; n/a not available. The values shown are the composite ozone concentration averages among trend sites based on the highest fourth daily maximum 8-hour concentration in parts per million. These trends are based on sites having an adequate record of monitoring data during the trend period. Data from exceptional events are included.
Source: U.S. Environmental Protection Agency, Air Quality Monitoring Information, "Air Quality Trends by City, 1990-2020"

Air Quality Index

Area	Percent of Days when Air Quality was...[2]					AQI Statistics[2]	
	Good	Moderate	Unhealthy for Sensitive Groups	Unhealthy	Very Unhealthy	Maximum	Median
MSA[1]	50.8	43.4	5.2	0.5	0.0	194	50

Note: (1) Data covers the Salt Lake City, UT Metropolitan Statistical Area; (2) Based on 366 days with AQI data in 2020. Air Quality Index (AQI) is an index for reporting daily air quality. EPA calculates the AQI for five major air pollutants regulated by the Clean Air Act: ground-level ozone, particle pollution (aka particulate matter), carbon monoxide, sulfur dioxide, and nitrogen dioxide. The AQI runs from 0 to 500. The higher the AQI value, the greater the level of air pollution and the greater the health concern. There are six AQI categories: "Good" AQI is between 0 and 50. Air quality is considered satisfactory; "Moderate" AQI is between 51 and 100. Air quality is acceptable; "Unhealthy for Sensitive Groups" When AQI values are between 101 and 150, members of sensitive groups may experience health effects; "Unhealthy" When AQI values are between 151 and 200 everyone may begin to experience health effects; "Very Unhealthy" AQI values between 201 and 300 trigger a health alert; "Hazardous" AQI values over 300 trigger warnings of emergency conditions (not shown).
Source: U.S. Environmental Protection Agency, Air Quality Index Report, 2020

Air Quality Index Pollutants

Area	Percent of Days when AQI Pollutant was...[2]					
	Carbon Monoxide	Nitrogen Dioxide	Ozone	Sulfur Dioxide	Particulate Matter 2.5	Particulate Matter 10
MSA[1]	0.0	13.1	51.4	0.0	34.7	0.8

Note: (1) Data covers the Salt Lake City, UT Metropolitan Statistical Area; (2) Based on 366 days with AQI data in 2020. The Air Quality Index (AQI) is an index for reporting daily air quality. EPA calculates the AQI for five major air pollutants regulated by the Clean Air Act: ground-level ozone, particle pollution (also known as particulate matter), carbon monoxide, sulfur dioxide, and nitrogen dioxide. The AQI runs from 0 to 500. The higher the AQI value, the greater the level of air pollution and the greater the health concern.
Source: U.S. Environmental Protection Agency, Air Quality Index Report, 2020

Maximum Air Pollutant Concentrations: Particulate Matter, Ozone, CO and Lead

	Particulate Matter 10 (ug/m³)	Particulate Matter 2.5 Wtd AM (ug/m³)	Particulate Matter 2.5 24-Hr (ug/m³)	Ozone (ppm)	Carbon Monoxide (ppm)	Lead (ug/m³)
MSA[1] Level	112	10.5	33	0.08	1	n/a
NAAQS[2]	150	15	35	0.075	9	0.15
Met NAAQS[2]	Yes	Yes	Yes	No	Yes	n/a

Note: (1) Data covers the Salt Lake City, UT Metropolitan Statistical Area; Data from exceptional events are included; (2) National Ambient Air Quality Standards; ppm = parts per million; ug/m³ = micrograms per cubic meter; n/a not available.
Concentrations: Particulate Matter 10 (coarse particulate)—highest second maximum 24-hour concentration; Particulate Matter 2.5 Wtd AM (fine particulate)—highest weighted annual mean concentration; Particulate Matter 2.5 24-Hour (fine particulate)—highest 98th percentile 24-hour concentration; Ozone—highest fourth daily maximum 8-hour concentration; Carbon Monoxide—highest second maximum non-overlapping 8-hour concentration; Lead—maximum running 3-month average
Source: U.S. Environmental Protection Agency, Air Quality Monitoring Information, "Air Quality Statistics by City, 2020"

Maximum Air Pollutant Concentrations: Nitrogen Dioxide and Sulfur Dioxide

	Nitrogen Dioxide AM (ppb)	Nitrogen Dioxide 1-Hr (ppb)	Sulfur Dioxide AM (ppb)	Sulfur Dioxide 1-Hr (ppb)	Sulfur Dioxide 24-Hr (ppb)
MSA[1] Level	17	51	n/a	5	n/a
NAAQS[2]	53	100	30	75	140
Met NAAQS[2]	Yes	Yes	n/a	Yes	n/a

Note: (1) Data covers the Salt Lake City, UT Metropolitan Statistical Area; Data from exceptional events are included; (2) National Ambient Air Quality Standards; ppm = parts per million; ug/m³ = micrograms per cubic meter; n/a not available.
Concentrations: Nitrogen Dioxide AM—highest arithmetic mean concentration; Nitrogen Dioxide 1-Hr—highest 98th percentile 1-hour daily maximum concentration; Sulfur Dioxide AM—highest annual mean concentration; Sulfur Dioxide 1-Hr—highest 99th percentile 1-hour daily maximum concentration; Sulfur Dioxide 24-Hr—highest second maximum 24-hour concentration
Source: U.S. Environmental Protection Agency, Air Quality Monitoring Information, "Air Quality Statistics by City, 2020"

San Diego, California

Background

San Diego is the archetypal southern California City. Located 100 miles south of Los Angeles, near the Mexican border, San Diego is characterized by sunny days, an excellent harbor, a populous citizenry influenced by its Spanish heritage, and recreational activities based on ideal weather conditions.

San Diego was first claimed in 1542 for Spain by Juan Rodríguez Cabrillo, a Portuguese navigator in the service of the Spanish crown. The site remained uneventful until 1769, when Spanish colonizer, Gaspar de Portola, established the first European settlement in California. Accompanying de Portola was a Franciscan monk named Junipero Serra, who established the Mission Basilica San Diego de Alcala, the first of a chain of missions along the California coast.

After San Diego fell under the U.S. flag during the Mexican War of 1846, the city existed in relative isolation, deferring status and importance to its sister cities in the north, Los Angeles and San Francisco. Even when San Francisco businessman Alonzo Horton bought 1,000 acres of land near the harbor to establish a downtown there, San Diego remained secondary to both these cities, and saw a decrease in population from 40,000 in 1880 to 17,000 at the turn of the century.

World War II repopulated the city, when the Navy moved one of its bases from Pearl Harbor to San Diego. The naval base brought personnel and several related industries, such as nuclear and oceanographic research, and aviation development. In celebration of this past, the famed *Midway*, a 1,000-foot World War II aircraft carrier, has undergone a $6.5 million reconstruction and has been moved to Navy Pier, where it opened in 2004 as a floating museum.

Today, San Diego is the second most populous city in California, with plenty of outdoor activities, jobs, fine educational institutions, theaters, and museums. Its downtown redevelopment agency has transformed what was largely an abandoned downtown into a glittering showcase of waterfront skyscrapers, live-work loft developments, five-star hotels, cafes, restaurants, and shops. The once-industrial East Village adjacent to PETCO ballpark is now the new frontier in San Diego's downtown urban renewal.

The western part of the U.S., from Seattle to the Silicon Valley, and from San Diego to Denver, is the center for hot growth industries, including telecommunications, biomedical products, software, and financial services. San Diego also leads the country in biotechnology companies.

The San Diego Convention Center underwent expansion in 2001, increasing exhibit space from 250,000 to 615,000 square feet. The water supply system, always a significant issue in this part of California, has been upgraded and improved in recent years.

Expansion of the city's trolley service was completed in 2021 and that same year renovations to San Diego International Airport began, promising to deliver a new terminal with 30 new gates, a new parking garage, and a new three-lane airport access road by 2030.

San Diego is a LGBTQ-friendly city, with the seventh-highest percentage of gay residents in the U.S. Additionally, San Diego State University (SDSU), one of the city's prominent universities, has been named one of the top LGBTQ-friendly campuses in the nation.

The city's Windansea Beach is known for its reef break and iconic palm frond shack, attracting some of the best surfers in the world. Windansea was the inspiration for the popular "Beach Party" movies in the 1960s. Today, the Windansea Surf Club continues to compete in surf contests and combines community involvement with its competitive heritage. Windansea's surf shack, originally built in 1946, has been rebuilt by surfers numerous times after storms destroyed it. Designated a Historical Landmark in 1998, it remains a symbol of San Diego's surfing heritage and Hawaiian roots.

San Diego summers are cool, and winters are warm in comparison with other locations along the same general latitude, due to the Pacific Ocean. A marked feature of the climate is the wide variation in temperature. In nearby valleys, for example, daytime temperatures are much warmer in summer and noticeably cooler on winter nights than in the city proper. As is usual on the Pacific Coast, nighttime and early morning cloudiness is the norm. Considerable fog occurs along the coast, especially during the winter months.

Rankings

General Rankings

- For its "Best for Vets: Places to Live 2019" rankings, *Military Times* evaluated 599 cities (83 large, 234 medium, 282 small) and compared the locations across three broad categories: veteran and military culture/services; economic indicators; and livability factors such as health, crime, traffic, and school quality. San Diego ranked #4 out of the top 25, in the large city category (population of more than 250,000). Data points more specific to veterans and the military weighed more heavily than others. *rebootcamp.militarytimes.com, "Military Times Best Places to Live 2019," September 10, 2018*
- In its eighth annual survey, *Travel + Leisure* readers nominated their favorite cities and towns in America—voting on numerous attractive features in categories including culture, food and drink, quality of life, style, and people. After 50,000 votes, San Diego was ranked #15 among the proposed favorites. *www.travelandleisure.com, "America's Favorite Cities," October 20, 2017*
- For its 34th annual "Readers' Choice Awards" survey, *Condé Nast Traveler* ranked its readers' favorite cities in the U.S. Whether it be a longed for visit or a first on the list, these are the places that inspired a return to travel. The list was broken into large cities and cities under 250,000. San Diego ranked #7 in the big city category. *Condé Nast Traveler, Readers' Choice Awards 2021, "Best Big Cities in the U.S." October 5, 2021*

Business/Finance Rankings

- The Brookings Institution ranked the nation's largest cities based on income inequality. San Diego was ranked #68 (#1 = greatest inequality). Criteria: the "95/20 ratio," a figure representing the income at which a household earns more than 95 percent of all other households, divided by the income at which a household earns more than only 20 percent of all other households. *Brookings Institution, "Household Income Inequality, Largest Cities of 97 Large U.S. Metro Areas, 2014-2016," February 5, 2018*
- The Brookings Institution ranked the 100 largest metro areas in the U.S. based on income inequality. San Diego was ranked #51 (#1 = greatest inequality). Criteria: the "95/20 ratio," a figure representing the income at which a household earns more than 95 percent of all other households, divided by the income at which a household earns more than only 20 percent of all other households. *Brookings Institution, "Household Income Inequality, 100 Largest U.S. Metro Areas, 2014-2016," February 5, 2018*
- Payscale.com ranked the 32 largest metro areas in terms of wage growth. The San Diego metro area ranked #6. Criteria: private-sector and education professional wage growth between the 4th quarter of 2019 and the 4th quarter of 2020. *PayScale, "Wage Trends by Metro Area-4th Quarter," January 11, 2021*
- The San Diego metro area was identified as one of the most debt-ridden places in America by the finance site Credit.com. The metro area was ranked #8. Criteria: residents' average credit card debt as well as median income. *Credit.com, "25 Cities With the Most Credit Card Debt," February 28, 2018*
- For its annual survey of the "Most Expensive U.S. Cities to Live In," Kiplinger applied Cost of Living Index statistics developed by the Council for Community and Economic Research to U.S. Census Bureau population and median household income data for 256 urban areas. San Diego was among the 20 most expensive in the country. *Kiplinger.com, "The 20 Most Expensive Cities in the U.S.," March 16, 2022*
- The San Diego metro area appeared on the Milken Institute "2021 Best Performing Cities" list. Rank: #49 out of 200 large metro areas (population over 250,000). Criteria: job growth; wage and salary growth; high-tech output growth; housing affordability; household broadband access. *Milken Institute, "Best-Performing Cities 2021," February 16, 2021*
- *Forbes* ranked the 200 most populous metro areas to determine the nation's "Best Places for Business and Careers." The San Diego metro area was ranked #45. Criteria: costs (business and living); job growth (past and projected); income growth; quality of life; educational attainment (college and high school); projected economic growth; cultural and leisure opportunities; workplace tolerance laws; net migration patterns. *Forbes, "The Best Places for Business and Careers 2019: Seattle Still On Top," October 30, 2019*

Children/Family Rankings

- San Diego was selected as one of the best cities for newlyweds by *Rent.com*. The city ranked #9 of 15. Criteria: cost of living; availability of affordable rental inventory; annual household income; activities and restaurant options; percentage of married couples; concentration of millennials; safety. *Rent.com, "The 15 Best Cities for Newlyweds," December 11, 2018*

Culture/Performing Arts Rankings

- San Diego was selected as one of the 25 best cities for moviemakers in North America. COVID-19 has spurred a quest for great film cities that offer more creative space, lower costs, and more great outdoors. NYC & LA were intentionally excluded. Criteria: longstanding reputations as film-friendly communities; film community and culture; work life balance; and efforts to deal with pandemic-specific challenges. The city was ranked #17. *MovieMaker Magazine, "Best Places to Live and Work as a Moviemaker in 2022," January 25, 2022*

Dating/Romance Rankings

- San Diego was selected as one of America's best cities for singles by the readers of *Travel + Leisure* in their annual "America's Favorite Cities" survey. Criteria included good-looking locals, cool shopping, an active bar scene and hipster-magnet coffee bars. *Travel + Leisure, "Best Cities in America for Singles," July 21, 2017*

Education Rankings

- Personal finance website *WalletHub* analyzed the 150 largest U.S. metropolitan statistical areas to determine where the most educated Americans are putting their degrees to work. Criteria: education levels; percentage of workers with degrees; education quality and attainment gap; public school quality rankings; quality and enrollment of each metro area's universities. San Diego was ranked #20 (#1 = most educated city). *www.WalletHub.com, "Most & Least Educated Cities in America," July 19, 2021*
- San Diego was selected as one of America's most literate cities. The city ranked #31 out of the 84 largest U.S. cities. Criteria: number of booksellers; library resources; Internet resources; educational attainment; periodical publishing resources; newspaper circulation. *Central Connecticut State University, "America's Most Literate Cities, 2018," February 2019*

Environmental Rankings

- The U.S. Environmental Protection Agency (EPA) released its list of U.S. metropolitan areas with the most ENERGY STAR certified buildings in 2020. The San Diego metro area was ranked #12 out of 25. *U.S. Environmental Protection Agency, "2021 Energy Star Top Cities," June 15, 2021*
- The U.S. Conference of Mayors and Walmart Stores sponsor the Mayors' Climate Protection Awards Program which recognize mayors for outstanding and innovative practices that mayors are taking to increase energy efficiency in their cities, reduce carbon emissions and expand renewable energy. San Diego received an Honorable Mention in the large city category. *U.S. Conference of Mayors, "2021 Mayors' Climate Protection Awards," December 17, 2021*
- San Diego was highlighted as one of the 25 most ozone-polluted metro areas in the U.S. during 2017 through 2019. The area ranked #7. *American Lung Association, "State of the Air 2021," April 21, 2021*

Health/Fitness Rankings

- For each of the 100 largest cities in the United States, the American Fitness Index®, published by the American College of Sports Medicine and the Anthem Foundation, evaluated community infrastructure and 34 health behaviors including preventive health, levels of chronic disease conditions, food insecurity, sleep quality, pedestrian safety, air quality, and community resources that support physical activity. San Diego ranked #15 for "community fitness." *americanfitnessindex.org, "2021 ACSM American Fitness Index Summary Report," July 13, 2021*
- Trulia analyzed the 100 largest U.S. metro areas to identify the nation's best cities for weight loss, based on the percentage of adults who bike or walk to work, sporting goods stores, grocery stores, access to outdoor activities, weight-loss centers, gyms, and average space reserved for parks. San Diego ranked #9. *Trulia.com, "Where to Live to Get in Shape in the New Year," January 4, 2018*
- San Diego was identified as a "2021 Spring Allergy Capital." The area ranked #88 out of 100. Three groups of factors were used to identify the most challenging cities for people with allergies during the spring season: annual spring pollen levels; over the counter medicine use; number of board-certified allergy specialists. *Asthma and Allergy Foundation of America, "Spring Allergy Capitals 2021," February 23, 2021*
- San Diego was identified as a "2021 Fall Allergy Capital." The area ranked #88 out of 100. Three groups of factors were used to identify the most challenging cities for people with allergies during the fall season: annual fall pollen levels; over the counter medicine use; number of board-certified allergy specialists. *Asthma and Allergy Foundation of America, "Fall Allergy Capitals 2021," February 23, 2021*

- San Diego was identified as a "2021 Asthma Capital." The area ranked #81 out of the nation's 100 largest metropolitan areas. Criteria: estimated asthma prevalence; asthma-related mortality; and ER visits due to asthma. Risk factors analyzed but not factored in the rankings: annual pollen score; annual air quality; public smoking laws; number of board-certified asthma specialists; rescue medication use; controller medication use; uninsured rate; poverty rate. *Asthma and Allergy Foundation of America, "Asthma Capitals 2021: The Most Challenging Places to Live With Asthma," May 5, 2021*

Real Estate Rankings

- *WalletHub* compared the most populated U.S. cities to determine which had the best markets for real estate agents. San Diego ranked #17 where demand was high and pay was the best. Criteria: sales per agent; annual median wage for real-estate agents; monthly average starting salary for real estate agents; real estate job density and competition; unemployment rate; home turnover rate; housing-market health index; and other relevant metrics. *www.WalletHub.com, "2021 Best Places to Be a Real Estate Agent," May 12, 2021*
- The San Diego metro area was identified as one of the 20 least affordable housing markets in the U.S. in 2021. The area ranked #179 out of 183 markets. Criteria: qualification for a mortgage loan with a 10 percent down payment on a typical home. *National Association of Realtors®, Qualifying Income Based on Sales Price of Existing Single-Family Homes for Metropolitan Areas, 2021*
- San Diego was ranked #233 out of 237 metro areas in terms of housing affordability in 2021 by the National Association of Home Builders (#1 = most affordable). Criteria: the share of homes sold in that area affordable to a family earning the local median income, based on standard mortgage underwriting criteria. *National Association of Home Builders®, NAHB-Wells Fargo Housing Opportunity Index, 4th Quarter 2021*

Safety Rankings

- Allstate ranked the 200 largest cities in America in terms of driver safety. San Diego ranked #119. Criteria: internal property damage claims over a two-year period from January 2016 to December 2017. The report helps increase the importance of safety and awareness behind the wheel. *Allstate, "Allstate America's Best Drivers Report, 2019" June 24, 2019*
- The National Insurance Crime Bureau ranked 390 metro areas in the U.S. in terms of per capita rates of vehicle theft. The San Diego metro area ranked #74 (#1 = highest rate). Criteria: number of vehicle theft offenses per 100,000 inhabitants in 2020. *National Insurance Crime Bureau, "Hot Spots 2020," August 31, 2021*

Seniors/Retirement Rankings

- From its Best Cities for Successful Aging indexes, the Milken Institute generated rankings for metropolitan areas, weighing data in nine categories—health care, wellness, living arrangements, transportation and convenience, financial characteristics, education, employment, community engagement, and overall livability. The San Diego metro area was ranked #22 overall in the large metro area category. *Milken Institute, "Best Cities for Successful Aging, 2017" March 14, 2017*

Transportation Rankings

- San Diego was identified as one of the most congested metro areas in the U.S. The area ranked #9 out of 10. Criteria: yearly delay per auto commuter in hours. *Texas A&M Transportation Institute, "2021 Urban Mobility Report," June 2021*
- According to the INRIX "2021 Global Traffic Scorecard," San Diego was identified as one of the most congested metro areas in the U.S. The area ranked #18 out of 25. Criteria: average annual time spent in traffic and average cost of congestion per motorist. *Inrix.com, "Americans Lost 3.4 Billion Hours Due to Congestion in 2021, 42% Below Pre-COVID," December 7, 2021*

Women/Minorities Rankings

- *Travel + Leisure* listed the best cities in and around the US for a memorable and fun girls' trip, even on a budget. Whether it is for a special occasion or just to get away, San Diego is sure to have something for all the ladies in your tribe. *Travel + Leisure, "25 Girls' Weekend Getaways That Won't Break the Bank," June 8, 2020*
- The *Houston Chronicle* listed the San Diego metro area as #9 in top places for young Latinos to live in the U.S, Research was largely based on housing and occupational data from the largest metropolitan areas performed by *Forbes* and NBC Universo. Criteria: percentage of 18-34 year-olds; Latino college grad rates; and diversity. *blog.chron.com, "The 15 Best Big Cities for Latino Millenials," January 26, 2016*

- Personal finance website *WalletHub* compared more than 180 U.S. cities across two key dimensions, "Hispanic Business-Friendliness" and "Hispanic Purchasing Power," to arrive at the most favorable conditions for Hispanic entrepreneurs. San Diego was ranked #120 out of 182. Criteria includes: share of Hispanic-Owned Businesses; Hispanic entrepreneurship rate to median annual income of Hispanics; Small Business-Friendliness score; cost of living; and number of Hispanics with at least a bachelor's degree. *WalletHub.com, "2019's Best Cities for Hispanic Entrepreneurs," May 1, 2019*

Miscellaneous Rankings

- While the majority of travel ground to a halt in 2020, plugged-in travel influencers and experts were able to rediscover their local regions. San Diego appeared on a *Forbes* list of 15 U.S. cities that provided solace as well as local inspiration. Whether it be quirky things to see and do, delicious take out, outdoor exploring and daytrips, these places are must-see destinations. *Forbes, "Bucket List Travel: The 15 Best U.S. Destinations For 2021," January 1, 2021*
- San Diego was selected as a 2021 Digital Cities Survey winner. The city ranked #2 in the large city (500,000 or more population) category. The survey examined and assessed how city governments are utilizing technology to continue innovation, engage with residents, and persevere through the challenges of the pandemic. Survey questions focused on ten initiatives: cybersecurity; citizen experience; disaster recovery; business intelligence; IT personnel; data governance; budget control; IT governance; infrastructure modernization; and broadband connectivity. *Center for Digital Government, "2021 Digital Cities Survey," November 16, 2021*
- In its roundup of St. Patrick's Day parades "Gayot" listed the best festivals and parades of all things Irish. The festivities in San Diego as among the best. *www.gayot.com, "Best St. Patrick's Day Parades," March 2022*
- The watchdog site, Charity Navigator, conducted a study of charities in major markets both to analyze statistical differences in their financial, accountability, and transparency practices and to track year-to-year variations in individual philanthropic communities. The San Diego metro area was ranked #1 among the 30 metro markets in the rating category of Overall Score. *www.charitynavigator.org, "2017 Metro Market Study," May 1, 2017*
- The financial planning site SmartAsset has compiled its annual study on the best places for Halloween in the U.S. for 2021. 210 cities were compared to determine that San Diego ranked #24 out of 35 for still being able to enjoy the festivities despite the COVID-19 pandemic. Metrics included: safety, family-friendliness, percentage of children in the population, concentration of candy and costume shops, weather and COVID infection rates. *www.smartasset.com, "2021 Edition-Best Places to Celebrate Halloween," October 20, 2021*
- *WalletHub* compared the 150 most populated U.S. cities to determine their operating efficiency. A "Quality of City Services" score was constructed for each city and then divided by the total budget per capita to reveal which were managed the best. San Diego ranked #62. Criteria: financial stability; economy; education; safety; health; infrastructure and pollution. *www.WalletHub.com, "2021's Best- & Worst-Run Cities in America," June 22, 2021*
- The National Alliance to End Homelessness listed the 25 most populous metro areas with the highest rate of homelessness. The San Diego metro area had a high rate of homelessness. Criteria: number of homeless people per 10,000 population in 2016. *National Alliance to End Homelessness, "Homelessness in the 25 Most Populous U.S. Metro Areas," September 1, 2017*

Business Environment

DEMOGRAPHICS

Population Growth

Area	1990 Census	2000 Census	2010 Census	2020* Estimate	Population Growth (%) 1990-2020	Population Growth (%) 2010-2020
City	1,111,048	1,223,400	1,307,402	1,414,545	27.3	8.2
MSA[1]	2,498,016	2,813,833	3,095,313	3,323,970	33.1	7.4
U.S.	248,709,873	281,421,906	308,745,538	326,569,308	31.3	5.8

Note: (1) Figures cover the San Diego-Carlsbad, CA Metropolitan Statistical Area; (*) 2016-2020 5-year estimated population
Source: U.S. Census Bureau, 1990 Census, Census 2000, Census 2010, 2016-2020 American Community Survey 5-Year Estimates

Household Size

Area	Persons in Household (%) One	Two	Three	Four	Five	Six	Seven or More	Average Household Size
City	27.6	34.1	15.8	13.0	5.6	2.3	1.6	2.70
MSA[1]	23.9	33.0	16.8	14.8	6.8	2.8	1.9	2.90
U.S.	28.0	33.9	15.5	12.9	6.0	2.3	1.4	2.60

Note: (1) Figures cover the San Diego-Carlsbad, CA Metropolitan Statistical Area
Source: U.S. Census Bureau, 2016-2020 American Community Survey 5-Year Estimates

Race

Area	White Alone[2] (%)	Black Alone[2] (%)	Asian Alone[2] (%)	AIAN[3] Alone[2] (%)	NHOPI[4] Alone[2] (%)	Other Race Alone[2] (%)	Two or More Races (%)
City	62.0	6.1	17.3	0.5	0.4	6.0	7.8
MSA[1]	66.6	4.9	12.0	0.7	0.4	6.7	8.6
U.S.	70.4	12.6	5.6	0.8	0.2	5.1	5.2

Note: (1) Figures cover the San Diego-Carlsbad, CA Metropolitan Statistical Area; (2) Alone is defined as not being in combination with one or more other races; (3) American Indian and Alaska Native; (4) Native Hawaiian and Other Pacific Islander
Source: U.S. Census Bureau, 2016-2020 American Community Survey 5-Year Estimates

Hispanic or Latino Origin

Area	Total (%)	Mexican (%)	Puerto Rican (%)	Cuban (%)	Other (%)
City	30.1	25.9	0.8	0.2	3.1
MSA[1]	33.9	29.7	0.8	0.2	3.2
U.S.	18.2	11.2	1.7	0.7	4.5

Note: Persons of Hispanic or Latino origin can be of any race; (1) Figures cover the San Diego-Carlsbad, CA Metropolitan Statistical Area
Source: U.S. Census Bureau, 2016-2020 American Community Survey 5-Year Estimates

Ancestry

Area	German	Irish	English	American	Italian	Polish	French[2]	Scottish	Dutch
City	8.2	7.0	5.9	2.4	4.2	1.8	1.7	1.4	0.8
MSA[1]	9.0	7.4	6.5	2.7	4.2	1.7	1.9	1.5	0.9
U.S.	13.0	9.7	7.7	5.9	5.1	2.7	2.3	1.6	1.1

Note: Figures are the percentage of the total population reporting a particular ancestry. The nine most commonly reported ancestries in the U.S. are shown. Figures include multiple ancestries (e.g. if a person reported being Irish and Italian, they were included in both columns); (1) Figures cover the San Diego-Carlsbad, CA Metropolitan Statistical Area; (2) Excludes Basque
Source: U.S. Census Bureau, 2016-2020 American Community Survey 5-Year Estimates

Foreign-born Population

Area	Percent of Population Born in: Any Foreign Country	Asia	Mexico	Europe	Caribbean	Central America[2]	South America	Africa	Canada
City	25.6	11.9	8.5	2.2	0.2	0.5	0.8	0.9	0.4
MSA[1]	22.9	8.9	9.7	1.8	0.2	0.6	0.6	0.6	0.4
U.S.	13.5	4.2	3.3	1.5	1.3	1.1	1.0	0.7	0.3

Note: (1) Figures cover the San Diego-Carlsbad, CA Metropolitan Statistical Area; (2) Excludes Mexico.
Source: U.S. Census Bureau, 2016-2020 American Community Survey 5-Year Estimates

Marital Status

Area	Never Married	Now Married[2]	Separated	Widowed	Divorced
City	40.2	44.4	1.6	4.1	9.7
MSA[1]	36.1	47.7	1.6	4.7	9.9
U.S.	33.5	48.1	1.8	5.7	10.8

Note: Figures are percentages and cover the population 15 years of age and older; (1) Figures cover the San Diego-Carlsbad, CA Metropolitan Statistical Area; (2) Excludes separated
Source: U.S. Census Bureau, 2016-2020 American Community Survey 5-Year Estimates

Disability by Age

Area	All Ages	Under 18 Years Old	18 to 64 Years Old	65 Years and Over
City	9.3	3.3	6.4	32.2
MSA[1]	10.0	3.2	7.3	32.7
U.S.	12.7	4.3	10.3	34.0

Note: Figures show percent of the civilian noninstitutionalized population that reported having a disability. Disability status is determined from six types of difficulty: vision, hearing, cognitive, ambulatory, self-care, and independent living. For children under 5 years old, hearing and vision difficulty are used to determine disability status. For children between the ages of 5 and 14, disability status is determined from hearing, vision, cognitive, ambulatory, and self-care difficulties. For people aged 15 years and older, they are considered to have a disability if they have difficulty with any one of the six difficulty types; Note: (1) Figures cover the San Diego-Carlsbad, CA Metropolitan Statistical Area
Source: U.S. Census Bureau, 2016-2020 American Community Survey 5-Year Estimates

Age

Area	Percent of Population									Median Age
	Under Age 5	Age 5–19	Age 20–34	Age 35–44	Age 45–54	Age 55–64	Age 65–74	Age 75–84	Age 85+	
City	5.8	16.6	27.3	14.1	12.2	10.8	7.7	3.8	1.8	35.2
MSA[1]	6.2	18.2	24.0	13.4	12.3	11.8	8.2	4.0	2.0	36.1
U.S.	6.0	19.1	20.6	12.7	12.7	12.9	9.4	4.7	2.0	38.2

Note: (1) Figures cover the San Diego-Carlsbad, CA Metropolitan Statistical Area
Source: U.S. Census Bureau, 2016-2020 American Community Survey 5-Year Estimates

Gender

Area	Males	Females	Males per 100 Females
City	714,965	699,580	102.2
MSA[1]	1,674,512	1,649,458	101.5
U.S.	160,818,530	165,750,778	97.0

Note: (1) Figures cover the San Diego-Carlsbad, CA Metropolitan Statistical Area
Source: U.S. Census Bureau, 2016-2020 American Community Survey 5-Year Estimates

Religious Groups by Family

Area	Catholic	Baptist	Non-Den.	Methodist[2]	Lutheran	LDS[3]	Pente-costal	Presby-terian[4]	Muslim[5]	Judaism
MSA[1]	25.9	2.0	4.8	1.1	1.0	2.3	1.0	0.9	0.7	0.5
U.S.	19.1	9.3	4.0	4.0	2.3	2.0	1.9	1.6	0.8	0.7

Note: Figures are the number of adherents as a percentage of the total population; (1) Figures cover the San Diego-Carlsbad, CA Metropolitan Statistical Area; (2) Methodist/Pietist; (3) Latter Day Saints; (4) Reformed; (5) Figures are estimates
Source: Association of Statisticians of American Religious Bodies, 2010 U.S. Religion Census: Religious Congregations & Membership Study

Religious Groups by Tradition

Area	Catholic	Evangelical Protestant	Mainline Protestant	Other Tradition	Black Protestant	Orthodox
MSA[1]	25.9	9.8	2.4	5.2	0.4	0.3
U.S.	19.1	16.2	7.3	4.3	1.6	0.3

Note: Figures are the number of adherents as a percentage of the total population; (1) Figures cover the San Diego-Carlsbad, CA Metropolitan Statistical Area
Source: Association of Statisticians of American Religious Bodies, 2010 U.S. Religion Census: Religious Congregations & Membership Study

ECONOMY

Gross Metropolitan Product

Area	2017	2018	2019	2020	Rank[2]
MSA[1]	237.2	249.4	260.3	272.1	17

Note: Figures are in billions of dollars; (1) Figures cover the San Diego-Carlsbad, CA Metropolitan Statistical Area; (2) Rank is based on 2018 data and ranges from 1 to 381
Source: U.S. Conference of Mayors, U.S. Metro Economies: GMP & Employment 2018-2020, September 2019

Economic Growth

Area	2015-17 (%)	2018 (%)	2019 (%)	2020 (%)	Rank[2]
MSA[1]	3.1	3.0	2.6	2.3	64
U.S.	1.9	2.9	2.3	2.1	–

Note: Figures are real gross metropolitan product (GMP) growth rates and represent average annual percent change; (1) Figures cover the San Diego-Carlsbad, CA Metropolitan Statistical Area; (2) Rank is based on 2017 2-year average annual percent change and ranges from 1 to 381
Source: U.S. Conference of Mayors, U.S. Metro Economies: GMP & Employment 2018-2020, September 2019

Metropolitan Area Exports

Area	2015	2016	2017	2018	2019	2020	Rank[2]
MSA[1]	17,439.7	18,086.6	18,637.1	20,156.8	19,774.1	18,999.7	19

Note: Figures are in millions of dollars; (1) Figures cover the San Diego-Carlsbad, CA Metropolitan Statistical Area; (2) Rank is based on 2020 data and ranges from 1 to 389
Source: U.S. Department of Commerce, International Trade Administration, Office of Trade and Economic Analysis, Industry and Analysis, Exports by Metropolitan Area, data extracted March 4, 2022

Building Permits

Area	Single-Family			Multi-Family			Total		
	2019	2020	Pct. Chg.	2019	2020	Pct. Chg.	2019	2020	Pct. Chg.
City	580	445	-23.3	3,361	4,237	26.1	3,941	4,682	18.8
MSA[1]	3,019	2,900	-3.9	5,197	6,572	26.5	8,216	9,472	15.3
U.S.	862,100	979,400	13.6	523,900	491,700	-6.1	1,386,000	1,471,100	6.1

Note: (1) Figures cover the San Diego-Carlsbad, CA Metropolitan Statistical Area; Figures represent new, privately-owned housing units authorized (unadjusted data); All permit data are based on estimates with imputation
Source: U.S. Census Bureau, Manufacturing, Mining, and Construction Statistics, Building Permits, 2019, 2020

Bankruptcy Filings

Area	Business Filings			Nonbusiness Filings		
	2020	2021	% Chg.	2020	2021	% Chg.
San Diego County	269	194	-27.9	5,848	4,533	-22.5
U.S.	21,655	14,347	-33.7	522,808	399,269	-23.6

Note: Business filings include Chapter 7, Chapter 9, Chapter 11, Chapter 12, Chapter 13, Chapter 15, and Section 304; Nonbusiness filings include Chapter 7, Chapter 11, and Chapter 13
Source: Administrative Office of the U.S. Courts, Business and Nonbusiness Bankruptcy, County Cases Commenced by Chapter of the Bankruptcy Code, During the 12-Month Period Ending December 31, 2020 and Business and Nonbusiness Bankruptcy, County Cases Commenced by Chapter of the Bankruptcy Code, During the 12-Month Period Ending December 31, 2021

Housing Vacancy Rates

Area	Gross Vacancy Rate[2] (%)			Year-Round Vacancy Rate[3] (%)			Rental Vacancy Rate[4] (%)			Homeowner Vacancy Rate[5] (%)		
	2019	2020	2021	2019	2020	2021	2019	2020	2021	2019	2020	2021
MSA[1]	7.5	6.0	6.9	7.3	5.6	6.7	5.8	3.9	3.1	0.8	0.8	0.7
U.S.	12.0	10.6	10.8	9.5	8.2	8.4	6.7	6.3	6.1	1.4	1.0	0.9

Note: (1) Figures cover the San Diego-Carlsbad, CA Metropolitan Statistical Area; (2) The percentage of the total housing inventory that is vacant; (3) The percentage of the housing inventory (excluding seasonal units) that is year-round vacant; (4) The percentage of rental inventory that is vacant for rent; (5) The percentage of homeowner inventory that is vacant for sale
Source: U.S. Census Bureau, Housing Vacancies and Homeownership Annual Statistics: 2019, 2020, 2021

INCOME

Income

Area	Per Capita ($)	Median Household ($)	Average Household ($)
City	43,090	83,454	113,681
MSA[1]	39,737	82,426	111,241
U.S.	35,384	64,994	91,547

Note: (1) Figures cover the San Diego-Carlsbad, CA Metropolitan Statistical Area
Source: U.S. Census Bureau, 2016-2020 American Community Survey 5-Year Estimates

Household Income Distribution

Area	Percent of Households Earning							
	Under $15,000	$15,000 -$24,999	$25,000 -$34,999	$35,000 -$49,999	$50,000 -$74,999	$75,000 -$99,999	$100,000 -$149,999	$150,000 and up
City	7.8	5.9	6.5	9.3	15.8	12.6	18.6	23.4
MSA[1]	7.3	6.2	6.8	9.7	15.8	12.7	18.4	23.0
U.S.	9.9	8.5	8.6	12.0	17.2	12.8	15.6	15.4

Note: (1) Figures cover the San Diego-Carlsbad, CA Metropolitan Statistical Area
Source: U.S. Census Bureau, 2016-2020 American Community Survey 5-Year Estimates

Poverty Rate

Area	All Ages	Under 18 Years Old	18 to 64 Years Old	65 Years and Over
City	11.8	13.8	11.7	9.5
MSA[1]	10.9	13.6	10.5	8.9
U.S.	12.8	17.5	12.1	9.3

Note: Figures are percentage of people whose income during the past 12 months was below the poverty level; (1) Figures cover the San Diego-Carlsbad, CA Metropolitan Statistical Area
Source: U.S. Census Bureau, 2016-2020 American Community Survey 5-Year Estimates

CITY FINANCES

City Government Finances

Component	2019 ($000)	2019 ($ per capita)
Total Revenues	3,953,539	2,785
Total Expenditures	3,579,653	2,522
Debt Outstanding	4,891,405	3,446
Cash and Securities[1]	2,126,087	1,498

Note: (1) Cash and security holdings of a government at the close of its fiscal year, including those of its dependent agencies, utilities, and liquor stores.
Source: U.S. Census Bureau, State & Local Government Finances 2019

City Government Revenue by Source

Source	2019 ($000)	2019 ($ per capita)	2019 (%)
General Revenue			
From Federal Government	290,975	205	7.4
From State Government	102,799	72	2.6
From Local Governments	3,048	2	0.1
Taxes			
Property	582,838	411	14.7
Sales and Gross Receipts	773,292	545	19.6
Personal Income	0	0	0.0
Corporate Income	0	0	0.0
Motor Vehicle License	0	0	0.0
Other Taxes	112,072	79	2.8
Current Charges	1,174,938	828	29.7
Liquor Store	0	0	0.0
Utility	549,254	387	13.9

Source: U.S. Census Bureau, State & Local Government Finances 2019

City Government Expenditures by Function

Function	2019 ($000)	2019 ($ per capita)	2019 (%)
General Direct Expenditures			
Air Transportation	10,471	7	0.3
Corrections	0	0	0.0
Education	0	0	0.0
Employment Security Administration	0	0	0.0
Financial Administration	65,809	46	1.8
Fire Protection	207,429	146	5.8
General Public Buildings	83,565	58	2.3
Governmental Administration, Other	39,790	28	1.1
Health	43,722	30	1.2
Highways	251,095	176	7.0
Hospitals	0	0	0.0
Housing and Community Development	397,790	280	11.1
Interest on General Debt	205,563	144	5.7
Judicial and Legal	77,950	54	2.2
Libraries	61,817	43	1.7
Parking	0	0	0.0
Parks and Recreation	365,092	257	10.2
Police Protection	383,743	270	10.7
Public Welfare	0	0	0.0
Sewerage	312,548	220	8.7
Solid Waste Management	66,134	46	1.8
Veterans' Services	0	0	0.0
Liquor Store	0	0	0.0
Utility	614,607	433	17.2

Source: U.S. Census Bureau, State & Local Government Finances 2019

EMPLOYMENT

Labor Force and Employment

Area	Civilian Labor Force			Workers Employed		
	Dec. 2020	Dec. 2021	% Chg.	Dec. 2020	Dec. 2021	% Chg.
City	696,144	704,246	1.2	641,244	675,861	5.4
MSA[1]	1,535,149	1,554,504	1.3	1,412,499	1,488,753	5.4
U.S.	160,017,000	161,696,000	1.0	149,613,000	155,732,000	4.1

Note: Data is not seasonally adjusted and covers workers 16 years of age and older; (1) Figures cover the San Diego-Carlsbad, CA Metropolitan Statistical Area
Source: Bureau of Labor Statistics, Local Area Unemployment Statistics

Unemployment Rate

Area	2021											
	Jan.	Feb.	Mar.	Apr.	May	Jun.	Jul.	Aug.	Sep.	Oct.	Nov.	Dec.
City	8.0	6.9	6.5	6.4	6.1	6.8	6.6	6.3	5.3	5.0	4.3	4.0
MSA[1]	8.0	7.2	6.8	6.7	6.3	7.0	6.9	6.6	5.6	5.3	4.6	4.2
U.S.	6.8	6.6	6.2	5.7	5.5	6.1	5.7	5.3	4.6	4.3	3.9	3.7

Note: Data is not seasonally adjusted and covers workers 16 years of age and older; (1) Figures cover the San Diego-Carlsbad, CA Metropolitan Statistical Area
Source: Bureau of Labor Statistics, Local Area Unemployment Statistics

Average Wages

Occupation	$/Hr.	Occupation	$/Hr.
Accountants and Auditors	42.08	Maintenance and Repair Workers	22.91
Automotive Mechanics	26.08	Marketing Managers	73.02
Bookkeepers	24.11	Network and Computer Systems Admin.	47.42
Carpenters	30.82	Nurses, Licensed Practical	30.59
Cashiers	15.26	Nurses, Registered	54.40
Computer Programmers	56.29	Nursing Assistants	18.55
Computer Systems Analysts	51.61	Office Clerks, General	19.99
Computer User Support Specialists	30.26	Physical Therapists	50.17
Construction Laborers	24.77	Physicians	131.06
Cooks, Restaurant	17.73	Plumbers, Pipefitters and Steamfitters	32.31
Customer Service Representatives	20.64	Police and Sheriff's Patrol Officers	47.50
Dentists	66.83	Postal Service Mail Carriers	26.70
Electricians	32.98	Real Estate Sales Agents	n/a
Engineers, Electrical	55.83	Retail Salespersons	16.97
Fast Food and Counter Workers	15.23	Sales Representatives, Technical/Scientific	52.16
Financial Managers	76.55	Secretaries, Exc. Legal/Medical/Executive	22.31
First-Line Supervisors of Office Workers	32.85	Security Guards	17.91
General and Operations Managers	58.95	Surgeons	n/a
Hairdressers/Cosmetologists	17.67	Teacher Assistants, Exc. Postsecondary*	17.81
Home Health and Personal Care Aides	15.28	Teachers, Secondary School, Exc. Sp. Ed.*	43.04
Janitors and Cleaners	17.07	Telemarketers	16.58
Landscaping/Groundskeeping Workers	18.39	Truck Drivers, Heavy/Tractor-Trailer	24.35
Lawyers	79.56	Truck Drivers, Light/Delivery Services	21.66
Maids and Housekeeping Cleaners	16.56	Waiters and Waitresses	17.31

Note: Wage data covers the San Diego-Carlsbad, CA Metropolitan Statistical Area; (*) Hourly wages were calculated from annual wage data based on a 40 hour work week; n/a not available.
Source: Bureau of Labor Statistics, Metro Area Occupational Employment & Wage Estimates, May 2021

Employment by Industry

Sector	MSA[1]		U.S.
	Number of Employees	Percent of Total	Percent of Total
Construction	83,300	5.6	5.0
Education and Health Services	217,200	14.5	16.0
Financial Activities	74,500	5.0	5.9
Government	244,600	16.3	14.9
Information	22,500	1.5	1.9
Leisure and Hospitality	182,600	12.2	9.8
Manufacturing	115,100	7.7	8.4
Mining and Logging	300	<0.1	0.4
Other Services	51,300	3.4	3.7
Professional and Business Services	279,000	18.6	14.6
Retail Trade	144,600	9.7	10.7
Transportation, Warehousing, and Utilities	40,500	2.7	4.8
Wholesale Trade	42,200	2.8	3.8

Note: Figures are non-farm employment as of December 2021. Figures are not seasonally adjusted and include workers 16 years of age and older; (1) Figures cover the San Diego-Carlsbad, CA Metropolitan Statistical Area
Source: Bureau of Labor Statistics, Current Employment Statistics, Employment, Hours, and Earnings

Employment by Occupation

Occupation Classification	City (%)	MSA[1] (%)	U.S. (%)
Management, Business, Science, and Arts	49.3	43.4	39.5
Natural Resources, Construction, and Maintenance	5.3	7.3	8.7
Production, Transportation, and Material Moving	8.7	9.6	13.1
Sales and Office	18.8	20.8	21.3
Service	17.9	18.9	17.4

Note: Figures cover employed civilians 16 years of age and older; (1) Figures cover the San Diego-Carlsbad, CA Metropolitan Statistical Area
Source: U.S. Census Bureau, 2016-2020 American Community Survey 5-Year Estimates

Occupations with Greatest Projected Employment Growth: 2021 – 2023

Occupation[1]	2021 Employment	2023 Projected Employment	Numeric Employment Change	Percent Employment Change
Fast Food and Counter Workers	383,500	457,000	73,500	19.2
Home Health and Personal Care Aides	663,400	716,600	53,200	8.0
Waiters and Waitresses	208,500	257,600	49,100	23.5
Cooks, Restaurant	136,700	175,300	38,600	28.2
Laborers and Freight, Stock, and Material Movers, Hand	401,500	431,600	30,100	7.5
Software Developers and Software Quality Assurance Analysts and Testers	311,600	336,800	25,200	8.1
Janitors and Cleaners, Except Maids and Housekeeping Cleaners	232,200	252,400	20,200	8.7
Cooks, Fast Food	109,600	128,200	18,600	17.0
Stockers and Order Fillers	273,000	290,400	17,400	6.4
First-Line Supervisors of Food Preparation and Serving Workers	81,700	98,600	16,900	20.7

Note: Projections cover California; (1) Sorted by numeric employment change
Source: www.projectionscentral.com, State Occupational Projections, 2021–2023 Short-Term Projections

Fastest-Growing Occupations: 2021 – 2023

Occupation[1]	2021 Employment	2023 Projected Employment	Numeric Employment Change	Percent Employment Change
Manicurists and Pedicurists	23,400	33,500	10,100	43.2
Cooks, All Other	3,900	5,400	1,500	38.5
Miscellaneous Entertainers and Performers, Sports and Related Workers	5,900	8,100	2,200	37.3
Barbers	1,900	2,600	700	36.8
Gaming Change Persons and Booth Cashiers	2,200	3,000	800	36.4
Gaming Service Workers, All Other	1,400	1,900	500	35.7
Gaming Dealers	12,200	16,500	4,300	35.2
First-Line Supervisors of Gambling Services Workers	2,900	3,900	1,000	34.5
Massage Therapists	18,000	24,200	6,200	34.4
Costume Attendants	1,500	2,000	500	33.3

Note: Projections cover California; (1) Sorted by percent employment change and excludes occupations with numeric employment change less than 50
Source: www.projectionscentral.com, State Occupational Projections, 2021–2023 Short-Term Projections

TAXES

State Corporate Income Tax Rates

State	Tax Rate (%)	Income Brackets ($)	Num. of Brackets	Financial Institution Tax Rate (%)[a]	Federal Income Tax Ded.
California	8.84 (b)	Flat rate	1	10.84 (b)	No

Note: Tax rates as of January 1, 2022; (a) Rates listed are the corporate income tax rate applied to financial institutions or excise taxes based on income. Some states have other taxes based upon the value of deposits or shares; (b) Minimum tax is $800 in California, $250 in District of Columbia, $50 in Arizona and North Dakota (banks), $400 ($100 banks) in Rhode Island, $200 per location in South Dakota (banks), $100 in Utah, $300 in Vermont.
Source: Federation of Tax Administrators, State Corporate Income Tax Rates, January 1, 2022

State Individual Income Tax Rates

State	Tax Rate (%)	Income Brackets ($)	Personal Exemptions ($) Single	Married	Depend.	Standard Ded. ($) Single	Married
California (a)	1.0 - 12.3 (g)	9,325 - 625,369 (b)	129	258	400 (c)	4,803	9,606 (a)

Note: Tax rates as of January 1, 2022; Local- and county-level taxes are not included; Federal income tax is not deductible on state income tax returns; (a) 19 states have statutory provision for automatically adjusting to the rate of inflation the dollar values of the income tax brackets, standard deductions, and/or personal exemptions. Michigan indexes the personal exemption only. Oregon does not index the income brackets for $125,000 and over; (b) For joint returns, taxes are twice the tax on half the couple's income; (c) The personal exemption takes the form of a tax credit instead of a deduction; (g) California imposes an additional 1% tax on taxable income over $1 million, making the maximum rate 13.3% over $1 million.
Source: Federation of Tax Administrators, State Individual Income Tax Rates, January 1, 2022

Various State Sales and Excise Tax Rates

State	State Sales Tax (%)	Gasoline[1] (¢/gal.)	Cigarette[2] ($/pack)	Spirits[3] ($/gal.)	Wine[4] ($/gal.)	Beer[5] ($/gal.)	Recreational Marijuana (%)
California	7.25	68.15	2.87	3.3	0.2	0.2	(c)

Note: All tax rates as of January 1, 2022; (1) The American Petroleum Institute has developed a methodology for determining the average tax rate on a gallon of fuel. Rates may include any of the following: excise taxes, environmental fees, storage tank fees, other fees or taxes, general sales tax, and local taxes; (2) The federal excise tax of $1.0066 per pack and local taxes are not included; (3) Rates are those applicable to off-premise sales of 40% alcohol by volume (a.b.v.) distilled spirits in 750ml containers. Local excise taxes are excluded; (4) Rates are those applicable to off-premise sales of 11% a.b.v. non-carbonated wine in 750ml containers; (5) Rates are those applicable to off-premise sales of 4.7% a.b.v. beer in 12 ounce containers; (c) 15% excise tax (levied on wholesale at average market rate); $10.08/oz. flowers & $3/oz. leaves cultivation tax; $1.41/oz fresh cannabis plant
Source: Tax Foundation, 2022 Facts & Figures: How Does Your State Compare?

State Business Tax Climate Index Rankings

State	Overall Rank	Corporate Tax Rank	Individual Income Tax Rank	Sales Tax Rank	Property Tax Rank	Unemployment Insurance Tax Rank
California	48	46	49	47	14	23

Note: The index is a measure of how each state's tax laws affect economic performance. The lower the rank, the more favorable a state's tax system is for business. States without a given tax are given a ranking of 1. The scores/rankings for the District of Columbia do not affect other states. The 2022 index represents the tax climate as of July 1, 2021.
Source: Tax Foundation, State Business Tax Climate Index 2022

TRANSPORTATION

Means of Transportation to Work

Area	Car/Truck/Van: Drove Alone	Car/Truck/Van: Car-pooled	Public Transportation: Bus	Public Transportation: Subway	Public Transportation: Railroad	Bicycle	Walked	Other Means	Worked at Home
City	72.0	8.5	3.2	0.1	0.1	0.8	2.9	1.8	10.5
MSA[1]	73.9	8.7	2.2	0.1	0.2	0.6	2.9	1.9	9.6
U.S.	74.9	8.9	2.2	1.7	0.5	0.5	2.6	1.4	7.3

Note: Figures are percentages and cover workers 16 years of age and older; (1) Figures cover the San Diego-Carlsbad, CA Metropolitan Statistical Area
Source: U.S. Census Bureau, 2016-2020 American Community Survey 5-Year Estimates

Travel Time to Work

Area	Less Than 10 Minutes	10 to 19 Minutes	20 to 29 Minutes	30 to 44 Minutes	45 to 59 Minutes	60 to 89 Minutes	90 Minutes or More
City	7.6	32.4	27.4	21.3	5.9	3.6	1.8
MSA[1]	8.2	29.2	24.2	23.5	7.7	5.1	2.2
U.S.	12.3	28.4	20.9	20.9	8.3	6.4	2.9

Note: Note: Figures are percentages and include workers 16 years old and over; (1) Figures cover the San Diego-Carlsbad, CA Metropolitan Statistical Area
Source: U.S. Census Bureau, 2016-2020 American Community Survey 5-Year Estimates

Key Congestion Measures

Measure	1990	2000	2010	2015	2020
Annual Hours of Delay, Total (000)	41,751	85,177	115,240	138,187	55,433
Annual Hours of Delay, Per Auto Commuter	29	41	54	63	24
Annual Congestion Cost, Per Auto Commuter ($)	864	1,324	1,426	1,577	665

Note: Covers the San Diego CA urban area
Source: Texas A&M Transportation Institute, 2021 Urban Mobility Report

Freeway Travel Time Index

Measure	1985	1990	1995	2000	2005	2010	2015	2020
Urban Area Index[1]	1.10	1.14	1.16	1.22	1.27	1.30	1.34	1.10
Urban Area Rank[1,2]	27	26	32	24	18	12	9	29

Note: Freeway Travel Time Index—the ratio of travel time in the peak period to the travel time at free-flow conditions. For example, a value of 1.30 indicates a 20-minute free-flow trip takes 26 minutes in the peak (20 minutes x 1.30 = 26 minutes); (1) Covers the San Diego CA urban area; (2) Rank is based on 101 larger urban areas (#1 = highest travel time index)
Source: Texas A&M Transportation Institute, 2021 Urban Mobility Report

Public Transportation

Agency Name / Mode of Transportation	Vehicles Operated in Maximum Service[1]	Annual Unlinked Passenger Trips[2] (in thous.)	Annual Passenger Miles[3] (in thous.)
San Diego Metropolitan Transit System (MTS)			
Bus (directly operated)	223	18,383.1	80,855.1
Bus (purchased transportation)	296	20,286.6	72,631.9
Commuter Bus (purchased transportation)	19	207.4	5,114.8
Demand Response (purchased transportation)	118	282.6	3,783.7
Demand Response - Taxi	147	61.4	642.3
Light Rail (directly operated)	103	32,003.0	194,284.9
North San Diego County Transit District (NCTD)			
Bus (purchased transportation)	140	5,166.2	22,231.9
Commuter Rail (purchased transportation)	24	944.1	24,963.4
Demand Response (purchased transportation)	33	116.4	1,889.1
Hybrid Rail (purchased transportation)	8	2,066.1	15,992.0
San Diego Association of Governments (SANDAG)			
Vanpool (purchased transportation)	642	1,494.0	75,951.4

Note: (1) Number of revenue vehicles operated by the given mode and type of service to meet the annual maximum service requirement. This is the revenue vehicle count during the peak season of the year; on the week and day that maximum service is provided. Vehicles operated in maximum service (VOMS) exclude atypical days and one-time special events; (2) Number of passengers who boarded public transportation vehicles. Passengers are counted each time they board a vehicle no matter how many vehicles they use to travel from their origin to their destination. (3) Sum of the distances ridden by all passengers during the entire fiscal year.
Source: Federal Transit Administration, National Transit Database, 2020

Air Transportation

Airport Name and Code / Type of Service	Passenger Airlines[1]	Passenger Enplanements	Freight Carriers[2]	Freight (lbs)
San Diego International-Lindbergh Field (SAN)				
Domestic service (U.S. carriers - 2021)	22	7,812,001	12	132,095,153
International service (U.S. carriers - 2020)	4	59,296	2	2,257,800

Note: (1) Includes all U.S.-based major, minor and commuter airlines that carried at least one passenger during the year; (2) Includes all U.S.-based airlines and freight carriers that transported at least one pound of freight during the year.
Source: Bureau of Transportation Statistics, The Intermodal Transportation Database, Air Carriers: T-100 Domestic Market (U.S. Carriers), 2021; Bureau of Transportation Statistics, The Intermodal Transportation Database, Air Carriers: T-100 International Market (U.S. Carriers), 2020

BUSINESSES

Major Business Headquarters

Company Name	Industry	Rankings	
		Fortune[1]	Forbes[2]
LPL Financial Holdings	Securities	466	-
Qualcomm	Network and Other Communications Equipment	124	-
Sempra	Electric and Gas Utilities	255	-

Note: (1) Companies that produce a 10-K are ranked 1 to 500 based on 2020 revenue; (2) All private companies with at least $2 billion in annual revenue through the end of their most current fiscal year are ranked 1 to 225; companies listed are headquartered in the city; dashes indicate no ranking
Source: Fortune, "Fortune 500," 2021; Forbes, "America's Largest Private Companies," 2021

Fastest-Growing Businesses

According to *Inc.*, San Diego is home to eight of America's 500 fastest-growing private companies: **NP Digital** (#21); **Big Block Realty** (#56); **Agnetix** (#207); **Tiled** (#220); **HazardHub** (#272); **Shield AI** (#287); **throtl** (#315); **NZS** (#481). Criteria: must be an independent, privately-held, for-profit, U.S. corporation, proprietorship or partnership as of December 31, 2020; revenues must be at least $100,000 in 2017 and $2 million in 2020; must have four-year operating/sales history. *Inc., "America's 500 Fastest-Growing Private Companies," 2021*

According to *Fortune*, San Diego is home to two of the 100 fastest-growing companies in the world: **Quidel** (#7); **Neurocrine Biosciences** (#15). Companies were ranked by their revenue growth rate; their EPS growth rate; and their three-year annualized total return to investors for the period ending June 30, 2021. Criteria for inclusion: a company, foreign or domestic, must trade on a major U.S. stock exchange; must file quarterly reports with the SEC; must have a minimum market capitalization of $250 million; must have a stock price of at least $5 on June 30, 2021; must have been trading continuously since June 30, 2018; must have revenue and net income for the four quarters ended on or before April 30, 2021, of at least $50 million and $10 million, respectively; and must have posted a compound annual growth in revenue and earnings per share of at least 15% annually over the three years ending on or before April 30, 2021. Real estate investment trusts, limited-liability companies, limited parterships, business development companies, closed-end investment firms, companies about to be acquired, and companies that lost money in the quarter ending April 30, 2021 were excluded. *Fortune, "100 Fastest-Growing Companies," 2021*

According to Deloitte, San Diego is home to eight of North America's 500 fastest-growing high-technology companies: **Regulus Therapeutics** (#15); **Fate Therapeutics** (#207); **AnaptysBio** (#211); **Quidel Corp.** (#261); **Tandem Diabetes Care** (#333); **Seismic** (#348); **Acadia Pharmaceuticals** (#441); **Cloudbeds** (#461). Companies are ranked by percentage growth in revenue over a four-year period. Criteria for inclusion: company must be headquartered within North America; must own proprietary intellectual property or technology that is sold to customers in products that contributes to a significant portion of the company's operating revenue; must have been in business for a minumum of four years with 2017 operating revenues of at least $50,000 USD/CD and 2020 operating revenues of at least $5 million USD/CD. *Deloitte, 2021 Technology Fast 500™*

Living Environment

COST OF LIVING

Cost of Living Index

Composite Index	Groceries	Housing	Utilities	Trans-portation	Health Care	Misc. Goods/ Services
147.3	112.4	220.4	120.9	131.6	108.4	110.3

Note: The Cost of Living Index measures regional differences in the cost of consumer goods and services, excluding taxes and non-consumer expenditures, for professional and managerial households in the top income quintile. It is based on more than 50,000 prices covering almost 60 different items for which prices are collected three times a year by chambers of commerce, economic development organizations or university applied economic centers in each participating urban area. The numbers shown should be read as a percentage above or below the national average of 100. For example, a value of 115.4 in the groceries column indicates that grocery prices are 15.4% higher than the national average. Small differences in the index numbers should not be interpreted as significant; Figures cover the San Diego CA urban area.
Source: The Council for Community and Economic Research, Cost of Living Index, 2021

Grocery Prices

Area[1]	T-Bone Steak ($/pound)	Frying Chicken ($/pound)	Whole Milk ($/half gal.)	Eggs ($/dozen)	Orange Juice ($/64 oz.)	Coffee ($/11.5 oz.)
City[2]	12.43	1.79	2.30	2.99	3.82	5.47
Avg.	12.82	1.40	2.22	1.57	3.59	4.30
Min.	8.91	0.91	1.29	0.75	2.87	3.02
Max.	21.35	2.69	3.92	3.86	5.49	8.11

Note: (1) Values for the local area are compared with the average, minimum and maximum values for all 285 areas in the Cost of Living Index; (2) Figures cover the San Diego CA urban area; ***T-Bone Steak*** *(price per pound);* ***Frying Chicken*** *(price per pound, whole fryer);* ***Whole Milk*** *(half gallon carton);* ***Eggs*** *(price per dozen, Grade A, large);* ***Orange Juice*** *(64 oz. Tropicana or Florida Natural);* ***Coffee*** *(11.5 oz. can, vacuum-packed, Maxwell House, Hills Bros, or Folgers).*
Source: The Council for Community and Economic Research, Cost of Living Index, 2021

Housing and Utility Costs

Area[1]	New Home Price ($)	Apartment Rent ($/month)	All Electric ($/month)	Part Electric ($/month)	Other Energy ($/month)	Telephone ($/month)
City[2]	897,154	2,579	-	165.29	74.36	179.39
Avg.	398,393	1,217	171.38	100.83	69.67	187.75
Min.	212,799	534	96.71	31.56	27.15	173.01
Max.	2,354,006	4,438	369.53	277.33	303.87	206.73

Note: (1) Values for the local area are compared with the average, minimum and maximum values for all 285 areas in the Cost of Living Index; (2) Figures cover the San Diego CA urban area; ***New Home Price*** *(2,400 sf living area, 8,000 sf lot, in urban area with full utilities);* ***Apartment Rent*** *(950 sf 2 bedroom/1.5 or 2 bath, unfurnished, excluding all utilities except water);* ***All Electric*** *(average monthly cost for an all-electric home);* ***Part Electric*** *(average monthly cost for a part-electric home);* ***Other Energy*** *(average monthly cost for natural gas, fuel oil, coal, wood, and any other forms of energy except electricity);* ***Telephone*** *(price includes the base monthly rate plus taxes and fees for three lines of mobile phone service).*
Source: The Council for Community and Economic Research, Cost of Living Index, 2021

Health Care, Transportation, and Other Costs

Area[1]	Doctor ($/visit)	Dentist ($/visit)	Optometrist ($/visit)	Gasoline ($/gallon)	Beauty Salon ($/visit)	Men's Shirt ($)
City[2]	125.00	109.73	123.80	3.97	65.72	35.00
Avg.	118.16	101.04	109.44	2.71	40.63	30.77
Min.	35.04	55.56	51.17	2.17	18.59	11.32
Max.	231.10	165.12	256.81	4.11	85.33	63.03

Note: (1) Values for the local area are compared with the average, minimum and maximum values for all 285 areas in the Cost of Living Index; (2) Figures cover the San Diego CA urban area; ***Doctor*** *(general practitioners routine exam of an established patient);* ***Dentist*** *(adult teeth cleaning and periodic oral examination);* ***Optometrist*** *(full vision eye exam for established adult patient);* ***Gasoline*** *(one gallon regular unleaded, national brand, including all taxes, cash price at self-service pump if available);* ***Beauty Salon*** *(woman's shampoo, trim, and blow-dry);* ***Men's Shirt*** *(cotton/polyester dress shirt, pinpoint weave, long sleeves).*
Source: The Council for Community and Economic Research, Cost of Living Index, 2021

HOUSING

Homeownership Rate

Area	2013 (%)	2014 (%)	2015 (%)	2016 (%)	2017 (%)	2018 (%)	2019 (%)	2020 (%)	2021 (%)
MSA[1]	55.0	57.4	51.8	53.3	56.0	56.1	56.7	57.8	52.6
U.S.	65.1	64.5	63.7	63.4	63.9	64.4	64.6	66.6	65.5

Note: (1) Figures cover the San Diego-Carlsbad, CA Metropolitan Statistical Area
Source: U.S. Census Bureau, Housing Vacancies and Homeownership Annual Statistics: 2013-2021

House Price Index (HPI)

Area	National Ranking[2]	Quarterly Change (%)	One-Year Change (%)	Five-Year Change (%)	Since 1991Q1 (%)
MSA[1]	80	4.24	20.55	47.78	305.27
U.S.[3]	–	3.33	17.54	54.45	258.04

Note: The HPI is a weighted repeat sales index. It measures average price changes in repeat sales or refinancings on the same properties. This information is obtained by reviewing repeat mortgage transactions on single-family properties whose mortgages have been purchased or securitized by Fannie Mae or Freddie Mac since January 1975; (1) Figures cover the San Diego-Carlsbad, CA Metropolitan Statistical Area; (2) Rankings are based on annual percentage change for all metro areas containing at least 15,000 transactions over the last 10 years and ranges from 1 to 268; (3) figures based on a weighted average of Census Division estimates using a seasonally adjusted, purchase-only index; all figures are for the period ending December 31, 2021
Source: Federal Housing Finance Agency, Change in FHFA Metropolitan Area House Price Indexes, 2021Q4

Median Single-Family Home Prices

Area	2019	2020	2021[p]	Percent Change 2020 to 2021
MSA[1]	645.0	710.0	830.0	16.9
U.S. Average	274.6	300.2	353.4	17.7

Note: Figures are median sales prices of existing single-family homes in thousands of dollars; (p) preliminary; (1) Figures cover the San Diego-Carlsbad, CA Metropolitan Statistical Area
Source: National Association of Realtors, Median Sales Price of Existing Single-Family Homes for Metropolitan Areas, 4th Quarter 2021

Qualifying Income Based on Median Sales Price of Existing Single-Family Homes

Area	With 5% Down ($)	With 10% Down ($)	With 20% Down ($)
MSA[1]	166,588	157,820	140,284
U.S. Average	70,699	66,978	59,536

Note: Figures are preliminary; Qualifying income is based on a mortgage rate of 3.13%. Monthly principal and interest payment is limited to 25% of income; (1) Figures cover the San Diego-Carlsbad, CA Metropolitan Statistical Area
Source: National Association of Realtors, Qualifying Income Based on Median Sales Price of Existing Single-Family Homes for Metropolitan Areas, 4th Quarter 2021

Home Value Distribution

Area	Under $50,000	$50,000 -$99,999	$100,000 -$149,999	$150,000 -$199,999	$200,000 -$299,999	$300,000 -$499,999	$500,000 -$999,999	$1,000,000 or more
City	1.5	1.0	0.8	0.8	3.9	25.0	50.2	16.8
MSA[1]	2.4	1.8	1.3	1.1	4.2	26.0	49.8	13.5
U.S.	6.6	11.0	12.3	13.6	20.0	20.5	12.3	3.7

Note: Figures are percentages and cover owner-occupied housing units; (1) Figures cover the San Diego-Carlsbad, CA Metropolitan Statistical Area
Source: U.S. Census Bureau, 2016-2020 American Community Survey 5-Year Estimates

Year Housing Structure Built

Area	2010 or Later	2000 -2009	1990 -1999	1980 -1989	1970 -1979	1960 -1969	1950 -1959	1940 -1949	Before 1940	Median Year
City	4.8	10.1	11.4	17.5	20.9	12.7	11.8	4.1	6.6	1977
MSA[1]	4.4	11.6	12.5	18.6	22.5	12.0	10.7	3.4	4.2	1979
U.S.	6.2	13.6	13.9	13.4	15.0	10.5	10.2	4.8	12.4	1978

Note: Figures are percentages except for Median Year; Note: (1) Figures cover the San Diego-Carlsbad, CA Metropolitan Statistical Area
Source: U.S. Census Bureau, 2016-2020 American Community Survey 5-Year Estimates

Gross Monthly Rent

Area	Under $500	$500 -$999	$1,000 -$1,499	$1,500 -$1,999	$2,000 -$2,499	$2,500 -$2,999	$3,000 and up	Median ($)
City	3.0	8.0	23.8	28.0	19.3	10.1	7.7	1,770
MSA[1]	3.3	7.8	25.5	28.9	17.7	9.1	7.7	1,732
U.S.	8.9	34.3	30.2	14.9	6.2	2.6	2.8	1,096

Note: Figures are percentages except for Median; Gross rent is the contract rent plus the estimated average monthly cost of utilities (electricity, gas, and water and sewer) and fuels (oil, coal, kerosene, wood, etc.) if these are paid by the renter (or paid for the renter by someone else); (1) Figures cover the San Diego-Carlsbad, CA Metropolitan Statistical Area
Source: U.S. Census Bureau, 2016-2020 American Community Survey 5-Year Estimates

HEALTH

Health Risk Factors

Category	MSA[1] (%)	U.S. (%)
Adults aged 18–64 who have any kind of health care coverage	n/a	86.8
Adults who reported being in good or better health	n/a	86.7
Adults who are current smokers	n/a	15.5
Adults who currently use chewing tobacco, snuff, or snus	n/a	3.7
Adults who are heavy drinkers[2]	n/a	6.7
Adults who are binge drinkers[3]	n/a	15.7
Adults who are overweight (BMI 25.0 - 29.9)	n/a	35.2
Adults who are obese (BMI 30.0 - 99.8)	n/a	31.9
Adults who participated in any physical activities in the past month	n/a	77.6
Adults who always or nearly always wears a seat belt	n/a	94.2

Note: (1) Figures for the San Diego-Carlsbad, CA Metropolitan Statistical Area were not available. (2) Heavy drinkers are classified as adult men having more than 14 drinks per week and adult women having more than 7 drinks per week; (3) Binge drinkers are classified as males having five or more drinks on one occasion or females having four or more drinks on one occasion
Source: Centers for Disease Control and Prevention, Behaviorial Risk Factor Surveillance System, SMART: Selected Metropolitan Area Risk Trends, 2020

Acute and Chronic Health Conditions

Category	MSA[1] (%)	U.S. (%)
Adults who have ever been told they had a heart attack	n/a	4.3
Adults who have ever been told they have angina or coronary heart disease	n/a	4.0
Adults who have ever been told they had a stroke	n/a	2.8
Adults who have ever been told they have asthma	n/a	14.2
Adults who have ever been told they have arthritis	n/a	24.5
Adults who have ever been told they have diabetes[2]	n/a	10.6
Adults who have ever been told they had skin cancer	n/a	6.4
Adults who have ever been told they had any other types of cancer	n/a	6.8
Adults who have ever been told they have COPD	n/a	6.2
Adults who have ever been told they have kidney disease	n/a	2.9
Adults who have ever been told they have a form of depression	n/a	19.6

Note: (1) Figures for the San Diego-Carlsbad, CA Metropolitan Statistical Area were not available. (2) Figures do not include pregnancy-related, borderline, or pre-diabetes
Source: Centers for Disease Control and Prevention, Behaviorial Risk Factor Surveillance System, SMART: Selected Metropolitan Area Risk Trends, 2020

Health Screening and Vaccination Rates

Category	MSA[1] (%)	U.S. (%)
Adults 50-75 who have had a blood stool test within the past year	n/a	9.3
Adults aged 65+ who have had flu shot within the past year	n/a	67.9
Adults aged 65+ who have ever had a pneumonia vaccination	n/a	72.2
Adults who have ever been tested for HIV	n/a	37.1
Women aged 21-65 who have had a pap test in the past three years	n/a	77.7
Men aged 40+ who have had a PSA test within the past two years	n/a	31.8
Women aged 40+ who have had a mammogram within the past two years	n/a	71.5

Note: (1) Figures for the San Diego-Carlsbad, CA Metropolitan Statistical Area were not available.
Source: Centers for Disease Control and Prevention, Behaviorial Risk Factor Surveillance System, SMART: Selected Metropolitan Area Risk Trends, 2020

Disability Status

Category	MSA[1] (%)	U.S. (%)
Adults who reported being deaf	n/a	6.8
Are you blind or have serious difficulty seeing, even when wearing glasses?	n/a	4.7
Do you have difficulty doing errands alone?	n/a	6.3
Do you have difficulty dressing or bathing?	n/a	3.0
Do you have serious difficulty concentrating/remembering/making decisions?	n/a	10.8
Do you have serious difficulty walking or climbing stairs?	n/a	11.9

Note: (1) Figures for the San Diego-Carlsbad, CA Metropolitan Statistical Area were not available.
Source: Centers for Disease Control and Prevention, Behaviorial Risk Factor Surveillance System, SMART: Selected Metropolitan Area Risk Trends, 2020

Mortality Rates for the Top 10 Causes of Death in the U.S.

ICD-10[a] Sub-Chapter	ICD-10[a] Code	Age-Adjusted Mortality Rate[1] per 100,000 population	
		County[2]	U.S.
Malignant neoplasms	C00-C97	133.2	146.4
Ischaemic heart diseases	I20-I25	67.3	90.2
Other forms of heart disease	I30-I51	41.9	51.9
Other degenerative diseases of the nervous system	G30-G31	46.3	39.7
Other external causes of accidental injury	W00-X59	29.0	38.7
Chronic lower respiratory diseases	J40-J47	26.2	38.1
Cerebrovascular diseases	I60-I69	42.0	37.6
Organic, including symptomatic, mental disorders	F01-F09	17.5	29.4
Hypertensive diseases	I10-I15	23.6	26.1
Diabetes mellitus	E10-E14	21.3	22.6

Note: (a) ICD-10 = International Classification of Diseases 10th Revision; (1) Mortality rates are a three-year average covering 2018-2020; (2) Figures cover San Diego County.
Source: Centers for Disease Control and Prevention, National Center for Health Statistics. Underlying Cause of Death 1999-2020 on CDC WONDER Online Database

Mortality Rates for Selected Causes of Death

ICD-10[a] Sub-Chapter	ICD-10[a] Code	Age-Adjusted Mortality Rate[1] per 100,000 population	
		County[2]	U.S.
Assault	X85-Y09	2.7	6.5
Diseases of the liver	K70-K76	11.7	15.3
Human immunodeficiency virus (HIV) disease	B20-B24	1.2	1.4
Influenza and pneumonia	J09-J18	9.2	13.4
Intentional self-harm	X60-X84	12.1	13.9
Malnutrition	E40-E46	2.9	2.9
Obesity and other hyperalimentation	E65-E68	1.7	2.4
Renal failure	N17-N19	3.0	12.5
Transport accidents	V01-V99	9.1	12.5
Viral hepatitis	B15-B19	1.4	1.0

Note: (a) ICD-10 = International Classification of Diseases 10th Revision; (1) Mortality rates are a three-year average covering 2018-2020; (2) Figures cover San Diego County; Data are suppressed when the data meet the criteria for confidentiality constraints; Mortality rates are flagged as unreliable when the rate would be calculated with a numerator of 20 or less.
Source: Centers for Disease Control and Prevention, National Center for Health Statistics. Underlying Cause of Death 1999-2020 on CDC WONDER Online Database

Health Insurance Coverage

Area	With Health Insurance	With Private Health Insurance	With Public Health Insurance	Without Health Insurance	Population Under Age 19 Without Health Insurance
City	92.5	70.6	31.4	7.5	3.6
MSA[1]	92.4	69.1	33.6	7.6	3.9
U.S.	91.3	68.1	35.3	8.7	5.2

Note: Figures are percentages that cover the civilian noninstitutionalized population; (1) Figures cover the San Diego-Carlsbad, CA Metropolitan Statistical Area
Source: U.S. Census Bureau, 2016-2020 American Community Survey 5-Year Estimates

Number of Medical Professionals

Area	MDs[3]	DOs[3,4]	Dentists	Podiatrists	Chiropractors	Optometrists
County[1] (number)	11,200	646	3,073	151	1,152	649
County[1] (rate[2])	339.5	19.6	93.2	4.6	34.9	19.7
U.S. (rate[2])	285.1	23.0	71.1	6.2	28.2	17.0

06073
Note: Data as of 2020 unless noted; (1) Data covers San Diego County; (2) Rate per 100,000 population; (3) Data as of 2019 and includes all active, non-federal physicians; (4) Doctor of Osteopathic Medicine
Source: U.S. Department of Health and Human Services, Health Resources and Services Administration, Bureau of Health Professions, Area Resource File (ARF) 2020-2021

Best Hospitals

According to *U.S. News*, the San Diego-Carlsbad, CA metro area is home to three of the best hospitals in the U.S.: **Scripps La Jolla Hospitals** (6 adult specialties); **Sharp Memorial Hospital** (1 adult specialty); **UC San Diego Health** (10 adult specialties). The hospitals listed were nationally ranked in at least one of 15 adult or 10 pediatric specialties. Only 175 U.S. hospitals performed well enough to be nationally ranked in one or more specialties. Twenty hospitals in the U.S. made the Honor Roll. The Best Hospitals Honor Roll takes both the national rankings and the procedure and condition ratings into account. Hospitals received points if they were nationally ranked in one of the 15 adult specialties—the higher they ranked, the more points they got—and how many ratings of "high performing" they earned in the 17 procedures and conditions. *U.S. News Online, "America's Best Hospitals 2021-22"*

According to *U.S. News,* the San Diego-Carlsbad, CA metro area is home to one of the best children's hospitals in the U.S.: **Rady Children's Hospital** (10 pediatric specialties). The hospital listed was highly ranked in at least one of 10 pediatric specialties. Ninety-two children's hospitals in the U.S. were nationally ranked in at least one specialty. Hospitals received points for being ranked in a specialty, and the 10 hospitals with the most points across the 10 specialties make up the Honor Roll. *U.S. News Online, "America's Best Children's Hospitals 2021-22"*

EDUCATION

Public School District Statistics

District Name	Schls	Pupils	Pupil/ Teacher Ratio	Minority Pupils[1] (%)	LEP/ELL[2] (%)	IEP[3] (%)
Del Mar Union Elementary	8	4,132	n/a	53.6	12.1	14.4
Poway Unified	38	36,586	n/a	58.9	11.1	13.0
San Diego Unified	176	102,270	n/a	75.8	21.1	14.8

Note: Table includes school districts with 2,000 or more students; (1) Percentage of students that are not non-Hispanic white; (2) Percentage of students that are Limited English Proficient (LEP) or English Language Learners (ELL) (2018-19); (3) Percentage of students that have an Individualized Education Program (IEP).
Source: U.S. Department of Education, National Center for Education Statistics, Common Core of Data, Local Education Agency (School District) Universe Survey: School Year 2019-2020

Best High Schools

According to *U.S. News,* San Diego is home to three of the top 500 high schools in the U.S.: **Canyon Crest Academy** (#161); **Del Norte High** (#228); **Westview High** (#429). Nearly 18,000 public, magnet and charter schools were ranked based on their performance on state assessments and how well they prepare students for college. *U.S. News & World Report, "Best High Schools 2021"*

Highest Level of Education

Area	Less than H.S.	H.S. Diploma	Some College, No Deg.	Associate Degree	Bachelor's Degree	Master's Degree	Prof. School Degree	Doctorate Degree
City	11.2	15.2	19.2	7.7	27.5	12.4	3.6	3.1
MSA[1]	12.0	18.2	22.0	8.3	24.2	10.2	2.9	2.2
U.S.	11.5	26.7	20.3	8.6	20.2	9.1	2.2	1.5

Note: Figures cover persons age 25 and over; (1) Figures cover the San Diego-Carlsbad, CA Metropolitan Statistical Area
Source: U.S. Census Bureau, 2016-2020 American Community Survey 5-Year Estimates

Educational Attainment by Race

Area	High School Graduate or Higher (%)					Bachelor's Degree or Higher (%)				
	Total	White	Black	Asian	Hisp.[2]	Total	White	Black	Asian	Hisp.[2]
City	88.8	90.4	91.4	88.9	71.8	46.7	49.7	27.7	53.7	21.7
MSA[1]	88.0	89.5	91.7	89.5	72.0	39.5	41.2	26.6	51.7	18.8
U.S.	88.5	90.7	86.7	87.3	70.3	32.9	34.4	22.6	55.0	17.6

Note: Figures shown cover persons 25 years old and over; (1) Figures cover the San Diego-Carlsbad, CA Metropolitan Statistical Area; (2) People of Hispanic origin can be of any race
Source: U.S. Census Bureau, 2016-2020 American Community Survey 5-Year Estimates

School Enrollment by Grade and Control

Area	Preschool (%)		Kindergarten (%)		Grades 1 - 4 (%)		Grades 5 - 8 (%)		Grades 9 - 12 (%)	
	Public	Private	Public	Private	Public	Private	Public	Private	Public	Private
City	48.8	51.2	92.2	7.8	90.4	9.6	91.9	8.1	91.7	8.3
MSA[1]	50.9	49.1	91.0	9.0	91.3	8.7	92.1	7.9	92.5	7.5
U.S.	58.9	41.1	86.9	13.1	89.0	11.0	89.0	11.0	89.7	10.3

Note: Figures shown cover persons 3 years old and over; (1) Figures cover the San Diego-Carlsbad, CA Metropolitan Statistical Area
Source: U.S. Census Bureau, 2016-2020 American Community Survey 5-Year Estimates

Higher Education

Four-Year Colleges			Two-Year Colleges			Medical Schools[1]	Law Schools[2]	Voc/ Tech[3]
Public	Private Non-profit	Private For-profit	Public	Private Non-profit	Private For-profit			
5	19	11	6	0	11	1	4	14

Note: Figures cover institutions located within the San Diego-Carlsbad, CA Metropolitan Statistical Area and include main campuses only; (1) includes schools accredited by the Liaison Committee on Medical Education and the American Osteopathic Association's Commission on Osteopathic College Accreditation; (2) includes ABA-accredited schools, schools with provisional ABA accreditation, and state accredited schools; (3) includes all schools with programs that are less than 2 years.
Source: National Center for Education Statistics, Integrated Postsecondary Education System (IPEDS), 2020-21; Wikipedia, List of Medical Schools in the United States, accessed April 11, 2022; Wikipedia, List of Law Schools in the United States, accessed April 11, 2022

According to *U.S. News & World Report,* the San Diego-Carlsbad, CA metro area is home to three of the top 200 national universities in the U.S.: **University of California—San Diego** (#34 tie); **University of San Diego** (#93 tie); **San Diego State University** (#148 tie). The indicators used to capture academic quality fall into a number of categories: assessment by administrators at peer institutions; retention of students; faculty resources; student selectivity; financial resources; alumni giving; high school counselor ratings of colleges; and graduation rate. *U.S. News & World Report, "America's Best Colleges 2022"*

According to *U.S. News & World Report,* the San Diego-Carlsbad, CA metro area is home to one of the top 100 law schools in the U.S.: **University of San Diego** (#86). The rankings are based on a weighted average of 12 measures of quality: peer assessment score; assessment score by lawyers/judges; median LSAT scores; median undergrad GPA; acceptance rate; employment rates for graduates; placement success; bar passage rate; faculty resources; expenditures per student; student/faculty ratio; and library resources. *U.S. News & World Report, "America's Best Graduate Schools, Law, 2022"*

According to *U.S. News & World Report,* the San Diego-Carlsbad, CA metro area is home to one of the top 75 medical schools for research in the U.S.: **University of California—San Diego** (#19 tie). The rankings are based on a weighted average of 11 measures of quality: quality assessment; peer assessment score; assessment score by residency directors; research activity; total research activity; average research activity per faculty member; student selectivity; median MCAT total score; median undergraduate GPA; acceptance rate; and faculty resources. *U.S. News & World Report, "America's Best Graduate Schools, Medical, 2022"*

EMPLOYERS

Major Employers

Company Name	Industry
Barona Resort & Casino	Resort hotels
CA Dept of Forestry and Fire Protection	Fire department, not including volunteer
CA Dept of Housing & Comm Dev	Housing agency, government
City of San Diego	Municipal government
Elite Show Services	Help supply services
Go-Staff	Temporary help services
Kaiser Foundation Hospitals	Trusts, nec
Palomar Community College District	Junior colleges
Qualcomm International	Patent buying, licensing, leasing
Risk Management Strategies	Employee programs administration
San Diego State University	Colleges & universities
Sharp Memorial Hospital	General medical & surgical hospitals
Solar Turbines Incorporated	Turbines & turbine generator sets
U.S. Marine Corps	Marine corps
U.S. Navy	U.S. military
University of California, San Diego	General medical & surgical hospitals
Veterans Health Administration	Administration of veterans' affairs

Note: Companies shown are located within the San Diego-Carlsbad, CA Metropolitan Statistical Area.
Source: Hoovers.com; Wikipedia

Best Companies to Work For

Scripps Health, headquartered in San Diego, is among "The 100 Best Companies to Work For." To pick the best companies, *Fortune* partnered with the Great Place to Work Institute. Two-thirds of a company's score is based on the results of the Institute's Trust Index survey, which is sent to a random sample of employees from each company. The questions related to attitudes about management's credibility, job satisfaction, and camaraderie. The other third of the scoring is based on the company's responses to the Institute's Culture Audit, which includes detailed questions about pay and benefit programs, and a series of open-ended questions about hiring practices, internal communication, training, recognition programs, and diversity efforts. Any company that is at least five years old with more than 1,000 U.S. employees is eligible. *Fortune, "The 100 Best Companies to Work For," 2021*

San Diego Gas & Electric and Southern California Gas Company; Sharp HealthCare, headquartered in San Diego, are among the "100 Best Places to Work in IT." To qualify, companies had to be U.S.-based organizations or be non-U.S.-based employers that met the following criteria: have a minimum of 300 total employees at a U.S. headquarters and a minimum of 30 IT employees in the U.S., with at least 50% of their IT employees based in the U.S. The best places to work were selected based on compensation, benefits, work/life balance, employee morale, and satisfaction with training and development programs. In addition, *InsiderPro* and *Computerworld* looked at retention efforts, programs for recognizing and rewarding outstanding performances, and benefits such as flextime, elder care and child care, and reimbursement for college tuition and the cost of pursuing technology certifications. *InsiderPro and Computerworld, "100 Best Places to Work in IT," 2021*

Aya Healthcare, headquartered in San Diego, is among "75 Best Large Workplaces for Women." To pick the best companies, *Fortune* partnered with the Great Place to Work Institute. Employees responded to over 60 survey questions describing the extent to which their organization creates a Great Place to Work For All. Eighty-five percent of the ranking is based on what women themselves report about their workplace, and how fairly those experiences compare to men's reports of the same workplaces. Fifteen percent of the remaining rank is based on how well represented women are in the workforce and throughout management, taking into account industry trends. To be considered, at a minimum, companies need to employ at least 50 women, at least 20% of their non-executive managers need to be female, and at least one of their executives needs to be female. *Fortune, "75 Best Large Workplaces for Women," 2021*

PUBLIC SAFETY

Crime Rate

Area	Total Crime	Violent Crime Rate				Property Crime Rate		
		Murder	Rape[3]	Robbery	Aggrav. Assault	Burglary	Larceny -Theft	Motor Vehicle Theft
City	2,060.6	3.9	33.7	84.0	247.3	231.2	1,116.0	344.5
Suburbs[1]	1,655.8	3.1	25.4	69.7	229.9	210.0	887.9	229.9
Metro[2]	1,830.5	3.4	29.0	75.8	237.4	219.1	986.3	279.3
U.S.	2,356.7	6.5	38.4	73.9	279.7	314.2	1,398.0	246.0

Note: Figures are crimes per 100,000 population; (1) All areas within the metro area that are located outside the city limits; (2) Figures cover the San Diego-Carlsbad, CA Metropolitan Statistical Area; (3) All figures shown were reported using the revised Uniform Crime Reporting (UCR) definition of rape.
Source: FBI Uniform Crime Reports, 2020

Hate Crimes

Area	Number of Quarters Reported	Number of Incidents per Bias Motivation					
		Race/Ethnicity/ Ancestry	Religion	Sexual Orientation	Disability	Gender	Gender Identity
City	4	17	1	7	0	0	1
U.S.	4	5,227	1,244	1,110	130	75	266

Source: Federal Bureau of Investigation, Hate Crime Statistics 2020

Identity Theft Consumer Reports

Area	Reports	Reports per 100,000 Population	Rank[2]
MSA[1]	8,561	256	164
U.S.	1,434,676	432	-

Note: (1) Figures cover the San Diego-Carlsbad, CA Metropolitan Statistical Area; (2) Rank ranges from 1 to 391 where 1 indicates greatest number of identity theft reports per 100,000 population
Source: Federal Trade Commission, Consumer Sentinel Network Data Book 2021

Fraud and Other Consumer Reports

Area	Reports	Reports per 100,000 Population	Rank[2]
MSA[1]	34,933	1,046	86
U.S.	4,328,977	1,304	-

Note: (1) Figures cover the San Diego-Carlsbad, CA Metropolitan Statistical Area; (2) Rank ranges from 1 to 391 where 1 indicates greatest number of fraud and other consumer reports per 100,000 population
Source: Federal Trade Commission, Consumer Sentinel Network Data Book 2021

POLITICS

2020 Presidential Election Results

Area	Biden	Trump	Jorgensen	Hawkins	Other
San Diego County	60.2	37.5	1.3	0.5	0.5
U.S.	51.3	46.8	1.2	0.3	0.5

Note: Results are percentages and may not add to 100% due to rounding
Source: Dave Leip's Atlas of U.S. Presidential Elections

SPORTS

Professional Sports Teams

Team Name	League	Year Established
San Diego Padres	Major League Baseball (MLB)	1969

Note: Includes teams located in the San Diego-Carlsbad, CA Metropolitan Statistical Area.
Source: Wikipedia, Major Professional Sports Teams of the United States and Canada, April 6, 2022

CLIMATE

Average and Extreme Temperatures

Temperature	Jan	Feb	Mar	Apr	May	Jun	Jul	Aug	Sep	Oct	Nov	Dec	Yr.
Extreme High (°F)	88	88	93	98	96	101	95	98	111	107	97	88	111
Average High (°F)	65	66	66	68	69	72	76	77	77	74	71	66	71
Average Temp. (°F)	57	58	59	62	64	67	71	72	71	67	62	58	64
Average Low (°F)	48	50	52	55	58	61	65	66	65	60	53	49	57
Extreme Low (°F)	29	36	39	44	48	51	55	58	51	43	38	34	29

Note: Figures cover the years 1948-1990
Source: National Climatic Data Center, International Station Meteorological Climate Summary, 9/96

Average Precipitation/Snowfall/Humidity

Precip./Humidity	Jan	Feb	Mar	Apr	May	Jun	Jul	Aug	Sep	Oct	Nov	Dec	Yr.
Avg. Precip. (in.)	1.9	1.4	1.7	0.8	0.2	0.1	Tr	0.1	0.2	0.4	1.2	1.4	9.5
Avg. Snowfall (in.)	Tr	0	0	0	0	0	0	0	0	0	0	Tr	Tr
Avg. Rel. Hum. 7am (%)	70	72	73	72	73	77	79	79	78	74	69	68	74
Avg. Rel. Hum. 4pm (%)	57	58	59	59	63	66	65	66	65	63	60	58	62

Note: Figures cover the years 1948-1990; Tr = Trace amounts (<0.05 in. of rain; <0.5 in. of snow)
Source: National Climatic Data Center, International Station Meteorological Climate Summary, 9/96

Weather Conditions

Temperature			Daytime Sky			Precipitation		
10°F & below	32°F & below	90°F & above	Clear	Partly cloudy	Cloudy	0.01 inch or more precip.	0.1 inch or more snow/ice	Thunder-storms
0	< 1	4	115	126	124	40	0	5

Note: Figures are average number of days per year and cover the years 1948-1990
Source: National Climatic Data Center, International Station Meteorological Climate Summary, 9/96

HAZARDOUS WASTE

Superfund Sites

The San Diego-Carlsbad, CA metro area is home to one site on the EPA's Superfund National Priorities List: **Camp Pendleton Marine Corps Base** (final). There are a total of 1,165 Superfund sites with a status of proposed or final on the list in the U.S. *U.S. Environmental Protection Agency, National Priorities List, April 6, 2022*

AIR QUALITY

Air Quality Trends: Ozone

	1990	1995	2000	2005	2010	2016	2017	2018	2019	2020
MSA[1]	0.112	0.093	0.084	0.079	0.075	0.070	0.077	0.069	0.071	0.077
U.S.	0.090	0.091	0.082	0.080	0.074	0.070	0.069	0.070	0.066	0.068

Note: (1) Data covers the San Diego-Carlsbad, CA Metropolitan Statistical Area. The values shown are the composite ozone concentration averages among trend sites based on the highest fourth daily maximum 8-hour concentration in parts per million. These trends are based on sites having an adequate record of monitoring data during the trend period. Data from exceptional events are included.
Source: U.S. Environmental Protection Agency, Air Quality Monitoring Information, "Air Quality Trends by City, 1990-2020"

Air Quality Index

Area	Percent of Days when Air Quality was...[2]					AQI Statistics[2]	
	Good	Moderate	Unhealthy for Sensitive Groups	Unhealthy	Very Unhealthy	Maximum	Median
MSA[1]	16.4	70.2	9.6	3.8	0.0	192	71

Note: (1) Data covers the San Diego-Carlsbad, CA Metropolitan Statistical Area; (2) Based on 366 days with AQI data in 2020. Air Quality Index (AQI) is an index for reporting daily air quality. EPA calculates the AQI for five major air pollutants regulated by the Clean Air Act: ground-level ozone, particle pollution (aka particulate matter), carbon monoxide, sulfur dioxide, and nitrogen dioxide. The AQI runs from 0 to 500. The higher the AQI value, the greater the level of air pollution and the greater the health concern. There are six AQI categories: "Good" AQI is between 0 and 50. Air quality is considered satisfactory; "Moderate" AQI is between 51 and 100. Air quality is acceptable; "Unhealthy for Sensitive Groups" When AQI values are between 101 and 150, members of sensitive groups may experience health effects; "Unhealthy" When AQI values are between 151 and 200 everyone may begin to experience health effects; "Very Unhealthy" AQI values between 201 and 300 trigger a health alert; "Hazardous" AQI values over 300 trigger warnings of emergency conditions (not shown).
Source: U.S. Environmental Protection Agency, Air Quality Index Report, 2020

Air Quality Index Pollutants

Area	Percent of Days when AQI Pollutant was...[2]					
	Carbon Monoxide	Nitrogen Dioxide	Ozone	Sulfur Dioxide	Particulate Matter 2.5	Particulate Matter 10
MSA[1]	0.0	0.5	32.2	0.0	66.4	0.8

Note: (1) Data covers the San Diego-Carlsbad, CA Metropolitan Statistical Area; (2) Based on 366 days with AQI data in 2020. The Air Quality Index (AQI) is an index for reporting daily air quality. EPA calculates the AQI for five major air pollutants regulated by the Clean Air Act: ground-level ozone, particle pollution (also known as particulate matter), carbon monoxide, sulfur dioxide, and nitrogen dioxide. The AQI runs from 0 to 500. The higher the AQI value, the greater the level of air pollution and the greater the health concern.
Source: U.S. Environmental Protection Agency, Air Quality Index Report, 2020

Maximum Air Pollutant Concentrations: Particulate Matter, Ozone, CO and Lead

	Particulate Matter 10 (ug/m^3)	Particulate Matter 2.5 Wtd AM (ug/m^3)	Particulate Matter 2.5 24-Hr (ug/m^3)	Ozone (ppm)	Carbon Monoxide (ppm)	Lead (ug/m^3)
MSA[1] Level	158	20.5	75	0.082	2	0.02
NAAQS[2]	150	15	35	0.075	9	0.15
Met NAAQS[2]	No	No	No	No	Yes	Yes

Note: (1) Data covers the San Diego-Carlsbad, CA Metropolitan Statistical Area; Data from exceptional events are included; (2) National Ambient Air Quality Standards; ppm = parts per million; ug/m^3 = micrograms per cubic meter; n/a not available.
Concentrations: Particulate Matter 10 (coarse particulate)—highest second maximum 24-hour concentration; Particulate Matter 2.5 Wtd AM (fine particulate)—highest weighted annual mean concentration; Particulate Matter 2.5 24-Hour (fine particulate)—highest 98th percentile 24-hour concentration; Ozone—highest fourth daily maximum 8-hour concentration; Carbon Monoxide—highest second maximum non-overlapping 8-hour concentration; Lead—maximum running 3-month average
Source: U.S. Environmental Protection Agency, Air Quality Monitoring Information, "Air Quality Statistics by City, 2020"

Maximum Air Pollutant Concentrations: Nitrogen Dioxide and Sulfur Dioxide

	Nitrogen Dioxide AM (ppb)	Nitrogen Dioxide 1-Hr (ppb)	Sulfur Dioxide AM (ppb)	Sulfur Dioxide 1-Hr (ppb)	Sulfur Dioxide 24-Hr (ppb)
MSA[1] Level	14	49	n/a	1	n/a
NAAQS[2]	53	100	30	75	140
Met NAAQS[2]	Yes	Yes	n/a	Yes	n/a

Note: (1) Data covers the San Diego-Carlsbad, CA Metropolitan Statistical Area; Data from exceptional events are included; (2) National Ambient Air Quality Standards; ppm = parts per million; ug/m^3 = micrograms per cubic meter; n/a not available.
Concentrations: Nitrogen Dioxide AM—highest arithmetic mean concentration; Nitrogen Dioxide 1-Hr—highest 98th percentile 1-hour daily maximum concentration; Sulfur Dioxide AM—highest annual mean concentration; Sulfur Dioxide 1-Hr—highest 99th percentile 1-hour daily maximum concentration; Sulfur Dioxide 24-Hr—highest second maximum 24-hour concentration
Source: U.S. Environmental Protection Agency, Air Quality Monitoring Information, "Air Quality Statistics by City, 2020"

San Francisco, California

Background

San Francisco is one of the most beautiful cities in the world. It is blessed with a mild climate, one of the best landlocked harbors in the world, and a strong sense of civic pride shaped by its unique history.

The hilly peninsula known today as San Francisco and its bay was largely ignored by explorers during the sixteenth and seventeenth centuries. Until the 1760s, Europeans had not seen the "Golden Gate" or the narrow strip of water leading into what was to become one of the greatest harbors in the world. San Francisco remained a quiet and pastoral settlement for nearly 90 years, until the discovery of gold in the Sierra Nevada foothills in 1848, which changed San Francisco forever. Every hopeful adventurer from around the world docked in San Francisco, aspiring to make his fortune, creating a rowdy, frontier, gold-prospecting town, with plenty of gambling houses and saloons.

When the supply of gold dwindled around 1855, many gold miners went back to their native countries. Those that stayed continued to live in the ethnic neighborhoods they had created—neighborhoods that still exist today, such as Chinatown, the Italian District, and Japan Center.

The present-day charm of San Francisco lies in its cosmopolitan, yet cohesive, flavor. The city has long embraced a significant gay community, and was home to the first lesbian-rights organization in the United States, Daughters of Bilitis; the first openly gay person to run for public office in the United States, José Sarria; the first openly gay man to be elected to public office in California, Harvey Milk; the first openly lesbian judge appointed in the U.S., Mary C. Morgan; and the first transgender police commissioner, Theresa Sparks.

The San Francisco Bay Area is part of the Silicon Valley—the region in Northern California that serves as a global center for high technology and innovation. As such, it is one of the major economic regions of the United States, with one of the highest percentages of college-educated adults and per-capita income in the nation. The Bay Area is home to seven Fortune 500 companies, and major employers include Lyft, Securitize, Wells Fargo, and Wanda. Twenty percent of California's environmental companies live in San Francisco, which has the largest concentration of biotech companies in the state. A former warehouse district in San Francisco has become the center for nearly 400 multimedia and technology companies. Silicon Valley accounts for about one-third of the nation's high-technology exports.

AT&T Park, home of the San Francisco Giants major league baseball team, was completed in 2000; the Giants won the World Series in 2010, 2012, and 2014. The city offers excellent convention facilities with its Moscone Center, which comprises 770,000 square feet of exhibit space. The center was named for Mayor George Moscone, who championed controversial causes and who was murdered in office in 1978, along with gay activist Harvey Milk. The film, *The Times of Harvey Milk* won the 2008 Academy Award for best picture.

The Fine Arts Museums of San Francisco include the de Young, the city's oldest museum, and the Legion of Honor, home to Rodin's *Thinker.* In 2005, the de Young reopened in a new space in Golden Gate Park, replacing a structure damaged by the 1989 earthquake.

Also damaged in that quake was the main facility of the California Academy of Sciences, which oversees the Steinhart Aquarium, the Morrison Planetarium, and the Natural History Museum and which also reopened in Golden Gate Park in 2008. Architect Renzo Piano designed the building to be seismically safe, green, and sustainable, which allows outside views from nearly anywhere inside.

San Francisco is known as the "Air-Conditioned City" with cool pleasant summers and mild winters. It has greater climatic variability than any other urban area of the same size in the country. Sea fogs and associated low stratus clouds are most common in the summertime.

Rankings

General Rankings

- *US News & World Report* conducted a survey of more than 3,600 people and analyzed the 150 largest metropolitan areas to determine what matters most when selecting the next place to live. San Francisco ranked #15 out of the top 25 as having the best combination of desirable factors. Criteria: cost of living; quality of life and education; net migration; job market; desirability; and other factors. *realestate.usnews.com, "The 25 Best Places to Live in the U.S. in 2021-2022," July 13, 2021*
- The San Francisco metro area was identified as one of America's fastest-growing areas in terms of population and business growth by *MagnifyMoney*. The area ranked #22 out of 35. The 100 most populous metro areas in the U.S. were evaluated on their change from 2011 to 2016 in the following categories: people and housing; workforce and employment opportunities; growing industry. *www.businessinsider.com, "The 35 Cities in the US with the Biggest Influx of People, the Most Work Opportunities, and the Hottest Business Growth," August 12, 2018*
- In its eighth annual survey, *Travel + Leisure* readers nominated their favorite cities and towns in America—voting on numerous attractive features in categories including culture, food and drink, quality of life, style, and people. After 50,000 votes, San Francisco was ranked #5 among the proposed favorites. *www.travelandleisure.com, "America's Favorite Cities," October 20, 2017*
- The human resources consulting firm Mercer ranked 231 major cities worldwide in terms of overall quality of life. San Francisco ranked #34. Criteria: political, social, economic, and socio-cultural factors; medical and health considerations; schools and education; public services and transportation; recreation; consumer goods; housing; and natural environment. *Mercer, "Mercer 2019 Quality of Living Survey," March 13, 2019*
- For its 34th annual "Readers' Choice Awards" survey, *Condé Nast Traveler* ranked its readers' favorite cities in the U.S. Whether it be a longed for visit or a first on the list, these are the places that inspired a return to travel. The list was broken into large cities and cities under 250,000. San Francisco ranked #5 in the big city category. *Condé Nast Traveler, Readers' Choice Awards 2021, "Best Big Cities in the U.S." October 5, 2021*

Business/Finance Rankings

- According to *Business Insider*, the San Francisco metro area is a prime place to run a startup or move an existing business to. The area ranked #2. More than 300 metro areas were analyzed for factors that were of top concern to new business owners. Data was based on the 2019 U.S. Census Bureau American Community Survey, statistics from the CDC, Bureau of Labor Statistics employment report, and University of Chicago analysis. Criteria: business formations; percentage of vaccinated population; percentage of households with internet subscriptions; median household income; and share of work that can be done from home. *www.businessinsider.com, "The 20 Best Cities for Starting a Business in 2022 Include Baltimore, Boulder, and Boston," January 5, 2022*
- The Brookings Institution ranked the nation's largest cities based on income inequality. San Francisco was ranked #6 (#1 = greatest inequality). Criteria: the "95/20 ratio," a figure representing the income at which a household earns more than 95 percent of all other households, divided by the income at which a household earns more than only 20 percent of all other households. *Brookings Institution, "Household Income Inequality, Largest Cities of 97 Large U.S. Metro Areas, 2014-2016," February 5, 2018*
- The Brookings Institution ranked the 100 largest metro areas in the U.S. based on income inequality. San Francisco was ranked #3 (#1 = greatest inequality). Criteria: the "95/20 ratio," a figure representing the income at which a household earns more than 95 percent of all other households, divided by the income at which a household earns more than only 20 percent of all other households. *Brookings Institution, "Household Income Inequality, 100 Largest U.S. Metro Areas, 2014-2016," February 5, 2018*
- Payscale.com ranked the 32 largest metro areas in terms of wage growth. The San Francisco metro area ranked #32. Criteria: private-sector and education professional wage growth between the 4th quarter of 2019 and the 4th quarter of 2020. *PayScale, "Wage Trends by Metro Area-4th Quarter," January 11, 2021*
- The San Francisco metro area was identified as one of the most debt-ridden places in America by the finance site Credit.com. The metro area was ranked #15. Criteria: residents' average credit card debt as well as median income. *Credit.com, "25 Cities With the Most Credit Card Debt," February 28, 2018*

- For its annual survey of the "Most Expensive U.S. Cities to Live In," Kiplinger applied Cost of Living Index statistics developed by the Council for Community and Economic Research to U.S. Census Bureau population and median household income data for 256 urban areas. San Francisco was among the 20 most expensive in the country. *Kiplinger.com, "The 20 Most Expensive Cities in the U.S.," March 16, 2022*
- San Francisco was identified as one of America's most frugal metro areas by *Coupons.com.* The city ranked #14 out of 25. Criteria: digital coupon usage. *Coupons.com, "America's Most Frugal Cities of 2017," March 22, 2018*
- San Francisco was identified as one of the happiest cities to work in by CareerBliss.com, an online community for career advancement. The city ranked #1 out of 10. Criteria: an employee's relationship with his or her boss and co-workers; daily tasks; general work environment; compensation; opportunities for advancement; company culture and job reputation; and resources. *Businesswire.com, "CareerBliss Happiest Cities to Work 2019," February 12, 2019*
- The San Francisco metro area appeared on the Milken Institute "2021 Best Performing Cities" list. Rank: #24 out of 200 large metro areas (population over 250,000). Criteria: job growth; wage and salary growth; high-tech output growth; housing affordability; household broadband access. *Milken Institute, "Best-Performing Cities 2021," February 16, 2021*
- *Forbes* ranked the 200 most populous metro areas to determine the nation's "Best Places for Business and Careers." The San Francisco metro area was ranked #18. Criteria: costs (business and living); job growth (past and projected); income growth; quality of life; educational attainment (college and high school); projected economic growth; cultural and leisure opportunities; workplace tolerance laws; net migration patterns. *Forbes, "The Best Places for Business and Careers 2019: Seattle Still On Top," October 30, 2019*
- Mercer Human Resources Consulting ranked 209 cities worldwide in terms of cost-of-living. San Francisco ranked #25 (the lower the ranking, the higher the cost-of-living). The survey measured the comparative cost of over 200 items (such as housing, food, clothing, household goods, transportation, and entertainment) in each location. *Mercer, "2021 Cost of Living City Ranking," June 22, 2021*

Children/Family Rankings

- San Francisco was selected as one of the most playful cities in the U.S. by KaBOOM! The organization's Playful City USA initiative honors cities and towns across the nation that have made their communities more playable. Criteria: pledging to integrate play as a solution to challenges in their communities; making it easy for children to get active and balanced play; creating more family-friendly and innovative communities as a result. *KaBOOM! National Campaign for Play, "2017 Playful City USA Communities"*

Culture/Performing Arts Rankings

- San Francisco was selected as one of the 25 best cities for moviemakers in North America. COVID-19 has spurred a quest for great film cities that offer more creative space, lower costs, and more great outdoors. NYC & LA were intentionally excluded. Criteria: longstanding reputations as film-friendly communities; film community and culture; work life balance; and efforts to deal with pandemic-specific challenges. The city was ranked #16. *MovieMaker Magazine, "Best Places to Live and Work as a Moviemaker in 2022," January 25, 2022*

Education Rankings

- Personal finance website *WalletHub* analyzed the 150 largest U.S. metropolitan statistical areas to determine where the most educated Americans are putting their degrees to work. Criteria: education levels; percentage of workers with degrees; education quality and attainment gap; public school quality rankings; quality and enrollment of each metro area's universities. San Francisco was ranked #4 (#1 = most educated city). *www.WalletHub.com, "Most & Least Educated Cities in America," July 19, 2021*
- San Francisco was selected as one of America's most literate cities. The city ranked #3 out of the 84 largest U.S. cities. Criteria: number of booksellers; library resources; Internet resources; educational attainment; periodical publishing resources; newspaper circulation. *Central Connecticut State University, "America's Most Literate Cities, 2018," February 2019*

Environmental Rankings

- Sperling's BestPlaces assessed the 50 largest metropolitan areas of the United States for the likelihood of dangerously extreme weather events or earthquakes. In general the Southeast and South-Central regions have the highest risk of weather extremes and earthquakes, while the Pacific Northwest enjoys the lowest risk. Of the least risky metropolitan areas, the San Francisco metro area was ranked #4. *www.bestplaces.net, "Avoid Natural Disasters: BestPlaces Reveals The Top 10 Safest Places to Live," October 25, 2017*

- The U.S. Environmental Protection Agency (EPA) released its list of U.S. metropolitan areas with the most ENERGY STAR certified buildings in 2020. The San Francisco metro area was ranked #3 out of 25. *U.S. Environmental Protection Agency, "2021 Energy Star Top Cities," June 15, 2021*

Food/Drink Rankings

- The U.S. Chamber of Commerce Foundation conducted an in-depth study on local food truck regulations, surveyed 288 food truck owners, and ranked 20 major American cities based on how friendly they are for operating a food truck. The compiled index assessed the following: procedures for obtaining permits and licenses; complying with restrictions; and financial obligations associated with operating a food truck. San Francisco ranked #18 overall (1 being the best). *www.foodtrucknation.us, "Food Truck Nation," March 20, 2018*
- Oracle Park was selected as one of PETA's "Top 10 Vegan-Friendly Ballparks" for 2019. The park ranked #4. *People for the Ethical Treatment of Animals, "Top 10 Vegan-Friendly Ballparks," May 23, 2019*

Health/Fitness Rankings

- For each of the 100 largest cities in the United States, the American Fitness Index®, published by the American College of Sports Medicine and the Anthem Foundation, evaluated community infrastructure and 34 health behaviors including preventive health, levels of chronic disease conditions, food insecurity, sleep quality, pedestrian safety, air quality, and community resources that support physical activity. San Francisco ranked #13 for "community fitness." *americanfitnessindex.org, "2021 ACSM American Fitness Index Summary Report," July 13, 2021*
- San Francisco was identified as one of the 10 most walkable cities in the U.S. by Walk Score. The city ranked #2. Walk Score measures walkability by analyzing hundreds of walking routes to nearby amenities, and also measures pedestrian friendliness by analyzing population density and road metrics such as block length and intersection density. *WalkScore.com, April 13, 2021*
- The San Francisco metro area was identified as one of the worst cities for bed bugs in America by pest control company Orkin. The area ranked #19 out of 50 based on the number of bed bug treatments Orkin performed from December 2020 to November 2021. *Orkin, "Chicago Takes Another Top Spot for Pests, This Time Ranking #1 On Orkin's Bed Bug Cities List," January 10, 2022*
- San Francisco was identified as a "2021 Spring Allergy Capital." The area ranked #94 out of 100. Three groups of factors were used to identify the most challenging cities for people with allergies during the spring season: annual spring pollen levels; over the counter medicine use; number of board-certified allergy specialists. *Asthma and Allergy Foundation of America, "Spring Allergy Capitals 2021," February 23, 2021*
- San Francisco was identified as a "2021 Fall Allergy Capital." The area ranked #99 out of 100. Three groups of factors were used to identify the most challenging cities for people with allergies during the fall season: annual fall pollen levels; over the counter medicine use; number of board-certified allergy specialists. *Asthma and Allergy Foundation of America, "Fall Allergy Capitals 2021," February 23, 2021*
- San Francisco was identified as a "2021 Asthma Capital." The area ranked #91 out of the nation's 100 largest metropolitan areas. Criteria: estimated asthma prevalence; asthma-related mortality; and ER visits due to asthma. Risk factors analyzed but not factored in the rankings: annual pollen score; annual air quality; public smoking laws; number of board-certified asthma specialists; rescue medication use; controller medication use; uninsured rate; poverty rate. *Asthma and Allergy Foundation of America, "Asthma Capitals 2021: The Most Challenging Places to Live With Asthma," May 5, 2021*
- The Sharecare Community Well-Being Index evaluates 10 individual and social health factors in order to measure what matters to Americans in the communities in which they live. The San Francisco metro area ranked #1 in the top 10 across all 10 domains. Criteria: access to healthcare, food, and community resources; housng and transportation; economic security; feeling of purpose; physical, financial, social, and community well-being. *www.sharecare.com, "Community Well-Being Index: 2020 Metro Area & County Rankings Report," August 30, 2021*

Real Estate Rankings

- *WalletHub* compared the most populated U.S. cities to determine which had the best markets for real estate agents. San Francisco ranked #24 where demand was high and pay was the best. Criteria: sales per agent; annual median wage for real-estate agents; monthly average starting salary for real estate agents; real estate job density and competition; unemployment rate; home turnover rate; housing-market health index; and other relevant metrics. *www.WalletHub.com, "2021 Best Places to Be a Real Estate Agent," May 12, 2021*

- The San Francisco metro area was identified as one of the 10 worst condo markets in the U.S. in 2021. The area ranked #59 out of 63 markets. Criteria: year-over-year change of median sales price of existing apartment condo-coop homes between the 4th quarter of 2020 and the 4th quarter of 2021. *National Association of Realtors®, Median Sales Price of Existing Apartment Condo-Coops Homes for Metropolitan Areas, 4th Quarter 2021*
- The San Francisco metro area was identified as one of the 20 least affordable housing markets in the U.S. in 2021. The area ranked #182 out of 183 markets. Criteria: qualification for a mortgage loan with a 10 percent down payment on a typical home. *National Association of Realtors®, Qualifying Income Based on Sales Price of Existing Single-Family Homes for Metropolitan Areas, 2021*
- San Francisco was ranked #234 out of 237 metro areas in terms of housing affordability in 2021 by the National Association of Home Builders (#1 = most affordable). Criteria: the share of homes sold in that area affordable to a family earning the local median income, based on standard mortgage underwriting criteria. *National Association of Home Builders®, NAHB-Wells Fargo Housing Opportunity Index, 4th Quarter 2021*

Safety Rankings

- Allstate ranked the 200 largest cities in America in terms of driver safety. San Francisco ranked #189. Criteria: internal property damage claims over a two-year period from January 2016 to December 2017. The report helps increase the importance of safety and awareness behind the wheel. *Allstate, "Allstate America's Best Drivers Report, 2019" June 24, 2019*
- The National Insurance Crime Bureau ranked 390 metro areas in the U.S. in terms of per capita rates of vehicle theft. The San Francisco metro area ranked #5 (#1 = highest rate). Criteria: number of vehicle theft offenses per 100,000 inhabitants in 2020. *National Insurance Crime Bureau, "Hot Spots 2020," August 31, 2021*

Seniors/Retirement Rankings

- From its Best Cities for Successful Aging indexes, the Milken Institute generated rankings for metropolitan areas, weighing data in nine categories—health care, wellness, living arrangements, transportation and convenience, financial characteristics, education, employment, community engagement, and overall livability. The San Francisco metro area was ranked #11 overall in the large metro area category. *Milken Institute, "Best Cities for Successful Aging, 2017" March 14, 2017*

Sports/Recreation Rankings

- San Francisco was chosen as one of America's best cities for bicycling. The city ranked #2 out of 50. Criteria: cycling infrastructure that is safe and friendly for all ages; energy and bike culture. The editors evaluated cities with populations of 100,000 or more. *Bicycling, "The 50 Best Bike Cities in America," October 10, 2018*

Transportation Rankings

- Business Insider presented an AllTransit Performance Score ranking of public transportation in major U.S. cities and towns, with populations over 250,000, in which San Francisco earned the #1-ranked "Transit Score," awarded for frequency of service, access to jobs, quality and number of stops, and affordability. *www.businessinsider.com, "The 17 Major U.S. Cities with the Best Public Transportation," April 17, 2018*
- The business website 24/7 Wall Street reviewed U.S. Census data to identify the 25 cities where the largest share of households do not own a vehicle. San Francisco held the #10 position. *247wallst.com, "Cities Where No One Wants to Drive," February 15, 2017*
- San Francisco was identified as one of the most congested metro areas in the U.S. The area ranked #3 out of 10. Criteria: yearly delay per auto commuter in hours. *Texas A&M Transportation Institute, "2021 Urban Mobility Report," June 2021*
- According to the INRIX "2021 Global Traffic Scorecard," San Francisco was identified as one of the most congested metro areas in the U.S. The area ranked #7 out of 25. Criteria: average annual time spent in traffic and average cost of congestion per motorist. *Inrix.com, "Americans Lost 3.4 Billion Hours Due to Congestion in 2021, 42% Below Pre-COVID," December 7, 2021*

Women/Minorities Rankings

- *24/7 Wall St.* compared median annual earnings for men and women who worked full-time, year-round, female employment in management roles, bachelor's degree attainment among women, female life expectancy, uninsured rates, and preschool enrollment to identify the best cities for women. The U.S. metropolitan area, San Francisco was ranked #4 in pay disparity and other gender gaps. *24/7 Wall St., "The Easiest (and Toughest) Cities to Be a Woman," January 11, 2020*

- San Francisco was selected as one of the gayest cities in America by *The Advocate.* The city ranked #17 out of 25. Criteria, among many: Trans Pride parades/festivals; gay rugby teams; lesbian bars; LGBT centers; theater screenings of "Moonlight"; LGBT-inclusive nondiscrimination ordinances; and gay bowling teams. *The Advocate, "Queerest Cities in America 2017" January 12, 2017*
- Personal finance website *WalletHub* compared more than 180 U.S. cities across two key dimensions, "Hispanic Business-Friendliness" and "Hispanic Purchasing Power," to arrive at the most favorable conditions for Hispanic entrepreneurs. San Francisco was ranked #87 out of 182. Criteria includes: share of Hispanic-Owned Businesses; Hispanic entrepreneurship rate to median annual income of Hispanics; Small Business-Friendliness score; cost of living; and number of Hispanics with at least a bachelor's degree. *WalletHub.com, "2019's Best Cities for Hispanic Entrepreneurs," May 1, 2019*

Miscellaneous Rankings

- *MoveHub* ranked 446 hipster cities across 20 countries, using its *alternative* Hipster Index and San Francisco came out as #15 among the top 50. Criteria: population over 150,000; number of vintage boutiques; density of tattoo parlors; vegan places to eat; coffee shops; and density of vinyl record stores. *www.movehub.com, "The Hipster Index: Brighton Pips Portland to Global Top Spot," July 28, 2021*
- San Francisco was selected as a 2021 Digital Cities Survey winner. The city ranked #3 in the large city (500,000 or more population) category. The survey examined and assessed how city governments are utilizing technology to continue innovation, engage with residents, and persevere through the challenges of the pandemic. Survey questions focused on ten initiatives: cybersecurity; citizen experience; disaster recovery; business intelligence; IT personnel; data governance; budget control; IT governance; infrastructure modernization; and broadband connectivity. *Center for Digital Government, "2021 Digital Cities Survey," November 16, 2021*
- In its roundup of St. Patrick's Day parades "Gayot" listed the best festivals and parades of all things Irish. The festivities in San Francisco as among the best. *www.gayot.com, "Best St. Patrick's Day Parades," March 2022*
- The watchdog site, Charity Navigator, conducted a study of charities in major markets both to analyze statistical differences in their financial, accountability, and transparency practices and to track year-to-year variations in individual philanthropic communities. The San Francisco metro area was ranked #16 among the 30 metro markets in the rating category of Overall Score. *www.charitynavigator.org, "2017 Metro Market Study," May 1, 2017*
- *WalletHub* compared the 150 most populated U.S. cities to determine their operating efficiency. A "Quality of City Services" score was constructed for each city and then divided by the total budget per capita to reveal which were managed the best. San Francisco ranked #149. Criteria: financial stability; economy; education; safety; health; infrastructure and pollution. *www.WalletHub.com, "2021's Best- & Worst-Run Cities in America," June 22, 2021*
- The National Alliance to End Homelessness listed the 25 most populous metro areas with the highest rate of homelessness. The San Francisco metro area had a high rate of homelessness. Criteria: number of homeless people per 10,000 population in 2016. *National Alliance to End Homelessness, "Homelessness in the 25 Most Populous U.S. Metro Areas," September 1, 2017*

Business Environment

DEMOGRAPHICS

Population Growth

Area	1990 Census	2000 Census	2010 Census	2020* Estimate	Population Growth (%) 1990-2020	Population Growth (%) 2010-2020
City	723,959	776,733	805,235	874,784	20.8	8.6
MSA[1]	3,686,592	4,123,740	4,335,391	4,709,220	27.7	8.6
U.S.	248,709,873	281,421,906	308,745,538	326,569,308	31.3	5.8

Note: (1) Figures cover the San Francisco-Oakland-Hayward, CA Metropolitan Statistical Area; (*) 2016-2020 5-year estimated population
Source: U.S. Census Bureau, 1990 Census, Census 2000, Census 2010, 2016-2020 American Community Survey 5-Year Estimates

Household Size

Area	Persons in Household (%): One	Two	Three	Four	Five	Six	Seven or More	Average Household Size
City	36.3	33.0	14.4	10.1	3.4	1.4	1.4	2.40
MSA[1]	26.3	31.8	17.0	14.9	6.1	2.2	1.6	2.70
U.S.	28.0	33.9	15.5	12.9	6.0	2.3	1.4	2.60

Note: (1) Figures cover the San Francisco-Oakland-Hayward, CA Metropolitan Statistical Area
Source: U.S. Census Bureau, 2016-2020 American Community Survey 5-Year Estimates

Race

Area	White Alone[2] (%)	Black Alone[2] (%)	Asian Alone[2] (%)	AIAN[3] Alone[2] (%)	NHOPI[4] Alone[2] (%)	Other Race Alone[2] (%)	Two or More Races (%)
City	44.9	5.1	34.3	0.4	0.4	7.7	7.2
MSA[1]	46.7	7.2	26.8	0.5	0.7	10.2	7.9
U.S.	70.4	12.6	5.6	0.8	0.2	5.1	5.2

Note: (1) Figures cover the San Francisco-Oakland-Hayward, CA Metropolitan Statistical Area; (2) Alone is defined as not being in combination with one or more other races; (3) American Indian and Alaska Native; (4) Native Hawaiian and Other Pacific Islander
Source: U.S. Census Bureau, 2016-2020 American Community Survey 5-Year Estimates

Hispanic or Latino Origin

Area	Total (%)	Mexican (%)	Puerto Rican (%)	Cuban (%)	Other (%)
City	15.2	7.7	0.6	0.3	6.7
MSA[1]	21.8	14.0	0.7	0.2	6.9
U.S.	18.2	11.2	1.7	0.7	4.5

Note: Persons of Hispanic or Latino origin can be of any race; (1) Figures cover the San Francisco-Oakland-Hayward, CA Metropolitan Statistical Area
Source: U.S. Census Bureau, 2016-2020 American Community Survey 5-Year Estimates

Ancestry

Area	German	Irish	English	American	Italian	Polish	French[2]	Scottish	Dutch
City	7.1	7.7	5.2	2.6	4.6	1.9	2.2	1.3	0.8
MSA[1]	7.5	7.2	6.0	2.4	4.6	1.5	1.9	1.4	0.8
U.S.	13.0	9.7	7.7	5.9	5.1	2.7	2.3	1.6	1.1

Note: Figures are the percentage of the total population reporting a particular ancestry. The nine most commonly reported ancestries in the U.S. are shown. Figures include multiple ancestries (e.g. if a person reported being Irish and Italian, they were included in both columns); (1) Figures cover the San Francisco-Oakland-Hayward, CA Metropolitan Statistical Area; (2) Excludes Basque
Source: U.S. Census Bureau, 2016-2020 American Community Survey 5-Year Estimates

Foreign-born Population

Area	Percent of Population Born in: Any Foreign Country	Asia	Mexico	Europe	Caribbean	Central America[2]	South America	Africa	Canada
City	34.2	22.1	2.3	4.6	0.2	2.4	1.1	0.5	0.6
MSA[1]	30.7	17.7	4.6	2.8	0.2	2.4	1.0	0.9	0.4
U.S.	13.5	4.2	3.3	1.5	1.3	1.1	1.0	0.7	0.3

Note: (1) Figures cover the San Francisco-Oakland-Hayward, CA Metropolitan Statistical Area; (2) Excludes Mexico.
Source: U.S. Census Bureau, 2016-2020 American Community Survey 5-Year Estimates

Marital Status

Area	Never Married	Now Married[2]	Separated	Widowed	Divorced
City	46.3	39.7	1.4	4.6	7.9
MSA[1]	36.6	48.5	1.5	4.7	8.8
U.S.	33.5	48.1	1.8	5.7	10.8

Note: Figures are percentages and cover the population 15 years of age and older; (1) Figures cover the San Francisco-Oakland-Hayward, CA Metropolitan Statistical Area; (2) Excludes separated
Source: U.S. Census Bureau, 2016-2020 American Community Survey 5-Year Estimates

Disability by Age

Area	All Ages	Under 18 Years Old	18 to 64 Years Old	65 Years and Over
City	10.1	2.5	6.3	34.1
MSA[1]	9.7	2.9	6.7	30.7
U.S.	12.7	4.3	10.3	34.0

Note: Figures show percent of the civilian noninstitutionalized population that reported having a disability. Disability status is determined from six types of difficulty: vision, hearing, cognitive, ambulatory, self-care, and independent living. For children under 5 years old, hearing and vision difficulty are used to determine disability status. For children between the ages of 5 and 14, disability status is determined from hearing, vision, cognitive, ambulatory, and self-care difficulties. For people aged 15 years and older, they are considered to have a disability if they have difficulty with any one of the six difficulty types; Note: (1) Figures cover the San Francisco-Oakland-Hayward, CA Metropolitan Statistical Area
Source: U.S. Census Bureau, 2016-2020 American Community Survey 5-Year Estimates

Age

Area	Percent of Population									Median Age
	Under Age 5	Age 5–19	Age 20–34	Age 35–44	Age 45–54	Age 55–64	Age 65–74	Age 75–84	Age 85+	
City	4.5	10.4	28.8	15.8	13.1	11.6	8.7	4.4	2.6	38.3
MSA[1]	5.4	16.4	21.9	14.5	13.6	12.6	9.0	4.4	2.2	39.1
U.S.	6.0	19.1	20.6	12.7	12.7	12.9	9.4	4.7	2.0	38.2

Note: (1) Figures cover the San Francisco-Oakland-Hayward, CA Metropolitan Statistical Area
Source: U.S. Census Bureau, 2016-2020 American Community Survey 5-Year Estimates

Gender

Area	Males	Females	Males per 100 Females
City	446,246	428,538	104.1
MSA[1]	2,330,358	2,378,862	98.0
U.S.	160,818,530	165,750,778	97.0

Note: (1) Figures cover the San Francisco-Oakland-Hayward, CA Metropolitan Statistical Area
Source: U.S. Census Bureau, 2016-2020 American Community Survey 5-Year Estimates

Religious Groups by Family

Area	Catholic	Baptist	Non-Den.	Methodist[2]	Lutheran	LDS[3]	Pente-costal	Presby-terian[4]	Muslim[5]	Judaism
MSA[1]	20.8	2.5	2.5	2.0	0.6	1.6	1.2	1.1	1.2	0.9
U.S.	19.1	9.3	4.0	4.0	2.3	2.0	1.9	1.6	0.8	0.7

Note: Figures are the number of adherents as a percentage of the total population; (1) Figures cover the San Francisco-Oakland-Hayward, CA Metropolitan Statistical Area; (2) Methodist/Pietist; (3) Latter Day Saints; (4) Reformed; (5) Figures are estimates
Source: Association of Statisticians of American Religious Bodies, 2010 U.S. Religion Census: Religious Congregations & Membership Study

Religious Groups by Tradition

Area	Catholic	Evangelical Protestant	Mainline Protestant	Other Tradition	Black Protestant	Orthodox
MSA[1]	20.8	6.2	3.8	5.2	1.1	0.7
U.S.	19.1	16.2	7.3	4.3	1.6	0.3

Note: Figures are the number of adherents as a percentage of the total population; (1) Figures cover the San Francisco-Oakland-Hayward, CA Metropolitan Statistical Area
Source: Association of Statisticians of American Religious Bodies, 2010 U.S. Religion Census: Religious Congregations & Membership Study

ECONOMY

Gross Metropolitan Product

Area	2017	2018	2019	2020	Rank[2]
MSA[1]	512.2	547.3	578.7	605.5	6

Note: Figures are in billions of dollars; (1) Figures cover the San Francisco-Oakland-Hayward, CA Metropolitan Statistical Area; (2) Rank is based on 2018 data and ranges from 1 to 381
Source: U.S. Conference of Mayors, U.S. Metro Economies: GMP & Employment 2018-2020, September 2019

Economic Growth

Area	2015-17 (%)	2018 (%)	2019 (%)	2020 (%)	Rank[2]
MSA[1]	4.8	5.1	4.3	2.5	18
U.S.	1.9	2.9	2.3	2.1	–

Note: Figures are real gross metropolitan product (GMP) growth rates and represent average annual percent change; (1) Figures cover the San Francisco-Oakland-Hayward, CA Metropolitan Statistical Area; (2) Rank is based on 2017 2-year average annual percent change and ranges from 1 to 381
Source: U.S. Conference of Mayors, U.S. Metro Economies: GMP & Employment 2018-2020, September 2019

Metropolitan Area Exports

Area	2015	2016	2017	2018	2019	2020	Rank[2]
MSA[1]	25,061.1	24,506.3	29,103.8	27,417.0	28,003.8	23,864.5	13

Note: Figures are in millions of dollars; (1) Figures cover the San Francisco-Oakland-Hayward, CA Metropolitan Statistical Area; (2) Rank is based on 2020 data and ranges from 1 to 389
Source: U.S. Department of Commerce, International Trade Administration, Office of Trade and Economic Analysis, Industry and Analysis, Exports by Metropolitan Area, data extracted March 4, 2022

Building Permits

Area	Single-Family			Multi-Family			Total		
	2019	2020	Pct. Chg.	2019	2020	Pct. Chg.	2019	2020	Pct. Chg.
City	22	21	-4.5	3,178	1,983	-37.6	3,200	2,004	-37.4
MSA[1]	4,076	3,386	-16.9	9,805	6,770	-31.0	13,881	10,156	-26.8
U.S.	862,100	979,400	13.6	523,900	491,700	-6.1	1,386,000	1,471,100	6.1

Note: (1) Figures cover the San Francisco-Oakland-Hayward, CA Metropolitan Statistical Area; Figures represent new, privately-owned housing units authorized (unadjusted data); All permit data are based on estimates with imputation
Source: U.S. Census Bureau, Manufacturing, Mining, and Construction Statistics, Building Permits, 2019, 2020

Bankruptcy Filings

Area	Business Filings			Nonbusiness Filings		
	2020	2021	% Chg.	2020	2021	% Chg.
San Francisco County	67	65	-3.0	384	334	-13.0
U.S.	21,655	14,347	-33.7	522,808	399,269	-23.6

Note: Business filings include Chapter 7, Chapter 9, Chapter 11, Chapter 12, Chapter 13, Chapter 15, and Section 304; Nonbusiness filings include Chapter 7, Chapter 11, and Chapter 13
Source: Administrative Office of the U.S. Courts, Business and Nonbusiness Bankruptcy, County Cases Commenced by Chapter of the Bankruptcy Code, During the 12-Month Period Ending December 31, 2020 and Business and Nonbusiness Bankruptcy, County Cases Commenced by Chapter of the Bankruptcy Code, During the 12-Month Period Ending December 31, 2021

Housing Vacancy Rates

Area	Gross Vacancy Rate[2] (%)			Year-Round Vacancy Rate[3] (%)			Rental Vacancy Rate[4] (%)			Homeowner Vacancy Rate[5] (%)		
	2019	2020	2021	2019	2020	2021	2019	2020	2021	2019	2020	2021
MSA[1]	7.1	6.4	7.6	6.9	6.2	7.3	3.8	5.3	6.5	0.9	0.5	1.1
U.S.	12.0	10.6	10.8	9.5	8.2	8.4	6.7	6.3	6.1	1.4	1.0	0.9

Note: (1) Figures cover the San Francisco-Oakland-Hayward, CA Metropolitan Statistical Area; (2) The percentage of the total housing inventory that is vacant; (3) The percentage of the housing inventory (excluding seasonal units) that is year-round vacant; (4) The percentage of rental inventory that is vacant for rent; (5) The percentage of homeowner inventory that is vacant for sale
Source: U.S. Census Bureau, Housing Vacancies and Homeownership Annual Statistics: 2019, 2020, 2021

INCOME

Income

Area	Per Capita ($)	Median Household ($)	Average Household ($)
City	72,041	119,136	167,663
MSA[1]	57,778	110,837	154,773
U.S.	35,384	64,994	91,547

Note: (1) Figures cover the San Francisco-Oakland-Hayward, CA Metropolitan Statistical Area
Source: U.S. Census Bureau, 2016-2020 American Community Survey 5-Year Estimates

Household Income Distribution

Area	Percent of Households Earning							
	Under $15,000	$15,000 -$24,999	$25,000 -$34,999	$35,000 -$49,999	$50,000 -$74,999	$75,000 -$99,999	$100,000 -$149,999	$150,000 and up
City	9.4	5.4	4.6	5.9	9.8	8.7	15.2	41.0
MSA[1]	6.9	4.8	4.8	6.7	11.4	10.7	17.4	37.2
U.S.	9.9	8.5	8.6	12.0	17.2	12.8	15.6	15.4

Note: (1) Figures cover the San Francisco-Oakland-Hayward, CA Metropolitan Statistical Area
Source: U.S. Census Bureau, 2016-2020 American Community Survey 5-Year Estimates

Poverty Rate

Area	All Ages	Under 18 Years Old	18 to 64 Years Old	65 Years and Over
City	10.1	9.8	9.3	13.9
MSA[1]	8.5	9.3	8.2	8.9
U.S.	12.8	17.5	12.1	9.3

Note: Figures are percentage of people whose income during the past 12 months was below the poverty level; (1) Figures cover the San Francisco-Oakland-Hayward, CA Metropolitan Statistical Area
Source: U.S. Census Bureau, 2016-2020 American Community Survey 5-Year Estimates

CITY FINANCES

City Government Finances

Component	2019 ($000)	2019 ($ per capita)
Total Revenues	14,153,040	16,004
Total Expenditures	14,670,763	16,589
Debt Outstanding	22,084,197	24,972
Cash and Securities[1]	10,233,455	11,572

Note: (1) Cash and security holdings of a government at the close of its fiscal year, including those of its dependent agencies, utilities, and liquor stores.
Source: U.S. Census Bureau, State & Local Government Finances 2019

City Government Revenue by Source

Source	2019 ($000)	2019 ($ per capita)	2019 (%)
General Revenue			
From Federal Government	574,662	650	4.1
From State Government	2,017,172	2,281	14.3
From Local Governments	785,188	888	5.5
Taxes			
Property	2,955,920	3,342	20.9
Sales and Gross Receipts	1,029,181	1,164	7.3
Personal Income	0	0	0.0
Corporate Income	0	0	0.0
Motor Vehicle License	4,376	5	0.0
Other Taxes	1,383,761	1,565	9.8
Current Charges	3,323,636	3,758	23.5
Liquor Store	0	0	0.0
Utility	1,064,786	1,204	7.5

Source: U.S. Census Bureau, State & Local Government Finances 2019

City Government Expenditures by Function

Function	2019 ($000)	2019 ($ per capita)	2019 (%)
General Direct Expenditures			
Air Transportation	1,995,559	2,256	13.6
Corrections	245,066	277	1.7
Education	0	0	0.0
Employment Security Administration	0	0	0.0
Financial Administration	79,772	90	0.5
Fire Protection	321,128	363	2.2
General Public Buildings	0	0	0.0
Governmental Administration, Other	421,003	476	2.9
Health	2,055,163	2,323	14.0
Highways	245,467	277	1.7
Hospitals	1,053,950	1,191	7.2
Housing and Community Development	410,422	464	2.8
Interest on General Debt	657,192	743	4.5
Judicial and Legal	139,377	157	1.0
Libraries	123,833	140	0.8
Parking	181,515	205	1.2
Parks and Recreation	399,216	451	2.7
Police Protection	577,814	653	3.9
Public Welfare	1,398,357	1,581	9.5
Sewerage	466,549	527	3.2
Solid Waste Management	0	0	0.0
Veterans' Services	0	0	0.0
Liquor Store	0	0	0.0
Utility	2,737,735	3,095	18.7

Source: U.S. Census Bureau, State & Local Government Finances 2019

EMPLOYMENT

Labor Force and Employment

Area	Civilian Labor Force			Workers Employed		
	Dec. 2020	Dec. 2021	% Chg.	Dec. 2020	Dec. 2021	% Chg.
City	541,641	566,632	4.6	506,712	549,426	8.4
MD[1]	966,070	1,012,179	4.8	906,405	982,508	8.4
U.S.	160,017,000	161,696,000	1.0	149,613,000	155,732,000	4.1

Note: Data is not seasonally adjusted and covers workers 16 years of age and older; (1) Figures cover the San Francisco-Redwood City-South San Francisco, CA Metropolitan Division
Source: Bureau of Labor Statistics, Local Area Unemployment Statistics

Unemployment Rate

Area	2021											
	Jan.	Feb.	Mar.	Apr.	May	Jun.	Jul.	Aug.	Sep.	Oct.	Nov.	Dec.
City	6.2	5.7	5.4	5.3	5.1	5.5	5.2	5.0	4.1	3.9	3.3	3.0
MD[1]	6.0	5.5	5.2	5.1	4.8	5.3	5.1	4.8	4.0	3.8	3.2	2.9
U.S.	6.8	6.6	6.2	5.7	5.5	6.1	5.7	5.3	4.6	4.3	3.9	3.7

Note: Data is not seasonally adjusted and covers workers 16 years of age and older; (1) Figures cover the San Francisco-Redwood City-South San Francisco, CA Metropolitan Division
Source: Bureau of Labor Statistics, Local Area Unemployment Statistics

Average Wages

Occupation	$/Hr.	Occupation	$/Hr.
Accountants and Auditors	51.70	Maintenance and Repair Workers	28.96
Automotive Mechanics	29.49	Marketing Managers	95.61
Bookkeepers	28.21	Network and Computer Systems Admin.	55.95
Carpenters	37.64	Nurses, Licensed Practical	36.26
Cashiers	17.74	Nurses, Registered	72.90
Computer Programmers	60.68	Nursing Assistants	22.84
Computer Systems Analysts	63.29	Office Clerks, General	24.03
Computer User Support Specialists	36.98	Physical Therapists	56.91
Construction Laborers	28.76	Physicians	125.00
Cooks, Restaurant	19.85	Plumbers, Pipefitters and Steamfitters	43.03
Customer Service Representatives	24.29	Police and Sheriff's Patrol Officers	56.95
Dentists	87.36	Postal Service Mail Carriers	27.32
Electricians	45.14	Real Estate Sales Agents	35.35
Engineers, Electrical	64.25	Retail Salespersons	19.78
Fast Food and Counter Workers	17.48	Sales Representatives, Technical/Scientific	57.95
Financial Managers	90.82	Secretaries, Exc. Legal/Medical/Executive	27.27
First-Line Supervisors of Office Workers	37.71	Security Guards	20.98
General and Operations Managers	73.32	Surgeons	n/a
Hairdressers/Cosmetologists	18.85	Teacher Assistants, Exc. Postsecondary*	20.59
Home Health and Personal Care Aides	16.97	Teachers, Secondary School, Exc. Sp. Ed.*	45.41
Janitors and Cleaners	20.21	Telemarketers	19.78
Landscaping/Groundskeeping Workers	22.91	Truck Drivers, Heavy/Tractor-Trailer	29.95
Lawyers	92.05	Truck Drivers, Light/Delivery Services	24.79
Maids and Housekeeping Cleaners	21.43	Waiters and Waitresses	18.09

Note: Wage data covers the San Francisco-Oakland-Hayward, CA Metropolitan Statistical Area; (*) Hourly wages were calculated from annual wage data based on a 40 hour work week; n/a not available.
Source: Bureau of Labor Statistics, Metro Area Occupational Employment & Wage Estimates, May 2021

Employment by Industry

Sector	MD[1]		U.S.
	Number of Employees	Percent of Total	Percent of Total
Construction	41,500	3.6	5.0
Education and Health Services	148,700	13.0	16.0
Financial Activities	84,800	7.4	5.9
Government	132,100	11.6	14.9
Information	117,500	10.3	1.9
Leisure and Hospitality	106,200	9.3	9.8
Manufacturing	37,900	3.3	8.4
Mining and Logging	200	<0.1	0.4
Other Services	37,500	3.3	3.7
Professional and Business Services	295,400	25.8	14.6
Retail Trade	71,000	6.2	10.7
Transportation, Warehousing, and Utilities	48,900	4.3	4.8
Wholesale Trade	22,000	1.9	3.8

Note: Figures are non-farm employment as of December 2021. Figures are not seasonally adjusted and include workers 16 years of age and older; (1) Figures cover the San Francisco-Redwood City-South San Francisco, CA Metropolitan Division
Source: Bureau of Labor Statistics, Current Employment Statistics, Employment, Hours, and Earnings

Employment by Occupation

Occupation Classification	City (%)	MSA[1] (%)	U.S. (%)
Management, Business, Science, and Arts	59.1	51.9	39.5
Natural Resources, Construction, and Maintenance	2.9	5.6	8.7
Production, Transportation, and Material Moving	5.6	8.1	13.1
Sales and Office	17.6	18.8	21.3
Service	14.9	15.6	17.4

Note: Figures cover employed civilians 16 years of age and older; (1) Figures cover the San Francisco-Oakland-Hayward, CA Metropolitan Statistical Area
Source: U.S. Census Bureau, 2016-2020 American Community Survey 5-Year Estimates

Occupations with Greatest Projected Employment Growth: 2021 – 2023

Occupation[1]	2021 Employment	2023 Projected Employment	Numeric Employment Change	Percent Employment Change
Fast Food and Counter Workers	383,500	457,000	73,500	19.2
Home Health and Personal Care Aides	663,400	716,600	53,200	8.0
Waiters and Waitresses	208,500	257,600	49,100	23.5
Cooks, Restaurant	136,700	175,300	38,600	28.2
Laborers and Freight, Stock, and Material Movers, Hand	401,500	431,600	30,100	7.5
Software Developers and Software Quality Assurance Analysts and Testers	311,600	336,800	25,200	8.1
Janitors and Cleaners, Except Maids and Housekeeping Cleaners	232,200	252,400	20,200	8.7
Cooks, Fast Food	109,600	128,200	18,600	17.0
Stockers and Order Fillers	273,000	290,400	17,400	6.4
First-Line Supervisors of Food Preparation and Serving Workers	81,700	98,600	16,900	20.7

Note: Projections cover California; (1) Sorted by numeric employment change
Source: www.projectionscentral.com, State Occupational Projections, 2021–2023 Short-Term Projections

Fastest-Growing Occupations: 2021 – 2023

Occupation[1]	2021 Employment	2023 Projected Employment	Numeric Employment Change	Percent Employment Change
Manicurists and Pedicurists	23,400	33,500	10,100	43.2
Cooks, All Other	3,900	5,400	1,500	38.5
Miscellaneous Entertainers and Performers, Sports and Related Workers	5,900	8,100	2,200	37.3
Barbers	1,900	2,600	700	36.8
Gaming Change Persons and Booth Cashiers	2,200	3,000	800	36.4
Gaming Service Workers, All Other	1,400	1,900	500	35.7
Gaming Dealers	12,200	16,500	4,300	35.2
First-Line Supervisors of Gambling Services Workers	2,900	3,900	1,000	34.5
Massage Therapists	18,000	24,200	6,200	34.4
Costume Attendants	1,500	2,000	500	33.3

Note: Projections cover California; (1) Sorted by percent employment change and excludes occupations with numeric employment change less than 50
Source: www.projectionscentral.com, State Occupational Projections, 2021–2023 Short-Term Projections

TAXES

State Corporate Income Tax Rates

State	Tax Rate (%)	Income Brackets ($)	Num. of Brackets	Financial Institution Tax Rate (%)[a]	Federal Income Tax Ded.
California	8.84 (b)	Flat rate	1	10.84 (b)	No

Note: Tax rates as of January 1, 2022; (a) Rates listed are the corporate income tax rate applied to financial institutions or excise taxes based on income. Some states have other taxes based upon the value of deposits or shares; (b) Minimum tax is $800 in California, $250 in District of Columbia, $50 in Arizona and North Dakota (banks), $400 ($100 banks) in Rhode Island, $200 per location in South Dakota (banks), $100 in Utah, $300 in Vermont.
Source: Federation of Tax Administrators, State Corporate Income Tax Rates, January 1, 2022

State Individual Income Tax Rates

State	Tax Rate (%)	Income Brackets ($)	Personal Exemptions ($)			Standard Ded. ($)	
			Single	Married	Depend.	Single	Married
California (a)	1.0 - 12.3 (g)	9,325 - 625,369 (b)	129	258	400 (c)	4,803	9,606 (a)

Note: Tax rates as of January 1, 2022; Local- and county-level taxes are not included; Federal income tax is not deductible on state income tax returns; (a) 19 states have statutory provision for automatically adjusting to the rate of inflation the dollar values of the income tax brackets, standard deductions, and/or personal exemptions. Michigan indexes the personal exemption only. Oregon does not index the income brackets for $125,000 and over; (b) For joint returns, taxes are twice the tax on half the couple's income; (c) The personal exemption takes the form of a tax credit instead of a deduction; (g) California imposes an additional 1% tax on taxable income over $1 million, making the maximum rate 13.3% over $1 million.
Source: Federation of Tax Administrators, State Individual Income Tax Rates, January 1, 2022

Various State Sales and Excise Tax Rates

State	State Sales Tax (%)	Gasoline[1] (¢/gal.)	Cigarette[2] ($/pack)	Spirits[3] ($/gal.)	Wine[4] ($/gal.)	Beer[5] ($/gal.)	Recreational Marijuana (%)
California	7.25	68.15	2.87	3.3	0.2	0.2	(c)

Note: All tax rates as of January 1, 2022; (1) The American Petroleum Institute has developed a methodology for determining the average tax rate on a gallon of fuel. Rates may include any of the following: excise taxes, environmental fees, storage tank fees, other fees or taxes, general sales tax, and local taxes; (2) The federal excise tax of $1.0066 per pack and local taxes are not included; (3) Rates are those applicable to off-premise sales of 40% alcohol by volume (a.b.v.) distilled spirits in 750ml containers. Local excise taxes are excluded; (4) Rates are those applicable to off-premise sales of 11% a.b.v. non-carbonated wine in 750ml containers; (5) Rates are those applicable to off-premise sales of 4.7% a.b.v. beer in 12 ounce containers; (c) 15% excise tax (levied on wholesale at average market rate); $10.08/oz. flowers & $3/oz. leaves cultivation tax; $1.41/oz fresh cannabis plant
Source: Tax Foundation, 2022 Facts & Figures: How Does Your State Compare?

State Business Tax Climate Index Rankings

State	Overall Rank	Corporate Tax Rank	Individual Income Tax Rank	Sales Tax Rank	Property Tax Rank	Unemployment Insurance Tax Rank
California	48	46	49	47	14	23

Note: The index is a measure of how each state's tax laws affect economic performance. The lower the rank, the more favorable a state's tax system is for business. States without a given tax are given a ranking of 1. The scores/rankings for the District of Columbia do not affect other states. The 2022 index represents the tax climate as of July 1, 2021.
Source: Tax Foundation, State Business Tax Climate Index 2022

TRANSPORTATION

Means of Transportation to Work

Area	Car/Truck/Van		Public Transportation			Bicycle	Walked	Other Means	Worked at Home
	Drove Alone	Car-pooled	Bus	Subway	Railroad				
City	30.5	6.8	19.9	8.2	1.5	3.7	11.7	6.0	11.8
MSA[1]	55.5	9.2	6.9	6.8	1.4	1.7	4.6	3.0	11.0
U.S.	74.9	8.9	2.2	1.7	0.5	0.5	2.6	1.4	7.3

Note: Figures are percentages and cover workers 16 years of age and older; (1) Figures cover the San Francisco-Oakland-Hayward, CA Metropolitan Statistical Area
Source: U.S. Census Bureau, 2016-2020 American Community Survey 5-Year Estimates

Travel Time to Work

Area	Less Than 10 Minutes	10 to 19 Minutes	20 to 29 Minutes	30 to 44 Minutes	45 to 59 Minutes	60 to 89 Minutes	90 Minutes or More
City	4.2	18.8	20.8	29.8	12.0	10.6	3.8
MSA[1]	6.6	22.3	17.4	23.7	12.3	12.6	5.1
U.S.	12.3	28.4	20.9	20.9	8.3	6.4	2.9

Note: Note: Figures are percentages and include workers 16 years old and over; (1) Figures cover the San Francisco-Oakland-Hayward, CA Metropolitan Statistical Area
Source: U.S. Census Bureau, 2016-2020 American Community Survey 5-Year Estimates

Key Congestion Measures

Measure	1990	2000	2010	2015	2020
Annual Hours of Delay, Total (000)	131,150	182,881	208,286	245,689	112,507
Annual Hours of Delay, Per Auto Commuter	68	79	90	101	46
Annual Congestion Cost, Per Auto Commuter ($)	2,590	2,713	2,456	2,675	1,301

Note: Covers the San Francisco-Oakland CA urban area
Source: Texas A&M Transportation Institute, 2021 Urban Mobility Report

Freeway Travel Time Index

Measure	1985	1990	1995	2000	2005	2010	2015	2020
Urban Area Index[1]	1.30	1.32	1.36	1.38	1.40	1.41	1.49	1.16
Urban Area Rank[1,2]	2	2	2	2	2	2	1	2

Note: Freeway Travel Time Index—the ratio of travel time in the peak period to the travel time at free-flow conditions. For example, a value of 1.30 indicates a 20-minute free-flow trip takes 26 minutes in the peak (20 minutes x 1.30 = 26 minutes); (1) Covers the San Francisco-Oakland CA urban area; (2) Rank is based on 101 larger urban areas (#1 = highest travel time index)
Source: Texas A&M Transportation Institute, 2021 Urban Mobility Report

Public Transportation

Agency Name / Mode of Transportation	Vehicles Operated in Maximum Service[1]	Annual Unlinked Passenger Trips[2] (in thous.)	Annual Passenger Miles[3] (in thous.)
San Francisco Municipal Railway (MUNI)			
Bus (directly operated)	469	86,174.8	176,249.3
Cable Car (directly operated)	27	4,012.5	5,213.3
Demand Response (purchased transportation)	134	309.1	2,105.7
Light Rail (directly operated)	149	37,419.4	102,607.8
Streetcar Rail (directly operated)	22	4,580.2	6,604.8
Trolleybus (directly operated)	195	38,098.3	52,097.8
San Francisco Bay Area Rapid Transit District (BART)			
Heavy Rail (directly operated)	599	88,698.9	1,238,506.2
Hybrid Rail (directly operated)	14	1,735.0	11,655.9
Monorail and Automated Guideway (purchased transportation)	3	573.1	1,822.5

Note: (1) Number of revenue vehicles operated by the given mode and type of service to meet the annual maximum service requirement. This is the revenue vehicle count during the peak season of the year; on the week and day that maximum service is provided. Vehicles operated in maximum service (VOMS) exclude atypical days and one-time special events; (2) Number of passengers who boarded public transportation vehicles. Passengers are counted each time they board a vehicle no matter how many vehicles they use to travel from their origin to their destination. (3) Sum of the distances ridden by all passengers during the entire fiscal year.
Source: Federal Transit Administration, National Transit Database, 2020

Air Transportation

Airport Name and Code / Type of Service	Passenger Airlines[1]	Passenger Enplanements	Freight Carriers[2]	Freight (lbs)
San Francisco International (SFO)				
Domestic service (U.S. carriers - 2021)	20	10,255,569	15	210,298,298
International service (U.S. carriers - 2020)	6	612,075	3	68,829,230

Note: (1) Includes all U.S.-based major, minor and commuter airlines that carried at least one passenger during the year; (2) Includes all U.S.-based airlines and freight carriers that transported at least one pound of freight during the year.
Source: Bureau of Transportation Statistics, The Intermodal Transportation Database, Air Carriers: T-100 Domestic Market (U.S. Carriers), 2021; Bureau of Transportation Statistics, The Intermodal Transportation Database, Air Carriers: T-100 International Market (U.S. Carriers), 2020

BUSINESSES

Major Business Headquarters

Company Name	Industry	Rankings	
		Fortune[1]	Forbes[2]
Block	Consumer Credit Card and Related Services	323	-
Charles Schwab	Securities	251	-
Gap	Specialty Retailers, Apparel	221	-
McKesson	Wholesalers, Health Care	7	-
PG&E	Utilities, Gas and Electric	160	-
Salesforce	Computer Software	137	-
Swinerton	Construction	-	86
Uber Technologies	Internet Services and Retailing	281	-
Wells Fargo	Commercial Banks	37	-
Wilbur-Ellis	Chemicals	-	156
Williams-Sonoma	Specialty Retailers, Other	425	-

Note: (1) Companies that produce a 10-K are ranked 1 to 500 based on 2020 revenue; (2) All private companies with at least $2 billion in annual revenue through the end of their most current fiscal year are ranked 1 to 225; companies listed are headquartered in the city; dashes indicate no ranking
Source: Fortune, "Fortune 500," 2021; Forbes, "America's Largest Private Companies," 2021

Fastest-Growing Businesses

According to *Inc.*, San Francisco is home to 14 of America's 500 fastest-growing private companies: **Carbon Health** (#2); **Varo Bank** (#7); **Pilot** (#63); **Bolt** (#64); **Outschool** (#70); **Montaro** (#96);

Lattice (#145); **Affinity** (#156); **Arkose Labs** (#195); **Premise Data** (#286); **Velano Vascular** (#347); **Picsart** (#375); **Juniper Square** (#425); **Upgrade** (#482). Criteria: must be an independent, privately-held, for-profit, U.S. corporation, proprietorship or partnership as of December 31, 2020; revenues must be at least $100,000 in 2017 and $2 million in 2020; must have four-year operating/sales history. *Inc., "America's 500 Fastest-Growing Private Companies," 2021*

According to *Fortune*, San Francisco is home to one of the 100 fastest-growing companies in the world: **Salesforce** (#37). Companies were ranked by their revenue growth rate; their EPS growth rate; and their three-year annualized total return to investors for the period ending June 30, 2021. Criteria for inclusion: a company, foreign or domestic, must trade on a major U.S. stock exchange; must file quarterly reports with the SEC; must have a minimum market capitalization of $250 million; must have a stock price of at least $5 on June 30, 2021; must have been trading continuously since June 30, 2018; must have revenue and net income for the four quarters ended on or before April 30, 2021, of at least $50 million and $10 million, respectively; and must have posted a compound annual growth in revenue and earnings per share of at least 15% annually over the three years ending on or before April 30, 2021. Real estate investment trusts, limited-liability companies, limited parterships, business development companies, closed-end investment firms, companies about to be acquired, and companies that lost money in the quarter ending April 30, 2021 were excluded. *Fortune, "100 Fastest-Growing Companies," 2021*

According to Deloitte, San Francisco is home to 49 of North America's 500 fastest-growing high-technology companies: **Apollo GraphQL** (#20); **Pilot** (#33); **Voltus** (#37); **Bolt** (#39); **Discord** (#42); **Instabase** (#46); **Samsara** (#60); **Vir Biotechnology** (#70); **EarnUp** (#75); **Nozomi Networks** (#79); **Arkose Labs** (#83); **Premise Data** (#97); **Kong** (#104); **Vercel** (#114); **SingleStore** (#126); **Upgrade** (#135); **Benchling** (#139); **Sigmoid** (#145); **Domino Data Lab** (#177); **MindTickle** (#199); **Vyvo** (#202); **Blueshift** (#219); **Fieldwire** (#222); **Treez** (#225); **Rescale** (#227); **Innovaccer** (#240); **Sysdig** (#242); **Sentry** (#244); **Fountain** (#249); **MURAL** (#251); **Pipefy** (#256); **Everlance** (#285); **Sentieo** (#322); **CircleCI** (#336); **Reciprocity** (#341); **Amplitude** (#346); **Twilio** (#347); **IGEL** (#351); **Square** (#358); **Ease** (#360); **Bitmovin** (#363); **JFrog** (#408); **Front** (#420); **PandaDoc** (#421); **Okta** (#435); **Pinterest** (#438); **Ontra (FKA InCloudCounsel)** (#454); **Noodle.ai** (#458); **Cloudflare** (#494). Companies are ranked by percentage growth in revenue over a four-year period. Criteria for inclusion: company must be headquartered within North America; must own proprietary intellectual property or technology that is sold to customers in products that contributes to a significant portion of the company's operating revenue; must have been in business for a minumum of four years with 2017 operating revenues of at least $50,000 USD/CD and 2020 operating revenues of at least $5 million USD/CD. *Deloitte, 2021 Technology Fast 500*™

Living Environment

COST OF LIVING

Cost of Living Index

Composite Index	Groceries	Housing	Utilities	Trans-portation	Health Care	Misc. Goods/ Services
194.2	130.4	341.3	133.7	142.7	122.8	122.5

Note: The Cost of Living Index measures regional differences in the cost of consumer goods and services, excluding taxes and non-consumer expenditures, for professional and managerial households in the top income quintile. It is based on more than 50,000 prices covering almost 60 different items for which prices are collected three times a year by chambers of commerce, economic development organizations or university applied economic centers in each participating urban area. The numbers shown should be read as a percentage above or below the national average of 100. For example, a value of 115.4 in the groceries column indicates that grocery prices are 15.4% higher than the national average. Small differences in the index numbers should not be interpreted as significant; Figures cover the San Francisco CA urban area.
Source: The Council for Community and Economic Research, Cost of Living Index, 2021

Grocery Prices

Area[1]	T-Bone Steak ($/pound)	Frying Chicken ($/pound)	Whole Milk ($/half gal.)	Eggs ($/dozen)	Orange Juice ($/64 oz.)	Coffee ($/11.5 oz.)
City[2]	16.71	1.80	2.55	2.94	4.14	6.12
Avg.	12.82	1.40	2.22	1.57	3.59	4.30
Min.	8.91	0.91	1.29	0.75	2.87	3.02
Max.	21.35	2.69	3.92	3.86	5.49	8.11

*Note: (1) Values for the local area are compared with the average, minimum and maximum values for all 285 areas in the Cost of Living Index; (2) Figures cover the San Francisco CA urban area; **T-Bone Steak** (price per pound); **Frying Chicken** (price per pound, whole fryer); **Whole Milk** (half gallon carton); **Eggs** (price per dozen, Grade A, large); **Orange Juice** (64 oz. Tropicana or Florida Natural); **Coffee** (11.5 oz. can, vacuum-packed, Maxwell House, Hills Bros, or Folgers).*
Source: The Council for Community and Economic Research, Cost of Living Index, 2021

Housing and Utility Costs

Area[1]	New Home Price ($)	Apartment Rent ($/month)	All Electric ($/month)	Part Electric ($/month)	Other Energy ($/month)	Telephone ($/month)
City[2]	1,396,782	3,702	-	192.51	73.93	196.49
Avg.	398,393	1,217	171.38	100.83	69.67	187.75
Min.	212,799	534	96.71	31.56	27.15	173.01
Max.	2,354,006	4,438	369.53	277.33	303.87	206.73

*Note: (1) Values for the local area are compared with the average, minimum and maximum values for all 285 areas in the Cost of Living Index; (2) Figures cover the San Francisco CA urban area; **New Home Price** (2,400 sf living area, 8,000 sf lot, in urban area with full utilities); **Apartment Rent** (950 sf 2 bedroom/1.5 or 2 bath, unfurnished, excluding all utilities except water); **All Electric** (average monthly cost for an all-electric home); **Part Electric** (average monthly cost for a part-electric home); **Other Energy** (average monthly cost for natural gas, fuel oil, coal, wood, and any other forms of energy except electricity); **Telephone** (price includes the base monthly rate plus taxes and fees for three lines of mobile phone service).*
Source: The Council for Community and Economic Research, Cost of Living Index, 2021

Health Care, Transportation, and Other Costs

Area[1]	Doctor ($/visit)	Dentist ($/visit)	Optometrist ($/visit)	Gasoline ($/gallon)	Beauty Salon ($/visit)	Men's Shirt ($)
City[2]	148.50	133.23	136.56	4.03	76.38	41.04
Avg.	118.16	101.04	109.44	2.71	40.63	30.77
Min.	35.04	55.56	51.17	2.17	18.59	11.32
Max.	231.10	165.12	256.81	4.11	85.33	63.03

*Note: (1) Values for the local area are compared with the average, minimum and maximum values for all 285 areas in the Cost of Living Index; (2) Figures cover the San Francisco CA urban area; **Doctor** (general practitioners routine exam of an established patient); **Dentist** (adult teeth cleaning and periodic oral examination); **Optometrist** (full vision eye exam for established adult patient); **Gasoline** (one gallon regular unleaded, national brand, including all taxes, cash price at self-service pump if available); **Beauty Salon** (woman's shampoo, trim, and blow-dry); **Men's Shirt** (cotton/polyester dress shirt, pinpoint weave, long sleeves).*
Source: The Council for Community and Economic Research, Cost of Living Index, 2021

HOUSING

Homeownership Rate

Area	2013 (%)	2014 (%)	2015 (%)	2016 (%)	2017 (%)	2018 (%)	2019 (%)	2020 (%)	2021 (%)
MSA[1]	55.2	54.6	56.3	55.8	55.7	55.6	52.8	53.0	54.7
U.S.	65.1	64.5	63.7	63.4	63.9	64.4	64.6	66.6	65.5

Note: (1) Figures cover the San Francisco-Oakland-Hayward, CA Metropolitan Statistical Area
Source: U.S. Census Bureau, Housing Vacancies and Homeownership Annual Statistics: 2013-2021

House Price Index (HPI)

Area	National Ranking[2]	Quarterly Change (%)	One-Year Change (%)	Five-Year Change (%)	Since 1991Q1 (%)
MD[1]	268	3.76	5.73	13.06	316.44
U.S.[3]	–	3.33	17.54	54.45	258.04

Note: The HPI is a weighted repeat sales index. It measures average price changes in repeat sales or refinancings on the same properties. This information is obtained by reviewing repeat mortgage transactions on single-family properties whose mortgages have been purchased or securitized by Fannie Mae or Freddie Mac since January 1975; (1) Figures cover the San Francisco-Redwood City-South San Francisco, CA Metropolitan Division; (2) Rankings are based on annual percentage change for all metro areas containing at least 15,000 transactions over the last 10 years and ranges from 1 to 268; (3) figures based on a weighted average of Census Division estimates using a seasonally adjusted, purchase-only index; all figures are for the period ending December 31, 2021
Source: Federal Housing Finance Agency, Change in FHFA Metropolitan Area House Price Indexes, 2021Q4

Median Single-Family Home Prices

Area	2019	2020	2021[p]	Percent Change 2020 to 2021
MSA[1]	988.0	1,100.0	1,320.0	20.0
U.S. Average	274.6	300.2	353.4	17.7

Note: Figures are median sales prices of existing single-family homes in thousands of dollars; (p) preliminary; (1) Figures cover the San Francisco-Oakland-Hayward, CA Metropolitan Statistical Area
Source: National Association of Realtors, Median Sales Price of Existing Single-Family Homes for Metropolitan Areas, 4th Quarter 2021

Qualifying Income Based on Median Sales Price of Existing Single-Family Homes

Area	With 5% Down ($)	With 10% Down ($)	With 20% Down ($)
MSA[1]	258,260	244,668	217,482
U.S. Average	70,699	66,978	59,536

Note: Figures are preliminary; Qualifying income is based on a mortgage rate of 3.13%. Monthly principal and interest payment is limited to 25% of income; (1) Figures cover the San Francisco-Oakland-Hayward, CA Metropolitan Statistical Area
Source: National Association of Realtors, Qualifying Income Based on Median Sales Price of Existing Single-Family Homes for Metropolitan Areas, 4th Quarter 2021

Home Value Distribution

Area	Under $50,000	$50,000 -$99,999	$100,000 -$149,999	$150,000 -$199,999	$200,000 -$299,999	$300,000 -$499,999	$500,000 -$999,999	$1,000,000 or more
City	1.0	0.4	0.5	0.2	1.1	3.5	30.0	63.3
MSA[1]	1.2	0.8	0.8	0.7	2.1	11.4	42.7	40.4
U.S.	6.6	11.0	12.3	13.6	20.0	20.5	12.3	3.7

Note: Figures are percentages and cover owner-occupied housing units; (1) Figures cover the San Francisco-Oakland-Hayward, CA Metropolitan Statistical Area
Source: U.S. Census Bureau, 2016-2020 American Community Survey 5-Year Estimates

Year Housing Structure Built

Area	2010 or Later	2000 -2009	1990 -1999	1980 -1989	1970 -1979	1960 -1969	1950 -1959	1940 -1949	Before 1940	Median Year
City	4.7	6.3	4.2	5.3	7.3	8.2	8.5	9.0	46.4	1944
MSA[1]	3.9	7.6	8.3	11.1	14.8	13.4	13.6	7.7	19.7	1967
U.S.	6.2	13.6	13.9	13.4	15.0	10.5	10.2	4.8	12.4	1978

Note: Figures are percentages except for Median Year; Note: (1) Figures cover the San Francisco-Oakland-Hayward, CA Metropolitan Statistical Area
Source: U.S. Census Bureau, 2016-2020 American Community Survey 5-Year Estimates

Gross Monthly Rent

Area	Under $500	$500 -$999	$1,000 -$1,499	$1,500 -$1,999	$2,000 -$2,499	$2,500 -$2,999	$3,000 and up	Median ($)
City	9.1	11.4	14.6	14.7	13.2	11.8	25.2	2,010
MSA[1]	5.7	8.1	15.2	20.1	18.7	12.9	19.2	2,021
U.S.	8.9	34.3	30.2	14.9	6.2	2.6	2.8	1,096

Note: Figures are percentages except for Median; Gross rent is the contract rent plus the estimated average monthly cost of utilities (electricity, gas, and water and sewer) and fuels (oil, coal, kerosene, wood, etc.) if these are paid by the renter (or paid for the renter by someone else); (1) Figures cover the San Francisco-Oakland-Hayward, CA Metropolitan Statistical Area
Source: U.S. Census Bureau, 2016-2020 American Community Survey 5-Year Estimates

HEALTH

Health Risk Factors

Category	MSA[1] (%)	U.S. (%)
Adults aged 18–64 who have any kind of health care coverage	n/a	86.8
Adults who reported being in good or better health	n/a	86.7
Adults who are current smokers	n/a	15.5
Adults who currently use chewing tobacco, snuff, or snus	n/a	3.7
Adults who are heavy drinkers[2]	n/a	6.7
Adults who are binge drinkers[3]	n/a	15.7
Adults who are overweight (BMI 25.0 - 29.9)	n/a	35.2
Adults who are obese (BMI 30.0 - 99.8)	n/a	31.9
Adults who participated in any physical activities in the past month	n/a	77.6
Adults who always or nearly always wears a seat belt	n/a	94.2

Note: (1) Figures for the San Francisco-Oakland-Hayward, CA Metropolitan Statistical Area were not available.
(2) Heavy drinkers are classified as adult men having more than 14 drinks per week and adult women having more than 7 drinks per week; (3) Binge drinkers are classified as males having five or more drinks on one occasion or females having four or more drinks on one occasion
Source: Centers for Disease Control and Prevention, Behaviorial Risk Factor Surveillance System, SMART: Selected Metropolitan Area Risk Trends, 2020

Acute and Chronic Health Conditions

Category	MSA[1] (%)	U.S. (%)
Adults who have ever been told they had a heart attack	n/a	4.3
Adults who have ever been told they have angina or coronary heart disease	n/a	4.0
Adults who have ever been told they had a stroke	n/a	2.8
Adults who have ever been told they have asthma	n/a	14.2
Adults who have ever been told they have arthritis	n/a	24.5
Adults who have ever been told they have diabetes[2]	n/a	10.6
Adults who have ever been told they had skin cancer	n/a	6.4
Adults who have ever been told they had any other types of cancer	n/a	6.8
Adults who have ever been told they have COPD	n/a	6.2
Adults who have ever been told they have kidney disease	n/a	2.9
Adults who have ever been told they have a form of depression	n/a	19.6

Note: (1) Figures for the San Francisco-Oakland-Hayward, CA Metropolitan Statistical Area were not available.
(2) Figures do not include pregnancy-related, borderline, or pre-diabetes
Source: Centers for Disease Control and Prevention, Behaviorial Risk Factor Surveillance System, SMART: Selected Metropolitan Area Risk Trends, 2020

Health Screening and Vaccination Rates

Category	MSA[1] (%)	U.S. (%)
Adults 50-75 who have had a blood stool test within the past year	n/a	9.3
Adults aged 65+ who have had flu shot within the past year	n/a	67.9
Adults aged 65+ who have ever had a pneumonia vaccination	n/a	72.2
Adults who have ever been tested for HIV	n/a	37.1
Women aged 21-65 who have had a pap test in the past three years	n/a	77.7
Men aged 40+ who have had a PSA test within the past two years	n/a	31.8
Women aged 40+ who have had a mammogram within the past two years	n/a	71.5

Note: (1) Figures for the San Francisco-Oakland-Hayward, CA Metropolitan Statistical Area were not available.
Source: Centers for Disease Control and Prevention, Behaviorial Risk Factor Surveillance System, SMART: Selected Metropolitan Area Risk Trends, 2020

Disability Status

Category	MSA[1] (%)	U.S. (%)
Adults who reported being deaf	n/a	6.8
Are you blind or have serious difficulty seeing, even when wearing glasses?	n/a	4.7
Do you have difficulty doing errands alone?	n/a	6.3
Do you have difficulty dressing or bathing?	n/a	3.0
Do you have serious difficulty concentrating/remembering/making decisions?	n/a	10.8
Do you have serious difficulty walking or climbing stairs?	n/a	11.9

Note: (1) Figures for the San Francisco-Oakland-Hayward, CA Metropolitan Statistical Area were not available.
Source: Centers for Disease Control and Prevention, Behaviorial Risk Factor Surveillance System, SMART: Selected Metropolitan Area Risk Trends, 2020

Mortality Rates for the Top 10 Causes of Death in the U.S.

ICD-10[a] Sub-Chapter	ICD-10[a] Code	Age-Adjusted Mortality Rate[1] per 100,000 population	
		County[2]	U.S.
Malignant neoplasms	C00-C97	117.3	146.4
Ischaemic heart diseases	I20-I25	58.0	90.2
Other forms of heart disease	I30-I51	31.3	51.9
Other degenerative diseases of the nervous system	G30-G31	28.2	39.7
Other external causes of accidental injury	W00-X59	49.2	38.7
Chronic lower respiratory diseases	J40-J47	16.6	38.1
Cerebrovascular diseases	I60-I69	32.9	37.6
Organic, including symptomatic, mental disorders	F01-F09	16.9	29.4
Hypertensive diseases	I10-I15	24.6	26.1
Diabetes mellitus	E10-E14	12.2	22.6

Note: (a) ICD-10 = International Classification of Diseases 10th Revision; (1) Mortality rates are a three-year average covering 2018-2020; (2) Figures cover San Francisco County.
Source: Centers for Disease Control and Prevention, National Center for Health Statistics. Underlying Cause of Death 1999-2020 on CDC WONDER Online Database

Mortality Rates for Selected Causes of Death

ICD-10[a] Sub-Chapter	ICD-10[a] Code	Age-Adjusted Mortality Rate[1] per 100,000 population	
		County[2]	U.S.
Assault	X85-Y09	4.5	6.5
Diseases of the liver	K70-K76	9.7	15.3
Human immunodeficiency virus (HIV) disease	B20-B24	3.7	1.4
Influenza and pneumonia	J09-J18	9.2	13.4
Intentional self-harm	X60-X84	8.4	13.9
Malnutrition	E40-E46	1.1	2.9
Obesity and other hyperalimentation	E65-E68	Unreliable	2.4
Renal failure	N17-N19	7.2	12.5
Transport accidents	V01-V99	4.3	12.5
Viral hepatitis	B15-B19	1.8	1.0

Note: (a) ICD-10 = International Classification of Diseases 10th Revision; (1) Mortality rates are a three-year average covering 2018-2020; (2) Figures cover San Francisco County; Data are suppressed when the data meet the criteria for confidentiality constraints; Mortality rates are flagged as unreliable when the rate would be calculated with a numerator of 20 or less.
Source: Centers for Disease Control and Prevention, National Center for Health Statistics. Underlying Cause of Death 1999-2020 on CDC WONDER Online Database

Health Insurance Coverage

Area	With Health Insurance	With Private Health Insurance	With Public Health Insurance	Without Health Insurance	Population Under Age 19 Without Health Insurance
City	96.4	76.3	29.2	3.6	1.7
MSA[1]	95.8	76.0	30.4	4.2	2.2
U.S.	91.3	68.1	35.3	8.7	5.2

Note: Figures are percentages that cover the civilian noninstitutionalized population; (1) Figures cover the San Francisco-Oakland-Hayward, CA Metropolitan Statistical Area
Source: U.S. Census Bureau, 2016-2020 American Community Survey 5-Year Estimates

Number of Medical Professionals

Area	MDs[3]	DOs[3,4]	Dentists	Podiatrists	Chiropractors	Optometrists
County[1] (number)	7,200	116	1,387	94	352	258
County[1] (rate[2])	823.8	13.3	158.7	10.8	40.3	29.5
U.S. (rate[2])	285.1	23.0	71.1	6.2	28.2	17.0

06075
Note: Data as of 2020 unless noted; (1) Data covers San Francisco County; (2) Rate per 100,000 population; (3) Data as of 2019 and includes all active, non-federal physicians; (4) Doctor of Osteopathic Medicine
Source: U.S. Department of Health and Human Services, Health Resources and Services Administration, Bureau of Health Professions, Area Resource File (ARF) 2020-2021

Best Hospitals

According to *U.S. News*, the San Francisco-Redwood City-South San Francisco, CA metro area is home to one of the best hospitals in the U.S.: **UCSF Health-UCSF Medical Center** (Honor Roll/14 adult specialties and 10 pediatric specialties). The hospital listed was nationally ranked in at least one of 15 adult or 10 pediatric specialties. Only 175 U.S. hospitals performed well enough to be nationally ranked in one or more specialties. Twenty hospitals in the U.S. made the Honor Roll. The Best Hospitals Honor Roll takes both the national rankings and the procedure and condition ratings into account. Hospitals received points if they were nationally ranked in one of the 15 adult specialties—the higher they ranked, the more points they got—and how many ratings of "high performing"

they earned in the 17 procedures and conditions. *U.S. News Online, "America's Best Hospitals 2021-22"*

According to *U.S. News,* the San Francisco-Redwood City-South San Francisco, CA metro area is home to one of the best children's hospitals in the U.S.: **UCSF Benioff Children's Hospitals, San Francisco and Oakland** (10 pediatric specialties). The hospital listed was highly ranked in at least one of 10 pediatric specialties. Ninety-two children's hospitals in the U.S. were nationally ranked in at least one specialty. Hospitals received points for being ranked in a specialty, and the 10 hospitals with the most points across the 10 specialties make up the Honor Roll. *U.S. News Online, "America's Best Children's Hospitals 2021-22"*

EDUCATION

Public School District Statistics

District Name	Schls	Pupils	Pupil/ Teacher Ratio	Minority Pupils[1] (%)	LEP/ELL[2] (%)	IEP[3] (%)
Five Keys Independence HSD	1	3,738	n/a	89.6	25.9	2.8
San Francisco Unified	114	52,811	n/a	85.1	28.5	12.4

Note: Table includes school districts with 2,000 or more students; (1) Percentage of students that are not non-Hispanic white; (2) Percentage of students that are Limited English Proficient (LEP) or English Language Learners (ELL) (2018-19); (3) Percentage of students that have an Individualized Education Program (IEP).
Source: U.S. Department of Education, National Center for Education Statistics, Common Core of Data, Local Education Agency (School District) Universe Survey: School Year 2019-2020

Best High Schools

According to *U.S. News,* San Francisco is home to two of the top 500 high schools in the U.S.: **Lowell High School** (#78); **KIPP San Francisco College Preparatory** (#377). Nearly 18,000 public, magnet and charter schools were ranked based on their performance on state assessments and how well they prepare students for college. *U.S. News & World Report, "Best High Schools 2021"*

Highest Level of Education

Area	Less than H.S.	H.S. Diploma	Some College, No Deg.	Associate Degree	Bachelor's Degree	Master's Degree	Prof. School Degree	Doctorate Degree
City	11.4	11.6	13.1	5.1	35.0	15.9	5.1	2.8
MSA[1]	10.5	15.2	17.0	6.7	29.8	14.1	3.8	2.9
U.S.	11.5	26.7	20.3	8.6	20.2	9.1	2.2	1.5

Note: Figures cover persons age 25 and over; (1) Figures cover the San Francisco-Oakland-Hayward, CA Metropolitan Statistical Area
Source: U.S. Census Bureau, 2016-2020 American Community Survey 5-Year Estimates

Educational Attainment by Race

Area	High School Graduate or Higher (%)					Bachelor's Degree or Higher (%)				
	Total	White	Black	Asian	Hisp.[2]	Total	White	Black	Asian	Hisp.[2]
City	88.6	96.8	87.7	79.9	78.2	58.8	74.4	30.2	47.9	35.9
MSA[1]	89.5	94.4	91.3	87.6	72.9	50.7	57.3	30.9	56.6	23.0
U.S.	88.5	90.7	86.7	87.3	70.3	32.9	34.4	22.6	55.0	17.6

Note: Figures shown cover persons 25 years old and over; (1) Figures cover the San Francisco-Oakland-Hayward, CA Metropolitan Statistical Area; (2) People of Hispanic origin can be of any race
Source: U.S. Census Bureau, 2016-2020 American Community Survey 5-Year Estimates

School Enrollment by Grade and Control

Area	Preschool (%)		Kindergarten (%)		Grades 1 - 4 (%)		Grades 5 - 8 (%)		Grades 9 - 12 (%)	
	Public	Private	Public	Private	Public	Private	Public	Private	Public	Private
City	34.3	65.7	67.8	32.2	72.2	27.8	66.5	33.5	74.5	25.5
MSA[1]	40.6	59.4	83.1	16.9	85.8	14.2	84.9	15.1	86.6	13.4
U.S.	58.9	41.1	86.9	13.1	89.0	11.0	89.0	11.0	89.7	10.3

Note: Figures shown cover persons 3 years old and over; (1) Figures cover the San Francisco-Oakland-Hayward, CA Metropolitan Statistical Area
Source: U.S. Census Bureau, 2016-2020 American Community Survey 5-Year Estimates

Higher Education

Four-Year Colleges			Two-Year Colleges			Medical Schools[1]	Law Schools[2]	Voc/ Tech[3]
Public	Private Non-profit	Private For-profit	Public	Private Non-profit	Private For-profit			
5	32	5	15	0	6	1	7	14

Note: Figures cover institutions located within the San Francisco-Oakland-Hayward, CA Metropolitan Statistical Area and include main campuses only; (1) includes schools accredited by the Liaison Committee on Medical Education and the American Osteopathic Association's Commission on Osteopathic College Accreditation; (2) includes ABA-accredited schools, schools with provisional ABA accreditation, and state accredited schools; (3) includes all schools with programs that are less than 2 years.
Source: National Center for Education Statistics, Integrated Postsecondary Education System (IPEDS), 2020-21; Wikipedia, List of Medical Schools in the United States, accessed April 11, 2022; Wikipedia, List of Law Schools in the United States, accessed April 11, 2022

According to *U.S. News & World Report,* the San Francisco-Redwood City-South San Francisco, CA metro division is home to one of the top 200 national universities in the U.S.: **University of San Francisco** (#103 tie). The indicators used to capture academic quality fall into a number of categories: assessment by administrators at peer institutions; retention of students; faculty resources; student selectivity; financial resources; alumni giving; high school counselor ratings of colleges; and graduation rate. *U.S. News & World Report, "America's Best Colleges 2022"*

According to *U.S. News & World Report,* the San Francisco-Redwood City-South San Francisco, CA metro division is home to one of the top 100 law schools in the U.S.: **University of California (Hastings)** (#50 tie). The rankings are based on a weighted average of 12 measures of quality: peer assessment score; assessment score by lawyers/judges; median LSAT scores; median undergrad GPA; acceptance rate; employment rates for graduates; placement success; bar passage rate; faculty resources; expenditures per student; student/faculty ratio; and library resources. *U.S. News & World Report, "America's Best Graduate Schools, Law, 2022"*

According to *U.S. News & World Report,* the San Francisco-Redwood City-South San Francisco, CA metro division is home to one of the top 75 medical schools for research in the U.S.: **University of California—San Francisco** (#4 tie). The rankings are based on a weighted average of 11 measures of quality: quality assessment; peer assessment score; assessment score by residency directors; research activity; total research activity; average research activity per faculty member; student selectivity; median MCAT total score; median undergraduate GPA; acceptance rate; and faculty resources. *U.S. News & World Report, "America's Best Graduate Schools, Medical, 2022"*

EMPLOYERS

Major Employers

Company Name	Industry
All Hallows Preservation	Apartment building operators
AT&T	Telephone communication, except radio
AT&T Services	Telephone communication, except radio
California Pacific Medical Center	General medical & surgical hospitals
City & County of San Francisco	Public welfare administration: nonoperating, govt.
Edy's Grand Ice Cream	Ice cream & other frozen treats
Franklin Templeton Services	Investment advice
Lawrence Livermore National Laboratory	Noncommercial research organizations
Menlo Worldwide Forwarding	Letter delivery, private air
Oracle America	Minicomputers
Oracle Systems Corporation	Prepackaged software
Pacific Gas and Electric Company	Electric & other services combined
PACPIZZA	Pizzeria, chain
San Francisco Community College District	Colleges & universities
University of California, Berkeley	University
Veterans Health Administration	Administration of veterans' affairs
Wells Fargo	National commercial banks

Note: Companies shown are located within the San Francisco-Oakland-Hayward, CA Metropolitan Statistical Area.
Source: Hoovers.com; Wikipedia

Best Companies to Work For

Atlassian; Kimpton Hotels & Restaurants; Orrick; Salesforce; Splunk; Twilio, headquartered in San Francisco, are among "The 100 Best Companies to Work For." To pick the best companies, *Fortune* partnered with the Great Place to Work Institute. Two-thirds of a company's score is based on the results of the Institute's Trust Index survey, which is sent to a random sample of employees from each company. The questions related to attitudes about management's credibility, job satisfaction, and camaraderie. The other third of the scoring is based on the company's responses to the Institute's Culture Audit, which includes detailed questions about pay and benefit programs, and a series of open-ended questions about hiring practices, internal communication, training, recognition programs, and diversity efforts. Any company that is at least five years old with more than 1,000 U.S. employees is eligible. *Fortune, "The 100 Best Companies to Work For," 2021*

Kimpton Hotels & Restaurants; Salesforce; Twilio, headquartered in San Francisco, are among "75 Best Large Workplaces for Women." To pick the best companies, *Fortune* partnered with the Great Place to Work Institute. Employees responded to over 60 survey questions describing the extent to which their organization creates a Great Place to Work For All. Eighty-five percent of the ranking is based on what women themselves report about their workplace, and how fairly those experiences compare to men's reports of the same workplaces. Fifteen percent of the remaining rank is based on how well represented women are in the workforce and throughout management, taking into account industry trends. To be considered, at a minimum, companies need to employ at least 50 women, at least 20% of their non-executive managers need to be female, and at least one of their executives needs to be female. *Fortune, "75 Best Large Workplaces for Women," 2021*

Federal Reserve Bank of San Francisco, headquartered in San Francisco, is among the "10 Best Companies for Working Mothers." Criteria: paid time off and leaves; workforce profile; benefits; women's issues and advancement; flexible work; company culture and work life programs. *Seramount, "Best Companies for Working Mothers," 2021*

Federal Reserve Bank of San Francisco, headquartered in San Francisco, is among the "10 Best Companies for Dads." Seramount's newest list recognizes the growing importance companies place on giving dads time off and support for their families. Rankings are determined by measuring gender-neutral or paternity leave offered, as well as actual time taken, phase-back policies, child- and dependent-care benefits, and corporate support groups for men and dads. *Seramount, "Best Companies for Dads," 2021*

PUBLIC SAFETY

Crime Rate

Area	Total Crime	Violent Crime Rate				Property Crime Rate		
		Murder	Rape[3]	Robbery	Aggrav. Assault	Burglary	Larceny -Theft	Motor Vehicle Theft
City	4,938.4	5.4	22.5	270.9	245.3	845.4	2,872.2	676.8
Suburbs[1]	3,106.9	5.3	33.9	157.3	219.7	345.9	1,757.2	587.6
Metro[2]	3,448.3	5.3	31.8	178.5	224.5	439.0	1,965.0	604.2
U.S.	2,356.7	6.5	38.4	73.9	279.7	314.2	1,398.0	246.0

Note: Figures are crimes per 100,000 population; (1) All areas within the metro area that are located outside the city limits; (2) Figures cover the San Francisco-Redwood City-South San Francisco, CA Metropolitan Division; (3) All figures shown were reported using the revised Uniform Crime Reporting (UCR) definition of rape.
Source: FBI Uniform Crime Reports, 2020

Hate Crimes

Area	Number of Quarters Reported	Number of Incidents per Bias Motivation					
		Race/Ethnicity/ Ancestry	Religion	Sexual Orientation	Disability	Gender	Gender Identity
City	4	37	7	8	0	0	2
U.S.	4	5,227	1,244	1,110	130	75	266

Source: Federal Bureau of Investigation, Hate Crime Statistics 2020

Identity Theft Consumer Reports

Area	Reports	Reports per 100,000 Population	Rank[2]
MSA[1]	11,007	233	188
U.S.	1,434,676	432	-

Note: (1) Figures cover the San Francisco-Oakland-Hayward, CA Metropolitan Statistical Area; (2) Rank ranges from 1 to 391 where 1 indicates greatest number of identity theft reports per 100,000 population
Source: Federal Trade Commission, Consumer Sentinel Network Data Book 2021

Fraud and Other Consumer Reports

Area	Reports	Reports per 100,000 Population	Rank[2]
MSA[1]	48,657	1,028	96
U.S.	4,328,977	1,304	-

Note: (1) Figures cover the San Francisco-Oakland-Hayward, CA Metropolitan Statistical Area; (2) Rank ranges from 1 to 391 where 1 indicates greatest number of fraud and other consumer reports per 100,000 population
Source: Federal Trade Commission, Consumer Sentinel Network Data Book 2021

POLITICS

2020 Presidential Election Results

Area	Biden	Trump	Jorgensen	Hawkins	Other
San Francisco County	85.3	12.7	0.7	0.6	0.7
U.S.	51.3	46.8	1.2	0.3	0.5

Note: Results are percentages and may not add to 100% due to rounding
Source: Dave Leip's Atlas of U.S. Presidential Elections

SPORTS

Professional Sports Teams

Team Name	League	Year Established
Golden State Warriors	National Basketball Association (NBA)	1962
Oakland Athletics	Major League Baseball (MLB)	1968
San Francisco 49ers	National Football League (NFL)	1946
San Francisco Giants	Major League Baseball (MLB)	1958

Note: Includes teams located in the San Francisco-Oakland-Hayward, CA Metropolitan Statistical Area.
Source: Wikipedia, Major Professional Sports Teams of the United States and Canada, April 6, 2022

CLIMATE

Average and Extreme Temperatures

Temperature	Jan	Feb	Mar	Apr	May	Jun	Jul	Aug	Sep	Oct	Nov	Dec	Yr.
Extreme High (°F)	72	77	85	92	97	106	105	98	103	99	85	75	106
Average High (°F)	56	59	61	64	66	70	71	72	73	70	63	56	65
Average Temp. (°F)	49	52	53	56	58	61	63	63	64	61	55	50	57
Average Low (°F)	42	44	45	47	49	52	53	54	54	51	47	42	49
Extreme Low (°F)	26	30	31	36	39	43	44	45	41	37	31	24	24

Note: Figures cover the years 1948-1990
Source: National Climatic Data Center, International Station Meteorological Climate Summary, 9/96

Average Precipitation/Snowfall/Humidity

Precip./Humidity	Jan	Feb	Mar	Apr	May	Jun	Jul	Aug	Sep	Oct	Nov	Dec	Yr.
Avg. Precip. (in.)	4.3	3.1	2.9	1.4	0.3	0.1	Tr	Tr	0.2	1.0	2.5	3.4	19.3
Avg. Snowfall (in.)	Tr	Tr	Tr	0	0	0	0	0	0	0	0	Tr	Tr
Avg. Rel. Hum. 7am (%)	86	85	82	79	78	77	81	83	83	83	85	86	82
Avg. Rel. Hum. 4pm (%)	67	65	63	61	61	60	60	62	60	60	64	68	63

Note: Figures cover the years 1948-1990; Tr = Trace amounts (<0.05 in. of rain; <0.5 in. of snow)
Source: National Climatic Data Center, International Station Meteorological Climate Summary, 9/96

Weather Conditions

Temperature			Daytime Sky			Precipitation		
10°F & below	32°F & below	90°F & above	Clear	Partly cloudy	Cloudy	0.01 inch or more precip.	0.1 inch or more snow/ice	Thunder-storms
0	6	4	136	130	99	63	< 1	5

Note: Figures are average number of days per year and cover the years 1948-1990
Source: National Climatic Data Center, International Station Meteorological Climate Summary, 9/96

HAZARDOUS WASTE

Superfund Sites

The San Francisco-Redwood City-South San Francisco, CA metro division is home to one site on the EPA's Superfund National Priorities List: **Treasure Island Naval Station-Hunters Point Annex** (final). There are a total of 1,165 Superfund sites with a status of proposed or final on the list in the U.S.
U.S. Environmental Protection Agency, National Priorities List, April 6, 2022

AIR QUALITY

Air Quality Trends: Ozone

	1990	1995	2000	2005	2010	2016	2017	2018	2019	2020
MSA[1]	0.058	0.074	0.057	0.057	0.061	0.062	0.060	0.053	0.060	0.062
U.S.	0.090	0.091	0.082	0.080	0.074	0.070	0.069	0.070	0.066	0.068

Note: (1) Data covers the San Francisco-Oakland-Hayward, CA Metropolitan Statistical Area. The values shown are the composite ozone concentration averages among trend sites based on the highest fourth daily maximum 8-hour concentration in parts per million. These trends are based on sites having an adequate record of monitoring data during the trend period. Data from exceptional events are included.
Source: U.S. Environmental Protection Agency, Air Quality Monitoring Information, "Air Quality Trends by City, 1990-2020"

Air Quality Index

Area	Percent of Days when Air Quality was...[2]					AQI Statistics[2]	
	Good	Moderate	Unhealthy for Sensitive Groups	Unhealthy	Very Unhealthy	Maximum	Median
MSA[1]	61.7	32.0	2.7	3.3	0.3	218	45

Note: (1) Data covers the San Francisco-Oakland-Hayward, CA Metropolitan Statistical Area; (2) Based on 366 days with AQI data in 2020. Air Quality Index (AQI) is an index for reporting daily air quality. EPA calculates the AQI for five major air pollutants regulated by the Clean Air Act: ground-level ozone, particle pollution (aka particulate matter), carbon monoxide, sulfur dioxide, and nitrogen dioxide. The AQI runs from 0 to 500. The higher the AQI value, the greater the level of air pollution and the greater the health concern. There are six AQI categories: "Good" AQI is between 0 and 50. Air quality is considered satisfactory; "Moderate" AQI is between 51 and 100. Air quality is acceptable; "Unhealthy for Sensitive Groups" When AQI values are between 101 and 150, members of sensitive groups may experience health effects; "Unhealthy" When AQI values are between 151 and 200 everyone may begin to experience health effects; "Very Unhealthy" AQI values between 201 and 300 trigger a health alert; "Hazardous" AQI values over 300 trigger warnings of emergency conditions (not shown).
Source: U.S. Environmental Protection Agency, Air Quality Index Report, 2020

Air Quality Index Pollutants

Area	Percent of Days when AQI Pollutant was...[2]					
	Carbon Monoxide	Nitrogen Dioxide	Ozone	Sulfur Dioxide	Particulate Matter 2.5	Particulate Matter 10
MSA[1]	0.0	3.8	42.3	0.3	53.6	0.0

Note: (1) Data covers the San Francisco-Oakland-Hayward, CA Metropolitan Statistical Area; (2) Based on 366 days with AQI data in 2020. The Air Quality Index (AQI) is an index for reporting daily air quality. EPA calculates the AQI for five major air pollutants regulated by the Clean Air Act: ground-level ozone, particle pollution (also known as particulate matter), carbon monoxide, sulfur dioxide, and nitrogen dioxide. The AQI runs from 0 to 500. The higher the AQI value, the greater the level of air pollution and the greater the health concern.
Source: U.S. Environmental Protection Agency, Air Quality Index Report, 2020

Maximum Air Pollutant Concentrations: Particulate Matter, Ozone, CO and Lead

	Particulate Matter 10 (ug/m^3)	Particulate Matter 2.5 Wtd AM (ug/m^3)	Particulate Matter 2.5 24-Hr (ug/m^3)	Ozone (ppm)	Carbon Monoxide (ppm)	Lead (ug/m^3)
MSA[1] Level	43	11.8	66	0.071	2	n/a
NAAQS[2]	150	15	35	0.075	9	0.15
Met NAAQS[2]	Yes	Yes	No	Yes	Yes	n/a

Note: (1) Data covers the San Francisco-Oakland-Hayward, CA Metropolitan Statistical Area; Data from exceptional events are included; (2) National Ambient Air Quality Standards; ppm = parts per million; ug/m^3 = micrograms per cubic meter; n/a not available.
Concentrations: Particulate Matter 10 (coarse particulate)—highest second maximum 24-hour concentration; Particulate Matter 2.5 Wtd AM (fine particulate)—highest weighted annual mean concentration; Particulate Matter 2.5 24-Hour (fine particulate)—highest 98th percentile 24-hour concentration; Ozone—highest fourth daily maximum 8-hour concentration; Carbon Monoxide—highest second maximum non-overlapping 8-hour concentration; Lead—maximum running 3-month average
Source: U.S. Environmental Protection Agency, Air Quality Monitoring Information, "Air Quality Statistics by City, 2020"

Maximum Air Pollutant Concentrations: Nitrogen Dioxide and Sulfur Dioxide

	Nitrogen Dioxide AM (ppb)	Nitrogen Dioxide 1-Hr (ppb)	Sulfur Dioxide AM (ppb)	Sulfur Dioxide 1-Hr (ppb)	Sulfur Dioxide 24-Hr (ppb)
MSA[1] Level	14	48	n/a	14	n/a
NAAQS[2]	53	100	30	75	140
Met NAAQS[2]	Yes	Yes	n/a	Yes	n/a

Note: (1) Data covers the San Francisco-Oakland-Hayward, CA Metropolitan Statistical Area; Data from exceptional events are included; (2) National Ambient Air Quality Standards; ppm = parts per million; ug/m^3 = micrograms per cubic meter; n/a not available.
Concentrations: Nitrogen Dioxide AM—highest arithmetic mean concentration; Nitrogen Dioxide 1-Hr—highest 98th percentile 1-hour daily maximum concentration; Sulfur Dioxide AM—highest annual mean concentration; Sulfur Dioxide 1-Hr—highest 99th percentile 1-hour daily maximum concentration; Sulfur Dioxide 24-Hr—highest second maximum 24-hour concentration
Source: U.S. Environmental Protection Agency, Air Quality Monitoring Information, "Air Quality Statistics by City, 2020"

San Jose, California

Background

Like many cities in the valleys of northern California, San Jose is an abundant cornucopia of wine grapes and produce. It is part of the famed, high-tech Silicon Valley, and situated only seven miles from the southernmost tip of San Francisco Bay, San Jose is flanked by the Santa Cruz Mountains to the west, and the Mount Hamilton arm of the Diablo Range to the east. The Coyote and Guadalupe rivers gently cut through this landscape, carrying water only in the spring.

San Jose was founded on November 29, 1777, by Spanish colonizers, and can rightfully claim to be the oldest civic settlement in California. San Jose was established by the Spanish to be a produce and cattle supplier to the nearby communities and presidios of San Francisco and Monterey, a role that it still enjoys today.

After U.S. troops wrested the territory of California from Mexican rule, San Jose became its state capital. At the same time, the city served as a supply base to gold prospectors.

Today, San Jose retains much of its history, still a major shipping and processing center for agricultural produce, and the city produces some of the best table wines in the country. A replica of the Mission of Santa Clara stands on the grounds of the University of Santa Clara - a reminder of its Spanish heritage.

Due to annexation of surrounding communities after World War II, the population of San Jose increased more than tenfold, attracting residents with industries that included NASA research, electronic components, and motors production. San Jose rapidly became a family-oriented community of housing developments and shopping malls.

During the 1990s, San Jose was home to more than half of Silicon Valley's leading semiconductor, networking, and telecommunications companies, earning the nickname "Capital of Silicon Valley." The renovated downtown is headquarters for a number of major software developers.

At the turn of the 21st century, San Jose suffered from a downturn in electronics and computer industries, but the city has since rebounded, with lower unemployment numbers and plans to ensure that the city's economic future remains bright. The region has been cited as the happiest place to work in the United States, noting that technology jobs typically offer a high salary and opportunity for growth, and that tech companies usually provide a fun and innovative work environment.

The HP Pavilion, home of the San Jose Sharks hockey team, is one of the most active venues for non-sporting events in the world.

Public art is an evolving attraction in the city. The city was one of the first to adopt a public art ordinance at 2 percent of capital improvement building project budgets, a commitment that has affected the visual landscape of the city, with a considerable number of public art projects throughout the downtown area, and a growing collection in the newer civic locations in neighborhoods including libraries, parks, and fire stations. Of note, San Jose's Mineta Airport has incorporated a program of Art & Technology that includes a series of platforms for projection-based, digital and data-driven artwork throughout the airport, designed to be changed over time in keeping up with technological advances.

San Jose enjoys a Mediterranean, or dry summer subtropical, climate. The rain that does fall comes mostly November through March. Severe winter storms with gale winds and heavy rain occur occasionally. The summer weather is dominated by night and morning stratus clouds along with sea breezes blowing from the cold waters of the bay. During the winter months fog is common, causing difficult flying conditions.

Rankings

General Rankings

- The San Jose metro area was identified as one of America's fastest-growing areas in terms of population and business growth by *MagnifyMoney.* The area ranked #19 out of 35. The 100 most populous metro areas in the U.S. were evaluated on their change from 2011 to 2016 in the following categories: people and housing; workforce and employment opportunities; growing industry. *www.businessinsider.com, "The 35 Cities in the US with the Biggest Influx of People, the Most Work Opportunities, and the Hottest Business Growth," August 12, 2018*

Business/Finance Rankings

- According to *Business Insider*, the San Jose metro area is a prime place to run a startup or move an existing business to. The area ranked #1. More than 300 metro areas were analyzed for factors that were of top concern to new business owners. Data was based on the 2019 U.S. Census Bureau American Community Survey, statistics from the CDC, Bureau of Labor Statistics employment report, and University of Chicago analysis. Criteria: business formations; percentage of vaccinated population; percentage of households with internet subscriptions; median household income; and share of work that can be done from home. *www.businessinsider.com, "The 20 Best Cities for Starting a Business in 2022 Include Baltimore, Boulder, and Boston," January 5, 2022*
- 24/7 Wall Street used metro data from the Bureau of Labor Statistics' Occupational Employment database to identify the cities with the highest percentage of those employed in jobs requiring knowledge in the science, technology, engineering, and math (STEM) fields as well as average wages for STEM jobs. The San Jose metro area was #11. *247wallst.com, "15 Cities with the Most High-Tech Jobs," January 11, 2020*
- Based on metro area social media reviews, the employment opinion group Glassdoor surveyed 50 of the most populous U.S. metro areas and equally weighed cost of living, hiring opportunity, and job satisfaction to compose a list of "25 Best Cities for Jobs." Median pay and home value, and number of active job openings were also factored in. The San Jose metro area was ranked #16 in overall job satisfaction. *www.glassdoor.com, "Best Cities for Jobs," February 25, 2020*
- The Brookings Institution ranked the nation's largest cities based on income inequality. San Jose was ranked #56 (#1 = greatest inequality). Criteria: the "95/20 ratio," a figure representing the income at which a household earns more than 95 percent of all other households, divided by the income at which a household earns more than only 20 percent of all other households. *Brookings Institution, "Household Income Inequality, Largest Cities of 97 Large U.S. Metro Areas, 2014-2016," February 5, 2018*
- The Brookings Institution ranked the 100 largest metro areas in the U.S. based on income inequality. San Jose was ranked #6 (#1 = greatest inequality). Criteria: the "95/20 ratio," a figure representing the income at which a household earns more than 95 percent of all other households, divided by the income at which a household earns more than only 20 percent of all other households. *Brookings Institution, "Household Income Inequality, 100 Largest U.S. Metro Areas, 2014-2016," February 5, 2018*
- Payscale.com ranked the 32 largest metro areas in terms of wage growth. The San Jose metro area ranked #29. Criteria: private-sector and education professional wage growth between the 4th quarter of 2019 and the 4th quarter of 2020. *PayScale, "Wage Trends by Metro Area-4th Quarter," January 11, 2021*
- The San Jose metro area appeared on the Milken Institute "2021 Best Performing Cities" list. Rank: #22 out of 200 large metro areas (population over 250,000). Criteria: job growth; wage and salary growth; high-tech output growth; housing affordability; household broadband access. *Milken Institute, "Best-Performing Cities 2021," February 16, 2021*
- *Forbes* ranked the 200 most populous metro areas to determine the nation's "Best Places for Business and Careers." The San Jose metro area was ranked #42. Criteria: costs (business and living); job growth (past and projected); income growth; quality of life; educational attainment (college and high school); projected economic growth; cultural and leisure opportunities; workplace tolerance laws; net migration patterns. *Forbes, "The Best Places for Business and Careers 2019: Seattle Still On Top," October 30, 2019*

Education Rankings

- Personal finance website *WalletHub* analyzed the 150 largest U.S. metropolitan statistical areas to determine where the most educated Americans are putting their degrees to work. Criteria: education levels; percentage of workers with degrees; education quality and attainment gap; public school quality rankings; quality and enrollment of each metro area's universities. San Jose was ranked #2 (#1 = most educated city). *www.WalletHub.com, "Most & Least Educated Cities in America, " July 19, 2021*
- San Jose was selected as one of America's most literate cities. The city ranked #50 out of the 84 largest U.S. cities. Criteria: number of booksellers; library resources; Internet resources; educational attainment; periodical publishing resources; newspaper circulation. *Central Connecticut State University, "America's Most Literate Cities, 2018, " February 2019*

Environmental Rankings

- Sperling's BestPlaces assessed the 50 largest metropolitan areas of the United States for the likelihood of dangerously extreme weather events or earthquakes. In general the Southeast and South-Central regions have the highest risk of weather extremes and earthquakes, while the Pacific Northwest enjoys the lowest risk. Of the least risky metropolitan areas, the San Jose metro area was ranked #6. *www.bestplaces.net, "Avoid Natural Disasters: BestPlaces Reveals The Top 10 Safest Places to Live, " October 25, 2017*
- The U.S. Environmental Protection Agency (EPA) released its list of U.S. metropolitan areas with the most ENERGY STAR certified buildings in 2020. The San Jose metro area was ranked #18 out of 25. *U.S. Environmental Protection Agency, "2021 Energy Star Top Cities, " June 15, 2021*
- The U.S. Environmental Protection Agency (EPA) released its list of mid-size U.S. metropolitan areas with the most ENERGY STAR certified buildings in 2020. The San Jose metro area was ranked #1 out of 10. *U.S. Environmental Protection Agency, "2021 Energy Star Top Cities, " June 15, 2021*
- San Jose was highlighted as one of the 25 most ozone-polluted metro areas in the U.S. during 2017 through 2019. The area ranked #10. *American Lung Association, "State of the Air 2021, " April 21, 2021*
- San Jose was highlighted as one of the 25 metro areas most polluted by year-round particle pollution (Annual PM 2.5) in the U.S. during 2017 through 2019. The area ranked #7. *American Lung Association, "State of the Air 2021, " April 21, 2021*
- San Jose was highlighted as one of the 25 metro areas most polluted by short-term particle pollution (24-hour PM 2.5) in the U.S. during 2017 through 2019. The area ranked #4. *American Lung Association, "State of the Air 2021, " April 21, 2021*

Health/Fitness Rankings

- For each of the 100 largest cities in the United States, the American Fitness Index®, published by the American College of Sports Medicine and the Anthem Foundation, evaluated community infrastructure and 34 health behaviors including preventive health, levels of chronic disease conditions, food insecurity, sleep quality, pedestrian safety, air quality, and community resources that support physical activity. San Jose ranked #20 for "community fitness." *americanfitnessindex.org, "2021 ACSM American Fitness Index Summary Report, " July 13, 2021*
- Trulia analyzed the 100 largest U.S. metro areas to identify the nation's best cities for weight loss, based on the percentage of adults who bike or walk to work, sporting goods stores, grocery stores, access to outdoor activities, weight-loss centers, gyms, and average space reserved for parks. San Jose ranked #10. *Trulia.com, "Where to Live to Get in Shape in the New Year, " January 4, 2018*
- San Jose was identified as a "2021 Spring Allergy Capital." The area ranked #92 out of 100. Three groups of factors were used to identify the most challenging cities for people with allergies during the spring season: annual spring pollen levels; over the counter medicine use; number of board-certified allergy specialists. *Asthma and Allergy Foundation of America, "Spring Allergy Capitals 2021, " February 23, 2021*
- San Jose was identified as a "2021 Fall Allergy Capital." The area ranked #96 out of 100. Three groups of factors were used to identify the most challenging cities for people with allergies during the fall season: annual fall pollen levels; over the counter medicine use; number of board-certified allergy specialists. *Asthma and Allergy Foundation of America, "Fall Allergy Capitals 2021, " February 23, 2021*

- San Jose was identified as a "2021 Asthma Capital." The area ranked #82 out of the nation's 100 largest metropolitan areas. Criteria: estimated asthma prevalence; asthma-related mortality; and ER visits due to asthma. Risk factors analyzed but not factored in the rankings: annual pollen score; annual air quality; public smoking laws; number of board-certified asthma specialists; rescue medication use; controller medication use; uninsured rate; poverty rate. *Asthma and Allergy Foundation of America, "Asthma Capitals 2021: The Most Challenging Places to Live With Asthma," May 5, 2021*
- The Sharecare Community Well-Being Index evaluates 10 individual and social health factors in order to measure what matters to Americans in the communities in which they live. The San Jose metro area ranked #2 in the top 10 across all 10 domains. Criteria: access to healthcare, food, and community resources; housng and transportation; economic security; feeling of purpose; physical, financial, social, and community well-being. *www.sharecare.com, "Community Well-Being Index: 2020 Metro Area & County Rankings Report," August 30, 2021*

Real Estate Rankings

- *WalletHub* compared the most populated U.S. cities to determine which had the best markets for real estate agents. San Jose ranked #10 where demand was high and pay was the best. Criteria: sales per agent; annual median wage for real-estate agents; monthly average starting salary for real estate agents; real estate job density and competition; unemployment rate; home turnover rate; housing-market health index; and other relevant metrics. *www.WalletHub.com, "2021 Best Places to Be a Real Estate Agent," May 12, 2021*
- The San Jose metro area was identified as one of the top 5 housing markets to invest in for 2022 by *Forbes*. Criteria: ratio of sales-to-list price; days on the market; available inventory; median sales prices; and other factors. *Forbes.com, "The Hottest Housing Markets Going Into 2022," November 29, 2021*
- The San Jose metro area was identified as one of the 20 least affordable housing markets in the U.S. in 2021. The area ranked #183 out of 183 markets. Criteria: qualification for a mortgage loan with a 10 percent down payment on a typical home. *National Association of Realtors®, Qualifying Income Based on Sales Price of Existing Single-Family Homes for Metropolitan Areas, 2021*
- San Jose was ranked #226 out of 237 metro areas in terms of housing affordability in 2021 by the National Association of Home Builders (#1 = most affordable). Criteria: the share of homes sold in that area affordable to a family earning the local median income, based on standard mortgage underwriting criteria. *National Association of Home Builders®, NAHB-Wells Fargo Housing Opportunity Index, 4th Quarter 2021*

Safety Rankings

- Allstate ranked the 200 largest cities in America in terms of driver safety. San Jose ranked #170. Criteria: internal property damage claims over a two-year period from January 2016 to December 2017. The report helps increase the importance of safety and awareness behind the wheel. *Allstate, "Allstate America's Best Drivers Report, 2019" June 24, 2019*
- The National Insurance Crime Bureau ranked 390 metro areas in the U.S. in terms of per capita rates of vehicle theft. The San Jose metro area ranked #11 (#1 = highest rate). Criteria: number of vehicle theft offenses per 100,000 inhabitants in 2020. *National Insurance Crime Bureau, "Hot Spots 2020," August 31, 2021*

Seniors/Retirement Rankings

- From its Best Cities for Successful Aging indexes, the Milken Institute generated rankings for metropolitan areas, weighing data in nine categories—health care, wellness, living arrangements, transportation and convenience, financial characteristics, education, employment, community engagement, and overall livability. The San Jose metro area was ranked #10 overall in the large metro area category. *Milken Institute, "Best Cities for Successful Aging, 2017" March 14, 2017*

Sports/Recreation Rankings

- San Jose was chosen as one of America's best cities for bicycling. The city ranked #43 out of 50. Criteria: cycling infrastructure that is safe and friendly for all ages; energy and bike culture. The editors evaluated cities with populations of 100,000 or more. *Bicycling, "The 50 Best Bike Cities in America," October 10, 2018*

Transportation Rankings

- San Jose was identified as one of the most congested metro areas in the U.S. The area ranked #4 out of 10. Criteria: yearly delay per auto commuter in hours. *Texas A&M Transportation Institute, "2021 Urban Mobility Report," June 2021*

Women/Minorities Rankings

- The *Houston Chronicle* listed the San Jose metro area as #12 in top places for young Latinos to live in the U.S. Research was largely based on housing and occupational data from the largest metropolitan areas performed by *Forbes* and NBC Universo. Criteria: percentage of 18-34 year-olds; Latino college grad rates; and diversity. *blog.chron.com, "The 15 Best Big Cities for Latino Millenials," January 26, 2016*
- Personal finance website *WalletHub* compared more than 180 U.S. cities across two key dimensions, "Hispanic Business-Friendliness" and "Hispanic Purchasing Power," to arrive at the most favorable conditions for Hispanic entrepreneurs. San Jose was ranked #103 out of 182. Criteria includes: share of Hispanic-Owned Businesses; Hispanic entrepreneurship rate to median annual income of Hispanics; Small Business-Friendliness score; cost of living; and number of Hispanics with at least a bachelor's degree. *WalletHub.com, "2019's Best Cities for Hispanic Entrepreneurs," May 1, 2019*

Miscellaneous Rankings

- San Jose was selected as a 2021 Digital Cities Survey winner. The city ranked #1 in the large city (500,000 or more population) category. The survey examined and assessed how city governments are utilizing technology to continue innovation, engage with residents, and persevere through the challenges of the pandemic. Survey questions focused on ten initiatives: cybersecurity; citizen experience; disaster recovery; business intelligence; IT personnel; data governance; budget control; IT governance; infrastructure modernization; and broadband connectivity. *Center for Digital Government, "2021 Digital Cities Survey," November 16, 2021*
- The financial planning site SmartAsset has compiled its annual study on the best places for Halloween in the U.S. for 2021. 210 cities were compared to determine that San Jose ranked #31 out of 35 for still being able to enjoy the festivities despite the COVID-19 pandemic. Metrics included: safety, family-friendliness, percentage of children in the population, concentration of candy and costume shops, weather and COVID infection rates. *www.smartasset.com, "2021 Edition-Best Places to Celebrate Halloween," October 20, 2021*
- *WalletHub* compared the 150 most populated U.S. cities to determine their operating efficiency. A "Quality of City Services" score was constructed for each city and then divided by the total budget per capita to reveal which were managed the best. San Jose ranked #94. Criteria: financial stability; economy; education; safety; health; infrastructure and pollution. *www.WalletHub.com, "2021's Best- & Worst-Run Cities in America," June 22, 2021*
- The National Alliance to End Homelessness listed the 25 most populous metro areas with the highest rate of homelessness. The San Jose metro area had a high rate of homelessness. Criteria: number of homeless people per 10,000 population in 2016. *National Alliance to End Homelessness, "Homelessness in the 25 Most Populous U.S. Metro Areas," September 1, 2017*

Business Environment

DEMOGRAPHICS

Population Growth

Area	1990 Census	2000 Census	2010 Census	2020* Estimate	Population Growth (%) 1990-2020	Population Growth (%) 2010-2020
City	784,324	894,943	945,942	1,029,409	31.2	8.8
MSA[1]	1,534,280	1,735,819	1,836,911	1,985,926	29.4	8.1
U.S.	248,709,873	281,421,906	308,745,538	326,569,308	31.3	5.8

Note: (1) Figures cover the San Jose-Sunnyvale-Santa Clara, CA Metropolitan Statistical Area; (*) 2016-2020 5-year estimated population
Source: U.S. Census Bureau, 1990 Census, Census 2000, Census 2010, 2016-2020 American Community Survey 5-Year Estimates

Household Size

Area	Persons in Household (%) One	Two	Three	Four	Five	Six	Seven or More	Average Household Size
City	19.5	28.8	18.9	17.9	8.2	3.2	3.3	3.10
MSA[1]	20.2	30.5	19.0	17.8	7.3	2.8	2.4	3.00
U.S.	28.0	33.9	15.5	12.9	6.0	2.3	1.4	2.60

Note: (1) Figures cover the San Jose-Sunnyvale-Santa Clara, CA Metropolitan Statistical Area
Source: U.S. Census Bureau, 2016-2020 American Community Survey 5-Year Estimates

Race

Area	White Alone[2] (%)	Black Alone[2] (%)	Asian Alone[2] (%)	AIAN[3] Alone[2] (%)	NHOPI[4] Alone[2] (%)	Other Race Alone[2] (%)	Two or More Races (%)
City	37.5	2.9	37.2	0.6	0.5	13.4	7.9
MSA[1]	42.6	2.4	36.6	0.5	0.4	9.9	7.6
U.S.	70.4	12.6	5.6	0.8	0.2	5.1	5.2

Note: (1) Figures cover the San Jose-Sunnyvale-Santa Clara, CA Metropolitan Statistical Area; (2) Alone is defined as not being in combination with one or more other races; (3) American Indian and Alaska Native; (4) Native Hawaiian and Other Pacific Islander
Source: U.S. Census Bureau, 2016-2020 American Community Survey 5-Year Estimates

Hispanic or Latino Origin

Area	Total (%)	Mexican (%)	Puerto Rican (%)	Cuban (%)	Other (%)
City	31.0	26.1	0.5	0.1	4.2
MSA[1]	26.1	21.5	0.5	0.2	4.0
U.S.	18.2	11.2	1.7	0.7	4.5

Note: Persons of Hispanic or Latino origin can be of any race; (1) Figures cover the San Jose-Sunnyvale-Santa Clara, CA Metropolitan Statistical Area
Source: U.S. Census Bureau, 2016-2020 American Community Survey 5-Year Estimates

Ancestry

Area	German	Irish	English	American	Italian	Polish	French[2]	Scottish	Dutch
City	4.8	4.0	3.6	1.9	3.3	0.8	1.1	0.8	0.5
MSA[1]	5.9	4.7	4.7	1.9	3.7	1.1	1.4	1.0	0.7
U.S.	13.0	9.7	7.7	5.9	5.1	2.7	2.3	1.6	1.1

Note: Figures are the percentage of the total population reporting a particular ancestry. The nine most commonly reported ancestries in the U.S. are shown. Figures include multiple ancestries (e.g. if a person reported being Irish and Italian, they were included in both columns); (1) Figures cover the San Jose-Sunnyvale-Santa Clara, CA Metropolitan Statistical Area; (2) Excludes Basque
Source: U.S. Census Bureau, 2016-2020 American Community Survey 5-Year Estimates

Foreign-born Population

Area	Percent of Population Born in: Any Foreign Country	Asia	Mexico	Europe	Caribbean	Central America[2]	South America	Africa	Canada
City	40.5	26.4	8.6	2.2	0.1	1.2	0.7	0.8	0.3
MSA[1]	39.1	26.1	6.7	3.1	0.1	0.9	0.8	0.7	0.5
U.S.	13.5	4.2	3.3	1.5	1.3	1.1	1.0	0.7	0.3

Note: (1) Figures cover the San Jose-Sunnyvale-Santa Clara, CA Metropolitan Statistical Area; (2) Excludes Mexico.
Source: U.S. Census Bureau, 2016-2020 American Community Survey 5-Year Estimates

Marital Status

Area	Never Married	Now Married[2]	Separated	Widowed	Divorced
City	35.8	50.6	1.5	4.3	7.8
MSA[1]	34.1	52.8	1.4	4.2	7.5
U.S.	33.5	48.1	1.8	5.7	10.8

Note: Figures are percentages and cover the population 15 years of age and older; (1) Figures cover the San Jose-Sunnyvale-Santa Clara, CA Metropolitan Statistical Area; (2) Excludes separated
Source: U.S. Census Bureau, 2016-2020 American Community Survey 5-Year Estimates

Disability by Age

Area	All Ages	Under 18 Years Old	18 to 64 Years Old	65 Years and Over
City	8.8	2.7	5.9	33.5
MSA[1]	8.2	2.5	5.3	31.3
U.S.	12.7	4.3	10.3	34.0

Note: Figures show percent of the civilian noninstitutionalized population that reported having a disability. Disability status is determined from six types of difficulty: vision, hearing, cognitive, ambulatory, self-care, and independent living. For children under 5 years old, hearing and vision difficulty are used to determine disability status. For children between the ages of 5 and 14, disability status is determined from hearing, vision, cognitive, ambulatory, and self-care difficulties. For people aged 15 years and older, they are considered to have a disability if they have difficulty with any one of the six difficulty types; Note: (1) Figures cover the San Jose-Sunnyvale-Santa Clara, CA Metropolitan Statistical Area
Source: U.S. Census Bureau, 2016-2020 American Community Survey 5-Year Estimates

Age

Area	Percent of Population									Median Age
	Under Age 5	Age 5–19	Age 20–34	Age 35–44	Age 45–54	Age 55–64	Age 65–74	Age 75–84	Age 85+	
City	5.9	18.3	22.6	14.6	13.7	12.0	7.5	3.8	1.7	37.1
MSA[1]	5.9	18.5	22.3	14.4	13.7	11.8	7.5	4.0	2.0	37.2
U.S.	6.0	19.1	20.6	12.7	12.7	12.9	9.4	4.7	2.0	38.2

Note: (1) Figures cover the San Jose-Sunnyvale-Santa Clara, CA Metropolitan Statistical Area
Source: U.S. Census Bureau, 2016-2020 American Community Survey 5-Year Estimates

Gender

Area	Males	Females	Males per 100 Females
City	521,180	508,229	102.5
MSA[1]	1,005,726	980,200	102.6
U.S.	160,818,530	165,750,778	97.0

Note: (1) Figures cover the San Jose-Sunnyvale-Santa Clara, CA Metropolitan Statistical Area
Source: U.S. Census Bureau, 2016-2020 American Community Survey 5-Year Estimates

Religious Groups by Family

Area	Catholic	Baptist	Non-Den.	Methodist[2]	Lutheran	LDS[3]	Pente-costal	Presby-terian[4]	Muslim[5]	Judaism
MSA[1]	26.0	1.4	4.3	1.1	0.6	1.4	1.2	0.7	1.0	0.7
U.S.	19.1	9.3	4.0	4.0	2.3	2.0	1.9	1.6	0.8	0.7

Note: Figures are the number of adherents as a percentage of the total population; (1) Figures cover the San Jose-Sunnyvale-Santa Clara, CA Metropolitan Statistical Area; (2) Methodist/Pietist; (3) Latter Day Saints; (4) Reformed; (5) Figures are estimates
Source: Association of Statisticians of American Religious Bodies, 2010 U.S. Religion Census: Religious Congregations & Membership Study

Religious Groups by Tradition

Area	Catholic	Evangelical Protestant	Mainline Protestant	Other Tradition	Black Protestant	Orthodox
MSA[1]	26.0	8.2	2.5	6.9	0.1	0.4
U.S.	19.1	16.2	7.3	4.3	1.6	0.3

Note: Figures are the number of adherents as a percentage of the total population; (1) Figures cover the San Jose-Sunnyvale-Santa Clara, CA Metropolitan Statistical Area
Source: Association of Statisticians of American Religious Bodies, 2010 U.S. Religion Census: Religious Congregations & Membership Study

ECONOMY

Gross Metropolitan Product

Area	2017	2018	2019	2020	Rank[2]
MSA[1]	281.6	303.1	321.2	334.7	13

Note: Figures are in billions of dollars; (1) Figures cover the San Jose-Sunnyvale-Santa Clara, CA Metropolitan Statistical Area; (2) Rank is based on 2018 data and ranges from 1 to 381
Source: U.S. Conference of Mayors, U.S. Metro Economies: GMP & Employment 2018-2020, September 2019

Economic Growth

Area	2015-17 (%)	2018 (%)	2019 (%)	2020 (%)	Rank[2]
MSA[1]	7.0	6.0	4.6	2.2	5
U.S.	1.9	2.9	2.3	2.1	–

Note: Figures are real gross metropolitan product (GMP) growth rates and represent average annual percent change; (1) Figures cover the San Jose-Sunnyvale-Santa Clara, CA Metropolitan Statistical Area; (2) Rank is based on 2017 2-year average annual percent change and ranges from 1 to 381
Source: U.S. Conference of Mayors, U.S. Metro Economies: GMP & Employment 2018-2020, September 2019

Metropolitan Area Exports

Area	2015	2016	2017	2018	2019	2020	Rank[2]
MSA[1]	19,827.2	21,716.8	21,464.7	22,224.2	20,909.4	19,534.5	18

Note: Figures are in millions of dollars; (1) Figures cover the San Jose-Sunnyvale-Santa Clara, CA Metropolitan Statistical Area; (2) Rank is based on 2020 data and ranges from 1 to 389
Source: U.S. Department of Commerce, International Trade Administration, Office of Trade and Economic Analysis, Industry and Analysis, Exports by Metropolitan Area, data extracted March 4, 2022

Building Permits

Area	Single-Family			Multi-Family			Total		
	2019	2020	Pct. Chg.	2019	2020	Pct. Chg.	2019	2020	Pct. Chg.
City	514	312	-39.3	1,831	1,057	-42.3	2,345	1,369	-41.6
MSA[1]	2,603	1,814	-30.3	3,627	4,037	11.3	6,230	5,851	-6.1
U.S.	862,100	979,400	13.6	523,900	491,700	-6.1	1,386,000	1,471,100	6.1

Note: (1) Figures cover the San Jose-Sunnyvale-Santa Clara, CA Metropolitan Statistical Area; Figures represent new, privately-owned housing units authorized (unadjusted data); All permit data are based on estimates with imputation
Source: U.S. Census Bureau, Manufacturing, Mining, and Construction Statistics, Building Permits, 2019, 2020

Bankruptcy Filings

Area	Business Filings			Nonbusiness Filings		
	2020	2021	% Chg.	2020	2021	% Chg.
Santa Clara County	86	80	-7.0	1,018	868	-14.7
U.S.	21,655	14,347	-33.7	522,808	399,269	-23.6

Note: Business filings include Chapter 7, Chapter 9, Chapter 11, Chapter 12, Chapter 13, Chapter 15, and Section 304; Nonbusiness filings include Chapter 7, Chapter 11, and Chapter 13
Source: Administrative Office of the U.S. Courts, Business and Nonbusiness Bankruptcy, County Cases Commenced by Chapter of the Bankruptcy Code, During the 12-Month Period Ending December 31, 2020 and Business and Nonbusiness Bankruptcy, County Cases Commenced by Chapter of the Bankruptcy Code, During the 12-Month Period Ending December 31, 2021

Housing Vacancy Rates

Area	Gross Vacancy Rate[2] (%)			Year-Round Vacancy Rate[3] (%)			Rental Vacancy Rate[4] (%)			Homeowner Vacancy Rate[5] (%)		
	2019	2020	2021	2019	2020	2021	2019	2020	2021	2019	2020	2021
MSA[1]	5.6	4.7	5.9	5.6	4.7	5.6	3.7	4.4	6.6	0.5	0.0	0.4
U.S.	12.0	10.6	10.8	9.5	8.2	8.4	6.7	6.3	6.1	1.4	1.0	0.9

Note: (1) Figures cover the San Jose-Sunnyvale-Santa Clara, CA Metropolitan Statistical Area; (2) The percentage of the total housing inventory that is vacant; (3) The percentage of the housing inventory (excluding seasonal units) that is year-round vacant; (4) The percentage of rental inventory that is vacant for rent; (5) The percentage of homeowner inventory that is vacant for sale
Source: U.S. Census Bureau, Housing Vacancies and Homeownership Annual Statistics: 2019, 2020, 2021

INCOME

Income

Area	Per Capita ($)	Median Household ($)	Average Household ($)
City	49,207	117,324	150,601
MSA[1]	58,508	129,343	172,472
U.S.	35,384	64,994	91,547

Note: (1) Figures cover the San Jose-Sunnyvale-Santa Clara, CA Metropolitan Statistical Area
Source: U.S. Census Bureau, 2016-2020 American Community Survey 5-Year Estimates

Household Income Distribution

Area	Percent of Households Earning							
	Under $15,000	$15,000 -$24,999	$25,000 -$34,999	$35,000 -$49,999	$50,000 -$74,999	$75,000 -$99,999	$100,000 -$149,999	$150,000 and up
City	5.6	4.6	4.4	6.9	11.2	10.3	18.4	38.6
MSA[1]	5.1	4.0	4.1	6.1	10.4	9.5	17.6	43.1
U.S.	9.9	8.5	8.6	12.0	17.2	12.8	15.6	15.4

Note: (1) Figures cover the San Jose-Sunnyvale-Santa Clara, CA Metropolitan Statistical Area
Source: U.S. Census Bureau, 2016-2020 American Community Survey 5-Year Estimates

Poverty Rate

Area	All Ages	Under 18 Years Old	18 to 64 Years Old	65 Years and Over
City	8.3	8.9	7.8	9.5
MSA[1]	7.2	7.5	6.9	8.2
U.S.	12.8	17.5	12.1	9.3

Note: Figures are percentage of people whose income during the past 12 months was below the poverty level; (1) Figures cover the San Jose-Sunnyvale-Santa Clara, CA Metropolitan Statistical Area
Source: U.S. Census Bureau, 2016-2020 American Community Survey 5-Year Estimates

CITY FINANCES

City Government Finances

Component	2019 ($000)	2019 ($ per capita)
Total Revenues	2,723,499	2,631
Total Expenditures	1,952,516	1,886
Debt Outstanding	4,853,835	4,688
Cash and Securities[1]	2,693,548	2,602

Note: (1) Cash and security holdings of a government at the close of its fiscal year, including those of its dependent agencies, utilities, and liquor stores.
Source: U.S. Census Bureau, State & Local Government Finances 2019

City Government Revenue by Source

Source	2019 ($000)	2019 ($ per capita)	2019 (%)
General Revenue			
From Federal Government	36,462	35	1.3
From State Government	108,207	105	4.0
From Local Governments	5,723	6	0.2
Taxes			
Property	583,045	563	21.4
Sales and Gross Receipts	408,849	395	15.0
Personal Income	0	0	0.0
Corporate Income	0	0	0.0
Motor Vehicle License	0	0	0.0
Other Taxes	242,680	234	8.9
Current Charges	783,806	757	28.8
Liquor Store	0	0	0.0
Utility	153,871	149	5.6

Source: U.S. Census Bureau, State & Local Government Finances 2019

City Government Expenditures by Function

Function	2019 ($000)	2019 ($ per capita)	2019 (%)
General Direct Expenditures			
Air Transportation	177,595	171	9.1
Corrections	0	0	0.0
Education	0	0	0.0
Employment Security Administration	0	0	0.0
Financial Administration	0	0	0.0
Fire Protection	154,483	149	7.9
General Public Buildings	0	0	0.0
Governmental Administration, Other	96,156	92	4.9
Health	152	< 1	< 0.1
Highways	84,815	81	4.3
Hospitals	0	0	0.0
Housing and Community Development	31,273	30	1.6
Interest on General Debt	238,821	230	12.2
Judicial and Legal	0	0	0.0
Libraries	31,426	30	1.6
Parking	15,470	14	0.8
Parks and Recreation	200,585	193	10.3
Police Protection	260,006	251	13.3
Public Welfare	0	0	0.0
Sewerage	291,762	281	14.9
Solid Waste Management	117,717	113	6.0
Veterans' Services	0	0	0.0
Liquor Store	0	0	0.0
Utility	140,972	136	7.2

Source: U.S. Census Bureau, State & Local Government Finances 2019

EMPLOYMENT

Labor Force and Employment

Area	Civilian Labor Force			Workers Employed		
	Dec. 2020	Dec. 2021	% Chg.	Dec. 2020	Dec. 2021	% Chg.
City	534,723	549,109	2.7	499,062	531,565	6.5
MSA[1]	1,041,226	1,074,395	3.2	979,012	1,042,538	6.5
U.S.	160,017,000	161,696,000	1.0	149,613,000	155,732,000	4.1

Note: Data is not seasonally adjusted and covers workers 16 years of age and older; (1) Figures cover the San Jose-Sunnyvale-Santa Clara, CA Metropolitan Statistical Area
Source: Bureau of Labor Statistics, Local Area Unemployment Statistics

Unemployment Rate

Area	2021											
	Jan.	Feb.	Mar.	Apr.	May	Jun.	Jul.	Aug.	Sep.	Oct.	Nov.	Dec.
City	6.4	5.9	5.6	5.5	5.3	5.8	5.5	5.3	4.4	4.1	3.5	3.2
MSA[1]	5.8	5.4	5.1	5.0	4.7	5.2	5.0	4.8	4.0	3.8	3.2	3.0
U.S.	6.8	6.6	6.2	5.7	5.5	6.1	5.7	5.3	4.6	4.3	3.9	3.7

Note: Data is not seasonally adjusted and covers workers 16 years of age and older; (1) Figures cover the San Jose-Sunnyvale-Santa Clara, CA Metropolitan Statistical Area
Source: Bureau of Labor Statistics, Local Area Unemployment Statistics

Average Wages

Occupation	$/Hr.	Occupation	$/Hr.
Accountants and Auditors	54.25	Maintenance and Repair Workers	28.79
Automotive Mechanics	30.20	Marketing Managers	101.10
Bookkeepers	28.72	Network and Computer Systems Admin.	65.12
Carpenters	37.83	Nurses, Licensed Practical	36.48
Cashiers	18.20	Nurses, Registered	74.63
Computer Programmers	69.29	Nursing Assistants	22.93
Computer Systems Analysts	67.93	Office Clerks, General	23.92
Computer User Support Specialists	36.78	Physical Therapists	59.22
Construction Laborers	29.80	Physicians	117.95
Cooks, Restaurant	20.86	Plumbers, Pipefitters and Steamfitters	45.47
Customer Service Representatives	25.30	Police and Sheriff's Patrol Officers	60.56
Dentists	80.79	Postal Service Mail Carriers	27.07
Electricians	43.79	Real Estate Sales Agents	36.34
Engineers, Electrical	71.57	Retail Salespersons	19.79
Fast Food and Counter Workers	17.83	Sales Representatives, Technical/Scientific	72.48
Financial Managers	96.79	Secretaries, Exc. Legal/Medical/Executive	26.31
First-Line Supervisors of Office Workers	39.45	Security Guards	21.00
General and Operations Managers	79.49	Surgeons	n/a
Hairdressers/Cosmetologists	18.04	Teacher Assistants, Exc. Postsecondary*	21.67
Home Health and Personal Care Aides	15.57	Teachers, Secondary School, Exc. Sp. Ed.*	50.00
Janitors and Cleaners	19.48	Telemarketers	20.25
Landscaping/Groundskeeping Workers	22.71	Truck Drivers, Heavy/Tractor-Trailer	29.59
Lawyers	111.15	Truck Drivers, Light/Delivery Services	24.93
Maids and Housekeeping Cleaners	21.60	Waiters and Waitresses	19.36

Note: Wage data covers the San Jose-Sunnyvale-Santa Clara, CA Metropolitan Statistical Area; (*) Hourly wages were calculated from annual wage data based on a 40 hour work week; n/a not available.
Source: Bureau of Labor Statistics, Metro Area Occupational Employment & Wage Estimates, May 2021

Employment by Industry

Sector	MSA[1]		U.S.
	Number of Employees	Percent of Total	Percent of Total
Construction	52,600	4.6	5.0
Education and Health Services	183,600	16.0	16.0
Financial Activities	37,600	3.3	5.9
Government	95,800	8.4	14.9
Information	109,700	9.6	1.9
Leisure and Hospitality	92,100	8.0	9.8
Manufacturing	172,800	15.1	8.4
Mining and Logging	200	<0.1	0.4
Other Services	23,300	2.0	3.7
Professional and Business Services	252,200	22.0	14.6
Retail Trade	77,800	6.8	10.7
Transportation, Warehousing, and Utilities	18,900	1.7	4.8
Wholesale Trade	28,400	2.5	3.8

Note: Figures are non-farm employment as of December 2021. Figures are not seasonally adjusted and include workers 16 years of age and older; (1) Figures cover the San Jose-Sunnyvale-Santa Clara, CA Metropolitan Statistical Area
Source: Bureau of Labor Statistics, Current Employment Statistics, Employment, Hours, and Earnings

Employment by Occupation

Occupation Classification	City (%)	MSA[1] (%)	U.S. (%)
Management, Business, Science, and Arts	48.2	54.8	39.5
Natural Resources, Construction, and Maintenance	6.9	6.1	8.7
Production, Transportation, and Material Moving	9.7	8.2	13.1
Sales and Office	17.8	16.5	21.3
Service	17.4	14.4	17.4

Note: Figures cover employed civilians 16 years of age and older; (1) Figures cover the San Jose-Sunnyvale-Santa Clara, CA Metropolitan Statistical Area
Source: U.S. Census Bureau, 2016-2020 American Community Survey 5-Year Estimates

Occupations with Greatest Projected Employment Growth: 2021 – 2023

Occupation[1]	2021 Employment	2023 Projected Employment	Numeric Employment Change	Percent Employment Change
Fast Food and Counter Workers	383,500	457,000	73,500	19.2
Home Health and Personal Care Aides	663,400	716,600	53,200	8.0
Waiters and Waitresses	208,500	257,600	49,100	23.5
Cooks, Restaurant	136,700	175,300	38,600	28.2
Laborers and Freight, Stock, and Material Movers, Hand	401,500	431,600	30,100	7.5
Software Developers and Software Quality Assurance Analysts and Testers	311,600	336,800	25,200	8.1
Janitors and Cleaners, Except Maids and Housekeeping Cleaners	232,200	252,400	20,200	8.7
Cooks, Fast Food	109,600	128,200	18,600	17.0
Stockers and Order Fillers	273,000	290,400	17,400	6.4
First-Line Supervisors of Food Preparation and Serving Workers	81,700	98,600	16,900	20.7

Note: Projections cover California; (1) Sorted by numeric employment change
Source: www.projectionscentral.com, State Occupational Projections, 2021–2023 Short-Term Projections

Fastest-Growing Occupations: 2021 – 2023

Occupation[1]	2021 Employment	2023 Projected Employment	Numeric Employment Change	Percent Employment Change
Manicurists and Pedicurists	23,400	33,500	10,100	43.2
Cooks, All Other	3,900	5,400	1,500	38.5
Miscellaneous Entertainers and Performers, Sports and Related Workers	5,900	8,100	2,200	37.3
Barbers	1,900	2,600	700	36.8
Gaming Change Persons and Booth Cashiers	2,200	3,000	800	36.4
Gaming Service Workers, All Other	1,400	1,900	500	35.7
Gaming Dealers	12,200	16,500	4,300	35.2
First-Line Supervisors of Gambling Services Workers	2,900	3,900	1,000	34.5
Massage Therapists	18,000	24,200	6,200	34.4
Costume Attendants	1,500	2,000	500	33.3

Note: Projections cover California; (1) Sorted by percent employment change and excludes occupations with numeric employment change less than 50
Source: www.projectionscentral.com, State Occupational Projections, 2021–2023 Short-Term Projections

TAXES

State Corporate Income Tax Rates

State	Tax Rate (%)	Income Brackets ($)	Num. of Brackets	Financial Institution Tax Rate (%)[a]	Federal Income Tax Ded.
California	8.84 (b)	Flat rate	1	10.84 (b)	No

Note: Tax rates as of January 1, 2022; (a) Rates listed are the corporate income tax rate applied to financial institutions or excise taxes based on income. Some states have other taxes based upon the value of deposits or shares; (b) Minimum tax is $800 in California, $250 in District of Columbia, $50 in Arizona and North Dakota (banks), $400 ($100 banks) in Rhode Island, $200 per location in South Dakota (banks), $100 in Utah, $300 in Vermont.
Source: Federation of Tax Administrators, State Corporate Income Tax Rates, January 1, 2022

State Individual Income Tax Rates

State	Tax Rate (%)	Income Brackets ($)	Personal Exemptions ($)			Standard Ded. ($)	
			Single	Married	Depend.	Single	Married
California (a)	1.0 - 12.3 (g)	9,325 - 625,369 (b)	129	258	400 (c)	4,803	9,606 (a)

Note: Tax rates as of January 1, 2022; Local- and county-level taxes are not included; Federal income tax is not deductible on state income tax returns; (a) 19 states have statutory provision for automatically adjusting to the rate of inflation the dollar values of the income tax brackets, standard deductions, and/or personal exemptions. Michigan indexes the personal exemption only. Oregon does not index the income brackets for $125,000 and over; (b) For joint returns, taxes are twice the tax on half the couple's income; (c) The personal exemption takes the form of a tax credit instead of a deduction; (g) California imposes an additional 1% tax on taxable income over $1 million, making the maximum rate 13.3% over $1 million.
Source: Federation of Tax Administrators, State Individual Income Tax Rates, January 1, 2022

Various State Sales and Excise Tax Rates

State	State Sales Tax (%)	Gasoline[1] (¢/gal.)	Cigarette[2] ($/pack)	Spirits[3] ($/gal.)	Wine[4] ($/gal.)	Beer[5] ($/gal.)	Recreational Marijuana (%)
California	7.25	68.15	2.87	3.3	0.2	0.2	(c)

Note: All tax rates as of January 1, 2022; (1) The American Petroleum Institute has developed a methodology for determining the average tax rate on a gallon of fuel. Rates may include any of the following: excise taxes, environmental fees, storage tank fees, other fees or taxes, general sales tax, and local taxes; (2) The federal excise tax of $1.0066 per pack and local taxes are not included; (3) Rates are those applicable to off-premise sales of 40% alcohol by volume (a.b.v.) distilled spirits in 750ml containers. Local excise taxes are excluded; (4) Rates are those applicable to off-premise sales of 11% a.b.v. non-carbonated wine in 750ml containers; (5) Rates are those applicable to off-premise sales of 4.7% a.b.v. beer in 12 ounce containers; (c) 15% excise tax (levied on wholesale at average market rate); $10.08/oz. flowers & $3/oz. leaves cultivation tax; $1.41/oz fresh cannabis plant
Source: Tax Foundation, 2022 Facts & Figures: How Does Your State Compare?

State Business Tax Climate Index Rankings

State	Overall Rank	Corporate Tax Rank	Individual Income Tax Rank	Sales Tax Rank	Property Tax Rank	Unemployment Insurance Tax Rank
California	48	46	49	47	14	23

Note: The index is a measure of how each state's tax laws affect economic performance. The lower the rank, the more favorable a state's tax system is for business. States without a given tax are given a ranking of 1. The scores/rankings for the District of Columbia do not affect other states. The 2022 index represents the tax climate as of July 1, 2021.
Source: Tax Foundation, State Business Tax Climate Index 2022

TRANSPORTATION

Means of Transportation to Work

Area	Car/Truck/Van		Public Transportation			Bicycle	Walked	Other Means	Worked at Home
	Drove Alone	Car-pooled	Bus	Subway	Railroad				
City	72.6	11.3	2.4	0.3	1.1	0.6	1.7	1.8	8.2
MSA[1]	71.2	10.3	2.1	0.3	1.2	1.5	2.1	1.7	9.6
U.S.	74.9	8.9	2.2	1.7	0.5	0.5	2.6	1.4	7.3

Note: Figures are percentages and cover workers 16 years of age and older; (1) Figures cover the San Jose-Sunnyvale-Santa Clara, CA Metropolitan Statistical Area
Source: U.S. Census Bureau, 2016-2020 American Community Survey 5-Year Estimates

Travel Time to Work

Area	Less Than 10 Minutes	10 to 19 Minutes	20 to 29 Minutes	30 to 44 Minutes	45 to 59 Minutes	60 to 89 Minutes	90 Minutes or More
City	5.3	23.3	22.2	26.9	10.6	8.4	3.4
MSA[1]	6.7	25.4	22.5	25.1	9.4	7.6	3.3
U.S.	12.3	28.4	20.9	20.9	8.3	6.4	2.9

Note: Note: Figures are percentages and include workers 16 years old and over; (1) Figures cover the San Jose-Sunnyvale-Santa Clara, CA Metropolitan Statistical Area
Source: U.S. Census Bureau, 2016-2020 American Community Survey 5-Year Estimates

Key Congestion Measures

Measure	1990	2000	2010	2015	2020
Annual Hours of Delay, Total (000)	33,232	59,026	87,229	114,375	46,377
Annual Hours of Delay, Per Auto Commuter	37	49	63	78	31
Annual Congestion Cost, Per Auto Commuter ($)	859	1,147	1,347	1,630	712

Note: Covers the San Jose CA urban area
Source: Texas A&M Transportation Institute, 2021 Urban Mobility Report

Freeway Travel Time Index

Measure	1985	1990	1995	2000	2005	2010	2015	2020
Urban Area Index[1]	1.15	1.21	1.23	1.28	1.32	1.34	1.43	1.12
Urban Area Rank[1,2]	15	7	8	9	8	6	3	10

Note: Freeway Travel Time Index—the ratio of travel time in the peak period to the travel time at free-flow conditions. For example, a value of 1.30 indicates a 20-minute free-flow trip takes 26 minutes in the peak (20 minutes x 1.30 = 26 minutes); (1) Covers the San Jose CA urban area; (2) Rank is based on 101 larger urban areas (#1 = highest travel time index)

Source: Texas A&M Transportation Institute, 2021 Urban Mobility Report

Public Transportation

Agency Name / Mode of Transportation	Vehicles Operated in Maximum Service[1]	Annual Unlinked Passenger Trips[2] (in thous.)	Annual Passenger Miles[3] (in thous.)
Santa Clara Valley Transportation Authority (VTA)			
Bus (directly operated)	377	21,702.5	110,906.8
Bus (purchased transportation)	12	307.0	1,118.4
Demand Response (purchased transportation)	154	351.0	4,032.9
Demand Response - Taxi	31	65.4	424.4
Light Rail (directly operated)	61	6,281.6	33,535.1

Note: (1) Number of revenue vehicles operated by the given mode and type of service to meet the annual maximum service requirement. This is the revenue vehicle count during the peak season of the year; on the week and day that maximum service is provided. Vehicles operated in maximum service (VOMS) exclude atypical days and one-time special events; (2) Number of passengers who boarded public transportation vehicles. Passengers are counted each time they board a vehicle no matter how many vehicles they use to travel from their origin to their destination. (3) Sum of the distances ridden by all passengers during the entire fiscal year.

Source: Federal Transit Administration, National Transit Database, 2020

Air Transportation

Airport Name and Code / Type of Service	Passenger Airlines[1]	Passenger Enplanements	Freight Carriers[2]	Freight (lbs)
San Jose International (SJC)				
Domestic service (U.S. carriers - 2021)	21	3,458,498	9	39,332,530
International service (U.S. carriers - 2020)	5	45,229	2	78,318

Note: (1) Includes all U.S.-based major, minor and commuter airlines that carried at least one passenger during the year; (2) Includes all U.S.-based airlines and freight carriers that transported at least one pound of freight during the year.

Source: Bureau of Transportation Statistics, The Intermodal Transportation Database, Air Carriers: T-100 Domestic Market (U.S. Carriers), 2021; Bureau of Transportation Statistics, The Intermodal Transportation Database, Air Carriers: T-100 International Market (U.S. Carriers), 2020

BUSINESSES

Major Business Headquarters

Company Name	Industry	Rankings	
		Fortune[1]	Forbes[2]
Adobe	Computer Software	234	-
Broadcom	Semiconductors and Other Electronic Components	121	-
Cisco Systems	Network and Other Communications Equipment	63	-
PayPal Holdings	Financial Data Services	134	-
Sanmina	Semiconductors and Other Electronic Components	418	-
eBay	Internet Services and Retailing	276	-

Note: (1) Companies that produce a 10-K are ranked 1 to 500 based on 2020 revenue; (2) All private companies with at least $2 billion in annual revenue through the end of their most current fiscal year are ranked 1 to 225; companies listed are headquartered in the city; dashes indicate no ranking

Source: Fortune, "Fortune 500," 2021; Forbes, "America's Largest Private Companies," 2021

Fastest-Growing Businesses

According to *Inc.*, San Jose is home to five of America's 500 fastest-growing private companies: **AppZen** (#171); **Balbix** (#251); **InstaMortgage** (#394); **The Pipeline Group** (#415); **Health at Scale Corporation** (#421). Criteria: must be an independent, privately-held, for-profit, U.S. corporation, proprietorship or partnership as of December 31, 2020; revenues must be at least $100,000 in 2017 and $2 million in 2020; must have four-year operating/sales history. *Inc., "America's 500 Fastest-Growing Private Companies," 2021*

According to *Fortune*, San Jose is home to two of the 100 fastest-growing companies in the world: **Adobe** (#56); **PayPal Holdings** (#74). Companies were ranked by their revenue growth rate; their EPS growth rate; and their three-year annualized total return to investors for the period ending June 30, 2021. Criteria for inclusion: a company, foreign or domestic, must trade on a major U.S. stock exchange; must file quarterly reports with the SEC; must have a minimum market capitalization of $250 million; must have a stock price of at least $5 on June 30, 2021; must have been trading continuously since June 30, 2018; must have revenue and net income for the four quarters ended on or before April 30, 2021, of at least $50 million and $10 million, respectively; and must have posted a compound annual growth in revenue and earnings per share of at least 15% annually over the three years ending on or before April 30, 2021. Real estate investment trusts, limited-liability companies, limited parterships, business development companies, closed-end investment firms, companies about to be acquired, and companies that lost money in the quarter ending April 30, 2021 were excluded. *Fortune, "100 Fastest-Growing Companies," 2021*

According to Deloitte, San Jose is home to 12 of North America's 500 fastest-growing high-technology companies: **Balbix** (#32); **AppZen** (#67); **InstaMortgage** (#110); **Whatfix** (#143); **Zoom Video Communications** (#149); **Kyligence** (#223); **Vectra AI** (#329); **Automation Anywhere** (#357); **TapClassifieds** (#389); **Iterate.ai** (#407); **Roku** (#450); **Zscaler** (#457). Companies are ranked by percentage growth in revenue over a four-year period. Criteria for inclusion: company must be headquartered within North America; must own proprietary intellectual property or technology that is sold to customers in products that contributes to a significant portion of the company's operating revenue; must have been in business for a minumum of four years with 2017 operating revenues of at least $50,000 USD/CD and 2020 operating revenues of at least $5 million USD/CD. *Deloitte, 2021 Technology Fast 500™*

Living Environment

COST OF LIVING

Cost of Living Index

Composite Index	Groceries	Housing	Utilities	Trans-portation	Health Care	Misc. Goods/ Services
n/a	n/a	n/a	n/a	n/a	n/a	n/a

Note: The Cost of Living Index measures regional differences in the cost of consumer goods and services, excluding taxes and non-consumer expenditures, for professional and managerial households in the top income quintile. It is based on more than 50,000 prices covering almost 60 different items for which prices are collected three times a year by chambers of commerce, economic development organizations or university applied economic centers in each participating urban area. The numbers shown should be read as a percentage above or below the national average of 100. For example, a value of 115.4 in the groceries column indicates that grocery prices are 15.4% higher than the national average. Small differences in the index numbers should not be interpreted as significant; n/a not available.
Source: The Council for Community and Economic Research, Cost of Living Index, 2021

Grocery Prices

Area[1]	T-Bone Steak ($/pound)	Frying Chicken ($/pound)	Whole Milk ($/half gal.)	Eggs ($/dozen)	Orange Juice ($/64 oz.)	Coffee ($/11.5 oz.)
City[2]	n/a	n/a	n/a	n/a	n/a	n/a
Avg.	12.82	1.40	2.22	1.57	3.59	4.30
Min.	8.91	0.91	1.29	0.75	2.87	3.02
Max.	21.35	2.69	3.92	3.86	5.49	8.11

Note: (1) Values for the local area are compared with the average, minimum and maximum values for all 285 areas in the Cost of Living Index; (2) Figures cover the San Jose CA urban area; n/a not available; ***T-Bone Steak*** *(price per pound);* ***Frying Chicken*** *(price per pound, whole fryer);* ***Whole Milk*** *(half gallon carton);* ***Eggs*** *(price per dozen, Grade A, large);* ***Orange Juice*** *(64 oz. Tropicana or Florida Natural);* ***Coffee*** *(11.5 oz. can, vacuum-packed, Maxwell House, Hills Bros, or Folgers).*
Source: The Council for Community and Economic Research, Cost of Living Index, 2021

Housing and Utility Costs

Area[1]	New Home Price ($)	Apartment Rent ($/month)	All Electric ($/month)	Part Electric ($/month)	Other Energy ($/month)	Telephone ($/month)
City[2]	n/a	n/a	n/a	n/a	n/a	n/a
Avg.	398,393	1,217	171.38	100.83	69.67	187.75
Min.	212,799	534	96.71	31.56	27.15	173.01
Max.	2,354,006	4,438	369.53	277.33	303.87	206.73

Note: (1) Values for the local area are compared with the average, minimum and maximum values for all 285 areas in the Cost of Living Index; (2) Figures cover the San Jose CA urban area; n/a not available; ***New Home Price*** *(2,400 sf living area, 8,000 sf lot, in urban area with full utilities);* ***Apartment Rent*** *(950 sf 2 bedroom/1.5 or 2 bath, unfurnished, excluding all utilities except water);* ***All Electric*** *(average monthly cost for an all-electric home);* ***Part Electric*** *(average monthly cost for a part-electric home);* ***Other Energy*** *(average monthly cost for natural gas, fuel oil, coal, wood, and any other forms of energy except electricity);* ***Telephone*** *(price includes the base monthly rate plus taxes and fees for three lines of mobile phone service).*
Source: The Council for Community and Economic Research, Cost of Living Index, 2021

Health Care, Transportation, and Other Costs

Area[1]	Doctor ($/visit)	Dentist ($/visit)	Optometrist ($/visit)	Gasoline ($/gallon)	Beauty Salon ($/visit)	Men's Shirt ($)
City[2]	n/a	n/a	n/a	n/a	n/a	n/a
Avg.	118.16	101.04	109.44	2.71	40.63	30.77
Min.	35.04	55.56	51.17	2.17	18.59	11.32
Max.	231.10	165.12	256.81	4.11	85.33	63.03

Note: (1) Values for the local area are compared with the average, minimum and maximum values for all 285 areas in the Cost of Living Index; (2) Figures cover the San Jose CA urban area; n/a not available; ***Doctor*** *(general practitioners routine exam of an established patient);* ***Dentist*** *(adult teeth cleaning and periodic oral examination);* ***Optometrist*** *(full vision eye exam for established adult patient);* ***Gasoline*** *(one gallon regular unleaded, national brand, including all taxes, cash price at self-service pump if available);* ***Beauty Salon*** *(woman's shampoo, trim, and blow-dry);* ***Men's Shirt*** *(cotton/polyester dress shirt, pinpoint weave, long sleeves).*
Source: The Council for Community and Economic Research, Cost of Living Index, 2021

HOUSING

Homeownership Rate

Area	2013 (%)	2014 (%)	2015 (%)	2016 (%)	2017 (%)	2018 (%)	2019 (%)	2020 (%)	2021 (%)
MSA[1]	56.4	56.4	50.7	49.9	50.4	50.4	52.4	52.6	48.4
U.S.	65.1	64.5	63.7	63.4	63.9	64.4	64.6	66.6	65.5

Note: (1) Figures cover the San Jose-Sunnyvale-Santa Clara, CA Metropolitan Statistical Area
Source: U.S. Census Bureau, Housing Vacancies and Homeownership Annual Statistics: 2013-2021

House Price Index (HPI)

Area	National Ranking[2]	Quarterly Change (%)	One-Year Change (%)	Five-Year Change (%)	Since 1991Q1 (%)
MSA[1]	259	3.85	10.13	23.40	334.40
U.S.[3]	–	3.33	17.54	54.45	258.04

Note: The HPI is a weighted repeat sales index. It measures average price changes in repeat sales or refinancings on the same properties. This information is obtained by reviewing repeat mortgage transactions on single-family properties whose mortgages have been purchased or securitized by Fannie Mae or Freddie Mac since January 1975; (1) Figures cover the San Jose-Sunnyvale-Santa Clara, CA Metropolitan Statistical Area; (2) Rankings are based on annual percentage change for all metro areas containing at least 15,000 transactions over the last 10 years and ranges from 1 to 268; (3) figures based on a weighted average of Census Division estimates using a seasonally adjusted, purchase-only index; all figures are for the period ending December 31, 2021
Source: Federal Housing Finance Agency, Change in FHFA Metropolitan Area House Price Indexes, 2021Q4

Median Single-Family Home Prices

Area	2019	2020	2021[p]	Percent Change 2020 to 2021
MSA[1]	1,265.0	1,385.0	1,640.0	18.4
U.S. Average	274.6	300.2	353.4	17.7

Note: Figures are median sales prices of existing single-family homes in thousands of dollars; (p) preliminary; (1) Figures cover the San Jose-Sunnyvale-Santa Clara, CA Metropolitan Statistical Area
Source: National Association of Realtors, Median Sales Price of Existing Single-Family Homes for Metropolitan Areas, 4th Quarter 2021

Qualifying Income Based on Median Sales Price of Existing Single-Family Homes

Area	With 5% Down ($)	With 10% Down ($)	With 20% Down ($)
MSA[1]	330,218	312,838	278,079
U.S. Average	70,699	66,978	59,536

Note: Figures are preliminary; Qualifying income is based on a mortgage rate of 3.13%. Monthly principal and interest payment is limited to 25% of income; (1) Figures cover the San Jose-Sunnyvale-Santa Clara, CA Metropolitan Statistical Area
Source: National Association of Realtors, Qualifying Income Based on Median Sales Price of Existing Single-Family Homes for Metropolitan Areas, 4th Quarter 2021

Home Value Distribution

Area	Under $50,000	$50,000 -$99,999	$100,000 -$149,999	$150,000 -$199,999	$200,000 -$299,999	$300,000 -$499,999	$500,000 -$999,999	$1,000,000 or more
City	1.4	1.1	1.5	1.0	2.0	5.3	45.7	42.0
MSA[1]	1.2	0.8	1.2	0.9	1.8	4.8	36.4	52.9
U.S.	6.6	11.0	12.3	13.6	20.0	20.5	12.3	3.7

Note: Figures are percentages and cover owner-occupied housing units; (1) Figures cover the San Jose-Sunnyvale-Santa Clara, CA Metropolitan Statistical Area
Source: U.S. Census Bureau, 2016-2020 American Community Survey 5-Year Estimates

Year Housing Structure Built

Area	2010 or Later	2000 -2009	1990 -1999	1980 -1989	1970 -1979	1960 -1969	1950 -1959	1940 -1949	Before 1940	Median Year
City	5.6	9.2	10.4	12.8	24.4	18.3	11.2	2.8	5.3	1975
MSA[1]	6.5	8.8	10.4	12.3	21.6	17.9	14.0	3.5	5.1	1974
U.S.	6.2	13.6	13.9	13.4	15.0	10.5	10.2	4.8	12.4	1978

Note: Figures are percentages except for Median Year; Note: (1) Figures cover the San Jose-Sunnyvale-Santa Clara, CA Metropolitan Statistical Area
Source: U.S. Census Bureau, 2016-2020 American Community Survey 5-Year Estimates

Gross Monthly Rent

Area	Under $500	$500 -$999	$1,000 -$1,499	$1,500 -$1,999	$2,000 -$2,499	$2,500 -$2,999	$3,000 and up	Median ($)
City	4.1	6.2	11.5	19.2	19.7	17.8	21.6	2,232
MSA[1]	3.3	5.3	9.7	17.0	20.1	18.3	26.2	2,365
U.S.	8.9	34.3	30.2	14.9	6.2	2.6	2.8	1,096

Note: Figures are percentages except for Median; Gross rent is the contract rent plus the estimated average monthly cost of utilities (electricity, gas, and water and sewer) and fuels (oil, coal, kerosene, wood, etc.) if these are paid by the renter (or paid for the renter by someone else); (1) Figures cover the San Jose-Sunnyvale-Santa Clara, CA Metropolitan Statistical Area
Source: U.S. Census Bureau, 2016-2020 American Community Survey 5-Year Estimates

HEALTH

Health Risk Factors

Category	MSA[1] (%)	U.S. (%)
Adults aged 18–64 who have any kind of health care coverage	n/a	86.8
Adults who reported being in good or better health	n/a	86.7
Adults who are current smokers	n/a	15.5
Adults who currently use chewing tobacco, snuff, or snus	n/a	3.7
Adults who are heavy drinkers[2]	n/a	6.7
Adults who are binge drinkers[3]	n/a	15.7
Adults who are overweight (BMI 25.0 - 29.9)	n/a	35.2
Adults who are obese (BMI 30.0 - 99.8)	n/a	31.9
Adults who participated in any physical activities in the past month	n/a	77.6
Adults who always or nearly always wears a seat belt	n/a	94.2

Note: (1) Figures for the San Jose-Sunnyvale-Santa Clara, CA Metropolitan Statistical Area were not available. (2) Heavy drinkers are classified as adult men having more than 14 drinks per week and adult women having more than 7 drinks per week; (3) Binge drinkers are classified as males having five or more drinks on one occasion or females having four or more drinks on one occasion
Source: Centers for Disease Control and Prevention, Behaviorial Risk Factor Surveillance System, SMART: Selected Metropolitan Area Risk Trends, 2020

Acute and Chronic Health Conditions

Category	MSA[1] (%)	U.S. (%)
Adults who have ever been told they had a heart attack	n/a	4.3
Adults who have ever been told they have angina or coronary heart disease	n/a	4.0
Adults who have ever been told they had a stroke	n/a	2.8
Adults who have ever been told they have asthma	n/a	14.2
Adults who have ever been told they have arthritis	n/a	24.5
Adults who have ever been told they have diabetes[2]	n/a	10.6
Adults who have ever been told they had skin cancer	n/a	6.4
Adults who have ever been told they had any other types of cancer	n/a	6.8
Adults who have ever been told they have COPD	n/a	6.2
Adults who have ever been told they have kidney disease	n/a	2.9
Adults who have ever been told they have a form of depression	n/a	19.6

Note: (1) Figures for the San Jose-Sunnyvale-Santa Clara, CA Metropolitan Statistical Area were not available. (2) Figures do not include pregnancy-related, borderline, or pre-diabetes
Source: Centers for Disease Control and Prevention, Behaviorial Risk Factor Surveillance System, SMART: Selected Metropolitan Area Risk Trends, 2020

Health Screening and Vaccination Rates

Category	MSA[1] (%)	U.S. (%)
Adults 50-75 who have had a blood stool test within the past year	n/a	9.3
Adults aged 65+ who have had flu shot within the past year	n/a	67.9
Adults aged 65+ who have ever had a pneumonia vaccination	n/a	72.2
Adults who have ever been tested for HIV	n/a	37.1
Women aged 21-65 who have had a pap test in the past three years	n/a	77.7
Men aged 40+ who have had a PSA test within the past two years	n/a	31.8
Women aged 40+ who have had a mammogram within the past two years	n/a	71.5

Note: (1) Figures for the San Jose-Sunnyvale-Santa Clara, CA Metropolitan Statistical Area were not available.
Source: Centers for Disease Control and Prevention, Behaviorial Risk Factor Surveillance System, SMART: Selected Metropolitan Area Risk Trends, 2020

Disability Status

Category	MSA[1] (%)	U.S. (%)
Adults who reported being deaf	n/a	6.8
Are you blind or have serious difficulty seeing, even when wearing glasses?	n/a	4.7
Do you have difficulty doing errands alone?	n/a	6.3
Do you have difficulty dressing or bathing?	n/a	3.0
Do you have serious difficulty concentrating/remembering/making decisions?	n/a	10.8
Do you have serious difficulty walking or climbing stairs?	n/a	11.9

Note: (1) Figures for the San Jose-Sunnyvale-Santa Clara, CA Metropolitan Statistical Area were not available.
Source: Centers for Disease Control and Prevention, Behaviorial Risk Factor Surveillance System, SMART: Selected Metropolitan Area Risk Trends, 2020

Mortality Rates for the Top 10 Causes of Death in the U.S.

ICD-10[a] Sub-Chapter	ICD-10[a] Code	Age-Adjusted Mortality Rate[1] per 100,000 population	
		County[2]	U.S.
Malignant neoplasms	C00-C97	110.5	146.4
Ischaemic heart diseases	I20-I25	51.4	90.2
Other forms of heart disease	I30-I51	22.1	51.9
Other degenerative diseases of the nervous system	G30-G31	52.4	39.7
Other external causes of accidental injury	W00-X59	20.2	38.7
Chronic lower respiratory diseases	J40-J47	15.3	38.1
Cerebrovascular diseases	I60-I69	30.4	37.6
Organic, including symptomatic, mental disorders	F01-F09	3.0	29.4
Hypertensive diseases	I10-I15	35.1	26.1
Diabetes mellitus	E10-E14	22.5	22.6

Note: (a) ICD-10 = International Classification of Diseases 10th Revision; (1) Mortality rates are a three-year average covering 2018-2020; (2) Figures cover Santa Clara County.
Source: Centers for Disease Control and Prevention, National Center for Health Statistics. Underlying Cause of Death 1999-2020 on CDC WONDER Online Database

Mortality Rates for Selected Causes of Death

ICD-10[a] Sub-Chapter	ICD-10[a] Code	Age-Adjusted Mortality Rate[1] per 100,000 population	
		County[2]	U.S.
Assault	X85-Y09	2.2	6.5
Diseases of the liver	K70-K76	8.9	15.3
Human immunodeficiency virus (HIV) disease	B20-B24	0.4	1.4
Influenza and pneumonia	J09-J18	9.3	13.4
Intentional self-harm	X60-X84	8.3	13.9
Malnutrition	E40-E46	0.7	2.9
Obesity and other hyperalimentation	E65-E68	1.6	2.4
Renal failure	N17-N19	2.9	12.5
Transport accidents	V01-V99	7.2	12.5
Viral hepatitis	B15-B19	1.3	1.0

Note: (a) ICD-10 = International Classification of Diseases 10th Revision; (1) Mortality rates are a three-year average covering 2018-2020; (2) Figures cover Santa Clara County; Data are suppressed when the data meet the criteria for confidentiality constraints; Mortality rates are flagged as unreliable when the rate would be calculated with a numerator of 20 or less.
Source: Centers for Disease Control and Prevention, National Center for Health Statistics. Underlying Cause of Death 1999-2020 on CDC WONDER Online Database

Health Insurance Coverage

Area	With Health Insurance	With Private Health Insurance	With Public Health Insurance	Without Health Insurance	Population Under Age 19 Without Health Insurance
City	94.9	72.7	30.0	5.1	2.0
MSA[1]	95.7	77.1	27.0	4.3	1.9
U.S.	91.3	68.1	35.3	8.7	5.2

Note: Figures are percentages that cover the civilian noninstitutionalized population; (1) Figures cover the San Jose-Sunnyvale-Santa Clara, CA Metropolitan Statistical Area
Source: U.S. Census Bureau, 2016-2020 American Community Survey 5-Year Estimates

Number of Medical Professionals

Area	MDs[3]	DOs[3,4]	Dentists	Podiatrists	Chiropractors	Optometrists
County[1] (number)	8,465	220	2,305	128	826	532
County[1] (rate[2])	437.2	11.4	119.0	6.6	42.7	27.5
U.S. (rate[2])	285.1	23.0	71.1	6.2	28.2	17.0

06085
Note: Data as of 2020 unless noted; (1) Data covers Santa Clara County; (2) Rate per 100,000 population; (3) Data as of 2019 and includes all active, non-federal physicians; (4) Doctor of Osteopathic Medicine
Source: U.S. Department of Health and Human Services, Health Resources and Services Administration, Bureau of Health Professions, Area Resource File (ARF) 2020-2021

Best Hospitals

According to *U.S. News*, the San Jose-Sunnyvale-Santa Clara, CA metro area is home to two of the best hospitals in the U.S.: **Santa Clara Valley Medical Center** (1 adult specialty); **Stanford Health Care-Stanford Hospital** (Honor Roll/11 adult specialties). The hospitals listed were nationally ranked in at least one of 15 adult or 10 pediatric specialties. Only 175 U.S. hospitals performed well enough to be nationally ranked in one or more specialties. Twenty hospitals in the U.S. made the Honor Roll. The Best Hospitals Honor Roll takes both the national rankings and the procedure and condition ratings into account. Hospitals received points if they were nationally ranked in one of the 15 adult specialties—the higher they ranked, the more points they got—and how many ratings of "high performing" they earned in the 17 procedures and conditions. *U.S. News Online, "America's Best Hospitals 2021-22"*

According to *U.S. News,* the San Jose-Sunnyvale-Santa Clara, CA metro area is home to one of the best children's hospitals in the U.S.: **Lucile Packard Children's Hospital Stanford** (Honor Roll/10 pediatric specialties). The hospital listed was highly ranked in at least one of 10 pediatric specialties. Ninety-two children's hospitals in the U.S. were nationally ranked in at least one specialty. Hospitals received points for being ranked in a specialty, and the 10 hospitals with the most points across the 10 specialties make up the Honor Roll. *U.S. News Online, "America's Best Children's Hospitals 2021-22"*

EDUCATION

Public School District Statistics

District Name	Schls	Pupils	Pupil/ Teacher Ratio	Minority Pupils[1] (%)	LEP/ELL[2] (%)	IEP[3] (%)
Alum Rock Union Elementary	25	9,118	n/a	98.4	42.8	12.7
Berryessa Union Elementary	14	6,842	n/a	95.3	34.2	10.8
Cambrian	6	3,366	n/a	60.2	13.5	12.5
Campbell Union High	6	8,465	n/a	63.5	6.6	13.2
East Side Union High	16	22,576	n/a	94.7	15.5	10.9
Evergreen Elementary	18	10,426	n/a	94.7	25.2	9.4
Franklin-Mckinley Elementary	16	6,872	n/a	97.8	48.3	13.2
Moreland	7	4,683	n/a	76.7	29.1	11.5
Mount Pleasant Elementary	5	2,110	n/a	97.3	49.0	14.7
Oak Grove Elementary	18	9,757	n/a	84.0	25.5	13.5
San Jose Unified	42	28,830	n/a	76.0	22.9	12.2
Union Elementary	8	5,860	n/a	59.6	12.0	9.9

Note: Table includes school districts with 2,000 or more students; (1) Percentage of students that are not non-Hispanic white; (2) Percentage of students that are Limited English Proficient (LEP) or English Language Learners (ELL) (2018-19); (3) Percentage of students that have an Individualized Education Program (IEP).
Source: U.S. Department of Education, National Center for Education Statistics, Common Core of Data, Local Education Agency (School District) Universe Survey: School Year 2019-2020

Best High Schools

According to *U.S. News,* San Jose is home to four of the top 500 high schools in the U.S.: **Lynbrook High** (#131); **University Preparatory Academy Charter** (#138); **KIPP San Jose Collegiate** (#337); **Leland High School** (#499). Nearly 18,000 public, magnet and charter schools were ranked based on their performance on state assessments and how well they prepare students for college. *U.S. News & World Report, "Best High Schools 2021"*

Highest Level of Education

Area	Less than H.S.	H.S. Diploma	Some College, No Deg.	Associate Degree	Bachelor's Degree	Master's Degree	Prof. School Degree	Doctorate Degree
City	15.0	16.5	16.3	7.4	26.1	14.0	2.1	2.6
MSA[1]	11.5	14.3	14.9	6.8	27.5	18.0	2.8	4.2
U.S.	11.5	26.7	20.3	8.6	20.2	9.1	2.2	1.5

Note: Figures cover persons age 25 and over; (1) Figures cover the San Jose-Sunnyvale-Santa Clara, CA Metropolitan Statistical Area
Source: U.S. Census Bureau, 2016-2020 American Community Survey 5-Year Estimates

Educational Attainment by Race

Area	High School Graduate or Higher (%)					Bachelor's Degree or Higher (%)				
	Total	White	Black	Asian	Hisp.[2]	Total	White	Black	Asian	Hisp.[2]
City	85.0	89.6	91.4	87.0	68.7	44.8	46.4	37.3	56.5	16.5
MSA[1]	88.5	91.4	92.3	91.0	70.6	52.5	51.2	40.7	66.4	18.5
U.S.	88.5	90.7	86.7	87.3	70.3	32.9	34.4	22.6	55.0	17.6

Note: Figures shown cover persons 25 years old and over; (1) Figures cover the San Jose-Sunnyvale-Santa Clara, CA Metropolitan Statistical Area; (2) People of Hispanic origin can be of any race
Source: U.S. Census Bureau, 2016-2020 American Community Survey 5-Year Estimates

School Enrollment by Grade and Control

Area	Preschool (%)		Kindergarten (%)		Grades 1 - 4 (%)		Grades 5 - 8 (%)		Grades 9 - 12 (%)	
	Public	Private	Public	Private	Public	Private	Public	Private	Public	Private
City	43.2	56.8	81.5	18.5	87.8	12.2	87.5	12.5	86.2	13.8
MSA[1]	36.3	63.7	80.1	19.9	86.1	13.9	86.0	14.0	85.8	14.2
U.S.	58.9	41.1	86.9	13.1	89.0	11.0	89.0	11.0	89.7	10.3

Note: Figures shown cover persons 3 years old and over; (1) Figures cover the San Jose-Sunnyvale-Santa Clara, CA Metropolitan Statistical Area
Source: U.S. Census Bureau, 2016-2020 American Community Survey 5-Year Estimates

Higher Education

Four-Year Colleges			Two-Year Colleges			Medical Schools[1]	Law Schools[2]	Voc/ Tech[3]
Public	Private Non-profit	Private For-profit	Public	Private Non-profit	Private For-profit			
2	4	3	6	0	2	1	3	4

Note: Figures cover institutions located within the San Jose-Sunnyvale-Santa Clara, CA Metropolitan Statistical Area and include main campuses only; (1) includes schools accredited by the Liaison Committee on Medical Education and the American Osteopathic Association's Commission on Osteopathic College Accreditation; (2) includes ABA-accredited schools, schools with provisional ABA accreditation, and state accredited schools; (3) includes all schools with programs that are less than 2 years.
Source: National Center for Education Statistics, Integrated Postsecondary Education System (IPEDS), 2020-21; Wikipedia, List of Medical Schools in the United States, accessed April 11, 2022; Wikipedia, List of Law Schools in the United States, accessed April 11, 2022

According to *U.S. News & World Report,* the San Jose-Sunnyvale-Santa Clara, CA metro area is home to two of the top 200 national universities in the U.S.: **Stanford University** (#6 tie); **Santa Clara University** (#55 tie). The indicators used to capture academic quality fall into a number of categories: assessment by administrators at peer institutions; retention of students; faculty resources; student selectivity; financial resources; alumni giving; high school counselor ratings of colleges; and graduation rate. *U.S. News & World Report, "America's Best Colleges 2022"*

According to *U.S. News & World Report,* the San Jose-Sunnyvale-Santa Clara, CA metro area is home to one of the top 100 law schools in the U.S.: **Stanford University** (#2). The rankings are based on a weighted average of 12 measures of quality: peer assessment score; assessment score by lawyers/judges; median LSAT scores; median undergrad GPA; acceptance rate; employment rates for graduates; placement success; bar passage rate; faculty resources; expenditures per student; student/faculty ratio; and library resources. *U.S. News & World Report, "America's Best Graduate Schools, Law, 2022"*

According to *U.S. News & World Report,* the San Jose-Sunnyvale-Santa Clara, CA metro area is home to one of the top 75 medical schools for research in the U.S.: **Stanford University** (#4 tie). The rankings are based on a weighted average of 11 measures of quality: quality assessment; peer assessment score; assessment score by residency directors; research activity; total research activity; average research activity per faculty member; student selectivity; median MCAT total score; median undergraduate GPA; acceptance rate; and faculty resources. *U.S. News & World Report, "America's Best Graduate Schools, Medical, 2022"*

According to *U.S. News & World Report,* the San Jose-Sunnyvale-Santa Clara, CA metro area is home to one of the top 75 business schools in the U.S.: **Stanford University** (#1). The rankings are based on a weighted average of the following nine measures: quality assessment; peer assessment; recruiter assessment; placement success; mean starting salary and bonus; student selectivity; mean GMAT and GRE scores; mean undergraduate GPA; and acceptance rate. *U.S. News & World Report, "America's Best Graduate Schools, Business, 2022"*

EMPLOYERS

Major Employers

Company Name	Industry
Adobe Systems Inc	Publishers-computer software, mfg
Advanced Micro Devices Inc	Semiconductor devices, mfg
Apple Inc	Computers-electronic-manufacturers
Applied Materials	Semiconductor manufacturing equip, mfg
Bon Appetit-Cafe Adobe	Restaurant management
California's Great America	Amusement & theme parks
Christopher Ranch	Garlic manufacturers
Cisco Systems Inc	Computer peripherals
Ebay	E-commerce
Flextronics	Solar energy equipment-manufacturers
General Motors Advanced Tech	Automobile manufacturing
Hewlett-Packard Co.	Computers-electronic-manufacturers
Intel Corporation	Semiconductor devices, mfg
Kaiser Permanente Medical Ctr	General medical & surgical hospitals
Lockheed Martin Space Systems	Satellite equipment & systems, mfg
Microsoft	Computer software-manufacturers
NASA	Government offices, federal
Net App Inc	Computer storage devices

Note: Companies shown are located within the San Jose-Sunnyvale-Santa Clara, CA Metropolitan Statistical Area.
Source: Hoovers.com; Wikipedia

Best Companies to Work For

Adobe; Cadence Design Systems; Cisco Systems, headquartered in San Jose, are among "The 100 Best Companies to Work For." To pick the best companies, *Fortune* partnered with the Great Place to Work Institute. Two-thirds of a company's score is based on the results of the Institute's Trust Index survey, which is sent to a random sample of employees from each company. The questions related to attitudes about management's credibility, job satisfaction, and camaraderie. The other third of the scoring is based on the company's responses to the Institute's Culture Audit, which includes detailed questions about pay and benefit programs, and a series of open-ended questions about hiring practices, internal communication, training, recognition programs, and diversity efforts. Any company that is at least five years old with more than 1,000 U.S. employees is eligible. *Fortune, "The 100 Best Companies to Work For," 2021*

Align Technology, headquartered in San Jose, is among the "100 Best Places to Work in IT." To qualify, companies had to be U.S.-based organizations or be non-U.S.-based employers that met the following criteria: have a minimum of 300 total employees at a U.S. headquarters and a minimum of 30 IT employees in the U.S., with at least 50% of their IT employees based in the U.S. The best places to work were selected based on compensation, benefits, work/life balance, employee morale, and satisfaction with training and development programs. In addition, *InsiderPro* and *Computerworld* looked at retention efforts, programs for recognizing and rewarding outstanding performances, and benefits such as flextime, elder care and child care, and reimbursement for college tuition and the cost of pursuing technology certifications. *InsiderPro and Computerworld, "100 Best Places to Work in IT," 2021*

Cisco, headquartered in San Jose, is among "75 Best Large Workplaces for Women." To pick the best companies, *Fortune* partnered with the Great Place to Work Institute. Employees responded to over 60 survey questions describing the extent to which their organization creates a Great Place to Work For All. Eighty-five percent of the ranking is based on what women themselves report about their workplace, and how fairly those experiences compare to men's reports of the same workplaces. Fifteen percent of the remaining rank is based on how well represented women are in the workforce and throughout management, taking into account industry trends. To be considered, at a minimum, companies need to employ at least 50 women, at least 20% of their non-executive managers need to be female, and at least one of their executives needs to be female. *Fortune, "75 Best Large Workplaces for Women," 2021*

Adobe, headquartered in San Jose, is among the "10 Best Companies for Working Mothers." Criteria: paid time off and leaves; workforce profile; benefits; women's issues and advancement; flexible work; company culture and work life programs. *Seramount, "Best Companies for Working Mothers," 2021*

PUBLIC SAFETY

Crime Rate

Area	Total Crime	Violent Crime Rate				Property Crime Rate		
		Murder	Rape[3]	Robbery	Aggrav. Assault	Burglary	Larceny -Theft	Motor Vehicle Theft
City	2,741.2	3.9	55.0	115.1	251.0	392.9	1,237.2	686.2
Suburbs[1]	2,331.9	1.7	27.1	56.1	116.6	343.6	1,474.4	312.3
Metro[2]	2,543.9	2.8	41.6	86.7	186.2	369.1	1,351.5	506.0
U.S.	2,356.7	6.5	38.4	73.9	279.7	314.2	1,398.0	246.0

Note: Figures are crimes per 100,000 population; (1) All areas within the metro area that are located outside the city limits; (2) Figures cover the San Jose-Sunnyvale-Santa Clara, CA Metropolitan Statistical Area; (3) All figures shown were reported using the revised Uniform Crime Reporting (UCR) definition of rape.
Source: FBI Uniform Crime Reports, 2020

Hate Crimes

Area	Number of Quarters Reported	Number of Incidents per Bias Motivation					
		Race/Ethnicity/ Ancestry	Religion	Sexual Orientation	Disability	Gender	Gender Identity
City	4	75	9	9	0	0	1
U.S.	4	5,227	1,244	1,110	130	75	266

Source: Federal Bureau of Investigation, Hate Crime Statistics 2020

Identity Theft Consumer Reports

Area	Reports	Reports per 100,000 Population	Rank[2]
MSA[1]	4,271	215	205
U.S.	1,434,676	432	-

Note: (1) Figures cover the San Jose-Sunnyvale-Santa Clara, CA Metropolitan Statistical Area; (2) Rank ranges from 1 to 391 where 1 indicates greatest number of identity theft reports per 100,000 population
Source: Federal Trade Commission, Consumer Sentinel Network Data Book 2021

Fraud and Other Consumer Reports

Area	Reports	Reports per 100,000 Population	Rank[2]
MSA[1]	19,009	955	140
U.S.	4,328,977	1,304	-

Note: (1) Figures cover the San Jose-Sunnyvale-Santa Clara, CA Metropolitan Statistical Area; (2) Rank ranges from 1 to 391 where 1 indicates greatest number of fraud and other consumer reports per 100,000 population
Source: Federal Trade Commission, Consumer Sentinel Network Data Book 2021

POLITICS

2020 Presidential Election Results

Area	Biden	Trump	Jorgensen	Hawkins	Other
Santa Clara County	72.6	25.2	1.1	0.5	0.6
U.S.	51.3	46.8	1.2	0.3	0.5

Note: Results are percentages and may not add to 100% due to rounding
Source: Dave Leip's Atlas of U.S. Presidential Elections

SPORTS

Professional Sports Teams

Team Name	League	Year Established
San Jose Earthquakes	Major League Soccer (MLS)	1996
San Jose Sharks	National Hockey League (NHL)	1991

Note: Includes teams located in the San Jose-Sunnyvale-Santa Clara, CA Metropolitan Statistical Area.
Source: Wikipedia, Major Professional Sports Teams of the United States and Canada, April 6, 2022

CLIMATE

Average and Extreme Temperatures

Temperature	Jan	Feb	Mar	Apr	May	Jun	Jul	Aug	Sep	Oct	Nov	Dec	Yr.
Extreme High (°F)	76	82	83	95	103	104	105	101	105	100	87	76	105
Average High (°F)	57	61	63	67	70	74	75	75	76	72	65	58	68
Average Temp. (°F)	50	53	55	58	61	65	66	67	66	63	56	50	59
Average Low (°F)	42	45	46	48	51	55	57	58	57	53	47	42	50
Extreme Low (°F)	21	26	30	32	38	43	45	47	41	33	29	23	21

Note: Figures cover the years 1945-1993
Source: National Climatic Data Center, International Station Meteorological Climate Summary, 9/96

Average Precipitation/Snowfall/Humidity

Precip./Humidity	Jan	Feb	Mar	Apr	May	Jun	Jul	Aug	Sep	Oct	Nov	Dec	Yr.
Avg. Precip. (in.)	2.7	2.3	2.2	0.9	0.3	0.1	Tr	Tr	0.2	0.7	1.7	2.3	13.5
Avg. Snowfall (in.)	Tr	Tr	Tr	0	0	0	0	0	0	0	0	Tr	Tr
Avg. Rel. Hum. 7am (%)	82	82	80	76	74	73	77	79	79	79	81	82	79
Avg. Rel. Hum. 4pm (%)	62	59	56	52	53	54	58	58	55	54	59	63	57

Note: Figures cover the years 1945-1993; Tr = Trace amounts (<0.05 in. of rain; <0.5 in. of snow)
Source: National Climatic Data Center, International Station Meteorological Climate Summary, 9/96

Weather Conditions

Temperature			Daytime Sky			Precipitation		
10°F & below	32°F & below	90°F & above	Clear	Partly cloudy	Cloudy	0.01 inch or more precip.	0.1 inch or more snow/ice	Thunderstorms
0	5	5	106	180	79	57	< 1	6

Note: Figures are average number of days per year and cover the years 1945-1993
Source: National Climatic Data Center, International Station Meteorological Climate Summary, 9/96

HAZARDOUS WASTE

Superfund Sites

The San Jose-Sunnyvale-Santa Clara, CA metro area is home to 17 sites on the EPA's Superfund National Priorities List: **Advanced Micro Devices, Inc.** (final); **Advanced Micro Devices, Inc. (Building 915)** (final); **Applied Materials** (final); **CTS Printex, Inc.** (final); **Fairchild Semiconductor Corp. (Mountain View Plant)** (final); **Fairchild Semiconductor Corp. (South San Jose Plant)** (final); **Hewlett-Packard (620-640 Page Mill Road)** (final); **Intel Corp. (Mountain View Plant)** (final); **Intel Magnetics** (final); **Intersil Inc./Siemens Components** (final); **Lorentz Barrel & Drum Co.** (final); **Moffett Field Naval Air Station** (final); **Monolithic Memories** (final); **National Semiconductor Corp.** (final); **New Idria Mercury Mine** (final); **Raytheon Corp.** (final); **South Bay Asbestos Area** (final). There are a total of 1,165 Superfund sites with a status of proposed or final on the list in the U.S. *U.S. Environmental Protection Agency, National Priorities List, April 6, 2022*

AIR QUALITY

Air Quality Trends: Ozone

	1990	1995	2000	2005	2010	2016	2017	2018	2019	2020
MSA[1]	0.079	0.085	0.070	0.065	0.073	0.067	0.065	0.061	0.062	0.066
U.S.	0.090	0.091	0.082	0.080	0.074	0.070	0.069	0.070	0.066	0.068

Note: (1) Data covers the San Jose-Sunnyvale-Santa Clara, CA Metropolitan Statistical Area. The values shown are the composite ozone concentration averages among trend sites based on the highest fourth daily maximum 8-hour concentration in parts per million. These trends are based on sites having an adequate record of monitoring data during the trend period. Data from exceptional events are included.
Source: U.S. Environmental Protection Agency, Air Quality Monitoring Information, "Air Quality Trends by City, 1990-2020"

Air Quality Index

Area	Percent of Days when Air Quality was...[2]					AQI Statistics[2]	
	Good	Moderate	Unhealthy for Sensitive Groups	Unhealthy	Very Unhealthy	Maximum	Median
MSA[1]	62.0	32.0	3.0	3.0	0.0	186	45

Note: (1) Data covers the San Jose-Sunnyvale-Santa Clara, CA Metropolitan Statistical Area; (2) Based on 366 days with AQI data in 2020. Air Quality Index (AQI) is an index for reporting daily air quality. EPA calculates the AQI for five major air pollutants regulated by the Clean Air Act: ground-level ozone, particle pollution (aka particulate matter), carbon monoxide, sulfur dioxide, and nitrogen dioxide. The AQI runs from 0 to 500. The higher the AQI value, the greater the level of air pollution and the greater the health concern. There are six AQI categories: "Good" AQI is between 0 and 50. Air quality is considered satisfactory; "Moderate" AQI is between 51 and 100. Air quality is acceptable; "Unhealthy for Sensitive Groups" When AQI values are between 101 and 150, members of sensitive groups may experience health effects; "Unhealthy" When AQI values are between 151 and 200 everyone may begin to experience health effects; "Very Unhealthy" AQI values between 201 and 300 trigger a health alert; "Hazardous" AQI values over 300 trigger warnings of emergency conditions (not shown).
Source: U.S. Environmental Protection Agency, Air Quality Index Report, 2020

Air Quality Index Pollutants

Area	Percent of Days when AQI Pollutant was...[2]					
	Carbon Monoxide	Nitrogen Dioxide	Ozone	Sulfur Dioxide	Particulate Matter 2.5	Particulate Matter 10
MSA[1]	0.0	1.1	51.9	0.0	45.9	1.1

Note: (1) Data covers the San Jose-Sunnyvale-Santa Clara, CA Metropolitan Statistical Area; (2) Based on 366 days with AQI data in 2020. The Air Quality Index (AQI) is an index for reporting daily air quality. EPA calculates the AQI for five major air pollutants regulated by the Clean Air Act: ground-level ozone, particle pollution (also known as particulate matter), carbon monoxide, sulfur dioxide, and nitrogen dioxide. The AQI runs from 0 to 500. The higher the AQI value, the greater the level of air pollution and the greater the health concern.
Source: U.S. Environmental Protection Agency, Air Quality Index Report, 2020

Maximum Air Pollutant Concentrations: Particulate Matter, Ozone, CO and Lead

	Particulate Matter 10 (ug/m^3)	Particulate Matter 2.5 Wtd AM (ug/m^3)	Particulate Matter 2.5 24-Hr (ug/m^3)	Ozone (ppm)	Carbon Monoxide (ppm)	Lead (ug/m^3)
MSA[1] Level	116	12.5	59	0.069	2	n/a
NAAQS[2]	150	15	35	0.075	9	0.15
Met NAAQS[2]	Yes	Yes	No	Yes	Yes	n/a

Note: (1) Data covers the San Jose-Sunnyvale-Santa Clara, CA Metropolitan Statistical Area; Data from exceptional events are included; (2) National Ambient Air Quality Standards; ppm = parts per million; ug/m^3 = micrograms per cubic meter; n/a not available.
Concentrations: Particulate Matter 10 (coarse particulate)—highest second maximum 24-hour concentration; Particulate Matter 2.5 Wtd AM (fine particulate)—highest weighted annual mean concentration; Particulate Matter 2.5 24-Hour (fine particulate)—highest 98th percentile 24-hour concentration; Ozone—highest fourth daily maximum 8-hour concentration; Carbon Monoxide—highest second maximum non-overlapping 8-hour concentration; Lead—maximum running 3-month average
Source: U.S. Environmental Protection Agency, Air Quality Monitoring Information, "Air Quality Statistics by City, 2020"

Maximum Air Pollutant Concentrations: Nitrogen Dioxide and Sulfur Dioxide

	Nitrogen Dioxide AM (ppb)	Nitrogen Dioxide 1-Hr (ppb)	Sulfur Dioxide AM (ppb)	Sulfur Dioxide 1-Hr (ppb)	Sulfur Dioxide 24-Hr (ppb)
MSA[1] Level	14	49	n/a	2	n/a
NAAQS[2]	53	100	30	75	140
Met NAAQS[2]	Yes	Yes	n/a	Yes	n/a

Note: (1) Data covers the San Jose-Sunnyvale-Santa Clara, CA Metropolitan Statistical Area; Data from exceptional events are included; (2) National Ambient Air Quality Standards; ppm = parts per million; ug/m³ = micrograms per cubic meter; n/a not available.
Concentrations: Nitrogen Dioxide AM—highest arithmetic mean concentration; Nitrogen Dioxide 1-Hr—highest 98th percentile 1-hour daily maximum concentration; Sulfur Dioxide AM—highest annual mean concentration; Sulfur Dioxide 1-Hr—highest 99th percentile 1-hour daily maximum concentration; Sulfur Dioxide 24-Hr—highest second maximum 24-hour concentration
Source: U.S. Environmental Protection Agency, Air Quality Monitoring Information, "Air Quality Statistics by City, 2020"

Santa Rosa, California

Background

Santa Rosa is located 55 miles north of San Francisco in the county seat of Sonoma County and home to one-third of the county's residents. The city is part of both the San Francisco Bay Area and the region known as California wine country. The popularity of the vineyards, especially among tourists, has helped the city evolve from a small farming town during the California gold rush to a thriving, modern city known for its climate, location, and natural beauty.

During the early days of European exploration, the area that is now Santa Rosa was a homestead for wealthy and prominent families, both under Mexican and Spanish rule. In 1852, the Mexican American War ended, and the territory of California became part of the United States. Around this time, the California Gold Rush brought large numbers of new settlers to the area. As the gold rush waned, explorers found they could make more money farming than they could digging for gold. The community began to grow, and the city was officially incorporated 1868. That same year, the first railroad line reached the city helping Santa Rosa's population to increase tenfold in just seven years.

During the twentieth century, population began to level off, and Santa Rosa settled into a medium-sized city that affords residents the benefits of a larger urban center.

Population began increasing rapidly at the end of the twentieth century. The city is planning for future growth via the *Santa Rosa 2030 Vision* and in 2017 annexed the community of Roseland in its quest for more land.

The city has two Sonoma-Marin Area Rail transit (SMART) stations—one downtown and the other in North Santa Rosa—enhancing pedestrian-friendly neighborhoods.

Downtown Santa Rosa, including the central Old Courthouse Square and historic Railroad Square is an area of shopping, restaurants, nightclubs, and theaters. The city's health care facilities include a Kaiser Permanente medical hub, and Sutter Medical Center.

Largely because of the city's natural beauty and highly regarded vineyards, Santa Rosa is a popular destination for tourists and wine enthusiasts. In addition to wine production, major attractions in Santa Rosa include the Luther Burbank Home and Gardens, Redwood Empire Ice Arena, Sonoma County Museum, and 6th Street Playhouse. The city is also home to the Charles M. Schulz Museum and Research Center, which celebrates the life and work of the Peanuts comic strip and its creator, who lived in Santa Rosa for over 30 years. In 2000, the city renamed its airport "Charles M. Schulz Sonoma County Airport," which is served by Alaska Airlines, with destinations that include San Diego, Los Angeles, Portland, and Seattle.

Institutions of higher learning in the city include the University of San Francisco Santa Rosa, Empire College, and Santa Rosa Junior College.

The city has the same comfortable northern California climate as other Bay Area cities with hot average temperatures and low humidity, ideal for wine grape production. Most of the city's precipitation falls during the spring and winter months, when temperatures are generally much cooler. Summer and fall hold potential for wildfires, and the October 2017 firestorm in the region was the most destructive and third deadliest in California history.

Rankings

Business/Finance Rankings

- According to *Business Insider*, the Santa Rosa metro area is a prime place to run a startup or move an existing business to. The area ranked #8. More than 300 metro areas were analyzed for factors that were of top concern to new business owners. Data was based on the 2019 U.S. Census Bureau American Community Survey, statistics from the CDC, Bureau of Labor Statistics employment report, and University of Chicago analysis. Criteria: business formations; percentage of vaccinated population; percentage of households with internet subscriptions; median household income; and share of work that can be done from home. *www.businessinsider.com, "The 20 Best Cities for Starting a Business in 2022 Include Baltimore, Boulder, and Boston," January 5, 2022*
- The Santa Rosa metro area appeared on the Milken Institute "2021 Best Performing Cities" list. Rank: #59 out of 200 large metro areas (population over 250,000). Criteria: job growth; wage and salary growth; high-tech output growth; housing affordability; household broadband access. *Milken Institute, "Best-Performing Cities 2021," February 16, 2021*
- *Forbes* ranked the 200 most populous metro areas to determine the nation's "Best Places for Business and Careers." The Santa Rosa metro area was ranked #110. Criteria: costs (business and living); job growth (past and projected); income growth; quality of life; educational attainment (college and high school); projected economic growth; cultural and leisure opportunities; workplace tolerance laws; net migration patterns. *Forbes, "The Best Places for Business and Careers 2019: Seattle Still On Top," October 30, 2019*

Education Rankings

- Personal finance website *WalletHub* analyzed the 150 largest U.S. metropolitan statistical areas to determine where the most educated Americans are putting their degrees to work. Criteria: education levels; percentage of workers with degrees; education quality and attainment gap; public school quality rankings; quality and enrollment of each metro area's universities. Santa Rosa was ranked #31 (#1 = most educated city). *www.WalletHub.com, "Most & Least Educated Cities in America, " July 19, 2021*

Real Estate Rankings

- *WalletHub* compared the most populated U.S. cities to determine which had the best markets for real estate agents. Santa Rosa ranked #43 where demand was high and pay was the best. Criteria: sales per agent; annual median wage for real-estate agents; monthly average starting salary for real estate agents; real estate job density and competition; unemployment rate; home turnover rate; housing-market health index; and other relevant metrics. *www.WalletHub.com, "2021 Best Places to Be a Real Estate Agent," May 12, 2021*
- Santa Rosa was ranked #218 out of 237 metro areas in terms of housing affordability in 2021 by the National Association of Home Builders (#1 = most affordable). Criteria: the share of homes sold in that area affordable to a family earning the local median income, based on standard mortgage underwriting criteria. *National Association of Home Builders®, NAHB-Wells Fargo Housing Opportunity Index, 4th Quarter 2021*

Safety Rankings

- Allstate ranked the 200 largest cities in America in terms of driver safety. Santa Rosa ranked #90. Criteria: internal property damage claims over a two-year period from January 2016 to December 2017. The report helps increase the importance of safety and awareness behind the wheel. *Allstate, "Allstate America's Best Drivers Report, 2019" June 24, 2019*
- The National Insurance Crime Bureau ranked 390 metro areas in the U.S. in terms of per capita rates of vehicle theft. The Santa Rosa metro area ranked #167 (#1 = highest rate). Criteria: number of vehicle theft offenses per 100,000 inhabitants in 2020. *National Insurance Crime Bureau, "Hot Spots 2020," August 31, 2021*

Seniors/Retirement Rankings

- From its Best Cities for Successful Aging indexes, the Milken Institute generated rankings for metropolitan areas, weighing data in nine categories—health care, wellness, living arrangements, transportation and convenience, financial characteristics, education, employment, community engagement, and overall livability. The Santa Rosa metro area was ranked #148 overall in the small metro area category. *Milken Institute, "Best Cities for Successful Aging, 2017" March 14, 2017*

Women/Minorities Rankings

- Personal finance website *WalletHub* compared more than 180 U.S. cities across two key dimensions, "Hispanic Business-Friendliness" and "Hispanic Purchasing Power," to arrive at the most favorable conditions for Hispanic entrepreneurs. Santa Rosa was ranked #114 out of 182. Criteria includes: share of Hispanic-Owned Businesses; Hispanic entrepreneurship rate to median annual income of Hispanics; Small Business-Friendliness score; cost of living; and number of Hispanics with at least a bachelor's degree. *WalletHub.com, "2019's Best Cities for Hispanic Entrepreneurs," May 1, 2019*

Business Environment

DEMOGRAPHICS

Population Growth

Area	1990 Census	2000 Census	2010 Census	2020* Estimate	Population Growth (%) 1990-2020	Population Growth (%) 2010-2020
City	123,297	147,595	167,815	178,391	44.7	6.3
MSA[1]	388,222	458,614	483,878	496,801	28.0	2.7
U.S.	248,709,873	281,421,906	308,745,538	326,569,308	31.3	5.8

Note: (1) Figures cover the Santa Rosa, CA Metropolitan Statistical Area; (*) 2016-2020 5-year estimated population
Source: U.S. Census Bureau, 1990 Census, Census 2000, Census 2010, 2016-2020 American Community Survey 5-Year Estimates

Household Size

Area	Persons in Household (%) One	Two	Three	Four	Five	Six	Seven or More	Average Household Size
City	28.4	32.4	15.4	13.4	6.6	2.0	1.8	2.60
MSA[1]	27.0	34.7	15.6	13.1	6.3	2.0	1.2	2.60
U.S.	28.0	33.9	15.5	12.9	6.0	2.3	1.4	2.60

Note: (1) Figures cover the Santa Rosa, CA Metropolitan Statistical Area
Source: U.S. Census Bureau, 2016-2020 American Community Survey 5-Year Estimates

Race

Area	White Alone[2] (%)	Black Alone[2] (%)	Asian Alone[2] (%)	AIAN[3] Alone[2] (%)	NHOPI[4] Alone[2] (%)	Other Race Alone[2] (%)	Two or More Races (%)
City	64.0	2.5	6.0	1.1	0.5	18.9	6.9
MSA[1]	72.5	1.7	4.3	0.9	0.3	13.3	7.0
U.S.	70.4	12.6	5.6	0.8	0.2	5.1	5.2

Note: (1) Figures cover the Santa Rosa, CA Metropolitan Statistical Area; (2) Alone is defined as not being in combination with one or more other races; (3) American Indian and Alaska Native; (4) Native Hawaiian and Other Pacific Islander
Source: U.S. Census Bureau, 2016-2020 American Community Survey 5-Year Estimates

Hispanic or Latino Origin

Area	Total (%)	Mexican (%)	Puerto Rican (%)	Cuban (%)	Other (%)
City	32.7	28.6	0.5	0.2	3.3
MSA[1]	27.0	22.7	0.5	0.2	3.6
U.S.	18.2	11.2	1.7	0.7	4.5

Note: Persons of Hispanic or Latino origin can be of any race; (1) Figures cover the Santa Rosa, CA Metropolitan Statistical Area
Source: U.S. Census Bureau, 2016-2020 American Community Survey 5-Year Estimates

Ancestry

Area	German	Irish	English	American	Italian	Polish	French[2]	Scottish	Dutch
City	10.8	10.0	9.3	2.6	6.8	1.6	2.7	1.9	1.2
MSA[1]	12.5	12.4	10.1	2.5	8.5	1.8	3.1	2.5	1.3
U.S.	13.0	9.7	7.7	5.9	5.1	2.7	2.3	1.6	1.1

Note: Figures are the percentage of the total population reporting a particular ancestry. The nine most commonly reported ancestries in the U.S. are shown. Figures include multiple ancestries (e.g. if a person reported being Irish and Italian, they were included in both columns); (1) Figures cover the Santa Rosa, CA Metropolitan Statistical Area; (2) Excludes Basque
Source: U.S. Census Bureau, 2016-2020 American Community Survey 5-Year Estimates

Foreign-born Population

Area	Percent of Population Born in: Any Foreign Country	Asia	Mexico	Europe	Caribbean	Central America[2]	South America	Africa	Canada
City	20.9	4.6	11.4	1.9	0.0	0.9	0.3	0.9	0.3
MSA[1]	16.6	3.0	9.2	1.9	0.1	0.8	0.4	0.5	0.4
U.S.	13.5	4.2	3.3	1.5	1.3	1.1	1.0	0.7	0.3

Note: (1) Figures cover the Santa Rosa, CA Metropolitan Statistical Area; (2) Excludes Mexico.
Source: U.S. Census Bureau, 2016-2020 American Community Survey 5-Year Estimates

Marital Status

Area	Never Married	Now Married[2]	Separated	Widowed	Divorced
City	33.1	46.7	1.9	5.7	12.7
MSA[1]	31.8	48.7	1.5	5.2	12.8
U.S.	33.5	48.1	1.8	5.7	10.8

Note: Figures are percentages and cover the population 15 years of age and older; (1) Figures cover the Santa Rosa, CA Metropolitan Statistical Area; (2) Excludes separated
Source: U.S. Census Bureau, 2016-2020 American Community Survey 5-Year Estimates

Disability by Age

Area	All Ages	Under 18 Years Old	18 to 64 Years Old	65 Years and Over
City	11.8	3.2	9.8	29.5
MSA[1]	11.7	3.5	9.0	28.6
U.S.	12.7	4.3	10.3	34.0

Note: Figures show percent of the civilian noninstitutionalized population that reported having a disability. Disability status is determined from six types of difficulty: vision, hearing, cognitive, ambulatory, self-care, and independent living. For children under 5 years old, hearing and vision difficulty are used to determine disability status. For children between the ages of 5 and 14, disability status is determined from hearing, vision, cognitive, ambulatory, and self-care difficulties. For people aged 15 years and older, they are considered to have a disability if they have difficulty with any one of the six difficulty types; Note: (1) Figures cover the Santa Rosa, CA Metropolitan Statistical Area
Source: U.S. Census Bureau, 2016-2020 American Community Survey 5-Year Estimates

Age

Area	Percent of Population									Median Age
	Under Age 5	Age 5–19	Age 20–34	Age 35–44	Age 45–54	Age 55–64	Age 65–74	Age 75–84	Age 85+	
City	5.5	18.2	19.9	13.5	12.5	12.6	10.2	4.9	2.6	39.6
MSA[1]	4.9	17.2	18.5	12.6	12.7	14.4	12.0	5.1	2.5	42.4
U.S.	6.0	19.1	20.6	12.7	12.7	12.9	9.4	4.7	2.0	38.2

Note: (1) Figures cover the Santa Rosa, CA Metropolitan Statistical Area
Source: U.S. Census Bureau, 2016-2020 American Community Survey 5-Year Estimates

Gender

Area	Males	Females	Males per 100 Females
City	85,637	92,754	92.3
MSA[1]	242,657	254,144	95.5
U.S.	160,818,530	165,750,778	97.0

Note: (1) Figures cover the Santa Rosa, CA Metropolitan Statistical Area
Source: U.S. Census Bureau, 2016-2020 American Community Survey 5-Year Estimates

Religious Groups by Family

Area	Catholic	Baptist	Non-Den.	Methodist[2]	Lutheran	LDS[3]	Pente-costal	Presby-terian[4]	Muslim[5]	Judaism
MSA[1]	22.3	1.4	1.5	0.9	1.0	1.9	0.7	0.9	0.5	0.4
U.S.	19.1	9.3	4.0	4.0	2.3	2.0	1.9	1.6	0.8	0.7

Note: Figures are the number of adherents as a percentage of the total population; (1) Figures cover the Santa Rosa, CA Metropolitan Statistical Area; (2) Methodist/Pietist; (3) Latter Day Saints; (4) Reformed; (5) Figures are estimates
Source: Association of Statisticians of American Religious Bodies, 2010 U.S. Religion Census: Religious Congregations & Membership Study

Religious Groups by Tradition

Area	Catholic	Evangelical Protestant	Mainline Protestant	Other Tradition	Black Protestant	Orthodox
MSA[1]	22.3	5.3	2.4	4.8	<0.1	0.3
U.S.	19.1	16.2	7.3	4.3	1.6	0.3

Note: Figures are the number of adherents as a percentage of the total population; (1) Figures cover the Santa Rosa, CA Metropolitan Statistical Area
Source: Association of Statisticians of American Religious Bodies, 2010 U.S. Religion Census: Religious Congregations & Membership Study

ECONOMY

Gross Metropolitan Product

Area	2017	2018	2019	2020	Rank[2]
MSA[1]	29.3	30.4	31.4	32.5	91

Note: Figures are in billions of dollars; (1) Figures cover the Santa Rosa, CA Metropolitan Statistical Area; (2) Rank is based on 2018 data and ranges from 1 to 381
Source: U.S. Conference of Mayors, U.S. Metro Economies: GMP & Employment 2018-2020, September 2019

Economic Growth

Area	2015-17 (%)	2018 (%)	2019 (%)	2020 (%)	Rank[2]
MSA[1]	2.5	1.2	1.7	1.1	100
U.S.	1.9	2.9	2.3	2.1	–

Note: Figures are real gross metropolitan product (GMP) growth rates and represent average annual percent change; (1) Figures cover the Santa Rosa, CA Metropolitan Statistical Area; (2) Rank is based on 2017 2-year average annual percent change and ranges from 1 to 381
Source: U.S. Conference of Mayors, U.S. Metro Economies: GMP & Employment 2018-2020, September 2019

Metropolitan Area Exports

Area	2015	2016	2017	2018	2019	2020	Rank[2]
MSA[1]	1,119.8	1,194.3	1,168.2	1,231.7	1,234.5	1,131.4	138

Note: Figures are in millions of dollars; (1) Figures cover the Santa Rosa, CA Metropolitan Statistical Area; (2) Rank is based on 2020 data and ranges from 1 to 389
Source: U.S. Department of Commerce, International Trade Administration, Office of Trade and Economic Analysis, Industry and Analysis, Exports by Metropolitan Area, data extracted March 4, 2022

Building Permits

Area	Single-Family			Multi-Family			Total		
	2019	2020	Pct. Chg.	2019	2020	Pct. Chg.	2019	2020	Pct. Chg.
City	939	440	-53.1	251	188	-25.1	1,190	628	-47.2
MSA[1]	2,079	1,171	-43.7	350	224	-36.0	2,429	1,395	-42.6
U.S.	862,100	979,400	13.6	523,900	491,700	-6.1	1,386,000	1,471,100	6.1

Note: (1) Figures cover the Santa Rosa, CA Metropolitan Statistical Area; Figures represent new, privately-owned housing units authorized (unadjusted data); All permit data are based on estimates with imputation
Source: U.S. Census Bureau, Manufacturing, Mining, and Construction Statistics, Building Permits, 2019, 2020

Bankruptcy Filings

Area	Business Filings			Nonbusiness Filings		
	2020	2021	% Chg.	2020	2021	% Chg.
Sonoma County	29	23	-20.7	388	329	-15.2
U.S.	21,655	14,347	-33.7	522,808	399,269	-23.6

Note: Business filings include Chapter 7, Chapter 9, Chapter 11, Chapter 12, Chapter 13, Chapter 15, and Section 304; Nonbusiness filings include Chapter 7, Chapter 11, and Chapter 13
Source: Administrative Office of the U.S. Courts, Business and Nonbusiness Bankruptcy, County Cases Commenced by Chapter of the Bankruptcy Code, During the 12-Month Period Ending December 31, 2020 and Business and Nonbusiness Bankruptcy, County Cases Commenced by Chapter of the Bankruptcy Code, During the 12-Month Period Ending December 31, 2021

Housing Vacancy Rates

Area	Gross Vacancy Rate[2] (%)			Year-Round Vacancy Rate[3] (%)			Rental Vacancy Rate[4] (%)			Homeowner Vacancy Rate[5] (%)		
	2019	2020	2021	2019	2020	2021	2019	2020	2021	2019	2020	2021
MSA[1]	n/a	n/a	n/a	n/a	n/a	n/a	n/a	n/a	n/a	n/a	n/a	n/a
U.S.	12.0	10.6	10.8	9.5	8.2	8.4	6.7	6.3	6.1	1.4	1.0	0.9

Note: (1) Figures cover the Santa Rosa, CA Metropolitan Statistical Area; (2) The percentage of the total housing inventory that is vacant; (3) The percentage of the housing inventory (excluding seasonal units) that is year-round vacant; (4) The percentage of rental inventory that is vacant for rent; (5) The percentage of homeowner inventory that is vacant for sale; n/a not available
Source: U.S. Census Bureau, Housing Vacancies and Homeownership Annual Statistics: 2019, 2020, 2021

INCOME

Income

Area	Per Capita ($)	Median Household ($)	Average Household ($)
City	38,773	80,472	101,066
MSA[1]	44,071	86,173	113,067
U.S.	35,384	64,994	91,547

Note: (1) Figures cover the Santa Rosa, CA Metropolitan Statistical Area
Source: U.S. Census Bureau, 2016-2020 American Community Survey 5-Year Estimates

Household Income Distribution

Area	Percent of Households Earning							
	Under $15,000	$15,000 -$24,999	$25,000 -$34,999	$35,000 -$49,999	$50,000 -$74,999	$75,000 -$99,999	$100,000 -$149,999	$150,000 and up
City	7.5	5.6	6.4	9.7	17.0	14.4	20.2	19.2
MSA[1]	6.6	5.7	6.4	9.3	15.5	14.1	19.3	23.2
U.S.	9.9	8.5	8.6	12.0	17.2	12.8	15.6	15.4

Note: (1) Figures cover the Santa Rosa, CA Metropolitan Statistical Area
Source: U.S. Census Bureau, 2016-2020 American Community Survey 5-Year Estimates

Poverty Rate

Area	All Ages	Under 18 Years Old	18 to 64 Years Old	65 Years and Over
City	10.0	13.0	9.2	9.1
MSA[1]	8.8	10.5	8.8	7.3
U.S.	12.8	17.5	12.1	9.3

Note: Figures are percentage of people whose income during the past 12 months was below the poverty level; (1) Figures cover the Santa Rosa, CA Metropolitan Statistical Area
Source: U.S. Census Bureau, 2016-2020 American Community Survey 5-Year Estimates

CITY FINANCES

City Government Finances

Component	2019 ($000)	2019 ($ per capita)
Total Revenues	420,662	2,400
Total Expenditures	434,016	2,476
Debt Outstanding	302,976	1,729
Cash and Securities[1]	112,787	644

Note: (1) Cash and security holdings of a government at the close of its fiscal year, including those of its dependent agencies, utilities, and liquor stores.
Source: U.S. Census Bureau, State & Local Government Finances 2019

City Government Revenue by Source

Source	2019 ($000)	2019 ($ per capita)	2019 (%)
General Revenue			
From Federal Government	10,211	58	2.4
From State Government	44,897	256	10.7
From Local Governments	4,115	23	1.0
Taxes			
Property	44,801	256	10.7
Sales and Gross Receipts	68,957	393	16.4
Personal Income	0	0	0.0
Corporate Income	0	0	0.0
Motor Vehicle License	0	0	0.0
Other Taxes	40,641	232	9.7
Current Charges	119,350	681	28.4
Liquor Store	0	0	0.0
Utility	45,228	258	10.8

Source: U.S. Census Bureau, State & Local Government Finances 2019

City Government Expenditures by Function

Function	2019 ($000)	2019 ($ per capita)	2019 (%)
General Direct Expenditures			
Air Transportation	0	0	0.0
Corrections	0	0	0.0
Education	0	0	0.0
Employment Security Administration	0	0	0.0
Financial Administration	9,876	56	2.3
Fire Protection	45,404	259	10.5
General Public Buildings	0	0	0.0
Governmental Administration, Other	37,968	216	8.7
Health	1,978	11	0.5
Highways	37,545	214	8.7
Hospitals	0	0	0.0
Housing and Community Development	23,377	133	5.4
Interest on General Debt	12,015	68	2.8
Judicial and Legal	2,341	13	0.5
Libraries	0	0	0.0
Parking	5,472	31	1.3
Parks and Recreation	20,257	115	4.7
Police Protection	60,343	344	13.9
Public Welfare	0	0	0.0
Sewerage	61,791	352	14.2
Solid Waste Management	0	0	0.0
Veterans' Services	0	0	0.0
Liquor Store	0	0	0.0
Utility	74,024	422	17.1

Source: U.S. Census Bureau, State & Local Government Finances 2019

EMPLOYMENT

Labor Force and Employment

Area	Civilian Labor Force			Workers Employed		
	Dec. 2020	Dec. 2021	% Chg.	Dec. 2020	Dec. 2021	% Chg.
City	83,192	86,619	4.1	77,343	83,335	7.7
MSA[1]	236,250	246,346	4.3	220,659	237,754	7.7
U.S.	160,017,000	161,696,000	1.0	149,613,000	155,732,000	4.1

Note: Data is not seasonally adjusted and covers workers 16 years of age and older; (1) Figures cover the Santa Rosa, CA Metropolitan Statistical Area
Source: Bureau of Labor Statistics, Local Area Unemployment Statistics

Unemployment Rate

Area	2021											
	Jan.	Feb.	Mar.	Apr.	May	Jun.	Jul.	Aug.	Sep.	Oct.	Nov.	Dec.
City	7.4	6.6	6.2	6.1	5.6	6.2	6.0	5.7	4.9	4.6	4.1	3.8
MSA[1]	7.1	6.3	5.9	5.7	5.2	5.8	5.6	5.3	4.4	4.2	3.7	3.5
U.S.	6.8	6.6	6.2	5.7	5.5	6.1	5.7	5.3	4.6	4.3	3.9	3.7

Note: Data is not seasonally adjusted and covers workers 16 years of age and older; (1) Figures cover the Santa Rosa, CA Metropolitan Statistical Area
Source: Bureau of Labor Statistics, Local Area Unemployment Statistics

Average Wages

Occupation	$/Hr.	Occupation	$/Hr.
Accountants and Auditors	44.54	Maintenance and Repair Workers	24.85
Automotive Mechanics	27.43	Marketing Managers	76.63
Bookkeepers	25.55	Network and Computer Systems Admin.	47.92
Carpenters	35.07	Nurses, Licensed Practical	34.22
Cashiers	16.65	Nurses, Registered	68.00
Computer Programmers	50.47	Nursing Assistants	19.60
Computer Systems Analysts	51.42	Office Clerks, General	21.66
Computer User Support Specialists	31.73	Physical Therapists	54.88
Construction Laborers	26.28	Physicians	99.53
Cooks, Restaurant	19.53	Plumbers, Pipefitters and Steamfitters	34.59
Customer Service Representatives	21.86	Police and Sheriff's Patrol Officers	50.99
Dentists	73.46	Postal Service Mail Carriers	26.07
Electricians	34.81	Real Estate Sales Agents	32.32
Engineers, Electrical	58.39	Retail Salespersons	18.54
Fast Food and Counter Workers	15.93	Sales Representatives, Technical/Scientific	52.27
Financial Managers	76.02	Secretaries, Exc. Legal/Medical/Executive	23.86
First-Line Supervisors of Office Workers	32.97	Security Guards	19.28
General and Operations Managers	57.86	Surgeons	n/a
Hairdressers/Cosmetologists	19.08	Teacher Assistants, Exc. Postsecondary*	19.50
Home Health and Personal Care Aides	15.52	Teachers, Secondary School, Exc. Sp. Ed.*	44.60
Janitors and Cleaners	18.25	Telemarketers	n/a
Landscaping/Groundskeeping Workers	20.53	Truck Drivers, Heavy/Tractor-Trailer	27.26
Lawyers	77.19	Truck Drivers, Light/Delivery Services	23.77
Maids and Housekeeping Cleaners	19.22	Waiters and Waitresses	17.99

Note: Wage data covers the Santa Rosa, CA Metropolitan Statistical Area; (*) Hourly wages were calculated from annual wage data based on a 40 hour work week; n/a not available.
Source: Bureau of Labor Statistics, Metro Area Occupational Employment & Wage Estimates, May 2021

Employment by Industry

Sector	MSA[1]		U.S.
	Number of Employees	Percent of Total	Percent of Total
Construction	15,700	7.9	5.0
Education and Health Services	33,700	16.9	16.0
Financial Activities	8,000	4.0	5.9
Government	26,200	13.1	14.9
Information	2,300	1.2	1.9
Leisure and Hospitality	23,500	11.8	9.8
Manufacturing	23,100	11.6	8.4
Mining and Logging	200	0.1	0.4
Other Services	6,800	3.4	3.7
Professional and Business Services	24,000	12.0	14.6
Retail Trade	23,700	11.9	10.7
Transportation, Warehousing, and Utilities	4,900	2.5	4.8
Wholesale Trade	7,500	3.8	3.8

Note: Figures are non-farm employment as of December 2021. Figures are not seasonally adjusted and include workers 16 years of age and older; (1) Figures cover the Santa Rosa, CA Metropolitan Statistical Area
Source: Bureau of Labor Statistics, Current Employment Statistics, Employment, Hours, and Earnings

Employment by Occupation

Occupation Classification	City (%)	MSA[1] (%)	U.S. (%)
Management, Business, Science, and Arts	36.9	39.6	39.5
Natural Resources, Construction, and Maintenance	9.6	9.8	8.7
Production, Transportation, and Material Moving	12.2	10.1	13.1
Sales and Office	21.8	21.1	21.3
Service	19.6	19.4	17.4

Note: Figures cover employed civilians 16 years of age and older; (1) Figures cover the Santa Rosa, CA Metropolitan Statistical Area
Source: U.S. Census Bureau, 2016-2020 American Community Survey 5-Year Estimates

Occupations with Greatest Projected Employment Growth: 2021 – 2023

Occupation[1]	2021 Employment	2023 Projected Employment	Numeric Employment Change	Percent Employment Change
Fast Food and Counter Workers	383,500	457,000	73,500	19.2
Home Health and Personal Care Aides	663,400	716,600	53,200	8.0
Waiters and Waitresses	208,500	257,600	49,100	23.5
Cooks, Restaurant	136,700	175,300	38,600	28.2
Laborers and Freight, Stock, and Material Movers, Hand	401,500	431,600	30,100	7.5
Software Developers and Software Quality Assurance Analysts and Testers	311,600	336,800	25,200	8.1
Janitors and Cleaners, Except Maids and Housekeeping Cleaners	232,200	252,400	20,200	8.7
Cooks, Fast Food	109,600	128,200	18,600	17.0
Stockers and Order Fillers	273,000	290,400	17,400	6.4
First-Line Supervisors of Food Preparation and Serving Workers	81,700	98,600	16,900	20.7

Note: Projections cover California; (1) Sorted by numeric employment change
Source: www.projectionscentral.com, State Occupational Projections, 2021–2023 Short-Term Projections

Fastest-Growing Occupations: 2021 – 2023

Occupation[1]	2021 Employment	2023 Projected Employment	Numeric Employment Change	Percent Employment Change
Manicurists and Pedicurists	23,400	33,500	10,100	43.2
Cooks, All Other	3,900	5,400	1,500	38.5
Miscellaneous Entertainers and Performers, Sports and Related Workers	5,900	8,100	2,200	37.3
Barbers	1,900	2,600	700	36.8
Gaming Change Persons and Booth Cashiers	2,200	3,000	800	36.4
Gaming Service Workers, All Other	1,400	1,900	500	35.7
Gaming Dealers	12,200	16,500	4,300	35.2
First-Line Supervisors of Gambling Services Workers	2,900	3,900	1,000	34.5
Massage Therapists	18,000	24,200	6,200	34.4
Costume Attendants	1,500	2,000	500	33.3

Note: Projections cover California; (1) Sorted by percent employment change and excludes occupations with numeric employment change less than 50
Source: www.projectionscentral.com, State Occupational Projections, 2021–2023 Short-Term Projections

TAXES

State Corporate Income Tax Rates

State	Tax Rate (%)	Income Brackets ($)	Num. of Brackets	Financial Institution Tax Rate (%)[a]	Federal Income Tax Ded.
California	8.84 (b)	Flat rate	1	10.84 (b)	No

Note: Tax rates as of January 1, 2022; (a) Rates listed are the corporate income tax rate applied to financial institutions or excise taxes based on income. Some states have other taxes based upon the value of deposits or shares; (b) Minimum tax is $800 in California, $250 in District of Columbia, $50 in Arizona and North Dakota (banks), $400 ($100 banks) in Rhode Island, $200 per location in South Dakota (banks), $100 in Utah, $300 in Vermont.
Source: Federation of Tax Administrators, State Corporate Income Tax Rates, January 1, 2022

State Individual Income Tax Rates

State	Tax Rate (%)	Income Brackets ($)	Personal Exemptions ($)			Standard Ded. ($)	
			Single	Married	Depend.	Single	Married
California (a)	1.0 - 12.3 (g)	9,325 - 625,369 (b)	129	258	400 (c)	4,803	9,606 (a)

Note: Tax rates as of January 1, 2022; Local- and county-level taxes are not included; Federal income tax is not deductible on state income tax returns; (a) 19 states have statutory provision for automatically adjusting to the rate of inflation the dollar values of the income tax brackets, standard deductions, and/or personal exemptions. Michigan indexes the personal exemption only. Oregon does not index the income brackets for $125,000 and over; (b) For joint returns, taxes are twice the tax on half the couple's income; (c) The personal exemption takes the form of a tax credit instead of a deduction; (g) California imposes an additional 1% tax on taxable income over $1 million, making the maximum rate 13.3% over $1 million.
Source: Federation of Tax Administrators, State Individual Income Tax Rates, January 1, 2022

Various State Sales and Excise Tax Rates

State	State Sales Tax (%)	Gasoline[1] (¢/gal.)	Cigarette[2] ($/pack)	Spirits[3] ($/gal.)	Wine[4] ($/gal.)	Beer[5] ($/gal.)	Recreational Marijuana (%)
California	7.25	68.15	2.87	3.3	0.2	0.2	(c)

Note: All tax rates as of January 1, 2022; (1) The American Petroleum Institute has developed a methodology for determining the average tax rate on a gallon of fuel. Rates may include any of the following: excise taxes, environmental fees, storage tank fees, other fees or taxes, general sales tax, and local taxes; (2) The federal excise tax of $1.0066 per pack and local taxes are not included; (3) Rates are those applicable to off-premise sales of 40% alcohol by volume (a.b.v.) distilled spirits in 750ml containers. Local excise taxes are excluded; (4) Rates are those applicable to off-premise sales of 11% a.b.v. non-carbonated wine in 750ml containers; (5) Rates are those applicable to off-premise sales of 4.7% a.b.v. beer in 12 ounce containers; (c) 15% excise tax (levied on wholesale at average market rate); $10.08/oz. flowers & $3/oz. leaves cultivation tax; $1.41/oz fresh cannabis plant
Source: Tax Foundation, 2022 Facts & Figures: How Does Your State Compare?

State Business Tax Climate Index Rankings

State	Overall Rank	Corporate Tax Rank	Individual Income Tax Rank	Sales Tax Rank	Property Tax Rank	Unemployment Insurance Tax Rank
California	48	46	49	47	14	23

Note: The index is a measure of how each state's tax laws affect economic performance. The lower the rank, the more favorable a state's tax system is for business. States without a given tax are given a ranking of 1. The scores/rankings for the District of Columbia do not affect other states. The 2022 index represents the tax climate as of July 1, 2021.
Source: Tax Foundation, State Business Tax Climate Index 2022

TRANSPORTATION

Means of Transportation to Work

Area	Car/Truck/Van		Public Transportation			Bicycle	Walked	Other Means	Worked at Home
	Drove Alone	Car-pooled	Bus	Subway	Railroad				
City	77.2	10.9	1.6	0.0	0.1	1.0	1.8	1.3	6.1
MSA[1]	74.2	10.4	1.3	0.1	0.2	0.7	2.5	1.5	9.1
U.S.	74.9	8.9	2.2	1.7	0.5	0.5	2.6	1.4	7.3

Note: Figures are percentages and cover workers 16 years of age and older; (1) Figures cover the Santa Rosa, CA Metropolitan Statistical Area
Source: U.S. Census Bureau, 2016-2020 American Community Survey 5-Year Estimates

Travel Time to Work

Area	Less Than 10 Minutes	10 to 19 Minutes	20 to 29 Minutes	30 to 44 Minutes	45 to 59 Minutes	60 to 89 Minutes	90 Minutes or More
City	12.7	40.3	21.6	13.3	4.5	4.3	3.2
MSA[1]	14.2	32.9	20.4	16.6	6.3	5.8	3.7
U.S.	12.3	28.4	20.9	20.9	8.3	6.4	2.9

Note: Note: Figures are percentages and include workers 16 years old and over; (1) Figures cover the Santa Rosa, CA Metropolitan Statistical Area
Source: U.S. Census Bureau, 2016-2020 American Community Survey 5-Year Estimates

Key Congestion Measures

Measure	1990	2000	2010	2015	2020
Annual Hours of Delay, Total (000)	n/a	n/a	n/a	18,462	7,830
Annual Hours of Delay, Per Auto Commuter	n/a	n/a	n/a	53	22
Annual Congestion Cost, Per Auto Commuter ($)	n/a	n/a	n/a	1,100	512

Note: n/a not available
Source: Texas A&M Transportation Institute, 2021 Urban Mobility Report

Freeway Travel Time Index

Measure	1985	1990	1995	2000	2005	2010	2015	2020
Urban Area Index[1]	n/a	n/a	n/a	n/a	n/a	n/a	1.22	1.11
Urban Area Rank[1,2]	n/a	n/a	n/a	n/a	n/a	n/a	n/a	n/a

Note: Freeway Travel Time Index—the ratio of travel time in the peak period to the travel time at free-flow conditions. For example, a value of 1.30 indicates a 20-minute free-flow trip takes 26 minutes in the peak (20 minutes x 1.30 = 26 minutes); (1) Covers the Santa Rosa CA urban area; (2) Rank is based on 101 larger urban areas (#1 = highest travel time index); n/a not available
Source: Texas A&M Transportation Institute, 2021 Urban Mobility Report

Public Transportation

Agency Name / Mode of Transportation	Vehicles Operated in Maximum Service[1]	Annual Unlinked Passenger Trips[2] (in thous.)	Annual Passenger Miles[3] (in thous.)
City of Santa Rosa (Santa Rosa CityBus)			
Bus (directly operated)	24	1,473.1	5,686.1
Bus (purchased transportation)	1	4.5	15.9
Demand Response (purchased transportation)	12	29.8	178.7
Sonoma County Transit			
Bus (purchased transportation)	45	722.1	6,013.7
Demand Response (purchased transportation)	25	47.8	582.0

Note: (1) Number of revenue vehicles operated by the given mode and type of service to meet the annual maximum service requirement. This is the revenue vehicle count during the peak season of the year; on the week and day that maximum service is provided. Vehicles operated in maximum service (VOMS) exclude atypical days and one-time special events; (2) Number of passengers who boarded public transportation vehicles. Passengers are counted each time they board a vehicle no matter how many vehicles they use to travel from their origin to their destination. (3) Sum of the distances ridden by all passengers during the entire fiscal year.
Source: Federal Transit Administration, National Transit Database, 2020

Air Transportation

Airport Name and Code / Type of Service	Passenger Airlines[1]	Passenger Enplanements	Freight Carriers[2]	Freight (lbs)
San Francisco International (SFO)				
Domestic service (U.S. carriers - 2021)	20	10,255,569	15	210,298,298
International service (U.S. carriers - 2020)	6	612,075	3	68,829,230

Note: (1) Includes all U.S.-based major, minor and commuter airlines that carried at least one passenger during the year; (2) Includes all U.S.-based airlines and freight carriers that transported at least one pound of freight during the year.
Source: Bureau of Transportation Statistics, The Intermodal Transportation Database, Air Carriers: T-100 Domestic Market (U.S. Carriers), 2021; Bureau of Transportation Statistics, The Intermodal Transportation Database, Air Carriers: T-100 International Market (U.S. Carriers), 2020

BUSINESSES

Major Business Headquarters

Company Name	Industry	Rankings	
		Fortune[1]	Forbes[2]
No companies listed	-	-	-

Note: (1) Companies that produce a 10-K are ranked 1 to 500 based on 2020 revenue; (2) All private companies with at least $2 billion in annual revenue through the end of their most current fiscal year are ranked 1 to 225; companies listed are headquartered in the city; dashes indicate no ranking
Source: Fortune, "Fortune 500," 2021; Forbes, "America's Largest Private Companies," 2021

Living Environment

COST OF LIVING

Cost of Living Index

Composite Index	Groceries	Housing	Utilities	Transportation	Health Care	Misc. Goods/ Services
n/a	n/a	n/a	n/a	n/a	n/a	n/a

Note: The Cost of Living Index measures regional differences in the cost of consumer goods and services, excluding taxes and non-consumer expenditures, for professional and managerial households in the top income quintile. It is based on more than 50,000 prices covering almost 60 different items for which prices are collected three times a year by chambers of commerce, economic development organizations or university applied economic centers in each participating urban area. The numbers shown should be read as a percentage above or below the national average of 100. For example, a value of 115.4 in the groceries column indicates that grocery prices are 15.4% higher than the national average. Small differences in the index numbers should not be interpreted as significant; n/a not available.
Source: The Council for Community and Economic Research, Cost of Living Index, 2021

Grocery Prices

Area[1]	T-Bone Steak ($/pound)	Frying Chicken ($/pound)	Whole Milk ($/half gal.)	Eggs ($/dozen)	Orange Juice ($/64 oz.)	Coffee ($/11.5 oz.)
City[2]	n/a	n/a	n/a	n/a	n/a	n/a
Avg.	12.82	1.40	2.22	1.57	3.59	4.30
Min.	8.91	0.91	1.29	0.75	2.87	3.02
Max.	21.35	2.69	3.92	3.86	5.49	8.11

Note: (1) Values for the local area are compared with the average, minimum and maximum values for all 285 areas in the Cost of Living Index; (2) Figures cover the Santa Rosa CA urban area; n/a not available; ***T-Bone Steak*** *(price per pound);* ***Frying Chicken*** *(price per pound, whole fryer);* ***Whole Milk*** *(half gallon carton);* ***Eggs*** *(price per dozen, Grade A, large);* ***Orange Juice*** *(64 oz. Tropicana or Florida Natural);* ***Coffee*** *(11.5 oz. can, vacuum-packed, Maxwell House, Hills Bros, or Folgers).*
Source: The Council for Community and Economic Research, Cost of Living Index, 2021

Housing and Utility Costs

Area[1]	New Home Price ($)	Apartment Rent ($/month)	All Electric ($/month)	Part Electric ($/month)	Other Energy ($/month)	Telephone ($/month)
City[2]	n/a	n/a	n/a	n/a	n/a	n/a
Avg.	398,393	1,217	171.38	100.83	69.67	187.75
Min.	212,799	534	96.71	31.56	27.15	173.01
Max.	2,354,006	4,438	369.53	277.33	303.87	206.73

Note: (1) Values for the local area are compared with the average, minimum and maximum values for all 285 areas in the Cost of Living Index; (2) Figures cover the Santa Rosa CA urban area; n/a not available; ***New Home Price*** *(2,400 sf living area, 8,000 sf lot, in urban area with full utilities);* ***Apartment Rent*** *(950 sf 2 bedroom/1.5 or 2 bath, unfurnished, excluding all utilities except water);* ***All Electric*** *(average monthly cost for an all-electric home);* ***Part Electric*** *(average monthly cost for a part-electric home);* ***Other Energy*** *(average monthly cost for natural gas, fuel oil, coal, wood, and any other forms of energy except electricity);* ***Telephone*** *(price includes the base monthly rate plus taxes and fees for three lines of mobile phone service).*
Source: The Council for Community and Economic Research, Cost of Living Index, 2021

Health Care, Transportation, and Other Costs

Area[1]	Doctor ($/visit)	Dentist ($/visit)	Optometrist ($/visit)	Gasoline ($/gallon)	Beauty Salon ($/visit)	Men's Shirt ($)
City[2]	n/a	n/a	n/a	n/a	n/a	n/a
Avg.	118.16	101.04	109.44	2.71	40.63	30.77
Min.	35.04	55.56	51.17	2.17	18.59	11.32
Max.	231.10	165.12	256.81	4.11	85.33	63.03

Note: (1) Values for the local area are compared with the average, minimum and maximum values for all 285 areas in the Cost of Living Index; (2) Figures cover the Santa Rosa CA urban area; n/a not available; ***Doctor*** *(general practitioners routine exam of an established patient);* ***Dentist*** *(adult teeth cleaning and periodic oral examination);* ***Optometrist*** *(full vision eye exam for established adult patient);* ***Gasoline*** *(one gallon regular unleaded, national brand, including all taxes, cash price at self-service pump if available);* ***Beauty Salon*** *(woman's shampoo, trim, and blow-dry);* ***Men's Shirt*** *(cotton/polyester dress shirt, pinpoint weave, long sleeves).*
Source: The Council for Community and Economic Research, Cost of Living Index, 2021

HOUSING

Homeownership Rate

Area	2013 (%)	2014 (%)	2015 (%)	2016 (%)	2017 (%)	2018 (%)	2019 (%)	2020 (%)	2021 (%)
MSA[1]	n/a	n/a	n/a	n/a	n/a	n/a	n/a	n/a	n/a
U.S.	65.1	64.5	63.7	63.4	63.9	64.4	64.6	66.6	65.5

Note: (1) Figures cover the Santa Rosa, CA Metropolitan Statistical Area; n/a not available
Source: U.S. Census Bureau, Housing Vacancies and Homeownership Annual Statistics: 2013-2021

House Price Index (HPI)

Area	National Ranking[2]	Quarterly Change (%)	One-Year Change (%)	Five-Year Change (%)	Since 1991Q1 (%)
MSA[1]	243	1.78	12.39	32.17	263.96
U.S.[3]	–	3.33	17.54	54.45	258.04

Note: The HPI is a weighted repeat sales index. It measures average price changes in repeat sales or refinancings on the same properties. This information is obtained by reviewing repeat mortgage transactions on single-family properties whose mortgages have been purchased or securitized by Fannie Mae or Freddie Mac since January 1975; (1) Figures cover the Santa Rosa, CA Metropolitan Statistical Area; (2) Rankings are based on annual percentage change for all metro areas containing at least 15,000 transactions over the last 10 years and ranges from 1 to 268; (3) figures based on a weighted average of Census Division estimates using a seasonally adjusted, purchase-only index; all figures are for the period ending December 31, 2021
Source: Federal Housing Finance Agency, Change in FHFA Metropolitan Area House Price Indexes, 2021Q4

Median Single-Family Home Prices

Area	2019	2020	2021[p]	Percent Change 2020 to 2021
MSA[1]	n/a	n/a	n/a	n/a
U.S. Average	274.6	300.2	353.4	17.7

Note: Figures are median sales prices of existing single-family homes in thousands of dollars; (p) preliminary; n/a not available; (1) Figures cover the Santa Rosa, CA Metropolitan Statistical Area
Source: National Association of Realtors, Median Sales Price of Existing Single-Family Homes for Metropolitan Areas, 4th Quarter 2021

Qualifying Income Based on Median Sales Price of Existing Single-Family Homes

Area	With 5% Down ($)	With 10% Down ($)	With 20% Down ($)
MSA[1]	n/a	n/a	n/a
U.S. Average	70,699	66,978	59,536

Note: Figures are preliminary; Qualifying income is based on a mortgage rate of 3.13%. Monthly principal and interest payment is limited to 25% of income; n/a not available; (1) Figures cover the Santa Rosa, CA Metropolitan Statistical Area
Source: National Association of Realtors, Qualifying Income Based on Median Sales Price of Existing Single-Family Homes for Metropolitan Areas, 4th Quarter 2021

Home Value Distribution

Area	Under $50,000	$50,000 -$99,999	$100,000 -$149,999	$150,000 -$199,999	$200,000 -$299,999	$300,000 -$499,999	$500,000 -$999,999	$1,000,000 or more
City	2.3	2.1	1.9	1.1	4.8	25.5	55.0	7.3
MSA[1]	2.1	2.5	1.7	1.1	3.4	18.3	55.2	15.6
U.S.	6.6	11.0	12.3	13.6	20.0	20.5	12.3	3.7

Note: Figures are percentages and cover owner-occupied housing units; (1) Figures cover the Santa Rosa, CA Metropolitan Statistical Area
Source: U.S. Census Bureau, 2016-2020 American Community Survey 5-Year Estimates

Year Housing Structure Built

Area	2010 or Later	2000 -2009	1990 -1999	1980 -1989	1970 -1979	1960 -1969	1950 -1959	1940 -1949	Before 1940	Median Year
City	3.2	13.1	13.3	18.7	20.7	12.9	7.7	4.6	5.8	1979
MSA[1]	3.1	10.8	14.1	18.1	20.3	11.8	8.7	4.8	8.3	1978
U.S.	6.2	13.6	13.9	13.4	15.0	10.5	10.2	4.8	12.4	1978

Note: Figures are percentages except for Median Year; Note: (1) Figures cover the Santa Rosa, CA Metropolitan Statistical Area
Source: U.S. Census Bureau, 2016-2020 American Community Survey 5-Year Estimates

Gross Monthly Rent

Area	Under $500	$500 -$999	$1,000 -$1,499	$1,500 -$1,999	$2,000 -$2,499	$2,500 -$2,999	$3,000 and up	Median ($)
City	6.1	5.3	26.0	27.6	19.5	9.8	5.6	1,728
MSA[1]	5.5	8.4	23.0	26.9	19.6	9.6	7.0	1,743
U.S.	8.9	34.3	30.2	14.9	6.2	2.6	2.8	1,096

Note: Figures are percentages except for Median; Gross rent is the contract rent plus the estimated average monthly cost of utilities (electricity, gas, and water and sewer) and fuels (oil, coal, kerosene, wood, etc.) if these are paid by the renter (or paid for the renter by someone else); (1) Figures cover the Santa Rosa, CA Metropolitan Statistical Area
Source: U.S. Census Bureau, 2016-2020 American Community Survey 5-Year Estimates

HEALTH

Health Risk Factors

Category	MSA[1] (%)	U.S. (%)
Adults aged 18–64 who have any kind of health care coverage	n/a	86.8
Adults who reported being in good or better health	n/a	86.7
Adults who are current smokers	n/a	15.5
Adults who currently use chewing tobacco, snuff, or snus	n/a	3.7
Adults who are heavy drinkers[2]	n/a	6.7
Adults who are binge drinkers[3]	n/a	15.7
Adults who are overweight (BMI 25.0 - 29.9)	n/a	35.2
Adults who are obese (BMI 30.0 - 99.8)	n/a	31.9
Adults who participated in any physical activities in the past month	n/a	77.6
Adults who always or nearly always wears a seat belt	n/a	94.2

Note: (1) Figures for the Santa Rosa, CA Metropolitan Statistical Area were not available. (2) Heavy drinkers are classified as adult men having more than 14 drinks per week and adult women having more than 7 drinks per week; (3) Binge drinkers are classified as males having five or more drinks on one occasion or females having four or more drinks on one occasion
Source: Centers for Disease Control and Prevention, Behaviorial Risk Factor Surveillance System, SMART: Selected Metropolitan Area Risk Trends, 2020

Acute and Chronic Health Conditions

Category	MSA[1] (%)	U.S. (%)
Adults who have ever been told they had a heart attack	n/a	4.3
Adults who have ever been told they have angina or coronary heart disease	n/a	4.0
Adults who have ever been told they had a stroke	n/a	2.8
Adults who have ever been told they have asthma	n/a	14.2
Adults who have ever been told they have arthritis	n/a	24.5
Adults who have ever been told they have diabetes[2]	n/a	10.6
Adults who have ever been told they had skin cancer	n/a	6.4
Adults who have ever been told they had any other types of cancer	n/a	6.8
Adults who have ever been told they have COPD	n/a	6.2
Adults who have ever been told they have kidney disease	n/a	2.9
Adults who have ever been told they have a form of depression	n/a	19.6

Note: (1) Figures for the Santa Rosa, CA Metropolitan Statistical Area were not available. (2) Figures do not include pregnancy-related, borderline, or pre-diabetes
Source: Centers for Disease Control and Prevention, Behaviorial Risk Factor Surveillance System, SMART: Selected Metropolitan Area Risk Trends, 2020

Health Screening and Vaccination Rates

Category	MSA[1] (%)	U.S. (%)
Adults 50-75 who have had a blood stool test within the past year	n/a	9.3
Adults aged 65+ who have had flu shot within the past year	n/a	67.9
Adults aged 65+ who have ever had a pneumonia vaccination	n/a	72.2
Adults who have ever been tested for HIV	n/a	37.1
Women aged 21-65 who have had a pap test in the past three years	n/a	77.7
Men aged 40+ who have had a PSA test within the past two years	n/a	31.8
Women aged 40+ who have had a mammogram within the past two years	n/a	71.5

Note: (1) Figures for the Santa Rosa, CA Metropolitan Statistical Area were not available.
Source: Centers for Disease Control and Prevention, Behaviorial Risk Factor Surveillance System, SMART: Selected Metropolitan Area Risk Trends, 2020

Disability Status

Category	MSA[1] (%)	U.S. (%)
Adults who reported being deaf	n/a	6.8
Are you blind or have serious difficulty seeing, even when wearing glasses?	n/a	4.7
Do you have difficulty doing errands alone?	n/a	6.3
Do you have difficulty dressing or bathing?	n/a	3.0
Do you have serious difficulty concentrating/remembering/making decisions?	n/a	10.8
Do you have serious difficulty walking or climbing stairs?	n/a	11.9

Note: (1) Figures for the Santa Rosa, CA Metropolitan Statistical Area were not available.
Source: Centers for Disease Control and Prevention, Behaviorial Risk Factor Surveillance System, SMART: Selected Metropolitan Area Risk Trends, 2020

Mortality Rates for the Top 10 Causes of Death in the U.S.

ICD-10[a] Sub-Chapter	ICD-10[a] Code	Age-Adjusted Mortality Rate[1] per 100,000 population	
		County[2]	U.S.
Malignant neoplasms	C00-C97	132.2	146.4
Ischaemic heart diseases	I20-I25	63.3	90.2
Other forms of heart disease	I30-I51	41.6	51.9
Other degenerative diseases of the nervous system	G30-G31	40.6	39.7
Other external causes of accidental injury	W00-X59	31.6	38.7
Chronic lower respiratory diseases	J40-J47	24.2	38.1
Cerebrovascular diseases	I60-I69	35.2	37.6
Organic, including symptomatic, mental disorders	F01-F09	22.5	29.4
Hypertensive diseases	I10-I15	16.3	26.1
Diabetes mellitus	E10-E14	17.0	22.6

Note: (a) ICD-10 = International Classification of Diseases 10th Revision; (1) Mortality rates are a three-year average covering 2018-2020; (2) Figures cover Sonoma County.
Source: Centers for Disease Control and Prevention, National Center for Health Statistics. Underlying Cause of Death 1999-2020 on CDC WONDER Online Database

Mortality Rates for Selected Causes of Death

ICD-10[a] Sub-Chapter	ICD-10[a] Code	Age-Adjusted Mortality Rate[1] per 100,000 population	
		County[2]	U.S.
Assault	X85-Y09	2.2	6.5
Diseases of the liver	K70-K76	11.8	15.3
Human immunodeficiency virus (HIV) disease	B20-B24	Unreliable	1.4
Influenza and pneumonia	J09-J18	9.2	13.4
Intentional self-harm	X60-X84	14.1	13.9
Malnutrition	E40-E46	2.4	2.9
Obesity and other hyperalimentation	E65-E68	2.1	2.4
Renal failure	N17-N19	4.8	12.5
Transport accidents	V01-V99	9.6	12.5
Viral hepatitis	B15-B19	1.2	1.0

Note: (a) ICD-10 = International Classification of Diseases 10th Revision; (1) Mortality rates are a three-year average covering 2018-2020; (2) Figures cover Sonoma County; Data are suppressed when the data meet the criteria for confidentiality constraints; Mortality rates are flagged as unreliable when the rate would be calculated with a numerator of 20 or less.
Source: Centers for Disease Control and Prevention, National Center for Health Statistics. Underlying Cause of Death 1999-2020 on CDC WONDER Online Database

Health Insurance Coverage

Area	With Health Insurance	With Private Health Insurance	With Public Health Insurance	Without Health Insurance	Population Under Age 19 Without Health Insurance
City	92.5	68.9	36.5	7.5	5.2
MSA[1]	94.0	72.4	36.3	6.0	3.6
U.S.	91.3	68.1	35.3	8.7	5.2

Note: Figures are percentages that cover the civilian noninstitutionalized population; (1) Figures cover the Santa Rosa, CA Metropolitan Statistical Area
Source: U.S. Census Bureau, 2016-2020 American Community Survey 5-Year Estimates

Number of Medical Professionals

Area	MDs[3]	DOs[3,4]	Dentists	Podiatrists	Chiropractors	Optometrists
County[1] (number)	1,395	89	466	34	205	88
County[1] (rate[2])	285.4	18.2	95.3	7.0	41.9	18.0
U.S. (rate[2])	285.1	23.0	71.1	6.2	28.2	17.0

06097
Note: Data as of 2020 unless noted; (1) Data covers Sonoma County; (2) Rate per 100,000 population; (3) Data as of 2019 and includes all active, non-federal physicians; (4) Doctor of Osteopathic Medicine
Source: U.S. Department of Health and Human Services, Health Resources and Services Administration, Bureau of Health Professions, Area Resource File (ARF) 2020-2021

EDUCATION

Public School District Statistics

District Name	Schls	Pupils	Pupil/ Teacher Ratio	Minority Pupils[1] (%)	LEP/ELL[2] (%)	IEP[3] (%)
Rincon Valley Union Elementary	9	3,241	n/a	45.9	13.6	13.0
Santa Rosa Elementary	12	4,903	n/a	73.6	40.4	14.4
Santa Rosa High	12	10,941	n/a	66.0	13.8	16.9

Note: Table includes school districts with 2,000 or more students; (1) Percentage of students that are not non-Hispanic white; (2) Percentage of students that are Limited English Proficient (LEP) or English Language Learners (ELL) (2018-19); (3) Percentage of students that have an Individualized Education Program (IEP).
Source: U.S. Department of Education, National Center for Education Statistics, Common Core of Data, Local Education Agency (School District) Universe Survey: School Year 2019-2020

Highest Level of Education

Area	Less than H.S.	H.S. Diploma	Some College, No Deg.	Associate Degree	Bachelor's Degree	Master's Degree	Prof. School Degree	Doctorate Degree
City	13.8	18.4	24.0	10.0	20.8	8.6	3.0	1.4
MSA[1]	10.9	18.2	24.9	9.5	22.9	8.9	3.2	1.5
U.S.	11.5	26.7	20.3	8.6	20.2	9.1	2.2	1.5

Note: Figures cover persons age 25 and over; (1) Figures cover the Santa Rosa, CA Metropolitan Statistical Area
Source: U.S. Census Bureau, 2016-2020 American Community Survey 5-Year Estimates

Educational Attainment by Race

Area	High School Graduate or Higher (%)					Bachelor's Degree or Higher (%)				
	Total	White	Black	Asian	Hisp.[2]	Total	White	Black	Asian	Hisp.[2]
City	86.2	92.3	86.7	85.7	62.8	33.8	38.9	28.8	46.7	13.9
MSA[1]	89.1	93.7	87.8	87.7	65.5	36.4	40.6	31.3	47.8	14.7
U.S.	88.5	90.7	86.7	87.3	70.3	32.9	34.4	22.6	55.0	17.6

Note: Figures shown cover persons 25 years old and over; (1) Figures cover the Santa Rosa, CA Metropolitan Statistical Area; (2) People of Hispanic origin can be of any race
Source: U.S. Census Bureau, 2016-2020 American Community Survey 5-Year Estimates

School Enrollment by Grade and Control

Area	Preschool (%)		Kindergarten (%)		Grades 1 - 4 (%)		Grades 5 - 8 (%)		Grades 9 - 12 (%)	
	Public	Private	Public	Private	Public	Private	Public	Private	Public	Private
City	49.3	50.7	92.1	7.9	94.1	5.9	90.9	9.1	93.3	6.7
MSA[1]	47.8	52.2	90.7	9.3	92.9	7.1	90.1	9.9	92.4	7.6
U.S.	58.9	41.1	86.9	13.1	89.0	11.0	89.0	11.0	89.7	10.3

Note: Figures shown cover persons 3 years old and over; (1) Figures cover the Santa Rosa, CA Metropolitan Statistical Area
Source: U.S. Census Bureau, 2016-2020 American Community Survey 5-Year Estimates

Higher Education

Four-Year Colleges			Two-Year Colleges			Medical Schools[1]	Law Schools[2]	Voc/ Tech[3]
Public	Private Non-profit	Private For-profit	Public	Private Non-profit	Private For-profit			
1	1	2	1	0	0	0	1	1

Note: Figures cover institutions located within the Santa Rosa, CA Metropolitan Statistical Area and include main campuses only; (1) includes schools accredited by the Liaison Committee on Medical Education and the American Osteopathic Association's Commission on Osteopathic College Accreditation; (2) includes ABA-accredited schools, schools with provisional ABA accreditation, and state accredited schools; (3) includes all schools with programs that are less than 2 years.
Source: National Center for Education Statistics, Integrated Postsecondary Education System (IPEDS), 2020-21; Wikipedia, List of Medical Schools in the United States, accessed April 11, 2022; Wikipedia, List of Law Schools in the United States, accessed April 11, 2022

EMPLOYERS

Major Employers

Company Name	Industry
Amy's Kitchen	Food manufacturing
AT&T	Utility company
Bear Republic Brewing Co.	Brewing company
Empire College	Education
Exchange Bank	Financial services
G&G Supermarket	Grocery stores
Ghilotti Construction Co.	Construction
Graton Resort & Casino	Casino resort
Hansel Auto Group	Auto sales
Hyatt Vineyard Creek Hotel & Spa	Hotels & motels
Jackson Family Wines	Winery
JDSU	Optical communications networks, communications equip
Kaiser Permanente	Healthcare
Keysight Technologies	Test equipment for labratories
Korbel	Korbel
La Tortilla Factory	Grocery stores
Mary's Pizza Shack	Grocery stores
Medtronic	Medical device manufacturer
Redwood Credit Union	Credit union
River Rock Casino	Casino resort
Sonoma Media Investments	Financial services
St. Joseph Health, Sonoma County	Healthcare
Sutter Santa Rosa Regional Hospital	Healthcare

Note: Companies shown are located within the Santa Rosa, CA Metropolitan Statistical Area.
Source: Hoovers.com; Wikipedia

PUBLIC SAFETY

Crime Rate

Area	Total Crime	Violent Crime Rate				Property Crime Rate		
		Murder	Rape[3]	Robbery	Aggrav. Assault	Burglary	Larceny -Theft	Motor Vehicle Theft
City	2,120.0	2.3	62.2	76.3	375.3	306.3	1,059.7	237.9
Suburbs[1]	1,554.3	1.9	41.1	41.8	329.5	232.8	807.9	99.2
Metro[2]	1,758.4	2.0	48.7	54.2	346.0	259.4	898.8	149.2
U.S.	2,356.7	6.5	38.4	73.9	279.7	314.2	1,398.0	246.0

Note: Figures are crimes per 100,000 population; (1) All areas within the metro area that are located outside the city limits; (2) Figures cover the Santa Rosa, CA Metropolitan Statistical Area; (3) All figures shown were reported using the revised Uniform Crime Reporting (UCR) definition of rape.
Source: FBI Uniform Crime Reports, 2020

Hate Crimes

Area	Number of Quarters Reported	Number of Incidents per Bias Motivation					
		Race/Ethnicity/ Ancestry	Religion	Sexual Orientation	Disability	Gender	Gender Identity
City	4	6	4	1	0	0	0
U.S.	4	5,227	1,244	1,110	130	75	266

Source: Federal Bureau of Investigation, Hate Crime Statistics 2020

Identity Theft Consumer Reports

Area	Reports	Reports per 100,000 Population	Rank[2]
MSA[1]	702	142	318
U.S.	1,434,676	432	-

Note: (1) Figures cover the Santa Rosa, CA Metropolitan Statistical Area; (2) Rank ranges from 1 to 391 where 1 indicates greatest number of identity theft reports per 100,000 population
Source: Federal Trade Commission, Consumer Sentinel Network Data Book 2021

Fraud and Other Consumer Reports

Area	Reports	Reports per 100,000 Population	Rank[2]
MSA[1]	4,300	870	201
U.S.	4,328,977	1,304	-

Note: (1) Figures cover the Santa Rosa, CA Metropolitan Statistical Area; (2) Rank ranges from 1 to 391 where 1 indicates greatest number of fraud and other consumer reports per 100,000 population
Source: Federal Trade Commission, Consumer Sentinel Network Data Book 2021

POLITICS

2020 Presidential Election Results

Area	Biden	Trump	Jorgensen	Hawkins	Other
Sonoma County	74.5	23.0	1.3	0.6	0.6
U.S.	51.3	46.8	1.2	0.3	0.5

Note: Results are percentages and may not add to 100% due to rounding
Source: Dave Leip's Atlas of U.S. Presidential Elections

SPORTS

Professional Sports Teams

Team Name	League	Year Established

No teams are located in the metro area
Source: Wikipedia, Major Professional Sports Teams of the United States and Canada, April 6, 2022

CLIMATE

Average and Extreme Temperatures

Temperature	Jan	Feb	Mar	Apr	May	Jun	Jul	Aug	Sep	Oct	Nov	Dec	Yr.
Extreme High (°F)	69	72	83	89	99	102	103	105	109	94	85	73	109
Average High (°F)	56	61	65	69	74	79	81	84	84	75	65	58	71
Average Temp. (°F)	46	50	51	55	60	63	65	66	65	60	52	47	57
Average Low (°F)	35	38	36	41	45	47	49	47	46	44	39	35	42
Extreme Low (°F)	24	26	25	29	32	36	41	40	36	32	28	23	23

Note: Figures cover the years 1948-1990
Source: National Climatic Data Center, International Station Meteorological Climate Summary, 9/96

Average Precipitation/Snowfall/Humidity

Precip./Humidity	Jan	Feb	Mar	Apr	May	Jun	Jul	Aug	Sep	Oct	Nov	Dec	Yr.
Avg. Precip. (in.)	5.6	6.2	4.5	0.7	0.9	0.1	0.0	0.0	0.0	2.3	4.7	4.0	29.0
Avg. Snowfall (in.)	n/a	n/a	n/a	0	0	0	0	0	0	0	n/a	n/a	n/a
Avg. Rel. Hum. (%)	85	74	70	69	68	63	71	68	66	74	81	82	73

Note: Figures cover the years 1948-1990
Source: National Climatic Data Center, International Station Meteorological Climate Summary, 9/96

Weather Conditions

Temperature			Daytime Sky			Precipitation		
0°F & below	32°F & below	90°F & above	Clear	Partly cloudy	Cloudy	0.01 inch or more precip.	0.1 inch or more snow/ice	Thunder-storms
0	43	30	n/a	n/a	n/a	n/a	n/a	2

Note: Figures are average number of days per year and cover the years 1948-1990
Source: National Climatic Data Center, International Station Meteorological Climate Summary, 9/96

HAZARDOUS WASTE

Superfund Sites

The Santa Rosa, CA metro area has no sites on the EPA's Superfund Final National Priorities List. There are a total of 1,165 Superfund sites with a status of proposed or final on the list in the U.S. *U.S. Environmental Protection Agency, National Priorities List, April 6, 2022*

AIR QUALITY

Air Quality Trends: Ozone

	1990	1995	2000	2005	2010	2016	2017	2018	2019	2020
MSA[1]	0.063	0.071	0.061	0.050	0.053	0.059	0.062	0.055	0.052	0.052
U.S.	0.090	0.091	0.082	0.080	0.074	0.070	0.069	0.070	0.066	0.068

Note: (1) Data covers the Santa Rosa, CA Metropolitan Statistical Area. The values shown are the composite ozone concentration averages among trend sites based on the highest fourth daily maximum 8-hour concentration in parts per million. These trends are based on sites having an adequate record of monitoring data during the trend period. Data from exceptional events are included.
Source: U.S. Environmental Protection Agency, Air Quality Monitoring Information, "Air Quality Trends by City, 1990-2020"

Air Quality Index

Area	Percent of Days when Air Quality was...[2]					AQI Statistics[2]	
	Good	Moderate	Unhealthy for Sensitive Groups	Unhealthy	Very Unhealthy	Maximum	Median
MSA[1]	87.2	10.9	0.3	1.6	0.0	187	33

Note: (1) Data covers the Santa Rosa, CA Metropolitan Statistical Area; (2) Based on 366 days with AQI data in 2020. Air Quality Index (AQI) is an index for reporting daily air quality. EPA calculates the AQI for five major air pollutants regulated by the Clean Air Act: ground-level ozone, particle pollution (aka particulate matter), carbon monoxide, sulfur dioxide, and nitrogen dioxide. The AQI runs from 0 to 500. The higher the AQI value, the greater the level of air pollution and the greater the health concern. There are six AQI categories: "Good" AQI is between 0 and 50. Air quality is considered satisfactory; "Moderate" AQI is between 51 and 100. Air quality is acceptable; "Unhealthy for Sensitive Groups" When AQI values are between 101 and 150, members of sensitive groups may experience health effects; "Unhealthy" When AQI values are between 151 and 200 everyone may begin to experience health effects; "Very Unhealthy" AQI values between 201 and 300 trigger a health alert; "Hazardous" AQI values over 300 trigger warnings of emergency conditions (not shown).
Source: U.S. Environmental Protection Agency, Air Quality Index Report, 2020

Air Quality Index Pollutants

Area	Percent of Days when AQI Pollutant was...[2]					
	Carbon Monoxide	Nitrogen Dioxide	Ozone	Sulfur Dioxide	Particulate Matter 2.5	Particulate Matter 10
MSA[1]	0.0	0.3	58.7	0.0	38.0	3.0

Note: (1) Data covers the Santa Rosa, CA Metropolitan Statistical Area; (2) Based on 366 days with AQI data in 2020. The Air Quality Index (AQI) is an index for reporting daily air quality. EPA calculates the AQI for five major air pollutants regulated by the Clean Air Act: ground-level ozone, particle pollution (also known as particulate matter), carbon monoxide, sulfur dioxide, and nitrogen dioxide. The AQI runs from 0 to 500. The higher the AQI value, the greater the level of air pollution and the greater the health concern.
Source: U.S. Environmental Protection Agency, Air Quality Index Report, 2020

Maximum Air Pollutant Concentrations: Particulate Matter, Ozone, CO and Lead

	Particulate Matter 10 (ug/m^3)	Particulate Matter 2.5 Wtd AM (ug/m^3)	Particulate Matter 2.5 24-Hr (ug/m^3)	Ozone (ppm)	Carbon Monoxide (ppm)	Lead (ug/m^3)
MSA[1] Level	134	8.3	34	0.052	2	n/a
NAAQS[2]	150	15	35	0.075	9	0.15
Met NAAQS[2]	Yes	Yes	Yes	Yes	Yes	n/a

Note: (1) Data covers the Santa Rosa, CA Metropolitan Statistical Area; Data from exceptional events are included; (2) National Ambient Air Quality Standards; ppm = parts per million; ug/m^3 = micrograms per cubic meter; n/a not available.
Concentrations: Particulate Matter 10 (coarse particulate)—highest second maximum 24-hour concentration; Particulate Matter 2.5 Wtd AM (fine particulate)—highest weighted annual mean concentration; Particulate Matter 2.5 24-Hour (fine particulate)—highest 98th percentile 24-hour concentration; Ozone—highest fourth daily maximum 8-hour concentration; Carbon Monoxide—highest second maximum non-overlapping 8-hour concentration; Lead—maximum running 3-month average
Source: U.S. Environmental Protection Agency, Air Quality Monitoring Information, "Air Quality Statistics by City, 2020"

Maximum Air Pollutant Concentrations: Nitrogen Dioxide and Sulfur Dioxide

	Nitrogen Dioxide AM (ppb)	Nitrogen Dioxide 1-Hr (ppb)	Sulfur Dioxide AM (ppb)	Sulfur Dioxide 1-Hr (ppb)	Sulfur Dioxide 24-Hr (ppb)
MSA[1] Level	4	25	n/a	n/a	n/a
NAAQS[2]	53	100	30	75	140
Met NAAQS[2]	Yes	Yes	n/a	n/a	n/a

Note: (1) Data covers the Santa Rosa, CA Metropolitan Statistical Area; Data from exceptional events are included; (2) National Ambient Air Quality Standards; ppm = parts per million; ug/m^3 = micrograms per cubic meter; n/a not available.
Concentrations: Nitrogen Dioxide AM—highest arithmetic mean concentration; Nitrogen Dioxide 1-Hr—highest 98th percentile 1-hour daily maximum concentration; Sulfur Dioxide AM—highest annual mean concentration; Sulfur Dioxide 1-Hr—highest 99th percentile 1-hour daily maximum concentration; Sulfur Dioxide 24-Hr—highest second maximum 24-hour concentration
Source: U.S. Environmental Protection Agency, Air Quality Monitoring Information, "Air Quality Statistics by City, 2020"

Seattle, Washington

Background

Believe it or not, the virgin hinterlands and wide curving arch of Elliot Bay in present-day Seattle were once named New York. The city was renamed Seattle in 1853, for the Native American Indian Chief Seattle, two years after its first five families from Illinois had settled into the narrow strip of land between Puget Sound and Lake Washington.

The lush, green forests of the "Emerald City," created by frequent rain and its many natural waterways, gave birth to Seattle's first major industry—lumber, which also bred a society of bearded, rabble-rousing bachelors. To alleviate that problem, Asa Mercer, president of the Territorial University, which later became the University of Washington, trekked back east, and recruited marriageable women, aka "Mercer girls."

Today, the city does not rely on lumber as its major industry, but boasts commercial aircraft production and missile research, importing and exporting, and technology. As the closest U.S. mainland port to Asia, Seattle has become a key trade center for goods such as cars, forest products, electronic equipment, bananas, and petroleum products. The city is home to ten Fortune 500 companies including Amazon, Microsoft, Costco, and Starbucks. Other major employers in Seattle are Nordstrom, Avanade, and Alaska Airlines.

Seattle continues to move toward becoming the next Silicon Valley. It is predominantly a software town dominated by Microsoft, in nearby Redmond, announced that expansion of their campus—17 new buildings and a parking facility for 6,500 cars—will open in 2023.

The Seattle Seaport Terminal Project, comprised of small-and-large-scale projects designed to improve the port's facilities for businesses, passengers, residents, and tourists, included a major renovation of Terminal 5, construction of a Cruise Ship Terminal improvement, and port facilities improvements. Seattle is the fourth largest container port in North America.

Seattle has undergone a cultural and commercial reemergence of its downtown. Tourists and locals are drawn by luxury hotels, restaurants, a 16-screen movie theater, and other entertainment-oriented businesses, including the first in a nationwide chain of Game Works, computerized playgrounds for adults. Center City Seattle continues to see renovation and development projects, as city planners try to deal with more people living, working, and visiting in the city.

The arts are a vital part of Seattle life. The world-famous Seattle Opera, now performing in a state-of-the-art hall dedicated in 2003, is well known for its summer presentations of Wagner's *Ring* cycle. The Seattle Philharmonic Orchestra celebrated its 50th anniversary in 2004; its annual Bushnell Concerto Competition features promising new area musicians. The city's jazz scene developed the early careers of Ray Charles and Quincy Jones, and is the birthplace of rocker Jimi Hendrix, the bands Nirvana, Pearl Jam, Soundgarden and Foo Fighters, and the alternative rock movement grunge.

The Seattle Museum constructed in Olympic Sculpture Park turned disused waterfront property into a permanent green space with plantings native to Puget Sound. The Seattle Museum of Flight's remarkable collection—the largest on the West Coast—includes a Concorde and the Boeing 707 used as Air Force One by presidents from Eisenhower to Nixon.

Seattle's professional sports teams are popular and many. Football's Seattle Seahawks are Super Bowl XLVIII champions. Major league rugby team, Seattle Seawolves won back-to-back championships in 2018 and 2019.

Seattle has a distinctly marine climate. The city's location on Puget Sound and between two mountain ranges ensures a mild climate year-round with moderate variations in temperature, and also puts it in a major earthquake zone. Summers are generally sunny and, while winters are rainy, most of the rain falls between October and March.

Rankings

General Rankings

- For its "Best for Vets: Places to Live 2019" rankings, *Military Times* evaluated 599 cities (83 large, 234 medium, 282 small) and compared the locations across three broad categories: veteran and military culture/services; economic indicators; and livability factors such as health, crime, traffic, and school quality. Seattle ranked #7 out of the top 25, in the large city category (population of more than 250,000). Data points more specific to veterans and the military weighed more heavily than others. *rebootcamp.militarytimes.com, "Military Times Best Places to Live 2019," September 10, 2018*
- *US News & World Report* conducted a survey of more than 3,600 people and analyzed the 150 largest metropolitan areas to determine what matters most when selecting the next place to live. Seattle ranked #19 out of the top 25 as having the best combination of desirable factors. Criteria: cost of living; quality of life and education; net migration; job market; desirability; and other factors. *realestate.usnews.com, "The 25 Best Places to Live in the U.S. in 2021-2022," July 13, 2021*
- The Seattle metro area was identified as one of America's fastest-growing areas in terms of population and business growth by *MagnifyMoney.* The area ranked #20 out of 35. The 100 most populous metro areas in the U.S. were evaluated on their change from 2011 to 2016 in the following categories: people and housing; workforce and employment opportunities; growing industry. *www.businessinsider.com, "The 35 Cities in the US with the Biggest Influx of People, the Most Work Opportunities, and the Hottest Business Growth," August 12, 2018*
- The Seattle metro area was identified as one of America's fastest-growing areas in terms of population and economy by *Forbes.* The area ranked #2 out of 25. The 100 most populous metro areas in the U.S. were evaluated on the following criteria: estimated population growth; employment; economic output; wages; home values. *Forbes, "America's Fastest-Growing Cities 2018," February 28, 2018*
- The human resources consulting firm Mercer ranked 231 major cities worldwide in terms of overall quality of life. Seattle ranked #46. Criteria: political, social, economic, and socio-cultural factors; medical and health considerations; schools and education; public services and transportation; recreation; consumer goods; housing; and natural environment. *Mercer, "Mercer 2019 Quality of Living Survey," March 13, 2019*

Business/Finance Rankings

- According to *Business Insider,* the Seattle metro area is a prime place to run a startup or move an existing business to. The area ranked #5. More than 300 metro areas were analyzed for factors that were of top concern to new business owners. Data was based on the 2019 U.S. Census Bureau American Community Survey, statistics from the CDC, Bureau of Labor Statistics employment report, and University of Chicago analysis. Criteria: business formations; percentage of vaccinated population; percentage of households with internet subscriptions; median household income; and share of work that can be done from home. *www.businessinsider.com, "The 20 Best Cities for Starting a Business in 2022 Include Baltimore, Boulder, and Boston," January 5, 2022*
- Based on metro area social media reviews, the employment opinion group Glassdoor surveyed 50 of the most populous U.S. metro areas and equally weighed cost of living, hiring opportunity, and job satisfaction to compose a list of "25 Best Cities for Jobs." Median pay and home value, and number of active job openings were also factored in. The Seattle metro area was ranked #23 in overall job satisfaction. *www.glassdoor.com, "Best Cities for Jobs," February 25, 2020*
- The Brookings Institution ranked the nation's largest cities based on income inequality. Seattle was ranked #34 (#1 = greatest inequality). Criteria: the "95/20 ratio," a figure representing the income at which a household earns more than 95 percent of all other households, divided by the income at which a household earns more than only 20 percent of all other households. *Brookings Institution, "Household Income Inequality, Largest Cities of 97 Large U.S. Metro Areas, 2014-2016," February 5, 2018*
- The Brookings Institution ranked the 100 largest metro areas in the U.S. based on income inequality. Seattle was ranked #71 (#1 = greatest inequality). Criteria: the "95/20 ratio," a figure representing the income at which a household earns more than 95 percent of all other households, divided by the income at which a household earns more than only 20 percent of all other households. *Brookings Institution, "Household Income Inequality, 100 Largest U.S. Metro Areas, 2014-2016," February 5, 2018*
- Payscale.com ranked the 32 largest metro areas in terms of wage growth. The Seattle metro area ranked #31. Criteria: private-sector and education professional wage growth between the 4th quarter of 2019 and the 4th quarter of 2020. *PayScale, "Wage Trends by Metro Area-4th Quarter," January 11, 2021*

- The Seattle metro area was identified as one of the most debt-ridden places in America by the finance site Credit.com. The metro area was ranked #9. Criteria: residents' average credit card debt as well as median income. *Credit.com, "25 Cities With the Most Credit Card Debt," February 28, 2018*
- For its annual survey of the "Most Expensive U.S. Cities to Live In," Kiplinger applied Cost of Living Index statistics developed by the Council for Community and Economic Research to U.S. Census Bureau population and median household income data for 256 urban areas. Seattle was among the 20 most expensive in the country. *Kiplinger.com, "The 20 Most Expensive Cities in the U.S.," March 16, 2022*
- The Seattle metro area appeared on the Milken Institute "2021 Best Performing Cities" list. Rank: #13 out of 200 large metro areas (population over 250,000). Criteria: job growth; wage and salary growth; high-tech output growth; housing affordability; household broadband access. *Milken Institute, "Best-Performing Cities 2021," February 16, 2021*
- *Forbes* ranked the 200 most populous metro areas to determine the nation's "Best Places for Business and Careers." The Seattle metro area was ranked #1. Criteria: costs (business and living); job growth (past and projected); income growth; quality of life; educational attainment (college and high school); projected economic growth; cultural and leisure opportunities; workplace tolerance laws; net migration patterns. *Forbes, "The Best Places for Business and Careers 2019: Seattle Still On Top," October 30, 2019*
- Mercer Human Resources Consulting ranked 209 cities worldwide in terms of cost-of-living. Seattle ranked #67 (the lower the ranking, the higher the cost-of-living). The survey measured the comparative cost of over 200 items (such as housing, food, clothing, household goods, transportation, and entertainment) in each location. *Mercer, "2021 Cost of Living City Ranking," June 22, 2021*

Dating/Romance Rankings

- Seattle was selected as one of the nation's most romantic cities with 100,000 or more residents by Amazon.com. The city ranked #14 of 20. Criteria: per capita sales of romance novels, relationship books, romantic comedy movies, romantic music, and sexual wellness products. *Amazon.com, "Top 20 Most Romantic Cities in the U.S.," February 1, 2017*

Education Rankings

- Personal finance website *WalletHub* analyzed the 150 largest U.S. metropolitan statistical areas to determine where the most educated Americans are putting their degrees to work. Criteria: education levels; percentage of workers with degrees; education quality and attainment gap; public school quality rankings; quality and enrollment of each metro area's universities. Seattle was ranked #8 (#1 = most educated city). *www.WalletHub.com, "Most & Least Educated Cities in America," July 19, 2021*
- Seattle was selected as one of the best cities for post grads by *Rent.com*. The city ranked among the top 10. Criteria: jobs per capita; unemployment rate; mean annual income; cost of living; rental inventory. *Rent.com, "Best Cities for College Grads," December 11, 2018*
- Seattle was selected as one of America's most literate cities. The city ranked #1 out of the 84 largest U.S. cities. Criteria: number of booksellers; library resources; Internet resources; educational attainment; periodical publishing resources; newspaper circulation. *Central Connecticut State University, "America's Most Literate Cities, 2018," February 2019*

Environmental Rankings

- Sperling's BestPlaces assessed the 50 largest metropolitan areas of the United States for the likelihood of dangerously extreme weather events or earthquakes. In general the Southeast and South-Central regions have the highest risk of weather extremes and earthquakes, while the Pacific Northwest enjoys the lowest risk. Of the least risky metropolitan areas, the Seattle metro area was ranked #5. *www.bestplaces.net, "Avoid Natural Disasters: BestPlaces Reveals The Top 10 Safest Places to Live," October 25, 2017*
- The U.S. Environmental Protection Agency (EPA) released its list of U.S. metropolitan areas with the most ENERGY STAR certified buildings in 2020. The Seattle metro area was ranked #11 out of 25. *U.S. Environmental Protection Agency, "2021 Energy Star Top Cities," June 15, 2021*
- Seattle was highlighted as one of the 25 metro areas most polluted by short-term particle pollution (24-hour PM 2.5) in the U.S. during 2017 through 2019. The area ranked #14. *American Lung Association, "State of the Air 2021," April 21, 2021*

Food/Drink Rankings

- The U.S. Chamber of Commerce Foundation conducted an in-depth study on local food truck regulations, surveyed 288 food truck owners, and ranked 20 major American cities based on how friendly they are for operating a food truck. The compiled index assessed the following: procedures for obtaining permits and licenses; complying with restrictions; and financial obligations associated with operating a food truck. Seattle ranked #17 overall (1 being the best). *www.foodtrucknation.us, "Food Truck Nation," March 20, 2018*
- T-Mobile Park was selected as one of PETA's "Top 10 Vegan-Friendly Ballparks" for 2019. The park ranked #8. *People for the Ethical Treatment of Animals, "Top 10 Vegan-Friendly Ballparks, " May 23, 2019*

Health/Fitness Rankings

- For each of the 100 largest cities in the United States, the American Fitness Index®, published by the American College of Sports Medicine and the Anthem Foundation, evaluated community infrastructure and 34 health behaviors including preventive health, levels of chronic disease conditions, food insecurity, sleep quality, pedestrian safety, air quality, and community resources that support physical activity. Seattle ranked #3 for "community fitness." *americanfitnessindex.org, "2021 ACSM American Fitness Index Summary Report," July 13, 2021*
- Seattle was identified as one of the 10 most walkable cities in the U.S. by Walk Score. The city ranked #8. Walk Score measures walkability by analyzing hundreds of walking routes to nearby amenities, and also measures pedestrian friendliness by analyzing population density and road metrics such as block length and intersection density. *WalkScore.com, April 13, 2021*
- The Seattle metro area was identified as one of the worst cities for bed bugs in America by pest control company Orkin. The area ranked #44 out of 50 based on the number of bed bug treatments Orkin performed from December 2020 to November 2021. *Orkin, "Chicago Takes Another Top Spot for Pests, This Time Ranking #1 On Orkin's Bed Bug Cities List," January 10, 2022*
- Seattle was identified as a "2021 Spring Allergy Capital." The area ranked #99 out of 100. Three groups of factors were used to identify the most challenging cities for people with allergies during the spring season: annual spring pollen levels; over the counter medicine use; number of board-certified allergy specialists. *Asthma and Allergy Foundation of America, "Spring Allergy Capitals 2021," February 23, 2021*
- Seattle was identified as a "2021 Fall Allergy Capital." The area ranked #100 out of 100. Three groups of factors were used to identify the most challenging cities for people with allergies during the fall season: annual fall pollen levels; over the counter medicine use; number of board-certified allergy specialists. *Asthma and Allergy Foundation of America, "Fall Allergy Capitals 2021," February 23, 2021*
- Seattle was identified as a "2021 Asthma Capital." The area ranked #64 out of the nation's 100 largest metropolitan areas. Criteria: estimated asthma prevalence; asthma-related mortality; and ER visits due to asthma. Risk factors analyzed but not factored in the rankings: annual pollen score; annual air quality; public smoking laws; number of board-certified asthma specialists; rescue medication use; controller medication use; uninsured rate; poverty rate. *Asthma and Allergy Foundation of America, "Asthma Capitals 2021: The Most Challenging Places to Live With Asthma," May 5, 2021*
- The Sharecare Community Well-Being Index evaluates 10 individual and social health factors in order to measure what matters to Americans in the communities in which they live. The Seattle metro area ranked #9 in the top 10 across all 10 domains. Criteria: access to healthcare, food, and community resources; housng and transportation; economic security; feeling of purpose; physical, financial, social, and community well-being. *www.sharecare.com, "Community Well-Being Index: 2020 Metro Area & County Rankings Report," August 30, 2021*

Real Estate Rankings

- *WalletHub* compared the most populated U.S. cities to determine which had the best markets for real estate agents. Seattle ranked #1 where demand was high and pay was the best. Criteria: sales per agent; annual median wage for real-estate agents; monthly average starting salary for real estate agents; real estate job density and competition; unemployment rate; home turnover rate; housing-market health index; and other relevant metrics. *www.WalletHub.com, "2021 Best Places to Be a Real Estate Agent," May 12, 2021*
- The Seattle metro area appeared on Realtor.com's list of hot housing markets to watch in 2022. The area ranked #8. Criteria: forecasted home price and sales growth; overall economy; population trends. *Realtor.com®, "Top 10 Housing Markets Positioned for Growth in 2022," December 7, 2021*

- The Seattle metro area was identified as one of the 20 least affordable housing markets in the U.S. in 2021. The area ranked #176 out of 183 markets. Criteria: qualification for a mortgage loan with a 10 percent down payment on a typical home. *National Association of Realtors®, Qualifying Income Based on Sales Price of Existing Single-Family Homes for Metropolitan Areas, 2021*
- Seattle was ranked #205 out of 237 metro areas in terms of housing affordability in 2021 by the National Association of Home Builders (#1 = most affordable). Criteria: the share of homes sold in that area affordable to a family earning the local median income, based on standard mortgage underwriting criteria. *National Association of Home Builders®, NAHB-Wells Fargo Housing Opportunity Index, 4th Quarter 2021*

Safety Rankings

- Allstate ranked the 200 largest cities in America in terms of driver safety. Seattle ranked #155. Criteria: internal property damage claims over a two-year period from January 2016 to December 2017. The report helps increase the importance of safety and awareness behind the wheel. *Allstate, "Allstate America's Best Drivers Report, 2019" June 24, 2019*
- The National Insurance Crime Bureau ranked 390 metro areas in the U.S. in terms of per capita rates of vehicle theft. The Seattle metro area ranked #26 (#1 = highest rate). Criteria: number of vehicle theft offenses per 100,000 inhabitants in 2020. *National Insurance Crime Bureau, "Hot Spots 2020," August 31, 2021*

Seniors/Retirement Rankings

- From its Best Cities for Successful Aging indexes, the Milken Institute generated rankings for metropolitan areas, weighing data in nine categories—health care, wellness, living arrangements, transportation and convenience, financial characteristics, education, employment, community engagement, and overall livability. The Seattle metro area was ranked #35 overall in the large metro area category. *Milken Institute, "Best Cities for Successful Aging, 2017" March 14, 2017*

Sports/Recreation Rankings

- Seattle was chosen as one of America's best cities for bicycling. The city ranked #1 out of 50. Criteria: cycling infrastructure that is safe and friendly for all ages; energy and bike culture. The editors evaluated cities with populations of 100,000 or more. *Bicycling, "The 50 Best Bike Cities in America," October 10, 2018*

Transportation Rankings

- Business Insider presented an AllTransit Performance Score ranking of public transportation in major U.S. cities and towns, with populations over 250,000, in which Seattle earned the #16-ranked "Transit Score," awarded for frequency of service, access to jobs, quality and number of stops, and affordability. *www.businessinsider.com, "The 17 Major U.S. Cities with the Best Public Transportation," April 17, 2018*
- Seattle was identified as one of the most congested metro areas in the U.S. The area ranked #6 out of 10. Criteria: yearly delay per auto commuter in hours. *Texas A&M Transportation Institute, "2021 Urban Mobility Report," June 2021*
- According to the INRIX "2021 Global Traffic Scorecard," Seattle was identified as one of the most congested metro areas in the U.S. The area ranked #21 out of 25. Criteria: average annual time spent in traffic and average cost of congestion per motorist. *Inrix.com, "Americans Lost 3.4 Billion Hours Due to Congestion in 2021, 42% Below Pre-COVID," December 7, 2021*

Women/Minorities Rankings

- Seattle was selected as one of the gayest cities in America by *The Advocate.* The city ranked #24 out of 25. Criteria, among many: Trans Pride parades/festivals; gay rugby teams; lesbian bars; LGBT centers; theater screenings of "Moonlight"; LGBT-inclusive nondiscrimination ordinances; and gay bowling teams. *The Advocate, "Queerest Cities in America 2017" January 12, 2017*
- Personal finance website *WalletHub* compared more than 180 U.S. cities across two key dimensions, "Hispanic Business-Friendliness" and "Hispanic Purchasing Power," to arrive at the most favorable conditions for Hispanic entrepreneurs. Seattle was ranked #107 out of 182. Criteria includes: share of Hispanic-Owned Businesses; Hispanic entrepreneurship rate to median annual income of Hispanics; Small Business-Friendliness score; cost of living; and number of Hispanics with at least a bachelor's degree. *WalletHub.com, "2019's Best Cities for Hispanic Entrepreneurs," May 1, 2019*

Miscellaneous Rankings

- *MoveHub* ranked 446 hipster cities across 20 countries, using its *alternative* Hipster Index and Seattle came out as #4 among the top 50. Criteria: population over 150,000; number of vintage boutiques; density of tattoo parlors; vegan places to eat; coffee shops; and density of vinyl record stores. *www.movehub.com, "The Hipster Index: Brighton Pips Portland to Global Top Spot," July 28, 2021*
- The watchdog site, Charity Navigator, conducted a study of charities in major markets both to analyze statistical differences in their financial, accountability, and transparency practices and to track year-to-year variations in individual philanthropic communities. The Seattle metro area was ranked #25 among the 30 metro markets in the rating category of Overall Score. *www.charitynavigator.org, "2017 Metro Market Study," May 1, 2017*
- *WalletHub* compared the 150 most populated U.S. cities to determine their operating efficiency. A "Quality of City Services" score was constructed for each city and then divided by the total budget per capita to reveal which were managed the best. Seattle ranked #114. Criteria: financial stability; economy; education; safety; health; infrastructure and pollution. *www.WalletHub.com, "2021's Best- & Worst-Run Cities in America," June 22, 2021*
- The National Alliance to End Homelessness listed the 25 most populous metro areas with the highest rate of homelessness. The Seattle metro area had a high rate of homelessness. Criteria: number of homeless people per 10,000 population in 2016. *National Alliance to End Homelessness, "Homelessness in the 25 Most Populous U.S. Metro Areas," September 1, 2017*

Business Environment

DEMOGRAPHICS

Population Growth

Area	1990 Census	2000 Census	2010 Census	2020* Estimate	Population Growth (%)	
					1990-2020	2010-2020
City	516,262	563,374	608,660	741,251	43.6	21.8
MSA[1]	2,559,164	3,043,878	3,439,809	3,928,498	53.5	14.2
U.S.	248,709,873	281,421,906	308,745,538	326,569,308	31.3	5.8

Note: (1) Figures cover the Seattle-Tacoma-Bellevue, WA Metropolitan Statistical Area; (*) 2016-2020 5-year estimated population
Source: U.S. Census Bureau, 1990 Census, Census 2000, Census 2010, 2016-2020 American Community Survey 5-Year Estimates

Household Size

Area	Persons in Household (%)							Average Household Size
	One	Two	Three	Four	Five	Six	Seven or More	
City	39.9	34.7	12.3	9.0	2.8	0.8	0.6	2.10
MSA[1]	27.4	34.1	15.9	13.9	5.3	2.0	1.3	2.50
U.S.	28.0	33.9	15.5	12.9	6.0	2.3	1.4	2.60

Note: (1) Figures cover the Seattle-Tacoma-Bellevue, WA Metropolitan Statistical Area
Source: U.S. Census Bureau, 2016-2020 American Community Survey 5-Year Estimates

Race

Area	White Alone[2] (%)	Black Alone[2] (%)	Asian Alone[2] (%)	AIAN[3] Alone[2] (%)	NHOPI[4] Alone[2] (%)	Other Race Alone[2] (%)	Two or More Races (%)
City	65.8	7.1	16.3	0.5	0.3	2.4	7.6
MSA[1]	66.5	5.9	14.2	0.8	0.9	3.9	7.8
U.S.	70.4	12.6	5.6	0.8	0.2	5.1	5.2

Note: (1) Figures cover the Seattle-Tacoma-Bellevue, WA Metropolitan Statistical Area; (2) Alone is defined as not being in combination with one or more other races; (3) American Indian and Alaska Native; (4) Native Hawaiian and Other Pacific Islander
Source: U.S. Census Bureau, 2016-2020 American Community Survey 5-Year Estimates

Hispanic or Latino Origin

Area	Total (%)	Mexican (%)	Puerto Rican (%)	Cuban (%)	Other (%)
City	7.1	4.1	0.4	0.2	2.5
MSA[1]	10.3	7.1	0.6	0.2	2.5
U.S.	18.2	11.2	1.7	0.7	4.5

Note: Persons of Hispanic or Latino origin can be of any race; (1) Figures cover the Seattle-Tacoma-Bellevue, WA Metropolitan Statistical Area
Source: U.S. Census Bureau, 2016-2020 American Community Survey 5-Year Estimates

Ancestry

Area	German	Irish	English	American	Italian	Polish	French[2]	Scottish	Dutch
City	14.6	11.0	10.5	2.2	4.3	2.6	2.9	2.9	1.4
MSA[1]	14.1	9.4	9.7	3.0	3.6	1.9	2.7	2.5	1.4
U.S.	13.0	9.7	7.7	5.9	5.1	2.7	2.3	1.6	1.1

Note: Figures are the percentage of the total population reporting a particular ancestry. The nine most commonly reported ancestries in the U.S. are shown. Figures include multiple ancestries (e.g. if a person reported being Irish and Italian, they were included in both columns); (1) Figures cover the Seattle-Tacoma-Bellevue, WA Metropolitan Statistical Area; (2) Excludes Basque
Source: U.S. Census Bureau, 2016-2020 American Community Survey 5-Year Estimates

Foreign-born Population

Area	Percent of Population Born in								
	Any Foreign Country	Asia	Mexico	Europe	Caribbean	Central America[2]	South America	Africa	Canada
City	19.4	11.0	1.3	2.5	0.1	0.5	0.5	2.2	1.0
MSA[1]	19.2	10.2	2.3	2.7	0.2	0.5	0.5	1.6	0.7
U.S.	13.5	4.2	3.3	1.5	1.3	1.1	1.0	0.7	0.3

Note: (1) Figures cover the Seattle-Tacoma-Bellevue, WA Metropolitan Statistical Area; (2) Excludes Mexico.
Source: U.S. Census Bureau, 2016-2020 American Community Survey 5-Year Estimates

Marital Status

Area	Never Married	Now Married[2]	Separated	Widowed	Divorced
City	45.4	40.3	1.2	3.2	9.9
MSA[1]	33.0	50.6	1.4	4.2	10.8
U.S.	33.5	48.1	1.8	5.7	10.8

Note: Figures are percentages and cover the population 15 years of age and older; (1) Figures cover the Seattle-Tacoma-Bellevue, WA Metropolitan Statistical Area; (2) Excludes separated
Source: U.S. Census Bureau, 2016-2020 American Community Survey 5-Year Estimates

Disability by Age

Area	All Ages	Under 18 Years Old	18 to 64 Years Old	65 Years and Over
City	9.3	2.4	6.9	31.5
MSA[1]	10.9	3.7	8.7	33.4
U.S.	12.7	4.3	10.3	34.0

Note: Figures show percent of the civilian noninstitutionalized population that reported having a disability. Disability status is determined from six types of difficulty: vision, hearing, cognitive, ambulatory, self-care, and independent living. For children under 5 years old, hearing and vision difficulty are used to determine disability status. For children between the ages of 5 and 14, disability status is determined from hearing, vision, cognitive, ambulatory, and self-care difficulties. For people aged 15 years and older, they are considered to have a disability if they have difficulty with any one of the six difficulty types; Note: (1) Figures cover the Seattle-Tacoma-Bellevue, WA Metropolitan Statistical Area
Source: U.S. Census Bureau, 2016-2020 American Community Survey 5-Year Estimates

Age

Area	Percent of Population									Median Age
	Under Age 5	Age 5–19	Age 20–34	Age 35–44	Age 45–54	Age 55–64	Age 65–74	Age 75–84	Age 85+	
City	4.6	12.4	32.6	15.5	12.2	10.3	7.6	3.2	1.7	35.2
MSA[1]	6.1	17.5	23.1	14.5	13.1	12.3	8.1	3.5	1.7	37.0
U.S.	6.0	19.1	20.6	12.7	12.7	12.9	9.4	4.7	2.0	38.2

Note: (1) Figures cover the Seattle-Tacoma-Bellevue, WA Metropolitan Statistical Area
Source: U.S. Census Bureau, 2016-2020 American Community Survey 5-Year Estimates

Gender

Area	Males	Females	Males per 100 Females
City	374,764	366,487	102.3
MSA[1]	1,969,246	1,959,252	100.5
U.S.	160,818,530	165,750,778	97.0

Note: (1) Figures cover the Seattle-Tacoma-Bellevue, WA Metropolitan Statistical Area
Source: U.S. Census Bureau, 2016-2020 American Community Survey 5-Year Estimates

Religious Groups by Family

Area	Catholic	Baptist	Non-Den.	Methodist[2]	Lutheran	LDS[3]	Pente-costal	Presby-terian[4]	Muslim[5]	Judaism
MSA[1]	12.3	2.2	5.0	1.2	2.1	3.3	2.8	1.4	0.5	0.5
U.S.	19.1	9.3	4.0	4.0	2.3	2.0	1.9	1.6	0.8	0.7

Note: Figures are the number of adherents as a percentage of the total population; (1) Figures cover the Seattle-Tacoma-Bellevue, WA Metropolitan Statistical Area; (2) Methodist/Pietist; (3) Latter Day Saints; (4) Reformed; (5) Figures are estimates
Source: Association of Statisticians of American Religious Bodies, 2010 U.S. Religion Census: Religious Congregations & Membership Study

Religious Groups by Tradition

Area	Catholic	Evangelical Protestant	Mainline Protestant	Other Tradition	Black Protestant	Orthodox
MSA[1]	12.3	11.9	4.7	5.9	0.4	0.4
U.S.	19.1	16.2	7.3	4.3	1.6	0.3

Note: Figures are the number of adherents as a percentage of the total population; (1) Figures cover the Seattle-Tacoma-Bellevue, WA Metropolitan Statistical Area
Source: Association of Statisticians of American Religious Bodies, 2010 U.S. Religion Census: Religious Congregations & Membership Study

ECONOMY

Gross Metropolitan Product

Area	2017	2018	2019	2020	Rank[2]
MSA[1]	367.9	397.5	416.9	435.0	11

Note: Figures are in billions of dollars; (1) Figures cover the Seattle-Tacoma-Bellevue, WA Metropolitan Statistical Area; (2) Rank is based on 2018 data and ranges from 1 to 381
Source: U.S. Conference of Mayors, U.S. Metro Economies: GMP & Employment 2018-2020, September 2019

Economic Growth

Area	2015-17 (%)	2018 (%)	2019 (%)	2020 (%)	Rank[2]
MSA[1]	4.3	6.3	3.4	2.4	29
U.S.	1.9	2.9	2.3	2.1	–

Note: Figures are real gross metropolitan product (GMP) growth rates and represent average annual percent change; (1) Figures cover the Seattle-Tacoma-Bellevue, WA Metropolitan Statistical Area; (2) Rank is based on 2017 2-year average annual percent change and ranges from 1 to 381
Source: U.S. Conference of Mayors, U.S. Metro Economies: GMP & Employment 2018-2020, September 2019

Metropolitan Area Exports

Area	2015	2016	2017	2018	2019	2020	Rank[2]
MSA[1]	67,226.4	61,881.0	59,007.0	59,742.9	41,249.0	23,851.0	14

Note: Figures are in millions of dollars; (1) Figures cover the Seattle-Tacoma-Bellevue, WA Metropolitan Statistical Area; (2) Rank is based on 2020 data and ranges from 1 to 389
Source: U.S. Department of Commerce, International Trade Administration, Office of Trade and Economic Analysis, Industry and Analysis, Exports by Metropolitan Area, data extracted March 4, 2022

Building Permits

Area	Single-Family			Multi-Family			Total		
	2019	2020	Pct. Chg.	2019	2020	Pct. Chg.	2019	2020	Pct. Chg.
City	507	247	-51.3	10,277	5,479	-46.7	10,784	5,726	-46.9
MSA[1]	8,737	8,860	1.4	17,862	14,179	-20.6	26,599	23,039	-13.4
U.S.	862,100	979,400	13.6	523,900	491,700	-6.1	1,386,000	1,471,100	6.1

Note: (1) Figures cover the Seattle-Tacoma-Bellevue, WA Metropolitan Statistical Area; Figures represent new, privately-owned housing units authorized (unadjusted data); All permit data are based on estimates with imputation
Source: U.S. Census Bureau, Manufacturing, Mining, and Construction Statistics, Building Permits, 2019, 2020

Bankruptcy Filings

Area	Business Filings			Nonbusiness Filings		
	2020	2021	% Chg.	2020	2021	% Chg.
King County	96	56	-41.7	1,516	1,094	-27.8
U.S.	21,655	14,347	-33.7	522,808	399,269	-23.6

Note: Business filings include Chapter 7, Chapter 9, Chapter 11, Chapter 12, Chapter 13, Chapter 15, and Section 304; Nonbusiness filings include Chapter 7, Chapter 11, and Chapter 13
Source: Administrative Office of the U.S. Courts, Business and Nonbusiness Bankruptcy, County Cases Commenced by Chapter of the Bankruptcy Code, During the 12-Month Period Ending December 31, 2020 and Business and Nonbusiness Bankruptcy, County Cases Commenced by Chapter of the Bankruptcy Code, During the 12-Month Period Ending December 31, 2021

Housing Vacancy Rates

Area	Gross Vacancy Rate[2] (%)			Year-Round Vacancy Rate[3] (%)			Rental Vacancy Rate[4] (%)			Homeowner Vacancy Rate[5] (%)		
	2019	2020	2021	2019	2020	2021	2019	2020	2021	2019	2020	2021
MSA[1]	5.5	4.7	6.2	5.2	4.5	5.5	4.4	3.6	5.3	1.0	0.6	0.7
U.S.	12.0	10.6	10.8	9.5	8.2	8.4	6.7	6.3	6.1	1.4	1.0	0.9

Note: (1) Figures cover the Seattle-Tacoma-Bellevue, WA Metropolitan Statistical Area; (2) The percentage of the total housing inventory that is vacant; (3) The percentage of the housing inventory (excluding seasonal units) that is year-round vacant; (4) The percentage of rental inventory that is vacant for rent; (5) The percentage of homeowner inventory that is vacant for sale
Source: U.S. Census Bureau, Housing Vacancies and Homeownership Annual Statistics: 2019, 2020, 2021

INCOME

Income

Area	Per Capita ($)	Median Household ($)	Average Household ($)
City	63,610	97,185	134,355
MSA[1]	48,157	90,790	121,379
U.S.	35,384	64,994	91,547

Note: (1) Figures cover the Seattle-Tacoma-Bellevue, WA Metropolitan Statistical Area
Source: U.S. Census Bureau, 2016-2020 American Community Survey 5-Year Estimates

Household Income Distribution

Area	Percent of Households Earning							
	Under $15,000	$15,000 -$24,999	$25,000 -$34,999	$35,000 -$49,999	$50,000 -$74,999	$75,000 -$99,999	$100,000 -$149,999	$150,000 and up
City	8.4	4.8	5.0	8.3	13.5	11.0	18.5	30.5
MSA[1]	6.3	5.1	5.5	8.9	15.5	13.1	19.8	25.8
U.S.	9.9	8.5	8.6	12.0	17.2	12.8	15.6	15.4

Note: (1) Figures cover the Seattle-Tacoma-Bellevue, WA Metropolitan Statistical Area
Source: U.S. Census Bureau, 2016-2020 American Community Survey 5-Year Estimates

Poverty Rate

Area	All Ages	Under 18 Years Old	18 to 64 Years Old	65 Years and Over
City	10.2	9.6	10.2	11.0
MSA[1]	8.4	9.9	8.1	7.6
U.S.	12.8	17.5	12.1	9.3

Note: Figures are percentage of people whose income during the past 12 months was below the poverty level; (1) Figures cover the Seattle-Tacoma-Bellevue, WA Metropolitan Statistical Area
Source: U.S. Census Bureau, 2016-2020 American Community Survey 5-Year Estimates

CITY FINANCES

City Government Finances

Component	2019 ($000)	2019 ($ per capita)
Total Revenues	4,380,499	6,044
Total Expenditures	4,031,304	5,562
Debt Outstanding	5,528,580	7,628
Cash and Securities[1]	2,549,803	3,518

Note: (1) Cash and security holdings of a government at the close of its fiscal year, including those of its dependent agencies, utilities, and liquor stores.
Source: U.S. Census Bureau, State & Local Government Finances 2019

City Government Revenue by Source

Source	2019 ($000)	2019 ($ per capita)	2019 (%)
General Revenue			
From Federal Government	52,498	72	1.2
From State Government	177,837	245	4.1
From Local Governments	14,851	20	0.3
Taxes			
Property	647,419	893	14.8
Sales and Gross Receipts	728,048	1,005	16.6
Personal Income	0	0	0.0
Corporate Income	0	0	0.0
Motor Vehicle License	67,880	94	1.5
Other Taxes	235,035	324	5.4
Current Charges	967,662	1,335	22.1
Liquor Store	0	0	0.0
Utility	1,257,787	1,735	28.7

Source: U.S. Census Bureau, State & Local Government Finances 2019

City Government Expenditures by Function

Function	2019 ($000)	2019 ($ per capita)	2019 (%)
General Direct Expenditures			
Air Transportation	0	0	0.0
Corrections	0	0	0.0
Education	63,936	88	1.6
Employment Security Administration	0	0	0.0
Financial Administration	11,061	15	0.3
Fire Protection	188,944	260	4.7
General Public Buildings	0	0	0.0
Governmental Administration, Other	71,688	98	1.8
Health	13,434	18	0.3
Highways	364,581	503	9.0
Hospitals	0	0	0.0
Housing and Community Development	106,968	147	2.7
Interest on General Debt	94,394	130	2.3
Judicial and Legal	53,603	74	1.3
Libraries	75,842	104	1.9
Parking	8,543	11	0.2
Parks and Recreation	277,520	382	6.9
Police Protection	276,755	381	6.9
Public Welfare	129,774	179	3.2
Sewerage	186,798	257	4.6
Solid Waste Management	162,725	224	4.0
Veterans' Services	0	0	0.0
Liquor Store	0	0	0.0
Utility	1,421,816	1,961	35.3

Source: U.S. Census Bureau, State & Local Government Finances 2019

EMPLOYMENT

Labor Force and Employment

Area	Civilian Labor Force			Workers Employed		
	Dec. 2020	Dec. 2021	% Chg.	Dec. 2020	Dec. 2021	% Chg.
City	473,538	485,328	2.5	448,865	472,509	5.3
MD[1]	1,695,895	1,736,759	2.4	1,595,578	1,681,651	5.4
U.S.	160,017,000	161,696,000	1.0	149,613,000	155,732,000	4.1

Note: Data is not seasonally adjusted and covers workers 16 years of age and older; (1) Figures cover the Seattle-Bellevue-Everett, WA Metropolitan Division
Source: Bureau of Labor Statistics, Local Area Unemployment Statistics

Unemployment Rate

Area	2021											
	Jan.	Feb.	Mar.	Apr.	May	Jun.	Jul.	Aug.	Sep.	Oct.	Nov.	Dec.
City	5.6	4.7	4.9	4.3	4.0	4.4	4.4	4.2	3.8	3.8	2.5	2.6
MD[1]	6.1	5.4	5.2	4.5	4.5	5.0	4.7	4.2	4.0	3.6	3.1	3.2
U.S.	6.8	6.6	6.2	5.7	5.5	6.1	5.7	5.3	4.6	4.3	3.9	3.7

Note: Data is not seasonally adjusted and covers workers 16 years of age and older; (1) Figures cover the Seattle-Bellevue-Everett, WA Metropolitan Division
Source: Bureau of Labor Statistics, Local Area Unemployment Statistics

Average Wages

Occupation	$/Hr.	Occupation	$/Hr.
Accountants and Auditors	44.02	Maintenance and Repair Workers	26.02
Automotive Mechanics	27.19	Marketing Managers	81.22
Bookkeepers	26.01	Network and Computer Systems Admin.	48.53
Carpenters	33.71	Nurses, Licensed Practical	31.91
Cashiers	17.02	Nurses, Registered	47.74
Computer Programmers	n/a	Nursing Assistants	19.51
Computer Systems Analysts	56.28	Office Clerks, General	22.87
Computer User Support Specialists	31.52	Physical Therapists	48.79
Construction Laborers	28.00	Physicians	129.27
Cooks, Restaurant	20.04	Plumbers, Pipefitters and Steamfitters	41.37
Customer Service Representatives	21.98	Police and Sheriff's Patrol Officers	48.24
Dentists	83.65	Postal Service Mail Carriers	26.76
Electricians	40.77	Real Estate Sales Agents	31.66
Engineers, Electrical	59.69	Retail Salespersons	18.65
Fast Food and Counter Workers	16.46	Sales Representatives, Technical/Scientific	59.77
Financial Managers	83.91	Secretaries, Exc. Legal/Medical/Executive	24.41
First-Line Supervisors of Office Workers	38.23	Security Guards	21.09
General and Operations Managers	70.61	Surgeons	147.59
Hairdressers/Cosmetologists	21.29	Teacher Assistants, Exc. Postsecondary*	22.30
Home Health and Personal Care Aides	18.34	Teachers, Secondary School, Exc. Sp. Ed.*	42.38
Janitors and Cleaners	19.20	Telemarketers	23.09
Landscaping/Groundskeeping Workers	21.55	Truck Drivers, Heavy/Tractor-Trailer	28.86
Lawyers	69.59	Truck Drivers, Light/Delivery Services	22.70
Maids and Housekeeping Cleaners	17.71	Waiters and Waitresses	22.64

Note: Wage data covers the Seattle-Tacoma-Bellevue, WA Metropolitan Statistical Area; (*) Hourly wages were calculated from annual wage data based on a 40 hour work week; n/a not available.
Source: Bureau of Labor Statistics, Metro Area Occupational Employment & Wage Estimates, May 2021

Employment by Industry

Sector	MD[1]		U.S.
	Number of Employees	Percent of Total	Percent of Total
Construction	105,100	6.0	5.0
Education and Health Services	222,200	12.8	16.0
Financial Activities	88,500	5.1	5.9
Government	213,100	12.2	14.9
Information	144,300	8.3	1.9
Leisure and Hospitality	141,500	8.1	9.8
Manufacturing	139,300	8.0	8.4
Mining and Logging	700	<0.1	0.4
Other Services	56,200	3.2	3.7
Professional and Business Services	284,200	16.3	14.6
Retail Trade	216,400	12.4	10.7
Transportation, Warehousing, and Utilities	60,900	3.5	4.8
Wholesale Trade	68,000	3.9	3.8

Note: Figures are non-farm employment as of December 2021. Figures are not seasonally adjusted and include workers 16 years of age and older; (1) Figures cover the Seattle-Bellevue-Everett, WA Metropolitan Division
Source: Bureau of Labor Statistics, Current Employment Statistics, Employment, Hours, and Earnings

Employment by Occupation

Occupation Classification	City (%)	MSA[1] (%)	U.S. (%)
Management, Business, Science, and Arts	62.7	47.6	39.5
Natural Resources, Construction, and Maintenance	3.0	7.4	8.7
Production, Transportation, and Material Moving	5.4	10.8	13.1
Sales and Office	15.8	18.9	21.3
Service	13.2	15.3	17.4

Note: Figures cover employed civilians 16 years of age and older; (1) Figures cover the Seattle-Tacoma-Bellevue, WA Metropolitan Statistical Area
Source: U.S. Census Bureau, 2016-2020 American Community Survey 5-Year Estimates

Occupations with Greatest Projected Employment Growth: 2021 – 2023

Occupation[1]	2021 Employment	2023 Projected Employment	Numeric Employment Change	Percent Employment Change
Fast Food and Counter Workers	95,060	113,360	18,300	19.3
Software Developers and Software Quality Assurance Analysts and Testers	143,010	154,090	11,080	7.7
Waiters and Waitresses	39,640	48,240	8,600	21.7
Cooks, Restaurant	25,990	31,700	5,710	22.0
First-Line Supervisors of Food Preparation and Serving Workers	21,430	25,830	4,400	20.5
Maids and Housekeeping Cleaners	23,090	27,280	4,190	18.1
General and Operations Managers	54,350	58,300	3,950	7.3
Office Clerks, General	74,360	78,270	3,910	5.3
Project Management Specialists and Business Operations Specialists, All Other	64,070	67,930	3,860	6.0
Teaching Assistants, Except Postsecondary	41,510	45,300	3,790	9.1

Note: Projections cover Washington; (1) Sorted by numeric employment change
Source: www.projectionscentral.com, State Occupational Projections, 2021–2023 Short-Term Projections

Fastest-Growing Occupations: 2021 – 2023

Occupation[1]	2021 Employment	2023 Projected Employment	Numeric Employment Change	Percent Employment Change
Lodging Managers	1,090	1,540	450	41.3
Hotel, Motel, and Resort Desk Clerks	3,880	5,480	1,600	41.2
Baggage Porters and Bellhops	460	590	130	28.3
Aircraft Structure, Surfaces, Rigging, and Systems Assemblers	8,790	10,930	2,140	24.3
Cooks, Fast Food	9,610	11,760	2,150	22.4
Hosts and Hostesses, Restaurant, Lounge, and Coffee Shop	6,960	8,520	1,560	22.4
Cooks, Restaurant	25,990	31,700	5,710	22.0
Waiters and Waitresses	39,640	48,240	8,600	21.7
Bartenders	12,500	15,140	2,640	21.1
Dining Room and Cafeteria Attendants and Bartender Helpers	6,160	7,460	1,300	21.1

Note: Projections cover Washington; (1) Sorted by percent employment change and excludes occupations with numeric employment change less than 50
Source: www.projectionscentral.com, State Occupational Projections, 2021–2023 Short-Term Projections

TAXES

State Corporate Income Tax Rates

State	Tax Rate (%)	Income Brackets ($)	Num. of Brackets	Financial Institution Tax Rate (%)[a]	Federal Income Tax Ded.
Washington	None	–	–	–	–

Note: Tax rates as of January 1, 2022; (a) Rates listed are the corporate income tax rate applied to financial institutions or excise taxes based on income. Some states have other taxes based upon the value of deposits or shares.
Source: Federation of Tax Administrators, State Corporate Income Tax Rates, January 1, 2022

State Individual Income Tax Rates

State	Tax Rate (%)	Income Brackets ($)	Personal Exemptions ($)			Standard Ded. ($)	
			Single	Married	Depend.	Single	Married
Washington	– No state income tax –						

Note: Tax rates as of January 1, 2022; Local- and county-level taxes are not included
Source: Federation of Tax Administrators, State Individual Income Tax Rates, January 1, 2022

Various State Sales and Excise Tax Rates

State	State Sales Tax (%)	Gasoline[1] (¢/gal.)	Cigarette[2] ($/pack)	Spirits[3] ($/gal.)	Wine[4] ($/gal.)	Beer[5] ($/gal.)	Recreational Marijuana (%)
Washington	6.5	49.4	3.025	37.81	0.87	0.26	(s)

Note: All tax rates as of January 1, 2022; (1) The American Petroleum Institute has developed a methodology for determining the average tax rate on a gallon of fuel. Rates may include any of the following: excise taxes, environmental fees, storage tank fees, other fees or taxes, general sales tax, and local taxes; (2) The federal excise tax of $1.0066 per pack and local taxes are not included; (3) Rates are those applicable to off-premise sales of 40% alcohol by volume (a.b.v.) distilled spirits in 750ml containers. Local excise taxes are excluded; (4) Rates are those applicable to off-premise sales of 11% a.b.v. non-carbonated wine in 750ml containers; (5) Rates are those applicable to off-premise sales of 4.7% a.b.v. beer in 12 ounce containers; (s) 37% excise tax (retail price)
Source: Tax Foundation, 2022 Facts & Figures: How Does Your State Compare?

State Business Tax Climate Index Rankings

State	Overall Rank	Corporate Tax Rank	Individual Income Tax Rank	Sales Tax Rank	Property Tax Rank	Unemployment Insurance Tax Rank
Washington	15	39	7	49	20	24

Note: The index is a measure of how each state's tax laws affect economic performance. The lower the rank, the more favorable a state's tax system is for business. States without a given tax are given a ranking of 1. The scores/rankings for the District of Columbia do not affect other states. The 2022 index represents the tax climate as of July 1, 2021.
Source: Tax Foundation, State Business Tax Climate Index 2022

TRANSPORTATION

Means of Transportation to Work

Area	Car/Truck/Van		Public Transportation			Bicycle	Walked	Other Means	Worked at Home
	Drove Alone	Car-pooled	Bus	Subway	Railroad				
City	43.4	6.6	18.0	1.3	0.1	3.1	10.8	2.8	14.0
MSA[1]	64.9	9.8	7.8	0.4	0.5	1.0	4.0	1.6	10.1
U.S.	74.9	8.9	2.2	1.7	0.5	0.5	2.6	1.4	7.3

Note: Figures are percentages and cover workers 16 years of age and older; (1) Figures cover the Seattle-Tacoma-Bellevue, WA Metropolitan Statistical Area
Source: U.S. Census Bureau, 2016-2020 American Community Survey 5-Year Estimates

Travel Time to Work

Area	Less Than 10 Minutes	10 to 19 Minutes	20 to 29 Minutes	30 to 44 Minutes	45 to 59 Minutes	60 to 89 Minutes	90 Minutes or More
City	7.1	23.5	24.7	28.0	10.4	4.8	1.5
MSA[1]	7.8	22.2	21.0	25.2	11.5	8.8	3.5
U.S.	12.3	28.4	20.9	20.9	8.3	6.4	2.9

Note: Note: Figures are percentages and include workers 16 years old and over; (1) Figures cover the Seattle-Tacoma-Bellevue, WA Metropolitan Statistical Area
Source: U.S. Census Bureau, 2016-2020 American Community Survey 5-Year Estimates

Key Congestion Measures

Measure	1990	2000	2010	2015	2020
Annual Hours of Delay, Total (000)	53,681	92,925	137,010	162,517	69,016
Annual Hours of Delay, Per Auto Commuter	43	55	64	74	31
Annual Congestion Cost, Per Auto Commuter ($)	946	1,231	1,442	1,580	685

Note: Covers the Seattle WA urban area
Source: Texas A&M Transportation Institute, 2021 Urban Mobility Report

Freeway Travel Time Index

Measure	1985	1990	1995	2000	2005	2010	2015	2020
Urban Area Index[1]	1.22	1.26	1.29	1.33	1.37	1.36	1.37	1.11
Urban Area Rank[1,2]	4	3	3	3	3	4	5	20

Note: Freeway Travel Time Index—the ratio of travel time in the peak period to the travel time at free-flow conditions. For example, a value of 1.30 indicates a 20-minute free-flow trip takes 26 minutes in the peak (20 minutes x 1.30 = 26 minutes); (1) Covers the Seattle WA urban area; (2) Rank is based on 101 larger urban areas (#1 = highest travel time index)
Source: Texas A&M Transportation Institute, 2021 Urban Mobility Report

Public Transportation

Agency Name / Mode of Transportation	Vehicles Operated in Maximum Service[1]	Annual Unlinked Passenger Trips[2] (in thous.)	Annual Passenger Miles[3] (in thous.)
King County Department of Transportation (KC Metro)			
Bus (directly operated)	1,080	48,865.8	210,354.2
Bus (purchased transportation)	29	391.9	1,514.6
Demand Response (purchased transportation)	327	455.4	4,551.8
Demand Response - Taxi	126	86.5	1,003.8
Ferryboat (directly operated)	2	146.9	896.1
Streetcar Rail (directly operated)	10	749.4	932.7
Trolleybus (directly operated)	127	8,385.2	15,704.8
Vanpool (directly operated)	1,670	1,084.8	24,936.5
Central Puget Sound Regional Transit Authority (Sound Transit)			
Commuter Bus (directly operated)	213	4,943.7	70,981.0
Commuter Bus (purchased transportation)	48	1,321.0	21,751.8
Commuter Rail (purchased transportation)	70	1,265.9	31,890.7
Light Rail (directly operated)	48	7,900.1	49,794.6
Streetcar Rail (directly operated)	2	439.3	390.1
Washington State Ferries			
Ferryboat (directly operated)	19	19,376.3	146,367.0
City of Seattle (Seattle Center Monorail)			
Monorail and Automated Guideway (purchased transportation)	8	298.3	268.5

Note: (1) Number of revenue vehicles operated by the given mode and type of service to meet the annual maximum service requirement. This is the revenue vehicle count during the peak season of the year; on the week and day that maximum service is provided. Vehicles operated in maximum service (VOMS) exclude atypical days and one-time special events; (2) Number of passengers who boarded public transportation vehicles. Passengers are counted each time they board a vehicle no matter how many vehicles they use to travel from their origin to their destination. (3) Sum of the distances ridden by all passengers during the entire fiscal year.
Source: Federal Transit Administration, National Transit Database, 2020

Air Transportation

Airport Name and Code / Type of Service	Passenger Airlines[1]	Passenger Enplanements	Freight Carriers[2]	Freight (lbs)
Seattle-Tacoma International (SEA)				
Domestic service (U.S. carriers - 2021)	16	16,666,000	19	361,649,417
International service (U.S. carriers - 2020)	5	336,057	6	24,241,885

Note: (1) Includes all U.S.-based major, minor and commuter airlines that carried at least one passenger during the year; (2) Includes all U.S.-based airlines and freight carriers that transported at least one pound of freight during the year.
Source: Bureau of Transportation Statistics, The Intermodal Transportation Database, Air Carriers: T-100 Domestic Market (U.S. Carriers), 2021; Bureau of Transportation Statistics, The Intermodal Transportation Database, Air Carriers: T-100 International Market (U.S. Carriers), 2020

BUSINESSES

Major Business Headquarters

Company Name	Industry	Rankings	
		Fortune[1]	Forbes[2]
Amazon	Internet Services and Retailing	2	-
Expeditors Intl. of Washington	Transportation and Logistics	299	-
Nordstrom	General Merchandisers	289	-
Saltchuk	Transportation	-	167
Starbucks	Food Services	125	-
Trident Seafoods	Food, Drink & Tobacco	-	194

Note: (1) Companies that produce a 10-K are ranked 1 to 500 based on 2020 revenue; (2) All private companies with at least $2 billion in annual revenue through the end of their most current fiscal year are ranked 1 to 225; companies listed are headquartered in the city; dashes indicate no ranking
Source: Fortune, "Fortune 500," 2021; Forbes, "America's Largest Private Companies," 2021

Fastest-Growing Businesses

According to *Inc.*, Seattle is home to five of America's 500 fastest-growing private companies: **GrowFlow Corp** (#312); **Spees Design Build** (#334); **Spees Design Build** (#334); **Amperity** (#360); **Knock** (#369). Criteria: must be an independent, privately-held, for-profit, U.S. corporation, proprietorship or partnership as of December 31, 2020; revenues must be at least $100,000 in 2017 and $2 million in 2020; must have four-year operating/sales history. *Inc., "America's 500 Fastest-Growing Private Companies," 2021*

According to *Fortune*, Seattle is home to one of the 100 fastest-growing companies in the world: **Amazon** (#30). Companies were ranked by their revenue growth rate; their EPS growth rate; and their three-year annualized total return to investors for the period ending June 30, 2021. Criteria for inclusion: a company, foreign or domestic, must trade on a major U.S. stock exchange; must file quarterly reports with the SEC; must have a minimum market capitalization of $250 million; must have a stock price of at least $5 on June 30, 2021; must have been trading continuously since June 30, 2018; must have revenue and net income for the four quarters ended on or before April 30, 2021, of at least $50 million and $10 million, respectively; and must have posted a compound annual growth in revenue and earnings per share of at least 15% annually over the three years ending on or before April 30, 2021. Real estate investment trusts, limited-liability companies, limited parterships, business development companies, closed-end investment firms, companies about to be acquired, and companies that lost money in the quarter ending April 30, 2021 were excluded. *Fortune, "100 Fastest-Growing Companies," 2021*

According to Deloitte, Seattle is home to 12 of North America's 500 fastest-growing high-technology companies: **Coinme** (#78); **Outreach** (#136); **Highspot** (#146); **Qumulo** (#163); **Flexe** (#166); **Mason** (#209); **Remitly** (#245); **Textio** (#268); **Hiya** (#306); **doxo** (#352); **HeadLight** (#354); **Skilljar** (#437). Companies are ranked by percentage growth in revenue over a four-year period. Criteria for inclusion: company must be headquartered within North America; must own proprietary intellectual property or technology that is sold to customers in products that contributes to a significant portion of the company's operating revenue; must have been in business for a minumum of four years with 2017 operating revenues of at least $50,000 USD/CD and 2020 operating revenues of at least $5 million USD/CD. *Deloitte, 2021 Technology Fast 500™*

Living Environment

COST OF LIVING

Cost of Living Index

Composite Index	Groceries	Housing	Utilities	Trans-portation	Health Care	Misc. Goods/ Services
152.7	129.7	209.4	108.1	134.6	121.9	131.5

Note: The Cost of Living Index measures regional differences in the cost of consumer goods and services, excluding taxes and non-consumer expenditures, for professional and managerial households in the top income quintile. It is based on more than 50,000 prices covering almost 60 different items for which prices are collected three times a year by chambers of commerce, economic development organizations or university applied economic centers in each participating urban area. The numbers shown should be read as a percentage above or below the national average of 100. For example, a value of 115.4 in the groceries column indicates that grocery prices are 15.4% higher than the national average. Small differences in the index numbers should not be interpreted as significant; Figures cover the Seattle WA urban area.
Source: The Council for Community and Economic Research, Cost of Living Index, 2021

Grocery Prices

Area[1]	T-Bone Steak ($/pound)	Frying Chicken ($/pound)	Whole Milk ($/half gal.)	Eggs ($/dozen)	Orange Juice ($/64 oz.)	Coffee ($/11.5 oz.)
City[2]	16.53	2.57	2.21	1.98	4.23	6.20
Avg.	12.82	1.40	2.22	1.57	3.59	4.30
Min.	8.91	0.91	1.29	0.75	2.87	3.02
Max.	21.35	2.69	3.92	3.86	5.49	8.11

Note: (1) Values for the local area are compared with the average, minimum and maximum values for all 285 areas in the Cost of Living Index; (2) Figures cover the Seattle WA urban area; ***T-Bone Steak*** *(price per pound);* ***Frying Chicken*** *(price per pound, whole fryer);* ***Whole Milk*** *(half gallon carton);* ***Eggs*** *(price per dozen, Grade A, large);* ***Orange Juice*** *(64 oz. Tropicana or Florida Natural);* ***Coffee*** *(11.5 oz. can, vacuum-packed, Maxwell House, Hills Bros, or Folgers).*
Source: The Council for Community and Economic Research, Cost of Living Index, 2021

Housing and Utility Costs

Area[1]	New Home Price ($)	Apartment Rent ($/month)	All Electric ($/month)	Part Electric ($/month)	Other Energy ($/month)	Telephone ($/month)
City[2]	826,291	2,621	188.34	-	-	197.61
Avg.	398,393	1,217	171.38	100.83	69.67	187.75
Min.	212,799	534	96.71	31.56	27.15	173.01
Max.	2,354,006	4,438	369.53	277.33	303.87	206.73

Note: (1) Values for the local area are compared with the average, minimum and maximum values for all 285 areas in the Cost of Living Index; (2) Figures cover the Seattle WA urban area; ***New Home Price*** *(2,400 sf living area, 8,000 sf lot, in urban area with full utilities);* ***Apartment Rent*** *(950 sf 2 bedroom/1.5 or 2 bath, unfurnished, excluding all utilities except water);* ***All Electric*** *(average monthly cost for an all-electric home);* ***Part Electric*** *(average monthly cost for a part-electric home);* ***Other Energy*** *(average monthly cost for natural gas, fuel oil, coal, wood, and any other forms of energy except electricity);* ***Telephone*** *(price includes the base monthly rate plus taxes and fees for three lines of mobile phone service).*
Source: The Council for Community and Economic Research, Cost of Living Index, 2021

Health Care, Transportation, and Other Costs

Area[1]	Doctor ($/visit)	Dentist ($/visit)	Optometrist ($/visit)	Gasoline ($/gallon)	Beauty Salon ($/visit)	Men's Shirt ($)
City[2]	150.37	125.24	153.67	3.61	56.95	41.05
Avg.	118.16	101.04	109.44	2.71	40.63	30.77
Min.	35.04	55.56	51.17	2.17	18.59	11.32
Max.	231.10	165.12	256.81	4.11	85.33	63.03

Note: (1) Values for the local area are compared with the average, minimum and maximum values for all 285 areas in the Cost of Living Index; (2) Figures cover the Seattle WA urban area; ***Doctor*** *(general practitioners routine exam of an established patient);* ***Dentist*** *(adult teeth cleaning and periodic oral examination);* ***Optometrist*** *(full vision eye exam for established adult patient);* ***Gasoline*** *(one gallon regular unleaded, national brand, including all taxes, cash price at self-service pump if available);* ***Beauty Salon*** *(woman's shampoo, trim, and blow-dry);* ***Men's Shirt*** *(cotton/polyester dress shirt, pinpoint weave, long sleeves).*
Source: The Council for Community and Economic Research, Cost of Living Index, 2021

HOUSING

Homeownership Rate

Area	2013 (%)	2014 (%)	2015 (%)	2016 (%)	2017 (%)	2018 (%)	2019 (%)	2020 (%)	2021 (%)
MSA[1]	61.0	61.3	59.5	57.7	59.5	62.5	61.5	59.4	58.0
U.S.	65.1	64.5	63.7	63.4	63.9	64.4	64.6	66.6	65.5

Note: (1) Figures cover the Seattle-Tacoma-Bellevue, WA Metropolitan Statistical Area
Source: U.S. Census Bureau, Housing Vacancies and Homeownership Annual Statistics: 2013-2021

House Price Index (HPI)

Area	National Ranking[2]	Quarterly Change (%)	One-Year Change (%)	Five-Year Change (%)	Since 1991Q1 (%)
MD[1]	99	3.07	19.15	57.91	404.34
U.S.[3]	–	3.33	17.54	54.45	258.04

Note: The HPI is a weighted repeat sales index. It measures average price changes in repeat sales or refinancings on the same properties. This information is obtained by reviewing repeat mortgage transactions on single-family properties whose mortgages have been purchased or securitized by Fannie Mae or Freddie Mac since January 1975; (1) Figures cover the Seattle-Bellevue-Everett, WA Metropolitan Division; (2) Rankings are based on annual percentage change for all metro areas containing at least 15,000 transactions over the last 10 years and ranges from 1 to 268; (3) figures based on a weighted average of Census Division estimates using a seasonally adjusted, purchase-only index; all figures are for the period ending December 31, 2021
Source: Federal Housing Finance Agency, Change in FHFA Metropolitan Area House Price Indexes, 2021Q4

Median Single-Family Home Prices

Area	2019	2020	2021p	Percent Change 2020 to 2021
MSA[1]	524.7	596.9	698.6	17.0
U.S. Average	274.6	300.2	353.4	17.7

Note: Figures are median sales prices of existing single-family homes in thousands of dollars; (p) preliminary; (1) Figures cover the Seattle-Tacoma-Bellevue, WA Metropolitan Statistical Area
Source: National Association of Realtors, Median Sales Price of Existing Single-Family Homes for Metropolitan Areas, 4th Quarter 2021

Qualifying Income Based on Median Sales Price of Existing Single-Family Homes

Area	With 5% Down ($)	With 10% Down ($)	With 20% Down ($)
MSA[1]	138,002	130,738	116,212
U.S. Average	70,699	66,978	59,536

Note: Figures are preliminary; Qualifying income is based on a mortgage rate of 3.13%. Monthly principal and interest payment is limited to 25% of income; (1) Figures cover the Seattle-Tacoma-Bellevue, WA Metropolitan Statistical Area
Source: National Association of Realtors, Qualifying Income Based on Median Sales Price of Existing Single-Family Homes for Metropolitan Areas, 4th Quarter 2021

Home Value Distribution

Area	Under $50,000	$50,000 -$99,999	$100,000 -$149,999	$150,000 -$199,999	$200,000 -$299,999	$300,000 -$499,999	$500,000 -$999,999	$1,000,000 or more
City	0.6	0.4	0.3	0.5	3.7	18.6	54.7	21.2
MSA[1]	2.3	1.1	1.5	3.0	12.3	34.2	35.5	10.1
U.S.	6.6	11.0	12.3	13.6	20.0	20.5	12.3	3.7

Note: Figures are percentages and cover owner-occupied housing units; (1) Figures cover the Seattle-Tacoma-Bellevue, WA Metropolitan Statistical Area
Source: U.S. Census Bureau, 2016-2020 American Community Survey 5-Year Estimates

Year Housing Structure Built

Area	2010 or Later	2000 -2009	1990 -1999	1980 -1989	1970 -1979	1960 -1969	1950 -1959	1940 -1949	Before 1940	Median Year
City	12.9	12.1	8.7	7.5	8.1	8.7	9.3	8.1	24.6	1969
MSA[1]	9.3	14.7	15.5	14.1	13.8	10.9	7.3	4.3	10.0	1983
U.S.	6.2	13.6	13.9	13.4	15.0	10.5	10.2	4.8	12.4	1978

Note: Figures are percentages except for Median Year; Note: (1) Figures cover the Seattle-Tacoma-Bellevue, WA Metropolitan Statistical Area
Source: U.S. Census Bureau, 2016-2020 American Community Survey 5-Year Estimates

Gross Monthly Rent

Area	Under $500	$500 -$999	$1,000 -$1,499	$1,500 -$1,999	$2,000 -$2,499	$2,500 -$2,999	$3,000 and up	Median ($)
City	5.7	8.1	24.9	28.0	17.7	7.9	7.7	1,702
MSA[1]	4.7	11.2	28.9	29.0	15.3	5.7	5.1	1,589
U.S.	8.9	34.3	30.2	14.9	6.2	2.6	2.8	1,096

Note: Figures are percentages except for Median; Gross rent is the contract rent plus the estimated average monthly cost of utilities (electricity, gas, and water and sewer) and fuels (oil, coal, kerosene, wood, etc.) if these are paid by the renter (or paid for the renter by someone else); (1) Figures cover the Seattle-Tacoma-Bellevue, WA Metropolitan Statistical Area
Source: U.S. Census Bureau, 2016-2020 American Community Survey 5-Year Estimates

HEALTH

Health Risk Factors

Category	MD[1] (%)	U.S. (%)
Adults aged 18–64 who have any kind of health care coverage	89.2	86.8
Adults who reported being in good or better health	89.8	86.7
Adults who are current smokers	9.5	15.5
Adults who currently use chewing tobacco, snuff, or snus	1.9	3.7
Adults who are heavy drinkers[2]	7.7	6.7
Adults who are binge drinkers[3]	16.3	15.7
Adults who are overweight (BMI 25.0 - 29.9)	36.1	35.2
Adults who are obese (BMI 30.0 - 99.8)	22.6	31.9
Adults who participated in any physical activities in the past month	84.1	77.6
Adults who always or nearly always wears a seat belt	97.7	94.2

Note: (1) Figures cover the Seattle-Bellevue-Everett, WA Metropolitan Division; (2) Heavy drinkers are classified as adult men having more than 14 drinks per week and adult women having more than 7 drinks per week; (3) Binge drinkers are classified as males having five or more drinks on one occasion or females having four or more drinks on one occasion
Source: Centers for Disease Control and Prevention, Behaviorial Risk Factor Surveillance System, SMART: Selected Metropolitan Area Risk Trends, 2020

Acute and Chronic Health Conditions

Category	MD[1] (%)	U.S. (%)
Adults who have ever been told they had a heart attack	2.5	4.3
Adults who have ever been told they have angina or coronary heart disease	2.9	4.0
Adults who have ever been told they had a stroke	2.5	2.8
Adults who have ever been told they have asthma	14.9	14.2
Adults who have ever been told they have arthritis	19.8	24.5
Adults who have ever been told they have diabetes[2]	7.3	10.6
Adults who have ever been told they had skin cancer	5.8	6.4
Adults who have ever been told they had any other types of cancer	6.7	6.8
Adults who have ever been told they have COPD	3.4	6.2
Adults who have ever been told they have kidney disease	2.3	2.9
Adults who have ever been told they have a form of depression	21.7	19.6

Note: (1) Figures cover the Seattle-Bellevue-Everett, WA Metropolitan Division; (2) Figures do not include pregnancy-related, borderline, or pre-diabetes
Source: Centers for Disease Control and Prevention, Behaviorial Risk Factor Surveillance System, SMART: Selected Metropolitan Area Risk Trends, 2020

Health Screening and Vaccination Rates

Category	MD[1] (%)	U.S. (%)
Adults 50-75 who have had a blood stool test within the past year	12.0	9.3
Adults aged 65+ who have had flu shot within the past year	76.0	67.9
Adults aged 65+ who have ever had a pneumonia vaccination	77.2	72.2
Adults who have ever been tested for HIV	38.4	37.1
Women aged 21-65 who have had a pap test in the past three years	72.6	77.7
Men aged 40+ who have had a PSA test within the past two years	24.0	31.8
Women aged 40+ who have had a mammogram within the past two years	65.6	71.5

Note: (1) Figures cover the Seattle-Bellevue-Everett, WA Metropolitan Division.
Source: Centers for Disease Control and Prevention, Behaviorial Risk Factor Surveillance System, SMART: Selected Metropolitan Area Risk Trends, 2020

Disability Status

Category	MD[1] (%)	U.S. (%)
Adults who reported being deaf	4.0	6.8
Are you blind or have serious difficulty seeing, even when wearing glasses?	2.8	4.7
Do you have difficulty doing errands alone?	5.1	6.3
Do you have difficulty dressing or bathing?	2.1	3.0
Do you have serious difficulty concentrating/remembering/making decisions?	8.6	10.8
Do you have serious difficulty walking or climbing stairs?	7.4	11.9

Note: (1) Figures cover the Seattle-Bellevue-Everett, WA Metropolitan Division.
Source: Centers for Disease Control and Prevention, Behaviorial Risk Factor Surveillance System, SMART: Selected Metropolitan Area Risk Trends, 2020

Mortality Rates for the Top 10 Causes of Death in the U.S.

ICD-10[a] Sub-Chapter	ICD-10[a] Code	Age-Adjusted Mortality Rate[1] per 100,000 population	
		County[2]	U.S.
Malignant neoplasms	C00-C97	123.1	146.4
Ischaemic heart diseases	I20-I25	67.0	90.2
Other forms of heart disease	I30-I51	28.6	51.9
Other degenerative diseases of the nervous system	G30-G31	48.9	39.7
Other external causes of accidental injury	W00-X59	30.9	38.7
Chronic lower respiratory diseases	J40-J47	20.0	38.1
Cerebrovascular diseases	I60-I69	28.2	37.6
Organic, including symptomatic, mental disorders	F01-F09	17.2	29.4
Hypertensive diseases	I10-I15	23.3	26.1
Diabetes mellitus	E10-E14	17.3	22.6

Note: (a) ICD-10 = International Classification of Diseases 10th Revision; (1) Mortality rates are a three-year average covering 2018-2020; (2) Figures cover King County.
Source: Centers for Disease Control and Prevention, National Center for Health Statistics. Underlying Cause of Death 1999-2020 on CDC WONDER Online Database

Mortality Rates for Selected Causes of Death

ICD-10[a] Sub-Chapter	ICD-10[a] Code	Age-Adjusted Mortality Rate[1] per 100,000 population	
		County[2]	U.S.
Assault	X85-Y09	3.7	6.5
Diseases of the liver	K70-K76	12.3	15.3
Human immunodeficiency virus (HIV) disease	B20-B24	0.9	1.4
Influenza and pneumonia	J09-J18	8.1	13.4
Intentional self-harm	X60-X84	12.6	13.9
Malnutrition	E40-E46	1.5	2.9
Obesity and other hyperalimentation	E65-E68	1.7	2.4
Renal failure	N17-N19	3.6	12.5
Transport accidents	V01-V99	6.2	12.5
Viral hepatitis	B15-B19	1.2	1.0

Note: (a) ICD-10 = International Classification of Diseases 10th Revision; (1) Mortality rates are a three-year average covering 2018-2020; (2) Figures cover King County; Data are suppressed when the data meet the criteria for confidentiality constraints; Mortality rates are flagged as unreliable when the rate would be calculated with a numerator of 20 or less.
Source: Centers for Disease Control and Prevention, National Center for Health Statistics. Underlying Cause of Death 1999-2020 on CDC WONDER Online Database

Health Insurance Coverage

Area	With Health Insurance	With Private Health Insurance	With Public Health Insurance	Without Health Insurance	Population Under Age 19 Without Health Insurance
City	95.6	80.7	23.5	4.4	1.5
MSA[1]	94.4	76.1	29.1	5.6	2.5
U.S.	91.3	68.1	35.3	8.7	5.2

Note: Figures are percentages that cover the civilian noninstitutionalized population; (1) Figures cover the Seattle-Tacoma-Bellevue, WA Metropolitan Statistical Area
Source: U.S. Census Bureau, 2016-2020 American Community Survey 5-Year Estimates

Number of Medical Professionals

Area	MDs[3]	DOs[3,4]	Dentists	Podiatrists	Chiropractors	Optometrists
County[1] (number)	11,203	370	2,493	142	1,063	499
County[1] (rate[2])	493.6	16.3	109.8	6.3	46.8	22.0
U.S. (rate[2])	285.1	23.0	71.1	6.2	28.2	17.0

53033
Note: Data as of 2020 unless noted; (1) Data covers King County; (2) Rate per 100,000 population; (3) Data as of 2019 and includes all active, non-federal physicians; (4) Doctor of Osteopathic Medicine
Source: U.S. Department of Health and Human Services, Health Resources and Services Administration, Bureau of Health Professions, Area Resource File (ARF) 2020-2021

Best Hospitals

According to *U.S. News*, the Seattle-Bellevue-Everett, WA metro area is home to four of the best hospitals in the U.S.: **Seattle Cancer Care Alliance/University of Washington Medical Center** (1 adult specialty); **Swedish Medical Center-Cherry Hill** (1 adult specialty); **UW Medicine-Harborview Medical Center** (1 adult specialty); **UW Medicine-University of Washington Medical Center** (6 adult specialties). The hospitals listed were nationally ranked in at least one of 15 adult or 10 pediatric specialties. Only 175 U.S. hospitals performed well enough to be nationally ranked in one or more specialties. Twenty hospitals in the U.S. made the Honor Roll. The Best Hospitals Honor Roll takes both the national rankings and the procedure and condition ratings into account. Hospitals received points if they were nationally ranked in one of the 15 adult specialties—the higher they ranked, the more points they got—and how many ratings of "high performing" they earned in the 17 procedures and conditions. *U.S. News Online, "America's Best Hospitals 2021-22"*

According to *U.S. News,* the Seattle-Bellevue-Everett, WA metro area is home to one of the best children's hospitals in the U.S.: **Seattle Children's Hospital** (10 pediatric specialties). The hospital listed was highly ranked in at least one of 10 pediatric specialties. Ninety-two children's hospitals in the U.S. were nationally ranked in at least one specialty. Hospitals received points for being ranked in a specialty, and the 10 hospitals with the most points across the 10 specialties make up the Honor Roll. *U.S. News Online, "America's Best Children's Hospitals 2021-22"*

EDUCATION

Public School District Statistics

District Name	Schls	Pupils	Pupil/ Teacher Ratio	Minority Pupils[1] (%)	LEP/ELL[2] (%)	IEP[3] (%)
Seattle Public Schools	110	55,986	17.3	53.6	11.7	13.9

Note: Table includes school districts with 2,000 or more students; (1) Percentage of students that are not non-Hispanic white; (2) Percentage of students that are Limited English Proficient (LEP) or English Language Learners (ELL) (2018-19); (3) Percentage of students that have an Individualized Education Program (IEP).
Source: U.S. Department of Education, National Center for Education Statistics, Common Core of Data, Local Education Agency (School District) Universe Survey: School Year 2019-2020

Highest Level of Education

Area	Less than H.S.	H.S. Diploma	Some College, No Deg.	Associate Degree	Bachelor's Degree	Master's Degree	Prof. School Degree	Doctorate Degree
City	4.8	9.5	14.4	6.3	37.0	18.9	5.4	3.8
MSA[1]	7.1	19.2	20.7	9.4	26.8	12.1	2.7	1.9
U.S.	11.5	26.7	20.3	8.6	20.2	9.1	2.2	1.5

Note: Figures cover persons age 25 and over; (1) Figures cover the Seattle-Tacoma-Bellevue, WA Metropolitan Statistical Area
Source: U.S. Census Bureau, 2016-2020 American Community Survey 5-Year Estimates

Educational Attainment by Race

Area	High School Graduate or Higher (%)					Bachelor's Degree or Higher (%)				
	Total	White	Black	Asian	Hisp.[2]	Total	White	Black	Asian	Hisp.[2]
City	95.2	98.0	88.2	89.6	85.7	65.0	70.0	34.5	64.6	45.2
MSA[1]	92.9	95.3	89.8	89.5	75.2	43.6	44.3	27.6	56.9	24.5
U.S.	88.5	90.7	86.7	87.3	70.3	32.9	34.4	22.6	55.0	17.6

Note: Figures shown cover persons 25 years old and over; (1) Figures cover the Seattle-Tacoma-Bellevue, WA Metropolitan Statistical Area; (2) People of Hispanic origin can be of any race
Source: U.S. Census Bureau, 2016-2020 American Community Survey 5-Year Estimates

School Enrollment by Grade and Control

Area	Preschool (%)		Kindergarten (%)		Grades 1 - 4 (%)		Grades 5 - 8 (%)		Grades 9 - 12 (%)	
	Public	Private	Public	Private	Public	Private	Public	Private	Public	Private
City	33.5	66.5	78.4	21.6	80.0	20.0	75.1	24.9	77.9	22.1
MSA[1]	40.9	59.1	83.4	16.6	87.3	12.7	87.8	12.2	90.4	9.6
U.S.	58.9	41.1	86.9	13.1	89.0	11.0	89.0	11.0	89.7	10.3

Note: Figures shown cover persons 3 years old and over; (1) Figures cover the Seattle-Tacoma-Bellevue, WA Metropolitan Statistical Area
Source: U.S. Census Bureau, 2016-2020 American Community Survey 5-Year Estimates

Higher Education

Four-Year Colleges			Two-Year Colleges			Medical Schools[1]	Law Schools[2]	Voc/ Tech[3]
Public	Private Non-profit	Private For-profit	Public	Private Non-profit	Private For-profit			
16	12	5	3	1	3	1	2	9

Note: Figures cover institutions located within the Seattle-Tacoma-Bellevue, WA Metropolitan Statistical Area and include main campuses only; (1) includes schools accredited by the Liaison Committee on Medical Education and the American Osteopathic Association's Commission on Osteopathic College Accreditation; (2) includes ABA-accredited schools, schools with provisional ABA accreditation, and state accredited schools; (3) includes all schools with programs that are less than 2 years.
Source: National Center for Education Statistics, Integrated Postsecondary Education System (IPEDS), 2020-21; Wikipedia, List of Medical Schools in the United States, accessed April 11, 2022; Wikipedia, List of Law Schools in the United States, accessed April 11, 2022

According to *U.S. News & World Report,* the Seattle-Bellevue-Everett, WA metro division is home to two of the top 200 national universities in the U.S.: **University of Washington** (#59 tie); **Seattle University** (#127 tie). The indicators used to capture academic quality fall into a number of categories: assessment by administrators at peer institutions; retention of students; faculty resources; student selectivity; financial resources; alumni giving; high school counselor ratings of colleges; and graduation rate. *U.S. News & World Report, "America's Best Colleges 2022"*

According to *U.S. News & World Report,* the Seattle-Bellevue-Everett, WA metro division is home to one of the top 100 law schools in the U.S.: **University of Washington** (#45). The rankings are based on a weighted average of 12 measures of quality: peer assessment score; assessment score by lawyers/judges; median LSAT scores; median undergrad GPA; acceptance rate; employment rates for graduates; placement success; bar passage rate; faculty resources; expenditures per student; student/faculty ratio; and library resources. *U.S. News & World Report, "America's Best Graduate Schools, Law, 2022"*

According to *U.S. News & World Report,* the Seattle-Bellevue-Everett, WA metro division is home to one of the top 75 medical schools for research in the U.S.: **University of Washington** (#7 tie). The rankings are based on a weighted average of 11 measures of quality: quality assessment; peer assessment score; assessment score by residency directors; research activity; total research activity; average research activity per faculty member; student selectivity; median MCAT total score; median undergraduate GPA; acceptance rate; and faculty resources. *U.S. News & World Report, "America's Best Graduate Schools, Medical, 2022"*

According to *U.S. News & World Report,* the Seattle-Bellevue-Everett, WA metro division is home to one of the top 75 business schools in the U.S.: **University of Washington (Foster)** (#22). The rankings are based on a weighted average of the following nine measures: quality assessment; peer assessment; recruiter assessment; placement success; mean starting salary and bonus; student selectivity; mean GMAT and GRE scores; mean undergraduate GPA; and acceptance rate. *U.S. News & World Report, "America's Best Graduate Schools, Business, 2022"*

EMPLOYERS

Major Employers

Company Name	Industry
City of Tacoma	Municipal government
Costco Wholesale Corporation	Miscellaneous general merchandise stores
County of Snohomish	County government
Evergreen Healthcare	General medical & surgical hospitals
Harborview Medical Center	General medical & surgical hospitals
King County Public Hospital Dist No. 2	Hospital & health services consultant
Microsoft	Prepackaged software
Prologix Distribution Services	General merchandise, non-durable
R U Corporation	American restaurant
SNC-Lavalin Constructors	Heavy construction, nec
Swedish Health Services	General medical & surgical hospitals
T-Mobile USA	Radio, telephone communication
The Boeing Company	Airplanes, fixed or rotary wing
Tulalip Resort Casino	Casino hotels
United States Department of the Army	Medical centers
University of Washington	Colleges & universities
Virginia Mason Medical Center	General medical & surgical hospitals
Virginia Mason Seattle Main Clinic	Clinic, operated by physicians
Washington Dept of Social & Health Svcs	General medical & surgical hospitals

Note: Companies shown are located within the Seattle-Tacoma-Bellevue, WA Metropolitan Statistical Area.
Source: Hoovers.com; Wikipedia

Best Companies to Work For

Perkins Coie; Slalom, headquartered in Seattle, are among "The 100 Best Companies to Work For." To pick the best companies, *Fortune* partnered with the Great Place to Work Institute. Two-thirds of a company's score is based on the results of the Institute's Trust Index survey, which is sent to a random sample of employees from each company. The questions related to attitudes about management's credibility, job satisfaction, and camaraderie. The other third of the scoring is based on the company's responses to the Institute's Culture Audit, which includes detailed questions about pay and benefit programs, and a series of open-ended questions about hiring practices, internal communication, training, recognition programs, and diversity efforts. Any company that is at least five years old with more than 1,000 U.S. employees is eligible. *Fortune, "The 100 Best Companies to Work For," 2021*

Perkins Coie; Slalom Consulting, headquartered in Seattle, are among "75 Best Large Workplaces for Women." To pick the best companies, *Fortune* partnered with the Great Place to Work Institute. Employees responded to over 60 survey questions describing the extent to which their organization creates a Great Place to Work For All. Eighty-five percent of the ranking is based on what women themselves report about their workplace, and how fairly those experiences compare to men's reports of the same workplaces. Fifteen percent of the remaining rank is based on how well represented women are in the workforce and throughout management, taking into account industry trends. To be considered, at a minimum, companies need to employ at least 50 women, at least 20% of their non-executive managers need to be female, and at least one of their executives needs to be female. *Fortune, "75 Best Large Workplaces for Women," 2021*

PUBLIC SAFETY

Crime Rate

Area	Total Crime	Violent Crime Rate				Property Crime Rate		
		Murder	Rape[3]	Robbery	Aggrav. Assault	Burglary	Larceny -Theft	Motor Vehicle Theft
City	5,498.9	6.7	39.0	190.7	389.9	1,351.5	2,884.6	636.5
Suburbs[1]	3,022.6	4.0	29.2	70.5	168.3	442.6	1,893.4	414.8
Metro[2]	3,496.7	4.5	31.1	93.5	210.7	616.6	2,083.1	457.2
U.S.	2,356.7	6.5	38.4	73.9	279.7	314.2	1,398.0	246.0

Note: Figures are crimes per 100,000 population; (1) All areas within the metro area that are located outside the city limits; (2) Figures cover the Seattle-Bellevue-Everett, WA Metropolitan Division; (3) All figures shown were reported using the revised Uniform Crime Reporting (UCR) definition of rape.
Source: FBI Uniform Crime Reports, 2020

Hate Crimes

Area	Number of Quarters Reported	Number of Incidents per Bias Motivation					
		Race/Ethnicity/ Ancestry	Religion	Sexual Orientation	Disability	Gender	Gender Identity
City[1]	4	100	6	27	3	4	8
U.S.	4	5,227	1,244	1,110	130	75	266

Note: (1) Figures include one incident reported with more than one bias motivation.
Source: Federal Bureau of Investigation, Hate Crime Statistics 2020

Identity Theft Consumer Reports

Area	Reports	Reports per 100,000 Population	Rank[2]
MSA[1]	7,568	190	241
U.S.	1,434,676	432	-

Note: (1) Figures cover the Seattle-Tacoma-Bellevue, WA Metropolitan Statistical Area; (2) Rank ranges from 1 to 391 where 1 indicates greatest number of identity theft reports per 100,000 population
Source: Federal Trade Commission, Consumer Sentinel Network Data Book 2021

Fraud and Other Consumer Reports

Area	Reports	Reports per 100,000 Population	Rank[2]
MSA[1]	42,255	1,062	79
U.S.	4,328,977	1,304	-

Note: (1) Figures cover the Seattle-Tacoma-Bellevue, WA Metropolitan Statistical Area; (2) Rank ranges from 1 to 391 where 1 indicates greatest number of fraud and other consumer reports per 100,000 population
Source: Federal Trade Commission, Consumer Sentinel Network Data Book 2021

POLITICS

2020 Presidential Election Results

Area	Biden	Trump	Jorgensen	Hawkins	Other
King County	75.0	22.2	1.5	0.5	0.8
U.S.	51.3	46.8	1.2	0.3	0.5

Note: Results are percentages and may not add to 100% due to rounding
Source: Dave Leip's Atlas of U.S. Presidential Elections

SPORTS

Professional Sports Teams

Team Name	League	Year Established
Seattle Kraken	National Hockey League (NHL)	2021
Seattle Mariners	Major League Baseball (MLB)	1977
Seattle Seahawks	National Football League (NFL)	1976
Seattle Sounders FC	Major League Soccer (MLS)	2009

Note: Includes teams located in the Seattle-Tacoma-Bellevue, WA Metropolitan Statistical Area.
Source: Wikipedia, Major Professional Sports Teams of the United States and Canada, April 6, 2022

CLIMATE

Average and Extreme Temperatures

Temperature	Jan	Feb	Mar	Apr	May	Jun	Jul	Aug	Sep	Oct	Nov	Dec	Yr.
Extreme High (°F)	64	70	75	85	93	96	98	99	98	89	74	63	99
Average High (°F)	44	48	52	57	64	69	75	74	69	59	50	45	59
Average Temp. (°F)	39	43	45	49	55	61	65	65	60	52	45	41	52
Average Low (°F)	34	36	38	41	46	51	54	55	51	45	39	36	44
Extreme Low (°F)	0	1	11	29	28	38	43	44	35	28	6	6	0

Note: Figures cover the years 1948-1990
Source: National Climatic Data Center, International Station Meteorological Climate Summary, 9/96

Average Precipitation/Snowfall/Humidity

Precip./Humidity	Jan	Feb	Mar	Apr	May	Jun	Jul	Aug	Sep	Oct	Nov	Dec	Yr.
Avg. Precip. (in.)	5.7	4.2	3.7	2.4	1.7	1.4	0.8	1.1	1.9	3.5	5.9	5.9	38.4
Avg. Snowfall (in.)	5	2	1	Tr	Tr	0	0	0	0	Tr	1	3	13
Avg. Rel. Hum. 7am (%)	83	83	84	83	80	79	79	84	87	88	85	85	83
Avg. Rel. Hum. 4pm (%)	76	69	63	57	54	54	49	51	57	68	76	79	63

Note: Figures cover the years 1948-1990; Tr = Trace amounts (<0.05 in. of rain; <0.5 in. of snow)
Source: National Climatic Data Center, International Station Meteorological Climate Summary, 9/96

Weather Conditions

Temperature			Daytime Sky			Precipitation		
5°F & below	32°F & below	90°F & above	Clear	Partly cloudy	Cloudy	0.01 inch or more precip.	0.1 inch or more snow/ice	Thunder-storms
< 1	38	3	57	120	188	157	8	8

Note: Figures are average number of days per year and cover the years 1948-1990
Source: National Climatic Data Center, International Station Meteorological Climate Summary, 9/96

HAZARDOUS WASTE

Superfund Sites

The Seattle-Bellevue-Everett, WA metro division is home to nine sites on the EPA's Superfund National Priorities List: **Harbor Island (Lead)** (final); **Lockheed West Seattle** (final); **Lower Duwamish Waterway** (final); **Midway Landfill** (final); **Pacific Car & Foundry Co.** (final); **Pacific Sound Resources** (final); **Queen City Farms** (final); **Quendall Terminals** (final); **Seattle Municipal Landfill (Kent Highlands)** (final). There are a total of 1,165 Superfund sites with a status of proposed or final on the list in the U.S. *U.S. Environmental Protection Agency, National Priorities List, April 6, 2022*

AIR QUALITY

Air Quality Trends: Ozone

	1990	1995	2000	2005	2010	2016	2017	2018	2019	2020
MSA[1]	0.082	0.062	0.056	0.053	0.053	0.059	0.076	0.067	0.052	0.060
U.S.	0.090	0.091	0.082	0.080	0.074	0.070	0.069	0.070	0.066	0.068

Note: (1) Data covers the Seattle-Tacoma-Bellevue, WA Metropolitan Statistical Area. The values shown are the composite ozone concentration averages among trend sites based on the highest fourth daily maximum 8-hour concentration in parts per million. These trends are based on sites having an adequate record of monitoring data during the trend period. Data from exceptional events are included.
Source: U.S. Environmental Protection Agency, Air Quality Monitoring Information, "Air Quality Trends by City, 1990-2020"

Air Quality Index

Area	Percent of Days when Air Quality was...[2]					AQI Statistics[2]	
	Good	Moderate	Unhealthy for Sensitive Groups	Unhealthy	Very Unhealthy	Maximum	Median
MSA[1]	73.0	23.2	1.4	1.1	1.4	275	43

Note: (1) Data covers the Seattle-Tacoma-Bellevue, WA Metropolitan Statistical Area; (2) Based on 366 days with AQI data in 2020. Air Quality Index (AQI) is an index for reporting daily air quality. EPA calculates the AQI for five major air pollutants regulated by the Clean Air Act: ground-level ozone, particle pollution (aka particulate matter), carbon monoxide, sulfur dioxide, and nitrogen dioxide. The AQI runs from 0 to 500. The higher the AQI value, the greater the level of air pollution and the greater the health concern. There are six AQI categories: "Good" AQI is between 0 and 50. Air quality is considered satisfactory; "Moderate" AQI is between 51 and 100. Air quality is acceptable; "Unhealthy for Sensitive Groups" When AQI values are between 101 and 150, members of sensitive groups may experience health effects; "Unhealthy" When AQI values are between 151 and 200 everyone may begin to experience health effects; "Very Unhealthy" AQI values between 201 and 300 trigger a health alert; "Hazardous" AQI values over 300 trigger warnings of emergency conditions (not shown).
Source: U.S. Environmental Protection Agency, Air Quality Index Report, 2020

Air Quality Index Pollutants

Area	Percent of Days when AQI Pollutant was...[2]					
	Carbon Monoxide	Nitrogen Dioxide	Ozone	Sulfur Dioxide	Particulate Matter 2.5	Particulate Matter 10
MSA[1]	0.0	4.6	54.4	0.0	41.0	0.0

Note: (1) Data covers the Seattle-Tacoma-Bellevue, WA Metropolitan Statistical Area; (2) Based on 366 days with AQI data in 2020. The Air Quality Index (AQI) is an index for reporting daily air quality. EPA calculates the AQI for five major air pollutants regulated by the Clean Air Act: ground-level ozone, particle pollution (also known as particulate matter), carbon monoxide, sulfur dioxide, and nitrogen dioxide. The AQI runs from 0 to 500. The higher the AQI value, the greater the level of air pollution and the greater the health concern.
Source: U.S. Environmental Protection Agency, Air Quality Index Report, 2020

Maximum Air Pollutant Concentrations: Particulate Matter, Ozone, CO and Lead

	Particulate Matter 10 (ug/m^3)	Particulate Matter 2.5 Wtd AM (ug/m^3)	Particulate Matter 2.5 24-Hr (ug/m^3)	Ozone (ppm)	Carbon Monoxide (ppm)	Lead (ug/m^3)
MSA[1] Level	38	10.6	61	0.06	2	n/a
NAAQS[2]	150	15	35	0.075	9	0.15
Met NAAQS[2]	Yes	Yes	No	Yes	Yes	n/a

Note: (1) Data covers the Seattle-Tacoma-Bellevue, WA Metropolitan Statistical Area; Data from exceptional events are included; (2) National Ambient Air Quality Standards; ppm = parts per million; ug/m^3 = micrograms per cubic meter; n/a not available.

Concentrations: Particulate Matter 10 (coarse particulate)—highest second maximum 24-hour concentration; Particulate Matter 2.5 Wtd AM (fine particulate)—highest weighted annual mean concentration; Particulate Matter 2.5 24-Hour (fine particulate)—highest 98th percentile 24-hour concentration; Ozone—highest fourth daily maximum 8-hour concentration; Carbon Monoxide—highest second maximum non-overlapping 8-hour concentration; Lead—maximum running 3-month average

Source: U.S. Environmental Protection Agency, Air Quality Monitoring Information, "Air Quality Statistics by City, 2020"

Maximum Air Pollutant Concentrations: Nitrogen Dioxide and Sulfur Dioxide

	Nitrogen Dioxide AM (ppb)	Nitrogen Dioxide 1-Hr (ppb)	Sulfur Dioxide AM (ppb)	Sulfur Dioxide 1-Hr (ppb)	Sulfur Dioxide 24-Hr (ppb)
MSA[1] Level	16	57	n/a	4	n/a
NAAQS[2]	53	100	30	75	140
Met NAAQS[2]	Yes	Yes	n/a	Yes	n/a

Note: (1) Data covers the Seattle-Tacoma-Bellevue, WA Metropolitan Statistical Area; Data from exceptional events are included; (2) National Ambient Air Quality Standards; ppm = parts per million; ug/m^3 = micrograms per cubic meter; n/a not available.

Concentrations: Nitrogen Dioxide AM—highest arithmetic mean concentration; Nitrogen Dioxide 1-Hr—highest 98th percentile 1-hour daily maximum concentration; Sulfur Dioxide AM—highest annual mean concentration; Sulfur Dioxide 1-Hr—highest 99th percentile 1-hour daily maximum concentration; Sulfur Dioxide 24-Hr—highest second maximum 24-hour concentration

Source: U.S. Environmental Protection Agency, Air Quality Monitoring Information, "Air Quality Statistics by City, 2020"

Tucson, Arizona

Background

Tucson lies in a high desert valley that was once the floor of an ancient inland sea. Its name derives from the Papago tribe's term for the ancient settlement, Stukshon, which in Spanish is Tuquison. It is believed that the Spanish Jesuit Eusebio Francesco Kino, who established the San Xavier Mission, was the first European to visit the area in 1700. Spanish prospectors who came after Father Kino were driven out by the native tribes trying to protect their territory.

Tucson came under Mexican jurisdiction in 1821, when Mexico was no longer ruled by Spain. In 1853 Mexico sold the area to the U.S. and soon, overland stage service from San Antonio was instituted. The Civil War interrupted travel along this route to California. After the war, Tucson continued as a supply and distribution point, first for the army and then for miners. From 1867 to 1877, it was the capital of the territory.

Tucson grew slowly until World War II when it became more industrialized. Today, the city is both an industrial center and a health resort. Aircraft and missile manufacturing, optics, electronics research, tourism, and education are chief industries. The University of Arizona is the city's largest employer while Raytheon Missile Systems, Davis-Monthan Air Force Base, the state of Arizona, and Wal-Mart are other top employers.

Recreation in Tucson revolves around its breathtaking natural beauty. Its attractions include the Arizona-Sonoran Desert Museum—21 acres of wild desert inhabited by over 300 animal species and 1,200 types of plants—and Kitt Peak National Observatory atop a 6,882-foot mountain, where visitors can take peek through its many optical telescopes and radio telescopes and enjoy exhibits and tours. Saguaro National Park is a 91,000-acre park featuring one of the world's largest saguaro, or tall cactus, stands. Mount Lemmon, over 9,000 feet high, offers hiking, camping, picnicking, and skiing. Biosphere 2, the world's largest controlled environment dedicated to understanding the impact of climate change is in nearby Oracle. This 3.14-acre laboratory is home to world-class research and education programs under the stewardship of the University of Arizona and a popular tourist attraction.

To deal with its ever-present water scarcity, the city embarked on a water harvesting program which saved 52.1 million gallons of water in 2018-2019. Today, Tucson is offering financial incentives to residents who harvest their rainwater as the city works to become carbon-neutral by 2030.

Arizona State Museum features extensive basketry and fiber arts exhibits, celebrating the Southwest United States' ancient fiber-weaving traditions. The unparalleled collections of basketry and pottery have been named National Treasures by the National Endowment for the Humanities. Other notable museums include the University of Arizona Museum of Art, Arizona-Sonora Desert Museum, and Pima Air & Space Museum. The city is home to numerous annual events, including the Tucson Gem & Mineral Show, the Tucson Festival of Books, the Tucson Folk Festival, and the All-Souls Procession Weekend.

The college scene in Tucson includes the University of Arizona, one of the top research universities in the U.S., with 45,000 national and international students, and Pima Community College, serving 75,000 students on six campuses with occupational and special interest courses. Tucson's sports focuses on the University of Arizona, with competitive men's basketball women's softball teams. A 2018 addition to the city was the Indoor Football League expansion team, the Tucson Sugar Skulls, playing in the renovated Tucson Arena.

Nightlife in Tucson abounds with music of all kinds—blues, jazz, country, folk, Latino, and reggae. The diverse restaurant scene, including Japanese, Southwestern, and Italian, is world-renowned.

The region is known for its nearly perfect climate. Surrounded by four mountain ranges, Tucson has much sunshine, dry air, and rich desert vegetation.

Rankings

Business/Finance Rankings

- The Brookings Institution ranked the nation's largest cities based on income inequality. Tucson was ranked #58 (#1 = greatest inequality). Criteria: the "95/20 ratio," a figure representing the income at which a household earns more than 95 percent of all other households, divided by the income at which a household earns more than only 20 percent of all other households. *Brookings Institution, "Household Income Inequality, Largest Cities of 97 Large U.S. Metro Areas, 2014-2016," February 5, 2018*
- The Brookings Institution ranked the 100 largest metro areas in the U.S. based on income inequality. Tucson was ranked #24 (#1 = greatest inequality). Criteria: the "95/20 ratio," a figure representing the income at which a household earns more than 95 percent of all other households, divided by the income at which a household earns more than only 20 percent of all other households. *Brookings Institution, "Household Income Inequality, 100 Largest U.S. Metro Areas, 2014-2016," February 5, 2018*
- The Tucson metro area appeared on the Milken Institute "2021 Best Performing Cities" list. Rank: #41 out of 200 large metro areas (population over 250,000). Criteria: job growth; wage and salary growth; high-tech output growth; housing affordability; household broadband access. *Milken Institute, "Best-Performing Cities 2021," February 16, 2021*
- *Forbes* ranked the 200 most populous metro areas to determine the nation's "Best Places for Business and Careers." The Tucson metro area was ranked #107. Criteria: costs (business and living); job growth (past and projected); income growth; quality of life; educational attainment (college and high school); projected economic growth; cultural and leisure opportunities; workplace tolerance laws; net migration patterns. *Forbes, "The Best Places for Business and Careers 2019: Seattle Still On Top," October 30, 2019*

Children/Family Rankings

- Tucson was selected as one of the most playful cities in the U.S. by KaBOOM! The organization's Playful City USA initiative honors cities and towns across the nation that have made their communities more playable. Criteria: pledging to integrate play as a solution to challenges in their communities; making it easy for children to get active and balanced play; creating more family-friendly and innovative communities as a result. *KaBOOM! National Campaign for Play, "2017 Playful City USA Communities"*

Education Rankings

- Personal finance website *WalletHub* analyzed the 150 largest U.S. metropolitan statistical areas to determine where the most educated Americans are putting their degrees to work. Criteria: education levels; percentage of workers with degrees; education quality and attainment gap; public school quality rankings; quality and enrollment of each metro area's universities. Tucson was ranked #50 (#1 = most educated city). *www.WalletHub.com, "Most & Least Educated Cities in America," July 19, 2021*
- Tucson was selected as one of America's most literate cities. The city ranked #56 out of the 84 largest U.S. cities. Criteria: number of booksellers; library resources; Internet resources; educational attainment; periodical publishing resources; newspaper circulation. *Central Connecticut State University, "America's Most Literate Cities, 2018," February 2019*

Health/Fitness Rankings

- For each of the 100 largest cities in the United States, the American Fitness Index®, published by the American College of Sports Medicine and the Anthem Foundation, evaluated community infrastructure and 34 health behaviors including preventive health, levels of chronic disease conditions, food insecurity, sleep quality, pedestrian safety, air quality, and community resources that support physical activity. Tucson ranked #36 for "community fitness." *americanfitnessindex.org, "2021 ACSM American Fitness Index Summary Report," July 13, 2021*
- Tucson was identified as a "2021 Spring Allergy Capital." The area ranked #49 out of 100. Three groups of factors were used to identify the most challenging cities for people with allergies during the spring season: annual spring pollen levels; over the counter medicine use; number of board-certified allergy specialists. *Asthma and Allergy Foundation of America, "Spring Allergy Capitals 2021," February 23, 2021*

- Tucson was identified as a "2021 Fall Allergy Capital." The area ranked #39 out of 100. Three groups of factors were used to identify the most challenging cities for people with allergies during the fall season: annual fall pollen levels; over the counter medicine use; number of board-certified allergy specialists. *Asthma and Allergy Foundation of America, "Fall Allergy Capitals 2021," February 23, 2021*
- Tucson was identified as a "2021 Asthma Capital." The area ranked #10 out of the nation's 100 largest metropolitan areas. Criteria: estimated asthma prevalence; asthma-related mortality; and ER visits due to asthma. Risk factors analyzed but not factored in the rankings: annual pollen score; annual air quality; public smoking laws; number of board-certified asthma specialists; rescue medication use; controller medication use; uninsured rate; poverty rate. *Asthma and Allergy Foundation of America, "Asthma Capitals 2021: The Most Challenging Places to Live With Asthma," May 5, 2021*

Real Estate Rankings

- *WalletHub* compared the most populated U.S. cities to determine which had the best markets for real estate agents. Tucson ranked #67 where demand was high and pay was the best. Criteria: sales per agent; annual median wage for real-estate agents; monthly average starting salary for real estate agents; real estate job density and competition; unemployment rate; home turnover rate; housing-market health index; and other relevant metrics. *www.WalletHub.com, "2021 Best Places to Be a Real Estate Agent," May 12, 2021*
- Tucson was ranked #18 in the top 20 out of the 100 largest metro areas in terms of house price appreciation in 2021 (#1 = highest rate). *Federal Housing Finance Agency, House Price Index, 4th Quarter 2021*
- The Tucson metro area was identified as one of the 20 best housing markets in the U.S. in 2021. The area ranked #6 out of 184 markets. Criteria: year-over-year change of median sales price of existing single-family homes between the 4th quarter of 2020 and the 4th quarter of 2021. *National Association of Realtors®, Median Sales Price of Existing Single-Family Homes for Metropolitan Areas, 4th Quarter 2021*
- Tucson was ranked #139 out of 237 metro areas in terms of housing affordability in 2021 by the National Association of Home Builders (#1 = most affordable). Criteria: the share of homes sold in that area affordable to a family earning the local median income, based on standard mortgage underwriting criteria. *National Association of Home Builders®, NAHB-Wells Fargo Housing Opportunity Index, 4th Quarter 2021*

Safety Rankings

- Allstate ranked the 200 largest cities in America in terms of driver safety. Tucson ranked #40. Criteria: internal property damage claims over a two-year period from January 2016 to December 2017. The report helps increase the importance of safety and awareness behind the wheel. *Allstate, "Allstate America's Best Drivers Report, 2019" June 24, 2019*
- The National Insurance Crime Bureau ranked 390 metro areas in the U.S. in terms of per capita rates of vehicle theft. The Tucson metro area ranked #119 (#1 = highest rate). Criteria: number of vehicle theft offenses per 100,000 inhabitants in 2020. *National Insurance Crime Bureau, "Hot Spots 2020," August 31, 2021*

Seniors/Retirement Rankings

- From its Best Cities for Successful Aging indexes, the Milken Institute generated rankings for metropolitan areas, weighing data in nine categories—health care, wellness, living arrangements, transportation and convenience, financial characteristics, education, employment, community engagement, and overall livability. The Tucson metro area was ranked #60 overall in the large metro area category. *Milken Institute, "Best Cities for Successful Aging, 2017" March 14, 2017*
- Tucson was identified as #4 of 20 most popular places to retire in the Southwest region by *Topretirements.com*. The site separated its annual "Best Places to Retire" list by major U.S. regions for 2019. The list reflects the 20 cities that visitors to the website are most interested in for retirement, based on the number of times a city's review was viewed on the website. *Topretirements.com, "20 Most Popular Places to Retire in the Southwest for 2019," October 2, 2019*

Sports/Recreation Rankings

- Tucson was chosen as a bicycle friendly community by the League of American Bicyclists. A "Bicycle Friendly Community" welcomes cyclists by providing safe and supportive accommodation for cycling and encouraging people to bike for transportation and recreation. There are five award levels: Diamond; Platinum; Gold; Silver; and Bronze. The community achieved an award level of Gold. *League of American Bicyclists, "Fall 2021 Awards-New & Renewing Bicycle Friendly Communities List," December 8, 2021*

- Tucson was chosen as one of America's best cities for bicycling. The city ranked #24 out of 50. Criteria: cycling infrastructure that is safe and friendly for all ages; energy and bike culture. The editors evaluated cities with populations of 100,000 or more. *Bicycling, "The 50 Best Bike Cities in America," October 10, 2018*

Women/Minorities Rankings

- The *Houston Chronicle* listed the Tucson metro area as #10 in top places for young Latinos to live in the U.S. Research was largely based on housing and occupational data from the largest metropolitan areas performed by *Forbes* and NBC Universo. Criteria: percentage of 18-34 year-olds; Latino college grad rates; and diversity. *blog.chron.com, "The 15 Best Big Cities for Latino Millenials," January 26, 2016*

- Personal finance website *WalletHub* compared more than 180 U.S. cities across two key dimensions, "Hispanic Business-Friendliness" and "Hispanic Purchasing Power," to arrive at the most favorable conditions for Hispanic entrepreneurs. Tucson was ranked #92 out of 182. Criteria includes: share of Hispanic-Owned Businesses; Hispanic entrepreneurship rate to median annual income of Hispanics; Small Business-Friendliness score; cost of living; and number of Hispanics with at least a bachelor's degree. *WalletHub.com, "2019's Best Cities for Hispanic Entrepreneurs," May 1, 2019*

Miscellaneous Rankings

- *WalletHub* compared the 150 most populated U.S. cities to determine their operating efficiency. A "Quality of City Services" score was constructed for each city and then divided by the total budget per capita to reveal which were managed the best. Tucson ranked #32. Criteria: financial stability; economy; education; safety; health; infrastructure and pollution. *www.WalletHub.com, "2021's Best- & Worst-Run Cities in America," June 22, 2021*

Business Environment

DEMOGRAPHICS

Population Growth

Area	1990 Census	2000 Census	2010 Census	2020* Estimate	Population Growth (%)	
					1990-2020	2010-2020
City	417,942	486,699	520,116	545,340	30.5	4.8
MSA[1]	666,880	843,746	980,263	1,038,476	55.7	5.9
U.S.	248,709,873	281,421,906	308,745,538	326,569,308	31.3	5.8

Note: (1) Figures cover the Tucson, AZ Metropolitan Statistical Area; (*) 2016-2020 5-year estimated population
Source: U.S. Census Bureau, 1990 Census, Census 2000, Census 2010, 2016-2020 American Community Survey 5-Year Estimates

Household Size

Area	Persons in Household (%)							Average Household Size
	One	Two	Three	Four	Five	Six	Seven or More	
City	35.1	31.1	14.3	11.2	5.0	1.9	1.4	2.40
MSA[1]	31.0	35.6	13.3	11.5	5.1	2.1	1.4	2.50
U.S.	28.0	33.9	15.5	12.9	6.0	2.3	1.4	2.60

Note: (1) Figures cover the Tucson, AZ Metropolitan Statistical Area
Source: U.S. Census Bureau, 2016-2020 American Community Survey 5-Year Estimates

Race

Area	White Alone[2] (%)	Black Alone[2] (%)	Asian Alone[2] (%)	AIAN[3] Alone[2] (%)	NHOPI[4] Alone[2] (%)	Other Race Alone[2] (%)	Two or More Races (%)
City	69.3	4.9	3.2	3.3	0.2	10.3	8.7
MSA[1]	73.3	3.5	2.9	3.6	0.2	8.7	7.8
U.S.	70.4	12.6	5.6	0.8	0.2	5.1	5.2

Note: (1) Figures cover the Tucson, AZ Metropolitan Statistical Area; (2) Alone is defined as not being in combination with one or more other races; (3) American Indian and Alaska Native; (4) Native Hawaiian and Other Pacific Islander
Source: U.S. Census Bureau, 2016-2020 American Community Survey 5-Year Estimates

Hispanic or Latino Origin

Area	Total (%)	Mexican (%)	Puerto Rican (%)	Cuban (%)	Other (%)
City	44.2	39.6	0.8	0.2	3.6
MSA[1]	37.5	33.4	0.8	0.2	3.1
U.S.	18.2	11.2	1.7	0.7	4.5

Note: Persons of Hispanic or Latino origin can be of any race; (1) Figures cover the Tucson, AZ Metropolitan Statistical Area
Source: U.S. Census Bureau, 2016-2020 American Community Survey 5-Year Estimates

Ancestry

Area	German	Irish	English	American	Italian	Polish	French[2]	Scottish	Dutch
City	11.1	8.1	7.2	2.8	3.5	1.9	2.0	1.5	0.9
MSA[1]	13.1	9.0	8.9	3.2	3.9	2.3	2.3	1.9	1.1
U.S.	13.0	9.7	7.7	5.9	5.1	2.7	2.3	1.6	1.1

Note: Figures are the percentage of the total population reporting a particular ancestry. The nine most commonly reported ancestries in the U.S. are shown. Figures include multiple ancestries (e.g. if a person reported being Irish and Italian, they were included in both columns); (1) Figures cover the Tucson, AZ Metropolitan Statistical Area; (2) Excludes Basque
Source: U.S. Census Bureau, 2016-2020 American Community Survey 5-Year Estimates

Foreign-born Population

Area	Percent of Population Born in								
	Any Foreign Country	Asia	Mexico	Europe	Caribbean	Central America[2]	South America	Africa	Canada
City	14.6	2.5	9.0	1.1	0.2	0.4	0.3	0.9	0.2
MSA[1]	12.5	2.2	7.2	1.3	0.2	0.3	0.3	0.6	0.4
U.S.	13.5	4.2	3.3	1.5	1.3	1.1	1.0	0.7	0.3

Note: (1) Figures cover the Tucson, AZ Metropolitan Statistical Area; (2) Excludes Mexico.
Source: U.S. Census Bureau, 2016-2020 American Community Survey 5-Year Estimates

Marital Status

Area	Never Married	Now Married[2]	Separated	Widowed	Divorced
City	42.5	35.7	2.3	5.3	14.3
MSA[1]	34.7	44.8	1.8	5.7	13.0
U.S.	33.5	48.1	1.8	5.7	10.8

Note: Figures are percentages and cover the population 15 years of age and older; (1) Figures cover the Tucson, AZ Metropolitan Statistical Area; (2) Excludes separated
Source: U.S. Census Bureau, 2016-2020 American Community Survey 5-Year Estimates

Disability by Age

Area	All Ages	Under 18 Years Old	18 to 64 Years Old	65 Years and Over
City	15.2	5.8	12.8	38.8
MSA[1]	15.2	5.2	12.3	34.4
U.S.	12.7	4.3	10.3	34.0

Note: Figures show percent of the civilian noninstitutionalized population that reported having a disability. Disability status is determined from six types of difficulty: vision, hearing, cognitive, ambulatory, self-care, and independent living. For children under 5 years old, hearing and vision difficulty are used to determine disability status. For children between the ages of 5 and 14, disability status is determined from hearing, vision, cognitive, ambulatory, and self-care difficulties. For people aged 15 years and older, they are considered to have a disability if they have difficulty with any one of the six difficulty types; Note: (1) Figures cover the Tucson, AZ Metropolitan Statistical Area
Source: U.S. Census Bureau, 2016-2020 American Community Survey 5-Year Estimates

Age

Area	Percent of Population									Median Age
	Under Age 5	Age 5–19	Age 20–34	Age 35–44	Age 45–54	Age 55–64	Age 65–74	Age 75–84	Age 85+	
City	5.7	18.9	26.8	12.0	10.8	11.0	8.4	4.5	2.0	34.0
MSA[1]	5.5	18.3	21.5	11.4	11.0	12.4	11.2	6.3	2.3	38.7
U.S.	6.0	19.1	20.6	12.7	12.7	12.9	9.4	4.7	2.0	38.2

Note: (1) Figures cover the Tucson, AZ Metropolitan Statistical Area
Source: U.S. Census Bureau, 2016-2020 American Community Survey 5-Year Estimates

Gender

Area	Males	Females	Males per 100 Females
City	270,117	275,223	98.1
MSA[1]	510,875	527,601	96.8
U.S.	160,818,530	165,750,778	97.0

Note: (1) Figures cover the Tucson, AZ Metropolitan Statistical Area
Source: U.S. Census Bureau, 2016-2020 American Community Survey 5-Year Estimates

Religious Groups by Family

Area	Catholic	Baptist	Non-Den.	Methodist[2]	Lutheran	LDS[3]	Pente-costal	Presby-terian[4]	Muslim[5]	Judaism
MSA[1]	20.8	3.3	3.8	1.4	1.5	3.0	1.6	1.0	<0.1	0.6
U.S.	19.1	9.3	4.0	4.0	2.3	2.0	1.9	1.6	0.8	0.7

Note: Figures are the number of adherents as a percentage of the total population; (1) Figures cover the Tucson, AZ Metropolitan Statistical Area; (2) Methodist/Pietist; (3) Latter Day Saints; (4) Reformed; (5) Figures are estimates
Source: Association of Statisticians of American Religious Bodies, 2010 U.S. Religion Census: Religious Congregations & Membership Study

Religious Groups by Tradition

Area	Catholic	Evangelical Protestant	Mainline Protestant	Other Tradition	Black Protestant	Orthodox
MSA[1]	20.8	10.0	3.8	4.6	0.4	0.2
U.S.	19.1	16.2	7.3	4.3	1.6	0.3

Note: Figures are the number of adherents as a percentage of the total population; (1) Figures cover the Tucson, AZ Metropolitan Statistical Area
Source: Association of Statisticians of American Religious Bodies, 2010 U.S. Religion Census: Religious Congregations & Membership Study

ECONOMY

Gross Metropolitan Product

Area	2017	2018	2019	2020	Rank[2]
MSA[1]	39.9	41.7	43.6	45.5	74

Note: Figures are in billions of dollars; (1) Figures cover the Tucson, AZ Metropolitan Statistical Area; (2) Rank is based on 2018 data and ranges from 1 to 381
Source: U.S. Conference of Mayors, U.S. Metro Economies: GMP & Employment 2018-2020, September 2019

Economic Growth

Area	2015-17 (%)	2018 (%)	2019 (%)	2020 (%)	Rank[2]
MSA[1]	2.0	2.7	2.8	2.0	133
U.S.	1.9	2.9	2.3	2.1	-

Note: Figures are real gross metropolitan product (GMP) growth rates and represent average annual percent change; (1) Figures cover the Tucson, AZ Metropolitan Statistical Area; (2) Rank is based on 2017 2-year average annual percent change and ranges from 1 to 381
Source: U.S. Conference of Mayors, U.S. Metro Economies: GMP & Employment 2018-2020, September 2019

Metropolitan Area Exports

Area	2015	2016	2017	2018	2019	2020	Rank[2]
MSA[1]	2,485.9	2,563.9	2,683.9	2,824.8	2,943.7	2,640.7	82

Note: Figures are in millions of dollars; (1) Figures cover the Tucson, AZ Metropolitan Statistical Area; (2) Rank is based on 2020 data and ranges from 1 to 389
Source: U.S. Department of Commerce, International Trade Administration, Office of Trade and Economic Analysis, Industry and Analysis, Exports by Metropolitan Area, data extracted March 4, 2022

Building Permits

Area	Single-Family			Multi-Family			Total		
	2019	2020	Pct. Chg.	2019	2020	Pct. Chg.	2019	2020	Pct. Chg.
City	999	1,043	4.4	817	712	-12.9	1,816	1,755	-3.4
MSA[1]	3,490	4,242	21.5	823	716	-13.0	4,313	4,958	15.0
U.S.	862,100	979,400	13.6	523,900	491,700	-6.1	1,386,000	1,471,100	6.1

Note: (1) Figures cover the Tucson, AZ Metropolitan Statistical Area; Figures represent new, privately-owned housing units authorized (unadjusted data); All permit data are based on estimates with imputation
Source: U.S. Census Bureau, Manufacturing, Mining, and Construction Statistics, Building Permits, 2019, 2020

Bankruptcy Filings

Area	Business Filings			Nonbusiness Filings		
	2020	2021	% Chg.	2020	2021	% Chg.
Pima County	32	21	-34.4	1,727	1,379	-20.2
U.S.	21,655	14,347	-33.7	522,808	399,269	-23.6

Note: Business filings include Chapter 7, Chapter 9, Chapter 11, Chapter 12, Chapter 13, Chapter 15, and Section 304; Nonbusiness filings include Chapter 7, Chapter 11, and Chapter 13
Source: Administrative Office of the U.S. Courts, Business and Nonbusiness Bankruptcy, County Cases Commenced by Chapter of the Bankruptcy Code, During the 12-Month Period Ending December 31, 2020 and Business and Nonbusiness Bankruptcy, County Cases Commenced by Chapter of the Bankruptcy Code, During the 12-Month Period Ending December 31, 2021

Housing Vacancy Rates

Area	Gross Vacancy Rate[2] (%)			Year-Round Vacancy Rate[3] (%)			Rental Vacancy Rate[4] (%)			Homeowner Vacancy Rate[5] (%)		
	2019	2020	2021	2019	2020	2021	2019	2020	2021	2019	2020	2021
MSA[1]	14.8	12.1	10.0	9.2	7.7	6.9	7.3	8.6	5.0	1.5	0.5	0.6
U.S.	12.0	10.6	10.8	9.5	8.2	8.4	6.7	6.3	6.1	1.4	1.0	0.9

Note: (1) Figures cover the Tucson, AZ Metropolitan Statistical Area; (2) The percentage of the total housing inventory that is vacant; (3) The percentage of the housing inventory (excluding seasonal units) that is year-round vacant; (4) The percentage of rental inventory that is vacant for rent; (5) The percentage of homeowner inventory that is vacant for sale
Source: U.S. Census Bureau, Housing Vacancies and Homeownership Annual Statistics: 2019, 2020, 2021

INCOME

Income

Area	Per Capita ($)	Median Household ($)	Average Household ($)
City	24,468	45,227	59,650
MSA[1]	30,747	55,023	75,662
U.S.	35,384	64,994	91,547

Note: (1) Figures cover the Tucson, AZ Metropolitan Statistical Area
Source: U.S. Census Bureau, 2016-2020 American Community Survey 5-Year Estimates

Household Income Distribution

Area	Percent of Households Earning							
	Under $15,000	$15,000 -$24,999	$25,000 -$34,999	$35,000 -$49,999	$50,000 -$74,999	$75,000 -$99,999	$100,000 -$149,999	$150,000 and up
City	15.1	12.6	11.2	15.6	18.3	11.4	10.2	5.6
MSA[1]	11.4	10.3	9.7	14.2	18.1	12.7	13.4	10.2
U.S.	9.9	8.5	8.6	12.0	17.2	12.8	15.6	15.4

Note: (1) Figures cover the Tucson, AZ Metropolitan Statistical Area
Source: U.S. Census Bureau, 2016-2020 American Community Survey 5-Year Estimates

Poverty Rate

Area	All Ages	Under 18 Years Old	18 to 64 Years Old	65 Years and Over
City	20.8	27.4	20.5	12.7
MSA[1]	15.9	22.2	16.2	8.5
U.S.	12.8	17.5	12.1	9.3

Note: Figures are percentage of people whose income during the past 12 months was below the poverty level; (1) Figures cover the Tucson, AZ Metropolitan Statistical Area
Source: U.S. Census Bureau, 2016-2020 American Community Survey 5-Year Estimates

CITY FINANCES

City Government Finances

Component	2019 ($000)	2019 ($ per capita)
Total Revenues	1,000,069	1,867
Total Expenditures	1,162,446	2,170
Debt Outstanding	627,643	1,172
Cash and Securities[1]	486,435	908

Note: (1) Cash and security holdings of a government at the close of its fiscal year, including those of its dependent agencies, utilities, and liquor stores.
Source: U.S. Census Bureau, State & Local Government Finances 2019

City Government Revenue by Source

Source	2019 ($000)	2019 ($ per capita)	2019 (%)
General Revenue			
From Federal Government	70,056	131	7.0
From State Government	210,840	394	21.1
From Local Governments	0	0	0.0
Taxes			
Property	57,399	107	5.7
Sales and Gross Receipts	284,000	530	28.4
Personal Income	0	0	0.0
Corporate Income	0	0	0.0
Motor Vehicle License	0	0	0.0
Other Taxes	12,921	24	1.3
Current Charges	118,204	221	11.8
Liquor Store	0	0	0.0
Utility	225,561	421	22.6

Source: U.S. Census Bureau, State & Local Government Finances 2019

City Government Expenditures by Function

Function	2019 ($000)	2019 ($ per capita)	2019 (%)
General Direct Expenditures			
Air Transportation	59,552	111	5.1
Corrections	0	0	0.0
Education	0	0	0.0
Employment Security Administration	0	0	0.0
Financial Administration	25,236	47	2.2
Fire Protection	111,210	207	9.6
General Public Buildings	1,096	2	0.1
Governmental Administration, Other	24,620	46	2.1
Health	0	0	0.0
Highways	131,703	245	11.3
Hospitals	0	0	0.0
Housing and Community Development	75,818	141	6.5
Interest on General Debt	9,633	18	0.8
Judicial and Legal	31,799	59	2.7
Libraries	0	0	0.0
Parking	5,938	11	0.5
Parks and Recreation	44,453	83	3.8
Police Protection	235,851	440	20.3
Public Welfare	0	0	0.0
Sewerage	0	0	0.0
Solid Waste Management	64,631	120	5.6
Veterans' Services	0	0	0.0
Liquor Store	0	0	0.0
Utility	313,618	585	27.0

Source: U.S. Census Bureau, State & Local Government Finances 2019

EMPLOYMENT

Labor Force and Employment

Area	Civilian Labor Force			Workers Employed		
	Dec. 2020	Dec. 2021	% Chg.	Dec. 2020	Dec. 2021	% Chg.
City	265,991	267,731	0.7	245,743	259,401	5.6
MSA[1]	493,760	499,312	1.1	459,909	485,470	5.6
U.S.	160,017,000	161,696,000	1.0	149,613,000	155,732,000	4.1

Note: Data is not seasonally adjusted and covers workers 16 years of age and older; (1) Figures cover the Tucson, AZ Metropolitan Statistical Area
Source: Bureau of Labor Statistics, Local Area Unemployment Statistics

Unemployment Rate

Area	2021											
	Jan.	Feb.	Mar.	Apr.	May	Jun.	Jul.	Aug.	Sep.	Oct.	Nov.	Dec.
City	7.9	8.2	7.4	7.3	7.5	8.1	7.1	5.9	4.8	4.1	3.5	3.1
MSA[1]	7.1	7.3	6.6	6.6	6.7	7.3	6.4	5.2	4.3	3.7	3.2	2.8
U.S.	6.8	6.6	6.2	5.7	5.5	6.1	5.7	5.3	4.6	4.3	3.9	3.7

Note: Data is not seasonally adjusted and covers workers 16 years of age and older; (1) Figures cover the Tucson, AZ Metropolitan Statistical Area
Source: Bureau of Labor Statistics, Local Area Unemployment Statistics

Average Wages

Occupation	$/Hr.	Occupation	$/Hr.
Accountants and Auditors	34.25	Maintenance and Repair Workers	19.33
Automotive Mechanics	21.26	Marketing Managers	63.88
Bookkeepers	20.48	Network and Computer Systems Admin.	37.41
Carpenters	21.27	Nurses, Licensed Practical	27.25
Cashiers	13.89	Nurses, Registered	37.89
Computer Programmers	41.57	Nursing Assistants	16.08
Computer Systems Analysts	45.36	Office Clerks, General	19.95
Computer User Support Specialists	26.04	Physical Therapists	44.18
Construction Laborers	18.23	Physicians	117.15
Cooks, Restaurant	15.44	Plumbers, Pipefitters and Steamfitters	25.33
Customer Service Representatives	16.57	Police and Sheriff's Patrol Officers	29.53
Dentists	75.94	Postal Service Mail Carriers	26.69
Electricians	23.78	Real Estate Sales Agents	20.03
Engineers, Electrical	46.97	Retail Salespersons	15.89
Fast Food and Counter Workers	14.38	Sales Representatives, Technical/Scientific	48.74
Financial Managers	56.29	Secretaries, Exc. Legal/Medical/Executive	18.46
First-Line Supervisors of Office Workers	25.93	Security Guards	15.90
General and Operations Managers	42.09	Surgeons	n/a
Hairdressers/Cosmetologists	20.03	Teacher Assistants, Exc. Postsecondary*	14.23
Home Health and Personal Care Aides	13.79	Teachers, Secondary School, Exc. Sp. Ed.*	22.24
Janitors and Cleaners	14.71	Telemarketers	15.30
Landscaping/Groundskeeping Workers	15.16	Truck Drivers, Heavy/Tractor-Trailer	22.41
Lawyers	56.04	Truck Drivers, Light/Delivery Services	20.30
Maids and Housekeeping Cleaners	14.26	Waiters and Waitresses	18.90

Note: Wage data covers the Tucson, AZ Metropolitan Statistical Area; (*) Hourly wages were calculated from annual wage data based on a 40 hour work week; n/a not available.
Source: Bureau of Labor Statistics, Metro Area Occupational Employment & Wage Estimates, May 2021

Employment by Industry

Sector	MSA[1]		U.S.
	Number of Employees	Percent of Total	Percent of Total
Construction	18,200	4.6	5.0
Education and Health Services	68,400	17.4	16.0
Financial Activities	19,100	4.9	5.9
Government	77,300	19.7	14.9
Information	5,100	1.3	1.9
Leisure and Hospitality	43,000	10.9	9.8
Manufacturing	27,800	7.1	8.4
Mining and Logging	1,800	0.5	0.4
Other Services	13,800	3.5	3.7
Professional and Business Services	45,500	11.6	14.6
Retail Trade	43,100	11.0	10.7
Transportation, Warehousing, and Utilities	22,100	5.6	4.8
Wholesale Trade	7,500	1.9	3.8

Note: Figures are non-farm employment as of December 2021. Figures are not seasonally adjusted and include workers 16 years of age and older; (1) Figures cover the Tucson, AZ Metropolitan Statistical Area
Source: Bureau of Labor Statistics, Current Employment Statistics, Employment, Hours, and Earnings

Employment by Occupation

Occupation Classification	City (%)	MSA[1] (%)	U.S. (%)
Management, Business, Science, and Arts	34.5	38.4	39.5
Natural Resources, Construction, and Maintenance	8.8	8.3	8.7
Production, Transportation, and Material Moving	10.2	9.5	13.1
Sales and Office	23.4	23.0	21.3
Service	23.1	20.8	17.4

Note: Figures cover employed civilians 16 years of age and older; (1) Figures cover the Tucson, AZ Metropolitan Statistical Area
Source: U.S. Census Bureau, 2016-2020 American Community Survey 5-Year Estimates

Occupations with Greatest Projected Employment Growth: 2021 – 2023

Occupation[1]	2021 Employment	2023 Projected Employment	Numeric Employment Change	Percent Employment Change
Home Health and Personal Care Aides	73,830	83,930	10,100	13.7
Laborers and Freight, Stock, and Material Movers, Hand	61,750	68,460	6,710	10.9
Customer Service Representatives	108,520	114,910	6,390	5.9
Stockers and Order Fillers	56,260	62,630	6,370	11.3
Waiters and Waitresses	45,830	51,130	5,300	11.6
Fast Food and Counter Workers	54,000	59,140	5,140	9.5
Cooks, Restaurant	31,160	36,290	5,130	16.5
Software Developers and Software Quality Assurance Analysts and Testers	40,110	45,180	5,070	12.6
Registered Nurses	58,640	63,090	4,450	7.6
General and Operations Managers	54,050	58,370	4,320	8.0

Note: Projections cover Arizona; (1) Sorted by numeric employment change
Source: www.projectionscentral.com, State Occupational Projections, 2021–2023 Short-Term Projections

Fastest-Growing Occupations: 2021 – 2023

Occupation[1]	2021 Employment	2023 Projected Employment	Numeric Employment Change	Percent Employment Change
Hotel, Motel, and Resort Desk Clerks	4,850	6,120	1,270	26.2
Ushers, Lobby Attendants, and Ticket Takers	1,000	1,250	250	25.0
Lodging Managers	1,300	1,620	320	24.6
Baggage Porters and Bellhops	750	910	160	21.3
Locker Room, Coatroom, and Dressing Room Attendants	240	290	50	20.8
Conveyor Operators and Tenders	290	350	60	20.7
Athletes and Sports Competitors	830	1,000	170	20.5
Barbers	780	940	160	20.5
Fine Artists, Including Painters, Sculptors, and Illustrators	490	590	100	20.4
Musicians and Singers	1,620	1,950	330	20.4

Note: Projections cover Arizona; (1) Sorted by percent employment change and excludes occupations with numeric employment change less than 50
Source: www.projectionscentral.com, State Occupational Projections, 2021–2023 Short-Term Projections

TAXES

State Corporate Income Tax Rates

State	Tax Rate (%)	Income Brackets ($)	Num. of Brackets	Financial Institution Tax Rate (%)[a]	Federal Income Tax Ded.
Arizona	4.9 (b)	Flat rate	1	4.9 (b)	No

Note: Tax rates as of January 1, 2022; (a) Rates listed are the corporate income tax rate applied to financial institutions or excise taxes based on income. Some states have other taxes based upon the value of deposits or shares; (b) Minimum tax is $800 in California, $250 in District of Columbia, $50 in Arizona and North Dakota (banks), $400 ($100 banks) in Rhode Island, $200 per location in South Dakota (banks), $100 in Utah, $300 in Vermont.
Source: Federation of Tax Administrators, State Corporate Income Tax Rates, January 1, 2022

State Individual Income Tax Rates

State	Tax Rate (%)	Income Brackets ($)	Personal Exemptions ($)			Standard Ded. ($)	
			Single	Married	Depend.	Single	Married
Arizona (a)	2.59 - 4.5	27,808 - 166,843 (b)	–	–	100 (c)	12,550	25,100

Note: Tax rates as of January 1, 2022; Local- and county-level taxes are not included; Federal income tax is not deductible on state income tax returns; (a) 19 states have statutory provision for automatically adjusting to the rate of inflation the dollar values of the income tax brackets, standard deductions, and/or personal exemptions. Michigan indexes the personal exemption only. Oregon does not index the income brackets for $125,000 and over; (b) For joint returns, taxes are twice the tax on half the couple's income; (c) The personal exemption takes the form of a tax credit instead of a deduction
Source: Federation of Tax Administrators, State Individual Income Tax Rates, January 1, 2022

Various State Sales and Excise Tax Rates

State	State Sales Tax (%)	Gasoline[1] (¢/gal.)	Cigarette[2] ($/pack)	Spirits[3] ($/gal.)	Wine[4] ($/gal.)	Beer[5] ($/gal.)	Recreational Marijuana (%)
Arizona	5.6	19	2	3	0.84	0.16	(b)

Note: All tax rates as of January 1, 2022; (1) The American Petroleum Institute has developed a methodology for determining the average tax rate on a gallon of fuel. Rates may include any of the following: excise taxes, environmental fees, storage tank fees, other fees or taxes, general sales tax, and local taxes; (2) The federal excise tax of $1.0066 per pack and local taxes are not included; (3) Rates are those applicable to off-premise sales of 40% alcohol by volume (a.b.v.) distilled spirits in 750ml containers. Local excise taxes are excluded; (4) Rates are those applicable to off-premise sales of 11% a.b.v. non-carbonated wine in 750ml containers; (5) Rates are those applicable to off-premise sales of 4.7% a.b.v. beer in 12 ounce containers; (b) 16% excise tax (retail price)
Source: Tax Foundation, 2022 Facts & Figures: How Does Your State Compare?

State Business Tax Climate Index Rankings

State	Overall Rank	Corporate Tax Rank	Individual Income Tax Rank	Sales Tax Rank	Property Tax Rank	Unemployment Insurance Tax Rank
Arizona	23	23	18	40	11	11

Note: The index is a measure of how each state's tax laws affect economic performance. The lower the rank, the more favorable a state's tax system is for business. States without a given tax are given a ranking of 1. The scores/rankings for the District of Columbia do not affect other states. The 2022 index represents the tax climate as of July 1, 2021.
Source: Tax Foundation, State Business Tax Climate Index 2022

TRANSPORTATION

Means of Transportation to Work

Area	Car/Truck/Van		Public Transportation			Bicycle	Walked	Other Means	Worked at Home
	Drove Alone	Car-pooled	Bus	Subway	Railroad				
City	73.1	10.5	2.8	0.0	0.0	2.2	3.0	1.7	6.7
MSA[1]	75.2	9.9	1.9	0.0	0.0	1.4	2.1	1.8	7.8
U.S.	74.9	8.9	2.2	1.7	0.5	0.5	2.6	1.4	7.3

Note: Figures are percentages and cover workers 16 years of age and older; (1) Figures cover the Tucson, AZ Metropolitan Statistical Area
Source: U.S. Census Bureau, 2016-2020 American Community Survey 5-Year Estimates

Travel Time to Work

Area	Less Than 10 Minutes	10 to 19 Minutes	20 to 29 Minutes	30 to 44 Minutes	45 to 59 Minutes	60 to 89 Minutes	90 Minutes or More
City	11.8	34.6	25.3	19.8	4.7	2.2	1.6
MSA[1]	10.6	29.2	24.7	23.9	7.2	2.6	1.8
U.S.	12.3	28.4	20.9	20.9	8.3	6.4	2.9

Note: Note: Figures are percentages and include workers 16 years old and over; (1) Figures cover the Tucson, AZ Metropolitan Statistical Area
Source: U.S. Census Bureau, 2016-2020 American Community Survey 5-Year Estimates

Key Congestion Measures

Measure	1990	2000	2010	2015	2020
Annual Hours of Delay, Total (000)	9,594	18,225	27,738	30,850	13,189
Annual Hours of Delay, Per Auto Commuter	28	40	43	49	21
Annual Congestion Cost, Per Auto Commuter ($)	470	673	816	836	381

Note: Covers the Tucson AZ urban area
Source: Texas A&M Transportation Institute, 2021 Urban Mobility Report

Freeway Travel Time Index

Measure	1985	1990	1995	2000	2005	2010	2015	2020
Urban Area Index[1]	1.10	1.14	1.16	1.20	1.21	1.20	1.21	1.07
Urban Area Rank[1,2]	27	26	32	29	35	36	36	57

Note: Freeway Travel Time Index—the ratio of travel time in the peak period to the travel time at free-flow conditions. For example, a value of 1.30 indicates a 20-minute free-flow trip takes 26 minutes in the peak (20 minutes x 1.30 = 26 minutes); (1) Covers the Tucson AZ urban area; (2) Rank is based on 101 larger urban areas (#1 = highest travel time index)
Source: Texas A&M Transportation Institute, 2021 Urban Mobility Report

Public Transportation

Agency Name / Mode of Transportation	Vehicles Operated in Maximum Service[1]	Annual Unlinked Passenger Trips[2] (in thous.)	Annual Passenger Miles[3] (in thous.)
City of Tucson (COT)			
Bus (purchased transportation)	198	12,346.8	47,142.3
Demand Response (purchased transportation)	121	423.0	3,342.0
Streetcar Rail (purchased transportation)	6	682.3	989.3

Note: (1) Number of revenue vehicles operated by the given mode and type of service to meet the annual maximum service requirement. This is the revenue vehicle count during the peak season of the year; on the week and day that maximum service is provided. Vehicles operated in maximum service (VOMS) exclude atypical days and one-time special events; (2) Number of passengers who boarded public transportation vehicles. Passengers are counted each time they board a vehicle no matter how many vehicles they use to travel from their origin to their destination. (3) Sum of the distances ridden by all passengers during the entire fiscal year.
Source: Federal Transit Administration, National Transit Database, 2020

Air Transportation

Airport Name and Code / Type of Service	Passenger Airlines[1]	Passenger Enplanements	Freight Carriers[2]	Freight (lbs)
Tucson International (TUS)				
Domestic service (U.S. carriers - 2021)	22	1,349,990	11	30,049,961
International service (U.S. carriers - 2020)	3	143	1	4,056

Note: (1) Includes all U.S.-based major, minor and commuter airlines that carried at least one passenger during the year; (2) Includes all U.S.-based airlines and freight carriers that transported at least one pound of freight during the year.
Source: Bureau of Transportation Statistics, The Intermodal Transportation Database, Air Carriers: T-100 Domestic Market (U.S. Carriers), 2021; Bureau of Transportation Statistics, The Intermodal Transportation Database, Air Carriers: T-100 International Market (U.S. Carriers), 2020

BUSINESSES

Major Business Headquarters

Company Name	Industry	Rankings	
		Fortune[1]	Forbes[2]
No companies listed	-	-	-

Note: (1) Companies that produce a 10-K are ranked 1 to 500 based on 2020 revenue; (2) All private companies with at least $2 billion in annual revenue through the end of their most current fiscal year are ranked 1 to 225; companies listed are headquartered in the city; dashes indicate no ranking
Source: Fortune, "Fortune 500," 2021; Forbes, "America's Largest Private Companies," 2021

Living Environment

COST OF LIVING

Cost of Living Index

Composite Index	Groceries	Housing	Utilities	Trans-portation	Health Care	Misc. Goods/ Services
103.9	101.0	105.6	103.7	103.8	104.4	104.0

Note: The Cost of Living Index measures regional differences in the cost of consumer goods and services, excluding taxes and non-consumer expenditures, for professional and managerial households in the top income quintile. It is based on more than 50,000 prices covering almost 60 different items for which prices are collected three times a year by chambers of commerce, economic development organizations or university applied economic centers in each participating urban area. The numbers shown should be read as a percentage above or below the national average of 100. For example, a value of 115.4 in the groceries column indicates that grocery prices are 15.4% higher than the national average. Small differences in the index numbers should not be interpreted as significant; Figures cover the Tucson AZ urban area.
Source: The Council for Community and Economic Research, Cost of Living Index, 2021

Grocery Prices

Area[1]	T-Bone Steak ($/pound)	Frying Chicken ($/pound)	Whole Milk ($/half gal.)	Eggs ($/dozen)	Orange Juice ($/64 oz.)	Coffee ($/11.5 oz.)
City[2]	13.02	1.48	1.70	1.58	3.65	5.12
Avg.	12.82	1.40	2.22	1.57	3.59	4.30
Min.	8.91	0.91	1.29	0.75	2.87	3.02
Max.	21.35	2.69	3.92	3.86	5.49	8.11

Note: (1) Values for the local area are compared with the average, minimum and maximum values for all 285 areas in the Cost of Living Index; (2) Figures cover the Tucson AZ urban area; ***T-Bone Steak*** *(price per pound);* ***Frying Chicken*** *(price per pound, whole fryer);* ***Whole Milk*** *(half gallon carton);* ***Eggs*** *(price per dozen, Grade A, large);* ***Orange Juice*** *(64 oz. Tropicana or Florida Natural);* ***Coffee*** *(11.5 oz. can, vacuum-packed, Maxwell House, Hills Bros, or Folgers).*
Source: The Council for Community and Economic Research, Cost of Living Index, 2021

Housing and Utility Costs

Area[1]	New Home Price ($)	Apartment Rent ($/month)	All Electric ($/month)	Part Electric ($/month)	Other Energy ($/month)	Telephone ($/month)
City[2]	445,261	1,150	-	125.25	60.60	181.82
Avg.	398,393	1,217	171.38	100.83	69.67	187.75
Min.	212,799	534	96.71	31.56	27.15	173.01
Max.	2,354,006	4,438	369.53	277.33	303.87	206.73

Note: (1) Values for the local area are compared with the average, minimum and maximum values for all 285 areas in the Cost of Living Index; (2) Figures cover the Tucson AZ urban area; ***New Home Price*** *(2,400 sf living area, 8,000 sf lot, in urban area with full utilities);* ***Apartment Rent*** *(950 sf 2 bedroom/1.5 or 2 bath, unfurnished, excluding all utilities except water);* ***All Electric*** *(average monthly cost for an all-electric home);* ***Part Electric*** *(average monthly cost for a part-electric home);* ***Other Energy*** *(average monthly cost for natural gas, fuel oil, coal, wood, and any other forms of energy except electricity);* ***Telephone*** *(price includes the base monthly rate plus taxes and fees for three lines of mobile phone service).*
Source: The Council for Community and Economic Research, Cost of Living Index, 2021

Health Care, Transportation, and Other Costs

Area[1]	Doctor ($/visit)	Dentist ($/visit)	Optometrist ($/visit)	Gasoline ($/gallon)	Beauty Salon ($/visit)	Men's Shirt ($)
City[2]	140.19	102.09	104.16	2.63	47.35	49.50
Avg.	118.16	101.04	109.44	2.71	40.63	30.77
Min.	35.04	55.56	51.17	2.17	18.59	11.32
Max.	231.10	165.12	256.81	4.11	85.33	63.03

Note: (1) Values for the local area are compared with the average, minimum and maximum values for all 285 areas in the Cost of Living Index; (2) Figures cover the Tucson AZ urban area; ***Doctor*** *(general practitioners routine exam of an established patient);* ***Dentist*** *(adult teeth cleaning and periodic oral examination);* ***Optometrist*** *(full vision eye exam for established adult patient);* ***Gasoline*** *(one gallon regular unleaded, national brand, including all taxes, cash price at self-service pump if available);* ***Beauty Salon*** *(woman's shampoo, trim, and blow-dry);* ***Men's Shirt*** *(cotton/polyester dress shirt, pinpoint weave, long sleeves).*
Source: The Council for Community and Economic Research, Cost of Living Index, 2021

HOUSING

Homeownership Rate

Area	2013 (%)	2014 (%)	2015 (%)	2016 (%)	2017 (%)	2018 (%)	2019 (%)	2020 (%)	2021 (%)
MSA[1]	66.1	66.7	61.4	56.0	60.1	63.8	60.1	67.1	63.5
U.S.	65.1	64.5	63.7	63.4	63.9	64.4	64.6	66.6	65.5

Note: (1) Figures cover the Tucson, AZ Metropolitan Statistical Area
Source: U.S. Census Bureau, Housing Vacancies and Homeownership Annual Statistics: 2013-2021

House Price Index (HPI)

Area	National Ranking[2]	Quarterly Change (%)	One-Year Change (%)	Five-Year Change (%)	Since 1991Q1 (%)
MSA[1]	29	4.00	24.59	64.46	277.21
U.S.[3]	–	3.33	17.54	54.45	258.04

Note: The HPI is a weighted repeat sales index. It measures average price changes in repeat sales or refinancings on the same properties. This information is obtained by reviewing repeat mortgage transactions on single-family properties whose mortgages have been purchased or securitized by Fannie Mae or Freddie Mac since January 1975; (1) Figures cover the Tucson, AZ Metropolitan Statistical Area; (2) Rankings are based on annual percentage change for all metro areas containing at least 15,000 transactions over the last 10 years and ranges from 1 to 268; (3) figures based on a weighted average of Census Division estimates using a seasonally adjusted, purchase-only index; all figures are for the period ending December 31, 2021
Source: Federal Housing Finance Agency, Change in FHFA Metropolitan Area House Price Indexes, 2021Q4

Median Single-Family Home Prices

Area	2019	2020	2021p	Percent Change 2020 to 2021
MSA[1]	238.9	265.1	331.2	24.9
U.S. Average	274.6	300.2	353.4	17.7

Note: Figures are median sales prices of existing single-family homes in thousands of dollars; (p) preliminary; (1) Figures cover the Tucson, AZ Metropolitan Statistical Area
Source: National Association of Realtors, Median Sales Price of Existing Single-Family Homes for Metropolitan Areas, 4th Quarter 2021

Qualifying Income Based on Median Sales Price of Existing Single-Family Homes

Area	With 5% Down ($)	With 10% Down ($)	With 20% Down ($)
MSA[1]	68,961	65,332	58,073
U.S. Average	70,699	66,978	59,536

Note: Figures are preliminary; Qualifying income is based on a mortgage rate of 3.13%. Monthly principal and interest payment is limited to 25% of income; (1) Figures cover the Tucson, AZ Metropolitan Statistical Area
Source: National Association of Realtors, Qualifying Income Based on Median Sales Price of Existing Single-Family Homes for Metropolitan Areas, 4th Quarter 2021

Home Value Distribution

Area	Under $50,000	$50,000 -$99,999	$100,000 -$149,999	$150,000 -$199,999	$200,000 -$299,999	$300,000 -$499,999	$500,000 -$999,999	$1,000,000 or more
City	9.7	10.8	20.2	25.0	23.2	8.4	2.1	0.6
MSA[1]	8.2	8.8	14.3	18.9	24.8	17.5	6.3	1.2
U.S.	6.6	11.0	12.3	13.6	20.0	20.5	12.3	3.7

Note: Figures are percentages and cover owner-occupied housing units; (1) Figures cover the Tucson, AZ Metropolitan Statistical Area
Source: U.S. Census Bureau, 2016-2020 American Community Survey 5-Year Estimates

Year Housing Structure Built

Area	2010 or Later	2000 -2009	1990 -1999	1980 -1989	1970 -1979	1960 -1969	1950 -1959	1940 -1949	Before 1940	Median Year
City	2.8	12.7	13.5	17.2	20.6	11.3	14.0	4.3	3.4	1978
MSA[1]	5.4	18.0	17.8	17.8	19.4	8.6	8.3	2.6	2.1	1985
U.S.	6.2	13.6	13.9	13.4	15.0	10.5	10.2	4.8	12.4	1978

Note: Figures are percentages except for Median Year; Note: (1) Figures cover the Tucson, AZ Metropolitan Statistical Area
Source: U.S. Census Bureau, 2016-2020 American Community Survey 5-Year Estimates

Gross Monthly Rent

Area	Under $500	$500 -$999	$1,000 -$1,499	$1,500 -$1,999	$2,000 -$2,499	$2,500 -$2,999	$3,000 and up	Median ($)
City	7.2	56.9	27.9	6.1	0.9	0.5	0.6	861
MSA[1]	6.5	50.0	32.2	7.9	1.6	0.8	1.0	931
U.S.	8.9	34.3	30.2	14.9	6.2	2.6	2.8	1,096

Note: Figures are percentages except for Median; Gross rent is the contract rent plus the estimated average monthly cost of utilities (electricity, gas, and water and sewer) and fuels (oil, coal, kerosene, wood, etc.) if these are paid by the renter (or paid for the renter by someone else); (1) Figures cover the Tucson, AZ Metropolitan Statistical Area
Source: U.S. Census Bureau, 2016-2020 American Community Survey 5-Year Estimates

HEALTH

Health Risk Factors

Category	MSA[1] (%)	U.S. (%)
Adults aged 18–64 who have any kind of health care coverage	n/a	86.8
Adults who reported being in good or better health	n/a	86.7
Adults who are current smokers	n/a	15.5
Adults who currently use chewing tobacco, snuff, or snus	n/a	3.7
Adults who are heavy drinkers[2]	n/a	6.7
Adults who are binge drinkers[3]	n/a	15.7
Adults who are overweight (BMI 25.0 - 29.9)	n/a	35.2
Adults who are obese (BMI 30.0 - 99.8)	n/a	31.9
Adults who participated in any physical activities in the past month	n/a	77.6
Adults who always or nearly always wears a seat belt	n/a	94.2

Note: (1) Figures for the Tucson, AZ Metropolitan Statistical Area were not available.
(2) Heavy drinkers are classified as adult men having more than 14 drinks per week and adult women having more than 7 drinks per week; (3) Binge drinkers are classified as males having five or more drinks on one occasion or females having four or more drinks on one occasion
Source: Centers for Disease Control and Prevention, Behaviorial Risk Factor Surveillance System, SMART: Selected Metropolitan Area Risk Trends, 2020

Acute and Chronic Health Conditions

Category	MSA[1] (%)	U.S. (%)
Adults who have ever been told they had a heart attack	n/a	4.3
Adults who have ever been told they have angina or coronary heart disease	n/a	4.0
Adults who have ever been told they had a stroke	n/a	2.8
Adults who have ever been told they have asthma	n/a	14.2
Adults who have ever been told they have arthritis	n/a	24.5
Adults who have ever been told they have diabetes[2]	n/a	10.6
Adults who have ever been told they had skin cancer	n/a	6.4
Adults who have ever been told they had any other types of cancer	n/a	6.8
Adults who have ever been told they have COPD	n/a	6.2
Adults who have ever been told they have kidney disease	n/a	2.9
Adults who have ever been told they have a form of depression	n/a	19.6

Note: (1) Figures for the Tucson, AZ Metropolitan Statistical Area were not available.
(2) Figures do not include pregnancy-related, borderline, or pre-diabetes
Source: Centers for Disease Control and Prevention, Behaviorial Risk Factor Surveillance System, SMART: Selected Metropolitan Area Risk Trends, 2020

Health Screening and Vaccination Rates

Category	MSA[1] (%)	U.S. (%)
Adults 50-75 who have had a blood stool test within the past year	n/a	9.3
Adults aged 65+ who have had flu shot within the past year	n/a	67.9
Adults aged 65+ who have ever had a pneumonia vaccination	n/a	72.2
Adults who have ever been tested for HIV	n/a	37.1
Women aged 21-65 who have had a pap test in the past three years	n/a	77.7
Men aged 40+ who have had a PSA test within the past two years	n/a	31.8
Women aged 40+ who have had a mammogram within the past two years	n/a	71.5

Note: (1) Figures for the Tucson, AZ Metropolitan Statistical Area were not available.
Source: Centers for Disease Control and Prevention, Behaviorial Risk Factor Surveillance System, SMART: Selected Metropolitan Area Risk Trends, 2020

Disability Status

Category	MSA[1] (%)	U.S. (%)
Adults who reported being deaf	n/a	6.8
Are you blind or have serious difficulty seeing, even when wearing glasses?	n/a	4.7
Do you have difficulty doing errands alone?	n/a	6.3
Do you have difficulty dressing or bathing?	n/a	3.0
Do you have serious difficulty concentrating/remembering/making decisions?	n/a	10.8
Do you have serious difficulty walking or climbing stairs?	n/a	11.9

Note: (1) Figures for the Tucson, AZ Metropolitan Statistical Area were not available.
Source: Centers for Disease Control and Prevention, Behaviorial Risk Factor Surveillance System, SMART: Selected Metropolitan Area Risk Trends, 2020

Mortality Rates for the Top 10 Causes of Death in the U.S.

ICD-10[a] Sub-Chapter	ICD-10[a] Code	Age-Adjusted Mortality Rate[1] per 100,000 population	
		County[2]	U.S.
Malignant neoplasms	C00-C97	135.0	146.4
Ischaemic heart diseases	I20-I25	83.1	90.2
Other forms of heart disease	I30-I51	31.9	51.9
Other degenerative diseases of the nervous system	G30-G31	50.2	39.7
Other external causes of accidental injury	W00-X59	49.8	38.7
Chronic lower respiratory diseases	J40-J47	37.1	38.1
Cerebrovascular diseases	I60-I69	34.4	37.6
Organic, including symptomatic, mental disorders	F01-F09	13.6	29.4
Hypertensive diseases	I10-I15	25.8	26.1
Diabetes mellitus	E10-E14	25.9	22.6

Note: (a) ICD-10 = International Classification of Diseases 10th Revision; (1) Mortality rates are a three-year average covering 2018-2020; (2) Figures cover Pima County.
Source: Centers for Disease Control and Prevention, National Center for Health Statistics. Underlying Cause of Death 1999-2020 on CDC WONDER Online Database

Mortality Rates for Selected Causes of Death

ICD-10[a] Sub-Chapter	ICD-10[a] Code	Age-Adjusted Mortality Rate[1] per 100,000 population	
		County[2]	U.S.
Assault	X85-Y09	7.2	6.5
Diseases of the liver	K70-K76	21.9	15.3
Human immunodeficiency virus (HIV) disease	B20-B24	1.0	1.4
Influenza and pneumonia	J09-J18	12.3	13.4
Intentional self-harm	X60-X84	20.6	13.9
Malnutrition	E40-E46	4.8	2.9
Obesity and other hyperalimentation	E65-E68	3.2	2.4
Renal failure	N17-N19	8.4	12.5
Transport accidents	V01-V99	14.7	12.5
Viral hepatitis	B15-B19	1.7	1.0

Note: (a) ICD-10 = International Classification of Diseases 10th Revision; (1) Mortality rates are a three-year average covering 2018-2020; (2) Figures cover Pima County; Data are suppressed when the data meet the criteria for confidentiality constraints; Mortality rates are flagged as unreliable when the rate would be calculated with a numerator of 20 or less.
Source: Centers for Disease Control and Prevention, National Center for Health Statistics. Underlying Cause of Death 1999-2020 on CDC WONDER Online Database

Health Insurance Coverage

Area	With Health Insurance	With Private Health Insurance	With Public Health Insurance	Without Health Insurance	Population Under Age 19 Without Health Insurance
City	88.7	57.1	42.4	11.3	8.0
MSA[1]	91.1	62.6	42.7	8.9	6.8
U.S.	91.3	68.1	35.3	8.7	5.2

Note: Figures are percentages that cover the civilian noninstitutionalized population; (1) Figures cover the Tucson, AZ Metropolitan Statistical Area
Source: U.S. Census Bureau, 2016-2020 American Community Survey 5-Year Estimates

Number of Medical Professionals

Area	MDs[3]	DOs[3,4]	Dentists	Podiatrists	Chiropractors	Optometrists
County[1] (number)	3,857	261	687	60	197	171
County[1] (rate[2])	369.6	25.0	65.8	5.8	18.9	16.4
U.S. (rate[2])	285.1	23.0	71.1	6.2	28.2	17.0

04019
Note: Data as of 2020 unless noted; (1) Data covers Pima County; (2) Rate per 100,000 population; (3) Data as of 2019 and includes all active, non-federal physicians; (4) Doctor of Osteopathic Medicine
Source: U.S. Department of Health and Human Services, Health Resources and Services Administration, Bureau of Health Professions, Area Resource File (ARF) 2020-2021

EDUCATION

Public School District Statistics

District Name	Schls	Pupils	Pupil/ Teacher Ratio	Minority Pupils[1] (%)	LEP/ELL[2] (%)	IEP[3] (%)
Amphitheater Unified District	23	13,410	17.0	54.3	5.9	18.1
Catalina Foothills Unified District	8	5,508	19.2	40.6	1.6	8.9
Flowing Wells Unified District	11	5,655	19.3	72.9	7.6	16.4
Leman Academy of Excellence	6	3,432	n/a	48.5	1.3	7.9
Sunnyside Unified District	22	15,610	19.1	91.6	16.1	12.6
Tanque Verde Unified District	4	2,180	17.4	27.7	0.3	13.1
Tucson Unified District	100	45,036	17.0	80.1	8.6	14.6

Note: Table includes school districts with 2,000 or more students; (1) Percentage of students that are not non-Hispanic white; (2) Percentage of students that are Limited English Proficient (LEP) or English Language Learners (ELL) (2018-19); (3) Percentage of students that have an Individualized Education Program (IEP).
Source: U.S. Department of Education, National Center for Education Statistics, Common Core of Data, Local Education Agency (School District) Universe Survey: School Year 2019-2020

Best High Schools

According to *U.S. News,* Tucson is home to two of the top 500 high schools in the U.S.: **University High School (Tucson)** (#17); **BASIS Tucson North** (#47). Nearly 18,000 public, magnet and charter schools were ranked based on their performance on state assessments and how well they prepare students for college. *U.S. News & World Report, "Best High Schools 2021"*

Highest Level of Education

Area	Less than H.S.	H.S. Diploma	Some College, No Deg.	Associate Degree	Bachelor's Degree	Master's Degree	Prof. School Degree	Doctorate Degree
City	14.1	23.0	26.0	8.8	17.2	8.1	1.4	1.6
MSA[1]	11.0	21.5	25.0	8.9	19.3	9.9	2.2	2.1
U.S.	11.5	26.7	20.3	8.6	20.2	9.1	2.2	1.5

Note: Figures cover persons age 25 and over; (1) Figures cover the Tucson, AZ Metropolitan Statistical Area
Source: U.S. Census Bureau, 2016-2020 American Community Survey 5-Year Estimates

Educational Attainment by Race

Area	High School Graduate or Higher (%)					Bachelor's Degree or Higher (%)				
	Total	White	Black	Asian	Hisp.[2]	Total	White	Black	Asian	Hisp.[2]
City	85.9	89.2	84.2	86.8	74.6	28.2	31.3	20.6	49.4	14.8
MSA[1]	89.0	91.8	87.5	88.3	77.3	33.6	36.7	27.3	54.7	17.4
U.S.	88.5	90.7	86.7	87.3	70.3	32.9	34.4	22.6	55.0	17.6

Note: Figures shown cover persons 25 years old and over; (1) Figures cover the Tucson, AZ Metropolitan Statistical Area; (2) People of Hispanic origin can be of any race
Source: U.S. Census Bureau, 2016-2020 American Community Survey 5-Year Estimates

School Enrollment by Grade and Control

Area	Preschool (%)		Kindergarten (%)		Grades 1 - 4 (%)		Grades 5 - 8 (%)		Grades 9 - 12 (%)	
	Public	Private	Public	Private	Public	Private	Public	Private	Public	Private
City	69.9	30.1	85.4	14.6	88.5	11.5	90.0	10.0	93.5	6.5
MSA[1]	66.5	33.5	88.1	11.9	89.1	10.9	88.7	11.3	91.4	8.6
U.S.	58.9	41.1	86.9	13.1	89.0	11.0	89.0	11.0	89.7	10.3

Note: Figures shown cover persons 3 years old and over; (1) Figures cover the Tucson, AZ Metropolitan Statistical Area
Source: U.S. Census Bureau, 2016-2020 American Community Survey 5-Year Estimates

Higher Education

Four-Year Colleges			Two-Year Colleges			Medical Schools[1]	Law Schools[2]	Voc/ Tech[3]
Public	Private Non-profit	Private For-profit	Public	Private Non-profit	Private For-profit			
1	1	4	2	0	1	1	1	7

Note: Figures cover institutions located within the Tucson, AZ Metropolitan Statistical Area and include main campuses only; (1) includes schools accredited by the Liaison Committee on Medical Education and the American Osteopathic Association's Commission on Osteopathic College Accreditation; (2) includes ABA-accredited schools, schools with provisional ABA accreditation, and state accredited schools; (3) includes all schools with programs that are less than 2 years.
Source: National Center for Education Statistics, Integrated Postsecondary Education System (IPEDS), 2020-21; Wikipedia, List of Medical Schools in the United States, accessed April 11, 2022; Wikipedia, List of Law Schools in the United States, accessed April 11, 2022

According to *U.S. News & World Report,* the Tucson, AZ metro area is home to one of the top 200 national universities in the U.S.: **University of Arizona** (#103 tie). The indicators used to capture academic quality fall into a number of categories: assessment by administrators at peer institutions; retention of students; faculty resources; student selectivity; financial resources; alumni giving; high school counselor ratings of colleges; and graduation rate. *U.S. News & World Report, "America's Best Colleges 2022"*

According to *U.S. News & World Report,* the Tucson, AZ metro area is home to one of the top 100 law schools in the U.S.: **University of Arizona (Rogers)** (#46 tie). The rankings are based on a weighted average of 12 measures of quality: peer assessment score; assessment score by lawyers/judges; median LSAT scores; median undergrad GPA; acceptance rate; employment rates for graduates; placement success; bar passage rate; faculty resources; expenditures per student; student/faculty ratio; and library resources. *U.S. News & World Report, "America's Best Graduate Schools, Law, 2022"*

According to *U.S. News & World Report,* the Tucson, AZ metro area is home to one of the top 75 medical schools for research in the U.S.: **University of Arizona—Tucson** (#70 tie). The rankings are based on a weighted average of 11 measures of quality: quality assessment; peer assessment score; assessment score by residency directors; research activity; total research activity; average research activity per faculty member; student selectivity; median MCAT total score; median undergraduate GPA; acceptance rate; and faculty resources. *U.S. News & World Report, "America's Best Graduate Schools, Medical, 2022"*

According to *U.S. News & World Report,* the Tucson, AZ metro area is home to one of the top 75 business schools in the U.S.: **University of Arizona (Eller)** (#64 tie). The rankings are based on a weighted average of the following nine measures: quality assessment; peer assessment; recruiter assessment; placement success; mean starting salary and bonus; student selectivity; mean GMAT and GRE scores; mean undergraduate GPA; and acceptance rate. *U.S. News & World Report, "America's Best Graduate Schools, Business, 2022"*

EMPLOYERS

Major Employers

Company Name	Industry
Banner University Medical Center Tucson	General medical & surgical hospitals
Davis-Monthan Air Force Base	U.S. military
Freeport-McMoran Copper & Gold	Mining
Pima County	County government
Raytheon Missile Systems	Missile systems
State of Arizona	State government
Tucson Unified School District	School districts
U.S. Customs and Border Protection	Federal government
University of Arizona	Public research university
Wal-Mart Stores	Retail stores

Note: Companies shown are located within the Tucson, AZ Metropolitan Statistical Area.
Source: Hoovers.com; Wikipedia

PUBLIC SAFETY

Crime Rate

Area	Total Crime	Violent Crime Rate				Property Crime Rate		
		Murder	Rape[3]	Robbery	Aggrav. Assault	Burglary	Larceny -Theft	Motor Vehicle Theft
City	4,319.0	11.1	84.1	177.7	425.3	381.0	2,898.7	341.2
Suburbs[1]	2,196.1	4.9	16.1	37.5	172.4	257.0	1,582.6	125.6
Metro[2]	3,298.3	8.1	51.4	110.3	303.7	321.4	2,265.9	237.5
U.S.	2,356.7	6.5	38.4	73.9	279.7	314.2	1,398.0	246.0

Note: Figures are crimes per 100,000 population; (1) All areas within the metro area that are located outside the city limits; (2) Figures cover the Tucson, AZ Metropolitan Statistical Area; (3) All figures shown were reported using the revised Uniform Crime Reporting (UCR) definition of rape.
Source: FBI Uniform Crime Reports, 2020

Hate Crimes

Area	Number of Quarters Reported	Number of Incidents per Bias Motivation					
		Race/Ethnicity/ Ancestry	Religion	Sexual Orientation	Disability	Gender	Gender Identity
City	n/a	n/a	n/a	n/a	n/a	n/a	n/a
U.S.	4	5,227	1,244	1,110	130	75	266

Note: n/a not available.
Source: Federal Bureau of Investigation, Hate Crime Statistics 2020

Identity Theft Consumer Reports

Area	Reports	Reports per 100,000 Population	Rank[2]
MSA[1]	3,729	356	95
U.S.	1,434,676	432	-

Note: (1) Figures cover the Tucson, AZ Metropolitan Statistical Area; (2) Rank ranges from 1 to 391 where 1 indicates greatest number of identity theft reports per 100,000 population
Source: Federal Trade Commission, Consumer Sentinel Network Data Book 2021

Fraud and Other Consumer Reports

Area	Reports	Reports per 100,000 Population	Rank[2]
MSA[1]	10,664	1,018	99
U.S.	4,328,977	1,304	-

Note: (1) Figures cover the Tucson, AZ Metropolitan Statistical Area; (2) Rank ranges from 1 to 391 where 1 indicates greatest number of fraud and other consumer reports per 100,000 population
Source: Federal Trade Commission, Consumer Sentinel Network Data Book 2021

POLITICS

2020 Presidential Election Results

Area	Biden	Trump	Jorgensen	Hawkins	Other
Pima County	58.4	39.8	1.5	0.0	0.3
U.S.	51.3	46.8	1.2	0.3	0.5

Note: Results are percentages and may not add to 100% due to rounding
Source: Dave Leip's Atlas of U.S. Presidential Elections

SPORTS

Professional Sports Teams

Team Name	League	Year Established
No teams are located in the metro area		

Source: Wikipedia, Major Professional Sports Teams of the United States and Canada, April 6, 2022

CLIMATE

Average and Extreme Temperatures

Temperature	Jan	Feb	Mar	Apr	May	Jun	Jul	Aug	Sep	Oct	Nov	Dec	Yr.
Extreme High (°F)	87	92	99	104	107	117	114	108	107	101	90	84	117
Average High (°F)	64	68	73	81	89	99	99	96	94	84	73	65	82
Average Temp. (°F)	51	54	59	66	74	84	86	84	81	71	59	52	69
Average Low (°F)	38	40	44	51	58	68	74	72	67	57	45	39	55
Extreme Low (°F)	16	20	20	33	38	47	62	61	44	26	24	16	16

Note: Figures cover the years 1946-1990
Source: National Climatic Data Center, International Station Meteorological Climate Summary, 9/96

Average Precipitation/Snowfall/Humidity

Precip./Humidity	Jan	Feb	Mar	Apr	May	Jun	Jul	Aug	Sep	Oct	Nov	Dec	Yr.
Avg. Precip. (in.)	0.9	0.7	0.7	0.3	0.1	0.2	2.5	2.2	1.4	0.9	0.6	0.9	11.6
Avg. Snowfall (in.)	Tr	Tr	Tr	Tr	0	0	0	0	0	0	Tr	Tr	2
Avg. Rel. Hum. 5am (%)	62	58	52	41	34	32	58	65	55	52	54	61	52
Avg. Rel. Hum. 5pm (%)	31	26	22	16	13	13	29	32	26	24	27	33	24

Note: Figures cover the years 1946-1990; Tr = Trace amounts (<0.05 in. of rain; <0.5 in. of snow)
Source: National Climatic Data Center, International Station Meteorological Climate Summary, 9/96

Weather Conditions

Temperature			Daytime Sky			Precipitation		
10°F & below	32°F & below	90°F & above	Clear	Partly cloudy	Cloudy	0.01 inch or more precip.	0.1 inch or more snow/ice	Thunder-storms
0	18	140	177	119	69	54	2	42

Note: Figures are average number of days per year and cover the years 1946-1990
Source: National Climatic Data Center, International Station Meteorological Climate Summary, 9/96

HAZARDOUS WASTE

Superfund Sites

The Tucson, AZ metro area has no sites on the EPA's Superfund Final National Priorities List. There are a total of 1,165 Superfund sites with a status of proposed or final on the list in the U.S. *U.S. Environmental Protection Agency, National Priorities List, April 6, 2022*

AIR QUALITY

Air Quality Trends: Ozone

	1990	1995	2000	2005	2010	2016	2017	2018	2019	2020
MSA[1]	0.073	0.078	0.074	0.075	0.068	0.065	0.070	0.069	0.065	0.070
U.S.	0.090	0.091	0.082	0.080	0.074	0.070	0.069	0.070	0.066	0.068

Note: (1) Data covers the Tucson, AZ Metropolitan Statistical Area. The values shown are the composite ozone concentration averages among trend sites based on the highest fourth daily maximum 8-hour concentration in parts per million. These trends are based on sites having an adequate record of monitoring data during the trend period. Data from exceptional events are included.
Source: U.S. Environmental Protection Agency, Air Quality Monitoring Information, "Air Quality Trends by City, 1990-2020"

Air Quality Index

Area	Percent of Days when Air Quality was...[2]					AQI Statistics[2]	
	Good	Moderate	Unhealthy for Sensitive Groups	Unhealthy	Very Unhealthy	Maximum	Median
MSA[1]	42.1	54.4	3.3	0.0	0.3	277	53

Note: (1) Data covers the Tucson, AZ Metropolitan Statistical Area; (2) Based on 366 days with AQI data in 2020. Air Quality Index (AQI) is an index for reporting daily air quality. EPA calculates the AQI for five major air pollutants regulated by the Clean Air Act: ground-level ozone, particle pollution (aka particulate matter), carbon monoxide, sulfur dioxide, and nitrogen dioxide. The AQI runs from 0 to 500. The higher the AQI value, the greater the level of air pollution and the greater the health concern. There are six AQI categories: "Good" AQI is between 0 and 50. Air quality is considered satisfactory; "Moderate" AQI is between 51 and 100. Air quality is acceptable; "Unhealthy for Sensitive Groups" When AQI values are between 101 and 150, members of sensitive groups may experience health effects; "Unhealthy" When AQI values are between 151 and 200 everyone may begin to experience health effects; "Very Unhealthy" AQI values between 201 and 300 trigger a health alert; "Hazardous" AQI values over 300 trigger warnings of emergency conditions (not shown).
Source: U.S. Environmental Protection Agency, Air Quality Index Report, 2020

Air Quality Index Pollutants

Area	Percent of Days when AQI Pollutant was...[2]					
	Carbon Monoxide	Nitrogen Dioxide	Ozone	Sulfur Dioxide	Particulate Matter 2.5	Particulate Matter 10
MSA[1]	0.0	0.0	55.2	0.0	12.3	32.5

Note: (1) Data covers the Tucson, AZ Metropolitan Statistical Area; (2) Based on 366 days with AQI data in 2020. The Air Quality Index (AQI) is an index for reporting daily air quality. EPA calculates the AQI for five major air pollutants regulated by the Clean Air Act: ground-level ozone, particle pollution (also known as particulate matter), carbon monoxide, sulfur dioxide, and nitrogen dioxide. The AQI runs from 0 to 500. The higher the AQI value, the greater the level of air pollution and the greater the health concern.
Source: U.S. Environmental Protection Agency, Air Quality Index Report, 2020

Maximum Air Pollutant Concentrations: Particulate Matter, Ozone, CO and Lead

	Particulate Matter 10 (ug/m^3)	Particulate Matter 2.5 Wtd AM (ug/m^3)	Particulate Matter 2.5 24-Hr (ug/m^3)	Ozone (ppm)	Carbon Monoxide (ppm)	Lead (ug/m^3)
MSA[1] Level	211	5.9	14	0.072	1	n/a
NAAQS[2]	150	15	35	0.075	9	0.15
Met NAAQS[2]	No	Yes	Yes	Yes	Yes	n/a

Note: (1) Data covers the Tucson, AZ Metropolitan Statistical Area; Data from exceptional events are included; (2) National Ambient Air Quality Standards; ppm = parts per million; ug/m^3 = micrograms per cubic meter; n/a not available.
Concentrations: Particulate Matter 10 (coarse particulate)—highest second maximum 24-hour concentration; Particulate Matter 2.5 Wtd AM (fine particulate)—highest weighted annual mean concentration; Particulate Matter 2.5 24-Hour (fine particulate)—highest 98th percentile 24-hour concentration; Ozone—highest fourth daily maximum 8-hour concentration; Carbon Monoxide—highest second maximum non-overlapping 8-hour concentration; Lead—maximum running 3-month average
Source: U.S. Environmental Protection Agency, Air Quality Monitoring Information, "Air Quality Statistics by City, 2020"

Maximum Air Pollutant Concentrations: Nitrogen Dioxide and Sulfur Dioxide

	Nitrogen Dioxide AM (ppb)	Nitrogen Dioxide 1-Hr (ppb)	Sulfur Dioxide AM (ppb)	Sulfur Dioxide 1-Hr (ppb)	Sulfur Dioxide 24-Hr (ppb)
MSA[1] Level	8	37	n/a	1	n/a
NAAQS[2]	53	100	30	75	140
Met NAAQS[2]	Yes	Yes	n/a	Yes	n/a

Note: (1) Data covers the Tucson, AZ Metropolitan Statistical Area; Data from exceptional events are included; (2) National Ambient Air Quality Standards; ppm = parts per million; ug/m^3 = micrograms per cubic meter; n/a not available.

Concentrations: Nitrogen Dioxide AM—highest arithmetic mean concentration; Nitrogen Dioxide 1-Hr—highest 98th percentile 1-hour daily maximum concentration; Sulfur Dioxide AM—highest annual mean concentration; Sulfur Dioxide 1-Hr—highest 99th percentile 1-hour daily maximum concentration; Sulfur Dioxide 24-Hr—highest second maximum 24-hour concentration

Source: U.S. Environmental Protection Agency, Air Quality Monitoring Information, "Air Quality Statistics by City, 2020"

Appendixes

Appendix A: Comparative Statistics

Table of Contents

Population Growth: City

Area	1990 Census	2000 Census	2010 Census	2020* Estimate	Population Growth (%) 1990-2020	Population Growth (%) 2010-2020
Albuquerque, NM	388,375	448,607	545,852	560,447	44.3	2.7
Allentown, PA	105,066	106,632	118,032	121,156	15.3	2.6
Anchorage, AK	226,338	260,283	291,826	292,090	29.1	0.1
Ann Arbor, MI	111,018	114,024	113,934	121,093	9.1	6.3
Athens, GA	86,561	100,266	115,452	124,962	44.4	8.2
Atlanta, GA	394,092	416,474	420,003	497,642	26.3	18.5
Austin, TX	499,053	656,562	790,390	965,872	93.5	22.2
Baltimore, MD	736,014	651,154	620,961	602,274	-18.2	-3.0
Baton Rouge, LA	223,299	227,818	229,493	222,191	-0.5	-3.2
Boise City, ID	144,317	185,787	205,671	228,057	58.0	10.9
Boston, MA	574,283	589,141	617,594	689,326	20.0	11.6
Boulder, CO	87,737	94,673	97,385	108,777	24.0	11.7
Buffalo, NY	328,123	292,648	261,310	255,805	-22.0	-2.1
Cape Coral, FL	75,507	102,286	154,305	189,633	151.1	22.9
Cedar Rapids, IA	110,829	120,758	126,326	133,125	20.1	5.4
Charleston, SC	96,102	96,650	120,083	137,041	42.6	14.1
Charlotte, NC	428,283	540,828	731,424	873,570	104.0	19.4
Chicago, IL	2,783,726	2,896,016	2,695,598	2,699,347	-3.0	0.1
Cincinnati, OH	363,974	331,285	296,943	302,687	-16.8	1.9
Clarksville, TN	78,569	103,455	132,929	156,092	98.7	17.4
Cleveland, OH	505,333	478,403	396,815	383,331	-24.1	-3.4
College Station, TX	53,318	67,890	93,857	115,802	117.2	23.4
Colorado Springs, CO	283,798	360,890	416,427	471,686	66.2	13.3
Columbia, MO	71,069	84,531	108,500	122,659	72.6	13.0
Columbia, SC	115,475	116,278	129,272	134,057	16.1	3.7
Columbus, OH	648,656	711,470	787,033	889,079	37.1	13.0
Dallas, TX	1,006,971	1,188,580	1,197,816	1,338,846	33.0	11.8
Davenport, IA	95,705	98,359	99,685	102,199	6.8	2.5
Denver, CO	467,153	554,636	600,158	715,878	53.2	19.3
Des Moines, IA	193,569	198,682	203,433	215,408	11.3	5.9
Durham, NC	151,737	187,035	228,330	276,341	82.1	21.0
Edison, NJ	88,680	97,687	99,967	99,876	12.6	-0.1
El Paso, TX	515,541	563,662	649,121	679,879	31.9	4.7
Fargo, ND	74,372	90,599	105,549	123,550	66.1	17.1
Fort Collins, CO	89,555	118,652	143,986	166,069	85.4	15.3
Fort Wayne, IN	205,671	205,727	253,691	268,378	30.5	5.8
Fort Worth, TX	448,311	534,694	741,206	892,221	99.0	20.4
Grand Rapids, MI	189,145	197,800	188,040	199,417	5.4	6.1
Green Bay, WI	96,466	102,313	104,057	104,508	8.3	0.4
Honolulu, HI	376,465	371,657	337,256	347,181	-7.8	2.9
Houston, TX	1,697,610	1,953,631	2,099,451	2,313,238	36.3	10.2
Huntsville, AL	161,842	158,216	180,105	199,845	23.5	11.0
Indianapolis, IN	730,993	781,870	820,445	869,387	18.9	6.0
Jacksonville, FL	635,221	735,617	821,784	902,488	42.1	9.8
Kansas City, MO	434,967	441,545	459,787	491,158	12.9	6.8
Lafayette, LA	104,735	110,257	120,623	126,674	20.9	5.0
Las Cruces, NM	63,267	74,267	97,618	102,950	62.7	5.5
Las Vegas, NV	261,374	478,434	583,756	644,594	146.6	10.4
Lexington, KY	225,366	260,512	295,803	322,200	43.0	8.9
Lincoln, NE	193,629	225,581	258,379	286,388	47.9	10.8
Little Rock, AR	177,519	183,133	193,524	198,067	11.6	2.3
Los Angeles, CA	3,487,671	3,694,820	3,792,621	3,973,278	13.9	4.8
Louisville, KY	269,160	256,231	597,337	618,733	129.9	3.6
Madison, WI	193,451	208,054	233,209	258,366	33.6	10.8
Manchester, NH	99,567	107,006	109,565	112,441	12.9	2.6

Table continued on following page.

Area	1990 Census	2000 Census	2010 Census	2020* Estimate	Population Growth (%)	
					1990-2020	2010-2020
Memphis, TN	660,536	650,100	646,889	650,910	-1.5	0.6
Miami, FL	358,843	362,470	399,457	461,080	28.5	15.4
Midland, TX	89,358	94,996	111,147	141,194	58.0	27.0
Milwaukee, WI	628,095	596,974	594,833	592,649	-5.6	-0.4
Minneapolis, MN	368,383	382,618	382,578	424,536	15.2	11.0
Nashville, TN	488,364	545,524	601,222	667,070	36.6	11.0
New Haven, CT	130,474	123,626	129,779	130,381	-0.1	0.5
New Orleans, LA	496,938	484,674	343,829	391,249	-21.3	13.8
New York, NY	7,322,552	8,008,278	8,175,133	8,379,552	14.4	2.5
Oklahoma City, OK	445,065	506,132	579,999	649,821	46.0	12.0
Omaha, NE	371,972	390,007	408,958	479,529	28.9	17.3
Orlando, FL	161,172	185,951	238,300	284,817	76.7	19.5
Philadelphia, PA	1,585,577	1,517,550	1,526,006	1,581,531	-0.3	3.6
Phoenix, AZ	989,873	1,321,045	1,445,632	1,658,422	67.5	14.7
Pittsburgh, PA	369,785	334,563	305,704	301,286	-18.5	-1.4
Portland, OR	485,833	529,121	583,776	650,380	33.9	11.4
Providence, RI	160,734	173,618	178,042	179,472	11.7	0.8
Provo, UT	87,148	105,166	112,488	116,886	34.1	3.9
Raleigh, NC	226,841	276,093	403,892	469,698	107.1	16.3
Reno, NV	139,950	180,480	225,221	250,903	79.3	11.4
Richmond, VA	202,783	197,790	204,214	229,233	13.0	12.3
Riverside, CA	226,232	255,166	303,871	327,569	44.8	7.8
Rochester, MN	74,151	85,806	106,769	117,134	58.0	9.7
Rochester, NY	231,642	219,773	210,565	206,357	-10.9	-2.0
Sacramento, CA	368,923	407,018	466,488	503,482	36.5	7.9
St. Louis, MO	396,685	348,189	319,294	304,709	-23.2	-4.6
Salt Lake City, UT	159,796	181,743	186,440	200,133	25.2	7.3
San Antonio, TX	997,258	1,144,646	1,327,407	1,529,133	53.3	15.2
San Diego, CA	1,111,048	1,223,400	1,307,402	1,414,545	27.3	8.2
San Francisco, CA	723,959	776,733	805,235	874,784	20.8	8.6
San Jose, CA	784,324	894,943	945,942	1,029,409	31.2	8.8
Santa Rosa, CA	123,297	147,595	167,815	178,391	44.7	6.3
Savannah, GA	138,038	131,510	136,286	145,492	5.4	6.8
Seattle, WA	516,262	563,374	608,660	741,251	43.6	21.8
Sioux Falls, SD	102,262	123,975	153,888	180,927	76.9	17.6
Springfield, IL	108,997	111,454	116,250	115,075	5.6	-1.0
Tampa, FL	279,960	303,447	335,709	395,912	41.4	17.9
Tucson, AZ	417,942	486,699	520,116	545,340	30.5	4.8
Tulsa, OK	367,241	393,049	391,906	402,441	9.6	2.7
Tuscaloosa, AL	81,075	77,906	90,468	100,633	24.1	11.2
Virginia Beach, VA	393,069	425,257	437,994	450,882	14.7	2.9
Washington, DC	606,900	572,059	601,723	701,974	15.7	16.7
Wichita, KS	313,693	344,284	382,368	390,566	24.5	2.1
Wilmington, NC	64,609	75,838	106,476	122,162	89.1	14.7
Winston-Salem, NC	168,139	185,776	229,617	245,787	46.2	7.0
U.S.	248,709,873	281,421,906	308,745,538	326,569,308	31.3	5.8

Note: (*) 2016-2020 5-year estimated population

Source: U.S. Census Bureau, 1990 Census, Census 2000, Census 2010, 2016-2020 American Community Survey 5-Year Estimates

Population Growth: Metro Area

Area	1990 Census	2000 Census	2010 Census	2020* Estimate	Population Growth (%)	
					1990-2020	2010-2020
Albuquerque, NM	599,416	729,649	887,077	915,986	52.8	3.3
Allentown, PA	686,666	740,395	821,173	841,265	22.5	2.4
Anchorage, AK	266,021	319,605	380,821	399,450	50.2	4.9
Ann Arbor, MI	282,937	322,895	344,791	368,385	30.2	6.8
Athens, GA	136,025	166,079	192,541	210,810	55.0	9.5
Atlanta, GA	3,069,411	4,247,981	5,268,860	5,947,008	93.8	12.9
Austin, TX	846,217	1,249,763	1,716,289	2,173,804	156.9	26.7
Baltimore, MD	2,382,172	2,552,994	2,710,489	2,800,427	17.6	3.3
Baton Rouge, LA	623,853	705,973	802,484	856,779	37.3	6.8
Boise City, ID	319,596	464,840	616,561	730,483	128.6	18.5
Boston, MA	4,133,895	4,391,344	4,552,402	4,854,808	17.4	6.6
Boulder, CO	208,898	269,758	294,567	324,682	55.4	10.2
Buffalo, NY	1,189,288	1,170,111	1,135,509	1,129,018	-5.1	-0.6
Cape Coral, FL	335,113	440,888	618,754	756,570	125.8	22.3
Cedar Rapids, IA	210,640	237,230	257,940	271,734	29.0	5.3
Charleston, SC	506,875	549,033	664,607	790,955	56.0	19.0
Charlotte, NC	1,024,331	1,330,448	1,758,038	2,595,027	153.3	47.6
Chicago, IL	8,182,076	9,098,316	9,461,105	9,478,801	15.8	0.2
Cincinnati, OH	1,844,917	2,009,632	2,130,151	2,214,265	20.0	3.9
Clarksville, TN	189,277	232,000	273,949	304,584	60.9	11.2
Cleveland, OH	2,102,219	2,148,143	2,077,240	2,053,137	-2.3	-1.2
College Station, TX	150,998	184,885	228,660	261,701	73.3	14.4
Colorado Springs, CO	409,482	537,484	645,613	735,480	79.6	13.9
Columbia, MO	122,010	145,666	172,786	207,248	69.9	19.9
Columbia, SC	548,325	647,158	767,598	832,925	51.9	8.5
Columbus, OH	1,405,176	1,612,694	1,836,536	2,101,543	49.6	14.4
Dallas, TX	3,989,294	5,161,544	6,371,773	7,451,858	86.8	17.0
Davenport, IA	368,151	376,019	379,690	380,274	3.3	0.2
Denver, CO	1,666,935	2,179,296	2,543,482	2,928,437	75.7	15.1
Des Moines, IA	416,346	481,394	569,633	690,585	65.9	21.2
Durham, NC	344,646	426,493	504,357	636,256	84.6	26.2
Edison, NJ	16,845,992	18,323,002	18,897,109	19,261,570	14.3	1.9
El Paso, TX	591,610	679,622	800,647	841,602	42.3	5.1
Fargo, ND	153,296	174,367	208,777	243,966	59.1	16.9
Fort Collins, CO	186,136	251,494	299,630	350,523	88.3	17.0
Fort Wayne, IN	354,435	390,156	416,257	409,419	15.5	-1.6
Fort Worth, TX	3,989,294	5,161,544	6,371,773	7,451,858	86.8	17.0
Grand Rapids, MI	645,914	740,482	774,160	1,069,696	65.6	38.2
Green Bay, WI	243,698	282,599	306,241	320,827	31.6	4.8
Honolulu, HI	836,231	876,156	953,207	979,682	17.2	2.8
Houston, TX	3,767,335	4,715,407	5,946,800	6,979,613	85.3	17.4
Huntsville, AL	293,047	342,376	417,593	464,607	58.5	11.3
Indianapolis, IN	1,294,217	1,525,104	1,756,241	2,050,933	58.5	16.8
Jacksonville, FL	925,213	1,122,750	1,345,596	1,533,796	65.8	14.0
Kansas City, MO	1,636,528	1,836,038	2,035,334	2,144,129	31.0	5.3
Lafayette, LA	208,740	239,086	273,738	490,220	134.8	79.1
Las Cruces, NM	135,510	174,682	209,233	217,696	60.6	4.0
Las Vegas, NV	741,459	1,375,765	1,951,269	2,228,866	200.6	14.2
Lexington, KY	348,428	408,326	472,099	514,273	47.6	8.9
Lincoln, NE	229,091	266,787	302,157	333,193	45.4	10.3
Little Rock, AR	535,034	610,518	699,757	740,602	38.4	5.8
Los Angeles, CA	11,273,720	12,365,627	12,828,837	13,211,027	17.2	3.0
Louisville, KY	1,055,973	1,161,975	1,283,566	1,262,287	19.5	-1.7
Madison, WI	432,323	501,774	568,593	660,212	52.7	16.1
Manchester, NH	336,073	380,841	400,721	415,305	23.6	3.6

Table continued on following page.

Area	1990 Census	2000 Census	2010 Census	2020* Estimate	Population Growth (%) 1990-2020	2010-2020
Memphis, TN	1,067,263	1,205,204	1,316,100	1,343,150	25.8	2.1
Miami, FL	4,056,100	5,007,564	5,564,635	6,129,858	51.1	10.2
Midland, TX	106,611	116,009	136,872	176,914	65.9	29.3
Milwaukee, WI	1,432,149	1,500,741	1,555,908	1,576,525	10.1	1.3
Minneapolis, MN	2,538,834	2,968,806	3,279,833	3,605,450	42.0	9.9
Nashville, TN	1,048,218	1,311,789	1,589,934	1,904,186	81.7	19.8
New Haven, CT	804,219	824,008	862,477	855,733	6.4	-0.8
New Orleans, LA	1,264,391	1,316,510	1,167,764	1,271,651	0.6	8.9
New York, NY	16,845,992	18,323,002	18,897,109	19,261,570	14.3	1.9
Oklahoma City, OK	971,042	1,095,421	1,252,987	1,397,040	43.9	11.5
Omaha, NE	685,797	767,041	865,350	940,163	37.1	8.6
Orlando, FL	1,224,852	1,644,561	2,134,411	2,560,260	109.0	20.0
Philadelphia, PA	5,435,470	5,687,147	5,965,343	6,092,403	12.1	2.1
Phoenix, AZ	2,238,480	3,251,876	4,192,887	4,860,338	117.1	15.9
Pittsburgh, PA	2,468,289	2,431,087	2,356,285	2,324,447	-5.8	-1.4
Portland, OR	1,523,741	1,927,881	2,226,009	2,472,774	62.3	11.1
Providence, RI	1,509,789	1,582,997	1,600,852	1,621,099	7.4	1.3
Provo, UT	269,407	376,774	526,810	633,129	135.0	20.2
Raleigh, NC	541,081	797,071	1,130,490	1,362,997	151.9	20.6
Reno, NV	257,193	342,885	425,417	468,268	82.1	10.1
Richmond, VA	949,244	1,096,957	1,258,251	1,282,067	35.1	1.9
Riverside, CA	2,588,793	3,254,821	4,224,851	4,600,396	77.7	8.9
Rochester, MN	141,945	163,618	186,011	219,848	54.9	18.2
Rochester, NY	1,002,410	1,037,831	1,054,323	1,071,784	6.9	1.7
Sacramento, CA	1,481,126	1,796,857	2,149,127	2,338,866	57.9	8.8
St. Louis, MO	2,580,897	2,698,687	2,812,896	2,806,349	8.7	-0.2
Salt Lake City, UT	768,075	968,858	1,124,197	1,215,955	58.3	8.2
San Antonio, TX	1,407,745	1,711,703	2,142,508	2,510,211	78.3	17.2
San Diego, CA	2,498,016	2,813,833	3,095,313	3,323,970	33.1	7.4
San Francisco, CA	3,686,592	4,123,740	4,335,391	4,709,220	27.7	8.6
San Jose, CA	1,534,280	1,735,819	1,836,911	1,985,926	29.4	8.1
Santa Rosa, CA	388,222	458,614	483,878	496,801	28.0	2.7
Savannah, GA	258,060	293,000	347,611	390,211	51.2	12.3
Seattle, WA	2,559,164	3,043,878	3,439,809	3,928,498	53.5	14.2
Sioux Falls, SD	153,500	187,093	228,261	264,437	72.3	15.8
Springfield, IL	189,550	201,437	210,170	208,224	9.9	-0.9
Tampa, FL	2,067,959	2,395,997	2,783,243	3,152,928	52.5	13.3
Tucson, AZ	666,880	843,746	980,263	1,038,476	55.7	5.9
Tulsa, OK	761,019	859,532	937,478	996,141	30.9	6.3
Tuscaloosa, AL	176,123	192,034	219,461	251,878	43.0	14.8
Virginia Beach, VA	1,449,389	1,576,370	1,671,683	1,768,956	22.0	5.8
Washington, DC	4,122,914	4,796,183	5,582,170	6,250,309	51.6	12.0
Wichita, KS	511,111	571,166	623,061	639,668	25.2	2.7
Wilmington, NC	200,124	274,532	362,315	293,339	46.6	-19.0
Winston-Salem, NC	361,091	421,961	477,717	671,156	85.9	40.5
U.S.	248,709,873	281,421,906	308,745,538	326,569,308	31.3	5.8

Note: (*) 2016-2020 5-year estimated population; Figures cover the Metropolitan Statistical Area (MSA)
Source: U.S. Census Bureau, 1990 Census, Census 2000, Census 2010, 2016-2020 American Community Survey 5-Year Estimates

Household Size: City

City	Persons in Household (%)							Average Household Size
	One	Two	Three	Four	Five	Six	Seven or More	
Albuquerque, NM	35.9	33.2	13.7	10.3	4.7	1.2	0.6	2.42
Allentown, PA	28.6	28.9	14.7	13.6	8.2	3.4	2.3	2.70
Anchorage, AK	25.9	33.3	16.1	13.6	6.3	2.4	2.1	2.66
Ann Arbor, MI	34.2	37.9	12.1	10.6	2.8	1.6	0.5	2.25
Athens, GA	34.6	34.1	15.1	10.9	3.3	1.2	0.4	2.29
Atlanta, GA	45.9	31.6	10.6	7.0	2.6	1.2	0.7	2.14
Austin, TX	33.9	33.9	14.4	10.7	4.3	1.6	0.8	2.39
Baltimore, MD	40.8	29.7	14.0	8.5	4.0	1.6	1.0	2.39
Baton Rouge, LA	38.8	31.1	14.5	9.1	4.4	1.1	0.7	2.51
Boise City, ID	33.3	35.6	14.2	10.3	4.4	1.1	0.6	2.38
Boston, MA	35.9	32.5	15.4	9.6	3.8	1.6	0.8	2.35
Boulder, CO	36.1	35.3	14.4	10.3	2.8	0.5	0.3	2.26
Buffalo, NY	40.4	28.7	14.0	9.8	3.8	1.8	1.2	2.23
Cape Coral, FL	25.8	43.0	13.3	10.7	4.8	1.3	0.7	2.70
Cedar Rapids, IA	33.0	34.4	14.7	11.0	4.1	1.5	0.8	2.33
Charleston, SC	35.8	38.2	13.6	9.1	2.5	0.5	0.1	2.29
Charlotte, NC	33.5	31.8	15.0	12.1	4.9	1.5	0.9	2.54
Chicago, IL	37.5	29.8	13.6	10.1	5.0	2.2	1.5	2.44
Cincinnati, OH	44.6	30.3	11.3	7.9	3.3	1.4	0.8	2.09
Clarksville, TN	24.2	31.9	18.3	15.7	6.3	2.2	1.1	2.64
Cleveland, OH	45.0	27.9	12.8	7.6	3.9	1.6	0.9	2.12
College Station, TX	30.4	32.1	15.3	15.5	3.6	2.3	0.4	2.50
Colorado Springs, CO	28.0	35.4	14.8	12.4	5.8	2.1	1.1	2.51
Columbia, MO	34.7	32.2	14.6	11.2	5.2	1.1	0.7	2.31
Columbia, SC	39.2	33.2	13.3	8.8	3.6	1.2	0.4	2.22
Columbus, OH	35.9	32.6	13.4	10.1	4.8	1.6	1.2	2.39
Dallas, TX	35.5	29.7	13.3	10.8	6.4	2.4	1.6	2.52
Davenport, IA	33.6	35.3	13.2	9.3	5.6	1.9	0.7	2.46
Denver, CO	38.4	33.0	11.8	9.6	4.1	1.5	1.2	2.44
Des Moines, IA	34.7	30.0	15.0	10.8	4.9	2.5	1.7	2.46
Durham, NC	34.9	33.6	14.1	9.8	4.9	1.7	0.7	2.31
Edison, NJ	17.8	28.9	20.8	21.9	6.4	2.2	1.7	2.90
El Paso, TX	25.4	27.9	17.3	16.1	8.2	3.3	1.6	2.92
Fargo, ND	37.1	34.2	13.2	9.1	4.3	1.5	0.3	2.14
Fort Collins, CO	25.0	37.4	17.5	14.4	3.9	1.0	0.4	2.56
Fort Wayne, IN	32.7	33.1	13.9	10.7	5.7	2.5	1.1	2.44
Fort Worth, TX	26.2	29.4	16.6	14.9	7.2	3.1	2.1	2.85
Grand Rapids, MI	33.0	31.0	14.4	10.7	6.3	2.3	2.1	2.51
Green Bay, WI	34.7	32.5	12.9	10.4	6.2	1.5	1.4	2.37
Honolulu, HI	34.6	30.7	14.2	10.4	5.0	2.1	2.6	2.55
Houston, TX	32.7	29.1	15.1	12.1	6.3	2.6	1.6	2.61
Huntsville, AL	36.5	34.7	14.8	8.2	3.9	1.1	0.5	2.20
Indianapolis, IN	37.2	31.9	12.9	9.9	4.9	1.8	1.0	2.49
Jacksonville, FL	31.6	33.2	16.3	10.9	5.2	1.6	0.8	2.53
Kansas City, MO	37.0	31.7	12.7	10.6	4.6	1.9	1.0	2.34
Lafayette, LA	31.9	37.1	15.3	8.1	4.2	1.8	1.2	2.43
Las Cruces, NM	31.4	31.8	16.4	12.6	4.7	1.7	0.9	2.45
Las Vegas, NV	30.0	31.5	15.3	12.1	6.4	2.7	1.7	2.68
Lexington, KY	32.3	34.2	15.0	11.3	4.5	1.7	0.7	2.36
Lincoln, NE	31.0	34.2	13.9	11.9	5.3	2.4	0.9	2.36
Little Rock, AR	37.7	32.2	12.9	10.1	4.4	1.7	0.7	2.33
Los Angeles, CA	30.4	28.8	15.2	13.0	6.8	2.9	2.5	2.77
Louisville, KY	34.0	32.8	15.2	10.4	4.7	1.5	0.8	2.40
Madison, WI	37.3	35.2	12.6	9.6	3.4	1.1	0.4	2.20

Table continued on following page.

City	Persons in Household (%)							Average Household Size
	One	Two	Three	Four	Five	Six	Seven or More	
Manchester, NH	33.7	33.6	15.8	10.2	3.7	1.8	0.8	2.33
Memphis, TN	37.9	30.2	14.7	9.4	4.2	2.0	1.3	2.49
Miami, FL	36.5	31.6	16.0	9.1	4.1	1.4	1.0	2.50
Midland, TX	26.8	28.2	16.8	15.6	7.7	3.4	1.2	2.93
Milwaukee, WI	37.4	28.6	13.6	10.4	5.7	2.4	1.6	2.51
Minneapolis, MN	40.3	31.2	12.1	9.4	3.5	1.6	1.6	2.28
Nashville, TN	35.0	33.2	14.6	9.7	4.7	1.4	1.0	2.31
New Haven, CT	37.2	28.4	15.5	9.5	5.6	2.3	1.1	2.47
New Orleans, LA	46.4	28.5	13.0	7.5	2.3	1.4	0.5	2.43
New York, NY	32.1	28.6	16.4	12.3	5.8	2.4	2.0	2.57
Oklahoma City, OK	31.8	31.6	14.8	11.5	6.5	2.5	1.0	2.58
Omaha, NE	33.2	31.7	13.9	10.6	6.0	2.7	1.5	2.46
Orlando, FL	33.2	33.5	16.5	9.9	4.1	1.6	1.0	2.50
Philadelphia, PA	37.2	29.4	15.0	10.1	4.8	1.9	1.3	2.50
Phoenix, AZ	28.2	29.6	15.1	12.9	7.2	3.8	2.9	2.82
Pittsburgh, PA	44.1	32.4	12.5	6.8	2.3	1.0	0.5	1.98
Portland, OR	34.0	35.2	14.2	10.4	3.7	1.3	0.8	2.29
Providence, RI	33.6	29.3	14.9	11.2	7.2	2.1	1.4	2.57
Provo, UT	14.5	34.3	17.8	15.4	7.3	7.1	3.2	3.14
Raleigh, NC	34.0	32.7	14.7	12.1	4.6	1.1	0.5	2.40
Reno, NV	32.4	33.9	14.4	11.1	5.0	1.5	1.3	2.33
Richmond, VA	43.0	32.9	11.7	7.5	2.7	1.3	0.4	2.40
Riverside, CA	18.8	27.4	18.2	16.4	10.1	5.0	3.8	3.44
Rochester, MN	30.6	34.6	13.2	12.1	5.3	2.2	1.6	2.37
Rochester, NY	41.7	29.0	12.7	9.8	3.9	1.6	1.0	2.24
Sacramento, CA	30.7	30.3	14.2	13.3	6.1	2.7	2.3	2.63
St. Louis, MO	45.4	30.4	11.1	7.4	3.2	1.1	1.0	2.05
Salt Lake City, UT	37.3	32.9	12.3	9.5	4.0	2.0	1.8	2.37
San Antonio, TX	30.7	29.2	15.6	12.8	6.9	2.8	1.7	2.96
San Diego, CA	27.5	34.1	15.8	12.9	5.6	2.2	1.5	2.69
San Francisco, CA	36.2	33.0	14.3	10.0	3.3	1.4	1.4	2.36
San Jose, CA	19.5	28.7	18.9	17.9	8.2	3.2	3.3	3.13
Santa Rosa, CA	28.4	32.4	15.3	13.4	6.5	1.9	1.7	2.63
Savannah, GA	33.1	35.4	14.8	9.6	4.3	1.5	0.9	2.55
Seattle, WA	39.8	34.6	12.2	9.0	2.7	0.7	0.5	2.08
Sioux Falls, SD	32.7	33.5	13.2	11.4	5.9	1.9	1.1	2.37
Springfield, IL	38.4	33.1	13.3	9.2	3.4	1.4	0.9	2.18
Tampa, FL	35.7	31.6	15.6	10.5	4.2	1.3	0.6	2.45
Tucson, AZ	35.0	31.1	14.2	11.2	5.0	1.9	1.3	2.40
Tulsa, OK	35.9	31.7	13.2	10.5	5.1	2.2	1.1	2.42
Tuscaloosa, AL	36.3	33.3	14.9	9.7	3.8	1.3	0.2	2.49
Virginia Beach, VA	24.0	35.3	17.6	14.1	6.1	1.9	0.7	2.56
Washington, DC	45.1	30.6	11.9	7.4	3.0	1.1	0.7	2.30
Wichita, KS	33.1	32.1	13.2	11.4	6.1	2.4	1.5	2.49
Wilmington, NC	39.1	36.5	12.5	7.5	3.3	0.4	0.4	2.17
Winston-Salem, NC	35.4	32.0	14.5	9.2	4.9	2.5	1.0	2.44
U.S.	27.9	33.9	15.5	12.8	5.9	2.2	1.4	2.60

U.S. Census Bureau, 2016-2020 American Community Survey 5-Year Estimates

Household Size: Metro Area

Metro Area	Persons in Household (%)							Average Household Size
	One	Two	Three	Four	Five	Six	Seven or More	
Albuquerque, NM	31.7	35.2	14.3	10.7	5.0	1.7	1.1	2.53
Allentown, PA	26.2	35.8	15.2	13.5	5.9	2.0	1.1	2.52
Anchorage, AK	25.3	33.7	15.8	13.4	6.6	2.6	2.3	2.81
Ann Arbor, MI	30.3	36.9	13.9	11.9	4.2	1.8	0.8	2.43
Athens, GA	28.9	34.8	16.1	12.9	4.6	1.4	0.8	2.48
Atlanta, GA	26.8	31.6	17.0	14.3	6.3	2.4	1.4	2.72
Austin, TX	27.4	33.8	15.7	13.5	6.0	2.2	1.2	2.68
Baltimore, MD	28.9	32.6	16.2	13.1	5.7	2.0	1.1	2.57
Baton Rouge, LA	28.0	34.4	16.8	12.1	5.8	1.7	0.9	2.68
Boise City, ID	26.1	35.8	14.7	12.4	6.4	2.8	1.5	2.67
Boston, MA	27.6	33.1	16.6	14.3	5.5	1.8	0.9	2.53
Boulder, CO	29.3	35.9	15.5	13.0	4.4	1.3	0.4	2.46
Buffalo, NY	34.0	33.9	14.1	11.2	4.3	1.4	0.8	2.27
Cape Coral, FL	28.8	44.6	11.1	8.6	4.4	1.5	0.7	2.58
Cedar Rapids, IA	28.9	36.6	14.3	12.3	4.9	1.6	0.9	2.42
Charleston, SC	29.4	35.7	16.3	11.4	4.7	1.4	0.7	2.58
Charlotte, NC	27.2	34.1	16.1	13.9	5.6	1.8	0.9	2.62
Chicago, IL	29.0	31.2	15.5	13.6	6.6	2.4	1.4	2.63
Cincinnati, OH	28.8	34.2	15.0	12.8	5.7	2.1	1.1	2.49
Clarksville, TN	24.7	32.8	17.9	14.3	6.5	2.5	1.1	2.63
Cleveland, OH	34.5	33.7	14.2	10.5	4.4	1.5	0.8	2.31
College Station, TX	29.5	32.3	15.4	13.5	5.2	2.5	1.3	2.58
Colorado Springs, CO	24.8	35.4	15.8	13.2	6.7	2.2	1.5	2.62
Columbia, MO	30.3	35.2	14.5	12.2	5.0	1.4	0.9	2.40
Columbia, SC	29.7	34.5	15.5	11.9	5.2	2.0	0.9	2.50
Columbus, OH	28.9	33.8	15.3	12.8	5.8	2.0	1.1	2.54
Dallas, TX	25.0	30.7	16.6	15.1	7.6	2.9	1.8	2.82
Davenport, IA	30.9	36.2	13.2	11.5	5.3	1.8	0.7	2.40
Denver, CO	28.4	34.1	15.0	13.3	5.5	2.2	1.3	2.64
Des Moines, IA	28.8	33.8	14.2	13.7	6.0	2.1	1.0	2.50
Durham, NC	30.4	35.7	15.2	11.3	5.0	1.4	0.7	2.41
Edison, NJ	27.9	29.5	17.0	14.5	6.5	2.4	1.9	2.67
El Paso, TX	23.8	27.5	17.5	16.7	8.9	3.7	1.7	3.01
Fargo, ND	32.2	34.0	14.3	11.4	5.4	1.6	0.8	2.31
Fort Collins, CO	24.5	39.9	15.8	12.3	4.9	1.3	0.9	2.54
Fort Wayne, IN	29.5	34.2	14.0	12.0	6.2	2.4	1.3	2.51
Fort Worth, TX	25.0	30.7	16.6	15.1	7.6	2.9	1.8	2.82
Grand Rapids, MI	24.7	34.1	15.2	14.4	7.3	2.5	1.5	2.63
Green Bay, WI	28.3	38.0	13.6	11.5	5.9	1.5	0.8	2.40
Honolulu, HI	24.4	30.5	16.7	13.2	7.4	3.5	3.9	2.98
Houston, TX	24.1	29.7	17.1	15.7	8.1	3.1	1.9	2.87
Huntsville, AL	30.1	35.7	15.4	11.7	4.7	1.6	0.6	2.46
Indianapolis, IN	29.5	33.9	14.9	12.8	5.7	1.8	1.0	2.55
Jacksonville, FL	27.6	35.2	16.3	12.1	5.7	1.8	0.9	2.60
Kansas City, MO	29.0	34.4	14.4	12.9	5.7	2.1	1.2	2.51
Lafayette, LA	26.6	33.1	17.9	12.8	5.8	2.3	1.1	2.63
Las Cruces, NM	26.4	32.5	16.8	14.0	5.7	2.4	1.8	2.67
Las Vegas, NV	28.2	32.8	15.2	12.3	6.8	2.6	1.8	2.73
Lexington, KY	29.0	35.1	15.8	12.4	4.7	1.8	0.7	2.44
Lincoln, NE	29.3	35.6	13.7	12.1	5.5	2.4	1.0	2.39
Little Rock, AR	30.7	34.1	15.4	11.6	5.2	1.8	0.8	2.51
Los Angeles, CA	24.6	28.6	17.0	15.3	7.9	3.4	2.8	2.97
Louisville, KY	30.5	34.2	15.7	11.6	5.1	1.7	0.8	2.49
Madison, WI	31.0	36.6	14.0	11.6	4.3	1.4	0.7	2.33

Table continued on following page.

Metro Area	Persons in Household (%)							Average Household Size
	One	Two	Three	Four	Five	Six	Seven or More	
Manchester, NH	26.9	35.8	16.4	13.0	5.0	1.9	0.8	2.50
Memphis, TN	30.1	32.3	16.3	11.9	5.5	2.2	1.4	2.61
Miami, FL	28.4	32.4	16.8	13.2	5.8	2.0	1.1	2.78
Midland, TX	26.6	28.1	16.5	15.7	8.3	3.0	1.5	2.94
Milwaukee, WI	32.1	34.3	13.6	11.7	5.2	1.8	0.9	2.44
Minneapolis, MN	28.1	34.1	14.7	13.6	5.8	2.0	1.4	2.55
Nashville, TN	26.5	34.8	16.5	13.2	5.7	1.9	1.0	2.57
New Haven, CT	31.0	32.9	16.2	12.3	4.8	1.6	0.8	2.49
New Orleans, LA	34.4	31.8	15.4	11.1	4.3	1.8	0.8	2.57
New York, NY	27.9	29.5	17.0	14.5	6.5	2.4	1.9	2.67
Oklahoma City, OK	28.7	33.5	15.6	12.1	6.1	2.4	1.1	2.61
Omaha, NE	28.8	33.7	14.5	12.1	6.5	2.6	1.5	2.53
Orlando, FL	24.3	34.3	17.3	14.0	6.3	2.3	1.2	2.82
Philadelphia, PA	29.0	32.2	16.1	13.5	5.7	2.0	1.0	2.57
Phoenix, AZ	26.3	34.5	14.3	12.5	6.8	3.0	2.3	2.74
Pittsburgh, PA	33.5	35.5	14.2	10.7	4.0	1.2	0.5	2.22
Portland, OR	26.7	35.5	15.5	13.4	5.3	2.1	1.3	2.54
Providence, RI	29.7	33.1	16.5	12.7	5.1	1.7	0.8	2.46
Provo, UT	12.2	28.8	15.6	15.6	12.5	8.8	6.1	3.52
Raleigh, NC	25.6	33.6	16.9	14.7	6.2	1.8	0.8	2.64
Reno, NV	27.7	35.3	15.2	12.2	5.6	2.2	1.5	2.46
Richmond, VA	29.3	34.5	15.7	12.5	5.3	1.7	0.7	2.56
Riverside, CA	19.9	28.3	16.5	16.3	10.0	4.8	3.7	3.28
Rochester, MN	26.9	36.9	13.4	13.1	5.9	2.2	1.2	2.43
Rochester, NY	30.9	35.8	14.4	11.7	4.6	1.4	0.8	2.35
Sacramento, CA	24.9	33.0	15.9	14.7	6.8	2.7	1.8	2.74
St. Louis, MO	30.1	34.5	15.1	12.4	5.1	1.6	0.8	2.42
Salt Lake City, UT	22.8	30.8	15.6	14.1	8.3	4.8	3.2	2.97
San Antonio, TX	26.8	30.9	16.2	13.7	7.4	2.9	1.8	2.99
San Diego, CA	23.8	32.9	16.7	14.8	6.8	2.8	1.9	2.86
San Francisco, CA	26.3	31.8	16.9	14.8	6.1	2.2	1.6	2.72
San Jose, CA	20.2	30.5	18.9	17.8	7.3	2.7	2.3	2.98
Santa Rosa, CA	27.0	34.7	15.6	13.1	6.2	1.9	1.2	2.58
Savannah, GA	28.3	36.4	15.7	12.2	4.6	1.6	0.9	2.60
Seattle, WA	27.4	34.0	15.9	13.9	5.3	1.9	1.3	2.52
Sioux Falls, SD	29.1	34.8	13.7	12.3	6.7	2.0	1.1	2.46
Springfield, IL	33.2	35.5	13.9	10.6	4.4	1.3	0.8	2.28
Tampa, FL	30.7	36.5	14.9	10.9	4.4	1.5	0.8	2.50
Tucson, AZ	30.9	35.5	13.3	11.4	5.1	2.1	1.3	2.45
Tulsa, OK	29.0	33.4	15.1	12.2	6.3	2.5	1.2	2.56
Tuscaloosa, AL	29.8	34.6	16.2	11.5	5.5	1.3	0.7	2.63
Virginia Beach, VA	27.3	34.7	17.0	12.7	5.4	1.8	0.8	2.53
Washington, DC	27.5	30.7	16.2	14.6	6.5	2.6	1.5	2.74
Wichita, KS	29.6	33.5	14.1	11.7	6.6	2.7	1.6	2.55
Wilmington, NC	33.3	36.7	14.1	10.0	3.8	1.2	0.5	2.36
Winston-Salem, NC	29.6	35.8	15.6	11.0	4.8	1.9	0.9	2.46
U.S.	27.9	33.9	15.5	12.8	5.9	2.2	1.4	2.60

Note: Figures cover the Metropolitan Statistical Area (MSA)
Source: U.S. Census Bureau, 2016-2020 American Community Survey 5-Year Estimates

Race: City

City	White Alone[1] (%)	Black Alone[1] (%)	Asian Alone[1] (%)	AIAN[2] Alone[1] (%)	NHOPI[3] Alone[1] (%)	Other Race Alone[1] (%)	Two or More Races (%)
Albuquerque, NM	70.3	3.1	3.0	4.5	0.1	9.8	9.2
Allentown, PA	57.4	13.8	3.0	0.8	0.0	13.9	11.0
Anchorage, AK	61.2	5.3	9.8	7.5	2.9	2.4	11.0
Ann Arbor, MI	69.5	7.0	17.4	0.3	0.1	1.0	4.7
Athens, GA	61.9	28.2	3.9	0.2	0.0	2.4	3.3
Atlanta, GA	40.4	49.8	4.8	0.4	0.0	1.4	3.2
Austin, TX	69.4	7.8	7.7	0.7	0.1	7.8	6.5
Baltimore, MD	29.7	62.3	2.5	0.3	0.0	2.0	3.2
Baton Rouge, LA	38.1	53.5	3.7	0.3	0.1	2.0	2.3
Boise City, ID	88.0	1.6	3.1	0.7	0.2	2.1	4.3
Boston, MA	52.1	24.2	9.8	0.3	0.1	6.3	7.2
Boulder, CO	86.3	1.1	5.9	0.3	0.1	1.7	4.8
Buffalo, NY	47.1	35.2	6.3	0.5	0.1	5.5	5.3
Cape Coral, FL	85.5	4.3	1.9	0.1	0.0	2.4	5.8
Cedar Rapids, IA	83.1	8.1	3.0	0.2	0.2	0.9	4.5
Charleston, SC	73.9	20.8	2.1	0.1	0.2	1.0	2.0
Charlotte, NC	46.7	35.5	6.6	0.4	0.0	6.7	4.1
Chicago, IL	47.7	29.2	6.8	0.3	0.0	10.5	5.3
Cincinnati, OH	50.3	41.4	2.2	0.1	0.1	1.4	4.6
Clarksville, TN	65.1	22.9	2.6	0.6	0.4	2.2	6.3
Cleveland, OH	39.7	47.6	2.5	0.4	0.1	3.9	5.8
College Station, TX	75.0	7.7	10.2	0.3	0.0	1.7	5.1
Colorado Springs, CO	77.3	6.3	2.8	0.9	0.3	4.6	7.9
Columbia, MO	76.0	11.1	6.1	0.4	0.1	0.7	5.6
Columbia, SC	52.6	39.6	2.8	0.1	0.2	1.2	3.4
Columbus, OH	57.4	29.2	5.9	0.2	0.0	2.3	4.9
Dallas, TX	57.7	24.3	3.6	0.3	0.0	7.6	6.4
Davenport, IA	79.9	11.0	2.5	0.4	0.0	1.2	5.0
Denver, CO	72.2	9.2	3.6	0.8	0.2	6.9	7.1
Des Moines, IA	73.3	11.4	6.5	0.3	0.1	3.2	5.3
Durham, NC	48.4	37.5	5.4	0.3	0.1	3.3	5.1
Edison, NJ	33.2	9.1	48.6	0.1	0.1	3.9	4.9
El Paso, TX	69.6	3.4	1.4	0.5	0.2	12.5	12.3
Fargo, ND	83.1	7.8	4.2	1.2	0.0	0.5	3.1
Fort Collins, CO	86.3	1.5	3.4	0.9	0.1	1.7	6.1
Fort Wayne, IN	72.0	15.0	5.0	0.2	0.0	2.7	5.1
Fort Worth, TX	60.1	18.5	4.8	0.5	0.1	9.9	6.1
Grand Rapids, MI	65.5	18.1	2.6	0.4	0.0	5.5	7.9
Green Bay, WI	74.9	4.3	4.2	3.4	0.0	6.0	7.2
Honolulu, HI	16.9	2.0	53.1	0.2	8.3	1.0	18.6
Houston, TX	51.5	22.8	6.9	0.3	0.0	11.3	7.0
Huntsville, AL	59.7	31.8	2.6	0.4	0.1	2.3	3.0
Indianapolis, IN	59.0	29.0	3.7	0.2	0.0	3.9	4.2
Jacksonville, FL	56.3	30.9	4.8	0.2	0.1	2.6	5.2
Kansas City, MO	60.3	27.7	2.8	0.3	0.3	3.9	4.8
Lafayette, LA	62.8	30.5	2.3	0.2	0.1	0.7	3.4
Las Cruces, NM	78.7	2.8	1.7	1.1	0.1	7.5	8.1
Las Vegas, NV	58.5	12.1	6.7	1.0	0.9	12.6	8.2
Lexington, KY	73.7	14.6	4.0	0.2	0.0	3.1	4.4
Lincoln, NE	84.0	4.3	4.6	0.7	0.1	1.5	4.9
Little Rock, AR	49.9	40.9	3.1	0.3	0.1	2.8	2.8
Los Angeles, CA	48.9	8.8	11.8	0.7	0.2	22.7	7.0
Louisville, KY	68.3	24.0	2.7	0.1	0.1	1.3	3.5
Madison, WI	77.5	6.6	9.1	0.4	0.1	1.4	5.0

Table continued on following page.

City	White Alone[1] (%)	Black Alone[1] (%)	Asian Alone[1] (%)	AIAN[2] Alone[1] (%)	NHOPI[3] Alone[1] (%)	Other Race Alone[1] (%)	Two or More Races (%)
Manchester, NH	82.1	5.9	5.3	0.1	0.1	1.4	5.2
Memphis, TN	27.9	64.4	1.8	0.2	0.0	3.5	2.2
Miami, FL	65.4	16.0	1.3	0.3	0.0	4.4	12.6
Midland, TX	75.0	7.6	2.3	0.7	0.0	7.4	7.0
Milwaukee, WI	42.0	38.8	4.6	0.5	0.0	8.4	5.6
Minneapolis, MN	62.9	18.9	5.9	1.4	0.0	5.0	6.0
Nashville, TN	62.3	27.3	3.6	0.2	0.1	2.8	3.7
New Haven, CT	43.6	33.6	5.2	0.4	0.0	11.6	5.7
New Orleans, LA	33.4	59.2	2.9	0.2	0.0	1.8	2.6
New York, NY	41.3	23.8	14.3	0.4	0.1	14.4	5.6
Oklahoma City, OK	65.9	14.4	4.4	2.9	0.1	4.3	7.9
Omaha, NE	75.5	12.1	4.0	0.5	0.0	2.9	5.0
Orlando, FL	57.4	24.2	4.7	0.1	0.0	5.5	8.1
Philadelphia, PA	39.3	41.4	7.4	0.3	0.0	7.3	4.3
Phoenix, AZ	68.2	7.1	3.9	2.0	0.2	10.3	8.3
Pittsburgh, PA	66.4	23.0	5.8	0.2	0.1	1.0	3.6
Portland, OR	75.3	5.9	8.7	0.8	0.7	2.3	6.4
Providence, RI	53.2	16.1	5.6	0.7	0.2	16.4	7.8
Provo, UT	85.6	1.1	2.8	1.0	1.3	2.8	5.5
Raleigh, NC	57.5	28.9	4.8	0.3	0.0	4.2	4.2
Reno, NV	72.2	3.2	7.2	1.1	0.8	9.2	6.3
Richmond, VA	45.2	46.1	2.1	0.2	0.0	2.3	4.1
Riverside, CA	52.8	5.9	8.7	0.8	0.3	24.1	7.3
Rochester, MN	78.4	8.6	7.4	0.4	0.1	1.1	4.0
Rochester, NY	45.4	39.4	3.3	0.7	0.2	4.9	6.2
Sacramento, CA	43.5	13.5	19.3	0.8	1.7	11.6	9.6
St. Louis, MO	46.4	45.7	3.4	0.3	0.0	1.1	3.1
Salt Lake City, UT	73.3	2.6	5.3	1.3	1.8	11.2	4.6
San Antonio, TX	71.9	6.8	3.0	0.7	0.1	7.4	10.1
San Diego, CA	62.0	6.1	17.3	0.5	0.4	6.0	7.8
San Francisco, CA	44.9	5.1	34.3	0.4	0.4	7.7	7.2
San Jose, CA	37.5	2.9	37.2	0.6	0.5	13.4	7.9
Santa Rosa, CA	64.0	2.5	6.0	1.1	0.5	18.9	6.9
Savannah, GA	38.1	54.4	2.7	0.2	0.1	1.7	2.9
Seattle, WA	65.8	7.1	16.3	0.5	0.3	2.4	7.6
Sioux Falls, SD	83.7	6.7	2.5	1.8	0.0	1.1	4.1
Springfield, IL	72.3	20.1	3.0	0.2	0.1	0.3	4.1
Tampa, FL	61.6	23.3	4.5	0.2	0.1	2.9	7.3
Tucson, AZ	69.3	4.9	3.2	3.3	0.2	10.3	8.7
Tulsa, OK	63.3	15.0	3.5	4.5	0.1	4.6	8.9
Tuscaloosa, AL	50.9	44.1	2.5	0.3	0.0	0.8	1.5
Virginia Beach, VA	65.1	18.8	7.1	0.3	0.1	2.1	6.5
Washington, DC	41.1	45.4	4.1	0.3	0.0	4.8	4.2
Wichita, KS	72.6	10.3	4.9	0.9	0.1	4.7	6.4
Wilmington, NC	76.0	17.7	1.2	0.3	0.2	2.0	2.7
Winston-Salem, NC	54.9	34.2	2.5	0.3	0.1	3.1	5.0
U.S.	70.4	12.6	5.6	0.8	0.2	5.1	5.2

Note: (1) Alone is defined as not being in combination with one or more other races; (2) American Indian and Alaska Native; (3) Native Hawaiian and Other Pacific Islander
Source: U.S. Census Bureau, 2016-2020 American Community Survey 5-Year Estimates

Race: Metro Area

Metro Area	White Alone[1] (%)	Black Alone[1] (%)	Asian Alone[1] (%)	AIAN[2] Alone[1] (%)	NHOPI[3] Alone[1] (%)	Other Race Alone[1] (%)	Two or More Races (%)
Albuquerque, NM	70.7	2.6	2.3	5.8	0.1	9.5	9.0
Allentown, PA	81.4	6.1	2.9	0.2	0.0	3.9	5.4
Anchorage, AK	66.7	4.3	7.6	7.1	2.2	1.9	10.3
Ann Arbor, MI	72.7	11.8	9.2	0.4	0.0	1.0	5.0
Athens, GA	71.1	20.4	3.3	0.2	0.0	2.1	3.0
Atlanta, GA	51.7	34.2	6.1	0.4	0.0	3.5	4.1
Austin, TX	72.4	7.3	6.0	0.5	0.1	6.7	7.0
Baltimore, MD	58.7	29.3	5.6	0.2	0.1	2.0	4.0
Baton Rouge, LA	58.6	35.1	2.0	0.2	0.0	1.6	2.4
Boise City, ID	86.5	0.9	1.9	0.7	0.2	4.9	4.7
Boston, MA	74.7	8.1	8.2	0.2	0.0	4.1	4.7
Boulder, CO	87.2	0.9	4.9	0.5	0.1	2.1	4.4
Buffalo, NY	78.8	11.9	3.3	0.6	0.0	2.0	3.4
Cape Coral, FL	81.3	8.3	1.7	0.2	0.1	3.6	5.0
Cedar Rapids, IA	88.9	4.8	2.0	0.2	0.1	0.6	3.4
Charleston, SC	66.9	25.2	1.9	0.3	0.1	2.3	3.4
Charlotte, NC	65.4	22.9	3.9	0.4	0.0	3.8	3.5
Chicago, IL	63.6	16.4	6.8	0.3	0.0	8.0	4.8
Cincinnati, OH	80.9	12.0	2.7	0.1	0.0	1.0	3.3
Clarksville, TN	71.6	18.5	2.0	0.4	0.4	1.6	5.4
Cleveland, OH	72.5	19.6	2.3	0.2	0.0	1.6	3.8
College Station, TX	75.3	11.6	5.3	0.2	0.1	2.6	4.9
Colorado Springs, CO	78.8	6.1	2.6	0.8	0.3	3.7	7.7
Columbia, MO	81.6	8.5	3.9	0.4	0.1	0.9	4.7
Columbia, SC	58.7	33.5	2.2	0.3	0.1	2.1	3.1
Columbus, OH	74.2	15.7	4.4	0.2	0.0	1.4	4.0
Dallas, TX	64.5	15.8	7.2	0.5	0.1	5.8	6.0
Davenport, IA	83.7	7.6	2.3	0.3	0.1	1.8	4.3
Denver, CO	78.0	5.7	4.3	0.7	0.1	4.8	6.3
Des Moines, IA	85.6	5.3	4.1	0.2	0.1	1.4	3.3
Durham, NC	61.6	26.0	4.6	0.3	0.1	3.0	4.4
Edison, NJ	55.7	17.0	11.5	0.3	0.0	10.3	5.1
El Paso, TX	69.2	3.2	1.3	0.6	0.1	13.4	12.2
Fargo, ND	87.0	5.5	2.8	1.1	0.1	0.5	3.0
Fort Collins, CO	89.2	1.0	2.2	0.7	0.1	1.8	5.0
Fort Wayne, IN	79.1	10.4	3.9	0.2	0.0	2.1	4.3
Fort Worth, TX	64.5	15.8	7.2	0.5	0.1	5.8	6.0
Grand Rapids, MI	82.8	6.5	2.6	0.4	0.0	2.8	4.8
Green Bay, WI	86.0	2.2	2.7	2.2	0.0	3.0	4.0
Honolulu, HI	20.2	2.5	42.6	0.2	10.0	1.2	23.3
Houston, TX	60.1	17.2	7.9	0.4	0.0	7.5	6.8
Huntsville, AL	69.7	22.3	2.4	0.6	0.1	1.7	3.2
Indianapolis, IN	75.3	15.4	3.4	0.2	0.0	2.3	3.4
Jacksonville, FL	67.6	21.3	3.8	0.2	0.1	2.1	4.9
Kansas City, MO	77.1	12.2	3.0	0.4	0.2	2.9	4.2
Lafayette, LA	69.7	24.4	1.6	0.3	0.0	0.9	3.0
Las Cruces, NM	78.5	1.8	1.1	1.0	0.1	9.0	8.5
Las Vegas, NV	56.6	11.9	9.9	0.9	0.8	11.9	8.1
Lexington, KY	79.8	10.9	2.9	0.2	0.0	2.4	3.8
Lincoln, NE	85.8	3.7	4.0	0.6	0.1	1.3	4.4
Little Rock, AR	69.3	23.5	1.7	0.3	0.1	1.9	3.2
Los Angeles, CA	50.1	6.5	16.3	0.7	0.3	18.9	7.2
Louisville, KY	78.3	14.9	2.2	0.1	0.0	1.1	3.4
Madison, WI	84.9	4.2	5.0	0.3	0.1	1.6	4.0

Table continued on following page.

Metro Area	White Alone[1] (%)	Black Alone[1] (%)	Asian Alone[1] (%)	AIAN[2] Alone[1] (%)	NHOPI[3] Alone[1] (%)	Other Race Alone[1] (%)	Two or More Races (%)
Manchester, NH	87.9	2.7	4.2	0.1	0.0	1.1	4.0
Memphis, TN	45.4	47.4	2.2	0.2	0.0	2.4	2.4
Miami, FL	64.0	21.0	2.5	0.2	0.0	3.8	8.3
Midland, TX	77.6	6.3	2.0	0.7	0.0	7.1	6.2
Milwaukee, WI	70.9	16.5	3.9	0.4	0.0	4.3	4.0
Minneapolis, MN	77.4	8.5	6.7	0.6	0.0	2.4	4.3
Nashville, TN	76.3	15.2	2.9	0.2	0.0	1.9	3.5
New Haven, CT	71.6	13.6	4.1	0.2	0.0	5.9	4.6
New Orleans, LA	56.1	35.0	2.9	0.4	0.0	2.6	3.1
New York, NY	55.7	17.0	11.5	0.3	0.0	10.3	5.1
Oklahoma City, OK	72.3	10.3	3.1	3.6	0.1	3.0	7.7
Omaha, NE	82.4	7.5	3.1	0.5	0.1	2.3	4.2
Orlando, FL	65.9	16.5	4.4	0.3	0.1	5.9	7.0
Philadelphia, PA	65.3	20.8	6.1	0.2	0.0	3.7	3.8
Phoenix, AZ	74.1	5.6	4.0	2.2	0.2	6.9	7.1
Pittsburgh, PA	85.9	8.2	2.5	0.1	0.0	0.6	2.7
Portland, OR	79.3	2.9	6.9	0.7	0.5	3.3	6.4
Providence, RI	80.3	5.7	3.0	0.3	0.1	5.6	4.9
Provo, UT	90.2	0.6	1.4	0.6	0.8	2.1	4.3
Raleigh, NC	65.6	19.8	6.0	0.4	0.0	3.9	4.3
Reno, NV	74.2	2.4	5.5	1.5	0.7	9.0	6.7
Richmond, VA	60.2	29.4	4.0	0.3	0.1	2.3	3.8
Riverside, CA	55.9	7.3	7.1	0.8	0.3	20.1	8.5
Rochester, MN	86.5	4.8	4.4	0.3	0.1	1.2	2.8
Rochester, NY	79.9	11.3	2.9	0.3	0.1	1.9	3.7
Sacramento, CA	62.6	6.9	14.1	0.6	0.8	6.6	8.4
St. Louis, MO	74.9	18.1	2.7	0.2	0.0	0.9	3.2
Salt Lake City, UT	78.2	1.9	3.9	0.8	1.5	9.0	4.7
San Antonio, TX	73.8	6.8	2.6	0.6	0.1	6.5	9.6
San Diego, CA	66.6	4.9	12.0	0.7	0.4	6.7	8.6
San Francisco, CA	46.7	7.2	26.8	0.5	0.7	10.2	7.9
San Jose, CA	42.6	2.4	36.6	0.5	0.4	9.9	7.6
Santa Rosa, CA	72.5	1.7	4.3	0.9	0.3	13.3	7.0
Savannah, GA	58.3	33.5	2.3	0.3	0.1	1.9	3.6
Seattle, WA	66.5	5.9	14.2	0.8	0.9	3.9	7.8
Sioux Falls, SD	87.3	4.8	1.8	1.5	0.0	0.9	3.7
Springfield, IL	82.1	12.0	1.9	0.1	0.1	0.4	3.4
Tampa, FL	75.2	12.2	3.5	0.3	0.1	2.9	5.9
Tucson, AZ	73.3	3.5	2.9	3.6	0.2	8.7	7.8
Tulsa, OK	70.1	7.9	2.7	7.4	0.1	2.6	9.2
Tuscaloosa, AL	59.9	36.0	1.4	0.2	0.0	0.8	1.7
Virginia Beach, VA	58.0	30.3	4.0	0.3	0.1	1.9	5.5
Washington, DC	51.9	25.2	10.4	0.3	0.1	6.6	5.6
Wichita, KS	79.2	7.1	3.6	0.9	0.1	3.4	5.7
Wilmington, NC	80.0	13.4	1.2	0.2	0.1	2.4	2.7
Winston-Salem, NC	74.2	17.8	1.8	0.4	0.0	2.0	3.7
U.S.	70.4	12.6	5.6	0.8	0.2	5.1	5.2

Note: Figures cover the Metropolitan Statistical Area (MSA); (1) Alone is defined as not being in combination with one or more other races; (2) American Indian and Alaska Native; (3) Native Hawaiian & Other Pacific Islander
Source: U.S. Census Bureau, 2016-2020 American Community Survey 5-Year Estimates

Hispanic Origin: City

City	Hispanic or Latino (%)	Mexican (%)	Puerto Rican (%)	Cuban (%)	Other Hispanic or Latino (%)
Albuquerque, NM	49.2	28.8	0.6	0.4	19.4
Allentown, PA	54.3	2.3	28.7	0.7	22.5
Anchorage, AK	9.4	5.0	1.4	0.2	2.8
Ann Arbor, MI	4.6	2.4	0.3	0.3	1.6
Athens, GA	10.9	6.4	0.5	0.6	3.4
Atlanta, GA	4.9	1.9	0.7	0.4	2.0
Austin, TX	33.3	26.4	0.9	0.7	5.3
Baltimore, MD	5.4	1.1	0.8	0.3	3.3
Baton Rouge, LA	4.1	1.1	0.3	0.2	2.5
Boise City, ID	9.0	6.8	0.4	0.0	1.8
Boston, MA	19.5	1.2	5.2	0.5	12.7
Boulder, CO	10.3	6.3	0.3	0.4	3.3
Buffalo, NY	12.2	0.9	9.2	0.4	1.8
Cape Coral, FL	22.6	1.8	5.0	9.3	6.5
Cedar Rapids, IA	4.1	2.9	0.2	0.0	0.9
Charleston, SC	3.6	1.4	0.6	0.2	1.5
Charlotte, NC	14.6	5.4	1.1	0.6	7.5
Chicago, IL	28.6	21.2	3.5	0.3	3.6
Cincinnati, OH	4.2	1.4	0.6	0.2	1.9
Clarksville, TN	11.6	5.8	2.9	0.3	2.7
Cleveland, OH	11.9	1.4	8.4	0.2	1.9
College Station, TX	17.2	12.4	0.6	0.2	3.9
Colorado Springs, CO	18.0	11.6	1.3	0.4	4.7
Columbia, MO	3.4	2.0	0.3	0.0	1.0
Columbia, SC	5.8	2.6	1.2	0.4	1.7
Columbus, OH	6.3	3.0	1.0	0.1	2.2
Dallas, TX	41.5	34.6	0.6	0.3	6.0
Davenport, IA	8.9	8.2	0.3	0.1	0.3
Denver, CO	29.5	22.9	0.6	0.2	5.8
Des Moines, IA	14.0	10.7	0.5	0.2	2.6
Durham, NC	13.8	6.6	0.9	0.3	6.0
Edison, NJ	10.8	1.7	2.1	0.7	6.2
El Paso, TX	81.5	76.9	1.0	0.2	3.4
Fargo, ND	3.2	1.9	0.6	0.0	0.7
Fort Collins, CO	12.3	8.8	0.4	0.1	2.9
Fort Wayne, IN	9.1	7.0	0.5	0.1	1.6
Fort Worth, TX	35.1	30.1	1.2	0.3	3.6
Grand Rapids, MI	16.3	9.9	1.6	0.2	4.5
Green Bay, WI	16.4	13.1	1.4	0.1	1.8
Honolulu, HI	7.2	2.1	1.8	0.1	3.1
Houston, TX	44.5	30.6	0.7	0.8	12.3
Huntsville, AL	6.3	3.5	1.1	0.2	1.5
Indianapolis, IN	10.4	7.1	0.6	0.2	2.5
Jacksonville, FL	10.4	1.9	3.2	1.4	3.9
Kansas City, MO	10.6	8.1	0.4	0.4	1.7
Lafayette, LA	3.7	1.3	0.2	0.2	2.0
Las Cruces, NM	60.2	51.1	0.6	0.3	8.2
Las Vegas, NV	33.2	24.9	1.1	1.4	5.8
Lexington, KY	7.2	4.9	0.6	0.2	1.6
Lincoln, NE	7.8	5.4	0.3	0.2	1.9
Little Rock, AR	7.5	4.9	0.2	0.2	2.2
Los Angeles, CA	48.1	31.6	0.5	0.4	15.5
Louisville, KY	6.1	2.1	0.4	2.2	1.4
Madison, WI	7.2	4.0	0.7	0.1	2.4
Manchester, NH	10.7	1.5	4.1	0.1	5.0

Table continued on following page.

City	Hispanic or Latino (%)	Mexican (%)	Puerto Rican (%)	Cuban (%)	Other Hispanic or Latino (%)
Memphis, TN	7.4	5.1	0.3	0.2	1.8
Miami, FL	72.5	2.0	3.5	34.5	32.5
Midland, TX	45.4	41.3	0.5	1.4	2.2
Milwaukee, WI	19.4	13.3	4.7	0.2	1.2
Minneapolis, MN	9.6	5.4	0.5	0.2	3.5
Nashville, TN	10.5	6.1	0.5	0.4	3.4
New Haven, CT	30.8	5.3	17.2	0.3	8.0
New Orleans, LA	5.5	1.3	0.2	0.5	3.5
New York, NY	28.9	3.8	8.0	0.5	16.6
Oklahoma City, OK	20.0	16.5	0.3	0.1	3.1
Omaha, NE	14.1	10.7	0.4	0.2	2.9
Orlando, FL	32.7	2.0	14.5	2.9	13.2
Philadelphia, PA	15.1	1.2	8.8	0.3	4.8
Phoenix, AZ	42.6	38.0	0.8	0.3	3.5
Pittsburgh, PA	3.4	1.1	0.7	0.2	1.5
Portland, OR	9.8	6.8	0.5	0.4	2.1
Providence, RI	43.5	1.7	9.0	0.4	32.5
Provo, UT	17.7	11.3	0.7	0.1	5.6
Raleigh, NC	10.9	5.0	1.5	0.4	4.1
Reno, NV	24.0	18.5	0.6	0.3	4.6
Richmond, VA	7.1	1.5	0.8	0.3	4.5
Riverside, CA	53.6	46.2	0.9	0.3	6.2
Rochester, MN	6.0	3.9	0.4	0.2	1.5
Rochester, NY	19.4	0.8	14.8	1.0	2.8
Sacramento, CA	28.3	23.9	0.8	0.2	3.4
St. Louis, MO	4.1	2.5	0.3	0.2	1.2
Salt Lake City, UT	21.2	15.6	0.4	0.3	4.8
San Antonio, TX	64.7	56.5	1.3	0.3	6.6
San Diego, CA	30.1	25.9	0.8	0.2	3.1
San Francisco, CA	15.2	7.7	0.6	0.3	6.7
San Jose, CA	31.0	26.1	0.5	0.1	4.2
Santa Rosa, CA	32.7	28.6	0.5	0.2	3.3
Savannah, GA	5.8	1.9	1.9	0.2	1.8
Seattle, WA	7.1	4.1	0.4	0.2	2.5
Sioux Falls, SD	5.5	2.9	0.4	0.1	2.2
Springfield, IL	3.1	1.5	0.7	0.1	0.7
Tampa, FL	26.2	2.8	7.3	7.7	8.4
Tucson, AZ	44.2	39.6	0.8	0.2	3.6
Tulsa, OK	17.1	13.4	0.6	0.2	2.9
Tuscaloosa, AL	2.8	1.2	0.3	0.1	1.2
Virginia Beach, VA	8.4	2.8	2.1	0.3	3.2
Washington, DC	11.1	2.0	0.8	0.4	7.9
Wichita, KS	17.4	14.7	0.4	0.2	2.1
Wilmington, NC	6.6	2.6	0.8	0.6	2.6
Winston-Salem, NC	15.1	9.1	1.4	0.2	4.4
U.S.	18.2	11.2	1.7	0.7	4.5

Note: Persons of Hispanic or Latino origin can be of any race
Source: U.S. Census Bureau, 2016-2020 American Community Survey 5-Year Estimates

Hispanic Origin: Metro Area

Metro Area	Hispanic or Latino (%)	Mexican (%)	Puerto Rican (%)	Cuban (%)	Other Hispanic or Latino (%)
Albuquerque, NM	49.4	28.5	0.6	0.4	20.0
Allentown, PA	17.7	1.3	9.2	0.3	6.8
Anchorage, AK	8.3	4.3	1.2	0.2	2.5
Ann Arbor, MI	4.9	2.7	0.3	0.2	1.6
Athens, GA	8.7	5.0	0.7	0.4	2.6
Atlanta, GA	10.7	5.5	1.1	0.4	3.8
Austin, TX	32.4	26.3	0.9	0.5	4.7
Baltimore, MD	6.0	1.3	1.0	0.2	3.4
Baton Rouge, LA	4.1	1.4	0.3	0.2	2.4
Boise City, ID	13.9	11.5	0.4	0.1	1.9
Boston, MA	11.3	0.7	2.8	0.3	7.5
Boulder, CO	13.8	10.0	0.4	0.3	3.1
Buffalo, NY	5.2	0.6	3.4	0.2	1.1
Cape Coral, FL	21.9	5.7	4.5	5.4	6.3
Cedar Rapids, IA	3.1	2.3	0.1	0.0	0.7
Charleston, SC	5.7	2.6	0.8	0.1	2.3
Charlotte, NC	10.3	4.6	1.0	0.4	4.4
Chicago, IL	22.2	17.3	2.2	0.3	2.5
Cincinnati, OH	3.3	1.5	0.4	0.1	1.3
Clarksville, TN	9.1	4.8	2.2	0.2	1.8
Cleveland, OH	6.0	1.3	3.5	0.1	1.1
College Station, TX	25.2	21.5	0.4	0.3	3.0
Colorado Springs, CO	17.1	10.4	1.6	0.4	4.7
Columbia, MO	3.3	2.2	0.2	0.0	0.8
Columbia, SC	5.7	2.9	1.0	0.3	1.5
Columbus, OH	4.3	2.1	0.7	0.1	1.5
Dallas, TX	29.0	23.6	0.8	0.3	4.3
Davenport, IA	8.9	7.8	0.4	0.1	0.6
Denver, CO	23.1	17.4	0.6	0.2	4.9
Des Moines, IA	7.2	5.3	0.4	0.1	1.4
Durham, NC	11.1	5.6	0.8	0.3	4.4
Edison, NJ	24.7	2.9	6.1	0.8	14.9
El Paso, TX	82.6	78.1	1.0	0.2	3.5
Fargo, ND	3.3	2.2	0.4	0.0	0.6
Fort Collins, CO	11.7	8.5	0.4	0.2	2.6
Fort Wayne, IN	7.2	5.4	0.4	0.1	1.3
Fort Worth, TX	29.0	23.6	0.8	0.3	4.3
Grand Rapids, MI	9.8	6.8	0.9	0.3	1.8
Green Bay, WI	7.8	6.1	0.7	0.1	0.9
Honolulu, HI	10.0	3.0	3.3	0.1	3.6
Houston, TX	37.4	27.2	0.7	0.6	8.9
Huntsville, AL	5.2	3.1	0.8	0.1	1.1
Indianapolis, IN	6.9	4.5	0.5	0.1	1.8
Jacksonville, FL	9.3	1.8	2.9	1.2	3.4
Kansas City, MO	9.2	7.0	0.4	0.2	1.6
Lafayette, LA	4.0	2.0	0.2	0.1	1.7
Las Cruces, NM	68.6	61.7	0.3	0.2	6.3
Las Vegas, NV	31.3	23.1	1.1	1.5	5.6
Lexington, KY	6.2	4.2	0.5	0.1	1.3
Lincoln, NE	7.0	4.9	0.3	0.2	1.7
Little Rock, AR	5.3	3.8	0.2	0.1	1.3
Los Angeles, CA	44.8	34.5	0.5	0.4	9.5
Louisville, KY	5.1	2.4	0.4	1.2	1.1
Madison, WI	5.9	3.6	0.5	0.1	1.7
Manchester, NH	7.1	1.1	2.5	0.2	3.3

Table continued on following page.

Metro Area	Hispanic or Latino (%)	Mexican (%)	Puerto Rican (%)	Cuban (%)	Other Hispanic or Latino (%)
Memphis, TN	5.6	3.9	0.3	0.1	1.3
Miami, FL	45.1	2.5	3.7	18.8	20.2
Midland, TX	45.5	41.9	0.4	1.2	1.9
Milwaukee, WI	11.0	7.4	2.5	0.2	0.9
Minneapolis, MN	5.9	3.8	0.3	0.1	1.7
Nashville, TN	7.4	4.4	0.5	0.3	2.2
New Haven, CT	18.6	2.1	10.6	0.4	5.5
New Orleans, LA	8.9	1.8	0.5	0.6	6.0
New York, NY	24.7	2.9	6.1	0.8	14.9
Oklahoma City, OK	13.6	11.0	0.3	0.1	2.2
Omaha, NE	10.7	8.0	0.4	0.1	2.1
Orlando, FL	31.2	2.7	15.1	2.5	11.0
Philadelphia, PA	9.7	1.8	4.6	0.3	3.0
Phoenix, AZ	31.1	27.0	0.7	0.3	3.1
Pittsburgh, PA	1.8	0.6	0.5	0.1	0.7
Portland, OR	12.2	9.4	0.4	0.2	2.2
Providence, RI	13.3	0.8	4.3	0.2	7.9
Provo, UT	11.8	7.6	0.3	0.1	3.9
Raleigh, NC	10.6	5.5	1.4	0.4	3.3
Reno, NV	24.5	18.9	0.6	0.4	4.7
Richmond, VA	6.5	1.6	1.1	0.2	3.6
Riverside, CA	51.5	44.5	0.8	0.4	5.8
Rochester, MN	4.5	2.9	0.3	0.2	1.2
Rochester, NY	7.7	0.7	5.0	0.4	1.6
Sacramento, CA	21.8	17.6	0.7	0.2	3.3
St. Louis, MO	3.1	2.0	0.3	0.1	0.8
Salt Lake City, UT	18.2	13.1	0.5	0.1	4.5
San Antonio, TX	55.6	48.4	1.3	0.3	5.6
San Diego, CA	33.9	29.7	0.8	0.2	3.2
San Francisco, CA	21.8	14.0	0.7	0.2	6.9
San Jose, CA	26.1	21.5	0.5	0.2	4.0
Santa Rosa, CA	27.0	22.7	0.5	0.2	3.6
Savannah, GA	6.3	2.9	1.5	0.3	1.6
Seattle, WA	10.3	7.1	0.6	0.2	2.5
Sioux Falls, SD	4.4	2.3	0.3	0.0	1.8
Springfield, IL	2.3	1.3	0.4	0.1	0.5
Tampa, FL	20.0	3.5	6.4	4.1	5.9
Tucson, AZ	37.5	33.4	0.8	0.2	3.1
Tulsa, OK	10.2	7.9	0.4	0.1	1.8
Tuscaloosa, AL	3.6	2.2	0.2	0.1	1.1
Virginia Beach, VA	7.0	2.3	1.9	0.3	2.4
Washington, DC	15.9	2.3	1.2	0.3	12.1
Wichita, KS	13.4	11.2	0.4	0.1	1.7
Wilmington, NC	6.0	2.6	0.9	0.4	2.2
Winston-Salem, NC	10.5	6.4	1.0	0.3	2.8
U.S.	18.2	11.2	1.7	0.7	4.5

Note: Persons of Hispanic or Latino origin can be of any race; Figures cover the Metropolitan Statistical Area (MSA)
Source: U.S. Census Bureau, 2016-2020 American Community Survey 5-Year Estimates

Age: City

City	Percent of Population									Median Age
	Under Age 5	Age 5–19	Age 20–34	Age 35–44	Age 45–54	Age 55–64	Age 65–74	Age 75–84	Age 85+	
Albuquerque, NM	5.7	18.8	22.4	13.1	11.9	12.4	9.3	4.3	2.0	37.1
Allentown, PA	7.8	22.6	25.1	11.6	10.7	10.4	6.7	3.3	1.9	31.2
Anchorage, AK	7.1	19.4	25.0	13.1	12.2	12.0	7.3	2.8	1.0	33.9
Ann Arbor, MI	3.9	17.8	40.3	9.9	8.0	8.1	6.8	3.5	1.6	27.5
Athens, GA	5.1	20.7	34.2	11.3	8.9	8.9	6.6	3.2	1.1	28.1
Atlanta, GA	5.4	16.4	31.6	13.8	11.6	9.7	7.0	3.2	1.4	33.2
Austin, TX	6.2	16.4	29.9	16.4	11.8	9.8	6.0	2.3	1.1	33.7
Baltimore, MD	6.3	16.9	25.8	12.6	11.6	12.7	8.4	3.9	1.7	35.5
Baton Rouge, LA	6.9	18.9	28.0	10.1	10.0	11.4	8.4	4.4	1.9	32.0
Boise City, ID	4.8	18.2	23.3	13.9	12.8	12.4	8.6	4.2	1.8	37.5
Boston, MA	4.9	15.4	34.6	12.5	10.6	10.1	6.8	3.3	1.7	32.4
Boulder, CO	3.0	18.3	37.5	10.2	10.1	9.4	6.8	3.0	1.8	28.8
Buffalo, NY	6.6	19.1	26.8	11.6	10.9	12.1	7.9	3.3	1.8	33.4
Cape Coral, FL	4.4	15.1	15.4	11.2	13.8	16.3	14.0	6.9	3.0	47.8
Cedar Rapids, IA	6.2	18.8	22.6	13.0	11.5	11.7	8.9	4.5	2.7	36.5
Charleston, SC	5.7	14.4	29.5	12.2	10.4	12.4	9.1	4.1	2.2	35.3
Charlotte, NC	6.7	19.1	25.3	14.8	12.9	10.8	6.4	2.7	1.2	34.4
Chicago, IL	6.1	16.7	27.5	14.0	11.9	11.1	7.3	3.7	1.6	34.8
Cincinnati, OH	7.1	18.8	27.9	11.5	10.5	11.6	7.5	3.3	1.7	32.4
Clarksville, TN	9.0	20.5	30.2	13.4	9.8	8.7	5.5	2.0	0.9	30.0
Cleveland, OH	6.1	18.2	23.8	11.6	12.1	13.8	8.1	4.2	2.0	36.3
College Station, TX	5.1	23.0	41.9	10.3	6.8	6.3	4.2	1.9	0.6	23.1
Colorado Springs, CO	6.3	19.3	24.9	12.7	11.7	11.5	8.2	3.6	1.8	34.7
Columbia, MO	5.6	19.4	33.8	11.5	9.2	9.4	6.0	3.5	1.5	28.8
Columbia, SC	5.3	22.5	33.3	9.9	10.3	8.5	6.3	2.8	1.1	28.2
Columbus, OH	7.2	18.4	29.3	13.1	11.2	10.7	6.4	2.7	1.3	32.4
Dallas, TX	7.4	19.7	26.3	13.8	11.8	10.5	6.3	2.9	1.4	32.9
Davenport, IA	6.4	18.7	22.4	12.4	11.9	13.1	9.0	4.0	2.3	37.0
Denver, CO	5.9	15.5	29.4	16.1	11.6	9.8	7.2	3.1	1.5	34.6
Des Moines, IA	7.0	19.9	24.7	12.7	11.8	11.9	7.3	3.1	1.6	34.0
Durham, NC	6.6	18.0	27.0	13.7	11.8	10.8	7.5	3.0	1.4	34.1
Edison, NJ	6.7	19.3	17.2	15.8	13.9	12.5	8.3	3.9	2.3	39.3
El Paso, TX	7.4	22.1	23.3	12.3	11.4	10.7	7.2	3.8	1.9	33.0
Fargo, ND	6.8	17.4	31.1	12.4	9.4	10.0	7.3	3.8	1.8	31.4
Fort Collins, CO	4.6	18.9	34.1	11.9	9.7	9.8	6.5	2.9	1.5	29.9
Fort Wayne, IN	7.1	20.2	22.4	12.3	11.8	12.2	8.4	3.7	2.1	35.3
Fort Worth, TX	7.8	22.2	23.6	14.2	12.1	10.2	6.1	2.7	1.2	33.0
Grand Rapids, MI	6.9	18.9	30.5	11.3	9.9	10.2	7.2	3.1	2.0	31.2
Green Bay, WI	7.7	20.1	22.2	12.8	12.2	12.1	7.2	3.8	1.9	35.1
Honolulu, HI	5.0	14.3	21.6	13.2	12.7	12.8	10.8	5.7	3.9	41.7
Houston, TX	7.5	19.6	25.8	14.0	11.7	10.5	6.6	3.0	1.4	33.3
Huntsville, AL	6.0	17.1	24.4	11.7	11.7	12.8	9.2	5.0	2.2	36.8
Indianapolis, IN	7.2	19.8	24.1	12.8	11.6	11.9	7.4	3.4	1.6	34.2
Jacksonville, FL	6.9	18.4	23.3	12.8	12.4	12.5	8.4	3.8	1.6	35.9
Kansas City, MO	6.6	18.4	24.4	13.1	11.8	12.3	8.0	3.5	1.8	35.4
Lafayette, LA	5.8	18.4	23.5	11.9	11.1	13.7	9.3	4.2	2.0	36.4
Las Cruces, NM	5.9	20.4	26.9	11.1	9.9	9.7	9.2	4.6	2.3	32.5
Las Vegas, NV	6.3	19.5	20.4	13.6	13.1	12.1	9.0	4.3	1.5	37.7
Lexington, KY	6.0	18.4	25.8	13.1	11.7	11.5	8.0	3.9	1.5	34.8
Lincoln, NE	6.3	20.0	26.7	12.5	10.4	10.7	7.9	3.8	1.7	32.9
Little Rock, AR	6.7	18.9	22.3	13.3	11.9	12.3	8.7	3.2	2.5	36.5
Los Angeles, CA	5.7	17.3	25.6	14.4	13.0	11.2	7.3	3.6	1.9	35.9
Louisville, KY	6.4	18.4	21.6	12.6	12.5	13.4	9.0	4.3	1.9	37.7
Madison, WI	5.0	16.0	35.4	12.2	9.7	9.6	7.1	3.3	1.5	31.2

Table continued on following page.

City	Percent of Population									Median Age
	Under Age 5	Age 5–19	Age 20–34	Age 35–44	Age 45–54	Age 55–64	Age 65–74	Age 75–84	Age 85+	
Manchester, NH	5.2	15.4	26.8	13.0	12.9	13.0	7.2	4.1	2.4	36.7
Memphis, TN	7.5	19.8	23.8	12.1	11.5	12.0	8.1	3.6	1.7	34.2
Miami, FL	5.8	13.3	23.1	14.7	14.4	12.2	8.2	5.8	2.6	40.1
Midland, TX	8.8	21.3	25.5	13.7	10.2	10.0	5.8	2.9	1.5	31.4
Milwaukee, WI	7.6	22.0	25.7	12.6	10.9	10.6	6.4	2.7	1.4	31.4
Minneapolis, MN	6.4	16.9	32.2	14.0	10.5	10.1	6.3	2.4	1.2	32.3
Nashville, TN	6.7	16.7	27.7	13.8	11.6	11.4	7.4	3.3	1.3	34.2
New Haven, CT	6.5	20.9	29.4	12.7	10.9	8.8	6.3	2.9	1.6	30.7
New Orleans, LA	5.9	16.5	24.0	13.7	11.9	13.1	9.2	3.8	1.8	37.2
New York, NY	6.4	16.4	24.2	13.6	12.5	11.8	8.4	4.5	2.1	36.9
Oklahoma City, OK	7.4	20.5	23.0	13.6	11.4	11.6	7.5	3.7	1.4	34.4
Omaha, NE	7.2	20.3	22.6	13.0	11.7	11.9	8.0	3.6	1.7	34.9
Orlando, FL	6.7	16.3	29.2	15.8	11.6	10.3	6.2	2.8	1.1	33.9
Philadelphia, PA	6.6	17.9	26.2	12.6	11.4	11.6	7.9	4.0	1.9	34.6
Phoenix, AZ	7.0	21.3	23.3	13.9	12.6	10.9	6.8	3.0	1.3	33.9
Pittsburgh, PA	4.7	14.8	33.2	11.0	9.7	11.6	8.5	4.2	2.4	33.4
Portland, OR	4.9	14.5	25.6	17.3	13.3	11.1	8.3	3.4	1.5	37.5
Providence, RI	6.1	21.0	28.5	12.0	11.0	9.8	6.4	3.4	1.8	31.2
Provo, UT	6.6	20.2	48.0	8.3	5.6	5.0	3.3	2.0	0.9	23.7
Raleigh, NC	5.7	18.5	27.5	14.3	12.8	10.4	6.6	2.9	1.3	34.0
Reno, NV	5.9	17.5	24.8	12.8	11.7	12.3	9.4	4.1	1.5	36.1
Richmond, VA	5.8	15.3	30.4	12.1	10.9	12.4	8.0	3.4	1.7	34.1
Riverside, CA	6.1	22.5	25.8	12.8	11.7	10.0	6.6	3.1	1.4	31.8
Rochester, MN	7.2	18.8	22.6	13.3	11.1	12.0	8.1	4.2	2.7	35.9
Rochester, NY	6.4	19.1	28.7	11.7	10.9	11.4	7.0	3.3	1.3	32.4
Sacramento, CA	6.5	18.6	25.2	13.7	11.5	11.2	8.0	3.6	1.8	34.9
St. Louis, MO	6.3	15.1	26.9	13.3	11.6	13.1	8.3	3.6	1.7	36.0
Salt Lake City, UT	5.9	16.5	32.0	14.1	9.8	10.0	6.9	3.4	1.3	32.5
San Antonio, TX	6.9	20.9	24.0	13.4	11.9	10.7	7.2	3.4	1.6	33.8
San Diego, CA	5.8	16.6	27.3	14.1	12.2	10.8	7.7	3.8	1.8	35.2
San Francisco, CA	4.5	10.4	28.8	15.8	13.1	11.6	8.7	4.4	2.6	38.3
San Jose, CA	5.9	18.3	22.6	14.6	13.7	12.0	7.5	3.8	1.7	37.1
Santa Rosa, CA	5.5	18.2	19.9	13.5	12.5	12.6	10.2	4.9	2.6	39.6
Savannah, GA	6.5	18.5	28.4	11.9	9.9	11.1	7.8	4.0	1.8	32.9
Seattle, WA	4.6	12.4	32.6	15.5	12.2	10.3	7.6	3.2	1.7	35.2
Sioux Falls, SD	7.6	20.0	23.8	13.3	11.1	11.4	8.0	3.3	1.7	34.2
Springfield, IL	6.0	18.5	19.8	11.4	12.2	14.1	10.4	5.2	2.4	39.9
Tampa, FL	6.3	18.4	24.1	13.5	13.2	11.9	7.4	3.8	1.5	35.9
Tucson, AZ	5.7	18.9	26.8	12.0	10.8	11.0	8.4	4.5	2.0	34.0
Tulsa, OK	7.0	20.2	22.6	12.5	11.3	12.1	8.6	4.1	1.7	35.2
Tuscaloosa, AL	5.4	22.3	29.0	10.5	9.7	10.0	7.7	3.9	1.4	29.5
Virginia Beach, VA	6.3	18.2	23.6	13.2	12.4	12.3	8.4	4.2	1.6	36.4
Washington, DC	6.4	14.6	30.8	15.1	10.8	10.0	7.0	3.6	1.6	34.1
Wichita, KS	6.7	20.7	22.2	12.2	11.4	12.2	8.7	3.8	2.0	35.3
Wilmington, NC	4.7	17.0	26.0	11.6	10.7	12.6	9.8	4.7	2.7	37.1
Winston-Salem, NC	6.2	21.1	21.6	12.1	12.2	12.4	8.3	4.4	1.8	35.9
U.S.	6.0	19.1	20.6	12.7	12.7	12.9	9.4	4.7	2.0	38.2

Source: U.S. Census Bureau, 2016-2020 American Community Survey 5-Year Estimates

Age: Metro Area

Metro Area	Percent of Population									Median Age
	Under Age 5	Age 5–19	Age 20–34	Age 35–44	Age 45–54	Age 55–64	Age 65–74	Age 75–84	Age 85+	
Albuquerque, NM	5.5	19.0	20.5	12.8	12.1	13.1	10.1	4.7	1.9	38.5
Allentown, PA	5.3	18.5	18.6	11.9	13.4	14.1	10.1	5.1	2.8	41.3
Anchorage, AK	7.1	20.1	23.8	13.2	12.2	12.4	7.5	2.8	1.0	34.3
Ann Arbor, MI	4.9	19.4	27.4	11.5	11.6	11.4	8.5	3.8	1.6	33.9
Athens, GA	5.3	21.0	26.7	12.0	11.1	10.9	7.9	3.9	1.2	32.5
Atlanta, GA	6.2	20.9	20.7	13.9	14.2	11.9	7.8	3.3	1.2	36.6
Austin, TX	6.3	19.4	24.3	15.7	12.8	10.6	7.0	2.7	1.2	35.0
Baltimore, MD	6.0	18.4	20.6	12.7	13.2	13.5	9.1	4.4	2.0	38.5
Baton Rouge, LA	6.5	19.9	22.4	12.8	12.0	12.2	8.8	4.0	1.4	35.9
Boise City, ID	6.2	21.5	20.0	13.5	12.4	11.9	9.0	4.2	1.4	36.6
Boston, MA	5.3	17.5	22.2	12.5	13.4	13.3	9.1	4.4	2.3	38.8
Boulder, CO	4.4	18.8	24.3	12.6	12.9	12.6	8.9	3.7	1.8	36.9
Buffalo, NY	5.4	17.4	20.3	11.2	12.8	14.6	10.3	5.1	2.8	40.8
Cape Coral, FL	4.6	15.0	15.8	10.3	11.7	14.0	15.5	9.5	3.5	48.8
Cedar Rapids, IA	6.2	19.4	19.4	12.8	12.6	13.0	9.3	4.7	2.4	38.6
Charleston, SC	6.0	18.4	22.0	13.2	12.5	12.8	9.5	4.1	1.5	37.4
Charlotte, NC	6.2	20.0	20.2	13.8	14.1	12.1	8.4	3.8	1.5	37.6
Chicago, IL	6.0	19.2	20.9	13.3	13.1	12.7	8.5	4.1	1.9	37.7
Cincinnati, OH	6.2	20.0	19.9	12.4	12.8	13.4	9.1	4.3	1.9	38.0
Clarksville, TN	8.4	20.7	26.8	12.5	10.6	9.9	6.7	3.2	1.2	31.2
Cleveland, OH	5.5	18.0	19.0	11.6	12.9	14.5	10.5	5.4	2.6	41.4
College Station, TX	6.1	20.8	32.6	11.1	9.5	9.2	6.4	3.0	1.3	28.1
Colorado Springs, CO	6.5	20.0	23.7	12.7	11.8	12.0	8.2	3.5	1.5	34.8
Columbia, MO	5.8	19.3	28.2	11.8	10.6	11.3	7.8	3.8	1.5	32.4
Columbia, SC	5.7	19.9	21.7	12.5	12.5	12.7	9.2	4.2	1.5	36.9
Columbus, OH	6.6	19.7	22.2	13.5	12.8	12.0	8.1	3.7	1.5	36.1
Dallas, TX	6.9	21.7	21.4	14.1	13.3	11.4	7.0	3.1	1.2	35.0
Davenport, IA	6.1	19.3	18.2	12.4	12.2	13.7	10.3	5.3	2.5	39.9
Denver, CO	5.9	18.7	22.7	14.7	13.0	12.0	8.1	3.4	1.5	36.7
Des Moines, IA	6.9	20.4	20.7	13.9	12.5	11.9	8.1	3.9	1.7	36.4
Durham, NC	5.6	18.4	22.4	12.9	12.8	12.6	9.4	4.2	1.8	37.7
Edison, NJ	6.1	17.7	21.1	13.0	13.4	12.9	8.9	4.7	2.3	38.8
El Paso, TX	7.5	22.7	23.4	12.5	11.4	10.4	6.9	3.5	1.7	32.4
Fargo, ND	7.0	19.7	27.1	13.1	10.3	10.6	7.0	3.5	1.8	32.7
Fort Collins, CO	5.0	18.3	25.2	12.4	11.0	12.5	9.7	4.0	1.9	36.2
Fort Wayne, IN	6.9	20.9	20.2	12.3	12.2	12.5	8.9	3.9	2.1	36.5
Fort Worth, TX	6.9	21.7	21.4	14.1	13.3	11.4	7.0	3.1	1.2	35.0
Grand Rapids, MI	6.4	20.5	21.9	12.4	12.1	12.4	8.4	4.0	2.0	35.9
Green Bay, WI	6.1	19.6	19.2	12.5	12.9	13.9	9.4	4.6	1.9	38.8
Honolulu, HI	6.4	16.9	22.3	12.7	11.9	11.9	9.6	5.1	3.1	38.2
Houston, TX	7.2	21.9	21.5	14.3	12.8	11.2	7.0	3.0	1.1	34.5
Huntsville, AL	5.8	18.7	20.5	12.4	13.7	13.8	8.8	4.6	1.6	38.8
Indianapolis, IN	6.6	20.4	20.8	13.3	12.9	12.4	8.2	3.8	1.7	36.6
Jacksonville, FL	6.2	18.4	20.6	12.7	13.0	13.3	9.7	4.4	1.7	38.6
Kansas City, MO	6.5	20.0	20.1	13.2	12.6	12.9	8.8	4.2	1.9	37.5
Lafayette, LA	6.8	20.1	21.0	12.7	12.2	13.0	8.5	3.9	1.7	36.3
Las Cruces, NM	6.4	21.9	23.7	11.0	10.2	11.1	9.0	5.0	1.7	33.3
Las Vegas, NV	6.2	19.0	21.0	13.8	13.2	11.8	9.1	4.3	1.4	37.5
Lexington, KY	6.1	19.0	23.1	13.0	12.4	12.1	8.6	4.1	1.5	36.2
Lincoln, NE	6.3	20.3	24.9	12.4	10.7	11.3	8.4	3.9	1.8	33.9
Little Rock, AR	6.3	19.6	21.1	13.0	12.2	12.4	9.2	4.2	1.9	37.1
Los Angeles, CA	5.9	18.4	22.7	13.5	13.5	12.1	7.9	4.0	2.0	37.1
Louisville, KY	6.1	18.8	19.8	12.8	13.0	13.6	9.6	4.4	1.9	39.1
Madison, WI	5.6	18.0	24.3	13.1	12.1	12.4	8.9	3.9	1.8	36.3

Table continued on following page.

Metro Area	Percent of Population									Median Age
	Under Age 5	Age 5–19	Age 20–34	Age 35–44	Age 45–54	Age 55–64	Age 65–74	Age 75–84	Age 85+	
Manchester, NH	5.2	17.6	20.1	12.2	14.4	14.9	9.3	4.4	2.0	40.8
Memphis, TN	6.7	20.7	20.7	12.7	12.7	12.6	8.6	3.8	1.5	36.5
Miami, FL	5.6	17.0	19.2	13.1	14.0	12.9	9.6	5.8	2.9	41.2
Midland, TX	8.7	22.5	23.8	14.0	10.3	10.4	5.9	2.8	1.5	31.8
Milwaukee, WI	6.2	19.4	20.3	12.6	12.5	13.4	9.0	4.3	2.3	38.0
Minneapolis, MN	6.4	19.6	20.7	13.4	12.9	13.0	8.3	3.8	1.8	37.2
Nashville, TN	6.3	19.2	22.2	13.7	13.0	12.3	8.2	3.7	1.4	36.5
New Haven, CT	5.2	18.1	20.3	11.8	13.4	14.0	9.8	4.9	2.7	40.5
New Orleans, LA	6.2	18.2	20.6	13.0	12.5	13.6	9.7	4.2	1.9	38.6
New York, NY	6.1	17.7	21.1	13.0	13.4	12.9	8.9	4.7	2.3	38.8
Oklahoma City, OK	6.7	20.5	22.1	13.2	11.6	12.0	8.4	4.1	1.5	35.5
Omaha, NE	7.1	20.9	20.7	13.3	12.1	12.2	8.2	3.8	1.7	35.9
Orlando, FL	5.8	18.5	22.1	13.8	13.1	11.8	8.7	4.4	1.8	37.4
Philadelphia, PA	5.8	18.4	20.7	12.4	13.1	13.5	9.2	4.6	2.2	38.9
Phoenix, AZ	6.2	20.1	21.0	13.0	12.4	11.5	9.1	4.8	1.8	36.9
Pittsburgh, PA	5.1	16.3	19.2	11.6	12.8	15.1	11.2	5.7	3.1	43.1
Portland, OR	5.6	17.9	21.4	14.7	13.2	12.3	9.2	3.9	1.8	38.3
Providence, RI	5.2	17.7	20.4	11.9	13.5	14.1	9.7	4.9	2.5	40.4
Provo, UT	9.3	28.1	26.9	12.7	8.5	6.7	4.6	2.4	0.8	25.0
Raleigh, NC	6.1	20.6	20.5	14.6	14.3	11.7	7.6	3.1	1.4	36.9
Reno, NV	5.9	18.0	21.6	12.4	12.5	13.2	10.4	4.5	1.6	38.6
Richmond, VA	5.8	18.4	20.6	12.8	13.3	13.4	9.5	4.3	1.8	38.9
Riverside, CA	6.7	21.9	21.8	12.9	12.3	11.3	7.7	3.9	1.5	34.8
Rochester, MN	6.6	19.8	19.0	12.8	12.0	13.3	9.1	4.8	2.6	38.5
Rochester, NY	5.3	18.3	20.1	11.2	12.9	14.3	10.3	5.0	2.5	40.3
Sacramento, CA	6.0	19.5	21.0	13.0	12.5	12.6	9.1	4.3	2.0	37.6
St. Louis, MO	5.9	18.5	19.6	12.5	12.7	14.1	9.6	4.8	2.2	39.5
Salt Lake City, UT	7.4	22.5	23.3	14.7	11.2	10.0	6.6	3.1	1.1	32.9
San Antonio, TX	6.8	21.2	22.1	13.4	12.2	11.2	7.8	3.6	1.6	34.9
San Diego, CA	6.2	18.2	24.0	13.4	12.3	11.8	8.2	4.0	2.0	36.1
San Francisco, CA	5.4	16.4	21.9	14.5	13.6	12.6	9.0	4.4	2.2	39.1
San Jose, CA	5.9	18.5	22.3	14.4	13.7	11.8	7.5	4.0	2.0	37.2
Santa Rosa, CA	4.9	17.2	18.5	12.6	12.7	14.4	12.0	5.1	2.5	42.4
Savannah, GA	6.5	19.4	22.9	13.1	11.8	11.8	8.8	4.0	1.7	35.7
Seattle, WA	6.1	17.5	23.1	14.5	13.1	12.3	8.1	3.5	1.7	37.0
Sioux Falls, SD	7.4	20.7	21.3	13.6	11.5	12.0	8.2	3.4	1.8	35.3
Springfield, IL	5.7	18.9	18.2	12.3	12.8	14.2	10.5	5.1	2.3	40.7
Tampa, FL	5.3	16.7	18.9	12.4	13.3	13.7	11.0	6.1	2.6	42.2
Tucson, AZ	5.5	18.3	21.5	11.4	11.0	12.4	11.2	6.3	2.3	38.7
Tulsa, OK	6.7	20.3	20.0	12.7	12.2	12.6	9.1	4.7	1.7	37.2
Tuscaloosa, AL	6.0	20.3	24.3	11.7	11.4	11.9	8.6	4.1	1.6	34.6
Virginia Beach, VA	6.2	18.5	23.1	12.5	12.1	12.9	8.7	4.4	1.6	36.5
Washington, DC	6.4	19.0	21.1	14.4	13.8	12.2	7.9	3.7	1.5	37.2
Wichita, KS	6.7	21.4	20.4	12.2	11.5	12.8	8.7	4.1	2.2	36.2
Wilmington, NC	5.0	17.5	21.0	12.8	12.6	13.5	10.7	4.9	2.1	39.8
Winston-Salem, NC	5.6	19.4	18.4	11.7	13.8	13.8	10.1	5.3	1.9	40.6
U.S.	6.0	19.1	20.6	12.7	12.7	12.9	9.4	4.7	2.0	38.2

Note: Figures cover the Metropolitan Statistical Area (MSA)
Source: U.S. Census Bureau, 2016-2020 American Community Survey 5-Year Estimates

Religious Groups by Family

Area[1]	Catholic	Baptist	Non-Den.	Methodist[2]	Lutheran	LDS[3]	Pente-costal	Presby-terian[4]	Muslim[5]	Judaism
Albuquerque, NM	27.1	3.7	4.2	1.4	0.9	2.3	1.4	1.0	0.2	0.2
Allentown, PA	23.1	0.4	1.9	3.9	7.9	0.3	0.4	6.2	0.6	0.6
Anchorage, AK	6.9	5.0	6.4	1.3	1.9	5.1	1.8	0.6	0.2	0.1
Ann Arbor, MI	12.3	2.2	1.5	3.0	2.8	0.8	1.9	2.9	1.2	0.9
Athens, GA	4.4	16.2	2.2	8.3	0.3	0.8	2.8	2.0	0.3	0.2
Atlanta, GA	7.4	17.4	6.8	7.8	0.5	0.7	2.6	1.8	0.7	0.5
Austin, TX	16.0	10.3	4.5	3.6	1.9	1.1	0.8	1.0	1.2	0.2
Baltimore, MD	16.6	4.1	4.8	6.0	2.1	0.5	1.0	1.3	0.5	1.8
Baton Rouge, LA	22.5	18.2	9.6	4.6	0.2	0.7	1.1	0.6	0.2	0.1
Boise City, ID	8.0	2.9	4.1	2.1	1.1	15.8	2.3	0.6	0.1	0.1
Boston, MA	44.3	1.1	1.0	0.9	0.3	0.4	0.6	1.6	0.4	1.4
Boulder, CO	20.1	2.3	4.7	1.7	3.0	2.9	0.4	2.0	0.1	0.7
Buffalo, NY	35.6	2.7	2.0	2.3	3.3	0.3	1.0	1.9	1.6	0.7
Cape Coral, FL	16.2	4.9	3.0	2.5	1.1	0.5	4.3	1.4	0.9	0.2
Cedar Rapids, IA	18.8	2.3	3.0	7.3	11.3	0.8	1.8	3.2	0.5	0.1
Charleston, SC	6.1	12.4	7.0	10.0	1.1	0.9	2.0	2.3	0.1	0.3
Charlotte, NC	5.9	17.2	6.7	8.6	1.3	0.7	3.2	4.5	0.2	0.3
Chicago, IL	34.2	3.2	4.4	1.9	3.0	0.3	1.2	1.9	3.2	0.8
Cincinnati, OH	19.0	9.5	3.6	3.8	1.1	0.5	2.2	1.5	0.2	0.5
Clarksville, TN	4.0	30.9	2.2	6.1	0.5	1.5	1.8	1.0	0.1	<0.1
Cleveland, OH	28.8	4.3	3.3	2.8	2.5	0.3	1.1	2.0	0.1	1.4
College Station, TX	11.7	15.6	3.9	4.7	1.5	1.2	0.6	0.9	1.1	<0.1
Colorado Springs, CO	8.3	4.3	7.4	2.4	1.9	3.0	1.0	2.0	<0.1	0.1
Columbia, MO	6.6	14.6	5.4	4.3	1.7	1.3	1.0	2.3	0.3	0.2
Columbia, SC	3.1	18.0	5.2	9.3	3.4	1.0	2.6	3.3	0.1	0.2
Columbus, OH	11.7	5.3	3.5	4.7	2.4	0.7	1.9	2.0	0.8	0.5
Dallas, TX	13.3	18.7	7.7	5.2	0.7	1.1	2.1	0.9	2.4	0.3
Davenport, IA	14.9	4.9	2.7	5.3	8.6	0.8	1.4	2.9	0.9	0.1
Denver, CO	16.0	2.9	4.6	1.7	2.1	2.4	1.2	1.5	0.5	0.6
Des Moines, IA	13.6	4.7	3.3	6.9	8.2	0.9	2.3	2.9	0.3	0.3
Durham, NC	5.0	13.8	5.6	8.1	0.4	0.7	1.3	2.5	0.4	0.5
Edison, NJ	36.9	1.8	1.7	1.3	0.7	0.3	0.8	1.0	2.3	4.7
El Paso, TX	43.2	3.7	4.9	0.8	0.3	1.5	1.4	0.2	<0.1	0.2
Fargo, ND	17.4	0.4	0.4	3.3	32.5	0.6	1.5	1.8	0.1	<0.1
Fort Collins, CO	11.8	2.2	6.3	4.3	3.4	2.9	4.7	1.9	0.1	<0.1
Fort Wayne, IN	14.2	6.0	6.8	5.1	8.5	0.4	1.4	1.6	0.2	0.1
Fort Worth, TX	13.3	18.7	7.7	5.2	0.7	1.1	2.1	0.9	2.4	0.3
Grand Rapids, MI	17.1	1.7	8.3	3.0	2.1	0.5	1.1	9.9	1.0	0.1
Green Bay, WI	42.0	0.7	3.4	2.2	12.7	0.3	0.6	1.0	0.1	<0.1
Honolulu, HI	18.2	1.9	2.2	0.8	0.3	5.1	4.1	1.4	<0.1	<0.1
Houston, TX	17.0	16.0	7.2	4.8	1.0	1.1	1.5	0.8	2.6	0.3
Huntsville, AL	3.9	27.6	3.1	7.5	0.7	1.1	1.2	1.7	0.2	0.1
Indianapolis, IN	10.5	10.2	7.1	4.9	1.6	0.7	1.6	1.6	0.2	0.3
Jacksonville, FL	9.8	18.5	7.7	4.5	0.6	1.1	1.9	1.6	0.6	0.4
Kansas City, MO	12.6	13.1	5.2	5.8	2.2	2.4	2.6	1.6	0.3	0.4
Lafayette, LA	47.0	14.7	3.9	2.5	0.2	0.4	2.9	0.1	0.1	<0.1
Las Cruces, NM	31.7	5.7	1.2	2.0	0.5	2.1	2.7	0.6	0.2	0.2
Las Vegas, NV	18.1	2.9	3.0	0.4	0.7	6.3	1.5	0.2	<0.1	0.3
Lexington, KY	6.7	24.9	2.3	5.9	0.4	1.0	2.1	1.3	0.1	0.3
Lincoln, NE	14.7	2.4	1.9	7.1	11.2	1.1	1.4	3.9	0.2	0.1
Little Rock, AR	4.5	25.9	6.0	7.3	0.5	0.9	2.8	0.8	0.1	0.1
Los Angeles, CA	33.8	2.7	3.6	1.0	0.6	1.7	1.7	0.9	0.7	0.9
Louisville, KY	13.6	25.0	1.7	3.7	0.6	0.8	0.9	1.1	0.5	0.4
Madison, WI	21.8	1.1	1.5	3.6	12.7	0.5	0.3	2.1	0.4	0.4
Manchester, NH	31.1	1.3	2.3	1.1	0.5	0.6	0.4	2.0	0.3	0.5

Table continued on following page.

Area[1]	Catholic	Baptist	Non-Den.	Methodist[2]	Lutheran	LDS[3]	Pente-costal	Presby-terian[4]	Muslim[5]	Judaism
Memphis, TN	5.2	30.8	5.4	6.2	0.3	0.6	4.7	2.4	0.3	0.6
Miami, FL	18.5	5.3	4.1	1.2	0.4	0.5	1.7	0.6	0.9	1.5
Midland, TX	22.4	25.2	8.8	4.2	0.6	1.2	1.6	1.8	3.7	<0.1
Milwaukee, WI	24.6	3.1	3.8	1.5	10.7	0.4	1.9	1.5	0.5	0.5
Minneapolis, MN	21.7	2.4	2.9	2.7	14.4	0.6	1.7	1.8	0.4	0.7
Nashville, TN	4.1	25.2	5.8	6.1	0.3	0.7	2.1	2.1	0.3	0.1
New Haven, CT	35.3	1.4	1.9	1.5	0.6	0.3	1.0	2.2	0.5	1.2
New Orleans, LA	31.5	8.4	3.7	2.6	0.8	0.5	2.1	0.5	0.4	0.5
New York, NY	36.9	1.8	1.7	1.3	0.7	0.3	0.8	1.0	2.3	4.7
Oklahoma City, OK	6.3	25.3	7.0	10.6	0.7	1.2	3.1	0.9	0.2	0.1
Omaha, NE	21.6	4.5	1.8	3.9	7.8	1.7	1.2	2.2	0.5	0.4
Orlando, FL	13.2	6.9	5.6	2.9	0.9	0.9	3.2	1.3	1.3	0.2
Philadelphia, PA	33.4	3.9	2.8	2.9	1.8	0.3	0.8	2.1	1.2	1.3
Phoenix, AZ	13.3	3.4	5.1	1.0	1.6	6.1	2.9	0.6	0.1	0.3
Pittsburgh, PA	32.8	2.3	2.8	5.6	3.3	0.3	1.1	4.6	0.3	0.7
Portland, OR	10.5	2.3	4.5	1.0	1.6	3.7	2.0	0.9	0.1	0.3
Providence, RI	47.0	1.4	1.2	0.8	0.5	0.3	0.5	1.0	0.1	0.7
Provo, UT	1.3	<0.1	<0.1	0.1	<0.1	88.5	0.1	<0.1	<0.1	<0.1
Raleigh, NC	9.1	12.1	5.9	6.7	0.9	0.8	2.2	2.2	0.9	0.3
Reno, NV	14.3	1.5	3.1	0.9	0.7	4.6	1.9	0.4	<0.1	0.1
Richmond, VA	5.9	19.9	5.4	6.1	0.6	0.9	1.8	2.1	2.7	0.3
Riverside, CA	24.8	2.6	5.5	0.6	0.5	2.4	1.5	0.6	0.5	<0.1
Rochester, MN	23.3	1.6	4.6	4.8	21.0	1.1	1.2	2.9	0.2	0.2
Rochester, NY	24.0	2.7	4.0	3.2	1.8	0.6	0.6	2.3	0.8	0.9
Sacramento, CA	16.1	3.1	4.0	1.7	0.7	3.3	2.0	0.8	0.8	0.2
St. Louis, MO	19.8	10.0	3.8	3.4	4.1	0.6	1.2	3.0	0.4	0.7
Salt Lake City, UT	8.9	0.8	0.5	0.5	0.5	58.9	0.6	0.3	0.4	0.1
San Antonio, TX	28.4	8.5	6.0	3.0	1.6	1.4	1.3	0.7	0.9	0.2
San Diego, CA	25.9	2.0	4.8	1.1	0.9	2.3	1.0	0.9	0.7	0.5
San Francisco, CA	20.7	2.5	2.4	1.9	0.5	1.5	1.2	1.1	1.2	0.8
San Jose, CA	26.0	1.3	4.2	1.0	0.5	1.4	1.1	0.7	1.0	0.6
Santa Rosa, CA	22.2	1.3	1.5	0.9	0.9	1.9	0.6	0.9	0.4	0.4
Savannah, GA	7.0	19.6	6.9	8.9	1.6	0.9	2.3	1.0	0.1	0.8
Seattle, WA	12.3	2.1	5.0	1.2	2.0	3.3	2.8	1.4	0.4	0.4
Sioux Falls, SD	14.9	3.0	1.5	3.8	21.4	0.7	1.0	6.2	0.3	<0.1
Springfield, IL	15.5	11.7	2.7	6.8	5.6	0.7	4.9	2.0	1.5	0.2
Tampa, FL	10.8	7.0	3.7	3.4	0.9	0.6	2.1	0.9	1.2	0.4
Tucson, AZ	20.7	3.3	3.7	1.3	1.5	2.9	1.5	1.0	<0.1	0.5
Tulsa, OK	5.8	22.9	7.6	9.2	0.7	1.1	3.3	1.2	0.3	0.2
Tuscaloosa, AL	1.7	32.2	4.5	8.3	<0.1	0.6	1.5	1.3	0.1	<0.1
Virginia Beach, VA	6.4	11.5	6.1	5.2	0.7	0.9	1.9	2.0	2.0	0.3
Washington, DC	14.5	7.3	4.8	4.5	1.2	1.1	1.0	1.3	2.3	1.1
Wichita, KS	14.5	13.4	3.1	7.1	1.7	1.4	1.9	1.6	0.1	<0.1
Wilmington, NC	6.1	14.4	4.6	8.4	0.9	1.0	1.1	2.5	0.2	0.1
Winston-Salem, NC	3.5	17.4	9.3	12.4	0.7	0.6	2.5	2.2	0.3	0.1
U.S.	19.1	9.3	4.0	4.0	2.3	2.0	1.9	1.6	0.8	0.7

Note: Figures are the number of adherents as a percentage of the total population; (1) Figures cover the Metropolitan Statistical Area; (2) Methodist/Pietist; (3) Latter Day Saints; (4) Reformed; (5) Figures are estimates
Source: Association of Statisticians of American Religious Bodies, 2010 U.S. Religion Census: Religious Congregations & Membership Study

Religious Groups by Tradition

Area	Catholic	Evangelical Protestant	Mainline Protestant	Other Tradition	Black Protestant	Orthodox
Albuquerque, NM	27.1	11.2	3.2	3.9	0.2	0.1
Allentown, PA	23.1	5.3	17.7	3.0	0.1	0.6
Anchorage, AK	6.9	15.6	3.5	6.8	0.3	0.6
Ann Arbor, MI	12.3	7.3	7.5	3.7	1.5	0.2
Athens, GA	4.4	21.1	9.7	1.7	2.4	0.1
Atlanta, GA	7.4	26.0	9.8	2.9	3.1	0.2
Austin, TX	16.0	16.1	6.3	3.9	1.3	0.1
Baltimore, MD	16.6	9.9	8.2	3.1	3.5	0.4
Baton Rouge, LA	22.5	24.8	5.6	1.5	5.1	<0.1
Boise City, ID	8.0	12.9	4.3	16.7	<0.1	<0.1
Boston, MA	44.3	3.2	4.5	3.4	0.1	1.0
Boulder, CO	20.1	9.7	6.4	4.8	<0.1	0.2
Buffalo, NY	35.6	5.8	7.1	3.2	2.2	0.4
Cape Coral, FL	16.2	14.3	4.6	2.0	0.3	0.1
Cedar Rapids, IA	18.8	13.7	17.5	1.9	0.1	0.2
Charleston, SC	6.1	19.6	11.1	1.8	7.3	0.1
Charlotte, NC	5.9	27.5	13.3	1.6	2.7	0.4
Chicago, IL	34.2	9.7	5.1	5.0	2.0	0.9
Cincinnati, OH	19.0	15.5	7.1	1.5	1.1	0.1
Clarksville, TN	4.0	35.3	7.2	1.6	2.4	<0.1
Cleveland, OH	28.8	9.0	7.5	2.6	2.1	0.8
College Station, TX	11.7	20.6	6.6	2.5	0.9	<0.1
Colorado Springs, CO	8.3	15.2	5.3	3.7	0.4	0.1
Columbia, MO	6.6	19.9	10.4	2.3	0.4	0.1
Columbia, SC	3.1	25.5	13.4	2.1	5.4	0.1
Columbus, OH	11.7	11.8	9.5	3.1	1.1	0.2
Dallas, TX	13.3	28.3	6.9	4.7	1.7	0.1
Davenport, IA	14.9	11.3	15.1	2.3	1.5	0.1
Denver, CO	16.0	11.0	4.5	4.6	0.3	0.3
Des Moines, IA	13.6	12.3	16.8	1.8	0.9	0.1
Durham, NC	5.0	19.3	11.7	2.9	3.1	<0.1
Edison, NJ	36.9	3.9	4.1	8.3	1.2	0.9
El Paso, TX	43.2	10.8	1.2	2.0	0.2	<0.1
Fargo, ND	17.4	10.7	30.8	0.8	<0.1	<0.1
Fort Collins, CO	11.8	18.8	5.9	3.9	<0.1	0.1
Fort Wayne, IN	14.2	24.6	9.1	0.9	2.4	0.2
Fort Worth, TX	13.3	28.3	6.9	4.7	1.7	0.1
Grand Rapids, MI	17.1	20.7	7.5	2.1	1.0	0.2
Green Bay, WI	42.0	14.1	8.1	0.6	<0.1	<0.1
Honolulu, HI	18.2	9.6	2.9	8.4	<0.1	<0.1
Houston, TX	17.0	24.9	6.6	4.9	1.3	0.2
Huntsville, AL	3.9	33.3	9.6	1.8	1.8	<0.1
Indianapolis, IN	10.5	18.2	9.6	1.6	1.8	0.2
Jacksonville, FL	9.8	27.1	5.6	2.9	4.2	0.2
Kansas City, MO	12.6	20.5	9.9	3.6	2.6	0.1
Lafayette, LA	47.0	12.7	3.2	0.7	9.2	<0.1
Las Cruces, NM	31.7	10.5	3.1	3.2	0.1	<0.1
Las Vegas, NV	18.1	7.7	1.3	7.6	0.4	0.4
Lexington, KY	6.7	28.3	10.2	1.7	2.0	0.1
Lincoln, NE	14.7	14.8	16.2	2.0	0.1	<0.1
Little Rock, AR	4.5	33.9	8.1	1.7	3.4	<0.1
Los Angeles, CA	33.8	9.0	2.3	4.6	0.8	0.6
Louisville, KY	13.6	24.5	7.1	2.0	2.9	<0.1
Madison, WI	21.8	7.2	15.3	2.2	0.1	<0.1
Manchester, NH	31.1	5.1	4.4	1.8	<0.1	0.7

Table continued on following page.

Area	Catholic	Evangelical Protestant	Mainline Protestant	Other Tradition	Black Protestant	Orthodox
Memphis, TN	5.2	29.4	8.3	2.1	13.4	<0.1
Miami, FL	18.5	11.4	2.4	3.5	1.7	0.2
Midland, TX	22.4	35.4	7.2	5.3	1.0	<0.1
Milwaukee, WI	24.6	14.6	7.1	2.3	2.4	0.6
Minneapolis, MN	21.7	12.8	14.5	2.2	0.4	0.2
Nashville, TN	4.1	32.9	8.0	1.7	3.3	0.4
New Haven, CT	35.3	3.8	6.1	2.3	0.7	0.4
New Orleans, LA	31.5	12.7	4.0	2.1	2.9	0.1
New York, NY	36.9	3.9	4.1	8.3	1.2	0.9
Oklahoma City, OK	6.3	39.0	9.8	2.7	1.9	0.1
Omaha, NE	21.6	12.1	10.7	3.2	1.4	0.1
Orlando, FL	13.2	17.8	4.7	3.2	1.2	0.3
Philadelphia, PA	33.4	6.3	8.9	3.7	1.7	0.4
Phoenix, AZ	13.3	13.2	2.6	7.8	0.1	0.3
Pittsburgh, PA	32.8	7.3	13.8	2.0	0.8	0.6
Portland, OR	10.5	11.6	3.6	5.2	0.1	0.3
Providence, RI	47.0	2.8	4.7	1.6	<0.1	0.5
Provo, UT	1.3	0.4	<0.1	88.8	<0.1	<0.1
Raleigh, NC	9.1	19.9	10.1	3.2	1.7	0.2
Reno, NV	14.3	7.6	1.9	5.1	0.2	0.1
Richmond, VA	5.9	23.6	13.3	4.5	2.4	0.1
Riverside, CA	24.8	11.4	1.3	3.7	0.8	0.1
Rochester, MN	23.3	18.9	21.0	2.0	<0.1	0.1
Rochester, NY	24.0	7.3	8.5	2.9	0.9	0.2
Sacramento, CA	16.1	11.3	2.2	5.8	0.5	0.3
St. Louis, MO	19.8	17.4	7.3	2.3	2.1	0.2
Salt Lake City, UT	8.9	2.6	1.2	60.0	0.1	0.4
San Antonio, TX	28.4	16.9	5.0	3.1	0.4	<0.1
San Diego, CA	25.9	9.7	2.4	5.2	0.3	0.2
San Francisco, CA	20.7	6.1	3.8	5.2	1.0	0.6
San Jose, CA	26.0	8.2	2.4	6.8	0.1	0.4
Santa Rosa, CA	22.2	5.3	2.3	4.8	<0.1	0.2
Savannah, GA	7.0	25.0	9.4	2.6	8.5	0.1
Seattle, WA	12.3	11.9	4.6	5.9	0.3	0.4
Sioux Falls, SD	14.9	12.9	28.0	1.2	0.1	0.1
Springfield, IL	15.5	21.4	11.6	3.1	2.1	0.1
Tampa, FL	10.8	13.6	5.1	3.1	1.1	0.8
Tucson, AZ	20.7	10.0	3.7	4.5	0.4	0.2
Tulsa, OK	5.8	34.6	11.2	2.1	1.5	<0.1
Tuscaloosa, AL	1.7	35.2	6.4	0.9	8.5	<0.1
Virginia Beach, VA	6.4	18.0	9.4	3.9	2.2	0.3
Washington, DC	14.5	12.4	8.7	5.9	2.3	0.6
Wichita, KS	14.5	20.7	11.0	2.4	1.8	0.2
Wilmington, NC	6.1	20.3	10.7	1.6	3.1	0.1
Winston-Salem, NC	3.5	29.1	15.6	1.2	2.2	0.2
U.S.	19.1	16.2	7.3	4.3	1.6	0.3

Note: Figures are the number of adherents as a percentage of the total population; (1) Figures cover the Metropolitan Statistical Area
Source: Association of Statisticians of American Religious Bodies, 2010 U.S. Religion Census: Religious Congregations & Membership Study

Ancestry: City

City	German	Irish	English	American	Italian	Polish	French[1]	Scottish	Dutch
Albuquerque, NM	9.4	7.7	7.5	3.6	3.1	1.4	1.8	1.4	0.8
Allentown, PA	9.9	4.9	2.0	2.5	4.2	1.6	0.9	0.4	0.9
Anchorage, AK	13.8	9.1	7.8	3.8	3.2	2.0	2.3	2.1	1.4
Ann Arbor, MI	16.9	10.2	9.1	2.9	4.8	6.1	2.7	2.6	2.2
Athens, GA	8.4	8.2	9.3	3.5	3.2	1.6	1.9	2.6	0.8
Atlanta, GA	6.5	5.7	7.5	5.3	2.8	1.4	1.7	1.7	0.5
Austin, TX	10.9	8.0	8.3	3.1	3.1	1.7	2.4	2.1	0.7
Baltimore, MD	6.1	5.6	3.2	2.9	3.1	2.4	0.9	0.7	0.3
Baton Rouge, LA	5.4	4.8	5.2	5.3	3.1	0.3	8.2	1.3	0.3
Boise City, ID	16.6	11.6	19.3	4.5	4.1	2.1	2.1	3.4	1.6
Boston, MA	4.8	13.6	4.7	2.3	7.6	2.1	1.8	1.1	0.4
Boulder, CO	16.8	11.8	11.4	2.5	6.1	3.5	2.5	3.2	1.3
Buffalo, NY	10.6	11.4	4.1	1.5	10.8	8.8	1.5	0.6	0.6
Cape Coral, FL	14.3	11.2	7.6	13.2	9.5	3.4	2.1	1.5	1.1
Cedar Rapids, IA	29.7	13.8	8.9	3.9	1.6	1.6	2.2	1.8	1.7
Charleston, SC	10.6	10.0	10.4	21.9	4.1	1.8	2.2	2.4	0.7
Charlotte, NC	8.0	6.8	6.7	5.0	3.4	1.6	1.3	1.7	0.6
Chicago, IL	7.4	7.4	2.7	2.1	3.9	5.5	1.0	0.7	0.5
Cincinnati, OH	17.5	9.7	5.7	4.0	3.7	1.7	1.6	1.2	0.8
Clarksville, TN	12.0	9.1	6.1	7.1	4.6	1.0	1.6	1.6	1.2
Cleveland, OH	9.6	8.5	3.1	2.2	4.7	4.0	0.8	0.6	0.6
College Station, TX	16.2	9.0	8.1	3.2	3.4	2.0	3.0	2.0	0.7
Colorado Springs, CO	18.1	10.6	10.8	4.3	4.8	2.3	2.8	2.7	1.5
Columbia, MO	23.2	12.1	10.1	5.2	3.4	2.2	2.1	2.2	1.4
Columbia, SC	10.5	7.1	7.9	5.4	3.4	1.2	2.1	2.2	0.6
Columbus, OH	15.6	10.2	6.6	3.9	4.9	2.1	1.5	1.5	0.9
Dallas, TX	5.1	4.1	4.8	4.1	1.7	0.8	1.2	1.1	0.4
Davenport, IA	28.5	15.6	6.9	3.3	2.1	2.0	1.4	1.8	1.6
Denver, CO	13.8	10.1	8.4	2.8	4.7	2.7	2.2	2.0	1.2
Des Moines, IA	19.7	12.0	7.4	3.4	4.1	1.2	1.6	1.1	2.4
Durham, NC	7.7	6.2	8.5	3.8	3.2	1.7	1.8	1.6	0.6
Edison, NJ	4.7	6.1	1.7	1.6	7.5	3.6	1.2	0.5	0.2
El Paso, TX	4.0	2.4	1.8	2.2	1.3	0.5	0.7	0.4	0.2
Fargo, ND	35.8	8.3	4.6	2.6	0.9	2.6	3.6	1.1	1.1
Fort Collins, CO	23.0	12.8	12.5	3.7	5.4	3.1	3.4	3.3	1.8
Fort Wayne, IN	23.7	9.7	7.2	5.7	2.4	2.1	3.0	1.7	1.2
Fort Worth, TX	7.4	6.4	6.1	4.6	1.8	1.0	1.4	1.4	0.7
Grand Rapids, MI	14.2	8.3	6.3	2.4	2.9	6.2	2.1	1.6	13.5
Green Bay, WI	28.9	8.6	4.0	3.2	2.1	7.9	3.9	0.9	2.8
Honolulu, HI	4.2	3.2	2.9	1.3	1.6	0.8	0.8	0.6	0.3
Houston, TX	4.8	3.6	4.1	3.7	1.5	0.9	1.5	0.9	0.4
Huntsville, AL	8.9	9.0	9.4	10.9	2.2	1.1	1.6	1.9	0.9
Indianapolis, IN	13.2	8.2	6.6	5.4	2.1	1.6	1.6	1.5	0.9
Jacksonville, FL	7.8	7.6	6.2	5.2	3.6	1.4	1.4	1.4	0.6
Kansas City, MO	15.3	10.2	7.3	3.9	3.5	1.6	1.7	1.5	1.0
Lafayette, LA	7.2	5.5	5.8	5.8	3.8	0.4	17.6	1.1	0.5
Las Cruces, NM	7.1	4.9	6.5	2.6	2.4	1.0	1.3	1.1	1.0
Las Vegas, NV	8.7	7.6	5.9	3.3	5.3	2.0	1.7	1.3	0.7
Lexington, KY	13.3	11.0	11.2	8.6	3.0	1.6	1.7	2.6	1.0
Lincoln, NE	31.9	11.5	8.6	3.6	2.1	2.6	1.9	1.4	1.6
Little Rock, AR	7.3	6.4	8.0	5.6	1.4	1.0	1.5	1.7	0.5
Los Angeles, CA	3.9	3.6	3.0	3.8	2.7	1.4	1.1	0.7	0.4
Louisville, KY	15.4	11.4	8.8	7.2	2.7	1.0	1.9	1.6	1.0
Madison, WI	30.3	11.8	8.6	2.1	3.9	5.6	2.7	1.6	1.9
Manchester, NH	6.3	19.1	9.3	3.2	8.5	3.9	12.2	3.0	0.4
Memphis, TN	3.2	4.0	3.9	3.9	1.6	0.6	0.9	1.0	0.3

Table continued on following page.

City	German	Irish	English	American	Italian	Polish	French[1]	Scottish	Dutch
Miami, FL	1.7	1.2	0.9	3.0	2.3	0.8	0.9	0.3	0.2
Midland, TX	6.1	6.2	6.7	4.4	1.2	0.5	2.0	1.8	0.4
Milwaukee, WI	15.7	5.7	2.1	1.3	2.7	6.2	1.4	0.5	0.6
Minneapolis, MN	20.5	10.2	6.0	1.7	2.7	3.9	2.6	1.4	1.4
Nashville, TN	8.5	7.8	8.2	7.2	2.5	1.4	1.7	1.8	0.7
New Haven, CT	3.7	6.5	3.2	1.9	8.1	2.2	1.1	0.5	0.5
New Orleans, LA	6.3	5.6	4.5	2.3	3.8	1.0	5.2	1.1	0.4
New York, NY	3.0	4.4	1.8	4.0	6.2	2.3	0.8	0.5	0.3
Oklahoma City, OK	10.2	7.9	6.9	5.4	1.8	0.7	1.5	1.6	0.9
Omaha, NE	25.1	13.3	7.6	3.0	4.1	3.5	2.1	1.5	1.4
Orlando, FL	6.1	5.5	5.1	5.6	4.8	1.6	1.8	1.1	0.6
Philadelphia, PA	6.7	10.1	2.8	2.4	7.1	3.1	0.8	0.6	0.3
Phoenix, AZ	10.0	7.4	6.0	2.8	3.9	1.8	1.6	1.2	0.9
Pittsburgh, PA	18.4	14.2	5.3	3.2	12.2	6.7	1.4	1.4	0.5
Portland, OR	15.7	11.1	11.2	4.6	4.4	2.2	2.9	2.9	1.9
Providence, RI	3.4	7.7	3.7	2.7	7.0	1.7	3.0	0.8	0.3
Provo, UT	10.1	4.5	24.0	2.6	1.8	0.8	1.5	4.4	1.4
Raleigh, NC	9.1	7.7	9.7	10.2	3.8	2.2	1.7	2.3	0.8
Reno, NV	12.5	10.4	9.6	4.0	6.1	1.9	2.5	2.0	1.3
Richmond, VA	7.2	6.8	8.1	4.4	3.5	1.3	1.6	2.0	0.5
Riverside, CA	5.8	4.9	4.5	3.3	3.0	1.0	1.3	0.8	0.7
Rochester, MN	29.1	10.5	6.4	2.5	1.6	3.2	1.8	1.3	1.7
Rochester, NY	8.5	7.6	5.0	2.9	7.2	2.6	1.3	0.9	1.0
Sacramento, CA	6.7	6.0	5.1	1.6	3.6	1.0	1.6	1.1	0.7
St. Louis, MO	15.8	9.5	5.0	3.9	3.8	1.8	2.2	1.2	0.8
Salt Lake City, UT	10.8	6.9	16.9	3.4	3.8	1.4	2.2	3.4	1.8
San Antonio, TX	6.9	4.3	3.8	3.2	1.7	1.0	1.3	0.9	0.3
San Diego, CA	8.2	7.0	5.9	2.4	4.2	1.8	1.7	1.4	0.8
San Francisco, CA	7.1	7.7	5.2	2.6	4.6	1.9	2.2	1.3	0.8
San Jose, CA	4.8	4.0	3.6	1.9	3.3	0.8	1.1	0.8	0.5
Santa Rosa, CA	10.8	10.0	9.3	2.6	6.8	1.6	2.7	1.9	1.2
Savannah, GA	6.1	7.5	4.8	3.4	2.9	1.4	1.6	1.5	0.7
Seattle, WA	14.6	11.0	10.5	2.2	4.3	2.6	2.9	2.9	1.4
Sioux Falls, SD	34.3	11.4	5.6	3.5	1.5	1.5	2.0	1.0	6.1
Springfield, IL	19.0	11.6	9.2	4.4	4.8	2.0	2.1	1.9	1.2
Tampa, FL	8.4	7.6	6.5	6.6	5.9	1.9	1.9	1.4	0.8
Tucson, AZ	11.1	8.1	7.2	2.8	3.5	1.9	2.0	1.5	0.9
Tulsa, OK	10.8	9.0	8.6	5.6	2.1	0.9	2.0	2.0	0.9
Tuscaloosa, AL	5.7	6.6	5.8	6.6	2.0	0.9	1.3	2.3	0.6
Virginia Beach, VA	11.1	10.3	9.9	8.0	5.6	2.1	2.3	2.3	0.8
Washington, DC	7.3	7.1	5.6	2.6	4.0	2.2	1.6	1.3	0.7
Wichita, KS	19.3	9.3	8.8	4.8	1.7	1.0	2.1	1.6	1.2
Wilmington, NC	9.8	9.1	11.1	4.8	4.9	1.9	1.9	2.5	0.7
Winston-Salem, NC	9.0	6.4	8.1	5.4	2.5	1.0	1.2	2.2	0.9
U.S.	13.0	9.7	7.7	5.9	5.1	2.7	2.3	1.6	1.1

Note: Figures are the percentage of the total population reporting a particular ancestry. The nine most commonly reported ancestries in the U.S. are shown. Figures include multiple ancestries (e.g. if a person reported being Irish and Italian, they were included in both columns); (1) Excludes Basque

Source: U.S. Census Bureau, 2016-2020 American Community Survey 5-Year Estimates

Ancestry: Metro Area

Metro Area	German	Irish	English	American	Italian	Polish	French[1]	Scottish	Dutch
Albuquerque, NM	9.0	7.1	7.3	4.2	3.0	1.3	1.7	1.5	0.7
Allentown, PA	23.4	13.2	6.1	4.6	12.3	5.0	1.5	1.1	2.0
Anchorage, AK	14.7	9.8	8.2	4.1	3.2	2.0	2.5	2.2	1.6
Ann Arbor, MI	18.8	10.6	10.2	6.0	4.6	6.4	2.9	2.5	2.1
Athens, GA	8.3	9.6	10.5	7.1	2.8	1.2	1.8	2.6	1.0
Atlanta, GA	6.5	6.5	7.6	8.4	2.6	1.2	1.4	1.7	0.6
Austin, TX	12.3	8.0	8.8	3.8	2.8	1.6	2.4	2.1	0.8
Baltimore, MD	14.5	11.6	7.6	4.7	6.0	4.0	1.6	1.5	0.7
Baton Rouge, LA	6.5	6.6	5.7	7.5	4.7	0.4	12.3	1.1	0.3
Boise City, ID	16.3	9.7	17.7	5.0	3.3	1.5	2.4	3.1	1.9
Boston, MA	5.8	20.8	9.6	3.5	12.8	3.2	4.3	2.2	0.6
Boulder, CO	19.0	11.7	12.5	3.1	5.3	3.2	2.7	3.2	1.7
Buffalo, NY	23.1	16.1	7.7	3.4	15.8	16.0	2.4	1.5	0.9
Cape Coral, FL	13.6	10.5	8.3	13.4	7.6	3.3	2.1	1.8	1.2
Cedar Rapids, IA	32.9	14.6	8.8	4.4	1.6	1.2	2.3	1.9	1.9
Charleston, SC	10.1	9.2	9.7	12.3	3.7	1.7	2.0	2.5	0.7
Charlotte, NC	10.7	8.3	8.3	9.1	3.8	1.8	1.5	2.1	0.8
Chicago, IL	14.0	10.6	4.4	2.5	6.6	8.6	1.4	0.9	1.2
Cincinnati, OH	26.5	13.4	9.1	6.6	4.2	1.6	1.9	1.8	1.1
Clarksville, TN	11.8	9.2	7.3	8.4	3.4	1.1	1.5	1.7	1.0
Cleveland, OH	18.8	13.3	7.3	4.1	9.6	7.7	1.5	1.4	0.9
College Station, TX	13.6	7.9	7.2	3.6	3.0	1.7	2.4	1.8	0.7
Colorado Springs, CO	18.2	10.6	10.3	4.4	4.7	2.3	2.6	2.7	1.5
Columbia, MO	24.5	12.0	10.5	6.7	2.8	1.6	2.1	2.1	1.4
Columbia, SC	10.1	7.1	7.7	8.0	2.3	1.3	1.5	1.8	0.6
Columbus, OH	21.1	12.7	9.2	5.8	5.4	2.3	1.8	2.0	1.2
Dallas, TX	8.4	6.5	7.2	6.1	2.1	1.1	1.6	1.5	0.7
Davenport, IA	27.1	13.9	7.8	4.2	2.4	2.1	1.7	1.5	1.9
Denver, CO	17.3	10.7	9.9	3.5	5.0	2.4	2.5	2.3	1.5
Des Moines, IA	26.6	13.1	9.2	4.2	3.3	1.3	1.7	1.6	3.7
Durham, NC	9.0	7.8	10.5	5.5	3.4	1.8	1.8	2.3	0.7
Edison, NJ	6.2	9.2	2.9	4.1	12.0	3.8	0.9	0.7	0.6
El Paso, TX	3.6	2.4	1.7	2.2	1.2	0.5	0.7	0.4	0.2
Fargo, ND	35.9	7.9	5.0	2.4	1.1	2.5	3.3	1.1	1.2
Fort Collins, CO	24.9	13.0	13.7	4.3	4.8	2.6	3.3	3.5	2.0
Fort Wayne, IN	26.8	9.5	7.7	6.6	2.5	2.1	3.3	1.6	1.3
Fort Worth, TX	8.4	6.5	7.2	6.1	2.1	1.1	1.6	1.5	0.7
Grand Rapids, MI	19.2	9.7	8.8	3.5	2.9	6.4	2.7	1.7	18.4
Green Bay, WI	35.7	9.5	4.4	3.6	2.0	10.1	4.2	0.8	4.1
Honolulu, HI	5.3	3.9	3.4	1.3	1.9	0.9	1.1	0.8	0.4
Houston, TX	7.5	5.2	5.6	4.0	2.0	1.1	2.0	1.1	0.6
Huntsville, AL	8.7	9.8	10.1	12.4	2.2	1.1	1.7	2.0	0.9
Indianapolis, IN	16.9	9.7	8.8	8.6	2.6	1.8	1.7	1.8	1.3
Jacksonville, FL	9.6	9.5	8.5	7.9	4.3	1.8	1.8	2.0	0.8
Kansas City, MO	20.3	12.4	10.5	4.9	3.2	1.6	2.2	1.9	1.3
Lafayette, LA	6.5	4.5	4.0	7.2	2.6	0.5	17.6	0.7	0.3
Las Cruces, NM	6.3	4.3	5.0	2.5	1.7	0.7	1.2	1.1	0.8
Las Vegas, NV	8.5	7.1	6.0	3.2	5.0	1.9	1.6	1.2	0.7
Lexington, KY	12.9	11.3	11.7	12.2	2.7	1.4	1.6	2.5	1.1
Lincoln, NE	33.3	11.3	8.3	3.7	2.1	2.5	1.9	1.3	1.9
Little Rock, AR	8.8	8.7	8.6	7.5	1.4	0.9	1.6	1.9	0.9
Los Angeles, CA	5.1	4.3	4.0	3.5	2.9	1.2	1.3	0.9	0.6
Louisville, KY	17.3	12.4	10.1	8.8	2.5	1.1	2.1	1.8	1.1
Madison, WI	36.3	12.8	8.9	2.7	3.6	5.3	2.5	1.6	1.9
Manchester, NH	8.3	20.8	13.7	3.5	9.9	4.1	11.6	3.4	0.7
Memphis, TN	5.1	6.1	6.1	7.5	2.1	0.7	1.2	1.3	0.5

Table continued on following page.

Metro Area	German	Irish	English	American	Italian	Polish	French[1]	Scottish	Dutch
Miami, FL	4.4	4.3	2.9	5.8	5.0	1.9	1.2	0.6	0.4
Midland, TX	6.1	5.9	6.3	4.7	1.3	0.5	1.8	1.6	0.4
Milwaukee, WI	32.4	9.8	4.5	2.1	4.2	10.6	2.3	0.8	1.2
Minneapolis, MN	28.5	10.8	6.0	3.0	2.6	4.2	3.3	1.3	1.4
Nashville, TN	9.9	9.4	10.3	10.3	2.7	1.4	1.8	2.1	0.8
New Haven, CT	7.7	14.7	6.9	2.8	20.3	5.9	3.2	1.1	0.5
New Orleans, LA	9.6	7.7	5.1	4.8	7.3	0.7	11.2	1.0	0.4
New York, NY	6.2	9.2	2.9	4.1	12.0	3.8	0.9	0.7	0.6
Oklahoma City, OK	11.8	9.1	8.1	7.2	1.9	0.8	1.6	1.8	1.0
Omaha, NE	28.8	13.5	8.7	3.5	3.9	3.8	2.1	1.5	1.7
Orlando, FL	8.4	7.6	6.3	7.7	5.2	1.8	1.8	1.3	0.7
Philadelphia, PA	14.4	17.8	7.3	3.3	12.7	4.9	1.3	1.3	0.7
Phoenix, AZ	12.6	8.5	8.2	3.8	4.5	2.3	2.0	1.6	1.1
Pittsburgh, PA	25.6	17.2	8.2	3.4	15.5	8.3	1.7	1.9	1.1
Portland, OR	17.0	10.6	11.0	4.6	3.8	1.8	2.7	2.8	1.8
Providence, RI	4.6	17.4	10.6	3.3	13.6	3.6	8.9	1.6	0.4
Provo, UT	10.4	5.0	28.2	4.2	2.3	0.6	1.7	4.7	1.5
Raleigh, NC	10.0	8.9	10.8	9.1	4.6	2.1	1.9	2.4	0.9
Reno, NV	13.2	10.6	10.2	3.8	6.6	1.8	2.6	2.0	1.3
Richmond, VA	9.0	7.8	11.4	6.8	3.7	1.6	1.6	2.1	0.7
Riverside, CA	6.8	5.4	4.8	2.7	3.0	0.9	1.5	1.0	0.9
Rochester, MN	34.7	11.3	6.7	2.9	1.4	3.0	2.0	1.3	1.9
Rochester, NY	18.5	14.9	11.4	4.8	15.5	4.6	2.6	1.9	3.0
Sacramento, CA	10.3	8.1	8.3	2.6	4.7	1.3	2.1	1.6	1.0
St. Louis, MO	26.5	12.9	8.1	5.7	4.7	2.4	3.1	1.5	1.0
Salt Lake City, UT	9.9	5.6	20.6	4.1	2.9	0.9	1.9	3.6	1.8
San Antonio, TX	10.0	5.6	5.5	3.5	2.0	1.4	1.7	1.2	0.4
San Diego, CA	9.0	7.4	6.5	2.7	4.2	1.7	1.9	1.5	0.9
San Francisco, CA	7.5	7.2	6.0	2.4	4.6	1.5	1.9	1.4	0.8
San Jose, CA	5.9	4.7	4.7	1.9	3.7	1.1	1.4	1.0	0.7
Santa Rosa, CA	12.5	12.4	10.1	2.5	8.5	1.8	3.1	2.5	1.3
Savannah, GA	9.2	10.1	8.3	7.7	3.4	1.3	1.8	1.8	0.7
Seattle, WA	14.1	9.4	9.7	3.0	3.6	1.9	2.7	2.5	1.4
Sioux Falls, SD	36.1	10.8	5.6	4.4	1.3	1.4	2.0	0.9	6.6
Springfield, IL	22.2	12.6	10.2	5.7	5.1	2.0	2.4	1.9	1.4
Tampa, FL	11.9	10.5	8.1	8.7	7.4	2.9	2.6	1.7	1.0
Tucson, AZ	13.1	9.0	8.9	3.2	3.9	2.3	2.3	1.9	1.1
Tulsa, OK	12.7	10.6	9.0	5.9	2.0	1.0	2.1	2.0	1.2
Tuscaloosa, AL	5.0	6.6	5.8	11.5	1.5	0.6	0.9	2.1	0.5
Virginia Beach, VA	9.7	8.6	9.4	8.6	4.0	1.7	1.9	1.9	0.7
Washington, DC	9.1	8.4	7.2	4.0	4.3	2.2	1.5	1.5	0.7
Wichita, KS	21.5	9.7	9.1	6.1	1.7	1.0	2.1	1.8	1.4
Wilmington, NC	11.2	10.7	11.0	5.6	5.5	2.2	1.9	3.0	0.8
Winston-Salem, NC	11.5	8.0	10.4	9.2	2.2	1.0	1.2	2.3	0.9
U.S.	13.0	9.7	7.7	5.9	5.1	2.7	2.3	1.6	1.1

Note: Figures are the percentage of the total population reporting a particular ancestry. The nine most commonly reported ancestries in the U.S. are shown. Figures include multiple ancestries (e.g. if a person reported being Irish and Italian, they were included in both columns); Figures cover the Metropolitan Statistical Area; (1) Excludes Basque

Source: U.S. Census Bureau, 2016-2020 American Community Survey 5-Year Estimates

Foreign-Born Population: City

City	Percent of Population Born in								
	Any Foreign Country	Asia	Mexico	Europe	Caribbean	Central America[1]	South America	Africa	Canada
Albuquerque, NM	9.8	2.6	4.9	1.0	0.3	0.1	0.4	0.4	0.1
Allentown, PA	18.8	3.2	1.0	0.7	9.9	0.9	2.1	0.9	0.0
Anchorage, AK	10.8	6.0	0.8	1.1	0.5	0.1	0.5	0.6	0.4
Ann Arbor, MI	19.7	13.1	0.5	3.0	0.2	0.1	0.7	1.1	0.8
Athens, GA	9.6	2.9	2.6	0.8	0.4	0.9	1.0	0.8	0.2
Atlanta, GA	8.0	3.3	0.6	1.3	0.8	0.1	0.7	0.8	0.3
Austin, TX	18.0	6.0	6.6	1.4	0.6	1.5	0.7	0.8	0.3
Baltimore, MD	8.1	2.2	0.3	0.9	1.4	1.0	0.5	1.7	0.1
Baton Rouge, LA	5.5	2.8	0.3	0.5	0.2	1.1	0.1	0.3	0.1
Boise City, ID	6.6	2.8	1.0	1.3	0.0	0.1	0.2	0.6	0.4
Boston, MA	28.2	7.6	0.4	3.3	8.4	2.5	2.4	3.0	0.4
Boulder, CO	10.5	4.5	1.2	2.8	0.1	0.3	0.8	0.2	0.4
Buffalo, NY	10.4	5.4	0.2	0.8	1.0	0.1	0.4	2.2	0.3
Cape Coral, FL	16.6	1.4	0.7	2.2	7.6	0.8	3.2	0.1	0.5
Cedar Rapids, IA	6.2	2.9	0.7	0.5	0.0	0.2	0.1	1.7	0.1
Charleston, SC	5.1	1.8	0.5	1.4	0.4	0.1	0.5	0.2	0.2
Charlotte, NC	17.2	5.4	2.6	1.3	1.2	2.9	1.4	2.1	0.2
Chicago, IL	20.3	5.1	8.2	3.4	0.3	0.8	1.1	1.0	0.2
Cincinnati, OH	6.1	1.8	0.4	0.8	0.2	0.7	0.3	1.8	0.2
Clarksville, TN	5.8	1.7	1.2	0.9	0.3	0.6	0.4	0.4	0.2
Cleveland, OH	6.1	2.4	0.3	1.1	0.7	0.4	0.3	0.7	0.1
College Station, TX	12.2	7.6	1.4	0.9	0.1	0.3	0.9	0.7	0.2
Colorado Springs, CO	7.5	2.1	2.0	1.5	0.3	0.3	0.4	0.4	0.3
Columbia, MO	8.6	5.3	0.6	0.9	0.1	0.3	0.2	1.0	0.2
Columbia, SC	5.0	2.3	0.4	0.6	0.4	0.3	0.4	0.4	0.1
Columbus, OH	12.8	5.0	1.1	0.8	0.4	0.7	0.4	4.3	0.1
Dallas, TX	23.9	2.9	14.2	0.8	0.4	2.8	0.7	2.0	0.1
Davenport, IA	4.9	1.8	2.2	0.4	0.2	0.0	0.0	0.2	0.1
Denver, CO	14.0	2.9	6.8	1.4	0.2	0.6	0.6	1.2	0.3
Des Moines, IA	12.9	4.6	3.3	0.8	0.1	1.2	0.2	2.7	0.1
Durham, NC	14.7	4.3	2.8	1.3	0.7	3.1	0.6	1.5	0.4
Edison, NJ	46.0	36.7	0.8	2.3	1.8	0.5	1.6	1.9	0.3
El Paso, TX	23.0	1.0	20.4	0.5	0.2	0.2	0.2	0.3	0.0
Fargo, ND	9.9	3.9	0.1	0.5	0.2	0.1	0.3	4.5	0.4
Fort Collins, CO	6.9	3.1	1.2	1.4	0.1	0.2	0.4	0.3	0.2
Fort Wayne, IN	8.1	4.0	1.8	0.7	0.1	0.6	0.2	0.6	0.1
Fort Worth, TX	16.3	3.7	9.2	0.6	0.3	0.8	0.5	1.1	0.1
Grand Rapids, MI	11.1	2.4	3.5	1.0	0.5	1.6	0.2	1.5	0.2
Green Bay, WI	9.7	2.1	5.6	0.4	0.1	0.4	0.3	0.7	0.1
Honolulu, HI	27.5	22.9	0.2	0.9	0.2	0.1	0.2	0.1	0.2
Houston, TX	28.9	5.9	10.8	1.1	1.0	6.4	1.4	2.0	0.2
Huntsville, AL	6.4	2.2	1.5	0.7	0.4	0.6	0.2	0.6	0.1
Indianapolis, IN	9.7	2.9	2.9	0.5	0.4	0.8	0.4	1.7	0.0
Jacksonville, FL	11.7	4.2	0.6	1.7	2.2	0.8	1.4	0.6	0.2
Kansas City, MO	8.0	2.4	2.2	0.5	0.6	0.5	0.2	1.4	0.1
Lafayette, LA	4.6	2.0	0.3	0.7	0.2	0.8	0.2	0.2	0.1
Las Cruces, NM	11.5	2.5	7.6	0.5	0.1	0.1	0.1	0.4	0.1
Las Vegas, NV	20.6	5.3	8.8	1.5	1.1	2.2	0.7	0.4	0.4
Lexington, KY	10.0	3.8	2.1	1.1	0.3	0.5	0.5	1.5	0.2
Lincoln, NE	9.0	4.9	1.3	0.9	0.4	0.4	0.3	0.7	0.1
Little Rock, AR	7.3	2.7	1.9	0.6	0.2	1.1	0.3	0.4	0.1
Los Angeles, CA	36.3	11.0	12.1	2.4	0.3	8.2	1.1	0.7	0.4
Louisville, KY	8.1	2.5	0.7	0.8	1.8	0.4	0.3	1.4	0.1
Madison, WI	11.9	6.5	1.2	1.5	0.2	0.2	1.1	0.9	0.3

Table continued on following page.

City	Percent of Population Born in								
	Any Foreign Country	Asia	Mexico	Europe	Caribbean	Central America[1]	South America	Africa	Canada
Manchester, NH	14.6	5.0	0.5	2.5	1.4	1.3	0.8	2.2	1.0
Memphis, TN	6.0	1.5	2.1	0.3	0.3	0.9	0.2	0.7	0.0
Miami, FL	58.1	1.2	1.1	1.8	31.9	11.8	9.8	0.3	0.1
Midland, TX	14.9	2.1	8.5	0.3	1.5	0.5	0.4	1.0	0.6
Milwaukee, WI	10.2	3.0	4.8	0.7	0.3	0.3	0.2	0.8	0.1
Minneapolis, MN	15.2	4.0	1.9	1.2	0.3	0.4	1.3	5.7	0.3
Nashville, TN	13.2	4.0	3.0	0.9	0.3	1.7	0.3	2.7	0.3
New Haven, CT	17.4	4.7	2.8	2.1	2.7	1.2	2.2	1.3	0.3
New Orleans, LA	5.4	1.9	0.3	0.7	0.2	1.5	0.4	0.3	0.1
New York, NY	36.4	10.9	1.9	5.2	10.1	1.4	4.8	1.7	0.3
Oklahoma City, OK	11.7	3.2	5.7	0.5	0.2	1.0	0.4	0.6	0.2
Omaha, NE	10.7	3.3	3.6	0.7	0.1	1.1	0.3	1.4	0.1
Orlando, FL	23.0	3.2	0.6	1.9	6.7	1.4	8.3	0.6	0.3
Philadelphia, PA	14.3	5.5	0.4	2.1	2.8	0.7	0.9	1.6	0.1
Phoenix, AZ	19.3	3.3	11.8	1.4	0.3	0.8	0.4	0.8	0.4
Pittsburgh, PA	9.0	4.7	0.3	1.8	0.3	0.1	0.6	0.9	0.2
Portland, OR	13.4	6.0	2.0	2.7	0.2	0.3	0.3	1.0	0.5
Providence, RI	30.2	3.8	0.6	2.7	13.5	4.9	1.5	2.8	0.3
Provo, UT	11.2	2.1	4.1	0.4	0.3	0.8	2.4	0.3	0.3
Raleigh, NC	12.8	3.9	2.5	1.2	1.0	1.0	0.7	2.2	0.2
Reno, NV	16.4	5.6	5.9	1.5	0.2	1.6	0.5	0.5	0.4
Richmond, VA	7.3	1.4	0.7	0.8	0.4	2.5	0.4	0.9	0.1
Riverside, CA	22.7	5.7	12.5	0.8	0.2	1.9	0.8	0.5	0.2
Rochester, MN	13.5	5.2	1.2	1.6	0.2	0.2	0.4	4.5	0.2
Rochester, NY	9.4	3.0	0.1	1.2	2.4	0.4	0.4	1.6	0.2
Sacramento, CA	21.3	10.8	6.0	1.5	0.1	0.7	0.2	0.6	0.1
St. Louis, MO	6.9	2.9	0.7	1.2	0.2	0.3	0.2	1.2	0.1
Salt Lake City, UT	16.3	4.3	5.7	2.0	0.2	0.7	1.5	0.8	0.4
San Antonio, TX	14.0	2.6	8.8	0.6	0.2	0.8	0.5	0.4	0.1
San Diego, CA	25.6	11.9	8.5	2.2	0.2	0.5	0.8	0.9	0.4
San Francisco, CA	34.2	22.1	2.3	4.6	0.2	2.4	1.1	0.5	0.6
San Jose, CA	40.5	26.4	8.6	2.2	0.1	1.2	0.7	0.8	0.3
Santa Rosa, CA	20.9	4.6	11.4	1.9	0.0	0.9	0.3	0.9	0.3
Savannah, GA	6.0	2.7	0.7	0.9	0.4	0.4	0.4	0.3	0.2
Seattle, WA	19.4	11.0	1.3	2.5	0.1	0.5	0.5	2.2	1.0
Sioux Falls, SD	9.2	2.1	0.5	1.2	0.1	1.1	0.1	3.9	0.1
Springfield, IL	4.2	2.3	0.4	0.5	0.2	0.1	0.2	0.5	0.1
Tampa, FL	17.8	3.7	1.0	1.6	7.2	1.2	2.1	0.6	0.3
Tucson, AZ	14.6	2.5	9.0	1.1	0.2	0.4	0.3	0.9	0.2
Tulsa, OK	11.2	2.7	5.5	0.6	0.3	1.0	0.4	0.6	0.1
Tuscaloosa, AL	4.1	2.2	0.5	0.4	0.1	0.5	0.1	0.2	0.1
Virginia Beach, VA	9.7	5.1	0.6	1.5	0.5	0.6	0.7	0.5	0.2
Washington, DC	13.4	3.0	0.6	2.4	1.1	2.6	1.4	2.0	0.3
Wichita, KS	9.9	3.7	4.3	0.4	0.1	0.5	0.3	0.5	0.1
Wilmington, NC	4.7	1.1	0.9	1.0	0.3	0.6	0.4	0.2	0.2
Winston-Salem, NC	9.9	2.1	4.0	0.7	0.4	1.4	0.6	0.7	0.1
U.S.	13.5	4.2	3.3	1.5	1.3	1.1	1.0	0.7	0.3

Note: (1) Excludes Mexico
Source: U.S. Census Bureau, 2016-2020 American Community Survey 5-Year Estimates

Foreign-Born Population: Metro Area

Metro Area	Percent of Population Born in								
	Any Foreign Country	Asia	Mexico	Europe	Caribbean	Central America[1]	South America	Africa	Canada
Albuquerque, NM	8.9	1.9	4.9	0.8	0.2	0.1	0.4	0.4	0.1
Allentown, PA	9.5	2.7	0.4	1.5	2.4	0.6	1.1	0.6	0.1
Anchorage, AK	8.8	4.7	0.7	1.1	0.4	0.1	0.4	0.4	0.4
Ann Arbor, MI	12.6	7.4	0.5	2.3	0.2	0.2	0.4	0.9	0.6
Athens, GA	7.5	2.5	1.9	0.7	0.3	0.7	0.7	0.6	0.2
Atlanta, GA	13.9	4.7	2.3	1.1	1.5	1.1	1.2	1.6	0.2
Austin, TX	14.8	4.6	5.9	1.2	0.4	1.2	0.6	0.7	0.3
Baltimore, MD	10.3	4.2	0.4	1.3	0.9	1.1	0.5	1.8	0.1
Baton Rouge, LA	4.0	1.5	0.6	0.3	0.2	1.0	0.1	0.2	0.1
Boise City, ID	6.4	1.6	2.6	1.1	0.0	0.2	0.3	0.3	0.3
Boston, MA	18.9	6.2	0.2	3.2	3.4	1.6	2.0	1.7	0.4
Boulder, CO	10.1	3.6	2.5	2.2	0.1	0.3	0.6	0.2	0.4
Buffalo, NY	6.6	3.1	0.1	1.4	0.5	0.1	0.3	0.7	0.5
Cape Coral, FL	16.6	1.3	2.4	2.0	6.0	1.7	2.2	0.1	1.0
Cedar Rapids, IA	3.9	1.8	0.4	0.4	0.1	0.1	0.1	0.9	0.1
Charleston, SC	5.6	1.5	1.0	1.1	0.3	0.6	0.7	0.2	0.2
Charlotte, NC	10.4	3.1	2.0	1.1	0.7	1.4	0.9	0.9	0.2
Chicago, IL	17.6	5.2	6.3	3.7	0.3	0.5	0.6	0.6	0.2
Cincinnati, OH	5.0	2.2	0.5	0.7	0.1	0.4	0.2	0.7	0.2
Clarksville, TN	4.5	1.4	0.9	0.7	0.3	0.4	0.2	0.4	0.1
Cleveland, OH	6.0	2.2	0.3	2.2	0.2	0.2	0.2	0.4	0.2
College Station, TX	11.8	4.0	5.2	0.7	0.2	0.5	0.5	0.5	0.1
Colorado Springs, CO	6.8	1.8	1.7	1.5	0.3	0.3	0.4	0.3	0.3
Columbia, MO	5.9	3.3	0.6	0.8	0.1	0.2	0.2	0.6	0.2
Columbia, SC	5.2	1.8	1.1	0.7	0.4	0.5	0.3	0.3	0.1
Columbus, OH	8.4	3.7	0.6	0.7	0.3	0.4	0.3	2.3	0.1
Dallas, TX	18.5	5.5	7.9	0.8	0.3	1.5	0.6	1.5	0.2
Davenport, IA	5.2	1.7	1.9	0.5	0.1	0.1	0.1	0.8	0.1
Denver, CO	11.8	3.3	4.7	1.3	0.1	0.5	0.5	1.0	0.3
Des Moines, IA	7.8	3.1	1.4	1.0	0.0	0.6	0.2	1.4	0.1
Durham, NC	11.6	3.5	2.5	1.4	0.5	1.9	0.5	1.0	0.3
Edison, NJ	29.3	8.7	1.4	4.4	6.9	1.9	4.4	1.4	0.2
El Paso, TX	24.0	0.9	21.7	0.4	0.2	0.3	0.2	0.3	0.0
Fargo, ND	6.9	2.8	0.1	0.5	0.1	0.0	0.2	2.9	0.3
Fort Collins, CO	5.7	1.9	1.4	1.2	0.1	0.2	0.4	0.3	0.2
Fort Wayne, IN	6.4	3.1	1.4	0.6	0.1	0.5	0.2	0.4	0.1
Fort Worth, TX	18.5	5.5	7.9	0.8	0.3	1.5	0.6	1.5	0.2
Grand Rapids, MI	6.6	2.1	1.7	1.0	0.4	0.5	0.1	0.6	0.2
Green Bay, WI	5.0	1.5	2.3	0.4	0.0	0.3	0.1	0.2	0.1
Honolulu, HI	19.5	15.7	0.2	0.7	0.2	0.1	0.2	0.1	0.2
Houston, TX	23.3	6.0	8.5	1.0	0.9	3.7	1.4	1.5	0.3
Huntsville, AL	4.9	1.8	1.1	0.7	0.3	0.4	0.2	0.4	0.2
Indianapolis, IN	7.1	2.7	1.6	0.6	0.2	0.5	0.3	1.0	0.1
Jacksonville, FL	9.4	3.1	0.5	1.7	1.6	0.6	1.2	0.4	0.2
Kansas City, MO	6.8	2.4	2.0	0.5	0.2	0.5	0.2	0.7	0.1
Lafayette, LA	3.3	1.2	0.5	0.3	0.2	0.6	0.2	0.1	0.1
Las Cruces, NM	16.5	1.5	14.0	0.5	0.1	0.1	0.1	0.2	0.1
Las Vegas, NV	22.1	7.3	7.9	1.6	1.2	1.9	0.8	0.9	0.4
Lexington, KY	7.7	2.7	1.8	1.0	0.2	0.4	0.4	1.0	0.2
Lincoln, NE	7.9	4.2	1.1	0.9	0.3	0.4	0.3	0.6	0.1
Little Rock, AR	4.2	1.3	1.2	0.5	0.1	0.5	0.2	0.2	0.1
Los Angeles, CA	32.7	12.8	11.7	1.7	0.3	4.2	0.9	0.6	0.3
Louisville, KY	6.0	2.0	0.9	0.7	1.0	0.3	0.2	0.8	0.1
Madison, WI	7.4	3.5	1.1	1.0	0.1	0.2	0.7	0.5	0.2

Table continued on following page.

Metro Area	Percent of Population Born in								
	Any Foreign Country	Asia	Mexico	Europe	Caribbean	Central America[1]	South America	Africa	Canada
Manchester, NH	9.9	3.6	0.4	1.8	1.1	0.4	0.8	0.9	0.9
Memphis, TN	5.3	1.8	1.6	0.4	0.2	0.6	0.2	0.5	0.1
Miami, FL	40.9	2.2	1.1	2.3	21.0	4.1	9.2	0.4	0.6
Midland, TX	13.8	1.8	8.5	0.2	1.3	0.4	0.3	0.8	0.5
Milwaukee, WI	7.5	2.8	2.3	1.3	0.2	0.2	0.2	0.4	0.1
Minneapolis, MN	10.6	4.1	1.2	1.0	0.2	0.4	0.6	2.9	0.2
Nashville, TN	8.2	2.6	1.9	0.7	0.2	0.9	0.3	1.2	0.2
New Haven, CT	13.0	3.3	1.0	2.9	2.0	0.6	1.9	1.0	0.3
New Orleans, LA	7.6	2.1	0.5	0.5	0.8	2.7	0.4	0.4	0.1
New York, NY	29.3	8.7	1.4	4.4	6.9	1.9	4.4	1.4	0.2
Oklahoma City, OK	7.8	2.4	3.3	0.4	0.1	0.6	0.3	0.4	0.2
Omaha, NE	7.6	2.4	2.4	0.6	0.1	0.7	0.3	0.9	0.1
Orlando, FL	18.8	3.0	1.0	1.6	5.6	1.2	5.5	0.6	0.3
Philadelphia, PA	11.1	4.6	0.8	1.8	1.4	0.5	0.7	1.1	0.2
Phoenix, AZ	14.2	3.3	7.1	1.4	0.3	0.6	0.3	0.5	0.7
Pittsburgh, PA	4.0	2.0	0.1	0.9	0.2	0.1	0.2	0.3	0.1
Portland, OR	12.7	5.1	3.1	2.4	0.2	0.4	0.3	0.6	0.4
Providence, RI	13.6	2.3	0.2	4.2	2.4	1.4	1.2	1.6	0.2
Provo, UT	7.2	1.1	2.5	0.5	0.1	0.5	1.6	0.2	0.4
Raleigh, NC	12.0	4.6	2.5	1.3	0.6	0.9	0.6	1.3	0.3
Reno, NV	14.3	4.0	6.0	1.2	0.2	1.4	0.4	0.3	0.4
Richmond, VA	8.0	3.1	0.6	1.0	0.4	1.5	0.5	0.7	0.1
Riverside, CA	21.1	4.9	12.1	0.9	0.2	1.6	0.6	0.4	0.3
Rochester, MN	8.3	3.1	0.8	1.1	0.1	0.2	0.3	2.4	0.2
Rochester, NY	6.8	2.5	0.2	1.9	0.8	0.2	0.3	0.6	0.3
Sacramento, CA	18.5	9.0	4.4	2.7	0.1	0.6	0.3	0.5	0.3
St. Louis, MO	4.8	2.2	0.5	1.1	0.1	0.2	0.2	0.4	0.1
Salt Lake City, UT	12.3	3.1	4.3	1.2	0.1	0.7	1.5	0.5	0.3
San Antonio, TX	11.6	2.2	7.0	0.6	0.2	0.7	0.4	0.3	0.1
San Diego, CA	22.9	8.9	9.7	1.8	0.2	0.6	0.6	0.6	0.4
San Francisco, CA	30.7	17.7	4.6	2.8	0.2	2.4	1.0	0.9	0.4
San Jose, CA	39.1	26.1	6.7	3.1	0.1	0.9	0.8	0.7	0.5
Santa Rosa, CA	16.6	3.0	9.2	1.9	0.1	0.8	0.4	0.5	0.4
Savannah, GA	6.0	2.0	1.3	0.9	0.4	0.3	0.4	0.3	0.2
Seattle, WA	19.2	10.2	2.3	2.7	0.2	0.5	0.5	1.6	0.7
Sioux Falls, SD	6.8	1.5	0.4	1.0	0.1	0.9	0.1	2.7	0.1
Springfield, IL	2.9	1.5	0.3	0.4	0.1	0.1	0.1	0.3	0.1
Tampa, FL	14.2	2.9	1.2	2.2	3.9	0.8	2.1	0.5	0.6
Tucson, AZ	12.5	2.2	7.2	1.3	0.2	0.3	0.3	0.6	0.4
Tulsa, OK	6.6	1.9	2.8	0.5	0.2	0.5	0.3	0.3	0.1
Tuscaloosa, AL	3.3	1.2	1.0	0.3	0.1	0.4	0.1	0.2	0.1
Virginia Beach, VA	6.7	2.9	0.4	1.1	0.6	0.6	0.4	0.5	0.1
Washington, DC	22.8	8.3	0.8	1.9	1.1	4.8	2.2	3.5	0.2
Wichita, KS	7.3	2.7	3.0	0.4	0.1	0.4	0.2	0.4	0.1
Wilmington, NC	4.5	1.1	0.9	1.0	0.2	0.6	0.4	0.2	0.3
Winston-Salem, NC	6.8	1.4	2.8	0.6	0.3	1.0	0.4	0.3	0.1
U.S.	13.5	4.2	3.3	1.5	1.3	1.1	1.0	0.7	0.3

Note: Figures cover the Metropolitan Statistical Area—see Appendix B for areas included; (1) Excludes Mexico
Source: U.S. Census Bureau, 2016-2020 American Community Survey 5-Year Estimates

Marital Status: City

City	Never Married	Now Married[1]	Separated	Widowed	Divorced
Albuquerque, NM	38.2	39.8	1.4	5.6	15.1
Allentown, PA	48.0	33.2	4.0	5.2	9.7
Anchorage, AK	33.8	49.5	1.7	3.5	11.5
Ann Arbor, MI	56.4	34.8	0.3	2.5	5.9
Athens, GA	54.5	31.0	1.8	3.8	9.0
Atlanta, GA	55.4	28.0	1.8	4.6	10.2
Austin, TX	43.3	41.3	1.6	3.1	10.7
Baltimore, MD	52.7	26.6	3.1	6.2	11.4
Baton Rouge, LA	50.2	30.9	2.0	6.1	10.8
Boise City, ID	34.9	46.6	1.0	4.3	13.2
Boston, MA	55.7	30.7	2.5	3.8	7.3
Boulder, CO	55.5	31.6	0.7	2.7	9.6
Buffalo, NY	51.4	29.3	2.6	6.0	10.7
Cape Coral, FL	24.9	52.9	1.4	7.6	13.3
Cedar Rapids, IA	35.0	46.3	1.1	5.7	11.9
Charleston, SC	41.4	42.3	1.6	5.5	9.3
Charlotte, NC	41.2	42.2	2.4	4.1	10.1
Chicago, IL	48.6	35.6	2.3	5.2	8.2
Cincinnati, OH	52.0	29.5	2.2	4.7	11.7
Clarksville, TN	29.7	51.4	2.3	3.9	12.7
Cleveland, OH	52.3	24.7	3.4	6.1	13.5
College Station, TX	59.2	32.0	0.9	2.2	5.7
Colorado Springs, CO	31.1	49.9	1.5	4.5	13.0
Columbia, MO	48.0	39.4	1.1	3.3	8.2
Columbia, SC	56.4	28.1	2.2	4.3	9.0
Columbus, OH	45.4	36.0	2.1	4.3	12.3
Dallas, TX	41.9	40.6	2.9	4.4	10.3
Davenport, IA	36.5	43.8	1.3	5.8	12.5
Denver, CO	44.4	37.8	1.8	3.9	12.1
Des Moines, IA	39.8	39.6	2.0	5.3	13.4
Durham, NC	43.4	40.5	2.3	3.9	9.9
Edison, NJ	25.4	62.0	0.6	5.4	6.5
El Paso, TX	35.5	44.3	3.5	5.7	10.9
Fargo, ND	42.4	44.6	0.9	4.3	7.8
Fort Collins, CO	47.2	39.7	0.7	3.4	9.0
Fort Wayne, IN	36.1	44.0	1.6	6.0	12.3
Fort Worth, TX	35.8	46.2	2.3	4.5	11.2
Grand Rapids, MI	46.1	38.0	1.2	4.8	9.9
Green Bay, WI	37.8	42.3	1.3	5.2	13.5
Honolulu, HI	37.0	45.0	1.3	7.0	9.7
Houston, TX	40.8	41.5	3.0	4.5	10.2
Huntsville, AL	36.2	43.6	2.0	6.1	12.1
Indianapolis, IN	42.7	38.6	1.8	4.9	12.0
Jacksonville, FL	35.8	42.3	2.2	5.6	14.0
Kansas City, MO	39.7	39.7	2.2	5.2	13.3
Lafayette, LA	41.5	40.4	1.8	6.0	10.4
Las Cruces, NM	41.8	39.3	1.9	4.7	12.3
Las Vegas, NV	35.3	43.8	2.0	5.2	13.8
Lexington, KY	38.6	43.4	1.6	4.6	11.7
Lincoln, NE	39.2	45.9	0.8	4.2	9.9
Little Rock, AR	37.9	39.7	2.3	5.9	14.3
Los Angeles, CA	45.7	39.1	2.5	4.6	8.1
Louisville, KY	36.6	41.9	2.0	6.5	13.0
Madison, WI	50.4	37.0	0.7	3.3	8.7
Manchester, NH	39.4	38.8	1.8	5.7	14.3
Memphis, TN	47.7	31.7	3.3	5.8	11.5

Table continued on following page.

City	Never Married	Now Married[1]	Separated	Widowed	Divorced
Miami, FL	39.8	36.8	3.5	6.5	13.5
Midland, TX	31.0	50.1	2.1	5.0	11.7
Milwaukee, WI	53.8	29.8	1.8	4.5	10.2
Minneapolis, MN	51.6	34.2	1.5	2.8	10.0
Nashville, TN	41.1	40.8	1.8	4.7	11.6
New Haven, CT	58.8	25.9	1.9	4.4	9.0
New Orleans, LA	50.3	28.5	2.7	5.7	12.8
New York, NY	43.3	40.6	2.9	5.4	7.9
Oklahoma City, OK	34.2	45.1	2.3	5.5	12.9
Omaha, NE	36.8	46.1	1.5	4.8	10.8
Orlando, FL	43.2	37.1	2.8	4.1	12.8
Philadelphia, PA	50.8	30.8	3.2	6.0	9.2
Phoenix, AZ	38.9	42.3	2.1	4.3	12.3
Pittsburgh, PA	52.6	30.5	2.0	5.7	9.2
Portland, OR	41.3	41.2	1.4	3.7	12.5
Providence, RI	53.7	31.4	2.0	4.3	8.6
Provo, UT	48.6	44.0	0.9	2.2	4.3
Raleigh, NC	43.3	39.9	2.2	3.8	10.8
Reno, NV	35.3	42.9	2.0	4.9	14.8
Richmond, VA	52.4	27.2	2.9	5.5	12.0
Riverside, CA	42.6	42.0	2.2	4.5	8.6
Rochester, MN	33.1	52.1	1.0	4.8	9.0
Rochester, NY	55.7	24.7	3.5	4.8	11.3
Sacramento, CA	40.1	41.2	2.6	5.1	11.1
St. Louis, MO	48.4	31.1	3.0	5.3	12.3
Salt Lake City, UT	43.0	41.3	1.4	3.4	10.9
San Antonio, TX	39.5	39.7	3.0	5.3	12.5
San Diego, CA	40.2	44.4	1.6	4.1	9.7
San Francisco, CA	46.3	39.7	1.4	4.6	7.9
San Jose, CA	35.8	50.6	1.5	4.3	7.8
Santa Rosa, CA	33.1	46.7	1.9	5.7	12.7
Savannah, GA	48.5	30.5	2.5	5.9	12.5
Seattle, WA	45.4	40.3	1.2	3.2	9.9
Sioux Falls, SD	34.9	47.9	1.3	4.6	11.3
Springfield, IL	37.3	40.0	1.5	6.3	14.9
Tampa, FL	40.5	38.5	2.4	5.1	13.5
Tucson, AZ	42.5	35.7	2.3	5.3	14.3
Tulsa, OK	34.7	42.2	2.5	5.9	14.6
Tuscaloosa, AL	51.6	33.0	1.7	4.0	9.6
Virginia Beach, VA	30.5	51.7	2.2	5.0	10.7
Washington, DC	57.0	29.1	1.9	3.8	8.3
Wichita, KS	33.4	45.9	1.9	5.3	13.5
Wilmington, NC	43.1	37.4	2.4	5.5	11.6
Winston-Salem, NC	40.9	39.9	2.7	5.8	10.7
U.S.	33.5	48.1	1.8	5.7	10.8

Note: Figures are percentages and cover the population 15 years of age and older; (1) Excludes separated
Source: U.S. Census Bureau, 2016-2020 American Community Survey 5-Year Estimates

Marital Status: Metro Area

Metro Area	Never Married	Now Married[1]	Separated	Widowed	Divorced
Albuquerque, NM	35.5	43.4	1.4	5.7	14.0
Allentown, PA	32.3	49.4	2.0	6.5	9.8
Anchorage, AK	33.3	49.4	1.7	3.8	11.8
Ann Arbor, MI	43.2	44.2	0.8	3.8	8.1
Athens, GA	42.7	41.4	1.7	4.6	9.6
Atlanta, GA	35.6	47.4	1.8	4.6	10.7
Austin, TX	36.5	47.7	1.5	3.7	10.6
Baltimore, MD	36.0	45.9	2.1	5.9	10.1
Baton Rouge, LA	36.9	44.0	2.0	5.7	11.4
Boise City, ID	29.1	53.2	1.1	4.4	12.3
Boston, MA	37.3	47.4	1.6	5.1	8.7
Boulder, CO	38.2	45.8	0.9	3.8	11.3
Buffalo, NY	35.8	44.9	1.8	6.9	10.6
Cape Coral, FL	26.2	50.9	1.6	8.3	13.0
Cedar Rapids, IA	30.3	51.8	1.1	5.7	11.2
Charleston, SC	34.7	47.0	2.3	5.6	10.5
Charlotte, NC	32.9	49.3	2.4	5.3	10.2
Chicago, IL	36.9	47.1	1.6	5.4	8.9
Cincinnati, OH	32.4	49.1	1.6	5.7	11.3
Clarksville, TN	28.4	52.6	2.1	4.9	11.9
Cleveland, OH	35.4	44.6	1.6	6.6	11.8
College Station, TX	45.7	40.4	1.9	3.9	8.1
Colorado Springs, CO	29.5	53.2	1.4	4.1	11.8
Columbia, MO	40.0	45.2	1.2	4.2	9.5
Columbia, SC	36.2	44.5	2.8	5.7	10.8
Columbus, OH	34.9	47.0	1.7	5.0	11.5
Dallas, TX	33.0	50.3	2.0	4.4	10.4
Davenport, IA	29.9	50.6	1.3	6.3	11.9
Denver, CO	34.0	48.7	1.4	4.0	11.8
Des Moines, IA	30.6	51.4	1.2	5.0	11.7
Durham, NC	37.1	46.0	2.2	4.8	9.9
Edison, NJ	37.6	46.6	2.2	5.6	8.0
El Paso, TX	35.5	45.1	3.5	5.5	10.4
Fargo, ND	37.0	50.2	0.8	4.2	7.8
Fort Collins, CO	35.6	49.2	0.8	4.0	10.4
Fort Wayne, IN	31.9	49.3	1.3	5.7	11.8
Fort Worth, TX	33.0	50.3	2.0	4.4	10.4
Grand Rapids, MI	32.2	52.1	0.9	4.6	10.2
Green Bay, WI	30.3	52.9	0.8	5.2	10.9
Honolulu, HI	34.2	49.7	1.2	6.4	8.5
Houston, TX	33.7	50.1	2.3	4.4	9.5
Huntsville, AL	30.3	50.5	1.7	5.8	11.8
Indianapolis, IN	33.2	48.8	1.4	5.0	11.5
Jacksonville, FL	31.4	47.6	1.9	5.9	13.2
Kansas City, MO	30.7	50.3	1.6	5.3	12.1
Lafayette, LA	34.3	47.2	2.0	5.9	10.7
Las Cruces, NM	38.2	44.2	2.1	4.8	10.6
Las Vegas, NV	34.9	44.1	2.2	5.1	13.7
Lexington, KY	34.1	47.1	1.6	5.1	12.2
Lincoln, NE	36.8	48.7	0.8	4.2	9.5
Little Rock, AR	30.7	47.2	2.1	6.1	13.9
Los Angeles, CA	40.1	44.6	2.0	4.9	8.4
Louisville, KY	31.7	47.5	1.8	6.3	12.8
Madison, WI	37.0	48.0	0.8	4.4	9.8
Manchester, NH	30.7	50.6	1.4	5.4	12.0
Memphis, TN	38.4	42.4	2.6	5.7	11.0

Table continued on following page.

Metro Area	Never Married	Now Married[1]	Separated	Widowed	Divorced
Miami, FL	34.5	43.5	2.6	6.4	13.0
Midland, TX	30.1	50.7	2.0	5.1	12.2
Milwaukee, WI	37.4	46.0	1.1	5.2	10.3
Minneapolis, MN	33.6	51.1	1.0	4.3	10.1
Nashville, TN	32.3	50.1	1.6	5.0	11.0
New Haven, CT	38.1	44.0	1.4	6.0	10.6
New Orleans, LA	37.9	41.1	2.4	6.3	12.2
New York, NY	37.6	46.6	2.2	5.6	8.0
Oklahoma City, OK	31.8	48.1	2.0	5.5	12.7
Omaha, NE	31.9	51.4	1.3	4.8	10.6
Orlando, FL	34.9	46.2	2.1	5.1	11.7
Philadelphia, PA	37.2	45.7	2.0	5.9	9.1
Phoenix, AZ	34.0	47.4	1.6	5.0	11.9
Pittsburgh, PA	31.9	49.3	1.7	7.2	9.9
Portland, OR	32.3	49.9	1.3	4.5	12.0
Providence, RI	36.2	45.1	1.5	6.1	11.1
Provo, UT	32.5	58.4	0.9	2.6	5.5
Raleigh, NC	32.3	51.6	2.1	4.2	9.8
Reno, NV	31.1	48.6	1.8	5.0	13.5
Richmond, VA	34.9	46.2	2.3	5.8	10.8
Riverside, CA	36.1	47.3	2.2	4.9	9.5
Rochester, MN	28.4	56.7	0.8	4.9	9.2
Rochester, NY	35.3	46.1	2.1	5.8	10.7
Sacramento, CA	33.5	48.5	2.0	5.1	10.8
St. Louis, MO	32.1	48.9	1.7	6.1	11.3
Salt Lake City, UT	32.3	52.1	1.6	3.7	10.3
San Antonio, TX	35.5	45.0	2.5	5.2	11.7
San Diego, CA	36.1	47.7	1.6	4.7	9.9
San Francisco, CA	36.6	48.5	1.5	4.7	8.8
San Jose, CA	34.1	52.8	1.4	4.2	7.5
Santa Rosa, CA	31.8	48.7	1.5	5.2	12.8
Savannah, GA	35.9	44.5	2.1	5.7	11.8
Seattle, WA	33.0	50.6	1.4	4.2	10.8
Sioux Falls, SD	30.9	52.7	1.1	4.7	10.7
Springfield, IL	32.1	46.9	1.3	6.2	13.6
Tampa, FL	31.2	46.0	2.0	7.0	13.8
Tucson, AZ	34.7	44.8	1.8	5.7	13.0
Tulsa, OK	28.6	50.2	2.0	6.3	13.0
Tuscaloosa, AL	40.0	42.5	1.8	5.4	10.2
Virginia Beach, VA	33.6	47.7	2.4	5.5	10.7
Washington, DC	36.3	48.7	1.8	4.4	8.8
Wichita, KS	29.8	50.7	1.5	5.5	12.4
Wilmington, NC	34.0	46.6	2.5	5.8	11.1
Winston-Salem, NC	30.3	49.7	2.5	6.6	10.9
U.S.	33.5	48.1	1.8	5.7	10.8

Note: Figures are percentages and cover the population 15 years of age and older; Figures cover the Metropolitan Statistical Area; (1) Excludes separated

Source: U.S. Census Bureau, 2016-2020 American Community Survey 5-Year Estimates

Disability by Age: City

City	All Ages	Under 18 Years Old	18 to 64 Years Old	65 Years and Over
Albuquerque, NM	14.0	4.5	12.0	35.5
Allentown, PA	16.5	9.7	16.0	35.1
Anchorage, AK	11.2	3.4	10.0	35.2
Ann Arbor, MI	6.9	3.4	4.9	23.2
Athens, GA	12.2	7.9	10.0	34.5
Atlanta, GA	11.5	4.7	9.5	34.5
Austin, TX	8.6	4.1	7.1	29.1
Baltimore, MD	15.5	6.1	13.6	38.6
Baton Rouge, LA	16.9	7.8	14.4	41.9
Boise City, ID	11.1	4.1	9.3	29.3
Boston, MA	11.8	5.7	8.8	39.3
Boulder, CO	6.3	2.7	4.4	22.9
Buffalo, NY	16.9	7.3	15.7	40.2
Cape Coral, FL	13.5	4.1	9.3	30.5
Cedar Rapids, IA	10.2	2.9	8.1	28.7
Charleston, SC	10.3	3.1	6.9	33.5
Charlotte, NC	7.9	2.5	6.6	28.4
Chicago, IL	10.8	3.1	8.5	35.8
Cincinnati, OH	12.8	5.1	11.9	32.2
Clarksville, TN	15.7	5.9	16.5	42.4
Cleveland, OH	19.5	8.2	18.4	42.3
College Station, TX	6.6	5.3	5.2	26.7
Colorado Springs, CO	13.0	4.8	11.8	32.2
Columbia, MO	10.9	5.0	8.8	35.4
Columbia, SC	12.6	5.2	10.4	38.6
Columbus, OH	12.1	5.0	10.9	36.1
Dallas, TX	10.1	4.0	8.5	34.9
Davenport, IA	12.0	4.4	10.2	30.9
Denver, CO	9.7	3.4	7.6	33.0
Des Moines, IA	14.2	5.5	13.3	36.8
Durham, NC	9.1	2.6	7.2	32.3
Edison, NJ	8.1	3.6	5.2	28.4
El Paso, TX	13.6	5.3	11.0	42.6
Fargo, ND	10.7	4.6	8.3	33.6
Fort Collins, CO	8.4	2.6	6.4	30.9
Fort Wayne, IN	13.9	5.6	12.7	34.2
Fort Worth, TX	10.0	3.6	8.7	35.5
Grand Rapids, MI	12.6	4.5	11.9	32.4
Green Bay, WI	13.3	6.6	11.8	33.5
Honolulu, HI	11.4	2.9	6.9	32.5
Houston, TX	9.8	3.6	7.8	35.3
Huntsville, AL	13.4	4.6	10.8	34.3
Indianapolis, IN	13.5	5.1	12.4	36.0
Jacksonville, FL	13.1	4.6	11.0	36.8
Kansas City, MO	12.5	3.6	11.0	35.1
Lafayette, LA	13.0	3.5	10.9	34.7
Las Cruces, NM	15.5	6.9	12.8	38.1
Las Vegas, NV	12.8	3.8	10.8	35.1
Lexington, KY	12.5	4.5	10.7	34.4
Lincoln, NE	10.5	4.2	8.4	31.2
Little Rock, AR	13.3	4.5	11.6	35.8
Los Angeles, CA	10.3	3.2	7.4	37.3
Louisville, KY	15.1	4.7	13.6	36.9
Madison, WI	8.3	3.7	6.3	27.1
Manchester, NH	14.4	6.9	12.0	37.8

Table continued on following page.

City	All Ages	Under 18 Years Old	18 to 64 Years Old	65 Years and Over
Memphis, TN	13.7	5.5	12.3	35.8
Miami, FL	11.7	4.5	7.4	36.8
Midland, TX	9.6	2.4	8.1	38.9
Milwaukee, WI	12.7	5.3	11.3	39.8
Minneapolis, MN	10.9	4.9	9.9	31.4
Nashville, TN	11.5	4.6	9.4	35.3
New Haven, CT	9.9	3.9	8.3	33.0
New Orleans, LA	13.7	5.0	12.1	32.6
New York, NY	10.9	3.6	7.9	34.6
Oklahoma City, OK	13.1	4.1	12.1	36.9
Omaha, NE	10.9	3.4	9.4	32.1
Orlando, FL	9.3	5.1	7.5	31.1
Philadelphia, PA	16.7	6.3	14.8	42.8
Phoenix, AZ	10.8	4.3	9.5	34.0
Pittsburgh, PA	14.2	7.3	11.1	36.1
Portland, OR	11.9	4.4	9.6	34.0
Providence, RI	13.6	6.2	12.1	37.5
Provo, UT	8.7	4.4	7.1	41.9
Raleigh, NC	9.1	4.3	7.3	30.3
Reno, NV	11.8	4.5	10.0	29.8
Richmond, VA	14.5	5.8	12.7	35.8
Riverside, CA	11.2	4.2	8.7	41.6
Rochester, MN	10.2	4.0	7.6	31.5
Rochester, NY	18.6	9.4	19.0	35.9
Sacramento, CA	11.8	3.2	9.5	37.9
St. Louis, MO	15.3	5.8	13.4	38.7
Salt Lake City, UT	11.0	3.5	9.1	35.7
San Antonio, TX	15.1	6.3	13.3	42.4
San Diego, CA	9.3	3.3	6.4	32.2
San Francisco, CA	10.1	2.5	6.3	34.1
San Jose, CA	8.8	2.7	5.9	33.5
Santa Rosa, CA	11.8	3.2	9.8	29.5
Savannah, GA	15.7	7.0	12.8	42.8
Seattle, WA	9.3	2.4	6.9	31.5
Sioux Falls, SD	10.0	2.9	9.1	28.5
Springfield, IL	15.0	6.0	12.8	33.6
Tampa, FL	12.1	3.7	9.7	39.0
Tucson, AZ	15.2	5.8	12.8	38.8
Tulsa, OK	14.3	4.7	13.4	34.6
Tuscaloosa, AL	10.7	2.8	9.4	28.4
Virginia Beach, VA	11.4	4.3	9.1	32.5
Washington, DC	11.4	4.5	9.2	34.3
Wichita, KS	14.3	5.3	13.0	35.8
Wilmington, NC	12.7	4.6	9.7	32.5
Winston-Salem, NC	10.9	3.2	9.6	29.1
U.S.	12.7	4.3	10.3	34.0

Note: Figures show percent of the civilian noninstitutionalized population that reported having a disability. Disability status is determined from from six types of difficulty: vision, hearing, cognitive, ambulatory, self-care, and independent living. For children under 5 years old, hearing and vision difficulty are used to determine disability status. For children between the ages of 5 and 14, disability status is determined from hearing, vision, cognitive, ambulatory, and self-care difficulties. For people aged 15 years and older, they are considered to have a disability if they have difficulty with any one of the six difficulty types.
Source: U.S. Census Bureau, 2016-2020 American Community Survey 5-Year Estimates

Disability by Age: Metro Area

Metro Area	All Ages	Under 18 Years Old	18 to 64 Years Old	65 Years and Over
Albuquerque, NM	15.0	4.3	12.9	36.9
Allentown, PA	12.9	5.4	10.3	31.1
Anchorage, AK	12.0	3.6	11.0	36.1
Ann Arbor, MI	9.6	3.7	7.6	27.1
Athens, GA	12.9	6.6	10.6	34.8
Atlanta, GA	10.3	3.9	8.6	31.7
Austin, TX	9.2	3.8	7.8	30.2
Baltimore, MD	11.8	4.6	9.5	31.4
Baton Rouge, LA	14.5	6.3	12.2	38.8
Boise City, ID	11.9	4.1	10.5	31.5
Boston, MA	10.7	4.2	7.9	30.8
Boulder, CO	8.1	2.9	6.0	25.4
Buffalo, NY	13.5	5.0	11.1	31.5
Cape Coral, FL	13.8	3.9	9.7	27.6
Cedar Rapids, IA	10.3	3.5	8.0	28.5
Charleston, SC	12.0	4.1	9.6	33.3
Charlotte, NC	10.6	3.4	8.7	32.1
Chicago, IL	10.1	3.1	7.8	31.2
Cincinnati, OH	12.4	4.8	10.6	32.2
Clarksville, TN	16.8	6.4	16.5	44.2
Cleveland, OH	14.0	5.1	11.6	32.8
College Station, TX	9.7	5.2	7.2	34.6
Colorado Springs, CO	12.5	4.8	11.3	31.9
Columbia, MO	12.1	4.7	10.2	34.3
Columbia, SC	14.4	4.5	12.5	37.3
Columbus, OH	12.1	4.7	10.4	33.9
Dallas, TX	9.5	3.6	7.8	33.3
Davenport, IA	12.5	5.1	9.9	30.7
Denver, CO	9.7	3.2	7.7	30.6
Des Moines, IA	10.7	3.8	9.1	30.9
Durham, NC	11.0	3.4	8.5	31.8
Edison, NJ	10.1	3.2	7.3	31.2
El Paso, TX	13.5	5.7	11.1	43.4
Fargo, ND	10.0	3.9	7.9	33.3
Fort Collins, CO	10.1	2.7	7.8	29.5
Fort Wayne, IN	12.8	5.0	11.3	32.7
Fort Worth, TX	9.5	3.6	7.8	33.3
Grand Rapids, MI	11.2	3.9	9.6	31.0
Green Bay, WI	11.1	4.3	9.2	28.3
Honolulu, HI	11.2	3.0	7.4	33.6
Houston, TX	9.5	3.7	7.8	33.6
Huntsville, AL	13.5	4.5	11.1	36.7
Indianapolis, IN	12.3	4.5	10.8	33.8
Jacksonville, FL	13.0	4.6	10.8	33.9
Kansas City, MO	11.7	3.8	9.8	32.9
Lafayette, LA	14.5	5.4	12.9	37.6
Las Cruces, NM	14.6	5.6	12.6	36.3
Las Vegas, NV	12.1	3.9	9.9	34.5
Lexington, KY	13.6	4.9	11.8	35.2
Lincoln, NE	10.4	3.9	8.1	31.6
Little Rock, AR	15.8	5.7	13.9	39.3
Los Angeles, CA	9.8	3.1	6.9	33.8
Louisville, KY	14.2	4.6	12.4	35.6
Madison, WI	9.3	4.1	6.9	27.7
Manchester, NH	11.8	4.5	9.6	31.2

Table continued on following page.

Metro Area	All Ages	Under 18 Years Old	18 to 64 Years Old	65 Years and Over
Memphis, TN	13.3	5.1	11.6	35.8
Miami, FL	11.0	3.7	7.3	31.8
Midland, TX	9.5	2.2	8.1	39.6
Milwaukee, WI	11.3	4.1	8.9	31.6
Minneapolis, MN	10.0	3.8	8.1	29.4
Nashville, TN	11.9	4.0	9.9	35.4
New Haven, CT	11.5	3.5	8.9	31.0
New Orleans, LA	14.6	5.2	12.6	36.1
New York, NY	10.1	3.2	7.3	31.2
Oklahoma City, OK	14.1	4.3	12.4	39.0
Omaha, NE	10.9	3.5	9.4	32.0
Orlando, FL	12.4	5.6	9.7	34.4
Philadelphia, PA	12.7	4.8	10.5	32.8
Phoenix, AZ	11.8	4.1	9.6	32.3
Pittsburgh, PA	14.5	5.5	11.2	33.5
Portland, OR	11.9	4.0	9.6	33.3
Providence, RI	13.8	5.4	11.4	32.8
Provo, UT	8.2	3.6	7.5	32.6
Raleigh, NC	9.7	3.8	8.0	30.6
Reno, NV	12.1	4.6	9.8	30.7
Richmond, VA	12.7	5.1	10.5	32.3
Riverside, CA	11.5	4.0	9.1	37.6
Rochester, MN	10.0	3.6	7.4	29.4
Rochester, NY	14.0	5.9	12.0	30.6
Sacramento, CA	11.7	3.4	9.0	34.7
St. Louis, MO	12.9	4.5	10.7	33.0
Salt Lake City, UT	9.5	3.7	8.3	31.3
San Antonio, TX	14.3	5.7	12.5	39.9
San Diego, CA	10.0	3.2	7.3	32.7
San Francisco, CA	9.7	2.9	6.7	30.7
San Jose, CA	8.2	2.5	5.3	31.3
Santa Rosa, CA	11.7	3.5	9.0	28.6
Savannah, GA	14.0	5.2	12.1	37.0
Seattle, WA	10.9	3.7	8.7	33.4
Sioux Falls, SD	9.7	2.7	8.8	28.0
Springfield, IL	13.9	5.8	11.4	32.6
Tampa, FL	14.3	4.8	11.0	34.4
Tucson, AZ	15.2	5.2	12.3	34.4
Tulsa, OK	14.6	4.6	13.0	37.4
Tuscaloosa, AL	14.8	4.5	12.8	39.0
Virginia Beach, VA	13.2	5.1	11.0	34.1
Washington, DC	8.8	3.2	6.7	28.6
Wichita, KS	14.2	5.4	12.5	36.6
Wilmington, NC	13.3	4.7	10.8	31.5
Winston-Salem, NC	13.1	4.1	10.6	33.8
U.S.	12.7	4.3	10.3	34.0

Note: Figures show percent of the civilian noninstitutionalized population that reported having a disability. Disability status is determined from from six types of difficulty: vision, hearing, cognitive, ambulatory, self-care, and independent living. For children under 5 years old, hearing and vision difficulty are used to determine disability status. For children between the ages of 5 and 14, disability status is determined from hearing, vision, cognitive, ambulatory, and self-care difficulties. For people aged 15 years and older, they are considered to have a disability if they have difficulty with any one of the six difficulty types; Figures cover the Metropolitan Statistical Area
Source: U.S. Census Bureau, 2016-2020 American Community Survey 5-Year Estimates

Male/Female Ratio: City

City	Males	Females	Males per 100 Females
Albuquerque, NM	273,056	287,391	95.0
Allentown, PA	58,626	62,530	93.8
Anchorage, AK	148,954	143,136	104.1
Ann Arbor, MI	59,870	61,223	97.8
Athens, GA	59,474	65,488	90.8
Atlanta, GA	242,321	255,321	94.9
Austin, TX	490,573	475,299	103.2
Baltimore, MD	282,388	319,886	88.3
Baton Rouge, LA	104,674	117,517	89.1
Boise City, ID	114,385	113,672	100.6
Boston, MA	330,560	358,766	92.1
Boulder, CO	56,091	52,686	106.5
Buffalo, NY	121,700	134,105	90.7
Cape Coral, FL	93,932	95,701	98.2
Cedar Rapids, IA	65,799	67,326	97.7
Charleston, SC	64,293	72,748	88.4
Charlotte, NC	419,246	454,324	92.3
Chicago, IL	1,310,878	1,388,469	94.4
Cincinnati, OH	146,522	156,165	93.8
Clarksville, TN	78,420	77,672	101.0
Cleveland, OH	184,050	199,281	92.4
College Station, TX	58,686	57,116	102.7
Colorado Springs, CO	236,066	235,620	100.2
Columbia, MO	59,211	63,448	93.3
Columbia, SC	67,946	66,111	102.8
Columbus, OH	433,751	455,328	95.3
Dallas, TX	663,950	674,896	98.4
Davenport, IA	50,404	51,795	97.3
Denver, CO	358,669	357,209	100.4
Des Moines, IA	105,826	109,582	96.6
Durham, NC	129,730	146,611	88.5
Edison, NJ	49,641	50,235	98.8
El Paso, TX	333,286	346,593	96.2
Fargo, ND	62,270	61,280	101.6
Fort Collins, CO	83,149	82,920	100.3
Fort Wayne, IN	130,013	138,365	94.0
Fort Worth, TX	437,310	454,911	96.1
Grand Rapids, MI	97,685	101,732	96.0
Green Bay, WI	52,048	52,460	99.2
Honolulu, HI	174,117	173,064	100.6
Houston, TX	1,152,063	1,161,175	99.2
Huntsville, AL	97,179	102,666	94.7
Indianapolis, IN	418,738	450,649	92.9
Jacksonville, FL	436,884	465,604	93.8
Kansas City, MO	238,194	252,964	94.2
Lafayette, LA	60,989	65,685	92.9
Las Cruces, NM	50,889	52,061	97.7
Las Vegas, NV	321,537	323,057	99.5
Lexington, KY	157,812	164,388	96.0
Lincoln, NE	143,731	142,657	100.8
Little Rock, AR	93,997	104,070	90.3
Los Angeles, CA	1,966,568	2,006,710	98.0
Louisville, KY	299,458	319,275	93.8
Madison, WI	127,882	130,484	98.0
Manchester, NH	57,098	55,343	103.2

Table continued on following page.

City	Males	Females	Males per 100 Females
Memphis, TN	307,896	343,014	89.8
Miami, FL	229,929	231,151	99.5
Midland, TX	71,831	69,363	103.6
Milwaukee, WI	285,959	306,690	93.2
Minneapolis, MN	215,075	209,461	102.7
Nashville, TN	321,584	345,486	93.1
New Haven, CT	60,781	69,600	87.3
New Orleans, LA	185,252	205,997	89.9
New York, NY	3,997,959	4,381,593	91.2
Oklahoma City, OK	320,348	329,473	97.2
Omaha, NE	236,260	243,269	97.1
Orlando, FL	136,773	148,044	92.4
Philadelphia, PA	748,846	832,685	89.9
Phoenix, AZ	828,085	830,337	99.7
Pittsburgh, PA	147,610	153,676	96.1
Portland, OR	322,445	327,935	98.3
Providence, RI	86,036	93,436	92.1
Provo, UT	57,710	59,176	97.5
Raleigh, NC	226,994	242,704	93.5
Reno, NV	126,469	124,434	101.6
Richmond, VA	108,709	120,524	90.2
Riverside, CA	163,233	164,336	99.3
Rochester, MN	57,244	59,890	95.6
Rochester, NY	99,809	106,548	93.7
Sacramento, CA	247,126	256,356	96.4
St. Louis, MO	147,692	157,017	94.1
Salt Lake City, UT	102,985	97,148	106.0
San Antonio, TX	754,815	774,318	97.5
San Diego, CA	714,965	699,580	102.2
San Francisco, CA	446,246	428,538	104.1
San Jose, CA	521,180	508,229	102.5
Santa Rosa, CA	85,637	92,754	92.3
Savannah, GA	69,716	75,776	92.0
Seattle, WA	374,764	366,487	102.3
Sioux Falls, SD	90,354	90,573	99.8
Springfield, IL	54,705	60,370	90.6
Tampa, FL	195,017	200,895	97.1
Tucson, AZ	270,117	275,223	98.1
Tulsa, OK	195,185	207,256	94.2
Tuscaloosa, AL	48,571	52,062	93.3
Virginia Beach, VA	221,526	229,356	96.6
Washington, DC	333,137	368,837	90.3
Wichita, KS	192,835	197,731	97.5
Wilmington, NC	56,744	65,418	86.7
Winston-Salem, NC	114,992	130,795	87.9
U.S.	160,818,530	165,750,778	97.0

Source: U.S. Census Bureau, 2016-2020 American Community Survey 5-Year Estimates

Male/Female Ratio: Metro Area

Metro Area	Males	Females	Males per 100 Females
Albuquerque, NM	450,378	465,608	96.7
Allentown, PA	412,757	428,508	96.3
Anchorage, AK	204,725	194,725	105.1
Ann Arbor, MI	182,543	185,842	98.2
Athens, GA	101,866	108,944	93.5
Atlanta, GA	2,873,826	3,073,182	93.5
Austin, TX	1,089,474	1,084,330	100.5
Baltimore, MD	1,349,193	1,451,234	93.0
Baton Rouge, LA	418,924	437,855	95.7
Boise City, ID	364,989	365,494	99.9
Boston, MA	2,360,061	2,494,747	94.6
Boulder, CO	163,343	161,339	101.2
Buffalo, NY	547,127	581,891	94.0
Cape Coral, FL	370,506	386,064	96.0
Cedar Rapids, IA	134,477	137,257	98.0
Charleston, SC	386,101	404,854	95.4
Charlotte, NC	1,258,821	1,336,206	94.2
Chicago, IL	4,640,471	4,838,330	95.9
Cincinnati, OH	1,085,972	1,128,293	96.2
Clarksville, TN	153,852	150,732	102.1
Cleveland, OH	991,337	1,061,800	93.4
College Station, TX	131,589	130,112	101.1
Colorado Springs, CO	371,410	364,070	102.0
Columbia, MO	101,311	105,937	95.6
Columbia, SC	404,117	428,808	94.2
Columbus, OH	1,034,609	1,066,934	97.0
Dallas, TX	3,666,414	3,785,444	96.9
Davenport, IA	187,258	193,016	97.0
Denver, CO	1,464,957	1,463,480	100.1
Des Moines, IA	341,251	349,334	97.7
Durham, NC	305,678	330,578	92.5
Edison, NJ	9,316,130	9,945,440	93.7
El Paso, TX	415,461	426,141	97.5
Fargo, ND	122,300	121,666	100.5
Fort Collins, CO	174,652	175,871	99.3
Fort Wayne, IN	200,447	208,972	95.9
Fort Worth, TX	3,666,414	3,785,444	96.9
Grand Rapids, MI	532,155	537,541	99.0
Green Bay, WI	159,901	160,926	99.4
Honolulu, HI	493,534	486,148	101.5
Houston, TX	3,461,935	3,517,678	98.4
Huntsville, AL	227,902	236,705	96.3
Indianapolis, IN	1,002,546	1,048,387	95.6
Jacksonville, FL	748,095	785,701	95.2
Kansas City, MO	1,052,929	1,091,200	96.5
Lafayette, LA	239,197	251,023	95.3
Las Cruces, NM	106,990	110,706	96.6
Las Vegas, NV	1,111,677	1,117,189	99.5
Lexington, KY	250,845	263,428	95.2
Lincoln, NE	167,357	165,836	100.9
Little Rock, AR	357,568	383,034	93.4
Los Angeles, CA	6,514,142	6,696,885	97.3
Louisville, KY	616,008	646,279	95.3
Madison, WI	329,421	330,791	99.6
Manchester, NH	206,540	208,765	98.9

Table continued on following page.

Metro Area	Males	Females	Males per 100 Females
Memphis, TN	641,630	701,520	91.5
Miami, FL	2,980,001	3,149,857	94.6
Midland, TX	89,446	87,468	102.3
Milwaukee, WI	768,888	807,637	95.2
Minneapolis, MN	1,787,858	1,817,592	98.4
Nashville, TN	929,313	974,873	95.3
New Haven, CT	412,404	443,329	93.0
New Orleans, LA	612,408	659,243	92.9
New York, NY	9,316,130	9,945,440	93.7
Oklahoma City, OK	688,854	708,186	97.3
Omaha, NE	465,794	474,369	98.2
Orlando, FL	1,250,887	1,309,373	95.5
Philadelphia, PA	2,946,671	3,145,732	93.7
Phoenix, AZ	2,414,389	2,445,949	98.7
Pittsburgh, PA	1,132,419	1,192,028	95.0
Portland, OR	1,224,427	1,248,347	98.1
Providence, RI	787,186	833,913	94.4
Provo, UT	320,120	313,009	102.3
Raleigh, NC	664,626	698,371	95.2
Reno, NV	236,059	232,209	101.7
Richmond, VA	619,328	662,739	93.4
Riverside, CA	2,291,834	2,308,562	99.3
Rochester, MN	108,357	111,491	97.2
Rochester, NY	520,784	551,000	94.5
Sacramento, CA	1,144,264	1,194,602	95.8
St. Louis, MO	1,361,671	1,444,678	94.3
Salt Lake City, UT	610,556	605,399	100.9
San Antonio, TX	1,241,729	1,268,482	97.9
San Diego, CA	1,674,512	1,649,458	101.5
San Francisco, CA	2,330,358	2,378,862	98.0
San Jose, CA	1,005,726	980,200	102.6
Santa Rosa, CA	242,657	254,144	95.5
Savannah, GA	189,136	201,075	94.1
Seattle, WA	1,969,246	1,959,252	100.5
Sioux Falls, SD	132,469	131,968	100.4
Springfield, IL	99,926	108,298	92.3
Tampa, FL	1,530,176	1,622,752	94.3
Tucson, AZ	510,875	527,601	96.8
Tulsa, OK	489,186	506,955	96.5
Tuscaloosa, AL	121,024	130,854	92.5
Virginia Beach, VA	870,959	897,997	97.0
Washington, DC	3,055,672	3,194,637	95.7
Wichita, KS	316,961	322,707	98.2
Wilmington, NC	141,224	152,115	92.8
Winston-Salem, NC	322,379	348,777	92.4
U.S.	160,818,530	165,750,778	97.0

Note: Figures cover the Metropolitan Statistical Area (MSA)
Source: U.S. Census Bureau, 2016-2020 American Community Survey 5-Year Estimates

Gross Metropolitan Product

MSA[1]	2017	2018	2019	2020	Rank[2]
Albuquerque, NM	42.8	44.4	46.3	48.6	68
Allentown, PA	43.9	46.2	48.1	49.9	64
Anchorage, AK	27.4	28.3	29.3	30.6	102
Ann Arbor, MI	23.5	24.6	25.5	26.4	112
Athens, GA	10.1	10.5	10.8	11.2	205
Atlanta, GA	391.0	409.9	431.6	452.0	10
Austin, TX	145.1	156.6	164.6	174.0	25
Baltimore, MD	194.5	202.3	210.8	219.5	19
Baton Rouge, LA	53.2	56.3	58.3	61.0	59
Boise City, ID	33.9	36.5	38.7	40.8	79
Boston, MA	449.5	472.7	493.6	515.0	8
Boulder, CO	25.6	27.2	28.7	29.9	107
Buffalo, NY	62.0	64.3	66.5	68.8	53
Cape Coral, FL	28.3	30.0	31.8	33.4	93
Cedar Rapids, IA	17.8	18.4	18.8	19.4	141
Charleston, SC	42.5	44.6	46.7	49.0	67
Charlotte, NC	174.1	185.6	195.5	205.3	20
Chicago, IL	683.3	716.3	743.3	770.7	3
Cincinnati, OH	137.2	143.5	150.7	156.1	29
Clarksville, TN	11.0	11.6	12.2	12.6	194
Cleveland, OH	138.3	145.9	152.3	157.1	28
College Station, TX	9.9	10.6	11.2	11.7	204
Colorado Springs, CO	33.1	34.9	36.6	38.5	84
Columbia, MO	9.2	9.6	9.9	10.3	220
Columbia, SC	41.4	42.3	43.9	45.8	73
Columbus, OH	135.6	142.2	148.6	154.7	32
Dallas, TX	522.3	556.9	586.7	620.6	5
Davenport, IA	19.8	20.7	21.6	22.3	124
Denver, CO	211.6	225.3	235.8	246.9	18
Des Moines, IA	55.0	57.7	60.3	62.8	58
Durham, NC	43.4	45.5	48.0	50.7	65
Edison, NJ	1,765.5	1,851.9	1,932.1	2,007.4	1
El Paso, TX	28.3	29.4	30.5	31.5	97
Fargo, ND	15.3	16.1	16.8	17.5	156
Fort Collins, CO	17.4	18.4	19.7	20.7	139
Fort Wayne, IN	21.9	22.9	23.9	24.8	117
Fort Worth, TX	522.3	556.9	586.7	620.6	5
Grand Rapids, MI	60.6	63.6	66.2	68.3	54
Green Bay, WI	19.4	20.4	21.3	22.1	128
Honolulu, HI	68.2	70.5	73.2	75.5	50
Houston, TX	478.1	513.9	546.1	583.7	7
Huntsville, AL	25.9	27.2	28.4	29.8	106
Indianapolis, IN	140.6	147.0	152.8	159.1	27
Jacksonville, FL	77.6	82.8	86.5	90.6	45
Kansas City, MO	131.8	138.2	144.1	149.7	33
Lafayette, LA	21.4	23.0	24.0	25.4	116
Las Cruces, NM	7.0	7.3	7.7	8.1	257
Las Vegas, NV	112.8	119.1	124.1	130.3	36
Lexington, KY	29.7	30.8	31.9	33.0	90
Lincoln, NE	19.7	20.6	21.2	22.0	125
Little Rock, AR	38.5	39.8	41.1	42.7	76
Los Angeles, CA	1,067.7	1,125.5	1,164.2	1,207.3	2
Louisville, KY	75.3	78.1	81.3	83.9	48
Madison, WI	49.5	52.1	54.5	56.5	61
Manchester, NH	28.7	30.0	31.2	32.5	94
Memphis, TN	72.9	76.2	79.4	82.2	49

Table continued on following page.

MSA[1]	2017	2018	2019	2020	Rank[2]
Miami, FL	349.2	369.5	386.7	403.4	12
Midland, TX	27.1	35.0	38.1	44.4	83
Milwaukee, WI	104.6	109.2	112.8	116.2	37
Minneapolis, MN	260.9	273.1	284.6	296.0	14
Nashville, TN	134.3	142.5	149.8	156.5	30
New Haven, CT	46.1	47.8	49.7	51.2	62
New Orleans, LA	76.7	81.0	83.8	87.5	46
New York, NY	1,765.5	1,851.9	1,932.1	2,007.4	1
Oklahoma City, OK	74.2	79.6	83.2	88.3	47
Omaha, NE	63.3	65.9	68.5	71.0	52
Orlando, FL	134.1	142.4	150.7	158.6	31
Philadelphia, PA	445.1	465.5	485.8	504.6	9
Phoenix, AZ	248.0	264.9	280.3	294.0	16
Pittsburgh, PA	147.4	156.4	162.8	168.5	26
Portland, OR	165.9	175.7	183.8	191.1	21
Providence, RI	84.0	86.8	89.5	93.0	44
Provo, UT	25.7	27.9	29.5	31.2	104
Raleigh, NC	83.2	88.3	92.8	97.8	42
Reno, NV	26.8	28.8	30.8	32.3	99
Richmond, VA	83.0	87.2	91.0	94.7	43
Riverside, CA	161.6	171.0	178.3	186.9	22
Rochester, MN	12.6	13.2	13.9	14.4	182
Rochester, NY	58.4	60.7	62.0	64.0	56
Sacramento, CA	129.3	137.0	144.3	151.5	34
St. Louis, MO	161.1	167.8	174.6	180.1	23
Salt Lake City, UT	87.9	93.6	97.8	102.5	41
San Antonio, TX	126.1	134.5	140.1	148.6	35
San Diego, CA	237.2	249.4	260.3	272.1	17
San Francisco, CA	512.2	547.3	578.7	605.5	6
San Jose, CA	281.6	303.1	321.2	334.7	13
Santa Rosa, CA	29.3	30.4	31.4	32.5	91
Savannah, GA	18.8	19.7	20.6	21.2	134
Seattle, WA	367.9	397.5	416.9	435.0	11
Sioux Falls, SD	19.6	20.5	21.5	22.4	127
Springfield, IL	10.3	10.7	11.0	11.4	202
Tampa, FL	148.2	156.6	164.0	172.0	24
Tucson, AZ	39.9	41.7	43.6	45.5	74
Tulsa, OK	57.2	60.9	63.7	67.4	55
Tuscaloosa, AL	11.8	12.4	13.0	13.4	190
Virginia Beach, VA	95.2	99.3	103.6	107.4	39
Washington, DC	539.6	562.6	585.8	612.1	4
Wichita, KS	34.3	35.7	37.0	38.0	81
Wilmington, NC	14.3	15.0	15.7	16.4	165
Winston-Salem, NC	29.7	31.2	32.5	33.8	88

Note: Figures are in billions of dollars; (1) Metropolitan Statistical Area; (2) Rank is based on 2018 data and ranges from 1 to 381.
Source: The U.S. Conference of Mayors, U.S. Metro Economies: GMP & Employment 2018-2020, September 2019

Economic Growth

MSA[1]	2015-17 (%)	2018 (%)	2019 (%)	2020 (%)	Rank[2]
Albuquerque, NM	0.7	1.4	2.6	2.5	252
Allentown, PA	1.2	2.6	2.3	1.6	210
Anchorage, AK	-1.5	-0.9	2.4	0.6	353
Ann Arbor, MI	2.1	2.5	1.9	1.3	123
Athens, GA	6.8	1.5	1.3	1.4	6
Atlanta, GA	3.7	2.8	3.6	2.6	47
Austin, TX	6.3	4.4	3.5	2.6	9
Baltimore, MD	2.1	2.0	2.3	1.9	125
Baton Rouge, LA	1.6	0.8	1.2	2.4	170
Boise City, ID	3.7	5.5	4.1	3.2	45
Boston, MA	2.0	3.0	2.8	2.1	134
Boulder, CO	2.5	4.1	3.9	2.1	98
Buffalo, NY	1.5	1.2	1.5	1.3	178
Cape Coral, FL	2.7	3.7	3.7	3.0	83
Cedar Rapids, IA	-1.6	0.9	0.8	1.0	354
Charleston, SC	5.0	2.4	2.9	2.6	16
Charlotte, NC	3.4	4.2	3.7	2.8	51
Chicago, IL	0.8	2.3	2.0	1.6	247
Cincinnati, OH	2.0	1.7	3.3	1.4	132
Clarksville, TN	-0.6	3.0	3.0	1.6	331
Cleveland, OH	1.7	1.9	2.8	0.9	160
College Station, TX	1.0	3.4	3.3	1.4	224
Colorado Springs, CO	2.9	3.1	3.0	2.8	73
Columbia, MO	0.9	1.6	1.5	1.8	242
Columbia, SC	0.8	-0.1	1.9	2.3	245
Columbus, OH	2.0	2.1	2.6	1.9	130
Dallas, TX	2.7	2.8	3.7	2.7	87
Davenport, IA	-0.2	2.4	2.4	1.2	311
Denver, CO	2.6	3.7	3.0	1.9	89
Des Moines, IA	2.8	1.8	2.7	1.9	78
Durham, NC	-2.0	2.9	3.7	3.5	363
Edison, NJ	1.3	2.6	2.6	1.6	196
El Paso, TX	0.9	1.5	1.6	1.4	244
Fargo, ND	0.4	2.1	2.6	2.0	283
Fort Collins, CO	5.3	3.7	4.7	3.1	14
Fort Wayne, IN	1.9	2.5	2.5	1.3	149
Fort Worth, TX	2.7	2.8	3.7	2.7	87
Grand Rapids, MI	1.9	3.4	2.3	1.2	139
Green Bay, WI	1.2	3.2	2.6	1.2	203
Honolulu, HI	1.6	1.0	1.9	0.9	165
Houston, TX	-1.7	2.9	4.6	3.1	360
Huntsville, AL	1.8	3.0	2.5	2.7	155
Indianapolis, IN	2.5	1.9	2.1	2.0	101
Jacksonville, FL	4.1	4.3	2.6	2.5	34
Kansas City, MO	0.6	2.6	2.4	1.7	263
Lafayette, LA	-4.9	2.6	3.0	2.0	380
Las Cruces, NM	1.0	1.7	2.7	2.5	228
Las Vegas, NV	1.5	3.1	2.3	2.7	182
Lexington, KY	1.6	1.3	2.0	1.1	167
Lincoln, NE	0.3	2.1	1.3	1.5	287
Little Rock, AR	0.4	0.9	1.6	1.5	286
Los Angeles, CA	2.3	3.5	1.8	1.6	110
Louisville, KY	0.7	1.4	2.3	1.2	254
Madison, WI	2.4	3.2	2.8	1.7	107
Manchester, NH	2.7	2.6	2.3	1.8	84
Memphis, TN	0.1	2.3	2.3	1.4	299

Table continued on following page.

MSA[1]	2015-17 (%)	2018 (%)	2019 (%)	2020 (%)	Rank[2]
Miami, FL	3.2	3.5	2.9	2.1	56
Midland, TX	1.0	13.0	9.2	3.6	231
Milwaukee, WI	0.9	2.1	1.5	0.9	243
Minneapolis, MN	1.9	2.3	2.5	1.9	144
Nashville, TN	4.0	3.9	3.3	2.3	39
New Haven, CT	1.2	1.7	2.1	0.9	204
New Orleans, LA	-0.6	1.2	1.3	2.0	329
New York, NY	1.3	2.6	2.6	1.6	196
Oklahoma City, OK	0.7	2.8	2.9	2.2	259
Omaha, NE	0.6	1.7	2.2	1.5	272
Orlando, FL	2.4	3.8	4.0	3.0	109
Philadelphia, PA	1.4	1.9	2.7	1.7	188
Phoenix, AZ	3.3	4.5	4.0	2.7	54
Pittsburgh, PA	2.0	2.6	2.5	1.3	137
Portland, OR	3.9	3.5	2.6	1.6	42
Providence, RI	0.7	1.0	1.3	1.7	262
Provo, UT	6.6	6.5	4.0	3.7	7
Raleigh, NC	3.1	3.9	3.4	3.3	62
Reno, NV	4.3	5.3	4.9	2.5	27
Richmond, VA	1.5	3.0	2.6	1.8	179
Riverside, CA	3.0	3.4	2.3	2.6	65
Rochester, MN	3.6	2.9	3.1	1.1	48
Rochester, NY	0.4	1.6	0.2	1.0	280
Sacramento, CA	2.6	3.6	3.4	2.7	90
St. Louis, MO	-0.3	2.0	2.3	1.0	317
Salt Lake City, UT	2.3	3.7	2.6	2.7	114
San Antonio, TX	4.2	2.0	2.7	1.7	30
San Diego, CA	3.1	3.0	2.6	2.3	64
San Francisco, CA	4.8	5.1	4.3	2.5	18
San Jose, CA	7.0	6.0	4.6	2.2	5
Santa Rosa, CA	2.5	1.2	1.7	1.1	100
Savannah, GA	2.3	2.7	2.4	1.2	115
Seattle, WA	4.3	6.3	3.4	2.4	29
Sioux Falls, SD	1.2	1.6	3.2	2.2	206
Springfield, IL	-0.8	0.8	1.4	0.9	337
Tampa, FL	2.7	3.5	2.9	2.6	85
Tucson, AZ	2.0	2.7	2.8	2.0	133
Tulsa, OK	-3.3	1.3	3.1	1.7	373
Tuscaloosa, AL	1.0	2.8	3.4	1.5	227
Virginia Beach, VA	-0.4	2.2	2.5	1.4	323
Washington, DC	2.0	2.3	2.4	2.1	131
Wichita, KS	1.9	1.5	1.8	0.5	141
Wilmington, NC	1.0	2.6	3.0	2.1	229
Winston-Salem, NC	-0.2	2.6	2.6	1.6	314
U.S.	1.9	2.9	2.3	2.1	–

Note: Figures are real gross metropolitan product (GMP) growth rates and represent annual average percent change; (1) Metropolitan Statistical Area; (2) Rank is based on 2017 2-year average annual percent change and ranges from 1 to 381

Source: The U.S. Conference of Mayors, U.S. Metro Economies: GMP & Employment 2018-2020, September 2019

Metropolitan Area Exports

MSA[1]	2015	2016	2017	2018	2019	2020	Rank[2]
Albuquerque, NM	1,761.2	999.7	624.2	771.5	1,629.7	1,265.3	127
Allentown, PA	3,439.9	3,657.2	3,639.4	3,423.2	3,796.3	3,207.4	70
Anchorage, AK	421.9	1,215.4	1,675.9	1,510.8	1,348.0	990.9	145
Ann Arbor, MI	1,053.0	1,207.9	1,447.4	1,538.7	1,432.7	1,183.1	133
Athens, GA	327.4	332.1	297.7	378.1	442.1	338.7	232
Atlanta, GA	19,163.9	20,480.1	21,748.0	24,091.6	25,800.8	25,791.0	12
Austin, TX	10,094.5	10,682.7	12,451.5	12,929.9	12,509.0	13,041.5	26
Baltimore, MD	6,047.2	5,288.6	4,674.3	6,039.2	7,081.8	6,084.6	49
Baton Rouge, LA	6,505.4	6,580.5	8,830.3	10,506.1	8,981.2	8,023.5	39
Boise City, ID	2,668.0	3,021.7	2,483.3	2,771.7	2,062.8	1,632.9	109
Boston, MA	21,329.5	21,168.0	23,116.2	24,450.1	23,505.8	23,233.8	15
Boulder, CO	1,039.1	956.3	1,012.0	1,044.1	1,014.9	1,110.4	139
Buffalo, NY	4,684.6	4,783.4	5,018.2	5,292.0	5,210.5	4,399.1	61
Cape Coral, FL	487.3	540.3	592.3	668.0	694.9	654.8	185
Cedar Rapids, IA	873.5	945.0	1,071.6	1,025.0	1,028.4	832.0	163
Charleston, SC	6,457.5	9,508.1	8,845.2	10,943.2	16,337.9	6,110.5	48
Charlotte, NC	13,985.8	11,944.1	13,122.5	14,083.2	13,892.4	8,225.6	37
Chicago, IL	44,820.9	43,932.7	46,140.2	47,287.8	42,438.8	41,279.4	4
Cincinnati, OH	24,127.0	26,326.2	28,581.8	27,396.3	28,778.3	21,002.2	17
Clarksville, TN	296.5	376.1	360.2	435.5	341.8	246.8	270
Cleveland, OH	9,629.7	8,752.9	8,944.9	9,382.9	8,829.9	7,415.8	42
College Station, TX	122.5	113.2	145.4	153.0	160.5	114.9	331
Colorado Springs, CO	832.4	786.9	819.7	850.6	864.2	979.2	146
Columbia, MO	214.0	213.7	224.0	238.6	291.4	256.2	264
Columbia, SC	2,011.8	2,007.7	2,123.9	2,083.8	2,184.6	2,058.8	92
Columbus, OH	6,201.6	5,675.4	5,962.2	7,529.5	7,296.6	6,304.8	47
Dallas, TX	27,372.9	27,187.8	30,269.1	36,260.9	39,474.0	35,642.0	5
Davenport, IA	5,711.8	4,497.6	5,442.7	6,761.9	6,066.3	5,097.5	52
Denver, CO	3,909.5	3,649.3	3,954.7	4,544.3	4,555.6	4,604.4	57
Des Moines, IA	1,047.8	1,052.2	1,141.2	1,293.7	1,437.8	1,414.0	119
Durham, NC	2,807.2	2,937.4	3,128.4	3,945.8	4,452.9	3,359.3	69
Edison, NJ	95,645.4	89,649.5	93,693.7	97,692.4	87,365.7	75,745.4	2
El Paso, TX	24,560.9	26,452.8	25,814.1	30,052.0	32,749.6	27,154.4	11
Fargo, ND	543.2	474.5	519.5	553.5	515.0	438.3	216
Fort Collins, CO	990.7	993.8	1,034.1	1,021.8	1,060.0	1,092.5	140
Fort Wayne, IN	1,529.0	1,322.2	1,422.8	1,593.3	1,438.5	1,144.6	136
Fort Worth, TX	27,372.9	27,187.8	30,269.1	36,260.9	39,474.0	35,642.0	5
Grand Rapids, MI	5,143.0	5,168.5	5,385.8	5,420.9	5,214.1	4,488.3	60
Green Bay, WI	968.1	1,044.0	1,054.8	1,044.3	928.2	736.4	176
Honolulu, HI	446.4	330.3	393.6	438.9	308.6	169.0	296
Houston, TX	97,054.3	84,105.5	95,760.3	120,714.3	129,656.0	104,538.2	1
Huntsville, AL	1,344.7	1,827.3	1,889.2	1,608.7	1,534.2	1,263.0	129
Indianapolis, IN	9,809.4	9,655.4	10,544.2	11,069.9	11,148.7	11,100.4	28
Jacksonville, FL	2,564.4	2,159.0	2,141.7	2,406.7	2,975.5	2,473.3	86
Kansas City, MO	6,723.2	6,709.8	7,015.0	7,316.9	7,652.6	7,862.7	40
Lafayette, LA	1,165.2	1,335.2	954.8	1,001.7	1,086.2	946.2	151
Las Cruces, NM	1,593.7	1,568.6	1,390.2	1,467.5	n/a	2,149.5	91
Las Vegas, NV	2,916.2	2,312.3	2,710.6	2,240.6	2,430.8	1,705.9	106
Lexington, KY	2,065.7	2,069.6	2,119.8	2,148.0	2,093.8	1,586.3	112
Lincoln, NE	1,189.3	796.9	860.9	885.6	807.0	726.3	178
Little Rock, AR	1,777.5	1,871.0	2,146.1	1,607.4	1,642.5	n/a	n/a
Los Angeles, CA	61,758.7	61,245.7	63,752.9	64,814.6	61,041.1	50,185.4	3
Louisville, KY	8,037.9	7,793.3	8,925.9	8,987.0	9,105.5	8,360.3	36
Madison, WI	2,280.4	2,204.8	2,187.7	2,460.2	2,337.6	2,450.5	87
Manchester, NH	1,556.6	1,465.2	1,714.7	1,651.4	1,587.1	1,704.9	107
Memphis, TN	11,819.5	11,628.7	11,233.9	12,695.4	13,751.7	13,350.3	25

Table continued on following page.

MSA[1]	2015	2016	2017	2018	2019	2020	Rank[2]
Miami, FL	33,258.5	32,734.5	34,780.5	35,650.2	35,498.9	29,112.1	8
Midland, TX	110.1	69.6	69.4	63.6	63.7	57.7	361
Milwaukee, WI	7,953.6	7,256.2	7,279.1	7,337.6	6,896.3	6,624.0	45
Minneapolis, MN	19,608.6	18,329.2	19,070.9	20,016.2	18,633.0	17,109.5	20
Nashville, TN	9,353.0	9,460.1	10,164.3	8,723.7	7,940.7	6,569.9	46
New Haven, CT	1,756.3	1,819.8	1,876.3	2,082.3	2,133.8	2,330.5	88
New Orleans, LA	27,023.3	29,518.8	31,648.5	36,570.4	34,109.6	31,088.4	6
New York, NY	95,645.4	89,649.5	93,693.7	97,692.4	87,365.7	75,745.4	2
Oklahoma City, OK	1,353.1	1,260.0	1,278.8	1,489.4	1,434.5	1,326.6	124
Omaha, NE	3,753.4	3,509.7	3,756.2	4,371.6	3,725.7	3,852.5	66
Orlando, FL	3,082.7	3,363.9	3,196.7	3,131.7	3,363.9	2,849.8	76
Philadelphia, PA	24,236.1	21,359.9	21,689.7	23,663.2	24,721.3	23,022.1	16
Phoenix, AZ	13,821.5	12,838.2	13,223.1	13,614.9	15,136.6	11,073.9	29
Pittsburgh, PA	9,137.1	7,971.0	9,322.7	9,824.2	9,672.9	7,545.1	41
Portland, OR	18,847.8	20,256.8	20,788.8	21,442.9	23,761.9	27,824.7	10
Providence, RI	5,048.8	6,595.7	7,125.4	6,236.6	7,424.8	6,685.2	44
Provo, UT	2,216.4	1,894.8	2,065.3	1,788.1	1,783.7	1,888.5	100
Raleigh, NC	2,553.4	2,620.4	2,865.8	3,193.2	3,546.8	3,372.0	68
Reno, NV	1,943.3	2,382.1	2,517.3	2,631.7	2,598.3	4,553.3	59
Richmond, VA	3,325.9	3,525.7	3,663.7	3,535.0	3,203.2	2,719.1	80
Riverside, CA	8,970.0	10,211.6	8,782.3	9,745.7	9,737.6	8,459.8	35
Rochester, MN	530.2	398.0	495.3	537.6	390.1	194.0	287
Rochester, NY	5,038.4	4,627.5	4,719.2	4,688.3	4,321.5	3,867.0	65
Sacramento, CA	8,101.2	7,032.1	6,552.6	6,222.8	5,449.2	4,980.9	54
St. Louis, MO	8,913.7	8,346.5	9,662.9	10,866.8	10,711.1	9,089.4	32
Salt Lake City, UT	10,380.5	8,653.7	7,916.9	9,748.6	13,273.9	13,565.5	23
San Antonio, TX	15,919.2	5,621.2	9,184.1	11,678.1	11,668.0	10,987.9	30
San Diego, CA	17,439.7	18,086.6	18,637.1	20,156.8	19,774.1	18,999.7	19
San Francisco, CA	25,061.1	24,506.3	29,103.8	27,417.0	28,003.8	23,864.5	13
San Jose, CA	19,827.2	21,716.8	21,464.7	22,224.2	20,909.4	19,534.5	18
Santa Rosa, CA	1,119.8	1,194.3	1,168.2	1,231.7	1,234.5	1,131.4	138
Savannah, GA	5,447.5	4,263.4	4,472.0	5,407.8	4,925.5	4,557.0	58
Seattle, WA	67,226.4	61,881.0	59,007.0	59,742.9	41,249.0	23,851.0	14
Sioux Falls, SD	375.0	334.3	386.8	400.0	431.5	524.9	202
Springfield, IL	111.7	88.3	107.5	91.2	99.8	90.5	342
Tampa, FL	5,660.4	5,702.9	6,256.0	4,966.7	6,219.7	5,082.2	53
Tucson, AZ	2,485.9	2,563.9	2,683.9	2,824.8	2,943.7	2,640.7	82
Tulsa, OK	2,699.7	2,363.0	2,564.7	3,351.7	3,399.2	2,567.8	84
Tuscaloosa, AL	n/a	n/a	n/a	n/a	n/a	5,175.0	51
Virginia Beach, VA	3,556.4	3,291.1	3,307.2	3,950.6	3,642.4	4,284.3	62
Washington, DC	13,900.4	13,582.4	12,736.1	13,602.7	14,563.8	13,537.3	24
Wichita, KS	3,717.6	3,054.9	3,299.2	3,817.0	3,494.7	2,882.1	75
Wilmington, NC	617.3	598.7	759.8	634.4	526.4	553.6	199
Winston-Salem, NC	1,267.4	1,234.6	1,131.7	1,107.5	1,209.1	913.1	154

Note: Figures are in millions of dollars; (1) Metropolitan Statistical Area; (2) Rank is based on 2020 data and ranges from 1 to 389
Source: U.S. Department of Commerce, International Trade Administration, Office of Trade and Economic Analysis, Industry and Analysis, Exports by Metropolitan Area, extracted March 4, 2022

Building Permits: City

City	Single-Family			Multi-Family			Total		
	2019	2020	Pct. Chg.	2019	2020	Pct. Chg.	2019	2020	Pct. Chg.
Albuquerque, NM	906	865	-4.5	188	0	-100.0	1,094	865	-20.9
Allentown, PA	0	0	0.0	0	0	0.0	0	0	0.0
Anchorage, AK	838	735	-12.3	221	235	6.3	1,059	970	-8.4
Ann Arbor, MI	96	96	0.0	0	158	–	96	254	164.6
Athens, GA	517	294	-43.1	766	341	-55.5	1,283	635	-50.5
Atlanta, GA	728	373	-48.8	2,555	1,301	-49.1	3,283	1,674	-49.0
Austin, TX	4,568	4,113	-10.0	10,141	13,577	33.9	14,709	17,690	20.3
Baltimore, MD	130	101	-22.3	380	1,520	300.0	510	1,621	217.8
Baton Rouge, LA	354	306	-13.6	0	0	0.0	354	306	-13.6
Boise City, ID	698	756	8.3	883	369	-58.2	1,581	1,125	-28.8
Boston, MA	37	24	-35.1	2,956	3,508	18.7	2,993	3,532	18.0
Boulder, CO	41	40	-2.4	286	276	-3.5	327	316	-3.4
Buffalo, NY	29	30	3.4	262	210	-19.8	291	240	-17.5
Cape Coral, FL	1,878	2,693	43.4	810	834	3.0	2,688	3,527	31.2
Cedar Rapids, IA	173	130	-24.9	197	106	-46.2	370	236	-36.2
Charleston, SC	828	959	15.8	360	322	-10.6	1,188	1,281	7.8
Charlotte, NC	n/a	n/a	n/a	n/a	n/a	n/a	n/a	n/a	n/a
Chicago, IL	410	248	-39.5	7,504	3,885	-48.2	7,914	4,133	-47.8
Cincinnati, OH	135	128	-5.2	992	778	-21.6	1,127	906	-19.6
Clarksville, TN	1,428	1,927	34.9	160	321	100.6	1,588	2,248	41.6
Cleveland, OH	78	95	21.8	19	22	15.8	97	117	20.6
College Station, TX	398	484	21.6	219	681	211.0	617	1,165	88.8
Colorado Springs, CO	n/a	n/a	n/a	n/a	n/a	n/a	n/a	n/a	n/a
Columbia, MO	338	412	21.9	166	110	-33.7	504	522	3.6
Columbia, SC	464	541	16.6	10	4	-60.0	474	545	15.0
Columbus, OH	512	834	62.9	2,258	5,467	142.1	2,770	6,301	127.5
Dallas, TX	2,093	1,475	-29.5	6,000	2,216	-63.1	8,093	3,691	-54.4
Davenport, IA	122	95	-22.1	196	0	-100.0	318	95	-70.1
Denver, CO	2,257	1,167	-48.3	5,073	3,892	-23.3	7,330	5,059	-31.0
Des Moines, IA	391	219	-44.0	279	222	-20.4	670	441	-34.2
Durham, NC	1,945	1,972	1.4	1,884	1,860	-1.3	3,829	3,832	0.1
Edison, NJ	55	93	69.1	175	10	-94.3	230	103	-55.2
El Paso, TX	1,873	1,570	-16.2	413	192	-53.5	2,286	1,762	-22.9
Fargo, ND	311	450	44.7	172	674	291.9	483	1,124	132.7
Fort Collins, CO	316	453	43.4	632	174	-72.5	948	627	-33.9
Fort Wayne, IN	n/a	n/a	n/a	n/a	n/a	n/a	n/a	n/a	n/a
Fort Worth, TX	5,063	7,286	43.9	6,276	2,282	-63.6	11,339	9,568	-15.6
Grand Rapids, MI	153	54	-64.7	183	251	37.2	336	305	-9.2
Green Bay, WI	63	71	12.7	0	252	–	63	323	412.7
Honolulu, HI	n/a	n/a	n/a	n/a	n/a	n/a	n/a	n/a	n/a
Houston, TX	5,120	5,923	15.7	10,343	10,662	3.1	15,463	16,585	7.3
Huntsville, AL	1,436	1,705	18.7	167	84	-49.7	1,603	1,789	11.6
Indianapolis, IN	1,153	1,108	-3.9	1,229	1,004	-18.3	2,382	2,112	-11.3
Jacksonville, FL	4,155	5,549	33.5	2,650	3,485	31.5	6,805	9,034	32.8
Kansas City, MO	619	900	45.4	879	1,550	76.3	1,498	2,450	63.6
Lafayette, LA	n/a	n/a	n/a	n/a	n/a	n/a	n/a	n/a	n/a
Las Cruces, NM	584	737	26.2	102	76	-25.5	686	813	18.5
Las Vegas, NV	1,885	1,941	3.0	780	1,415	81.4	2,665	3,356	25.9
Lexington, KY	579	702	21.2	804	735	-8.6	1,383	1,437	3.9
Lincoln, NE	863	964	11.7	864	778	-10.0	1,727	1,742	0.9
Little Rock, AR	480	415	-13.5	539	418	-22.4	1,019	833	-18.3
Los Angeles, CA	2,647	1,854	-30.0	11,740	10,438	-11.1	14,387	12,292	-14.6
Louisville, KY	1,207	1,194	-1.1	2,204	29	-98.7	3,411	1,223	-64.1
Madison, WI	426	406	-4.7	1,232	1,779	44.4	1,658	2,185	31.8

Table continued on following page.

City	Single-Family			Multi-Family			Total		
	2019	2020	Pct. Chg.	2019	2020	Pct. Chg.	2019	2020	Pct. Chg.
Manchester, NH	106	133	25.5	26	14	-46.2	132	147	11.4
Memphis, TN	n/a	n/a	n/a	n/a	n/a	n/a	n/a	n/a	n/a
Miami, FL	107	81	-24.3	4,361	3,502	-19.7	4,468	3,583	-19.8
Midland, TX	1,290	1,289	-0.1	0	0	0.0	1,290	1,289	-0.1
Milwaukee, WI	15	34	126.7	178	78	-56.2	193	112	-42.0
Minneapolis, MN	122	79	-35.2	4,691	3,261	-30.5	4,813	3,340	-30.6
Nashville, TN	3,830	3,533	-7.8	5,935	9,616	62.0	9,765	13,149	34.7
New Haven, CT	4	16	300.0	695	722	3.9	699	738	5.6
New Orleans, LA	558	621	11.3	748	739	-1.2	1,306	1,360	4.1
New York, NY	332	217	-34.6	26,215	19,190	-26.8	26,547	19,407	-26.9
Oklahoma City, OK	3,243	3,800	17.2	128	116	-9.4	3,371	3,916	16.2
Omaha, NE	1,179	1,686	43.0	965	1,363	41.2	2,144	3,049	42.2
Orlando, FL	747	956	28.0	1,887	3,645	93.2	2,634	4,601	74.7
Philadelphia, PA	894	983	10.0	3,672	4,682	27.5	4,566	5,665	24.1
Phoenix, AZ	4,175	4,666	11.8	5,723	6,981	22.0	9,898	11,647	17.7
Pittsburgh, PA	78	167	114.1	582	453	-22.2	660	620	-6.1
Portland, OR	703	584	-16.9	4,391	1,195	-72.8	5,094	1,779	-65.1
Providence, RI	14	18	28.6	183	195	6.6	197	213	8.1
Provo, UT	174	219	25.9	140	138	-1.4	314	357	13.7
Raleigh, NC	380	1,162	205.8	827	2,317	180.2	1,207	3,479	188.2
Reno, NV	1,176	1,330	13.1	2,144	1,871	-12.7	3,320	3,201	-3.6
Richmond, VA	353	294	-16.7	887	729	-17.8	1,240	1,023	-17.5
Riverside, CA	170	180	5.9	509	164	-67.8	679	344	-49.3
Rochester, MN	296	296	0.0	478	129	-73.0	774	425	-45.1
Rochester, NY	9	58	544.4	337	741	119.9	346	799	130.9
Sacramento, CA	1,538	935	-39.2	1,463	2,649	81.1	3,001	3,584	19.4
St. Louis, MO	115	124	7.8	266	298	12.0	381	422	10.8
Salt Lake City, UT	127	168	32.3	3,359	2,499	-25.6	3,486	2,667	-23.5
San Antonio, TX	3,890	4,275	9.9	5,306	4,950	-6.7	9,196	9,225	0.3
San Diego, CA	580	445	-23.3	3,361	4,237	26.1	3,941	4,682	18.8
San Francisco, CA	22	21	-4.5	3,178	1,983	-37.6	3,200	2,004	-37.4
San Jose, CA	514	312	-39.3	1,831	1,057	-42.3	2,345	1,369	-41.6
Santa Rosa, CA	939	440	-53.1	251	188	-25.1	1,190	628	-47.2
Savannah, GA	339	349	2.9	0	0	0.0	339	349	2.9
Seattle, WA	507	247	-51.3	10,277	5,479	-46.7	10,784	5,726	-46.9
Sioux Falls, SD	1,013	1,190	17.5	643	1,577	145.3	1,656	2,767	67.1
Springfield, IL	57	61	7.0	112	94	-16.1	169	155	-8.3
Tampa, FL	1,159	1,308	12.9	3,618	2,025	-44.0	4,777	3,333	-30.2
Tucson, AZ	999	1,043	4.4	817	712	-12.9	1,816	1,755	-3.4
Tulsa, OK	629	521	-17.2	580	310	-46.6	1,209	831	-31.3
Tuscaloosa, AL	321	411	28.0	844	613	-27.4	1,165	1,024	-12.1
Virginia Beach, VA	667	493	-26.1	683	445	-34.8	1,350	938	-30.5
Washington, DC	168	139	-17.3	5,777	7,231	25.2	5,945	7,370	24.0
Wichita, KS	618	662	7.1	364	174	-52.2	982	836	-14.9
Wilmington, NC	n/a	n/a	n/a	n/a	n/a	n/a	n/a	n/a	n/a
Winston-Salem, NC	1,185	1,554	31.1	0	28	–	1,185	1,582	33.5
U.S.	862,100	979,400	13.6	523,900	491,700	-6.1	1,386,000	1,471,100	6.1

Note: Figures represent new, privately-owned housing units authorized (unadjusted data); All permit data are based on estimates with imputation
Source: U.S. Census Bureau, Manufacturing, Mining, and Construction Statistics, Building Permits, 2019, 2020

Building Permits: Metro Area

Metro Area	Single-Family			Multi-Family			Total		
	2019	2020	Pct. Chg.	2019	2020	Pct. Chg.	2019	2020	Pct. Chg.
Albuquerque, NM	1,872	1,925	2.8	276	89	-67.8	2,148	2,014	-6.2
Allentown, PA	1,078	1,110	3.0	267	578	116.5	1,345	1,688	25.5
Anchorage, AK	878	771	-12.2	285	259	-9.1	1,163	1,030	-11.4
Ann Arbor, MI	608	711	16.9	207	354	71.0	815	1,065	30.7
Athens, GA	821	857	4.4	770	361	-53.1	1,591	1,218	-23.4
Atlanta, GA	26,261	28,632	9.0	6,575	3,714	-43.5	32,836	32,346	-1.5
Austin, TX	18,426	22,570	22.5	13,611	19,694	44.7	32,037	42,264	31.9
Baltimore, MD	4,802	5,010	4.3	2,165	3,084	42.4	6,967	8,094	16.2
Baton Rouge, LA	3,612	3,766	4.3	10	14	40.0	3,622	3,780	4.4
Boise City, ID	7,570	8,158	7.8	3,062	1,604	-47.6	10,632	9,762	-8.2
Boston, MA	4,299	4,457	3.7	10,789	9,791	-9.3	15,088	14,248	-5.6
Boulder, CO	742	573	-22.8	908	1,061	16.9	1,650	1,634	-1.0
Buffalo, NY	912	912	0.0	781	532	-31.9	1,693	1,444	-14.7
Cape Coral, FL	5,633	6,828	21.2	3,472	3,845	10.7	9,105	10,673	17.2
Cedar Rapids, IA	509	453	-11.0	305	191	-37.4	814	644	-20.9
Charleston, SC	4,758	5,791	21.7	1,937	2,813	45.2	6,695	8,604	28.5
Charlotte, NC	16,253	19,690	21.1	8,384	6,858	-18.2	24,637	26,548	7.8
Chicago, IL	7,598	8,122	6.9	10,487	6,873	-34.5	18,085	14,995	-17.1
Cincinnati, OH	4,488	5,392	20.1	1,535	1,905	24.1	6,023	7,297	21.2
Clarksville, TN	2,332	3,043	30.5	325	762	134.5	2,657	3,805	43.2
Cleveland, OH	2,584	2,814	8.9	448	560	25.0	3,032	3,374	11.3
College Station, TX	1,091	1,392	27.6	389	711	82.8	1,480	2,103	42.1
Colorado Springs, CO	4,051	5,039	24.4	1,457	1,893	29.9	5,508	6,932	25.9
Columbia, MO	633	806	27.3	166	128	-22.9	799	934	16.9
Columbia, SC	4,209	4,787	13.7	215	85	-60.5	4,424	4,872	10.1
Columbus, OH	4,389	5,481	24.9	3,701	6,877	85.8	8,090	12,358	52.8
Dallas, TX	34,939	44,005	25.9	27,769	16,807	-39.5	62,708	60,812	-3.0
Davenport, IA	533	431	-19.1	268	151	-43.7	801	582	-27.3
Denver, CO	11,081	11,234	1.4	8,227	8,498	3.3	19,308	19,732	2.2
Des Moines, IA	3,915	4,740	21.1	1,354	1,768	30.6	5,269	6,508	23.5
Durham, NC	3,561	3,528	-0.9	2,234	1,977	-11.5	5,795	5,505	-5.0
Edison, NJ	11,072	10,993	-0.7	50,096	43,842	-12.5	61,168	54,835	-10.4
El Paso, TX	2,433	2,330	-4.2	633	232	-63.3	3,066	2,562	-16.4
Fargo, ND	939	1,200	27.8	486	776	59.7	1,425	1,976	38.7
Fort Collins, CO	1,580	2,190	38.6	910	375	-58.8	2,490	2,565	3.0
Fort Wayne, IN	1,330	1,520	14.3	626	266	-57.5	1,956	1,786	-8.7
Fort Worth, TX	34,939	44,005	25.9	27,769	16,807	-39.5	62,708	60,812	-3.0
Grand Rapids, MI	2,531	2,510	-0.8	1,624	926	-43.0	4,155	3,436	-17.3
Green Bay, WI	723	832	15.1	407	601	47.7	1,130	1,433	26.8
Honolulu, HI	912	862	-5.5	1,367	759	-44.5	2,279	1,621	-28.9
Houston, TX	39,507	49,915	26.3	24,165	20,625	-14.6	63,672	70,540	10.8
Huntsville, AL	3,399	4,210	23.9	167	131	-21.6	3,566	4,341	21.7
Indianapolis, IN	7,120	8,405	18.0	2,601	2,593	-0.3	9,721	10,998	13.1
Jacksonville, FL	11,583	13,210	14.0	3,104	4,036	30.0	14,687	17,246	17.4
Kansas City, MO	4,811	6,173	28.3	4,536	4,555	0.4	9,347	10,728	14.8
Lafayette, LA	1,632	2,526	54.8	34	24	-29.4	1,666	2,550	53.1
Las Cruces, NM	876	1,033	17.9	102	76	-25.5	978	1,109	13.4
Las Vegas, NV	10,042	10,038	0.0	3,861	4,062	5.2	13,903	14,100	1.4
Lexington, KY	1,308	1,451	10.9	938	879	-6.3	2,246	2,330	3.7
Lincoln, NE	1,088	1,230	13.1	1,010	808	-20.0	2,098	2,038	-2.9
Little Rock, AR	1,921	2,188	13.9	1,084	893	-17.6	3,005	3,081	2.5
Los Angeles, CA	9,306	9,737	4.6	21,248	17,193	-19.1	30,554	26,930	-11.9
Louisville, KY	3,122	3,667	17.5	2,644	884	-66.6	5,766	4,551	-21.1
Madison, WI	1,536	1,723	12.2	1,807	3,545	96.2	3,343	5,268	57.6

Table continued on following page.

Metro Area	Single-Family			Multi-Family			Total		
	2019	2020	Pct. Chg.	2019	2020	Pct. Chg.	2019	2020	Pct. Chg.
Manchester, NH	691	666	-3.6	561	202	-64.0	1,252	868	-30.7
Memphis, TN	3,319	3,887	17.1	355	910	156.3	3,674	4,797	30.6
Miami, FL	7,241	7,808	7.8	13,447	13,950	3.7	20,688	21,758	5.2
Midland, TX	1,306	1,292	-1.1	0	0	0.0	1,306	1,292	-1.1
Milwaukee, WI	1,494	1,571	5.2	925	1,127	21.8	2,419	2,698	11.5
Minneapolis, MN	9,610	10,277	6.9	12,804	12,064	-5.8	22,414	22,341	-0.3
Nashville, TN	14,460	15,549	7.5	8,242	11,609	40.9	22,702	27,158	19.6
New Haven, CT	399	419	5.0	1,054	954	-9.5	1,453	1,373	-5.5
New Orleans, LA	3,241	3,563	9.9	785	785	0.0	4,026	4,348	8.0
New York, NY	11,072	10,993	-0.7	50,096	43,842	-12.5	61,168	54,835	-10.4
Oklahoma City, OK	5,924	6,842	15.5	633	589	-7.0	6,557	7,431	13.3
Omaha, NE	2,633	3,454	31.2	1,467	2,019	37.6	4,100	5,473	33.5
Orlando, FL	14,995	15,343	2.3	9,475	9,156	-3.4	24,470	24,499	0.1
Philadelphia, PA	6,963	7,999	14.9	8,644	8,202	-5.1	15,607	16,201	3.8
Phoenix, AZ	25,026	31,658	26.5	10,847	16,561	52.7	35,873	48,219	34.4
Pittsburgh, PA	2,830	3,441	21.6	1,154	1,383	19.8	3,984	4,824	21.1
Portland, OR	7,688	7,513	-2.3	9,127	5,933	-35.0	16,815	13,446	-20.0
Providence, RI	1,592	1,621	1.8	456	447	-2.0	2,048	2,068	1.0
Provo, UT	5,423	6,800	25.4	1,524	1,167	-23.4	6,947	7,967	14.7
Raleigh, NC	11,142	12,697	14.0	2,178	4,261	95.6	13,320	16,958	27.3
Reno, NV	2,157	2,629	21.9	3,106	1,875	-39.6	5,263	4,504	-14.4
Richmond, VA	4,481	5,330	18.9	3,859	2,860	-25.9	8,340	8,190	-1.8
Riverside, CA	11,147	12,897	15.7	3,452	2,335	-32.4	14,599	15,232	4.3
Rochester, MN	614	642	4.6	497	264	-46.9	1,111	906	-18.5
Rochester, NY	1,116	1,149	3.0	905	1,093	20.8	2,021	2,242	10.9
Sacramento, CA	7,184	7,279	1.3	2,247	3,885	72.9	9,431	11,164	18.4
St. Louis, MO	5,179	5,719	10.4	1,875	2,144	14.3	7,054	7,863	11.5
Salt Lake City, UT	4,760	5,203	9.3	5,920	5,830	-1.5	10,680	11,033	3.3
San Antonio, TX	9,103	10,541	15.8	6,792	6,156	-9.4	15,895	16,697	5.0
San Diego, CA	3,019	2,900	-3.9	5,197	6,572	26.5	8,216	9,472	15.3
San Francisco, CA	4,076	3,386	-16.9	9,805	6,770	-31.0	13,881	10,156	-26.8
San Jose, CA	2,603	1,814	-30.3	3,627	4,037	11.3	6,230	5,851	-6.1
Santa Rosa, CA	2,079	1,171	-43.7	350	224	-36.0	2,429	1,395	-42.6
Savannah, GA	2,151	2,061	-4.2	440	965	119.3	2,591	3,026	16.8
Seattle, WA	8,737	8,860	1.4	17,862	14,179	-20.6	26,599	23,039	-13.4
Sioux Falls, SD	1,376	1,597	16.1	743	1,953	162.9	2,119	3,550	67.5
Springfield, IL	149	197	32.2	180	138	-23.3	329	335	1.8
Tampa, FL	14,670	16,088	9.7	8,870	4,260	-52.0	23,540	20,348	-13.6
Tucson, AZ	3,490	4,242	21.5	823	716	-13.0	4,313	4,958	15.0
Tulsa, OK	3,377	4,039	19.6	929	885	-4.7	4,306	4,924	14.4
Tuscaloosa, AL	630	656	4.1	844	613	-27.4	1,474	1,269	-13.9
Virginia Beach, VA	4,345	5,242	20.6	1,563	1,709	9.3	5,908	6,951	17.7
Washington, DC	12,977	13,991	7.8	13,827	11,175	-19.2	26,804	25,166	-6.1
Wichita, KS	1,389	1,553	11.8	737	471	-36.1	2,126	2,024	-4.8
Wilmington, NC	1,950	2,248	15.3	1,625	1,609	-1.0	3,575	3,857	7.9
Winston-Salem, NC	3,160	4,126	30.6	174	90	-48.3	3,334	4,216	26.5
U.S.	862,100	979,400	13.6	523,900	491,700	-6.1	1,386,000	1,471,100	6.1

Note: Figures cover the Metropolitan Statistical Area; Figures represent new, privately-owned housing units authorized (unadjusted data); All permit data are based on estimates with imputation
Source: U.S. Census Bureau, Manufacturing, Mining, and Construction Statistics, Building Permits, 2019, 2020

Housing Vacancy Rates

MSA[1]	Gross Vacancy Rate[2] (%)			Year-Round Vacancy Rate[3] (%)			Rental Vacancy Rate[4] (%)			Homeowner Vacancy Rate[5] (%)		
	2019	2020	2021	2019	2020	2021	2019	2020	2021	2019	2020	2021
Albuquerque, NM	7.9	5.1	5.3	7.4	4.9	5.1	6.5	5.4	6.4	1.9	1.4	0.5
Allentown, PA	7.7	4.9	5.2	5.8	4.8	4.3	4.0	3.9	4.0	1.4	0.7	0.1
Anchorage, AK	n/a	n/a	n/a	n/a	n/a	n/a	n/a	n/a	n/a	n/a	n/a	n/a
Ann Arbor, MI	n/a	n/a	n/a	n/a	n/a	n/a	n/a	n/a	n/a	n/a	n/a	n/a
Athens, GA	n/a	n/a	n/a	n/a	n/a	n/a	n/a	n/a	n/a	n/a	n/a	n/a
Atlanta, GA	7.6	5.8	6.1	7.3	5.4	5.7	7.0	6.4	5.2	1.3	0.8	1.0
Austin, TX	10.7	7.0	6.5	10.3	6.8	6.2	8.2	6.6	8.5	1.8	2.0	1.3
Baltimore, MD	9.7	7.2	6.8	9.6	7.0	6.6	8.8	7.0	6.1	2.3	1.0	1.0
Baton Rouge, LA	13.9	12.6	12.4	13.0	11.8	11.7	10.2	7.4	8.1	1.9	1.7	0.7
Boise City, ID	n/a	n/a	n/a	n/a	n/a	n/a	n/a	n/a	n/a	n/a	n/a	n/a
Boston, MA	7.1	6.8	7.4	6.2	5.6	6.2	3.6	4.7	4.5	0.8	0.4	0.5
Boulder, CO	n/a	n/a	n/a	n/a	n/a	n/a	n/a	n/a	n/a	n/a	n/a	n/a
Buffalo, NY	7.2	6.9	7.7	7.2	6.9	7.6	6.4	5.0	6.0	1.2	0.6	0.2
Cape Coral, FL	40.0	35.1	36.4	17.9	15.8	13.0	8.5	15.5	10.7	2.3	1.9	2.4
Cedar Rapids, IA	n/a	n/a	n/a	n/a	n/a	n/a	n/a	n/a	n/a	n/a	n/a	n/a
Charleston, SC	18.4	18.1	12.9	16.6	16.5	10.5	16.7	27.7	15.4	2.2	2.3	1.3
Charlotte, NC	9.3	6.6	7.7	9.0	6.3	7.4	7.6	5.6	6.8	1.8	1.0	1.3
Chicago, IL	7.6	7.4	8.7	7.6	7.2	8.6	5.7	7.4	8.0	1.5	1.2	1.3
Cincinnati, OH	8.6	6.6	7.9	8.4	6.2	7.3	10.7	7.9	7.2	1.1	0.7	0.5
Clarksville, TN	n/a	n/a	n/a	n/a	n/a	n/a	n/a	n/a	n/a	n/a	n/a	n/a
Cleveland, OH	10.1	9.3	7.7	9.9	8.8	7.5	3.8	5.5	3.6	1.1	0.7	0.4
College Station, TX	n/a	n/a	n/a	n/a	n/a	n/a	n/a	n/a	n/a	n/a	n/a	n/a
Colorado Springs, CO	n/a	n/a	n/a	n/a	n/a	n/a	n/a	n/a	n/a	n/a	n/a	n/a
Columbia, MO	n/a	n/a	n/a	n/a	n/a	n/a	n/a	n/a	n/a	n/a	n/a	n/a
Columbia, SC	10.6	7.2	7.6	10.4	7.1	7.6	9.3	4.5	4.7	1.5	0.7	1.1
Columbus, OH	4.5	4.7	6.8	4.2	4.5	6.6	4.3	5.9	6.5	0.8	0.3	0.8
Dallas, TX	7.6	6.4	6.6	7.3	6.4	6.5	6.9	7.2	7.0	1.5	0.7	0.7
Davenport, IA	n/a	n/a	n/a	n/a	n/a	n/a	n/a	n/a	n/a	n/a	n/a	n/a
Denver, CO	7.5	5.8	6.5	7.0	5.1	5.3	4.7	4.8	4.6	1.0	0.5	1.0
Des Moines, IA	n/a	n/a	n/a	n/a	n/a	n/a	n/a	n/a	n/a	n/a	n/a	n/a
Durham, NC	n/a	n/a	n/a	n/a	n/a	n/a	n/a	n/a	n/a	n/a	n/a	n/a
Edison, NJ	9.2	9.1	9.8	7.8	7.8	8.7	4.3	4.5	5.2	1.4	1.3	1.2
El Paso, TX	n/a	n/a	n/a	n/a	n/a	n/a	n/a	n/a	n/a	n/a	n/a	n/a
Fargo, ND	n/a	n/a	n/a	n/a	n/a	n/a	n/a	n/a	n/a	n/a	n/a	n/a
Fort Collins, CO	n/a	n/a	n/a	n/a	n/a	n/a	n/a	n/a	n/a	n/a	n/a	n/a
Fort Wayne, IN	n/a	n/a	n/a	n/a	n/a	n/a	n/a	n/a	n/a	n/a	n/a	n/a
Fort Worth, TX	7.6	6.4	6.6	7.3	6.4	6.5	6.9	7.2	7.0	1.5	0.7	0.7
Grand Rapids, MI	7.4	7.1	7.0	5.1	4.7	4.2	4.5	4.6	3.4	0.5	1.1	0.7
Green Bay, WI	n/a	n/a	n/a	n/a	n/a	n/a	n/a	n/a	n/a	n/a	n/a	n/a
Honolulu, HI	11.7	10.0	10.6	10.9	9.6	10.1	5.7	5.5	5.1	1.8	1.0	0.6
Houston, TX	9.8	6.8	7.2	9.1	6.3	6.6	11.4	9.7	8.8	1.9	1.1	0.8
Huntsville, AL	n/a	n/a	n/a	n/a	n/a	n/a	n/a	n/a	n/a	n/a	n/a	n/a
Indianapolis, IN	7.2	7.3	6.2	6.7	7.0	6.1	7.0	10.4	8.2	1.5	0.8	0.7
Jacksonville, FL	10.1	9.5	8.3	9.8	9.3	7.6	5.2	7.5	5.6	1.0	1.5	0.4
Kansas City, MO	8.9	9.1	8.3	8.7	9.1	8.2	10.0	9.4	8.9	1.4	0.7	1.2
Lafayette, LA	n/a	n/a	n/a	n/a	n/a	n/a	n/a	n/a	n/a	n/a	n/a	n/a
Las Cruces, NM	n/a	n/a	n/a	n/a	n/a	n/a	n/a	n/a	n/a	n/a	n/a	n/a
Las Vegas, NV	10.2	7.8	7.7	9.5	7.1	7.1	5.5	5.0	3.7	2.0	1.1	0.9
Lexington, KY	n/a	n/a	n/a	n/a	n/a	n/a	n/a	n/a	n/a	n/a	n/a	n/a
Lincoln, NE	n/a	n/a	n/a	n/a	n/a	n/a	n/a	n/a	n/a	n/a	n/a	n/a
Little Rock, AR	9.9	9.4	11.4	9.6	9.1	11.2	11.4	9.1	10.0	1.7	1.3	1.2
Los Angeles, CA	6.3	5.5	6.4	5.8	4.8	5.9	4.0	3.6	4.6	1.1	0.6	0.7
Louisville, KY	7.9	6.9	8.3	7.8	6.9	8.3	10.6	6.4	8.5	0.7	1.4	0.7
Madison, WI	n/a	n/a	n/a	n/a	n/a	n/a	n/a	n/a	n/a	n/a	n/a	n/a

Table continued on following page.

MSA[1]	Gross Vacancy Rate[2] (%)			Year-Round Vacancy Rate[3] (%)			Rental Vacancy Rate[4] (%)			Homeowner Vacancy Rate[5] (%)		
	2019	2020	2021	2019	2020	2021	2019	2020	2021	2019	2020	2021
Manchester, NH	n/a	n/a	n/a	n/a	n/a	n/a	n/a	n/a	n/a	n/a	n/a	n/a
Memphis, TN	9.9	7.3	7.7	9.9	7.0	7.6	10.6	6.6	6.9	1.4	1.0	0.8
Miami, FL	14.1	12.6	12.2	7.4	6.8	6.8	7.0	5.4	5.5	1.8	1.4	1.0
Midland, TX	n/a	n/a	n/a	n/a	n/a	n/a	n/a	n/a	n/a	n/a	n/a	n/a
Milwaukee, WI	8.0	6.6	5.2	7.8	6.3	5.1	6.6	4.6	2.2	0.6	0.6	0.5
Minneapolis, MN	4.4	4.7	5.3	3.8	3.7	4.6	4.1	4.0	4.9	0.5	0.5	0.6
Nashville, TN	7.8	6.5	7.1	7.5	6.1	6.8	8.6	7.3	7.9	1.2	0.7	1.0
New Haven, CT	11.9	9.4	7.9	11.1	8.4	7.2	8.3	7.8	5.4	1.5	0.2	0.5
New Orleans, LA	12.9	10.7	12.6	12.8	9.8	11.1	9.4	6.1	7.2	1.8	1.3	1.0
New York, NY	9.2	9.1	9.8	7.8	7.8	8.7	4.3	4.5	5.2	1.4	1.3	1.2
Oklahoma City, OK	10.8	7.5	6.1	10.4	7.3	6.0	8.6	6.4	5.7	2.7	0.9	0.8
Omaha, NE	5.6	5.6	6.0	4.8	5.3	5.7	6.3	6.5	5.1	0.6	0.5	0.7
Orlando, FL	16.0	12.9	9.5	12.7	9.8	7.5	8.3	8.6	7.5	2.5	1.2	0.5
Philadelphia, PA	8.3	6.0	6.1	8.1	5.8	5.9	7.1	5.4	4.8	1.3	0.7	0.5
Phoenix, AZ	10.3	8.9	9.0	6.2	5.3	5.6	5.0	4.9	4.9	1.0	0.7	0.6
Pittsburgh, PA	10.6	11.5	11.4	10.3	11.3	10.8	7.3	9.3	9.4	1.2	1.0	0.4
Portland, OR	6.6	5.5	6.0	5.6	4.9	5.6	4.4	4.3	5.2	0.9	0.8	0.9
Providence, RI	9.8	8.7	7.9	8.2	6.6	5.8	4.2	3.5	2.7	0.9	0.8	0.7
Provo, UT	n/a	n/a	n/a	n/a	n/a	n/a	n/a	n/a	n/a	n/a	n/a	n/a
Raleigh, NC	6.6	4.6	6.3	6.5	4.5	6.3	7.0	2.3	2.9	0.8	0.4	1.1
Reno, NV	n/a	n/a	n/a	n/a	n/a	n/a	n/a	n/a	n/a	n/a	n/a	n/a
Richmond, VA	8.5	6.0	5.8	8.5	6.0	5.8	9.5	2.7	1.8	1.3	0.9	1.0
Riverside, CA	14.9	11.8	10.9	9.6	7.5	6.6	4.5	4.4	3.1	1.7	0.8	0.8
Rochester, MN	n/a	n/a	n/a	n/a	n/a	n/a	n/a	n/a	n/a	n/a	n/a	n/a
Rochester, NY	8.6	4.2	5.0	7.2	3.4	4.2	5.9	2.0	3.1	0.9	1.0	0.5
Sacramento, CA	7.8	6.1	6.7	7.1	5.8	6.5	4.2	4.2	3.6	0.8	1.0	0.7
St. Louis, MO	9.5	6.4	7.0	9.2	6.3	7.0	8.8	5.3	6.5	1.2	0.7	0.5
Salt Lake City, UT	4.8	5.7	4.1	4.8	5.6	3.9	5.0	6.2	4.1	0.8	0.3	0.8
San Antonio, TX	9.0	7.4	7.6	8.2	6.7	6.9	10.1	7.2	8.4	2.0	1.0	1.1
San Diego, CA	7.5	6.0	6.9	7.3	5.6	6.7	5.8	3.9	3.1	0.8	0.8	0.7
San Francisco, CA	7.1	6.4	7.6	6.9	6.2	7.3	3.8	5.3	6.5	0.9	0.5	1.1
San Jose, CA	5.6	4.7	5.9	5.6	4.7	5.6	3.7	4.4	6.6	0.5	n/a	0.4
Santa Rosa, CA	n/a	n/a	n/a	n/a	n/a	n/a	n/a	n/a	n/a	n/a	n/a	n/a
Savannah, GA	n/a	n/a	n/a	n/a	n/a	n/a	n/a	n/a	n/a	n/a	n/a	n/a
Seattle, WA	5.5	4.7	6.2	5.2	4.5	5.5	4.4	3.6	5.3	1.0	0.6	0.7
Sioux Falls, SD	n/a	n/a	n/a	n/a	n/a	n/a	n/a	n/a	n/a	n/a	n/a	n/a
Springfield, IL	n/a	n/a	n/a	n/a	n/a	n/a	n/a	n/a	n/a	n/a	n/a	n/a
Tampa, FL	16.2	13.0	14.2	12.7	10.1	10.5	10.7	8.9	7.3	1.6	1.5	1.0
Tucson, AZ	14.8	12.1	10.0	9.2	7.7	6.9	7.3	8.6	5.0	1.5	0.5	0.6
Tulsa, OK	8.4	9.4	11.0	8.0	8.8	10.0	8.5	8.6	5.3	1.6	0.8	1.5
Tuscaloosa, AL	n/a	n/a	n/a	n/a	n/a	n/a	n/a	n/a	n/a	n/a	n/a	n/a
Virginia Beach, VA	10.4	7.9	7.7	9.3	7.0	6.9	7.1	5.5	5.5	2.2	0.6	0.6
Washington, DC	7.1	6.5	5.5	6.7	6.2	5.3	5.6	5.5	5.9	1.1	0.7	0.5
Wichita, KS	n/a	n/a	n/a	n/a	n/a	n/a	n/a	n/a	n/a	n/a	n/a	n/a
Wilmington, NC	n/a	n/a	n/a	n/a	n/a	n/a	n/a	n/a	n/a	n/a	n/a	n/a
Winston-Salem, NC	n/a	n/a	n/a	n/a	n/a	n/a	n/a	n/a	n/a	n/a	n/a	n/a
U.S.	12.0	10.6	10.8	9.5	8.2	8.4	6.7	6.3	6.1	1.4	1.0	0.9

Note: (1) Metropolitan Statistical Area; (2) The percentage of the total housing inventory that is vacant; (3) The percentage of the housing inventory (excluding seasonal units) that is year-round vacant; (4) The percentage of rental inventory that is vacant for rent; (5) The percentage of homeowner inventory that is vacant for sale; n/a not available

Source: U.S. Census Bureau, Housing Vacancies and Homeownership Annual Statistics: 2019, 2020, 2021

Bankruptcy Filings

City	Area Covered	Business Filings			Nonbusiness Filings		
		2020	2021	% Chg.	2020	2021	% Chg.
Albuquerque, NM	Bernalillo County	33	21	-36.4	872	560	-35.8
Allentown, PA	Lehigh County	10	5	-50.0	433	346	-20.1
Anchorage, AK	Anchorage Borough	20	12	-40.0	137	116	-15.3
Ann Arbor, MI	Washtenaw County	13	8	-38.5	454	352	-22.5
Athens, GA	Clarke County	5	10	100.0	228	162	-28.9
Atlanta, GA	Fulton County	152	87	-42.8	2,591	2,072	-20.0
Austin, TX	Travis County	175	113	-35.4	529	443	-16.3
Baltimore, MD	Baltimore City	28	18	-35.7	1,701	1,323	-22.2
Baton Rouge, LA	East Baton Rouge Parish	49	9	-81.6	435	321	-26.2
Boise City, ID	Ada County	19	13	-31.6	589	393	-33.3
Boston, MA	Suffolk County	37	23	-37.8	279	224	-19.7
Boulder, CO	Boulder County	42	13	-69.0	286	216	-24.5
Buffalo, NY	Erie County	39	31	-20.5	1,036	788	-23.9
Cape Coral, FL	Lee County	79	39	-50.6	1,112	928	-16.5
Cedar Rapids, IA	Linn County	9	6	-33.3	285	193	-32.3
Charleston, SC	Charleston County	21	8	-61.9	261	176	-32.6
Charlotte, NC	Mecklenburg County	45	56	24.4	639	460	-28.0
Chicago, IL	Cook County	335	270	-19.4	16,384	10,430	-36.3
Cincinnati, OH	Hamilton County	25	28	12.0	1,845	1,500	-18.7
Clarksville, TN	Montgomery County	6	11	83.3	579	333	-42.5
Cleveland, OH	Cuyahoga County	96	48	-50.0	4,189	3,240	-22.7
College Station, TX	Brazos County	6	8	33.3	87	66	-24.1
Colorado Springs, CO	El Paso County	30	22	-26.7	1,154	728	-36.9
Columbia, MO	Boone County	8	1	-87.5	263	193	-26.6
Columbia, SC	Richland County	12	8	-33.3	520	348	-33.1
Columbus, OH	Franklin County	86	128	48.8	2,960	2,223	-24.9
Dallas, TX	Dallas County	568	186	-67.3	2,452	1,797	-26.7
Davenport, IA	Scott County	7	5	-28.6	246	163	-33.7
Denver, CO	Denver County	91	72	-20.9	1,029	764	-25.8
Des Moines, IA	Polk County	12	22	83.3	782	550	-29.7
Durham, NC	Durham County	18	10	-44.4	223	175	-21.5
Edison, NJ	Middlesex County	31	45	45.2	1,097	843	-23.2
El Paso, TX	El Paso County	42	46	9.5	1,290	961	-25.5
Fargo, ND	Cass County	5	4	-20.0	183	131	-28.4
Fort Collins, CO	Larimer County	28	14	-50.0	404	306	-24.3
Fort Wayne, IN	Allen County	15	6	-60.0	1,057	872	-17.5
Fort Worth, TX	Tarrant County	271	151	-44.3	2,937	2,277	-22.5
Grand Rapids, MI	Kent County	47	8	-83.0	613	469	-23.5
Green Bay, WI	Brown County	9	2	-77.8	418	388	-7.2
Honolulu, HI	Honolulu County	46	28	-39.1	1,106	830	-25.0
Houston, TX	Harris County	608	269	-55.8	2,967	2,310	-22.1
Huntsville, AL	Madison County	42	18	-57.1	1,024	894	-12.7
Indianapolis, IN	Marion County	39	45	15.4	3,319	2,705	-18.5
Jacksonville, FL	Duval County	57	58	1.8	1,604	1,336	-16.7
Kansas City, MO	Jackson County	26	22	-15.4	1,394	1,027	-26.3
Lafayette, LA	Lafayette Parish	22	17	-22.7	306	263	-14.1
Las Cruces, NM	Dona Ana County	6	8	33.3	322	187	-41.9
Las Vegas, NV	Clark County	204	181	-11.3	6,529	5,825	-10.8
Lexington, KY	Fayette County	54	8	-85.2	520	450	-13.5
Lincoln, NE	Lancaster County	11	6	-45.5	485	430	-11.3
Little Rock, AR	Pulaski County	30	23	-23.3	1,519	1,157	-23.8
Los Angeles, CA	Los Angeles County	857	672	-21.6	13,323	11,316	-15.1
Louisville, KY	Jefferson County	39	19	-51.3	2,174	1,918	-11.8
Madison, WI	Dane County	28	26	-7.1	527	436	-17.3
Manchester, NH	Hillsborough County	27	19	-29.6	339	253	-25.4

Table continued on following page.

City	Area Covered	Business Filings			Nonbusiness Filings		
		2020	2021	% Chg.	2020	2021	% Chg.
Memphis, TN	Shelby County	41	29	-29.3	5,523	4,063	-26.4
Miami, FL	Miami-Dade County	322	201	-37.6	7,108	6,432	-9.5
Midland, TX	Midland County	11	18	63.6	48	64	33.3
Milwaukee, WI	Milwaukee County	48	20	-58.3	4,019	3,237	-19.5
Minneapolis, MN	Hennepin County	92	52	-43.5	1,552	1,240	-20.1
Nashville, TN	Davidson County	60	37	-38.3	1,330	959	-27.9
New Haven, CT	New Haven County	33	14	-57.6	1,258	864	-31.3
New Orleans, LA	Orleans Parish	21	31	47.6	391	263	-32.7
New York, NY	Bronx County	24	23	-4.2	1,498	1,219	-18.6
New York, NY	Kings County	182	108	-40.7	1,710	1,238	-27.6
New York, NY	New York County	480	398	-17.1	854	721	-15.6
New York, NY	Queens County	127	82	-35.4	1,990	1,447	-27.3
New York, NY	Richmond County	19	24	26.3	459	310	-32.5
Oklahoma City, OK	Oklahoma County	139	52	-62.6	1,679	1,424	-15.2
Omaha, NE	Douglas County	16	20	25.0	1,064	807	-24.2
Orlando, FL	Orange County	167	100	-40.1	2,477	1,909	-22.9
Philadelphia, PA	Philadelphia County	116	31	-73.3	1,162	741	-36.2
Phoenix, AZ	Maricopa County	261	223	-14.6	8,954	6,402	-28.5
Pittsburgh, PA	Allegheny County	116	79	-31.9	1,700	1,266	-25.5
Portland, OR	Multnomah County	59	33	-44.1	1,147	802	-30.1
Providence, RI	Providence County	29	16	-44.8	887	638	-28.1
Provo, UT	Utah County	31	22	-29.0	1,151	814	-29.3
Raleigh, NC	Wake County	75	53	-29.3	882	614	-30.4
Reno, NV	Washoe County	44	25	-43.2	765	592	-22.6
Richmond, VA	Richmond city	21	21	0.0	695	590	-15.1
Riverside, CA	Riverside County	145	105	-27.6	4,455	3,583	-19.6
Rochester, MN	Olmsted County	4	0	-100.0	138	90	-34.8
Rochester, NY	Monroe County	33	17	-48.5	582	428	-26.5
Sacramento, CA	Sacramento County	124	80	-35.5	2,300	1,731	-24.7
St. Louis, MO	Saint Louis City	53	12	-77.4	1,748	1,395	-20.2
Salt Lake City, UT	Salt Lake County	60	27	-55.0	3,232	2,389	-26.1
San Antonio, TX	Bexar County	128	143	11.7	1,445	1,102	-23.7
San Diego, CA	San Diego County	269	194	-27.9	5,848	4,533	-22.5
San Francisco, CA	San Francisco County	67	65	-3.0	384	334	-13.0
San Jose, CA	Santa Clara County	86	80	-7.0	1,018	868	-14.7
Santa Rosa, CA	Sonoma County	29	23	-20.7	388	329	-15.2
Savannah, GA	Chatham County	13	9	-30.8	729	546	-25.1
Seattle, WA	King County	96	56	-41.7	1,516	1,094	-27.8
Sioux Falls, SD	Minnehaha County	11	7	-36.4	268	221	-17.5
Springfield, IL	Sangamon County	8	6	-25.0	311	221	-28.9
Tampa, FL	Hillsborough County	110	87	-20.9	2,538	2,061	-18.8
Tucson, AZ	Pima County	32	21	-34.4	1,727	1,379	-20.2
Tulsa, OK	Tulsa County	45	30	-33.3	1,163	874	-24.8
Tuscaloosa, AL	Tuscaloosa County	10	4	-60.0	799	679	-15.0
Virginia Beach, VA	Virginia Beach City	14	11	-21.4	1,206	788	-34.7
Washington, DC	District of Columbia	50	36	-28.0	449	264	-41.2
Wichita, KS	Sedgwick County	15	20	33.3	941	760	-19.2
Wilmington, NC	New Hanover County	8	12	50.0	173	144	-16.8
Winston-Salem, NC	Forsyth County	15	10	-33.3	363	240	-33.9
U.S.	U.S.	21,655	14,347	-33.7	522,808	399,269	-23.6

Note: Business filings include Chapter 7, Chapter 9, Chapter 11, Chapter 12, Chapter 13, Chapter 15, and Section 304; Nonbusiness filings include Chapter 7, Chapter 11, and Chapter 13

Source: Administrative Office of the U.S. Courts, Business and Nonbusiness Bankruptcy, County Cases Commenced by Chapter of the Bankruptcy Code, During the 12-Month Period Ending December 31, 2020 and Business and Nonbusiness Bankruptcy, County Cases Commenced by Chapter of the Bankruptcy Code, During the 12-Month Period Ending December 31, 2021

Income: City

City	Per Capita ($)	Median Household ($)	Average Household ($)
Albuquerque, NM	31,103	53,936	72,426
Allentown, PA	21,144	43,816	57,795
Anchorage, AK	41,127	84,813	108,393
Ann Arbor, MI	44,710	69,456	101,571
Athens, GA	25,203	39,713	61,850
Atlanta, GA	50,032	64,179	111,013
Austin, TX	44,829	75,752	105,709
Baltimore, MD	32,699	52,164	76,395
Baton Rouge, LA	30,726	44,177	74,900
Boise City, ID	37,191	63,778	86,841
Boston, MA	46,845	76,298	113,307
Boulder, CO	49,050	72,279	117,554
Buffalo, NY	25,654	39,677	57,853
Cape Coral, FL	31,440	61,780	78,434
Cedar Rapids, IA	34,019	60,787	79,677
Charleston, SC	46,575	72,071	104,916
Charlotte, NC	39,834	65,359	98,462
Chicago, IL	39,068	62,097	94,733
Cincinnati, OH	32,159	42,663	68,877
Clarksville, TN	26,312	55,819	68,193
Cleveland, OH	22,442	31,838	47,716
College Station, TX	28,008	47,456	73,916
Colorado Springs, CO	35,506	67,719	88,315
Columbia, MO	31,341	53,447	77,067
Columbia, SC	30,863	47,416	76,760
Columbus, OH	30,056	54,902	70,667
Dallas, TX	35,487	54,747	87,999
Davenport, IA	29,530	53,140	70,917
Denver, CO	45,636	72,661	105,901
Des Moines, IA	29,064	54,843	70,393
Durham, NC	36,136	61,962	85,619
Edison, NJ	44,177	102,913	126,837
El Paso, TX	23,450	48,866	66,117
Fargo, ND	35,450	57,520	78,742
Fort Collins, CO	35,489	70,528	91,635
Fort Wayne, IN	27,593	51,454	66,777
Fort Worth, TX	30,374	64,567	84,769
Grand Rapids, MI	26,556	51,333	66,387
Green Bay, WI	28,092	52,214	67,863
Honolulu, HI	39,235	72,454	99,703
Houston, TX	33,626	53,600	86,249
Huntsville, AL	36,762	56,758	82,580
Indianapolis, IN	29,839	50,813	71,733
Jacksonville, FL	30,906	55,531	76,190
Kansas City, MO	33,215	56,179	77,114
Lafayette, LA	33,362	54,139	79,216
Las Cruces, NM	24,674	45,140	60,220
Las Vegas, NV	31,521	58,377	81,840
Lexington, KY	35,466	58,954	85,507
Lincoln, NE	32,345	60,063	79,255
Little Rock, AR	37,188	53,620	85,272
Los Angeles, CA	37,143	65,290	101,006
Louisville, KY	32,187	54,929	76,735
Madison, WI	39,595	67,565	89,404
Manchester, NH	34,096	62,087	78,636
Memphis, TN	26,704	41,864	64,439

Table continued on following page.

City	Per Capita ($)	Median Household ($)	Average Household ($)
Miami, FL	31,437	44,268	74,731
Midland, TX	41,077	83,616	115,667
Milwaukee, WI	24,167	43,125	59,318
Minneapolis, MN	40,368	66,068	93,145
Nashville, TN	36,716	62,087	86,197
New Haven, CT	27,607	44,507	69,282
New Orleans, LA	32,764	43,258	73,963
New York, NY	41,625	67,046	107,000
Oklahoma City, OK	30,976	56,456	78,057
Omaha, NE	34,449	62,213	85,535
Orlando, FL	34,033	55,183	80,986
Philadelphia, PA	29,644	49,127	72,419
Phoenix, AZ	31,427	60,914	85,527
Pittsburgh, PA	35,093	50,536	73,913
Portland, OR	43,811	73,159	100,369
Providence, RI	28,733	49,065	74,501
Provo, UT	21,607	50,072	70,832
Raleigh, NC	40,520	69,720	98,016
Reno, NV	36,358	61,860	85,808
Richmond, VA	35,682	51,421	80,218
Riverside, CA	27,144	72,738	90,520
Rochester, MN	40,789	76,034	98,609
Rochester, NY	24,916	37,395	55,801
Sacramento, CA	33,503	65,847	87,213
St. Louis, MO	31,930	45,782	65,863
Salt Lake City, UT	39,126	63,156	92,248
San Antonio, TX	26,328	53,420	71,917
San Diego, CA	43,090	83,454	113,681
San Francisco, CA	72,041	119,136	167,663
San Jose, CA	49,207	117,324	150,601
Santa Rosa, CA	38,773	80,472	101,066
Savannah, GA	26,102	46,149	65,818
Seattle, WA	63,610	97,185	134,355
Sioux Falls, SD	33,276	61,738	80,371
Springfield, IL	33,978	54,164	75,497
Tampa, FL	37,834	55,634	91,281
Tucson, AZ	24,468	45,227	59,650
Tulsa, OK	31,753	49,474	75,714
Tuscaloosa, AL	26,891	44,507	68,382
Virginia Beach, VA	39,788	78,136	101,686
Washington, DC	58,659	90,842	133,587
Wichita, KS	29,812	53,466	73,424
Wilmington, NC	35,329	51,137	77,843
Winston-Salem, NC	29,130	47,269	71,747
U.S.	35,384	64,994	91,547

Source: U.S. Census Bureau, 2016-2020 American Community Survey 5-Year Estimates

Income: Metro Area

Metro Area	Per Capita ($)	Median Household ($)	Average Household ($)
Albuquerque, NM	30,397	55,370	74,226
Allentown, PA	36,053	69,769	91,520
Anchorage, AK	38,664	82,890	105,130
Ann Arbor, MI	42,855	75,730	104,918
Athens, GA	29,718	49,503	76,015
Atlanta, GA	36,867	71,193	98,643
Austin, TX	41,283	80,852	108,042
Baltimore, MD	42,782	83,811	109,773
Baton Rouge, LA	32,252	60,043	83,907
Boise City, ID	32,704	64,717	85,592
Boston, MA	49,528	93,537	127,262
Boulder, CO	48,776	87,476	121,262
Buffalo, NY	34,438	59,079	79,277
Cape Coral, FL	34,818	59,608	84,303
Cedar Rapids, IA	35,423	66,620	86,435
Charleston, SC	36,925	65,894	92,599
Charlotte, NC	36,155	65,725	92,924
Chicago, IL	39,625	74,621	103,463
Cincinnati, OH	35,861	66,435	89,920
Clarksville, TN	27,022	54,911	70,402
Cleveland, OH	34,743	57,263	80,726
College Station, TX	28,843	51,261	74,718
Colorado Springs, CO	35,155	71,171	91,541
Columbia, MO	31,056	57,980	77,719
Columbia, SC	30,681	56,680	76,539
Columbus, OH	35,394	66,715	89,381
Dallas, TX	36,368	72,882	100,451
Davenport, IA	32,570	59,876	78,172
Denver, CO	43,427	83,289	110,927
Des Moines, IA	37,089	71,734	92,399
Durham, NC	37,943	64,745	93,338
Edison, NJ	45,049	81,951	120,401
El Paso, TX	22,439	48,193	64,952
Fargo, ND	36,064	65,995	86,531
Fort Collins, CO	38,142	76,366	97,178
Fort Wayne, IN	30,123	57,693	75,286
Fort Worth, TX	36,368	72,882	100,451
Grand Rapids, MI	32,489	66,297	86,260
Green Bay, WI	33,727	64,951	82,285
Honolulu, HI	38,288	87,722	112,641
Houston, TX	35,125	69,328	99,268
Huntsville, AL	36,211	66,450	88,920
Indianapolis, IN	34,755	63,545	87,488
Jacksonville, FL	34,228	63,064	86,676
Kansas City, MO	36,728	69,240	91,638
Lafayette, LA	29,448	52,827	74,136
Las Cruces, NM	22,772	44,024	60,780
Las Vegas, NV	31,651	61,048	83,343
Lexington, KY	34,203	60,769	84,976
Lincoln, NE	33,329	62,883	82,659
Little Rock, AR	31,654	55,983	77,700
Los Angeles, CA	37,452	76,399	108,889
Louisville, KY	33,589	60,891	82,683
Madison, WI	40,627	73,807	95,827
Manchester, NH	42,081	82,099	104,497
Memphis, TN	30,423	53,896	78,029

Table continued on following page.

Metro Area	Per Capita ($)	Median Household ($)	Average Household ($)
Miami, FL	33,759	59,030	89,252
Midland, TX	40,214	82,768	113,424
Milwaukee, WI	36,617	63,739	88,332
Minneapolis, MN	42,614	82,887	108,282
Nashville, TN	36,626	68,406	93,607
New Haven, CT	39,134	71,370	97,361
New Orleans, LA	32,727	54,388	78,882
New York, NY	45,049	81,951	120,401
Oklahoma City, OK	32,065	60,476	82,061
Omaha, NE	35,722	69,439	90,823
Orlando, FL	30,941	61,229	83,866
Philadelphia, PA	40,420	74,825	103,846
Phoenix, AZ	34,378	67,068	91,834
Pittsburgh, PA	37,195	61,969	84,195
Portland, OR	40,138	77,511	101,594
Providence, RI	37,294	70,676	92,573
Provo, UT	27,293	76,864	96,434
Raleigh, NC	39,968	78,706	104,264
Reno, NV	37,707	68,214	93,405
Richmond, VA	39,237	71,223	98,618
Riverside, CA	28,263	68,331	89,733
Rochester, MN	40,088	76,787	99,134
Rochester, NY	34,501	61,747	82,434
Sacramento, CA	37,122	75,533	100,554
St. Louis, MO	36,995	65,725	89,659
Salt Lake City, UT	34,242	77,102	99,517
San Antonio, TX	29,695	61,437	83,695
San Diego, CA	39,737	82,426	111,241
San Francisco, CA	57,778	110,837	154,773
San Jose, CA	58,508	129,343	172,472
Santa Rosa, CA	44,071	86,173	113,067
Savannah, GA	32,999	60,851	84,276
Seattle, WA	48,157	90,790	121,379
Sioux Falls, SD	34,076	67,713	85,045
Springfield, IL	35,765	62,590	82,422
Tampa, FL	33,448	57,097	81,178
Tucson, AZ	30,747	55,023	75,662
Tulsa, OK	33,780	57,341	80,237
Tuscaloosa, AL	26,507	50,871	68,357
Virginia Beach, VA	35,927	68,454	89,417
Washington, DC	51,515	106,415	138,719
Wichita, KS	30,212	58,333	76,654
Wilmington, NC	35,130	57,488	82,665
Winston-Salem, NC	29,693	52,607	72,782
U.S.	35,384	64,994	91,547

Note: Figures cover the Metropolitan Statistical Area (MSA)
Source: U.S. Census Bureau, 2016-2020 American Community Survey 5-Year Estimates

Household Income Distribution: City

City	Percent of Households Earning							
	Under $15,000	$15,000 -$24,999	$25,000 -$34,999	$35,000 -$49,999	$50,000 -$74,999	$75,000 -$99,999	$100,000 -$149,999	$150,000 and up
Albuquerque, NM	13.3	9.9	10.0	13.4	18.1	12.3	13.6	9.4
Allentown, PA	14.7	13.0	12.6	15.5	18.8	11.5	9.4	4.6
Anchorage, AK	5.3	4.9	6.3	9.2	18.2	14.3	20.2	21.6
Ann Arbor, MI	14.8	6.9	7.2	9.1	14.6	11.2	15.3	21.0
Athens, GA	19.8	14.4	11.6	12.3	14.4	9.2	10.5	7.9
Atlanta, GA	14.9	8.9	7.6	10.0	15.0	10.9	12.6	20.1
Austin, TX	8.5	5.9	7.0	11.1	16.9	12.7	17.9	19.9
Baltimore, MD	16.9	9.7	9.3	12.4	16.9	10.9	12.5	11.6
Baton Rouge, LA	17.2	14.8	10.2	12.5	15.2	9.0	11.6	9.4
Boise City, ID	8.6	8.2	9.4	12.9	19.2	12.9	14.9	13.9
Boston, MA	15.3	7.7	5.7	8.4	12.2	10.6	15.9	24.1
Boulder, CO	13.9	7.1	7.2	9.4	13.4	9.9	13.7	25.4
Buffalo, NY	21.5	13.4	10.9	13.1	16.2	9.6	9.2	6.2
Cape Coral, FL	8.0	7.4	9.7	13.8	20.4	15.8	15.9	9.0
Cedar Rapids, IA	7.8	8.4	9.4	14.5	19.8	15.0	14.5	10.6
Charleston, SC	10.3	7.3	6.3	10.8	17.0	12.2	17.7	18.3
Charlotte, NC	8.2	7.2	9.1	13.2	18.4	12.7	14.9	16.3
Chicago, IL	13.5	9.4	8.4	10.7	15.3	11.5	14.3	16.9
Cincinnati, OH	18.6	12.8	11.2	12.9	15.6	9.3	9.9	9.7
Clarksville, TN	9.9	7.8	11.0	15.6	20.3	15.3	14.0	6.2
Cleveland, OH	26.5	14.7	12.5	13.7	14.6	8.0	6.3	3.8
College Station, TX	20.7	10.6	8.8	11.4	15.0	9.7	12.1	11.7
Colorado Springs, CO	8.5	7.7	8.2	12.3	18.7	13.9	16.7	14.1
Columbia, MO	13.6	11.0	9.9	13.3	16.7	10.9	12.3	12.4
Columbia, SC	18.1	10.8	10.3	12.3	15.5	10.6	10.9	11.3
Columbus, OH	11.7	9.2	10.1	14.6	19.4	13.2	13.8	7.9
Dallas, TX	11.4	9.6	10.4	14.2	18.3	11.0	11.4	13.7
Davenport, IA	12.0	10.1	9.5	14.9	19.6	11.9	13.8	8.2
Denver, CO	8.9	6.7	7.2	10.9	17.5	12.3	16.4	20.1
Des Moines, IA	11.0	9.3	10.8	14.6	19.9	13.5	13.0	7.9
Durham, NC	9.8	7.4	10.0	13.0	17.7	12.7	15.1	14.4
Edison, NJ	4.7	4.0	4.1	7.8	13.7	14.4	21.5	29.9
El Paso, TX	14.5	12.0	10.7	13.7	18.7	11.1	12.0	7.3
Fargo, ND	10.2	10.3	9.4	12.5	20.0	12.9	14.4	10.3
Fort Collins, CO	9.7	7.7	7.6	11.5	16.4	13.7	16.6	16.8
Fort Wayne, IN	10.8	11.6	11.3	15.1	20.0	13.0	11.5	6.7
Fort Worth, TX	9.4	7.6	8.9	12.0	19.2	13.3	16.8	12.8
Grand Rapids, MI	13.1	11.6	9.2	14.4	19.6	12.9	12.5	6.5
Green Bay, WI	11.1	10.7	9.9	15.8	21.2	12.5	13.0	5.8
Honolulu, HI	9.6	6.4	6.4	12.1	17.4	12.9	16.7	18.5
Houston, TX	12.1	10.5	10.6	13.6	16.9	10.8	11.7	13.8
Huntsville, AL	12.5	10.4	10.9	11.2	16.1	10.6	13.7	14.5
Indianapolis, IN	13.0	10.3	11.0	15.0	18.5	11.3	11.9	9.0
Jacksonville, FL	11.0	9.2	9.9	14.3	19.4	13.1	13.3	9.7
Kansas City, MO	11.8	9.5	10.6	13.3	17.2	12.7	14.0	10.7
Lafayette, LA	14.2	10.2	9.5	12.5	17.0	11.7	12.7	12.1
Las Cruces, NM	18.7	13.4	10.5	11.7	17.7	10.6	11.7	5.8
Las Vegas, NV	11.6	8.7	9.4	13.6	17.7	12.8	14.6	11.6
Lexington, KY	10.9	9.0	10.1	12.8	17.5	12.1	14.4	13.2
Lincoln, NE	9.0	8.3	10.6	13.4	20.0	13.0	15.1	10.5
Little Rock, AR	11.8	11.0	10.6	13.6	17.3	10.9	11.6	13.1
Los Angeles, CA	12.1	8.6	8.1	11.1	15.4	11.4	14.9	18.3
Louisville, KY	11.8	9.4	10.4	13.6	18.6	12.4	13.3	10.5
Madison, WI	9.9	7.2	8.2	11.8	18.0	13.7	16.8	14.4

Table continued on following page.

City	Percent of Households Earning							
	Under $15,000	$15,000 -$24,999	$25,000 -$34,999	$35,000 -$49,999	$50,000 -$74,999	$75,000 -$99,999	$100,000 -$149,999	$150,000 and up
Manchester, NH	8.7	8.6	10.5	12.0	20.0	13.8	15.7	10.7
Memphis, TN	18.2	12.7	12.1	14.6	16.6	9.4	9.1	7.3
Miami, FL	19.1	12.4	10.8	12.3	15.2	8.9	10.3	10.9
Midland, TX	7.4	6.1	6.4	9.4	16.0	13.6	18.4	22.8
Milwaukee, WI	17.4	12.6	11.5	14.7	17.7	11.0	10.1	5.1
Minneapolis, MN	12.5	7.7	7.5	11.3	16.3	12.4	15.4	16.9
Nashville, TN	9.3	7.7	8.9	13.8	19.3	13.4	15.0	12.5
New Haven, CT	19.2	11.7	10.2	12.4	17.2	8.9	9.9	10.4
New Orleans, LA	20.4	12.7	10.5	10.8	14.5	9.6	9.9	11.5
New York, NY	13.9	8.5	7.5	10.0	14.1	11.2	14.8	20.1
Oklahoma City, OK	11.6	8.7	9.9	14.1	18.7	12.6	13.4	11.0
Omaha, NE	9.9	8.2	8.7	13.4	19.0	13.5	14.6	12.9
Orlando, FL	11.6	10.1	9.4	13.5	18.9	11.5	12.4	12.3
Philadelphia, PA	17.8	10.7	9.7	12.5	16.1	11.2	11.6	10.4
Phoenix, AZ	9.2	8.3	9.3	14.2	19.0	13.0	14.1	12.9
Pittsburgh, PA	16.9	10.8	10.0	11.9	16.1	11.8	11.7	10.8
Portland, OR	10.1	6.8	7.4	10.3	16.4	12.6	16.9	19.5
Providence, RI	17.5	11.6	8.7	12.8	17.0	11.3	10.8	10.3
Provo, UT	12.0	11.4	13.1	13.5	18.8	11.9	10.7	8.6
Raleigh, NC	6.9	6.9	8.7	13.0	18.1	13.4	16.1	16.8
Reno, NV	8.8	9.4	8.7	13.7	18.1	12.5	16.0	12.8
Richmond, VA	15.4	10.4	10.0	13.2	17.5	10.2	11.7	11.6
Riverside, CA	8.3	7.0	8.0	11.0	17.3	13.8	19.0	15.6
Rochester, MN	7.4	6.6	6.3	11.4	17.5	14.9	17.6	18.3
Rochester, NY	21.4	14.1	11.9	13.4	16.2	9.0	8.7	5.3
Sacramento, CA	10.8	7.8	8.0	11.4	17.6	13.2	16.2	14.9
St. Louis, MO	17.8	10.8	11.2	13.5	17.3	10.4	10.8	8.1
Salt Lake City, UT	12.0	7.7	8.4	12.3	17.5	12.7	14.9	14.4
San Antonio, TX	12.8	9.9	10.4	13.9	19.0	12.0	12.8	9.1
San Diego, CA	7.8	5.9	6.5	9.3	15.8	12.6	18.6	23.4
San Francisco, CA	9.4	5.4	4.6	5.9	9.8	8.7	15.2	41.0
San Jose, CA	5.6	4.6	4.4	6.9	11.2	10.3	18.4	38.6
Santa Rosa, CA	7.5	5.6	6.4	9.7	17.0	14.4	20.2	19.2
Savannah, GA	16.0	12.1	9.9	15.6	16.8	11.9	10.3	7.4
Seattle, WA	8.4	4.8	5.0	8.3	13.5	11.0	18.5	30.5
Sioux Falls, SD	8.3	8.0	10.7	12.8	19.0	14.8	15.7	10.8
Springfield, IL	13.4	10.0	10.0	12.8	17.2	13.1	13.5	10.0
Tampa, FL	13.7	9.7	9.9	12.4	16.0	10.8	12.3	15.3
Tucson, AZ	15.1	12.6	11.2	15.6	18.3	11.4	10.2	5.6
Tulsa, OK	13.1	11.5	10.7	15.3	17.1	10.7	10.8	10.8
Tuscaloosa, AL	19.8	10.8	11.1	12.2	15.7	8.5	12.5	9.3
Virginia Beach, VA	5.3	5.2	6.5	11.8	19.1	14.9	20.3	16.9
Washington, DC	12.3	5.4	5.5	7.2	12.4	10.6	16.4	30.1
Wichita, KS	11.7	10.0	11.0	14.5	18.2	12.4	13.2	9.1
Wilmington, NC	15.4	11.0	9.9	12.6	18.2	10.0	11.6	11.3
Winston-Salem, NC	14.7	10.9	11.3	15.3	16.8	12.1	10.3	8.6
U.S.	9.9	8.5	8.6	12.0	17.2	12.8	15.6	15.4

Source: U.S. Census Bureau, 2016-2020 American Community Survey 5-Year Estimates

Household Income Distribution: Metro Area

Metro Area	Percent of Households Earning							
	Under $15,000	$15,000 -$24,999	$25,000 -$34,999	$35,000 -$49,999	$50,000 -$74,999	$75,000 -$99,999	$100,000 -$149,999	$150,000 and up
Albuquerque, NM	12.4	9.8	9.7	13.4	18.2	12.7	13.7	10.0
Allentown, PA	7.5	8.2	8.4	11.9	17.5	13.7	17.7	15.2
Anchorage, AK	6.2	5.4	6.5	9.3	17.9	14.0	20.1	20.8
Ann Arbor, MI	10.3	6.5	7.2	10.1	15.5	13.0	16.7	20.7
Athens, GA	15.3	11.7	10.9	12.5	15.4	10.4	13.0	10.9
Atlanta, GA	8.1	7.2	8.0	11.7	17.6	13.3	16.6	17.6
Austin, TX	7.2	5.4	6.6	10.5	16.7	13.5	19.2	21.0
Baltimore, MD	8.1	5.9	6.3	9.8	15.2	12.8	18.9	23.0
Baton Rouge, LA	11.5	9.9	9.0	11.6	16.5	12.2	16.1	13.3
Boise City, ID	8.0	7.5	8.4	13.1	21.2	13.8	16.0	12.1
Boston, MA	8.4	5.9	5.4	8.1	13.1	11.8	18.5	28.7
Boulder, CO	8.5	5.9	6.1	9.2	14.0	12.1	17.7	26.5
Buffalo, NY	11.6	9.7	9.2	12.5	17.5	12.9	14.9	11.8
Cape Coral, FL	9.2	8.6	9.8	13.8	19.7	13.3	13.9	11.6
Cedar Rapids, IA	7.3	7.3	8.7	13.4	18.7	15.3	16.3	12.9
Charleston, SC	9.4	8.1	8.2	12.2	18.0	12.8	16.3	14.9
Charlotte, NC	8.5	7.9	8.8	12.6	18.0	13.1	15.5	15.4
Chicago, IL	9.1	7.3	7.4	10.4	16.0	12.8	17.5	19.4
Cincinnati, OH	9.6	8.4	8.4	11.6	17.4	13.5	16.6	14.6
Clarksville, TN	11.0	8.3	10.8	15.0	19.8	14.1	13.4	7.5
Cleveland, OH	12.3	9.4	9.4	13.0	17.6	12.3	14.2	11.8
College Station, TX	16.6	10.2	8.9	13.1	17.0	10.8	12.7	10.7
Colorado Springs, CO	7.6	6.9	7.7	11.7	18.8	14.1	17.7	15.3
Columbia, MO	11.1	9.7	9.8	13.1	18.1	13.1	13.8	11.2
Columbia, SC	12.1	9.0	9.9	13.2	18.5	13.0	13.8	10.6
Columbus, OH	8.8	7.6	8.4	12.4	18.2	13.4	16.5	14.7
Dallas, TX	7.4	6.6	7.9	11.7	17.7	13.2	17.3	18.2
Davenport, IA	10.0	9.0	9.2	13.3	19.0	13.4	15.9	10.3
Denver, CO	6.2	5.4	6.3	10.1	16.9	13.5	19.6	21.8
Des Moines, IA	6.8	6.8	8.1	11.9	18.6	14.3	18.4	15.0
Durham, NC	9.7	7.6	9.1	12.4	17.1	12.5	15.2	16.4
Edison, NJ	10.0	7.1	6.6	9.0	13.7	11.5	16.7	25.3
El Paso, TX	14.6	11.9	10.8	14.1	18.8	11.1	11.8	6.9
Fargo, ND	8.9	8.7	7.7	11.8	18.9	14.4	16.9	12.7
Fort Collins, CO	7.9	7.2	7.0	10.5	16.5	14.8	18.4	17.6
Fort Wayne, IN	8.7	10.0	10.2	14.2	20.2	14.2	13.8	8.8
Fort Worth, TX	7.4	6.6	7.9	11.7	17.7	13.2	17.3	18.2
Grand Rapids, MI	7.5	8.4	8.1	12.9	19.7	14.6	16.9	11.9
Green Bay, WI	7.7	8.2	8.8	13.3	19.4	15.0	17.6	10.0
Honolulu, HI	6.8	4.7	5.7	9.6	15.9	13.5	19.9	24.0
Houston, TX	8.6	7.8	8.5	11.6	16.9	12.3	16.2	18.2
Huntsville, AL	9.7	8.6	8.9	11.8	15.8	12.7	16.3	16.2
Indianapolis, IN	9.2	8.1	9.0	12.7	18.6	13.1	15.7	13.6
Jacksonville, FL	9.2	7.8	8.8	13.2	18.9	13.6	15.1	13.3
Kansas City, MO	7.9	7.6	8.7	12.0	17.5	14.1	17.2	14.9
Lafayette, LA	13.3	11.3	10.5	12.4	16.2	12.8	13.8	9.7
Las Cruces, NM	17.5	14.6	10.7	12.0	17.9	9.5	12.1	5.7
Las Vegas, NV	9.8	8.4	9.3	13.7	18.4	13.6	15.0	11.8
Lexington, KY	10.3	8.6	9.8	13.1	17.5	13.1	15.2	12.5
Lincoln, NE	8.4	8.0	10.0	13.0	19.6	13.4	16.3	11.4
Little Rock, AR	11.4	10.2	10.3	13.4	18.0	12.4	14.0	10.4
Los Angeles, CA	9.2	7.1	7.2	10.2	15.4	12.4	17.1	21.4
Louisville, KY	9.8	8.4	9.5	13.2	18.8	13.4	15.0	11.9
Madison, WI	7.1	6.6	7.4	11.7	18.0	14.3	18.7	16.1

Table continued on following page.

Metro Area	Percent of Households Earning							
	Under $15,000	$15,000 -$24,999	$25,000 -$34,999	$35,000 -$49,999	$50,000 -$74,999	$75,000 -$99,999	$100,000 -$149,999	$150,000 and up
Manchester, NH	5.8	6.2	7.5	9.7	16.4	13.4	20.1	20.9
Memphis, TN	13.1	10.2	10.2	13.2	17.3	11.7	13.4	11.0
Miami, FL	11.4	9.3	9.5	12.9	17.2	12.0	13.7	14.1
Midland, TX	7.1	6.1	6.8	9.7	15.9	13.4	18.2	22.7
Milwaukee, WI	10.1	8.8	8.7	12.2	17.2	13.0	15.9	14.0
Minneapolis, MN	6.5	5.7	6.4	10.3	16.4	13.9	19.9	20.8
Nashville, TN	7.9	7.1	8.1	12.7	18.7	14.0	16.8	14.7
New Haven, CT	9.8	8.0	7.4	10.7	16.3	12.6	16.6	18.6
New Orleans, LA	13.6	11.1	9.8	11.7	16.8	11.7	13.3	12.1
New York, NY	10.0	7.1	6.6	9.0	13.7	11.5	16.7	25.3
Oklahoma City, OK	9.9	9.0	9.3	13.4	18.8	13.2	14.8	11.6
Omaha, NE	8.0	7.2	8.1	12.1	18.4	14.3	17.5	14.4
Orlando, FL	9.0	8.3	9.6	13.8	18.9	13.3	15.0	12.1
Philadelphia, PA	9.6	7.3	7.5	10.2	15.5	12.5	17.0	20.4
Phoenix, AZ	8.2	7.4	8.3	12.8	18.6	13.6	16.5	14.6
Pittsburgh, PA	10.2	9.3	9.1	12.3	17.7	13.0	15.6	12.9
Portland, OR	7.3	6.2	6.9	10.7	17.2	13.6	19.0	19.0
Providence, RI	10.3	8.3	7.8	10.6	15.7	13.2	18.0	16.1
Provo, UT	5.7	5.8	7.3	11.1	18.7	16.0	20.1	15.3
Raleigh, NC	6.3	6.6	7.2	11.1	16.6	13.5	18.7	20.0
Reno, NV	7.4	8.1	8.1	12.2	18.5	13.9	16.9	14.9
Richmond, VA	8.3	7.1	7.6	12.0	17.3	13.2	17.9	16.6
Riverside, CA	8.9	8.0	8.2	11.6	17.6	13.3	17.0	15.4
Rochester, MN	6.4	6.5	6.7	11.1	17.9	15.1	18.9	17.5
Rochester, NY	10.2	9.3	9.0	12.4	17.9	13.1	16.1	12.1
Sacramento, CA	8.7	6.9	7.3	10.3	16.5	13.0	17.8	19.5
St. Louis, MO	9.0	8.1	8.6	12.4	17.8	13.3	16.4	14.3
Salt Lake City, UT	6.2	5.5	6.8	11.1	18.8	15.0	19.8	16.8
San Antonio, TX	10.3	8.4	9.2	12.6	18.6	13.0	15.1	12.7
San Diego, CA	7.3	6.2	6.8	9.7	15.8	12.7	18.4	23.0
San Francisco, CA	6.9	4.8	4.8	6.7	11.4	10.7	17.4	37.2
San Jose, CA	5.1	4.0	4.1	6.1	10.4	9.5	17.6	43.1
Santa Rosa, CA	6.6	5.7	6.4	9.3	15.5	14.1	19.3	23.2
Savannah, GA	10.0	8.3	8.8	13.7	17.8	14.0	15.3	12.0
Seattle, WA	6.3	5.1	5.5	8.9	15.5	13.1	19.8	25.8
Sioux Falls, SD	7.0	7.2	9.6	12.1	19.2	15.7	17.6	11.6
Springfield, IL	10.5	8.4	9.4	12.1	17.1	14.0	16.5	12.0
Tampa, FL	10.5	9.3	10.1	14.0	18.1	12.5	13.6	12.0
Tucson, AZ	11.4	10.3	9.7	14.2	18.1	12.7	13.4	10.2
Tulsa, OK	10.0	9.9	10.1	13.9	18.1	12.9	14.1	11.0
Tuscaloosa, AL	15.8	10.2	10.5	12.8	17.1	11.4	14.2	7.9
Virginia Beach, VA	8.2	7.3	7.9	12.2	18.8	14.1	17.7	13.8
Washington, DC	5.7	4.0	4.6	7.2	13.1	12.3	20.0	33.1
Wichita, KS	10.3	9.0	10.1	13.9	18.8	13.1	15.1	9.7
Wilmington, NC	11.8	9.8	9.1	12.9	18.0	12.2	13.9	12.3
Winston-Salem, NC	11.7	10.5	10.8	14.5	18.4	13.0	12.2	8.8
U.S.	9.9	8.5	8.6	12.0	17.2	12.8	15.6	15.4

Note: Figures cover the Metropolitan Statistical Area (MSA)
Source: Source: U.S. Census Bureau, 2016-2020 American Community Survey 5-Year Estimates

Poverty Rate: City

City	All Ages	Under 18 Years Old	18 to 64 Years Old	65 Years and Over
Albuquerque, NM	16.0	21.7	15.2	10.9
Allentown, PA	25.6	38.0	21.9	16.0
Anchorage, AK	8.8	11.5	8.3	6.1
Ann Arbor, MI	23.4	10.0	28.5	8.3
Athens, GA	26.9	24.3	30.5	9.6
Atlanta, GA	19.2	29.4	17.1	15.4
Austin, TX	12.5	16.4	11.8	10.1
Baltimore, MD	20.0	27.8	18.0	17.7
Baton Rouge, LA	24.4	36.4	23.9	9.1
Boise City, ID	12.0	14.1	12.0	9.3
Boston, MA	18:0	25.0	16.0	19.8
Boulder, CO	20.3	5.6	25.1	7.4
Buffalo, NY	28.3	42.3	25.8	16.2
Cape Coral, FL	9.7	14.2	9.3	7.4
Cedar Rapids, IA	11.2	15.6	10.9	6.4
Charleston, SC	12.6	15.4	13.3	6.9
Charlotte, NC	11.9	18.0	10.3	8.4
Chicago, IL	17.3	24.9	15.3	15.7
Cincinnati, OH	24.3	36.3	22.3	13.4
Clarksville, TN	13.8	18.3	12.7	7.5
Cleveland, OH	32.0	46.6	29.1	22.1
College Station, TX	28.3	13.0	34.3	6.1
Colorado Springs, CO	11.3	14.7	11.0	7.1
Columbia, MO	20.2	15.7	24.0	5.2
Columbia, SC	22.8	27.2	22.5	17.5
Columbus, OH	19.1	28.4	17.1	11.9
Dallas, TX	18.1	27.8	15.0	14.3
Davenport, IA	15.9	24.4	14.5	8.8
Denver, CO	11.9	16.2	10.8	10.6
Des Moines, IA	16.0	24.3	14.1	9.8
Durham, NC	14.2	21.1	13.0	8.1
Edison, NJ	5.9	6.8	5.1	7.8
El Paso, TX	18.8	25.8	15.8	18.9
Fargo, ND	13.2	14.4	14.3	5.3
Fort Collins, CO	15.9	9.3	19.0	7.4
Fort Wayne, IN	15.5	23.6	14.0	7.5
Fort Worth, TX	13.6	19.4	11.5	10.9
Grand Rapids, MI	19.9	27.2	18.6	12.8
Green Bay, WI	15.5	20.5	14.6	9.9
Honolulu, HI	10.7	13.3	9.9	10.9
Houston, TX	19.6	30.1	16.4	14.8
Huntsville, AL	15.2	23.3	14.6	7.7
Indianapolis, IN	16.9	24.8	15.3	9.8
Jacksonville, FL	15.0	21.4	13.3	12.1
Kansas City, MO	15.3	22.9	13.7	9.6
Lafayette, LA	18.4	26.8	17.9	9.2
Las Cruces, NM	23.6	30.0	24.3	11.6
Las Vegas, NV	14.9	21.3	13.5	10.8
Lexington, KY	15.8	19.0	16.6	7.2
Lincoln, NE	12.8	13.4	14.1	6.2
Little Rock, AR	15.3	22.2	14.1	9.3
Los Angeles, CA	16.9	23.6	15.0	15.8
Louisville, KY	15.2	23.1	13.8	9.4
Madison, WI	16.4	11.3	19.3	6.4
Manchester, NH	13.1	21.0	12.0	7.9

Table continued on following page.

City	All Ages	Under 18 Years Old	18 to 64 Years Old	65 Years and Over
Memphis, TN	24.6	39.6	20.8	13.9
Miami, FL	21.5	29.7	17.3	29.8
Midland, TX	9.4	11.9	8.0	10.7
Milwaukee, WI	24.6	35.1	21.8	14.5
Minneapolis, MN	18.3	23.8	17.5	13.1
Nashville, TN	14.4	22.3	12.7	9.7
New Haven, CT	25.2	34.4	23.1	17.4
New Orleans, LA	23.0	33.5	20.8	18.3
New York, NY	17.3	23.8	15.0	18.1
Oklahoma City, OK	15.2	21.6	13.9	8.5
Omaha, NE	12.0	15.6	11.4	7.8
Orlando, FL	16.1	22.9	14.2	14.1
Philadelphia, PA	23.1	32.2	21.0	18.1
Phoenix, AZ	16.2	24.0	14.0	10.5
Pittsburgh, PA	19.7	26.2	19.7	13.3
Portland, OR	13.1	15.1	12.9	11.1
Providence, RI	23.0	31.8	20.6	19.3
Provo, UT	25.8	19.2	29.3	10.4
Raleigh, NC	11.8	16.5	11.2	6.4
Reno, NV	12.6	14.5	12.9	8.9
Richmond, VA	20.9	32.9	19.2	13.5
Riverside, CA	13.2	16.0	12.7	10.4
Rochester, MN	9.5	11.4	9.6	6.2
Rochester, NY	30.4	48.2	26.4	17.3
Sacramento, CA	15.7	20.4	14.8	11.7
St. Louis, MO	20.4	30.0	18.9	14.5
Salt Lake City, UT	15.2	16.5	15.8	9.4
San Antonio, TX	17.6	25.7	15.2	13.2
San Diego, CA	11.8	13.8	11.7	9.5
San Francisco, CA	10.1	9.8	9.3	13.9
San Jose, CA	8.3	8.9	7.8	9.5
Santa Rosa, CA	10.0	13.0	9.2	9.1
Savannah, GA	20.4	30.3	19.1	11.6
Seattle, WA	10.2	9.6	10.2	11.0
Sioux Falls, SD	10.1	10.7	10.3	7.8
Springfield, IL	17.9	27.9	17.2	8.0
Tampa, FL	17.5	24.4	15.1	18.4
Tucson, AZ	20.8	27.4	20.5	12.7
Tulsa, OK	18.3	27.8	16.9	8.1
Tuscaloosa, AL	23.2	22.5	25.3	14.4
Virginia Beach, VA	7.2	9.8	6.9	4.3
Washington, DC	15.5	22.8	13.8	13.7
Wichita, KS	15.5	21.4	14.8	8.7
Wilmington, NC	19.2	24.9	20.2	9.9
Winston-Salem, NC	19.2	29.1	17.5	10.1
U.S.	12.8	17.5	12.1	9.3

Note: Figures are percentage of people whose income during the past 12 months was below the poverty level; Source: U.S. Census Bureau, 2016-2020 American Community Survey 5-Year Estimates

Poverty Rate: Metro Area

Metro Area	All Ages	Under 18 Years Old	18 to 64 Years Old	65 Years and Over
Albuquerque, NM	15.5	21.0	14.8	10.8
Allentown, PA	10.5	16.5	9.4	7.0
Anchorage, AK	9.2	11.6	8.7	7.0
Ann Arbor, MI	13.9	11.1	16.3	6.5
Athens, GA	20.5	21.1	22.9	7.9
Atlanta, GA	11.4	16.0	10.2	8.5
Austin, TX	10.2	11.9	9.9	8.0
Baltimore, MD	9.8	12.6	9.1	8.6
Baton Rouge, LA	15.3	20.6	14.7	8.9
Boise City, ID	10.5	11.8	10.5	8.2
Boston, MA	9.0	10.5	8.5	9.0
Boulder, CO	11.2	6.4	13.6	6.3
Buffalo, NY	13.5	19.1	12.9	9.0
Cape Coral, FL	11.8	18.9	11.4	8.2
Cedar Rapids, IA	9.3	11.9	9.2	6.3
Charleston, SC	12.4	18.3	11.3	8.6
Charlotte, NC	11.1	15.6	9.9	8.3
Chicago, IL	11.3	15.5	10.2	9.2
Cincinnati, OH	11.7	15.8	11.0	7.9
Clarksville, TN	13.8	17.9	12.8	9.7
Cleveland, OH	14.0	20.0	13.3	9.4
College Station, TX	22.3	20.3	25.3	8.3
Colorado Springs, CO	9.8	12.6	9.5	6.5
Columbia, MO	16.3	15.4	18.7	5.9
Columbia, SC	14.8	19.7	14.3	10.0
Columbus, OH	12.7	17.5	11.9	8.0
Dallas, TX	11.1	15.8	9.6	8.6
Davenport, IA	12.6	19.1	11.7	7.1
Denver, CO	8.3	10.3	7.8	7.1
Des Moines, IA	9.2	11.8	8.7	6.6
Durham, NC	13.2	18.3	12.9	7.3
Edison, NJ	12.4	16.8	10.9	12.0
El Paso, TX	19.5	26.4	16.3	19.7
Fargo, ND	11.2	12.1	11.9	5.7
Fort Collins, CO	11.1	8.6	13.0	6.4
Fort Wayne, IN	12.4	18.4	11.3	6.4
Fort Worth, TX	11.1	15.8	9.6	8.6
Grand Rapids, MI	10.3	12.5	10.2	7.3
Green Bay, WI	9.4	12.0	9.1	6.7
Honolulu, HI	8.4	10.8	7.7	8.1
Houston, TX	13.5	19.2	11.6	10.3
Huntsville, AL	11.7	16.8	10.7	8.3
Indianapolis, IN	11.5	16.0	10.7	7.2
Jacksonville, FL	12.3	17.3	11.4	8.9
Kansas City, MO	9.9	13.8	9.1	6.8
Lafayette, LA	18.5	25.9	17.0	11.8
Las Cruces, NM	24.8	34.7	23.5	14.4
Las Vegas, NV	13.4	18.7	12.3	9.3
Lexington, KY	14.5	18.4	14.7	7.7
Lincoln, NE	11.6	11.8	12.9	5.8
Little Rock, AR	14.1	19.0	13.6	8.7
Los Angeles, CA	13.2	17.9	11.8	12.2
Louisville, KY	12.1	17.4	11.2	8.0
Madison, WI	10.4	9.0	11.6	7.1
Manchester, NH	7.4	9.9	6.9	6.1

Table continued on following page.

Metro Area	All Ages	Under 18 Years Old	18 to 64 Years Old	65 Years and Over
Memphis, TN	17.3	27.2	14.9	10.0
Miami, FL	13.9	18.6	11.9	15.3
Midland, TX	9.8	13.9	7.8	9.9
Milwaukee, WI	13.0	18.7	11.9	8.7
Minneapolis, MN	8.3	10.6	7.8	6.5
Nashville, TN	11.0	15.0	10.2	7.9
New Haven, CT	11.2	15.8	10.6	7.5
New Orleans, LA	16.9	24.7	15.2	12.2
New York, NY	12.4	16.8	10.9	12.0
Oklahoma City, OK	13.5	18.1	13.0	7.3
Omaha, NE	9.3	11.2	9.0	6.9
Orlando, FL	12.8	17.6	11.8	10.0
Philadelphia, PA	11.9	16.1	11.2	8.9
Phoenix, AZ	12.7	18.1	11.7	8.1
Pittsburgh, PA	10.7	14.1	10.5	7.9
Portland, OR	10.1	12.2	9.9	8.0
Providence, RI	11.3	15.5	10.4	9.2
Provo, UT	10.1	8.7	11.5	5.6
Raleigh, NC	9.2	12.2	8.5	7.2
Reno, NV	10.9	13.4	10.7	8.5
Richmond, VA	10.4	14.6	9.6	7.8
Riverside, CA	13.7	18.5	12.3	10.7
Rochester, MN	7.8	9.4	7.7	5.9
Rochester, NY	13.2	19.6	12.7	7.6
Sacramento, CA	12.7	15.8	12.6	8.6
St. Louis, MO	10.7	14.7	10.2	7.3
Salt Lake City, UT	8.4	9.7	8.3	6.3
San Antonio, TX	14.2	20.0	12.5	10.8
San Diego, CA	10.9	13.6	10.5	8.9
San Francisco, CA	8.5	9.3	8.2	8.9
San Jose, CA	7.2	7.5	6.9	8.2
Santa Rosa, CA	8.8	10.5	8.8	7.3
Savannah, GA	12.8	17.7	12.0	8.6
Seattle, WA	8.4	9.9	8.1	7.6
Sioux Falls, SD	8.2	8.6	8.4	6.8
Springfield, IL	13.6	20.7	13.1	6.7
Tampa, FL	13.0	17.6	12.3	10.5
Tucson, AZ	15.9	22.2	16.2	8.5
Tulsa, OK	13.6	19.5	12.8	7.5
Tuscaloosa, AL	18.9	25.0	18.4	11.7
Virginia Beach, VA	10.6	15.8	9.7	7.0
Washington, DC	7.6	9.6	6.9	7.1
Wichita, KS	12.7	16.5	12.1	8.7
Wilmington, NC	14.5	18.3	15.1	8.1
Winston-Salem, NC	15.3	23.6	14.0	9.0
U.S.	12.8	17.5	12.1	9.3

Note: Figures are percentage of people whose income during the past 12 months was below the poverty level; Figures cover the Metropolitan Statistical Area
Source: U.S. Census Bureau, 2016-2020 American Community Survey 5-Year Estimates

Employment by Industry

Metro Area[1]	(A)	(B)	(C)	(D)	(E)	(F)	(G)	(H)	(I)	(J)	(K)	(L)	(M)	(N)
Albuquerque, NM	6.6	n/a	16.7	4.8	20.5	1.4	10.3	4.2	n/a	2.8	15.9	10.9	3.2	2.8
Allentown, PA	3.5	n/a	19.7	3.5	10.2	1.5	8.5	10.5	n/a	3.6	13.7	10.6	10.9	3.8
Anchorage, AK	6.5	5.3	19.0	4.6	20.1	2.0	10.0	1.4	1.1	3.6	10.6	11.6	7.7	3.0
Ann Arbor, MI	2.2	n/a	12.9	3.0	38.1	2.7	6.5	6.1	n/a	2.7	13.7	7.0	2.1	3.0
Athens, GA	n/a	n/a	n/a	n/a	28.4	n/a	11.0	n/a	n/a	n/a	9.1	11.4	n/a	n/a
Atlanta, GA	4.6	4.6	13.1	6.5	11.4	3.9	9.4	6.0	0.1	3.4	19.6	10.5	6.3	5.2
Austin, TX	6.2	n/a	11.4	6.3	15.3	3.9	10.6	5.5	n/a	3.7	20.6	9.8	2.7	4.1
Baltimore, MD	5.7	n/a	18.8	5.5	16.3	1.2	8.4	4.3	n/a	3.4	17.7	9.3	6.0	3.5
Baton Rouge, LA	10.6	10.4	13.8	4.5	18.4	1.3	9.5	7.2	0.2	3.9	13.0	10.2	4.3	3.3
Boise City, ID	8.0	n/a	14.5	5.8	13.2	1.1	9.8	7.7	n/a	3.4	15.3	11.3	5.0	5.0
Boston, MA[4]	4.1	n/a	23.3	8.0	10.4	3.5	8.3	4.1	n/a	3.4	21.9	7.4	2.5	3.1
Boulder, CO	2.8	n/a	12.9	3.8	18.5	4.6	9.3	10.6	n/a	3.2	20.7	9.1	1.1	3.4
Buffalo, NY	3.9	n/a	17.4	6.4	15.4	1.1	9.7	9.7	n/a	4.4	12.8	11.1	4.2	3.8
Cape Coral, FL	11.8	n/a	11.4	5.0	15.2	1.1	14.7	2.5	n/a	4.0	14.1	15.0	2.4	2.8
Cedar Rapids, IA	6.4	n/a	14.6	7.9	11.6	2.1	7.8	13.6	n/a	3.4	10.3	10.8	7.3	4.1
Charleston, SC	5.7	n/a	11.6	4.3	18.5	1.9	12.9	7.4	n/a	4.0	15.3	11.1	4.5	2.9
Charlotte, NC	5.5	n/a	10.1	9.0	12.3	1.9	10.0	8.3	n/a	3.6	17.3	10.7	6.4	4.7
Chicago, IL[2]	3.5	3.5	16.0	7.4	11.0	1.8	8.9	7.3	<0.1	4.1	19.1	9.2	6.5	5.0
Cincinnati, OH	4.6	n/a	15.0	7.0	11.4	1.2	9.8	10.5	n/a	3.4	15.8	9.8	6.2	5.2
Clarksville, TN	3.8	n/a	12.8	3.3	19.8	1.1	12.9	12.1	n/a	3.3	9.9	14.4	3.4	n/a
Cleveland, OH	3.6	n/a	18.8	6.6	12.6	1.3	8.6	11.2	n/a	3.6	15.1	9.5	4.0	4.9
College Station, TX	5.7	n/a	9.7	3.2	35.9	1.1	13.5	4.5	n/a	2.7	9.0	10.7	2.0	2.2
Colorado Springs, CO	6.0	n/a	13.9	6.1	17.8	1.7	12.2	3.8	n/a	6.0	16.6	11.0	2.9	2.0
Columbia, MO	n/a	n/a	n/a	n/a	28.3	n/a	n/a	n/a	n/a	n/a	n/a	11.1	n/a	n/a
Columbia, SC	4.1	n/a	12.6	8.5	20.4	1.3	9.2	8.0	n/a	4.0	12.8	10.9	4.4	3.8
Columbus, OH	4.0	n/a	14.3	7.7	15.8	1.5	8.8	6.4	n/a	3.6	16.3	9.3	8.7	3.7
Dallas, TX[2]	5.3	n/a	11.4	9.8	11.0	2.6	9.0	6.5	n/a	3.0	20.6	9.4	5.8	5.6
Davenport, IA	n/a	n/a	n/a	n/a	n/a	n/a	n/a	n/a	n/a	n/a	n/a	n/a	n/a	n/a
Denver, CO	7.0	n/a	12.4	7.6	12.9	3.4	10.1	4.6	n/a	3.8	19.2	9.1	5.0	4.9
Des Moines, IA	5.8	n/a	13.9	15.0	12.6	1.6	8.7	5.7	n/a	3.4	13.6	10.7	4.2	4.7
Durham, NC	2.7	n/a	22.4	5.0	20.4	1.9	7.0	10.1	n/a	3.3	14.6	7.2	2.8	2.5
Edison, NJ[2]	3.6	n/a	22.2	8.9	13.1	4.0	8.1	2.7	n/a	3.9	16.7	8.7	4.3	3.7
El Paso, TX	5.4	n/a	14.4	4.1	21.2	1.4	12.0	5.3	n/a	2.7	11.3	12.6	5.6	3.8
Fargo, ND	5.8	n/a	19.0	8.0	13.6	2.0	9.1	7.2	n/a	3.3	10.6	10.6	5.0	5.9
Fort Collins, CO	6.9	n/a	10.6	4.0	24.0	1.5	11.5	8.6	n/a	3.9	11.8	11.7	2.5	3.1
Fort Wayne, IN	5.2	n/a	18.3	5.4	9.6	0.9	8.9	16.5	n/a	5.0	10.2	10.9	4.5	4.6
Fort Worth, TX[2]	6.5	n/a	12.7	6.3	12.2	0.9	11.0	8.9	n/a	3.7	11.6	11.6	9.5	5.0
Grand Rapids, MI	4.7	n/a	17.0	4.9	8.7	1.1	8.0	20.0	n/a	4.0	13.4	8.9	3.5	5.8
Green Bay, WI	4.2	n/a	15.2	6.6	11.4	0.9	8.4	18.0	n/a	4.5	10.8	9.9	5.2	4.8
Honolulu, HI	6.0	n/a	14.6	4.9	21.6	1.6	14.4	2.1	n/a	4.2	12.2	10.0	5.3	3.0
Houston, TX	8.8	6.8	13.4	5.4	13.8	1.0	10.0	6.9	2.0	3.5	16.2	10.2	5.7	5.2
Huntsville, AL	4.1	n/a	8.4	3.0	20.9	0.9	8.2	11.6	n/a	3.4	24.9	10.4	1.6	2.5
Indianapolis, IN	5.3	5.2	14.8	6.7	12.3	1.1	9.1	8.3	0.1	3.9	16.6	9.5	7.9	4.5
Jacksonville, FL	6.5	6.4	15.0	9.6	10.4	1.2	10.7	4.3	0.1	3.7	16.1	11.3	7.2	3.8
Kansas City, MO	5.2	n/a	14.2	7.2	13.6	1.5	9.6	7.3	n/a	3.8	16.8	10.3	5.8	4.7
Lafayette, LA	10.3	5.3	16.6	5.3	13.4	1.2	10.6	7.4	4.9	3.4	10.8	13.4	3.1	4.2
Las Cruces, NM	5.2	n/a	22.3	3.1	26.5	0.7	11.4	4.0	n/a	1.9	9.4	10.1	3.6	2.0
Las Vegas, NV	6.5	6.4	10.8	5.4	10.2	1.1	25.6	2.6	<0.1	2.7	14.9	11.2	6.8	2.3
Lexington, KY	4.7	n/a	13.1	3.8	19.3	1.0	10.9	10.1	n/a	4.1	14.0	10.5	4.6	4.0
Lincoln, NE	5.3	n/a	16.4	5.9	21.9	1.8	9.2	7.2	n/a	3.8	10.9	9.9	5.8	2.1
Little Rock, AR	5.0	n/a	15.9	6.2	18.6	1.5	8.8	5.3	n/a	4.9	13.0	10.7	5.6	4.4
Los Angeles, CA[2]	3.5	3.4	19.3	4.7	12.7	5.1	10.6	7.0	<0.1	3.2	14.7	9.5	5.1	4.6
Louisville, KY	4.5	n/a	14.5	7.1	10.7	1.3	9.1	11.9	n/a	3.4	13.4	9.5	9.9	4.7
Madison, WI	4.5	n/a	12.4	5.8	21.5	4.4	8.1	9.4	n/a	4.9	12.9	10.0	2.6	3.5
Manchester, NH[3]	4.9	n/a	22.9	6.7	10.5	2.4	8.4	7.0	n/a	4.0	15.1	11.0	3.1	4.0
Memphis, TN	3.8	n/a	14.2	4.2	12.8	0.8	9.5	6.6	n/a	4.1	15.0	9.8	13.7	5.6

Table continued on following page.

Metro Area[1]	(A)	(B)	(C)	(D)	(E)	(F)	(G)	(H)	(I)	(J)	(K)	(L)	(M)	(N)
Miami, FL[2]	4.3	4.3	15.9	7.0	11.4	1.7	11.0	3.4	<0.1	3.9	16.2	11.5	7.7	6.1
Midland, TX	30.2	n/a	6.6	4.7	9.4	0.7	10.8	3.8	n/a	3.6	9.5	9.9	5.1	5.7
Milwaukee, WI	4.1	4.0	19.8	5.9	9.7	1.5	8.7	13.6	0.1	5.1	13.9	9.1	4.1	4.5
Minneapolis, MN	4.3	n/a	17.3	8.0	12.3	1.7	7.9	10.2	n/a	3.8	16.5	9.4	4.1	4.6
Nashville, TN	4.9	n/a	14.6	6.8	11.1	2.5	10.7	7.6	n/a	4.0	17.5	9.7	6.5	4.0
New Haven, CT[3]	3.7	n/a	28.9	4.0	12.2	1.3	7.4	7.8	n/a	3.6	10.8	9.7	6.9	3.8
New Orleans, LA	6.0	5.4	18.4	5.3	12.3	1.6	13.6	5.2	0.7	3.9	14.1	10.9	5.1	3.5
New York, NY[2]	3.6	n/a	22.2	8.9	13.1	4.0	8.1	2.7	n/a	3.9	16.7	8.7	4.3	3.7
Oklahoma City, OK	6.1	4.6	15.2	5.3	19.4	0.9	11.1	5.1	1.4	4.2	13.0	11.0	5.5	3.3
Omaha, NE	6.1	n/a	16.2	8.5	13.4	2.2	9.7	6.7	n/a	3.7	13.9	10.8	5.4	3.3
Orlando, FL	6.3	6.3	12.2	6.4	9.3	2.0	18.6	3.8	<0.1	3.1	18.7	11.5	4.5	3.5
Philadelphia, PA[2]	2.4	n/a	31.2	6.1	13.3	1.7	8.8	3.4	n/a	3.9	14.6	7.7	4.4	2.5
Phoenix, AZ	6.2	6.1	15.4	9.5	10.7	1.8	9.8	6.1	0.1	3.1	16.9	11.4	5.4	3.8
Pittsburgh, PA	5.8	5.1	21.2	6.6	9.9	1.9	9.2	7.1	0.7	4.0	15.8	10.6	4.4	3.5
Portland, OR	6.4	6.3	15.0	6.2	12.4	2.3	9.1	10.3	0.1	3.2	15.7	10.1	4.5	4.8
Providence, RI[3]	4.4	4.3	20.8	6.3	12.8	1.2	10.6	8.6	<0.1	4.4	13.0	11.1	3.6	3.3
Provo, UT	9.2	n/a	19.9	4.4	11.5	5.3	8.4	7.4	n/a	2.1	14.1	13.2	1.9	2.6
Raleigh, NC	6.5	n/a	12.6	5.5	14.6	3.6	10.1	4.7	n/a	3.9	19.7	10.8	3.8	4.1
Reno, NV	7.8	7.6	11.0	4.4	11.9	1.2	13.6	11.4	0.1	2.5	12.9	9.9	9.4	3.9
Richmond, VA	6.0	n/a	14.3	7.7	16.5	0.9	9.2	4.6	n/a	4.4	17.6	10.0	4.8	3.9
Riverside, CA	6.5	6.5	15.6	2.8	15.5	0.6	10.6	5.9	0.1	2.7	10.5	11.5	13.6	4.1
Rochester, MN	4.1	n/a	43.5	2.3	10.2	1.0	8.4	7.7	n/a	3.2	5.6	9.7	2.2	2.2
Rochester, NY	4.3	4.1	24.7	4.3	14.7	1.2	8.2	10.6	0.1	3.4	12.3	10.4	2.9	3.1
Sacramento, CA	7.1	7.0	16.5	5.1	23.6	1.0	9.6	3.7	0.1	3.1	13.4	10.3	3.9	2.6
Salt Lake City, UT	6.9	n/a	11.6	8.2	13.7	2.9	7.9	7.9	n/a	2.8	17.2	10.6	5.8	4.5
San Antonio, TX	5.8	5.2	15.0	8.8	16.2	1.6	12.0	4.8	0.5	3.6	14.3	11.0	3.7	3.4
San Diego, CA	5.6	5.6	14.5	5.0	16.3	1.5	12.2	7.7	<0.1	3.4	18.6	9.7	2.7	2.8
San Francisco, CA[2]	3.6	3.6	13.0	7.4	11.6	10.3	9.3	3.3	<0.1	3.3	25.8	6.2	4.3	1.9
San Jose, CA	4.6	4.6	16.0	3.3	8.4	9.6	8.0	15.1	<0.1	2.0	22.0	6.8	1.7	2.5
Santa Rosa, CA	8.0	7.9	16.9	4.0	13.1	1.2	11.8	11.6	0.1	3.4	12.0	11.9	2.5	3.8
Savannah, GA	4.2	n/a	13.4	3.4	12.0	1.9	13.3	9.2	n/a	3.8	14.0	11.9	9.3	3.5
Seattle, WA[2]	6.1	6.0	12.8	5.1	12.2	8.3	8.1	8.0	<0.1	3.2	16.3	12.4	3.5	3.9
Sioux Falls, SD	6.3	n/a	21.7	9.3	9.2	1.6	9.1	8.8	n/a	3.7	9.3	11.8	3.7	5.3
Springfield, IL	3.2	n/a	19.4	5.5	24.6	2.8	8.7	3.1	n/a	5.5	11.3	11.1	2.2	2.7
St. Louis, MO	5.2	n/a	18.4	6.5	11.2	1.9	9.6	8.3	n/a	3.7	15.5	10.1	5.0	4.7
Tampa, FL	6.1	6.0	15.3	9.2	10.7	1.9	10.8	4.9	<0.1	3.3	18.9	11.7	3.3	4.0
Tucson, AZ	5.1	4.6	17.4	4.9	19.7	1.3	10.9	7.1	0.5	3.5	11.6	11.0	5.6	1.9
Tulsa, OK	6.6	5.5	15.8	5.1	12.5	1.3	10.2	10.4	1.1	4.3	13.6	11.3	5.3	3.5
Tuscaloosa, AL	5.4	n/a	8.3	3.5	26.6	0.8	10.1	15.9	n/a	4.1	9.1	10.9	3.2	2.0
Virginia Beach, VA	4.9	n/a	14.1	4.9	20.1	1.2	11.4	7.2	n/a	4.2	14.7	11.0	3.8	2.4
Washington, DC[2]	4.7	n/a	12.6	4.4	22.4	2.4	8.9	1.4	n/a	6.4	24.3	8.0	2.8	1.9
Wichita, KS	5.9	n/a	15.0	3.9	14.3	1.1	11.0	15.8	n/a	3.9	11.6	10.7	3.9	2.9
Wilmington, NC	7.1	n/a	16.1	4.7	13.8	1.9	14.2	4.3	n/a	4.3	14.1	13.0	3.0	3.5
Winston-Salem, NC	4.4	n/a	21.2	4.9	11.3	0.6	10.0	12.5	n/a	3.2	12.7	11.5	4.7	3.0
U.S.	5.3	5.0	16.0	5.9	14.9	1.9	9.8	8.4	0.4	3.7	14.6	10.7	4.8	3.8

Note: All figures are percentages covering non-farm employment as of December 2021 and are not seasonally adjusted; (1) Figures cover the Metropolitan Statistical Area (MSA) except where noted. See Appendix B for areas included; (2) Metropolitan Division; (3) New England City and Town Area; (4) New England City and Town Area Division; (A) Construction, Mining, and Logging (some areas report Construction separate from Mining and Logging); (B) Construction; (C) Education and Health Services; (D) Financial Activities; (E) Government; (F) Information; (G) Leisure and Hospitality; (H) Manufacturing; (I) Mining and Logging; (J) Other Services; (K) Professional and Business Services; (L) Retail Trade; (M) Transportation and Utilities; (N) Wholesale Trade; n/a not available
Source: Bureau of Labor Statistics, Current Employment Statistics, Employment, Hours, and Earnings, December 2021

Labor Force, Employment and Job Growth: City

City	Civilian Labor Force			Workers Employed		
	Dec. 2020	Dec. 2021	% Chg.	Dec. 2020	Dec. 2021	% Chg.
Albuquerque, NM	283,911	282,488	-0.5	260,865	269,987	3.5
Allentown, PA	56,044	53,643	-4.2	49,932	50,666	1.4
Anchorage, AK	152,457	152,303	-0.1	143,093	145,581	1.7
Ann Arbor, MI	63,458	62,930	-0.8	60,833	61,271	0.7
Athens, GA	58,797	59,018	0.3	55,584	57,571	3.5
Atlanta, GA	267,337	269,277	0.7	247,331	261,628	5.7
Austin, TX	598,704	629,228	5.1	570,326	612,094	7.3
Baltimore, MD	278,897	276,076	-1.0	254,092	261,111	2.7
Baton Rouge, LA	113,763	111,853	-1.6	104,552	107,513	2.8
Boise City, ID	133,110	133,310	0.1	127,984	131,155	2.4
Boston, MA	387,348	388,169	0.2	358,020	375,383	4.8
Boulder, CO	63,840	65,584	2.7	60,404	63,755	5.5
Buffalo, NY	110,602	104,205	-5.7	98,333	99,908	1.6
Cape Coral, FL	89,945	96,733	7.5	86,987	93,448	7.4
Cedar Rapids, IA	68,110	68,956	1.2	64,384	66,443	3.2
Charleston, SC	73,473	75,515	2.7	69,599	73,387	5.4
Charlotte, NC	498,058	504,138	1.2	466,137	487,236	4.5
Chicago, IL	1,291,653	1,362,918	5.5	1,161,549	1,289,886	11.0
Cincinnati, OH	146,500	147,528	0.7	138,003	142,550	3.2
Clarksville, TN	64,250	65,166	1.4	59,973	62,676	4.5
Cleveland, OH	155,985	151,569	-2.8	138,503	143,494	3.6
College Station, TX	60,837	61,614	1.2	58,242	59,747	2.5
Colorado Springs, CO	243,833	249,831	2.4	225,146	239,206	6.2
Columbia, MO	66,768	67,046	0.4	64,502	65,816	2.0
Columbia, SC	57,417	58,067	1.1	53,659	56,104	4.5
Columbus, OH	480,615	478,019	-0.5	457,099	463,757	1.4
Dallas, TX	703,517	720,484	2.4	655,483	691,872	5.5
Davenport, IA	48,131	49,514	2.8	45,031	47,572	5.6
Denver, CO	428,037	436,110	1.8	394,814	416,130	5.4
Des Moines, IA	107,234	111,329	3.8	101,253	107,403	6.0
Durham, NC	151,495	155,432	2.6	142,896	151,263	5.8
Edison, NJ	53,162	53,901	1.3	50,465	52,089	3.2
El Paso, TX	308,094	306,886	-0.3	286,276	293,153	2.4
Fargo, ND	71,050	72,237	1.6	68,350	70,758	3.5
Fort Collins, CO	102,741	102,230	-0.5	96,111	99,065	3.0
Fort Wayne, IN	128,478	125,552	-2.2	122,088	123,812	1.4
Fort Worth, TX	453,183	463,124	2.1	423,632	444,860	5.0
Grand Rapids, MI	104,928	102,005	-2.7	96,823	97,216	0.4
Green Bay, WI	52,907	53,700	1.5	50,790	52,659	3.6
Honolulu, HI	446,117	449,039	0.6	408,943	428,507	4.7
Houston, TX	1,137,893	1,161,569	2.0	1,051,938	1,107,766	5.3
Huntsville, AL	101,874	101,617	-0.2	98,693	99,295	0.6
Indianapolis, IN	457,610	447,590	-2.1	431,378	440,366	2.0
Jacksonville, FL	459,202	489,301	6.5	442,882	471,893	6.5
Kansas City, MO	261,431	262,192	0.2	247,274	254,562	2.9
Lafayette, LA	59,183	58,683	-0.8	55,470	56,902	2.5
Las Cruces, NM	48,527	47,528	-2.0	44,666	45,495	1.8
Las Vegas, NV	303,291	310,246	2.2	274,574	291,433	6.1
Lexington, KY	170,085	172,085	1.1	161,892	167,567	3.5
Lincoln, NE	156,049	158,828	1.7	151,110	156,988	3.8
Little Rock, AR	97,273	95,339	-1.9	91,639	92,348	0.7
Los Angeles, CA	1,982,385	2,049,462	3.3	1,741,791	1,919,116	10.1
Louisville, KY	383,791	393,917	2.6	362,475	380,365	4.9
Madison, WI	155,372	159,742	2.8	150,703	157,841	4.7
Manchester, NH	64,625	62,551	-3.2	61,813	61,059	-1.2

Table continued on following page.

City	Civilian Labor Force			Workers Employed		
	Dec. 2020	Dec. 2021	% Chg.	Dec. 2020	Dec. 2021	% Chg.
Memphis, TN	304,572	301,839	-0.9	277,335	285,969	3.1
Miami, FL	222,722	224,579	0.8	204,304	221,636	8.4
Midland, TX	78,994	81,136	2.7	72,968	77,829	6.6
Milwaukee, WI	267,096	269,983	1.0	249,725	261,173	4.5
Minneapolis, MN	238,399	238,591	0.0	226,183	232,384	2.7
Nashville, TN	403,329	412,373	2.2	382,329	400,833	4.8
New Haven, CT	65,472	65,139	-0.5	59,291	61,754	4.1
New Orleans, LA	183,513	175,871	-4.1	161,751	165,683	2.4
New York, NY	3,964,116	3,971,798	0.1	3,471,464	3,707,265	6.7
Oklahoma City, OK	326,033	328,813	0.8	310,832	323,099	3.9
Omaha, NE	243,497	245,740	0.9	234,537	241,847	3.1
Orlando, FL	153,390	166,869	8.7	145,738	160,386	10.0
Philadelphia, PA	695,374	679,395	-2.3	624,715	639,771	2.4
Phoenix, AZ	879,665	899,909	2.3	817,499	876,739	7.2
Pittsburgh, PA	150,408	146,592	-2.5	139,456	141,344	1.3
Portland, OR	381,311	390,784	2.4	355,432	376,716	5.9
Providence, RI	84,268	86,112	2.1	76,894	82,166	6.8
Provo, UT	67,158	70,473	4.9	65,654	69,726	6.2
Raleigh, NC	257,719	262,887	2.0	242,594	255,387	5.2
Reno, NV	142,120	142,480	0.2	135,813	138,462	1.9
Richmond, VA	115,901	112,381	-3.0	106,540	108,084	1.4
Riverside, CA	155,946	157,686	1.1	143,359	150,678	5.1
Rochester, MN	66,476	66,974	0.7	63,761	65,533	2.7
Rochester, NY	91,915	88,067	-4.1	80,961	83,981	3.7
Sacramento, CA	237,986	238,610	0.2	216,868	226,597	4.4
Salt Lake City, UT	116,271	119,804	3.0	112,477	118,246	5.1
San Antonio, TX	739,191	751,698	1.6	694,043	723,866	4.3
San Diego, CA	696,144	704,246	1.1	641,244	675,861	5.4
San Francisco, CA	541,641	566,632	4.6	506,712	549,426	8.4
San Jose, CA	534,723	549,109	2.6	499,062	531,565	6.5
Santa Rosa, CA	83,192	86,619	4.1	77,343	83,335	7.7
Savannah, GA	69,474	70,699	1.7	64,158	68,643	6.9
Seattle, WA	473,538	485,328	2.4	448,865	472,509	5.2
Sioux Falls, SD	108,144	108,646	0.4	104,561	106,310	1.6
Springfield, IL	54,163	53,308	-1.5	49,652	51,085	2.8
St. Louis, MO	151,343	149,342	-1.3	141,167	143,569	1.7
Tampa, FL	202,879	217,923	7.4	195,033	210,530	7.9
Tucson, AZ	265,991	267,731	0.6	245,743	259,401	5.5
Tulsa, OK	196,233	195,638	-0.3	185,549	191,763	3.3
Tuscaloosa, AL	46,558	46,072	-1.0	44,429	44,554	0.2
Virginia Beach, VA	223,694	221,431	-1.0	211,774	215,866	1.9
Washington, DC	379,196	383,122	1.0	352,794	363,416	3.0
Wichita, KS	189,992	187,117	-1.5	179,598	180,628	0.5
Wilmington, NC	63,883	66,678	4.3	60,149	64,808	7.7
Winston-Salem, NC	118,047	118,917	0.7	109,899	114,688	4.3
U.S.	160,017,000	161,696,000	1.0	149,613,000	155,732,000	4.1

Note: Data is not seasonally adjusted and covers workers 16 years of age and older
Source: Bureau of Labor Statistics, Local Area Unemployment Statistics

Labor Force, Employment and Job Growth: Metro Area

Metro Area[1]	Civilian Labor Force			Workers Employed		
	Dec. 2020	Dec. 2021	% Chg.	Dec. 2020	Dec. 2021	% Chg.
Albuquerque, NM	440,283	438,957	-0.3	404,900	418,975	3.4
Allentown, PA	434,896	430,272	-1.0	406,276	413,035	1.6
Anchorage, AK	201,421	201,824	0.2	188,820	192,144	1.7
Ann Arbor, MI	192,619	190,379	-1.1	182,951	184,269	0.7
Athens, GA	98,163	99,130	0.9	93,473	96,931	3.7
Atlanta, GA	3,092,660	3,157,316	2.0	2,914,291	3,083,242	5.8
Austin, TX	1,264,319	1,328,683	5.0	1,202,616	1,290,031	7.2
Baltimore, MD	1,459,168	1,463,271	0.2	1,367,956	1,407,083	2.8
Baton Rouge, LA	422,223	420,154	-0.4	395,398	406,530	2.8
Boise City, ID	385,310	386,259	0.2	369,979	379,345	2.5
Boston, MA[4]	1,631,293	1,644,008	0.7	1,521,449	1,595,235	4.8
Boulder, CO	194,211	199,627	2.7	182,991	193,142	5.5
Buffalo, NY	539,853	522,318	-3.2	497,217	505,001	1.5
Cape Coral, FL	339,999	364,988	7.3	328,487	352,886	7.4
Cedar Rapids, IA	136,883	138,983	1.5	130,421	134,382	3.0
Charleston, SC	389,778	399,797	2.5	368,189	388,147	5.4
Charlotte, NC	1,366,797	1,387,855	1.5	1,284,503	1,343,680	4.6
Chicago, IL[2]	3,629,415	3,779,864	4.1	3,345,319	3,620,502	8.2
Cincinnati, OH	1,103,118	1,122,132	1.7	1,052,423	1,090,310	3.6
Clarksville, TN	117,910	120,451	2.1	110,783	115,996	4.7
Cleveland, OH	985,745	1,011,298	2.5	918,459	964,969	5.0
College Station, TX	133,664	134,733	0.8	127,114	130,377	2.5
Colorado Springs, CO	362,171	372,478	2.8	335,526	356,536	6.2
Columbia, MO	97,720	98,231	0.5	94,439	96,363	2.0
Columbia, SC	398,888	405,975	1.7	376,883	393,562	4.4
Columbus, OH	1,105,510	1,104,231	-0.1	1,057,275	1,072,944	1.4
Dallas, TX[2]	2,742,934	2,825,340	3.0	2,581,381	2,723,577	5.5
Davenport, IA	181,138	184,365	1.7	170,121	177,606	4.4
Denver, CO	1,688,119	1,725,927	2.2	1,568,519	1,653,017	5.3
Des Moines, IA	344,970	360,388	4.4	330,749	350,431	5.9
Durham, NC	305,680	314,304	2.8	289,594	306,408	5.8
Edison, NJ[2]	6,736,786	6,811,725	1.1	6,091,324	6,379,796	4.7
El Paso, TX	371,554	369,595	-0.5	343,878	352,108	2.3
Fargo, ND	140,806	142,676	1.3	135,688	139,730	2.9
Fort Collins, CO	207,120	207,229	0.0	193,967	199,929	3.0
Fort Wayne, IN	215,671	211,787	-1.8	206,458	209,225	1.3
Fort Worth, TX[2]	1,325,035	1,356,864	2.4	1,244,323	1,306,502	5.0
Grand Rapids, MI	573,470	562,570	-1.9	540,903	542,923	0.3
Green Bay, WI	170,349	173,117	1.6	164,280	170,046	3.5
Honolulu, HI	446,117	449,039	0.6	408,943	428,507	4.7
Houston, TX	3,409,040	3,482,713	2.1	3,148,520	3,314,497	5.2
Huntsville, AL	235,387	235,643	0.1	229,292	230,686	0.6
Indianapolis, IN	1,077,936	1,064,327	-1.2	1,030,409	1,051,034	2.0
Jacksonville, FL	780,452	831,643	6.5	755,957	805,154	6.5
Kansas City, MO	1,150,324	1,153,717	0.3	1,098,793	1,124,687	2.3
Lafayette, LA	210,736	208,862	-0.8	196,809	201,880	2.5
Las Cruces, NM	99,084	97,888	-1.2	91,359	93,054	1.8
Las Vegas, NV	1,097,286	1,120,967	2.1	992,442	1,053,379	6.1
Lexington, KY	265,734	269,114	1.2	253,162	262,015	3.5
Lincoln, NE	181,684	184,809	1.7	175,892	182,686	3.8
Little Rock, AR	355,832	349,105	-1.8	338,136	340,428	0.6
Los Angeles, CA[2]	4,894,787	4,980,229	1.7	4,354,871	4,701,381	7.9
Louisville, KY	648,505	663,130	2.2	616,374	644,099	4.5
Madison, WI	384,189	394,822	2.7	372,181	389,231	4.5
Manchester, NH[3]	120,409	117,035	-2.8	115,996	114,582	-1.2

Table continued on following page.

Metro Area[1]	Civilian Labor Force			Workers Employed		
	Dec. 2020	Dec. 2021	% Chg.	Dec. 2020	Dec. 2021	% Chg.
Memphis, TN	651,858	651,646	0.0	606,594	625,187	3.0
Miami, FL[2]	1,300,892	1,320,238	1.4	1,200,212	1,281,048	6.7
Midland, TX	98,752	101,007	2.2	90,805	96,819	6.6
Milwaukee, WI	791,895	807,693	2.0	755,226	789,570	4.5
Minneapolis, MN	1,962,193	1,970,209	0.4	1,867,593	1,920,386	2.8
Nashville, TN	1,080,130	1,107,763	2.5	1,029,442	1,078,329	4.7
New Haven, CT[3]	324,654	327,329	0.8	301,308	313,875	4.1
New Orleans, LA	593,773	580,966	-2.1	542,181	555,480	2.4
New York, NY[2]	6,736,786	6,811,725	1.1	6,091,324	6,379,796	4.7
Oklahoma City, OK	694,008	701,756	1.1	663,947	690,277	3.9
Omaha, NE	485,780	492,402	1.3	469,511	484,411	3.1
Orlando, FL	1,235,272	1,349,896	9.2	1,179,958	1,299,042	10.0
Philadelphia, PA[2]	984,461	961,709	-2.3	894,382	910,961	1.8
Phoenix, AZ	2,529,507	2,601,855	2.8	2,367,440	2,538,519	7.2
Pittsburgh, PA	1,155,318	1,132,268	-2.0	1,073,061	1,087,300	1.3
Portland, OR	1,323,921	1,372,904	3.7	1,241,677	1,325,954	6.7
Providence, RI[3]	671,467	683,283	1.7	619,481	657,278	6.1
Provo, UT	322,546	337,804	4.7	314,394	333,883	6.2
Raleigh, NC	727,584	744,531	2.3	689,136	725,155	5.2
Reno, NV	264,095	264,813	0.2	252,360	257,292	1.9
Richmond, VA	658,975	647,057	-1.8	618,135	626,567	1.3
Riverside, CA	2,097,412	2,121,275	1.1	1,914,226	2,012,478	5.1
Rochester, MN	125,119	125,644	0.4	120,001	122,805	2.3
Rochester, NY	515,660	512,248	-0.6	481,210	497,460	3.3
Sacramento, CA	1,089,088	1,099,258	0.9	1,005,859	1,051,043	4.4
Salt Lake City, UT	674,466	696,167	3.2	653,349	686,805	5.1
San Antonio, TX	1,218,490	1,240,624	1.8	1,145,131	1,194,319	4.3
San Diego, CA	1,535,149	1,554,504	1.2	1,412,499	1,488,753	5.4
San Francisco, CA[2]	966,070	1,012,179	4.7	906,405	982,508	8.4
San Jose, CA	1,041,226	1,074,395	3.1	979,012	1,042,538	6.4
Santa Rosa, CA	236,250	246,346	4.2	220,659	237,754	7.7
Savannah, GA	195,727	201,932	3.1	184,365	197,238	6.9
Seattle, WA[2]	1,695,895	1,736,759	2.4	1,595,578	1,681,651	5.3
Sioux Falls, SD	157,606	158,401	0.5	152,715	155,169	1.6
Springfield, IL	100,651	99,900	-0.7	93,308	95,989	2.8
St. Louis, MO	1,443,527	1,438,375	-0.3	1,369,424	1,394,513	1.8
Tampa, FL	1,535,085	1,654,474	7.7	1,482,746	1,600,427	7.9
Tucson, AZ	493,760	499,312	1.1	459,909	485,470	5.5
Tulsa, OK	480,973	481,610	0.1	457,111	472,459	3.3
Tuscaloosa, AL	114,823	114,012	-0.7	110,323	110,628	0.2
Virginia Beach, VA	829,771	815,888	-1.6	775,820	790,400	1.8
Washington, DC[2]	2,669,261	2,682,839	0.5	2,494,750	2,595,093	4.0
Wichita, KS	316,350	311,160	-1.6	299,958	301,603	0.5
Wilmington, NC	150,192	156,857	4.4	141,812	152,659	7.6
Winston-Salem, NC	325,141	328,533	1.0	305,408	318,543	4.3
U.S.	160,017,000	161,696,000	1.0	149,613,000	155,732,000	4.1

Note: Data is not seasonally adjusted and covers workers 16 years of age and older; (1) Figures cover the Metropolitan Statistical Area (MSA) except where noted. See Appendix B for areas included; (2) Metropolitan Division; (3) New England City and Town Area; (4) New England City and Town Area Division

Source: Bureau of Labor Statistics, Local Area Unemployment Statistics

Unemployment Rate: City

City	2021											
	Jan.	Feb.	Mar.	Apr.	May	Jun.	Jul.	Aug.	Sep.	Oct.	Nov.	Dec.
Albuquerque, NM	8.6	7.7	7.3	7.1	6.9	7.9	7.3	5.9	5.4	4.9	4.9	4.4
Allentown, PA	12.6	13.0	12.5	11.7	11.3	12.1	12.5	10.6	8.8	7.3	6.3	5.5
Anchorage, AK	6.3	6.5	6.8	6.5	5.9	6.1	5.6	4.8	4.9	4.7	4.7	4.4
Ann Arbor, MI	3.9	3.4	3.5	3.3	3.8	3.9	3.9	3.1	3.8	3.2	2.8	2.6
Athens, GA	4.9	4.4	3.9	3.7	4.0	4.6	3.1	3.1	2.4	2.4	2.1	2.5
Atlanta, GA	6.4	5.8	5.3	5.2	5.3	6.0	4.2	4.1	3.2	3.1	2.6	2.8
Austin, TX	5.2	5.4	5.1	4.4	4.1	4.5	3.9	3.5	3.3	3.2	3.0	2.7
Baltimore, MD	8.7	8.1	8.0	7.7	7.7	8.5	7.3	7.3	7.1	6.8	6.1	5.4
Baton Rouge, LA	8.6	7.9	7.0	7.5	7.8	8.8	7.5	6.4	5.2	4.6	4.3	3.9
Boise City, ID	4.1	4.1	3.6	3.1	2.8	3.0	2.7	2.5	2.0	1.8	1.8	1.6
Boston, MA	7.5	7.0	6.3	6.0	5.2	5.8	6.0	5.6	5.5	5.2	4.6	3.3
Boulder, CO	5.4	5.1	5.1	4.8	4.4	5.3	4.4	4.0	3.2	3.1	3.1	2.8
Buffalo, NY	10.9	10.5	9.5	8.3	7.7	8.1	8.7	8.3	7.2	6.7	5.9	4.1
Cape Coral, FL	4.4	4.3	4.6	4.8	4.7	5.4	4.8	4.5	4.0	3.9	3.6	3.4
Cedar Rapids, IA	6.0	6.2	6.1	5.7	5.6	6.4	5.4	5.3	4.2	3.8	3.6	3.6
Charleston, SC	5.1	4.4	4.0	3.6	2.9	3.6	3.7	3.6	2.7	2.6	2.5	2.8
Charlotte, NC	6.3	5.9	4.9	4.7	4.7	5.1	4.7	4.6	3.9	3.9	3.6	3.4
Chicago, IL	10.4	10.1	9.0	9.4	9.4	10.7	9.7	9.2	7.1	6.7	5.9	5.4
Cincinnati, OH	6.8	6.2	4.9	5.5	5.7	6.9	6.7	5.8	5.0	4.3	3.6	3.4
Clarksville, TN	6.3	5.7	6.3	5.5	5.5	6.5	5.6	5.2	4.1	4.0	3.6	3.8
Cleveland, OH	10.4	7.0	6.8	6.8	7.4	9.2	8.3	7.6	6.2	5.3	5.1	5.3
College Station, TX	4.8	5.0	4.6	4.1	3.9	5.1	4.4	3.9	3.6	3.6	3.3	3.0
Colorado Springs, CO	7.2	7.0	6.7	6.4	5.8	6.4	6.2	5.5	4.9	4.6	4.5	4.3
Columbia, MO	3.8	3.3	3.0	2.6	3.2	3.7	2.6	2.4	1.8	2.1	1.9	1.8
Columbia, SC	5.8	5.6	5.2	5.1	4.2	5.0	4.8	4.5	3.5	3.2	3.1	3.4
Columbus, OH	5.9	5.9	5.7	5.3	5.4	6.3	6.0	5.1	4.4	3.8	3.3	3.0
Dallas, TX	7.3	7.6	7.4	6.5	6.0	6.4	5.9	5.2	4.8	4.6	4.3	4.0
Davenport, IA	7.2	6.9	6.2	6.4	6.4	7.1	6.2	5.8	4.4	4.2	3.9	3.9
Denver, CO	7.7	7.3	7.1	7.0	6.4	6.7	6.6	5.9	5.2	5.0	4.8	4.6
Des Moines, IA	6.5	6.8	6.0	5.5	5.5	6.1	5.0	4.8	3.7	3.5	3.2	3.5
Durham, NC	5.3	5.0	4.1	3.8	4.0	4.3	4.0	3.8	3.2	3.2	2.9	2.7
Edison, NJ	5.4	5.8	5.4	4.9	5.1	5.9	5.7	5.1	4.5	3.9	3.8	3.4
El Paso, TX	7.6	7.9	7.4	6.6	6.1	6.9	6.1	5.5	5.1	5.0	4.7	4.5
Fargo, ND	3.8	4.4	3.6	3.1	2.7	3.5	2.6	2.3	2.0	1.7	1.9	2.0
Fort Collins, CO	6.1	5.7	5.6	5.3	4.8	5.5	5.0	4.4	3.6	3.5	3.4	3.1
Fort Wayne, IN	5.2	4.9	5.1	4.7	5.0	5.1	4.6	5.3	3.2	2.8	2.3	1.4
Fort Worth, TX	7.1	7.5	7.3	6.4	6.0	6.7	6.0	5.3	4.9	4.6	4.3	3.9
Grand Rapids, MI	7.5	6.4	6.3	5.8	6.5	6.5	6.2	5.5	6.3	5.4	4.9	4.7
Green Bay, WI	4.5	4.9	4.9	4.6	4.3	4.8	4.2	4.2	2.9	2.4	1.9	1.9
Honolulu, HI	8.9	7.7	7.7	7.1	6.7	7.1	6.2	6.1	5.9	5.4	5.0	4.6
Houston, TX	8.0	8.3	8.0	7.2	6.6	7.2	6.7	6.0	5.5	5.3	5.0	4.6
Huntsville, AL	3.6	3.4	3.0	2.5	2.4	3.1	2.9	2.9	2.5	2.2	2.5	2.3
Indianapolis, IN	6.1	5.6	5.7	5.4	5.6	5.7	5.2	4.8	3.6	3.1	2.6	1.6
Jacksonville, FL	4.6	4.7	4.9	4.9	4.8	5.5	5.0	4.7	4.1	4.1	3.7	3.6
Kansas City, MO	5.6	5.8	5.3	5.4	6.3	6.6	4.9	4.3	3.6	3.3	2.9	2.9
Lafayette, LA	6.8	6.2	6.0	5.8	6.0	6.6	5.6	4.8	4.1	3.7	3.4	3.0
Las Cruces, NM	8.5	7.4	7.1	6.9	6.7	7.9	7.6	6.2	5.8	5.3	4.8	4.3
Las Vegas, NV	9.7	9.3	8.9	9.1	8.9	9.7	9.5	8.2	7.4	6.6	6.4	6.1
Lexington, KY	4.4	4.4	4.4	3.2	3.4	4.6	3.9	3.2	3.3	3.1	2.4	2.6
Lincoln, NE	3.3	3.2	2.9	2.2	2.2	2.6	1.9	1.7	1.3	1.3	1.1	1.2
Little Rock, AR	6.2	6.4	5.9	5.5	5.8	6.2	5.7	5.1	4.1	3.2	2.9	3.1
Los Angeles, CA	12.6	10.6	10.8	11.1	10.2	10.3	10.2	9.7	8.2	7.9	7.2	6.4
Louisville, KY	5.7	5.0	5.0	4.2	3.8	5.8	4.8	3.6	3.7	3.6	3.4	3.4
Madison, WI	3.2	3.3	3.3	3.2	3.1	3.6	3.1	3.1	2.1	1.7	1.4	1.2
Manchester, NH	4.8	3.8	3.7	3.2	2.8	3.5	3.7	3.1	2.5	2.3	2.3	2.4

Table continued on following page.

City	2021											
	Jan.	Feb.	Mar.	Apr.	May	Jun.	Jul.	Aug.	Sep.	Oct.	Nov.	Dec.
Memphis, TN	9.2	8.1	8.3	8.2	8.1	9.6	9.1	8.1	6.3	5.8	5.1	5.3
Miami, FL	8.5	7.9	8.3	6.9	6.7	7.0	6.5	6.7	5.7	3.7	3.4	1.3
Midland, TX	7.9	7.9	7.3	6.8	6.2	6.6	5.9	5.3	4.9	4.7	4.4	4.1
Milwaukee, WI	6.8	7.3	7.4	7.7	7.1	8.0	7.5	7.4	5.0	4.2	3.3	3.3
Minneapolis, MN	4.9	4.6	4.4	4.8	4.6	5.4	4.2	4.1	3.5	3.0	2.5	2.6
Nashville, TN	4.9	4.4	4.6	4.4	4.3	5.2	4.3	3.8	3.1	2.9	2.7	2.8
New Haven, CT	9.8	9.6	9.6	9.3	8.8	9.0	8.9	7.9	6.9	6.7	5.8	5.2
New Orleans, LA	12.4	11.8	9.7	11.2	11.2	12.0	10.3	8.9	7.9	6.5	6.2	5.8
New York, NY	13.3	12.8	11.3	10.9	10.2	10.6	10.1	9.5	8.2	7.7	7.0	6.7
Oklahoma City, OK	5.1	5.3	4.4	4.2	3.7	4.1	3.2	2.9	2.0	2.0	1.8	1.7
Omaha, NE	4.0	3.9	3.5	2.9	2.8	3.3	2.7	2.3	1.8	1.7	1.5	1.6
Orlando, FL	7.3	5.7	5.8	6.1	6.0	6.2	5.5	5.3	4.8	4.7	4.2	3.9
Philadelphia, PA	11.2	11.2	10.6	9.5	8.5	9.4	9.5	9.4	8.1	7.2	6.5	5.8
Phoenix, AZ	7.2	7.3	6.6	6.6	6.7	7.1	6.2	5.2	4.2	3.5	3.0	2.6
Pittsburgh, PA	8.1	7.8	7.1	6.3	5.7	6.2	6.7	6.1	5.0	4.6	4.0	3.6
Portland, OR	7.4	6.9	7.0	6.2	5.5	5.4	5.0	4.6	4.3	3.5	3.5	3.6
Providence, RI	9.4	9.2	8.6	5.9	6.1	6.3	7.3	7.7	5.5	5.1	5.1	4.6
Provo, UT	2.6	2.7	2.1	2.1	2.1	2.7	2.1	2.1	1.1	1.1	1.1	1.1
Raleigh, NC	5.5	5.2	4.2	4.1	4.2	4.5	4.3	4.1	3.5	3.4	3.1	2.9
Reno, NV	4.8	4.9	4.6	4.9	4.7	5.0	5.0	4.3	3.6	3.2	2.9	2.8
Richmond, VA	8.0	7.7	7.1	5.8	5.8	6.2	5.6	5.4	4.8	4.5	4.1	3.8
Riverside, CA	7.9	7.5	7.0	6.9	6.6	7.4	7.2	6.8	5.8	5.4	4.7	4.4
Rochester, MN	4.1	3.9	3.6	3.4	3.3	3.9	3.0	3.0	2.6	2.2	1.9	2.2
Rochester, NY	11.7	10.9	9.8	8.2	7.9	8.3	8.7	8.5	7.5	6.9	6.4	4.6
Sacramento, CA	8.6	8.1	7.6	7.4	7.0	7.8	7.7	7.4	6.4	6.2	5.3	5.0
Salt Lake City, UT	3.6	3.7	2.9	2.9	2.8	3.1	2.9	2.5	1.6	1.4	1.4	1.3
San Antonio, TX	6.7	6.9	6.6	5.7	5.3	6.0	5.4	4.9	4.5	4.3	4.1	3.7
San Diego, CA	8.0	6.9	6.5	6.4	6.1	6.8	6.6	6.3	5.3	5.0	4.3	4.0
San Francisco, CA	6.2	5.7	5.4	5.3	5.1	5.5	5.2	5.0	4.1	3.9	3.3	3.0
San Jose, CA	6.4	5.9	5.6	5.5	5.3	5.8	5.5	5.3	4.4	4.1	3.5	3.2
Santa Rosa, CA	7.4	6.6	6.2	6.1	5.6	6.2	6.0	5.7	4.9	4.6	4.1	3.8
Savannah, GA	6.8	6.0	5.5	5.4	5.4	6.1	4.2	4.0	3.3	3.0	2.8	2.9
Seattle, WA	5.6	4.7	4.9	4.3	4.0	4.4	4.4	4.2	3.8	3.8	2.5	2.6
Sioux Falls, SD	3.2	3.5	3.2	2.8	2.7	3.0	2.3	2.5	2.0	2.1	1.9	2.2
Springfield, IL	8.5	6.8	7.0	6.8	5.9	6.9	6.1	6.7	5.0	5.0	4.6	4.2
St. Louis, MO	7.0	7.0	6.3	6.2	6.7	7.4	6.0	5.5	4.1	4.2	3.7	3.9
Tampa, FL	5.1	4.9	5.0	5.1	4.9	5.5	4.9	4.7	4.1	4.1	3.6	3.4
Tucson, AZ	7.9	8.2	7.4	7.3	7.5	8.1	7.1	5.9	4.8	4.1	3.5	3.1
Tulsa, OK	5.9	5.9	4.8	4.3	4.0	4.4	3.6	3.2	2.3	2.4	2.1	2.0
Tuscaloosa, AL	5.3	4.9	4.0	3.4	3.5	4.7	4.4	4.2	3.5	3.2	3.3	3.3
Virginia Beach, VA	5.4	5.0	4.7	3.7	3.8	4.2	3.7	3.6	3.2	2.9	2.6	2.5
Washington, DC	6.0	6.6	6.6	6.5	6.6	8.1	7.6	7.3	6.5	6.2	5.7	5.1
Wichita, KS	7.3	6.0	5.9	5.4	5.8	6.5	6.8	5.8	5.1	5.0	4.0	3.5
Wilmington, NC	5.7	5.3	4.3	4.2	4.3	4.7	4.3	4.1	3.4	3.3	3.1	2.8
Winston-Salem, NC	6.7	6.3	5.1	5.0	5.1	5.5	5.3	5.0	4.3	4.2	3.8	3.6
U.S.	6.8	6.6	6.2	5.7	5.5	6.1	5.7	5.3	4.6	4.3	3.9	3.7

Note: Data is not seasonally adjusted and covers workers 16 years of age and older; All figures are percentages
Source: Bureau of Labor Statistics, Local Area Unemployment Statistics

Unemployment Rate: Metro Area

Metro Area[1]	2021											
	Jan.	Feb.	Mar.	Apr.	May	Jun.	Jul.	Aug.	Sep.	Oct.	Nov.	Dec.
Albuquerque, NM	8.6	7.8	7.4	7.2	7.0	8.0	7.4	6.0	5.6	5.0	5.0	4.6
Allentown, PA	7.7	7.9	7.3	6.5	5.9	6.7	6.9	6.7	5.5	5.0	4.5	4.0
Anchorage, AK	6.6	6.8	7.1	6.7	6.1	6.3	5.8	4.9	5.0	4.9	5.0	4.8
Ann Arbor, MI	4.8	4.2	4.3	4.0	4.6	4.7	4.7	3.8	4.6	3.8	3.4	3.2
Athens, GA	4.2	3.8	3.4	3.2	3.5	4.0	2.7	2.8	2.2	2.2	1.9	2.2
Atlanta, GA	5.1	4.5	4.1	3.9	4.0	4.5	3.2	3.1	2.5	2.4	2.2	2.3
Austin, TX	5.4	5.6	5.3	4.6	4.3	4.8	4.2	3.8	3.5	3.4	3.2	2.9
Baltimore, MD	6.1	5.9	5.8	5.5	5.6	6.4	5.4	5.4	5.1	4.8	4.3	3.8
Baton Rouge, LA	6.7	6.2	5.8	5.9	6.1	6.8	5.8	5.0	4.2	3.7	3.5	3.2
Boise City, ID	4.3	4.3	3.8	3.3	2.9	3.3	3.0	2.7	2.2	2.0	1.9	1.8
Boston, MA[4]	6.7	6.4	5.8	5.3	4.5	4.9	5.2	4.9	4.8	4.6	4.1	3.0
Boulder, CO	6.0	5.6	5.5	5.3	4.8	5.5	4.9	4.4	3.7	3.5	3.5	3.2
Buffalo, NY	7.9	8.0	7.2	6.0	5.4	5.7	5.8	5.7	4.7	4.6	4.3	3.3
Cape Coral, FL	4.4	4.3	4.6	4.6	4.6	5.3	4.8	4.6	4.0	3.8	3.5	3.3
Cedar Rapids, IA	5.4	5.7	5.4	4.8	4.9	5.6	4.8	4.6	3.6	3.4	3.1	3.3
Charleston, SC	5.0	4.8	4.4	4.0	3.3	4.0	3.9	3.8	2.9	2.8	2.7	2.9
Charlotte, NC	5.8	5.4	4.6	4.4	4.3	4.7	4.4	4.3	3.7	3.6	3.3	3.2
Chicago, IL[2]	7.9	7.5	6.8	7.0	6.8	8.1	7.3	6.6	5.3	5.1	4.5	4.2
Cincinnati, OH	5.3	5.0	4.2	4.1	4.3	5.5	5.2	4.4	3.9	3.5	3.0	2.8
Clarksville, TN	5.7	5.3	5.7	4.8	4.9	6.1	5.1	4.6	4.0	3.8	3.3	3.7
Cleveland, OH	7.3	7.4	6.5	6.0	6.0	7.0	6.3	5.7	5.0	4.6	4.4	4.6
College Station, TX	5.5	5.6	5.2	4.7	4.5	5.5	4.8	4.2	3.8	3.7	3.5	3.2
Colorado Springs, CO	7.1	7.0	6.7	6.4	5.8	6.5	6.2	5.6	4.9	4.6	4.6	4.3
Columbia, MO	3.8	3.5	3.0	2.6	3.1	3.6	2.5	2.4	1.8	2.2	1.9	1.9
Columbia, SC	5.0	4.8	4.4	4.1	3.3	4.2	4.0	4.0	3.0	2.8	2.8	3.1
Columbus, OH	5.3	5.4	5.0	4.5	4.7	5.7	5.4	4.6	4.0	3.5	3.0	2.8
Dallas, TX[2]	6.4	6.7	6.4	5.7	5.3	5.9	5.2	4.6	4.3	4.1	3.9	3.6
Davenport, IA	7.0	6.3	6.0	5.7	5.1	5.8	5.1	5.2	3.8	4.0	3.7	3.7
Denver, CO	7.0	6.7	6.7	6.4	5.9	6.3	6.1	5.5	4.8	4.6	4.5	4.2
Des Moines, IA	4.8	5.0	4.4	4.0	4.2	4.7	4.0	3.7	2.9	2.9	2.6	2.8
Durham, NC	4.9	4.6	3.8	3.5	3.7	4.1	3.9	3.7	3.1	3.0	2.7	2.5
Edison, NJ[2]	10.7	10.9	9.6	9.0	8.4	8.8	8.8	8.4	7.6	7.0	6.6	6.3
El Paso, TX	8.0	8.3	7.8	7.0	6.5	7.3	6.5	5.8	5.3	5.2	5.0	4.7
Fargo, ND	4.0	4.4	3.8	3.2	2.8	3.6	2.7	2.5	2.0	1.8	1.8	2.1
Fort Collins, CO	6.4	6.0	5.8	5.4	4.9	5.5	5.2	4.7	3.9	3.8	3.8	3.5
Fort Wayne, IN	4.5	4.4	4.5	4.1	4.3	4.4	3.9	4.9	2.7	2.4	2.0	1.2
Fort Worth, TX[2]	6.7	7.0	6.7	5.9	5.5	6.2	5.5	4.9	4.5	4.3	4.0	3.7
Grand Rapids, MI	5.5	4.7	4.7	4.2	4.8	4.8	4.5	3.9	4.6	4.0	3.6	3.5
Green Bay, WI	4.0	4.4	4.4	3.8	3.5	4.0	3.6	3.6	2.4	2.0	1.7	1.8
Honolulu, HI	8.9	7.7	7.7	7.1	6.7	7.1	6.2	6.1	5.9	5.4	5.0	4.6
Houston, TX	8.2	8.4	8.0	7.2	6.7	7.4	6.8	6.1	5.6	5.4	5.1	4.8
Huntsville, AL	2.9	2.7	2.6	2.2	2.2	2.8	2.5	2.6	2.3	2.0	2.4	2.1
Indianapolis, IN	4.7	4.5	4.5	4.2	4.4	4.5	4.1	3.8	2.8	2.5	2.0	1.2
Jacksonville, FL	4.1	4.2	4.4	4.4	4.2	5.0	4.5	4.3	3.7	3.7	3.3	3.2
Kansas City, MO	5.1	4.8	4.2	4.1	5.0	5.4	4.4	3.8	3.5	3.0	2.7	2.5
Lafayette, LA	7.0	6.5	6.4	6.0	6.0	6.6	5.6	4.9	4.3	3.8	3.6	3.3
Las Cruces, NM	8.7	8.0	8.0	7.6	7.2	8.4	7.8	6.3	5.7	5.2	5.4	4.9
Las Vegas, NV	9.8	9.2	8.8	9.1	8.9	9.6	9.3	8.2	7.4	6.6	6.3	6.0
Lexington, KY	4.4	4.3	4.3	3.2	3.3	4.5	3.9	3.2	3.3	3.2	2.4	2.6
Lincoln, NE	3.3	3.2	2.9	2.2	2.2	2.5	1.9	1.7	1.3	1.3	1.1	1.1
Little Rock, AR	5.3	5.4	4.9	4.5	4.7	5.1	4.7	4.0	3.3	2.5	2.3	2.5
Los Angeles, CA[2]	11.2	10.7	10.4	10.3	9.5	10.0	9.6	8.9	7.6	7.1	6.2	5.6
Louisville, KY	5.2	4.6	4.7	3.9	3.7	5.4	4.5	3.4	3.3	3.2	3.0	2.9
Madison, WI	3.5	3.7	3.7	3.3	3.1	3.6	3.1	3.1	2.1	1.8	1.4	1.4
Manchester, NH[3]	4.0	3.1	3.1	2.6	2.4	3.1	3.3	2.8	2.3	2.1	2.0	2.1

Table continued on following page.

Metro Area[1]	2021											
	Jan.	Feb.	Mar.	Apr.	May	Jun.	Jul.	Aug.	Sep.	Oct.	Nov.	Dec.
Memphis, TN	7.0	6.3	6.5	6.3	6.3	7.6	6.9	6.1	4.9	4.5	3.9	4.1
Miami, FL[2]	7.1	6.6	6.8	6.1	5.6	5.8	5.3	5.1	4.5	3.8	3.3	3.0
Midland, TX	8.2	8.3	7.6	6.9	6.2	6.7	5.9	5.3	4.9	4.7	4.4	4.1
Milwaukee, WI	5.0	5.2	5.3	5.2	4.8	5.5	5.0	4.9	3.3	2.8	2.2	2.2
Minneapolis, MN	4.8	4.6	4.3	4.1	3.8	4.5	3.5	3.5	2.9	2.6	2.2	2.5
Nashville, TN	4.4	4.0	4.3	4.1	3.8	4.6	3.7	3.5	3.0	2.8	2.6	2.7
New Haven, CT[3]	7.9	7.7	7.6	7.1	6.5	6.5	6.6	5.8	5.1	4.9	4.4	4.1
New Orleans, LA	9.1	8.6	7.5	8.2	8.2	8.9	7.6	6.6	6.2	5.0	4.8	4.4
New York, NY[2]	10.7	10.9	9.6	9.0	8.4	8.8	8.8	8.4	7.6	7.0	6.6	6.3
Oklahoma City, OK	4.8	4.9	4.1	3.7	3.4	3.7	2.9	2.7	1.9	1.9	1.8	1.6
Omaha, NE	3.6	3.7	3.3	2.7	2.7	3.2	2.6	2.3	1.7	1.7	1.5	1.6
Orlando, FL	6.5	5.2	5.4	5.6	5.4	6.0	5.3	5.0	4.4	4.4	4.0	3.8
Philadelphia, PA[2]	10.2	10.1	9.6	8.5	7.7	8.5	8.6	8.6	7.3	6.6	5.9	5.3
Phoenix, AZ	6.6	6.7	6.1	6.1	6.2	6.6	5.7	4.7	3.8	3.2	2.8	2.4
Pittsburgh, PA	8.3	8.2	7.4	6.3	5.7	6.2	6.6	6.5	5.3	4.8	4.3	4.0
Portland, OR	6.7	6.4	6.4	5.7	5.1	5.0	4.6	4.4	4.0	3.4	3.3	3.4
Providence, RI[3]	8.4	7.9	7.2	5.4	5.4	5.8	5.9	6.0	4.7	4.5	4.3	3.8
Provo, UT	2.9	3.1	2.4	2.4	2.3	2.8	2.3	2.3	1.4	1.2	1.2	1.2
Raleigh, NC	5.0	4.7	3.8	3.7	3.8	4.2	3.9	3.7	3.2	3.0	2.8	2.6
Reno, NV	4.8	4.8	4.7	4.9	4.6	4.9	5.0	4.3	3.5	3.2	2.9	2.8
Richmond, VA	6.1	5.8	5.5	4.4	4.5	4.9	4.3	4.1	3.6	3.4	3.1	3.2
Riverside, CA	8.6	8.1	7.7	7.5	7.2	8.0	7.9	7.6	6.6	6.3	5.4	5.1
Rochester, MN	4.4	4.4	3.9	3.3	3.0	3.6	2.7	2.8	2.3	2.0	1.8	2.3
Rochester, NY	7.0	7.1	6.4	5.5	4.9	5.3	5.3	5.2	4.3	4.1	3.7	2.9
Sacramento, CA	7.6	7.1	6.8	6.6	6.2	6.9	6.7	6.4	5.5	5.3	4.7	4.4
Salt Lake City, UT	3.5	3.7	3.0	3.0	2.8	3.2	2.8	2.6	1.6	1.5	1.4	1.3
San Antonio, TX	6.6	6.8	6.5	5.7	5.3	6.0	5.4	4.8	4.5	4.3	4.1	3.7
San Diego, CA	8.0	7.2	6.8	6.7	6.3	7.0	6.9	6.6	5.6	5.3	4.6	4.2
San Francisco, CA[2]	6.0	5.5	5.2	5.1	4.8	5.3	5.1	4.8	4.0	3.8	3.2	2.9
San Jose, CA	5.8	5.4	5.1	5.0	4.7	5.2	5.0	4.8	4.0	3.8	3.2	3.0
Santa Rosa, CA	7.1	6.3	5.9	5.7	5.2	5.8	5.6	5.3	4.4	4.2	3.7	3.5
Savannah, GA	5.1	4.5	4.1	3.9	4.0	4.5	3.1	3.1	2.5	2.4	2.1	2.3
Seattle, WA[2]	6.1	5.4	5.2	4.5	4.5	5.0	4.7	4.2	4.0	3.6	3.1	3.2
Sioux Falls, SD	3.0	3.3	3.0	2.6	2.5	2.9	2.2	2.4	1.9	2.0	1.8	2.0
Springfield, IL	7.6	6.2	6.2	5.9	5.1	6.0	5.4	5.8	4.3	4.3	4.2	3.9
St. Louis, MO	5.5	5.3	4.7	4.4	4.6	5.3	4.4	4.2	3.2	3.2	2.9	3.0
Tampa, FL	4.5	4.4	4.6	4.7	4.6	5.2	4.7	4.5	3.9	3.8	3.5	3.3
Tucson, AZ	7.1	7.3	6.6	6.6	6.7	7.3	6.4	5.2	4.3	3.7	3.2	2.8
Tulsa, OK	5.4	5.4	4.2	3.7	3.5	3.9	3.2	2.9	2.1	2.2	2.0	1.9
Tuscaloosa, AL	4.4	4.1	3.6	3.1	3.2	4.1	3.9	3.7	3.2	3.0	3.1	3.0
Virginia Beach, VA	6.5	6.1	5.8	4.6	4.7	5.0	4.5	4.4	3.8	3.6	3.3	3.1
Washington, DC[2]	6.1	5.8	5.6	4.9	4.9	5.4	5.0	4.9	4.1	3.7	3.5	3.3
Wichita, KS	6.7	5.4	5.3	4.8	5.1	5.9	6.2	5.2	4.6	4.5	3.5	3.1
Wilmington, NC	5.5	5.0	4.1	3.9	4.0	4.4	4.0	3.8	3.3	3.1	2.9	2.7
Winston-Salem, NC	5.8	5.4	4.4	4.3	4.4	4.8	4.5	4.3	3.7	3.6	3.2	3.0
U.S.	6.8	6.6	6.2	5.7	5.5	6.1	5.7	5.3	4.6	4.3	3.9	3.7

Note: Data is not seasonally adjusted and covers workers 16 years of age and older; All figures are percentages; (1) Figures cover the Metropolitan Statistical Area (MSA) except where noted. See Appendix B for areas included; (2) Metropolitan Division; (3) New England City and Town Area; (4) New England City and Town Area Division

Source: Bureau of Labor Statistics, Local Area Unemployment Statistics

Average Hourly Wages: Occupations A – C

Metro Area[1]	Accountants/ Auditors	Automotive Mechanics	Book- keepers	Carpenters	Cashiers	Computer Program- mers	Computer Systems Analysts
Albuquerque, NM	35.64	21.75	19.93	22.11	12.69	37.36	37.61
Allentown, PA	37.50	22.65	21.03	24.54	11.76	44.57	43.99
Anchorage, AK	37.91	28.37	24.38	34.05	15.16	43.83	46.58
Ann Arbor, MI	37.78	25.73	21.73	24.80	12.70	39.84	42.42
Athens, GA	32.54	20.99	19.21	20.19	10.74	40.11	39.79
Atlanta, GA	39.93	22.85	21.65	23.07	11.18	52.00	49.21
Austin, TX	41.99	26.03	21.88	21.30	12.82	40.22	47.24
Baltimore, MD	39.78	24.72	22.68	25.54	13.33	44.48	49.17
Baton Rouge, LA	34.06	23.32	20.21	23.00	10.49	38.93	39.12
Boise City, ID	34.78	20.64	19.42	19.72	12.23	36.09	41.20
Boston, MA[2]	45.15	26.41	26.25	32.40	14.96	53.08	54.62
Boulder, CO	43.69	26.64	23.39	26.61	15.73	57.20	53.93
Buffalo, NY	39.93	21.80	21.30	27.86	13.68	40.61	45.05
Cape Coral, FL	35.62	22.70	20.34	20.04	12.27	50.52	41.73
Cedar Rapids, IA	35.94	21.87	21.65	21.98	12.29	39.78	41.97
Charleston, SC	36.20	21.07	20.20	22.39	11.59	41.41	42.63
Charlotte, NC	44.69	23.76	20.50	21.40	11.79	52.85	50.01
Chicago, IL	39.06	24.85	22.98	33.35	13.40	50.54	44.34
Cincinnati, OH	38.10	21.75	20.72	25.06	11.95	40.64	46.45
Clarksville, TN	30.80	19.52	18.95	20.08	10.93	33.34	42.74
Cleveland, OH	38.55	22.04	21.06	26.41	12.09	35.19	45.76
College Station, TX	32.54	20.97	17.76	18.17	10.91	n/a	36.21
Colorado Springs, CO	38.11	24.49	20.35	23.91	14.30	43.09	50.29
Columbia, MO	30.99	20.57	19.32	24.01	11.74	34.10	41.19
Columbia, SC	31.93	20.78	18.97	21.62	10.76	44.74	39.38
Columbus, OH	37.32	22.53	21.33	24.92	11.94	41.88	46.18
Dallas, TX	42.17	24.34	21.93	21.43	12.20	42.36	51.34
Davenport, IA	34.28	21.08	20.50	23.64	12.13	42.25	44.62
Denver, CO	42.42	25.21	23.30	25.29	15.03	51.14	53.87
Des Moines, IA	37.03	22.53	22.88	23.52	12.60	38.49	45.13
Durham, NC	41.51	23.74	22.20	20.65	11.68	51.76	47.49
Edison, NJ	52.56	26.14	25.39	34.58	15.43	51.10	56.08
El Paso, TX	34.15	18.34	17.69	17.10	10.15	30.14	36.48
Fargo, ND	32.75	23.40	20.54	23.42	13.17	41.83	45.90
Fort Collins, CO	38.19	25.13	21.49	24.18	14.83	30.17	46.29
Fort Wayne, IN	34.84	19.76	19.47	23.20	11.49	38.50	39.31
Fort Worth, TX	42.17	24.34	21.93	21.43	12.20	42.36	51.34
Grand Rapids, MI	35.64	22.99	20.50	23.19	12.59	37.07	42.12
Green Bay, WI	35.71	21.94	20.94	25.63	12.16	52.93	45.03
Honolulu, HI	33.88	25.18	22.42	39.29	14.60	45.28	42.10
Houston, TX	44.33	24.19	21.63	23.10	12.08	44.93	56.14
Huntsville, AL	38.18	21.49	18.78	21.04	11.36	47.66	57.06
Indianapolis, IN	36.76	22.69	20.74	24.92	11.86	51.50	44.85
Jacksonville, FL	34.69	21.14	20.34	20.06	11.86	39.48	44.87
Kansas City, MO	35.44	21.80	21.31	26.69	12.47	43.58	41.90
Lafayette, LA	33.47	21.89	18.67	20.48	10.01	37.41	38.66
Las Cruces, NM	30.88	19.20	17.90	19.98	11.62	33.37	35.38
Las Vegas, NV	30.92	23.43	20.47	29.70	12.21	39.00	44.90
Lexington, KY	34.39	20.31	20.40	23.15	11.95	34.87	42.02
Lincoln, NE	32.69	24.92	19.47	20.44	12.37	36.87	35.93
Little Rock, AR	34.12	21.71	18.89	20.56	12.05	41.00	34.83
Los Angeles, CA	43.13	25.40	24.26	30.58	15.34	50.13	55.04
Louisville, KY	35.97	21.01	20.59	23.32	11.85	43.63	42.69
Madison, WI	37.23	22.03	21.22	26.68	12.98	50.98	44.70
Manchester, NH[2]	36.59	24.38	21.93	24.12	12.40	34.82	52.06

Table continued on following page.

Metro Area[1]	Accountants/ Auditors	Automotive Mechanics	Book-keepers	Carpenters	Cashiers	Computer Program-mers	Computer Systems Analysts
Memphis, TN	33.68	22.88	20.26	21.87	11.23	42.85	40.42
Miami, FL	38.05	22.41	20.64	22.13	12.05	43.37	44.94
Midland, TX	45.85	24.36	22.98	23.44	12.79	46.75	51.04
Milwaukee, WI	38.93	22.19	21.60	26.79	12.40	44.85	46.46
Minneapolis, MN	39.63	26.18	23.70	29.06	13.93	47.72	49.61
Nashville, TN	34.74	22.61	20.90	21.32	11.83	46.53	41.65
New Haven, CT[2]	37.36	24.30	23.82	30.03	13.89	41.25	47.20
New Orleans, LA	35.27	23.96	20.94	22.55	10.61	37.62	43.52
New York, NY	52.56	26.14	25.39	34.58	15.43	51.10	56.08
Oklahoma City, OK	35.83	22.67	19.72	19.64	11.62	39.90	43.24
Omaha, NE	35.17	23.85	20.99	21.47	12.68	42.81	43.50
Orlando, FL	36.66	20.74	20.50	22.66	11.95	42.65	45.10
Philadelphia, PA	42.24	24.27	23.20	29.26	12.53	44.65	50.48
Phoenix, AZ	38.88	23.07	21.64	23.77	14.34	39.02	47.79
Pittsburgh, PA	36.39	21.78	20.77	26.79	11.34	42.12	43.80
Portland, OR	39.17	25.93	23.24	28.95	15.55	50.00	51.45
Providence, RI[2]	42.31	23.13	23.16	28.77	13.61	47.30	50.41
Provo, UT	33.20	22.18	20.57	21.23	12.38	45.65	55.42
Raleigh, NC	39.39	22.91	20.64	21.59	11.75	48.15	48.56
Reno, NV	33.07	24.44	21.88	28.25	12.55	43.95	46.69
Richmond, VA	38.86	24.01	20.93	21.21	11.76	41.70	47.87
Riverside, CA	38.52	25.03	22.34	28.56	14.92	42.54	45.59
Rochester, MN	36.59	23.20	22.07	27.19	13.32	n/a	42.43
Rochester, NY	39.35	22.65	21.63	26.46	13.75	36.45	47.18
Sacramento, CA	40.35	25.92	23.84	30.30	15.42	49.68	50.24
Salt Lake City, UT	35.97	24.99	22.18	24.24	12.62	48.03	44.89
San Antonio, TX	39.22	22.72	20.78	21.04	12.13	38.95	46.80
San Diego, CA	42.08	26.08	24.11	30.82	15.26	56.29	51.61
San Francisco, CA	51.70	29.49	28.21	37.64	17.74	60.68	63.29
San Jose, CA	54.25	30.20	28.72	37.83	18.20	69.29	67.93
Santa Rosa, CA	44.54	27.43	25.55	35.07	16.65	50.47	51.42
Savannah, GA	34.81	22.02	20.59	21.98	10.76	43.23	53.49
Seattle, WA	44.02	27.19	26.01	33.71	17.02	n/a	56.28
Sioux Falls, SD	35.30	24.05	18.52	20.41	12.41	29.12	38.51
Springfield, IL	35.05	24.03	21.24	28.45	12.42	44.39	45.94
St. Louis, MO	36.22	21.78	22.36	29.16	12.63	39.66	45.35
Tampa, FL	38.64	22.28	21.08	20.68	11.81	39.01	43.18
Tucson, AZ	34.25	21.26	20.48	21.27	13.89	41.57	45.36
Tulsa, OK	39.45	23.24	20.22	21.11	11.75	38.22	41.81
Tuscaloosa, AL	34.39	22.37	18.42	19.96	10.99	n/a	40.74
Virginia Beach, VA	36.17	22.76	20.18	21.02	11.61	43.06	46.53
Washington, DC	47.91	28.03	25.54	26.98	14.21	56.67	55.62
Wichita, KS	34.89	20.75	18.56	20.44	11.23	38.85	40.34
Wilmington, NC	37.18	20.06	19.26	20.33	11.01	50.30	42.84
Winston-Salem, NC	36.85	21.64	19.67	19.66	11.19	45.00	45.20

Notes: (1) Figures cover the Metropolitan Statistical Area (MSA) except where noted. See Appendix B for areas included; (2) New England City and Town Area; n/a not available
Source: Bureau of Labor Statistics, May 2021 Metro Area Occupational Employment and Wage Estimates

Average Hourly Wages: Occupations C – E

Metro Area	Comp. User Support Specialists	Construction Laborers	Cooks, Restaurant	Customer Service Reps.	Dentists	Electricians	Engineers, Electrical
Albuquerque, NM	23.60	16.88	14.15	16.91	90.15	25.39	56.62
Allentown, PA	27.28	22.69	14.48	18.12	82.97	33.07	50.28
Anchorage, AK	29.27	25.56	16.22	20.25	79.32	37.45	50.53
Ann Arbor, MI	24.67	21.14	15.07	18.30	72.84	32.76	46.24
Athens, GA	22.88	16.45	12.68	15.57	78.89	25.06	51.23
Atlanta, GA	29.29	18.13	13.87	18.33	81.29	26.90	54.95
Austin, TX	26.94	17.92	14.83	18.60	69.79	26.18	58.10
Baltimore, MD	28.43	18.21	15.56	19.35	80.63	29.10	56.95
Baton Rouge, LA	24.06	18.09	13.46	16.92	86.62	27.65	58.57
Boise City, ID	24.62	17.84	13.20	16.69	57.66	25.20	55.32
Boston, MA[2]	34.64	29.11	18.01	22.83	85.75	36.95	57.85
Boulder, CO	34.92	19.55	18.13	20.40	96.97	27.79	54.64
Buffalo, NY	26.48	22.71	15.57	19.71	79.34	31.66	48.49
Cape Coral, FL	24.26	17.48	15.21	17.61	84.41	23.02	41.50
Cedar Rapids, IA	25.34	21.49	14.11	19.71	92.44	28.74	n/a
Charleston, SC	26.24	17.67	14.67	17.23	63.34	24.08	51.45
Charlotte, NC	26.66	17.38	14.18	18.73	99.87	23.69	49.89
Chicago, IL	26.93	31.69	15.85	20.26	64.79	41.64	48.70
Cincinnati, OH	25.27	22.80	14.11	19.07	89.86	27.32	45.51
Clarksville, TN	21.58	16.91	12.92	15.66	n/a	23.14	38.73
Cleveland, OH	25.25	24.25	14.38	19.52	72.80	29.07	46.04
College Station, TX	20.22	15.31	12.04	15.28	62.90	24.09	21.35
Colorado Springs, CO	30.02	18.94	16.32	18.23	77.91	25.94	49.66
Columbia, MO	23.95	24.65	13.45	17.06	73.06	24.28	41.48
Columbia, SC	24.52	17.16	13.62	16.79	60.12	24.20	43.43
Columbus, OH	25.21	24.29	14.23	19.04	92.77	27.30	49.65
Dallas, TX	26.32	17.83	14.57	19.09	70.53	25.59	52.35
Davenport, IA	24.87	21.28	13.67	18.20	79.73	29.37	46.60
Denver, CO	31.72	19.70	17.67	20.48	60.38	28.78	49.49
Des Moines, IA	26.59	20.91	14.45	21.02	74.24	27.38	46.34
Durham, NC	31.62	17.54	14.39	19.49	98.85	25.50	52.36
Edison, NJ	32.68	31.05	18.10	22.52	87.59	40.90	53.39
El Paso, TX	20.60	14.55	11.84	14.66	67.50	21.40	39.80
Fargo, ND	25.29	21.25	15.06	19.45	76.45	29.47	43.65
Fort Collins, CO	28.95	19.71	16.66	17.87	92.60	27.54	52.55
Fort Wayne, IN	24.01	21.45	13.57	18.66	78.66	30.05	48.19
Fort Worth, TX	26.32	17.83	14.57	19.09	70.53	25.59	52.35
Grand Rapids, MI	25.31	19.74	14.62	18.53	94.41	25.91	42.99
Green Bay, WI	27.42	21.50	14.15	19.41	86.36	28.90	42.94
Honolulu, HI	30.11	28.96	17.56	19.59	82.15	38.72	52.64
Houston, TX	26.08	17.96	14.05	17.95	76.91	26.96	52.91
Huntsville, AL	25.10	16.08	12.85	16.26	83.27	24.40	52.79
Indianapolis, IN	25.23	21.68	14.32	18.99	72.14	30.68	48.25
Jacksonville, FL	24.88	17.06	14.58	17.83	101.75	22.88	44.38
Kansas City, MO	26.50	21.58	14.21	18.56	93.36	30.36	45.30
Lafayette, LA	25.06	16.46	12.27	15.84	58.11	25.18	41.99
Las Cruces, NM	20.62	16.10	12.73	14.45	81.76	22.49	45.77
Las Vegas, NV	22.84	20.72	15.84	17.99	80.56	32.48	48.49
Lexington, KY	24.18	19.02	13.76	16.88	75.63	24.64	45.88
Lincoln, NE	23.46	18.60	15.45	16.94	76.88	24.90	45.92
Little Rock, AR	24.15	16.05	13.15	17.65	98.36	21.24	46.76
Los Angeles, CA	31.32	24.70	18.32	20.84	72.86	34.83	59.67
Louisville, KY	24.70	19.97	14.06	18.33	68.53	27.92	45.41
Madison, WI	28.09	22.32	14.84	19.81	91.84	31.47	45.67
Manchester, NH[2]	28.48	19.59	16.65	20.46	132.94	28.57	53.93

Table continued on following page.

Metro Area	Comp. User Support Specialists	Construction Laborers	Cooks, Restaurant	Customer Service Reps.	Dentists	Electricians	Engineers, Electrical
Memphis, TN	23.44	17.49	13.30	17.38	90.16	24.68	48.05
Miami, FL	25.14	17.81	15.49	17.75	70.89	25.16	43.62
Midland, TX	26.20	18.19	14.53	19.04	75.22	28.05	42.47
Milwaukee, WI	26.48	22.67	14.80	20.21	90.78	33.51	45.37
Minneapolis, MN	28.57	25.28	17.04	21.59	91.22	34.82	49.61
Nashville, TN	24.34	18.15	14.83	17.90	79.22	25.53	45.82
New Haven, CT[2]	28.58	23.66	16.79	21.53	109.32	31.69	49.08
New Orleans, LA	25.25	17.62	12.68	16.78	68.34	28.01	57.17
New York, NY	32.68	31.05	18.10	22.52	87.59	40.90	53.39
Oklahoma City, OK	25.09	17.15	13.71	16.50	83.82	26.59	48.05
Omaha, NE	25.72	19.92	15.54	18.08	65.07	25.80	44.16
Orlando, FL	24.76	16.55	15.16	17.12	87.85	22.73	47.34
Philadelphia, PA	29.35	24.83	15.61	20.18	90.97	36.02	54.35
Phoenix, AZ	26.83	19.70	16.11	18.74	87.75	24.53	48.89
Pittsburgh, PA	27.87	23.21	13.67	18.69	66.14	32.75	50.70
Portland, OR	29.02	23.45	17.48	20.24	104.00	40.05	50.79
Providence, RI[2]	n/a	26.11	15.87	20.05	90.21	29.44	54.22
Provo, UT	25.51	18.10	14.67	17.07	62.68	26.19	44.41
Raleigh, NC	28.78	17.42	14.60	18.73	89.60	23.31	51.13
Reno, NV	23.61	21.87	14.96	17.78	58.47	30.31	47.85
Richmond, VA	26.51	16.50	13.48	17.51	68.02	27.26	49.73
Riverside, CA	28.71	23.87	16.31	19.92	79.35	33.67	47.98
Rochester, MN	28.20	22.75	15.68	19.69	86.86	31.10	51.27
Rochester, NY	26.46	23.50	15.84	19.26	85.39	32.95	47.57
Sacramento, CA	43.50	25.27	17.88	20.44	96.67	35.72	59.94
Salt Lake City, UT	28.49	18.79	15.20	19.08	66.94	28.52	51.10
San Antonio, TX	24.43	17.07	13.77	17.78	70.98	25.15	45.83
San Diego, CA	30.26	24.77	17.73	20.64	66.83	32.98	55.83
San Francisco, CA	36.98	28.76	19.85	24.29	87.36	45.14	64.25
San Jose, CA	36.78	29.80	20.86	25.30	80.79	43.79	71.57
Santa Rosa, CA	31.73	26.28	19.53	21.86	73.46	34.81	58.39
Savannah, GA	24.96	16.41	13.23	15.70	76.02	25.83	52.28
Seattle, WA	31.52	28.00	20.04	21.98	83.65	40.77	59.69
Sioux Falls, SD	20.79	17.32	14.10	17.48	74.64	25.78	48.11
Springfield, IL	25.85	26.78	14.25	18.24	87.79	34.26	46.38
St. Louis, MO	28.54	26.20	14.28	18.60	84.74	33.00	49.22
Tampa, FL	25.86	17.21	14.43	17.96	75.85	23.61	47.02
Tucson, AZ	26.04	18.23	15.44	16.57	75.94	23.78	46.97
Tulsa, OK	24.46	17.70	13.74	16.79	n/a	28.06	49.80
Tuscaloosa, AL	29.47	15.34	12.80	17.17	89.44	25.46	50.75
Virginia Beach, VA	25.60	16.67	13.07	16.57	78.01	25.90	46.79
Washington, DC	32.03	20.02	16.67	21.08	83.65	32.85	58.52
Wichita, KS	24.19	17.75	12.85	16.12	84.13	26.95	40.89
Wilmington, NC	25.80	16.83	13.61	17.36	86.55	21.70	53.17
Winston-Salem, NC	25.27	16.53	13.50	17.55	98.00	22.33	47.66

Notes: (1) Figures cover the Metropolitan Statistical Area (MSA) except where noted. See Appendix B for areas included; (2) New England City and Town Area; n/a not available
Source: Bureau of Labor Statistics, May 2021 Metro Area Occupational Employment and Wage Estimates

Average Hourly Wages: Occupations F – H

Metro Area	Fast Food and Counter Workers	Financial Managers	First-Line Supervisors/ of Office Workers	General and Operations Managers	Hair-dressers/ Cosme-tologists	Home Health and Personal Care Aides	Janitors/ Cleaners
Albuquerque, NM	11.91	59.98	26.92	52.87	12.14	12.66	13.25
Allentown, PA	11.57	72.81	30.10	54.83	16.51	13.63	15.57
Anchorage, AK	13.37	58.02	31.62	50.16	13.55	16.58	16.77
Ann Arbor, MI	12.62	65.75	28.89	60.05	18.88	13.89	16.92
Athens, GA	10.23	62.49	26.67	43.79	15.86	12.36	13.54
Atlanta, GA	11.60	74.05	30.34	52.93	19.05	12.43	13.95
Austin, TX	11.50	78.13	32.58	53.26	15.43	11.81	14.00
Baltimore, MD	13.49	74.39	30.98	56.04	18.02	14.08	15.43
Baton Rouge, LA	9.78	59.15	26.85	57.79	14.00	9.90	11.70
Boise City, ID	10.42	56.49	27.13	38.16	14.36	13.37	13.47
Boston, MA[2]	15.00	80.24	34.91	71.94	20.90	16.85	19.83
Boulder, CO	15.17	87.34	33.09	68.52	20.61	16.65	17.63
Buffalo, NY	14.14	76.80	31.35	55.20	16.75	14.96	15.66
Cape Coral, FL	11.83	60.80	28.97	45.61	17.73	14.42	13.88
Cedar Rapids, IA	11.72	59.93	30.30	48.33	15.31	14.72	15.21
Charleston, SC	10.90	66.65	28.48	48.82	15.41	12.23	12.27
Charlotte, NC	11.34	84.22	29.61	58.51	16.89	11.85	13.33
Chicago, IL	12.77	72.09	33.47	60.57	20.39	14.37	16.33
Cincinnati, OH	11.49	69.00	29.94	52.96	15.45	13.09	15.06
Clarksville, TN	9.83	50.89	24.52	43.97	14.39	11.86	12.80
Cleveland, OH	11.67	69.24	30.54	55.84	15.94	12.65	15.29
College Station, TX	9.65	57.77	24.25	42.51	12.39	10.43	12.35
Colorado Springs, CO	14.04	77.12	30.14	59.45	18.13	15.18	15.58
Columbia, MO	11.71	60.26	27.11	42.55	17.70	12.34	14.58
Columbia, SC	10.06	59.15	28.62	44.62	14.46	11.30	12.11
Columbus, OH	11.42	68.41	30.25	55.03	15.72	13.09	15.20
Dallas, TX	11.35	77.64	30.60	54.42	15.05	11.70	13.92
Davenport, IA	11.64	56.77	27.99	45.53	15.57	13.75	15.43
Denver, CO	14.67	86.86	33.52	66.83	17.65	15.58	16.38
Des Moines, IA	12.07	67.56	31.64	48.71	15.57	14.18	14.72
Durham, NC	12.06	82.38	31.65	66.73	21.62	12.44	15.64
Edison, NJ	15.12	100.53	37.23	76.54	19.67	16.11	19.22
El Paso, TX	9.35	59.11	23.80	40.25	12.36	9.42	11.32
Fargo, ND	12.68	67.10	29.59	46.76	17.41	15.67	15.61
Fort Collins, CO	14.28	77.74	30.32	59.28	18.64	15.57	16.06
Fort Wayne, IN	10.92	57.13	29.19	52.83	15.92	12.47	13.45
Fort Worth, TX	11.35	77.64	30.60	54.42	15.05	11.70	13.92
Grand Rapids, MI	11.98	62.79	29.31	54.01	22.15	13.42	14.33
Green Bay, WI	10.90	61.78	31.76	60.52	14.80	12.84	14.77
Honolulu, HI	13.62	59.93	29.39	53.15	21.03	14.60	15.99
Houston, TX	11.04	77.65	29.92	55.18	13.99	11.24	13.00
Huntsville, AL	9.75	66.09	26.45	65.15	16.83	10.45	12.04
Indianapolis, IN	11.50	65.03	30.85	56.90	15.11	12.74	14.32
Jacksonville, FL	10.86	64.74	29.59	48.39	15.94	13.09	12.85
Kansas City, MO	11.87	70.81	30.78	50.02	18.10	13.01	15.11
Lafayette, LA	9.26	56.27	25.29	55.14	12.85	9.81	11.18
Las Cruces, NM	11.42	48.61	25.05	45.03	12.51	11.38	12.50
Las Vegas, NV	11.20	54.48	26.95	48.61	12.37	12.24	14.65
Lexington, KY	10.72	58.51	30.01	44.11	11.71	13.99	13.71
Lincoln, NE	11.98	57.55	26.88	44.36	17.14	13.41	14.26
Little Rock, AR	11.82	58.53	25.50	41.90	15.64	12.14	12.71
Los Angeles, CA	15.33	77.35	33.40	63.48	20.20	15.02	17.58
Louisville, KY	10.93	66.88	30.90	46.56	13.41	14.98	13.57
Madison, WI	11.49	71.94	33.43	63.62	16.77	13.76	15.19

Table continued on following page.

Metro Area	Fast Food and Counter Workers	Financial Managers	First-Line Supervisors/ of Office Workers	General and Operations Managers	Hair-dressers/ Cosme-tologists	Home Health and Personal Care Aides	Janitors/ Cleaners
Manchester, NH[2]	12.30	68.11	32.08	60.65	15.82	14.91	15.49
Memphis, TN	10.45	62.46	28.67	56.55	15.89	11.57	12.66
Miami, FL	11.40	71.30	31.01	49.18	14.70	12.45	13.07
Midland, TX	11.58	73.09	31.35	56.37	15.21	12.15	14.04
Milwaukee, WI	11.08	75.64	33.43	66.39	16.42	12.87	14.92
Minneapolis, MN	13.66	71.57	33.66	54.11	17.68	14.71	17.11
Nashville, TN	10.72	66.88	29.79	61.56	17.34	12.46	13.38
New Haven, CT[2]	13.72	68.81	31.76	67.70	16.08	15.92	17.29
New Orleans, LA	10.34	61.87	26.00	56.48	13.46	10.80	12.13
New York, NY	15.12	100.53	37.23	76.54	19.67	16.11	19.22
Oklahoma City, OK	10.12	61.10	27.36	47.42	13.35	11.22	12.77
Omaha, NE	12.14	63.91	27.76	46.18	19.08	13.43	14.47
Orlando, FL	11.17	67.48	28.83	46.74	15.71	12.42	12.81
Philadelphia, PA	12.33	81.57	33.01	63.48	17.53	13.90	16.09
Phoenix, AZ	15.27	66.61	29.45	50.20	19.51	14.23	15.02
Pittsburgh, PA	11.03	74.14	29.73	53.97	16.62	13.36	15.12
Portland, OR	15.10	67.59	31.56	56.48	17.10	15.92	16.88
Providence, RI[2]	13.94	78.00	33.43	61.49	16.13	15.40	16.95
Provo, UT	11.73	58.84	27.36	42.31	13.30	13.94	13.28
Raleigh, NC	11.37	74.10	29.59	61.04	17.80	12.21	13.47
Reno, NV	11.60	55.75	27.64	50.41	13.98	12.22	14.01
Richmond, VA	11.29	74.83	29.55	54.80	17.60	11.51	13.20
Riverside, CA	15.06	66.09	30.12	53.12	18.17	14.59	17.66
Rochester, MN	13.03	64.22	31.26	47.57	16.89	14.82	16.56
Rochester, NY	13.87	75.91	31.74	56.54	17.13	15.16	15.33
Sacramento, CA	15.35	71.93	34.08	57.73	17.82	15.11	17.50
Salt Lake City, UT	12.37	62.34	28.73	43.88	14.78	15.25	13.94
San Antonio, TX	10.65	68.65	29.32	50.15	13.99	10.63	13.28
San Diego, CA	15.23	76.55	32.85	58.95	17.67	15.28	17.07
San Francisco, CA	17.48	90.82	37.71	73.32	18.85	16.97	20.21
San Jose, CA	17.83	96.79	39.45	79.49	18.04	15.57	19.48
Santa Rosa, CA	15.93	76.02	32.97	57.86	19.08	15.52	18.25
Savannah, GA	11.94	61.27	25.90	45.63	17.41	11.76	13.15
Seattle, WA	16.46	83.91	38.23	70.61	21.29	18.34	19.20
Sioux Falls, SD	12.34	74.05	27.23	66.94	16.38	13.70	14.47
Springfield, IL	11.94	60.54	30.00	50.32	20.67	12.82	15.57
St. Louis, MO	12.11	67.56	31.71	51.98	17.84	12.25	15.01
Tampa, FL	11.20	67.26	29.38	49.23	17.02	12.44	12.90
Tucson, AZ	14.38	56.29	25.93	42.09	20.03	13.79	14.71
Tulsa, OK	10.11	68.25	28.46	50.14	13.40	11.75	12.91
Tuscaloosa, AL	10.05	61.26	26.37	52.12	17.24	10.82	13.93
Virginia Beach, VA	11.35	70.85	27.92	51.82	15.67	11.33	13.03
Washington, DC	13.99	83.20	35.36	71.43	21.83	14.66	16.50
Wichita, KS	10.42	66.29	27.55	44.05	15.34	11.08	13.59
Wilmington, NC	10.38	71.28	26.23	51.35	15.79	11.59	13.27
Winston-Salem, NC	11.27	74.11	27.54	53.98	14.83	11.69	12.58

Notes: (1) Figures cover the Metropolitan Statistical Area (MSA) except where noted. See Appendix B for areas included; (2) New England City and Town Area; n/a not available
Source: Bureau of Labor Statistics, May 2021 Metro Area Occupational Employment and Wage Estimates

Average Hourly Wages: Occupations L – N

Metro Area	Landscapers	Lawyers	Maids/ House-keepers	Main-tenance/ Repairers	Marketing Managers	Network Admin.	Nurses, Licensed Practical
Albuquerque, NM	15.74	57.83	12.04	19.77	53.28	38.85	27.06
Allentown, PA	16.90	60.85	13.89	22.47	65.90	37.52	24.91
Anchorage, AK	19.32	54.45	14.52	24.74	50.92	42.14	30.49
Ann Arbor, MI	16.71	57.57	14.22	20.92	61.46	39.98	26.62
Athens, GA	14.83	44.97	11.80	18.84	49.59	34.54	22.07
Atlanta, GA	16.45	69.41	12.42	20.33	70.55	46.73	24.81
Austin, TX	16.08	67.69	13.18	19.80	71.32	43.33	25.39
Baltimore, MD	17.58	67.14	14.12	22.23	69.07	52.00	26.56
Baton Rouge, LA	14.87	53.75	11.37	20.29	57.98	34.28	21.78
Boise City, ID	16.81	51.74	12.99	19.25	51.68	37.62	24.66
Boston, MA[2]	20.88	82.53	18.00	25.63	78.95	50.60	30.04
Boulder, CO	20.13	n/a	16.02	23.65	81.78	45.72	27.32
Buffalo, NY	17.19	57.88	15.37	21.37	77.60	42.11	23.25
Cape Coral, FL	15.64	59.67	12.93	19.11	60.04	39.53	23.50
Cedar Rapids, IA	16.00	58.23	13.05	22.10	64.00	41.97	23.41
Charleston, SC	16.09	50.80	12.30	20.16	60.38	41.81	23.67
Charlotte, NC	16.50	69.92	12.74	21.50	69.79	41.61	24.42
Chicago, IL	17.26	74.01	15.13	24.56	68.61	45.98	27.64
Cincinnati, OH	16.04	58.62	12.96	22.05	70.54	41.85	24.04
Clarksville, TN	15.09	42.81	10.86	20.69	42.53	33.22	21.20
Cleveland, OH	16.71	62.40	13.16	22.58	68.33	43.34	24.48
College Station, TX	14.38	58.31	11.86	16.53	55.88	35.32	21.56
Colorado Springs, CO	19.21	51.23	15.00	21.14	77.39	43.42	26.52
Columbia, MO	14.37	55.94	12.07	19.14	51.38	37.51	21.82
Columbia, SC	14.66	49.86	11.53	19.77	63.97	41.23	22.31
Columbus, OH	16.61	60.51	13.12	21.71	69.51	43.48	23.43
Dallas, TX	16.30	77.72	13.09	20.14	70.97	46.83	25.69
Davenport, IA	14.86	56.61	12.73	21.27	60.13	42.00	22.83
Denver, CO	19.22	69.18	15.89	22.84	78.36	46.41	27.98
Des Moines, IA	16.53	59.72	13.44	21.19	63.89	43.85	24.27
Durham, NC	16.45	70.15	13.69	23.15	72.88	48.01	24.90
Edison, NJ	19.94	88.40	19.44	25.73	91.98	53.33	28.47
El Paso, TX	12.93	61.74	10.48	16.24	47.56	34.95	21.82
Fargo, ND	18.46	55.20	14.08	20.45	63.54	38.76	23.12
Fort Collins, CO	18.81	63.75	15.57	21.76	80.61	40.88	25.82
Fort Wayne, IN	15.53	62.34	11.98	21.08	58.43	35.88	24.15
Fort Worth, TX	16.30	77.72	13.09	20.14	70.97	46.83	25.69
Grand Rapids, MI	16.59	59.29	13.77	20.06	63.36	38.10	25.11
Green Bay, WI	16.33	62.82	13.30	22.31	61.97	37.30	22.07
Honolulu, HI	18.67	49.23	19.61	23.94	54.25	43.34	26.08
Houston, TX	15.56	76.98	13.22	20.41	68.32	43.70	25.46
Huntsville, AL	15.05	63.18	10.74	19.61	71.62	41.84	20.40
Indianapolis, IN	16.70	64.61	12.85	21.12	65.50	40.70	25.47
Jacksonville, FL	15.29	58.73	12.58	19.68	60.23	38.60	22.76
Kansas City, MO	16.92	64.37	13.10	21.16	64.44	42.08	23.63
Lafayette, LA	14.34	51.19	10.45	18.03	49.61	35.43	20.10
Las Cruces, NM	14.80	56.69	11.23	17.22	n/a	38.34	25.10
Las Vegas, NV	16.40	65.53	16.12	21.01	58.31	45.09	29.09
Lexington, KY	15.40	50.88	12.29	20.97	52.18	35.33	22.91
Lincoln, NE	16.14	53.44	13.68	21.00	46.22	37.62	23.26
Little Rock, AR	14.33	47.57	12.09	17.47	53.87	35.95	21.85
Los Angeles, CA	18.89	85.36	17.03	23.74	77.77	46.28	30.77
Louisville, KY	15.51	51.13	12.85	21.87	72.47	37.91	24.15
Madison, WI	18.05	61.31	14.47	22.09	67.89	39.95	24.98
Manchester, NH[2]	18.35	66.05	14.32	22.93	73.62	44.07	28.68

Table continued on following page.

Metro Area	Landscapers	Lawyers	Maids/ House-keepers	Main-tenance/ Repairers	Marketing Managers	Network Admin.	Nurses, Licensed Practical
Memphis, TN	15.13	53.92	12.05	20.42	56.12	38.90	21.90
Miami, FL	15.67	66.53	13.06	19.66	69.74	40.22	23.68
Midland, TX	16.62	77.81	13.39	19.50	79.34	42.88	26.21
Milwaukee, WI	16.82	70.71	13.85	22.49	64.98	41.01	25.43
Minneapolis, MN	19.14	66.45	16.16	24.64	76.99	44.74	25.39
Nashville, TN	16.04	60.64	12.38	20.87	60.23	38.85	21.96
New Haven, CT[2]	20.32	67.58	14.70	23.41	72.74	44.21	28.43
New Orleans, LA	14.84	57.06	11.45	18.52	56.29	36.90	22.24
New York, NY	19.94	88.40	19.44	25.73	91.98	53.33	28.47
Oklahoma City, OK	15.35	47.38	11.55	17.97	61.02	37.87	22.12
Omaha, NE	16.78	53.18	14.08	21.46	53.56	42.11	23.90
Orlando, FL	15.20	67.91	13.37	19.12	67.20	40.68	23.04
Philadelphia, PA	17.82	70.06	14.58	22.63	73.34	41.13	26.75
Phoenix, AZ	16.57	63.06	14.71	21.54	63.45	43.62	28.14
Pittsburgh, PA	15.95	60.51	13.74	20.84	68.31	37.40	23.72
Portland, OR	19.37	71.10	16.43	22.93	64.96	45.42	29.52
Providence, RI[2]	19.52	69.93	16.27	23.90	78.23	45.23	28.68
Provo, UT	16.62	69.48	13.58	20.67	56.64	41.93	23.55
Raleigh, NC	16.42	62.22	13.32	21.82	70.94	44.45	25.41
Reno, NV	16.69	65.89	14.51	23.16	54.05	38.60	28.90
Richmond, VA	15.00	68.51	12.31	20.82	70.18	43.17	23.52
Riverside, CA	17.93	72.68	16.24	23.19	63.83	43.39	28.97
Rochester, MN	18.27	52.98	15.72	22.35	61.34	43.73	25.24
Rochester, NY	17.44	61.05	15.10	21.72	75.14	40.93	22.72
Sacramento, CA	19.08	75.74	18.59	23.52	73.18	46.15	31.77
Salt Lake City, UT	17.21	63.20	14.47	22.76	59.66	44.66	26.56
San Antonio, TX	15.05	64.38	12.61	18.80	62.90	40.94	24.68
San Diego, CA	18.39	79.56	16.56	22.91	73.02	47.42	30.59
San Francisco, CA	22.91	92.05	21.43	28.96	95.61	55.95	36.26
San Jose, CA	22.71	111.15	21.60	28.79	101.10	65.12	36.48
Santa Rosa, CA	20.53	77.19	19.22	24.85	76.63	47.92	34.22
Savannah, GA	15.32	58.77	11.19	19.24	64.88	41.84	22.67
Seattle, WA	21.55	69.59	17.71	26.02	81.22	48.53	31.91
Sioux Falls, SD	16.02	49.48	12.48	19.71	64.32	33.79	20.32
Springfield, IL	16.84	53.86	13.87	21.97	59.74	37.63	23.37
St. Louis, MO	16.96	61.86	13.61	22.67	59.69	44.94	23.91
Tampa, FL	14.84	60.84	12.62	19.09	n/a	40.38	23.02
Tucson, AZ	15.16	56.04	14.26	19.33	63.88	37.41	27.25
Tulsa, OK	15.30	61.50	11.69	18.79	63.98	38.56	23.03
Tuscaloosa, AL	15.21	51.10	10.61	16.77	45.67	38.97	20.32
Virginia Beach, VA	15.16	54.74	12.38	20.43	67.69	41.35	22.32
Washington, DC	18.36	89.72	15.51	24.42	82.81	52.13	27.15
Wichita, KS	15.18	46.87	11.70	19.18	59.25	38.07	21.64
Wilmington, NC	15.41	54.92	11.67	18.85	65.50	38.06	23.64
Winston-Salem, NC	15.62	66.04	12.54	21.02	63.94	41.63	23.52

Notes: (1) Figures cover the Metropolitan Statistical Area (MSA) except where noted. See Appendix B for areas included; (2) New England City and Town Area; n/a not available
Source: Bureau of Labor Statistics, May 2021 Metro Area Occupational Employment and Wage Estimates

Average Hourly Wages: Occupations N – P

Metro Area	Nurses, Registered	Nursing Assistants	Office Clerks	Physical Therapists	Physicians	Plumbers	Police Officers
Albuquerque, NM	38.25	15.54	14.66	46.27	124.08	24.80	27.32
Allentown, PA	36.64	16.66	19.56	46.11	78.67	32.37	36.70
Anchorage, AK	46.23	19.99	20.94	45.65	123.16	41.42	46.53
Ann Arbor, MI	40.79	18.31	17.99	42.74	117.95	31.37	34.64
Athens, GA	35.28	13.44	16.57	41.85	106.88	24.67	23.49
Atlanta, GA	38.83	16.13	17.98	46.59	130.62	27.09	26.72
Austin, TX	39.15	15.51	18.78	48.51	108.58	26.81	35.97
Baltimore, MD	39.94	16.12	18.59	43.18	118.32	28.97	38.71
Baton Rouge, LA	33.80	13.11	14.31	47.39	128.50	30.30	23.18
Boise City, ID	36.30	15.18	17.28	41.63	144.79	24.58	31.03
Boston, MA[2]	48.05	18.69	22.16	44.21	105.03	41.03	36.53
Boulder, CO	40.88	17.84	23.23	43.04	139.68	27.80	40.99
Buffalo, NY	38.82	16.32	18.34	38.46	57.17	31.50	35.47
Cape Coral, FL	35.30	15.55	17.78	42.36	153.03	23.91	30.65
Cedar Rapids, IA	31.68	15.49	18.61	38.63	n/a	31.25	31.91
Charleston, SC	34.94	15.23	16.14	39.99	138.87	24.44	25.30
Charlotte, NC	35.22	14.62	18.18	42.70	119.40	24.47	28.92
Chicago, IL	39.09	16.53	19.88	45.58	122.31	42.88	41.85
Cincinnati, OH	34.81	15.52	19.08	43.70	94.10	30.28	33.01
Clarksville, TN	31.34	13.31	15.63	42.15	107.46	22.42	23.62
Cleveland, OH	36.01	15.77	19.18	45.57	77.71	30.82	33.81
College Station, TX	33.85	13.15	12.87	42.62	77.31	21.38	28.91
Colorado Springs, CO	37.75	16.32	21.32	41.33	143.62	25.37	34.59
Columbia, MO	31.88	14.44	18.16	36.79	n/a	27.37	25.58
Columbia, SC	33.34	14.25	15.45	39.93	145.20	22.88	24.09
Columbus, OH	35.23	14.95	19.52	46.23	102.68	30.27	36.86
Dallas, TX	39.55	15.57	17.92	46.63	112.79	25.01	36.31
Davenport, IA	31.50	14.94	17.06	40.76	137.02	31.29	31.58
Denver, CO	39.84	17.45	23.49	44.51	118.01	28.56	42.33
Des Moines, IA	32.19	16.05	18.91	40.12	115.75	30.01	34.80
Durham, NC	35.10	15.76	19.03	38.24	55.15	24.82	26.66
Edison, NJ	47.34	20.17	20.84	47.54	113.19	39.86	41.69
El Paso, TX	33.29	12.96	14.87	42.01	120.81	20.47	30.68
Fargo, ND	34.93	16.69	20.19	38.45	92.94	28.06	33.51
Fort Collins, CO	37.82	16.55	21.42	40.46	130.44	27.57	42.17
Fort Wayne, IN	33.06	14.47	17.85	41.71	152.29	31.11	31.15
Fort Worth, TX	39.55	15.57	17.92	46.63	112.79	25.01	36.31
Grand Rapids, MI	34.60	15.93	18.97	39.94	130.21	28.48	31.69
Green Bay, WI	35.00	16.12	18.31	41.78	150.97	35.45	34.16
Honolulu, HI	51.77	17.68	19.62	44.80	126.41	35.40	39.26
Houston, TX	40.33	15.54	18.51	48.82	103.91	27.11	32.58
Huntsville, AL	30.54	13.41	13.52	45.06	138.55	24.68	25.18
Indianapolis, IN	34.13	15.40	18.44	45.63	141.28	30.25	33.31
Jacksonville, FL	33.87	14.42	17.48	42.73	133.34	22.72	30.06
Kansas City, MO	34.52	15.36	19.17	42.75	96.78	30.19	29.55
Lafayette, LA	31.78	11.78	13.40	42.38	115.69	23.90	20.54
Las Cruces, NM	34.07	13.30	13.47	45.42	134.17	22.00	27.10
Las Vegas, NV	43.38	17.45	18.91	50.32	126.33	31.03	37.51
Lexington, KY	32.19	14.78	17.09	41.74	133.06	29.15	24.01
Lincoln, NE	33.39	15.55	16.00	44.06	133.63	25.53	33.55
Little Rock, AR	33.49	13.98	16.83	41.21	74.47	21.70	22.90
Los Angeles, CA	55.82	18.60	21.13	45.64	113.29	32.17	49.72
Louisville, KY	33.66	15.09	17.70	42.83	134.17	28.55	25.55
Madison, WI	40.09	17.95	20.02	42.72	141.45	36.15	35.33
Manchester, NH[2]	37.68	17.00	20.71	41.26	n/a	28.32	32.17

Table continued on following page.

Metro Area	Nurses, Registered	Nursing Assistants	Office Clerks	Physical Therapists	Physicians	Plumbers	Police Officers
Memphis, TN	32.94	14.27	16.32	44.69	75.54	25.35	25.94
Miami, FL	35.69	14.42	17.87	43.97	110.95	23.78	36.57
Midland, TX	35.58	16.21	19.42	56.19	n/a	26.80	34.24
Milwaukee, WI	37.59	16.49	19.33	44.50	135.65	35.25	38.61
Minneapolis, MN	41.68	18.63	20.94	41.82	129.14	40.18	39.63
Nashville, TN	34.09	14.72	16.89	43.58	123.40	27.01	25.10
New Haven, CT[2]	43.05	17.28	20.03	47.54	107.28	30.95	35.47
New Orleans, LA	35.47	12.91	14.54	45.02	134.63	26.31	23.45
New York, NY	47.34	20.17	20.84	47.54	113.19	39.86	41.69
Oklahoma City, OK	33.62	13.85	16.18	42.50	106.67	24.77	32.72
Omaha, NE	34.41	16.26	17.68	41.49	142.05	30.59	33.14
Orlando, FL	34.99	14.41	17.94	42.62	116.76	23.03	30.95
Philadelphia, PA	39.35	17.14	20.52	47.50	109.94	34.40	38.17
Phoenix, AZ	39.72	16.94	20.37	45.87	123.85	27.19	34.65
Pittsburgh, PA	35.18	16.39	19.16	43.07	73.72	31.73	35.01
Portland, OR	48.90	19.04	20.23	44.33	93.93	40.80	40.26
Providence, RI[2]	40.96	17.03	20.51	46.63	93.60	32.39	33.96
Provo, UT	33.61	14.42	17.38	42.30	108.18	24.27	28.08
Raleigh, NC	34.75	14.76	18.29	40.20	123.42	24.63	27.05
Reno, NV	40.67	16.54	19.54	49.12	n/a	31.87	35.24
Richmond, VA	36.99	14.82	17.25	43.82	91.99	25.16	28.27
Riverside, CA	53.70	17.39	19.41	51.63	81.89	31.48	46.85
Rochester, MN	41.57	18.12	20.14	42.17	134.34	38.17	36.08
Rochester, NY	36.57	16.37	17.79	38.62	99.68	29.85	37.10
Sacramento, CA	65.14	19.19	20.76	52.79	135.69	34.10	47.89
Salt Lake City, UT	36.33	15.28	18.21	43.21	117.34	28.79	31.31
San Antonio, TX	37.92	14.84	17.45	47.90	120.50	23.65	31.74
San Diego, CA	54.40	18.55	19.99	50.17	131.06	32.31	47.50
San Francisco, CA	72.90	22.84	24.03	56.91	125.00	43.03	56.95
San Jose, CA	74.63	22.93	23.92	59.22	117.95	45.47	60.56
Santa Rosa, CA	68.00	19.60	21.66	54.88	99.53	34.59	50.99
Savannah, GA	34.35	13.89	17.13	45.03	110.08	26.62	23.63
Seattle, WA	47.74	19.51	22.87	48.79	129.27	41.37	48.24
Sioux Falls, SD	28.35	14.32	15.13	39.51	n/a	23.48	31.18
Springfield, IL	35.27	15.24	19.45	43.68	135.25	37.76	37.13
St. Louis, MO	33.96	14.78	19.24	40.96	136.59	33.35	31.29
Tampa, FL	35.28	14.74	18.13	44.44	120.95	23.44	31.29
Tucson, AZ	37.89	16.08	19.95	44.18	117.15	25.33	29.53
Tulsa, OK	32.75	13.83	16.19	42.22	92.42	25.24	27.94
Tuscaloosa, AL	29.51	13.25	13.60	46.80	111.95	23.53	27.37
Virginia Beach, VA	36.23	14.29	16.92	41.73	100.40	25.87	27.26
Washington, DC	42.82	17.06	22.17	47.01	103.73	30.44	37.43
Wichita, KS	30.41	13.98	13.77	43.98	90.22	25.50	25.40
Wilmington, NC	32.90	13.65	16.70	38.89	109.01	22.45	23.33
Winston-Salem, NC	35.11	14.07	17.21	44.36	52.85	21.76	23.50

Notes: (1) Figures cover the Metropolitan Statistical Area (MSA) except where noted. See Appendix B for areas included; (2) New England City and Town Area; n/a not available
Source: Bureau of Labor Statistics, May 2021 Metro Area Occupational Employment and Wage Estimates

Average Hourly Wages: Occupations P – S

Metro Area	Postal Mail Carriers	R.E. Sales Agents	Retail Sales-persons	Sales Reps., Technical/ Scientific	Secretaries, Exc. Leg./ Med./Exec.	Security Guards	Surgeons
Albuquerque, NM	25.43	22.51	14.34	36.71	19.08	15.54	154.18
Allentown, PA	26.73	27.06	14.90	40.42	19.31	15.53	n/a
Anchorage, AK	25.28	33.30	17.29	39.23	20.55	23.15	n/a
Ann Arbor, MI	25.93	36.04	15.83	47.28	21.68	18.32	45.70
Athens, GA	25.45	21.53	13.27	44.42	16.71	15.79	n/a
Atlanta, GA	25.92	28.33	14.14	47.50	18.54	15.93	158.56
Austin, TX	26.66	30.89	15.44	45.78	19.61	17.49	n/a
Baltimore, MD	26.50	30.55	15.10	51.39	20.80	18.98	167.56
Baton Rouge, LA	25.77	28.18	13.37	43.99	17.62	16.93	n/a
Boise City, ID	26.37	18.41	15.99	37.00	17.54	16.62	n/a
Boston, MA[2]	26.97	44.46	17.42	58.86	24.38	19.35	171.23
Boulder, CO	26.37	37.69	17.87	56.70	21.25	20.67	169.91
Buffalo, NY	25.94	31.05	16.11	47.00	19.67	17.80	113.00
Cape Coral, FL	26.15	19.79	14.22	40.21	17.59	14.29	n/a
Cedar Rapids, IA	26.31	24.10	14.67	53.89	19.65	18.18	n/a
Charleston, SC	25.79	24.77	13.65	36.53	18.88	14.59	n/a
Charlotte, NC	26.22	32.43	14.44	49.26	19.40	15.05	n/a
Chicago, IL	26.53	23.35	15.83	51.31	21.92	17.69	n/a
Cincinnati, OH	26.96	25.67	14.58	50.36	19.27	15.18	158.18
Clarksville, TN	25.52	19.67	13.39	33.26	16.67	15.49	n/a
Cleveland, OH	26.53	19.31	14.72	54.91	18.92	15.81	n/a
College Station, TX	25.52	24.31	12.65	39.23	16.41	12.49	n/a
Colorado Springs, CO	25.23	29.87	16.01	45.53	18.76	16.96	132.43
Columbia, MO	25.19	19.44	14.15	45.34	17.36	16.24	n/a
Columbia, SC	25.46	24.52	12.85	33.34	17.87	13.67	n/a
Columbus, OH	26.32	22.95	14.65	52.99	19.70	16.30	n/a
Dallas, TX	26.53	29.16	14.95	49.25	19.42	17.45	137.74
Davenport, IA	25.30	29.37	14.89	56.77	18.20	18.83	n/a
Denver, CO	26.13	36.10	17.22	53.64	20.99	18.52	135.07
Des Moines, IA	26.27	28.26	15.34	56.14	21.93	17.19	n/a
Durham, NC	26.73	28.03	14.46	68.02	20.89	23.13	n/a
Edison, NJ	26.46	41.66	17.86	57.83	22.13	19.81	128.39
El Paso, TX	25.63	22.35	12.55	n/a	15.52	15.01	n/a
Fargo, ND	26.39	27.05	16.48	48.83	19.57	15.58	n/a
Fort Collins, CO	25.64	32.04	16.16	44.82	19.46	17.41	n/a
Fort Wayne, IN	25.90	25.77	13.92	47.83	17.44	17.65	121.20
Fort Worth, TX	26.53	29.16	14.95	49.25	19.42	17.45	137.74
Grand Rapids, MI	26.36	26.10	15.24	42.28	19.18	14.76	78.90
Green Bay, WI	25.74	27.54	15.32	36.04	19.39	15.56	n/a
Honolulu, HI	26.11	24.72	16.88	44.50	22.86	17.49	146.73
Houston, TX	26.04	28.02	15.04	47.22	18.96	16.54	123.50
Huntsville, AL	25.75	35.33	13.50	44.00	19.25	15.47	n/a
Indianapolis, IN	26.41	26.04	14.45	53.75	18.81	16.52	106.71
Jacksonville, FL	26.76	21.30	13.99	46.44	18.51	14.64	n/a
Kansas City, MO	26.16	30.11	15.17	51.19	18.48	18.61	144.75
Lafayette, LA	26.01	23.18	12.64	35.69	16.22	12.99	n/a
Las Cruces, NM	25.53	21.37	13.23	43.89	17.34	14.98	n/a
Las Vegas, NV	26.19	30.73	14.95	46.38	20.02	15.30	n/a
Lexington, KY	26.01	21.76	13.97	36.11	19.52	13.20	155.58
Lincoln, NE	26.34	29.56	13.93	39.60	18.56	15.95	n/a
Little Rock, AR	26.19	n/a	13.88	41.98	16.94	14.99	n/a
Los Angeles, CA	27.29	35.97	17.29	46.52	22.40	17.75	n/a
Louisville, KY	26.45	25.81	14.17	41.30	19.12	14.20	140.14
Madison, WI	25.43	27.68	15.97	34.70	20.88	16.61	n/a
Manchester, NH[2]	26.26	22.20	15.57	42.74	19.50	17.42	n/a

Table continued on following page.

Metro Area	Postal Mail Carriers	R.E. Sales Agents	Retail Sales-persons	Sales Reps., Technical/ Scientific	Secretaries, Exc. Leg./ Med./Exec.	Security Guards	Surgeons
Memphis, TN	26.43	22.61	14.13	40.81	18.32	14.62	n/a
Miami, FL	26.15	27.18	14.62	43.48	18.95	14.68	n/a
Midland, TX	24.56	48.11	16.03	53.51	19.75	17.88	n/a
Milwaukee, WI	26.18	24.84	15.48	39.09	20.98	15.22	n/a
Minneapolis, MN	26.35	24.15	16.39	52.59	22.20	18.34	172.24
Nashville, TN	26.31	20.12	14.47	38.30	19.07	14.77	134.53
New Haven, CT[2]	26.08	35.06	16.44	48.71	23.53	17.71	n/a
New Orleans, LA	25.61	35.04	13.23	39.56	17.53	15.42	n/a
New York, NY	26.46	41.66	17.86	57.83	22.13	19.81	128.39
Oklahoma City, OK	26.57	32.82	13.85	37.67	16.90	15.63	n/a
Omaha, NE	26.27	n/a	14.28	38.73	18.75	16.99	140.01
Orlando, FL	26.17	24.37	14.02	42.12	17.88	14.09	n/a
Philadelphia, PA	26.26	25.26	15.45	47.99	20.92	16.44	151.92
Phoenix, AZ	26.85	24.19	16.62	45.15	19.83	16.17	n/a
Pittsburgh, PA	25.96	31.32	14.35	42.66	18.68	15.20	n/a
Portland, OR	26.00	27.87	17.03	54.99	23.43	17.34	147.47
Providence, RI[2]	26.05	24.77	16.67	44.05	21.90	17.11	n/a
Provo, UT	25.82	22.96	14.94	34.68	18.18	16.06	130.48
Raleigh, NC	26.63	25.79	14.94	52.35	19.12	15.37	n/a
Reno, NV	26.10	26.33	15.14	49.73	20.93	15.79	n/a
Richmond, VA	26.10	30.87	13.85	47.70	18.80	16.00	n/a
Riverside, CA	26.31	24.46	16.43	49.34	21.59	17.26	n/a
Rochester, MN	25.95	24.06	16.01	38.69	20.94	17.84	n/a
Rochester, NY	26.10	37.27	16.14	63.92	19.76	18.02	109.22
Sacramento, CA	27.18	28.61	17.18	48.77	22.33	18.04	n/a
Salt Lake City, UT	26.51	31.65	16.05	50.78	19.19	17.58	158.20
San Antonio, TX	26.42	26.18	14.72	43.15	18.62	15.96	128.89
San Diego, CA	26.70	n/a	16.97	52.16	22.31	17.91	n/a
San Francisco, CA	27.32	35.35	19.78	57.95	27.27	20.98	n/a
San Jose, CA	27.07	36.34	19.79	72.48	26.31	21.00	n/a
Santa Rosa, CA	26.07	32.32	18.54	52.27	23.86	19.28	n/a
Savannah, GA	26.18	23.44	13.22	40.16	17.54	13.84	n/a
Seattle, WA	26.76	31.66	18.65	59.77	24.41	21.09	147.59
Sioux Falls, SD	26.53	36.84	16.12	51.92	16.16	16.08	n/a
Springfield, IL	25.72	25.95	14.72	40.38	19.11	17.61	n/a
St. Louis, MO	25.92	28.66	15.57	49.90	18.64	17.32	n/a
Tampa, FL	26.23	27.77	14.31	41.24	18.13	14.75	n/a
Tucson, AZ	26.69	20.03	15.89	48.74	18.46	15.90	n/a
Tulsa, OK	26.35	38.12	14.22	38.17	17.22	15.27	n/a
Tuscaloosa, AL	25.85	28.20	13.04	n/a	18.51	15.12	n/a
Virginia Beach, VA	25.59	33.57	13.81	46.93	18.99	15.92	148.64
Washington, DC	26.30	35.85	16.37	62.64	23.41	22.69	112.99
Wichita, KS	25.70	27.55	14.44	45.64	17.05	15.28	n/a
Wilmington, NC	25.46	25.70	14.36	58.42	18.58	15.11	n/a
Winston-Salem, NC	26.52	34.31	14.00	41.66	19.41	16.95	n/a

Notes: (1) Figures cover the Metropolitan Statistical Area (MSA) except where noted. See Appendix B for areas included; (2) New England City and Town Area; n/a not available
Source: Bureau of Labor Statistics, May 2021 Metro Area Occupational Employment and Wage Estimates

Average Hourly Wages: Occupations T – W

Metro Area	Teacher Assistants[3]	Teachers, Secondary School[3]	Telemarketers	Truck Drivers, Heavy	Truck Drivers, Light	Waiters/ Waitresses
Albuquerque, NM	12.11	28.98	18.27	21.54	19.08	13.13
Allentown, PA	14.02	34.04	n/a	24.42	20.84	13.33
Anchorage, AK	16.48	37.13	n/a	26.31	24.05	13.74
Ann Arbor, MI	14.88	30.65	n/a	24.06	21.44	16.28
Athens, GA	10.40	29.00	n/a	26.78	20.74	10.11
Atlanta, GA	12.84	36.41	13.50	25.00	19.29	11.51
Austin, TX	13.54	29.37	15.22	23.04	21.81	12.96
Baltimore, MD	18.38	35.52	14.98	24.65	21.25	14.61
Baton Rouge, LA	10.83	26.88	n/a	23.70	19.00	10.62
Boise City, ID	13.12	26.51	n/a	24.17	22.32	11.86
Boston, MA[2]	18.47	41.63	18.97	26.44	22.68	17.99
Boulder, CO	17.55	34.47	15.29	26.75	22.94	18.30
Buffalo, NY	15.08	37.73	14.47	24.42	18.86	18.46
Cape Coral, FL	14.60	31.13	n/a	21.31	18.03	14.03
Cedar Rapids, IA	13.89	28.82	14.66	27.67	18.60	12.06
Charleston, SC	12.94	29.97	8.99	23.86	17.84	11.48
Charlotte, NC	13.13	26.17	16.03	24.03	19.68	11.36
Chicago, IL	15.67	37.75	14.75	27.33	23.12	12.48
Cincinnati, OH	14.52	33.91	15.95	24.38	20.80	11.74
Clarksville, TN	14.62	34.50	n/a	21.82	18.08	9.90
Cleveland, OH	14.80	35.60	12.92	23.61	20.26	11.27
College Station, TX	10.28	24.49	n/a	20.19	19.92	10.58
Colorado Springs, CO	14.73	26.79	18.92	23.88	20.28	17.43
Columbia, MO	12.90	22.95	n/a	25.30	21.76	12.83
Columbia, SC	12.52	28.19	n/a	22.39	18.43	10.47
Columbus, OH	14.97	34.64	13.68	23.50	21.46	11.91
Dallas, TX	12.53	30.12	15.89	24.39	21.04	12.13
Davenport, IA	14.27	29.34	13.59	24.59	19.66	12.05
Denver, CO	16.83	32.01	16.66	26.77	21.78	16.59
Des Moines, IA	13.63	30.23	16.78	25.30	19.62	12.45
Durham, NC	13.27	26.64	n/a	23.39	20.23	11.46
Edison, NJ	17.08	45.65	19.04	28.17	22.79	18.06
El Paso, TX	12.13	27.51	12.06	20.16	17.89	10.41
Fargo, ND	15.26	28.90	n/a	26.27	21.41	13.87
Fort Collins, CO	15.88	29.95	17.07	23.54	20.90	17.45
Fort Wayne, IN	13.17	25.99	14.01	23.48	19.69	12.19
Fort Worth, TX	12.53	30.12	15.89	24.39	21.04	12.13
Grand Rapids, MI	14.66	30.06	13.55	24.04	19.77	16.51
Green Bay, WI	15.38	29.04	n/a	23.93	20.32	11.78
Honolulu, HI	15.46	31.27	16.72	26.14	19.61	19.46
Houston, TX	11.94	30.49	15.39	23.73	20.85	12.49
Huntsville, AL	10.80	27.36	n/a	22.45	18.11	10.32
Indianapolis, IN	13.80	28.44	16.15	25.27	21.80	12.25
Jacksonville, FL	13.95	30.80	13.65	22.27	19.38	13.81
Kansas City, MO	13.98	27.63	17.80	27.21	21.74	12.59
Lafayette, LA	9.97	25.49	n/a	21.73	16.02	9.80
Las Cruces, NM	11.72	28.83	n/a	20.14	18.37	12.31
Las Vegas, NV	16.02	30.04	11.60	24.20	19.49	11.59
Lexington, KY	16.19	29.56	n/a	24.54	20.64	11.92
Lincoln, NE	15.68	32.32	11.61	26.53	19.56	11.12
Little Rock, AR	11.92	26.55	14.76	24.39	18.23	11.61
Los Angeles, CA	19.48	46.47	16.92	24.61	21.93	17.49
Louisville, KY	15.56	28.12	14.20	24.44	22.97	11.65
Madison, WI	16.18	30.07	n/a	24.09	20.52	12.92
Manchester, NH[2]	16.00	30.12	n/a	25.10	19.39	14.85

Table continued on following page.

Metro Area	Teacher Assistants[3]	Teachers, Secondary School[3]	Telemarketers	Truck Drivers, Heavy	Truck Drivers, Light	Waiters/ Waitresses
Memphis, TN	13.21	27.53	11.77	25.75	22.87	9.93
Miami, FL	14.83	33.24	15.11	22.13	19.63	14.00
Midland, TX	11.63	29.62	n/a	24.58	21.55	12.74
Milwaukee, WI	16.17	31.03	15.08	25.12	20.42	12.45
Minneapolis, MN	18.20	32.03	22.23	27.57	23.00	14.71
Nashville, TN	13.41	26.65	12.70	25.41	19.40	10.29
New Haven, CT[2]	16.46	35.25	23.41	25.21	20.55	15.97
New Orleans, LA	12.67	26.77	n/a	23.88	18.52	9.89
New York, NY	17.08	45.65	19.04	28.17	22.79	18.06
Oklahoma City, OK	11.70	27.80	12.15	23.60	18.77	12.25
Omaha, NE	14.20	31.00	11.29	26.81	20.31	11.85
Orlando, FL	13.83	30.57	13.34	22.14	19.12	14.21
Philadelphia, PA	15.20	36.03	17.57	25.63	21.28	14.07
Phoenix, AZ	14.59	27.99	15.88	24.44	21.56	19.59
Pittsburgh, PA	14.42	39.71	13.73	23.97	19.41	13.01
Portland, OR	18.49	41.20	17.77	26.96	21.32	17.10
Providence, RI[2]	17.21	35.38	n/a	25.81	21.12	14.02
Provo, UT	13.94	31.63	14.48	23.79	18.92	13.77
Raleigh, NC	12.03	27.14	15.03	23.03	18.69	12.53
Reno, NV	10.75	27.00	13.24	24.77	19.76	11.87
Richmond, VA	13.77	n/a	16.12	21.99	19.42	13.85
Riverside, CA	18.60	49.03	16.07	24.78	21.58	15.69
Rochester, MN	16.52	29.66	n/a	25.52	20.98	14.02
Rochester, NY	14.74	32.22	14.29	24.35	18.60	19.95
Sacramento, CA	18.57	41.43	16.78	25.32	22.16	16.81
Salt Lake City, UT	15.44	31.75	14.70	25.50	20.36	13.92
San Antonio, TX	14.05	29.86	15.28	22.62	19.69	11.82
San Diego, CA	17.81	43.04	16.58	24.35	21.66	17.31
San Francisco, CA	20.59	45.41	19.78	29.95	24.79	18.09
San Jose, CA	21.67	50.00	20.25	29.59	24.93	19.36
Santa Rosa, CA	19.50	44.60	n/a	27.26	23.77	17.99
Savannah, GA	14.32	29.63	n/a	25.42	20.26	10.74
Seattle, WA	22.30	42.38	23.09	28.86	22.70	22.64
Sioux Falls, SD	12.77	24.02	n/a	23.48	19.69	11.94
Springfield, IL	12.69	28.17	n/a	23.57	20.38	11.61
St. Louis, MO	14.17	26.97	16.08	25.83	22.31	13.67
Tampa, FL	13.32	31.25	14.72	21.24	17.76	14.13
Tucson, AZ	14.23	22.24	15.30	22.41	20.30	18.90
Tulsa, OK	12.46	28.25	12.45	26.10	18.97	11.10
Tuscaloosa, AL	10.27	26.43	n/a	22.99	17.61	10.03
Virginia Beach, VA	15.63	33.67	16.20	21.52	18.26	13.02
Washington, DC	19.21	41.72	16.42	25.33	23.01	17.06
Wichita, KS	13.91	26.88	n/a	23.40	19.80	10.42
Wilmington, NC	12.58	25.51	n/a	21.17	19.60	10.73
Winston-Salem, NC	11.66	24.46	10.99	23.46	18.07	10.90

Notes: (1) Figures cover the Metropolitan Statistical Area (MSA) except where noted. See Appendix B for areas included; (2) New England City and Town Area; (3) Hourly wages were calculated from annual wage data assuming a 40 hour work week; n/a not available

Source: Bureau of Labor Statistics, May 2021 Metro Area Occupational Employment and Wage Estimates

Means of Transportation to Work: City

City	Car/Truck/Van		Public Transportation			Bicycle	Walked	Other Means	Worked at Home
	Drove Alone	Car-pooled	Bus	Subway	Railroad				
Albuquerque, NM	78.5	9.5	1.6	0.0	0.1	1.0	1.9	1.1	6.5
Allentown, PA	68.5	15.7	4.0	0.0	0.0	0.2	5.2	1.5	4.9
Anchorage, AK	75.0	12.4	1.5	0.0	0.0	1.1	2.6	1.9	5.5
Ann Arbor, MI	51.5	5.5	9.2	0.2	0.0	3.5	17.1	0.7	12.4
Athens, GA	72.5	8.4	3.4	0.0	0.0	1.3	5.3	1.2	7.9
Atlanta, GA	63.0	5.6	5.9	3.6	0.2	1.1	4.9	2.8	12.8
Austin, TX	70.1	8.5	2.7	0.1	0.1	1.2	2.6	1.4	13.4
Baltimore, MD	59.2	8.6	13.2	1.3	1.2	0.9	6.2	2.3	7.1
Baton Rouge, LA	79.1	10.0	2.0	0.0	0.0	0.7	3.4	1.1	3.7
Boise City, ID	76.5	7.1	0.5	0.0	0.0	2.7	3.2	1.5	8.5
Boston, MA	37.5	5.7	12.0	16.9	1.1	2.2	14.6	2.6	7.3
Boulder, CO	48.5	4.7	7.5	0.0	0.0	9.1	10.2	1.4	18.7
Buffalo, NY	67.9	10.0	9.4	0.4	0.0	0.9	5.8	1.5	4.1
Cape Coral, FL	80.9	7.9	0.1	0.0	0.0	0.2	1.0	1.5	8.3
Cedar Rapids, IA	82.6	7.4	0.5	0.0	0.0	0.5	2.0	1.1	5.9
Charleston, SC	76.3	6.4	0.9	0.0	0.0	1.8	4.2	1.3	9.1
Charlotte, NC	72.6	9.5	2.2	0.3	0.1	0.1	2.0	1.8	11.4
Chicago, IL	48.1	7.6	12.2	12.1	1.6	1.5	6.1	2.1	8.5
Cincinnati, OH	70.6	8.6	6.6	0.0	0.0	0.3	5.5	1.4	6.9
Clarksville, TN	85.8	7.5	0.8	0.0	0.0	0.0	1.0	1.3	3.5
Cleveland, OH	68.8	10.1	8.0	0.5	0.1	0.6	4.8	1.5	5.6
College Station, TX	76.3	8.2	2.4	0.0	0.0	2.2	2.5	1.0	7.4
Colorado Springs, CO	76.2	10.4	0.8	0.1	0.0	0.5	1.9	1.0	9.1
Columbia, MO	75.8	9.4	1.0	0.0	0.0	1.3	6.1	0.7	5.6
Columbia, SC	63.4	5.8	1.6	0.0	0.0	0.5	22.0	1.8	4.9
Columbus, OH	77.7	7.6	2.7	0.0	0.0	0.4	3.0	1.2	7.4
Dallas, TX	74.3	11.2	2.5	0.4	0.3	0.2	2.1	1.5	7.5
Davenport, IA	85.2	5.9	0.6	0.0	0.0	0.3	2.3	0.7	4.9
Denver, CO	66.1	7.3	4.1	0.8	0.5	2.1	4.7	2.2	12.4
Des Moines, IA	78.6	9.7	1.8	0.1	0.0	0.3	2.7	1.3	5.5
Durham, NC	74.8	8.3	3.3	0.0	0.0	0.5	2.3	1.2	9.6
Edison, NJ	66.9	8.7	0.7	0.6	11.2	0.2	1.4	1.4	9.0
El Paso, TX	80.2	10.8	1.5	0.0	0.0	0.2	1.0	2.2	4.2
Fargo, ND	81.3	8.1	1.2	0.0	0.0	0.6	3.4	1.6	3.8
Fort Collins, CO	69.7	6.7	1.9	0.0	0.0	4.9	4.2	0.9	11.6
Fort Wayne, IN	82.0	9.7	1.0	0.0	0.0	0.4	1.3	0.7	4.9
Fort Worth, TX	79.1	11.3	0.5	0.0	0.1	0.2	1.3	1.0	6.5
Grand Rapids, MI	73.1	10.4	3.4	0.1	0.0	1.0	4.4	0.9	6.8
Green Bay, WI	79.4	9.8	1.3	0.0	0.0	0.5	2.5	1.4	5.2
Honolulu, HI	57.9	12.8	10.4	0.0	0.0	1.7	8.3	3.9	5.0
Houston, TX	75.9	10.0	3.4	0.1	0.0	0.4	1.9	2.1	6.2
Huntsville, AL	84.1	6.6	0.3	0.0	0.0	0.2	1.2	0.9	6.7
Indianapolis, IN	79.8	9.2	1.6	0.0	0.0	0.4	2.0	1.0	6.0
Jacksonville, FL	78.7	8.8	1.7	0.0	0.0	0.5	1.6	1.9	6.7
Kansas City, MO	79.9	7.5	2.4	0.0	0.0	0.2	1.8	1.4	6.7
Lafayette, LA	83.1	5.1	0.9	0.0	0.0	0.9	2.3	1.3	6.4
Las Cruces, NM	77.1	11.5	0.6	0.0	0.0	1.7	2.2	0.8	6.0
Las Vegas, NV	76.7	10.3	3.1	0.0	0.0	0.2	1.4	2.7	5.6
Lexington, KY	77.9	8.2	1.8	0.0	0.0	0.5	3.7	1.3	6.7
Lincoln, NE	79.7	9.2	1.1	0.0	0.0	1.0	3.2	0.7	5.1
Little Rock, AR	80.8	9.4	0.7	0.0	0.0	0.2	1.8	1.4	5.8
Los Angeles, CA	67.7	8.9	7.1	0.9	0.1	0.8	3.3	2.0	9.2
Louisville, KY	78.0	8.7	2.9	0.0	0.0	0.3	2.0	1.6	6.4
Madison, WI	62.5	6.9	8.1	0.0	0.1	4.0	9.0	1.3	8.1

Table continued on following page.

City	Car/Truck/Van		Public Transportation			Bicycle	Walked	Other Means	Worked at Home
	Drove Alone	Car-pooled	Bus	Subway	Railroad				
Manchester, NH	79.2	9.5	0.6	0.0	0.0	0.3	3.3	1.2	6.0
Memphis, TN	81.6	10.4	1.3	0.0	0.0	0.2	1.4	1.2	3.8
Miami, FL	67.9	8.0	6.9	1.1	0.2	0.7	4.6	3.2	7.4
Midland, TX	83.4	10.1	0.2	0.0	0.0	0.2	0.8	1.1	4.2
Milwaukee, WI	71.9	10.0	6.6	0.0	0.1	0.7	4.3	1.0	5.4
Minneapolis, MN	59.0	6.4	10.2	0.7	0.2	3.3	7.1	2.6	10.6
Nashville, TN	75.3	9.2	1.8	0.0	0.1	0.2	2.3	1.2	9.9
New Haven, CT	59.1	8.8	8.4	0.1	1.1	2.5	11.5	1.5	7.1
New Orleans, LA	66.5	9.8	5.0	0.0	0.0	2.8	5.4	2.8	7.7
New York, NY	22.3	4.5	9.8	41.2	1.3	1.3	9.8	2.4	7.4
Oklahoma City, OK	81.4	10.1	0.5	0.0	0.0	0.2	1.6	1.2	5.0
Omaha, NE	79.2	9.1	1.4	0.0	0.0	0.3	2.1	1.2	6.8
Orlando, FL	77.0	8.1	2.8	0.1	0.0	0.6	1.6	2.8	7.0
Philadelphia, PA	49.5	8.2	14.6	5.5	2.5	2.1	7.9	2.7	7.0
Phoenix, AZ	72.9	12.2	2.4	0.1	0.0	0.6	1.5	2.0	8.3
Pittsburgh, PA	53.6	7.3	16.2	0.4	0.0	1.6	10.2	1.6	9.0
Portland, OR	55.7	7.9	8.6	0.7	0.3	5.4	5.5	3.2	12.7
Providence, RI	65.1	11.4	4.0	0.1	1.2	0.9	8.1	1.9	7.2
Provo, UT	59.8	11.5	3.1	0.2	1.1	2.1	13.1	1.4	7.7
Raleigh, NC	75.3	7.4	1.9	0.1	0.0	0.3	1.6	1.4	12.1
Reno, NV	73.0	11.9	2.8	0.0	0.0	0.8	3.1	1.8	6.5
Richmond, VA	70.2	8.5	4.9	0.1	0.0	2.1	5.0	1.6	7.7
Riverside, CA	76.1	12.0	1.6	0.0	0.8	0.6	2.5	1.1	5.3
Rochester, MN	68.7	11.9	5.8	0.0	0.0	0.9	4.3	1.0	7.4
Rochester, NY	68.1	10.3	7.2	0.1	0.1	1.4	5.5	1.5	5.9
Sacramento, CA	71.9	10.1	1.8	0.2	0.3	1.8	3.0	2.0	8.9
St. Louis, MO	71.0	7.5	6.6	0.4	0.1	0.9	4.6	1.3	7.6
Salt Lake City, UT	66.0	9.5	4.3	0.3	0.7	2.1	4.9	3.1	9.1
San Antonio, TX	76.3	11.7	2.5	0.0	0.0	0.2	1.9	1.6	5.8
San Diego, CA	72.0	8.5	3.2	0.1	0.1	0.8	2.9	1.8	10.5
San Francisco, CA	30.5	6.8	19.9	8.2	1.5	3.7	11.7	6.0	11.8
San Jose, CA	72.6	11.3	2.4	0.3	1.1	0.6	1.7	1.8	8.2
Santa Rosa, CA	77.2	10.9	1.6	0.0	0.1	1.0	1.8	1.3	6.1
Savannah, GA	71.3	10.3	4.0	0.1	0.0	1.4	4.7	1.8	6.4
Seattle, WA	43.4	6.6	18.0	1.3	0.1	3.1	10.8	2.8	14.0
Sioux Falls, SD	83.5	8.1	0.6	0.0	0.0	0.3	2.3	0.5	4.7
Springfield, IL	80.3	7.0	1.7	0.1	0.0	0.6	1.7	1.7	6.9
Tampa, FL	74.0	9.0	2.2	0.0	0.0	1.0	2.4	1.8	9.7
Tucson, AZ	73.1	10.5	2.8	0.0	0.0	2.2	3.0	1.7	6.7
Tulsa, OK	79.7	10.2	0.7	0.0	0.0	0.2	1.8	1.8	5.5
Tuscaloosa, AL	81.5	9.1	1.3	0.0	0.0	0.5	1.6	0.5	5.5
Virginia Beach, VA	80.3	8.3	0.7	0.0	0.1	0.5	2.4	1.6	6.1
Washington, DC	32.1	4.9	11.8	19.3	0.3	4.2	12.5	2.6	12.3
Wichita, KS	82.5	9.9	0.6	0.0	0.0	0.4	1.3	1.1	4.1
Wilmington, NC	77.8	7.2	0.7	0.0	0.0	0.6	2.7	0.6	10.3
Winston-Salem, NC	79.3	9.1	1.2	0.0	0.0	0.3	2.3	1.3	6.4
U.S.	74.9	8.9	2.2	1.7	0.5	0.5	2.6	1.4	7.3

Note: Figures are percentages and cover workers 16 years of age and older
Source: U.S. Census Bureau, 2016-2020 American Community Survey 5-Year Estimates

Means of Transportation to Work: Metro Area

Metro Area	Car/Truck/Van		Public Transportation			Bicycle	Walked	Other Means	Worked at Home
	Drove Alone	Car-pooled	Bus	Subway	Railroad				
Albuquerque, NM	78.8	9.7	1.2	0.0	0.2	0.7	1.6	1.1	6.8
Allentown, PA	80.3	8.1	1.4	0.1	0.1	0.2	2.4	1.1	6.3
Anchorage, AK	74.6	11.9	1.3	0.0	0.0	0.9	2.5	2.8	6.0
Ann Arbor, MI	69.6	7.1	4.6	0.1	0.0	1.5	7.4	0.7	9.1
Athens, GA	76.1	8.6	2.0	0.0	0.0	0.8	3.6	1.1	7.8
Atlanta, GA	75.2	9.0	1.8	0.8	0.1	0.2	1.3	1.7	10.0
Austin, TX	73.1	8.8	1.5	0.1	0.1	0.7	1.9	1.2	12.5
Baltimore, MD	74.7	7.9	3.9	0.9	0.9	0.3	2.4	1.4	7.9
Baton Rouge, LA	84.2	8.4	0.7	0.0	0.0	0.3	1.5	1.0	3.8
Boise City, ID	78.1	8.3	0.3	0.0	0.0	1.2	1.9	1.3	8.9
Boston, MA	64.4	6.9	3.7	6.2	2.1	1.0	5.3	1.7	8.8
Boulder, CO	62.7	7.0	4.6	0.0	0.0	4.0	4.6	1.0	16.1
Buffalo, NY	80.6	7.3	2.7	0.2	0.0	0.4	2.5	1.0	5.3
Cape Coral, FL	77.8	9.8	0.6	0.0	0.0	0.8	1.1	2.3	7.5
Cedar Rapids, IA	82.3	7.4	0.3	0.0	0.0	0.4	2.0	0.8	6.9
Charleston, SC	80.9	7.6	0.7	0.0	0.0	0.6	2.0	1.2	7.0
Charlotte, NC	77.6	9.0	1.0	0.2	0.1	0.1	1.4	1.3	9.4
Chicago, IL	68.3	7.7	4.1	4.1	3.0	0.6	2.9	1.4	7.8
Cincinnati, OH	80.6	7.9	1.6	0.0	0.0	0.2	1.9	0.8	7.0
Clarksville, TN	83.6	8.3	0.6	0.0	0.0	0.1	2.8	1.2	3.4
Cleveland, OH	79.7	7.4	2.5	0.2	0.0	0.3	2.1	1.1	6.6
College Station, TX	79.1	9.7	1.4	0.0	0.0	1.4	1.9	1.2	5.5
Colorado Springs, CO	75.1	10.2	0.6	0.0	0.0	0.4	3.4	1.0	9.2
Columbia, MO	77.3	10.4	0.7	0.0	0.0	0.8	4.1	0.8	5.9
Columbia, SC	79.5	8.4	0.6	0.0	0.0	0.1	4.4	1.7	5.2
Columbus, OH	80.0	7.1	1.5	0.0	0.0	0.3	2.2	1.0	8.0
Dallas, TX	78.1	9.7	0.7	0.2	0.2	0.1	1.2	1.3	8.4
Davenport, IA	85.1	6.5	0.8	0.0	0.0	0.2	2.2	0.7	4.4
Denver, CO	72.7	7.9	2.5	0.5	0.3	0.8	2.2	1.6	11.4
Des Moines, IA	81.4	7.7	0.8	0.0	0.0	0.2	1.8	0.9	7.2
Durham, NC	74.2	7.8	3.0	0.0	0.0	0.6	2.7	1.4	10.2
Edison, NJ	48.5	6.3	7.1	18.7	3.6	0.7	5.7	2.1	7.4
El Paso, TX	79.7	10.9	1.2	0.0	0.0	0.1	1.4	2.2	4.4
Fargo, ND	81.0	8.4	0.9	0.0	0.0	0.5	2.5	1.3	5.3
Fort Collins, CO	73.0	7.3	1.3	0.1	0.0	2.7	2.8	1.1	11.7
Fort Wayne, IN	82.8	9.1	0.7	0.0	0.0	0.3	1.2	0.7	5.2
Fort Worth, TX	78.1	9.7	0.7	0.2	0.2	0.1	1.2	1.3	8.4
Grand Rapids, MI	80.3	8.8	1.4	0.0	0.0	0.4	2.2	0.7	6.2
Green Bay, WI	82.8	7.7	0.6	0.0	0.0	0.2	1.9	0.8	6.1
Honolulu, HI	65.2	13.4	7.1	0.0	0.0	0.9	5.6	2.7	5.1
Houston, TX	78.9	9.6	1.8	0.0	0.0	0.3	1.2	1.4	6.7
Huntsville, AL	86.0	6.1	0.2	0.0	0.0	0.1	0.7	0.9	6.0
Indianapolis, IN	80.8	8.2	0.8	0.0	0.0	0.2	1.6	0.9	7.5
Jacksonville, FL	78.7	8.3	1.1	0.0	0.0	0.5	1.4	1.8	8.1
Kansas City, MO	81.4	7.6	0.8	0.0	0.0	0.1	1.2	1.0	7.9
Lafayette, LA	83.8	7.2	0.4	0.0	0.0	0.3	2.0	1.2	5.0
Las Cruces, NM	79.2	11.2	0.4	0.0	0.0	0.9	1.8	0.8	5.6
Las Vegas, NV	77.5	10.1	3.0	0.0	0.0	0.2	1.3	2.2	5.6
Lexington, KY	78.9	8.8	1.2	0.0	0.0	0.3	3.0	1.2	6.6
Lincoln, NE	80.1	9.0	0.9	0.0	0.0	0.9	3.1	0.7	5.3
Little Rock, AR	82.7	9.6	0.4	0.0	0.0	0.2	1.3	1.1	4.7
Los Angeles, CA	73.1	9.5	3.7	0.4	0.2	0.6	2.4	1.7	8.3
Louisville, KY	80.5	8.3	1.7	0.0	0.0	0.2	1.5	1.2	6.6
Madison, WI	72.9	7.2	3.8	0.0	0.0	2.0	4.9	0.9	8.2

Table continued on following page.

Metro Area	Car/Truck/Van		Public Transportation			Bicycle	Walked	Other Means	Worked at Home
	Drove Alone	Car-pooled	Bus	Subway	Railroad				
Manchester, NH	80.3	7.4	0.7	0.0	0.1	0.2	2.1	0.9	8.3
Memphis, TN	83.8	9.4	0.6	0.0	0.0	0.1	0.9	1.0	4.1
Miami, FL	76.7	9.2	2.5	0.3	0.1	0.5	1.5	2.0	7.1
Midland, TX	83.1	10.1	0.2	0.0	0.0	0.1	1.3	0.9	4.3
Milwaukee, WI	79.2	7.6	2.8	0.0	0.1	0.4	2.4	0.8	6.7
Minneapolis, MN	75.0	7.8	3.7	0.1	0.1	0.7	2.1	1.2	9.2
Nashville, TN	79.1	8.7	0.8	0.0	0.1	0.1	1.2	1.1	8.9
New Haven, CT	77.0	8.1	2.6	0.1	0.8	0.5	3.3	1.1	6.5
New Orleans, LA	77.2	10.0	1.9	0.0	0.0	1.0	2.3	1.7	5.8
New York, NY	48.5	6.3	7.1	18.7	3.6	0.7	5.7	2.1	7.4
Oklahoma City, OK	81.9	9.4	0.3	0.0	0.0	0.3	1.6	1.1	5.4
Omaha, NE	81.7	8.2	0.8	0.0	0.0	0.2	1.7	1.0	6.5
Orlando, FL	77.8	9.7	1.3	0.0	0.1	0.4	1.1	1.8	7.8
Philadelphia, PA	70.4	7.5	4.6	1.9	2.0	0.6	3.4	1.4	8.2
Phoenix, AZ	73.9	10.8	1.5	0.0	0.0	0.6	1.5	1.9	9.7
Pittsburgh, PA	75.0	7.8	4.8	0.2	0.0	0.3	3.1	1.2	7.5
Portland, OR	68.6	8.8	4.2	0.5	0.2	2.0	3.3	2.1	10.4
Providence, RI	79.8	8.2	1.3	0.2	0.9	0.3	2.9	0.9	5.5
Provo, UT	71.6	10.6	1.1	0.2	0.8	0.7	3.8	1.1	10.1
Raleigh, NC	77.0	7.7	0.8	0.0	0.0	0.2	1.1	1.1	12.1
Reno, NV	75.1	11.8	2.1	0.0	0.0	0.5	2.2	1.5	6.7
Richmond, VA	78.8	8.2	1.3	0.0	0.1	0.5	1.6	1.1	8.4
Riverside, CA	78.2	11.5	0.7	0.1	0.3	0.2	1.4	1.4	6.3
Rochester, MN	72.7	11.1	3.6	0.0	0.0	0.6	3.5	0.9	7.7
Rochester, NY	79.2	7.9	1.8	0.1	0.0	0.5	3.0	0.9	6.7
Sacramento, CA	74.7	9.1	1.4	0.1	0.2	1.3	1.7	1.6	9.9
St. Louis, MO	81.3	7.0	1.6	0.2	0.1	0.2	1.6	1.0	7.1
Salt Lake City, UT	73.2	10.7	1.8	0.3	0.5	0.6	2.0	1.6	9.2
San Antonio, TX	77.2	10.9	1.7	0.0	0.0	0.2	1.8	1.5	6.7
San Diego, CA	73.9	8.7	2.2	0.1	0.2	0.6	2.9	1.9	9.6
San Francisco, CA	55.5	9.2	6.9	6.8	1.4	1.7	4.6	3.0	11.0
San Jose, CA	71.2	10.3	2.1	0.3	1.2	1.5	2.1	1.7	9.6
Santa Rosa, CA	74.2	10.4	1.3	0.1	0.2	0.7	2.5	1.5	9.1
Savannah, GA	79.5	8.7	1.6	0.1	0.0	0.6	2.3	1.7	5.5
Seattle, WA	64.9	9.8	7.8	0.4	0.5	1.0	4.0	1.6	10.1
Sioux Falls, SD	83.3	7.7	0.4	0.0	0.0	0.2	2.3	0.5	5.6
Springfield, IL	82.4	7.0	1.0	0.1	0.0	0.5	1.4	1.2	6.5
Tampa, FL	77.1	8.5	1.1	0.0	0.0	0.6	1.4	1.6	9.7
Tucson, AZ	75.2	9.9	1.9	0.0	0.0	1.4	2.1	1.8	7.8
Tulsa, OK	82.1	9.3	0.3	0.0	0.0	0.2	1.2	1.3	5.6
Tuscaloosa, AL	82.9	10.2	0.6	0.0	0.0	0.2	1.0	0.4	4.6
Virginia Beach, VA	79.6	8.3	1.4	0.0	0.0	0.3	3.3	1.6	5.4
Washington, DC	63.4	8.9	4.3	6.9	0.7	0.8	3.1	1.6	10.2
Wichita, KS	82.8	9.1	0.4	0.0	0.0	0.4	1.6	1.1	4.6
Wilmington, NC	79.8	7.5	0.3	0.0	0.1	0.3	1.6	0.5	9.9
Winston-Salem, NC	82.0	9.1	0.6	0.0	0.0	0.1	1.4	0.9	5.9
U.S.	74.9	8.9	2.2	1.7	0.5	0.5	2.6	1.4	7.3

Note: Figures are percentages and cover workers 16 years of age and older; (1) Figures cover the Metropolitan Statistical Area
Source: U.S. Census Bureau, 2016-2020 American Community Survey 5-Year Estimates

Travel Time to Work: City

City	Less Than 10 Minutes	10 to 19 Minutes	20 to 29 Minutes	30 to 44 Minutes	45 to 59 Minutes	60 to 89 Minutes	90 Minutes or More
Albuquerque, NM	11.0	35.6	27.9	18.0	3.2	2.8	1.4
Allentown, PA	11.1	32.9	30.4	14.9	4.0	4.6	2.1
Anchorage, AK	16.0	45.2	23.6	10.4	2.2	1.3	1.3
Ann Arbor, MI	12.7	45.9	20.0	13.2	5.4	2.1	0.6
Athens, GA	17.5	46.9	16.9	9.5	3.6	3.3	2.3
Atlanta, GA	6.6	29.6	25.7	22.1	7.5	5.3	3.3
Austin, TX	9.6	31.8	24.4	21.9	7.3	3.6	1.5
Baltimore, MD	6.3	23.6	23.1	25.2	9.0	7.8	4.9
Baton Rouge, LA	12.0	39.9	26.1	14.0	3.7	2.3	2.0
Boise City, ID	13.7	46.0	25.7	10.6	1.5	1.3	1.3
Boston, MA	6.7	19.7	19.9	30.4	12.1	9.1	2.1
Boulder, CO	18.9	44.3	16.4	10.2	5.6	3.6	1.1
Buffalo, NY	15.7	39.8	25.0	13.0	2.7	2.3	1.4
Cape Coral, FL	8.0	25.0	22.0	27.6	10.0	5.1	2.3
Cedar Rapids, IA	19.4	48.8	17.0	9.3	2.4	1.6	1.5
Charleston, SC	11.5	32.1	25.8	20.7	7.1	1.6	1.1
Charlotte, NC	8.2	29.2	26.8	23.6	6.9	3.4	2.0
Chicago, IL	4.4	16.0	18.0	30.6	15.4	12.2	3.3
Cincinnati, OH	11.0	33.2	27.1	19.0	4.2	3.3	2.1
Clarksville, TN	10.0	34.4	25.0	13.8	7.0	7.9	1.8
Cleveland, OH	9.9	33.3	27.3	19.8	4.3	3.3	2.2
College Station, TX	17.5	54.9	17.4	6.2	0.5	2.1	1.4
Colorado Springs, CO	11.3	35.5	28.1	16.3	3.4	2.9	2.6
Columbia, MO	20.3	55.0	12.6	7.4	2.6	1.0	1.2
Columbia, SC	30.8	35.8	18.1	10.2	2.0	1.8	1.2
Columbus, OH	10.1	33.9	30.4	18.9	3.4	2.0	1.3
Dallas, TX	8.1	26.7	23.2	26.4	8.0	5.8	1.8
Davenport, IA	17.5	47.1	21.2	8.9	2.9	1.5	1.0
Denver, CO	7.7	28.8	24.7	25.8	7.6	3.9	1.5
Des Moines, IA	13.3	42.8	27.2	12.2	2.2	1.3	1.0
Durham, NC	8.8	37.8	25.9	18.3	4.7	3.0	1.6
Edison, NJ	7.1	22.6	17.9	18.0	11.6	13.2	9.6
El Paso, TX	9.5	33.9	28.4	19.5	4.7	2.1	1.9
Fargo, ND	20.8	56.1	16.4	3.1	1.2	1.7	0.7
Fort Collins, CO	15.7	43.3	20.9	10.2	4.8	3.6	1.5
Fort Wayne, IN	12.3	39.4	28.0	13.0	3.0	2.3	1.9
Fort Worth, TX	7.7	28.1	22.8	24.4	8.6	6.2	2.1
Grand Rapids, MI	14.2	43.4	24.1	11.8	3.6	2.2	0.8
Green Bay, WI	18.6	47.2	19.8	8.0	3.6	1.8	1.0
Honolulu, HI	8.5	36.6	23.0	21.6	5.3	3.6	1.4
Houston, TX	7.1	25.9	22.7	27.5	8.7	6.2	1.9
Huntsville, AL	13.0	41.9	25.8	15.0	2.5	0.8	0.9
Indianapolis, IN	9.4	30.4	29.3	22.3	4.2	2.5	1.8
Jacksonville, FL	8.7	28.3	26.9	25.3	6.3	3.0	1.5
Kansas City, MO	11.3	33.6	28.0	20.2	4.2	1.6	1.2
Lafayette, LA	15.6	43.6	20.6	11.7	2.6	3.3	2.6
Las Cruces, NM	17.0	49.0	17.3	8.6	3.5	4.0	0.7
Las Vegas, NV	7.3	24.6	29.7	27.8	6.2	2.6	1.8
Lexington, KY	12.7	39.6	26.5	14.1	3.0	2.5	1.6
Lincoln, NE	16.3	44.5	23.4	9.9	2.4	2.2	1.2
Little Rock, AR	15.2	45.3	24.2	11.3	1.9	1.3	0.9
Los Angeles, CA	5.8	21.8	19.2	28.3	10.8	10.3	3.8
Louisville, KY	9.4	32.2	30.5	20.1	4.2	2.2	1.5
Madison, WI	14.9	39.4	24.8	15.0	3.2	1.9	0.8
Manchester, NH	12.8	36.4	22.1	14.3	6.5	5.3	2.6

Table continued on following page.

City	Less Than 10 Minutes	10 to 19 Minutes	20 to 29 Minutes	30 to 44 Minutes	45 to 59 Minutes	60 to 89 Minutes	90 Minutes or More
Memphis, TN	9.8	32.3	32.1	20.0	3.4	1.4	1.0
Miami, FL	5.5	21.4	23.9	31.2	9.4	7.0	1.7
Midland, TX	16.4	48.4	17.8	11.4	2.3	1.9	1.8
Milwaukee, WI	10.0	36.9	26.0	19.1	3.5	2.8	1.7
Minneapolis, MN	7.8	32.4	30.6	21.0	4.3	2.8	1.1
Nashville, TN	8.9	28.6	25.7	24.0	7.4	3.9	1.6
New Haven, CT	14.2	40.3	21.1	13.0	4.3	4.3	2.8
New Orleans, LA	10.2	33.8	26.0	19.4	4.6	3.9	2.0
New York, NY	3.9	12.2	13.5	27.2	16.3	19.3	7.6
Oklahoma City, OK	10.9	36.4	29.1	17.5	3.3	1.4	1.4
Omaha, NE	14.2	41.1	27.0	12.7	2.4	1.8	0.9
Orlando, FL	7.3	26.4	26.3	26.6	7.3	4.0	2.2
Philadelphia, PA	6.1	18.8	20.1	28.0	12.7	10.1	4.3
Phoenix, AZ	8.8	26.5	25.7	24.9	7.6	4.8	1.9
Pittsburgh, PA	9.5	31.3	26.6	22.4	4.7	3.9	1.6
Portland, OR	7.9	27.0	26.6	24.6	7.7	4.5	1.7
Providence, RI	10.8	41.0	19.5	13.7	6.2	5.7	3.1
Provo, UT	20.8	44.9	16.5	9.8	3.5	3.0	1.5
Raleigh, NC	9.3	31.8	26.5	21.2	6.0	3.3	1.9
Reno, NV	15.1	41.3	22.2	12.8	4.4	2.7	1.5
Richmond, VA	10.7	37.2	28.1	17.0	3.0	2.6	1.5
Riverside, CA	8.4	26.1	18.9	22.4	7.8	10.1	6.4
Rochester, MN	19.0	54.5	14.0	7.0	2.0	2.0	1.5
Rochester, NY	13.8	45.9	21.9	11.2	2.7	2.7	1.8
Sacramento, CA	8.1	31.2	25.7	22.0	5.7	4.1	3.2
St. Louis, MO	9.2	33.8	26.5	20.5	4.7	3.0	2.2
Salt Lake City, UT	12.7	44.8	22.5	13.1	3.5	2.1	1.2
San Antonio, TX	8.9	31.3	26.5	22.0	6.1	3.4	1.8
San Diego, CA	7.6	32.4	27.4	21.3	5.9	3.6	1.8
San Francisco, CA	4.2	18.8	20.8	29.8	12.0	10.6	3.8
San Jose, CA	5.3	23.3	22.2	26.9	10.6	8.4	3.4
Santa Rosa, CA	12.7	40.3	21.6	13.3	4.5	4.3	3.2
Savannah, GA	15.9	39.7	22.9	12.8	4.3	2.8	1.6
Seattle, WA	7.1	23.5	24.7	28.0	10.4	4.8	1.5
Sioux Falls, SD	17.1	51.9	21.8	5.9	1.3	1.0	1.0
Springfield, IL	17.2	52.5	18.2	6.1	2.1	2.3	1.6
Tampa, FL	10.9	30.3	22.5	23.1	7.0	4.4	1.9
Tucson, AZ	11.8	34.6	25.3	19.8	4.7	2.2	1.6
Tulsa, OK	14.3	45.2	25.5	10.4	1.9	1.5	1.2
Tuscaloosa, AL	16.4	44.5	24.0	7.6	3.4	2.9	1.3
Virginia Beach, VA	10.6	30.3	27.7	22.0	5.4	2.7	1.4
Washington, DC	4.9	18.2	22.3	33.2	12.2	6.9	2.2
Wichita, KS	13.9	45.0	26.7	9.9	1.8	1.4	1.3
Wilmington, NC	15.1	47.3	23.0	9.2	2.3	2.0	1.2
Winston-Salem, NC	14.9	39.5	23.3	13.8	4.5	2.4	1.6
U.S.	12.3	28.4	20.9	20.9	8.3	6.4	2.9

Note: Figures are percentages and include workers 16 years old and over
Source: U.S. Census Bureau, 2016-2020 American Community Survey 5-Year Estimates

Travel Time to Work: Metro Area

Metro Area	Less Than 10 Minutes	10 to 19 Minutes	20 to 29 Minutes	30 to 44 Minutes	45 to 59 Minutes	60 to 89 Minutes	90 Minutes or More
Albuquerque, NM	10.7	31.5	26.0	20.5	5.9	3.7	1.7
Allentown, PA	12.5	27.2	23.2	18.3	7.6	7.2	4.0
Anchorage, AK	15.3	41.3	21.9	10.8	4.4	4.0	2.3
Ann Arbor, MI	10.9	32.4	24.9	19.1	7.5	4.1	1.2
Athens, GA	14.0	39.4	21.9	13.2	5.3	3.7	2.6
Atlanta, GA	7.0	22.2	19.5	25.0	12.3	10.2	3.8
Austin, TX	9.5	26.9	22.0	23.3	10.1	6.2	2.0
Baltimore, MD	7.5	22.9	20.8	24.8	11.3	8.8	3.9
Baton Rouge, LA	9.6	28.1	22.4	22.1	8.7	6.7	2.6
Boise City, ID	12.7	34.2	25.4	18.7	5.1	2.3	1.5
Boston, MA	8.9	22.3	18.3	24.4	11.9	10.6	3.5
Boulder, CO	14.2	33.6	21.3	17.5	7.1	4.9	1.4
Buffalo, NY	14.1	33.8	26.1	18.5	4.4	1.9	1.2
Cape Coral, FL	9.0	25.3	22.5	26.2	9.7	5.1	2.2
Cedar Rapids, IA	18.4	39.8	21.1	12.9	4.3	2.1	1.5
Charleston, SC	8.8	26.2	23.8	25.5	9.2	4.9	1.7
Charlotte, NC	9.4	27.6	22.6	23.5	9.6	5.3	2.0
Chicago, IL	8.3	21.6	18.6	25.2	12.4	10.5	3.3
Cincinnati, OH	10.7	28.0	25.3	23.2	7.6	3.6	1.6
Clarksville, TN	14.5	32.3	21.8	16.0	6.8	6.2	2.4
Cleveland, OH	11.5	28.0	25.6	23.1	7.1	3.2	1.6
College Station, TX	16.0	49.0	19.2	9.9	2.3	2.2	1.4
Colorado Springs, CO	11.8	32.2	26.9	18.2	4.9	3.5	2.5
Columbia, MO	17.3	44.9	18.3	12.3	3.9	1.7	1.6
Columbia, SC	13.0	29.0	23.5	22.1	7.0	3.3	2.1
Columbus, OH	11.3	29.3	26.6	21.8	6.3	3.2	1.4
Dallas, TX	8.6	24.9	21.5	25.7	10.4	6.8	2.1
Davenport, IA	18.7	36.7	24.0	13.6	3.6	2.2	1.2
Denver, CO	8.2	24.9	23.0	26.5	9.9	5.7	1.8
Des Moines, IA	14.8	34.9	27.6	16.5	3.7	1.4	1.1
Durham, NC	9.6	31.2	24.8	21.2	7.2	4.4	1.5
Edison, NJ	6.8	18.3	16.2	23.9	12.7	15.0	7.0
El Paso, TX	10.5	32.4	27.2	20.6	5.1	2.3	2.0
Fargo, ND	17.7	52.2	18.5	6.3	2.2	1.9	1.2
Fort Collins, CO	13.7	35.5	22.0	15.8	5.9	5.0	2.1
Fort Wayne, IN	12.8	36.2	28.3	15.2	3.5	2.2	1.8
Fort Worth, TX	8.6	24.9	21.5	25.7	10.4	6.8	2.1
Grand Rapids, MI	14.7	35.4	24.8	16.3	4.9	2.6	1.5
Green Bay, WI	18.0	39.9	22.0	12.8	4.0	2.0	1.4
Honolulu, HI	9.7	25.4	19.8	25.0	9.6	7.7	2.8
Houston, TX	7.6	23.4	19.9	26.4	11.8	8.5	2.4
Huntsville, AL	10.4	32.0	27.5	21.6	5.5	1.7	1.3
Indianapolis, IN	11.3	27.8	24.0	24.2	7.5	3.6	1.7
Jacksonville, FL	9.1	25.5	24.0	26.1	8.9	4.6	1.8
Kansas City, MO	12.0	30.8	25.3	21.6	6.6	2.5	1.2
Lafayette, LA	14.5	32.7	21.2	18.5	5.5	3.7	3.8
Las Cruces, NM	14.5	39.0	21.5	13.5	5.3	4.5	1.7
Las Vegas, NV	7.7	27.6	29.1	25.7	5.4	2.6	1.9
Lexington, KY	14.2	35.7	24.6	17.2	4.3	2.5	1.5
Lincoln, NE	16.6	41.6	24.0	11.7	2.8	2.1	1.2
Little Rock, AR	12.8	33.1	22.5	20.2	7.1	2.8	1.4
Los Angeles, CA	7.0	24.5	19.6	25.4	10.2	9.6	3.7
Louisville, KY	9.6	29.8	27.8	22.6	6.2	2.5	1.4
Madison, WI	15.7	32.0	24.9	18.3	5.4	2.6	1.1
Manchester, NH	10.9	29.8	20.8	19.5	8.4	7.2	3.5

Table continued on following page.

Metro Area	Less Than 10 Minutes	10 to 19 Minutes	20 to 29 Minutes	30 to 44 Minutes	45 to 59 Minutes	60 to 89 Minutes	90 Minutes or More
Memphis, TN	10.0	27.7	27.1	24.3	6.9	2.6	1.3
Miami, FL	6.4	22.6	22.4	27.7	10.2	7.9	2.7
Midland, TX	16.7	44.4	19.7	12.8	2.6	2.1	1.7
Milwaukee, WI	11.9	32.1	25.6	21.3	5.1	2.6	1.4
Minneapolis, MN	10.3	27.4	25.1	23.6	8.0	4.2	1.4
Nashville, TN	9.2	26.0	21.5	23.6	10.9	6.8	2.0
New Haven, CT	11.7	31.5	23.2	19.7	6.2	4.8	2.9
New Orleans, LA	10.7	30.6	22.3	20.4	7.8	5.7	2.6
New York, NY	6.8	18.3	16.2	23.9	12.7	15.0	7.0
Oklahoma City, OK	12.2	32.4	25.5	20.3	5.6	2.4	1.5
Omaha, NE	13.9	36.2	27.3	16.0	3.7	1.8	1.0
Orlando, FL	7.1	22.7	22.3	28.3	11.5	5.8	2.4
Philadelphia, PA	9.4	23.5	20.5	24.0	11.1	8.3	3.2
Phoenix, AZ	9.9	26.1	23.7	23.7	8.9	5.8	1.9
Pittsburgh, PA	11.8	26.7	20.9	23.1	9.3	6.0	2.1
Portland, OR	10.5	26.9	22.8	22.9	9.3	5.5	2.1
Providence, RI	11.8	30.1	21.6	19.5	7.8	6.2	3.0
Provo, UT	17.1	35.8	19.7	15.9	6.0	3.9	1.6
Raleigh, NC	8.8	26.8	24.4	24.4	9.0	4.8	1.9
Reno, NV	12.6	36.6	24.4	17.0	4.9	2.9	1.5
Richmond, VA	9.1	28.6	26.9	23.5	6.6	3.0	2.2
Riverside, CA	9.0	25.9	18.6	20.0	8.8	10.5	7.3
Rochester, MN	18.5	40.9	18.6	13.4	3.9	2.8	1.9
Rochester, NY	15.0	33.5	26.8	16.6	4.5	2.4	1.1
Sacramento, CA	9.7	28.3	22.4	23.1	7.9	4.9	3.6
St. Louis, MO	10.8	27.0	24.2	24.1	8.1	4.0	1.7
Salt Lake City, UT	10.7	33.2	27.0	19.6	5.6	2.9	1.1
San Antonio, TX	9.2	28.2	24.1	23.2	8.4	4.8	2.2
San Diego, CA	8.2	29.2	24.2	23.5	7.7	5.1	2.2
San Francisco, CA	6.6	22.3	17.4	23.7	12.3	12.6	5.1
San Jose, CA	6.7	25.4	22.5	25.1	9.4	7.6	3.3
Santa Rosa, CA	14.2	32.9	20.4	16.6	6.3	5.8	3.7
Savannah, GA	11.2	29.8	24.6	21.4	7.8	3.7	1.6
Seattle, WA	7.8	22.2	21.0	25.2	11.5	8.8	3.5
Sioux Falls, SD	17.3	43.8	24.0	10.2	2.2	1.2	1.2
Springfield, IL	15.0	43.3	23.1	11.8	3.0	2.1	1.8
Tampa, FL	9.4	27.0	21.2	23.5	10.1	6.4	2.3
Tucson, AZ	10.6	29.2	24.7	23.9	7.2	2.6	1.8
Tulsa, OK	13.3	33.8	26.6	18.1	4.6	2.1	1.4
Tuscaloosa, AL	11.5	32.9	24.5	17.3	6.8	5.0	1.9
Virginia Beach, VA	11.7	30.6	23.4	21.3	7.1	4.1	1.7
Washington, DC	5.9	18.9	17.9	26.1	14.0	12.7	4.5
Wichita, KS	15.9	37.3	26.1	14.9	2.9	1.5	1.4
Wilmington, NC	12.1	38.7	23.5	15.8	5.7	2.3	1.9
Winston-Salem, NC	12.5	32.2	24.4	19.5	6.2	3.1	2.1
U.S.	12.3	28.4	20.9	20.9	8.3	6.4	2.9

Note: Figures are percentages and include workers 16 years old and over; Figures cover the Metropolitan Statistical Area
Source: U.S. Census Bureau, 2016-2020 American Community Survey 5-Year Estimates

2020 Presidential Election Results

City	Area Covered	Biden	Trump	Jorgensen	Hawkins	Other
Albuquerque, NM	Bernalillo County	61.0	36.6	1.5	0.5	0.4
Allentown, PA	Lehigh County	53.1	45.5	1.2	0.1	0.2
Anchorage, AK	State of Alaska	42.8	52.8	2.5	0.0	1.9
Ann Arbor, MI	Washtenaw County	72.4	25.9	0.9	0.3	0.4
Athens, GA	Clarke County	70.1	28.1	1.6	0.1	0.1
Atlanta, GA	Fulton County	72.6	26.2	1.2	0.0	0.0
Austin, TX	Travis County	71.4	26.4	1.5	0.3	0.4
Baltimore, MD	Baltimore City	87.3	10.7	0.7	0.6	0.7
Baton Rouge, LA	East Baton Rouge Parish	55.5	42.5	1.2	0.0	0.8
Boise City, ID	Ada County	46.1	50.0	2.0	0.1	1.8
Boston, MA	Suffolk County	80.6	17.5	0.9	0.5	0.5
Boulder, CO	Boulder County	77.2	20.6	1.2	0.3	0.6
Buffalo, NY	Erie County	56.5	41.7	0.9	0.4	0.5
Cape Coral, FL	Lee County	39.9	59.1	0.5	0.1	0.3
Cedar Rapids, IA	Linn County	55.6	41.9	1.6	0.3	0.7
Charleston, SC	Charleston County	55.5	42.6	1.5	0.3	0.1
Charlotte, NC	Mecklenburg County	66.7	31.6	1.0	0.3	0.5
Chicago, IL	Cook County	74.2	24.0	0.8	0.5	0.5
Cincinnati, OH	Hamilton County	57.1	41.3	1.2	0.3	0.0
Clarksville, TN	Montgomery County	42.3	55.0	1.9	0.2	0.7
Cleveland, OH	Cuyahoga County	66.4	32.3	0.7	0.3	0.3
College Station, TX	Brazos County	41.4	55.7	2.1	0.3	0.4
Colorado Springs, CO	El Paso County	42.7	53.5	2.4	0.3	1.0
Columbia, MO	Boone County	54.8	42.3	2.2	0.3	0.4
Columbia, SC	Richland County	68.4	30.1	1.0	0.4	0.1
Columbus, OH	Franklin County	64.7	33.4	1.2	0.3	0.4
Dallas, TX	Dallas County	64.9	33.3	1.0	0.4	0.4
Davenport, IA	Scott County	50.7	47.2	1.2	0.2	0.7
Denver, CO	Denver County	79.6	18.2	1.2	0.3	0.7
Des Moines, IA	Polk County	56.5	41.3	1.3	0.2	0.7
Durham, NC	Durham County	80.4	18.0	0.8	0.3	0.4
Edison, NJ	Middlesex County	60.2	38.2	0.7	0.3	0.6
El Paso, TX	El Paso County	66.7	31.6	1.0	0.5	0.2
Fargo, ND	Cass County	46.8	49.5	2.9	0.0	0.7
Fort Collins, CO	Larimer County	56.2	40.8	1.8	0.3	0.9
Fort Wayne, IN	Allen County	43.2	54.3	2.2	0.0	0.3
Fort Worth, TX	Tarrant County	49.3	49.1	1.2	0.3	0.0
Grand Rapids, MI	Kent County	51.9	45.8	1.5	0.3	0.5
Green Bay, WI	Brown County	45.5	52.7	1.3	0.0	0.5
Honolulu, HI	Honolulu County	62.5	35.7	0.9	0.6	0.4
Houston, TX	Harris County	55.9	42.7	1.0	0.3	0.0
Huntsville, AL	Madison County	44.8	52.8	1.9	0.0	0.5
Indianapolis, IN	Marion County	63.3	34.3	1.8	0.1	0.4
Jacksonville, FL	Duval County	51.1	47.3	1.0	0.2	0.5
Kansas City, MO	Jackson County	59.8	37.9	1.4	0.4	0.5
Lafayette, LA	Lafayette Parish	34.7	63.3	1.3	0.0	0.7
Las Cruces, NM	Dona Ana County	58.0	39.7	1.4	0.5	0.4
Las Vegas, NV	Clark County	53.7	44.3	0.9	0.0	1.1
Lexington, KY	Fayette County	59.2	38.5	1.6	0.1	0.6
Lincoln, NE	Lancaster County	52.3	44.6	2.4	0.0	0.7
Little Rock, AR	Pulaski County	60.0	37.5	1.0	0.3	1.3
Los Angeles, CA	Los Angeles County	71.0	26.9	0.8	0.5	0.8
Louisville, KY	Jefferson County	58.9	38.8	1.2	0.1	1.0
Madison, WI	Dane County	75.5	22.9	1.1	0.1	0.6
Manchester, NH	Hillsborough County	52.8	45.2	1.7	0.0	0.3
Memphis, TN	Shelby County	64.4	34.0	0.6	0.2	0.8

Table continued on following page.

City	Area Covered	Biden	Trump	Jorgensen	Hawkins	Other
Miami, FL	Miami-Dade County	53.3	46.0	0.3	0.1	0.3
Midland, TX	Midland County	20.9	77.3	1.3	0.2	0.2
Milwaukee, WI	Milwaukee County	69.1	29.3	0.9	0.0	0.7
Minneapolis, MN	Hennepin County	70.5	27.2	1.0	0.3	1.0
Nashville, TN	Davidson County	64.5	32.4	1.1	0.2	1.8
New Haven, CT	New Haven County	58.0	40.6	0.9	0.4	0.0
New Orleans, LA	Orleans Parish	83.1	15.0	0.9	0.0	1.0
New York, NY	Bronx County	83.3	15.9	0.2	0.3	0.3
New York, NY	Kings County	76.8	22.1	0.3	0.4	0.4
New York, NY	New York County	86.4	12.2	0.5	0.4	0.5
New York, NY	Queens County	72.0	26.9	0.3	0.4	0.4
New York, NY	Richmond County	42.0	56.9	0.4	0.3	0.4
Oklahoma City, OK	Oklahoma County	48.1	49.2	1.8	0.0	0.9
Omaha, NE	Douglas County	54.4	43.1	2.0	0.0	0.6
Orlando, FL	Orange County	60.9	37.8	0.7	0.2	0.4
Philadelphia, PA	Philadelphia County	81.2	17.9	0.7	0.1	0.2
Phoenix, AZ	Maricopa County	50.1	48.0	1.5	0.0	0.3
Pittsburgh, PA	Allegheny County	59.4	39.0	1.2	0.0	0.4
Portland, OR	Multnomah County	79.2	17.9	1.2	0.6	1.0
Providence, RI	Providence County	60.5	37.6	0.8	0.0	1.0
Provo, UT	Utah County	26.3	66.7	3.6	0.3	3.1
Raleigh, NC	Wake County	62.3	35.8	1.2	0.3	0.5
Reno, NV	Washoe County	50.8	46.3	1.4	0.0	1.5
Richmond, VA	Richmond City	82.9	14.9	1.5	0.0	0.6
Riverside, CA	Riverside County	53.0	45.0	1.0	0.3	0.6
Rochester, MN	Olmsted County	54.2	43.4	1.2	0.3	0.9
Rochester, NY	Monroe County	59.3	38.2	1.3	0.4	0.8
Sacramento, CA	Sacramento County	61.4	36.1	1.4	0.5	0.7
St. Louis, MO	St. Louis City	81.9	16.0	1.1	0.4	0.5
Salt Lake City, UT	Salt Lake County	53.0	42.1	2.2	0.4	2.2
San Antonio, TX	Bexar County	58.2	40.1	1.1	0.4	0.2
San Diego, CA	San Diego County	60.2	37.5	1.3	0.5	0.5
San Francisco, CA	San Francisco County	85.3	12.7	0.7	0.6	0.7
San Jose, CA	Santa Clara County	72.6	25.2	1.1	0.5	0.6
Santa Rosa, CA	Sonoma County	74.5	23.0	1.3	0.6	0.6
Savannah, GA	Chatham County	58.6	39.9	1.4	0.0	0.0
Seattle, WA	King County	75.0	22.2	1.5	0.5	0.8
Sioux Falls, SD	Minnehaha County	43.8	53.3	2.8	0.0	0.0
Springfield, IL	Sangamon County	46.5	50.9	1.4	0.6	0.6
Tampa, FL	Hillsborough County	52.7	45.8	0.8	0.2	0.5
Tucson, AZ	Pima County	58.4	39.8	1.5	0.0	0.3
Tulsa, OK	Tulsa County	40.9	56.5	1.8	0.0	0.8
Tuscaloosa, AL	Tuscaloosa County	41.9	56.7	1.0	0.0	0.4
Virginia Beach, VA	Virginia Beach City	51.6	46.2	1.8	0.0	0.4
Washington, DC	District of Columbia	92.1	5.4	0.6	0.5	1.4
Wichita, KS	Sedgwick County	42.6	54.4	2.4	0.0	0.5
Wilmington, NC	New Hanover County	50.2	48.0	1.2	0.3	0.4
Winston-Salem, NC	Forsyth County	56.2	42.3	0.9	0.2	0.4
U.S.	U.S.	51.3	46.8	1.2	0.3	0.5

Note: Results are percentages and may not add to 100% due to rounding
Source: Dave Leip's Atlas of U.S. Presidential Elections

House Price Index (HPI)

Metro Area[1]	National Ranking[3]	Quarterly Change (%)	One-Year Change (%)	Five-Year Change (%)	Since 1991Q1 (%)
Albuquerque, NM	109	3.52	18.66	43.07	212.14
Allentown, PA	144	2.70	16.98	41.01	136.63
Anchorage, AK	261	0.74	9.95	19.44	210.38
Ann Arbor, MI	244	1.69	12.33	39.57	195.86
Athens, GA	65	5.42	21.56	61.54	243.08
Atlanta, GA	61	5.13	21.84	59.09	221.18
Austin, TX	2	3.12	32.31	73.38	566.23
Baltimore, MD	242	1.69	12.50	27.10	189.07
Baton Rouge, LA	262	2.05	9.49	23.05	214.49
Boise City, ID	4	2.08	31.29	117.06	493.84
Boston, MA[2]	196	1.99	14.86	40.34	277.23
Boulder, CO	153	1.19	16.72	43.62	521.25
Buffalo, NY	143	1.79	16.99	49.97	173.69
Cape Coral, FL	8	6.85	30.12	61.31	276.13
Cedar Rapids, IA	246	0.93	11.89	27.95	157.09
Charleston, SC	81	3.93	20.47	51.97	360.39
Charlotte, NC	54	4.96	22.05	60.54	244.45
Chicago, IL[2]	254	2.04	11.32	24.85	147.60
Cincinnati, OH	178	2.66	15.64	45.44	166.70
Clarksville, TN	(a)	n/a	23.48	54.95	n/a
Cleveland, OH	207	2.06	14.43	42.09	132.86
College Station, TX	(a)	n/a	16.27	37.12	n/a
Colorado Springs, CO	48	3.24	22.26	71.49	392.05
Columbia, MO	145	3.35	16.90	35.93	192.66
Columbia, SC	161	2.38	16.34	40.51	161.36
Columbus, OH	165	2.27	16.23	51.07	205.18
Dallas, TX[2]	71	4.24	21.21	52.03	266.50
Davenport, IA	250	1.03	11.58	22.60	181.26
Denver, CO	95	2.51	19.44	53.94	500.40
Des Moines, IA	230	1.94	13.37	31.33	188.55
Durham, NC	85	3.80	20.30	53.02	238.34
Edison, NJ[2]	253	2.21	11.32	30.31	231.51
El Paso, TX	150	4.26	16.83	37.15	155.25
Fargo, ND	260	1.48	10.11	21.06	233.06
Fort Collins, CO	126	2.95	17.86	47.46	448.11
Fort Wayne, IN	123	2.09	18.03	53.46	150.59
Fort Worth, TX[2]	70	4.17	21.31	58.26	252.35
Grand Rapids, MI	124	2.05	17.91	58.02	223.99
Green Bay, WI	192	2.49	15.06	41.47	196.03
Honolulu, HI	219	5.43	14.02	23.26	189.27
Houston, TX	218	3.56	14.05	34.96	253.54
Huntsville, AL	33	6.46	23.82	57.66	177.15
Indianapolis, IN	135	3.48	17.47	52.94	175.57
Jacksonville, FL	30	5.00	24.14	62.76	302.33
Kansas City, MO	181	2.28	15.53	50.33	217.95
Lafayette, LA	265	1.52	8.47	16.45	203.48
Las Cruces, NM	97	3.27	19.28	42.47	157.99
Las Vegas, NV	32	5.02	23.96	74.24	226.18
Lexington, KY	160	3.19	16.41	42.80	195.19
Lincoln, NE	191	0.59	15.10	41.74	219.19
Little Rock, AR	186	4.23	15.33	30.46	165.64
Los Angeles, CA[2]	141	3.58	17.03	43.63	266.91
Louisville, KY	208	2.76	14.42	40.36	218.00
Madison, WI	229	1.53	13.38	37.82	261.17
Manchester, NH	128	2.23	17.82	50.92	214.99

Table continued on following page.

Metro Area[1]	National Ranking[3]	Quarterly Change (%)	One-Year Change (%)	Five-Year Change (%)	Since 1991Q1 (%)
Memphis, TN	108	3.83	18.68	50.45	160.38
Miami, FL[2]	74	4.87	21.05	54.02	424.33
Midland, TX	267	2.48	6.65	33.79	327.50
Milwaukee, WI	235	1.14	12.84	37.11	205.36
Minneapolis, MN	223	1.32	13.80	41.13	252.32
Nashville, TN	36	5.90	23.67	63.19	351.79
New Haven, CT	140	2.11	17.04	33.74	111.07
New Orleans, LA	251	2.18	11.51	29.18	261.07
New York, NY[2]	253	2.21	11.32	30.31	231.51
Oklahoma City, OK	177	3.29	15.68	36.80	221.26
Omaha, NE	180	2.28	15.58	45.06	218.52
Orlando, FL	82	4.34	20.44	59.63	258.46
Philadelphia, PA[2]	236	1.31	12.84	41.78	226.96
Phoenix, AZ	11	5.33	29.26	77.70	397.18
Pittsburgh, PA	232	1.41	13.35	37.78	202.08
Portland, OR	116	2.32	18.40	46.02	467.52
Providence, RI	119	2.58	18.21	47.19	200.71
Provo, UT	15	3.82	28.09	75.93	464.66
Raleigh, NC	40	5.33	23.31	56.13	244.83
Reno, NV	24	3.85	25.10	68.22	312.60
Richmond, VA	179	2.25	15.60	42.09	212.89
Riverside, CA	31	4.57	24.04	57.79	235.21
Rochester, MN	217	1.23	14.09	42.99	214.24
Rochester, NY	188	0.85	15.15	41.39	115.43
Sacramento, CA	76	3.18	20.94	53.71	223.68
St. Louis, MO	237	1.74	12.79	33.77	169.28
Salt Lake City, UT	23	3.19	25.65	74.98	540.19
San Antonio, TX	102	4.27	18.96	49.74	285.62
San Diego, CA	80	4.24	20.55	47.78	305.27
San Francisco, CA[2]	268	3.76	5.73	13.06	316.44
San Jose, CA	259	3.85	10.13	23.40	334.40
Santa Rosa, CA	243	1.78	12.39	32.17	263.96
Savannah, GA	89	5.79	19.82	48.96	282.71
Seattle, WA[2]	99	3.07	19.15	57.91	404.34
Sioux Falls, SD	114	3.47	18.48	46.25	269.05
Springfield, IL	256	2.85	10.74	16.13	104.64
Tampa, FL	21	5.64	26.20	72.93	346.50
Tucson, AZ	29	4.00	24.59	64.46	277.21
Tulsa, OK	155	3.19	16.62	38.68	193.48
Tuscaloosa, AL	(a)	n/a	11.82	31.86	n/a
Virginia Beach, VA	205	2.22	14.49	31.58	208.89
Washington, DC[2]	241	1.93	12.65	31.53	233.58
Wichita, KS	213	1.97	14.25	37.10	168.59
Wilmington, NC	87	4.21	20.27	56.21	285.45
Winston-Salem, NC	110	3.46	18.60	46.34	157.92
U.S.[4]	–	3.33	17.54	54.45	258.04

Note: The HPI is a weighted repeat sales index. It measures average price changes in repeat sales or refinancings on the same properties. This information is obtained by reviewing repeat mortgage transactions on single-family properties whose mortgages have been purchased or securitized by Fannie Mae or Freddie Mac since January 1975; all figures are for the period ended December 31, 2021; (1) figures cover the Metropolitan Statistical Area (MSA) unless noted otherwise; (2) Metropolitan Division; (3) Rankings are based on annual percentage change, for all MSAs containing at least 15,000 transactions over the last 10 years and ranges from 1 to 268; (4) figures based on a weighted division average; (a) Not ranked because of increased index variability due to smaller sample size; n/a not available
Source: Federal Housing Finance Agency, Change in FHFA Metropolitan Area House Price Indexes, 2021Q4

Home Value Distribution: City

Area	Under $50,000	$50,000 -$99,999	$100,000 -$149,999	$150,000 -$199,999	$200,000 -$299,999	$300,000 -$499,999	$500,000 -$999,999	$1,000,000 or more
Albuquerque, NM	4.6	4.0	15.5	24.4	31.2	16.6	3.4	0.4
Allentown, PA	3.4	20.0	36.0	24.0	11.0	4.2	1.2	0.3
Anchorage, AK	5.3	1.9	4.2	6.2	26.7	41.1	13.3	1.1
Ann Arbor, MI	1.0	2.2	4.8	7.5	22.9	40.9	18.0	2.7
Athens, GA	6.7	10.8	17.6	19.9	23.3	14.4	6.6	0.7
Atlanta, GA	3.8	7.9	9.1	10.4	17.0	21.8	21.1	8.9
Austin, TX	2.1	1.6	3.6	7.3	22.6	36.7	21.3	4.9
Baltimore, MD	6.9	16.5	19.4	17.5	19.7	13.4	5.5	1.0
Baton Rouge, LA	4.7	15.7	14.2	20.1	23.6	14.1	6.0	1.7
Boise City, ID	3.7	1.4	5.8	13.5	30.8	31.6	11.9	1.3
Boston, MA	1.7	0.5	0.3	1.1	6.6	29.2	45.3	15.3
Boulder, CO	3.1	2.3	1.4	2.1	4.1	13.3	47.1	26.5
Buffalo, NY	17.4	32.2	15.9	10.3	11.3	7.8	4.5	0.6
Cape Coral, FL	1.3	2.5	8.2	23.1	34.4	22.2	7.2	1.0
Cedar Rapids, IA	5.6	14.0	34.6	20.8	17.3	6.0	1.5	0.2
Charleston, SC	1.6	2.1	3.3	6.6	25.0	34.0	20.2	7.2
Charlotte, NC	2.2	7.1	14.4	17.5	22.3	21.1	11.9	3.6
Chicago, IL	3.0	6.1	9.9	14.4	24.3	24.9	13.4	4.1
Cincinnati, OH	6.0	22.4	22.1	13.0	15.8	12.3	6.8	1.5
Clarksville, TN	3.2	11.7	25.3	28.5	23.1	5.9	1.8	0.4
Cleveland, OH	28.1	41.5	15.6	6.4	4.6	2.3	1.2	0.4
College Station, TX	1.5	0.8	4.8	17.2	39.3	29.9	5.7	0.8
Colorado Springs, CO	3.0	1.9	4.6	11.0	31.3	36.7	10.3	1.2
Columbia, MO	3.0	7.0	15.7	21.4	28.1	19.4	5.1	0.3
Columbia, SC	4.0	15.7	17.7	17.0	17.0	17.0	10.1	1.5
Columbus, OH	5.4	17.1	22.7	20.7	21.7	9.6	2.3	0.4
Dallas, TX	5.4	16.0	14.9	12.4	14.3	18.2	13.9	4.9
Davenport, IA	6.8	22.7	29.4	14.4	17.1	7.8	1.5	0.3
Denver, CO	1.2	1.0	2.0	4.7	16.1	37.1	31.3	6.4
Des Moines, IA	5.3	18.8	31.5	23.0	14.5	5.0	1.8	0.3
Durham, NC	1.5	4.7	11.2	18.9	31.2	24.5	7.1	0.9
Edison, NJ	1.8	2.0	2.0	2.4	17.0	47.3	25.5	2.0
El Paso, TX	4.9	23.0	31.8	20.2	13.5	5.1	1.3	0.3
Fargo, ND	3.9	4.1	10.0	22.7	35.0	19.3	4.2	0.8
Fort Collins, CO	2.9	0.9	1.3	2.4	13.9	55.5	21.6	1.5
Fort Wayne, IN	9.6	27.3	28.4	17.4	11.9	4.2	1.1	0.1
Fort Worth, TX	5.0	14.2	15.2	18.8	27.5	14.4	4.0	1.0
Grand Rapids, MI	4.0	15.8	25.9	27.4	19.7	5.7	1.3	0.2
Green Bay, WI	3.0	17.4	35.1	23.3	13.6	5.6	1.8	0.3
Honolulu, HI	1.0	0.6	0.8	1.0	6.4	22.3	42.2	25.7
Houston, TX	4.9	16.9	16.9	14.2	15.9	16.8	10.7	3.8
Huntsville, AL	6.0	16.8	14.9	16.7	22.4	17.3	4.8	1.1
Indianapolis, IN	6.2	20.7	25.5	19.4	15.3	8.9	3.4	0.7
Jacksonville, FL	6.8	13.0	15.8	18.7	26.5	13.7	4.1	1.5
Kansas City, MO	10.6	15.5	18.2	18.2	19.9	12.4	4.3	0.8
Lafayette, LA	4.4	7.9	14.8	24.0	24.2	16.6	6.4	1.7
Las Cruces, NM	7.2	11.7	24.6	26.3	20.6	7.7	1.7	0.3
Las Vegas, NV	2.5	2.7	6.5	12.4	32.5	31.0	10.6	1.8
Lexington, KY	2.2	7.8	19.0	20.7	23.5	18.6	6.9	1.3
Lincoln, NE	3.4	7.7	22.4	24.4	25.6	13.2	2.6	0.7
Little Rock, AR	6.1	16.9	17.0	17.7	17.2	16.7	7.1	1.4
Los Angeles, CA	1.2	0.9	0.6	0.6	3.3	21.6	47.6	24.2
Louisville, KY	5.5	14.0	23.2	18.9	18.6	14.2	4.6	0.8
Madison, WI	1.6	2.1	7.1	15.4	36.5	29.3	7.1	1.0
Manchester, NH	1.8	3.3	6.7	18.8	43.8	23.4	1.9	0.3

Table continued on following page.

Area	Under $50,000	$50,000 -$99,999	$100,000 -$149,999	$150,000 -$199,999	$200,000 -$299,999	$300,000 -$499,999	$500,000 -$999,999	$1,000,000 or more
Memphis, TN	13.0	34.2	16.6	12.0	11.8	7.3	3.8	1.3
Miami, FL	1.7	3.8	4.7	7.8	22.8	34.3	17.2	7.7
Midland, TX	4.4	7.8	10.9	14.9	30.9	20.7	8.4	2.0
Milwaukee, WI	8.3	25.1	28.7	19.7	11.8	4.0	1.8	0.5
Minneapolis, MN	1.6	3.2	8.7	14.4	31.5	27.2	11.2	2.2
Nashville, TN	2.2	3.4	9.7	15.2	29.2	26.7	11.4	2.3
New Haven, CT	2.4	8.0	13.4	24.3	29.6	14.7	5.9	1.7
New Orleans, LA	2.5	7.1	12.5	17.6	21.3	21.6	14.1	3.3
New York, NY	3.0	1.3	1.7	2.1	6.1	21.1	43.1	21.7
Oklahoma City, OK	7.8	17.3	19.1	20.7	19.7	10.7	3.7	1.0
Omaha, NE	4.0	13.4	23.5	21.6	21.3	12.1	3.5	0.7
Orlando, FL	2.3	8.0	11.4	12.7	24.9	28.6	10.1	1.9
Philadelphia, PA	6.0	17.9	17.5	17.6	21.4	12.5	5.9	1.3
Phoenix, AZ	4.2	4.4	8.4	16.2	28.8	24.8	11.3	1.9
Pittsburgh, PA	11.1	26.0	17.5	13.9	13.2	11.0	6.3	1.0
Portland, OR	1.7	0.8	0.8	3.0	13.0	42.6	34.4	3.7
Providence, RI	2.0	4.0	11.8	23.4	30.4	16.7	9.3	2.4
Provo, UT	3.8	1.3	4.1	9.4	32.1	35.7	11.4	2.3
Raleigh, NC	2.1	2.1	8.4	17.4	28.2	27.4	12.2	2.1
Reno, NV	3.4	2.7	3.1	4.9	19.1	45.5	18.6	2.7
Richmond, VA	1.7	9.6	12.6	14.9	21.7	23.2	12.8	3.5
Riverside, CA	2.8	1.7	1.2	1.9	11.7	58.6	20.0	1.9
Rochester, MN	2.8	3.5	13.2	23.4	29.3	21.5	5.8	0.4
Rochester, NY	14.7	45.8	18.3	8.0	6.0	4.2	2.6	0.4
Sacramento, CA	2.6	1.6	2.6	4.8	22.9	42.9	20.1	2.5
St. Louis, MO	12.1	20.3	19.9	17.2	15.9	10.5	3.3	0.9
Salt Lake City, UT	2.6	1.2	5.1	9.4	23.4	31.7	22.3	4.3
San Antonio, TX	6.1	21.7	19.3	19.3	19.6	10.7	2.7	0.6
San Diego, CA	1.5	1.0	0.8	0.8	3.9	25.0	50.2	16.8
San Francisco, CA	1.0	0.4	0.5	0.2	1.1	3.5	30.0	63.3
San Jose, CA	1.4	1.1	1.5	1.0	2.0	5.3	45.7	42.0
Santa Rosa, CA	2.3	2.1	1.9	1.1	4.8	25.5	55.0	7.3
Savannah, GA	6.1	16.0	20.9	21.2	20.0	9.5	5.0	1.3
Seattle, WA	0.6	0.4	0.3	0.5	3.7	18.6	54.7	21.2
Sioux Falls, SD	5.2	6.0	14.8	22.1	29.9	16.6	4.7	0.8
Springfield, IL	8.9	26.0	23.8	15.5	15.9	7.8	1.9	0.1
Tampa, FL	3.2	8.2	11.3	14.6	21.5	22.4	13.4	5.4
Tucson, AZ	9.7	10.8	20.2	25.0	23.2	8.4	2.1	0.6
Tulsa, OK	8.0	22.2	22.5	15.3	14.3	11.2	5.0	1.3
Tuscaloosa, AL	4.9	10.4	17.8	20.4	19.3	16.5	9.0	1.7
Virginia Beach, VA	2.3	1.2	5.3	11.5	34.0	31.5	11.8	2.5
Washington, DC	1.1	0.8	1.0	1.4	8.5	25.6	41.3	20.3
Wichita, KS	8.0	25.6	21.6	19.2	15.0	7.7	2.7	0.3
Wilmington, NC	2.1	4.3	12.4	15.3	24.2	25.3	13.2	3.2
Winston-Salem, NC	5.9	17.9	25.0	22.0	14.2	9.1	5.1	0.7
U.S.	6.6	11.0	12.3	13.6	20.0	20.5	12.3	3.7

Note: Figures are percentages and cover owner-occupied housing units.
Source: U.S. Census Bureau, 2016-2020 American Community Survey 5-Year Estimates

Home Value Distribution: Metro Area

MSA[1]	Under $50,000	$50,000 -$99,999	$100,000 -$149,999	$150,000 -$199,999	$200,000 -$299,999	$300,000 -$499,999	$500,000 -$999,999	$1,000,000 or more
Albuquerque, NM	6.0	6.7	15.3	22.2	27.4	16.4	5.1	1.0
Allentown, PA	3.6	6.9	13.9	19.5	28.5	22.5	4.4	0.6
Anchorage, AK	4.8	2.5	4.7	8.2	29.5	38.0	11.3	1.0
Ann Arbor, MI	4.9	5.3	7.4	12.6	24.8	30.6	12.7	1.8
Athens, GA	8.5	10.5	14.9	18.0	22.1	17.8	6.7	1.5
Atlanta, GA	3.5	7.2	12.8	17.5	24.0	23.0	10.2	1.9
Austin, TX	3.0	3.0	5.3	10.2	27.8	31.9	15.2	3.5
Baltimore, MD	3.0	4.0	6.8	10.3	24.4	32.4	16.8	2.2
Baton Rouge, LA	8.6	11.0	13.7	20.1	25.7	15.6	4.3	1.0
Boise City, ID	4.2	3.2	7.7	14.4	29.6	29.6	9.9	1.4
Boston, MA	1.6	0.9	1.5	3.0	12.5	37.2	34.9	8.4
Boulder, CO	2.7	1.2	0.9	1.8	7.7	31.3	41.6	12.7
Buffalo, NY	6.6	17.2	23.4	19.4	18.9	10.6	3.3	0.6
Cape Coral, FL	5.5	7.8	10.2	16.3	26.3	21.7	9.4	2.8
Cedar Rapids, IA	6.2	12.3	27.1	18.9	21.6	10.6	2.8	0.6
Charleston, SC	6.0	6.1	9.9	14.2	24.5	22.6	12.6	4.2
Charlotte, NC	4.7	10.0	14.6	16.6	22.9	20.6	8.6	2.1
Chicago, IL	3.3	6.2	11.3	16.0	26.2	24.3	10.2	2.4
Cincinnati, OH	4.6	13.7	20.5	19.1	21.8	14.8	4.8	0.8
Clarksville, TN	5.8	15.3	21.0	22.1	22.5	9.9	2.7	0.7
Cleveland, OH	7.3	18.7	21.4	17.7	19.4	11.7	3.3	0.6
College Station, TX	8.6	12.7	11.6	16.5	24.8	18.2	6.6	0.9
Colorado Springs, CO	3.1	1.7	4.4	10.9	29.9	36.2	12.6	1.4
Columbia, MO	5.5	10.3	17.3	20.1	24.0	17.0	5.1	0.6
Columbia, SC	8.1	16.2	21.2	19.1	17.8	12.4	4.3	0.9
Columbus, OH	4.6	11.6	16.8	18.3	24.0	18.6	5.4	0.7
Dallas, TX	4.1	8.9	12.1	15.4	25.0	23.6	8.8	2.2
Davenport, IA	7.2	21.9	24.6	17.4	16.2	10.0	2.3	0.5
Denver, CO	2.0	1.0	1.5	3.6	15.3	44.9	27.5	4.0
Des Moines, IA	4.3	10.2	18.0	19.8	25.8	16.7	4.6	0.5
Durham, NC	4.3	7.5	11.6	15.4	23.9	24.8	11.0	1.6
Edison, NJ	2.1	1.4	2.2	3.6	12.2	34.2	33.8	10.5
El Paso, TX	7.2	24.7	30.6	19.1	12.6	4.6	1.1	0.3
Fargo, ND	3.8	4.7	10.6	22.1	32.2	20.5	5.5	0.7
Fort Collins, CO	3.8	1.3	1.1	2.9	15.7	49.5	23.0	2.6
Fort Wayne, IN	7.8	22.4	25.5	18.3	15.7	7.8	2.1	0.4
Fort Worth, TX	4.1	8.9	12.1	15.4	25.0	23.6	8.8	2.2
Grand Rapids, MI	6.4	9.5	17.7	21.4	24.8	15.2	4.0	1.0
Green Bay, WI	3.6	10.7	21.7	22.6	25.3	12.7	3.0	0.5
Honolulu, HI	0.7	0.6	0.7	0.9	4.3	18.9	54.3	19.5
Houston, TX	5.0	10.4	14.6	17.8	23.9	18.5	7.3	2.4
Huntsville, AL	6.3	12.2	17.4	18.6	23.9	16.9	4.1	0.7
Indianapolis, IN	5.1	14.2	20.6	19.1	20.4	15.0	4.8	0.9
Jacksonville, FL	5.4	9.9	12.6	16.6	26.1	20.2	7.3	2.0
Kansas City, MO	5.9	11.2	16.2	18.0	23.7	18.1	5.9	1.0
Lafayette, LA	12.7	15.4	16.6	19.9	19.9	10.9	3.9	0.7
Las Cruces, NM	11.4	17.2	19.8	20.1	18.5	9.9	2.9	0.3
Las Vegas, NV	3.4	3.0	6.2	10.9	31.4	33.4	9.8	1.9
Lexington, KY	3.0	8.8	20.1	20.4	22.7	17.2	6.6	1.2
Lincoln, NE	3.2	7.5	20.7	23.1	25.2	15.5	4.0	0.9
Little Rock, AR	7.9	16.5	21.9	19.5	19.6	10.5	3.3	0.8
Los Angeles, CA	1.8	1.4	0.9	1.0	3.9	22.2	50.3	18.5
Louisville, KY	4.8	12.5	20.4	19.5	21.9	15.0	5.0	0.9
Madison, WI	2.1	3.2	9.4	14.8	32.2	29.0	8.0	1.4
Manchester, NH	2.1	2.5	5.3	10.7	34.0	36.6	8.1	0.7

Table continued on following page.

MSA[1]	Under $50,000	$50,000 -$99,999	$100,000 -$149,999	$150,000 -$199,999	$200,000 -$299,999	$300,000 -$499,999	$500,000 -$999,999	$1,000,000 or more
Memphis, TN	8.2	20.3	17.2	16.3	20.1	12.6	4.2	0.9
Miami, FL	3.6	6.1	7.5	10.5	22.8	31.5	13.4	4.6
Midland, TX	8.1	9.5	10.4	13.4	27.9	21.1	8.0	1.8
Milwaukee, WI	3.5	8.0	14.1	17.5	27.3	21.8	6.7	1.2
Minneapolis, MN	2.6	2.2	6.2	14.6	33.2	29.8	9.9	1.5
Nashville, TN	2.8	4.8	9.9	14.6	27.4	25.9	12.1	2.5
New Haven, CT	1.9	4.6	11.1	16.3	29.2	27.8	7.9	1.2
New Orleans, LA	4.3	7.7	16.0	20.5	25.7	17.4	7.0	1.4
New York, NY	2.1	1.4	2.2	3.6	12.2	34.2	33.8	10.5
Oklahoma City, OK	7.4	16.2	20.4	20.0	19.2	11.7	3.9	1.1
Omaha, NE	4.0	11.0	20.9	20.6	23.4	15.6	3.9	0.7
Orlando, FL	5.6	6.5	9.1	15.0	31.1	24.3	6.7	1.7
Philadelphia, PA	3.3	6.9	9.5	14.1	26.1	27.4	10.9	1.7
Phoenix, AZ	5.4	4.0	6.8	13.3	28.9	28.1	11.0	2.5
Pittsburgh, PA	8.2	19.2	18.3	17.8	18.7	12.9	4.1	0.7
Portland, OR	2.9	1.2	1.6	3.5	16.5	46.2	25.2	3.0
Providence, RI	2.1	1.6	4.5	11.7	33.2	34.2	11.0	1.8
Provo, UT	2.2	0.9	2.2	6.9	28.0	43.5	14.3	2.0
Raleigh, NC	3.7	4.2	9.5	14.0	25.9	30.4	10.9	1.3
Reno, NV	3.1	2.5	3.5	5.3	20.4	41.1	19.1	4.9
Richmond, VA	2.4	4.5	10.5	16.8	30.3	25.2	9.1	1.3
Riverside, CA	4.7	3.3	3.3	5.5	18.8	42.7	19.6	2.2
Rochester, MN	4.0	6.0	13.5	20.7	25.6	22.0	7.0	1.1
Rochester, NY	5.8	18.1	27.2	19.9	17.5	8.5	2.5	0.5
Sacramento, CA	2.7	1.5	1.8	3.1	14.7	43.5	29.1	3.6
St. Louis, MO	6.6	14.9	16.9	17.8	22.1	15.3	5.2	1.0
Salt Lake City, UT	2.7	1.1	3.7	8.3	27.3	38.4	16.5	2.1
San Antonio, TX	6.1	16.0	15.5	17.8	22.5	15.4	5.4	1.3
San Diego, CA	2.4	1.8	1.3	1.1	4.2	26.0	49.8	13.5
San Francisco, CA	1.2	0.8	0.8	0.7	2.1	11.4	42.7	40.4
San Jose, CA	1.2	0.8	1.2	0.9	1.8	4.8	36.4	52.9
Santa Rosa, CA	2.1	2.5	1.7	1.1	3.4	18.3	55.2	15.6
Savannah, GA	5.4	9.7	16.2	18.6	25.3	14.8	8.1	1.8
Seattle, WA	2.3	1.1	1.5	3.0	12.3	34.2	35.5	10.1
Sioux Falls, SD	5.1	6.9	14.3	20.7	28.7	18.2	5.3	0.8
Springfield, IL	7.5	23.2	21.6	17.9	19.2	8.6	1.8	0.3
Tampa, FL	8.0	10.6	12.2	16.1	25.6	18.8	6.9	1.8
Tucson, AZ	8.2	8.8	14.3	18.9	24.8	17.5	6.3	1.2
Tulsa, OK	8.9	17.4	21.4	19.4	18.0	10.5	3.6	0.9
Tuscaloosa, AL	12.8	14.0	15.7	20.7	19.6	11.8	4.7	0.8
Virginia Beach, VA	3.5	3.5	9.5	15.9	31.4	26.7	8.3	1.3
Washington, DC	1.4	0.9	1.7	4.0	15.9	36.4	32.5	7.1
Wichita, KS	8.2	22.8	21.5	19.8	16.2	8.7	2.4	0.4
Wilmington, NC	4.0	6.3	11.4	16.6	25.0	24.2	10.3	2.2
Winston-Salem, NC	6.7	15.6	23.7	20.9	17.8	10.8	3.9	0.5
U.S.	6.6	11.0	12.3	13.6	20.0	20.5	12.3	3.7

Note: (1) Figures cover the Metropolitan Statistical Area (MSA); Figures are percentages and cover owner-occupied housing units.
Source: U.S. Census Bureau, 2016-2020 American Community Survey 5-Year Estimates

Homeownership Rate

Metro Area	2013	2014	2015	2016	2017	2018	2019	2020	2021
Albuquerque, NM	65.9	64.4	64.3	66.9	67.0	67.9	70.0	69.5	66.5
Allentown, PA	71.5	68.2	69.2	68.9	73.1	72.1	67.8	68.8	70.4
Anchorage, AK	n/a	n/a	n/a	n/a	n/a	n/a	n/a	n/a	n/a
Ann Arbor, MI	n/a	n/a	n/a	n/a	n/a	n/a	n/a	n/a	n/a
Athens, GA	n/a	n/a	n/a	n/a	n/a	n/a	n/a	n/a	n/a
Atlanta, GA	61.6	61.6	61.7	61.5	62.4	64.0	64.2	66.4	64.2
Austin, TX	59.6	61.1	57.5	56.5	55.6	56.1	59.0	65.4	62.2
Baltimore, MD	66.0	64.1	65.3	68.5	67.5	63.5	66.5	70.7	67.5
Baton Rouge, LA	66.6	64.8	64.2	64.8	66.9	66.6	66.2	72.1	70.4
Boise City, ID	n/a	n/a	n/a	n/a	n/a	n/a	n/a	n/a	n/a
Boston, MA	66.3	62.8	59.3	58.9	58.8	61.0	60.9	61.2	60.7
Boulder, CO	n/a	n/a	n/a	n/a	n/a	n/a	n/a	n/a	n/a
Buffalo, NY	65.5	64.1	63.9	62.6	62.4	63.1	66.5	70.1	63.7
Cape Coral, FL	n/a	n/a	62.9	66.5	65.5	75.1	72.0	77.4	76.1
Cedar Rapids, IA	n/a	n/a	n/a	n/a	n/a	n/a	n/a	n/a	n/a
Charleston, SC	n/a	n/a	65.8	62.1	67.7	68.8	70.7	75.5	73.2
Charlotte, NC	58.9	58.1	62.3	66.2	64.6	67.9	72.3	73.3	70.0
Chicago, IL	68.2	66.3	64.3	64.5	64.1	64.6	63.4	66.0	67.5
Cincinnati, OH	63.3	65.5	65.9	64.9	65.7	67.3	67.4	71.1	72.1
Clarksville, TN	n/a	n/a	n/a	n/a	n/a	n/a	n/a	n/a	n/a
Cleveland, OH	65.8	69.2	68.4	64.8	66.6	66.7	64.4	66.3	64.7
College Station, TX	n/a	n/a	n/a	n/a	n/a	n/a	n/a	n/a	n/a
Colorado Springs, CO	n/a	n/a	n/a	n/a	n/a	n/a	n/a	n/a	n/a
Columbia, MO	n/a	n/a	n/a	n/a	n/a	n/a	n/a	n/a	n/a
Columbia, SC	68.9	69.5	66.1	63.9	70.7	69.3	65.9	69.7	69.4
Columbus, OH	60.5	60.0	59.0	57.5	57.9	64.8	65.7	65.6	64.6
Dallas, TX	59.9	57.7	57.8	59.7	61.8	62.0	60.6	64.7	61.8
Davenport, IA	n/a	n/a	n/a	n/a	n/a	n/a	n/a	n/a	n/a
Denver, CO	61.0	61.9	61.6	61.6	59.3	60.1	63.5	62.9	62.8
Des Moines, IA	n/a	n/a	n/a	n/a	n/a	n/a	n/a	n/a	n/a
Durham, NC	n/a	n/a	n/a	n/a	n/a	n/a	n/a	n/a	n/a
Edison, NJ	50.6	50.7	49.9	50.4	49.9	49.7	50.4	50.9	50.7
El Paso, TX	n/a	n/a	n/a	n/a	n/a	n/a	n/a	n/a	n/a
Fargo, ND	n/a	n/a	n/a	n/a	n/a	n/a	n/a	n/a	n/a
Fort Collins, CO	n/a	n/a	n/a	n/a	n/a	n/a	n/a	n/a	n/a
Fort Wayne, IN	n/a	n/a	n/a	n/a	n/a	n/a	n/a	n/a	n/a
Fort Worth, TX	59.9	57.7	57.8	59.7	61.8	62.0	60.6	64.7	61.8
Grand Rapids, MI	73.7	71.6	75.8	76.2	71.7	73.0	75.2	71.8	65.0
Green Bay, WI	n/a	n/a	n/a	n/a	n/a	n/a	n/a	n/a	n/a
Honolulu, HI	57.9	58.2	59.6	57.9	53.8	57.7	59.0	56.9	55.9
Houston, TX	60.5	60.4	60.3	59.0	58.9	60.1	61.3	65.3	64.1
Huntsville, AL	n/a	n/a	n/a	n/a	n/a	n/a	n/a	n/a	n/a
Indianapolis, IN	67.5	66.9	64.6	63.9	63.9	64.3	66.2	70.0	70.1
Jacksonville, FL	69.9	65.3	62.5	61.8	65.2	61.4	63.1	64.8	68.1
Kansas City, MO	65.6	66.1	65.0	62.4	62.4	64.3	65.0	66.7	63.8
Lafayette, LA	n/a	n/a	n/a	n/a	n/a	n/a	n/a	n/a	n/a
Las Cruces, NM	n/a	n/a	n/a	n/a	n/a	n/a	n/a	n/a	n/a
Las Vegas, NV	52.8	53.2	52.1	51.3	54.4	58.1	56.0	57.3	57.7
Lexington, KY	n/a	n/a	n/a	n/a	n/a	n/a	n/a	n/a	n/a
Lincoln, NE	n/a	n/a	n/a	n/a	n/a	n/a	n/a	n/a	n/a
Little Rock, AR	n/a	n/a	65.8	64.9	61.0	62.2	65.0	67.7	64.6
Los Angeles, CA	48.7	49.0	49.1	47.1	49.1	49.5	48.2	48.5	47.9
Louisville, KY	64.5	68.9	67.7	67.6	71.7	67.9	64.9	69.3	71.4
Madison, WI	n/a	n/a	n/a	n/a	n/a	n/a	n/a	n/a	n/a
Manchester, NH	n/a	n/a	n/a	n/a	n/a	n/a	n/a	n/a	n/a
Memphis, TN	56.2	57.2	59.6	61.8	62.4	63.5	63.7	62.5	60.7

Table continued on following page.

Metro Area	2013	2014	2015	2016	2017	2018	2019	2020	2021
Miami, FL	60.1	58.8	58.6	58.4	57.9	59.9	60.4	60.6	59.4
Midland, TX	n/a	n/a	n/a	n/a	n/a	n/a	n/a	n/a	n/a
Milwaukee, WI	60.0	55.9	57.0	60.4	63.9	62.3	56.9	58.5	56.8
Minneapolis, MN	71.7	69.7	67.9	69.1	70.1	67.8	70.2	73.0	75.0
Nashville, TN	63.9	67.1	67.4	65.0	69.4	68.3	69.8	69.8	65.7
New Haven, CT	62.0	62.4	64.6	59.4	58.7	65.0	65.1	63.4	61.0
New Orleans, LA	61.4	60.6	62.8	59.3	61.7	62.6	61.1	66.3	66.2
New York, NY	50.6	50.7	49.9	50.4	49.9	49.7	50.4	50.9	50.7
Oklahoma City, OK	67.6	65.7	61.4	63.1	64.7	64.6	64.3	68.3	61.9
Omaha, NE	70.6	68.7	69.6	69.2	65.5	67.8	66.9	68.6	68.6
Orlando, FL	65.5	62.3	58.4	58.5	59.5	58.5	56.1	64.2	63.0
Philadelphia, PA	69.1	67.0	67.0	64.7	65.6	67.4	67.4	69.2	69.8
Phoenix, AZ	62.2	61.9	61.0	62.6	64.0	65.3	65.9	67.9	65.2
Pittsburgh, PA	68.3	69.1	71.0	72.2	72.7	71.7	71.5	69.8	69.1
Portland, OR	60.9	59.8	58.9	61.8	61.1	59.2	60.0	62.5	64.1
Providence, RI	60.1	61.6	60.0	57.5	58.6	61.3	63.5	64.8	64.1
Provo, UT	n/a	n/a	n/a	n/a	n/a	n/a	n/a	n/a	n/a
Raleigh, NC	65.5	65.5	67.4	65.9	68.2	64.9	63.0	68.2	62.7
Reno, NV	n/a	n/a	n/a	n/a	n/a	n/a	n/a	n/a	n/a
Richmond, VA	65.4	72.6	67.4	61.7	63.1	62.9	66.4	66.5	64.9
Riverside, CA	56.3	56.8	61.1	62.9	59.9	62.3	64.4	65.8	62.4
Rochester, MN	n/a	n/a	n/a	n/a	n/a	n/a	n/a	n/a	n/a
Rochester, NY	69.3	68.0	64.9	58.0	63.1	62.5	65.3	67.5	69.1
Sacramento, CA	60.4	60.1	60.8	60.5	60.1	64.1	61.6	63.4	63.2
St. Louis, MO	72.7	71.1	68.7	66.4	65.6	65.8	68.1	71.1	73.8
Salt Lake City, UT	66.8	68.2	69.1	69.2	68.1	69.5	69.2	68.0	64.1
San Antonio, TX	70.1	70.2	66.0	61.6	62.5	64.4	62.6	64.2	62.7
San Diego, CA	55.0	57.4	51.8	53.3	56.0	56.1	56.7	57.8	52.6
San Francisco, CA	55.2	54.6	56.3	55.8	55.7	55.6	52.8	53.0	54.7
San Jose, CA	56.4	56.4	50.7	49.9	50.4	50.4	52.4	52.6	48.4
Santa Rosa, CA	n/a	n/a	n/a	n/a	n/a	n/a	n/a	n/a	n/a
Savannah, GA	n/a	n/a	n/a	n/a	n/a	n/a	n/a	n/a	n/a
Seattle, WA	61.0	61.3	59.5	57.7	59.5	62.5	61.5	59.4	58.0
Sioux Falls, SD	n/a	n/a	n/a	n/a	n/a	n/a	n/a	n/a	n/a
Springfield, IL	n/a	n/a	n/a	n/a	n/a	n/a	n/a	n/a	n/a
Tampa, FL	65.3	64.9	64.9	62.9	60.4	64.9	68.0	72.2	68.3
Tucson, AZ	66.1	66.7	61.4	56.0	60.1	63.8	60.1	67.1	63.5
Tulsa, OK	64.1	65.3	65.2	65.4	66.8	68.3	70.5	70.1	63.8
Tuscaloosa, AL	n/a	n/a	n/a	n/a	n/a	n/a	n/a	n/a	n/a
Virginia Beach, VA	63.3	64.1	59.4	59.6	65.3	62.8	63.0	65.8	64.4
Washington, DC	66.0	65.0	64.6	63.1	63.3	62.9	64.7	67.9	65.8
Wichita, KS	n/a	n/a	n/a	n/a	n/a	n/a	n/a	n/a	n/a
Wilmington, NC	n/a	n/a	n/a	n/a	n/a	n/a	n/a	n/a	n/a
Winston-Salem, NC	n/a	n/a	n/a	n/a	n/a	n/a	n/a	n/a	n/a
U.S.	65.1	64.5	63.7	63.4	63.9	64.4	64.6	66.6	65.5

Note: Figures are percentages and cover the Metropolitan Statistical Area; n/a not available
Source: U.S. Census Bureau, Housing Vacancies and Homeownership Annual Statistics: 2012-2021

Year Housing Structure Built: City

City	2010 or Later	2000 -2009	1990 -1999	1980 -1989	1970 -1979	1960 -1969	1950 -1959	1940 -1949	Before 1940	Median Year
Albuquerque, NM	4.8	15.7	15.4	15.2	19.3	10.1	11.8	4.5	3.0	1981
Allentown, PA	2.2	5.1	3.7	4.8	10.0	11.9	16.4	7.2	38.6	1953
Anchorage, AK	3.9	11.9	12.2	26.4	27.7	10.2	6.0	1.2	0.5	1982
Ann Arbor, MI	4.8	5.8	11.1	11.0	17.0	18.4	11.7	5.2	15.0	1970
Athens, GA	5.2	16.9	18.4	16.6	15.9	13.0	6.9	2.1	5.1	1984
Atlanta, GA	10.7	21.6	11.1	7.5	7.8	11.8	11.3	6.0	12.2	1981
Austin, TX	15.2	17.4	15.6	18.8	15.5	7.8	4.6	2.4	2.8	1989
Baltimore, MD	2.9	3.5	3.9	4.2	5.5	8.4	15.6	11.8	44.3	1945
Baton Rouge, LA	6.7	9.1	8.6	12.6	21.3	16.7	12.6	6.4	6.0	1974
Boise City, ID	7.9	10.9	23.4	15.9	17.7	7.6	6.8	3.9	6.0	1985
Boston, MA	6.0	6.1	4.4	5.7	7.7	7.6	7.4	5.7	49.3	1941
Boulder, CO	7.6	7.3	11.3	16.3	19.9	18.2	9.5	1.7	7.9	1976
Buffalo, NY	1.9	1.4	3.0	2.5	3.4	4.9	10.8	10.4	61.7	<1940
Cape Coral, FL	6.4	35.1	18.3	22.3	11.9	4.7	0.9	0.2	0.1	1995
Cedar Rapids, IA	7.0	10.9	11.5	7.7	14.8	15.1	12.3	4.1	16.6	1971
Charleston, SC	15.0	19.5	12.3	13.2	10.3	8.1	5.8	3.7	12.2	1988
Charlotte, NC	11.2	22.0	19.7	14.7	11.4	9.1	6.6	2.6	2.8	1991
Chicago, IL	3.3	7.8	5.1	4.8	7.7	9.9	12.1	9.0	40.3	1951
Cincinnati, OH	2.7	3.6	4.2	5.5	9.4	12.9	11.7	8.7	41.1	1950
Clarksville, TN	14.6	21.5	21.2	12.9	12.7	7.8	4.5	3.0	1.9	1993
Cleveland, OH	2.4	3.5	3.3	2.9	5.4	7.8	12.4	11.4	50.9	<1940
College Station, TX	19.0	21.3	20.0	17.4	15.8	3.6	2.0	0.6	0.4	1995
Colorado Springs, CO	8.2	14.9	15.6	19.1	17.7	9.5	7.3	1.9	5.7	1984
Columbia, MO	14.0	20.7	18.0	12.0	12.3	10.7	4.5	2.4	5.5	1991
Columbia, SC	7.9	15.2	11.7	9.9	9.7	10.9	14.5	10.2	10.0	1975
Columbus, OH	6.8	11.3	15.3	13.4	14.4	11.8	10.7	4.7	11.7	1978
Dallas, TX	8.6	10.5	10.8	16.8	16.8	12.9	13.4	5.1	5.2	1978
Davenport, IA	4.0	8.2	8.3	6.3	15.5	12.8	11.5	5.8	27.6	1964
Denver, CO	10.8	11.1	6.6	7.6	13.5	11.0	14.8	6.1	18.6	1970
Des Moines, IA	4.6	6.9	7.4	6.7	13.4	10.3	15.1	8.0	27.7	1959
Durham, NC	14.8	19.2	16.4	15.0	10.6	8.1	6.2	3.7	5.9	1990
Edison, NJ	1.9	4.8	9.3	23.6	12.7	19.3	18.5	4.2	5.7	1972
El Paso, TX	11.2	14.3	13.4	14.3	16.3	10.7	11.4	3.5	5.0	1982
Fargo, ND	17.8	14.0	15.4	13.8	14.6	6.4	7.4	2.7	8.0	1988
Fort Collins, CO	11.6	18.4	22.2	14.9	16.8	7.0	2.9	1.6	4.7	1991
Fort Wayne, IN	1.8	6.7	13.7	11.5	16.6	15.4	13.1	6.3	14.9	1970
Fort Worth, TX	12.6	22.5	12.1	13.7	9.4	7.9	10.8	5.1	5.9	1988
Grand Rapids, MI	3.0	4.4	6.4	7.2	8.6	9.5	14.9	9.3	36.6	1953
Green Bay, WI	1.9	6.8	10.8	12.3	18.0	13.0	15.3	6.3	15.5	1970
Honolulu, HI	5.0	6.7	8.2	10.1	25.5	21.6	12.2	5.5	5.1	1972
Houston, TX	10.3	12.8	10.2	14.4	20.4	13.0	10.3	4.4	4.2	1979
Huntsville, AL	13.1	11.8	11.1	16.2	12.9	21.0	9.0	2.3	2.6	1981
Indianapolis, IN	4.2	9.0	12.8	11.8	13.1	13.6	12.7	6.3	16.4	1971
Jacksonville, FL	7.5	18.3	15.4	15.5	12.5	10.0	10.9	4.7	5.1	1984
Kansas City, MO	5.6	9.6	9.2	8.7	12.0	12.8	14.0	6.2	21.8	1966
Lafayette, LA	8.5	12.2	9.7	18.8	21.6	14.0	8.6	3.7	2.8	1980
Las Cruces, NM	10.2	20.0	14.7	17.8	14.9	8.2	9.6	2.2	2.3	1987
Las Vegas, NV	6.0	21.9	32.2	16.3	10.0	7.5	4.3	1.3	0.5	1993
Lexington, KY	7.3	14.5	16.1	13.3	15.3	13.7	9.5	3.3	7.0	1981
Lincoln, NE	9.2	13.1	14.9	10.2	15.3	9.8	10.7	3.2	13.6	1978
Little Rock, AR	7.1	11.0	12.7	14.2	19.3	14.1	9.1	5.1	7.3	1977
Los Angeles, CA	4.0	5.4	6.0	10.6	13.7	13.9	17.1	9.5	19.8	1963
Louisville, KY	5.4	11.0	11.5	7.1	12.6	13.9	14.7	6.9	17.0	1968
Madison, WI	8.4	14.3	13.0	10.0	13.5	11.8	10.1	4.8	14.1	1977
Manchester, NH	2.5	6.3	8.3	15.5	11.9	7.1	10.4	7.4	30.5	1962

Table continued on following page.

City	2010 or Later	2000 -2009	1990 -1999	1980 -1989	1970 -1979	1960 -1969	1950 -1959	1940 -1949	Before 1940	Median Year
Memphis, TN	2.6	6.5	10.1	12.2	17.9	14.4	19.2	9.4	7.7	1970
Miami, FL	9.5	18.0	6.3	7.8	13.4	10.5	14.7	10.6	9.2	1974
Midland, TX	15.9	8.4	14.3	17.7	11.6	10.5	18.1	2.4	1.1	1984
Milwaukee, WI	2.0	3.2	3.2	4.1	8.5	11.3	19.9	10.2	37.5	1951
Minneapolis, MN	6.5	6.5	4.1	6.7	8.8	7.5	9.2	7.0	43.8	1949
Nashville, TN	11.7	14.3	12.3	14.9	14.1	11.8	10.3	4.2	6.3	1982
New Haven, CT	3.6	4.8	3.0	7.1	9.0	11.0	9.5	6.9	45.2	1947
New Orleans, LA	3.7	6.6	3.3	7.3	14.1	11.3	12.2	7.4	34.1	1957
New York, NY	3.5	5.5	3.9	4.8	7.0	12.6	12.9	9.7	40.2	1950
Oklahoma City, OK	10.4	12.7	9.6	14.8	15.9	12.1	10.5	5.6	8.5	1978
Omaha, NE	4.0	7.4	12.9	11.2	15.3	14.7	11.1	4.5	18.9	1971
Orlando, FL	12.2	20.8	15.6	15.5	14.3	7.4	8.3	3.0	3.0	1989
Philadelphia, PA	3.2	2.9	3.3	3.8	7.2	11.0	16.0	11.2	41.3	1948
Phoenix, AZ	5.3	16.3	16.2	17.3	19.6	11.5	9.6	2.4	1.9	1983
Pittsburgh, PA	3.1	2.8	3.6	4.6	6.6	8.9	13.2	8.7	48.5	1942
Portland, OR	7.5	10.1	8.5	6.7	10.7	8.8	11.5	8.1	28.1	1963
Providence, RI	0.7	4.7	4.5	5.1	8.6	6.2	7.7	6.1	56.4	<1940
Provo, UT	6.1	10.9	19.9	14.6	18.3	10.2	7.7	5.0	7.3	1981
Raleigh, NC	13.4	23.9	18.8	16.8	10.2	7.8	4.2	1.9	3.1	1993
Reno, NV	8.8	19.7	18.2	13.4	18.2	9.0	6.4	2.9	3.4	1988
Richmond, VA	5.7	5.3	5.1	7.1	10.5	12.2	14.8	8.8	30.5	1957
Riverside, CA	3.2	12.4	10.7	16.5	17.8	11.6	16.3	4.4	7.1	1976
Rochester, MN	10.3	18.2	14.7	13.1	12.4	10.6	9.3	3.6	7.7	1985
Rochester, NY	1.7	1.6	3.4	4.9	7.8	8.0	10.1	8.4	54.2	<1940
Sacramento, CA	3.3	14.9	9.1	15.5	14.3	11.7	12.4	7.4	11.4	1975
St. Louis, MO	1.9	4.2	3.0	3.1	4.1	6.6	10.5	8.3	58.2	<1940
Salt Lake City, UT	6.7	6.8	6.4	8.2	11.7	9.9	13.2	8.9	28.2	1960
San Antonio, TX	8.6	15.2	13.5	16.3	14.8	10.3	10.2	5.6	5.4	1982
San Diego, CA	4.8	10.1	11.4	17.5	20.9	12.7	11.8	4.1	6.6	1977
San Francisco, CA	4.7	6.3	4.2	5.3	7.3	8.2	8.5	9.0	46.4	1944
San Jose, CA	5.6	9.2	10.4	12.8	24.4	18.3	11.2	2.8	5.3	1975
Santa Rosa, CA	3.2	13.1	13.3	18.7	20.7	12.9	7.7	4.6	5.8	1979
Savannah, GA	7.6	10.2	6.6	10.7	12.1	12.7	14.7	8.2	17.1	1968
Seattle, WA	12.9	12.1	8.7	7.5	8.1	8.7	9.3	8.1	24.6	1969
Sioux Falls, SD	14.8	17.9	15.0	9.9	13.5	7.5	9.1	3.2	9.1	1988
Springfield, IL	2.5	9.0	13.8	8.9	16.5	12.3	11.4	6.6	19.1	1970
Tampa, FL	9.3	17.4	12.6	12.3	11.9	9.5	13.3	4.8	8.9	1981
Tucson, AZ	2.8	12.7	13.5	17.2	20.6	11.3	14.0	4.3	3.4	1978
Tulsa, OK	4.0	6.1	9.5	13.5	20.6	14.6	16.4	6.5	8.6	1972
Tuscaloosa, AL	14.7	16.6	15.4	11.2	15.7	10.2	8.1	4.2	3.9	1987
Virginia Beach, VA	5.4	11.1	13.7	27.5	21.4	12.5	6.1	1.2	1.2	1983
Washington, DC	9.1	8.2	3.3	4.5	6.9	11.0	12.1	11.3	33.6	1954
Wichita, KS	5.3	9.7	12.7	12.3	12.9	9.6	19.8	7.5	10.2	1972
Wilmington, NC	9.0	13.7	19.2	15.9	14.0	6.9	6.6	5.4	9.3	1985
Winston-Salem, NC	5.4	13.8	12.5	14.4	16.2	12.3	12.9	5.3	7.2	1978
U.S.	6.2	13.6	13.9	13.4	15.0	10.5	10.2	4.8	12.4	1978

Note: Figures are percentages except for Median Year
Source: U.S. Census Bureau, 2016-2020 American Community Survey 5-Year Estimates

Year Housing Structure Built: Metro Area

Metro Area	2010 or Later	2000 -2009	1990 -1999	1980 -1989	1970 -1979	1960 -1969	1950 -1959	1940 -1949	Before 1940	Median Year
Albuquerque, NM	4.9	16.9	18.1	16.8	18.0	9.0	9.3	3.8	3.2	1984
Allentown, PA	3.7	11.7	10.6	10.9	11.8	9.6	11.2	5.1	25.4	1969
Anchorage, AK	5.1	16.7	13.5	25.6	24.0	8.6	4.9	1.0	0.5	1984
Ann Arbor, MI	4.4	13.3	17.4	11.2	15.8	12.2	9.7	4.4	11.5	1978
Athens, GA	6.0	17.6	20.8	17.7	15.1	10.2	5.5	1.8	5.0	1987
Atlanta, GA	7.9	23.8	21.4	17.4	12.7	7.4	4.6	1.9	2.9	1991
Austin, TX	19.5	23.5	17.5	16.0	11.2	5.1	3.1	1.7	2.3	1996
Baltimore, MD	5.4	9.3	13.5	13.5	13.0	10.4	12.8	6.2	15.9	1974
Baton Rouge, LA	11.5	18.7	14.8	15.3	16.7	9.7	6.6	2.8	3.8	1987
Boise City, ID	12.6	23.6	21.3	10.2	14.9	5.1	4.4	2.8	5.0	1994
Boston, MA	4.9	7.5	7.5	10.5	11.0	10.2	10.8	5.1	32.6	1962
Boulder, CO	8.0	11.8	19.6	16.3	20.0	11.2	5.1	1.4	6.6	1984
Buffalo, NY	3.0	4.6	7.1	6.6	10.2	11.1	18.0	8.9	30.4	1956
Cape Coral, FL	7.2	30.0	18.1	21.3	14.8	5.2	2.4	0.4	0.6	1993
Cedar Rapids, IA	7.6	13.6	13.5	7.5	13.6	12.5	10.2	3.6	18.0	1974
Charleston, SC	13.7	20.8	16.3	15.9	14.1	8.0	5.2	2.4	3.6	1990
Charlotte, NC	11.4	22.9	19.6	13.2	11.2	8.1	6.4	3.0	4.1	1992
Chicago, IL	2.9	11.3	11.4	9.1	14.2	11.7	13.0	5.9	20.5	1969
Cincinnati, OH	4.4	12.1	14.1	10.7	13.9	10.7	11.8	5.0	17.4	1974
Clarksville, TN	12.5	19.2	21.1	12.1	15.0	8.5	6.1	2.6	2.9	1991
Cleveland, OH	2.8	6.8	8.8	6.8	12.4	13.4	17.8	7.7	23.4	1961
College Station, TX	14.5	19.2	18.2	17.7	15.3	5.9	4.8	2.1	2.2	1991
Colorado Springs, CO	9.2	18.0	16.7	17.9	16.6	8.2	6.5	1.6	5.3	1987
Columbia, MO	10.5	18.7	17.9	13.1	14.9	10.0	4.8	2.7	7.4	1988
Columbia, SC	9.9	19.0	18.9	13.7	15.3	9.4	7.0	3.1	3.6	1988
Columbus, OH	6.8	14.2	16.3	11.7	14.0	10.9	10.0	3.9	12.3	1979
Dallas, TX	12.0	19.4	16.1	17.7	13.7	8.5	7.4	2.6	2.7	1989
Davenport, IA	4.0	7.5	8.5	6.7	16.4	13.0	12.1	7.1	24.7	1965
Denver, CO	9.0	16.2	15.4	14.1	17.9	9.2	9.1	2.7	6.5	1983
Des Moines, IA	12.6	16.1	12.9	8.3	13.3	8.3	9.0	4.1	15.3	1980
Durham, NC	11.5	18.8	18.4	15.8	12.1	8.6	6.4	3.0	5.4	1989
Edison, NJ	3.5	6.5	6.2	7.8	9.7	13.6	15.7	8.6	28.3	1958
El Paso, TX	12.5	15.7	14.4	14.8	15.5	9.5	9.9	3.2	4.5	1985
Fargo, ND	16.6	17.2	13.7	11.1	15.1	7.2	7.5	2.7	8.9	1988
Fort Collins, CO	11.9	18.7	20.3	12.8	18.4	7.0	3.5	1.8	5.6	1990
Fort Wayne, IN	4.3	11.1	14.6	10.7	15.0	13.1	11.5	5.3	14.3	1974
Fort Worth, TX	12.0	19.4	16.1	17.7	13.7	8.5	7.4	2.6	2.7	1989
Grand Rapids, MI	5.6	12.4	16.0	11.9	14.0	9.3	10.1	5.2	15.4	1977
Green Bay, WI	6.3	13.9	16.6	12.1	14.9	9.7	9.6	4.3	12.6	1979
Honolulu, HI	6.0	9.7	11.5	12.6	24.2	18.4	10.4	4.0	3.3	1976
Houston, TX	13.9	20.7	14.3	15.4	16.4	8.2	6.1	2.5	2.4	1989
Huntsville, AL	12.9	18.2	17.4	16.8	11.1	13.5	6.1	1.7	2.2	1989
Indianapolis, IN	7.7	15.0	16.6	10.5	12.2	10.9	10.1	4.5	12.6	1980
Jacksonville, FL	9.9	21.7	16.5	16.5	12.3	7.9	7.8	3.3	4.1	1989
Kansas City, MO	5.9	13.3	14.3	12.1	15.1	11.8	11.2	4.4	11.8	1977
Lafayette, LA	11.2	15.9	12.5	15.7	15.6	11.0	9.2	3.9	4.9	1983
Las Cruces, NM	9.6	17.5	19.9	19.1	14.7	7.4	6.7	2.2	2.8	1988
Las Vegas, NV	8.6	29.0	28.8	14.6	10.6	5.0	2.2	0.7	0.4	1996
Lexington, KY	7.6	16.5	17.1	13.7	15.0	11.4	7.9	3.3	7.6	1984
Lincoln, NE	9.1	13.4	14.9	9.9	15.6	9.9	9.9	3.0	14.2	1978
Little Rock, AR	10.9	17.0	17.0	14.1	16.7	10.3	7.0	3.3	3.7	1986
Los Angeles, CA	3.6	5.9	7.7	12.4	16.1	15.8	18.5	8.2	11.8	1967
Louisville, KY	5.5	12.9	14.1	9.3	15.0	12.3	12.4	5.8	12.6	1975
Madison, WI	7.7	15.8	16.4	10.6	14.4	9.8	7.6	3.6	14.1	1981
Manchester, NH	3.7	9.8	10.8	20.3	15.7	9.4	7.0	4.0	19.3	1977

Table continued on following page.

Metro Area	2010 or Later	2000 -2009	1990 -1999	1980 -1989	1970 -1979	1960 -1969	1950 -1959	1940 -1949	Before 1940	Median Year
Memphis, TN	5.3	14.9	17.2	13.5	16.0	10.7	11.8	5.7	4.9	1981
Miami, FL	5.0	12.8	15.1	19.2	21.2	12.1	9.8	2.7	2.1	1981
Midland, TX	17.3	10.9	14.9	17.5	11.0	9.5	15.2	2.4	1.4	1986
Milwaukee, WI	3.5	8.3	10.9	8.0	12.7	11.5	16.0	6.7	22.5	1964
Minneapolis, MN	6.1	13.8	14.3	14.3	14.5	9.7	9.5	3.8	13.9	1979
Nashville, TN	13.1	19.0	17.5	14.1	13.0	9.0	6.8	2.9	4.6	1990
New Haven, CT	2.1	5.8	7.3	12.3	13.5	12.4	14.9	7.3	24.3	1963
New Orleans, LA	4.4	11.8	10.2	13.0	18.9	13.6	10.1	4.5	13.4	1974
New York, NY	3.5	6.5	6.2	7.8	9.7	13.6	15.7	8.6	28.3	1958
Oklahoma City, OK	10.5	14.6	11.0	14.8	17.0	11.7	9.5	4.8	6.1	1981
Omaha, NE	7.8	14.1	12.9	10.1	14.2	11.9	8.6	3.6	16.8	1976
Orlando, FL	11.0	22.6	20.4	19.5	12.7	6.0	5.1	1.2	1.5	1992
Philadelphia, PA	3.7	7.9	9.7	9.7	12.1	12.1	15.4	7.3	22.0	1964
Phoenix, AZ	8.1	24.7	20.0	17.1	15.9	7.2	4.8	1.2	0.9	1991
Pittsburgh, PA	3.4	6.2	7.6	7.7	11.8	11.5	16.5	8.8	26.3	1959
Portland, OR	7.9	14.0	18.1	11.4	16.9	8.3	7.0	4.6	11.9	1981
Providence, RI	2.2	6.3	8.2	11.1	12.3	11.0	11.6	6.2	31.1	1961
Provo, UT	16.8	24.6	18.8	8.9	13.3	5.0	5.1	3.0	4.3	1995
Raleigh, NC	15.5	24.6	22.7	14.8	9.1	5.7	3.5	1.5	2.8	1996
Reno, NV	7.6	20.9	19.5	14.8	18.9	8.8	5.0	2.1	2.5	1989
Richmond, VA	7.3	14.6	15.4	15.8	14.9	9.6	9.1	4.2	9.0	1982
Riverside, CA	5.2	20.2	14.6	21.5	15.6	8.9	8.5	2.7	2.8	1985
Rochester, MN	8.2	18.4	14.6	11.2	13.1	9.4	7.8	3.5	13.8	1982
Rochester, NY	3.6	6.8	9.6	10.9	12.7	12.3	11.3	5.3	27.5	1965
Sacramento, CA	4.4	17.1	15.3	16.7	18.2	10.7	9.8	3.5	4.3	1982
St. Louis, MO	4.5	11.4	12.2	11.1	13.1	12.8	12.7	5.6	16.6	1972
Salt Lake City, UT	11.1	14.8	15.4	12.1	18.0	8.9	8.6	3.5	7.7	1983
San Antonio, TX	13.3	19.2	14.5	15.1	13.1	8.4	7.7	4.1	4.5	1988
San Diego, CA	4.4	11.6	12.5	18.6	22.5	12.0	10.7	3.4	4.2	1979
San Francisco, CA	3.9	7.6	8.3	11.1	14.8	13.4	13.6	7.7	19.7	1967
San Jose, CA	6.5	8.8	10.4	12.3	21.6	17.9	14.0	3.5	5.1	1974
Santa Rosa, CA	3.1	10.8	14.1	18.1	20.3	11.8	8.7	4.8	8.3	1978
Savannah, GA	10.9	21.1	15.4	12.8	11.6	7.9	8.1	4.3	8.0	1988
Seattle, WA	9.3	14.7	15.5	14.1	13.8	10.9	7.3	4.3	10.0	1983
Sioux Falls, SD	13.2	18.2	15.3	8.8	13.8	7.0	8.0	3.3	12.4	1986
Springfield, IL	3.6	10.2	13.7	8.9	16.4	11.6	11.5	6.4	17.5	1972
Tampa, FL	6.9	16.0	14.3	19.8	20.5	9.3	8.5	2.0	2.7	1984
Tucson, AZ	5.4	18.0	17.8	17.8	19.4	8.6	8.3	2.6	2.1	1985
Tulsa, OK	8.0	14.1	12.5	14.3	18.9	10.7	10.4	4.4	6.7	1979
Tuscaloosa, AL	10.7	18.3	19.3	13.3	15.0	9.7	6.7	3.3	3.7	1989
Virginia Beach, VA	6.9	12.6	15.3	18.7	15.6	11.6	9.5	4.1	5.7	1982
Washington, DC	7.8	14.3	14.4	15.6	13.9	11.9	9.1	4.9	8.2	1981
Wichita, KS	5.7	11.3	14.0	12.4	13.2	8.8	17.6	6.2	10.8	1975
Wilmington, NC	10.3	19.9	22.1	15.8	13.0	5.6	4.7	3.4	5.3	1991
Winston-Salem, NC	5.6	15.1	16.8	15.3	16.7	10.5	9.4	4.3	6.3	1982
U.S.	6.2	13.6	13.9	13.4	15.0	10.5	10.2	4.8	12.4	1978

Note: Figures are percentages except for Median Year; Figures cover the Metropolitan Statistical Area
Source: U.S. Census Bureau, 2016-2020 American Community Survey 5-Year Estimates

Gross Monthly Rent: City

City	Under $500	$500 -$999	$1,000 -$1,499	$1,500 -$1,999	$2,000 -$2,499	$2,500 -$2,999	$3,000 and up	Median ($)
Albuquerque, NM	8.5	52.7	30.1	6.9	1.0	0.3	0.4	889
Allentown, PA	8.8	37.4	41.3	10.9	1.2	0.2	0.2	1,035
Anchorage, AK	4.4	21.8	37.4	19.5	11.8	3.4	1.6	1,310
Ann Arbor, MI	4.2	19.7	38.5	24.1	6.9	2.8	3.8	1,299
Athens, GA	7.3	57.5	26.0	6.4	1.8	0.9	0.2	871
Atlanta, GA	10.9	22.9	33.5	21.3	7.5	2.1	1.8	1,227
Austin, TX	3.0	15.1	44.7	24.2	8.5	2.6	1.9	1,346
Baltimore, MD	15.6	26.6	35.7	15.1	4.4	1.6	0.9	1,094
Baton Rouge, LA	9.1	56.4	26.1	5.4	2.3	0.3	0.4	886
Boise City, ID	4.3	44.8	38.0	10.2	1.4	0.6	0.7	1,009
Boston, MA	15.4	11.0	15.6	21.7	16.5	9.0	10.7	1,685
Boulder, CO	2.8	8.2	34.4	26.5	14.2	6.2	7.8	1,588
Buffalo, NY	15.7	58.1	21.4	3.3	0.8	0.3	0.3	801
Cape Coral, FL	0.9	19.0	42.0	30.3	4.9	0.9	2.0	1,367
Cedar Rapids, IA	14.4	60.2	20.9	2.2	0.7	0.2	1.2	791
Charleston, SC	5.8	17.3	42.4	23.8	6.1	1.7	2.9	1,318
Charlotte, NC	3.4	26.0	48.7	16.2	3.5	1.1	1.1	1,185
Chicago, IL	9.1	29.3	31.7	16.3	7.7	3.4	2.4	1,154
Cincinnati, OH	18.3	54.9	18.9	5.4	1.4	0.6	0.6	760
Clarksville, TN	5.5	48.8	35.2	8.6	1.7	0.1	0.1	963
Cleveland, OH	21.3	56.7	16.8	3.3	1.1	0.5	0.2	735
College Station, TX	2.6	47.4	29.7	13.8	4.6	1.3	0.6	1,001
Colorado Springs, CO	3.5	28.9	40.0	19.8	4.7	2.3	0.9	1,196
Columbia, MO	5.0	58.8	26.4	6.5	2.9	0.3	0.2	890
Columbia, SC	10.8	44.7	32.7	9.6	1.8	0.2	0.2	956
Columbus, OH	6.2	45.2	38.6	7.6	1.7	0.4	0.4	989
Dallas, TX	3.7	35.7	40.0	13.4	4.2	1.6	1.4	1,111
Davenport, IA	8.8	66.1	18.8	4.0	0.7	0.7	0.9	786
Denver, CO	7.6	14.4	35.3	25.9	11.2	3.7	1.9	1,397
Des Moines, IA	8.9	57.0	26.9	5.7	1.0	0.3	0.2	881
Durham, NC	6.4	33.3	43.1	13.5	2.5	0.3	0.8	1,098
Edison, NJ	3.5	4.3	35.9	36.0	16.2	2.8	1.1	1,587
El Paso, TX	14.4	52.6	26.2	5.8	0.5	0.3	0.2	857
Fargo, ND	6.7	67.6	19.1	4.9	1.3	0.3	0.2	821
Fort Collins, CO	2.9	19.2	37.8	28.5	9.0	1.5	1.0	1,373
Fort Wayne, IN	11.3	68.8	17.3	1.7	0.6	0.2	0.1	777
Fort Worth, TX	4.2	35.1	37.6	17.1	4.0	1.1	1.0	1,115
Grand Rapids, MI	9.9	46.1	33.1	6.7	3.5	0.5	0.2	947
Green Bay, WI	10.9	70.4	17.3	1.0	0.2	0.1	0.2	768
Honolulu, HI	7.3	11.6	30.2	22.4	12.2	6.8	9.4	1,520
Houston, TX	3.7	38.5	37.3	13.9	3.5	1.5	1.5	1,086
Huntsville, AL	8.4	57.0	28.9	4.4	0.4	0.3	0.5	868
Indianapolis, IN	6.2	56.7	29.0	6.2	1.3	0.2	0.3	911
Jacksonville, FL	6.0	34.5	43.4	12.8	2.6	0.3	0.4	1,089
Kansas City, MO	8.3	43.9	35.7	9.2	1.7	0.6	0.5	979
Lafayette, LA	7.9	54.8	29.8	6.1	0.9	0.3	0.1	899
Las Cruces, NM	13.6	58.4	24.0	2.9	1.0	0.0	0.2	805
Las Vegas, NV	4.5	31.1	43.1	16.0	3.7	0.9	0.7	1,153
Lexington, KY	7.6	51.7	31.4	6.3	2.4	0.3	0.3	920
Lincoln, NE	8.3	56.6	27.2	5.5	1.2	0.2	1.1	871
Little Rock, AR	8.2	55.1	29.8	4.6	1.1	0.6	0.6	889
Los Angeles, CA	5.2	13.8	30.0	23.6	13.4	7.0	7.1	1,523
Louisville, KY	13.0	51.7	28.6	5.3	0.7	0.3	0.4	878
Madison, WI	3.8	30.7	44.3	14.0	4.6	1.5	1.1	1,147
Manchester, NH	7.1	26.9	44.8	16.5	3.2	1.1	0.4	1,160

Table continued on following page.

City	Under $500	$500 -$999	$1,000 -$1,499	$1,500 -$1,999	$2,000 -$2,499	$2,500 -$2,999	$3,000 and up	Median ($)
Memphis, TN	7.2	53.8	31.8	5.9	0.9	0.2	0.2	915
Miami, FL	10.0	23.1	31.2	18.0	9.9	3.9	3.9	1,242
Midland, TX	2.0	25.5	42.5	19.3	7.4	2.5	0.7	1,256
Milwaukee, WI	8.4	59.9	25.1	4.7	1.3	0.4	0.3	866
Minneapolis, MN	12.0	32.5	31.0	16.0	5.5	1.6	1.4	1,078
Nashville, TN	7.9	26.1	41.2	17.0	5.1	1.4	1.3	1,170
New Haven, CT	13.5	16.8	42.0	19.9	5.6	1.3	0.8	1,219
New Orleans, LA	11.5	36.3	34.5	12.0	4.3	0.7	0.6	1,025
New York, NY	10.1	13.9	26.6	22.5	11.9	5.9	9.1	1,489
Oklahoma City, OK	7.5	56.2	28.2	6.1	1.3	0.3	0.4	884
Omaha, NE	6.6	50.2	33.3	7.8	1.2	0.3	0.7	948
Orlando, FL	3.8	20.1	48.4	20.9	4.8	1.3	0.7	1,253
Philadelphia, PA	9.9	32.9	36.5	12.8	4.8	1.6	1.4	1,084
Phoenix, AZ	4.3	35.7	42.0	14.0	2.8	0.7	0.5	1,100
Pittsburgh, PA	13.1	38.5	29.6	12.2	4.3	1.6	0.7	984
Portland, OR	6.1	18.0	38.5	23.2	9.1	3.3	1.8	1,325
Providence, RI	19.0	29.6	35.0	11.1	3.1	1.0	1.1	1,015
Provo, UT	11.7	49.5	24.9	10.3	3.0	0.3	0.3	901
Raleigh, NC	3.2	26.9	49.9	15.8	2.8	0.7	0.8	1,175
Reno, NV	6.0	35.5	35.8	17.0	4.4	0.5	0.7	1,107
Richmond, VA	11.5	31.3	39.2	14.2	2.8	0.3	0.6	1,070
Riverside, CA	3.0	13.2	36.1	31.0	13.0	2.2	1.5	1,466
Rochester, MN	8.2	39.1	31.8	15.0	1.8	1.0	3.2	1,044
Rochester, NY	12.3	52.3	28.2	5.1	1.4	0.4	0.3	875
Sacramento, CA	5.8	20.7	36.4	26.7	8.0	1.7	0.8	1,328
St. Louis, MO	11.3	56.6	25.3	5.0	1.4	0.3	0.1	840
Salt Lake City, UT	8.4	37.6	34.6	14.6	3.4	0.8	0.6	1,050
San Antonio, TX	6.9	40.7	38.2	10.8	2.1	0.7	0.6	1,025
San Diego, CA	3.0	8.0	23.8	28.0	19.3	10.1	7.7	1,770
San Francisco, CA	9.1	11.4	14.6	14.7	13.2	11.8	25.2	2,010
San Jose, CA	4.1	6.2	11.5	19.2	19.7	17.8	21.6	2,232
Santa Rosa, CA	6.1	5.3	26.0	27.6	19.5	9.8	5.6	1,728
Savannah, GA	9.0	36.0	40.8	11.4	1.7	0.3	0.8	1,049
Seattle, WA	5.7	8.1	24.9	28.0	17.7	7.9	7.7	1,702
Sioux Falls, SD	7.6	65.5	20.7	4.4	0.6	0.4	0.8	838
Springfield, IL	12.3	61.6	20.4	3.7	0.8	1.0	0.2	820
Tampa, FL	7.5	26.6	38.6	17.6	6.0	2.0	1.6	1,178
Tucson, AZ	7.2	56.9	27.9	6.1	0.9	0.5	0.6	861
Tulsa, OK	9.8	59.2	25.3	3.6	1.1	0.4	0.6	839
Tuscaloosa, AL	12.4	56.3	23.0	5.0	1.6	0.7	0.9	858
Virginia Beach, VA	3.0	11.5	46.7	28.5	6.9	2.0	1.3	1,380
Washington, DC	10.1	12.2	23.2	21.1	14.6	8.6	10.3	1,607
Wichita, KS	10.3	61.9	22.5	4.0	0.5	0.2	0.5	821
Wilmington, NC	11.3	38.0	36.9	10.6	2.0	0.5	0.7	1,008
Winston-Salem, NC	10.2	60.0	24.4	3.9	0.9	0.2	0.4	827
U.S.	8.9	34.3	30.2	14.9	6.2	2.6	2.8	1,096

Note: Figures are percentages except for Median; Gross rent is the contract rent plus the estimated average monthly cost of utilities (electricity, gas, and water and sewer) and fuels (oil, coal, kerosene, wood, etc.) if these are paid by the renter (or paid for the renter by someone else).
Source: U.S. Census Bureau, 2016-2020 American Community Survey 5-Year Estimates

Gross Monthly Rent: Metro Area

MSA[1]	Under $500	$500 -$999	$1,000 -$1,499	$1,500 -$1,999	$2,000 -$2,499	$2,500 -2,999	$3,000 and up	Median ($)
Albuquerque, NM	8.5	50.9	31.2	7.7	1.1	0.3	0.4	908
Allentown, PA	9.4	32.1	39.2	14.8	2.8	0.8	0.9	1,090
Anchorage, AK	4.9	23.3	37.2	19.4	10.8	3.0	1.4	1,277
Ann Arbor, MI	5.7	28.6	39.5	17.2	4.5	1.6	2.8	1,161
Athens, GA	7.6	57.5	25.1	6.8	1.7	1.0	0.3	869
Atlanta, GA	4.5	24.7	45.7	18.8	4.3	1.0	1.0	1,205
Austin, TX	3.0	16.6	44.6	23.8	7.9	2.4	1.7	1,326
Baltimore, MD	8.9	17.3	36.1	24.3	9.1	2.7	1.6	1,324
Baton Rouge, LA	8.2	50.9	30.4	7.2	2.6	0.3	0.4	930
Boise City, ID	7.4	42.1	37.2	10.7	1.6	0.5	0.5	1,005
Boston, MA	11.6	12.3	23.4	23.9	14.8	7.2	6.7	1,555
Boulder, CO	3.7	9.5	32.0	29.2	13.7	5.7	6.1	1,582
Buffalo, NY	13.6	57.2	22.4	4.5	1.2	0.5	0.6	831
Cape Coral, FL	4.0	25.0	44.3	17.6	5.1	1.7	2.2	1,225
Cedar Rapids, IA	15.1	60.6	19.6	2.6	0.6	0.3	1.2	768
Charleston, SC	4.9	26.8	42.3	17.9	4.8	1.5	1.8	1,197
Charlotte, NC	5.4	37.5	40.2	12.4	2.8	1.0	0.8	1,073
Chicago, IL	7.3	29.7	35.1	16.9	6.6	2.4	2.0	1,155
Cincinnati, OH	11.8	53.2	25.9	6.4	1.6	0.5	0.7	859
Clarksville, TN	8.4	50.4	32.4	7.4	1.3	0.1	0.0	920
Cleveland, OH	12.4	56.4	24.2	4.7	1.2	0.4	0.6	837
College Station, TX	5.9	49.4	28.5	10.6	3.7	1.1	0.8	954
Colorado Springs, CO	3.5	27.4	37.6	23.6	5.1	2.1	0.8	1,232
Columbia, MO	6.9	59.2	25.8	5.3	2.4	0.3	0.2	875
Columbia, SC	7.2	48.1	33.4	8.7	1.7	0.4	0.5	955
Columbus, OH	7.2	45.3	36.6	8.0	2.0	0.5	0.4	981
Dallas, TX	3.0	28.7	41.8	18.1	5.7	1.6	1.2	1,188
Davenport, IA	14.3	61.4	18.0	4.1	0.8	0.5	0.8	773
Denver, CO	4.8	13.2	36.2	29.0	11.5	3.5	1.8	1,446
Des Moines, IA	7.2	50.8	32.3	7.1	1.7	0.3	0.7	935
Durham, NC	6.8	36.4	40.1	12.2	3.0	0.4	1.0	1,068
Edison, NJ	8.9	13.0	29.1	23.8	11.8	5.7	7.7	1,483
El Paso, TX	14.2	52.9	25.9	6.1	0.5	0.2	0.2	855
Fargo, ND	7.4	63.2	20.8	6.6	1.4	0.3	0.3	835
Fort Collins, CO	3.9	21.1	36.3	27.3	8.0	2.2	1.2	1,340
Fort Wayne, IN	10.8	67.7	18.3	2.4	0.6	0.1	0.1	788
Fort Worth, TX	3.0	28.7	41.8	18.1	5.7	1.6	1.2	1,188
Grand Rapids, MI	8.5	52.6	29.6	5.9	2.3	0.7	0.4	910
Green Bay, WI	8.8	69.2	19.0	2.0	0.4	0.1	0.5	807
Honolulu, HI	5.7	9.6	23.4	20.1	14.8	10.8	15.5	1,779
Houston, TX	3.7	33.6	38.6	16.8	4.6	1.4	1.3	1,136
Huntsville, AL	8.8	57.2	27.4	5.1	0.6	0.4	0.5	869
Indianapolis, IN	6.1	52.5	31.4	7.6	1.6	0.3	0.5	936
Jacksonville, FL	5.5	33.0	42.1	14.3	3.6	0.8	0.7	1,113
Kansas City, MO	7.4	43.9	35.8	9.3	2.3	0.6	0.7	989
Lafayette, LA	14.7	58.1	21.5	3.9	0.9	0.1	0.8	823
Las Cruces, NM	16.3	58.2	20.6	3.5	1.2	0.1	0.1	765
Las Vegas, NV	2.7	30.0	43.0	18.5	4.1	0.9	0.7	1,181
Lexington, KY	9.0	54.4	28.8	5.5	1.8	0.2	0.3	887
Lincoln, NE	8.7	56.1	27.3	5.3	1.3	0.2	1.1	870
Little Rock, AR	9.2	59.7	25.4	4.2	0.8	0.4	0.3	853
Los Angeles, CA	4.1	11.0	28.3	26.3	15.4	7.6	7.3	1,624
Louisville, KY	12.4	51.9	29.2	5.0	0.8	0.3	0.5	882
Madison, WI	4.9	37.1	40.6	12.4	3.2	1.0	0.8	1,080
Manchester, NH	7.0	22.9	42.5	20.5	4.7	1.5	0.8	1,217

Table continued on following page.

MSA[1]	Under $500	$500 -$999	$1,000 -$1,499	$1,500 -$1,999	$2,000 -$2,499	$2,500 -2,999	$3,000 and up	Median ($)
Memphis, TN	7.0	50.0	33.3	7.5	1.5	0.3	0.3	944
Miami, FL	5.0	14.8	37.3	26.0	10.4	3.9	2.7	1,408
Midland, TX	3.1	25.9	41.4	19.0	7.3	2.6	0.6	1,239
Milwaukee, WI	7.1	53.2	29.9	7.1	1.7	0.6	0.4	917
Minneapolis, MN	8.7	29.2	36.8	17.9	4.8	1.4	1.3	1,144
Nashville, TN	7.2	30.4	39.1	16.6	4.2	1.3	1.1	1,135
New Haven, CT	10.6	23.1	41.3	18.3	4.5	1.0	1.2	1,173
New Orleans, LA	8.5	39.8	37.0	10.5	2.9	0.5	0.8	1,017
New York, NY	8.9	13.0	29.1	23.8	11.8	5.7	7.7	1,483
Oklahoma City, OK	8.2	54.9	28.8	6.1	1.3	0.3	0.5	887
Omaha, NE	7.3	49.0	33.0	8.1	1.4	0.4	0.8	952
Orlando, FL	2.7	21.1	45.7	22.8	5.4	1.3	1.0	1,273
Philadelphia, PA	7.6	26.7	39.6	16.8	5.7	2.0	1.6	1,172
Phoenix, AZ	3.4	29.6	41.8	18.2	4.5	1.2	1.3	1,177
Pittsburgh, PA	14.8	50.7	24.2	6.6	2.1	0.8	0.9	850
Portland, OR	4.4	16.7	41.6	24.8	8.4	2.5	1.6	1,345
Providence, RI	15.8	35.0	32.6	12.0	3.0	0.8	0.9	993
Provo, UT	6.0	37.0	33.9	16.9	4.5	0.8	0.9	1,095
Raleigh, NC	4.3	28.7	45.5	15.9	3.8	0.9	1.0	1,162
Reno, NV	5.1	33.1	36.0	19.0	4.8	1.0	1.0	1,149
Richmond, VA	6.9	28.0	44.5	15.6	3.2	0.8	1.0	1,141
Riverside, CA	3.9	19.9	33.5	25.2	11.3	4.1	2.1	1,387
Rochester, MN	11.0	43.1	29.5	11.9	1.4	0.7	2.3	952
Rochester, NY	10.7	49.4	29.4	7.2	1.9	0.4	0.8	920
Sacramento, CA	4.4	18.9	36.6	25.7	10.2	2.7	1.6	1,364
St. Louis, MO	8.7	51.7	30.4	5.9	1.7	0.6	1.0	913
Salt Lake City, UT	5.0	28.2	43.4	17.8	3.8	1.0	0.8	1,171
San Antonio, TX	6.3	38.2	38.7	12.5	2.8	0.8	0.8	1,058
San Diego, CA	3.3	7.8	25.5	28.9	17.7	9.1	7.7	1,732
San Francisco, CA	5.7	8.1	15.2	20.1	18.7	12.9	19.2	2,021
San Jose, CA	3.3	5.3	9.7	17.0	20.1	18.3	26.2	2,365
Santa Rosa, CA	5.5	8.4	23.0	26.9	19.6	9.6	7.0	1,743
Savannah, GA	6.4	31.3	44.1	14.3	2.7	0.4	0.7	1,114
Seattle, WA	4.7	11.2	28.9	29.0	15.3	5.7	5.1	1,589
Sioux Falls, SD	8.4	64.5	20.8	4.5	0.6	0.4	0.8	836
Springfield, IL	11.7	61.5	21.3	3.8	0.6	0.7	0.3	826
Tampa, FL	4.4	30.0	41.4	17.2	4.2	1.6	1.2	1,160
Tucson, AZ	6.5	50.0	32.2	7.9	1.6	0.8	1.0	931
Tulsa, OK	9.8	56.0	27.1	5.1	1.0	0.4	0.6	863
Tuscaloosa, AL	16.5	54.7	21.9	4.5	1.3	0.6	0.6	833
Virginia Beach, VA	6.6	25.2	42.0	18.8	4.9	1.5	1.0	1,187
Washington, DC	4.5	7.3	24.1	32.3	17.3	7.6	6.8	1,718
Wichita, KS	10.3	60.4	22.7	4.7	1.0	0.3	0.5	829
Wilmington, NC	9.1	36.1	39.6	11.1	2.3	1.2	0.5	1,046
Winston-Salem, NC	12.8	61.2	21.7	3.1	0.8	0.2	0.2	790
U.S.	8.9	34.3	30.2	14.9	6.2	2.6	2.8	1,096

Note: (1) Figures cover the Metropolitan Statistical Area (MSA); Figures are percentages except for Median; Gross rent is the contract rent plus the estimated average monthly cost of utilities (electricity, gas, and water and sewer) and fuels (oil, coal, kerosene, wood, etc.) if these are paid by the renter (or paid for the renter by someone else).
Source: U.S. Census Bureau, 2016-2020 American Community Survey 5-Year Estimates

Highest Level of Education: City

City	Less than H.S.	H.S. Diploma	Some College, No Deg.	Associate Degree	Bachelors Degree	Masters Degree	Profess. School Degree	Doctorate Degree
Albuquerque, NM	9.1	22.3	23.3	8.8	20.4	10.9	2.7	2.4
Allentown, PA	19.4	38.3	18.4	7.3	11.1	3.7	1.0	0.8
Anchorage, AK	6.0	23.7	24.8	8.9	22.7	9.7	2.8	1.4
Ann Arbor, MI	2.4	7.1	9.5	3.8	30.0	27.2	8.3	11.7
Athens, GA	10.6	19.8	17.7	6.4	22.3	14.3	3.0	5.8
Atlanta, GA	8.3	18.6	14.5	5.2	29.8	15.7	5.3	2.6
Austin, TX	9.7	14.7	16.9	5.3	33.1	14.4	3.4	2.5
Baltimore, MD	14.5	28.5	19.2	4.9	16.7	10.7	3.0	2.4
Baton Rouge, LA	12.6	27.2	20.9	4.4	18.8	11.4	2.4	2.4
Boise City, ID	5.0	20.4	23.2	8.8	27.6	10.2	2.7	2.2
Boston, MA	12.1	18.9	13.0	4.6	27.8	15.1	5.0	3.4
Boulder, CO	2.7	5.7	11.2	3.6	37.1	24.6	6.4	8.6
Buffalo, NY	14.3	27.5	19.5	10.0	16.5	8.5	2.0	1.5
Cape Coral, FL	7.6	37.9	22.0	9.4	15.4	5.2	1.3	1.1
Cedar Rapids, IA	6.4	26.2	22.3	12.3	22.9	6.8	2.1	1.0
Charleston, SC	4.5	17.2	16.2	7.6	33.7	13.2	4.9	2.6
Charlotte, NC	10.6	16.8	19.7	8.1	29.2	11.6	2.8	1.1
Chicago, IL	14.1	22.0	17.2	5.7	24.0	11.8	3.5	1.7
Cincinnati, OH	11.6	23.7	18.9	7.2	22.5	10.5	3.4	2.2
Clarksville, TN	6.8	26.8	26.9	11.2	18.6	8.0	0.8	0.9
Cleveland, OH	17.8	33.1	23.5	7.1	11.1	5.1	1.6	0.8
College Station, TX	5.2	12.5	17.5	6.9	29.4	15.2	2.7	10.4
Colorado Springs, CO	6.0	19.4	24.1	10.8	23.9	11.9	2.2	1.6
Columbia, MO	4.8	17.1	18.3	6.5	28.1	14.8	5.1	5.2
Columbia, SC	10.0	19.9	19.2	7.5	23.7	12.3	4.0	3.4
Columbus, OH	10.2	25.2	20.4	7.3	23.8	9.7	1.9	1.5
Dallas, TX	21.0	21.7	17.9	4.7	21.6	8.7	3.1	1.2
Davenport, IA	8.5	31.6	21.5	11.9	17.7	6.4	1.6	0.8
Denver, CO	10.9	17.2	16.1	5.6	31.0	13.1	4.2	1.9
Des Moines, IA	13.3	29.3	20.4	9.0	19.5	5.8	1.7	0.9
Durham, NC	10.3	16.3	15.2	7.0	26.7	15.5	4.4	4.6
Edison, NJ	8.0	18.8	12.3	5.4	29.7	21.0	2.5	2.2
El Paso, TX	19.4	22.5	23.5	8.6	17.1	6.6	1.3	1.0
Fargo, ND	5.4	19.3	20.0	14.4	27.8	9.5	1.9	1.7
Fort Collins, CO	3.3	15.0	17.2	8.9	31.9	17.5	2.4	3.8
Fort Wayne, IN	11.0	28.8	21.9	10.1	18.9	7.2	1.3	0.9
Fort Worth, TX	16.8	24.9	21.2	7.1	19.9	7.5	1.6	1.1
Grand Rapids, MI	12.7	22.0	19.8	7.8	25.2	9.2	2.0	1.4
Green Bay, WI	12.5	31.4	19.9	11.8	17.6	4.9	1.1	0.8
Honolulu, HI	10.2	23.3	18.2	10.5	23.9	8.7	3.1	2.1
Houston, TX	20.3	22.1	17.5	5.9	20.7	9.0	2.9	1.7
Huntsville, AL	9.3	18.0	21.0	7.7	26.5	13.2	1.9	2.4
Indianapolis, IN	13.6	27.4	19.2	7.7	20.8	8.0	2.2	1.2
Jacksonville, FL	10.2	28.7	21.8	10.0	19.8	6.9	1.7	0.9
Kansas City, MO	9.3	25.2	22.4	7.4	22.5	9.6	2.5	1.2
Lafayette, LA	9.7	25.5	21.0	4.6	26.3	8.4	2.9	1.7
Las Cruces, NM	11.5	19.7	23.2	8.8	20.5	12.0	2.4	1.9
Las Vegas, NV	14.7	27.6	24.5	7.9	16.4	6.1	2.0	0.8
Lexington, KY	8.1	19.0	20.5	7.5	25.3	12.1	4.2	3.3
Lincoln, NE	7.1	20.8	21.0	11.2	24.9	9.8	2.4	2.8
Little Rock, AR	8.1	22.5	20.7	6.2	24.3	11.7	3.9	2.7
Los Angeles, CA	21.7	18.8	17.5	6.3	23.3	7.9	3.0	1.4
Louisville, KY	10.3	28.0	23.0	8.3	18.5	8.5	2.1	1.3
Madison, WI	4.1	14.0	15.7	7.8	32.3	16.2	4.2	5.8
Manchester, NH	12.5	28.7	18.8	9.2	20.6	7.9	1.4	0.9

Table continued on following page.

City	Less than H.S.	H.S. Diploma	Some College, No Deg.	Associate Degree	Bachelors Degree	Masters Degree	Profess. School Degree	Doctorate Degree
Memphis, TN	13.5	30.3	23.7	5.8	16.0	7.4	2.0	1.3
Miami, FL	21.7	27.0	12.2	7.6	18.9	7.5	4.0	1.1
Midland, TX	16.1	25.4	21.5	7.8	21.6	5.6	1.6	0.5
Milwaukee, WI	15.6	31.1	21.4	7.3	15.9	6.5	1.3	0.9
Minneapolis, MN	9.6	14.5	16.6	7.5	31.7	13.8	3.9	2.4
Nashville, TN	10.5	21.6	18.9	6.2	27.0	10.4	3.0	2.3
New Haven, CT	14.4	31.4	14.3	4.7	16.0	11.0	3.9	4.4
New Orleans, LA	12.3	22.7	21.5	5.4	21.0	10.6	4.3	2.0
New York, NY	17.2	23.6	13.6	6.4	22.6	11.7	3.3	1.6
Oklahoma City, OK	13.2	24.7	22.6	8.0	19.9	7.7	2.6	1.2
Omaha, NE	10.2	22.0	21.8	7.7	24.7	9.1	2.9	1.6
Orlando, FL	9.3	22.5	17.1	11.2	25.5	9.9	3.1	1.4
Philadelphia, PA	14.3	31.8	16.7	6.0	17.9	8.9	2.7	1.7
Phoenix, AZ	17.1	23.4	22.2	7.9	18.5	7.7	2.0	1.2
Pittsburgh, PA	6.8	24.9	15.0	7.9	23.5	13.2	4.6	4.1
Portland, OR	7.1	15.5	19.7	6.8	30.7	13.7	4.2	2.4
Providence, RI	17.3	31.2	14.3	5.0	17.3	8.9	3.3	2.7
Provo, UT	6.9	15.1	26.1	9.0	30.1	8.6	1.7	2.6
Raleigh, NC	7.8	15.8	17.5	7.5	32.6	13.3	3.3	2.3
Reno, NV	10.1	22.5	24.2	8.3	21.6	8.8	2.3	2.2
Richmond, VA	13.1	21.3	19.3	5.2	23.9	12.0	3.1	2.3
Riverside, CA	18.4	26.5	23.0	7.9	14.2	6.7	1.5	1.7
Rochester, MN	6.1	18.1	16.3	11.5	27.0	12.5	4.9	3.6
Rochester, NY	17.8	26.0	18.9	10.3	15.5	8.0	2.0	1.6
Sacramento, CA	14.1	20.6	22.6	8.4	21.9	8.1	3.1	1.3
St. Louis, MO	11.3	24.2	21.0	6.3	20.5	11.1	3.2	2.5
Salt Lake City, UT	10.0	16.5	18.0	6.7	27.3	13.1	4.6	3.7
San Antonio, TX	17.3	26.1	22.4	7.9	16.6	6.9	1.8	1.1
San Diego, CA	11.2	15.2	19.2	7.7	27.5	12.4	3.6	3.1
San Francisco, CA	11.4	11.6	13.1	5.1	35.0	15.9	5.1	2.8
San Jose, CA	15.0	16.5	16.3	7.4	26.1	14.0	2.1	2.6
Santa Rosa, CA	13.8	18.4	24.0	10.0	20.8	8.6	3.0	1.4
Savannah, GA	11.9	26.5	26.1	6.4	18.4	7.5	1.9	1.2
Seattle, WA	4.8	9.5	14.4	6.3	37.0	18.9	5.4	3.8
Sioux Falls, SD	7.0	25.7	20.3	11.9	23.6	8.3	2.1	1.1
Springfield, IL	8.5	26.2	22.4	8.1	20.7	9.6	3.4	1.2
Tampa, FL	11.6	24.9	15.7	7.9	24.1	10.1	3.9	1.8
Tucson, AZ	14.1	23.0	26.0	8.8	17.2	8.1	1.4	1.6
Tulsa, OK	12.2	25.6	22.5	8.4	20.2	7.4	2.6	1.1
Tuscaloosa, AL	9.1	26.4	19.4	6.7	21.8	10.6	2.3	3.5
Virginia Beach, VA	6.0	20.8	24.8	11.2	23.5	10.3	2.1	1.3
Washington, DC	8.1	16.6	12.6	2.9	25.3	21.3	9.1	4.1
Wichita, KS	11.5	26.5	23.4	7.9	19.6	8.3	1.8	1.1
Wilmington, NC	7.0	19.7	19.8	9.6	28.6	10.0	3.4	1.9
Winston-Salem, NC	12.1	24.6	21.6	7.5	20.2	9.0	2.8	2.2
U.S.	11.5	26.7	20.3	8.6	20.2	9.1	2.2	1.5

Note: Figures cover persons age 25 and over
Source: U.S. Census Bureau, 2016-2020 American Community Survey 5-Year Estimates

Highest Level of Education: Metro Area

Metro Area	Less than H.S.	H.S. Diploma	Some College, No Deg.	Associate Degree	Bachelors Degree	Masters Degree	Profess. School Degree	Doctorate Degree
Albuquerque, NM	10.4	24.3	23.4	8.9	18.5	10.1	2.3	2.1
Allentown, PA	9.4	33.9	16.7	9.4	19.2	8.5	1.6	1.3
Anchorage, AK	6.1	26.4	25.5	9.2	20.5	8.6	2.4	1.2
Ann Arbor, MI	4.3	14.7	17.5	6.8	26.7	18.8	5.1	6.1
Athens, GA	10.9	23.8	17.6	7.5	19.8	12.5	3.3	4.5
Atlanta, GA	9.8	23.7	19.2	7.7	24.5	10.8	2.6	1.6
Austin, TX	9.4	18.5	19.7	6.4	29.4	12.1	2.5	1.9
Baltimore, MD	8.7	24.4	19.1	6.8	22.6	13.2	3.0	2.3
Baton Rouge, LA	12.2	31.4	21.3	6.3	18.2	7.5	1.8	1.3
Boise City, ID	7.8	24.5	25.3	9.2	22.3	7.7	1.8	1.4
Boston, MA	8.0	21.6	14.3	7.1	26.6	15.5	3.5	3.3
Boulder, CO	4.5	11.3	14.8	6.4	34.6	19.0	4.2	5.2
Buffalo, NY	8.0	27.9	18.3	12.4	18.8	10.9	2.2	1.5
Cape Coral, FL	10.7	31.2	20.5	9.1	17.4	7.5	2.3	1.3
Cedar Rapids, IA	5.5	28.5	21.3	13.1	21.9	7.1	1.7	0.9
Charleston, SC	9.2	24.8	20.0	9.5	23.4	9.2	2.6	1.3
Charlotte, NC	10.6	23.1	21.0	9.5	23.8	9.2	1.9	0.9
Chicago, IL	10.9	23.6	19.3	7.3	23.6	11.2	2.7	1.5
Cincinnati, OH	8.5	29.4	19.1	8.4	21.5	9.5	2.0	1.5
Clarksville, TN	8.7	28.9	25.7	10.8	16.7	7.3	1.1	0.8
Cleveland, OH	9.0	28.7	21.7	8.7	19.2	8.9	2.5	1.3
College Station, TX	12.4	23.3	19.9	6.6	21.0	9.5	2.3	5.1
Colorado Springs, CO	5.4	20.2	24.5	11.3	23.3	11.8	1.9	1.6
Columbia, MO	6.2	22.8	19.0	7.6	25.3	11.9	3.5	3.7
Columbia, SC	9.8	26.4	21.5	9.2	20.1	9.2	1.9	1.8
Columbus, OH	8.3	27.3	19.5	7.5	23.6	9.9	2.4	1.5
Dallas, TX	13.8	22.2	20.9	7.1	23.4	9.5	1.9	1.2
Davenport, IA	8.4	30.1	22.9	11.1	17.6	7.4	1.5	0.9
Denver, CO	8.4	19.9	19.3	7.7	28.4	12.0	2.6	1.6
Des Moines, IA	7.0	25.8	19.7	10.5	25.6	8.2	2.2	1.2
Durham, NC	10.2	19.3	16.2	7.8	23.6	13.9	4.3	4.7
Edison, NJ	13.0	24.1	14.6	6.8	23.9	12.5	3.4	1.7
El Paso, TX	21.2	23.2	22.8	8.9	16.0	5.9	1.2	0.8
Fargo, ND	4.9	20.0	21.5	14.6	27.1	8.8	1.7	1.4
Fort Collins, CO	3.8	18.6	20.6	9.3	28.1	14.4	2.3	2.9
Fort Wayne, IN	10.0	29.3	21.4	11.0	19.2	6.9	1.5	0.8
Fort Worth, TX	13.8	22.2	20.9	7.1	23.4	9.5	1.9	1.2
Grand Rapids, MI	8.2	26.9	21.7	9.5	22.2	8.7	1.7	1.1
Green Bay, WI	7.6	32.0	19.8	12.7	19.8	6.0	1.4	0.8
Honolulu, HI	7.6	25.7	20.1	10.9	23.1	8.5	2.5	1.6
Houston, TX	15.7	22.8	20.5	7.4	21.3	8.6	2.2	1.5
Huntsville, AL	9.7	21.6	21.3	7.7	24.9	11.7	1.4	1.8
Indianapolis, IN	9.8	27.6	19.1	8.0	22.7	9.3	2.3	1.3
Jacksonville, FL	8.9	27.7	21.3	10.0	21.1	7.9	2.0	1.1
Kansas City, MO	7.5	25.4	21.8	7.8	23.6	10.3	2.3	1.2
Lafayette, LA	14.7	36.3	18.7	6.0	17.2	4.9	1.3	0.8
Las Cruces, NM	19.4	21.5	21.4	8.1	17.3	9.0	1.7	1.5
Las Vegas, NV	13.7	28.3	24.7	8.1	16.7	6.0	1.7	0.9
Lexington, KY	9.1	23.8	20.6	7.9	22.2	10.6	3.3	2.5
Lincoln, NE	6.7	21.5	20.9	11.6	24.7	9.7	2.3	2.6
Little Rock, AR	8.8	29.3	22.5	8.1	19.5	8.5	2.0	1.4
Los Angeles, CA	18.7	19.6	19.1	7.2	22.9	8.4	2.6	1.4
Louisville, KY	9.6	29.3	22.4	8.7	18.4	8.4	2.1	1.2
Madison, WI	4.3	20.4	17.9	10.3	28.5	12.2	3.0	3.4
Manchester, NH	7.6	25.7	17.9	10.2	24.6	11.1	1.6	1.4

Table continued on following page.

Metro Area	Less than H.S.	H.S. Diploma	Some College, No Deg.	Associate Degree	Bachelors Degree	Masters Degree	Profess. School Degree	Doctorate Degree
Memphis, TN	11.3	29.1	23.4	7.4	17.6	8.2	1.9	1.2
Miami, FL	14.1	26.1	17.2	9.5	20.6	8.1	3.1	1.2
Midland, TX	16.0	26.3	22.5	7.9	19.6	5.8	1.4	0.4
Milwaukee, WI	8.2	26.7	20.3	8.7	23.5	9.0	2.2	1.4
Minneapolis, MN	6.2	20.8	19.7	10.6	27.9	10.6	2.5	1.7
Nashville, TN	9.5	26.0	19.9	7.3	24.3	9.1	2.2	1.7
New Haven, CT	9.7	30.1	17.0	7.3	19.0	11.7	3.2	2.1
New Orleans, LA	12.5	27.4	22.6	6.4	19.3	7.7	2.8	1.2
New York, NY	13.0	24.1	14.6	6.8	23.9	12.5	3.4	1.7
Oklahoma City, OK	10.6	26.8	23.2	8.0	20.2	7.8	2.1	1.3
Omaha, NE	8.0	23.6	22.1	9.3	24.2	9.3	2.3	1.2
Orlando, FL	10.4	25.3	19.6	11.5	21.7	8.4	2.0	1.0
Philadelphia, PA	8.8	28.6	16.7	7.2	22.8	11.1	2.8	1.9
Phoenix, AZ	11.7	23.1	24.1	8.8	20.4	8.6	2.0	1.3
Pittsburgh, PA	5.7	31.8	16.3	10.3	21.8	10.0	2.3	1.8
Portland, OR	7.5	20.0	23.2	8.9	25.2	10.5	2.7	2.0
Providence, RI	11.9	28.8	17.8	8.6	20.2	9.2	2.0	1.5
Provo, UT	4.9	17.2	26.7	10.5	28.1	9.1	1.7	1.8
Raleigh, NC	7.7	17.5	18.0	9.0	30.1	13.1	2.5	2.1
Reno, NV	11.1	23.7	25.0	8.6	19.7	8.2	2.1	1.7
Richmond, VA	9.3	24.8	20.3	7.7	23.3	10.8	2.3	1.6
Riverside, CA	18.2	26.5	24.4	8.5	14.5	5.7	1.4	0.9
Rochester, MN	5.9	23.0	18.3	12.5	24.0	10.0	3.8	2.4
Rochester, NY	9.2	25.7	17.4	12.1	19.7	11.9	2.3	1.7
Sacramento, CA	10.3	20.9	24.5	10.0	22.0	8.1	2.8	1.5
St. Louis, MO	7.5	25.8	22.2	9.1	21.0	10.6	2.2	1.6
Salt Lake City, UT	8.5	22.9	23.6	9.3	23.0	9.0	2.3	1.6
San Antonio, TX	14.5	26.1	22.6	8.1	18.3	7.7	1.8	1.1
San Diego, CA	12.0	18.2	22.0	8.3	24.2	10.2	2.9	2.2
San Francisco, CA	10.5	15.2	17.0	6.7	29.8	14.1	3.8	2.9
San Jose, CA	11.5	14.3	14.9	6.8	27.5	18.0	2.8	4.2
Santa Rosa, CA	10.9	18.2	24.9	9.5	22.9	8.9	3.2	1.5
Savannah, GA	9.8	26.4	23.4	7.9	20.2	8.7	2.3	1.5
Seattle, WA	7.1	19.2	20.7	9.4	26.8	12.1	2.7	1.9
Sioux Falls, SD	6.5	26.5	20.3	12.8	23.4	7.6	1.9	1.0
Springfield, IL	7.3	28.0	22.6	8.6	20.6	9.2	2.5	1.1
Tampa, FL	10.1	28.7	20.2	9.9	20.1	7.8	2.1	1.1
Tucson, AZ	11.0	21.5	25.0	8.9	19.3	9.9	2.2	2.1
Tulsa, OK	10.0	29.2	23.6	9.3	18.8	6.5	1.7	0.9
Tuscaloosa, AL	11.9	30.7	21.1	8.3	16.6	7.8	1.3	2.3
Virginia Beach, VA	8.1	24.6	24.3	10.1	20.1	9.6	1.9	1.3
Washington, DC	8.7	17.9	15.8	5.9	26.1	17.9	4.5	3.2
Wichita, KS	9.7	26.6	24.0	8.7	20.1	8.4	1.6	1.0
Wilmington, NC	7.7	21.5	21.3	10.0	25.9	9.2	2.8	1.5
Winston-Salem, NC	12.5	29.0	22.2	9.5	17.2	6.5	1.7	1.4
U.S.	11.5	26.7	20.3	8.6	20.2	9.1	2.2	1.5

Note: Figures cover persons age 25 and over; Figures cover the Metropolitan Statistical Area
Source: U.S. Census Bureau, 2016-2020 American Community Survey 5-Year Estimates

School Enrollment by Grade and Control: City

City	Preschool (%)		Kindergarten (%)		Grades 1 - 4 (%)		Grades 5 - 8 (%)		Grades 9 - 12 (%)	
	Public	Private	Public	Private	Public	Private	Public	Private	Public	Private
Albuquerque, NM	59.5	40.5	84.5	15.5	89.3	10.7	91.1	8.9	91.3	8.7
Allentown, PA	79.9	20.1	86.5	13.5	88.8	11.2	87.0	13.0	88.5	11.5
Anchorage, AK	53.5	46.5	91.8	8.2	90.8	9.2	90.3	9.7	94.1	5.9
Ann Arbor, MI	34.7	65.3	95.5	4.5	91.6	8.4	90.7	9.3	94.6	5.4
Athens, GA	57.8	42.2	91.4	8.6	91.2	8.8	89.3	10.7	88.8	11.2
Atlanta, GA	51.1	48.9	78.9	21.1	87.0	13.0	81.2	18.8	81.1	18.9
Austin, TX	55.5	44.5	86.3	13.7	87.8	12.2	88.5	11.5	90.9	9.1
Baltimore, MD	68.9	31.1	85.3	14.7	84.2	15.8	84.3	15.7	86.5	13.5
Baton Rouge, LA	59.8	40.2	67.6	32.4	79.6	20.4	79.7	20.3	78.3	21.7
Boise City, ID	32.7	67.3	80.7	19.3	92.9	7.1	92.0	8.0	89.4	10.6
Boston, MA	46.5	53.5	85.0	15.0	85.7	14.3	84.2	15.8	88.8	11.2
Boulder, CO	49.7	50.3	87.0	13.0	87.8	12.2	93.2	6.8	92.2	7.8
Buffalo, NY	74.5	25.5	89.8	10.2	85.9	14.1	87.4	12.6	84.1	15.9
Cape Coral, FL	79.4	20.6	94.2	5.8	93.5	6.5	93.9	6.1	89.8	10.2
Cedar Rapids, IA	70.2	29.8	88.3	11.7	88.6	11.4	91.5	8.5	86.7	13.3
Charleston, SC	39.0	61.0	80.7	19.3	85.2	14.8	81.4	18.6	75.0	25.0
Charlotte, NC	49.4	50.6	86.8	13.2	89.8	10.2	87.6	12.4	89.6	10.4
Chicago, IL	55.4	44.6	79.4	20.6	84.3	15.7	84.3	15.7	85.9	14.1
Cincinnati, OH	64.9	35.1	65.9	34.1	76.6	23.4	80.2	19.8	81.0	19.0
Clarksville, TN	53.7	46.3	90.7	9.3	94.4	5.6	91.6	8.4	90.0	10.0
Cleveland, OH	74.8	25.2	80.9	19.1	82.3	17.7	77.9	22.1	78.6	21.4
College Station, TX	50.3	49.7	87.6	12.4	86.6	13.4	92.5	7.5	89.2	10.8
Colorado Springs, CO	55.7	44.3	88.8	11.2	89.7	10.3	90.6	9.4	91.9	8.1
Columbia, MO	39.8	60.2	86.1	13.9	86.7	13.3	85.5	14.5	91.7	8.3
Columbia, SC	56.4	43.6	68.4	31.6	88.0	12.0	86.9	13.1	85.6	14.4
Columbus, OH	60.8	39.2	83.3	16.7	86.2	13.8	86.3	13.7	87.3	12.7
Dallas, TX	70.9	29.1	91.0	9.0	91.2	8.8	91.3	8.7	90.8	9.2
Davenport, IA	61.3	38.7	87.8	12.2	87.3	12.7	84.7	15.3	93.2	6.8
Denver, CO	60.0	40.0	86.1	13.9	90.2	9.8	90.2	9.8	91.8	8.2
Des Moines, IA	75.3	24.7	90.0	10.0	90.8	9.2	90.1	9.9	92.7	7.3
Durham, NC	58.4	41.6	88.3	11.7	89.1	10.9	84.8	15.2	91.3	8.7
Edison, NJ	23.5	76.5	70.0	30.0	89.2	10.8	89.9	10.1	92.6	7.4
El Paso, TX	86.6	13.4	94.1	5.9	95.8	4.2	93.7	6.3	95.9	4.1
Fargo, ND	50.0	50.0	94.3	5.7	89.4	10.6	89.4	10.6	93.6	6.4
Fort Collins, CO	42.2	57.8	91.2	8.8	94.4	5.6	93.5	6.5	93.2	6.8
Fort Wayne, IN	47.7	52.3	79.8	20.2	80.3	19.7	81.7	18.3	81.2	18.8
Fort Worth, TX	63.2	36.8	86.2	13.8	91.5	8.5	90.2	9.8	93.1	6.9
Grand Rapids, MI	67.1	32.9	74.8	25.2	79.3	20.7	81.0	19.0	83.3	16.7
Green Bay, WI	74.5	25.5	80.9	19.1	87.6	12.4	84.2	15.8	90.6	9.4
Honolulu, HI	36.4	63.6	73.2	26.8	81.9	18.1	76.2	23.8	73.9	26.1
Houston, TX	65.5	34.5	88.2	11.8	93.3	6.7	92.7	7.3	92.8	7.2
Huntsville, AL	55.5	44.5	86.9	13.1	82.2	17.8	79.1	20.9	83.1	16.9
Indianapolis, IN	60.4	39.6	85.9	14.1	86.8	13.2	85.8	14.2	88.0	12.0
Jacksonville, FL	54.4	45.6	84.6	15.4	83.8	16.2	81.9	18.1	84.1	15.9
Kansas City, MO	58.1	41.9	86.4	13.6	89.0	11.0	87.5	12.5	83.5	16.5
Lafayette, LA	63.9	36.1	61.3	38.7	70.5	29.5	72.6	27.4	80.1	19.9
Las Cruces, NM	79.6	20.4	89.8	10.2	93.6	6.4	97.2	2.8	96.8	3.2
Las Vegas, NV	63.9	36.1	90.4	9.6	91.3	8.7	91.9	8.1	93.1	6.9
Lexington, KY	40.9	59.1	85.9	14.1	83.9	16.1	84.3	15.7	87.1	12.9
Lincoln, NE	49.4	50.6	76.4	23.6	85.8	14.2	83.0	17.0	86.7	13.3
Little Rock, AR	66.3	33.7	88.6	11.4	78.3	21.7	81.6	18.4	77.6	22.4
Los Angeles, CA	57.3	42.7	86.9	13.1	88.6	11.4	88.3	11.7	89.2	10.8
Louisville, KY	50.6	49.4	80.3	19.7	83.2	16.8	80.9	19.1	78.3	21.7
Madison, WI	41.8	58.2	87.7	12.3	89.9	10.1	86.1	13.9	90.8	9.2
Manchester, NH	56.3	43.7	86.2	13.8	91.4	8.6	93.7	6.3	91.5	8.5

Table continued on following page.

City	Preschool (%)		Kindergarten (%)		Grades 1 - 4 (%)		Grades 5 - 8 (%)		Grades 9 - 12 (%)	
	Public	Private	Public	Private	Public	Private	Public	Private	Public	Private
Memphis, TN	69.3	30.7	88.5	11.5	89.2	10.8	87.2	12.8	84.1	15.9
Miami, FL	55.6	44.4	87.6	12.4	87.7	12.3	84.1	15.9	89.4	10.6
Midland, TX	71.7	28.3	83.0	17.0	82.9	17.1	79.7	20.3	85.2	14.8
Milwaukee, WI	77.3	22.7	79.2	20.8	75.6	24.4	75.6	24.4	82.0	18.0
Minneapolis, MN	56.6	43.4	83.1	16.9	87.5	12.5	88.5	11.5	90.8	9.2
Nashville, TN	47.0	53.0	84.3	15.7	84.6	15.4	81.0	19.0	81.4	18.6
New Haven, CT	85.6	14.4	92.6	7.4	95.1	4.9	92.6	7.4	94.7	5.3
New Orleans, LA	49.2	50.8	81.0	19.0	82.2	17.8	80.7	19.3	79.9	20.1
New York, NY	62.3	37.7	79.3	20.7	82.7	17.3	81.3	18.7	81.4	18.6
Oklahoma City, OK	69.5	30.5	86.7	13.3	90.1	9.9	88.7	11.3	88.5	11.5
Omaha, NE	53.9	46.1	80.0	20.0	82.2	17.8	81.9	18.1	82.3	17.7
Orlando, FL	61.0	39.0	83.7	16.3	90.3	9.7	86.2	13.8	89.5	10.5
Philadelphia, PA	55.5	44.5	78.7	21.3	79.4	20.6	81.1	18.9	79.5	20.5
Phoenix, AZ	61.8	38.2	86.7	13.3	91.3	8.7	91.2	8.8	92.9	7.1
Pittsburgh, PA	48.0	52.0	74.0	26.0	74.9	25.1	73.5	26.5	77.6	22.4
Portland, OR	40.5	59.5	83.9	16.1	87.6	12.4	87.5	12.5	84.7	15.3
Providence, RI	48.6	51.4	83.7	16.3	86.7	13.3	83.6	16.4	87.6	12.4
Provo, UT	57.5	42.5	93.7	6.3	94.3	5.7	95.7	4.3	90.6	9.4
Raleigh, NC	38.0	62.0	87.6	12.4	88.7	11.3	88.7	11.3	89.0	11.0
Reno, NV	61.7	38.3	89.7	10.3	94.1	5.9	92.6	7.4	95.1	4.9
Richmond, VA	50.3	49.7	89.6	10.4	86.5	13.5	82.8	17.2	86.1	13.9
Riverside, CA	64.8	35.2	90.6	9.4	92.0	8.0	93.4	6.6	94.6	5.4
Rochester, MN	51.6	48.4	89.0	11.0	89.3	10.7	90.1	9.9	89.3	10.7
Rochester, NY	88.7	11.3	92.0	8.0	90.7	9.3	90.6	9.4	89.5	10.5
Sacramento, CA	66.4	33.6	92.9	7.1	93.6	6.4	92.9	7.1	91.4	8.6
St. Louis, MO	58.3	41.7	78.6	21.4	84.0	16.0	81.2	18.8	77.3	22.7
Salt Lake City, UT	43.9	56.1	88.1	11.9	90.5	9.5	90.1	9.9	94.1	5.9
San Antonio, TX	74.8	25.2	89.7	10.3	92.9	7.1	92.9	7.1	91.4	8.6
San Diego, CA	48.8	51.2	92.2	7.8	90.4	9.6	91.9	8.1	91.7	8.3
San Francisco, CA	34.3	65.7	67.8	32.2	72.2	27.8	66.5	33.5	74.5	25.5
San Jose, CA	43.2	56.8	81.5	18.5	87.8	12.2	87.5	12.5	86.2	13.8
Santa Rosa, CA	49.3	50.7	92.1	7.9	94.1	5.9	90.9	9.1	93.3	6.7
Savannah, GA	74.7	25.3	92.0	8.0	90.1	9.9	92.4	7.6	90.5	9.5
Seattle, WA	33.5	66.5	78.4	21.6	80.0	20.0	75.1	24.9	77.9	22.1
Sioux Falls, SD	55.9	44.1	90.7	9.3	87.2	12.8	89.1	10.9	78.7	21.3
Springfield, IL	57.8	42.2	81.8	18.2	83.6	16.4	82.6	17.4	82.9	17.1
Tampa, FL	54.4	45.6	82.1	17.9	89.6	10.4	85.2	14.8	82.5	17.5
Tucson, AZ	69.9	30.1	85.4	14.6	88.5	11.5	90.0	10.0	93.5	6.5
Tulsa, OK	66.5	33.5	84.3	15.7	86.7	13.3	83.9	16.1	83.6	16.4
Tuscaloosa, AL	70.5	29.5	93.7	6.3	83.9	16.1	93.1	6.9	92.7	7.3
Virginia Beach, VA	34.7	65.3	77.7	22.3	91.7	8.3	90.5	9.5	92.5	7.5
Washington, DC	74.2	25.8	90.4	9.6	88.3	11.7	84.4	15.6	81.2	18.8
Wichita, KS	62.8	37.2	85.1	14.9	86.5	13.5	83.7	16.3	84.1	15.9
Wilmington, NC	57.8	42.2	86.5	13.5	76.2	23.8	72.4	27.6	88.7	11.3
Winston-Salem, NC	52.3	47.7	93.0	7.0	92.5	7.5	91.2	8.8	93.7	6.3
U.S.	58.9	41.1	86.9	13.1	89.0	11.0	89.0	11.0	89.7	10.3

Note: Figures shown cover persons 3 years old and over
Source: U.S. Census Bureau, 2016-2020 American Community Survey 5-Year Estimates

School Enrollment by Grade and Control: Metro Area

Metro Area	Preschool (%)		Kindergarten (%)		Grades 1 - 4 (%)		Grades 5 - 8 (%)		Grades 9 - 12 (%)	
	Public	Private	Public	Private	Public	Private	Public	Private	Public	Private
Albuquerque, NM	60.9	39.1	82.9	17.1	87.7	12.3	89.9	10.1	91.0	9.0
Allentown, PA	51.1	48.9	86.9	13.1	90.2	9.8	90.3	9.7	91.5	8.5
Anchorage, AK	55.8	44.2	90.8	9.2	89.4	10.6	88.9	11.1	92.2	7.8
Ann Arbor, MI	51.0	49.0	90.4	9.6	86.9	13.1	88.5	11.5	92.1	7.9
Athens, GA	60.7	39.3	91.0	9.0	90.4	9.6	86.2	13.8	87.6	12.4
Atlanta, GA	54.1	45.9	86.2	13.8	90.3	9.7	88.7	11.3	89.1	10.9
Austin, TX	52.9	47.1	86.8	13.2	90.7	9.3	90.2	9.8	91.9	8.1
Baltimore, MD	48.6	51.4	84.7	15.3	86.4	13.6	84.2	15.8	84.1	15.9
Baton Rouge, LA	56.4	43.6	73.5	26.5	81.9	18.1	80.8	19.2	80.2	19.8
Boise City, ID	35.1	64.9	87.8	12.2	90.5	9.5	91.0	9.0	89.9	10.1
Boston, MA	45.6	54.4	88.5	11.5	91.0	9.0	89.4	10.6	86.6	13.4
Boulder, CO	54.1	45.9	86.9	13.1	90.3	9.7	90.8	9.2	95.0	5.0
Buffalo, NY	60.2	39.8	89.0	11.0	89.1	10.9	89.7	10.3	87.1	12.9
Cape Coral, FL	63.7	36.3	91.0	9.0	92.0	8.0	91.1	8.9	90.3	9.7
Cedar Rapids, IA	70.3	29.7	86.5	13.5	88.7	11.3	90.7	9.3	90.4	9.6
Charleston, SC	46.8	53.2	76.9	23.1	87.4	12.6	89.0	11.0	88.6	11.4
Charlotte, NC	49.9	50.1	87.6	12.4	90.3	9.7	88.6	11.4	89.9	10.1
Chicago, IL	56.2	43.8	84.4	15.6	88.8	11.2	89.0	11.0	90.2	9.8
Cincinnati, OH	53.0	47.0	77.6	22.4	83.1	16.9	84.1	15.9	82.3	17.7
Clarksville, TN	63.1	36.9	90.5	9.5	87.2	12.8	88.1	11.9	88.6	11.4
Cleveland, OH	54.0	46.0	79.1	20.9	82.1	17.9	82.1	17.9	83.3	16.7
College Station, TX	62.6	37.4	83.1	16.9	89.0	11.0	90.2	9.8	91.5	8.5
Colorado Springs, CO	58.9	41.1	88.0	12.0	89.7	10.3	90.9	9.1	91.4	8.6
Columbia, MO	52.9	47.1	89.5	10.5	85.4	14.6	86.5	13.5	90.6	9.4
Columbia, SC	56.2	43.8	88.0	12.0	92.0	8.0	92.7	7.3	93.0	7.0
Columbus, OH	56.8	43.2	84.2	15.8	88.0	12.0	88.2	11.8	89.3	10.7
Dallas, TX	59.0	41.0	89.7	10.3	91.7	8.3	91.7	8.3	92.0	8.0
Davenport, IA	68.6	31.4	91.6	8.4	91.5	8.5	91.6	8.4	92.6	7.4
Denver, CO	58.0	42.0	89.0	11.0	91.3	8.7	91.7	8.3	92.0	8.0
Des Moines, IA	65.6	34.4	88.5	11.5	92.2	7.8	90.5	9.5	92.5	7.5
Durham, NC	47.9	52.1	85.1	14.9	88.3	11.7	86.2	13.8	91.6	8.4
Edison, NJ	56.2	43.8	82.1	17.9	85.4	14.6	85.2	14.8	84.8	15.2
El Paso, TX	87.3	12.7	94.5	5.5	95.9	4.1	94.2	5.8	96.3	3.7
Fargo, ND	60.6	39.4	92.1	7.9	88.6	11.4	89.2	10.8	92.9	7.1
Fort Collins, CO	44.2	55.8	91.4	8.6	90.5	9.5	88.1	11.9	88.6	11.4
Fort Wayne, IN	42.9	57.1	76.8	23.2	77.9	22.1	77.7	22.3	81.7	18.3
Fort Worth, TX	59.0	41.0	89.7	10.3	91.7	8.3	91.7	8.3	92.0	8.0
Grand Rapids, MI	63.8	36.2	82.6	17.4	84.6	15.4	86.6	13.4	85.6	14.4
Green Bay, WI	71.4	28.6	85.2	14.8	88.7	11.3	88.4	11.6	92.4	7.6
Honolulu, HI	37.9	62.1	78.3	21.7	85.0	15.0	79.3	20.7	76.1	23.9
Houston, TX	56.6	43.4	88.9	11.1	92.3	7.7	92.7	7.3	92.8	7.2
Huntsville, AL	55.6	44.4	81.0	19.0	82.3	17.7	81.4	18.6	83.6	16.4
Indianapolis, IN	53.7	46.3	87.2	12.8	88.6	11.4	87.6	12.4	88.8	11.2
Jacksonville, FL	55.5	44.5	86.6	13.4	85.7	14.3	84.4	15.6	86.5	13.5
Kansas City, MO	59.4	40.6	88.5	11.5	89.0	11.0	89.1	10.9	88.8	11.2
Lafayette, LA	67.5	32.5	76.3	23.7	80.9	19.1	79.2	20.8	81.2	18.8
Las Cruces, NM	82.9	17.1	92.6	7.4	91.4	8.6	96.5	3.5	96.4	3.6
Las Vegas, NV	60.1	39.9	89.3	10.7	92.3	7.7	92.9	7.1	93.0	7.0
Lexington, KY	45.5	54.5	83.0	17.0	85.4	14.6	83.4	16.6	87.1	12.9
Lincoln, NE	47.7	52.3	76.6	23.4	83.7	16.3	83.6	16.4	87.0	13.0
Little Rock, AR	68.0	32.0	89.2	10.8	87.7	12.3	88.6	11.4	87.1	12.9
Los Angeles, CA	56.4	43.6	87.8	12.2	90.3	9.7	90.5	9.5	91.2	8.8
Louisville, KY	50.0	50.0	82.4	17.6	84.0	16.0	82.3	17.7	81.0	19.0
Madison, WI	61.4	38.6	87.6	12.4	90.5	9.5	90.2	9.8	94.7	5.3
Manchester, NH	46.5	53.5	84.5	15.5	87.4	12.6	89.1	10.9	88.9	11.1

Table continued on following page.

Metro Area	Preschool (%)		Kindergarten (%)		Grades 1 - 4 (%)		Grades 5 - 8 (%)		Grades 9 - 12 (%)	
	Public	Private	Public	Private	Public	Private	Public	Private	Public	Private
Memphis, TN	63.6	36.4	88.3	11.7	87.8	12.2	86.6	13.4	84.7	15.3
Miami, FL	50.0	50.0	83.7	16.3	85.8	14.2	86.1	13.9	86.6	13.4
Midland, TX	74.2	25.8	79.4	20.6	83.8	16.2	83.7	16.3	85.2	14.8
Milwaukee, WI	59.0	41.0	79.1	20.9	79.6	20.4	79.7	20.3	85.9	14.1
Minneapolis, MN	60.5	39.5	87.5	12.5	89.4	10.6	89.9	10.1	91.7	8.3
Nashville, TN	47.6	52.4	84.9	15.1	86.8	13.2	85.9	14.1	83.6	16.4
New Haven, CT	64.5	35.5	92.7	7.3	92.0	8.0	90.7	9.3	89.4	10.6
New Orleans, LA	52.3	47.7	76.5	23.5	78.4	21.6	77.6	22.4	76.1	23.9
New York, NY	56.2	43.8	82.1	17.9	85.4	14.6	85.2	14.8	84.8	15.2
Oklahoma City, OK	70.8	29.2	88.3	11.7	89.8	10.2	89.2	10.8	89.3	10.7
Omaha, NE	57.9	42.1	83.8	16.2	85.2	14.8	85.4	14.6	85.3	14.7
Orlando, FL	50.2	49.8	81.0	19.0	85.0	15.0	84.7	15.3	88.9	11.1
Philadelphia, PA	46.9	53.1	81.4	18.6	85.0	15.0	84.5	15.5	83.2	16.8
Phoenix, AZ	60.3	39.7	87.0	13.0	90.6	9.4	91.3	8.7	92.8	7.2
Pittsburgh, PA	49.7	50.3	83.6	16.4	88.7	11.3	88.6	11.4	89.5	10.5
Portland, OR	43.0	57.0	84.9	15.1	88.4	11.6	89.2	10.8	89.8	10.2
Providence, RI	54.7	45.3	88.1	11.9	91.0	9.0	89.3	10.7	88.7	11.3
Provo, UT	53.5	46.5	88.7	11.3	92.4	7.6	93.9	6.1	94.9	5.1
Raleigh, NC	34.6	65.4	85.3	14.7	88.2	11.8	87.3	12.7	89.1	10.9
Reno, NV	58.5	41.5	89.4	10.6	93.1	6.9	93.4	6.6	93.3	6.7
Richmond, VA	42.1	57.9	88.3	11.7	90.0	10.0	88.7	11.3	89.4	10.6
Riverside, CA	67.2	32.8	91.0	9.0	94.0	6.0	93.7	6.3	94.6	5.4
Rochester, MN	62.4	37.6	90.7	9.3	89.4	10.6	91.1	8.9	90.6	9.4
Rochester, NY	64.6	35.4	87.6	12.4	89.8	10.2	89.1	10.9	89.8	10.2
Sacramento, CA	61.8	38.2	90.6	9.4	92.4	7.6	92.4	7.6	91.8	8.2
St. Louis, MO	54.0	46.0	82.0	18.0	84.4	15.6	82.8	17.2	84.8	15.2
Salt Lake City, UT	54.5	45.5	87.0	13.0	91.1	8.9	93.4	6.6	93.4	6.6
San Antonio, TX	68.4	31.6	89.8	10.2	92.4	7.6	91.8	8.2	91.4	8.6
San Diego, CA	50.9	49.1	91.0	9.0	91.3	8.7	92.1	7.9	92.5	7.5
San Francisco, CA	40.6	59.4	83.1	16.9	85.8	14.2	84.9	15.1	86.6	13.4
San Jose, CA	36.3	63.7	80.1	19.9	86.1	13.9	86.0	14.0	85.8	14.2
Santa Rosa, CA	47.8	52.2	90.7	9.3	92.9	7.1	90.1	9.9	92.4	7.6
Savannah, GA	55.4	44.6	89.0	11.0	82.1	17.9	87.6	12.4	85.5	14.5
Seattle, WA	40.9	59.1	83.4	16.6	87.3	12.7	87.8	12.2	90.4	9.6
Sioux Falls, SD	56.7	43.3	90.0	10.0	87.9	12.1	90.4	9.6	83.0	17.0
Springfield, IL	60.5	39.5	86.9	13.1	87.0	13.0	88.0	12.0	88.2	11.8
Tampa, FL	55.3	44.7	82.6	17.4	85.7	14.3	86.4	13.6	87.5	12.5
Tucson, AZ	66.5	33.5	88.1	11.9	89.1	10.9	88.7	11.3	91.4	8.6
Tulsa, OK	67.9	32.1	87.5	12.5	87.7	12.3	87.2	12.8	87.1	12.9
Tuscaloosa, AL	70.2	29.8	88.2	11.8	86.7	13.3	91.2	8.8	88.1	11.9
Virginia Beach, VA	50.3	49.7	80.2	19.8	89.7	10.3	90.1	9.9	91.0	9.0
Washington, DC	45.2	54.8	85.7	14.3	88.4	11.6	87.5	12.5	88.1	11.9
Wichita, KS	63.7	36.3	85.5	14.5	87.1	12.9	85.9	14.1	86.5	13.5
Wilmington, NC	48.2	51.8	82.7	17.3	85.0	15.0	81.9	18.1	87.9	12.1
Winston-Salem, NC	51.5	48.5	88.6	11.4	90.9	9.1	89.5	10.5	90.1	9.9
U.S.	58.9	41.1	86.9	13.1	89.0	11.0	89.0	11.0	89.7	10.3

Note: Figures shown cover persons 3 years old and over; Figures cover the Metropolitan Statistical Area
Source: U.S. Census Bureau, 2016-2020 American Community Survey 5-Year Estimates

Educational Attainment by Race: City

City	High School Graduate or Higher (%)					Bachelor's Degree or Higher (%)				
	Total	White	Black	Asian	Hisp.[1]	Total	White	Black	Asian	Hisp.[1]
Albuquerque, NM	90.9	92.4	92.9	87.9	85.0	36.5	39.3	35.2	52.7	23.5
Allentown, PA	80.6	83.2	84.3	83.8	70.2	16.6	19.1	10.0	42.3	7.5
Anchorage, AK	94.0	96.4	92.5	85.8	84.5	36.6	43.6	20.1	25.5	23.3
Ann Arbor, MI	97.6	98.2	92.2	98.5	93.9	77.3	80.0	37.4	85.6	70.4
Athens, GA	89.4	93.1	83.0	95.8	63.6	45.4	56.1	22.2	75.4	24.4
Atlanta, GA	91.7	97.9	86.0	96.4	84.8	53.4	78.9	27.9	86.1	48.2
Austin, TX	90.3	92.4	89.0	93.3	74.9	53.4	56.9	29.9	76.6	29.1
Baltimore, MD	85.5	90.1	83.4	90.0	71.3	32.9	57.7	17.6	71.7	31.7
Baton Rouge, LA	87.4	96.1	81.6	80.5	71.6	34.9	55.2	16.9	55.4	25.7
Boise City, ID	95.0	95.8	81.0	91.5	82.9	42.7	42.9	34.0	55.1	22.3
Boston, MA	87.9	93.9	84.4	79.4	71.9	51.3	67.3	23.2	54.4	25.7
Boulder, CO	97.3	98.0	89.3	95.0	80.5	76.7	77.4	33.3	81.6	51.8
Buffalo, NY	85.7	90.4	83.0	67.8	74.4	28.6	38.1	15.6	34.1	18.8
Cape Coral, FL	92.4	93.2	87.7	89.5	87.5	23.1	23.5	20.1	33.7	17.3
Cedar Rapids, IA	93.6	95.2	80.1	88.6	81.5	32.9	33.4	15.2	55.4	22.6
Charleston, SC	95.5	97.8	87.5	96.8	86.9	54.4	62.8	21.9	63.9	44.4
Charlotte, NC	89.4	93.9	90.4	84.4	60.4	44.8	57.0	29.8	61.9	18.1
Chicago, IL	85.9	89.8	85.9	87.6	70.1	41.1	53.3	22.8	63.6	17.9
Cincinnati, OH	88.4	92.5	83.1	92.0	75.0	38.7	54.8	15.6	79.7	34.6
Clarksville, TN	93.2	93.9	92.9	86.2	87.7	28.3	29.9	24.0	35.7	16.7
Cleveland, OH	82.2	84.9	80.8	75.9	70.0	18.6	26.8	10.3	43.6	9.2
College Station, TX	94.8	95.3	91.2	94.9	86.3	57.8	57.2	33.0	80.3	43.3
Colorado Springs, CO	94.0	95.3	94.1	84.3	82.6	39.6	42.7	24.4	42.6	19.7
Columbia, MO	95.2	96.1	90.7	95.0	92.3	53.3	55.6	25.9	72.6	44.0
Columbia, SC	90.0	95.8	82.9	91.0	86.9	43.4	60.9	20.5	70.4	34.5
Columbus, OH	89.8	92.3	86.5	85.2	73.7	36.8	43.0	19.4	59.1	25.2
Dallas, TX	79.0	78.2	88.2	85.6	54.0	34.7	41.6	21.2	65.5	12.7
Davenport, IA	91.5	93.5	84.0	74.8	74.8	26.6	28.6	9.6	34.1	14.2
Denver, CO	89.1	92.0	88.2	85.5	67.4	50.3	56.8	27.3	54.7	16.8
Des Moines, IA	86.7	90.8	81.7	60.5	57.5	27.9	30.6	15.3	25.5	9.3
Durham, NC	89.7	91.9	89.6	91.6	51.7	51.2	62.7	34.9	77.0	15.5
Edison, NJ	92.0	92.8	96.1	92.7	81.8	55.4	37.1	38.7	76.7	24.3
El Paso, TX	80.6	82.3	96.6	89.1	76.8	25.9	27.2	30.3	53.6	21.9
Fargo, ND	94.6	96.2	82.8	77.6	93.1	40.9	42.8	18.5	52.3	14.6
Fort Collins, CO	96.7	97.3	94.0	91.4	85.9	55.6	56.7	33.9	69.7	33.6
Fort Wayne, IN	89.0	93.0	84.8	49.9	64.6	28.2	31.3	15.9	25.7	12.5
Fort Worth, TX	83.2	86.4	89.0	82.7	62.2	30.1	35.2	21.7	44.3	13.3
Grand Rapids, MI	87.3	91.4	84.8	79.8	53.7	37.7	44.5	19.2	44.2	12.3
Green Bay, WI	87.5	90.4	83.4	77.0	53.4	24.4	26.3	16.4	27.6	7.1
Honolulu, HI	89.8	97.7	95.1	86.7	92.9	37.8	53.0	31.1	37.5	29.8
Houston, TX	79.7	80.3	89.0	87.6	60.0	34.3	40.2	24.5	61.6	15.1
Huntsville, AL	90.7	93.3	86.5	90.5	66.9	44.0	50.5	29.5	57.8	26.3
Indianapolis, IN	86.4	89.3	85.1	71.3	58.5	32.1	38.0	19.0	44.9	14.2
Jacksonville, FL	89.8	91.4	87.5	88.1	82.9	29.3	31.8	20.6	49.1	26.8
Kansas City, MO	90.7	93.5	87.7	83.8	72.1	35.7	44.1	16.7	49.4	19.9
Lafayette, LA	90.3	94.9	79.4	92.6	73.4	39.3	48.7	15.9	60.4	29.3
Las Cruces, NM	88.5	89.8	86.9	89.6	82.9	36.8	37.5	48.4	66.3	23.6
Las Vegas, NV	85.3	88.6	88.7	91.5	65.4	25.2	27.9	18.6	42.6	10.5
Lexington, KY	91.9	94.0	87.3	90.2	65.1	45.0	49.2	20.7	69.3	22.3
Lincoln, NE	92.9	94.7	85.2	80.8	68.8	39.9	41.1	23.6	46.1	20.9
Little Rock, AR	91.9	95.0	89.2	87.2	65.9	42.6	56.4	24.2	57.6	10.0
Los Angeles, CA	78.3	82.8	89.0	90.7	57.8	35.6	42.3	28.4	55.6	13.5
Louisville, KY	89.7	91.4	86.7	78.9	77.9	30.4	33.9	17.3	49.8	25.9
Madison, WI	95.9	97.3	87.9	92.7	82.2	58.5	60.3	24.6	72.2	42.3
Manchester, NH	87.5	89.2	76.0	79.4	64.8	30.8	31.5	17.2	39.6	12.3

Table continued on following page.

City	High School Graduate or Higher (%)					Bachelor's Degree or Higher (%)				
	Total	White	Black	Asian	Hisp.[1]	Total	White	Black	Asian	Hisp.[1]
Memphis, TN	86.5	92.7	85.3	81.7	50.9	26.6	46.5	16.1	55.6	13.1
Miami, FL	78.3	79.2	75.9	91.4	75.5	31.5	34.2	15.0	69.2	28.0
Midland, TX	83.9	86.2	87.1	77.5	69.0	29.2	32.0	15.8	49.0	12.8
Milwaukee, WI	84.4	90.0	83.8	72.8	62.9	24.6	35.9	12.9	29.3	10.2
Minneapolis, MN	90.4	96.4	74.8	85.2	62.8	51.8	62.5	16.6	57.4	24.4
Nashville, TN	89.5	91.4	88.8	82.3	57.2	42.8	48.8	28.0	55.9	15.9
New Haven, CT	85.6	86.7	87.9	93.8	71.8	35.2	46.8	21.9	76.8	13.8
New Orleans, LA	87.7	96.0	83.0	76.7	80.0	38.0	64.4	19.9	42.8	37.8
New York, NY	82.8	89.5	84.2	76.5	70.2	39.1	53.1	25.2	43.5	19.7
Oklahoma City, OK	86.8	88.0	91.3	81.7	55.2	31.5	34.1	23.6	40.6	10.0
Omaha, NE	89.8	92.3	87.0	71.1	57.6	38.3	41.8	18.8	49.8	12.9
Orlando, FL	90.7	93.6	82.9	91.9	88.5	39.9	47.2	21.9	51.0	31.6
Philadelphia, PA	85.7	90.7	86.2	72.2	70.3	31.2	44.1	18.6	39.4	17.3
Phoenix, AZ	82.9	85.9	89.0	85.7	64.2	29.4	31.9	24.1	58.6	11.1
Pittsburgh, PA	93.2	94.7	88.7	92.6	86.3	45.4	50.8	20.1	77.7	48.6
Portland, OR	92.9	95.3	85.7	78.9	77.9	51.0	54.9	23.9	43.6	33.0
Providence, RI	82.7	87.4	84.9	84.7	72.3	32.3	40.5	23.2	52.9	11.7
Provo, UT	93.1	93.8	97.2	86.7	76.0	42.9	44.2	20.3	47.6	17.6
Raleigh, NC	92.2	96.3	90.5	89.0	64.1	51.4	63.0	31.3	58.4	23.8
Reno, NV	89.9	92.6	94.1	91.9	67.0	34.8	36.5	30.2	52.2	13.5
Richmond, VA	86.9	94.0	80.5	84.9	56.6	41.2	65.2	14.4	65.9	17.8
Riverside, CA	81.6	85.7	90.8	88.7	69.9	24.1	25.1	28.9	52.0	12.8
Rochester, MN	93.9	96.4	71.9	85.0	73.0	48.0	49.5	17.7	60.9	31.8
Rochester, NY	82.2	87.7	77.3	70.9	69.4	27.1	40.0	11.3	40.0	9.7
Sacramento, CA	85.9	90.5	91.1	80.6	73.8	34.3	41.2	24.0	38.4	19.9
St. Louis, MO	88.7	93.7	83.0	85.6	77.6	37.2	53.2	16.0	57.3	37.4
Salt Lake City, UT	90.0	94.7	85.0	82.9	65.1	48.7	53.3	34.2	61.4	20.6
San Antonio, TX	82.7	83.6	90.9	85.4	75.7	26.4	27.3	24.7	53.8	17.0
San Diego, CA	88.8	90.4	91.4	88.9	71.8	46.7	49.7	27.7	53.7	21.7
San Francisco, CA	88.6	96.8	87.7	79.9	78.2	58.8	74.4	30.2	47.9	35.9
San Jose, CA	85.0	89.6	91.4	87.0	68.7	44.8	46.4	37.3	56.5	16.5
Santa Rosa, CA	86.2	92.3	86.7	85.7	62.8	33.8	38.9	28.8	46.7	13.9
Savannah, GA	88.1	93.9	83.9	81.9	80.8	29.1	44.4	15.9	52.8	25.6
Seattle, WA	95.2	98.0	88.2	89.6	85.7	65.0	70.0	34.5	64.6	45.2
Sioux Falls, SD	93.0	95.3	79.9	72.4	68.5	35.1	37.3	18.3	36.8	13.3
Springfield, IL	91.5	93.6	81.0	93.3	88.0	34.8	37.4	17.0	67.8	37.0
Tampa, FL	88.4	91.1	84.2	87.2	78.4	39.9	46.7	18.2	64.9	24.8
Tucson, AZ	85.9	89.2	84.2	86.8	74.6	28.2	31.3	20.6	49.4	14.8
Tulsa, OK	87.8	90.5	89.6	74.4	59.0	31.3	36.1	17.2	37.0	11.1
Tuscaloosa, AL	90.9	95.5	86.9	90.0	77.0	38.3	57.1	17.3	64.2	9.5
Virginia Beach, VA	94.0	95.6	92.6	88.4	84.9	37.3	40.2	27.5	41.2	27.6
Washington, DC	91.9	98.2	87.8	95.2	75.7	59.8	89.8	29.1	83.4	47.6
Wichita, KS	88.5	91.1	88.3	76.6	64.1	30.7	33.5	17.3	36.9	13.7
Wilmington, NC	93.0	94.9	87.1	86.6	76.6	43.9	49.6	19.1	58.5	31.9
Winston-Salem, NC	87.9	89.9	87.9	88.0	58.6	34.3	41.8	21.3	71.1	15.4
U.S.	88.5	90.7	86.7	87.3	70.3	32.9	34.4	22.6	55.0	17.6

Note: Figures shown cover persons 25 years old and over; (1) People of Hispanic origin can be of any race
Source: U.S. Census Bureau, 2016-2020 American Community Survey 5-Year Estimates

Educational Attainment by Race: Metro Area

Metro Area	High School Graduate or Higher (%)					Bachelor's Degree or Higher (%)				
	Total	White	Black	Asian	Hisp.[1]	Total	White	Black	Asian	Hisp.[1]
Albuquerque, NM	89.6	91.5	91.5	89.4	83.1	33.0	36.1	34.0	52.3	20.7
Allentown, PA	90.6	91.8	88.9	87.6	76.7	30.6	31.2	21.6	59.4	15.1
Anchorage, AK	93.9	95.7	92.7	85.7	85.6	32.7	37.1	20.2	25.2	22.6
Ann Arbor, MI	95.7	96.7	90.3	96.4	88.5	56.7	58.4	28.2	82.7	46.6
Athens, GA	89.1	91.6	82.5	89.4	65.8	40.1	44.6	20.6	66.6	28.3
Atlanta, GA	90.2	91.9	91.1	87.1	66.6	39.5	43.5	31.6	59.1	22.1
Austin, TX	90.6	92.4	91.0	92.6	75.9	46.0	48.1	30.6	72.1	25.0
Baltimore, MD	91.3	93.3	88.5	89.2	76.6	41.0	45.4	27.4	63.1	32.2
Baton Rouge, LA	87.8	91.1	82.9	85.3	68.1	28.8	32.9	19.5	58.3	19.2
Boise City, ID	92.2	94.0	86.6	88.6	71.0	33.2	34.2	27.6	49.2	14.8
Boston, MA	92.0	94.8	85.9	86.2	73.3	48.9	51.5	27.9	63.1	23.9
Boulder, CO	95.5	96.6	88.7	93.4	75.1	63.0	64.0	24.7	73.3	30.2
Buffalo, NY	92.0	93.8	84.4	80.0	77.7	33.3	35.2	17.3	52.9	23.4
Cape Coral, FL	89.3	90.9	80.0	92.2	73.8	28.5	30.1	15.4	47.5	14.8
Cedar Rapids, IA	94.5	95.5	80.9	86.2	80.4	31.6	32.0	15.1	53.9	22.6
Charleston, SC	90.8	94.1	84.2	89.6	70.7	36.5	43.6	17.4	51.0	20.7
Charlotte, NC	89.4	91.5	88.9	86.1	64.4	35.9	38.6	26.6	60.8	19.1
Chicago, IL	89.1	92.1	88.4	91.0	69.5	39.0	42.9	24.0	66.4	16.0
Cincinnati, OH	91.5	92.3	87.3	89.9	76.8	34.5	35.6	20.5	65.3	29.5
Clarksville, TN	91.3	91.9	89.9	85.9	86.6	26.0	26.5	23.3	39.3	18.6
Cleveland, OH	91.0	92.8	85.9	86.9	76.0	31.9	35.1	16.2	62.9	16.9
College Station, TX	87.6	88.2	87.3	94.1	66.7	37.8	39.0	19.0	77.7	17.3
Colorado Springs, CO	94.6	95.6	94.9	86.0	84.7	38.6	40.8	27.4	41.5	20.8
Columbia, MO	93.8	94.4	89.5	94.4	86.6	44.3	45.4	22.4	70.6	36.5
Columbia, SC	90.2	92.1	88.1	90.4	68.2	33.0	37.2	24.3	58.3	22.3
Columbus, OH	91.7	93.1	87.2	87.8	76.7	37.3	39.1	21.9	62.8	28.3
Dallas, TX	86.2	87.5	91.3	88.7	62.7	36.0	37.3	28.4	62.0	15.5
Davenport, IA	91.6	93.5	78.0	81.6	75.0	27.5	28.4	12.6	49.5	15.8
Denver, CO	91.6	93.7	90.0	84.4	73.1	44.7	47.9	28.3	51.2	17.9
Des Moines, IA	93.0	94.9	84.3	74.3	64.8	37.1	38.3	19.8	41.3	15.1
Durham, NC	89.8	91.8	88.1	92.1	54.8	46.4	52.6	30.1	75.1	19.1
Edison, NJ	87.0	91.4	85.9	84.0	72.5	41.4	47.6	26.5	55.6	20.8
El Paso, TX	78.8	80.8	96.2	89.6	75.0	23.9	25.3	29.8	51.8	20.1
Fargo, ND	95.1	96.3	83.0	80.6	88.2	39.1	40.4	19.8	50.9	17.0
Fort Collins, CO	96.2	96.7	95.5	90.3	84.1	47.7	48.4	32.8	57.6	26.9
Fort Wayne, IN	90.0	92.7	85.5	56.3	67.0	28.4	30.2	16.5	30.3	11.9
Fort Worth, TX	86.2	87.5	91.3	88.7	62.7	36.0	37.3	28.4	62.0	15.5
Grand Rapids, MI	91.8	93.7	86.7	74.5	66.8	33.7	35.4	19.8	38.6	15.0
Green Bay, WI	92.4	94.1	83.2	84.7	58.2	27.9	28.6	20.1	47.2	10.2
Honolulu, HI	92.4	97.5	96.7	89.8	94.3	35.7	48.5	31.2	37.2	26.9
Houston, TX	84.3	85.2	91.4	87.2	65.9	33.6	34.8	28.9	56.8	16.0
Huntsville, AL	90.3	91.8	87.1	91.6	71.3	39.8	42.0	31.6	60.2	26.7
Indianapolis, IN	90.2	92.1	86.2	80.4	65.6	35.6	37.9	21.3	55.9	19.2
Jacksonville, FL	91.1	92.5	87.9	89.6	85.1	32.1	34.4	20.9	49.3	27.9
Kansas City, MO	92.5	94.0	89.5	87.6	71.0	37.5	40.1	20.5	56.9	18.7
Lafayette, LA	85.3	88.1	78.4	73.8	66.8	24.3	27.5	13.0	37.1	15.6
Las Cruces, NM	80.6	81.6	88.1	91.9	72.5	29.5	30.1	48.8	62.5	18.3
Las Vegas, NV	86.3	89.1	90.1	90.7	67.6	25.2	26.9	18.8	40.7	11.0
Lexington, KY	90.9	92.3	87.3	90.5	64.2	38.6	40.5	20.5	65.0	19.5
Lincoln, NE	93.3	94.9	85.4	80.5	69.4	39.3	40.3	23.6	45.8	21.3
Little Rock, AR	91.2	92.4	89.4	87.3	72.0	31.4	33.5	24.5	48.5	15.0
Los Angeles, CA	81.3	84.9	90.1	88.4	63.7	35.4	38.5	28.9	53.9	14.4
Louisville, KY	90.4	91.4	87.2	84.8	74.5	30.1	31.6	18.2	55.9	22.4
Madison, WI	95.7	96.6	89.3	90.9	77.8	47.1	47.4	25.9	68.9	31.0
Manchester, NH	92.4	93.0	82.9	89.5	73.0	38.6	38.5	24.1	60.7	17.6

Table continued on following page.

Metro Area	High School Graduate or Higher (%)					Bachelor's Degree or Higher (%)				
	Total	White	Black	Asian	Hisp.[1]	Total	White	Black	Asian	Hisp.[1]
Memphis, TN	88.7	92.6	86.2	85.9	57.9	28.8	36.5	19.5	59.5	15.8
Miami, FL	85.9	87.6	82.5	87.2	80.6	33.0	36.6	20.4	52.8	28.8
Midland, TX	84.0	85.9	87.6	79.5	69.3	27.2	29.4	15.5	52.3	11.8
Milwaukee, WI	91.8	94.8	84.6	84.8	69.6	36.1	40.7	14.1	51.5	15.4
Minneapolis, MN	93.8	96.4	82.9	82.1	72.2	42.7	45.0	23.2	46.5	22.6
Nashville, TN	90.5	91.5	89.4	86.3	63.7	37.3	38.5	29.1	56.1	17.9
New Haven, CT	90.3	92.2	88.1	91.1	74.8	36.0	38.6	22.2	66.8	15.4
New Orleans, LA	87.5	90.8	83.8	77.6	75.6	31.1	37.6	19.4	40.4	20.7
New York, NY	87.0	91.4	85.9	84.0	72.5	41.4	47.6	26.5	55.6	20.8
Oklahoma City, OK	89.4	90.5	91.7	84.7	60.6	31.5	33.2	23.8	45.3	12.8
Omaha, NE	92.0	93.6	88.0	76.1	64.2	37.0	38.5	21.2	49.2	16.4
Orlando, FL	89.6	91.4	84.9	89.0	84.6	33.1	35.1	23.9	52.1	24.7
Philadelphia, PA	91.2	93.8	88.4	84.2	72.2	38.7	43.1	22.2	56.6	20.0
Phoenix, AZ	88.3	90.5	90.9	88.4	70.5	32.2	33.7	26.2	58.9	14.0
Pittsburgh, PA	94.3	94.8	90.2	88.0	87.7	35.9	36.2	21.3	69.8	36.5
Portland, OR	92.5	94.1	88.7	87.2	70.8	40.4	40.9	28.8	53.7	20.5
Providence, RI	88.1	89.5	84.8	87.3	74.5	33.0	34.4	24.7	52.4	15.9
Provo, UT	95.1	95.5	96.1	93.5	78.8	40.7	41.2	29.4	54.3	22.0
Raleigh, NC	92.3	94.8	90.3	92.1	65.4	47.8	51.8	31.4	73.3	21.8
Reno, NV	88.9	91.9	92.2	91.3	64.7	31.7	33.4	27.2	49.0	12.4
Richmond, VA	90.7	93.6	86.4	89.4	69.2	38.0	44.3	21.7	66.2	21.8
Riverside, CA	81.8	85.1	89.9	90.2	69.1	22.4	23.0	24.2	49.2	11.7
Rochester, MN	94.1	95.6	73.1	85.1	72.0	40.3	40.4	17.9	59.1	28.9
Rochester, NY	90.8	93.1	78.9	80.5	75.1	35.6	38.2	15.2	52.8	17.9
Sacramento, CA	89.7	92.7	91.2	84.1	75.8	34.3	35.7	25.4	43.9	19.4
St. Louis, MO	92.5	93.9	87.2	90.3	81.1	35.4	37.8	19.5	66.9	30.4
Salt Lake City, UT	91.5	94.6	85.3	86.6	72.4	35.8	38.0	23.8	51.0	16.6
San Antonio, TX	85.5	86.5	92.0	86.8	77.1	28.8	29.7	29.1	52.3	17.9
San Diego, CA	88.0	89.5	91.7	89.5	72.0	39.5	41.2	26.6	51.7	18.8
San Francisco, CA	89.5	94.4	91.3	87.6	72.9	50.7	57.3	30.9	56.6	23.0
San Jose, CA	88.5	91.4	92.3	91.0	70.6	52.5	51.2	40.7	66.4	18.5
Santa Rosa, CA	89.1	93.7	87.8	87.7	65.5	36.4	40.6	31.3	47.8	14.7
Savannah, GA	90.2	92.8	86.8	83.3	82.2	32.6	38.6	20.0	50.8	25.6
Seattle, WA	92.9	95.3	89.8	89.5	75.2	43.6	44.3	27.6	56.9	24.5
Sioux Falls, SD	93.5	95.0	80.6	73.5	70.2	33.9	35.3	17.9	37.6	14.8
Springfield, IL	92.7	94.0	81.5	90.3	88.3	33.5	34.7	17.5	65.2	35.9
Tampa, FL	89.9	91.1	88.1	85.2	81.3	31.2	31.7	23.9	51.3	23.6
Tucson, AZ	89.0	91.8	87.5	88.3	77.3	33.6	36.7	27.3	54.7	17.4
Tulsa, OK	90.0	91.6	90.1	78.3	65.0	27.9	30.1	19.1	35.7	12.9
Tuscaloosa, AL	88.1	90.8	84.5	82.5	70.8	27.9	34.6	15.6	55.7	11.8
Virginia Beach, VA	91.9	94.5	87.9	87.7	84.1	32.9	37.3	22.9	43.5	26.8
Washington, DC	91.3	94.5	92.1	91.0	69.6	51.7	60.0	36.2	65.1	27.2
Wichita, KS	90.3	92.3	88.1	77.3	66.3	31.0	32.6	19.5	37.0	15.9
Wilmington, NC	92.3	93.9	86.6	83.5	78.5	39.4	42.5	20.8	60.6	27.0
Winston-Salem, NC	87.5	88.7	87.3	86.6	59.1	26.8	27.8	21.2	55.8	13.9
U.S.	88.5	90.7	86.7	87.3	70.3	32.9	34.4	22.6	55.0	17.6

Note: Figures shown cover persons 25 years old and over; Figures cover the Metropolitan Statistical Area; (1) People of Hispanic origin can be of any race
Source: U.S. Census Bureau, 2016-2020 American Community Survey 5-Year Estimates

Cost of Living Index

Urban Area	Composite	Groceries	Housing	Utilities	Transp.	Health	Misc.
Albuquerque, NM	93.8	104.8	84.5	87.7	97.2	99.8	96.6
Allentown, PA	104.4	98.4	114.0	103.4	104.8	94.6	100.6
Anchorage, AK	124.5	132.6	140.0	124.0	114.8	144.2	109.7
Ann Arbor, MI	n/a	n/a	n/a	n/a	n/a	n/a	n/a
Athens, GA	n/a	n/a	n/a	n/a	n/a	n/a	n/a
Atlanta, GA	102.8	103.4	103.5	85.1	103.6	107.1	106.0
Austin, TX	99.7	91.2	105.5	95.2	90.7	105.8	101.4
Baltimore, MD	n/a	n/a	n/a	n/a	n/a	n/a	n/a
Baton Rouge	99.4	102.6	92.3	85.4	100.5	104.5	106.5
Boise City, ID	98.7	94.5	97.5	81.9	108.5	103.0	102.8
Boston, MA	151.0	109.3	228.6	120.5	112.0	118.3	129.3
Boulder, CO	n/a	n/a	n/a	n/a	n/a	n/a	n/a
Buffalo, NY	n/a	n/a	n/a	n/a	n/a	n/a	n/a
Cape Coral, FL	100.6	107.8	89.6	98.8	98.7	108.5	106.3
Cedar Rapids, IA	96.2	94.8	83.0	102.1	96.6	107.0	103.9
Charleston, SC	97.2	99.7	93.2	120.4	86.6	97.5	95.9
Charlotte, NC	98.2	101.7	88.8	95.6	90.7	105.1	106.0
Chicago, IL	120.6	101.9	155.7	92.4	125.9	100.0	109.4
Cincinnati, OH	99.7	91.2	105.5	95.2	90.7	105.8	101.4
Clarksville, TN	n/a	n/a	n/a	n/a	n/a	n/a	n/a
Cleveland, OH	96.9	106.0	83.3	96.1	99.4	104.4	102.6
College Station, TX	n/a	n/a	n/a	n/a	n/a	n/a	n/a
Colorado Springs, CO	101.1	95.9	101.3	97.2	97.7	108.6	104.1
Columbia, MO	91.8	95.5	75.0	100.0	92.0	102.6	99.8
Columbia, SC	93.5	103.1	72.7	126.2	87.1	79.9	100.5
Columbus, OH	92.6	98.6	81.2	89.1	95.5	88.5	99.7
Dallas, TX	108.2	100.2	118.8	106.8	96.7	105.4	106.7
Davenport, IA	92.0	99.7	76.9	98.9	105.8	105.3	93.7
Denver, CO	111.3	98.3	139.3	80.5	100.9	103.6	106.6
Des Moines, IA	89.9	95.2	80.2	90.1	99.1	95.4	92.3
Durham, NC[1]	n/a	n/a	n/a	n/a	n/a	n/a	n/a
Edison, NJ[2]	120.6	108.7	149.3	105.8	107.8	102.5	112.4
El Paso, TX	87.7	102.3	73.7	85.7	99.0	99.3	89.0
Fargo, ND	98.6	111.5	77.6	90.5	100.4	120.1	108.9
Fort Collins, CO	n/a	n/a	n/a	n/a	n/a	n/a	n/a
Fort Wayne, IN	86.9	86.7	62.3	95.7	99.5	101.5	98.6
Fort Worth, TX	94.9	92.4	88.4	107.2	96.9	101.5	96.2
Grand Rapids, MI	94.1	92.8	87.4	98.5	104.1	92.3	96.3
Green Bay, WI	91.1	91.0	77.9	97.4	97.7	101.8	96.6
Honolulu, HI	192.9	165.0	332.6	172.3	138.2	118.8	124.2
Houston, TX	95.8	88.4	91.2	105.8	95.2	92.0	100.3
Huntsville, AL	91.3	95.1	66.6	99.0	97.3	96.4	104.7
Indianapolis, IN	92.4	94.1	78.4	105.4	97.9	90.6	98.0
Jacksonville, FL	91.7	98.4	88.0	97.7	86.0	83.7	92.7
Kansas City, MO	95.8	102.4	82.6	100.6	92.6	105.9	101.7
Lafayette, LA	88.9	101.8	72.0	88.0	104.7	88.0	93.3
Las Cruces, NM	n/a	n/a	n/a	n/a	n/a	n/a	n/a
Las Vegas, NV	103.6	95.8	118.3	98.6	114.0	100.2	94.2
Lexington, KY	92.7	89.9	83.7	95.6	96.7	78.9	100.7
Lincoln, NE	93.0	95.6	78.7	90.2	93.4	105.8	102.2
Little Rock, AR	96.0	95.1	88.1	97.4	94.7	89.6	103.2
Los Angeles, CA	146.7	116.3	230.6	106.2	134.8	110.8	112.0
Louisville, KY	94.1	91.8	79.8	94.6	98.1	105.2	103.7
Madison, WI	107.0	107.6	108.6	99.8	104.4	124.0	106.0
Manchester, NH	108.9	102.2	109.6	117.9	104.1	116.0	108.9
Memphis, TN	99.7	91.2	105.5	95.2	90.7	105.8	101.4

Table continued on following page.

Urban Area	Composite	Groceries	Housing	Utilities	Transp.	Health	Misc.
Miami, FL	115.0	110.5	144.3	102.0	101.5	100.6	102.7
Midland, TX	102.1	93.6	91.5	106.6	104.1	96.5	112.6
Milwaukee, WI	96.7	93.4	100.5	94.8	99.8	115.9	92.4
Minneapolis, MN	106.6	103.6	102.9	97.5	104.4	105.6	113.9
Nashville, TN	98.9	99.5	98.5	97.0	97.9	92.4	100.4
New Haven, CT	122.3	111.0	128.5	136.7	110.6	115.8	121.9
New Orleans, LA	105.0	102.6	125.5	81.5	101.3	115.1	96.1
New York, NY[3]	181.6	128.4	339.0	121.4	113.7	107.1	123.1
Oklahoma City, OK	86.0	93.3	69.6	95.3	86.2	95.0	92.1
Omaha, NE	92.3	96.8	83.6	99.4	98.3	96.4	93.3
Orlando, FL	92.1	100.7	85.1	97.2	89.3	88.3	94.1
Philadelphia, PA	110.9	118.7	116.5	105.6	116.1	101.8	104.8
Phoenix, AZ	99.3	99.7	103.8	109.5	107.2	90.1	91.9
Pittsburgh, PA	103.1	111.9	105.7	116.1	114.0	93.1	92.6
Portland, OR	134.7	112.4	186.4	87.1	131.0	115.6	119.4
Providence, RI	119.2	106.7	132.8	126.4	112.1	109.3	114.6
Provo, UT	98.2	93.0	96.1	84.7	100.7	94.5	105.4
Raleigh, NC	95.4	92.7	89.0	98.3	90.9	103.8	100.9
Reno, NV	114.1	118.7	125.8	85.9	126.3	113.9	107.6
Richmond, VA	94.2	89.0	86.0	97.6	86.9	106.7	102.1
Riverside, CA	99.7	91.2	105.5	95.2	90.7	105.8	101.4
Rochester, MN	n/a	n/a	n/a	n/a	n/a	n/a	n/a
Rochester, NY	n/a	n/a	n/a	n/a	n/a	n/a	n/a
Sacramento, CA	118.4	120.2	134.2	102.9	139.0	113.6	104.8
Saint Louis, MO	n/a	n/a	n/a	n/a	n/a	n/a	n/a
Salt Lake City, UT	103.6	108.0	106.7	87.8	103.6	105.7	103.6
San Antonio, TX	89.5	88.0	82.2	87.6	89.1	87.2	96.5
San Diego, CA	142.1	116.1	216.3	123.2	129.2	107.3	107.3
San Francisco, CA	197.9	131.3	368.9	123.0	145.3	129.6	133.4
San Jose, CA	n/a	n/a	n/a	n/a	n/a	n/a	n/a
Santa Rosa, CA	n/a	n/a	n/a	n/a	n/a	n/a	n/a
Savannah, GA	89.5	95.7	66.2	96.0	94.9	106.1	100.0
Seattle, WA	157.5	129.1	227.6	108.0	137.8	128.6	136.2
Sioux Falls, SD	92.5	96.3	86.3	84.7	91.9	107.7	96.3
Springfield, IL	n/a	n/a	n/a	n/a	n/a	n/a	n/a
Tampa, FL	91.2	104.8	79.2	85.9	99.4	98.3	93.7
Tucson, AZ	97.5	100.5	87.9	99.9	101.1	98.7	102.0
Tulsa, OK	86.0	96.2	62.7	99.5	84.4	91.6	96.1
Tuscaloosa, AL	n/a	n/a	n/a	n/a	n/a	n/a	n/a
Virginia Beach, VA[4]	94.1	92.7	89.1	97.4	92.2	90.4	98.7
Washington, DC	159.9	116.0	277.1	117.9	110.6	95.8	118.1
Wichita, KS	91.1	94.3	69.6	99.3	95.3	96.1	102.5
Wilmington, NC	n/a	n/a	n/a	n/a	n/a	n/a	n/a
Winston-Salem, NC	90.8	101.4	66.7	94.6	92.0	119.5	100.5
U.S.	100.0	100.0	100.0	100.0	100.0	100.0	100.0

Note: The Cost of Living Index measures regional differences in the cost of consumer goods and services, excluding taxes and non-consumer expenditures, for professional and managerial households in the top income quintile. It is based on more than 50,000 prices covering almost 60 different items for which prices are collected three times a year by chambers of commerce, economic development organizations or university applied economic centers in each participating urban area. The numbers shown should be read as a percentage above or below the national average of 100. For example, a value of 115.4 in the groceries column indicates that grocery prices are 15.4% higher than the national average. Small differences in the index numbers should not be interpreted as significant. In cases where data is not available for the city, data for the metro area or for a neighboring city has been provided and noted as follows: (1) Chapel Hill NC; (2) Middlesex-Monmouth NJ; (3) Brooklyn, NY; (4) Hampton Roads-SE Virginia

Source: The Council for Community and Economic Research, Cost of Living Index, 2021

Grocery Prices

Urban Area	T-Bone Steak ($/pound)	Frying Chicken ($/pound)	Whole Milk ($/half gal.)	Eggs ($/dozen)	Orange Juice ($/64 oz.)	Coffee ($/11.5 oz.)
Albuquerque, NM	12.04	1.09	1.81	1.49	3.60	4.14
Allentown, PA	13.54	1.34	2.12	1.39	3.39	3.47
Anchorage, AK	14.13	1.88	3.02	2.19	4.02	5.16
Ann Arbor, MI	n/a	n/a	n/a	n/a	n/a	n/a
Athens, GA	n/a	n/a	n/a	n/a	n/a	n/a
Atlanta, GA	12.56	1.02	1.66	1.14	3.82	4.87
Austin, TX	11.94	1.15	1.98	1.56	3.20	4.04
Baltimore, MD	13.47	1.53	2.57	2.01	3.58	4.45
Baton Rouge	11.76	1.15	2.29	1.44	3.42	4.00
Boise City, ID	13.01	1.55	1.90	1.17	3.49	4.45
Boston, MA	15.77	1.92	3.07	2.02	3.61	4.06
Boulder, CO	n/a	n/a	n/a	n/a	n/a	n/a
Buffalo, NY	14.42	1.26	2.34	1.41	3.34	4.27
Cape Coral, FL	13.34	2.05	2.81	1.74	3.86	3.83
Cedar Rapids, IA	16.35	1.46	2.43	1.52	3.39	4.98
Charleston, SC	9.95	1.40	1.73	1.22	3.43	4.09
Charlotte, NC	11.92	1.42	1.73	1.42	3.64	3.94
Chicago, IL	14.96	1.85	2.26	1.68	3.68	4.62
Cincinnati, OH	13.63	1.54	1.60	1.26	3.62	4.24
Clarksville, TN	n/a	n/a	n/a	n/a	n/a	n/a
Cleveland, OH	15.38	1.65	1.75	1.27	3.67	4.17
College Station, TX	n/a	n/a	n/a	n/a	n/a	n/a
Colorado Springs, CO	14.08	1.19	1.75	1.25	3.48	4.68
Columbia, MO	13.00	1.60	2.24	1.06	3.50	4.17
Columbia, SC	12.10	1.31	2.37	1.40	3.62	4.25
Columbus, OH	13.55	1.19	1.71	1.73	3.68	7.43
Dallas, TX	11.96	1.19	2.29	1.34	3.57	4.46
Davenport, IA	13.78	1.59	2.99	1.82	3.81	5.07
Denver, CO	12.86	1.24	1.79	1.49	3.58	4.10
Des Moines, IA	14.11	1.57	2.34	1.25	3.07	4.30
Durham, NC[1]	13.27	1.52	2.10	1.47	4.03	3.62
Edison, NJ[2]	14.36	1.97	2.56	1.75	3.34	4.30
El Paso, TX	14.97	1.82	2.31	1.65	3.55	5.71
Fargo, ND	n/a	n/a	n/a	n/a	n/a	n/a
Fort Collins, CO	n/a	n/a	n/a	n/a	n/a	n/a
Fort Wayne, IN	12.59	1.04	1.49	0.75	3.16	3.46
Fort Worth, TX	12.62	1.45	2.01	1.48	3.93	4.49
Grand Rapids, MI	13.62	1.16	1.72	1.48	3.19	3.11
Green Bay, WI	14.19	1.19	1.79	1.17	3.47	3.79
Honolulu, HI	16.01	2.24	3.92	3.86	5.09	8.11
Houston, TX	11.80	1.23	2.04	1.55	3.78	4.17
Huntsville, AL	12.21	1.52	1.92	1.15	3.81	4.13
Indianapolis, IN	13.08	1.34	1.73	1.29	3.41	4.04
Jacksonville, FL	11.92	1.71	2.61	1.83	3.69	4.82
Kansas City, MO	12.34	1.56	2.26	1.23	3.04	3.83
Lafayette, LA	12.07	1.33	2.46	2.59	3.63	4.34
Las Cruces, NM	13.27	1.05	3.31	1.97	3.64	4.63
Las Vegas, NV	12.62	1.70	2.79	2.22	3.76	6.03
Lexington, KY	12.65	1.04	1.67	1.36	3.38	3.85
Lincoln, NE	12.39	1.45	2.05	1.28	2.98	4.22
Little Rock, AR	11.20	1.10	1.85	1.38	3.25	3.86
Los Angeles, CA	12.66	1.79	2.30	2.95	3.76	5.47
Louisville, KY	14.79	1.15	1.41	1.00	3.39	3.54
Madison, WI	15.92	1.55	2.27	1.29	3.55	4.59
Manchester, NH	14.29	1.20	2.62	1.79	3.74	4.15

Table continued on following page.

Urban Area	T-Bone Steak ($/pound)	Frying Chicken ($/pound)	Whole Milk ($/half gal.)	Eggs ($/dozen)	Orange Juice ($/64 oz.)	Coffee ($/11.5 oz.)
Memphis, TN	12.74	1.01	1.90	1.25	3.26	4.05
Miami, FL	13.85	1.79	3.36	1.84	3.88	3.41
Midland, TX	11.20	1.02	1.74	1.53	3.53	4.14
Milwaukee, WI	12.29	1.32	2.32	1.49	3.32	4.28
Minneapolis, MN	13.31	2.02	2.52	1.85	3.74	4.70
Nashville, TN	13.73	1.09	2.09	1.14	3.91	4.49
New Haven, CT	14.03	1.41	2.85	1.93	3.16	3.68
New Orleans, LA	12.62	1.21	2.30	1.71	3.48	3.81
New York, NY[3]	15.49	1.89	2.72	2.46	3.88	4.60
Oklahoma City, OK	12.77	1.25	1.99	1.23	3.23	4.03
Omaha, NE	13.29	1.13	2.07	1.49	3.59	4.94
Orlando, FL	11.02	1.51	2.51	1.63	3.81	3.85
Philadelphia, PA	14.32	1.69	2.15	1.96	4.35	4.78
Phoenix, AZ	13.76	1.61	1.82	1.78	3.78	4.69
Pittsburgh, PA	15.37	1.71	2.04	1.38	3.36	4.53
Portland, OR	12.57	1.58	2.61	2.04	3.93	5.63
Providence, RI	13.95	1.75	2.62	2.14	3.82	3.33
Provo, UT	11.47	1.42	1.76	1.43	4.08	5.22
Raleigh, NC	11.32	1.05	1.74	1.17	3.59	3.46
Reno, NV	12.76	1.32	2.81	1.70	3.50	5.53
Richmond, VA	11.66	1.08	1.72	1.17	3.44	3.84
Riverside, CA	n/a	n/a	n/a	n/a	n/a	n/a
Rochester, MN	n/a	n/a	n/a	n/a	n/a	n/a
Rochester, NY	14.15	1.11	2.52	1.34	3.40	4.42
Sacramento, CA	11.52	1.59	3.79	2.54	3.84	4.84
Saint Louis, MO	18.02	1.64	1.78	1.34	3.47	4.17
Salt Lake City, UT	12.10	1.56	1.78	1.40	3.60	4.44
San Antonio, TX	10.38	1.00	2.06	2.01	3.16	3.83
San Diego, CA	12.43	1.79	2.30	2.99	3.82	5.47
San Francisco, CA	16.71	1.80	2.55	2.94	4.14	6.12
San Jose, CA	n/a	n/a	n/a	n/a	n/a	n/a
Santa Rosa, CA	n/a	n/a	n/a	n/a	n/a	n/a
Savannah, GA	12.39	1.27	1.94	1.39	3.28	3.95
Seattle, WA	16.53	2.57	2.21	1.98	4.23	6.20
Sioux Falls, SD	10.43	1.70	2.44	1.40	2.96	4.58
Springfield, IL	9.93	1.61	1.61	1.71	3.82	4.68
Tampa, FL	11.53	1.67	2.76	1.81	3.62	4.24
Tucson, AZ	13.02	1.48	1.70	1.58	3.65	5.12
Tulsa, OK	14.66	1.29	2.06	1.52	3.39	4.17
Tuscaloosa, AL	n/a	n/a	n/a	n/a	n/a	n/a
Virginia Beach, VA[4]	11.38	1.18	1.79	1.23	3.76	4.09
Washington, DC	13.82	1.68	2.91	1.89	3.40	4.38
Wichita, KS	12.91	1.20	1.97	1.19	3.88	4.33
Wilmington, NC	n/a	n/a	n/a	n/a	n/a	n/a
Winston-Salem, NC	13.32	1.27	1.48	1.19	4.01	3.73
Average*	12.82	1.40	2.22	1.57	3.59	4.30
Minimum*	8.91	0.91	1.29	0.75	2.87	3.02
Maximum*	21.35	2.69	3.92	3.86	5.49	8.11

Note: ***T-Bone Steak*** *(price per pound);* ***Frying Chicken*** *(price per pound, whole fryer);* ***Whole Milk*** *(half gallon carton);* ***Eggs*** *(price per dozen, Grade A, large);* ***Orange Juice*** *(64 oz. Tropicana or Florida Natural);* ***Coffee*** *(11.5 oz. can, vacuum-packed, Maxwell House, Hills Bros, or Folgers); (*) Average, minimum, and maximum values for all 285 areas in the Cost of Living Index report; n/a not available; In cases where data is not available for the city, data for the metro area or for a neighboring city has been provided and noted as follows: (1) Chapel Hill NC; (2) Middlesex-Monmouth NJ; (3) Brooklyn, NY; (4) Hampton Roads-SE Virginia*
Source: The Council for Community and Economic Research, Cost of Living Index, 2021

Housing and Utility Costs

Urban Area	New Home Price ($)	Apartment Rent ($/month)	All Electric ($/month)	Part Electric ($/month)	Other Energy ($/month)	Telephone ($/month)
Albuquerque, NM	365,948	951	-	106.17	44.01	187.47
Allentown, PA	426,283	1,469	-	99.25	82.35	192.45
Anchorage, AK	594,678	1,312	-	129.09	131.80	187.80
Ann Arbor, MI	n/a	n/a	n/a	n/a	n/a	n/a
Athens, GA	n/a	n/a	n/a	n/a	n/a	n/a
Atlanta, GA	449,444	1,377	-	84.93	37.58	188.46
Austin, TX	416,574	1,599	-	103.16	51.85	188.86
Baltimore, MD	417,557	1,648	-	87.81	94.03	195.41
Baton Rouge	358,085	1,139	100.84	-	-	182.36
Boise City, ID	437,890	1,410	-	63.81	63.35	173.61
Boston, MA	815,930	3,323	-	76.78	175.29	184.49
Boulder, CO	n/a	n/a	n/a	n/a	n/a	n/a
Buffalo, NY	398,950	917	-	85.91	72.51	192.72
Cape Coral, FL	404,669	1,278	167.21	-	-	191.25
Cedar Rapids, IA	339,249	836	-	134.19	49.87	184.20
Charleston, SC	384,108	1,395	222.79	-	-	190.91
Charlotte, NC	281,522	1,326	153.98	-	-	183.30
Chicago, IL	564,356	2,394	-	76.96	52.42	206.73
Cincinnati, OH	325,555	963	-	76.34	60.07	183.28
Clarksville, TN	n/a	n/a	n/a	n/a	n/a	n/a
Cleveland, OH	306,902	1,161	-	89.55	76.37	183.98
College Station, TX	n/a	n/a	n/a	n/a	n/a	n/a
Colorado Springs, CO	445,666	1,568	-	96.11	73.34	185.54
Columbia, MO	382,188	912	-	96.49	65.29	193.86
Columbia, SC	280,688	980	-	112.25	147.20	189.41
Columbus, OH	319,841	1,212	-	78.99	63.49	183.23
Dallas, TX	391,973	1,539	-	134.55	65.71	188.86
Davenport, IA	245,861	974	-	88.01	57.06	194.67
Denver, CO	575,410	1,619	-	60.85	57.04	186.45
Des Moines, IA	319,302	715	-	78.15	51.55	184.26
Durham, NC[1]	516,293	1,202	-	85.79	57.52	183.36
Edison, NJ[2]	524,043	1,618	-	98.22	91.61	183.25
El Paso, TX	263,095	953	-	93.81	47.74	188.86
Fargo, ND	n/a	n/a	n/a	n/a	n/a	n/a
Fort Collins, CO	n/a	n/a	n/a	n/a	n/a	n/a
Fort Wayne, IN	236,782	912	-	102.32	51.80	187.80
Fort Worth, TX	306,815	1,230	-	135.77	65.24	188.11
Grand Rapids, MI	338,439	1,194	-	106.54	71.51	184.56
Green Bay, WI	327,185	810	-	83.06	80.95	182.84
Honolulu, HI	1,399,439	3,190	369.53	-	-	181.65
Houston, TX	324,596	1,113	-	153.86	39.91	187.36
Huntsville, AL	282,992	751	161.54	-	-	185.19
Indianapolis, IN	296,783	1,141	-	111.24	71.09	187.80
Jacksonville, FL	314,537	1,313	159.06	-	-	191.90
Kansas City, MO	363,024	1,355	-	99.39	60.31	193.33
Lafayette, LA	249,560	988	-	94.39	53.25	183.56
Las Cruces, NM	316,391	814	-	77.22	40.12	188.36
Las Vegas, NV	439,033	1,325	-	116.97	42.69	178.82
Lexington, KY	321,402	866	-	84.79	99.27	195.91
Lincoln, NE	315,284	956	-	64.93	64.21	197.75
Little Rock, AR	389,088	886	-	84.45	63.83	200.68
Los Angeles, CA	917,683	2,770	-	120.13	71.51	187.64
Louisville, KY	296,691	1,228	-	84.83	99.27	183.02
Madison, WI	448,567	1,166	-	103.54	75.91	182.84
Manchester, NH	376,710	1,732	-	116.15	98.94	183.36

Table continued on following page.

Urban Area	New Home Price ($)	Apartment Rent ($/month)	All Electric ($/month)	Part Electric ($/month)	Other Energy ($/month)	Telephone ($/month)
Memphis, TN	305,002	1,031	-	88.04	42.99	189.02
Miami, FL	459,109	2,362	172.59	-	-	191.55
Midland, TX	327,254	859	-	114.32	45.10	187.73
Milwaukee, WI	387,279	1,387	-	104.40	70.09	182.09
Minneapolis, MN	393,526	1,240	-	96.59	66.21	184.36
Nashville, TN	364,246	1,199	-	90.80	51.95	189.02
New Haven, CT	414,217	2,080	-	166.18	115.11	182.20
New Orleans, LA	582,357	1,588	-	61.16	39.05	183.56
New York, NY[3]	1,264,254	3,533	-	100.66	82.79	192.91
Oklahoma City, OK	306,159	855	-	90.04	65.43	191.74
Omaha, NE	327,718	1,169	-	89.67	60.25	197.81
Orlando, FL	365,090	1,371	153.30	-	-	191.25
Philadelphia, PA	428,533	1,473	-	99.85	96.50	195.45
Phoenix, AZ	394,309	1,745	192.55	-	-	181.87
Pittsburgh, PA	390,296	1,228	-	111.56	123.58	193.95
Portland, OR	628,508	2,544	-	80.74	67.49	177.93
Providence, RI	436,045	1,837	-	132.22	119.10	192.37
Provo, UT	444,696	1,186	-	67.96	60.58	190.47
Raleigh, NC	323,846	1,398	-	104.92	59.94	183.30
Reno, NV	525,709	1,326	-	84.77	37.80	181.37
Richmond, VA	339,453	1,234	-	93.89	86.52	181.35
Riverside, CA	n/a	n/a	n/a	n/a	n/a	n/a
Rochester, MN	n/a	n/a	n/a	n/a	n/a	n/a
Rochester, NY	379,074	1,426	-	84.77	63.17	191.59
Sacramento, CA	514,667	2,051	-	152.89	43.30	184.64
Saint Louis, MO	292,549	950	-	86.72	59.87	197.28
Salt Lake City, UT	436,783	1,251	-	77.49	62.29	191.06
San Antonio, TX	288,739	1,369	-	99.94	37.03	187.73
San Diego, CA	897,154	2,579	-	165.29	74.36	179.39
San Francisco, CA	1,396,782	3,702	-	192.51	73.93	196.49
San Jose, CA	n/a	n/a	n/a	n/a	n/a	n/a
Santa Rosa, CA	n/a	n/a	n/a	n/a	n/a	n/a
Savannah, GA	238,921	971	151.42	-	-	185.61
Seattle, WA	826,291	2,621	188.34	-	-	197.61
Sioux Falls, SD	405,855	990	-	87.75	57.99	191.00
Springfield, IL	389,850	1,240	-	94.23	73.35	194.78
Tampa, FL	309,518	1,333	160.44	-	-	192.30
Tucson, AZ	445,261	1,150	-	125.25	60.60	181.82
Tulsa, OK	268,827	690	-	90.90	67.25	191.58
Tuscaloosa, AL	n/a	n/a	n/a	n/a	n/a	n/a
Virginia Beach, VA[4]	347,649	1,256	-	96.40	83.18	184.18
Washington, DC	1,045,070	2,986	-	117.06	82.44	188.30
Wichita, KS	269,985	839	-	97.01	65.66	194.61
Wilmington, NC	n/a	n/a	n/a	n/a	n/a	n/a
Winston-Salem, NC	288,299	1,539	156.30	-	-	173.01
Average*	398,393	1,217	171.38	100.83	69.67	187.75
Minimum*	212,799	534	96.71	31.56	27.15	173.01
Maximum*	2,354,006	4,438	369.53	277.33	303.87	206.73

*Note: **New Home Price** (2,400 sf living area, 8,000 sf lot, in urban area with full utilities); **Apartment Rent** (950 sf 2 bedroom/1.5 or 2 bath, unfurnished, excluding all utilities except water); **All Electric** (average monthly cost for an all-electric home); **Part Electric** (average monthly cost for a part-electric home); **Other Energy** (average monthly cost for natural gas, fuel oil, coal, wood, and any other forms of energy except electricity); **Telephone** (price includes the base monthly rate plus taxes and fees for three lines of mobile phone service); (*) Average, minimum, and maximum values for all 285 areas in the Cost of Living Index report; n/a not available; In cases where data is not available for the city, data for the metro area or for a neighboring city has been provided and noted as follows: (1) Chapel Hill NC; (2) Middlesex-Monmouth NJ; (3) Brooklyn, NY; (4) Hampton Roads-SE Virginia*
Source: The Council for Community and Economic Research, Cost of Living Index, 2021

Health Care, Transportation, and Other Costs

Urban Area	Doctor ($/visit)	Dentist ($/visit)	Optometrist ($/visit)	Gasoline ($/gallon)	Beauty Salon ($/visit)	Men's Shirt ($)
Albuquerque, NM	107.50	99.30	108.72	2.77	42.21	26.60
Allentown, PA	93.56	125.14	100.29	2.91	42.13	30.19
Anchorage, AK	211.00	145.68	228.22	3.12	50.83	19.59
Ann Arbor, MI	n/a	n/a	n/a	n/a	n/a	n/a
Athens, GA	n/a	n/a	n/a	n/a	n/a	n/a
Atlanta, GA	121.28	114.41	121.68	2.72	50.23	38.87
Austin, TX	111.36	119.12	118.24	2.39	49.66	22.56
Baltimore, MD	82.95	84.98	82.95	2.70	55.39	26.90
Baton Rouge	112.17	97.16	106.50	2.33	50.64	35.99
Boise City, ID	138.86	88.67	134.62	3.04	36.66	36.23
Boston, MA	194.00	108.00	102.75	2.70	64.22	32.92
Boulder, CO	n/a	n/a	n/a	n/a	n/a	n/a
Buffalo, NY	86.85	98.38	72.83	2.73	39.63	19.20
Cape Coral, FL	118.67	109.65	85.65	2.70	42.30	25.02
Cedar Rapids, IA	128.24	110.86	100.05	2.48	37.44	26.71
Charleston, SC	135.74	94.42	85.00	2.47	60.13	28.60
Charlotte, NC	127.19	121.04	111.50	2.63	35.13	45.70
Chicago, IL	105.52	102.17	97.30	3.39	59.38	35.09
Cincinnati, OH	112.13	101.55	101.13	2.70	40.87	30.63
Clarksville, TN	n/a	n/a	n/a	n/a	n/a	n/a
Cleveland, OH	116.73	110.67	90.58	2.74	32.55	42.00
College Station, TX	n/a	n/a	n/a	n/a	n/a	n/a
Colorado Springs, CO	119.60	100.70	112.79	2.81	45.60	31.79
Columbia, MO	124.13	88.17	112.03	2.52	42.31	29.28
Columbia, SC	113.17	73.17	66.33	2.35	50.00	24.28
Columbus, OH	124.42	80.85	56.01	2.72	41.93	32.77
Dallas, TX	132.09	126.71	112.55	2.50	51.54	31.69
Davenport, IA	120.89	82.00	83.72	2.60	30.25	33.15
Denver, CO	113.95	111.41	110.56	2.94	44.79	36.47
Des Moines, IA	115.47	80.69	115.02	2.38	32.12	18.18
Durham, NC[1]	151.38	121.99	122.49	2.63	52.03	11.67
Edison, NJ[2]	93.00	104.80	110.20	2.83	34.67	42.30
El Paso, TX	144.83	80.20	85.12	2.60	26.43	18.38
Fargo, ND	n/a	n/a	n/a	n/a	n/a	n/a
Fort Collins, CO	n/a	n/a	n/a	n/a	n/a	n/a
Fort Wayne, IN	134.78	94.00	90.94	2.61	33.00	31.49
Fort Worth, TX	92.61	106.16	97.41	2.45	63.06	42.56
Grand Rapids, MI	97.83	99.05	105.89	2.79	31.89	15.37
Green Bay, WI	176.50	81.33	72.11	2.56	21.31	26.89
Honolulu, HI	151.37	85.30	205.02	3.67	66.60	60.31
Houston, TX	91.80	107.85	100.03	2.41	61.97	28.04
Huntsville, AL	120.22	87.08	67.30	2.41	50.36	33.93
Indianapolis, IN	91.73	89.83	67.23	2.66	38.57	35.76
Jacksonville, FL	76.25	95.47	70.00	2.68	50.33	23.06
Kansas City, MO	87.49	97.13	89.00	2.38	32.79	25.42
Lafayette, LA	129.89	80.20	97.40	2.40	41.60	38.41
Las Cruces, NM	106.77	99.67	107.20	2.88	36.83	25.82
Las Vegas, NV	109.27	102.27	103.80	3.24	46.03	23.03
Lexington, KY	82.97	79.87	70.58	2.54	38.65	37.50
Lincoln, NE	156.08	96.23	111.85	2.68	39.00	38.07
Little Rock, AR	121.28	55.56	89.78	2.42	51.64	31.66
Los Angeles, CA	126.33	115.69	123.18	3.91	85.33	32.77
Louisville, KY	91.67	87.78	66.11	2.80	81.11	31.75
Madison, WI	205.50	120.55	66.22	2.60	53.17	36.55
Manchester, NH	158.77	129.12	102.92	2.46	41.83	35.04

Table continued on following page.

Urban Area	Doctor ($/visit)	Dentist ($/visit)	Optometrist ($/visit)	Gasoline ($/gallon)	Beauty Salon ($/visit)	Men's Shirt ($)
Memphis, TN	89.81	82.07	75.56	2.42	41.00	19.92
Miami, FL	116.25	105.00	116.43	2.72	74.42	23.55
Midland, TX	115.00	121.67	101.56	2.50	35.22	22.52
Milwaukee, WI	182.44	102.53	66.80	2.59	43.40	22.00
Minneapolis, MN	145.70	87.08	90.04	2.67	35.26	34.62
Nashville, TN	100.75	99.76	93.44	2.51	35.66	33.68
New Haven, CT	130.40	110.50	115.00	2.92	49.78	35.39
New Orleans, LA	158.33	118.89	102.44	2.45	48.33	28.55
New York, NY[3]	116.89	116.47	100.16	2.92	63.44	48.92
Oklahoma City, OK	101.62	101.84	105.39	2.31	43.06	22.66
Omaha, NE	127.69	87.99	108.92	2.77	30.86	19.50
Orlando, FL	91.11	109.61	98.02	2.57	51.44	26.77
Philadelphia, PA	135.61	96.25	114.00	2.95	61.70	33.14
Phoenix, AZ	99.00	92.00	111.72	2.88	40.00	25.85
Pittsburgh, PA	104.64	99.12	96.63	2.86	38.46	20.13
Portland, OR	168.67	101.75	146.25	3.31	60.28	43.30
Providence, RI	157.77	92.70	130.63	2.75	47.48	36.31
Provo, UT	95.10	90.16	98.09	3.06	38.90	33.86
Raleigh, NC	116.11	90.70	99.25	2.60	48.10	20.81
Reno, NV	124.17	109.89	103.33	3.26	36.39	20.46
Richmond, VA	147.87	106.38	113.52	2.54	49.83	26.74
Riverside, CA	n/a	n/a	n/a	n/a	n/a	n/a
Rochester, MN	n/a	n/a	n/a	n/a	n/a	n/a
Rochester, NY	110.93	106.79	130.85	2.72	41.28	28.54
Sacramento, CA	188.58	96.32	146.32	4.11	62.33	29.93
Saint Louis, MO	81.57	95.49	74.63	2.51	36.88	20.72
Salt Lake City, UT	107.40	96.11	96.64	3.10	38.87	28.98
San Antonio, TX	110.51	91.49	101.55	2.27	49.97	34.84
San Diego, CA	125.00	109.73	123.80	3.97	65.72	35.00
San Francisco, CA	148.50	133.23	136.56	4.03	76.38	41.04
San Jose, CA	n/a	n/a	n/a	n/a	n/a	n/a
Santa Rosa, CA	n/a	n/a	n/a	n/a	n/a	n/a
Savannah, GA	110.78	142.03	91.76	2.59	37.36	28.04
Seattle, WA	150.37	125.24	153.67	3.61	56.95	41.05
Sioux Falls, SD	160.93	101.20	122.03	2.61	28.58	27.20
Springfield, IL	120.02	103.71	121.40	3.01	26.28	18.49
Tampa, FL	93.96	105.33	96.40	2.54	35.05	23.87
Tucson, AZ	140.19	102.09	104.16	2.63	47.35	49.50
Tulsa, OK	122.06	103.49	99.86	2.29	37.11	25.06
Tuscaloosa, AL	n/a	n/a	n/a	n/a	n/a	n/a
Virginia Beach, VA[4]	85.23	102.83	112.56	2.53	38.41	34.67
Washington, DC	109.41	94.40	79.25	2.81	78.94	38.86
Wichita, KS	96.76	89.40	145.83	2.59	37.93	48.62
Wilmington, NC	n/a	n/a	n/a	n/a	n/a	n/a
Winston-Salem, NC	123.63	148.17	119.13	2.47	35.00	40.58
Average*	118.16	101.04	109.44	2.71	40.63	30.77
Minimum*	35.04	55.56	51.17	2.17	18.59	11.32
Maximum*	231.10	165.12	256.81	4.11	85.33	63.03

*Note: **Doctor** (general practitioners routine exam of an established patient); **Dentist** (adult teeth cleaning and periodic oral examination); **Optometrist** (full vision eye exam for established adult patient); **Gasoline** (one gallon regular unleaded, national brand, including all taxes, cash price at self-service pump if available); **Beauty Salon** (woman's shampoo, trim, and blow-dry); **Men's Shirt** (cotton/polyester dress shirt, pinpoint weave, long sleeves); (*) Average, minimum, and maximum values for all 285 areas in the Cost of Living Index report; n/a not available; In cases where data is not available for the city, data for the metro area or for a neighboring city has been provided and noted as follows: (1) Chapel Hill NC; (2) Middlesex-Monmouth NJ; (3) Brooklyn, NY; (4) Hampton Roads-SE Virginia*

Source: The Council for Community and Economic Research, Cost of Living Index, 2021

Number of Medical Professionals

City	Area Covered	MDs[1]	DOs[1,2]	Dentists	Podiatrists	Chiropractors	Optometrists
Albuquerque, NM	Bernalillo County	462.8	20.8	86.2	9.5	25.0	16.7
Allentown, PA	Lehigh County	358.8	86.6	86.8	12.3	29.1	20.6
Anchorage, AK	Anchorage Borough	375.3	45.8	127.0	5.2	63.5	30.9
Ann Arbor, MI	Washtenaw County	1,290.5	42.4	187.0	7.0	27.1	17.5
Athens, GA	Clarke County	321.8	14.8	53.6	4.7	21.0	15.5
Atlanta, GA	Fulton County	522.3	14.0	71.2	5.2	56.3	18.7
Austin, TX	Travis County	324.5	19.3	72.5	4.2	34.0	17.1
Baltimore, MD	Baltimore City	1,074.8	22.6	79.6	8.5	14.3	15.4
Baton Rouge, LA	East Baton Rouge Parish	401.1	7.3	73.6	3.9	12.0	13.6
Boise City, ID	Ada County	289.9	33.8	80.4	3.8	53.9	19.8
Boston, MA	Suffolk County	1,515.5	15.5	222.1	9.9	14.3	34.3
Boulder, CO	Boulder County	360.2	32.2	105.5	6.0	80.4	26.3
Buffalo, NY	Erie County	379.7	23.8	82.3	8.1	41.8	15.8
Cape Coral, FL	Lee County	196.0	30.6	52.3	8.3	27.6	13.5
Cedar Rapids, IA	Linn County	189.2	24.3	73.4	7.4	56.4	17.8
Charleston, SC	Charleston County	803.3	30.9	111.7	5.1	52.2	23.0
Charlotte, NC	Mecklenburg County	336.4	15.8	70.9	3.5	33.4	14.3
Chicago, IL	Cook County	440.6	23.2	92.6	12.3	28.2	20.4
Cincinnati, OH	Hamilton County	613.6	24.3	74.4	10.0	20.3	21.4
Clarksville, TN	Montgomery County	97.1	15.3	43.6	2.3	12.7	11.8
Cleveland, OH	Cuyahoga County	725.2	53.3	105.3	18.3	18.3	17.2
College Station, TX	Brazos County	262.6	17.9	54.3	3.4	16.7	16.2
Colorado Springs, CO	El Paso County	206.0	31.8	104.3	4.4	44.5	24.2
Columbia, MO	Boone County	808.5	58.7	70.3	6.0	35.4	26.7
Columbia, SC	Richland County	360.3	14.2	91.8	7.2	23.3	19.2
Columbus, OH	Franklin County	432.7	61.7	92.1	7.2	25.2	27.4
Dallas, TX	Dallas County	344.0	20.5	88.8	4.2	36.6	14.0
Davenport, IA	Scott County	241.7	54.4	78.4	4.0	180.9	17.2
Denver, CO	Denver County	591.3	32.0	79.7	6.3	37.2	16.9
Des Moines, IA	Polk County	215.2	99.4	75.3	11.2	57.7	20.9
Durham, NC	Durham County	1,127.3	15.2	74.2	4.3	20.6	15.1
Edison, NJ	Middlesex County	390.4	19.8	86.4	9.7	24.4	19.6
El Paso, TX	El Paso County	201.5	13.1	46.8	3.9	8.8	10.1
Fargo, ND	Cass County	404.6	18.7	80.2	4.3	75.3	33.1
Fort Collins, CO	Larimer County	246.8	31.4	82.2	6.1	55.1	21.4
Fort Wayne, IN	Allen County	264.4	29.5	65.6	5.7	22.8	25.9
Fort Worth, TX	Tarrant County	187.3	34.0	61.6	4.5	27.9	16.2
Grand Rapids, MI	Kent County	354.2	69.1	74.8	4.7	38.0	26.0
Green Bay, WI	Brown County	255.2	24.9	81.9	3.0	46.9	17.9
Honolulu, HI	Honolulu County	360.8	16.9	95.4	3.2	19.3	23.1
Houston, TX	Harris County	342.2	11.6	71.7	4.8	22.5	20.5
Huntsville, AL	Madison County	281.6	12.6	53.3	3.3	22.7	18.5
Indianapolis, IN	Marion County	444.9	21.0	89.7	6.1	16.3	20.2
Jacksonville, FL	Duval County	352.1	23.7	79.3	6.9	24.8	16.0
Kansas City, MO	Jackson County	319.6	60.5	90.6	6.4	45.7	20.2
Lafayette, LA	Lafayette Parish	370.7	9.8	70.7	3.3	33.1	14.5
Las Cruces, NM	Dona Ana County	168.2	13.7	61.9	5.9	18.2	9.1
Las Vegas, NV	Clark County	179.8	34.8	64.2	4.4	20.0	13.7
Lexington, KY	Fayette County	741.8	37.4	144.5	7.8	23.6	24.8
Lincoln, NE	Lancaster County	224.7	12.8	101.1	5.3	46.5	21.4
Little Rock, AR	Pulaski County	750.2	14.8	76.2	4.8	21.3	21.0
Los Angeles, CA	Los Angeles County	307.9	14.2	90.5	6.4	29.9	18.9
Louisville, KY	Jefferson County	483.6	14.9	103.6	7.8	28.0	15.5
Madison, WI	Dane County	611.9	20.9	72.1	4.5	43.6	21.2
Manchester, NH	Hillsborough County	243.2	25.4	81.6	5.4	26.0	20.6
Memphis, TN	Shelby County	413.6	10.4	75.5	3.8	14.0	32.4

Table continued on following page.

City	Area Covered	MDs[1]	DOs[1,2]	Dentists	Podiatrists	Chiropractors	Optometrists
Miami, FL	Miami-Dade County	361.0	18.0	71.4	10.1	18.4	15.0
Midland, TX	Midland County	149.9	7.4	60.0	2.4	13.5	12.4
Milwaukee, WI	Milwaukee County	379.5	20.9	85.2	7.5	20.8	11.0
Minneapolis, MN	Hennepin County	533.5	23.7	99.6	5.2	73.7	21.1
Nashville, TN	Davidson County	660.2	13.1	78.8	4.7	25.6	16.8
New Haven, CT	New Haven County	571.3	10.8	77.4	9.8	26.7	16.9
New Orleans, LA	Orleans Parish	838.4	19.0	77.1	3.9	9.4	7.3
New York, NY	New York City	493.5	17.4	84.0	12.7	15.5	16.9
Oklahoma City, OK	Oklahoma County	418.3	41.3	107.0	5.0	28.3	19.2
Omaha, NE	Douglas County	545.9	26.8	97.3	5.3	41.9	20.4
Orlando, FL	Orange County	323.2	23.7	50.2	3.5	27.7	13.0
Philadelphia, PA	Philadelphia County	578.0	44.7	79.1	16.6	15.3	17.6
Phoenix, AZ	Maricopa County	249.4	32.1	70.8	6.9	34.1	16.3
Pittsburgh, PA	Allegheny County	644.7	42.7	94.0	9.4	43.8	20.3
Portland, OR	Multnomah County	640.1	31.7	98.6	4.9	74.9	23.2
Providence, RI	Providence County	494.3	17.7	57.8	9.7	20.7	20.6
Provo, UT	Utah County	119.1	20.3	59.8	4.5	25.5	10.5
Raleigh, NC	Wake County	286.8	12.1	72.1	3.6	27.2	16.8
Reno, NV	Washoe County	299.9	20.4	68.4	3.9	29.0	23.6
Richmond, VA	Richmond City	754.2	30.8	147.4	11.9	7.5	17.2
Riverside, CA	Riverside County	130.1	15.2	55.1	2.7	17.2	13.0
Rochester, MN	Olmsted County	2,511.2	46.1	122.8	6.8	41.8	23.3
Rochester, NY	Monroe County	503.1	16.7	83.2	6.2	28.7	17.9
Sacramento, CA	Sacramento County	327.0	16.2	78.9	4.5	21.7	18.0
St. Louis, MO	St. Louis City	1,170.1	35.9	62.7	4.6	19.2	17.2
Salt Lake City, UT	Salt Lake County	383.7	17.9	77.8	6.1	27.9	13.5
San Antonio, TX	Bexar County	327.3	18.6	91.1	5.5	16.8	18.4
San Diego, CA	San Diego County	335.5	19.4	93.2	4.6	34.9	19.7
San Francisco, CA	San Francisco County	816.7	13.2	158.7	10.8	40.3	29.5
San Jose, CA	Santa Clara County	439.1	11.4	119.0	6.6	42.7	27.5
Santa Rosa, CA	Sonoma County	282.2	18.0	95.3	7.0	41.9	18.0
Savannah, GA	Chatham County	358.3	19.0	67.7	6.4	19.3	13.2
Seattle, WA	King County	497.3	16.4	109.8	6.3	46.8	22.0
Sioux Falls, SD	Minnehaha County	369.2	23.3	55.3	6.1	57.8	19.8
Springfield, IL	Sangamon County	626.7	25.2	85.1	5.6	38.7	21.9
Tampa, FL	Hillsborough County	355.1	28.9	60.6	5.5	27.0	14.8
Tucson, AZ	Pima County	368.3	24.9	65.8	5.8	18.9	16.4
Tulsa, OK	Tulsa County	270.4	117.4	68.6	4.2	37.8	23.5
Tuscaloosa, AL	Tuscaloosa County	234.1	8.1	45.4	4.4	18.9	16.7
Virginia Beach, VA	Virginia Beach City	261.6	14.7	77.5	6.7	26.8	16.5
Washington, DC	District of Columbia	792.6	18.6	125.2	9.0	9.7	14.4
Wichita, KS	Sedgwick County	257.9	34.9	65.7	2.3	43.3	28.6
Wilmington, NC	New Hanover County	339.9	30.3	81.1	8.9	36.8	23.9
Winston-Salem, NC	Forsyth County	669.6	28.8	63.8	6.0	18.0	18.3
U.S.	U.S.	287.9	23.2	71.1	6.2	28.2	17.0

Note: All figures are rates per 100,000 population; Data as of 2020 unless noted; (1) Data as of 2019 and includes all active, non-federal physicians; (2) Doctor of Osteopathic Medicine

Source: U.S. Department of Health and Human Services, Health Resources and Services Administration, Bureau of Health Professions, Area Resource File (ARF) 2020-2021

Health Insurance Coverage: City

City	With Health Insurance	With Private Health Insurance	With Public Health Insurance	Without Health Insurance	Population Under Age 19 Without Health Insurance
Albuquerque, NM	92.5	60.8	44.1	7.5	3.8
Allentown, PA	89.4	46.6	50.7	10.6	4.8
Anchorage, AK	89.4	70.4	31.5	10.6	7.6
Ann Arbor, MI	97.6	87.7	20.0	2.4	1.3
Athens, GA	87.5	70.4	25.4	12.5	7.8
Atlanta, GA	89.4	69.2	28.0	10.6	5.3
Austin, TX	87.2	74.2	20.5	12.8	8.2
Baltimore, MD	94.0	59.1	45.5	6.0	3.2
Baton Rouge, LA	89.9	57.7	42.4	10.1	5.0
Boise City, ID	91.3	76.4	26.7	8.7	4.3
Boston, MA	96.5	68.3	36.0	3.5	1.6
Boulder, CO	95.9	83.8	21.0	4.1	1.2
Buffalo, NY	95.7	51.4	54.7	4.3	1.5
Cape Coral, FL	87.0	64.7	37.8	13.0	9.5
Cedar Rapids, IA	95.4	74.0	33.9	4.6	2.3
Charleston, SC	92.7	79.6	25.2	7.3	3.0
Charlotte, NC	87.5	68.5	26.4	12.5	7.2
Chicago, IL	90.4	61.6	35.8	9.6	3.4
Cincinnati, OH	92.8	60.5	40.3	7.2	5.0
Clarksville, TN	91.5	71.6	34.6	8.5	3.6
Cleveland, OH	92.7	44.5	57.0	7.3	3.2
College Station, TX	92.3	85.3	14.0	7.7	5.0
Colorado Springs, CO	92.2	68.9	36.9	7.8	4.3
Columbia, MO	93.0	80.5	22.2	7.0	3.4
Columbia, SC	91.6	71.5	30.5	8.4	2.8
Columbus, OH	90.8	63.4	35.1	9.2	5.9
Dallas, TX	76.9	53.2	29.7	23.1	14.9
Davenport, IA	93.7	66.6	39.1	6.3	4.1
Denver, CO	90.4	65.8	32.4	9.6	4.9
Des Moines, IA	93.6	63.6	42.1	6.4	2.4
Durham, NC	87.7	69.5	27.9	12.3	8.0
Edison, NJ	94.8	80.4	23.9	5.2	1.8
El Paso, TX	80.6	54.8	33.9	19.4	9.7
Fargo, ND	93.8	80.2	25.4	6.2	3.8
Fort Collins, CO	94.0	78.5	24.2	6.0	4.7
Fort Wayne, IN	91.3	64.9	36.9	8.7	6.1
Fort Worth, TX	81.4	61.2	26.9	18.6	12.1
Grand Rapids, MI	91.4	61.8	39.3	8.6	4.5
Green Bay, WI	92.2	65.9	36.2	7.8	5.0
Honolulu, HI	96.3	77.6	35.5	3.7	2.2
Houston, TX	76.8	52.4	30.4	23.2	14.1
Huntsville, AL	90.0	72.3	33.3	10.0	3.7
Indianapolis, IN	90.3	63.0	37.2	9.7	5.8
Jacksonville, FL	88.0	64.6	33.9	12.0	6.5
Kansas City, MO	88.2	68.5	29.1	11.8	7.2
Lafayette, LA	91.7	67.1	36.6	8.3	3.8
Las Cruces, NM	93.1	56.1	51.3	6.9	2.0
Las Vegas, NV	87.5	61.4	35.9	12.5	7.9
Lexington, KY	93.3	71.4	32.8	6.7	3.6
Lincoln, NE	92.3	77.8	25.8	7.7	4.7
Little Rock, AR	91.5	64.4	38.5	8.5	4.2
Los Angeles, CA	89.3	55.2	40.7	10.7	3.8
Louisville, KY	94.8	67.2	40.7	5.2	3.0
Madison, WI	96.2	83.6	22.7	3.8	1.7
Manchester, NH	90.2	65.1	35.2	9.8	3.3

Table continued on following page.

City	With Health Insurance	With Private Health Insurance	With Public Health Insurance	Without Health Insurance	Population Under Age 19 Without Health Insurance
Memphis, TN	86.4	56.6	41.2	13.6	6.7
Miami, FL	80.5	48.0	35.6	19.5	8.2
Midland, TX	82.7	69.2	20.4	17.3	14.6
Milwaukee, WI	90.7	54.5	44.7	9.3	3.3
Minneapolis, MN	93.8	67.8	33.7	6.2	3.4
Nashville, TN	88.2	68.6	29.3	11.8	7.6
New Haven, CT	92.1	51.9	46.3	7.9	3.7
New Orleans, LA	90.8	54.5	44.6	9.2	4.8
New York, NY	93.0	59.2	43.1	7.0	2.4
Oklahoma City, OK	85.1	63.9	32.0	14.9	7.0
Omaha, NE	89.5	71.3	27.9	10.5	6.9
Orlando, FL	85.1	63.6	28.5	14.9	8.2
Philadelphia, PA	92.4	57.4	45.8	7.6	3.9
Phoenix, AZ	85.7	57.4	35.5	14.3	9.6
Pittsburgh, PA	94.7	73.6	33.5	5.3	3.9
Portland, OR	93.8	72.3	31.6	6.2	2.5
Providence, RI	92.7	54.7	46.1	7.3	3.6
Provo, UT	89.5	78.5	17.3	10.5	10.2
Raleigh, NC	89.9	74.4	24.8	10.1	5.6
Reno, NV	90.0	69.0	30.9	10.0	8.4
Richmond, VA	88.5	63.1	34.9	11.5	6.4
Riverside, CA	91.0	59.7	38.0	9.0	3.9
Rochester, MN	95.7	78.6	31.2	4.3	2.0
Rochester, NY	95.1	52.4	53.4	4.9	2.1
Sacramento, CA	94.3	63.6	41.2	5.7	2.3
St. Louis, MO	89.8	62.7	35.2	10.2	4.7
Salt Lake City, UT	87.7	73.0	22.3	12.3	11.2
San Antonio, TX	82.9	59.4	32.9	17.1	9.2
San Diego, CA	92.5	70.6	31.4	7.5	3.6
San Francisco, CA	96.4	76.3	29.2	3.6	1.7
San Jose, CA	94.9	72.7	30.0	5.1	2.0
Santa Rosa, CA	92.5	68.9	36.5	7.5	5.2
Savannah, GA	84.3	58.0	35.3	15.7	6.5
Seattle, WA	95.6	80.7	23.5	4.4	1.5
Sioux Falls, SD	92.3	78.0	26.1	7.7	5.0
Springfield, IL	96.1	70.2	41.3	3.9	1.3
Tampa, FL	88.5	62.9	33.0	11.5	5.6
Tucson, AZ	88.7	57.1	42.4	11.3	8.0
Tulsa, OK	83.3	58.7	35.5	16.7	8.4
Tuscaloosa, AL	92.5	72.3	32.0	7.5	2.0
Virginia Beach, VA	92.6	80.4	26.7	7.4	3.8
Washington, DC	96.3	70.8	35.5	3.7	2.0
Wichita, KS	88.2	67.2	32.7	11.8	5.6
Wilmington, NC	88.8	69.4	32.7	11.2	6.6
Winston-Salem, NC	87.9	63.0	36.4	12.1	4.7
U.S.	91.3	68.1	35.3	8.7	5.2

Note: Figures are percentages that cover the civilian noninstitutionalized population
Source: U.S. Census Bureau, 2016-2020 American Community Survey 5-Year Estimates

Health Insurance Coverage: Metro Area

Metro Area	With Health Insurance	With Private Health Insurance	With Public Health Insurance	Without Health Insurance	Population Under Age 19 Without Health Insurance
Albuquerque, NM	92.1	60.2	45.3	7.9	4.6
Allentown, PA	94.6	73.2	35.6	5.4	3.3
Anchorage, AK	88.4	68.1	32.8	11.6	8.9
Ann Arbor, MI	96.8	83.1	26.7	3.2	1.6
Athens, GA	88.4	70.2	28.0	11.6	6.1
Atlanta, GA	87.4	69.6	27.0	12.6	7.8
Austin, TX	87.9	75.2	21.7	12.1	8.0
Baltimore, MD	95.3	75.2	33.3	4.7	3.0
Baton Rouge, LA	92.2	66.5	36.0	7.8	3.8
Boise City, ID	90.1	72.6	29.9	9.9	4.8
Boston, MA	97.1	77.0	32.5	2.9	1.5
Boulder, CO	95.5	80.4	25.4	4.5	1.9
Buffalo, NY	96.9	71.8	40.7	3.1	1.6
Cape Coral, FL	86.6	62.6	43.2	13.4	9.5
Cedar Rapids, IA	96.3	76.6	33.1	3.7	1.8
Charleston, SC	89.6	70.9	32.0	10.4	5.9
Charlotte, NC	89.9	70.6	29.5	10.1	5.3
Chicago, IL	92.5	70.6	31.6	7.5	3.2
Cincinnati, OH	94.8	73.1	32.9	5.2	3.2
Clarksville, TN	92.0	70.1	37.2	8.0	5.7
Cleveland, OH	94.7	68.9	38.7	5.3	3.2
College Station, TX	87.7	73.7	23.5	12.3	8.2
Colorado Springs, CO	92.8	71.0	35.8	7.2	4.5
Columbia, MO	92.9	79.3	24.9	7.1	4.3
Columbia, SC	90.3	70.4	34.0	9.7	4.3
Columbus, OH	93.1	71.2	32.0	6.9	4.5
Dallas, TX	83.7	66.5	24.6	16.3	11.2
Davenport, IA	94.9	72.2	37.6	5.1	3.2
Denver, CO	92.3	72.5	29.3	7.7	4.5
Des Moines, IA	95.8	76.8	31.9	4.2	1.9
Durham, NC	89.9	72.3	29.6	10.1	5.9
Edison, NJ	93.2	67.8	36.1	6.8	3.0
El Paso, TX	79.4	53.0	33.9	20.6	10.3
Fargo, ND	94.7	81.2	25.3	5.3	4.4
Fort Collins, CO	94.0	75.7	29.6	6.0	4.5
Fort Wayne, IN	92.0	69.5	33.6	8.0	6.0
Fort Worth, TX	83.7	66.5	24.6	16.3	11.2
Grand Rapids, MI	94.8	75.7	31.6	5.2	3.2
Green Bay, WI	95.0	75.7	30.9	5.0	3.7
Honolulu, HI	96.6	80.0	33.3	3.4	2.3
Houston, TX	81.8	62.1	26.5	18.2	11.7
Huntsville, AL	91.8	76.8	29.8	8.2	3.1
Indianapolis, IN	92.4	71.9	31.5	7.6	5.3
Jacksonville, FL	89.3	68.6	33.1	10.7	6.3
Kansas City, MO	91.1	75.2	27.1	8.9	5.4
Lafayette, LA	91.1	61.8	40.4	8.9	3.5
Las Cruces, NM	89.4	48.6	52.4	10.6	5.5
Las Vegas, NV	88.3	63.9	34.3	11.7	7.6
Lexington, KY	94.0	71.3	34.6	6.0	3.5
Lincoln, NE	92.8	78.8	25.6	7.2	4.6
Little Rock, AR	92.5	66.5	39.4	7.5	3.7
Los Angeles, CA	91.3	61.1	37.6	8.7	3.6
Louisville, KY	94.8	71.6	36.8	5.2	3.4
Madison, WI	96.2	83.2	25.3	3.8	2.0
Manchester, NH	93.8	77.0	29.1	6.2	2.7

Table continued on following page.

Metro Area	With Health Insurance	With Private Health Insurance	With Public Health Insurance	Without Health Insurance	Population Under Age 19 Without Health Insurance
Memphis, TN	89.2	64.8	35.8	10.8	5.5
Miami, FL	85.1	59.4	33.3	14.9	7.9
Midland, TX	83.5	69.4	20.9	16.5	13.4
Milwaukee, WI	94.4	71.8	34.3	5.6	2.6
Minneapolis, MN	95.7	78.1	29.7	4.3	3.0
Nashville, TN	90.7	72.7	28.5	9.3	5.6
New Haven, CT	95.1	67.9	39.0	4.9	2.6
New Orleans, LA	90.7	59.5	41.5	9.3	4.3
New York, NY	93.2	67.8	36.1	6.8	3.0
Oklahoma City, OK	87.2	68.4	31.0	12.8	6.8
Omaha, NE	92.2	75.6	27.4	7.8	4.7
Orlando, FL	87.9	66.0	31.3	12.1	6.7
Philadelphia, PA	94.6	73.1	34.7	5.4	3.2
Phoenix, AZ	89.3	65.4	34.7	10.7	8.5
Pittsburgh, PA	96.3	76.7	36.2	3.7	1.9
Portland, OR	94.0	73.4	32.7	6.0	2.9
Providence, RI	96.2	70.9	39.0	3.8	2.1
Provo, UT	92.3	82.4	17.3	7.7	6.1
Raleigh, NC	90.9	75.7	25.2	9.1	4.8
Reno, NV	90.3	69.9	31.6	9.7	8.2
Richmond, VA	92.1	75.0	30.1	7.9	4.7
Riverside, CA	91.6	57.9	42.0	8.4	4.1
Rochester, MN	95.4	79.8	30.5	4.6	3.4
Rochester, NY	96.3	72.2	39.2	3.7	2.9
Sacramento, CA	95.0	69.9	38.2	5.0	2.5
St. Louis, MO	93.7	74.9	30.3	6.3	3.3
Salt Lake City, UT	90.1	77.6	20.4	9.9	7.9
San Antonio, TX	84.8	64.4	31.2	15.2	8.7
San Diego, CA	92.4	69.1	33.6	7.6	3.9
San Francisco, CA	95.8	76.0	30.4	4.2	2.2
San Jose, CA	95.7	77.1	27.0	4.3	1.9
Santa Rosa, CA	94.0	72.4	36.3	6.0	3.6
Savannah, GA	87.2	67.9	30.5	12.8	5.7
Seattle, WA	94.4	76.1	29.1	5.6	2.5
Sioux Falls, SD	93.0	79.5	25.2	7.0	4.4
Springfield, IL	96.4	74.9	37.1	3.6	1.5
Tampa, FL	88.3	63.6	36.7	11.7	6.0
Tucson, AZ	91.1	62.6	42.7	8.9	6.8
Tulsa, OK	86.3	65.6	32.9	13.7	7.8
Tuscaloosa, AL	92.5	70.5	34.6	7.5	2.4
Virginia Beach, VA	92.0	75.2	31.4	8.0	4.5
Washington, DC	92.6	78.0	25.9	7.4	4.5
Wichita, KS	90.1	71.6	30.9	9.9	5.0
Wilmington, NC	89.8	71.9	33.1	10.2	6.6
Winston-Salem, NC	89.1	65.9	35.9	10.9	5.0
U.S.	91.3	68.1	35.3	8.7	5.2

Note: Figures are percentages that cover the civilian noninstitutionalized population; Figures cover the Metropolitan Statistical Area (MSA)—see Appendix B for areas included
Source: U.S. Census Bureau, 2016-2020 American Community Survey 5-Year Estimates

Crime Rate: City

City	Total Crime Rate	Violent Crime Rate				Property Crime Rate		
		Murder	Rape	Robbery	Aggrav. Assault	Burglary	Larceny -Theft	Motor Vehicle Theft
Albuquerque, NM	6,355.7	14.2	78.5	256.0	994.9	902.9	3,225.8	883.3
Allentown, PA[1]	2,669.6	5.7	52.5	139.5	188.7	427.6	1,656.1	199.4
Anchorage, AK	4,659.4	6.3	194.8	194.8	816.4	504.2	2,541.7	401.2
Ann Arbor, MI	1,563.2	0.8	40.6	31.5	170.7	126.8	1,125.6	67.1
Athens, GA	3,463.9	3.1	81.9	79.6	345.7	465.9	2,213.8	273.9
Atlanta, GA[2]	5,423.2	17.7	49.4	221.5	480.1	621.2	3,366.4	666.8
Austin, TX	4,098.2	4.4	47.8	110.1	304.7	477.3	2,747.3	406.6
Baltimore, MD[1]	6,169.9	58.3	54.2	813.1	933.1	906.5	2,745.1	659.5
Baton Rouge, LA	5,777.6	46.5	25.1	208.4	671.9	865.7	3,582.3	377.7
Boise City, ID	1,933.2	1.7	73.5	23.8	193.8	207.2	1,312.6	120.7
Boston, MA	2,490.8	8.3	26.4	131.8	457.9	243.5	1,439.4	183.6
Boulder, CO	4,092.0	1.9	29.1	67.5	223.3	613.5	2,808.7	348.0
Buffalo, NY	4,098.5	24.0	20.8	267.1	706.1	450.1	2,163.2	467.4
Cape Coral, FL	1,195.5	0.5	9.0	10.0	108.3	152.9	848.1	66.7
Cedar Rapids, IA	3,488.4	8.2	11.9	75.9	225.6	619.4	2,132.8	414.7
Charleston, SC	2,771.1	12.2	38.7	71.6	343.2	233.6	1,747.4	324.5
Charlotte, NC	4,076.6	12.4	25.6	184.0	614.4	449.9	2,478.9	311.4
Chicago, IL	n/a	28.6	50.0	292.1	616.2	320.9	n/a	373.2
Cincinnati, OH	4,576.3	30.2	70.6	246.1	546.1	762.0	2,427.1	494.2
Clarksville, TN	2,852.9	9.3	52.1	48.4	500.1	273.6	1,715.6	253.8
Cleveland, OH	5,727.5	42.2	103.7	420.2	1,090.7	973.8	2,321.2	775.7
College Station, TX	2,082.2	1.7	45.5	22.3	110.1	265.7	1,463.2	173.8
Colorado Springs, CO	3,976.6	7.4	82.5	77.5	429.6	533.5	2,344.8	501.4
Columbia, MO	3,106.6	10.4	71.3	46.5	314.0	323.6	1,985.1	355.7
Columbia, SC	5,227.8	14.4	65.3	156.3	516.0	552.4	3,442.2	481.1
Columbus, OH	3,686.0	19.1	89.5	197.1	249.9	609.1	2,180.6	340.7
Dallas, TX	4,291.0	17.3	41.7	241.5	544.2	727.6	1,955.6	763.1
Davenport, IA	4,661.8	9.8	65.8	133.6	527.5	895.8	2,568.6	460.7
Denver, CO	5,506.6	13.1	90.8	165.1	588.9	708.0	2,800.8	1,139.9
Des Moines, IA	4,606.3	15.3	55.3	114.3	519.8	894.1	2,347.1	660.5
Durham, NC	4,596.6	12.6	43.9	219.7	582.6	668.9	2,730.2	338.7
Edison, NJ	1,242.2	1.0	9.0	31.1	62.3	131.5	889.7	117.5
El Paso, TX	1,557.6	4.1	38.1	42.2	231.9	123.6	1,057.2	60.6
Fargo, ND	3,929.0	5.5	84.3	48.1	322.2	800.5	2,302.1	366.4
Fort Collins, CO[1]	2,389.9	0.6	24.0	21.1	171.5	204.8	1,834.5	133.4
Fort Wayne, IN	2,659.5	14.3	35.6	90.0	272.9	240.6	1,818.8	187.3
Fort Worth, TX	3,274.2	11.8	48.0	93.3	387.9	366.9	1,988.9	377.4
Grand Rapids, MI	2,666.0	13.8	59.7	94.8	544.2	228.6	1,437.9	286.9
Green Bay, WI	2,056.4	5.7	67.8	43.0	410.9	196.8	1,222.2	109.9
Honolulu, HI	n/a	n/a	n/a	n/a	n/a	n/a	n/a	n/a
Houston, TX	5,435.1	17.0	48.5	373.2	817.5	672.9	2,875.9	630.0
Huntsville, AL	n/a	n/a	n/a	n/a	n/a	n/a	n/a	n/a
Indianapolis, IN	4,440.6	24.3	64.3	243.2	538.9	580.6	2,376.9	612.5
Jacksonville, FL	3,569.3	15.2	49.5	100.8	532.3	419.3	2,129.5	322.6
Kansas City, MO	5,705.4	35.2	76.5	257.3	1,216.8	615.2	2,595.1	909.2
Lafayette, LA	5,081.3	11.1	13.4	116.0	421.5	843.9	3,352.6	322.9
Las Cruces, NM[1]	4,077.5	9.7	61.8	55.1	370.0	631.8	2,652.6	296.6
Las Vegas, NV	2,738.2	5.7	63.1	100.8	358.1	416.8	1,390.7	403.0
Lexington, KY	3,191.6	8.6	54.6	102.8	154.1	445.0	2,108.3	318.2
Lincoln, NE[1]	3,133.7	1.7	110.9	57.0	213.3	339.4	2,255.4	155.9
Little Rock, AR	6,707.0	24.8	99.1	190.2	1,535.8	772.4	3,572.3	512.4
Los Angeles, CA	2,869.9	8.8	49.6	200.3	463.3	344.3	1,274.6	529.1
Louisville, KY[1]	4,578.4	13.9	29.8	149.2	494.0	638.9	2,670.2	582.4
Madison, WI	3,099.3	3.8	28.2	62.8	225.7	497.5	2,034.7	246.6

Table continued on following page.

City	Total Crime Rate	Violent Crime Rate				Property Crime Rate		
		Murder	Rape	Robbery	Aggrav. Assault	Burglary	Larceny -Theft	Motor Vehicle Theft
Manchester, NH	2,858.0	4.4	64.6	97.3	426.5	253.9	1,854.6	156.6
Memphis, TN	7,912.7	44.4	63.1	327.4	1,917.1	895.8	3,982.6	682.4
Miami, FL	3,305.4	12.8	19.7	128.1	394.9	305.2	2,104.0	340.7
Midland, TX	2,436.7	6.6	53.8	33.2	271.0	268.4	1,494.1	309.6
Milwaukee, WI	4,325.4	32.4	73.2	326.8	1,164.5	578.5	1,388.2	761.8
Minneapolis, MN	5,713.0	18.2	83.0	409.5	644.2	899.8	2,747.1	911.3
Nashville, TN	5,228.7	16.4	56.0	253.2	830.1	544.3	3,086.9	441.9
New Haven, CT	4,218.8	16.1	22.3	257.9	411.4	419.8	2,507.3	584.0
New Orleans, LA	5,863.9	51.0	180.8	280.9	811.6	506.4	3,138.3	894.9
New York, NY	2,136.3	5.6	27.1	158.8	386.2	167.5	1,279.4	111.5
Oklahoma City, OK	4,621.5	9.5	84.2	123.1	509.1	881.3	2,444.3	569.9
Omaha, NE	3,805.8	7.7	73.1	96.6	453.9	316.7	2,227.2	630.7
Orlando, FL	4,663.8	10.6	57.6	172.8	619.4	408.4	3,003.8	391.3
Philadelphia, PA[2]	4,005.6	22.1	69.0	331.6	486.0	409.4	2,329.5	357.9
Phoenix, AZ	3,788.0	10.9	62.5	191.8	533.2	433.4	2,121.4	434.7
Pittsburgh, PA[2]	3,594.8	18.8	40.0	230.0	289.9	443.2	2,331.9	241.0
Portland, OR	5,261.6	8.0	39.5	121.7	353.4	567.0	3,211.0	960.9
Providence, RI	2,900.8	9.5	36.7	101.9	338.0	335.2	1,776.7	302.9
Provo, UT[1]	1,623.0	0.9	37.5	11.1	65.7	139.1	1,259.5	109.2
Raleigh, NC	2,412.8	4.4	34.2	97.0	256.5	270.0	1,468.3	282.4
Reno, NV	2,710.2	6.6	108.4	110.4	338.0	426.4	1,345.1	375.4
Richmond, VA	3,269.8	28.3	8.6	117.4	194.6	330.4	2,328.7	261.8
Riverside, CA	3,430.6	6.0	45.5	117.8	276.6	490.2	1,930.8	563.7
Rochester, MN	2,172.3	4.2	61.5	36.6	147.1	275.9	1,519.1	128.0
Rochester, NY	4,175.0	23.4	41.9	203.7	549.7	676.9	2,233.4	445.9
Sacramento, CA	3,428.4	8.1	24.1	169.3	481.8	546.0	1,715.2	483.8
Saint Louis, MO	7,846.6	88.1	78.4	416.2	1,433.5	855.2	3,895.8	1,079.3
Salt Lake City, UT	8,274.5	8.4	137.0	240.9	536.1	764.1	5,503.8	1,084.1
San Antonio, TX	4,362.2	8.3	75.5	137.5	514.2	503.4	2,679.8	443.7
San Diego, CA	2,060.6	3.9	33.7	84.0	247.3	231.2	1,116.0	344.5
San Francisco, CA	4,938.4	5.4	22.5	270.9	245.3	845.4	2,872.2	676.8
San Jose, CA	2,741.2	3.9	55.0	115.1	251.0	392.9	1,237.2	686.2
Santa Rosa, CA	2,120.0	2.3	62.2	76.3	375.3	306.3	1,059.7	237.9
Savannah, GA[2]	2,865.5	11.6	35.1	110.2	248.5	364.9	1,824.4	270.8
Seattle, WA	5,498.9	6.7	39.0	190.7	389.9	1,351.5	2,884.6	636.5
Sioux Falls, SD	3,729.0	6.9	51.8	54.4	484.6	365.1	2,273.0	493.1
Springfield, IL	n/a	9.7	88.7	171.2	676.8	822.6	n/a	223.0
Tampa, FL	1,885.4	10.1	24.8	79.8	405.5	227.1	980.2	157.8
Tucson, AZ	4,319.0	11.1	84.1	177.7	425.3	381.0	2,898.7	341.2
Tulsa, OK	6,244.2	17.9	94.0	184.3	836.5	1,095.8	3,045.0	970.7
Tuscaloosa, AL[2]	4,843.6	4.9	46.2	137.6	316.4	739.9	3,289.0	309.5
Virginia Beach, VA	1,610.5	3.8	13.3	27.5	54.1	110.7	1,262.7	138.4
Washington, DC	4,389.2	27.8	43.1	309.8	577.3	275.4	2,683.2	472.8
Wichita, KS[1]	6,462.8	9.0	94.1	118.2	919.8	686.3	4,044.6	590.9
Wilmington, NC	3,175.8	17.5	52.5	113.7	445.2	473.0	1,915.8	158.2
Winston-Salem, NC	n/a	n/a	n/a	n/a	n/a	n/a	n/a	n/a
U.S.	2,356.7	6.5	38.4	73.9	279.7	314.2	1,398.0	246.0

Note: Figures are crimes per 100,000 population in 2020 except where noted; n/a not available; (1) 2019 data; (2) 2018 data
Source: FBI Uniform Crime Reports, 2018, 2019, 2020

Crime Rate: Suburbs

Suburbs[1]	Total Crime	Violent Crime Rate				Property Crime Rate		
		Murder	Rape	Robbery	Aggrav. Assault	Burglary	Larceny -Theft	Motor Vehicle Theft
Albuquerque, NM	2,025.9	1.9	34.6	40.4	405.3	354.2	870.1	319.4
Allentown, PA	n/a	n/a	n/a	n/a	n/a	n/a	n/a	n/a
Anchorage, AK	3,312.3	0.0	63.6	42.4	445.2	233.2	2,247.1	280.9
Ann Arbor, MI	1,734.3	3.2	74.1	38.7	378.3	167.6	942.7	129.7
Athens, GA	1,270.6	2.3	20.5	11.4	171.1	219.0	735.7	110.6
Atlanta, GA[3]	2,666.3	4.6	24.0	82.5	168.8	373.2	1,770.4	242.7
Austin, TX	1,578.6	2.3	40.3	25.2	129.8	227.0	1,028.7	125.3
Baltimore, MD[2]	2,213.3	3.9	31.8	88.1	260.3	217.8	1,485.2	126.1
Baton Rouge, LA	2,925.7	6.6	26.4	32.2	367.5	326.9	2,010.2	155.8
Boise City, ID	1,206.5	1.9	52.0	6.9	189.1	178.4	674.0	104.3
Boston, MA	1,043.0	1.2	21.0	22.6	147.3	96.5	677.6	76.8
Boulder, CO	2,552.6	0.9	66.0	30.7	181.8	304.8	1,686.2	282.2
Buffalo, NY	1,776.7	2.1	23.6	40.4	124.0	196.2	1,275.7	114.7
Cape Coral, FL	1,333.2	5.3	37.6	48.3	222.8	148.9	761.7	108.6
Cedar Rapids, IA	1,291.6	0.7	39.3	10.0	135.0	318.6	660.1	127.9
Charleston, SC	2,958.7	11.2	35.6	81.5	313.9	324.5	1,914.7	277.3
Charlotte, NC	n/a	n/a	n/a	n/a	n/a	n/a	n/a	n/a
Chicago, IL	n/a	n/a	n/a	n/a	n/a	n/a	n/a	n/a
Cincinnati, OH	1,469.5	1.9	27.0	24.3	78.3	177.6	1,049.2	111.1
Clarksville, TN	1,659.2	4.0	32.5	25.9	161.9	300.0	988.2	146.7
Cleveland, OH	1,328.9	3.0	20.9	35.0	104.7	154.4	907.3	103.7
College Station, TX	2,209.2	5.4	86.2	41.4	262.1	349.1	1,310.7	154.2
Colorado Springs, CO	1,620.4	4.1	66.6	24.3	191.2	193.8	966.8	173.6
Columbia, MO	1,789.7	2.3	52.8	19.9	179.4	218.1	1,128.2	188.8
Columbia, SC	3,572.6	8.2	37.6	61.2	415.2	504.0	2,183.1	363.3
Columbus, OH	1,664.0	1.5	28.2	27.2	77.2	205.1	1,223.7	101.1
Dallas, TX	n/a	n/a	n/a	n/a	n/a	n/a	n/a	n/a
Davenport, IA	n/a	5.8	57.2	48.2	268.5	345.6	n/a	174.3
Denver, CO	3,233.8	3.8	57.7	70.7	238.2	357.6	1,904.0	601.8
Des Moines, IA	1,384.2	2.2	25.9	9.9	141.1	218.8	859.4	126.9
Durham, NC	1,768.6	4.6	17.6	32.3	169.1	319.6	1,113.7	111.7
Edison, NJ	n/a	n/a	n/a	n/a	n/a	n/a	n/a	n/a
El Paso, TX	1,026.7	3.1	36.2	20.0	217.8	121.7	554.9	73.0
Fargo, ND	2,397.0	5.8	53.5	17.3	159.7	489.9	1,455.9	214.9
Fort Collins, CO[2]	1,855.9	1.1	44.9	14.6	189.3	184.4	1,296.7	124.9
Fort Wayne, IN	988.4	1.4	22.3	16.7	146.5	136.7	579.0	85.8
Fort Worth, TX	n/a	n/a	n/a	n/a	n/a	n/a	n/a	n/a
Grand Rapids, MI	1,390.3	2.5	70.8	21.3	172.1	149.8	837.9	135.8
Green Bay, WI	816.1	0.9	22.7	3.2	54.1	122.4	580.0	32.8
Honolulu, HI	n/a	n/a	n/a	n/a	n/a	n/a	n/a	n/a
Houston, TX	2,188.3	5.4	42.8	68.3	212.3	270.6	1,338.7	250.2
Huntsville, AL	n/a	n/a	n/a	n/a	n/a	n/a	n/a	n/a
Indianapolis, IN	n/a	n/a	n/a	n/a	n/a	n/a	n/a	n/a
Jacksonville, FL	1,375.4	2.4	28.0	23.8	169.5	172.0	880.2	99.5
Kansas City, MO	n/a	n/a	n/a	n/a	n/a	n/a	n/a	n/a
Lafayette, LA	2,189.8	7.4	23.9	35.5	344.1	400.2	1,210.2	168.4
Las Cruces, NM[2]	1,781.8	1.7	52.3	10.5	546.8	362.8	699.5	108.1
Las Vegas, NV	1,944.4	5.0	31.6	99.0	209.5	261.9	1,057.0	280.4
Lexington, KY	2,178.6	1.5	29.6	28.6	75.6	317.7	1,508.9	216.6
Lincoln, NE[2]	1,017.1	0.0	77.9	0.0	41.1	119.0	705.4	73.6
Little Rock, AR	3,185.5	8.9	56.1	52.4	493.6	457.2	1,830.0	287.2
Los Angeles, CA	2,435.2	4.2	28.0	102.7	228.4	355.9	1,303.4	412.7
Louisville, KY[2]	1,847.8	1.9	21.7	30.8	98.0	230.7	1,263.0	201.7
Madison, WI	1,304.6	1.7	21.3	17.4	85.0	157.7	930.9	90.6

Table continued on following page.

Suburbs[1]	Total Crime	Violent Crime Rate				Property Crime Rate		
		Murder	Rape	Robbery	Aggrav. Assault	Burglary	Larceny -Theft	Motor Vehicle Theft
Manchester, NH	801.4	0.0	34.0	8.8	36.6	64.3	609.1	48.6
Memphis, TN	2,431.4	5.4	34.0	36.3	356.4	285.4	1,490.5	223.5
Miami, FL	2,551.6	7.0	31.8	85.7	280.9	220.2	1,689.2	236.7
Midland, TX	2,973.5	8.2	30.0	13.6	360.1	349.2	1,606.8	605.6
Milwaukee, WI	1,624.3	1.5	20.3	29.8	78.2	114.7	1,274.1	105.6
Minneapolis, MN	n/a	n/a	n/a	n/a	n/a	n/a	n/a	n/a
Nashville, TN	1,755.3	3.0	29.0	27.7	266.9	199.9	1,090.1	138.6
New Haven, CT	2,076.3	4.2	20.2	61.1	82.9	193.7	1,413.6	300.7
New Orleans, LA	2,268.4	8.6	24.1	45.2	233.6	244.1	1,581.0	131.9
New York, NY	n/a	n/a	n/a	n/a	n/a	n/a	n/a	n/a
Oklahoma City, OK	2,313.8	6.3	37.1	28.2	177.5	392.7	1,432.3	239.8
Omaha, NE	1,602.2	1.5	37.1	23.2	163.9	191.7	977.7	207.1
Orlando, FL	1,994.4	5.4	40.1	59.7	267.8	251.1	1,217.2	153.1
Philadelphia, PA[3]	1,935.5	7.6	16.3	96.8	235.8	202.8	1,235.3	140.9
Phoenix, AZ	2,118.2	3.8	35.2	43.8	211.2	276.5	1,380.4	167.3
Pittsburgh, PA[3]	1,402.7	3.5	23.7	33.2	168.7	159.1	958.5	55.9
Portland, OR	n/a	n/a	41.7	37.9	150.0	262.3	1,381.0	296.2
Providence, RI	1,264.5	1.7	40.2	29.7	189.1	149.7	749.5	104.7
Provo, UT[2]	1,312.0	1.1	30.2	7.2	46.1	131.5	1,018.1	77.8
Raleigh, NC	1,376.5	2.8	12.2	21.8	100.3	201.3	956.0	82.2
Reno, NV	1,808.3	4.5	59.7	39.2	243.4	304.1	959.0	198.4
Richmond, VA	1,784.2	5.9	23.2	30.9	126.7	136.3	1,342.0	119.3
Riverside, CA	2,337.0	7.3	26.5	90.0	306.2	359.1	1,123.2	424.8
Rochester, MN	824.5	1.0	36.1	2.9	75.1	191.3	456.7	61.5
Rochester, NY	1,348.8	0.7	35.3	19.7	73.0	156.0	998.4	65.7
Sacramento, CA	2,102.6	3.8	27.9	64.5	196.3	323.1	1,274.4	212.6
Saint Louis, MO	n/a	5.6	29.6	39.0	241.8	262.7	n/a	283.8
Salt Lake City, UT	3,411.8	4.1	53.4	45.4	176.7	364.6	2,327.6	439.9
San Antonio, TX	1,759.0	3.9	36.2	22.5	151.5	297.8	1,074.4	172.6
San Diego, CA	1,655.8	3.1	25.4	69.7	229.9	210.0	887.9	229.9
San Francisco, CA	3,106.9	5.3	33.9	157.3	219.7	345.9	1,757.2	587.6
San Jose, CA	2,331.9	1.7	27.1	56.1	116.6	343.6	1,474.4	312.3
Santa Rosa, CA	1,554.3	1.9	41.1	41.8	329.5	232.8	807.9	99.2
Savannah, GA[3]	3,497.3	5.3	37.2	67.1	245.2	497.1	2,366.1	279.1
Seattle, WA	3,022.6	4.0	29.2	70.5	168.3	442.6	1,893.4	414.8
Sioux Falls, SD	1,410.7	2.3	31.5	8.2	172.8	462.4	597.9	135.5
Springfield, IL	n/a	1.1	36.1	21.9	259.1	349.8	n/a	122.4
Tampa, FL	1,648.1	3.1	34.5	42.4	204.3	176.5	1,068.6	118.6
Tucson, AZ	2,196.1	4.9	16.1	37.5	172.4	257.0	1,582.6	125.6
Tulsa, OK	2,005.9	3.6	31.0	21.9	174.2	380.7	1,150.1	244.3
Tuscaloosa, AL[3]	2,503.0	3.3	28.5	41.7	249.6	518.3	1,449.1	212.5
Virginia Beach, VA	2,536.3	12.5	30.6	67.3	327.6	197.9	1,701.5	198.8
Washington, DC	n/a	n/a	n/a	n/a	n/a	n/a	n/a	n/a
Wichita, KS[2]	n/a	1.6	42.3	14.5	156.8	271.8	n/a	129.8
Wilmington, NC	1,803.5	2.3	27.7	24.3	135.2	300.9	1,220.4	92.7
Winston-Salem, NC	n/a	n/a	n/a	n/a	n/a	n/a	n/a	n/a
U.S.	2,356.7	6.5	38.4	73.9	279.7	314.2	1,398.0	246.0

Note: Figures are crimes per 100,000 population in 2020 except where noted; n/a not available; (1) All areas within the metro area that are located outside the city limits; (2) 2019 data; (3) 2018 data
Source: FBI Uniform Crime Reports, 2018, 2019, 2020

Crime Rate: Metro Area

Metro Area[1]	Total Crime	Violent Crime Rate				Property Crime Rate		
		Murder	Rape	Robbery	Aggrav. Assault	Burglary	Larceny -Theft	Motor Vehicle Theft
Albuquerque, NM	4,660.5	9.4	61.3	171.6	764.1	688.1	2,303.5	662.5
Allentown, PA[3]	n/a	n/a	n/a	n/a	n/a	n/a	n/a	n/a
Anchorage, AK	4,576.1	5.9	186.7	185.4	793.4	487.5	2,523.4	393.8
Ann Arbor, MI	1,678.4	2.4	63.2	36.3	310.4	154.3	1,002.5	109.3
Athens, GA	2,572.9	2.8	57.0	51.9	274.8	365.6	1,613.3	207.6
Atlanta, GA[4]	2,895.7	5.7	26.1	94.1	194.7	393.9	1,903.2	278.0
Austin, TX	2,682.2	3.2	43.6	62.4	206.4	336.6	1,781.5	248.5
Baltimore, MD[3]	3,057.2	15.5	36.6	242.7	403.8	364.7	1,753.9	239.9
Baton Rouge, LA	3,656.9	16.8	26.1	77.4	445.5	465.1	2,413.3	212.7
Boise City, ID	1,424.4	1.8	58.5	11.9	190.5	187.0	865.5	109.2
Boston, MA[2]	1,249.7	2.2	21.8	38.2	191.6	117.5	786.3	92.1
Boulder, CO	3,053.3	1.2	54.0	42.7	195.3	405.2	2,051.3	303.6
Buffalo, NY	2,304.6	7.1	22.9	92.0	256.3	253.9	1,477.4	194.9
Cape Coral, FL	1,298.3	4.1	30.4	38.6	193.8	149.9	783.6	98.0
Cedar Rapids, IA	2,367.4	4.4	25.9	42.3	179.4	465.9	1,381.3	268.3
Charleston, SC	2,926.8	11.3	36.1	79.8	318.9	309.0	1,886.2	285.4
Charlotte, NC	n/a	n/a	n/a	n/a	n/a	n/a	n/a	n/a
Chicago, IL[2]	n/a	n/a	n/a	n/a	n/a	n/a	n/a	n/a
Cincinnati, OH	1,894.4	5.7	33.0	54.6	142.3	257.5	1,237.7	163.5
Clarksville, TN	2,276.1	6.7	42.6	37.5	336.7	286.4	1,364.1	202.0
Cleveland, OH	2,145.2	10.3	36.2	106.5	287.7	306.5	1,169.7	228.4
College Station, TX	2,152.0	3.7	67.9	32.8	193.6	311.5	1,379.4	163.0
Colorado Springs, CO	3,139.6	6.2	76.8	58.6	344.9	412.8	1,855.2	384.9
Columbia, MO	2,572.2	7.1	63.8	35.7	259.4	280.8	1,637.3	288.0
Columbia, SC	3,830.0	9.2	41.9	76.0	430.9	511.5	2,378.9	381.6
Columbus, OH	2,523.0	9.0	54.3	99.3	150.6	376.7	1,630.2	202.9
Dallas, TX[2]	n/a	n/a	n/a	n/a	n/a	n/a	n/a	n/a
Davenport, IA	n/a	6.9	59.6	71.2	338.3	493.9	n/a	251.4
Denver, CO	3,793.1	6.1	65.8	93.9	324.5	443.9	2,124.7	734.2
Des Moines, IA	2,362.1	6.2	34.8	41.6	256.0	423.8	1,310.9	288.8
Durham, NC	3,000.9	8.1	29.1	113.9	349.3	471.8	1,818.1	210.6
Edison, NJ[2]	n/a	n/a	n/a	n/a	n/a	n/a	n/a	n/a
El Paso, TX	1,457.0	3.9	37.7	38.0	229.2	123.2	962.0	62.9
Fargo, ND	3,180.0	5.6	69.3	33.0	242.8	648.6	1,888.3	292.3
Fort Collins, CO[3]	2,112.3	0.8	34.8	17.7	180.7	194.2	1,555.0	129.0
Fort Wayne, IN	2,083.1	9.9	31.0	64.7	229.3	204.7	1,391.1	152.3
Fort Worth, TX[2]	n/a	n/a	n/a	n/a	n/a	n/a	n/a	n/a
Grand Rapids, MI	1,628.8	4.6	68.8	35.1	241.6	164.6	950.1	164.0
Green Bay, WI	1,216.1	2.5	37.3	16.0	169.2	146.4	787.1	57.6
Honolulu, HI[3]	n/a	n/a	n/a	n/a	n/a	n/a	n/a	n/a
Houston, TX	3,249.2	9.2	44.7	167.9	410.0	402.1	1,841.0	374.3
Huntsville, AL	n/a	n/a	n/a	n/a	n/a	n/a	n/a	n/a
Indianapolis, IN	n/a	n/a	n/a	n/a	n/a	n/a	n/a	n/a
Jacksonville, FL	2,653.0	9.9	40.5	68.6	380.8	316.0	1,607.7	229.4
Kansas City, MO	n/a	n/a	n/a	n/a	n/a	n/a	n/a	n/a
Lafayette, LA	2,937.4	8.4	21.2	56.3	364.1	514.9	1,764.1	208.4
Las Cruces, NM[3]	2,871.0	5.5	56.8	31.6	462.9	490.4	1,626.2	197.5
Las Vegas, NV	2,525.2	5.5	54.6	100.3	318.2	375.2	1,301.2	370.1
Lexington, KY	2,811.4	5.9	45.2	75.0	124.6	397.2	1,883.4	280.1
Lincoln, NE[3]	2,843.7	1.5	106.4	49.2	189.7	309.2	2,043.0	144.7
Little Rock, AR	4,117.3	13.1	67.5	88.9	769.4	540.6	2,291.0	346.8
Los Angeles, CA[2]	2,567.7	5.6	34.6	132.5	300.0	352.3	1,294.6	448.2
Louisville, KY[3]	3,300.8	8.3	26.0	93.8	308.7	447.9	2,011.8	404.3
Madison, WI	2,007.2	2.5	24.0	35.2	140.1	290.7	1,363.0	151.7

Table continued on following page.

Metro Area[1]	Total Crime	Violent Crime Rate				Property Crime Rate		
		Murder	Rape	Robbery	Aggrav. Assault	Burglary	Larceny -Theft	Motor Vehicle Theft
Manchester, NH	1,355.7	1.2	42.2	32.7	141.6	115.4	944.8	77.7
Memphis, TN	5,077.3	24.2	48.1	176.8	1,109.7	580.0	2,693.4	445.0
Miami, FL[2]	2,609.4	7.5	30.9	88.9	289.6	226.7	1,721.0	244.7
Midland, TX	2,541.9	6.9	49.1	29.4	288.5	284.2	1,516.1	367.5
Milwaukee, WI	2,634.0	13.1	40.0	140.8	484.3	288.1	1,316.8	350.9
Minneapolis, MN	n/a	n/a	n/a	n/a	n/a	n/a	n/a	n/a
Nashville, TN	2,968.8	7.7	38.4	106.5	463.7	320.3	1,787.7	244.5
New Haven, CT	2,425.5	6.1	20.5	93.2	136.5	230.5	1,591.8	346.9
New Orleans, LA	3,378.9	21.7	72.5	118.0	412.2	325.1	2,061.9	367.5
New York, NY[2]	n/a	n/a	n/a	n/a	n/a	n/a	n/a	n/a
Oklahoma City, OK	3,387.0	7.8	59.0	72.3	331.7	619.9	1,902.9	393.3
Omaha, NE	2,710.6	4.6	55.2	60.1	309.8	254.6	1,606.2	420.2
Orlando, FL	2,288.9	5.9	42.0	72.2	306.6	268.4	1,414.3	179.4
Philadelphia, PA[2,4]	3,462.1	18.3	55.2	270.0	420.3	355.2	2,042.3	300.9
Phoenix, AZ	2,681.7	6.2	44.4	93.8	319.9	329.5	1,630.4	257.5
Pittsburgh, PA[4]	1,687.7	5.5	25.8	58.8	184.5	196.1	1,137.0	80.0
Portland, OR	n/a	n/a	41.1	60.0	203.7	342.7	1,864.0	471.6
Providence, RI	1,445.8	2.5	39.8	37.7	205.6	170.2	863.3	126.6
Provo, UT[3]	1,368.4	1.1	31.6	7.9	49.6	132.9	1,061.8	83.5
Raleigh, NC	1,727.9	3.3	19.7	47.3	153.3	224.6	1,129.7	150.1
Reno, NV	2,291.8	5.6	85.8	77.4	294.1	369.6	1,165.9	293.3
Richmond, VA	2,050.3	9.9	20.6	46.4	138.8	171.1	1,518.7	144.8
Riverside, CA	2,415.6	7.2	27.9	92.0	304.0	368.5	1,181.3	434.7
Rochester, MN	1,552.4	2.7	49.8	21.1	114.0	237.0	1,030.4	97.4
Rochester, NY	1,895.0	5.1	36.5	55.3	165.1	256.7	1,237.1	139.2
Sacramento, CA	2,393.6	4.8	27.0	87.5	259.0	372.0	1,371.2	272.1
Saint Louis, MO	n/a	14.3	34.8	79.2	368.7	325.8	n/a	368.6
Salt Lake City, UT	4,200.7	4.8	67.0	77.1	235.0	429.5	2,842.9	544.4
San Antonio, TX	3,339.5	6.6	60.1	92.3	371.7	422.6	2,049.1	337.2
San Diego, CA	1,830.5	3.4	29.0	75.8	237.4	219.1	986.3	279.3
San Francisco, CA[2]	3,448.3	5.3	31.8	178.5	224.5	439.0	1,965.0	604.2
San Jose, CA	2,543.9	2.8	41.6	86.7	186.2	369.1	1,351.5	506.0
Santa Rosa, CA	1,758.4	2.0	48.7	54.2	346.0	259.4	898.8	149.2
Savannah, GA[4]	3,107.5	9.2	35.9	93.7	247.2	415.6	2,032.0	274.0
Seattle, WA[2]	3,496.7	4.5	31.1	93.5	210.7	616.6	2,083.1	457.2
Sioux Falls, SD	3,001.8	5.5	45.4	39.9	386.8	395.6	1,747.6	381.0
Springfield, IL	n/a	5.8	65.2	104.7	490.8	612.0	n/a	178.2
Tampa, FL	1,678.0	4.0	33.3	47.1	229.7	182.8	1,057.5	123.6
Tucson, AZ	3,298.3	8.1	51.4	110.3	303.7	321.4	2,265.9	237.5
Tulsa, OK	3,701.1	9.3	56.2	86.8	439.1	666.7	1,908.0	534.9
Tuscaloosa, AL[4]	3,445.1	4.0	35.6	80.3	276.5	607.5	2,189.7	251.6
Virginia Beach, VA	2,301.0	10.3	26.2	57.2	258.1	175.7	1,590.0	183.5
Washington, DC[2]	n/a	n/a	n/a	n/a	n/a	n/a	n/a	n/a
Wichita, KS[3]	n/a	6.1	74.0	77.9	623.3	525.2	n/a	411.7
Wilmington, NC	2,373.9	8.6	38.0	61.5	264.0	372.4	1,509.5	120.0
Winston-Salem, NC	n/a	n/a	n/a	n/a	n/a	n/a	n/a	n/a
U.S.	2,356.7	6.5	38.4	73.9	279.7	314.2	1,398.0	246.0

Note: Figures are crimes per 100,000 population in 2020 except where noted; n/a not available; (1) Figures cover the Metropolitan Statistical Area except where noted; (2) Metropolitan Division (MD); (3) 2019 data; (4) 2018 data
Source: FBI Uniform Crime Reports, 2018, 2019, 2020

Temperature & Precipitation: Yearly Averages and Extremes

City	Extreme Low (°F)	Average Low (°F)	Average Temp. (°F)	Average High (°F)	Extreme High (°F)	Average Precip. (in.)	Average Snow (in.)
Albuquerque, NM	-17	43	57	70	105	8.5	11
Allentown, PA	-12	42	52	61	105	44.2	32
Anchorage, AK	-34	29	36	43	85	15.7	71
Ann Arbor, MI	-21	39	49	58	104	32.4	41
Athens, GA	-8	52	62	72	105	49.8	2
Atlanta, GA	-8	52	62	72	105	49.8	2
Austin, TX	-2	58	69	79	109	31.1	1
Baltimore, MD	-7	45	56	65	105	41.2	21
Baton Rouge, LA	8	57	68	78	103	58.5	Trace
Boise City, ID	-25	39	51	63	111	11.8	22
Boston, MA	-12	44	52	59	102	42.9	41
Boulder, CO	-25	37	51	64	103	15.5	63
Buffalo, NY	-20	40	48	56	99	38.1	90
Cape Coral, FL	26	65	75	84	103	53.9	0
Cedar Rapids, IA	-34	36	47	57	105	34.4	33
Charleston, SC	6	55	66	76	104	52.1	1
Charlotte, NC	-5	50	61	71	104	42.8	6
Chicago, IL	-27	40	49	59	104	35.4	39
Cincinnati, OH	-25	44	54	64	103	40.9	23
Clarksville, TN	-17	49	60	70	107	47.4	11
Cleveland, OH	-19	41	50	59	104	37.1	55
College Station, TX	-2	58	69	79	109	31.1	1
Colorado Springs, CO	-24	36	49	62	99	17.0	48
Columbia, MO	-20	44	54	64	111	40.6	25
Columbia, SC	-1	51	64	75	107	48.3	2
Columbus, OH	-19	42	52	62	104	37.9	28
Dallas, TX	-2	56	67	77	112	33.9	3
Davenport, IA	-24	40	50	60	108	31.8	33
Denver, CO	-25	37	51	64	103	15.5	63
Des Moines, IA	-24	40	50	60	108	31.8	33
Durham, NC	-9	48	60	71	105	42.0	8
Edison, NJ	-8	46	55	63	105	43.5	27
El Paso, TX	-8	50	64	78	114	8.6	6
Fargo, ND	-36	31	41	52	106	19.6	40
Fort Collins, CO	-25	37	51	64	103	15.5	63
Fort Wayne, IN	-22	40	50	60	106	35.9	33
Fort Worth, TX	-1	55	66	76	113	32.3	3
Grand Rapids, MI	-22	38	48	57	102	34.7	73
Green Bay, WI	-31	34	44	54	99	28.3	46
Honolulu, HI	52	70	77	84	94	22.4	0
Houston, TX	7	58	69	79	107	46.9	Trace
Huntsville, AL	-11	50	61	71	104	56.8	4
Indianapolis, IN	-23	42	53	62	104	40.2	25
Jacksonville, FL	7	58	69	79	103	52.0	0
Kansas City, MO	-23	44	54	64	109	38.1	21
Lafayette, LA	8	57	68	78	103	58.5	Trace
Las Cruces, NM	-8	50	64	78	114	8.6	6
Las Vegas, NV	8	53	67	80	116	4.0	1
Lexington, KY	-21	45	55	65	103	45.1	17
Lincoln, NE	-33	39	51	62	108	29.1	27
Little Rock, AR	-5	51	62	73	112	50.7	5
Los Angeles, CA	27	55	63	70	110	11.3	Trace
Louisville, KY	-20	46	57	67	105	43.9	17
Madison, WI	-37	35	46	57	104	31.1	42
Manchester, NH	-33	34	46	57	102	36.9	63

Table continued on following page.

City	Extreme Low (°F)	Average Low (°F)	Average Temp. (°F)	Average High (°F)	Extreme High (°F)	Average Precip. (in.)	Average Snow (in.)
Memphis, TN	0	52	65	77	107	54.8	1
Miami, FL	30	69	76	83	98	57.1	0
Midland, TX	-11	50	64	77	116	14.6	4
Milwaukee, WI	-26	38	47	55	103	32.0	49
Minneapolis, MN	-34	35	45	54	105	27.1	52
Nashville, TN	-17	49	60	70	107	47.4	11
New Haven, CT	-7	44	52	60	103	41.4	25
New Orleans, LA	11	59	69	78	102	60.6	Trace
New York, NY	-2	47	55	62	104	47.0	23
Oklahoma City, OK	-8	49	60	71	110	32.8	10
Omaha, NE	-23	40	51	62	110	30.1	29
Orlando, FL	19	62	72	82	100	47.7	Trace
Philadelphia, PA	-7	45	55	64	104	41.4	22
Phoenix, AZ	17	59	72	86	122	7.3	Trace
Pittsburgh, PA	-18	41	51	60	103	37.1	43
Portland, OR	-3	45	54	62	107	37.5	7
Providence, RI	-13	42	51	60	104	45.3	35
Provo, UT	-22	40	52	64	107	15.6	63
Raleigh, NC	-9	48	60	71	105	42.0	8
Reno, NV	-16	33	50	67	105	7.2	24
Richmond, VA	-8	48	58	69	105	43.0	13
Riverside, CA	24	53	66	78	114	n/a	n/a
Rochester, MN	-40	34	44	54	102	29.4	47
Rochester, NY	-19	39	48	57	100	31.8	92
Sacramento, CA	18	48	61	73	115	17.3	Trace
Saint Louis, MO	-18	46	56	66	115	36.8	20
Salt Lake City, UT	-22	40	52	64	107	15.6	63
San Antonio, TX	0	58	69	80	108	29.6	1
San Diego, CA	29	57	64	71	111	9.5	Trace
San Francisco, CA	24	49	57	65	106	19.3	Trace
San Jose, CA	21	50	59	68	105	13.5	Trace
Santa Rosa, CA	23	42	57	71	109	29.0	n/a
Savannah, GA	3	56	67	77	105	50.3	Trace
Seattle, WA	0	44	52	59	99	38.4	13
Sioux Falls, SD	-36	35	46	57	110	24.6	38
Springfield, IL	-24	44	54	63	112	34.9	21
Tampa, FL	18	63	73	82	99	46.7	Trace
Tucson, AZ	16	55	69	82	117	11.6	2
Tulsa, OK	-8	50	61	71	112	38.9	10
Tuscaloosa, AL	-6	51	63	74	106	53.5	2
Virginia Beach, VA	-3	51	60	69	104	44.8	8
Washington, DC	-5	49	58	67	104	39.5	18
Wichita, KS	-21	45	57	68	113	29.3	17
Wilmington, NC	0	53	64	74	104	55.0	2
Winston-Salem, NC	-8	47	58	69	103	42.5	10

Source: National Climatic Data Center, International Station Meteorological Climate Summary, 9/96; NOAA

Weather Conditions

City	Temperature			Daytime Sky			Precipitation		
	10°F & below	32°F & below	90°F & above	Clear	Partly cloudy	Cloudy	0.01 inch or more precip.	1.0 inch or more snow/ice	Thunder-storms
Albuquerque, NM	4	114	65	140	161	64	60	9	38
Allentown, PA	n/a	123	15	77	148	140	123	20	31
Anchorage, AK	n/a	194	n/a	50	115	200	113	49	2
Ann Arbor, MI	n/a	136	12	74	134	157	135	38	32
Athens, GA	1	49	38	98	147	120	116	3	48
Atlanta, GA	1	49	38	98	147	120	116	3	48
Austin, TX	< 1	20	111	105	148	112	83	1	41
Baltimore, MD	6	97	31	91	143	131	113	13	27
Baton Rouge, LA	< 1	21	86	99	150	116	113	< 1	73
Boise City, ID	n/a	124	45	106	133	126	91	22	14
Boston, MA	n/a	97	12	88	127	150	253	48	18
Boulder, CO	24	155	33	99	177	89	90	38	39
Buffalo, NY	n/a	131	4	47	144	174	169	65	30
Cape Coral, FL	n/a	n/a	115	93	220	52	110	0	92
Cedar Rapids, IA	n/a	156	16	89	132	144	109	28	42
Charleston, SC	< 1	33	53	89	162	114	114	1	59
Charlotte, NC	1	65	44	98	142	125	113	3	41
Chicago, IL	n/a	132	17	83	136	146	125	31	38
Cincinnati, OH	14	107	23	80	126	159	127	25	39
Clarksville, TN	5	76	51	98	135	132	119	8	54
Cleveland, OH	n/a	123	12	63	127	175	157	48	34
College Station, TX	< 1	20	111	105	148	112	83	1	41
Colorado Springs, CO	21	161	18	108	157	100	98	33	49
Columbia, MO	17	108	36	99	127	139	110	17	52
Columbia, SC	< 1	58	77	97	149	119	110	1	53
Columbus, OH	n/a	118	19	72	137	156	136	29	40
Dallas, TX	1	34	102	108	160	97	78	2	49
Davenport, IA	n/a	137	26	99	129	137	106	25	46
Denver, CO	24	155	33	99	177	89	90	38	39
Des Moines, IA	n/a	137	26	99	129	137	106	25	46
Durham, NC	n/a	n/a	39	98	143	124	110	3	42
Edison, NJ	n/a	90	24	80	146	139	122	16	46
El Paso, TX	1	59	106	147	164	54	49	3	35
Fargo, ND	n/a	180	15	81	145	139	100	38	31
Fort Collins, CO	24	155	33	99	177	89	90	38	39
Fort Wayne, IN	n/a	131	16	75	140	150	131	31	39
Fort Worth, TX	1	40	100	123	136	106	79	3	47
Grand Rapids, MI	n/a	146	11	67	119	179	142	57	34
Green Bay, WI	n/a	163	7	86	125	154	120	40	33
Honolulu, HI	n/a	n/a	23	25	286	54	98	0	7
Houston, TX	n/a	n/a	96	83	168	114	101	1	62
Huntsville, AL	2	66	49	70	118	177	116	2	54
Indianapolis, IN	19	119	19	83	128	154	127	24	43
Jacksonville, FL	< 1	16	83	86	181	98	114	1	65
Kansas City, MO	22	110	39	112	134	119	103	17	51
Lafayette, LA	< 1	21	86	99	150	116	113	< 1	73
Las Cruces, NM	1	59	106	147	164	54	49	3	35
Las Vegas, NV	< 1	37	134	185	132	48	27	2	13
Lexington, KY	11	96	22	86	136	143	129	17	44
Lincoln, NE	n/a	145	40	108	135	122	94	19	46
Little Rock, AR	1	57	73	110	142	113	104	4	57
Los Angeles, CA	0	< 1	5	131	125	109	34	0	1
Louisville, KY	8	90	35	82	143	140	125	15	45
Madison, WI	n/a	161	14	88	119	158	118	38	40

Table continued on following page.

City	Temperature			Daytime Sky			Precipitation		
	10°F & below	32°F & below	90°F & above	Clear	Partly cloudy	Cloudy	0.01 inch or more precip.	1.0 inch or more snow/ice	Thunder-storms
Manchester, NH	n/a	171	12	87	131	147	125	32	19
Memphis, TN	1	53	86	101	152	112	104	2	59
Miami, FL	n/a	n/a	55	48	263	54	128	0	74
Midland, TX	1	62	102	144	138	83	52	3	38
Milwaukee, WI	n/a	141	10	90	118	157	126	38	35
Minneapolis, MN	n/a	156	16	93	125	147	113	41	37
Nashville, TN	5	76	51	98	135	132	119	8	54
New Haven, CT	n/a	n/a	7	80	146	139	118	17	22
New Orleans, LA	0	13	70	90	169	106	114	1	69
New York, NY	n/a	n/a	18	85	166	114	120	11	20
Oklahoma City, OK	5	79	70	124	131	110	80	8	50
Omaha, NE	n/a	139	35	100	142	123	97	20	46
Orlando, FL	n/a	n/a	90	76	208	81	115	0	80
Philadelphia, PA	5	94	23	81	146	138	117	14	27
Phoenix, AZ	0	10	167	186	125	54	37	< 1	23
Pittsburgh, PA	n/a	121	8	62	137	166	154	42	35
Portland, OR	n/a	37	11	67	116	182	152	4	7
Providence, RI	n/a	117	9	85	134	146	123	21	21
Provo, UT	n/a	128	56	94	152	119	92	38	38
Raleigh, NC	n/a	n/a	39	98	143	124	110	3	42
Reno, NV	14	178	50	143	139	83	50	17	14
Richmond, VA	3	79	41	90	147	128	115	7	43
Riverside, CA	0	4	82	124	178	63	n/a	n/a	5
Rochester, MN	n/a	165	9	87	126	152	114	40	41
Rochester, NY	n/a	135	11	58	137	170	157	65	27
Sacramento, CA	0	21	73	175	111	79	58	< 1	2
Saint Louis, MO	13	100	43	97	138	130	109	14	46
Salt Lake City, UT	n/a	128	56	94	152	119	92	38	38
San Antonio, TX	n/a	n/a	112	97	153	115	81	1	36
San Diego, CA	0	< 1	4	115	126	124	40	0	5
San Francisco, CA	0	6	4	136	130	99	63	< 1	5
San Jose, CA	0	5	5	106	180	79	57	< 1	6
Santa Rosa, CA	n/a	43	30	n/a	365	n/a	n/a	n/a	2
Savannah, GA	< 1	29	70	97	155	113	111	< 1	63
Seattle, WA	n/a	38	3	57	121	187	157	8	8
Sioux Falls, SD	n/a	n/a	n/a	95	136	134	n/a	n/a	n/a
Springfield, IL	19	111	34	96	126	143	111	18	49
Tampa, FL	n/a	n/a	85	81	204	80	107	< 1	87
Tucson, AZ	0	18	140	177	119	69	54	2	42
Tulsa, OK	6	78	74	117	141	107	88	8	50
Tuscaloosa, AL	1	57	59	91	161	113	119	1	57
Virginia Beach, VA	< 1	53	33	89	149	127	115	5	38
Washington, DC	2	71	34	84	144	137	112	9	30
Wichita, KS	13	110	63	117	132	116	87	13	54
Wilmington, NC	< 1	42	46	96	150	119	115	1	47
Winston-Salem, NC	3	85	32	94	143	128	113	5	43

Note: Figures are average number of days per year
Source: National Climatic Data Center, International Station Meteorological Climate Summary, 9/96; NOAA

Air Quality Index

MSA[1] (Days[2])	Percent of Days when Air Quality was...					AQI Statistics	
	Good	Moderate	Unhealthy for Sensitive Groups	Unhealthy	Very Unhealthy	Maximum	Median
Albuquerque, NM (366)	35.8	61.5	2.2	0.3	0.3	214	54
Allentown, PA (366)	81.7	18.0	0.3	0.0	0.0	117	39
Anchorage, AK (366)	89.1	10.7	0.3	0.0	0.0	103	25
Ann Arbor, MI (366)	79.8	18.6	1.4	0.3	0.0	157	38
Athens, GA (366)	85.2	14.8	0.0	0.0	0.0	99	36
Atlanta, GA (366)	65.8	33.3	0.8	0.0	0.0	125	44
Austin, TX (366)	71.0	28.4	0.3	0.3	0.0	153	44
Baltimore, MD (365)	78.1	21.1	0.8	0.0	0.0	119	42
Baton Rouge, LA (366)	67.5	30.9	1.6	0.0	0.0	136	44
Boise City, ID (366)	57.7	36.6	2.7	3.0	0.0	198	47
Boston, MA (366)	80.3	19.7	0.0	0.0	0.0	97	42
Boulder, CO (366)	59.3	35.0	5.2	0.5	0.0	173	47
Buffalo, NY (366)	86.1	13.4	0.0	0.5	0.0	155	37
Cape Coral, FL (366)	90.2	9.8	0.0	0.0	0.0	100	36
Cedar Rapids, IA (366)	74.0	25.7	0.3	0.0	0.0	105	40
Charleston, SC (366)	89.6	10.1	0.3	0.0	0.0	117	35
Charlotte, NC (366)	77.0	22.4	0.5	0.0	0.0	112	42
Chicago, IL (366)	33.1	59.3	6.3	1.4	0.0	197	56
Cincinnati, OH (366)	53.0	44.8	2.2	0.0	0.0	126	50
Clarksville, TN (366)	88.0	11.5	0.5	0.0	0.0	116	39
Cleveland, OH (366)	57.9	38.0	3.8	0.3	0.0	154	48
College Station, TX (353)	88.7	11.3	0.0	0.0	0.0	99	28
Colorado Springs, CO (366)	69.7	28.4	1.6	0.3	0.0	151	45
Columbia, MO (244)	96.3	3.7	0.0	0.0	0.0	93	33
Columbia, SC (366)	87.7	12.0	0.3	0.0	0.0	117	38
Columbus, OH (366)	79.8	19.4	0.8	0.0	0.0	102	41
Dallas, TX (366)	55.2	38.3	5.7	0.8	0.0	159	48
Davenport, IA (366)	62.6	36.6	0.5	0.3	0.0	155	45
Denver, CO (366)	32.5	58.2	8.2	1.1	0.0	161	58
Des Moines, IA (366)	84.2	15.3	0.0	0.5	0.0	186	36
Durham, NC (366)	90.4	9.6	0.0	0.0	0.0	97	35
Edison, NJ (366)	60.4	36.6	3.0	0.0	0.0	140	47
El Paso, TX (366)	41.3	53.8	4.6	0.3	0.0	192	54
Fargo, ND (363)	92.6	7.4	0.0	0.0	0.0	80	34
Fort Collins, CO (366)	60.7	34.2	4.6	0.5	0.0	157	48
Fort Wayne, IN (366)	69.7	29.8	0.5	0.0	0.0	120	44
Fort Worth, TX (366)	55.2	38.3	5.7	0.8	0.0	159	48
Grand Rapids, MI (366)	82.2	15.6	1.9	0.3	0.0	153	36
Green Bay, WI (366)	84.2	15.6	0.3	0.0	0.0	119	35
Honolulu, HI (366)	97.0	3.0	0.0	0.0	0.0	92	26
Houston, TX (366)	47.3	46.2	5.7	0.8	0.0	182	52
Huntsville, AL (364)	84.3	15.7	0.0	0.0	0.0	88	40
Indianapolis, IN (366)	51.9	46.2	1.9	0.0	0.0	144	49
Jacksonville, FL (366)	71.9	26.5	1.4	0.3	0.0	157	43
Kansas City, MO (366)	56.8	41.8	1.1	0.3	0.0	157	48
Lafayette, LA (365)	75.1	24.7	0.3	0.0	0.0	120	41
Las Cruces, NM (366)	45.9	48.4	4.1	0.8	0.3	400	53
Las Vegas, NV (366)	29.5	63.7	6.0	0.8	0.0	174	61
Lexington, KY (366)	88.5	11.5	0.0	0.0	0.0	84	39
Lincoln, NE (366)	96.7	3.3	0.0	0.0	0.0	74	30
Little Rock, AR (366)	75.1	24.3	0.5	0.0	0.0	132	42
Los Angeles, CA (366)	16.4	44.8	21.6	12.8	4.4	235	84
Louisville, KY (366)	63.7	34.4	1.9	0.0	0.0	143	46
Madison, WI (366)	77.6	21.0	1.4	0.0	0.0	115	40

Table continued on following page.

MSA[1] (Days[2])	Percent of Days when Air Quality was...					AQI Statistics	
	Good	Moderate	Unhealthy for Sensitive Groups	Unhealthy	Very Unhealthy	Maximum	Median
Manchester, NH (366)	97.8	2.2	0.0	0.0	0.0	90	36
Memphis, TN (366)	67.8	31.1	0.8	0.3	0.0	152	45
Miami, FL (366)	71.3	28.1	0.5	0.0	0.0	142	43
Midland, TX (n/a)	n/a	n/a	n/a	n/a	n/a	n/a	n/a
Milwaukee, WI (366)	69.1	29.0	1.6	0.3	0.0	169	41
Minneapolis, MN (366)	70.8	28.4	0.5	0.3	0.0	160	44
Nashville, TN (366)	74.9	24.6	0.5	0.0	0.0	121	43
New Haven, CT (366)	72.7	23.8	3.0	0.5	0.0	174	42
New Orleans, LA (366)	68.0	32.0	0.0	0.0	0.0	91	44
New York, NY (366)	60.4	36.6	3.0	0.0	0.0	140	47
Oklahoma City, OK (366)	61.5	37.2	1.4	0.0	0.0	121	46
Omaha, NE (366)	77.6	21.9	0.3	0.3	0.0	156	41
Orlando, FL (366)	86.1	13.9	0.0	0.0	0.0	93	39
Philadelphia, PA (366)	56.3	41.5	2.2	0.0	0.0	143	48
Phoenix, AZ (366)	3.0	34.2	23.2	18.9	20.2	1,124	119
Pittsburgh, PA (366)	53.8	42.3	3.8	0.0	0.0	142	49
Portland, OR (366)	78.1	18.0	1.6	0.0	0.8	509	37
Providence, RI (366)	76.0	23.0	0.8	0.3	0.0	154	43
Provo, UT (366)	64.8	33.9	1.4	0.0	0.0	150	45
Raleigh, NC (365)	77.5	22.2	0.3	0.0	0.0	101	40
Reno, NV (366)	65.3	28.1	3.0	3.0	0.5	240	46
Richmond, VA (366)	89.9	10.1	0.0	0.0	0.0	77	38
Riverside, CA (366)	10.4	41.5	22.4	19.7	5.5	576	98
Rochester, MN (366)	88.8	10.9	0.3	0.0	0.0	111	35
Rochester, NY (366)	87.4	12.6	0.0	0.0	0.0	80	37
Sacramento, CA (366)	36.1	50.3	6.3	6.6	0.8	222	60
St. Louis, MO (366)	43.2	53.8	2.7	0.3	0.0	155	54
Salt Lake City, UT (366)	50.8	43.4	5.2	0.5	0.0	194	50
San Antonio, TX (366)	54.1	43.2	2.5	0.3	0.0	158	49
San Diego, CA (366)	16.4	70.2	9.6	3.8	0.0	192	71
San Francisco, CA (366)	61.7	32.0	2.7	3.3	0.3	218	45
San Jose, CA (366)	62.0	32.0	3.0	3.0	0.0	186	45
Santa Rosa, CA (366)	87.2	10.9	0.3	1.6	0.0	187	33
Savannah, GA (366)	80.9	18.6	0.5	0.0	0.0	131	39
Seattle, WA (366)	73.0	23.2	1.4	1.1	1.4	275	43
Sioux Falls, SD (366)	88.5	11.5	0.0	0.0	0.0	90	35
Springfield, IL (364)	85.7	14.3	0.0	0.0	0.0	97	39
Tampa, FL (366)	72.4	26.8	0.8	0.0	0.0	112	44
Tucson, AZ (366)	42.1	54.4	3.3	0.0	0.3	277	53
Tulsa, OK (366)	73.5	26.0	0.5	0.0	0.0	129	43
Tuscaloosa, AL (278)	96.0	4.0	0.0	0.0	0.0	97	31
Virginia Beach, VA (366)	94.8	5.2	0.0	0.0	0.0	71	34
Washington, DC (366)	77.9	21.3	0.5	0.3	0.0	166	43
Wichita, KS (366)	74.9	23.5	1.6	0.0	0.0	117	41
Wilmington, NC (357)	96.4	3.6	0.0	0.0	0.0	74	31
Winston-Salem, NC (366)	74.3	25.7	0.0	0.0	0.0	97	41

Note: The Air Quality Index (AQI) is an index for reporting daily air quality. EPA calculates the AQI for five major air pollutants regulated by the Clean Air Act: ground-level ozone, particle pollution (also known as particulate matter), carbon monoxide, sulfur dioxide, and nitrogen dioxide. The AQI runs from 0 to 500. The higher the AQI value, the greater the level of air pollution and the greater the health concern. There are six AQI categories: "Good" The AQI is between 0 and 50. Air quality is considered satisfactory; "Moderate" The AQI is between 51 and 100. Air quality is acceptable; "Unhealthy for Sensitive Groups" When AQI values are between 101 and 150, members of sensitive groups may experience health effects; "Unhealthy" When AQI values are between 151 and 200 everyone may begin to experience health effects; "Very Unhealthy" AQI values between 201 and 300 trigger a health alert; "Hazardous" AQI values over 300 trigger health warnings of emergency conditions; (1) Data covers the Metropolitan Statistical Area; (2) Number of days with AQI data in 2020
Source: U.S. Environmental Protection Agency, Air Quality Index Report, 2020

Air Quality Index Pollutants

MSA[1] (Days[2])	Percent of Days when AQI Pollutant was...					
	Carbon Monoxide	Nitrogen Dioxide	Ozone	Sulfur Dioxide	Particulate Matter 2.5	Particulate Matter 10
Albuquerque, NM (366)	0.0	0.0	55.2	0.0	22.1	22.7
Allentown, PA (366)	0.0	1.6	59.3	0.0	39.1	0.0
Anchorage, AK (366)	1.1	0.0	0.0	0.0	67.8	31.1
Ann Arbor, MI (366)	0.0	0.0	65.3	0.0	34.7	0.0
Athens, GA (366)	0.0	0.0	35.8	0.0	64.2	0.0
Atlanta, GA (366)	0.0	3.0	41.3	0.0	55.7	0.0
Austin, TX (366)	0.0	1.6	44.3	0.0	53.8	0.3
Baltimore, MD (365)	0.0	7.1	63.0	0.0	29.9	0.0
Baton Rouge, LA (366)	0.0	0.5	49.2	2.5	47.8	0.0
Boise City, ID (366)	0.0	0.5	39.9	0.0	57.7	1.9
Boston, MA (366)	0.0	5.2	47.3	0.0	47.5	0.0
Boulder, CO (366)	0.0	0.0	68.0	0.0	31.7	0.3
Buffalo, NY (366)	0.0	1.1	69.4	0.3	29.2	0.0
Cape Coral, FL (366)	0.0	0.0	70.5	0.0	29.5	0.0
Cedar Rapids, IA (366)	0.0	0.0	36.3	2.7	60.9	0.0
Charleston, SC (366)	0.0	0.3	47.3	0.0	52.5	0.0
Charlotte, NC (366)	0.0	0.0	55.7	0.0	44.3	0.0
Chicago, IL (366)	0.0	2.2	29.0	5.7	52.7	10.4
Cincinnati, OH (366)	0.0	3.6	38.0	3.3	54.4	0.8
Clarksville, TN (366)	0.0	0.0	63.9	0.0	36.1	0.0
Cleveland, OH (366)	0.0	0.3	42.6	3.3	52.5	1.4
College Station, TX (353)	0.0	0.0	0.0	14.4	85.6	0.0
Colorado Springs, CO (366)	0.0	0.0	92.9	0.0	7.1	0.0
Columbia, MO (244)	0.0	0.0	100.0	0.0	0.0	0.0
Columbia, SC (366)	0.0	0.5	54.1	0.0	45.4	0.0
Columbus, OH (366)	0.0	1.9	55.2	0.0	42.9	0.0
Dallas, TX (366)	0.0	2.2	54.9	0.0	42.9	0.0
Davenport, IA (366)	0.0	0.0	31.7	0.0	41.0	27.3
Denver, CO (366)	0.0	18.6	58.2	0.0	19.1	4.1
Des Moines, IA (366)	0.0	3.6	49.2	0.0	47.0	0.3
Durham, NC (366)	0.0	0.0	48.4	2.7	48.6	0.3
Edison, NJ (366)	0.0	10.7	44.0	0.3	45.1	0.0
El Paso, TX (366)	0.0	6.6	56.6	0.0	34.7	2.2
Fargo, ND (363)	0.0	1.9	69.1	0.0	28.9	0.0
Fort Collins, CO (366)	0.0	0.0	86.3	0.0	13.7	0.0
Fort Wayne, IN (366)	0.0	0.0	40.2	0.0	59.8	0.0
Fort Worth, TX (366)	0.0	2.2	54.9	0.0	42.9	0.0
Grand Rapids, MI (366)	0.3	1.4	77.0	0.0	21.3	0.0
Green Bay, WI (366)	0.0	0.0	47.5	0.0	52.5	0.0
Honolulu, HI (366)	0.0	0.3	76.0	9.6	13.4	0.8
Houston, TX (366)	0.0	4.9	46.2	0.0	48.6	0.3
Huntsville, AL (364)	0.0	0.0	36.3	0.0	62.4	1.4
Indianapolis, IN (366)	0.0	0.0	35.0	0.0	64.5	0.5
Jacksonville, FL (366)	0.0	0.0	33.6	5.2	61.2	0.0
Kansas City, MO (366)	0.0	1.1	33.3	0.0	54.6	10.9
Lafayette, LA (365)	0.0	0.0	55.3	0.0	44.7	0.0
Las Cruces, NM (366)	0.0	1.9	64.8	0.0	10.7	22.7
Las Vegas, NV (366)	0.0	4.6	58.5	0.0	33.6	3.3
Lexington, KY (366)	0.0	3.0	50.0	0.0	47.0	0.0
Lincoln, NE (366)	0.0	0.0	59.0	23.5	17.5	0.0
Little Rock, AR (366)	0.0	1.6	42.3	0.0	56.0	0.0
Los Angeles, CA (366)	0.0	6.3	57.4	0.0	35.0	1.4
Louisville, KY (366)	0.0	2.7	42.9	0.0	54.4	0.0
Madison, WI (366)	0.0	0.0	41.8	0.0	58.2	0.0

Table continued on following page.

MSA[1] (Days[2])	Percent of Days when AQI Pollutant was...					
	Carbon Monoxide	Nitrogen Dioxide	Ozone	Sulfur Dioxide	Particulate Matter 2.5	Particulate Matter 10
Manchester, NH (366)	0.0	0.0	97.0	0.0	3.0	0.0
Memphis, TN (366)	0.0	1.1	42.6	0.0	56.3	0.0
Miami, FL (366)	0.0	0.8	35.8	0.0	60.4	3.0
Midland, TX (n/a)	n/a	n/a	n/a	n/a	n/a	n/a
Milwaukee, WI (366)	0.0	3.3	51.9	0.0	44.8	0.0
Minneapolis, MN (366)	0.0	1.1	39.1	0.5	42.1	17.2
Nashville, TN (366)	0.0	4.9	39.9	0.0	55.2	0.0
New Haven, CT (366)	0.3	4.1	57.7	0.0	36.9	1.1
New Orleans, LA (366)	0.0	0.5	47.8	13.4	38.3	0.0
New York, NY (366)	0.0	10.7	44.0	0.3	45.1	0.0
Oklahoma City, OK (366)	0.0	1.9	45.1	0.0	52.5	0.5
Omaha, NE (366)	0.0	0.0	41.8	4.6	47.8	5.7
Orlando, FL (366)	0.0	0.0	66.9	0.0	32.2	0.8
Philadelphia, PA (366)	0.0	3.8	35.0	0.0	61.2	0.0
Phoenix, AZ (366)	0.0	0.0	61.5	0.0	16.7	21.9
Pittsburgh, PA (366)	0.0	0.3	40.7	4.4	54.1	0.5
Portland, OR (366)	0.0	0.5	59.6	0.0	39.9	0.0
Providence, RI (366)	0.0	1.1	57.7	0.0	41.3	0.0
Provo, UT (366)	0.0	2.5	69.4	0.0	27.6	0.5
Raleigh, NC (365)	0.3	0.5	46.8	0.0	52.3	0.0
Reno, NV (366)	0.0	1.1	70.8	0.0	26.2	1.9
Richmond, VA (366)	0.0	4.6	58.2	0.0	37.2	0.0
Riverside, CA (366)	0.0	2.5	59.0	0.0	29.0	9.6
Rochester, MN (366)	0.0	0.0	61.5	0.0	38.5	0.0
Rochester, NY (366)	0.0	0.0	70.2	0.0	29.8	0.0
Sacramento, CA (366)	0.0	0.3	54.6	0.0	42.6	2.5
St. Louis, MO (366)	0.0	1.4	31.7	1.6	56.3	9.0
Salt Lake City, UT (366)	0.0	13.1	51.4	0.0	34.7	0.8
San Antonio, TX (366)	0.0	0.3	48.6	0.0	50.8	0.3
San Diego, CA (366)	0.0	0.5	32.2	0.0	66.4	0.8
San Francisco, CA (366)	0.0	3.8	42.3	0.3	53.6	0.0
San Jose, CA (366)	0.0	1.1	51.9	0.0	45.9	1.1
Santa Rosa, CA (366)	0.0	0.3	58.7	0.0	38.0	3.0
Savannah, GA (366)	0.0	0.0	27.9	12.6	59.6	0.0
Seattle, WA (366)	0.0	4.6	54.4	0.0	41.0	0.0
Sioux Falls, SD (366)	0.0	1.6	69.1	0.0	24.6	4.6
Springfield, IL (364)	0.0	0.0	52.7	0.0	47.3	0.0
Tampa, FL (366)	0.0	0.0	44.0	2.7	52.2	1.1
Tucson, AZ (366)	0.0	0.0	55.2	0.0	12.3	32.5
Tulsa, OK (366)	0.0	0.0	58.2	0.0	41.0	0.8
Tuscaloosa, AL (278)	0.0	0.0	73.7	0.0	26.3	0.0
Virginia Beach, VA (366)	0.0	12.6	53.6	0.0	33.6	0.3
Washington, DC (366)	0.0	7.9	57.7	0.0	34.4	0.0
Wichita, KS (366)	0.0	0.5	56.0	0.0	37.2	6.3
Wilmington, NC (357)	0.0	0.0	62.2	0.0	37.8	0.0
Winston-Salem, NC (366)	0.0	1.4	41.3	0.0	57.4	0.0

Note: The Air Quality Index (AQI) is an index for reporting daily air quality. EPA calculates the AQI for five major air pollutants regulated by the Clean Air Act: ground-level ozone, particle pollution (also known as particulate matter), carbon monoxide, sulfur dioxide, and nitrogen dioxide. The AQI runs from 0 to 500. The higher the AQI value, the greater the level of air pollution and the greater the health concern; (1) Data covers the Metropolitan Statistical Area—see Appendix B for areas included; (2) Number of days with AQI data in 2020
Source: U.S. Environmental Protection Agency, Air Quality Index Report, 2020

Air Quality Trends: Ozone

MSA[1]	1990	1995	2000	2005	2010	2016	2017	2018	2019	2020
Albuquerque, NM	0.072	0.070	0.072	0.073	0.066	0.066	0.069	0.074	0.067	0.071
Allentown, PA	0.093	0.091	0.091	0.086	0.080	0.070	0.067	0.067	0.064	0.063
Anchorage, AK	n/a	n/a	n/a	n/a	n/a	n/a	n/a	n/a	n/a	n/a
Ann Arbor, MI	n/a	n/a	n/a	n/a	n/a	n/a	n/a	n/a	n/a	n/a
Athens, GA	n/a	n/a	n/a	n/a	n/a	n/a	n/a	n/a	n/a	n/a
Atlanta, GA	0.104	0.103	0.101	0.087	0.076	0.070	0.068	0.068	0.071	0.060
Austin, TX	0.088	0.089	0.088	0.082	0.074	0.073	0.070	0.072	0.065	0.065
Baltimore, MD	0.100	0.103	0.088	0.089	0.084	0.073	0.071	0.071	0.070	0.064
Baton Rouge, LA	0.105	0.091	0.090	0.090	0.075	0.069	0.069	0.069	0.066	0.065
Boise City, ID	n/a	n/a	n/a	n/a	n/a	n/a	n/a	n/a	n/a	n/a
Boston, MA	n/a	n/a	n/a	n/a	n/a	n/a	n/a	n/a	n/a	n/a
Boulder, CO	n/a	n/a	n/a	n/a	n/a	n/a	n/a	n/a	n/a	n/a
Buffalo, NY	0.089	0.088	0.083	0.090	0.072	0.069	0.064	0.069	0.061	0.065
Cape Coral, FL	n/a	n/a	n/a	n/a	n/a	n/a	n/a	n/a	n/a	n/a
Cedar Rapids, IA	n/a	n/a	n/a	n/a	n/a	n/a	n/a	n/a	n/a	n/a
Charleston, SC	0.068	0.071	0.078	0.073	0.067	0.054	0.062	0.058	0.064	0.059
Charlotte, NC	n/a	n/a	n/a	n/a	n/a	n/a	n/a	n/a	n/a	n/a
Chicago, IL	0.074	0.094	0.073	0.084	0.070	0.066	0.071	0.073	0.069	0.076
Cincinnati, OH	0.091	0.091	0.081	0.085	0.075	0.068	0.067	0.074	0.067	0.067
Clarksville, TN	n/a	n/a	n/a	n/a	n/a	n/a	n/a	n/a	n/a	n/a
Cleveland, OH	0.085	0.092	0.076	0.083	0.077	0.071	0.070	0.074	0.070	0.072
College Station, TX	n/a	n/a	n/a	n/a	n/a	n/a	n/a	n/a	n/a	n/a
Colorado Springs, CO	n/a	n/a	n/a	n/a	n/a	n/a	n/a	n/a	n/a	n/a
Columbia, MO	n/a	n/a	n/a	n/a	n/a	n/a	n/a	n/a	n/a	n/a
Columbia, SC	0.093	0.079	0.096	0.082	0.070	0.056	0.059	0.060	0.066	0.054
Columbus, OH	0.090	0.091	0.085	0.084	0.073	0.066	0.065	0.062	0.060	0.062
Dallas, TX	0.095	0.105	0.096	0.097	0.080	0.077	0.073	0.078	0.071	0.072
Davenport, IA	n/a	n/a	n/a	n/a	n/a	n/a	n/a	n/a	n/a	n/a
Denver, CO	0.077	0.070	0.069	0.072	0.070	0.073	0.072	0.071	0.068	0.079
Des Moines, IA	n/a	n/a	n/a	n/a	n/a	n/a	n/a	n/a	n/a	n/a
Durham, NC	n/a	n/a	n/a	n/a	n/a	n/a	n/a	n/a	n/a	n/a
Edison, NJ	0.101	0.106	0.089	0.090	0.081	0.074	0.070	0.073	0.067	0.063
El Paso, TX	0.080	0.078	0.082	0.074	0.072	0.071	0.073	0.077	0.074	0.076
Fargo, ND	n/a	n/a	n/a	n/a	n/a	n/a	n/a	n/a	n/a	n/a
Fort Collins, CO	0.066	0.072	0.074	0.076	0.072	0.069	0.067	0.073	0.065	0.070
Fort Wayne, IN	0.086	0.094	0.086	0.081	0.067	0.061	0.063	0.071	0.063	0.064
Fort Worth, TX	0.095	0.105	0.096	0.097	0.080	0.077	0.073	0.078	0.071	0.072
Grand Rapids, MI	0.102	0.089	0.073	0.085	0.071	0.066	0.065	0.072	0.065	0.077
Green Bay, WI	n/a	n/a	n/a	n/a	n/a	n/a	n/a	n/a	n/a	n/a
Honolulu, HI	0.034	0.049	0.044	0.042	0.046	0.048	0.046	0.046	0.053	0.044
Houston, TX	0.119	0.114	0.102	0.087	0.079	0.083	0.070	0.073	0.074	0.067
Huntsville, AL	0.079	0.080	0.088	0.075	0.071	0.063	0.063	0.065	0.063	0.057
Indianapolis, IN	0.085	0.095	0.081	0.081	0.070	0.065	0.066	0.076	0.066	0.065
Jacksonville, FL	0.080	0.068	0.072	0.076	0.068	0.060	0.059	0.060	0.062	0.057
Kansas City, MO	0.075	0.098	0.088	0.084	0.072	0.063	0.069	0.073	0.063	0.065
Lafayette, LA	n/a	n/a	n/a	n/a	n/a	n/a	n/a	n/a	n/a	n/a
Las Cruces, NM	0.073	0.075	0.075	0.070	0.060	0.070	0.071	0.072	0.068	0.071
Las Vegas, NV	n/a	n/a	n/a	n/a	n/a	n/a	n/a	n/a	n/a	n/a
Lexington, KY	0.078	0.088	0.077	0.078	0.070	0.069	0.063	0.063	0.059	0.060
Lincoln, NE	0.057	0.060	0.057	0.056	0.050	0.061	0.062	0.062	0.056	0.054
Little Rock, AR	0.080	0.086	0.090	0.083	0.072	0.063	0.060	0.066	0.059	0.062
Los Angeles, CA	0.134	0.114	0.091	0.085	0.076	0.083	0.093	0.084	0.080	0.100
Louisville, KY	0.078	0.087	0.088	0.085	0.076	0.070	0.064	0.069	0.064	0.063
Madison, WI	0.077	0.084	0.072	0.079	0.062	0.064	0.064	0.066	0.059	0.070
Manchester, NH	n/a	n/a	n/a	n/a	n/a	n/a	n/a	n/a	n/a	n/a
Memphis, TN	0.088	0.095	0.092	0.086	0.076	0.065	0.063	0.069	0.065	0.063

Table continued on following page.

MSA[1]	1990	1995	2000	2005	2010	2016	2017	2018	2019	2020
Miami, FL	0.068	0.072	0.075	0.065	0.064	0.061	0.064	0.064	0.058	0.058
Midland, TX	n/a	n/a	n/a	n/a	n/a	n/a	n/a	n/a	n/a	n/a
Milwaukee, WI	0.095	0.106	0.082	0.092	0.079	0.069	0.072	0.073	0.066	0.074
Minneapolis, MN	0.068	0.084	0.065	0.074	0.066	0.061	0.062	0.065	0.059	0.060
Nashville, TN	0.089	0.092	0.084	0.078	0.073	0.065	0.063	0.068	0.064	0.061
New Haven, CT	n/a	n/a	n/a	n/a	n/a	n/a	n/a	n/a	n/a	n/a
New Orleans, LA	0.082	0.088	0.091	0.079	0.074	0.067	0.063	0.065	0.062	0.061
New York, NY	0.101	0.106	0.089	0.090	0.081	0.074	0.070	0.073	0.067	0.063
Oklahoma City, OK	0.078	0.086	0.082	0.077	0.071	0.067	0.070	0.072	0.067	0.068
Omaha, NE	0.054	0.075	0.063	0.069	0.058	0.055	0.061	0.063	0.050	0.055
Orlando, FL	0.081	0.075	0.080	0.083	0.069	0.060	0.067	0.062	0.062	0.061
Philadelphia, PA	0.102	0.109	0.099	0.091	0.083	0.074	0.073	0.075	0.067	0.065
Phoenix, AZ	0.080	0.087	0.082	0.077	0.076	0.072	0.075	0.074	0.071	0.080
Pittsburgh, PA	0.080	0.097	0.083	0.082	0.076	0.069	0.067	0.070	0.062	0.065
Portland, OR	0.081	0.065	0.059	0.059	0.056	0.064	0.073	0.062	0.058	0.058
Providence, RI	0.106	0.107	0.087	0.090	0.072	0.070	0.076	0.074	0.064	0.065
Provo, UT	n/a	n/a	n/a	n/a	n/a	n/a	n/a	n/a	n/a	n/a
Raleigh, NC	0.093	0.081	0.087	0.082	0.071	0.065	0.066	0.063	0.064	0.054
Reno, NV	0.074	0.069	0.067	0.069	0.068	0.071	0.068	0.077	0.063	0.071
Richmond, VA	0.083	0.089	0.080	0.082	0.079	0.062	0.063	0.062	0.061	0.054
Riverside, CA	0.146	0.129	0.104	0.102	0.093	0.094	0.099	0.097	0.091	0.101
Rochester, MN	n/a	n/a	n/a	n/a	n/a	n/a	n/a	n/a	n/a	n/a
Rochester, NY	0.087	0.096	0.070	0.065	0.071	0.061	0.065	0.071	0.060	0.060
Sacramento, CA	0.087	0.093	0.086	0.085	0.074	0.074	0.072	0.075	0.067	0.073
St. Louis, MO	0.085	0.093	0.081	0.088	0.075	0.067	0.069	0.072	0.066	0.067
Salt Lake City, UT	n/a	n/a	n/a	n/a	n/a	n/a	n/a	n/a	n/a	n/a
San Antonio, TX	0.090	0.095	0.078	0.084	0.072	0.079	0.073	0.072	0.075	0.069
San Diego, CA	0.112	0.093	0.084	0.079	0.075	0.070	0.077	0.069	0.071	0.077
San Francisco, CA	0.058	0.074	0.057	0.057	0.061	0.062	0.060	0.053	0.060	0.062
San Jose, CA	0.079	0.085	0.070	0.065	0.073	0.067	0.065	0.061	0.062	0.066
Santa Rosa, CA	0.063	0.071	0.061	0.050	0.053	0.059	0.062	0.055	0.052	0.052
Savannah, GA	n/a	n/a	n/a	n/a	n/a	n/a	n/a	n/a	n/a	n/a
Seattle, WA	0.082	0.062	0.056	0.053	0.053	0.059	0.076	0.067	0.052	0.060
Sioux Falls, SD	n/a	n/a	n/a	n/a	n/a	n/a	n/a	n/a	n/a	n/a
Springfield, IL	n/a	n/a	n/a	n/a	n/a	n/a	n/a	n/a	n/a	n/a
Tampa, FL	0.080	0.075	0.081	0.075	0.067	0.062	0.064	0.065	0.065	0.063
Tucson, AZ	0.073	0.078	0.074	0.075	0.068	0.065	0.070	0.069	0.065	0.070
Tulsa, OK	0.086	0.091	0.081	0.072	0.069	0.061	0.065	0.067	0.062	0.061
Tuscaloosa, AL	n/a	n/a	n/a	n/a	n/a	n/a	n/a	n/a	n/a	n/a
Virginia Beach, VA	0.085	0.084	0.083	0.078	0.074	0.061	0.059	0.061	0.059	0.053
Washington, DC	0.088	0.093	0.082	0.081	0.077	0.067	0.065	0.066	0.061	0.056
Wichita, KS	0.077	0.069	0.080	0.074	0.075	0.064	0.063	0.064	0.062	0.059
Wilmington, NC	0.082	0.079	0.080	0.075	0.062	0.057	0.057	0.062	0.059	0.054
Winston-Salem, NC	0.084	0.086	0.089	0.080	0.078	0.065	0.066	0.064	0.062	0.058
U.S.	0.090	0.091	0.082	0.080	0.074	0.070	0.069	0.070	0.066	0.068

Note: (1) Data covers the Metropolitan Statistical Area; n/a not available. The values shown are the composite ozone concentration averages among trend sites based on the highest fourth daily maximum 8-hour concentration in parts per million. These trends are based on sites having an adequate record of monitoring data during the trend period. Data from exceptional events are included.
Source: U.S. Environmental Protection Agency, Air Quality Monitoring Information, "Air Quality Trends by City, 1990-2020"

Maximum Air Pollutant Concentrations: Particulate Matter, Ozone, CO and Lead

Metro Aea	PM 10 (ug/m^3)	PM 2.5 Wtd AM (ug/m^3)	PM 2.5 24-Hr (ug/m^3)	Ozone (ppm)	Carbon Monoxide (ppm)	Lead (ug/m^3)
Albuquerque, NM	349	9.4	25	0.074	1	n/a
Allentown, PA	34	7.2	18	0.063	n/a	0.06
Anchorage, AK	77	5.9	24	n/a	3	n/a
Ann Arbor, MI	n/a	8.2	20	0.072	n/a	n/a
Athens, GA	n/a	8.4	20	0.056	n/a	n/a
Atlanta, GA	68	9.5	25	0.066	2	n/a
Austin, TX	91	9.5	23	0.063	2	n/a
Baltimore, MD	32	7.5	21	0.069	2	n/a
Baton Rouge, LA	62	8.6	21	0.069	1	0.01
Boise City, ID	142	10.6	49	0.065	2	n/a
Boston, MA	33	8.2	16	0.06	1	n/a
Boulder, CO	74	9.5	52	0.076	n/a	n/a
Buffalo, NY	27	6.8	19	0.066	1	n/a
Cape Coral, FL	57	n/a	n/a	0.061	n/a	n/a
Cedar Rapids, IA	62	8.1	21	0.064	n/a	n/a
Charleston, SC	45	7.1	16	0.053	n/a	n/a
Charlotte, NC	49	8.4	18	0.06	1	n/a
Chicago, IL	149	10.8	23	0.079	1	0.05
Cincinnati, OH	48	10.7	25	0.071	2	n/a
Clarksville, TN	n/a	7.9	21	0.06	n/a	n/a
Cleveland, OH	73	9	22	0.075	2	0.05
College Station, TX	n/a	8.1	21	n/a	n/a	n/a
Colorado Springs, CO	50	6	21	0.079	1	n/a
Columbia, MO	n/a	n/a	n/a	0.057	n/a	n/a
Columbia, SC	42	7.1	17	0.055	0	n/a
Columbus, OH	28	7.8	18	0.067	1	n/a
Dallas, TX	73	9.8	23	0.077	1	0.04
Davenport, IA	159	8.2	20	0.063	1	n/a
Denver, CO	113	10.5	42	0.087	2	n/a
Des Moines, IA	61	7.6	17	0.057	n/a	n/a
Durham, NC	29	7.1	18	0.053	n/a	n/a
Edison, NJ	32	8.5	21	0.073	2	n/a
El Paso, TX	99	9.1	24	0.079	2	0.01
Fargo, ND	33	6.4	14	0.056	n/a	n/a
Fort Collins, CO	n/a	8.1	47	0.075	1	n/a
Fort Wayne, IN	n/a	8.9	20	0.065	n/a	n/a
Fort Worth, TX	73	9.8	23	0.077	1	0.04
Grand Rapids, MI	27	7.7	18	0.078	1	n/a
Green Bay, WI	n/a	7.3	18	0.064	n/a	n/a
Honolulu, HI	38	3.9	7	0.045	1	n/a
Houston, TX	101	11.6	34	0.075	2	n/a
Huntsville, AL	37	7.1	17	0.057	n/a	n/a
Indianapolis, IN	65	11	24	0.069	2	n/a
Jacksonville, FL	98	8.3	18	0.057	1	n/a
Kansas City, MO	138	11	27	0.066	1	n/a
Lafayette, LA	90	8.2	27	0.06	n/a	n/a
Las Cruces, NM	367	9	21	0.077	n/a	n/a
Las Vegas, NV	210	12.2	33	0.078	2	n/a
Lexington, KY	21	7.5	17	0.06	n/a	n/a
Lincoln, NE	n/a	6.1	17	0.054	n/a	n/a
Little Rock, AR	35	9.7	24	0.064	1	n/a
Los Angeles, CA	169	14.8	53	0.124	3	0.02
Louisville, KY	47	9.7	22	0.071	1	n/a
Madison, WI	33	8	18	0.071	n/a	n/a
Manchester, NH	n/a	3	9	0.058	0	n/a

Table continued on following page.

Metro Aea	PM 10 (ug/m^3)	PM 2.5 Wtd AM (ug/m^3)	PM 2.5 24-Hr (ug/m^3)	Ozone (ppm)	Carbon Monoxide (ppm)	Lead (ug/m^3)
Memphis, TN	64	9.1	20	0.069	1	n/a
Miami, FL	87	9.3	21	0.067	1	n/a
Midland, TX	n/a	n/a	n/a	n/a	n/a	n/a
Milwaukee, WI	46	9	21	0.075	1	n/a
Minneapolis, MN	108	8.7	20	0.063	1	0.08
Nashville, TN	58	8.8	20	0.063	1	n/a
New Haven, CT	66	8.2	23	0.08	1	n/a
New Orleans, LA	58	7.9	21	0.063	1	0.01
New York, NY	32	8.5	21	0.073	2	n/a
Oklahoma City, OK	120	9.9	25	0.069	1	n/a
Omaha, NE	90	8.3	22	0.061	2	0.05
Orlando, FL	43	7.3	17	0.062	1	n/a
Philadelphia, PA	40	9.7	25	0.071	2	0
Phoenix, AZ	624	15.5	41	0.087	3	n/a
Pittsburgh, PA	72	9.8	27	0.071	3	0
Portland, OR	35	13.9	147	0.07	14	n/a
Providence, RI	30	8.3	20	0.067	2	n/a
Provo, UT	90	7.9	26	0.07	1	n/a
Raleigh, NC	46	7.8	20	0.055	1	n/a
Reno, NV	220	11.1	75	0.079	2	n/a
Richmond, VA	24	6.9	15	0.055	1	n/a
Riverside, CA	359	15.1	43	0.125	2	n/a
Rochester, MN	n/a	5.6	17	0.067	n/a	n/a
Rochester, NY	25	6.3	15	0.061	1	n/a
Sacramento, CA	231	14.7	134	0.086	2	n/a
St. Louis, MO	122	10.1	26	0.074	2	0.12
Salt Lake City, UT	112	10.5	33	0.08	1	n/a
San Antonio, TX	80	8.6	23	0.074	1	n/a
San Diego, CA	158	20.5	75	0.082	2	0.02
San Francisco, CA	43	11.8	66	0.071	2	n/a
San Jose, CA	116	12.5	59	0.069	2	n/a
Santa Rosa, CA	134	8.3	34	0.052	2	n/a
Savannah, GA	n/a	8.9	18	0.054	n/a	n/a
Seattle, WA	38	10.6	61	0.06	2	n/a
Sioux Falls, SD	71	6	16	0.064	1	n/a
Springfield, IL	n/a	7.6	18	0.067	n/a	n/a
Tampa, FL	60	8.4	18	0.065	1	0.09
Tucson, AZ	211	5.9	14	0.072	1	n/a
Tulsa, OK	96	8.9	20	0.062	1	n/a
Tuscaloosa, AL	n/a	7.5	17	0.052	n/a	n/a
Virginia Beach, VA	21	5.9	13	0.054	1	n/a
Washington, DC	46	7.9	21	0.065	2	n/a
Wichita, KS	139	8.9	24	0.06	n/a	n/a
Wilmington, NC	24	3.7	13	0.054	n/a	n/a
Winston-Salem, NC	60	8.2	26	0.062	n/a	n/a
NAAQS[1]	150	15.0	35	0.075	9	0.15

Note: Data from exceptional events are included; Data covers the Metropolitan Statistical Area; (1) National Ambient Air Quality Standards; ppm = parts per million; ug/m^3 = micrograms per cubic meter; n/a not available
Concentrations: Particulate Matter 10 (coarse particulate)—highest second maximum 24-hour concentration; Particulate Matter 2.5 Wtd AM (fine particulate)—highest weighted annual mean concentration; Particulate Matter 2.5 24-Hour (fine particulate)—highest 98th percentile 24-hour concentration; Ozone—highest fourth daily maximum 8-hour concentration; Carbon Monoxide—highest second maximum non-overlapping 8-hour concentration; Lead—maximum running 3-month average
Source: U.S. Environmental Protection Agency, Air Quality Monitoring Information, "Air Quality Statistics by City, 2020"

Maximum Air Pollutant Concentrations: Nitrogen Dioxide and Sulfur Dioxide

Metro Area	Nitrogen Dioxide AM (ppb)	Nitrogen Dioxide 1-Hr (ppb)	Sulfur Dioxide AM (ppb)	Sulfur Dioxide 1-Hr (ppb)	Sulfur Dioxide 24-Hr (ppb)
Albuquerque, NM	8	41	n/a	3	n/a
Allentown, PA	10	37	n/a	7	n/a
Anchorage, AK	n/a	n/a	n/a	n/a	n/a
Ann Arbor, MI	n/a	n/a	n/a	n/a	n/a
Athens, GA	n/a	n/a	n/a	n/a	n/a
Atlanta, GA	16	42	n/a	3	n/a
Austin, TX	12	43	n/a	n/a	n/a
Baltimore, MD	14	48	n/a	5	n/a
Baton Rouge, LA	7	40	n/a	37	n/a
Boise City, ID	10	43	n/a	2	n/a
Boston, MA	12	46	n/a	6	n/a
Boulder, CO	n/a	n/a	n/a	n/a	n/a
Buffalo, NY	8	40	n/a	16	n/a
Cape Coral, FL	n/a	n/a	n/a	n/a	n/a
Cedar Rapids, IA	n/a	n/a	n/a	43	n/a
Charleston, SC	6	30	n/a	2	n/a
Charlotte, NC	9	32	n/a	2	n/a
Chicago, IL	16	50	n/a	81	n/a
Cincinnati, OH	17	49	n/a	41	n/a
Clarksville, TN	n/a	n/a	n/a	n/a	n/a
Cleveland, OH	8	36	n/a	80	n/a
College Station, TX	n/a	n/a	n/a	n/a	n/a
Colorado Springs, CO	n/a	n/a	n/a	9	n/a
Columbia, MO	n/a	n/a	n/a	n/a	n/a
Columbia, SC	3	n/a	n/a	2	n/a
Columbus, OH	8	39	n/a	n/a	n/a
Dallas, TX	12	45	n/a	8	n/a
Davenport, IA	n/a	n/a	n/a	4	n/a
Denver, CO	25	71	n/a	7	n/a
Des Moines, IA	6	33	n/a	n/a	n/a
Durham, NC	n/a	n/a	n/a	44	n/a
Edison, NJ	18	55	n/a	14	n/a
El Paso, TX	13	59	n/a	7	n/a
Fargo, ND	4	34	n/a	3	n/a
Fort Collins, CO	n/a	n/a	n/a	n/a	n/a
Fort Wayne, IN	n/a	n/a	n/a	n/a	n/a
Fort Worth, TX	12	45	n/a	8	n/a
Grand Rapids, MI	5	28	n/a	15	n/a
Green Bay, WI	n/a	n/a	n/a	6	n/a
Honolulu, HI	3	26	n/a	57	n/a
Houston, TX	16	55	n/a	14	n/a
Huntsville, AL	n/a	n/a	n/a	n/a	n/a
Indianapolis, IN	11	39	n/a	6	n/a
Jacksonville, FL	10	37	n/a	60	n/a
Kansas City, MO	10	42	n/a	7	n/a
Lafayette, LA	n/a	n/a	n/a	n/a	n/a
Las Cruces, NM	8	49	n/a	n/a	n/a
Las Vegas, NV	23	57	n/a	5	n/a
Lexington, KY	5	38	n/a	3	n/a
Lincoln, NE	n/a	n/a	n/a	25	n/a
Little Rock, AR	7	36	n/a	5	n/a
Los Angeles, CA	23	86	n/a	3	n/a
Louisville, KY	13	44	n/a	15	n/a
Madison, WI	n/a	n/a	n/a	2	n/a
Manchester, NH	n/a	n/a	n/a	1	n/a

Table continued on following page.

Metro Area	Nitrogen Dioxide AM (ppb)	Nitrogen Dioxide 1-Hr (ppb)	Sulfur Dioxide AM (ppb)	Sulfur Dioxide 1-Hr (ppb)	Sulfur Dioxide 24-Hr (ppb)
Memphis, TN	10	36	n/a	2	n/a
Miami, FL	13	39	n/a	1	n/a
Midland, TX	n/a	n/a	n/a	n/a	n/a
Milwaukee, WI	12	40	n/a	2	n/a
Minneapolis, MN	11	27	n/a	12	n/a
Nashville, TN	12	45	n/a	2	n/a
New Haven, CT	11	45	n/a	2	n/a
New Orleans, LA	8	43	n/a	56	n/a
New York, NY	18	55	n/a	14	n/a
Oklahoma City, OK	11	39	n/a	2	n/a
Omaha, NE	n/a	n/a	n/a	44	n/a
Orlando, FL	3	n/a	n/a	4	n/a
Philadelphia, PA	13	50	n/a	7	n/a
Phoenix, AZ	25	57	n/a	7	n/a
Pittsburgh, PA	9	36	n/a	65	n/a
Portland, OR	10	30	n/a	2	n/a
Providence, RI	15	45	n/a	3	n/a
Provo, UT	10	43	n/a	n/a	n/a
Raleigh, NC	8	30	n/a	2	n/a
Reno, NV	12	46	n/a	3	n/a
Richmond, VA	12	41	n/a	3	n/a
Riverside, CA	29	78	n/a	5	n/a
Rochester, MN	n/a	n/a	n/a	n/a	n/a
Rochester, NY	6	n/a	n/a	2	n/a
Sacramento, CA	11	46	n/a	3	n/a
St. Louis, MO	10	41	n/a	34	n/a
Salt Lake City, UT	17	51	n/a	5	n/a
San Antonio, TX	8	34	n/a	6	n/a
San Diego, CA	14	49	n/a	1	n/a
San Francisco, CA	14	48	n/a	14	n/a
San Jose, CA	14	49	n/a	2	n/a
Santa Rosa, CA	4	25	n/a	n/a	n/a
Savannah, GA	n/a	n/a	n/a	64	n/a
Seattle, WA	16	57	n/a	4	n/a
Sioux Falls, SD	4	31	n/a	4	n/a
Springfield, IL	n/a	n/a	n/a	n/a	n/a
Tampa, FL	9	35	n/a	42	n/a
Tucson, AZ	8	37	n/a	1	n/a
Tulsa, OK	6	n/a	n/a	7	n/a
Tuscaloosa, AL	n/a	n/a	n/a	n/a	n/a
Virginia Beach, VA	7	35	n/a	4	n/a
Washington, DC	14	45	n/a	4	n/a
Wichita, KS	6	34	n/a	3	n/a
Wilmington, NC	n/a	n/a	n/a	n/a	n/a
Winston-Salem, NC	5	30	n/a	3	n/a
NAAQS[1]	53	100	30	75	140

Note: Data from exceptional events are included; Data covers the Metropolitan Statistical Area; (1) National Ambient Air Quality Standards; ppb = parts per billion; n/a not available
Concentrations: Nitrogen Dioxide AM—highest arithmetic mean concentration; Nitrogen Dioxide 1-Hr—highest 98th percentile 1-hour daily maximum concentration; Sulfur Dioxide AM—highest annual mean concentration; Sulfur Dioxide 1-Hr—highest 99th percentile 1-hour daily maximum concentration; Sulfur Dioxide 24-Hr—highest second maximum 24-hour concentration
Source: U.S. Environmental Protection Agency, Air Quality Monitoring Information, "Air Quality Statistics by City, 2020"

Appendix B: Metropolitan Area Definitions

Metropolitan Statistical Areas (MSA), Metropolitan Divisions (MD), New England City and Town Areas (NECTA), and New England City and Town Area Divisions (NECTAD)

Note: *In March 2020, the Office of Management and Budget (OMB) announced changes to metropolitan and micropolitan statistical area definitions. Both current and historical definitions (December 2009) are shown below. If the change only affected the name of the metro area, the counties included were not repeated.*

Albuquerque, NM MSA
Bernalillo, Sandoval, Torrance, and Valencia Counties

Allentown-Bethlehem-Easton, PA-NJ MSA
Carbon, Lehigh, and Northampton Counties, PA; Warren County, NJ

Anchorage, AK MSA
Anchorage Municipality and Matanuska-Susitna Borough

Ann Arbor, MI MSA
Washtenaw County

Athens-Clarke County, GA MSA
Clarke, Madison, Oconee, and Oglethorpe Counties

Atlanta-Sandy Springs-Roswell, GA MSA
Barrow, Bartow, Butts, Carroll, Cherokee, Clayton, Cobb, Coweta, Dawson, DeKalb, Douglas, Fayette, Forsyth, Fulton, Gwinnett, Haralson, Heard, Henry, Jasper, Lamar, Meriwether, Morgan, Newton, Paulding, Pickens, Pike, Rockdale, Spalding, and Walton Counties
Previously Atlanta-Sandy Springs-Marietta, GA MSA
Barrow, Bartow, Butts, Carroll, Cherokee, Clayton, Cobb, Coweta, Dawson, DeKalb, Douglas, Fayette, Forsyth, Fulton, Gwinnett, Haralson, Heard, Henry, Jasper, Lamar, Meriwether, Newton, Paulding, Pickens, Pike, Rockdale, Spalding, and Walton Counties

Austin-Round Rock, TX MSA
Previously Austin-Round Rock-San Marcos, TX MSA
Bastrop, Caldwell, Hays, Travis, and Williamson Counties

Baltimore-Columbia-Towson, MD MSA
Previously Baltimore-Towson, MD MSA
Baltimore city; Anne Arundel, Baltimore, Carroll, Harford, Howard, and Queen Anne's Counties

Baton Rouge, LA MSA
Ascension, East Baton Rouge, East Feliciana, Iberville, Livingston, Pointe Coupee, St. Helena, West Baton Rouge, and West Feliciana Parishes
Previously Baton Rouge, LA MSA
Ascension, East Baton Rouge, Livingston, and West Baton Rouge Parishes

Boise City, ID MSA
Previously Boise City-Nampa, ID MSA
Ada, Boise, Canyon, Gem, and Owyhee Counties

Boston, MA

Boston-Cambridge-Newton, MA-NH MSA
Previously Boston-Cambridge-Quincy, MA-NH MSA
Essex, Middlesex, Norfolk, Plymouth, and Suffolk Counties, MA; Rockingham and Strafford Counties, NH

Boston, MA MD
Previously Boston-Quincy, MA MD
Norfolk, Plymouth, and Suffolk Counties

Boston-Cambridge-Nashua, MA-NH NECTA
Includes 157 cities and towns in Massachusetts and 34 cities and towns in New Hampshire
Previously Boston-Cambridge-Quincy, MA-NH NECTA
Includes 155 cities and towns in Massachusetts and 38 cities and towns in New Hampshire

Boston-Cambridge-Newton, MA NECTA Division
Includes 92 cities and towns in Massachusetts
Previously Boston-Cambridge-Quincy, MA NECTA Division
Includes 97 cities and towns in Massachusetts

Boulder, CO MSA
Boulder County

Buffalo-Niagara Falls, NY MSA
Erie and Niagara Counties

Cape Coral-Fort Myers, FL MSA
Lee County

Cedar Rapids, IA, MSA
Benton, Jones, and Linn Counties

Charleston-North Charleston, SC MSA
Previously Charleston-North Charleston-Summerville, SC MSA
Berkeley, Charleston, and Dorchester Counties

Charlotte-Concord-Gastonia, NC-SC MSA
Cabarrus, Gaston, Iredell, Lincoln, Mecklenburg, Rowan, and Union Counties, NC; Chester, Lancaster, and York Counties, SC
Previously Charlotte-Gastonia-Rock Hill, NC-SC MSA
Anson, Cabarrus, Gaston, Mecklenburg, and Union Counties, NC; York County, SC

Chicago, IL

Chicago-Naperville-Elgin, IL-IN-WI MSA
Previous name: Chicago-Joliet-Naperville, IL-IN-WI MSA
Cook, DeKalb, DuPage, Grundy, Kane, Kendall, Lake, McHenry, and Will Counties, IL; Jasper, Lake, Newton, and Porter Counties, IN; Kenosha County, WI

Chicago-Naperville-Arlington Heights, IL MD
Cook, DuPage, Grundy, Kendall, McHenry, and Will Counties
Previous name: Chicago-Joliet-Naperville, IL MD
Cook, DeKalb, DuPage, Grundy, Kane, Kendall, McHenry, and Will Counties

Elgin, IL MD
DeKalb and Kane Counties
Previously part of the Chicago-Joliet-Naperville, IL MD

Gary, IN MD
Jasper, Lake, Newton, and Porter Counties

Lake County-Kenosha County, IL-WI MD
Lake County, IL; Kenosha County, WI

Cincinnati, OH-KY-IN MSA
Brown, Butler, Clermont, Hamilton, and Warren Counties, OH; Boone, Bracken, Campbell, Gallatin, Grant, Kenton, and Pendleton County, KY; Dearborn, Franklin, Ohio, and Union Counties, IN
Previously Cincinnati-Middletown, OH-KY-IN MSA
Brown, Butler, Clermont, Hamilton, and Warren Counties, OH; Boone, Bracken, Campbell, Gallatin, Grant, Kenton, and Pendleton County, KY; Dearborn, Franklin, and Ohio Counties, IN

Clarksville, TN-KY MSA
Montgomery and Stewart Counties, TN; Christian and Trigg Counties, KY

Cleveland-Elyria-Mentor, OH MSA
Cuyahoga, Geauga, Lake, Lorain, and Medina Counties

College Station-Bryan, TX MSA
Brazos, Burleson and Robertson Counties

Colorado Springs, CO MSA
El Paso and Teller Counties

Columbia, MO MSA
Boone and Howard Counties

Columbia, SC MSA
Calhoun, Fairfield, Kershaw, Lexington, Richland and Saluda Counties

Columbus, OH MSA
Delaware, Fairfield, Franklin, Licking, Madison, Morrow, Pickaway, and Union Counties

Dallas, TX

Dallas-Fort Worth-Arlington, TX MSA
Collin, Dallas, Denton, Ellis, Hunt, Johnson, Kaufman, Parker, Rockwall, Tarrant, and Wise Counties

Dallas-Plano-Irving, TX MD
Collin, Dallas, Denton, Ellis, Hunt, Kaufman, and Rockwall Counties

Davenport-Moline-Rock Island, IA-IL MSA
Henry, Mercer, and Rock Island Counties, IA; Scott County

Denver-Aurora-Lakewood, CO MSA
Previously Denver-Aurora-Broomfield, CO MSA
Adams, Arapahoe, Broomfield, Clear Creek, Denver, Douglas, Elbert, Gilpin, Jefferson, and Park Counties

Des Moines-West Des Moines, IA MSA
Dallas, Guthrie, Madison, Polk, and Warren Counties

Durham-Chapel Hill, NC MSA
Chatham, Durham, Orange, and Person Counties

Edison, NJ
See New York, NY (New York-Jersey City-White Plains, NY-NJ MD)

El Paso, TX MSA
El Paso County

Fargo, ND-MN MSA
Cass County, ND; Clay County, MN

Fort Collins, CO MSA
Previously Fort Collins-Loveland, CO MSA
Larimer County

Fort Wayne, IN MSA
Allen, Wells, and Whitley Counties

Fort Worth, TX

Dallas-Fort Worth-Arlington, TX MSA
Collin, Dallas, Denton, Ellis, Hunt, Johnson, Kaufman, Parker, Rockwall, Tarrant, and Wise Counties

Fort Worth-Arlington, TX MD
Hood, Johnson, Parker, Somervell, Tarrant, and Wise Counties

Grand Rapids-Wyoming, MI MSA
Barry, Kent, Montcalm, and Ottawa Counties
Previously Grand Rapids-Wyoming, MI MSA
Barry, Ionia, Kent, and Newaygo Counties

Green Bay, WI MSA
Brown, Kewaunee, and Oconto Counties

Honolulu, HI MSA
Honolulu County

Houston-The Woodlands-Sugar Land-Baytown, TX MSA
Austin, Brazoria, Chambers, Fort Bend, Galveston, Harris, Liberty, Montgomery, and Waller Counties
Previously Houston-Sugar Land-Baytown, TX MSA
Austin, Brazoria, Chambers, Fort Bend, Galveston, Harris, Liberty, Montgomery, San Jacinto, and Waller Counties

Huntsville, AL MSA
Limestone and Madison Counties

Indianapolis-Carmel, IN MSA
Boone, Brown, Hamilton, Hancock, Hendricks, Johnson, Marion, Morgan, Putnam, and Shelby Counties

Jacksonville, FL MSA
Baker, Clay, Duval, Nassau, and St. Johns Counties

Kansas City, MO-KS MSA
Franklin, Johnson, Leavenworth, Linn, Miami, and Wyandotte Counties, KS; Bates, Caldwell, Cass, Clay, Clinton, Jackson, Lafayette, Platte, and Ray Counties, MO

Lafayette, LA MSA
Acadia, Iberia, Lafayette, St. Martin, and Vermilion Parishes

Las Cruces, NM MSA
Doña Ana County
Previously Las Cruces, NM MSA
Doña Ana and San Miguel Counties

Las Vegas-Henderson-Paradise, NV MSA
Previously Las Vegas-Paradise, NV MSA
Clark County

Lexington-Fayette, KY MSA
Bourbon, Clark, Fayette, Jessamine, Scott, and Woodford Counties

Lincoln, NE MSA
Lancaster and Seward Counties

Little Rock-North Little Rock-Conway, AR MSA
Faulkner, Grant, Lonoke, Perry, Pulaski, and Saline Counties

Los Angeles, CA

Los Angeles-Long Beach-Anaheim, CA MSA
Previously Los Angeles-Long Beach-Santa Ana, CA MSA
Los Angeles and Orange Counties

Los Angeles-Long Beach-Glendale, CA MD
Los Angeles County

Anaheim-Santa Ana-Irvine, CA MD
Previously Santa Ana-Anaheim-Irvine, CA MD
Orange County

Louisville/Jefferson, KY-IN MSA
Clark, Floyd, Harrison, Scott, and Washington Counties, IN; Bullitt, Henry, Jefferson, Oldham, Shelby, Spencer, and Trimble Counties, KY

Madison, WI MSA
Columbia, Dane, and Iowa Counties

Manchester, NH

Manchester-Nashua, NH MSA
Hillsborough County

Manchester, NH NECTA
Includes 11 cities and towns in New Hampshire
Previously Manchester, NH NECTA
Includes 9 cities and towns in New Hampshire

Memphis, TN-AR-MS MSA
Fayette, Shelby and Tipton Counties, TN; Crittenden County, AR; DeSoto, Marshall, Tate and Tunica Counties, MS

Miami, FL

Miami-Fort Lauderdale-West Palm Beach, FL MSA
Previously Miami-Fort Lauderdale-Pompano Beach, FL MSA
Broward, Miami-Dade, and Palm Beach Counties

Miami-Miami Beach-Kendall, FL MD
Miami-Dade County

Midland, TX MSA
Martin, and Midland Counties

Milwaukee-Waukesha-West Allis, WI MSA
Milwaukee, Ozaukee, Washington, and Waukesha Counties

Minneapolis-St. Paul-Bloomington, MN-WI MSA
Anoka, Carver, Chisago, Dakota, Hennepin, Isanti, Le Sueur, Mille Lacs, Ramsey, Scott, Sherburne, Sibley, Washington, and Wright Counties, MN; Pierce and St. Croix Counties, WI

Nashville-Davidson-Murfreesboro-Franklin, TN MSA
Cannon, Cheatham, Davidson, Dickson, Hickman, Macon, Robertson, Rutherford, Smith, Sumner, Trousdale, Williamson, and Wilson Counties

New Haven-Milford, CT MSA
New Haven County

New Orleans-Metarie-Kenner, LA MSA
Jefferson, Orleans, Plaquemines, St. Bernard, St. Charles, St. James, St. John the Baptist, and St. Tammany Parish
Previously New Orleans-Metarie-Kenner, LA MSA
Jefferson, Orleans, Plaquemines, St. Bernard, St. Charles, St. John the Baptist, and St. Tammany Parish

New York, NY

New York-Newark-Jersey City, NY-NJ-PA MSA
Bergen, Essex, Hudson, Hunterdon, Middlesex, Monmouth, Morris, Ocean, Passaic, Somerset, Sussex, and Union Counties, NJ; Bronx, Dutchess, Kings, Nassau, New York, Orange, Putnam, Queens, Richmond, Rockland, Suffolk, and Westchester Counties, NY; Pike County, PA
Previous name: New York-Northern New Jersey-Long Island, NY-NJ-PA MSA
Bergen, Essex, Hudson, Hunterdon, Middlesex, Monmouth, Morris, Ocean, Passaic, Somerset, Sussex, and Union Counties, NJ; Bronx, Kings, Nassau, New York, Putnam, Queens, Richmond, Rockland, Suffolk, and Westchester Counties, NY; Pike County, PA

Dutchess County-Putnam County, NY MD
Dutchess and Putnam Counties
Dutchess County was previously part of the Poughkeepsie-Newburgh-Middletown, NY MSA. Putnam County was previously part of the New York-Wayne-White Plains, NY-NJ MD

Nassau-Suffolk, NY MD
Nassau and Suffolk Counties

New York-Jersey City-White Plains, NY-NJ MD
Bergen, Hudson, Middlesex, Monmouth, Ocean, and Passaic Counties, NJ; Bronx, Kings, New York, Orange, Queens, Richmond, Rockland, and Westchester Counties, NY
Previous name: New York-Wayne-White Plains, NY-NJ MD
Bergen, Hudson, and Passaic Counties, NJ; Bronx, Kings, New York, Putnam, Queens, Richmond, Rockland, and Westchester Counties, NY

Newark, NJ-PA MD
Essex, Hunterdon, Morris, Somerset, Sussex, and Union Counties, NJ; Pike County, PA
Previous name: Newark-Union, NJ-PA MD
Essex, Hunterdon, Morris, Sussex, and Union Counties, NJ; Pike County, PA

Oklahoma City, OK MSA
Canadian, Cleveland, Grady, Lincoln, Logan, McClain, and Oklahoma Counties

Omaha-Council Bluffs, NE-IA MSA
Harrison, Mills, and Pottawattamie Counties, IA; Cass, Douglas, Sarpy, Saunders, and Washington Counties, NE

Orlando-Kissimmee-Sanford, FL MSA
Lake, Orange, Osceola, and Seminole Counties

Philadelphia, PA

Philadelphia-Camden-Wilmington, PA-NJ-DE-MD MSA
New Castle County, DE; Cecil County, MD; Burlington, Camden, Gloucester, and Salem Counties, NJ; Bucks, Chester, Delaware, Montgomery, and Philadelphia Counties, PA

Camden, NJ MD
Burlington, Camden, and Gloucester Counties

Montgomery County-Bucks County-Chester County, PA MD
Bucks, Chester, and Montgomery Counties
Previously part of the Philadelphia, PA MD

Philadelphia, PA MD
Delaware and Philadelphia Counties
Previous name: Philadelphia, PA MD
Bucks, Chester, Delaware, Montgomery, and Philadelphia Counties

Wilmington, DE-MD-NJ MD
New Castle County, DE; Cecil County, MD; Salem County, NJ

Phoenix-Mesa-Scottsdale, AZ MSA
Previously Phoenix-Mesa-Glendale, AZ MSA
Maricopa and Pinal Counties

Pittsburgh, PA MSA
Allegheny, Armstrong, Beaver, Butler, Fayette, Washington, and Westmoreland Counties

Portland-Vancouver-Hillsboro, OR-WA MSA
Clackamas, Columbia, Multnomah, Washington, and Yamhill Counties, OR; Clark and Skamania Counties, WA

Providence, RI

Providence-New Bedford-Fall River, RI-MA MSA
Previously Providence-New Bedford-Fall River, RI-MA MSA
Bristol County, MA; Bristol, Kent, Newport, Providence, and Washington Counties, RI

Providence-Warwick, RI-MA NECTA
Includes 12 cities and towns in Massachusetts and 36 cities and towns in Rhode Island
Previously Providence-Fall River-Warwick, RI-MA NECTA
Includes 12 cities and towns in Massachusetts and 37 cities and towns in Rhode Island

Provo-Orem, UT MSA
Juab and Utah Counties

Raleigh, NC MSA
Previously Raleigh-Cary, NC MSA
Franklin, Johnston, and Wake Counties

Reno, NV MSA
Previously Reno-Sparks, NV MSA
Storey and Washoe Counties

Richmond, VA MSA
Amelia, Caroline, Charles City, Chesterfield, Dinwiddie, Goochland, Hanover, Henrico, King William, New Kent, Powhatan, Prince George, and Sussex Counties; Colonial Heights, Hopewell, Petersburg, and Richmond Cities

Riverside-San Bernardino-Ontario, CA MSA
Riverside and San Bernardino Counties

Rochester, MN MSA
Dodge, Fillmore, Olmsted, and Wabasha Counties

Rochester, NY MSA
Livingston, Monroe, Ontario, Orleans, Wayne, and Yates Counties
Previously Rochester, NY MSA
Livingston, Monroe, Ontario, Orleans, and Wayne Counties

Sacramento—Roseville—Arden-Arcade, CA MSA
El Dorado, Placer, Sacramento, and Yolo Counties

Saint Louis, MO-IL MSA
Bond, Calhoun, Clinton, Jersey, Macoupin, Madison, Monroe, and St. Clair Counties, IL; St. Louis city; Franklin, Jefferson, Lincoln, St. Charles, St. Louis, and Warren Counties, MO
Previously Saint Louis, MO-IL MSA
Bond, Calhoun, Clinton, Jersey, Macoupin, Madison, Monroe, and St. Clair Counties, IL; St. Louis city; Crawford (part), Franklin, Jefferson, Lincoln, St. Charles, St. Louis, Warren, and Washington Counties, MO

Salt Lake City, UT MSA
Salt Lake and Tooele Counties

San Antonio-New Braunfels, TX MSA
Atascosa, Bandera, Bexar, Comal, Guadalupe, Kendall, Medina, and Wilson Counties

San Diego-Carlsbad, CA MSA
Previously San Diego-Carlsbad-San Marcos, CA MSA
San Diego County

San Francisco, CA

San Francisco-Oakland-Hayward, CA MSA
Previously San Francisco-Oakland- Fremont, CA MSA
Alameda, Contra Costa, Marin, San Francisco, and San Mateo Counties

San Francisco-Redwood City-South San Francisco, CA MD
San Francisco and San Mateo Counties

Previously San Francisco-San Mateo-Redwood City, CA MD
Marin, San Francisco, and San Mateo Counties

San Jose-Sunnyvale-Santa Clara, CA MSA
San Benito and Santa Clara Counties

Santa Rosa, CA MSA
Previously Santa Rosa-Petaluma, CA MSA
Sonoma County

Savannah, GA MSA
Bryan, Chatham, and Effingham Counties

Seattle, WA

Seattle-Tacoma-Bellevue, WA MSA
King, Pierce, and Snohomish Counties

Seattle-Bellevue-Everett, WA MD
King and Snohomish Counties

Sioux Falls, SD MSA
Lincoln, McCook, Minnehaha, and Turner Counties

Springfield, IL MSA
Menard and Sangamon Counties

Tampa-St. Petersburg-Clearwater, FL MSA
Hernando, Hillsborough, Pasco, and Pinellas Counties

Tucson, AZ MSA
Pima County

Tulsa, OK MSA
Creek, Okmulgee, Osage, Pawnee, Rogers, Tulsa, and Wagoner Counties

Tuscaloosa, AL MSA
Hale, Pickens, and Tuscaloosa Counties

Virginia Beach-Norfolk-Newport News, VA-NC MSA
Currituck County, NC; Chesapeake, Hampton, Newport News, Norfolk, Poquoson, Portsmouth, Suffolk, Virginia Beach and Williamsburg cities, VA; Gloucester, Isle of Wight, James City, Mathews, Surry, and York Counties, VA

Washington, DC

Washington-Arlington-Alexandria, DC-VA-MD-WV MSA
District of Columbia; Calvert, Charles, Frederick, Montgomery, and Prince George's Counties, MD; Alexandria, Fairfax, Falls Church, Fredericksburg, Manassas Park, and Manassas cities, VA; Arlington, Clarke, Culpepper, Fairfax, Fauquier, Loudoun, Prince William, Rappahannock, Spotsylvania, Stafford, and Warren Counties, VA; Jefferson County, WV
Previously Washington-Arlington-Alexandria, DC-VA-MD-WV MSA
District of Columbia; Calvert, Charles, Frederick, Montgomery, and Prince George's Counties, MD; Alexandria, Fairfax, Falls Church, Fredericksburg, Manassas Park, and Manassas cities, VA; Arlington, Clarke, Fairfax, Fauquier, Loudoun, Prince William, Spotsylvania, Stafford, and Warren Counties, VA; Jefferson County, WV

Washington-Arlington-Alexandria, DC-VA-MD-WV MD
District of Columbia; Calvert, Charles, and Prince George's Counties, MD; Alexandria, Fairfax, Falls Church, Fredericksburg, Manassas Park, and Manassas cities, VA; Arlington, Clarke, Culpepper, Fairfax, Fauquier, Loudoun, Prince William, Rappahannock, Spotsylvania, Stafford, and Warren Counties, VA; Jefferson County, WV
Previously Washington-Arlington-Alexandria, DC-VA-MD-WV MD
District of Columbia; Calvert, Charles, and Prince George's Counties, MD; Alexandria, Fairfax, Falls Church, Fredericksburg, Manassas Park, and Manassas cities, VA; Arlington, Clarke, Fairfax, Fauquier, Loudoun, Prince William, Spotsylvania, Stafford, and Warren Counties, VA; Jefferson County, WV

Wichita, KS MSA
Butler, Harvey, Kingman, Sedgwick, and Sumner Counties

Wilmington, NC MSA
New Hanover and Pender Counties
Previously Wilmington, NC MSA
Brunswick, New Hanover and Pender Counties

Winston-Salem, NC MSA
Davidson, Davie, Forsyth, Stokes, and Yadkin Counties

Appendix C: Government Type and Primary County

This appendix includes the government structure of each place included in this book. It also includes the county or county equivalent in which each place is located. If a place spans more than one county, the county in which the majority of the population resides is shown.

Albuquerque, NM
Government Type: City
County: Bernalillo

Allentown, PA
Government Type: City
County: Lehigh

Anchorage, AK
Government Type: Municipality
Borough: Anchorage

Ann Arbor, MI
Government Type: City
County: Washtenaw

Athens, GA
Government Type: Consolidated city-county
County: Clarke

Atlanta, GA
Government Type: City
County: Fulton

Austin, TX
Government Type: City
County: Travis

Baltimore, MD
Government Type: Independent city

Baton Rouge, LA
Government Type: Consolidated city-parish
Parish: East Baton Rouge

Boise City, ID
Government Type: City
County: Ada

Boston, MA
Government Type: City
County: Suffolk

Boulder, CO
Government Type: City
County: Boulder

Buffalo, NY
Government Type: City
County: Erie

Cape Coral, FL
Government Type: City
County: Lee

Cedar Rapids, IA
Government Type: City
County: Linn

Charleston, SC
Government Type: City
County: Charleston

Charlotte, NC
Government Type: City
County: Mecklenburg

Chicago, IL
Government Type: City
County: Cook

Cincinnati, OH
Government Type: City
County: Hamilton

Clarksville, TN
Government Type: City
County: Montgomery

Cleveland, OH
Government Type: City
County: Cuyahoga

College Station, TX
Government Type: City
County: Brazos

Colorado Springs, CO
Government Type: City
County: El Paso

Columbia, MO
Government Type: City
County: Boone

Columbia, SC
Government Type: City
County: Richland

Columbus, OH
Government Type: City
County: Franklin

Dallas, TX
Government Type: City
County: Dallas

Davenport, IA
Government Type: City
County: Scott

Denver, CO
Government Type: City
County: Denver

Des Moines, IA
Government Type: City
County: Polk

Durham, NC
Government Type: City
County: Durham

Edison, NJ
Government Type: Township
County: Middlesex

El Paso, TX
Government Type: City
County: El Paso

Fargo, ND
Government Type: City
County: Cass

Fort Collins, CO
Government Type: City
County: Larimer

Fort Wayne, IN
Government Type: City
County: Allen

Fort Worth, TX
Government Type: City
County: Tarrant

Grand Rapids, MI
Government Type: City
County: Kent

Green Bay, WI
Government Type: City
County: Brown

Honolulu, HI
Government Type: Census Designated Place (CDP)
County: Honolulu

Houston, TX
Government Type: City
County: Harris

Huntsville, AL
Government Type: City
County: Madison

Indianapolis, IN
Government Type: City
County: Marion

Jacksonville, FL
Government Type: City
County: Duval

Kansas City, MO
Government Type: City
County: Jackson

Lafayette, LA
Government Type: City
Parish: Lafayette

Las Cruces, NM
Government Type: City
County: Doña Ana

Las Vegas, NV
Government Type: City
County: Clark

Lexington, KY
Government Type: Consolidated city-county
County: Fayette

Lincoln, NE
Government Type: City
County: Lancaster

Little Rock, AR
Government Type: City
County: Pulaski

Los Angeles, CA
Government Type: City
County: Los Angeles

Louisville, KY
Government Type: Consolidated city-county
County: Jefferson

Madison, WI
Government Type: City
County: Dane

Manchester, NH
Government Type: City
County: Hillsborough

Memphis, TN
Government Type: City
County: Shelby

Miami, FL
Government Type: City
County: Miami-Dade

Midland, TX
Government Type: City
County: Midland

Milwaukee, WI
Government Type: City
County: Milwaukee

Minneapolis, MN
Government Type: City
County: Hennepin

Nashville, TN
Government Type: Consolidated city-county
County: Davidson

New Haven, CT
Government Type: City
County: New Haven

New Orleans, LA
Government Type: City
Parish: Orleans

New York, NY
Government Type: City
Counties: Bronx; Kings; New York; Queens; Staten Island

Oklahoma City, OK
Government Type: City
County: Oklahoma

Omaha, NE
Government Type: City
County: Douglas

Orlando, FL
Government Type: City
County: Orange

Philadelphia, PA
Government Type: City
County: Philadelphia

Phoenix, AZ
Government Type: City
County: Maricopa

Pittsburgh, PA
Government Type: City
County: Allegheny

Portland, OR
Government Type: City
County: Multnomah

Providence, RI
Government Type: City
County: Providence

Provo, UT
Government Type: City
County: Utah

Raleigh, NC
Government Type: City
County: Wake

Reno, NV
Government Type: City
County: Washoe

Richmond, VA
Government Type: Independent city

Riverside, CA
Government Type: City
County: Riverside

Rochester, MN
Government Type: City
County: Olmsted

Rochester, NY
Government Type: City
County: Monroe

Sacramento, CA
Government Type: City
County: Sacramento

Saint Louis, MO
Government Type: Independent city

Salt Lake City, UT
Government Type: City
County: Salt Lake

San Antonio, TX
Government Type: City
County: Bexar

San Diego, CA
Government Type: City
County: San Diego

San Francisco, CA
Government Type: City
County: San Francisco

San Jose, CA
Government Type: City
County: Santa Clara

Santa Rosa, CA
Government Type: City
County: Sonoma

Savannah, GA
Government Type: City
County: Chatham

Seattle, WA
Government Type: City
County: King

Sioux Falls, SD
Government Type: City
County: Minnehaha

Springfield, IL
Government Type: City
County: Sangamon

Tampa, FL
Government Type: City
County: Hillsborough

Tucson, AZ
Government Type: City
County: Pima

Tulsa, OK
Government Type: City
County: Tulsa

Tuscaloosa, AL
Government Type: City
County: Tuscaloosa

Virginia Beach, VA
Government Type: Independent city

Washington, DC
Government Type: City
County: District of Columbia

Wichita, KS
Government Type: City
County: Sedgwick

Wilmington, NC
Government Type: City
County: New Hanover

Winston-Salem, NC
Government Type: City
County: Forsyth

Appendix D: Chambers of Commerce

Albuquerque, NM
Albuquerque Chamber of Commerce
P.O. Box 25100
Albuquerque, NM 87125
Phone: (505) 764-3700
Fax: (505) 764-3714
http://www.abqchamber.com

Albuquerque Economic Development Dept
851 University Blvd SE, Suite 203
Albuquerque, NM 87106
Phone: (505) 246-6200
Fax: (505) 246-6219
http://www.cabq.gov/econdev

Allentown, PA
Greater Lehigh Valley Chamber of Commerce
Allentown Office
840 Hamilton Street, Suite 205
Allentown, PA 18101
Phone: (610) 751-4929
Fax: (610) 437-4907
http://www.lehighvalleychamber.org

Anchorage, AK
Anchorage Chamber of Commerce
1016 W Sixth Avenue
Suite 303
Anchorage, AK 99501
Phone: (907) 272-2401
Fax: (907) 272-4117
http://www.anchoragechamber.org

Anchorage Economic Development Department
900 W 5th Avenue
Suite 300
Anchorage, AK 99501
Phone: (907) 258-3700
Fax: (907) 258-6646
http://aedcweb.com

Ann Arbor, MI
Ann Arbor Area Chamber of Commerce
115 West Huron
3rd Floor
Ann Arbor, MI 48104
Phone: (734) 665-4433
Fax: (734) 665-4191
http://www.annarborchamber.org

Ann Arbor Economic Development Department
201 S Division
Suite 430
Ann Arbor, MI 48104
Phone: (734) 761-9317
http://www.annarborspark.org

Athens, GA
Athens Area Chamber of Commerce
246 W Hancock Avenue
Athens, GA 30601
Phone: (706) 549-6800
Fax: (706) 549-5636
http://www.aacoc.org

Athens-Clarke County Economic Development Department
246 W. Hancock Avenue
Athens, GA 30601
Phone: (706) 613-3233
Fax: (706) 613-3812
http://www.athensbusiness.org

Atlanta, GA
Metro Atlanta Chamber of Commerce
235 Andrew Young International Blvd NW
Atlanta, GA 30303
Phone: (404) 880-9000
Fax: (404) 586-8464
http://www.metroatlantachamber.com

Austin, TX
Greater Austin Chamber of Commerce
210 Barton Springs Road
Suite 400
Austin, TX 78704
Phone: (512) 478-9383
Fax: (512) 478-6389
http://www.austin-chamber.org

Baltimore, MD
Baltimore City Chamber of Commerce
P.O. Box 43121
Baltimore, MD 21236
443-860-2020
https://baltimorecitychamberofcommerceinc.wildapricot.org

Baltimore County Chamber of Commerce
102 W. Pennsylvania Avenue
Suite 305
Towson, MD, 21204
Phone: (410) 825-6200
Fax: (410) 821-9901
https://www.baltcountychamber.com

Baton Rouge, LA
Baton Rouge Area Chamber
451 Florida Street
Suite 1050
Baton Rouge, LA 70801
Phone (225) 381-7125
http://www.brac.org

Boise City, ID
Boise Metro Chamber of Commerce
250 S 5th Street
Suite 800
Boise City, ID 83701
Phone: (208) 472-5200
Fax: (208) 472-5201
http://www.boisechamber.org

Boston, MA
Greater Boston Chamber of Commerce
265 Franklin Street
12th Floor
Boston, MA 02110
Phone: (617) 227-4500
Fax: (617) 227-7505
http://www.bostonchamber.com

Boulder, CO
Boulder Chamber of Commerce
2440 Pearl Street
Boulder, CO 80302
Phone: (303) 442-1044
Fax: (303) 938-8837
http://www.boulderchamber.com

City of Boulder Economic Vitality Program
P.O. Box 791
Boulder, CO 80306
Phone: (303) 441-3090
http://www.bouldercolorado.gov

Buffalo, NY
Buffalo Niagara Partnership
257 West Genesee Street
Suite 600
Phone: (716) 852-7100
Fax: (716) 852-2761
https://www.thepartnership.org

Cape Coral, FL
Chamber of Commerce of Cape Coral
2051 Cape Coral Parkway East
Cape Coral, FL 33904
Phone: (239) 549-6900
Fax: (239) 549-9609
http://www.capecoralchamber.com

Cedar Rapids, IA
Cedar Rapids Chamber of Commerce
424 First Avenue NE
Cedar Rapids, IA 52401
Phone: (319) 398-5317
Fax: (319) 398-5228
http://www.cedarrapids.org

Cedar Rapids Economic Development
50 Second Avenue Bridge
Sixth Floor
Cedar Rapids, IA 52401-1256
Phone: (319) 286-5041
Fax: (319) 286-5141
http://www.cedar-rapids.org

Charleston, SC
Charleston Metro Chamber of Commerce
P.O. Box 975
Charleston, SC 29402
Phone: (843) 577-2510
http://www.charlestonchamber.net

Charlotte, NC
Charlotte Chamber of Commerce
330 S Tryon Street
P.O. Box 32785
Charlotte, NC 28232
Phone: (704) 378-1300
Fax: (704) 374-1903
http://www.charlottechamber.com

Charlotte Regional Partnership
1001 Morehead Square Drive
Suite 200
Charlotte, NC 28203
Phone: (704) 347-8942
Fax: (704) 347-8981
http://www.charlotteusa.com

Chicago, IL
Chicagoland Chamber of Commerce
200 E Randolph Street
Suite 2200
Chicago, IL 60601-6436
Phone: (312) 494-6700
Fax: (312) 861-0660
http://www.chicagolandchamber.org

City of Chicago Department of Planning and Development
City Hall, Room 1000
121 North La Salle Street
Chicago, IL 60602
Phone: (312) 744-4190
Fax: (312) 744-2271
https://www.cityofchicago.org/city/en/depts/dcd.html

Cincinnati, OH
Cincinnati USA Regional Chamber
3 East 4th Street
Suite 200
Cincinnati, Ohio 45202
Phone: (513) 579-3111
https://www.cincinnatichamber.com

Clarksville, TN
Clarksville Area Chamber of Commerce
25 Jefferson Street
Suite 300
Clarksville, TN 37040
Phone: (931) 647-2331
http://www.clarksvillechamber.com

Cleveland, OH
Greater Cleveland Partnership
1240 Huron Rd. E
Suite 300
Cleveland, OH 44115
Phone: (216) 621-3300
https://www.gcpartnership.com

College Station, TX
Bryan-College Station Chamber of Commerce
4001 East 29th St, Suite 175
Bryan, TX 77802
Phone: (979) 260-5200
http://www.bcschamber.org

Colorado Springs, CO
Colorado Springs Chamber and EDC
102 South Tejon Street
Suite 430
Colorado Springs, CO 80903
Phone: (719) 471-8183
https://coloradospringschamberedc.com

Columbia, MO
Columbia Chamber of Commerce
300 South Providence Rd.
P.O. Box 1016
Columbia, MO 65205-1016
Phone: (573) 874-1132
Fax: (573) 443-3986
http://www.columbiamochamber.com

Columbia, SC
The Columbia Chamber
930 Richland Street
Columbia, SC 29201
Phone: (803) 733-1110
Fax: (803) 733-1113
http://www.columbiachamber.com

Columbus, OH
Greater Columbus Chamber
37 North High Street
Columbus, OH 43215
Phone: (614) 221-1321
Fax: (614) 221-1408
http://www.columbus.org

Dallas, TX
City of Dallas Economic Development Department
1500 Marilla Street
5C South
Dallas, TX 75201
Phone: (214) 670-1685
Fax: (214) 670-0158
http://www.dallas-edd.org

Greater Dallas Chamber of Commerce
700 North Pearl Street
Suite1200
Dallas, TX 75201
Phone: (214) 746-6600
Fax: (214) 746-6799
http://www.dallaschamber.org

Davenport, IA
Quad Cities Chamber
331 W. 3rd Street
Suite 100
Davenport, IA 52801
Phone: (563) 322-1706
https://quadcitieschamber.com

Denver, CO
Denver Metro Chamber of Commerce
1445 Market Street
Denver, CO 80202
Phone: (303) 534-8500
Fax: (303) 534-3200
http://www.denverchamber.org

Downtown Denver Partnership
511 16th Street
Suite 200
Denver, CO 80202
Phone: (303) 534-6161
Fax: (303) 534-2803
http://www.downtowndenver.com

Des Moines, IA
Des Moines Downtown Chamber
301 Grand Ave
Des Moines, IA 50309
Phone: (515) 309-3229
http://desmoinesdowntownchamber.com

Greater Des Moines Partnership
700 Locust Street
Suite 100
Des Moines, IA 50309
Phone: (515) 286-4950
Fax: (515) 286-4974
http://www.desmoinesmetro.com

Durham, NC
Durham Chamber of Commerce
P.O. Box 3829
Durham, NC 27702
Phone: (919) 682-2133
Fax: (919) 688-8351
http://www.durhamchamber.org

North Carolina Institute of Minority Economic Development
114 W Parish Street
Durham, NC 27701
Phone: (919) 956-8889
Fax: (919) 688-7668
http://www.ncimed.com

Edison, NJ
Edison Chamber of Commerce
939 Amboy Avenue
Edison, NJ 08837
Phone: (732) 738-9482
http://www.edisonchamber.com

El Paso, TX
City of El Paso Department of Economic Development
2 Civic Center Plaza
El Paso, TX 79901
Phone: (915) 541-4000
Fax: (915) 541-1316
http://www.elpasotexas.gov

Greater El Paso Chamber of Commerce
10 Civic Center Plaza
El Paso, TX 79901
Phone: (915) 534-0500
Fax: (915) 534-0510
http://www.elpaso.org

Fargo, ND
Chamber of Commerce of Fargo Moorhead
202 First Avenue North
Fargo, ND 56560
Phone: (218) 233-1100
Fax: (218) 233-1200
http://www.fmchamber.com

Greater Fargo-Moorhead Economic Development Corporation
51 Broadway, Suite 500
Fargo, ND 58102
Phone: (701) 364-1900
Fax: (701) 293-7819
http://www.gfmedc.com

Fort Collins, CO
Fort Collins Chamber of Commerce
225 South Meldrum
Fort Collins, CO 80521
Phone: (970) 482-3746
Fax: (970) 482-3774
https://fortcollinschamber.com

Fort Wayne, IN
City of Fort Wayne Economic Development
1 Main St
1 Main Street
Fort Wayne, IN 46802
Phone: (260) 427-1111
Fax: (260) 427-1375
http://www.cityoffortwayne.org

Greater Fort Wayne Chamber of Commerce
826 Ewing Street
Fort Wayne, IN 46802
Phone: (260) 424-1435
Fax: (260) 426-7232
http://www.fwchamber.org

Fort Worth, TX
City of Fort Worth Economic Development
City Hall
900 Monroe Street
Suite 301
Fort Worth, TX 76102
Phone: (817) 392-6103
Fax: (817) 392-2431
http://www.fortworthgov.org

Fort Worth Chamber of Commerce
777 Taylor Street
Suite 900
Fort Worth, TX 76102-4997
Phone: (817) 336-2491
Fax: (817) 877-4034
http://www.fortworthchamber.com

Grand Rapids, MI
Grands Rapids Area Chamber of Commerce
111 Pearl Street N.W.
Grand Rapids, MI 49503
Phone: (616) 771-0300
Fax: (616) 771-0318
http://www.grandrapids.org

Green Bay, WI
Economic Development
100 N Jefferson St
Room 202
Green Bay, WI 54301
Phone: (920) 448-3397
Fax: (920) 448-3063
http://www.ci.green-bay.wi.us

Green Bay Area Chamber of Commerce
300 N. Broadway
Suite 3A
Green Bay, WI 54305-1660
Phone: (920) 437-8704
Fax: (920) 593-3468
http://www.titletown.org

Honolulu, HI
The Chamber of Commerce of Hawaii
1132 Bishop Street
Suite 402
Honolulu, HI 96813
Phone: (808) 545-4300
Fax: (808) 545-4369
http://www.cochawaii.com

Houston, TX
Greater Houston Partnership
1200 Smith Street
Suite 700
Houston, TX 77002-4400
Phone: (713) 844-3600
Fax: (713) 844-0200
http://www.houston.org

Huntsville, AL
Chamber of Commerce of
Huntsville/Madison County
225 Church Street
Huntsville, AL 35801
Phone: (256) 535-2000
Fax: (256) 535-2015
http://www.huntsvillealabamausa.com

Indianapolis, IN
Greater Indianapolis Chamber of Commerce
111 Monument Circle
Suite 1950
Indianapolis, IN 46204
Phone: (317) 464-2222
Fax: (317) 464-2217
http://www.indychamber.com

The Indy Partnership
111 Monument Circle
Suite 1800
Indianapolis, IN 46204
Phone: (317) 236-6262
Fax: (317) 236-6275
http://indypartnership.com

Jacksonville, FL
Jacksonville Chamber of Commerce
3 Independent Drive
Jacksonville, FL 32202
Phone: (904) 366-6600
Fax: (904) 632-0617
http://www.myjaxchamber.com

Kansas City, MO
Greater Kansas City Chamber of Commerce
2600 Commerce Tower
911 Main Street
Kansas City, MO 64105
Phone: (816) 221-2424
Fax: (816) 221-7440
http://www.kcchamber.com

Kansas City Area Development Council
2600 Commerce Tower
911 Main Street
Kansas City, MO 64105
Phone: (816) 221-2121
Fax: (816) 842-2865
http://www.thinkkc.com

Lafayette, LA
Greater Lafayette Chamber of Commerce
804 East Saint Mary Blvd.
Lafayette, LA 70503
Phone: (337) 233-2705
Fax: (337) 234-8671
http://www.lafchamber.org

Las Cruces, NM
Greater Las Cruces Chamber of Commerce
505 S Main Street
Suite 134
Las Cruces, NM 88001
Phone: (575) 524-1968
Fax: (575) 527-5546
http://www.lascruces.org

Las Vegas, NV
Las Vegas Chamber of Commerce
6671 Las Vegas Blvd South
Suite 300
Las Vegas, NV 89119
Phone: (702) 735-1616
Fax: (702) 735-0406
http://www.lvchamber.org

Las Vegas Office of Business Development
400 Stewart Avenue
City Hall
Las Vegas, NV 89101
Phone: (702) 229-6011
Fax: (702) 385-3128
http://www.lasvegasnevada.gov

Lexington, KY
Greater Lexington Chamber of Commerce
330 East Main Street
Suite 100
Lexington, KY 40507
Phone: (859) 254-4447
Fax: (859) 233-3304
http://www.commercelexington.com

Lexington Downtown Development
Authority
101 East Vine Street
Suite 500
Lexington, KY 40507
Phone: (859) 425-2296
Fax: (859) 425-2292
http://www.lexingtondda.com

Lincoln, NE
Lincoln Chamber of Commerce
1135 M Street
Suite 200
Lincoln, NE 68508
Phone: (402) 436-2350
Fax: (402) 436-2360
http://www.lcoc.com

Little Rock, AR
Little Rock Regional Chamber
One Chamber Plaza
Little Rock, AR 72201
Phone: (501) 374-2001
Fax: (501) 374-6018
http://www.littlerockchamber.com

Los Angeles, CA
Los Angeles Area Chamber of Commerce
350 South Bixel Street
Los Angeles, CA 90017
Phone: (213) 580-7500
Fax: (213) 580-7511
http://www.lachamber.org

Los Angeles County Economic Development Corporation
444 South Flower Street
34th Floor
Los Angeles, CA 90071
Phone: (213) 622-4300
Fax: (213) 622-7100
http://www.laedc.org

Louisville, KY
The Greater Louisville Chamber of Commerce
614 West Main Street
Suite 6000
Louisville, KY 40202
Phone: (502) 625-0000
Fax: (502) 625-0010
http://www.greaterlouisville.com

Madison, WI
Greater Madison Chamber of Commerce
615 East Washington Avenue
P.O. Box 71
Madison, WI 53701-0071
Phone: (608) 256-8348
Fax: (608) 256-0333
http://www.greatermadisonchamber.com

Manchester, NH
Greater Manchester Chamber of Commerce
889 Elm Street
Manchester, NH 03101
Phone: (603) 666-6600
Fax: (603) 626-0910
http://www.manchester-chamber.org

Manchester Economic Development Office
One City Hall Plaza
Manchester, NH 03101
Phone: (603) 624-6505
Fax: (603) 624-6308
http://www.yourmanchesternh.com

Memphis, TN
Greater Memphis Chamber
22 North Front Street, Suite 200
Memphis, TN 38103-2100
Phone: (901) 543-3500
https://memphischamber.com

Miami, FL
Greater Miami Chamber of Commerce
1601 Biscayne Boulevard
Ballroom Level
Miami, FL 33132-1260
Phone: (305) 350-7700
Fax: (305) 374-6902
http://www.miamichamber.com

The Beacon Council
80 Southwest 8th Street
Suite 2400
Miami, FL 33130
Phone: (305) 579-1300
Fax: (305) 375-0271
http://www.beaconcouncil.com

Midland, TX
Midland Chamber of Commerce
109 N. Main
Midland, TX 79701
Phone: (432) 683-3381
Fax: (432) 686-3556
http://www.midlandtxchamber.com

Milwaukee, WI
Greater Milwaukee Chamber of Commerce
6815 W. Capitol Drive
Suite 300
Milwaukee, WI 53216
Phone: (414) 465-2422
http://www.gmcofc.org

Metropolitan Milwaukee Association of Commerce
756 N. Milwaukee Street
Suite 400
Milwaukee, WI 53202
Phone: (414) 287-4100
Fax: (414) 271-7753
https://www.mmac.org

Minneapolis, MN
Minneapolis Community Development Agency
Crown Roller Mill
105 5th Avenue South
Suite 200
Minneapolis, MN 55401
Phone: (612) 673-5095
Fax: (612) 673-5100
http://www.ci.minneapolis.mn.us

Minneapolis Regional Chamber
81 South Ninth Street
Suite 200
Minneapolis, MN 55402
Phone: (612) 370-9100
Fax: (612) 370-9195
http://www.minneapolischamber.org

Nashville, TN
Nashville Area Chamber of Commerce
211 Commerce Street
Suite 100
Nashville, TN 37201
Phone: (615) 743-3000
Fax: (615) 256-3074
http://www.nashvillechamber.com

Tennessee Valley Authority Economic Development
400 West Summit Hill Drive
Knoxville TN 37902
Phone: (865) 632-2101
http://www.tvaed.com

New Haven, CT
Greater New Haven Chamber of Commerce
900 Chapel Street
10th Floor
New Haven, CT 06510
Phone: (203) 787-6735
https://www.gnhcc.com

New Orleans, LA
New Orleans Chamber of Commerce
1515 Poydras Street
Suite 1010
New Orleans, LA 70112
Phone: (504) 799-4260
Fax: (504) 799-4259
http://www.neworleanschamber.org

New York, NY
New York City Economic Development Corporation
110 William Street
New York, NY 10038
Phone: (212) 619-5000
http://www.nycedc.com

The Partnership for New York City
One Battery Park Plaza
5th Floor
New York, NY 10004
Phone: (212) 493-7400
Fax: (212) 344-3344
http://www.pfnyc.org

Oklahoma City, OK
Greater Oklahoma City Chamber of Commerce
123 Park Avenue
Oklahoma City, OK 73102
Phone: (405) 297-8900
Fax: (405) 297-8916
http://www.okcchamber.com

Omaha, NE
Omaha Chamber of Commerce
1301 Harney Street
Omaha, NE 68102
Phone: (402) 346-5000
Fax: (402) 346-7050
http://www.omahachamber.org

Orlando, FL
Metro Orlando Economic Development Commission of Mid-Florida
301 East Pine Street
Suite 900
Orlando, FL 32801
Phone: (407) 422-7159
Fax: (407) 425.6428
http://www.orlandoedc.com

Orlando Regional Chamber of Commerce
75 South Ivanhoe Boulevard
P.O. Box 1234
Orlando, FL 32802
Phone: (407) 425-1234
Fax: (407) 839-5020
http://www.orlando.org

Philadelphia, PA
Greater Philadelphia Chamber of Commerce
200 South Broad Street
Suite 700
Philadelphia, PA 19102
Phone: (215) 545-1234
Fax: (215) 790-3600
http://www.greaterphilachamber.com

Phoenix, AZ
Greater Phoenix Chamber of Commerce
201 North Central Avenue
27th Floor
Phoenix, AZ 85073
Phone: (602) 495-2195
Fax: (602) 495-8913
http://www.phoenixchamber.com

Greater Phoenix Economic Council
2 North Central Avenue
Suite 2500
Phoenix, AZ 85004
Phone: (602) 256-7700
Fax: (602) 256-7744
http://www.gpec.org

Pittsburgh, PA
Allegheny County Industrial Development Authority
425 6th Avenue
Suite 800
Pittsburgh, PA 15219
Phone: (412) 350-1067
Fax: (412) 642-2217
http://www.alleghenycounty.us

Greater Pittsburgh Chamber of Commerce
425 6th Avenue
12th Floor
Pittsburgh, PA 15219
Phone: (412) 392-4500
Fax: (412) 392-4520
http://www.alleghenyconference.org

Portland, OR
Portland Business Alliance
200 SW Market Street
Suite 1770
Portland, OR 97201
Phone: (503) 224-8684
Fax: (503) 323-9186
http://www.portlandalliance.com

Providence, RI
Greater Providence Chamber of Commerce
30 Exchange Terrace
Fourth Floor
Providence, RI 02903
Phone: (401) 521-5000
Fax: (401) 351-2090
http://www.provchamber.com

Rhode Island Economic Development Corporation
Providence City Hall
25 Dorrance Street
Providence, RI 02903
Phone: (401) 421-7740
Fax: (401) 751-0203
http://www.providenceri.com

Provo, UT
Provo-Orem Chamber of Commerce
51 South University Avenue
Suite 215
Provo, UT 84601
Phone: (801) 851-2555
Fax: (801) 851-2557
http://www.thechamber.org

Raleigh, NC
Greater Raleigh Chamber of Commerce
800 South Salisbury Street
Raleigh, NC 27601-2978
Phone: (919) 664-7000
Fax: (919) 664-7099
http://www.raleighchamber.org

Reno, NV
Greater Reno-Sparks Chamber of Commerce
1 East First Street
16th Floor
Reno, NV 89505
Phone: (775) 337-3030
Fax: (775) 337-3038
http://www.reno-sparkschamber.org

The Chamber Reno-Sparks-Northern Nevada
449 S. Virginia St.
2nd Floor
Reno, NV 89501
Phone: (775) 636-9550
http://www.thechambernv.org

Richmond, VA
Greater Richmond Chamber
600 East Main Street
Suite 700
Richmond, VA 23219
Phone: (804) 648-1234
http://www.grcc.com

Greater Richmond Partnership
901 East Byrd Street
Suite 801
Richmond, VA 23219-4070
Phone: (804) 643-3227
Fax: (804) 343-7167
http://www.grpva.com

Riverside, CA
Greater Riverside Chambers of Commerce
3985 University Avenue
Riverside, CA 92501
Phone: (951) 683-7100
https://www.riverside-chamber.com

Rochester, MN
Rochester Area Chamber of Commerce
220 South Broadway
Suite 100
Rochester, MN 55904
Phone: (507) 288-1122
Fax: (507) 282-8960
http://www.rochestermnchamber.com

Rochester, NY
Greater Rochester Chamber of Commerce
150 State Street
Suite 400
Rochester, NY 14614-1308
Phone: (585) 244-1800
https://www.greaterrochesterchamber.com

Sacramento, CA
Sacramento Metro Chamber
One Capitol Mall
Suite 700
Sacramento, CA 95814
Phone: (916) 552-6800
https://metrochamber.org

Saint Louis, MO
St. Louis Regional Chamber
One Metropolitan Square
Suite 1300
St. Louis, MO 63102
Phone: (314) 231-5555
https://www.stlregionalchamber.com

Salt Lake City, UT
Department of Economic Development
451 South State Street
Room 425
Salt Lake City, UT 84111
Phone: (801) 535-7240
Fax: (801) 535-6331
http://www.slcgov.com/economic-development

Salt Lake Chamber
175 E. University Blvd. (400 S)
Suite 600
Salt Lake City, UT 84111
Phone: (801) 364-3631
http://www.slchamber.com

San Antonio, TX
The Greater San Antonio Chamber of Commerce
602 E. Commerce Street
San Antonio, TX 78205
Phone: (210) 229-2100
Fax: (210) 229-1600
http://www.sachamber.org

San Antonio Economic Development Department
P.O. Box 839966
San Antonio, TX 78283-3966
Phone: (210) 207-8080
Fax: (210) 207-8151
http://www.sanantonio.gov/edd

San Diego, CA
San Diego Economic Development Corp.
401 B Street
Suite 1100
San Diego, CA 92101
Phone: (619) 234-8484
Fax: (619) 234-1935
http://www.sandiegobusiness.org

San Diego Regional Chamber of Commerce
402 West Broadway
Suite 1000
San Diego, CA 92101-3585
Phone: (619) 544-1300
Fax: (619) 744-7481
http://www.sdchamber.org

San Francisco, CA
San Francisco Chamber of Commerce
235 Montgomery Street
12th Floor
San Francisco, CA 94104
Phone: (415) 392-4520
Fax: (415) 392-0485
http://www.sfchamber.com

San Jose, CA
Office of Economic Development
60 South Market Street
Suite 470
San Jose, CA 95113
Phone: (408) 277-5880
Fax: (408) 277-3615
http://www.sba.gov

The Silicon Valley Organization
101 W Santa Clara Street
San Jose, CA 95113
Phone: (408) 291-5250
https://www.thesvo.com

Santa Rosa, CA
Santa Rosa Chamber of Commerce
1260 North Dutton Avenue
Suite 272
Santa Rosa, CA 95401
Phone: (707) 545-1414
http://www.santarosachamber.com

Savannah, GA
Economic Development Authority
131 Hutchinson Island Road
4th Floor
Savannah, GA 31421
Phone: (912) 447-8450
Fax: (912) 447-8455
http://www.seda.org

Savannah Chamber of Commerce
101 E. Bay Street
Savannah, GA 31402
Phone: (912) 644-6400
Fax: (912) 644-6499
http://www.savannahchamber.com

Seattle, WA
Greater Seattle Chamber of Commerce
1301 Fifth Avenue
Suite 2500
Seattle, WA 98101
Phone: (206) 389-7200
Fax: (206) 389-7288
http://www.seattlechamber.com

Sioux Falls, SD
Sioux Falls Area Chamber of Commerce
200 N. Phillips Avenue
Suite 102
Sioux Falls, SD 57104
Phone: (605) 336-1620
Fax: (605) 336-6499
http://www.siouxfallschamber.com

Springfield, IL
The Greater Springfield Chamber of Commerce
1011 S. Second Street
Springfield, IL 62704
Phone: (217) 525-1173
Fax: (217) 525-8768
http://www.gscc.org

Tampa, FL
Greater Tampa Chamber of Commerce
P.O. Box 420
Tampa, FL 33601-0420
Phone: (813) 276-9401
Fax: (813) 229-7855
http://www.tampachamber.com

Tucson, AZ
Tucson Metro Chamber
212 E. Broadway Blvd
Tucson, AZ 85701
Phone: (520) 792-1212
https://tucsonchamber.org

Tulsa, OK
Tulsa Regional Chamber
One West Third Street
Suite 100
Tulsa, OK 74103
Phone: (918) 585-1201
https://www.tulsachamber.com

Tuscaloosa, AL
The Chamber of Commerce of West Alabama
2201 Jack Warner Parkway
Building C
Tuscaloosa, AL 35401
Phone: (205) 758-7588
https://tuscaloosachamber.com

Virginia Beach, VA
Hampton Roads Chamber of Commerce
500 East Main Street
Suite 700
Virginia Beach, VA 23510
Phone: (757) 664-2531
http://www.hamptonroadschamber.com

Washington, DC
District of Columbia Chamber of Commerce
1213 K Street NW
Washington, DC 20005
Phone: (202) 347-7201
Fax: (202) 638-6762
http://www.dcchamber.org

District of Columbia Office of Planning and Economic Development
J.A. Wilson Building
1350 Pennsylvania Ave NW
Suite 317
Washington, DC 20004
Phone: (202) 727-6365
Fax: (202) 727-6703
http://www.dcbiz.dc.gov

Wichita, KS
Wichita Regional Chamber of Commerce
350 W Douglas Avenue
Wichita, KS 67202
Phone: (316) 265-7771
https://www.wichitachamber.org

Wilmington, NC
Wilmington Chamber of Commerce
One Estell Lee Place
Wilmington, NC 28401
Phone: (910) 762-2611
http://www.wilmingtonchamber.org

Winston-Salem, NC
Winston-Salem Chamber of Commerce
411 West Fourth Street
Suite 211
Winston-Salem, NC 27101
Phone: (336) 728-9200
http://www.winstonsalem.com

Appendix E: State Departments of Labor

Alabama
Alabama Department of Labor
P.O. Box 303500
Montgomery, AL 36130-3500
Phone: (334) 242-3072
https://www.labor.alabama.gov

Alaska
Dept of Labor and Workforce Devel.
P.O. Box 11149
Juneau, AK 99822-2249
Phone: (907) 465-2700
http://www.labor.state.ak.us

Arizona
Industrial Commission or Arizona
800 West Washington Street
Phoenix, AZ 85007
Phone: (602) 542-4411
https://www.azica.gov

Arkansas
Department of Labor
10421 West Markham
Little Rock, AR 72205
Phone: (501) 682-4500
http://www.labor.ar.gov

California
Labor and Workforce Development
445 Golden Gate Ave., 10th Floor
San Francisco, CA 94102
Phone: (916) 263-1811
http://www.labor.ca.gov

Colorado
Dept of Labor and Employment
633 17th St., 2nd Floor
Denver, CO 80202-3660
Phone: (888) 390-7936
https://www.colorado.gov/CDLE

Connecticut
Department of Labor
200 Folly Brook Blvd.
Wethersfield, CT 06109-1114
Phone: (860) 263-6000
http://www.ctdol.state.ct.us

Delaware
Department of Labor
4425 N. Market St., 4th Floor
Wilmington, DE 19802
Phone: (302) 451-3423
http://dol.delaware.gov

District of Columbia
Department of Employment Services
614 New York Ave., NE, Suite 300
Washington, DC 20002
Phone: (202) 671-1900
http://does.dc.gov

Florida
Florida Department of Economic Opportunity
The Caldwell Building
107 East Madison St. Suite 100
Tallahassee, FL 32399-4120
Phone: (800) 342-3450
http://www.floridajobs.org

Georgia
Department of Labor
Sussex Place, Room 600
148 Andrew Young Intl Blvd., NE
Atlanta, GA 30303
Phone: (404) 656-3011
http://dol.georgia.gov

Hawaii
Dept of Labor & Industrial Relations
830 Punchbowl Street
Honolulu, HI 96813
Phone: (808) 586-8842
http://labor.hawaii.gov

Idaho
Department of Labor
317 W. Main St.
Boise, ID 83735-0001
Phone: (208) 332-3579
http://www.labor.idaho.gov

Illinois
Department of Labor
160 N. LaSalle Street, 13th Floor
Suite C-1300
Chicago, IL 60601
Phone: (312) 793-2800
https://www.illinois.gov/idol

Indiana
Indiana Department of Labor
402 West Washington Street, Room W195
Indianapolis, IN 46204
Phone: (317) 232-2655
http://www.in.gov/dol

Iowa
Iowa Workforce Development
1000 East Grand Avenue
Des Moines, IA 50319-0209
Phone: (515) 242-5870
http://www.iowadivisionoflabor.gov

Kansas
Department of Labor
401 S.W. Topeka Blvd.
Topeka, KS 66603-3182
Phone: (785) 296-5000
http://www.dol.ks.gov

Kentucky
Department of Labor
1047 U.S. Hwy 127 South, Suite 4
Frankfort, KY 40601-4381
Phone: (502) 564-3070
http://www.labor.ky.gov

Louisiana
Louisiana Workforce Commission
1001 N. 23rd Street
Baton Rouge, LA 70804-9094
Phone: (225) 342-3111
http://www.laworks.net

Maine
Department of Labor
45 Commerce Street
Augusta, ME 04330
Phone: (207) 623-7900
http://www.state.me.us/labor

Maryland
Department of Labor, Licensing & Regulation
500 N. Calvert Street
Suite 401
Baltimore, MD 21202
Phone: (410) 767-2357
http://www.dllr.state.md.us

Massachusetts
Dept of Labor & Workforce Development
One Ashburton Place
Room 2112
Boston, MA 02108
Phone: (617) 626-7100
http://www.mass.gov/lwd

Michigan
Department of Licensing and Regulatory Affairs
611 W. Ottawa
P.O. Box 30004
Lansing, MI 48909
Phone: (517) 373-1820
http://www.michigan.gov/lara

Minnesota
Dept of Labor and Industry
443 Lafayette Road North
Saint Paul, MN 55155
Phone: (651) 284-5070
http://www.doli.state.mn.us

Mississippi
Dept of Employment Security
P.O. Box 1699
Jackson, MS 39215-1699
Phone: (601) 321-6000
http://www.mdes.ms.gov

Missouri
Labor and Industrial Relations
P.O. Box 599
3315 W. Truman Boulevard
Jefferson City, MO 65102-0599
Phone: (573) 751-7500
https://labor.mo.gov

Montana
Dept of Labor and Industry
P.O. Box 1728
Helena, MT 59624-1728
Phone: (406) 444-9091
http://www.dli.mt.gov

Nebraska
Department of Labor
550 S 16th Street
Lincoln, NE 68508
Phone: (402) 471-9000
https://dol.nebraska.gov

Nevada
Dept of Business and Industry
3300 W. Sahara Ave
Suite 425
Las Vegas, NV 89102
Phone: (702) 486-2750
http://business.nv.gov

New Hampshire
Department of Labor
State Office Park South
95 Pleasant Street
Concord, NH 03301
Phone: (603) 271-3176
https://www.nh.gov/labor

New Jersey
Department of Labor & Workforce Development
John Fitch Plaza, 13th Floor
Suite D
Trenton, NJ 08625-0110
Phone: (609) 777-3200
http://lwd.dol.state.nj.us/labor

New Mexico
Department of Workforce Solutions
401 Broadway, NE
Albuquerque, NM 87103-1928
Phone: (505) 841-8450
https://www.dws.state.nm.us

New York
Department of Labor
State Office Bldg. # 12
W.A. Harriman Campus
Albany, NY 12240
Phone: (518) 457-9000
https://www.labor.ny.gov

North Carolina
Department of Labor
4 West Edenton Street
Raleigh, NC 27601-1092
Phone: (919) 733-7166
https://www.labor.nc.gov

North Dakota
North Dakota Department of Labor and Human Rights
State Capitol Building
600 East Boulevard, Dept 406
Bismark, ND 58505-0340
Phone: (701) 328-2660
http://www.nd.gov/labor

Ohio
Department of Commerce
77 South High Street, 22nd Floor
Columbus, OH 43215
Phone: (614) 644-2239
http://www.com.state.oh.us

Oklahoma
Department of Labor
4001 N. Lincoln Blvd.
Oklahoma City, OK 73105-5212
Phone: (405) 528-1500
https://www.ok.gov/odol

Oregon
Bureau of Labor and Industries
800 NE Oregon St., #32
Portland, OR 97232
Phone: (971) 673-0761
http://www.oregon.gov/boli

Pennsylvania
Dept of Labor and Industry
1700 Labor and Industry Bldg
7th and Forster Streets
Harrisburg, PA 17120
Phone: (717) 787-5279
http://www.dli.pa.gov

Rhode Island
Department of Labor and Training
1511 Pontiac Avenue
Cranston, RI 02920
Phone: (401) 462-8000
http://www.dlt.state.ri.us

South Carolina
Dept of Labor, Licensing & Regulations
P.O. Box 11329
Columbia, SC 29211-1329
Phone: (803) 896-4300
http://www.llr.state.sc.us

South Dakota
Department of Labor & Regulation
700 Governors Drive
Pierre, SD 57501-2291
Phone: (605) 773-3682
http://dlr.sd.gov

Tennessee
Dept of Labor & Workforce Development
Andrew Johnson Tower
710 James Robertson Pkwy
Nashville, TN 37243-0655
Phone: (615) 741-6642
http://www.tn.gov/workforce

Texas
Texas Workforce Commission
101 East 15th St.
Austin, TX 78778
Phone: (512) 475-2670
http://www.twc.state.tx.us

Utah
Utah Labor Commission
160 East 300 South, 3rd Floor
Salt Lake City, UT 84114-6600
Phone: (801) 530-6800
https://laborcommission.utah.gov

Vermont
Department of Labor
5 Green Mountain Drive
P.O. Box 488
Montpelier, VT 05601-0488
Phone: (802) 828-4000
http://labor.vermont.gov

Virginia
Dept of Labor and Industry
Powers-Taylor Building
13 S. 13th Street
Richmond, VA 23219
Phone: (804) 371-2327
http://www.doli.virginia.gov

Washington
Dept of Labor and Industries
P.O. Box 44001
Olympia, WA 98504-4001
Phone: (360) 902-4200
http://www.lni.wa.gov

West Virginia
Division of Labor
749 B Building 6
Capitol Complex
Charleston, WV 25305
Phone: (304) 558-7890
https://labor.wv.gov

Wisconsin
Dept of Workforce Development
201 E. Washington Ave., #A400
P.O. Box 7946
Madison, WI 53707-7946
Phone: (608) 266-6861
http://dwd.wisconsin.gov

Wyoming
Department of Workforce Services
1510 East Pershing Blvd.
Cheyenne, WY 82002
Phone: (307) 777-7261
http://www.wyomingworkforce.org

Grey House Publishing

2022 Title List

Grey House Publishing

Visit www.GreyHouse.com for Product Information, Table of Contents, and Sample Pages.

Opinions Throughout History

Opinions Throughout History: Church & State
Opinions Throughout History: The Death Penalty
Opinions Throughout History: Diseases & Epidemics
Opinions Throughout History: Drug Use & Abuse
Opinions Throughout History: The Environment
Opinions Throughout History: Free Speech & Censorship
Opinions Throughout History: Gender: Roles & Rights
Opinions Throughout History: Globalization
Opinions Throughout History: Guns in America
Opinions Throughout History: Immigration
Opinions Throughout History: Law Enforcement in America
Opinions Throughout History: National Security vs. Civil & Privacy Rights
Opinions Throughout History: Presidential Authority
Opinions Throughout History: Robotics & Artificial Intelligence
Opinions Throughout History: Social Media Issues
Opinions Throughout History: Voters' Rights
Opinions Throughout History: War & the Military
Opinions Throughout History: Workers Rights & Wages

This is Who We Were

This is Who We Were: Colonial America (1492-1775)
This is Who We Were: 1880-1899
This is Who We Were: In the 1900s
This is Who We Were: In the 1910s
This is Who We Were: In the 1920s
This is Who We Were: A Companion to the 1940 Census
This is Who We Were: In the 1940s (1940-1949)
This is Who We Were: In the 1950s
This is Who We Were: In the 1960s
This is Who We Were: In the 1970s
This is Who We Were: In the 1980s
This is Who We Were: In the 1990s
This is Who We Were: In the 2000s
This is Who We Were: In the 2010s

Working Americans

Working Americans—Vol. 1: The Working Class
Working Americans—Vol. 2: The Middle Class
Working Americans—Vol. 3: The Upper Class
Working Americans—Vol. 4: Children
Working Americans—Vol. 5: At War
Working Americans—Vol. 6: Working Women
Working Americans—Vol. 7: Social Movements
Working Americans—Vol. 8: Immigrants
Working Americans—Vol. 9: Revolutionary War to the Civil War
Working Americans—Vol. 10: Sports & Recreation
Working Americans—Vol. 11: Inventors & Entrepreneurs
Working Americans—Vol. 12: Our History through Music
Working Americans—Vol. 13: Education & Educators
Working Americans—Vol. 14: African Americans
Working Americans—Vol. 15: Politics & Politicians
Working Americans—Vol. 16: Farming & Ranching
Working Americans—Vol. 17: Teens in America
Working Americans—Vol. 18: Health Care Workers

Grey House Health & Wellness Guides

The Autism Spectrum Handbook & Resource Guide
Autoimmune Disorders Handbook & Resource Guide
Cardiovascular Disease Handbook & Resource Guide
Dementia Handbook & Resource Guide
Diabetes Handbook & Resource Guide
Nutrition, Obesity & Eating Disorders Handbook & Resource Guide

Consumer Health

Complete Mental Health Resource Guide
Complete Resource Guide for Pediatric Disorders
Complete Resource Guide for People with Chronic Illness
Complete Resource Guide for People with Disabilities
Older Americans Information Resource
Parenting: Styles & Strategies

Education

Complete Learning Disabilities Resource Guide
Educators Resource Guide
The Comparative Guide to Elem. & Secondary Schools
Special Education: A Reference Book for Policy & Curriculum Development

General Reference

American Environmental Leaders
Constitutional Amendments
Encyclopedia of African-American Writing
Encyclopedia of Invasions & Conquests
Encyclopedia of Prisoners of War & Internment
Encyclopedia of the Continental Congresses
Encyclopedia of the United States Cabinet
Encyclopedia of War Journalism
The Environmental Debate
Financial Literacy Starter Kit
From Suffrage to the Senate
The Gun Debate: Gun Rights & Gun Control in the U.S.
Historical Warrior Peoples & Modern Fighting Groups
Human Rights and the United States
Political Corruption in America
Privacy Rights in the Digital Age
The Religious Right and American Politics
Speakers of the House of Representatives, 1789-2021
US Land & Natural Resources Policy
The Value of a Dollar 1600-1865 Colonial to Civil War
The Value of a Dollar 1860-2019

Business Information

Business Information Resources
The Complete Broadcasting Industry Guide: Television, Radio, Cable & Streaming
Directory of Mail Order Catalogs
Environmental Resource Handbook
Food & Beverage Market Place
The Grey House Guide to Homeland Security Resources
The Grey House Performing Arts Industry Guide
Guide to Healthcare Group Purchasing Organizations
Guide to U.S. HMOs and PPOs
Guide to Venture Capital & Private Equity Firms
Hudson's Washington News Media Contacts Guide
New York State Directory
Sports Market Place

2022 Title List

Visit www.GreyHouse.com for Product Information, Table of Contents, and Sample Pages.

Statistics & Demographics

America's Top-Rated Cities
America's Top-Rated Smaller Cities
The Comparative Guide to American Suburbs
Profiles of America
Profiles of California
Profiles of Florida
Profiles of Illinois
Profiles of Indiana
Profiles of Massachusetts
Profiles of Michigan
Profiles of New Jersey
Profiles of New York
Profiles of North Carolina & South Carolina
Profiles of Ohio
Profiles of Pennsylvania
Profiles of Texas
Profiles of Virginia
Profiles of Wisconsin

Canadian Resources

Associations Canada
Canadian Almanac & Directory
Canadian Environmental Resource Guide
Canadian Parliamentary Guide
Canadian Venture Capital & Private Equity Firms
Canadian Who's Who
Cannabis Canada
Careers & Employment Canada
Financial Post: Directory of Directors
Financial Services Canada
FP Bonds: Corporate
FP Bonds: Government
FP Equities: Preferreds & Derivatives
FP Survey: Industrials
FP Survey: Mines & Energy
FP Survey: Predecessor & Defunct
Health Guide Canada
Libraries Canada

Weiss Financial Ratings

Financial Literacy Basics
Financial Literacy: How to Become an Investor
Financial Literacy: Planning for the Future
Weiss Ratings Consumer Guides
Weiss Ratings Guide to Banks
Weiss Ratings Guide to Credit Unions
Weiss Ratings Guide to Health Insurers
Weiss Ratings Guide to Life & Annuity Insurers
Weiss Ratings Guide to Property & Casualty Insurers
Weiss Ratings Investment Research Guide to Bond & Money Market Mutual Funds
Weiss Ratings Investment Research Guide to Exchange-Traded Funds
Weiss Ratings Investment Research Guide to Stock Mutual Funds
Weiss Ratings Investment Research Guide to Stocks

Books in Print Series

American Book Publishing Record® Annual
American Book Publishing Record® Monthly
Books In Print®
Books In Print® Supplement
Books Out Loud™
Bowker's Complete Video Directory™
Children's Books In Print®
El-Hi Textbooks & Serials In Print®
Forthcoming Books®
Law Books & Serials In Print™
Medical & Health Care Books In Print™
Publishers, Distributors & Wholesalers of the US™
Subject Guide to Books In Print®
Subject Guide to Children's Books In Print®

SALEM PRESS

2022 Title List

SALEM PRESS

Visit www.SalemPress.com for Product Information, Table of Contents, and Sample Pages.

LITERATURE

Critical Insights: Authors

Louisa May Alcott
Sherman Alexie
Isabel Allende
Maya Angelou
Isaac Asimov
Margaret Atwood
Jane Austen
James Baldwin
Saul Bellow
Roberto Bolano
Ray Bradbury
The Brontë Sisters
Gwendolyn Brooks
Albert Camus
Raymond Carver
Willa Cather
Geoffrey Chaucer
John Cheever
Joseph Conrad
Charles Dickens
Emily Dickinson
Frederick Douglass
T. S. Eliot
George Eliot
Harlan Ellison
Louise Erdrich
William Faulkner
F. Scott Fitzgerald
Gustave Flaubert
Horton Foote
Benjamin Franklin
Robert Frost
Neil Gaiman
Gabriel Garcia Marquez
Thomas Hardy
Nathaniel Hawthorne
Robert A. Heinlein
Lillian Hellman
Ernest Hemingway
Langston Hughes
Zora Neale Hurston
Henry James
Thomas Jefferson
James Joyce
Jamaica Kincaid
Stephen King
Martin Luther King, Jr.
Barbara Kingsolver
Abraham Lincoln
Mario Vargas Llosa
Jack London
James McBride
Cormac McCarthy
Herman Melville
Arthur Miller
Toni Morrison
Alice Munro
Tim O'Brien
Flannery O'Connor
Eugene O'Neill
George Orwell
Sylvia Plath
Edgar Allan Poe
Philip Roth
Salman Rushdie
J.D. Salinger
Mary Shelley
John Steinbeck
Amy Tan
Leo Tolstoy
Mark Twain
John Updike
Kurt Vonnegut
Alice Walker
David Foster Wallace
Edith Wharton
Walt Whitman
Oscar Wilde
Tennessee Williams
Virginia Woolf
Richard Wright
Malcolm X

Critical Insights: Works

Absalom, Absalom!
Adventures of Huckleberry Finn
Adventures of Tom Sawyer
Aeneid
All Quiet on the Western Front
Animal Farm
Anna Karenina
The Awakening
The Bell Jar
Beloved
Billy Budd, Sailor
The Book Thief
Brave New World
The Canterbury Tales
Catch-22
The Catcher in the Rye
The Color Purple
The Crucible
Death of a Salesman
The Diary of a Young Girl
Dracula
Fahrenheit 451
The Grapes of Wrath
Great Expectations
The Great Gatsby
Hamlet
The Handmaid's Tale
Harry Potter Series
Heart of Darkness
The Hobbit
The House on Mango Street
How the Garcia Girls Lost Their Accents
The Hunger Games Trilogy
I Know Why the Caged Bird Sings
In Cold Blood
The Inferno
Invisible Man
Jane Eyre
The Joy Luck Club
Julius Caesar
King Lear
The Kite Runner
Life of Pi
Little Women
Lolita
Lord of the Flies
The Lord of the Rings
Macbeth
The Metamorphosis
Midnight's Children
A Midsummer Night's Dream
Moby-Dick
Mrs. Dalloway
Nineteen Eighty-Four
The Odyssey
Of Mice and Men
The Old Man and the Sea
On the Road
One Flew Over the Cuckoo's Nest
One Hundred Years of Solitude
Othello
The Outsiders
Paradise Lost
The Pearl
The Poetry of Baudelaire
The Poetry of Edgar Allan Poe
A Portrait of the Artist as a Young Man
Pride and Prejudice
The Red Badge of Courage
Romeo and Juliet
The Scarlet Letter
Short Fiction of Flannery O'Connor
Slaughterhouse-Five
The Sound and the Fury
A Streetcar Named Desire
The Sun Also Rises
A Tale of Two Cities
The Tales of Edgar Allan Poe
Their Eyes Were Watching God
Things Fall Apart
To Kill a Mockingbird
War and Peace
The Woman Warrior

Critical Insights: Themes

The American Comic Book
American Creative Non-Fiction
The American Dream
American Multicultural Identity
American Road Literature
American Short Story
American Sports Fiction
The American Thriller
American Writers in Exile
Censored & Banned Literature
Civil Rights Literature, Past & Present
Coming of Age
Conspiracies
Contemporary Canadian Fiction
Contemporary Immigrant Short Fiction
Contemporary Latin American Fiction
Contemporary Speculative Fiction
Crime and Detective Fiction
Crisis of Faith
Cultural Encounters
Dystopia
Family
The Fantastic
Feminism

SALEM PRESS

2022 Title List

SALEM PRESS

Visit www.SalemPress.com for Product Information, Table of Contents, and Sample Pages.

Flash Fiction
Gender, Sex and Sexuality
Good & Evil
The Graphic Novel
Greed
Harlem Renaissance
The Hero's Quest
Historical Fiction
Holocaust Literature
The Immigrant Experience
Inequality
LGBTQ Literature
Literature in Times of Crisis
Literature of Protest
Love
Magical Realism
Midwestern Literature
Modern Japanese Literature
Nature & the Environment
Paranoia, Fear & Alienation
Patriotism
Political Fiction
Postcolonial Literature
Pulp Fiction of the '20s and '30s
Rebellion
Russia's Golden Age
Satire
The Slave Narrative
Social Justice and American Literature
Southern Gothic Literature
Southwestern Literature
Survival
Technology & Humanity
Truth & Lies
Violence in Literature
Virginia Woolf & 20th Century Women Writers
War

Critical Insights: Film

Bonnie & Clyde
Casablanca
Alfred Hitchcock
Stanley Kubrick

Critical Approaches to Literature

Critical Approaches to Literature: Feminist
Critical Approaches to Literature: Moral
Critical Approaches to Literature: Multicultural
Critical Approaches to Literature: Psychological

Critical Surveys of Literature

Critical Survey of American Literature
Critical Survey of Drama
Critical Survey of Graphic Novels: Heroes & Superheroes
Critical Survey of Graphic Novels: History, Theme, and Technique
Critical Survey of Graphic Novels: Independents & Underground Classics
Critical Survey of Graphic Novels: Manga
Critical Survey of Long Fiction
Critical Survey of Mystery and Detective Fiction
Critical Survey of Mythology & Folklore: Gods & Goddesses
Critical Survey of Mythology & Folklore: Heroes and Heroines
Critical Survey of Mythology & Folklore: Love, Sexuality, and Desire
Critical Survey of Mythology & Folklore: World Mythology
Critical Survey of Poetry
Critical Survey of Poetry: Contemporary Poets
Critical Survey of Science Fiction & Fantasy Literature
Critical Survey of Shakespeare's Plays
Critical Survey of Shakespeare's Sonnets
Critical Survey of Short Fiction
Critical Survey of World Literature
Critical Survey of Young Adult Literature

Cyclopedia of Literary Characters & Places

Cyclopedia of Literary Characters
Cyclopedia of Literary Places

Introduction to Literary Context

American Poetry of the 20th Century
American Post-Modernist Novels
American Short Fiction
English Literature
Plays
World Literature

Magill's Literary Annual

Magill's Literary Annual, 2022
Magill's Literary Annual, 2021
Magill's Literary Annual, 2020
Magill's Literary Annual (Backlist Issues 2019-1977)

Masterplots

Masterplots, Fourth Edition
Masterplots, 2010-2018 Supplement

Notable Writers

Notable African American Writers
Notable American Women Writers
Notable Mystery & Detective Fiction Writers
Notable Writers of the American West & the Native American Experience
Novels into Film: Adaptations & Interpretation
Recommended Reading: 600 Classics Reviewed

SALEM PRESS

2022 Title List

SALEM PRESS

Visit www.SalemPress.com for Product Information, Table of Contents, and Sample Pages.

HISTORY

The Decades

The 1910s in America
The Twenties in America
The Thirties in America
The Forties in America
The Fifties in America
The Sixties in America
The Seventies in America
The Eighties in America
The Nineties in America
The 2000s in America
The 2010s in America

Defining Documents in American History

Defining Documents: The 1900s
Defining Documents: The 1910s
Defining Documents: The 1920s
Defining Documents: The 1930s
Defining Documents: The 1950s
Defining Documents: The 1960s
Defining Documents: The 1970s
Defining Documents: The 1980s
Defining Documents: American Citizenship
Defining Documents: The American Economy
Defining Documents: The American Revolution
Defining Documents: The American West
Defining Documents: Business Ethics
Defining Documents: Capital Punishment
Defining Documents: Civil Rights
Defining Documents: Civil War
Defining Documents: The Constitution
Defining Documents: The Cold War
Defining Documents: Dissent & Protest
Defining Documents: Domestic Terrorism
Defining Documents: Drug Policy
Defining Documents: The Emergence of Modern America
Defining Documents: Environment & Conservation
Defining Documents: Espionage & Intrigue
Defining Documents: Exploration and Colonial America
Defining Documents: The First Amendment
Defining Documents: The Free Press
Defining Documents: The Great Depression
Defining Documents: The Great Migration
Defining Documents: The Gun Debate
Defining Documents: Immigration & Immigrant Communities
Defining Documents: The Legacy of 9/11
Defining Documents: LGBTQ+
Defining Documents: Manifest Destiny and the New Nation
Defining Documents: Native Americans
Defining Documents: Political Campaigns, Candidates & Discourse
Defining Documents: Postwar 1940s
Defining Documents: Prison Reform
Defining Documents: Secrets, Leaks & Scandals
Defining Documents: Slavery
Defining Documents: Supreme Court Decisions
Defining Documents: Reconstruction Era
Defining Documents: The Vietnam War
Defining Documents: U.S. Involvement in the Middle East
Defining Documents: World War I
Defining Documents: World War II

Defining Documents in World History

Defining Documents: The 17th Century
Defining Documents: The 18th Century
Defining Documents: The 19th Century
Defining Documents: The 20th Century (1900-1950)
Defining Documents: The Ancient World
Defining Documents: Asia
Defining Documents: Genocide & the Holocaust
Defining Documents: Nationalism & Populism
Defining Documents: Pandemics, Plagues & Public Health
Defining Documents: Renaissance & Early Modern Era
Defining Documents: The Middle Ages
Defining Documents: The Middle East
Defining Documents: Women's Rights

Great Events from History

Great Events from History: The Ancient World
Great Events from History: The Middle Ages
Great Events from History: The Renaissance & Early Modern Era
Great Events from History: The 17th Century
Great Events from History: The 18th Century
Great Events from History: The 19th Century
Great Events from History: The 20th Century, 1901-1940
Great Events from History: The 20th Century, 1941-1970
Great Events from History: The 20th Century, 1971-2000
Great Events from History: Modern Scandals
Great Events from History: African American History
Great Events from History: The 21st Century, 2000-2016
Great Events from History: LGBTQ Events
Great Events from History: Human Rights
Great Events from History: Women's History

Great Lives from History

Computer Technology Innovators
Fashion Innovators
Great Athletes
Great Athletes of the Twenty-First Century
Great Lives from History: African Americans
Great Lives from History: American Heroes
Great Lives from History: American Women
Great Lives from History: Asian and Pacific Islander Americans
Great Lives from History: Inventors & Inventions
Great Lives from History: Jewish Americans
Great Lives from History: Latinos
Great Lives from History: Scientists and Science
Great Lives from History: The 17th Century
Great Lives from History: The 18th Century
Great Lives from History: The 19th Century
Great Lives from History: The 20th Century
Great Lives from History: The 21st Century, 2000-2017
Great Lives from History: The Ancient World
Great Lives from History: The Incredibly Wealthy
Great Lives from History: The Middle Ages
Great Lives from History: The Renaissance & Early Modern Era
Human Rights Innovators
Internet Innovators
Music Innovators
Musicians and Composers of the 20th Century
World Political Innovators

SALEM PRESS

2022 Title List

SALEM PRESS

Visit www.SalemPress.com for Product Information, Table of Contents, and Sample Pages.

History & Government

American First Ladies
American Presidents
The 50 States
The Ancient World: Extraordinary People in Extraordinary Societies
The Bill of Rights
The Criminal Justice System
The U.S. Supreme Court

SOCIAL SCIENCES

Civil Rights Movements: Past & Present
Countries, Peoples and Cultures
Countries: Their Wars & Conflicts: A World Survey
Education Today: Issues, Policies & Practices
Encyclopedia of American Immigration
Ethics: Questions & Morality of Human Actions
Issues in U.S. Immigration
Principles of Sociology: Group Relationships & Behavior
Principles of Sociology: Personal Relationships & Behavior
Principles of Sociology: Societal Issues & Behavior
Racial & Ethnic Relations in America
World Geography

HEALTH

Addictions, Substance Abuse & Alcoholism
Adolescent Health & Wellness
Aging
Cancer
Community & Family Health Issues
Integrative, Alternative & Complementary Medicine
Genetics and Inherited Conditions
Infectious Diseases and Conditions
Magill's Medical Guide
Nutrition
Parenting: Styles & Strategies
Psychology & Behavioral Health
Women's Health

Principles of Health

Principles of Health: Allergies & Immune Disorders
Principles of Health: Anxiety & Stress
Principles of Health: Depression
Principles of Health: Diabetes
Principles of Health: Nursing
Principles of Health: Obesity
Principles of Health: Pain Management
Principles of Health: Prescription Drug Abuse

SCIENCE

Ancient Creatures
Applied Science
Applied Science: Engineering & Mathematics
Applied Science: Science & Medicine
Applied Science: Technology
Biomes and Ecosystems
Earth Science: Earth Materials and Resources
Earth Science: Earth's Surface and History
Earth Science: Earth's Weather, Water and Atmosphere
Earth Science: Physics and Chemistry of the Earth
Encyclopedia of Climate Change
Encyclopedia of Energy
Encyclopedia of Environmental Issues
Encyclopedia of Global Resources
Encyclopedia of Mathematics and Society
Forensic Science
Notable Natural Disasters
The Solar System
USA in Space

Principles of Science

Principles of Anatomy
Principles of Astronomy
Principles of Behavioral Science
Principles of Biology
Principles of Biotechnology
Principles of Botany
Principles of Chemistry
Principles of Climatology
Principles of Computer-aided Design
Principles of Information Technology
Principles of Computer Science
Principles of Ecology
Principles of Energy
Principles of Fire Science
Principles of Geology
Principles of Marine Science
Principles of Mathematics
Principles of Microbiology
Principles of Modern Agriculture
Principles of Pharmacology
Principles of Physical Science
Principles of Physics
Principles of Programming & Coding
Principles of Robotics & Artificial Intelligence
Principles of Scientific Research
Principles of Sports Medicine & Kinesiology
Principles of Sustainability
Principles of Zoology

SALEM PRESS

2022 Title List

SALEM PRESS

Visit www.SalemPress.com for Product Information, Table of Contents, and Sample Pages.

CAREERS

Careers: Paths to Entrepreneurship
Careers in Artificial Intelligence
Careers in the Arts: Fine, Performing & Visual
Careers in the Automotive Industry
Careers in Biology
Careers in Building Construction
Careers in Business
Careers in Chemistry
Careers in Communications & Media
Careers in Education & Training
Careers in Engineering
Careers in Environment & Conservation
Careers in Financial Services
Careers in Forensic Science
Careers in Gaming
Careers in Green Energy
Careers in Healthcare
Careers in Hospitality & Tourism
Careers in Human Services
Careers in Information Technology
Careers in Law, Criminal Justice & Emergency Services
Careers in the Music Industry
Careers in Manufacturing & Production
Careers in Nursing
Careers in Physics
Careers in Protective Services
Careers in Psychology & Behavioral Health
Careers in Public Administration
Careers in Sales, Insurance & Real Estate
Careers in Science & Engineering
Careers in Social Media
Careers in Sports & Fitness
Careers in Sports Medicine & Training
Careers in Technical Services & Equipment Repair
Careers in Transportation
Careers in Writing & Editing
Careers Outdoors
Careers Overseas
Careers Working with Infants & Children
Careers Working with Animals

BUSINESS

Principles of Business: Accounting
Principles of Business: Economics
Principles of Business: Entrepreneurship
Principles of Business: Finance
Principles of Business: Globalization
Principles of Business: Leadership
Principles of Business: Management
Principles of Business: Marketing

2022 Title List

Visit www.HWWilsonInPrint.com for Product Information, Table of Contents, and Sample Pages.

Core Collections
Children's Core Collection
Fiction Core Collection
Graphic Novels Core Collection
Middle & Junior High School Core
Public Library Core Collection: Nonfiction
Senior High Core Collection
Young Adult Fiction Core Collection

The Reference Shelf
Affordable Housing
Aging in America
Alternative Facts, Post-Truth and the Information War
The American Dream
Artificial Intelligence
The Business of Food
Campaign Trends & Election Law
College Sports
Democracy Evolving
The Digital Age
Embracing New Paradigms in Education
Food Insecurity & Hunger in the United States
Future of U.S. Economic Relations: Mexico, Cuba, & Venezuela
Global Climate Change
Guns in America
Hate Crimes
Immigration
Income Inequality
Internet Abuses & Privacy Rights
Internet Law
LGBTQ in the 21st Century
Marijuana Reform
Mental Health Awareness
National Debate Topic 2014/2015: The Ocean
National Debate Topic 2015/2016: Surveillance
National Debate Topic 2016/2017: US/China Relations
National Debate Topic 2017/2018: Education Reform
National Debate Topic 2018/2019: Immigration
National Debate Topic 2019/2021: Arms Sales
National Debate Topic 2020/2021: Criminal Justice Reform
National Debate Topic 2021/2022: Water Resources
National Debate Topic 2022/2023
New Frontiers in Space
Policing in 2020
Pollution
Prescription Drug Abuse
Propaganda and Misinformation
Racial Tension in a Postracial Age
Reality Television
Representative American Speeches, Annual Editions
Rethinking Work
Revisiting Gender
The South China Sea Conflict
Sports in America
The Supreme Court
The Transformation of American Cities
The Two Koreas
UFOs
Vaccinations
Voters' Rights
Whistleblowers

Current Biography
Current Biography Cumulative Index 1946-2021
Current Biography Monthly Magazine
Current Biography Yearbook

Readers' Guide to Periodical Literature
Abridged Readers' Guide to Periodical Literature
Readers' Guide to Periodical Literature

Indexes
Index to Legal Periodicals & Books
Short Story Index
Book Review Digest

Sears List
Sears List of Subject Headings
Sears: Lista de Encabezamientos de Materia

History
American Game Changers: Invention, Innovation & Transformation
American Reformers
Speeches of the American Presidents

Facts About Series
Facts About the 20th Century
Facts About American Immigration
Facts About China
Facts About the Presidents
Facts About the World's Languages

Nobel Prize Winners
Nobel Prize Winners: 1901-1986
Nobel Prize Winners: 1987-1991
Nobel Prize Winners: 1992-1996
Nobel Prize Winners: 1997-2001
Nobel Prize Winners: 2002-2018

Famous First Facts
Famous First Facts
Famous First Facts About American Politics
Famous First Facts About Sports
Famous First Facts About the Environment
Famous First Facts: International Edition

American Book of Days
The American Book of Days
The International Book of Days